OPERATION
WORLD

The author and publishers gratefully acknowledge the assistance of the Research Team in the International Office of WEC at Bulstrode, Gerrards Cross, UK in the preparation of the text of *Operation World*.

You Can Change The World by Jill Johnstone, a children's version of *Operation World*, is available from your local Christian bookshop.

PATRICK JOHNSTONE

OPERATION
WORLD

The Day-by-Day Guide
To Praying For the World

ZondervanPublishingHouse
Grand Rapids, Michigan

A Division of HarperCollins*Publishers*

Copyright © 1993 Patrick J StG Johnstone

1st edition	Dorothea Mission	1974
2nd edition	STL	1978
revised	STL	1979
3rd edition	STL	1980
4th edition	STL & WEC International	1986
reprinted	STL & WEC International	1986
reprinted	STL & WEC International	1987
5th edition	OM Publishing	1993

First published in the USA by
Zondervan Publishing House, 5300 Patterson Ave. S.E., Grand Rapids, MI 49530,
by arrangement with OM Publishing.

Library of Congress Cataloging-in-Publication Data

Johnstone, Patrick J. St. G.
    Operation world : a day-to-day guide to praying for the world /
Patrick Johnstone. -- [Updated, U.S. ed.]
        p.   cm.
    ISBN 0–310–40031–7 (pbk.)
    1. Devotional calendars.   2. Religions--Handbooks, manuals, etc.
3. Christian sects--Handbooks, manuals, etc.   4. Geography-
-Handbooks, manuals, etc.   I. Title.
BV4811.J596   1993
266'.0021--dc20
                                                                    93-8006
                                                                    CIP

Typeset by Photoprint, Torquay, Devon, UK
and printed in the United States of America
for the publishers by R.R. Donnelley & Sons, Harrisonburg, Virginia.

CONTENTS

INDEX

Key to Index

1. **BOLD CAPITALS** – regions as defined in this book.

2. **Bold lower case** – states and territories included in the main body of the book.

3. Lower case – an alternative or commonly used name. The name used in the book follows in bold type.

4. *Lower case italics* – either a name no longer used or a territory that has been absorbed by the state in brackets following.

Note:

1. Territories without permanent inhabitants have not been listed – including Antarctica.

2. States formed since 1990 are retained as sub-sections of the original state because of ongoing political, military and statistical links and also because the statistical date-line is for June 1990. This includes the former Czechoslovakia, Ethiopia and Yugoslavia.

3. States under the occupation or jurisdiction of other states are included under the latter. For instance, the Western Sahara is under Morocco; the West Bank of the Jordan and the Gaza Strip under Israel. This is to represent the *de facto* situation and is not an expression of a political opinion.

Specialized ministries are included in the prayer calendar for the last three weeks of December.

The following have been selected from the many ministries and specific outreaches which operate worldwide.

Appendices

PREFACE
Fifth Edition

Operation World

It is with much thankfulness and praise to God that this edition ever came to completion. There were several times when I made the decision to stop – especially when my dear wife, Jill, became ill with cancer in 1990. Both she and my WEC Research Office colleagues encouraged me to continue. During the time of her illness Jill wrote a children's version of *Operation World*, entitled *You Can Change The World*, and she completed the text a few weeks before her Homecall in June 1992. The two books are being published simultaneously as companion volumes. The Lord wonderfully gave us joy, peace and grace through this intense, wrenching time. Many prayed faithfully for us; thank you all!

Operation World is one of a series of attempts to survey the world and portray its spiritual needs. I am honoured to follow in that succession – such as William Carey's *Enquiry* published in 1792 and more recently, my friend and co-researcher David Barrett's *World Christian Encyclopedia* published in 1980. To David I owe a debt of gratitude for his unstinting help and advice in the last two editions.

Perhaps the uniqueness of *Operation World* is its deliberate design as a prayer manual, and a highlighting of facts and figures that stimulate intercession. Although the information and statistics are fairly comprehensive, it is not intended as a complete reference book. I have had to limit ministries, agencies, bibliographies, sources and information to that which I considered absolutely essential to the main purpose of the book. Even so, I am embarrassed at the large size of the book and the small size of the type! Far more information is available in the electronic version carefully crafted by Global Mapping International in the USA.

Many have asked how I became involved in such a ministry. Had I known how costly, painful and demanding it would prove to be, I would probably have declined! It was not my idea. To accomplish the writing of the first and second editions in Africa was certainly the Lord's doing, for I had nearly every possible disadvantage. Maybe the Lord wanted to demonstrate that good postal services, telephones, faxes, computers and supportive team are not essential if he is in it! Here is a brief chronological account of how *Operation World* developed.

The Origin of *Operation World*

1900 **Dr Andrew Murray**, that great man of God in South Africa, wrote a book entitled **The Key to the Missionary Problem**. Its subject matter is still so relevant that **CLC** published an edition in 1983 contemporized by Leona Choy. In this book Andrew Murray put out a challenge for Christians and churches to hold a **Week of Prayer for the World**. As far as I know, that challenge was not taken up for decades.

1943 God called **Hans von Staden** to preach the gospel in the rapidly developing urban slums of Southern Africa. The Dorothea Mission, under his leadership, became one of the early urban evangelistic agencies in that part of the world. Many people turned from sin and bondage to the liberty there is in Jesus Christ. Prayer was a major emphasis in the work. As a result, all of us who were workers of the Dorothea Mission received a wider vision for the world, and for this I will be eternally grateful.

1962 The Dorothea Mission arranged the first of what became a series of over **100 Weeks of Prayer** for the World, which were convened in African and European countries. The author's first experience in his missionary career was to share in that first Week of Prayer.

1963 A small **Week of Prayer for the World** was arranged by Robert Footner and the author in **Nairobi, Kenya**. The pressing need for prayer information in written and visual form impelled me to compile some sheets of world facts and figures for use during that time. This was the forerunner of the present volume.

1964   Hans von Staden encouraged me to write a booklet with prayer information on 30 needy countries for use in subsequent Weeks of Prayer for the World. He suggested the title *Operation World*, which suitably expresses the vision of the book for spiritual warfare, active involvement and goal-oriented objectives we wanted to impart. That first publication was very simple and was produced on a Gestetner machine! It was later printed in West Germany.

1970   A new edition was proposed by Hans von Staden. I rashly said that any future edition would have to cover the world. I did not know what I was undertaking! The work began, using odd moments in a busy itinerant ministry of team evangelism and Bible translation in Zimbabwe (then Rhodesia). My office was the back of a van, or church vestries in dozens of towns and cities of that land. Two cardboard boxes served as a filing cabinet. There were frequent interruptions, mainly visits by African people seeking salvation or wanting to know more about the Christian life. My major problems were lack of any good missiological libraries and increasing postal isolation from the outside world. Rhodesia became ostracized by many countries around the world, and letters frequently had to be sent to informants via middlemen in other lands.

1974   The first full *Operation World* was lovingly and painstakingly typeset by the Dorothea Mission printer, **Kees Lugthart**. Unfortunately, it was not possible to sell the 3–4,000 copies that were printed. Nevertheless, copies of this book found their way around the world. **Dr Ralph Winter** in the USA arranged for a reprint in 1976 by the William Carey Library in an adapted form and under the title *World Handbook for the World Christian*.

1976   **Operation Mobilisation** became involved. **George Verwer** pressed for an updated version of the book. This was completed in Zimbabwe, and retyped and published by **STL Books (OM)** in Britain in 1978. The remarkable connection between the title of the book and that of the new publishers must have been planned by the Lord. It was certainly not premeditated.

1977   **Dave Hicks** of **OM**, then director of the MV *Logos*, was moved to condense the information from the 1974 edition to produce prayer cards on 52 needy nations. This has expanded into a ministry of challenge to Christians in about 20 languages which continued to this day. The number of prayer cards has increased to 74. A new set prepared with the information from this book is being published simultaneously with this edition.

1978   The multiplication of *Operation World* versions into other languages began. By 1986 editions had been published in German, French, Spanish, Portuguese and half the book in Korean. It is expected that the fifth edition may be translated into 8–10 languages. It has become a significant tool for mobilizing non-Western and non-English-speaking missions movements.

1979   Jill and I were released by the Dorothea Mission to become International Research Secretaries of WEC International based in the United Kingdom. We and our three children, Peter, Timothy and Ruth, travelled to Britain via the **OM** ship MV *Logos*, on which we ministered for a year in Asia and the Pacific. Timothy so appreciated this year that in 1993 he was in his third year serving on the sister ship MV *Doulos*.

1980–1993   This has been the most fulfilling and exciting period of our ministry as part of the leadership team of a large multi-national, multi-field mission agency committed to pioneer evangelism and church planting and part of an exciting restructuring and advance into many hitherto unreached areas. For six years Jill and I were also deputy leaders of WEC. It was within this context that the fourth and fifth editions have been written.

1990-1993   This has been the period over which the present edition has been written. Learning to use sophisticated technology and complex databases and communicating with over 220 lands has not been easy, especially with the rapid changes in our world during this period.

How can I thank all involved in such a complex operation?

1. **Our Research Office team**: My wife Jill, Robyn Erwin, David Phillips and Peter Yardley who tamed the vast flow of information; Margaret Bardsley, who typed the 650 or more pages of text and thousands of letters; John Bardsley who drew the maps; Marko Jauhiainen, whose programming delivered the results we needed; Darrell Dorr (**USCWM** and **Frontiers**), released one day/week for two years to assess information, edit and coordinate many aspects of the work; and also many others who gave days or weeks to help in the task.

2. **My WEC colleagues in the International Office** who lightened my administrative load to complete the book.

3. **Those who helped with computer programming and data entry.** The programming was started by Kathy Lannon of **Global Mapping International** with much of the data entry done by Sue Whitham (**SIM**) and John and Joan Woodman (**YWAM**), graciously released by their missions to help at critical junctures in the production of the book.

4. **Thousands of friends, advisers and information-providers** who supplied time and effort to fill information gaps and correct manuscripts.

May 1993   As this edition goes for publication, we send it out with fervent prayer that the Lord Jesus Christ may be glorified, the Church mobilized and world evangelization furthered. To him be all the praise, for it is only by his grace that the spiritual battles to bring this book to completion have been won.

Patrick Johnstone
WEC International
Gerrards Cross
Bucks SL9 8SZ
England

THE ETHOS OF *OPERATION WORLD*

There are certain fundamental assumptions I have made in compiling this book. I realize that I cannot satisfy all readers, but I trust that in this edition I have been more appreciative of other theological and political points of view. However, my own perspectives inevitably influence the selection of material and opinions expressed, and for these I must accept responsibility.

All views here expressed are my own and not necessarily those of the publishers or of any organization mentioned in this book. I value constructive advice for future revisions. However, I have made the following decisions:

1. **Readership.** I am writing for Bible-believing Christians who want to obey the last great command of the Lord Jesus by evangelizing the world. This means primarily Protestant Evangelical Christians (including Pentecostal and Charismatic Christians). However, I have received a number of letters from those of like persuasion in other Christian communions who lovingly suggested certain changes to make the book of wider appeal. I have sought to heed this plea without compromising my own theological position.

2. **Theology.** As an evangelical believer, I have sought to take a central position in more controversial issues that perplex Evangelicals, such as church government, baptism, the sovereignty of God, the work of the Holy Spirit and social involvement. The perceptive reader will, no doubt, see an unintended bias that reflects the author's own views.

3. **Politics.** I am a Western Christian and cannot divorce myself from the society of which I am a part. I am also a global Christian, so have sought as far as possible to write about each country with sensitivity as if I were of that country. However, I have had to make difficult decisions in referring to less good things in the political life of a country. How far does one condone perceived wrong for the sake of local sensitivities and the continuing ministry of the Lord's servants? Here I have sought to be balanced but probably have failed many times. My desire is that the book be of global value.

4. **Time validity.** The accelerating rate of change in the world can quickly date information. We have sought to cover events to April 1993 and for this edition to be valid through the '90s. I make no promises about a further edition but an AD2000 edition might be appropriate.

5. **An emphasis on the Church.** Early editions were rightly criticized for over-emphasizing mission agencies and the contribution of missionaries. I have sought to rectify this, but it is important to realize that it is often these very agencies that are the most efficient communicators of prayer information, hence the present system of highlighting mission initials. The churches planted by missions are often identified by the letters of that mission, but this does not signify continued mission control.

6. **The selection of agencies** mentioned is not intended to be a mark of validation or rejection. I have sought to draw attention to some of international and interdenominational interest to English-speaking readers. Hopefully, the other language versions will give greater place to agencies based in their own language areas.

7. **The burden.** My longing is that the book will be seen as a tool for prayer. The spiritual tone and vision that expresses the heart of our heavenly Father is what should be in the forefront. All other issues *must* be secondary.

PRAYER AND WORLD EVANGELIZATION

How often have you seen a wall-plaque with the words *Prayer Changes Things*? All believers readily give mental and verbal assent to this, but do we *really* believe it? What a difference there would be in our personal and corporate prayer life if we did. What a difference in the world too!

There is some confusion among believers about prayer. Is prayer just an act of obedience to a Sovereign God, or do we change his mind as did the importunate widow pleading her cause to the unjust judge? Unless we are utterly convinced of its essentiality and efficacy, we will never make prayer our central ministry as God intended.

Prayer is fundamental in the Kingdom of God. It is not an optional extra, nor is it a last resort when all other methods have failed. Prayerlessness is a sin (1 Samuel 12:23); without prayer God's plan for the world cannot be achieved. We do not just pray for the work; prayer is the work! Prayer lifts Christian activities from the realm of human effort to the divine. Someone made the statement *When man works*, man *works*; *when man prays*, God *works*. Through prayer we become co-workers with the Lord God Almighty. We move from time into eternity, sharing in the eternal counsels of God. Would that we could grasp the significance of the ministry of intercession! Some unusual Scriptures can help us.

In Revelation 5:1–8:5 there is the magnificent mystery of the opening of the seven seals. Whether their primary application is future, past or present is not relevant here, but certain principles are of abiding significance and can be applied today.

1. **Only the Lamb could open the seals.** All the earth-shaking, awesome forces unleashed on the world shown in the opening of the earlier six seals of Revelation 6 and 7 are released by the Lord Jesus Christ. He reigns today. He is in the control room of the universe. He is the only Ultimate Cause; all the sins of man and machinations of Satan ultimately have to enhance the glory and kingdom of our Saviour. This is true of our world today in wars, famines, earthquakes or the evil that apparently has the ascendancy. All God's actions are just and loving. We have become too enemy-conscious, and can overdo the spiritual warfare aspect of intercession. We need to be more God-conscious, so that we can laugh the laugh of faith *knowing* that we have power over all the power of the enemy (Luke 10:19). He has already lost control because of Calvary where the Lamb was slain. What confidence and rest of heart this gives us as we face a world in turmoil and in such spiritual need.

2. **Only through the prayers of the saints** will God's purposes be carried out (Revelation 5:8 and 8:1–5). The seventh seal, the final one, is unusual! Why was there silence in heaven for half an hour? It was not just for dramatic effect, or the silence before the storm. It was because God would not act until his people prayed. Once their prayers had risen to the throne, God poured out the fire from the altar upon the earth. The fire of the Spirit comes in answer to prayer (Acts 1:4, 2:1–8), but so does the fire of judgement. James and John wanted to call down fire from heaven on the Samaritans (Luke 9:54), but in rebuking them Jesus did not deny they could. How the Saviour longed to kindle that fire (Luke 12:49)! We now have that awesome authority as we pray in the Spirit! Let us use it.

As intercessors what power we wield! We reign in life with the Lord Jesus. He has raised us up to share his throne and his authority. From that vantage point we rejoice even as the earth-bound cry out their woes (Revelation 12:12). We have authority over Satan to thwart his plans, pull down his strongholds, release his captives. Our prayers change our world, open closed doors, make resistant people receptive, put down and raise up leaders and extend the kingdom of our Lord Jesus.

That fire we pray down mobilizes his Church, calls out labourers, empowers them for the ministry and brings in the missing disciples from peoples not yet represented before his throne (Revelation 7:9–10).

Is it any wonder the enemy would do all he can to distract or dismay us from commitment to intercession? Let us mobilize prayer! We can tip the scales of history. Christians can be the controlling factor in the unfolding drama of today's world. Let us not allow ourselves to be chased around by the enemy, but let us go up at once and take the kingdoms of this world for Jesus (Numbers 13:30; Daniel 7:18). He is delighted to give them to us (Daniel 7:22, 27; Luke 12:32).

In practical terms may these truths make our prayer lives as individuals and in prayer meetings outward-looking, Satan-shaking, captive-releasing, kingdom-taking, revival-giving, Christ-glorifying power channels for God!

Operation World is written to provide fuel for such prayer meetings. May fire from the altar fall on every place and people named in this volume.

Prayer not only changes things, situations and people. It also changes those who pray. Be open to all that God may say to you as an individual or as a church. You may have the privilege of becoming the answer to your own prayers. In Matthew 9:35–38 Jesus challenged his disciples to pray for labourers to be thrust out into the harvest. At the beginning of the next chapter they themselves were called to go. My prayer is that many of you may be changed through praying through this book – and many go as witnesses to those who have never heard of the Lord Jesus Christ.

HOW TO USE *OPERATION WORLD*

The book is written for two main purposes:

1. **To inform for prayer**; so the whole layout of the book is in the form of a prayer diary, with a section of prayer requests assigned for each day of the year.

2. **To mobilize for witness**; so information and relevant statistics are given to channel that witness to the least reached parts and peoples of our world. For many Christians this book is the only source of global information they will ever see. Earlier editions have become an essential resource for the growing missions movement around the world – in a particular way this has been true of the non-English editions.

Here are some suggestions on how to use this book. Otherwise the number of pages, size of print and the 5,000 or so prayer requests could overwhelm you!

In private

1. Pray through the book using the running calendar, perhaps taking one or two items only which the Holy Spirit lays on your heart. Why not mark those items covered in prayer and then later make note of God's answers?

2. Keep the book near your television, radio or newspaper. When news comes of major events in a far-off land, find out the spiritual dimensions and turn secular news into spiritual dynamite.

3. Use it together with prayer letters and mission magazines. Often the larger context is lacking – may the information in this book put depth and perspective into your intercession.

In the family

1. Read a small section at the meal table and pray for the country of the day. Why not use my wife's book *You Can Change The World* if you have younger children? It is written for 8–12-year-olds as a beautifully designed prayer diary.

2. The book can be the source of informative fun and quiz games and make missions meaningful in a roundabout way.

In your church

Missions and prayer for the world should be at the heart of every fellowship. This is sadly often not the case. *Operation World* can help to give praise and prayer points that stimulate this.

1. **In church services.** Use prayer items in the intercessory period in worship services. We have also produced numerous maps, diagrams and photographs on overhead transparencies which may help in this. Please refer to the last pages in the book which tell how you may obtain these.

2. **Prayer meetings.** Wise use of the information in this book can stimulate more informed prayer for the world and for your mission outreach.

3. **Church bulletins and magazines.** Use quotes from relevant sections of the book to gain interest and prayer. Please quote the source – perhaps for your own protection!

In teaching on missions

Some Bible schools have made praying through the book an obligatory part of their course. Many instructors have used it for teaching on missions. Many Christians have been led into specific missionary service as a result.

For Christian research

There is unique information contained in this book and much can be gleaned and moulded into new ways of expressing the world's need or the Church's growth. As a further help, Global Mapping International have published an electronic version of the book which will enable:

1. **Text searching, text retrieval** and printing in other documents; also access from the text into more detailed information in the databases.

2. **Database access.** All the sources and underlying data on which the facts of this book are based are made available in unique databases which include data on:
a) the world's denominations (over 5,500 denominations and information covering 30 years).
b) the world's missions and missionaries (over 4,100 missions mentioned by name with 16,600 entries for missionaries in specific countries).
c) the world's religions (between AD 1900 and AD 2000 as percentages and numbers for each country and region of the world).
d) relevant secular data for each country of the world: area, population, literacy, etc.

3. **Mapping facility.** Selecting data for inclusion on world and regional maps on screen or for printing.

Please look at the back of the book for more details.

For use in Prayer Days, Conferences, Concerts for Prayer, Praying through the 10/40 Window (see p. 27), etc.

The original purpose of this book was to provide prayer fuel for weeks of prayer for the world. Here are a few guidelines for prayer session leaders:

1. **Be brief.** The people are gathered to *pray* and not to be impressed by the amount of information presented. Only a quarter to one-third of the time should be set aside for reporting on the need.

2. **Be personal.** I have deliberately refrained from mentioning individuals, but rather have given the overall situation in a country. Personal information on individual workers and specific situations may be added by the leader.

3. **Be selective.** Too many facts will not be retained unless they are written down. Rather select those items for prayer that will challenge and burden believers long after the meeting.

4. **Be careful with statistics**: too many figures make any report very dull! This is why the statistical sections are in a smaller type. Only choose those statistics that specifically apply to the prayer items you mention. The many figures are given so that you may have the facts available.

5. **Be dependent on the leading of the Holy Spirit.** The burdens imparted by him will inspire others to pray in the Spirit and move them into God's will for their lives. This could mean commitment in intercession, financial giving, or going to a particular area or people for which prayer has been made.

Other resources

1. **Operation Mobilisation** have produced a new set of prayer cards based on the information in this edition. Why not order a set? Use the OM Publishing address at the front of the book.

2. **OM Publishing** have also a superb world map especially designed for use with *Operation World*.

EXPLANATION OF THE STATISTICS AND ABBREVIATIONS

The purpose of this book is to inspire God's people to prayer and action to change our world. Statistics are an important support in this in providing solid factual basis for action. In this I believe I am entirely scriptural. I follow in the footsteps of Moses, Joshua, Ezekiel, Luke and John in giving meticulous and carefully compiled statistics.

This book's description of each region and country is divided into two parts:

1. The two columns of statistical background information.

2. The specific items for prayer.

The statistics are included as background to the prayer information, hence the difference in type size.

A brief explanation of their significance is given below. A fuller explanation of the sources and how these figures were handled is given in appendices 6 and 7.

Availability, consistency and accuracy of secular, religious and Christian statistics vary enormously from country to country and among denominations. Some denominations do not even keep statistics. Inadequate sources, varying dates of publication and my further editing and compiling of the statistics all add to the margin of error. I have used the most recent and reliable information available to me. I therefore plead for the sympathy of the reader in any errors or discrepancies discovered. **Please send any corrections for inclusion in future editions to me at the address at the end of the *Preface*.**

My prayer is that these statistics may present a balanced account of what God is doing in our world and the extent of the unfinished task. I am only too aware of the many gaps in my knowledge and of statistics I was never able to locate.

Below is an explanation of how each category of statistics is handled in the order used throughout the book.

My statistical base date is June 1990. Most of the statistics used are compiled from data gathered between 1988 and 1993. Where no statistics were available I have had to extrapolate from earlier figures or make estimates. There is not the space to indicate dates and sources for each figure, but much of this is available in the electronic version of *Operation World*. (Please see the last pages of this book concerning its availability.)

Area in square kilometres. This is rounded to the nearest 1,000 sq.km in all but the smaller territories. The area given does not imply approval or disapproval of the *status quo* in April 1993, but is a reflection of the actual situation. Disputed territories, such as the West Bank of the Jordan (Palestine) and the Falkland Islands (Malvinas), are in this category; the West Bank and the Falklands are respectively included under Israel and as a British colony.

Population: Figures given for 1990 and 1995. Populations given rounded to the nearest 100,000 except for small states. Average annual growth rates for the previous five years are given in the second column, and population density in people/sq.km is given in the third column.

Peoples: The ethnic diversity is listed in a manner considered to be the most helpful for the reader.

1. Major groupings of peoples are given as a **percentage** of the country's total population. The larger ethnic groups within those groupings are

given in **absolute numbers**, and are valid for June 1990.

2. Smaller peoples are not mentioned by name unless there is a particular challenge or point of wider interest.

3. **The total number of ethno-linguistic peoples** given in the country text is derived from my own sources. Those in the regional tables (pages 20–81) are derived from more recent information gathered by David Barrett and made available shortly before this book went to press. There are therefore some discrepancies. In both sets of tallies, the totals represent the sum total of all identifiable **ethno-linguistic peoples within a country**. For instance, the Tamil are counted 23 times in the global totals because Tamil communities exist in at least 23 countries, likewise the Kurds 20 times, the Soninke of West Africa six times.

4. Refugees and temporarily resident communities are often listed but not included in national percentages.

Literacy: The highest publicized figure is given. **Functional literacy** may be much lower.

Official languages were those known to be recognized as such in June 1990.

All languages: This represents the total of all indigenous languages spoken within each nation. The figure is quoted from the *Ethnologue* (**SIL**) unless fuller information was available elsewhere.

Languages with Scriptures: The number of languages in which there is a full Bible (Bi), or only a New Testament (NT), or just portions (por) is given. Adding these three figures together and subtracting the total from the number of languages can give an approximate indication of the need for further translation ministry. Further information on translation needs is given in the points for prayer.

Capitals and cities: Statistics were derived from a number of sources. As far as possible, the conurbation figure is given and not just the population that may live within specific municipal boundaries. The figures given are often significantly higher than those officially quoted. Most world-class cities are mentioned by name, i.e. those with populations that exceed one million.

Economy:

1. **Public debt/person** represents the total public debt in US dollars divided by the population.

2. **Income/person** is the gross national product (GNP) in US dollars divided by the population. This is also given as a percentage of the USA figure. This gives a rough indication of living standards, but is not an indication of purchasing power within the country. Other more efficient indicators of this were not available to me when I started the writing of this book.
Comparing public debt/person with income/person is an indication of the health of the economy. If the former is close to or greater than the latter, the economy could be in serious problems.

Politics: The brief comments are intended to be aids to prayer and not a full political assessment. It is hopefully not too biased by the author's own viewpoint.

Religion:

1. **Non-Christian religions** are listed either in size or importance depending on the local situation.

2. **Six ecclesiological types of Christians** have been used: Protestant, Roman Catholic, Other Catholic, Orthodox, Foreign marginal, Indigenous marginal. Use of computer databases to derive the denominational tables and ease of layout and reading made it preferable to list them in this order irrespective of size. See Appendix 6 for explanation on why I have used a broad definition of "Christian" – for instance, even including Mormons.

3. **The percentage of Christians** represents the total number who are claimed to be Christian, either by individuals themselves in a government census, or by the churches to which they are affiliated, whichever percentage is the larger being the figure used.

4. Where the official or estimated percentage is higher than that claimed by the churches, both **professing** and **affiliated** percentages are given. If the difference is significant that is indicated as a **nominal** percentage.

5. The **professing** Christian percentage is the first percentage (if given) of each of the six ecclesiological types. The **affiliated** Christian percentage is the second percentage and is the percentage of the population of the final denominational total given at the end of the denominational list.

6. **Double counting** can seriously distort totals. Where this is known to be a factor a subtraction total is given to allow for those who have changed religion or denomination but are counted by both. This is an attempt to simplify the methodology of the *World Christian Encyclopedia*.

7. **Church attendance** is emphasized by saturation church planting (the **DAWN** movement) as a more objective way of measuring growth and commitment. At first I sought to include these figures throughout, but the inconsistency of results and the paucity of countries with such figures forced me to abandon this as a consistent practice. However, where possible I have given an **attendance** percentage as a percentage of the total population.

8. **Growth rates** are frequently given and represent average annual growth between 1985 and 1990.

9. **Denominational listings** contain a representative selection of the larger denominations with:
a) **number of congregations** (with widely differing denominational differences in what constitutes a congregation).
b) adult baptized/confirmed **members** (the figure usually used by Baptists, Pentecostals and Free Churches).
c) **Affiliated** – the whole Christian community, inclusive membership, which includes children, non-member adherents, etc. This is the figure usually used by Catholic, Anglican, Lutheran and many Reformed Churches.
I have sought to cross-calculate a derivation for all three figures when only one or two are given so that meaningful comparisons and totals can be made. I have also had to make projections to 1990 for denominations where recent statistics were not available. See a fuller explanation in Appendix 6, and all details in the electronic edition of *Operation World* (see last page of book).

10. **Evangelical** percentages for 1960–1990 and charismatic percentages for 1990 are carefully derived according to the methodology described in Appendix 6. The degree of accuracy is reduced and

assessment more subjective in lands where there are large state or traditional churches to which a majority of the population belongs (e.g. Scandinavia).

11. **Indentation** has been made for each sub-set. For instance, each ecclesiological family is a sub-set of Christianity, Evangelicals a sub-set of Protestants and Pentecostals (and Charismatics) a sub-set of Evangelicals.

12. **Missionary statistics** have been compiled after considerable effort to scour the world, so included here is a fairly comprehensive totalling of the global missionary force. Each country has a total for missionaries received and sent as well as the number of agencies involved. We have sought to overcome widely differing definitions of what constitutes a missionary so that like can be compared with like. This is how we have sought to do this:

frn. All missionaries serving in other lands whether cross-cultural or working among expatriate communities. This is the commonly used definition in North America.

xcul. All missionaries serving cross-culturally, whether at home or abroad. This is a more commonly used European and Latin American definition.

dom. All with an apostolic (missionary) calling to evangelize and plant churches in the same or a related culture. This is generally used in Africa and Asia.

The total missionary force = *xcul* + *dom*.

For the first time this enables us to give more objective figures for the world's missionary numbers and compare the growing non-Western missions movement with the older Western movements.

See Appendices 3 and 5 for a fuller analysis.

13. **Organizational abbreviations.**
a) Those in **bold type** are the 120 or more agencies for which we have given contact addresses. A fuller list of agencies with addresses is available in the electronic version of *Operation World*.
b) A full list of agency and other abbreviations used in the book is given in Appendices 2 and 4.

The graphs:

These tell a fascinating story of growth and decline in the world's religions and also of Evangelicals. Some have asked for explanations of the changes. Space unfortunately forbids!

1. **Religious changes**

The purpose of the graph is to show the growth of the missionary religions over this century.

Non-Christian religions and ideologies are shown from the **top downwards**.

Major Christian traditions are shown from the bottom upwards. Where the number of Christians

is very small, only the total Christian population is given.

Usually the population from where most converts are being drawn is indicated in the middle.

The smaller portions in between indicate the total of either non-Christian (unshaded) or Christian religions or traditions (black) too small in percentage to be of significance in the graph. Please refer to the accompanying statistics for that country to identify them.

Key to the figures:

The time scale on the bottom line is 1900–2000.

1990 is the year for which the statistics in this book are valid. 1990–2000 represents projections through that period.

The right-hand vertical scale allows the proportion of the major religious groups to be seen in comparison with each other, and as a percentage of the country's total population.

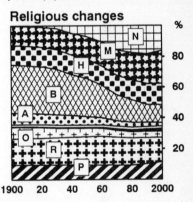

Religious changes

Key to shading

Non-Christian

N Non-religious/other

M Muslim

H Hindu

B Buddhist/Chinese/
   Japanese religions

J Jews

A Traditional religions/
   Animist/Spiritist/etc.

   Various, Other

Christian

S Marginal, Sects

O Orthodox

R Roman Catholic

P Protestant

   Christian (general)

The letter on the graph will help identify the religion without referring constantly to this key. It is usually the **first** letter of the religion listed under the **Religion** section. Only the more significant religions are shaded and labelled.

2. Evangelicals

The growth of **affiliated** evangelical Protestants is always given (not members, so as to compare percentages with other religions).

Frequently the growth of Evangelicals who are members of Pentecostal denominations is also given.

Occasionally another growing group or religion is given for comparison – usually Jehovah's Witnesses or Mormons.

The time scale is *different* from the Religions graph and only covers 1960–2000, the period of the most dramatic change in history for Evangelicals.

The percentage of the population indicated *varies* between countries, so carefully note the scale on the right-hand side before comparisons are made.

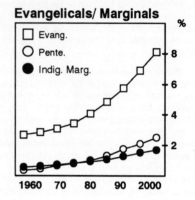

Evangelicals/ Marginals

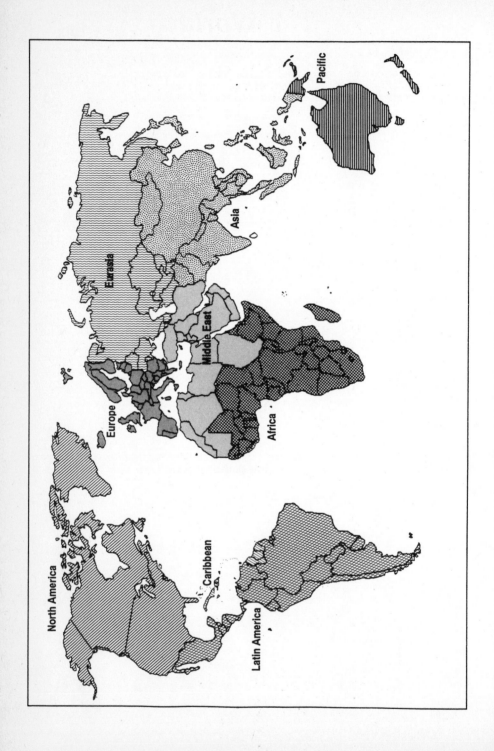

The World

The map on the opposite page shows the regions of the world as used in this book. These regions are not identical to the commonly accepted continents, which are a purely geographical concept. The regions here are classified according to socio-political commonalities that link the nations of each shaded area.

Area 135,294,000 sq.km excluding the 14 million sq.km of Antarctica.

There are 237 countries and territories listed in this book. Their populations vary greatly; see diagram below.

Region	Population in millions 1990	1995	Affiliated Christian Percentages Total	Prot	Evang	Total No. of Peoples	Peoples in Region World A	B	C
AFRICA	480.8	557.9	48.1	20.2	13.2	3,168	1,074	975	1,119
ASIA	2,940.3	3,209.3	7.3	3.9	3.1	2,658	1,607	503	548
CARIBBEAN	35.3	37.8	69.2	16.5	11.1	287	15	83	189
EURASIA	280.6	290.5	45.8	1.1	0.9	596	306	104	186
EUROPE	507.9	514.8	77.2	18.3	2.8	1,083	120	176	787
LATIN AMERICA	412.7	455.8	90.9	12.1	11.1	1,233	96	261	876
MIDDLE EAST	330.8	378.1	4.6	0.6	0.4	889	558	159	172
NORTH AMERICA	276.6	284.8	70.7	40.6	27.9	427	28	48	351
PACIFIC	26.5	28.4	66.8	37.0	15.8	1,533	111	237	1,185
WORLD	5,291.7	5,757.3	30.1	9.2	5.7	11,874	3,915	2,546	5,413

World A The unevangelized/unreached world where %E < 50% for constituent peoples.
World B The evangelized non-Christian world where %E > 50% and All Christians < 60%.
World C The broadly Christian world where All Christians in people are > 60%.
See Appendix 5 for fuller definitions.

Population:

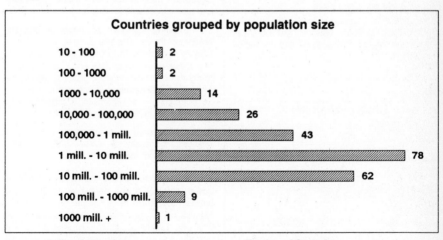

Countries grouped by population size

Population size	Number of Countries
10 - 100	2
100 - 1000	2
1000 - 10,000	14
10,000 - 100,000	26
100,000 - 1 mill.	43
1 mill. - 10 mill.	78
10 mill. - 100 mill.	62
100 mill. - 1000 mill.	9
1000 mill. +	1

Population (in millions)		Ann.Growth	Density
1950	2,516	1.73%	18.6/sq.km
1955	2,752	1.79%	20.3/sq.km
1960	3,019	1.86%	22.3/sq.km
1965	3,329	1.99%	24.6/sq.km
1970	3,690	2.06%	27.3/sq.km
1975	4,068	1.96%	30.1/sq.km
1980	4,436	1.73%	32.8/sq.km
1985	4,838	1.74%	35.8/sq.km
1990	5,292	1.74%	39.1/sq.km
1995	5,757	1.73%	42.8/sq.km
2000	6,236	1.63%	46.1/sq.km

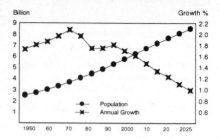

World Population 1950 - 2025

See p 108 for comparison of populations and growth rates between continental regions.

Peoples: For 20 years Christian researchers have argued and speculated on the definition of a people or people group, how many there are, and how many are unreached. Approximate figures were given in the 1986 *Operation World*. These have been refined and defined more accurately but are in broad agreement with the 1986 figures. They are derived from the Global Evangelization Database. See definitions and sources in Appendices.

Ethno-linguistic peoples 11,874.
  in World A (least evangelized) 3,915.
  in World B (evangelized non-Christians) 2,546.
  in World C (Christians) 5,413.

Their distribution in the world's regions are shown in the table above and graphs on pages 27 and 113. By using other narrower criteria of dialect, district and sub-grouping other researchers give estimates of the number of ethno-linguistic peoples as high as 24,000, but no list of the larger estimate exists.

Languages of the world 6,528.
Languages with Scriptures: total 1,964 in 1990; 276Bi 676NT 1,012por. *Note: In mid-1993, the Scriptures in the 2000th language were published by the **UBS**.*

Languages without Scriptures: 4,564.

Definite need	925
Needing revision	58
Probable need	227
Possible need	2,465
Unlikely need	100
Adequately bilingual	266
Nearly extinct	336
Other categories	187

Languages with translation in progress 1,199. See diagrams on Bible translation on page 117. See also more detailed graph on translation needs on p 134.

Global literacy 79%. This means that there are over 1.1 billion illiterates in the world.

Cities: World-class cities are defined as those of over one million inhabitants. There are 305 of these. This survey uses the (generally) higher figure for conurbations (i.e. satellite cities and suburbs) rather than the more strictly defined metropolitan areas. **Urbanization** 43%.

Significant politico-economic trends in the '90s and their implications for God's Kingdom.

1. **The ending of global super-power politics.** The collapse of the USSR is also being accompanied by USA retrenchment. The division of the world into two major power blocs has ended and a major realignment of the world's nations will gather momentum. US decline is in part due to economic developments – it will mean a proportionately smaller US contribution to world missions.

2. **Unprecedented uncertainty** with rapid changes, multiplicity of ethnic conflicts, border changes, and yet more new nations.

3. **The emergence of new economic and political power blocs** with the danger of protectionism between them – the EC in Europe, NAFTA in North America, the Muslim nations of the Middle East, East Asia with a dominant Japan. The emergence of a powerful and economically strong China within 10 years is a big unknown factor. This may force a greater regionalization of missions because of greater mobility within these blocs and visa restrictions between them.

4. **The Middle East** becoming once more centre-

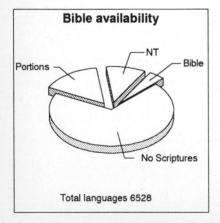

Bible availability

NT
Bible
Portions
No Scriptures

Total languages 6528

stage in the world. So much is bound up in the future of Jerusalem.

5. **The decade of unsettled politics** and possibly civil and national wars between the constituent nations of the former Communist bloc. Yugoslavia's bloody breakup could be only a beginning of sorrows. This has big implications for missions planning.

6. **The poor south** which is likely to become poorer and even more marginalized because of the richer north's control of electronic knowledge and communications. The increase in famines, diseases (including AIDS, malaria, tuberculosis) is likely to continue – particularly affecting Africa.

7. **Migrations of peoples** from poorer or war-torn areas to those with more wealth or relative peace; these will increase more than in the '80s.

The world's crises will be God's opportunities, the world's pain the opening for showing God's love.

Religion: There have been dramatic changes in religious profession during the 20th century. Graphs below and interspersed through the book indicate this. See graphs on p 159, 183 & 319.

Muslim 19.6%. 1,035 million. Most live in the great belt of territory stretching from West Africa to central and southeast Asia. It is the majority religion of 43 states and territories, over 10% of a further 31, and over 1% in 49 others. Growth 2.9% – significantly higher than global growth rates and increasing Islam from 12.4% of the world's population in 1900 to 19.6% in 1993. Growth has been largely through high birthrates but also through conversions, mainly in parts of Africa and Indonesia. Growth in the Americas, Europe and Pacific is almost entirely due to immigration. See graphs on p 159, 319 & 431.

Non-religious/other 18.3%. 969 million. Growth averaged 4.5% between 1960 and 1985 through secularization in the West and atheism propagated in the Communist world. The return of millions in the former Communist world to Christianity or other religions has halted this growth for a time. See graphs on p 159, 319 & 431.

Hindu 13.5%. 716 million. The majority religion of three nations, and a significant minority in 11 other lands. Hinduism has made notable missionary inroads in the West through the wide acceptance of transcendental meditation, Yoga, New Age thinking, sects such as Hare Krishna and Indian *gurus* who have gained significant followings among young people. Growth 2%. See graph on p 159.

Buddhist/Eastern religions 11.6%. 613 million. Buddhism is the state religion of five nations in Asia, the majority in a further four, and a significant minority in yet another 11. Over half of this total are followers of the mixture of the Chinese religions Taoism, Confucianism and Buddhism. The various religious systems are so intermingled that a clear differentiation is hard to make. Growth 2.1%; after years of gradual decline, the discrediting of Communism has caused a resurgence of these religions in China, Mongolia, Cambodia and Vietnam.

Animist/spiritist/traditional religions 2.7%. 144 million. Tribal religions decreasing, spiritism worldwide increasing. Overall growth 0.2%. In 1900, Animists were 7.4% of the world's population.

Sikh 0.3%. 17.2 million. Growth 2.3%. Mainly in India; many migrants in Britain and Canada.

Jews 0.25%. 13.4 million. Growth −1.3%. Major losses through the Holocaust, secularization and conversion to Christianity. In 1900, Jews were 0.8% of the world's population with a total of 12.2 million. Nearly 27% of Jews now live in Israel – increasing rapidly with immigration from the former USSR.

Baha'i 0.09%. Five million. A syncretic amalgam of Islam and other world religions. Declining in Middle East where it originated. A missionary religion that is expanding elsewhere. Growth 5.5%.

Other 0.8%. Numerous other religions. 48 million. Mainly new religious movements, also Jain 3.5 million, Parsee 170,000 and others.

Christian 32.8%. 1,734 million. Growth 2.3%. A majority in seven of the nine regions in this book and in 149 states and territories; over 10% in a further 23; over 1% in a further 35. Only in 29 states and territories is Christianity less than 1% of the population. Christianity has truly become a world religion in this century. Only a small proportion of this number would actually be born-again Christians, but God alone knows how many. The Lamb's book of life would make fascinating reading! Affiliated 30.1%. Growth 2.7%.

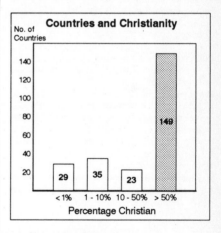

Countries and Christianity

Protestant 10.3%. 543 million. Protestants are in a majority in 43 states and territories, over 10% in a further 70, over 1% in another 69. Growth 3.3%. In the 1980s the growth of Protestantism in Latin America, Africa and Asia exceeded that of the decline in the West, giving a significant growth increase. Affiliated 9.2%. 488 million. Growth 3.5%. Evangelical growth 5.4% and Pentecostal growth 8.1% are significantly higher and are the fastest-growing major religious groupings in the world. See diagrams on pages 159, 183 & 254.

Missionaries in the world 138,492. 76,120frn 83,465xcul 55,027dom. (1:3,500 Protestants) in

2,576 agencies. See Appendix 3 for a full listing and graphs on pages 513 & 601.

Roman Catholic 16.8%. 892 million. Roman Catholics are strongest in Europe and Latin America, but losses to secularism in Europe and Protestants in Latin America have reduced the world Catholic percentage from 18.7% in 1960 to 16.8% in 1990. Growth 1.3%. In 1981 the number of Muslims surpassed that of the Catholics. Roman Catholics are a majority in 66 states and territories, more than 10% in a further 70 and over 1% in another 55. Affiliated 15.7%. 830 million. Growth 1.2%. Catholic Charismatics are hard to estimate, but there are possibly about 10 million active Catholic Charismatics, and a further 60 million post-Charismatics (those no longer actively involved in Charismatic gatherings). There is also a growing movement of Evangelical Catholics – involving anything from five to 20 million Catholics. See definitions in Appendix 5 & p 455.

Missionaries in the world 266,025. These figures are based on a variety of sources spread over 20 years, so are both partial and too high. There has been an overall decline in missionary workers.

Other Catholic 0.2%. 9.7 million. Breakaway denominations from the Roman Catholic Church. Growth 0.8%. Affiliated 0.18%. 9.4 million. Growth 1.2%.

Orthodox 4.1%. 215 million. A majority in 10 states and territories. Over 10% in a further 14 and over 1% in another 28. The majority of Orthodox are in Eurasia, central Europe, Middle East and Ethiopia. Growth 3.3%. Gradual decline as a percentage of world population until 1989 when possibly up to 20 million or more Slavic and other peoples returned to the faith of their forebears following the demise of Communism. Affiliated 3.8%. 200 million. Growth 7%. See graph on p 191.

Marginal groups 1.4%. 74 million. Growth 6.9% Affiliated 1.3%. 67 million. Diverse Western and non-Western marginal groups are included. World-wide movements of Western origin, such as the Mormons and Jehovah's Witnesses, and syncretic African groups are the largest. Between 1990 and 1992 Jehovah's Witnesses grew at 9.3% annually, and between 1981 and 1990 Mormons grew at 4.6% – but outside North America the growth rate was 11.3%, especially in the Pacific.

Church groupings

Church groupings	Cong	Members	Affiliated
Protestant	1,633,000	240,200,000	488,400,000
Evangelical 5.7% of pop		149,400,000	303,700,000
Pentecostal 1.8% of pop		43,100,000	93,100,000
Charismatic 1.2% of pop		30,800,000	65,200,000
Catholic (Latin & Eastern)	353,000	496,300,000	830,400,000
Charismatic		est. 5,700,000	9,700,000
Evangelical		est. 5,000,000	9,000,000
Other Catholic	13,000	5,400,000	9,400,000
Orthodox	93,000	131,000,000	200,000,000
Marginal	200,000	43,200,000	66,600,000
Total	2,292,000	916,100,000	1,594,800,000

Religious changes

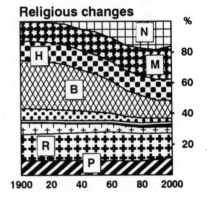

Evangelicals/ Marginals

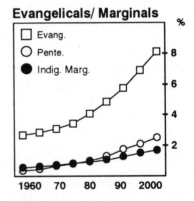

☐ Evang.
◯ Pente.
● Indig. Marg.

THE WORLDWIDE ADVANCE OF THE GOSPEL
Praise points and answers to prayer

The visual media have served to erode the faith of believers in God's present sovereignty in the world. Television cameramen, like vultures, swoop on the wars, famines, disasters and tragedies of this world. The beautiful, wholesome and good is less camera-worthy, so what God does and what God's servants are achieving are rarely noticed.

The view from a heavenly vantage point is very different! There is a titanic struggle going on in the heavenlies between the forces of the Lord Jesus and the hosts of darkness, and the effects in our world are dramatic. Yet the victory has already been won on the Cross. There are many evidences given in subsequent pages. Here are some of global significance. May these build up faith for the pulling down of spiritual strongholds that still resist the King of kings and Lord of lords.

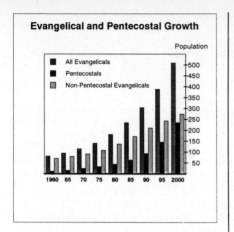

Evangelical and Pentecostal Growth

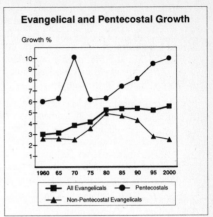

Evangelical and Pentecostal Growth

See graph on page 486 for regional distribution of Evangelicals and Pentecostals.

1. **The unprecedented harvest being won.** We are living in the time of the largest ingathering of people into the Kingdom of God that the world has ever seen. The information gathered for this edition reveals the astonishing growth in Africa and Asia today which more than counterbalances the serious decline in the Western world.

2. **The globalization of Christianity.** The growth in Eurasia, Asia and Africa has been such that the centre of gravity of Christianity moved away from the West in the early '70s. By 1985 that growth had even begun to compensate for the overall decline in Christianity between 1960 and 1985 as a percentage of the world's population. In 1960, about 58% of professing Christians lived in the West (Europe, North America and the Pacific). By 1990 this had fallen to 38% and by 2000 it will probably be 31%. See accompanying diagram.

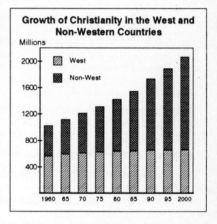

Growth of Christianity in the West and Non-Western Countries

3. **Evangelical growth.** This has been more dramatic. The post-war surge of evangelical mission thrusts has borne much fruit. In the West there has been a slow, but steady growth in contrast to the decline of the Church in general. In the so-called mission fields it has been a different story. Note the curves in the graphs below.

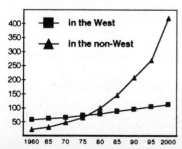

Number of Evangelicals in millions in the West and non-West

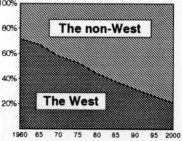

% of World's Evangelicals

a) Evangelicals in the West (North America, Europe and Pacific) grew from 57.7 million in 1960 to 95.9 million in 1990 with an average annual growth of 1.7%. In the rest of the world, the 1960 total of Evangelicals of 29 million grew to 208 million in 1990 – an average annual growth of 6.8%.

b) Overall Evangelical growth for the world averaged 4.5% annually. However, that rate reached a peak in the '80s at 5.4%, mainly because of the growth of Christianity in China.

c) Nearly 70% of the world's Evangelicals now live in the non-Western world and this is likely to rise to 77% by the end of the century.

4. **Pentecostal growth.** This has been even more spectacular. Lack of data makes it difficult to give reliable growth rates for the phenomenal growth of Charismatic Christianity, so these figures only cover Pentecostal denominations. In 1960 Pentecostals were 11 million (14% of all Evangelicals); by 1990 they reached 93 million. This is nearly 31% of all Evangelicals; but this rises to 52% if Charismatic Christians in other denominations are added. The average growth over these 30 years was 7.4%. The graph above tells the story. The most remarkable growth has been in Latin America where nearly 40% of the world's Pentecostals live. See graph on p 486.

5. **The manifest failure of human ideologies**, which became more obvious in the '80s.

a) **The collapse of Communism** as a global threat, and the bankruptcy of atheism has caused an unprecedented turning to Christ in answer to prayer.

b) **Fundamentalist Islam** has gained in political power and its ability to cause havoc in the world through subversion and sometimes terrorism, but has lost credibility in the minds of many Muslims (many of whom are becoming secularized). As a result many have become more open to the gospel and to receive Christ despite the danger. The last 15 years has been a time of more Muslims coming to Christ than ever before in history. These are the beginnings of what we believe could be a flood – if it is to be demonstrated Jesus is Lord even over Islam.

c) **The Buddhist world** has long proved a tough challenge with few major breakthroughs, but the rising tide of interest and concern for the Buddhist heartlands of Tibet and Mongolia is bearing fruit. Mongolia has opened and Tibet is increasingly surrounded – north, south and east – by an active Christian witness. Communism has been a means for preparing many Asian Buddhist cultures for the coming of the gospel.

6. **The globalization of the missions vision.** For the first time we have attempted a global synthesis of differing statistics of the Protestant missions force so that comparable totals could be derived to measure the growth of the world's missionary force.

See the statistics above and in Appendix 3, also the graphs on page 513 and page 601.

7. **The progress towards completion of world evangelization.** Much remains to be done, but the build-up of momentum is breathtaking.

a) **Global information** on the growth of the church and the extent of the unreached world has never before been so widely available.

b) **Global presence of churches and agencies** means that there are relatively few areas and peoples geographically distant from a Christian presence – though cultural and social barriers to acceptance may be high.

c) **Closing doors of the '70s and '80s are proving to be revolving doors!** In opening former Communist lands the biggest problem is not so much recruitment of workers but how to get the multiplicity of ministries to work together!

For the first time in history we can meaningfully talk of the real possibility of world evangelization in our generation. What a privilege, what a responsibility to be a Christian alive today!

THE WORLD EVANGELIZED
A Realizable Goal

Only a few broad outlines can be given, but there has been much progress towards the two major goals given to us by the Lord Jesus Christ:

1. The evangelistic challenge of Mark 16:15 to preach the gospel to every creature.

2. The discipling/church-planting challenge of Matthew 28:18–20 to make disciples from every nation (people) and to baptize and teach them.

Jesus gave the promise in Matthew 24:14 that when this task was accomplished, the end would come.

A growing number of Christians are committed to achieve this, if possible, by the year 2000. The AD2000 and Beyond Movement has the rallying cry:

A church for every people
and
the gospel for every person
by AD2000.

This is a close approximation to the Great Commission challenges of the Lord Jesus.

How close are we to achieving these goals?

The evangelistic commission.

How can exposure to the gospel be measured? Over the years Dr David Barrett and others have constructed models to assess this. All professing Christians are, by definition, evangelized even if many are deficient in understanding of the gospel. Exposure of non-Christians is derived by carefully assessing the extent and range of ministries directed towards their evangelization and thereby determining the percentage likely to have been exposed to the gospel. This is the %E used in the above world table and subsequent regional tables.

Almost all peoples of "World A" live in the band of territory extending from West Africa's Atlantic Coast through the Middle East and Asia to the Pacific Ocean, or have migrated from that area to other more evangelized parts of the world – for instance, Muslims moving to Europe. I have earlier described this as the **Resistant Belt**. It has been more recently described and popularized as the **10/40 Window** (the area of Africa and Asia between the 10th and 40th degrees of latitude). See map on page 82.

Depending on strictness of criteria used, we estimate that between 15% and 25% of the world's population is beyond the reach of the present proclamation of the gospel. This means that between 800 million and 1,300 million people still need to be given their first opportunity to respond to the gospel.

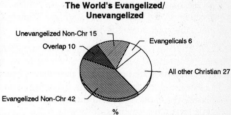

The World's Evangelized/ Unevangelized

Unevangelized Non-Chr 15
Overlap 10
Evangelicals 6
All other Christian 27
Evangelized Non-Chr 42
%

The discipling/church-planting commission.

For years there has been intense discussion among Christian researchers about definitions, categories and actual numbers of peoples and how far they have been reached (see Appendix 5). Below is a diagrammatic representation of the peoples table on p 21.

Revelation 7:9–10 tells us that there must be redeemed representatives of every race, tribe, people and tongue before the Throne of the Lamb. God alone knows when this *minimum* requirement is achieved. For us, a measurable minimum goal would therefore be at least one or two visible, functioning, viable, witnessing churches for every one of these peoples.

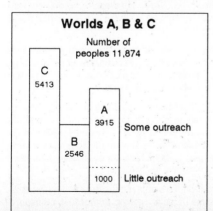

Worlds A, B & C

Number of peoples 11,874

C 5413

A 3915 Some outreach

B 2546

1000 Little outreach

Total peoples 11,874. A large proportion of these peoples are named in the Countries section of the book.

World A represents peoples less than 50% evangelized.
World B represents evangelized non-Christians: those peoples with a large proportion of non-Christians and also a significant Christian Church within their cultures.
World C represents Christianized peoples – those with over 60% professing Christian.

Pray for:

1. **The speediest possible completion of the goals given by the Lord Jesus to his Church.**

2. **All churches to make obedience to the Great Commission their primary ministry objective.** Only through this will the resources be available to bring the task to conclusion, or *closure*, in our generation.

3. **All leadership training institutions and programmes** to ensure that missions be a fundamental and essential core component of every course. It is failure to do this that has caused the centuries of neglect and marginalization of world evangelization in churches and agencies.

4. **Mission agency** prayer, planning and deployment to emphasize reaching unreached areas, peoples and cities. The Adopt-a-People Clearinghouse and the AD2000 and Beyond Movement have compiled a list of over 6,000 unreached and adoptable peoples submitted by agencies as targeted for entry. Many are those included in our World A totals, others are World B and C peoples.

See Appendix 2 for addresses of these organizations and agencies who can provide further information.

5. **The adoption of unreached peoples** by churches, Christian groups, prayer circles and individuals. The task can be completed only as Christians take responsibility in earnest intercession until believers are won and churches planted in each people.

THE CHURCH

The whole of God's plan of redemption centres round the Church of his beloved Son. This is why he called Abraham (Genesis 12:3; Galatians 3:8). Christ died for the Church (Ephesians 2:16) and he lives as its Head (Ephesians 1:22). As part of his Body, our longing should be for its upbuilding and perfection (Col. 1:24). One day soon the Bride of Christ, the Church, will be complete and perfect (Ephesians 5:27; Rev. 7:9–10)!

The Church on earth is only an imperfect manifestation of the one, true and invisible Church of the Lord Jesus Christ, yet we are promised by Jesus that the gates of hell will not prevail against it. In some lands there are hundreds of thousands of congregations and in others maybe only one or two. The wheat and the tares are mixed, the divisions and weaknesses are all too plain and obvious, yet the Holy Spirit is working in and through the Church in all its diversity of doctrines, denominations, languages and personalities. It is through the Church that God wants redemption to be proclaimed to mankind. Many prayer points through the book major on the needs of the Church. Here are a few suggested items of wider application:

1. **Maintaining a clear witness to the uniqueness of Christ** in the midst of a growth of religious pluralism, non-Christian religious revival, urbanization, modernity and relativism. Christians will be increasingly criticized for being "intolerant".

2. **Sustaining the centrality of the Scriptures** in today's world at a time when many Evangelicals in the West are becoming less firm in their convictions. Too often believers' thoughts, prejudices and fears are moulded more by the prevailing culture, philosophies, superstitions and religions of the society around them than by the Bible. Humanism in the West, Hinduism in India, etc., are examples. All such can rob Christians of their assurance, power and joy in the face of a hostile world, and sidetrack believers into secondary or irrelevant issues.

3. **The effective functioning of local congregations.** Each should be an organism, a body. Each member has gifts to contribute to the upbuilding of the whole, yet rarely do congregations function in this way. This emphasis on "body life" has come into prominence in the past two decades. May every congregation be an effective body through which the Holy Spirit can work!

4. **Leadership – the key.** Pastors, ministers and elders need constant upholding in prayer. There is a worldwide lack of men and women truly called of God and deeply taught in the Scriptures to lead the churches – people willing to suffer scorn, poverty and the shame of the Cross for the sake of the Saviour who redeemed them. Those who accurately and effectively expound the Scriptures are few, especially in areas where the churches are growing rapidly. May all leaders be an example to their flocks in holy living, evangelism and missionary concern for a lost world!

5. **Spiritual depth.** This is rare in many congregations. Superficiality, an inadequate devotional life and worldliness are common. This highlights the need for effective teaching, in the mother tongue, of the Bible's content, doctrines, and applicability to life and witness.

6. **Victorious optimism.** This is rare where evangelical believers are a small and despised minority. These believers are often introspective and timid, and hardly a mighty force for the pulling down of the fortifications of the devil. Believers need prayer that they may witness boldly and effectively.

7. **Young people.** In this modern age they are often lost to the church and become worldly, even after a Christian upbringing, because of a growing generation gap. Every new generation needs to be evangelized afresh, or the churches soon become nominal. Young people need prayer as never before.

8. **Revival.** This has occurred in various parts of the world this century (see Regions), but not on the scale, nor with the effect, for which believers long in this critical and momentous time of history.

9. **Missionary vision.** An Acts 1:8 strategy is needed for every church and denomination. Amazing results have been achieved by a dedicated few. How speedily the world would be evangelized if all believers and every congregation obeyed the commands of Jesus in Acts 1, and believed his promises for the enablement through the Holy Spirit! Pray for the awakening and growth of missionary concern. Pray for effective and practical missionary involvement in praying, giving and going.

THE HARVEST FORCE

The Church is God's means for evangelizing the world, and from New Testament times men and women as individuals and teams have been set apart and sent out with the apostolic task of preaching the gospel beyond the reach of local congregations. Those members of the Church who move out in this way constitute the missionary force of the world.

1. **Mission agencies.** There has been a multiplication of Protestant missionary sending and support agencies over the past two centuries; this has become a worldwide phenomenon of great significance. Pray for:
a) **Effective strategies** to evangelize the world and plant churches among its diverse peoples. Lack of such can lead to misuse of resources and frustration of personnel.
b) **Adaptability** in a rapidly changing world. Few agencies are easily able to change structures and strategies to cope with the new and challenging demands of such a changing world.
c) **Leadership** in mission agencies. These leaders need wisdom in setting clear objectives, guidance in the selection and placing of workers and ability to give pastoral care and to maintain good relationships with secular authorities.
d) **Harmonious cooperation and fellowship with missionary-sending and missionary-receiving churches.** The growing emphasis on local church responsibility for world evangelism can lead to tensions and misunderstandings unless mutual responsibilities and relationships are clearly understood. The local churches and mission agencies need each other. Neither can do the job alone.
e) **Effective cooperation**, rather than competitiveness, between missionary agencies over finances, personnel and areas of ministry. World recession in the early '90s has made these problems more real. There is often unnecessary duplication of effort, and a lack of corporate planning together about ways to get the job done. The manner of entry of agencies into the former Communist bloc after 1989 was a demonstration of how *not* to do it.
f) **Working networks** in areas difficult to enter overtly as missionaries. The development of non-residential missionary programmes advanced fast in the '80s. This and the tactful ministry of **Interdev**, a service agency dedicated to brokering such networks, are significant new advances into what are often called *creative-access nations*.

2. **Missionaries.** The old type of individualistic missionary of the colonial era is no longer acceptable. Teamwork and an ability to work with, and under, leaders of other nationalities make great demands. The modern missionary must be a self-effacing spiritual giant! The missionary's personal walk with God is vital. The harsh realities of the modern world soon dispel the imagined glamour of pioneer missionary work. Pray for:
a) **Vital, supportive home fellowships of believers** who are willing to pray the missionary out to the field and keep him or her there through the years of greatest effectiveness.
b) **The supply of his/her financial need.** Missionary ministries are more expensive to maintain than those at home. Many live sacrificially for Christ, yet their living standards may appear sumptuous to local people, and a wise balance is needed. The problems of exchange control, export of currency, inflation, artificial exchange rates, endemic bribery, etc. are constant time-wasting frustrations.

c) **Adequate preparation for missionary work.** This is arduous and long – theological training, ministry experience, language learning and adaptation to a new land may take years before an effective ministry can be exercised. Those years can be traumatic and discouraging for both single workers and young married couples. The rising number of missionaries who fail to return for a second term of service is indicative of possible deficiencies in selection, preparation, structure and pastoral care.

d) **Cultural adjustment.** Culture shock is the subject of much humour, but is very real. Many prospective missionaries cannot make the adjustment to new foods, life styles, languages, value systems and attitudes. Some return home disillusioned and with a sense of failure; others react wrongly on the field and hinder fellowship and witness; yet others go too far in their adaptation and compromise their health and sometimes their faith. Balance and objectivity are needed.

e) **Protection from Satan's attacks.** In many areas Satan's kingdom has never been challenged before. The powers of darkness are real. Missionaries need discernment and authority to resist attacks he makes through health, the mind, opponents of the gospel and even Christian workers. They need the victorious faith that will "bind the strong man and spoil his goods".

f) **Family life.** For some, especially single women, the missionary call may mean foregoing marriage for the sake of the gospel. The loneliness of single workers can be a heavy burden to bear. For others, family life may be made difficult by living conditions, inadequate amenities or lack of finance, or be disrupted by long separations, many visitors and excessive workloads. Missionaries' children may be separated from their parents for long periods because of education, and can become resentful or rebellious in their teens. Pray that missionary families may be an effective witness and example of all that a Christian family should be.

g) **Commitment to God's will.** The assurance that God has guided to a particular ministry is the only anchor to retain workers in difficult situations, misunderstandings, broken relationships and "impossible" crises. Pray that none may leave a place of calling for a negative or superficial reason, but only because of a positive leading from God.

h) **Fruitfulness.** All workers need the anointing of God on their lives, and an effective ministry that bears eternal fruit. For this they need clear objectives and time to achieve them. Too much time can be spent on survival and handling trivial interruptions, and too little on the real reason for being there. Only the Holy Spirit can give a worker that constraining love of Christ for sinners – human pity and love are inadequate.

i) **A sense of urgency.** Expulsions or enforced departure from the field could suddenly terminate a ministry. The missionary needs to work hard to train his successors and help local believers to maturity.

j) **Homecoming** for furlough, or for home ministry, which can be traumatic. Returning missionaries need the continued support of God's people for overcoming re-entry shock and establishment of an effective rapport with churches at home, and of an effective ministry.

THE LEADERS OF THE NATIONS OF THIS WORLD

The Scriptures clearly command that prayer be made for kings and all in authority (1 Tim. 2:1–2).

As we pray for the rulers of this world, remember that all authority *has* been given to the Lord Jesus Christ, the King of kings and Lord of lords (Psalm 2:1–12; Matthew 28:18–20; Revelation 17:14). In fact, all who rule can only do so because God placed them in their position of authority, whether they know it or not. He can just as easily remove them (Romans 13:1–7).

We live in an increasingly stormy and uncertain world. We are not flotsam blown hither and thither by these storms, but are raised with Christ and seated with him in heavenly places. We are world-changers in him. We can take authority in his name over spiritual and secular leaders of this world – to support the righteous, to challenge self-seeking sinners and bind or remove those who defy our God or persecute the body of Christ. Use this authority to pray for:

1. **Those who give just and godly leadership, many of whom are committed Christians.** They need to be upheld in prayer. They have to make difficult decisions for a majority who may not share their faith. Pray that they may continually stand firm for what is good, moral and just for the nations they rule and not give way to numerous pressure groups who would wish to gain advantage for vested interests, nor push for the relaxation of laws that forbid what the Bible names as sin.

2. **Those who face major crises.** Pray for courage to take the right decisions, however unpopular. It is easy to go for the soft or cheap option which ultimately proves hard and costly. The '90s will

provide an ever-multiplying number of these crises as the securities and rigidities of the cold war melt away.

3. **Those who rule by force** and with no accountability to the people they lead. Tyrannies and dictatorships did not end with the collapse of European Communism and the rise of the worldwide democracy movement. Many states in Eurasia and Africa have paid lip-service to democracy, but by ballot-rigging, intimidation and manipulation retain power for their own selfish ends. Many countries have leaders with foreign bank accounts large enough to settle their nation's indebtedness.

4. **Those who impose ethnic discrimination and genocide as official policy.** Neither *apartheid* nor discrimination were a South African invention nor did they cease with *apartheid's* ending there. In the last century Western nations deliberately decimated the indigenous American Indians and Australian Aborigines; in this century Turkey did the same with the Armenians, Russia the Crimean Tatars and Baltic peoples, Germany the Jews; and today the Serbs and Croats with the Bosnian Muslims, the Sudanese Arabs the southern Sudanese, Hindu Indians the Muslim minority, and many more. Few nations are blameless. *Ethnic cleansing* could increase in the '90s.

5. **Those who persecute Christians** and restrict the preaching of the gospel. Many have signed the UN Declaration of Human Rights which includes freedom of religion. Persecution can bring spiritual benefits – the purification of the Church, the stimulation of earnest prayer, an outpouring of the Spirit of God, and a more rapid spread of the gospel. Yet the people of God suffer under the cruelty or discrimination of national leaders. Countries where such leadership exists are:

Africa: Comoros, Somalia.
Asia: Afghanistan, Bhutan, Brunei, Cambodia, China, North Korea, Maldives, Myanmar, Pakistan, Vietnam.
Eurasia: Azerbaijan.
Middle East: There is not complete religious freedom in any of the 24 nations. In some, persecution is severe – especially for those converted from a Muslim background.

Thirty-one of these lands are Muslim. Muslims demand religious freedom and privileges in other lands but deny them to followers of other religions in their own lands.

6. **Leaders who oppose the entry of missionaries and the spread of the gospel.** Pray that the opposition may be used to actively prepare the hearts of those they rule for the coming of the gospel, or that their attitude may change, or that they be replaced by leaders more sympathetic to the gospel. Over the past 30 years there have been dramatic answers to prayer in closed doors being opened. Since 1985 and the writing of the last *Operation World* the following lands have opened up more for Christian workers in NGOs or even for mission agencies.

Africa: Angola, Benin, Burundi, Equatorial Guinea, Eritrea, Ethiopia.
Asia: Cambodia, Mongolia, Nepal.
Americas: Cuba.
Eurasia: Nearly all the new republics.
Europe: Albania, Bulgaria, Czech Republic, Estonia, Hungary, Latvia, Lithuania, Macedonia, Poland, Romania, Slovakia, Slovenia.
Middle East: Lebanon.

7. **Countries still closed to the entry or open proclamation of the gospel,** and also without a viable indigenous church. The many new open doors in these countries encourage us to believe the Lord for opening the following:

Africa: Comoros, Somalia.
Asia: Afghanistan, Bhutan, North Korea, Maldives.
Middle East: Algeria, Libya, Mauritania, Qatar, Saudi Arabia, Tunisia, Yemen.

In Appendix 1 on pages 622–626 is a list of the decision-making rulers of the nations and territories of the world. You may wish to pray for some by name. Keep the list up-to-date as leadership changes occur.

**January
7–9**

Africa

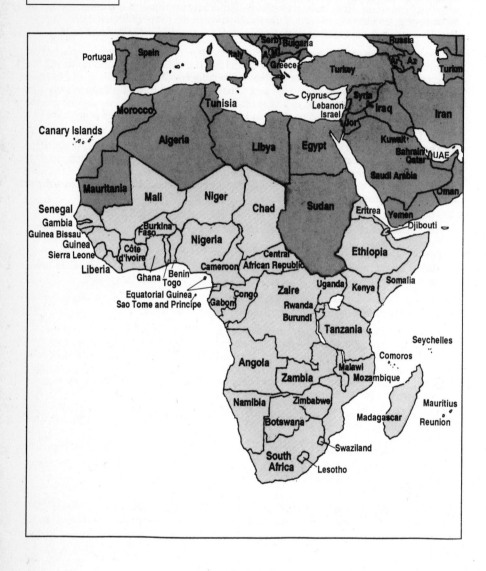

Area 30,000,000 sq.km. However, in this book we are including the seven mainly Arabic-speaking lands of North Africa in the Middle East, to which they culturally belong, and also the Spanish enclaves of Ceuta and Melilla on the Moroccan coast with Spain. The Sahara Desert separates the Arab north from the African south. Sudan, Chad, Mali, Niger and Mauritania straddle that cultural divide, and during the '80s were subject to inter-racial conflict – the most severe being that of Sudan.

Africa south of the Sahara has an area of 20,536,000 sq.km. (15.4% of the earth's surface).

Comments on countries included on map, in table and text.

1. All countries in sub-Saharan Africa – 48.

2. Only British Indian Ocean Territory is not described in this edition, but is mentioned under Mauritius.

3. Eritrea is included as a separate country, having overwhelmingly voted for independence from Ethiopia in the April 1993 referendum. Independence was achieved in May 1993.

4. The island of St Helena in the Atlantic is included for the first time in this volume.

5. During the lifetime of use of this edition of *Operation World* several countries may divide or fragment further. Possible countries: Ethiopia, Somalia (Somaliland has already declared its independence), South Africa, Tanzania (possibly Zanzibar), Zaire.

6. States and territories with superscript numbers are grouped together for prayer, and those with page numbers with lands in other continents.

Country	Population in millions 1990	Population in millions 1995	Affiliated Christian Percentages Total	Prot	Evang	Total No. of Peoples	Peoples in Country World A	B	C
Angola	10.0	11.5	68.6	14.4	8.4	59	8	17	34
Benin	4.7	5.6	24.0	3.4	2.0	43	22	15	6
Botswana	1.3	1.5	47.6	12.5	3.7	65	33	25	7
Brit Indian Ocean Terr[1]	0.0	0.0	n.a.	n.a.	n.a.	4	0	1	3
Burkina Faso	9.0	10.4	13.2	4.5	4.4	78	66	9	3
Burundi	5.5	6.3	74.7	14.6	14.0	13	3	1	9
Cameroon	11.2	12.9	46.2	14.9	4.9	286	78	80	128
Cape Verde Islands	0.4	0.4	96.0	3.5	3.0	6	0	0	6
Central African Rep	2.9	3.3	42.7	24.2	23.7	87	21	41	25
Chad	5.7	6.4	19.8	13.3	13.3	130	77	46	7
Comoros[2]	0.4	0.5	0.6	0.2	0.0	11	8	1	2
Congo	2.0	2.3	75.8	20.1	18.2	76	4	33	39
Côte d'Ivoire	12.6	15.3	20.8	5.3	4.3	95	42	28	25
Djibouti	0.4	0.5	2.8	0.1	0.0	9	3	3	3
Equatorial Guinea[3]	0.4	0.5	77.7	3.2	0.9	22	2	1	19
Eritrea[4]	3.7	4.6	32.5	1.5	1.5	0	Included in Ethiopia		
Ethiopia[4]	45.6	52.6	51.0	13.2	13.0	151	77	51	23
Gabon	1.2	1.4	82.2	17.5	5.1	49	4	3	42
Gambia	0.9	1.0	2.5	0.7	0.2	27	16	5	6
Ghana	15.0	17.5	44.3	20.3	8.9	105	37	23	45
Guinea	6.9	7.8	1.8	0.5	0.5	40	33	2	5
Guinea-Bissau	1.0	1.1	6.2	0.8	0.8	31	22	5	4
Kenya	25.1	30.8	69.6	37.3	34.0	121	51	39	31
Lesotho	1.8	2.0	77.1	21.0	3.9	12	0	3	9
Liberia	2.6	3.0	24.9	16.4	8.1	46	9	20	17
Madagascar	12.0	14.1	47.2	24.9	6.3	53	8	37	8
Malawi	8.4	10.0	67.9	28.7	11.3	28	1	12	15
Mali	9.4	10.9	1.8	0.7	0.7	35	30	3	2
Mauritius[1]	1.1	1.2	32.7	6.6	6.0	23	1	16	6
Mayotte[2]	0.1	0.1	2.0	0.2	0.0	9	6	1	2
Mozambique	15.7	17.9	27.8	10.8	8.9	49	9	30	10
Namibia	1.9	2.2	63.0	44.5	8.8	31	10	2	19
Niger	7.1	8.3	0.4	0.1	0.1	35	27	4	4
Nigeria	88.5	100.1	40.9	22.4	15.9	455	197	155	103
Réunion	0.6	0.6	83.5	4.8	4.3	16	2	5	9
Rwanda	7.2	8.6	76.0	28.6	20.1	12	3	1	8
São Tomé & Príncipe[3]	0.1	0.1	90.7	4.9	3.7	6	0	0	6
Senegal	7.4	8.4	5.1	0.1	0.1	54	38	10	6
Seychelles	0.1	0.1	92.4	9.5	4.1	9	1	2	6
Sierra Leone	4.2	4.7	7.1	5.1	2.2	30	18	6	6
Somalia	7.6	8.5	0.0	0.0	0.0	22	16	0	6
South Africa	35.2	39.2	72.6	38.4	16.5	70	7	36	27
St Helena (p 556)	0.0	0.0	76.6	70.5	3.3	3	0	0	3
Swaziland	0.8	0.9	70.4	16.7	11.9	11	1	4	6
Tanzania	27.3	32.9	36.6	14.7	9.7	161	46	55	60
Togo	3.5	4.0	28.9	5.4	1.8	48	20	16	12
Uganda	18.4	22.0	69.6	27.6	24.7	59	4	15	40
Zaire	36.0	42.3	92.3	35.4	21.1	258	5	58	195
Zambia	8.5	10.2	54.8	22.1	12.5	84	5	36	43
Zimbabwe	9.7	11.4	48.8	24.1	14.3	41	3	19	19
AFRICA	**480.8**	**557.9**	**48.1**	**20.2**	**13.2**	**3,168**	**1,074**	**975**	**1,119**

Superscripted countries are grouped together for prayer. St Helena is added to the prayer day of the United Kingdom.

World A The unevangelized/unreached world where %E < 50% for constituent peoples.
World B The evangelized non-Christian world where %E > 50% and All Christians < 60%.
World C The broadly Christian world where All Christians in people are > 60%.
See Appendix 5 for fuller definitions. See p 113 for diagrams.

Population	Ann.Gr.	Density
1985 415,100,000	2.9%	20/sq.km
1990 480,800,000	3.0%	23/sq.km
1995 557,900,000	3.0%	27/sq.km
2000 647,200,000	3.0%	32/sq.km

Africa is the continent with the highest growth rate. It had 9.1% of the world's population in 1990, but will have 10.4% by 2000 and 15.5% by 2024 – assuming no massive population loss with AIDS.

Peoples: Over 3,000 ethno-linguistic peoples in Africa.
Indigenous African 97.1%. Almost entirely Negroid peoples of three major types – West African, Sudanic and Bantu. There are remnants of the pre-negroid peoples: **Pygmies** in the rain forests of Central Africa (560,000), **Khoi-khoi** in Southern Africa (680,000).
European 1.3%. Nearly all in South Africa; significant minorities in most lands.
Mixed race 0.8%. Mainly South Africa, Réunion and Mauritius.
Asian 0.45%. Predominantly Indians in Mauritius, and Natal in South Africa. Significant minorities in East and Central Africa.
Berber/Arab 0.3%. Mainly Tuareg (1,700,000), Maures in Western Sahelian nations, and Arabs along the east coast of Africa, Chad and the Sahel.

Languages: 1,800 known languages are spoken. This rises to 1,995, or 30.5% of the world's total if North Africa is included.

Official languages: The increasing use of French (22 countries), English (18 countries), Portuguese (4) and Spanish (1) is often at the expense of indigenous languages. In only six nations is an African language officially used as the main means of conducting the nation's business.

Bible translation: Africa is the greatest remaining challenge for Bible translation with existing openings for missionary translators. **Languages with Scriptures:** 107Bi 196NT 277por. There is work in progress in 295 languages and a definite need for translators in 267 more. This latter number could rise to 1,200 after careful field research.

Cities: There are 21 or more world-class cities of over one million inhabitants. Vast squatter camps and slums with uncounted migrants would raise this number. Urbanization in 1990 was 27%; by the year 2000 this may rise to 45%.

Economy: No other continent has suffered such a series of natural, political and economic disasters over the past 25 years. Food production has declined in a time of rapid population growth. In 1992 famine gripped much of Africa – in part due to drought and in part war. At that time 60 million faced death through starvation. The worst-hit areas in the '80s were the Sahel extending from Senegal in the west to Ethiopia and Somalia in the east, and also southern Africa. The reasons for Africa's economic decline are:

1. **Uncontrolled population growth**, with rapid deforestation.

2. **Maladministration**, and the favouring of the educated elite and the more politically active urban population.

3. **Low investment in agriculture** and development of viable methods of food production, distribution and sale, with food aid distorting local marketing and diet patterns.

4. **Foreign debt.** The oil crises of the '70s and unwise borrowing by governments have increased sub-Saharan Africa's debt to $174 billion ($340/person – or 90% of the total annual earnings of the continent). Much of export earnings is used to service this debt.

5. **The ending of the cold war** which eclipsed Africa's UN influence in holding the balancing vote in the conflict between the superpowers. Africa has been marginalized and foreign aid diminished.

Of the world's 40 poorest nations, 32 are in Africa; of these about 13 are in almost complete collapse. Only 1.2% of the world's earnings are generated in Africa. All these pressures are bringing a new realism, self-reliance and growth of the informal economy in many countries.

Politics: Black Africa's isolation from the rest of the world ended in the "Scramble for Africa" by the European colonial powers in the last century. For all its faults, the 100 years of colonial rule brought peace, education, better health services and some economic development. In the short space of 35 years since 1957, all of the mainland states of Black Africa attained independence with the exception of South Africa. South Africa's ending of apartheid and commitment to non-racial elections in 1994 has enormous implications for Africa and possibly the world. Only the island territories of Réunion, Mayotte and St Helena remain administratively tied to Europe.

The post-"cold war" era has decisively affected Africa. Foreign interest and wooing of African governments for ideological support has waned and is beginning to free Africa from its colonial past with:

1. **A new sense of responsibility** for present difficulties and an acknowledgement that past colonial and neo-colonial influence cannot be blamed for everything.

2. **A new accountability to the people.** A groundswell of resentment at the exploitation and plunder of national wealth by the elite and pressure from aid donor countries are compelling a greater degree of multi-party democracy. Many countries have had democratic elections with varying degrees of success and failure. This follows 30 years of one-party or military rule and dictatorships with over 100 violent changes of leadership.

3. **A greater flexibility in handling ethnic diversity** and colonial divisions imposed in the last century

expressed through regional alliances, federalization and even (in the case of Eritrea) a redrawing of frontiers.

4. **The ending of apartheid** in South Africa and Namibia – inevitable once the ideological threat of Communism diminished.

There are few post-independence nations that have proved both politically and economically successful – one of these being Botswana. One of Africa's major problems has, arguably, been bad government.

Religion: Important trends:

1. **The sharpening of the contest for the soul of Africa between Islam and Christianity** – both making advances into each other's areas of influence. This has become violent with Muslims using force in Sudan and Nigeria to promote or protect their cause.

2. **The increase in religious freedom** since 1985. Nine states that leaned to or had turned to Marxism and often oppressed Christians have now rejected that ideology and proclaimed religious freedom – notably Ethiopia, Eritrea, Angola and Mozambique. In 11 states there is more religious freedom than in 1985; in only two has it become less – Somalia and Liberia; and only in Comoros and Somalia is there official pressure exerted on Christians.

3. **The continued growth in numbers and influence of evangelical Christianity** – especially of indigenous Pentecostal denominations.

4. **The multiplication and proliferation of indigenous syncretic movements** incorporating elements of Christianity and traditional religions.

Traditional religions 15.4%. 70 million. Growth −1.6%. The marked numerical decline belies the continuing hold of witchcraft, fear of spirits, fetishism and ancestor worship. Only three countries in Black Africa still have a majority of those following traditional religions – Benin, Liberia and Sierra Leone.

Muslim 26.7%. 129 million. Growth 4.5%. A further 130 million Muslims live in the seven North African lands which are included in the Middle East region here. There are nine African states south of the Sahara with a Muslim majority, though Muslims claim more than this. These are **Comoros** and Mayotte, Djibouti, Gambia, Guinea, Mali, Niger, Senegal, **Somalia**. Only the two highlighted are closed for conventional missionary work, though others impose quota, visa or ministry restrictions. **Baha'i** 0.30%. 1.5 million.

Hindu 0.29%. 1.4 million. Almost entirely in the Indian communities of southern and eastern Africa, and a majority in Mauritius.
Jews 0.02%. 90,000. Mainly in South Africa and some remaining in Ethiopia.
Christian 57.3%. 275 million. Growth 3.7%. Affil 48.1%. Christians are in a majority in 30 countries.
  Protestant 22.7%. 109 million. Affil 20.1%. Growth 6%. Evangelical growth is 7% and Pentecostal growth 8.4%.
  Missionaries:
    to Africa (expatriates) from African and other lands 17,646 (1:27,000 people).
    from Africa (home and expatriate) 12,829 (1:7,500 Protestants) 1,665 frn 3,713xcul 9,116dom.
  Roman Catholic 21.3%. 102 million. Affil 16.7%. Growth 3.4%.
  Missionaries:
    to Africa from African and other lands 28,044 (1:17,000 people).
    from Africa 2,269. [*Approximate figure based on 1973–1990 sources.*]
  Orthodox 4.6%. 22 million. Affil 3.9%. Growth −0.88%.
  Almost entirely in Ethiopia and Eritrea.
  Foreign Marginal 0.56%. 2.8 million. Affil 0.54%. Growth 7.3%. Mainly Jehovah's Witnesses.
  Indigenous Marginal 8.1%. 39 million. Affil 6.7%. Growth 4.1%. Predominantly in Anglophone countries and Zaire.

Church groupings	Cong	Members	Affiliated
Protestant	318,000	39,600,000	96,900,000
Evangelical 13.2% of pop		26,500,000	63,500,000
Pentecostal 4.1% of pop		9,100,000	19,900,000
Charismatic 1.4% of pop		2,300,000	6,600,000
Roman Catholic	78,400	46,300,000	80,400,000
Charismatic		180,000	313,000
Orthodox	15,700	10,900,000	18,700,000
Foreign Marginal	13,000	1,100,000	2,600,000
Indigenous Marginal	n.a.	15,300,000	32,400,000
Total	425,100	113,200,000	231,313,000

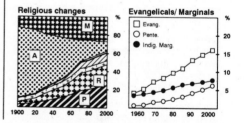

Religious changes

Evangelicals/ Marginals
□ Evang.
○ Pente.
● Indig. Marg.

PRAISE ITEMS AND ANSWERS TO PRAYER

During the 1980s God gave many remarkable breakthroughs, answers to prayer and continued growth. Specifically:

1. **Africa's turning to Christianity.** Christianity is professed by over half of sub-Saharan Africa's population. This is the first time in history that a continent has turned in this way. In 1900 African

Christians were eight million (2.5 million Protestants) and 10% of the population. In 1990 this had risen to 275 million and 57% and is likely to reach 396 million and 61% by 2000.

2. **The growth of Evangelicals** from 1.9% of Africans in 1900 to 13.2% in 1990. This is a seven-fold increase in percentage but a thirty-fold increase in numbers.

a) **Revivals and great turnings to Christ** in East Africa, Zaire and more recently in Zambia and Ethiopia have brought millions in mainline denominations to a warm personal faith in Christ. Many Anglican and Lutheran bishops in East Africa and Ethiopia are fervent Evangelicals.

b) **Major church growth has occurred in daughter churches founded by faith missions.** Churches related to **SIM** in Africa have an estimated 6,500,000 adherents, and those related to **AIM** a further 3 million adherents.

c) **Indigenous African Pentecostal denominations** have grown dramatically over the past 20 years. To name only two: The Deeper Life Bible Church in Nigeria has rapidly grown to 350,000 members with mission work in 42 countries of the world, and the Zimbabwe Assemblies of God, African to 600,000 members to become the largest Protestant denomination in the country.

3. **Opening of countries for the gospel.** In 1980 there were about 14 countries that were "closed" for the proclamation of the gospel and Christians restricted or persecuted; only four to five remain "closed" or restricted (parts of Angola, Comoros, parts of Gabon, parts of Liberia, Somalia). There are many opportunities for Christian service in some of these newly opened lands, such as Mozambique, Ethiopia, Eritrea, Guinea, Guinea-Bissau and Togo.

4. **The resilience of African Christians under persecution** which has been an example to the world. Times of persecution in Zaire, Mozambique, Angola, Zimbabwe, Nigeria, Ethiopia, Eritrea and Sudan during the '70s and '80s have put iron into the soul of the Church in these lands and increased subsequent outreach.

5. **The impact of the gospel on the educated.** The ministry of **SU**, **IFES** and others among students has been remarkable; through this and the ministry of churches and agencies a large proportion of Africa's professionals and leaders in Anglophone countries are committed Christians. Their influence is becoming decisive in addressing corruption and social evils and in affecting the power structures of society. The democracy movement, Zambia's change of government and pressure for positive change in Malawi, Zaire, South Africa, Uganda and other lands is much due to Christian involvement. May this impact grow!

6. **The saturation church-planting vision.** This was pioneered in Ghana and is spreading to many countries in Africa with the encouragement of the **DAWN** movement. Careful research of unreached areas, countries and peoples has been promoted by a growing band of talented African Christian researchers. The Nigeria Evangelical Missions Association-sponsored survey of the unreached peoples of Nigeria, conducted by Calvary Ministries, is an example of this.

7. **Missions vision.** This has grown, and the number of African missionaries and agencies is steadily increasing. Notable in this respect is the maturity and variety of Nigerian missions, many with a strong emphasis on Muslim and unreached people outreach. Also praiseworthy are missionary training initiatives all over Africa (AEAM), West Africa (Calvary Ministries) and East Africa (Africa Inland Church).

THE CHURCH IN AFRICA

January 10

There are many big challenges for African Christians to confront in the '90s. The colonial past is fading, the wrong of apartheid is being removed and these can no longer be used by African leaders to turn attention away from present realities. Specific challenges about which to intercede:

1. **Rapid growth** with inadequate discipling. So great has been the harvest that non-Christian customs, worldviews and attitudes have invaded the church. **Syncretism** is a major problem in many areas. Thoroughgoing repentance and renunciation of sin and the works of darkness is often lacking and many Christians are not free from the fear of witchcraft and evil spirits. The new generation or third wave of African Christianity takes a clear stand against these, but many churches are seriously compromised.

2. **Unity in diversity.** The profusion of denominations brings confusion. Pray for spiritual unity for all Bible-believing Christians. The role of the **Association of Evangelicals of Africa and Madagascar** (**AEAM**) is widely appreciated in linking national evangelical fellowships and individual

evangelical denominations in fellowship, stimulating vision and promoting leadership training, culturally relevant biblical theology and social action. Over 188 denominations and agencies are members and these represent a 50-million Christian constituency.

3. Morality and the AIDS crisis. The AIDS pandemic has spread through central and east Africa. Villages and towns along road and river trade routes are being decimated by the disease. No one really knows the level of infection with the virus – estimates in 1992 ranged from seven million to 20 million or more. Especially badly affected are Uganda, Zaire, Zambia, Zimbabwe and South Africa. The most economically active section of the population has the highest rate of infection, so the economic impact is already devastating. The two major challenges are:

a) **Ministry to the sick**, suffering and bereaved and care for the anticipated 5.5 million children in central Africa who will be orphaned in this decade.

b) **Teaching for Christians and especially young people.** God's standards of total morality must be shown to be and embraced as the highest, safest and best. **SU** and others are developing effective teaching programmes.

4. Leadership training – the critical bottleneck. There is a lack of funds – in a continent becoming poorer – for training and supporting full-time workers. Leadership is limited at every level: for village congregations, for the urban educated, for theological training. Pray for:

a) **Theological institutions.** These have multiplied for students with primary, secondary and post-secondary level. There are only two main interdenominational graduate-level theological schools – in Nairobi, Kenya, and Bangui, Central African Republic (both sponsored by AEAM). AEAM has set up an effective accreditation body, ACTEA. Its directory lists over 100 members and many more schools, over half being in four countries – Nigeria (130), South Africa (111), Zaire (85) and Kenya (66).

b) **A relevant curriculum** that is biblical yet Africa-oriented. Too much is geared to Western theological battles and perceptions.

c) **Harmony among staff.** Tensions among missionaries and between missionary and national staff have sometimes not been a spiritual example to the students they teach.

d) **Selection of students.** Discernment is needed to know who are anointed of the Spirit for future leadership and who apply for baser motives of prestige, desire for education, etc.

e) **Funds.** The poverty of the Church and lack of understanding among potential donors hampers the development of Bible training institutions. The needs for buildings, libraries, student grants and travel are endless. Western churches need to give as freely for providing spiritual food to the starving Christians as they have done to provide for Africa's famines.

f) **TEE programmes**, vital for training lay leadership. Over 100 programmes are in operation, but some are less than successful. Funding, difficulties in travel, low motivation and the failure to involve the real leaders have all been hindrances.

5. African theologians. There is a theological vacuum to be filled. A truly indigenous evangelical African theology has been slow to develop. A clear stand by African theologians to expound the universal and unchangeable truths of Scripture is needed which will also counteract:

a) **Western liberal theology** which never really took root in Africa. However, the deadening influence of missionaries who were affected by it is evident in many mainline denominations where nominal orthodoxy, compromise and power struggles for leadership have sapped spiritual life.

b) **African theology.** The term is used to describe attempts to find God in the pre-Christian religions of Africa rather than in the Bible. Syncretism (mixing Christianity with non-Christian religions) and universalism (the belief that all will ultimately be saved) are widespread.

c) **Black theology.** This is the Marxist-influenced Black Power expression of "liberation theology" which equates political liberation with salvation.

d) **Ignorance about spiritual warfare.** The spiritual nature of Africa's present conflicts needs to be understood, scripturally expounded and actively dealt with.

6. The expatriate missionary force. This is increasingly multi-continental and less Western, which makes spiritual unity and commonness of purpose an even greater challenge! Pray for this! The need for missionaries continues to be greater than the supply of those with the gifting and vision for:

a) **Pioneer areas.** These still abound; see below. A high degree of commitment and sacrifice will be required to reach present pioneer areas where conditions are sometimes very hard. In some cases missionaries will need to learn 2–4 languages before they can reach the least reached.

b) **Church support missionaries** for teaching, youth work, etc., which are needed as never before. Yet the willingness to work under African leadership and as part of the Church in Africa is essential.

c) **Specialists** for Bible translation, education, agriculture, health, radio, television, cassette ministries, etc. These are constantly requested by African Christians.

d) **Social projects and aid ministries** which are in ever-growing demand. In many countries governments have been unable to provide basic services to their people and Christian churches and agencies have had to take these up. Physical needs must be met, but such is the pressure that this can lead to neglect of spiritual needs that may be the ultimate cause of suffering and deprivation.

7. **Making missions central to the life of the church in Africa.** Few realize how much of the pioneer missionary work in Africa has actually been done by humble, dedicated African missionaries who have crossed cultural and national boundaries to evangelize peoples not their own. Pray for:

a) **Churches to see the importance of the missionary task.** Most Africans think missionary work to be the job of Europeans.

b) **Funds to be made available** to train and send out missionaries. Exchange controls and poverty prevent many churches from realizing their mission vision to the full.

c) **Adequate training facilities** for cross-cultural missionaries. Beginnings have been made in Nigeria, South Africa, Kenya, Zaire, Ghana and Côte d'Ivoire.

In 1989 Africa's first student missions congress was held – over 1,200 students came. In 1992 the Deeper Life Bible Church hosted a conference in Nigeria for 12,000 African pastors to launch the AD2000 and Beyond vision to complete the Great Commission requirements for world evangelization. Pray that this vision may be widely spread.

THE FINAL FRONTIERS FOR WORLD EVANGELIZATION IN AFRICA | January 11

1. **Islam** is the greatest challenge to be faced. Muslim advances have been liberally funded and sometimes well provided with military weapons. Muslims have been successful in winning non-Muslims in lands west of Ghana, in Francophone coastal cities and, in more recent years, in east and central Africa. Pray that African Christians may see the need to love and evangelize Muslims – in Nigeria, Chad, Cameroon and Ethiopia they are seen more as a threat.

a) There are 129 million Muslims in sub-Sahara Africa. Few Christians have been won from this background, but growing numbers are coming to Christ in some countries. Pray that the present trickle may become a flood.

b) There are 38 million people living in the Sahel belt across Africa who still follow traditional religions. Pray that they may be won to Christ before being ensnared by Islam.

2. **Least-evangelized countries.**

a) Those with less than 0.1% Evangelical Christian: Comoros, Djibouti, Niger, Senegal, Somalia. All these states are Muslim.

b) Others with less than 1% Evangelical Christian: Equatorial Guinea, Gambia, Guinea, Guinea-Bissau, Mali.

3. **Least-reached peoples** – study the table facing the Africa map.

a) Major transnational peoples: the Fula (14 million in 17 nations), Mandingo/Mande (13 million in 14 nations), Hausa (23 million in 18 nations), Somali (11 million in nine nations).

b) Of the world's 3,915 least-reached peoples, 1,074 are in sub-Saharan Africa. See the "World A" column in table above and refer to the relevant country for more detail.

c) **Africa's nomadic peoples** – mainly in the Sahel and the Horn of Africa: the Fulani, Chad Arabs, Somali, Galla and Tuareg are some of Africa's least-reached peoples. The adaptation and dedication needed for missionaries to disciple them are great.

4. **Making an impact on Africa's cities.** Africa's urban population may rise from 130 million in 1990 to 300 million by 2000. Most will live in dire poverty, unemployed and in many countries with a high proportion infected with the HIV virus. Christianity has grown best in rural areas and among the better educated. Few indigenous denominations and agencies have the skills, resources and spiritual gifts to make an impact where the need is greatest.

5. **Bible translation.** Pray for the provision of national and expatriate translators and literacy workers. Over 40 million Africans speaking 1,200 languages have nothing of the Scriptures, and nearly 200 million cannot read. The greatest challenges are in Nigeria (between 64 and 327 languages needing a New Testament), Cameroon (38–173), Zaire (29–158), Tanzania (61–89) and Chad (33–78).

January
12–15

Asia

Area 21,288,000 sq.km., 15.7% of the land area of the world. Countries excluded in this edition:

1. **Parts of the former USSR, usually considered in Asia,** such as Russia east of the Urals (Siberia), Kazakhstan, Kyrgyzstan, Tajikistan, Turkmenistan and Uzbekistan, are included under **Eurasia**.

2. **West Asia** (Asian Arab states, Israel, Iran and Turkey) is included in the Middle East.
NOTE: Afghanistan was also included in the Middle East in the last edition, but in this it is included with Asia.

Country	Population in millions		Affiliated Christian Percentages			Total No. of Peoples	Peoples in Country World		
	1990	1995	Total	Prot	Evang		A	B	C
Afghanistan	16.6	23.1	0.0	0.0	0.0	67	62	1	4
Bangladesh	115.6	132.2	0.4	0.2	0.1	57	32	15	10
Bhutan	0.6	0.7	0.3	0.3	0.3	21	17	3	1
Brunei	0.3	0.3	5.1	2.9	1.4	26	12	12	2
Cambodia	8.2	9.2	0.4	0.1	0.1	35	27	5	3
China, People's Rep	1,135.5	1,214.2	6.1	5.1	5.0	160	134	21	5
China, Taiwan	20.3	21.5	4.8	3.0	2.1	28	6	5	17
Hong Kong	5.8	6.2	14.1	8.5	6.9	32	5	15	12
India	853.4	947.3	3.9	1.9	1.0	432	318	58	56
Indonesia	181.3	195.6	12.6	9.4	4.5	702	288	130	284
Japan	123.5	126.3	1.6	0.5	0.3	27	15	8	4
Korea, North	22.9	25.5	0.6	0.4	0.4	6	3	1	2
Korea, South	43.5	44.9	34.6	27.1	21.1	8	0	5	3
Laos	4.1	4.6	1.5	0.7	0.7	111	101	8	2
Macao	0.4	0.4	7.3	1.8	1.5	9	1	4	4
Malaysia	17.3	19.2	7.3	4.0	3.1	173	103	51	19
Maldives	0.2	0.2	0.1	0.0	0.0	8	5	2	1
Mongolia	2.2	2.6	0.1	0.1	0.1	19	16	2	1
Myanmar	41.7	46.3	6.3	5.2	3.6	130	72	26	32
Nepal	19.1	21.5	0.6	0.6	0.6	105	92	9	4
Pakistan	122.7	141.6	1.7	1.1	0.2	88	79	7	2
Philippines	62.4	69.9	88.5	7.5	5.1	180	107	19	54
Singapore	2.7	2.8	12.3	7.8	6.8	43	12	22	9
Sri Lanka	17.2	18.3	7.6	0.9	0.4	21	8	9	4
Thailand	55.7	59.6	0.8	0.4	0.3	87	54	26	7
Vietnam	67.2	75.0	9.8	0.8	0.8	83	38	39	6
ASIA	2940.3	3209.3	7.3	3.9	3.1	2,658	1,607	503	548

World A The unevangelized/unreached world where %E < 50% for constituent peoples.
World B The evangelized non-Christian world where %E > 50% and All Christians < 60%.
World C The broadly Christian world where All Christians in people are > 60%.
See Appendix 5 for fuller definitions.

Population	Ann.Gr	Density
1985	2,689,500,000	1.8%	126/sq.km
1990	2,940,300,000	1.8%	138/sq.km
1995	3,209,300,000	1.8%	151/sq.km
2000	3,472,600,000	1.6%	163/sq.km

This was 55.6% of the world's population in 1990 and will be 55.7% by 2000.

Peoples: An estimated 2,658 ethno-linguistic people groups, of which 23% are in Indonesia.

Languages: Over 1,980 known languages are spoken, or 27% of the world's total. There are probably many more Indian languages not included in this **SIL** figure. **Languages with Scriptures** 91Bi 137NT 246por. There are 336 languages with a definite need for NT translation, but there could be as many as 1,362.

Cities: There are 89 world-class cities of over one million inhabitants. Nearly one billion people live in Asia's cities. Urbanization 39%.

Economy: Asia has become the continent of dynamic growth. Many perceive that the Pacific Rim nations will dominate the 21st century. Japan is now the world's wealthiest nation. The four little tiger states – South Korea, Taiwan, Hong Kong and Singapore – are fast catching up and other nations are not far behind. The long-stagnating economies of India, China and Indonesia are being transformed by market reforms and rapid growth. The contrast with stagnating and poor nations (Bangladesh, Cambodia, Laos, Myanmar, Philippines and Vietnam) is becoming more marked by the year.

Politics: Out of the ferment of the past 80 years has emerged a younger, stronger and more vigorous group of nations. Their growing economic and political influence is shifting the centre-stage of the world from the Atlantic nations to those of the Pacific Rim. Major factors to consider:

1. **The withdrawal of Western nations** meant that in 1946 only five nations were not under some form of Western control. The last two remaining territories of the colonial era, Hong Kong and Macao, revert to China by the end of the decade. US military power has steadily been withdrawn since the end of the Vietnam War in 1975 culminating in withdrawal from the Philippines in 1992. Only in South Korea is there still a US military presence.

2. **The Cold War confrontation** between Marxism and capitalism was not cold in Asia with a succession of destructive revolutions and wars in China, Korea, Indo-China and numerous smaller wars and guerrilla movements in nearly every Asian country. Fighting which still continues in Cambodia and Philippines and the dangerous confrontation between North and South Korea are the last pages of this violent story. These conflicts militarized Asia and provided the economic stimulus to modernize and develop. Communism is a spent force economically with its last proponents either wallowing in economic destitution (North Korea, Vietnam, Cambodia and Laos) or rapidly changing to a market-oriented economy (China).

3. **The growing political and economic power of Japan and China** will dominate the coming decades with new alignments developing in the region as Cold War divisions become irrelevant.

4. **Ancient hostilities and rivalries** have been renewed – between Muslims and Hindus in the Indian subcontinent, between China and India, Korea and Japan, Muslims and Christians in the Philippines, and Vietnamese and Cambodians in Indo-China.

5. **Modern multi-ethnic nation-states** have come under great strain as local nationalisms, ancient grievances and religious intolerance polarize the political scene. India, Pakistan, Afghanistan, Bhutan, Cambodia, China, Indonesia, Myanmar, Philippines and Sri Lanka have all suffered violence, rioting and ethnic wars in the past decade – some still active.

6. **Immigrant minorities** help the economies of their host nations through their business skills and initiative, but they can become an economic and potential political threat. **The Chinese** all over Southeast Asia form one such group; others include the Indians in Malaysia, and the many **Vietnamese**, **Laotian and Cambodian** refugees and migrants. There is a rapid increase in illegal immigrants from poorer Asian countries to the richer, such as Iranian, Bangladeshi, Pakistani, Thai and Filipino illegals in Japan.

Religion: Muslims, Hindus and Buddhists have moved centre-stage with the failure of secular, socialist and Marxist politics in many lands. This has led to increased discrimination against religious minorities and more finance for religious missionary endeavours to convert minorities and spread their beliefs worldwide. Religious intolerance is on the rise in south and southeast Asia.

Non-religious/other 25.4%. 742 million. There are five Asian states that remain Communist politically, but some are turning to market economics. Only Mongolia renounced Communism – but its leaders remain the same! Persecution of those with a religious faith varies from total repression in North Korea to persecution of unregistered churches in China and Vietnam and to a measure of tolerance in Laos and Cambodia.

Hindu 24.2%. 713 million. The majority in India, Nepal and Bali (Indonesia), and a significant minority in four other lands.

Buddhist/East Asian religions 20.9%. 609 million. The boundary between Buddhism and China's Taoism, Japan's Shinto and other religions is hard to define, so all are included in one total. Majority are in Bhutan, Cambodia, Japan, Laos, Myanmar, Sri Lanka, Thailand and Vietnam.

Muslim 17.9%. 527 million. Islam is the majority religion of seven countries: Afghanistan, Bangladesh, Brunei, Indonesia, Malaysia, Maldives and Pakistan. It is a significant minority in 14 others.

Animist 2%. 57 million. Predominantly among ethnic and tribal minorities scattered throughout Asia. Hinduism and Buddhism are much influenced by an animistic worldview.

New Religions 1.25%. 44 million. Numerous syncretic religions have sprung up in the 20th century in Japan, Korea and Vietnam.

Sikhs 0.56%. 16.5 million. **Baha'i** 0.08%. 2.2 million.

Christian 7.8%. 229 million. Affil 7.3%. 215 million. Growth 4.9%.
In a majority only in the Philippines, but rapidly growing in Korea, Indonesia, China and Singapore.

Protestant 4.3%. 127 million. Affil 3.9%. 115.2 million. Growth 6.1%. The largest Protestant percentages are in Korea and Indonesia but nearly half of Asia's Protestants are in China. Evangelical growth 7%. Pentecostal growth 6.7%.
Missionaries:
to Asia (expatriates from Asia and the world) 17,059 (1:172,000 people).
from Asia (to their own and other countries) 23,681 (1:4,900 Protestants) 3,461frn 9,593xcul 14,088dom.

Roman Catholic 2.9%. 85 million. Affil 2.8%. 82 million. Growth 3.5%. A majority in Philippines; large numbers in India, Vietnam and Sri Lanka.
Missionaries:
to Asia (expatriates from Asia and the world) 10,909 (1:154,000 people).
from Asia (to their own and other countries) 7,542 (1:10,800 Catholics).

Other Catholic 0.17%. 5 million. Growth 1.5%.
Orthodox 0.08%. 1.78 million. Growth 1.25%. Almost entirely Syrian Orthodox Indians in Kerala State, India.

Marginal groups 0.37%. 10.6 million. Growth 6%. Filipino and Chinese groups, also Mormons and Jehovah's Witnesses.

Church groups	Cong	Members	Affiliated
Protestant	45,900	52,105,000	115,260,000
Evangelical 3.1% of pop		40,160,000	90,700,000
Pentecostal 0.4% of pop		5,330,000	11,580,000
Charismatic 1.3% of pop		15,800,000	38,700,000
Roman Catholic	68,010	46,900,000	81,900,000
Charismatic		est. 150,000	260,000
Other Catholic	9,700	3,100,000	5,116,000
Orthodox	1,390	1,060,000	1,776,000
Marginal groups	33,000	5,600,000	10,400,000
Total	158,000	108,765,000	214,452,000

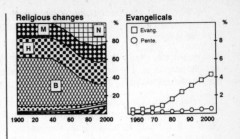

PRAISE ITEMS AND ANSWERS TO PRAYER

1. **Asia's most spectacular church growth** in history was probably the harvest won in the 1980s – most of this in China, Korea and Indonesia.
a) **Protestants** increased from 58 million in 1980 to 127 million in 1990. This is a doubling of the Protestant Church in a decade.
b) **Asian Evangelicals** probably surpassed the number in North America in about 1987 and in the entire Western world (North America, Europe and Australasia) in 1991.
c) **Roman Catholic** growth was less spectacular – from 69 to 82 million affiliated over the decade.

2. **The major growth has been in China** – three million Catholics and 1.5 million Protestants in 1949 had become an estimated 12 million and 63 million respectively by 1992. The world has never known a turning on such a scale before.

3. **South Korea is a land of Christian superlatives**. The largest Christian gatherings ever held, the world's largest congregations of Pentecostals, Presbyterians and Methodists, the largest theological seminaries and the largest non-Western missionary-sending nation! All this in a land that only opened up for the gospel just over a century ago.

4. **Indonesia's claim to renown** is being the first largely Muslim country to have many Muslims coming to Christ. Some estimate that a fifth of the population could be Christian today, though not all of these come from a Muslim background.

5. **Asia's doors are opening.** In 1980 there were five countries with no known groups of believers: Afghanistan, Cambodia, North Korea, Maldives and Mongolia. There are now only three; there are believers in Afghanistan and growing churches in Mongolia today. Countries with great restrictions on Christians have eased these and more Christian ministries are possible in Nepal, Laos, Vietnam and Cambodia. This stimulates faith for the opening of closed lands such as Bhutan, Brunei, Maldives, North Korea.

6. **Asia has has experienced revival.** In the last three decades there have been significant awakenings and revivals in Indonesia (West Timor, Java, Irian Jaya), India (Nagaland, Mizoram), China and elsewhere.

7. **Asia's missions movement** has gained in momentum, size, maturity and in fruitfulness around the world. Chinese, Korean, Filipino and Japanese missionaries are becoming an increasing component in the missionary force in many lands – see evidence of that in the countries that follow. The multiplication of Indian agencies and missionaries is cause for praise.

THE CHURCH IN ASIA

> **January 14**

There is much for which to praise God in Asia, but there are also major prayer needs. To name a few:

1. **Areas of decline.** For decades the church in Sri Lanka has been steadily going down as a percentage of the population – only recently reversed. Hong Kong is losing as many Christians through emigration as it is gaining through conversion. North India has a small Christian presence, but this is nominal and in decline in many areas. Pray for this to be reversed.

2. **Nominalism.** This has become a problem in some Christian communities in Indonesia, India, Myanmar and Philippines; yet in these same countries many denominations are growing vigorously. Pray for revival.

3. **Syncretism.** Evangelical theological education has expanded as nowhere else in the world in east and southeast Asia. Theology is being indigenized and losing some of the Western emphases, but is in danger of compromise – in universalism, evolution and veneration of ancestors and other areas.

4. **Persecution.** The collapse of Communism in other parts of the world has less affected Asia. Persecution of all believers is still acute in North Korea and persecution of unofficial Christianity in China and Vietnam remains harsh. Persecution of Christians by Muslims in Indonesia, Pakistan, Malaysia and Brunei has increased during the '80s. Buddhists in Bhutan and Sri Lanka have stepped up pressure on Christians. There is greater freedom in Hindu Nepal, but persecution of Christians has increased in some areas of India.

5. **Missions vision.** This has grown spectacularly during the '80s. At first most of this vision was for unreached ethnic groups within their own nations (especially India, Philippines, Myanmar, Indonesia) or to their own ethnic communities in other lands (Japanese, Koreans and Chinese especially). However, this has changed and the cross-cultural foreign missionary force is growing fast. Particular areas to cover in prayer:
   a) **Maturity in missions** and willingness to learn from mistakes of the past and not repeat them – for example in paternalism and use of funds.
   b) **Partnerships with Western missions to be mutually beneficial**, whether serving together in international agencies or through inter-agency cooperation on fields.
   c) **Effective local church and denominational support for missions.** Few understand the cost, long periods of time required for language and culture learning, the need for supportive ministries and the effort to see fruit in a pioneer field.
   d) **Retention of Asian missionaries** who are serving cross-culturally. This will be a big long-term problem unless issues such as the education of missionaries' children and retirement are tackled.

| January 15 | THE UNFINISHED TASK IN ASIA |

Here are a few broad assessments of needs.

1. **There are 2,658 ethno-linguistic peoples in Asia.** Of these, 1,607 are among the least evangelized (as defined in the above table). *[See the diagram on page 113.]*

2. **There are 15 countries of the 26 in Asia with less than 1% of population who are Evangelicals.** Of these, six have less than 0.1% – Afghanistan, Bangladesh, Bhutan, Cambodia, Maldives and Mongolia.

3. **The Muslim bloc** is almost untouched. Apart from Javanese Muslims in Indonesia, few have heard the gospel and even fewer have believed. There has been, until now, only a trickle of converts to Christ from Muslim Malays, Indians, Bengalis, Pakistanis, etc. Very few national or expatriate workers are even engaged in seeking to win them.

4. **The Hindus** have only been marginally evangelized. Some reckon that only 1–2% of all Christians in India are first-generation converts out of Hinduism. The higher castes and the millions of North India are some of the least reached groups of Asia. A new and concerted effort must be made to win Hindus to the Saviour. Much of present Indian cross-cultural outreach is to the tribal peoples. More should be done for the Hindus. Breakthroughs among Hindus in neighbouring Nepal give raised expectations for India too.

5. **The core of the Buddhist world is Tibet.** For a century or more there has been prayer and effort to reach Tibetans, but with meagre results and few openings. New efforts are bearing fruit – in Nepal, Mongolia, North India, Siberia and other lands. Pray Tibet open. Other Buddhist lands have been unyielding and few converts to Christ won. Especially pray for Bhutan, Thailand and Sri Lanka.

The missions input still needed – both from Asia and other parts of the Christian world:

1. **Provision of visas.** Many countries have made entry of missionaries more difficult. Yet some of the largest unreached peoples and least evangelized countries of the world are in Asia. Pray for the relaxation of restrictions for India, Indonesia and Myanmar.

2. **Effective use of the present missionary force** for pioneer work and to train national believers to pioneer among unreached peoples.

3. **Greater mobilization of indigenous churches and agencies** to send cross-cultural missionaries within their own country. India, Myanmar and Indonesia have achieved much in compensating for the loss of expatriate missionaries in many areas of their countries.

4. **Effective and innovative strategies** for non-residential missionary activity directed towards peoples and areas not so open for direct outreach – through training programmes, literature, radio and other means.

<table>
<tr><td>January
16–21</td><td></td></tr>
</table>

Caribbean

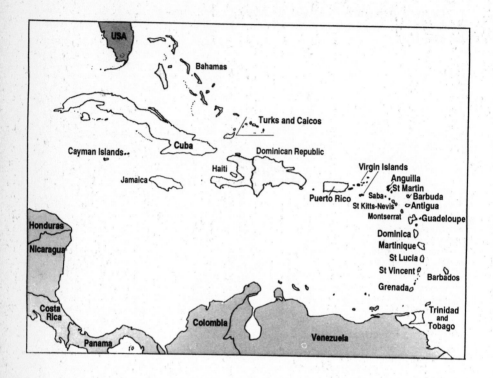

Area 730,000 sq.km. 0.5% of the land surface of the world.

The following included in this overview:
1. All the islands of the Caribbean:
a) The Greater Antilles: Cuba, Hispaniola (Dominican Republic and Haiti), Jamaica, Puerto Rico.
b) The Lesser Antilles (the Windward and Leeward Islands) comprising all the smaller islands.

2. The mainland states and territories that do not use Spanish (they are non-Latin enclaves in Latin America): Belize, French Guiana, Guyana and Suriname.

These countries are conveniently grouped together, though their commonalities may be limited to geography, spiritual history and, for the English-speaking states, a single international cricket team! The territories marked with * have no specific prayer calendar day. Please pray for them during the period assigned to this region. Territories marked with superscript numbers are grouped together for prayer.

Country	Population in millions		Affiliated Christian Percentages			Total No. of Peoples	Peoples in Country World		
	1990	1995	Total	Prot	Evang		A	B	C
Anguilla*	0.0	0.0	94.5	89.4	18.4	4	0	1	3
Antigua and Barbuda*	0.1	0.1	77.3	67.9	11.7	4	0	1	3
Aruba (2)	0.1	0.1	91.7	9.9	6.0	2	0	0	2
Bahamas*	0.3	0.3	71.6	53.4	33.2	6	0	2	4
Barbados*	0.3	0.3	71.7	64.4	24.5	9	1	4	4
Belize	0.2	0.2	92.1	25.7	11.6	15	0	5	10
Bermuda*	0.1	0.1	86.3	69.2	17.8	5	0	1	4
British Virgin Is*	0.0	0.0	90.2	83.9	25.2	7	0	2	5
Cayman Islands*	0.0	0.0	76.9	74.9	32.3	5	0	2	3
Cuba	10.3	10.8	44.1	2.8	2.5	14	0	8	6
Dominica*	0.1	0.1	86.3	16.9	9.6	12	3	3	6
Dominican Republic	7.2	7.9	84.4	6.1	5.1	13	0	4	9
French Guiana(1)	0.1	0.1	78.7	5.8	3.9	19	3	5	11
Grenada*	0.1	0.1	92.1	33.6	12.3	7	0	0	7
Guadeloupe(1)	0.3	0.3	94.4	6.1	4.1	6	0	1	5
Guyana	0.8	0.8	48.3	33.3	15.5	23	2	8	13
Haiti	6.5	7.1	88.3	25.5	20.7	8	0	3	5
Jamaica	2.5	2.7	50.4	38.0	18.5	12	0	7	5
Martinique(1)	0.3	0.3	87.8	8.0	5.1	8	0	3	5
Montserrat	0.0	0.0	81.1	68.6	21.2	7	0	1	6
Netherlands Antilles(2)	0.2	0.2	94.4	12.9	4.7	13	0	4	9
Puerto Rico	3.7	4.0	90.1	26.0	22.5	11	0	4	7
St Kitts and Nevis*	0.0	0.0	79.4	67.3	25.3	5	0	1	4
St Lucia*	0.2	0.2	92.9	18.2	10.3	6	0	0	6
St Vincent*	0.1	0.1	68.2	54.0	24.7	12	0	2	10
Suriname	0.4	0.4	39.5	17.6	2.9	26	5	6	15
Trinidad & Tobago	1.3	1.5	56.7	27.5	10.2	16	1	3	12
Turks and Caicos Is*	0.0	0.0	77.6	63.6	36.5	4	0	0	4
Virgin Is of the USA*	0.1	0.1	87.7	55.6	22.7	8	0	2	6
CARIBBEAN	35.3	37.8	69.2	16.5	11.1	287	15	83	189

World A The unevangelized/unreached world where %E < 50% for constituent peoples.
World B The evangelized non-Christian world where %E > 50% and All Christians < 60%.
World C The broadly Christian world where All Christians in people are > 60%.
See Appendix 5 for fuller definitions.

Population: About 0.67% of the world's population.

Population		Ann.Gr.	Density
1985	32,792,000	1.32%	42.4/sq.km
1990	35,266,000	1.47%	45.6/sq.km
1995	37,840,000	1.42%	49.0/sq.km
2000	40,442,000	1.34%	52.3/sq.km

These figures hide great disparities of population and population density.
Mainland territories (4) 1,456,000 and 3 people/sq.km.
Lesser Antilles 3,582,000 and 132 people/sq.km.
Greater Antilles (5) 30,228,000 and 142 people/sq.km.

Peoples:
Amerindians 0.18%. The original inhabitants have been virtually wiped out through disease and ill treatment: 26,000 in 10 tribes in the Guianas and 38,000 in three tribes in Belize.

Afro-Caribbean 35%. Introduced from Africa with great cruelty as slave labour for the sugar plantations.

Creole/Mulatto (Afro-European) 31.1%. Together with the Afro-Caribbean, a majority in all states but Cuba, Guyana and Suriname.

Europeans 30%. Predominantly Spanish (96%), some British, French, Dutch, etc. The majority originally came as sugar planters. The European component is a majority only in Cuba.
Asians 3.7% – brought in by the British and Dutch from India and Java (Indonesia) to Trinidad, Guyana and Suriname. There are about 91,000 Chinese in these three lands and Cuba. Asians are in the majority in Guyana and Suriname.

Cities: There are only four world-class cities of over one million. Urbanization 44%.

Economy: The mainland states are underdeveloped and underpopulated, with great economic potential if the political determination were there. Most islands are overpopulated, with limited possibilities for development; hence much poverty and emigration to North America and Europe. There is overdependence on sugar-growing and tourism. The economy is further held back by poor communications between the many and scattered islands, and the collapse of the oil refining industry. The poorer territories are heavily dependent on aid programmes and advantageous trade agreements with Europe and North America. The richer territories have often gained their wealth through off-shore banking and even drug-dealing with dire effects on public life and crime levels.

Politics: All but Puerto Rico of the Greater Antilles are independent, but with both Cuba and Haiti politically and economically isolated because of repressive dictatorships. Thirteen states remain dependent on larger powers – Britain (6), France (3), Netherlands (2), USA (2). Efforts to promote greater political unity have foundered on:

1. **Language divisions** – due to the haphazard acquisition of colonial possessions by the European powers. The Caribbean population is linguistically divided thus: Spanish 59%, French 21%, English 17%, Dutch 3%.

2. **The insularity of the island peoples.** Each island has its own character and is resentful of outside influence and control. There are 29 political entities in the region.

3. **Distance and smallness of populations** which make inter-island communication and trade uneconomic.

Religion: This has been largely determined by that of the original colonizing power.
Non-religious/other 10.8%. 3.8 million; mostly in Cuba, but in decline as Communism loses its dominance.
Spiritist/animist 8.4%. 3 million. Rapid increase in Cuba during the '70s and '80s. Much Voodooism in Haiti.
Hindu 1.9%. 664,000. Mainly East Indians and Javanese in the Guianas. Also **Sikh** 0.03%.

Muslim 0.68%. 240,000. East Indians and Javanese.
Baha'i 0.08%. 28,000.
Buddhist/other Asian 0.05%. 20,000. Mainly Chinese.
Jews 0.03%. 9,700.
Christian 78%. 27 million. Only in Cuba, Guyana and Suriname are Christians a minority.
   Protestant 19.4%. 6.8 million. Affil 16.5%. Growth 3.9%. A majority in most of the English-speaking territories except Dominica and St Lucia. Evangelical growth 5.7%. Pentecostal growth 5.8%.
   Missionaries:
      to Caribbean (expatriates from Caribbean and the world) 1,985 (1:17,800 people).
      from Caribbean 262 (1:22,200 Protestants) 125frn 83xcul 179dom.
   Roman Catholic 57.3%. 20 million. Affil 51.5%. Growth 0.69%. A majority in all Spanish- and French-speaking territories.
   Missionaries:
      to Caribbean 5,566 (1:6,300 people).
      from Caribbean 842 (1:21,500 Catholics).
   Orthodox 0.07%. 26,000.
Marginal 1.21%. 430,000. Affil 1.1%. Growth 3%.

Church groupings	Cong	Members	Affiliated
Protestant	24,100	2,585,000	5,816,000
Evangelical 11.1% of pop		1,780,000	3,900,000
Pentecostal 5.4%		942,000	1,918,000
Charismatic 0.6%		85,000	200,000
Roman Catholic	3,629	10,384,000	18,174,000
Charismatic	est.	100,000	210,000
Orthodox	98	16,700	26,000
Marginal	2,150	126,000	378,000
Total	29,977	13,112,000	24,394,000

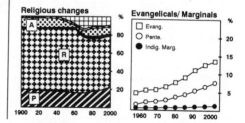

Religious changes

Evangelicals/ Marginals
□ Evang.
○ Pente.
● Indig. Marg.

PRAISE POINTS AND ANSWERS TO PRAYER

1. **Communism's collapse** has removed one of the major sources of tension and violent revolution in the region. Castro defiantly refuses to relinquish control in Cuba and continues to uphold the "revolution" despite disastrous economic decline and diplomatic isolation.

2. **A great turning to God in Cuba** is cause for praise. The failed ideology of Communism and broken economy has turned people to seek after God. An unprecedented growth in evangelical churches is under way.

THE CHURCH IN THE CARIBBEAN

The population has been Christian for centuries and a general stagnation, compromise with the world and loss of vision is widespread. The sad legacy of the past and difficult economic present hinder spiritual growth and vitality. Pray for:

1. **Revival** that will restore the church and rebuild family life. In many areas 80–85% of children are born out of wedlock and stable two-parent families are rare.

2. **Clear proclamation of the Truth.** Cults, spiritism and error have become a major problem with heavy losses of nominal Christians.

3. **Economic viability** for the small nations that will enable workers to be trained, missions vision to be encouraged and pastors to be supported.

4. **Leadership training.** There are nearly 60 accredited evangelical theological institutions in the area: Spanish (Puerto Rico 12; Dominican Republic 7; Cuba 1); French (Haiti 12; Guadeloupe 1); English (Jamaica 14; Trinidad 6; St Vincent 3). Funding for students is a critical issue. Few schools major on missions, so missions vision is limited.

5. **Ministry to young people.** Few churches have adequate programmes. High unemployment and limited prospects for advancement turn many to drugs, crime and immorality. The smaller islands and territories have fewer ministries for youth.

6. **Christian literature.** Larger islands are better served, but poverty and the cost of transport between the islands make it hard to provide affordable literature for the smaller islands. Pray for the work of **CLC** with 10 bookstores in eight countries and a ministry through correspondence courses and publication of the *Caribbean Challenge* magazine, an evangelistic and teaching magazine with a 29-nation circulation.

THE UNFINISHED TASK IN THE CARIBBEAN

1. **Less-reached islands and communities:**
a) **Many smaller islands** are neglected and isolated such as the Grenadines, Barbuda, Anguilla and St Martin.
b) **Rastafarians** reject the Western worldview and champion Black consciousness, exotic life styles and use of drugs. Many young people have turned to them. There are 250,000 in the Caribbean, UK and USA.
c) **The wealthy** are mostly unreached. Some islands have become rich through off-shore banking, laundering of drug money and trans-shipment of drugs from Latin America to the West. The corrupting influence of money and drugs has subverted governments, stimulated crime and damaged whole societies.
d) **East Indians** are a major section of the community in Trinidad, Suriname and Guyana and a minority on most islands. Most are Hindu, Muslim or Sikh and represent the largest non-Christian peoples of the Caribbean, yet there is a significant Christian minority among them.
e) **The Chinese** are scattered throughout the region, but with concentrations in Jamaica (31,000), Trinidad (6,500), Belize (2,500) and elsewhere. A number have become Christian but in some areas there is no witness among them.

2. **The greatest need is for a missions vision** to be rekindled in Caribbean churches. In the last century Caribbean missionaries played a decisive role in the evangelization of West Africa.

January 22–25

Eurasia

Countries included: All constituent republics of the former USSR (with the exception of the three Baltic states: Estonia, Latvia and Lithuania). These are:

1. The Russian Federation.

2. The three European republics: Byelarus, Moldova and Ukraine.

3. The three Caucasus republics: Armenia, Azerbaijan and Georgia.

4. The five Central Asian states: Kazakhstan, Kyrgyzstan, Tajikistan, Turkmenistan and Uzbekistan.
Note: During the lifetime of this edition of Operation World *other countries may fragment, such as Russia and Georgia.*

Area 22,100,000 sq.km. Extending from the Baltic to the Pacific, the Arctic Ocean to Central Asia.

Country	Population in millions 1990	Population in millions 1995	Affiliated Christian Percentages Total	Affiliated Christian Percentages Prot	Affiliated Christian Percentages Evang	Total No. of Peoples	Peoples in Country World A	Peoples in Country World B	Peoples in Country World C
Armenia	3.3	3.4	79.1	0.6	0.6	24	10	5	9
Azerbaijan	7.1	7.6	2.6	0.0	0.0	32	21	4	7
Byelarus	10.2	10.5	67.6	1.1	1.0	25	6	6	13
Georgia	5.4	5.6	56.2	0.4	0.3	32	16	5	11
Kazakhstan	16.7	17.6	11.2	1.0	0.7	48	26	8	14
Kyrgyzstan	4.3	4.7	7.4	0.2	0.2	41	24	7	10
Moldova	4.4	4.5	63.1	1.7	1.5	30	10	6	14
Russia	148.1	150.9	51.6	0.7	0.6	160	85	29	46
Tajikistan	5.2	6.0	2.3	0.0	0.0	39	22	7	10
Turkmenistan	3.6	4.1	3.7	0.0	0.0	37	20	6	11
Ukraine	51.8	52.5	65.1	3.2	2.7	65	27	12	26
Uzbekistan	20.4	23.0	1.5	0.1	0.1	63	39	9	15
EURASIA	280.6	290.5	45.8	1.1	0.9	596	306	104	186

World A The unevangelized/unreached world where %E < 50% for constituent peoples.
World B The evangelized non-Christian world where %E > 50% and All Christians < 60%.
World C The broadly Christian world where All Christians in people are > 60%.
See Appendix 5 for fuller definitions.

Population		Ann.Gr	Density
1985	269,800,000	1.03%	12.0/sq.km
1990	280,600,000	0.79%	12.7/sq.km
1995	290,500,000	0.70%	13.1/sq.km
2000	300,000,000	0.65%	13.6/sq.km

Peoples: Total 127 in USSR Census 1989; 596 peoples within countries.
Indo-European 78.9%.
  Slav 71.2%. Mainly Russian, Ukrainian and Byelorussian.
  Caucasus peoples 4.1%.
  Iranian 1.5%.
  Other 2.1%.
Turkic/Altaic 17.2%. Central Asians, Bashkir, Tatar, etc.
Finno/Ugric 1.2%.
Jews 0.5%.
Other 2.2%. German, Korean, etc.

Literacy 98%. **All languages:** over 145. **Languages with Scriptures** 30Bi 17NT 34por.

Urbanization 66%. There are 24 cities of over one million inhabitants.

Economy: Over 70 years of a highly centralized socialist command economy. The gross distortions, inefficiencies, and short-sightedness of the system ultimately led to the collapse of both the economy and the ideology that had spawned it. Only since 1989 has the extent of the damage to national infrastructure, ecology and work ethic of the population become plain. Only with much pain, a radical change in attitudes and wise investment of huge amounts of capital can a market economy and stability be attained. The vast mineral and agricultural wealth of these republics and also the high level of education of the population have hardly been tapped.

Politics: The awesome military power of the USSR obscured the rottenness within. The suddenness and completeness of the collapse of the Soviet Empire and the ideology of Marxist-Leninism that held it together astonished the world. This disintegration has been accompanied by:

1. Power struggles between the ex-Communists and emerging democrats intent on reforming their countries.

2. Civil wars in Azerbaijan, Georgia, Moldova and Tajikistan.

3. Inter-republic wars in the Caucasus.

4. Ethnic discrimination by local nationalist majorities of minorities (especially Russians).

5. Vast movements of population as the ethnic mixing encouraged for a lifetime is gradually unravelled.

6. Breakdowns in long-established trading patterns.

7. Uncertainty about the fate of the USSR's considerable stockpile of nuclear weapons.

The '90s may lead to the further disintegration of Russia, Georgia and other republics, enormous social and economic upheavals and major regional wars. Attempts to retain trading, economic and political links under the umbrella of the Commonwealth of Independent States have all failed and the CIS is likely to be temporary in status and a bridge between the dictatorial centralism of the USSR and total autonomy of national states.

Religion: The persecution of Christians and all religions under Communism was unprecedented in modern times. Especially severe were the devastating purges of Stalin in the 1930s. There were an estimated 12 million Christians martyred – Orthodox, Catholic and Protestant. Religious freedom since 1990 in most republics has restored the fortunes and much of the influence of the Orthodox Church as well as turning the whole region into a spiritual battlefield for the missionary faiths of the world.

1. The six predominantly Muslim states are being assiduously courted by Saudi Arabia, Iran and Turkey.

2. Every variety of cult, eastern religion and New Age movement has sought to gain a following.

3. Input by Western and Asian Evangelicals with heavy investment of money, materials and manpower has brought millions into contact with the gospel.

4. Ukraine and Byelarus are the scene of a confrontation between the Orthodox (who took over the churches of the banned Catholic Uniates) and the latter's claims for the return of what is rightfully theirs.

Non-religious/other 29.3%. 82 million.
Growth −6%. Millions of agnostics and former Communist Party members (supposedly atheist) have been turning to Christianity.
Muslim 18%. 50.3 million. Growth 2.5%. The majority religion of six countries.
Jews 0.52%. 1.5 million. Growth −5%. Steady decline through emigration. In 1970 there were 2.2 million Jews.
Animist/shamanist 0.42%. 1.2 million. Est. growth 6%.
Buddhist 0.34%. 960,000. Est. growth 8%.
New religions 0.3%. 900,000. Est. growth 30%.

Christian 51.1%. 143 million. Affil 45.8%. Growth 5.5%.
Protestant 1.1%. 3.2 million. Half in Ukraine. Christian statistics are considerably lower than those estimated a decade ago under Communism, but rapid growth since 1989, especially among Pentecostals. Growth est. 5.9%. Evangelical growth 7.7%. Pentecostal growth 13.3%.
Missionaries:
to Eurasia (expatriates from Eurasia and the world) est. 1,035.
from Eurasia est. 351 31frn 39xcul 312dom.
Catholic 3.9%. 11 million. Both Latin- and Eastern-rite Catholics. Predominantly in Byelarus and Ukraine. Rapid growth since the Communist suppression of the Eastern-rite Uniates ended. Est. growth 15%.
Orthodox 46.1%. 129 million. Predominantly Russian, Ukrainian, Byelorussian and Moldovan. Est. growth 5%.
Marginal groups est. 0.04%. 120,000.

Church

groupings	Cong	Members	Affiliated
Protestant	6,900	1,160,000	3,139,000
Evangelical 0.92% of pop		900,000	2,700,000
Pentecostal 0.41%		340,000	1,190,000
Catholic	2,500	6,045,000	9,067,000
Orthodox	17,200	77,000,000	116,000,000
Marginal	n.a.	93,000	240,000
Total	26,600	84,298,000	128,446,000

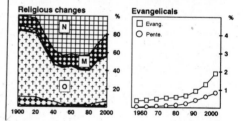

Religious changes

Evangelicals

PRAISE ITEMS AND ANSWERS TO PRAYER

1. **Communism's collapse** came with bewildering speed and little violence. What an answer to the prayers of millions! A seven-year campaign of prayer for the Soviet Union was launched in 1983 by **Open Doors** and others with the goal of complete religious liberty and Bibles available to all. The goals were achieved on time!

2. **Christianity's triumph** over its most implacable persecutor in the 20th century is cause for great rejoicing. May the battle won not become a peace lost in dissension and carnality.

3. **Disgust and rejection of all that Communism did and taught** has caused a search after spirituality and for God. Millions have turned to the faith of their forebears. Every evangelistic outreach creates a big response – even if understanding is limited.

4. **The multi-faceted efforts from Christians of other lands** to evangelize in nearly every city and district of the region has made a significant impact – evangelistic campaigns, extensive use of the media, literature and Bible distribution, establishing theological training programmes and material aid. It is reckoned that by 1993, 105 million people had seen the Russian version of the *Jesus* film.

5. **The rapid multiplication of indigenous agencies** for missions, evangelism and social concern, especially in Ukraine and to a lesser extent in Russia and Central Asia, is cause for much praise.

THE CHURCH

A new day of opportunity has opened up for Christian witness; it could so easily be lost. So pray for:

1. **Unity and understanding among Christians.** There have been tensions between the Orthodox and Protestants, Baptists and Pentecostals, and Uniate Catholics and Orthodox which have not helped in making an impact on the many who are sincerely seeking spiritual light.

2. **Healing of past wounds.** Under Communism, government interference in Church life, appointment of leaders, dispensing of privileges and persecution caused division in nearly every denomination between the legal and illegal, or registered and unregistered. Those divisions remain. Pray for revival.

3. **Training of leaders.** For so long forbidden, this is now being taken up with vigour. Numerous new seminaries, Bible schools and TEE programmes have sprung up across the region – many as cooperative efforts between indigenous churches and Western and Korean mission agencies. A 1993 survey revealed that by 1994 there will be up to 64 Protestant, 21 Orthodox and seven Catholic institutions – most launched since 1989. There are approximately 2,000 Protestant students doing formal courses and a further 4,600 in TEE or BEE informal courses. Pray that these institutions and students may give the theological depth and spiritual cutting edge to the Church for growth in the '90s.

4. **Sensitivity and wisdom for expatriate agencies in relating to indigenous believers.** The extraordinary and sudden changes stirred an enormous interest and commitment among Western and Asian Christians. Amidst much good, there was much that brought discredit and confusion. Many went in on short-term programmes with little cultural preparation and less humility in dispensing aid, advice and inappropriate Western programmes. Empire-building and media grandstanding was pursued by some. Pray for stabilization, long-term commitment and real support for indigenous leadership and initiatives.

5. **Vision for outreach and missions** in the day of opportunity. How long will that opportunity remain?

THE FUTURE   January 25

Events in Eurasia over the coming two decades will deeply affect the world. Pray for God's Kingdom to be extended whatever the future may bring. Specifically pray for:

1. **The leaders of these 12 nations.** Democracy is an untried experiment. Some have moved further in liberalizing politico-economic structures, others hesitate and shelter behind the old system with its controls. Pray for wisdom and big-heartedness among leaders in relating to both ethnic minorities within their borders and surrounding nations, without which little betterment can be expected. Inter-state wars could create a battlefield far bigger than the former Yugoslavia. New tyrannies could arise.

2. **The Central Asian republics.** For five centuries they were a global backwater, but they are regaining their strategic importance. Their vast oil, gas and mineral wealth, their dismaying lack of water but growing population, and the political and religious tug-of-war involving five surrounding nations that possess nuclear weapons could make the region one of the major world flashpoints in the '90s. Pray that impending events may lead to the rapid growth of the Church among these peoples.

3. **The millions of people** likely to be forced to move or become refugees as national identities and languages are enforced. Over 71 million people are living as minorities under the rule of an ethnic majority – 25 million Russians alone live in other republics of the former USSR. Pray that uncertainty and fear for the future may cause many to seek after peace in the Lord Jesus.

4. **Repair of ecological damage.** Millions live in areas severely contaminated by nuclear and biological accidents, irresponsible dumping of toxic chemicals and careless misuse of the environment. Health and quality of life will be affected for generations to come. Pray that Christians may both give aid to those affected and become leaders with the moral authority and integrity to address these horrendous wrongs.

THE UNREACHED

Only the broad outlines of the peoples and regions with the least gospel witness can be given here. See the individual countries for more detail.

1. **The Central Asian republics.** These are some of the least evangelized nations on earth. Especially needy are the rural areas.

2. **The Caucasus republics.** Azerbaijan and most of the small republics which are part of the Russian Federation have few, if any, indigenous believers.

3. **The medley of small peoples in the Caucasus** in both Russia and the Caucasus republics of Armenia, Azerbaijan and Georgia. Most are Muslim and without an indigenous witness.

4. **The Arctic and Siberian peoples.** Most were superficially evangelized in the last century but little living Christianity exists today.

5. **The Buddhist peoples** – the Kalmyk in Europe and other peoples along Russia's Siberian border with China and Mongolia.

6. **There is a total of 596 peoples** within the countries of Eurasia. Of these, 306 are in the less-reached category.

These areas have suddenly become one of the most spectacular open doors for pioneer evangelism after years of being some of the most inaccessible. Pray that this door may remain open and the opportunities be well used.

January
26–29

Europe

The new Europe is reflected in the classification used here which includes the following:

1. All the states of western and southern Europe, including Cyprus (see p 68 for map of Cyprus).

2. All the former non-USSR ex-Communist states of central Europe.

3. The Baltic states – Estonia, Latvia and Lithuania – which were annexed by the USSR for 50 years.

All the remaining European and Asian republics of the former USSR are grouped under Eurasia.

Area 4,499,000 sq.km. This is 3.3% of the earth's land surface area.

Country	Population in millions 1990	1995	Affiliated Christian Percentages Total	Prot	Evang	Total No. of Peoples	Peoples in Country World A	B	C
Albania	3.2	3.5	14.2	0.1	0.1	12	5	5	2
Andorra[1]	0.1	0.1	86.9	0.1	0.1	5	1	0	4
Austria	7.5	7.5	90.3	5.3	0.5	28	0	8	20
Belgium	9.9	10.0	89.5	0.9	0.3	29	2	11	16
Bosnia[2]	4.3	4.4	41.9	0.0	0.0	19	3	3	13
Bulgaria	9.0	9.0	69.0	1.3	1.2	34	7	3	24
Channel Islands[3]	0.1	0.1	See UK			5	0	2	3
Croatia[2]	4.7	4.8	88.1	0.6	0.2	26	2	4	20
Cyprus	0.7	0.7	77.9	1.0	0.4	11	4	1	6
Czech Republic[4]	15.7	15.9	54.3	5.1	1.4	24	1	4	19
Denmark[5]	5.1	5.1	91.3	90.1	4.8	25	0	6	19
Estonia	1.6	1.6	36.7	15.3	7.5	20	4	5	11
Faeroe Islands[5]	0.0	0.0	93.6	93.1	25.7	4	0	0	4
Finland	5.0	5.0	89.2	87.3	16.0	20	1	2	17
France[8]	56.2	57.2	71.1	1.8	0.6	90	13	15	62
Germany	79.1	80.0	73.7	37.0	3.2	80	9	14	57
Gibraltar[1]	0.0	0.0	75.4	7.9	1.5	6	0	3	3
Greece	10.0	10.1	96.2	0.2	0.1	23	4	2	17
Holy See (Vatican)[6]	0.0	0.0	100.0	0.0	0.0	3	0	0	3
Hungary	10.6	10.5	86.5	24.4	4.9	20	2	1	17
Iceland	0.3	0.3	98.2	97.0	2.8	6	0	0	6
Ireland	3.7	3.9	89.9	3.5	0.9	19	0	3	16
Isle of Man[3]	0.1	0.1	See UK			4	1	0	3
Italy[6]	57.3	57.6	80.4	1.1	1.0	54	3	5	46
Latvia	2.7	2.8	37.4	14.7	5.6	34	8	7	19
Liechtenstein[7]	0.0	0.0	84.8	7.2	0.3	4	1	0	3
Lithuania	3.7	3.8	74.7	1.0	0.3	23	8	4	11
Luxembourg	0.4	0.4	83.8	1.2	0.1	12	0	1	11
Macedonia[2]	2.0	2.1	62.8	0.2	0.1	23	5	3	15
Malta	0.4	0.4	95.2	0.5	0.1	9	1	2	6
Monaco[8]	0.0	0.0	90.1	3.6	0.2	12	0	1	11
Netherlands	15.0	15.3	64.1	27.7	5.0	39	3	13	23
Norway[9]	4.2	4.3	90.0	88.7	9.8	21	0	1	20
Poland	38.4	39.4	97.9	0.5	0.2	22	4	2	16
Portugal	10.3	10.4	91.4	1.2	1.0	22	0	3	19
Romania	23.3	23.8	85.0	7.9	4.9	29	6	3	20
San Marino[6]	0.0	0.0	92.5	0.0	0.0	3	0	0	3
Slovakia[4]	0.0	0.0	Incl with Czech Republic			5	0	0	5
Slovenia[2]	2.0	2.0	82.5	1.3	0.2	14	0	0	14
Spain[1]	39.3	40.1	87.7	0.9	0.8	31	2	4	25
Svalbard[9]	0.0	0.0	48.2	33.0	8.2	2	0	1	1
Sweden	8.3	8.3	59.2	55.6	6.8	45	2	4	39
Switzerland[7]	6.5	6.6	91.0	41.0	5.4	33	0	7	26
United Kingdom[3]	56.9	57.3	66.5	53.2	8.6	93	13	18	62
Yugoslavia[2]	10.2	10.3	74.0	0.8	0.2	40	5	5	30
EUROPE	507.9	514.8	77.2	18.3	2.8	1,083	120	176	787

Superscript numbering indicates countries grouped together under the same assigned prayer day.

World A The unevangelized/unreached world where %E < 50% for constituent peoples.
World B The evangelized non-Christian world where %E > 50% and All Christians < 60%.
World C The broadly Christian world where All Christians in people are > 60%.
See Appendix 5 for fuller definitions.

Population		Ann.Gr	Density
1985	483,516,000	0.3%	107/sq.km
1990	507,944,000	0.9%	112/sq.km
1995	514,781,000	0.3%	114/sq.km
2000	527,877,000	0.5%	116/sq.km

Peoples: Europe's ethnic diversity, strong national-isms and large migratory movements are a major factor in hindering stability and cooperation. All ethnic groups within Europe's countries: 1,083. See table on previous page and graph on p 113.
Germanic 34.9%. Predominantly central and north-western Europe. Majority in 15 states and territories.
Latin 33.7%. Southern and southwestern Europe, also Romania. Majority in 10 states.
Slavic 16.6%. Central and eastern Europe. Majority in nine states.
Finno/Ugric 3.6%. Finland, Estonia and Hungary.
Greek 2.2%. Greece and Cyprus.
Gypsy 1%. 5,200,000. In nearly every country of Europe.
Turks 0.7%. 3,600,000.
Jews 0.24%. 1,200,000.
Other Europeans 4.4%.
Other 2.7%. Middle Eastern 8,000,000; Asian 3,500,000; Caribbean 1,600,000; African 600,000.

Languages indigenous to Europe 124.

Urbanization 75%.

Economy: Western Europe's relative affluence is in contrast to central and eastern Europe's impover-ishment under Communism. The task of integrating East Germany with the West has proved so costly that it has helped plunge the continent into recession and imperilled painstaking efforts to build a united, integrated Europe. Europe's long industrial and technological dominance in the world has steadily given way to that of North America and Asian nations of the Pacific Rim. Income/person $12,990 (62% of USA and 51% of Japan).

Politics: Major forces in Europe of the 1990s.

1. **Political and economic integration.** The EC has done much to break down trade barriers and integrate the nations of Western Europe, but can the bureaucratic monster created prove flexible and innovative enough in the modern world?

2. **Ethnic fragmentation.** For 200 years ideology has masked Europe's ancient ethnic conflicts. These underlie the civil wars in the former Yugosla-via, tardiness in unifying Europe economically, guerrilla movements in Northern Ireland, Corsica and Spain, violence against immigrant communities and oppression of minorities in central Europe.

3. **The future direction of central Europe.** The economic, political and moral damage wreaked by Communism was far greater than realized, and made western Europe's welcome more cool than that needed. This could increase stresses in Europe in the '90s.

4. **Multiplied millions of illegal immigrants** who

could flood into Europe. These will be fleeing shortages of food and water and also economic stagnation in Africa, poverty in parts of the Middle East and Eurasia.

Religion: After the Muslim invasions of the 8th century, Christianity was virtually wiped out in the lands of the Middle East where the early Church first took root. For nearly 1,000 years the countries of the West became the last major refuge for Christianity. The encircling Muslim lands effectively prevented any missionary outreach to Africa and Asia. It was not until the Reformation in the 16th century that the Church was revitalized to eventually become a force for world evangelization. The last 250 years have been years of worldwide advance for the gospel. Yet in this time, a deadening secular humanism has effectually become the dominating force in Euro-pean society. This philosophy has corrupted every part of its culture – art, music, social values, morality and theology. The decline in churchgoing has been so disastrous that only about a tenth of Europe's population are regular worshippers in a church. The decline in Christian profession is shown in the graph on the opposite page.
Major religious trends:

1. **The sea-change in worldview** of younger Euro-peans away from the certainties of their Judeo-Christian heritage to New Age thinking, relative truth, reincarnation and the occult.

2. **Freedom of religion for all of Europe.** For the first time in history there is freedom to propagate one's faith, to change religion and worship unhin-dered. Residual legal restrictions remain in a few countries.

3. **The growth of Evangelicalism** both in mainline denominations and in smaller evangelical, Pente-costal and charismatic churches – the growing edge of the church in Europe despite the overall decline.

Non-religious/other 17.6%. There are 90 million openly non-religious people in Europe. Growth 3.7%. In the former Communist countries growth is probably −3.3%.
Muslim 3.3%. 16.8 million. Growth 4.2%. Much of the growth is through immigration from North Africa and the Middle East and also a higher birth rate. Albania is Europe's only majority Muslim country. In Bosnia, Muslims have been the largest religious group, but this may no longer be so with Serbian expulsions of Muslims. Other states with over one million Muslims are: Bulgaria, France, Germany, Italy, UK and Yugoslavia (Serbia and Montenegro). In seven European states Muslims are more than 10% of the population.
Jews 0.25%. 1.3 million. In 1960 it was three million. Losses through emigration and assimilation. Largest concentrations: France (620,000), UK (347,000), Hungary (63,000).
Hindu 0.11%. 565,000. Growth 8%. Major concen-trations in UK (originating from India, East Africa) and Netherlands (from Suriname). Rapid growth through immigration of Tamils from Sri Lanka.

Sikh 0.08%. Almost entirely in cities in England.
Buddhist 0.08%. Mainly Asians.
Other 0.07%.
Christian 78.5%. 397 million. Growth 0.3% – mainly central Europe's temporary increase concealing west Europe's continuing decline. Most "Christians" have retained few meaningful links with the Church.
  Protestant 18.7%. 95 million. A majority in nine lands and territories. Growth 0.5% (mainly through growth in central Europe). Evangelical growth 1.6%. Pentecostal growth 6%, but Pentecostals are proportionately the world's smallest community with relation to that of all Protestants.
  Missionaries:
    to Europe (expatriates from European and other countries) 9,685 (1:52,400 people).
    from Europe 19,564 (1:4,800 Protestants) 15,671frn 15,780xcul 3,784dom.
  Roman Catholic 49.8%. 253 million. Growth 0.1%. A majority in 21 states and territories.
  Missionaries:
    to Europe (from European and other countries) est. 35,764 (1:14,200 people).
    from Europe est 117,920 (mainly 1973 figures) (1:2,100 Catholics).
  Other Catholic 0.16%. 800,000.
  Orthodox 9%. 46 million. Majority in six states. Growth 0.8%. Growth mainly in former Communist states of southeast Europe.

Marginal groups 0.85%. 4.3 million. Growth 5.4%.

Church groupings

	Cong	Members	Affiliated
Protestant	120,000	41,200,000	93,100,000
Evangelical 2.8% of pop		6,600,000	14,400,000
Pentecostal 0.56%		1,400,000	2,800,000
Roman Catholic	134,000	137,800,000	248,600,000
Charismatics est. 0.45%		1,300,000	2,300,000
Other Catholic	1,500	310,000	490,000
Orthodox	52,000	31,700,000	45,800,000
Marginal	18,300	2,000,000	4,200,000
Total	325,800	213,000,000	392,200,000

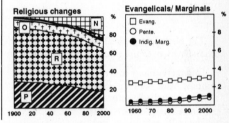

Religious changes

Evangelicals/ Marginals
□ Evang.
○ Pente.
● Indig. Marg.

PRAISE ITEMS AND ANSWERS TO PRAYER

1. **The sudden disappearance of the Iron Curtain** that had divided Europe for nearly half a century was a dramatic answer to prayer! Who could have expected it to happen so quickly, relatively peacefully and completely? Communism's sordid reality has been vividly portrayed and millions once tyrannized are seeking spiritual solutions.

2. **Freedom of religion** has become a reality for all of Europe – for the first time ever. Praise God for this, but pray that unprecedented windows of opportunity may be wisely used to proclaim the gospel of freedom in Christ.

3. **Europe's great spiritual heritage** has blessed the world. Five hundred years ago Christianity was a beleaguered remnant in western and northern Europe. God gave great movements – the Reformation, Pietism, revivals, men and women of God – which resulted in the world being penetrated with the gospel. Praise God for the past. May Europe's spiritual fortunes once more be restored, and the continent return to its Christian roots.

4. **Present movements of the Spirit** in Europe. Only a few salient points can be given.
a) **The steady growth in strength and confidence of Evangelicals.** In mainline denominations their proportion is increasing and newer evangelical, charismatic and Pentecostal denominations are growing and attracting young people.
b) **The increase in Evangelicals in theological training.** All over Europe liberal schools are empty, and evangelical seminaries and schools are multiplying and often full.
c) **The turning of Gypsy people to Christ.** Of the estimated 10 million Gypsies in Europe, over 200,000 are fervent Pentecostal Christians, and they are now the largest group of evangelical believers in both Spain and France.
d) **The responsiveness of some immigrant groups** – Antilleans in France and Caribbean peoples in the UK, Vietnamese and Chinese being examples.
e) **The growth of Evangelicals in central Europe**, especially Romania, Albania and Bulgaria. In Bulgaria over 5,000 Turkish-speaking people have come to Christ since 1990. Since the collapse of atheism in Albania evangelical churches have multiplied.

January 28
EUROPE'S LEADERS

The face of Europe was dramatically changed in 1989/90. The reverberations of the demise of Communism will take decades to subside. The leaders of Europe's nations need special prayer as they grapple with these changes. Pray for:

1. **Vision and generosity** in helping the newly-free nations to retain that freedom and to attain reasonable economic growth and integration into the developed economies of western Europe. Failure could have dire consequences.

2. **The European Community** – founded and developed with such expectation. The EC is floundering. Leaders need courage to set aside narrow, national self-interest and protectionism for the sake of the betterment of all and fulfil responsibilities both inside and outside the Community.

3. **Restoration of moral and spiritual values in society.** Leaders are bowing to anti-Christian pressure groups to dispense with the very standards that have undergirded Europe's culture and development.

THE CHURCH

1. **The church in general has lost the younger generation.** Christian profession is likely to decline dramatically over the coming two decades. Pray for continent-wide revival to reverse this trend.

2. **Liberal theology** rose to dominate theological institutions all over Europe by the beginning of this century. Most mainline Protestant denominations were spiritually crippled by the resulting loss in confidence in the Scriptures and uniqueness of the gospel. Liberal theological institutions are sparsely patronized by students today and this aberration is losing influence. In contrast, evangelical theological institutions are generally full and the proportion of Evangelicals in mainline denominations increasing. Pray for a return to relevant biblical theology, preaching and life style in the mainline denominations. Free Church and Pentecostal Christians are only a small proportion of the total Christian community.

3. **The Church in central Europe** has emerged from the long night of Communist oppression battered but alive. Since 1989 there has been a considerable return of people to the faith of their forefathers – mainly to Orthodox and Catholic Churches. Evangelical groups have seen a spurt of growth in most lands. Pray that this momentum might be maintained and that Christians may play a key role in restoring moral, ethical and spiritual standards in society.

4. **A renewed missions vision** is needed. The opportunities and challenges are enormous both in Europe and worldwide. Pray that Christians might regain a sense of victorious expectation that replaces a widespread negativism and defensiveness.

January 29
EUROPE'S NEED

1. **Great swathes of Europe are truly post-Christian** with a small, "irrelevant", committed Christian remnant, and need to be evangelized again – for example, North Germany, parts of Sweden, rural England and Wales and much of France. Many of these areas have not had much meaningful exposure to biblical Christianity for several generations.

2. **Evangelical churches are few in much of southern Europe,** and especially southeastern Europe. About 22 states in Europe have less than 1% Evangelicals, and of these 11 have less than 0.2%. Look prayerfully through the list after the Europe map. Pray for the planting of many vibrant, witnessing groups of believers in these lands.

3. **Major peoples in Europe with a Christian tradition** but very few Evangelicals. To name a few: Lithuanian, Serbian, Montenegrin, Macedonian, Greek, Basque.

4. **Young people** are a challenge. In few countries has Christianity any meaning. Christians are considered remnants of a past age that hinder "progress". New Age "spirituality", an eastern religious worldview and fascination with the occult have diverted millions from their Christian heritage and its absolutes. Pray for those involved in outreach and discipling ministries among youth.

5. **Unreached peoples.** Nearly 300 non-Christian peoples within Europe's countries are only partially evangelized at best. Many are immigrant or refugee peoples for whom specialized outreach is needed. Of particular challenge are:

a) **Muslim ethnic groups** from the Middle East, North Africa, Black Africa and southeast Europe (especially Bosnians, Albanians and Turks).

b) **Gypsy minorities** – especially those of the Balkan states.

c) **The Jewish remnant** – decimated in many lands in the Holocaust and through emigration to Israel, but still needing to be brought to the Messiah.

6. **Europe's ethnic and political ferment** will continue to cause great migrations of people as refugees from poverty, war and famine. Pray that new and unexpected opportunities to share love and the gospel may not be lost.

<table>
<tr><td>

January 30–
February 1

</td></tr>
</table>

Latin America

Country	Population in millions 1990	1995	Affiliated Christian Percentages Total	Prot	Evang	Total No. of Peoples	Peoples in Country World A	B	C
Argentina[1]	32.3	34.3	90.9	7.7	6.9	63	2	13	48
Bolivia	7.3	8.4	88.5	9.3	8.4	60	6	13	41
Brazil	150.4	165.1	91.7	19.2	17.8	257	31	109	117
Chile	13.2	14.2	89.0	27.8	26.9	27	3	6	18
Colombia	31.8	34.9	95.9	3.7	3.1	99	13	21	65
Costa Rica	3.0	3.4	91.8	10.7	9.7	20	0	5	15
Ecuador	10.8	12.3	92.5	3.5	3.4	32	3	8	21
El Salvador	5.3	5.9	94.6	20.6	19.8	14	1	3	10
Falkland Islands[1]	0.0	0.0	86.9	75.9	36.3	4	0	0	4
Guatemala	9.2	10.6	88.5	24.0	23.3	61	0	4	57
Honduras	5.1	6.0	94.7	11.0	10.4	25	1	4	20
Mexico	88.6	98.0	88.0	5.2	4.3	269	3	5	261
Nicaragua	3.9	4.5	91.0	17.3	15.1	23	1	7	15
Panama	2.4	2.7	90.0	16.7	13.7	32	2	10	20
Paraguay	4.3	4.9	97.0	5.4	4.3	40	2	10	28
Peru	22.3	25.1	93.0	7.0	5.6	107	20	18	69
Uruguay	3.1	3.2	56.2	3.5	2.2	31	1	1	29
Venezuela	19.7	22.2	91.0	5.3	4.8	69	7	24	38
LATIN AMERICA	412.7	455.8	90.9	12.1	11.1	1,233	96	261	876

World A The unevangelized/unreached world where %E < 50% for constituent peoples.
World B The evangelized non-Christian world where %E > 50% and All Christians < 60%.
World C The broadly Christian world where All Christians in people are > 60%.
See Appendix 5 for fuller definitions.

Area 19,807,000 sq.km. 14.6% of the world's land area.

Countries included:

1. All Spanish- and Portuguese-speaking states of mainland Central and South America.

2. The Falkland/Malvinas Islands – whose ownership is in dispute between Argentina and Britain.

Countries excluded:

1. Caribbean Islands (including Spanish-speaking states).

2. The three Guianas and Belize, which are included with the Caribbean Region.

Population		Ann.Gr	Density
1985	370,783,000	2.3%	19/sq.km
1990	412,742,000	2.2%	21/sq.km
1995	455,807,000	2.0%	23/sq.km
2000	499,134,000	1.8%	25/sq.km

7.8% of world's population.

Peoples: Total peoples within countries 1,233. Racial intermingling has been on such a scale that a breakdown of ethnic groups is only approximate. There is more class consciousness than colour consciousness in most countries, but there are wide differences in composition between the countries. There are five main components to the population:
Amerindians 11%. The original inhabitants. A majority in Guatemala and Bolivia, nearly half the population in Peru and Ecuador, and a large minority of Mexico and Paraguay. Two major types:
   Highland nations 9.7%, whose empires were crushed by the Spanish in the 16th century. Major peoples are the Quechua 18,300,000 and Aymara 3,400,000 of Peru, Bolivia, etc., and the Maya 7,300,000 and Aztec 5,600,000 of Central America – all with numerous ethnic and language subdivisions.
   Lowland tribes and smaller peoples 1.3%. Estimates as to the number of peoples vary between 800 and 1,200. Most are very small indeed.
Euro-American 41.4%. In the majority in Argentina, Brazil, Uruguay and Costa Rica and a large minority in Chile, Paraguay, Mexico and the Andean region. Politically dominant throughout the continent. Immigrant European minority communities have retained language and culture distinctives in many lands, but are steadily being absorbed into the host culture.
Afro-American 7%. Descendants of slaves brought from Africa. Most live in Brazil, but many live along the Caribbean and Pacific coasts of Venezuela, Colombia and Ecuador.
Mixed Race 39.8%. A majority in eight nations.
   Mestizos (in South America) and **Ladinos** (in Central America) are mixed European and Amerindian. Many Amerindians become Mestizos simply by adopting Spanish as their language.
   Mulattos are of mixed European and African origin.
Asians 0.8%. Considerable Japanese and Korean emigration to Brazil, and Chinese to all parts of the continent.

Literacy 85%. **All languages** approx. 670. **Indigenous languages with Scriptures** 9Bi 254NT 191por.

Cities: There are 27 cities of over one million inhabitants; Mexico City and Sao Paulo are the world's largest cities. Urbanization 71%.

Economy: In 1982–83 Latin America's economic woes threatened the world's banking system with massive debts and corrupt despotic regimes unwilling to make changes. The coming of more democratic rule instituting economic reforms has transformed the situation and many economies are growing rapidly. The rapid growth in population, the yawning gap between the rich elite and the poor, and the baleful influence of the narcotics "industry" are serious matters yet to be tackled.

Politics: Major trends in the '80s and '90s.

1. **The democratization of Latin America** which gathered pace in the '80s; by 1993 most countries had freely elected democratic governments. Much must be done to reform political and judicial structures that hitherto protected authoritarian rule, and also to make the democratic process more sensitive to the needs of the people.

2. **The decline in Marxist revolutionary guerrilla warfare** following the eclipse of Communism elsewhere. The underlying social inequalities that fuelled these insurrections are not yet adequately addressed. Only in Peru, and to a lesser degree Guatemala and Colombia, are there guerrilla wars in progress. However, in El Salvador and Nicaragua peace remains fragile.

3. **Narcotics empires** so powerful as to openly challenge national and local government and engage in destructive military action. This problem is particularly acute in Colombia, Panama and Peru.

4. **Regional economic alliances** which are emerging as the economies of most nations improve. Mexico is joining NAFTA (with USA and Canada), the Southern Cone nations are establishing *MERCOSUR*, and the Andean Pact is drawing together the Andes nations.

Religion: In 1900 almost the entire population was considered Catholic. The changes since then have been dramatic – from a narrow traditionalism, with strong opposition to Protestant missionary activity, to freedom of religion and a rapid growth of Evangelicals. The Catholic Church has responded with a vigorous drive to check these losses and regain the initiative and hearts of the people.
Non-religious/other 3.3%. 14 million. Growth 6.4%. Many young urban intellectuals have become secularists and Marxists.
Animist/spiritist 2.4%. 10 million. Both the original Amerindian beliefs and Afro-Spiritism. The latter is growing as fast as Pentecostalism in some areas – especially Brazil and Uruguay. Growth 2.5%.
Muslim 0.21%. 900,000. Growth 6.7%. Half in Argentina, most of the remainder in Brazil, Panama and Venezuela.
Baha'i 0.2%. 770,000. Growth 4%.
Jews 0.13%. 530,000. Growth −4%. Mainly in Argentina, Brazil, Mexico and Uruguay.
Buddhist/East Asian religions 0.1%. 400,000. Growth −3%.
Christian 93.7%. 387 million. Only in Uruguay and Bolivia are professing Christians less than 90% of the population. Growth 2.0%.
   Protestant 12.4%. 51 million. In 1960 Latin America was 3.4% Protestant with 6.7 million people. Growth 8.8%. In Guatemala, Chile and El Salvador over 20% of the population is Protestant, and in Brazil, Nicaragua and Panama it is over 15%.

Evangelical growth 8.8%.
Pentecostal growth 9.8%.
Missionaries:
 to Latin America (expatriates from Latin America
 and the world) 14,620 (1:28,200 people).
 from Latin America 4,482 (1:11,200 Protestants)
 1,364frn 2,126xcul 2,356dom.
Roman Catholic 79.2%. Growth 1.1%. 327
million. Many are baptized Catholic but practising
Spiritists or Christo-pagans. Practising Catholics
vary between 10% and 20% of national populations. Losses to other denominations or religions
is 3.7 million annually or 10,000 daily.
Missionaries:
 to Latin America 30,330 (1973–1990 figures).
 from Latin America 9,835 (mainly 1973 figures).
Other Catholic 0.76%. 3.1 million. Mainly in Brazil.
Growth 2%.
Orthodox 0.14%. 572,000. Mainly immigrants
from Europe and Middle East. Growth 2.9%.
Marginal groups 1.2%. 4.9 million. Predominantly
Mormons and Jehovah's Witnesses.
Growth 13.9%.

Church groupings	Cong	Members	Affiliated
Protestant	270,000	23,700,000	50,000,000
Evangelical 11.1% of pop		21,370,000	45,720,000
Pentecostal 8.7%		16,840,000	35,900,000
Roman Catholic	31,634	197,450,000	316,100,000
Charismatics est. 0.47%		1,200,000	1,900,000
Other Catholics	900	1,574,000	3,130,000
Orthodox	1,600	290,000	519,000
Marginal groups	26,400	2,364,000	5,000,000
Totals	330,534	225,380,000	374,749,000

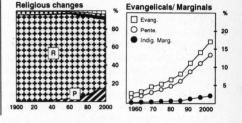

PRAISE ITEMS AND ANSWERS TO PRAYER

Praise the Lord for the powerful work of the Holy Spirit in Latin America this century. This has been one of the great evangelical missionary successes of the 20th century. Growth came slowly at first; opposition and persecution was normal. The first churches were planted by Protestant immigrants from Europe, then by expatriate agencies. However, in recent years the explosive growth has come from indigenous Pentecostal denominations. Specific items for praise:

1. **Evangelicals have grown** from an estimated 200–300,000 in 1900 to 21 million in 1980 and 46 million in 1990. This could rise to 80–90 million by 2000 if the high loss-rate can be reduced. Evangelicals have become a dynamic new force for the regeneration of Latin American political and economic structures.

2. **Over 11% of Latin Americans are Evangelicals.** Some have given even higher estimates which are hard to substantiate. Yet even figures used here tell an amazing story. Brazil has twice as many Evangelicals as there are in all of Europe. There are more Evangelicals in a worship service on Sunday than Catholics in this, the most Catholic of continents.

3. **National crises and disasters** have furthered the gospel. Economic stress, guerrilla warfare, earthquakes and tyrannies have all worked together to spur response to widespread proclamation of the gospel. This has been particularly true for Guatemala, Nicaragua and El Salvador, where earthquakes and war have been severe. Argentina, after military defeat in the Falklands/Malvinas, has seen revival.

4. **Pentecostal growth** has been spectacular. Nearly 40% of all members of the world's Pentecostal denominations are in Latin America. The growth has been marred by the fragmentation of denominations and, in some countries, large losses too.

5. **The impact of the Scriptures on Catholics** has opened the hearts of millions to a personal encounter with the Lord Jesus. Many have become fervent evangelical believers, both within the Catholic Church and, increasingly, outside it.

6. **People movements are growing among the Amerindians** who have been long resistant or indifferent to the gospel. The present growth of Quechua and Aymara churches in the Andes and Mayan peoples in Central America is exciting.

7. **The Bible translation achievements of WBT and UBS** have been remarkable. The pioneer work of **SIL** in providing New Testaments in indigenous languages has sparked ingatherings of peoples into churches across the continent. In some lands the work of translation has been virtually completed. Praise the Lord for a task well done!

8. There has been rapid growth and maturation of missions vision in Latin America. The COMIBAM Conference in Sao Paulo, Brazil, in 1987 generated continent-wide interest and sparked off numerous new initiatives to reach the unreached. Major missionary-contributing nations are Brazil, Costa Rica and Argentina.

9. The impact of the media has been significant. Widespread use of local, national and international radio and television networks by Christians has had a big impact. International Christian radio agencies broadcast nearly 3,000 hours/week in Spanish and 320 hours in Portuguese. In November 1991 Billy Graham preached to five million all over Latin America during his ministry in Argentina, with overwhelming response.

THE CHURCH

1. The Roman Catholic Church has passed through 30 years of tumultuous change, in part spurred by successes of Evangelicals. The traditional monolithic structure that once dominated the continent has gone for ever. Many regret the misused four centuries of monopoly which bred complacency and condoned syncretism so widespread among ordinary people. The impact of the Vatican II Council, theological diversity, emphasis on Bible reading and the charismatic movement have been enormous. Pope John Paul II has pulled the Church back from political and doctrinal extremes to a more traditional Catholicism. Various powerful movements are discernible:

a) **Concern for the poor and social justice.** Some priests have become revolutionaries espousing liberation theology. Over 200,000 Base Communities have brought lay leadership and social involvement to the fore all over the continent, but often seeking to interpret social issues exclusively in terms of class conflict.

b) **The charismatic movement.** This grew rapidly during the '70s, but is not growing at the same pace now. Millions have been involved; some joined evangelical churches, but others remained within the Catholic Church.

c) **Traditional Catholicism.** This has re-emerged as a strong force. This may lead to a further cooling of relationships with Evangelicals. Popular, and often syncretic, Catholicism is still widespread. Pray for Catholics to come to a personal faith in Christ. Millions still strive to earn their entrance into heaven and gain temporal blessings by their pilgrimages, works and ceremonies.

2. The challenges for Evangelicals in the '90s. Pray for:

a) **Wise handling of political power.** With democracy and their voting power, Evangelicals are thrust into participation. Such power can divert from evangelism or stifle the inclination to be a prophetic voice in a society in need of moral absolutes and ethical standards. Such power could also subvert Evangelicals to seek political power for selfish ends. Evangelicals are increasingly being voted into the highest offices of their respective countries.

b) **Willingness to confront social and economic injustices** in a biblical way. Pray that Latin Americans may develop their own biblical theology by keeping in balance faithfulness to the gospel and social involvement. The Latin American Theological Fraternity, founded in 1969, has an important role in this.

c) **Religious freedom** – this is still an issue despite legislation granting this in many Latin American countries. Discrimination against Evangelicals still occurs in Costa Rica and Venezuela. Localized persecution of Evangelicals has been reported in Mexico, Bolivia and elsewhere. Persecution of Evangelicals by Maoist guerrillas in Peru and Colombia is still very real.

d) **Adequate training for present and future pastors**, whether by informal TEE or church programmes or formal schools. Some reckon that there are 175,000 evangelical pastors with no formal training.

e) **Maturity in the churches.** Evangelistic outreach gains a large following, but many churches fail to conserve the fruit. In some churches the back door is used as much as the front. In Costa Rica there are estimated to be more ex-Evangelicals than Evangelicals.

f) **Denominationalism**, a major problem. The structure of society, encouraging powerful father-figure pastors, gives rise to partisan evangelism and divisions over personalities.

g) **The integration of Amerindian churches** into the mainstream of Christianity in their countries.

h) **Christians to face up to the challenge of the cults** – both Jehovah's Witnesses and Mormons and also Spiritism from Brazil. The latter is growing at a faster rate than even the Pentecostals.

THE UNFINISHED TASK

There are many challenges for outreach ministry in Latin America, but its relative need is less than most other regions of the world. Here are some of these challenges:

1. **Countries with the lowest number of Protestants.** Uruguay, Ecuador and Colombia all have below 4% Protestants, though in the latter two churches are growing fast.

2. **Upper and Middle classes.** These are generally less evangelized by Evangelicals, most of whom come from the poor. Specific strategies are needed to reach these other classes.

3. **The cities.** Some are ringed and permeated by slums and are the home of hundreds of thousands of unwanted street children, hotbeds of crime and drug-taking or -trafficking and, especially in Brazil, increasingly affected by AIDS.

4. **Students** in the universities. Only a small minority are Evangelicals, usually far smaller than the national average. **IFES** has a well established work in over 12 countries, with younger movements in others. Pray for all agencies concentrating on this strategic sector of the community. A clear, radiant, evangelical student witness in every university is a key target for prayer.

5. **Amerindian peoples.** In most of the smaller tribes there are Bible translation and church-planting ministries. However, among some tribes in Colombia, Venezuela and parts of Brazil and Mexico various factors have prevented the effective establishment of an ongoing work. These are: geographical inaccessibility, government restrictions, the assiduous activities of anti-Christian anthropologists and, increasingly, narcotics gangs who have taken over whole areas and terrorized local people to further their evil activities. The total population of unreached is relatively small, probably not exceeding one million, but found in numerous small tribes. Amerindian leaders are actively using the international media to expose their plight and gain recognition of their cultural, political and land rights.

6. **Immigrant communities** from all over the world which are often unreached. The **Chinese** in Central America (100,000) and Peru (60,000) are two such. **Japanese** in Brazil have been more influenced by Catholics than Evangelicals. **Muslims** are increasing in nearly all countries; their numbers are small but significant, most being from the Middle East, and especially Lebanon.

7. **The Jews** of the southern part of the continent. These are one of the least evangelized major concentrations of their people in the world.

8. **The world.** The growing Latin American missionary movement is extending to many parts of the world, but needs prayer for:
   a) **Churches to learn the privileges and responsibilities** of supporting cross-cultural outreach within their own lands and abroad.
   b) **Finance, which is a major limitation.** Lack of it will prevent the present trickle of cross-cultural missionaries from becoming a flood. High inflation in Brazil is a particularly acute problem.
   c) **Developing viable and locally applicable sending structures** and training programmes that result in fruitful long-term missions involvement.
   d) **The ability to relate to the international missions world** and to Western and Asian missionaries.

February
2–4

Middle East

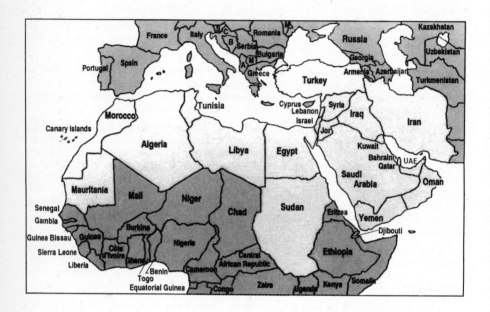

In this survey the Middle East is defined as the Arab lands of North Africa, and all lands of southwest Asia to the west of Pakistan and Afghanistan (the latter two countries being part of the Asian region).

Area 15,654,000 sq.km. 11.5% of the world's land surface. Only 5% of the land in the Middle East has sufficient water to support cultivation.

Country	Population in millions		Affiliated Christian Percentages			Total No. of Peoples	Peoples in Country World		
	1990	1995	Total	Prot	Evang		A	B	C
Algeria	25.4	29.3	0.3	0.1	0.1	41	31	5	5
Bahrain	0.5	0.6	5.0	1.3	0.7	11	5	4	2
Egypt	54.1	60.5	14.1	0.9	0.7	32	16	6	10
Gaza Strip[(1)]	0.6	0.7	Included with Israel			Included with Palestine			
Iran	56.6	64.5	0.4	0.0	0.0	85	73	4	8
Iraq	18.9	22.4	3.0	0.0	0.0	35	21	5	9
Israel[(1)]	6.1	7.2	2.3	0.2	0.2	42	21	12	9
Jordan	3.4	3.8	4.7	0.5	0.2	12	6	3	3
Kuwait	1.3	1.5	3.0	0.2	0.1	25	6	13	6
Lebanon	3.0	3.3	38.4	0.5	0.4	18	2	5	11
Libya	4.5	5.4	2.2	0.1	0.1	36	24	3	9
Mauritania	2.0	2.3	0.3	0.0	0.0	23	18	2	3
Morocco[(2)]	25.1	29.1	0.2	0.0	0.0	30	23	1	6
Oman	1.5	1.7	1.7	0.3	0.2	17	8	7	2
Palestine, West Bank[(1)]	0.9	1.0	Included with Israel			20	5	4	11
Qatar	0.4	0.5	2.5	1.1	0.5	17	5	6	6
Sahara[(2)]	0.2	0.2	0.0	0.0	0.0	11	9	0	2
Saudi Arabia	14.1	17.1	3.2	0.6	0.3	35	18	10	7
Sudan	25.2	29.1	14.4	5.0	3.1	240	184	34	22
Syria	12.5	14.9	6.4	0.2	0.1	26	8	7	11
Tunisia	8.2	9.0	0.2	0.0	0.0	23	13	3	7
Turkey	55.6	61.2	0.2	0.0	0.0	55	34	7	14
United Arab Emirates	1.9	2.2	8.4	0.7	0.3	35	16	14	5
Yemen	10.5	12.4	0.0	0.0	0.0	20	12	4	4
MIDDLE EAST	330.8	378.1	4.6	0.6	0.4	889	558	159	172

World A The unevangelized/unreached world where %E < 50% for constituent peoples.
World B The evangelized non-Christian world where %E > 50% and All Christians < 60%.
World C The broadly Christian world where All Christians in people are > 60%.
See Appendix 5 for fuller definitions.

Population	Ann.Gr	Density
1985	287,090,000	3.2%	18/sq.km
1990	330,828,000	2.9%	21/sq.km
1995	378,050,000	2.7%	24/sq.km
2000	430,057,000	2.6%	27/sq.km

Peoples: Total 889.
Semitic 50.6%. Arab 164,000,000; Jews 3,900,000; Assyrian 180,000. The Arabs conquered the entire region, except for Asia Minor (today's Turkey) in the seventh and eighth centuries, Arabizing the Egyptians and Arameans (Syrians).
Indo-European 20.8%. Iranian 43,900,000; Kurd 21,000,000; Gypsy 3,000,000; European 1,000,000.
Turkic 16.2%. 53,700,000. For centuries the Ottoman Turks ruled most of the countries in the Middle East and North Africa, ending at the turn of this century. Only 45% of Turkic peoples live in the Middle East; the majority live in Eurasia.

African 5.8%. 19,100,000. The great majority live in the Sudan, and culturally belong to Africa south of the Sahara, but are included here in the Middle East. Other African peoples live in Egypt (Nubians), Libya and southern Mauritania.
Berber 5.5%. 18,000,000. North Africa.
Asian 0.73%. 2,400,000. Guest-workers in oil-producing states of the Gulf and Libya.
Caucasus peoples 0.41%. 1,340,000. Armenian, Cherkess, Adygey, Georgian.

Cities: There are 23 world-class cities of over one million people. Urbanization 56%.

Economy: Over 70% of the world's proven oil reserves are in the Middle East. States with oil have become wealthy, and those without remained poor. Three major wars of the past 20 years have impacted the world's economy.

1. The 1973 Yom Kippur war between Israel and the Arab states.

2. The 1978 Iranian revolution with a subsequent eight-year war between Iraq and Iran. This caused massive oil price rises.

3. The oil glut of 1985 and the 1992 Gulf War to liberate Kuwait from Iraq, the effects of which caused a collapse of oil prices. The Gulf War cost Arab states an estimated $620 billion.

Rapid population growth and the politics of water and its distribution could cause immense unrest in the coming 20 years.

Politics: The ending of the Cold War has made the city of Jerusalem and its future the major focus of international instability and emotional involvement of three world religions. The 50-year confrontation between Israel and surrounding Arab nations, two rival forms of Islam battling for power, the concentration of oil wealth and military power and restive ethnic minorities (Kurds, Sudan Africans and North African Berbers) all point to the possibility of major upheavals and wars in the coming decade.

Religion: Three major world religions had their beginnings in the region: Judaism, Christianity and Islam. All claim spiritual descent from Abraham, but intense rivalry, persecution and warfare between them complicate present-day politics.
Muslim 92.5%. 306 million. Growth 3%. Over 30% of all Muslims live in the Middle East. Two major branches of Islam, Sunni and Shi'a, are vying for power and proof of their loyalty to Islam, further stimulating fundamentalist factions and intolerance of dissent or minority religions.
Jews 1.1%. 3.6 million. Growth 2%, mainly through large-scale immigration from the former USSR. About 27% of the Jews of the world live in the region – almost all in Israel.
African traditional religions 0.6%. Two million. Growth −7.2%. Almost entirely southern Sudan peoples. Rapidly decreasing.
Non-religious/other 0.64%. Baha'i 290,000; Hindu 254,000; Buddhist/Eastern religions 130,000.

Christian 5.2%. 17.1 million. Growth 2.4%. Rapid growth in southern Sudan obscures the decline elsewhere. In other areas a lower birthrate, relentless pressures from Muslims to convert Christians, and emigration to the West are causing decline. Note the differences in the graphs below.
Protestant 0.77%. 2.5 million, mostly in southern Sudan. Elsewhere distribution uneven – mainly Egypt, Lebanon and Syria. Growth 7.7%. Evangelical growth 7.2%. Pentecostal growth 4.8%.
Missionaries involved in Middle Eastern ministries (expatriates from Middle East and the world) 2,210 (1:150,000 people).
Missionaries from the Middle East 277 (1:7,100 Protestants) 70frn 61xcul 216dom.
Catholic 1.7%. 5.6 million. 2.2 million of these in southern Sudan, the majority of the rest in non-Latin Uniate churches which retain their own rites and traditions but acknowledge the authority of the Pope. Growth 5.1%.
Missionaries:
  to Middle East est. 4,532.
  from Middle East est. 558.
Orthodox 2.7%. 9 million. Growth −0.3%. Great majority in the Egyptian Coptic Church.
Major

church groups	Cong.	Members	Affiliated
Protestant	est. 2,700	654,000	1,975,000
Evangelical 0.4% of pop		430,000	1,325,000
Pentecostal 0.02% of pop	29,000		60,000
Catholic	2,760	2,660,000	4,600,000
Orthodox	2,600	5,036,000	8,750,000
Total	8,060	8,350,000	15,325,000

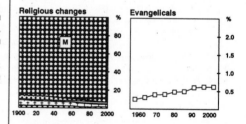

Religious changes

Evangelicals

PRAISE ITEMS AND ANSWERS TO PRAYER

1. **Islamic fundamentalism** has become a powerful force throughout the Muslim world. Rather than uniting Muslims and solving growing economic and social problems, it is dividing and confusing them everywhere with its harsh extremisms. Under an outward conformity is fear, dismay and a search for answers. The Islamic Revolution in Iran is a major factor in the conversion of thousands of Iranians to Christ – mostly among those who fled the country.

2. **Political upheavals** have further unsettled Muslims and eroded their confidence in Islam, with the unending confrontation with Israel, wars between Muslim nations and the disunity of the Arab world. The impact of modern technology only highlights the inadequacies of Islam in providing viable answers to life. As a result there is increased response as never before, though in the whole Middle East there may be no more than 15,000 believers from a Muslim background. Praise God that Muslims are reachable and winnable!

3. **The Gulf War opened up the Kurds** to the world's media and for Christian outreach, leading to the first concerted attempt to reach them. The Kurds are one of the largest unreached peoples in the world.

4. **The Bible Society's ministry (UBS)** has had an extraordinary impact. Every year distribution figures increase, and there is great demand, even at risk of life to obtain copies. Pray that no human barrier may prevent the dissemination of God's Word.

5. **Christian media ministries** have had a quiet but effective impact – radio, magazines, Christian videos and especially the *Jesus* film on video. The advent of satellite broadcasting and impossibility of shielding Muslim populations from hearing the gospel increase opportunities. Pray that a groundswell of interest may so increase that soon large-scale conversions to Christ may occur.

6. **The Church in southern Sudan** is growing fast with a great ingathering of people in the midst of terrible suffering through war, famine and persecution. Praise God for the faithful evangelists and pastors who continue to uplift Christ in evangelism and train new leaders in spite of the danger and suffering.

7. **There is growing concern for and commitment of Christians** to Muslim evangelism in the Middle East and to immigrant communities in other lands. The multiplying of prayer groups that concentrate on the spiritual need of Muslims is encouraging.

8. **The number of volunteers** for service among Middle Eastern peoples is increasing. Both long-term and short-term Christian workers are moving out as tentmaker missionaries and witnesses.

THE FUTURE OF THE MIDDLE EAST | February 3

Political events in the Middle East over the past three decades have already radically changed our world. The next decades could be even more traumatic. Whatever view Christians may have on circumstances that surround the return of the Lord Jesus Christ, all should be prayerfully watching the unfolding events. May the God of history work out his purposes and bring glory to his name! Pray specifically about:

1. **The confrontation between Israel and surrounding nations and the Palestinian population.** Events are heading towards a climax. Hopes for a fair, negotiated settlement are low. Pray for political leaders on all sides that moderation and balance may prevail. Pray for the peace of Jerusalem.

2. **Islamic fundamentalism** which is becoming a major political force. It is radically altering non-theocratic Muslim states through insurrection and terrorism, forcing the Islamization of national structures and life and extending Muslim mission work around the world. The rival systems promoted by Iran and Saudi Arabia are heavily funding these movements. Pray for the frustration of these aims and for these developments to become a means for opening up the Muslim world for the Lord Jesus.

3. **Population growth and lack of water** which are becoming major factors in the politics of the area. Wars and large movements of population are likely. Pray that other nations may respond to these wisely and sensitively. A global confrontation between "Christian" and Muslim nations could easily arise.

THE CHURCH IN THE MIDDLE EAST

1. **Praise God for the tenacity of Middle Eastern Christians.** The ancient Churches in the area have maintained a witness, even if often muted, through centuries of persecution and discrimination.

2. **Muslim pressure on the church** over the centuries caused its extinction in North Africa and decimation in Turkey and Iran; in Egypt and other lands the Church survived. In recent years discrimination and pressure on Christians has increased in a deliberate attempt to eliminate a Christian presence in the area. Inducements to convert to Islam, job discrimination and failure to check violence against Christians and churches have been particularly severe in Egypt. The wars in Lebanon and Sudan have been used to increase Muslim political power and marginalize Christians. Emigration of Christians to other lands has increased. Pray that these losses may be halted.

3. **Popular Muslim misconceptions** convince them that the Christian Church is divided, decadent and in decline. Pray that Christians may live exemplary lives in often difficult circumstances, and that God may grant revival. There are significant renewal and revival movements in Lebanon and Egypt.

4. **Protestant denominations** are generally small except in Egypt and southern Sudan. Relationships between them and the ancient churches have often been strained. Pray for spiritual unity and understanding at a time when all Christians are under threat. Most Protestants are converts from nominal Christianity.

5. **Believers from a Muslim background** are few and often scattered. Pressures on them are usually acute – from relatives, in employment and from the authorities. For many, emigration is the only way out of impossible situations. Pray for:
a) **All who have come to Christ out of Islam.** They need fellowship, but often cannot find it with Christians from a different background. They need to study the Word and become established, but rarely have the time or facilities. They need courage in the face of intimidation, threats, ostracism and even physical danger.
b) **The witness of believers.** They need deliverance from fear, a commendable life style, inspiration to witness wisely, and expectation of fruit from their witness.
c) **Christian homes.** These are few. Unequal marriages between Christians and Muslims are a major cause of backsliding. The Muslim world needs to see the beauty of a Christian home.
d) **Church planting.** Too few congregations of former Muslims exist.

6. **Trained leadership for the Protestant churches** is inadequate. There are few in training and few institutions in the Middle East that can provide it. Many of those who study in the West find good ministry opportunities there, and few return. Pray for the development of fellowship links between indigenous Christian workers.

7. **A missionary vision needs to develop.** Some Middle Eastern Christians work in lands closed to normal mission work: Libya, Saudi Arabia, etc. This vision needs to be encouraged. Pray for the excellent work done in this respect by **OM** and **YWAM** in mobilizing and training young people from Jordan, Sudan and Egypt.

February 4

THE UNFINISHED TASK
IN THE MIDDLE EAST

1. **The home of the early Church is now the most needy mission field in the world.** Islam is both the most zealous persecutor of Christians and the most resistant to the gospel of all the world's ideologies. Pray that the centuries of misunderstanding of the truths of the gospel and mistrust generated by negative interactions with Christians may be removed. Pray also for the love of Christ to constrain Christians to reach out to Muslims.

2. **The Muslim heartland** in the Middle East contains only 30% of the world's Muslims, yet the focal point of Islam is Mecca in Saudi Arabia. Pray for a visible manifestation of Christ's glory so that the whole Muslim world is affected.

3. **The opening up of the Muslim world for the gospel** cannot be organized by human effort or stratagems but only by prayer. Our weapons are spiritual, not carnal. Pray for an army of intercessors to be raised up that a breakthrough as decisive and sudden as that in China and the former USSR may also occur in the Muslim world. During the Muslim fasting month of Ramadan in 1993, many Christians round the world fasted and prayed for this. May this become an annual event until the breakthrough is given!

4. **The unreached.** So many could be named:
a) **Countless villages and towns** where the gospel has never been proclaimed.
b) **University students:** only in Egypt is there an established evangelical student work.
c) **The lands closed to the gospel and without a single known indigenous evangelical church:** Mauritania, Libya, Saudi Arabia, Qatar, Kuwait and UAE. In each of these lands there are, however, groups of expatriate believers.
d) **The 15 lands where indigenous evangelical believers number less than 1,000.** In addition to the above: Algeria, Bahrain, Morocco, Oman, Tunisia, Turkey, Yemen.

e) **The numerous ethnic minorities** without a single known believer or portion of God's Word in their own language, such as some of the Berber peoples of North Africa, the Beja and Darfur peoples of Sudan, the many minorities of Iran, the Nubians of Egypt and the Druze of Lebanon.

f) **Muslim women** who are virtually inaccessible in their prison-like seclusion in many lands.

5. **Effective means of reaching Muslims** must be used to the full:

a) **Medical work.** This opens up countries and hearts to the gospel, and is the only way in which missionary work can be done in some states. Pray for this ministry, that it may create opportunities for a witness to Muslims. There are openings for medical workers with Christian agencies and in government hospitals.

b) **Personal witness** by nationals and expatriates. This is the most effective way, but it needs a high degree of self-giving, much love and patience, and great faith. Pray for the many Asian Christians serving in secular employment and maintaining a courageous witness.

c) **Bible distribution.** The **UBS** has seen a considerable increase in Bible distribution – 37,000 Bibles and New Testaments in 1992 alone. Pray for effective and innovative ways of distributing Bibles in lands where all is done to prevent this.

d) **Christian literature.** This is especially important for both teaching Christians and winning Muslims. Pray for:

    i) **Producers of literature. MECO**, Carmel Mission and others have a region-wide ministry in producing good apologetic literature. Pray for all engaged in writing, publishing and distributing literature. **OM** has distributed much literature in various countries in recent years.

    ii) *Magalla* **Magazine** (**MEM**). With a circulation of 60,000 every month and up to 350,000 readers, this has had a significant impact on non-Christian young people. It has a broad interest presentation with a good Christian slant.

    iii) **Books.** Arabic Christian publishers bring out, on average, 25 new titles annually – few are written locally in Arabic. Pray that this number may increase.

e) **Radio**, the most effective (and sometimes the only) means of witnessing to Muslims in many areas. There are studios for the production of programmes in Spain (**GMU**) and France (**AWM**) for broadcasting by **TWR** in Monaco and Cyprus and **FEBA** in Seychelles. The response has been good and effective when follow-up is possible by BCCs and personal contacts with Christians. Television programming for satellite broadcasting gives many creative opportunities. Pray that these may be adequately used.

f) **Bible correspondence courses.** In combination with Christian radio, these have been used of the Lord to win more Muslims to Christ than any other ministry. This is especially true of North Africa, Turkey and Iran. Pray for missions involved in this ministry: **GMU**, **IFES** and others. This witness is subject to much opposition by Muslim authorities – postal censorship and harassment of students, etc. Pray for these students, that they may be won for Christ and brought into living fellowships of believers.

g) **Gospel recordings, and audio and video cassette tapes** which are proving ideal tools for evangelism and Christian teaching in areas that have not been visited by missionaries. There are over five million video cassette recorders in use in the region.

h) **Muslims in other lands** who are more accessible. Pray for all involved in ministry to students and workers in Europe and North America. Pray that converts from this ministry may become effective witnesses when they return home.

FURTHER PRAYER INFORMATION

For security reasons, little has been indicated in this book of specific Christian agencies in the nations of the region. There are many who would use such information to hinder or stop work now being done. If the Lord leads you, we suggest you contact:

a) **FFM**, a prayer fellowship of Christians worldwide which provides good prayer information covering the Muslim world. See Appendix 2 for address.

b) The agencies listed in Appendix 2: **AWM, CMA, Frontiers, Interserve, MECO, OM, WEC, YWAM,** who all have a deep concern for, and involvement in, the area.

c) **MEM**: Middle East Media, P.O. Box 1845, Limassol, Cyprus.

d) **Friends of Turkey**, PO Box 3098, Grand Junction, CO 81502, USA and PO Box 28, Ilkley, W. Yorks., LS29 6RB, England.

e) *Intercede*, Center for Ministry to Muslims, 1315 Portland Ave, Minneapolis MN 55404, USA.

f) *Muslim People's News*, People International, PO Box 26, Tunbridge Wells, Kent TN2 5AZ, England.

<table>
<tr><td>February
5</td><td></td></tr>
</table>

North America

Area 21,675,000 sq.km. North America contains three of the 13 largest countries of the world: Canada (2); USA (4) and Greenland (13). Nearly 16% of the world's land surface.

Country	Population in millions		Affiliated Christian Percentages			Total No. of Peoples	Peoples in Country World		
	1990	1995	Total	Prot	Evang		A	B	C
Canada	27.3	26.5	64.2	18.0	7.6	157	6	22	129
Greenland*	0.1	0.1	68.1	67.5	3.7	4	0	0	4
St Pierre & Miquelon*	0.0	0.0	96.0	0.9	0.1	2	0	0	2
United States of America	249.2	258.2	71.5	43.1	30.2	264	22	26	216
NORTH AMERICA	276.6	284.8	70.7	40.6	27.9	427	28	48	351

*These territories have no prayer calendar date. Include Greenland with Denmark; St Pierre and Miquelon with France.

World A The unevangelized/unreached world where %E < 50% for constituent peoples.
World B The evangelized non-Christian world where %E > 50% and All Christians < 60%.
World C The broadly Christian world where All Christians in people are > 60%.
See Appendix 5 for fuller definitions.

Population		Ann.Gr	Density
1985	264,721,000	1.0%	12/sq.km
1990	276,594,000	0.9%	13/sq.km
1995	284,793,000	0.6%	13/sq.km
2000	294,769,000	0.7%	14/sq.km

5.2% of the world's population.

Peoples:
Native Americans 1.1%. Only in Greenland are they in a majority; elsewhere often a marginalized under-class alongside a large majority that overran their continent.

Euro-American 72%. Communities from every ethnic group in Europe have settled in the New World.
Afro-American 11%. Almost entirely urban.
Hispanic 8.5%. Most are from Mexico, Central America and Caribbean.
Asian 3.1%. Majority are immigrants from east Asia and settled on North America's Pacific coast.
Jews 2.4%.
Middle Eastern 1.9%.

All languages 245. English is the major language of communication except for French in Quebec, Canada, and in St Pierre and Miquelon, and Danish in Greenland.

Cities: There are 47 cities of over one million inhabitants. Urbanization 74%.

Economy: Economically the world's wealthiest region despite decline in the '80s. The North American Free Trade Area finalized in 1993 makes Mexico, USA and Canada the most powerful trading bloc in the world.

Politics: The economic and political strength of the USA has the potential to overwhelm its neighbours, which encourages a defensive nationalism on the part of the latter.

Religion: Freedom of religion.
Non-religious/other 8.8%. 25 million.
Jews 2.3%. 6.3 million.
Muslim 1.7%. 4.7 million. Growth 6% – mostly through immigration from Middle East.
Buddhist/East Asian religions 0.4%. 1.1 million. Mostly Chinese and Japanese.
Hindu 0.25%. 700,000.

Other 0.4%. Sikh 260,000; Baha'i 100,000; Animist/spiritist 100,000.
Christian 86.2%. 238 million. Affil 70.7%. 196 million. Growth 0.35%.
  Protestant 49.4%. 137 million. Affil 40.6%. 112 million. Growth 0.22%. Evangelical growth 1.7%. Pentecostal growth 5.6%.
  Missionaries:
    to North America (expatriates from North America and the world) 2,942 (1:94,000 people).
    from North America 64,378 (1:6,300 Protestants) 43,554frn 44,168xcul 20,210 dom.
  Roman Catholic 29.7%. 82 million. Affil 23.4%. 64.8 million. Growth 0.1%.
  Missionaries:
    to North America 11,171 (1973 figure).
    from North America 8,554 (1:7,600 Catholics).
  Other Catholic 0.26%. 716,000. Affil 0.23%. 650,000. Growth −0.7%.
  Orthodox 3%. 8.3 million. Affil 2.8%. 7.7 million. Growth 0.5%.
  Marginal groups 3.8%. 10.6 million. Affil 3.7%. 10.3 million. Growth 4.3%.

Church groupings	Cong	Members	Affiliated
Protestant	400,000	76,100,000	112,283,000
Evangelical 27.9% of pop		50,200,000	77,260,000
Pentecostal 6.9%		8,800,000	19,000,000
Charismatic 5.6%		11,240,000	15,500,000
Roman Catholic	28,367	44,300,000	64,800,000
Charismatic 1% of pop		2,730,000	4,000,000
Other Catholic	1,100	400,000	650,000
Orthodox	2,300	5,300,000	7,700,000
Marginal	45,400	6,500,000	10,300,000
Total	477,167	132,600,000	195,733,000

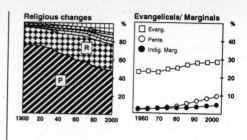

PRAISE POINTS AND ANSWERS TO PRAYER

1. **The spiritual impact of North America**, and especially the USA, on the world. Praise God for:
a) **Great evangelists** who have touched the world (Finney, Moody, Billy Graham and others).
b) **Great missionary statesmen** and visionaries who helped to lay the foundations for the present global harvest.
c) **Unstinting generosity** in giving for great causes – especially missions advances.
May this influence continue, and supplant the blatant secularism propagated by the media. The Hollywood view of American life is not the whole story!

2. **The missionary contribution of North Americans** in the 20th century. Increasingly the missionary enterprise is becoming global, but even in 1993 it is still predominantly North American – with over 57% of foreign missionaries and 46% of all missionaries (home and foreign).

THE CHURCH IN NORTH AMERICA

Please refer to the sections on USA and Canada. Generalizations for these two countries are superfluous here.

THE UNFINISHED TASK

No other continent has such a wealth of Christians, churches, agencies and available tools and means for evangelizing their own continent and the world. Yet there are real challenges where more needs to be done in the 1990s.

1. **The two smallest territories are the most needy** – **Greenland** with its small population, vast wilderness and few Evangelicals, and **St Pierre and Miquelon** in the St Lawrence estuary with no known congregation of evangelical believers.

2. **The inner-city urban underclass.** The appalling moral collapse, lack of family cohesion, drugs, unemployment and incidence of AIDS are symptoms of a section of society hardly touched by the gospel. Many are Afro-Americans, Hispanics and other recent immigrants.

3. **Both Canada and USA are nations of immigrants** (most of the 28 "World A" peoples of the table above are in this category). Almost every nation on earth and a high proportion of the world's ethnic and linguistic groups have representatives or even large communities in North America. These migrants are a vital component in reaching their own kin in their lands of origin – a resource inadequately researched and used.

Pacific

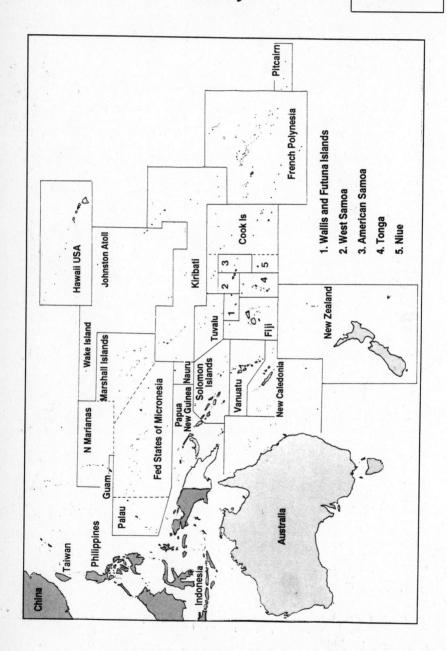

Pitcairn

French Polynesia

1. Wallis and Futuna Islands
2. West Samoa
3. American Samoa
4. Tonga
5. Niue

Hawaii USA

Johnston Atoll

Cook Is

Kiribati

New Zealand

Wake Island

Tuvalu

Fiji

Marshall Islands

N Marianas

Papua
New Guinea Nauru

Solomon
Islands

Vanuatu

New Caledonia

Guam

Fed States of Micronesia

Palau

Australia

Philippines

Taiwan

China

Indonesia

Area 8,501,000 sq.km. 6.3% of the land surface of the world. There are 25,000 islands scattered over 88 million sq.km. of ocean.

The region includes:

1. Australia and New Zealand.

2. Papua New Guinea. This is the eastern half of the island of New Guinea; the western half was annexed by Indonesia (see page 292).

3. The 27 island states and territories.

4. The smallest territories which are grouped with related states: Christmas Is, Cocos Is, Norfolk Is with **Australia**; Johnston Is, Wake Is with **Guam**; Niue, Pitcairn Is and Tokelau with **Cook Is**.

The countries marked with * have no specific prayer calendar day and should be included for prayer during the period assigned to the Pacific region. Territories marked with superscript numbers are grouped together for prayer. The three French territories marked with ⁰ are included for prayer under the day assigned to French Guiana.

Country	Population in millions		Affiliated Christian Percentages			Total No. of Peoples	Peoples in Country World		
	1990	1995	Total	Prot	Evang	Peoples	A	B	C
American Samoa*	0.0	0.0	89.4	44.4	23.9	5	0	0	5
Australia[1]	16.7	17.7	61.3	30.4	12.6	217	58	61	98
Christmas Island[1]	0.0	0.0	0.0	0.0	0.0	7	3	2	2
Cocos (Keeling) Is[1]	0.0	0.0	0.0	0.0	0.0	4	1	1	2
Cook Islands[2]*	0.0	0.0	90.0	72.2	5.2	7	0	0	7
Fiji	0.7	0.8	53.1	42.4	10.4	33	2	7	24
French Polynesia⁰	0.2	0.2	84.4	41.0	3.7	13	0	2	11
Guam[3]*	0.1	0.1	94.2	13.7	9.5	11	0	2	9
Johnston Island[3]*	0.0	0.0	0.0	0.0	0.0	2	0	0	2
Kiribati*	0.1	0.1	97.6	44.0	6.2	5	0	1	4
Marshall Islands[4]	0.0	0.1	73.1	61.3	34.6	2	0	0	2
Micronesia, Federated States[4]	0.1	0.1	81.0	37.6	14.5	22	0	2	20
Midway Islands[3]*	0.0	0.0	0.0	0.0	0.0	2	0	1	1
Nauru*	0.0	0.0	84.2	56.7	6.8	8	0	2	6
New Caledonia⁰	0.2	0.2	79.0	19.7	6.8	49	0	4	45
New Zealand	3.4	3.5	69.8	50.3	25.9	46	0	7	39
Niue Islands[2]*	0.0	0.0	94.7	70.4	3.5	3	0	1	2
Norfolk Island[1]	0.0	0.0	57.8	45.5	19.6	5	0	0	5
Northern Mariana Is[4]	0.1	0.1	66.2	9.4	8.5	1	0	0	1
Palau (4)	0.0	0.0	96.2	25.3	21.1	2	0	0	2
Papua New Guinea	4.0	4.6	81.6	48.6	22.3	869	45	122	702
Pitcairn Islands[2]*	0.0	0.0	0.0	0.0	0.0	2	0	0	2
Samoa	0.2	0.2	98.0	53.3	11.2	6	0	0	6
Solomon Islands	0.3	0.4	92.6	71.9	26.8	72	0	1	71
Tokelau Islands[2]*	0.0	0.0	94.9	61.8	3.1	2	0	0	2
Tonga*	0.1	0.1	98.1	49.7	11.9	9	0	1	8
Tuvalu*	0.0	0.0	96.6	93.8	5.0	6	0	0	6
Vanuatu*	0.2	0.2	74.2	59.2	21.7	120	2	20	98
Wallis and Futuna Is⁰	0.0	0.0	99.1	0.2	0.2	3	0	0	3
PACIFIC	26.5	28.4	66.8	37.0	15.8	1,533	111	237	1,185

World A The unevangelized/unreached world where %E < 50% for constituent peoples.
World B The evangelized non-Christian world where %E > 50% and All Christians < 60%.
World C The broadly Christian world where All Christians in people are > 60%.
See Appendix 5 for fuller definitions.

Population	Ann.Gr	Density
1985 24,636,000	1.6%	2.9/sq.km
1990 26,525,000	1.5%	3.1/sq.km
1995 28,376,000	1.4%	3.3/sq.km
2000 30,247,000	1.3%	3.6/sq.km

Many of the smaller island states are densely populated, but Australia, with 90% of the region's surface area, is sparsely populated.

Peoples: There are five major groupings and 1,533 ethno-linguistic peoples.
European 75%. The majority in Australia and New Zealand, where most are of British descent. Large French minority in New Caledonia.
Melanesian 18% (Melanesia means "black islands"). The majority of indigenous inhabitants in New Guinea, Solomon Islands, New Caledonia and Fiji. A significant minority in Australia. Melanesians are unique for the variety of languages spoken.
Polynesian 4% (Polynesia means "many islands"). The majority of indigenous inhabitants of New Zealand and islands of the central Pacific. The Polynesians are one of the most remarkable seafaring races in the world.
Micronesian 1% (Micronesia means "small islands"). The majority in island groups on, or north of, the equator.
Asian 2%. Indian majority in Fiji, and smaller communities in Australia and New Zealand. Chinese communities in many territories throughout the region.

Languages 1,341. **Languages with Scriptures** 16Bi 123NT 202por. There are between 155 and 650 languages in which Bible translation work may still be needed, most being spoken by a very small number of people.

Cities: There are six world-class cities in the region. Urbanization 71%.

Economy: The affluence and development of Australia and New Zealand are in contrast to the subsistence economies of most of the other territories. Overpopulation and lack of work opportunities have stimulated large migrations to the wealthier areas. Average income/person $13,190 (63% of USA).

Politics: All but a handful of the smaller territories are either independent or have internal self-government. There is growing concern to develop regional cooperation for protection of the island economies and cultures from abuse by Pacific Rim nations.

Religion: In every state and territory except Fiji the great majority of people are Christian, but nominalism and secularism have eroded commitment to the Church. The massive increase in the Mormons in the islands of Polynesia is a challenge to Evangelicals.

Non-religious/other 21%. 5.5 million. Rapid secularization in Australia and New Zealand. Growth 5.2%.
Muslim 1.2%. 320,000. Mainly Australia and Fiji. Growth 7.3%. Rapid growth in Australia through immigration from the Middle East. Indian Muslims in Fiji are not growing in numbers.
Hindu 1.1%. 300,000. Growth 1.8%. Indians in Fiji and New Zealand.
Buddhist/East Asian religions 0.63%. 177,000. Mainly Chinese, some Japanese and Koreans.
Animist 0.4%. 100,000. Growth 0.4%. Pockets of peoples in New Guinea, a few in Solomon Islands and in Australia.
Jews 0.33%. 87,000. Mainly in Australia.
Baha'i 0.15%. 40,000. Growth 2.7%. Majority in Papua New Guinea and Fiji.
Christian 75.2%. 20 million. Growth 0.5%. This is lower than population growth. Affiliated 66.8%.
 Protestant 45%. 11.9 million. Growth 0.2%. Affiliated 37%. Growth 0.3%.
 Evangelical growth 1.3%. Pentecostal growth 6.5%.
 Missionaries:
  to Pacific (expatriates from Pacific and the world) 3,941 (1:6,700 people).
  from Pacific 6,211 (1:2,850 Protestants) 3,672frn 3,773xcul 2,438dom.
Roman Catholic 25.6%. 6.8 million. Growth 1%. Affiliated 25.4%.
Missionaries:
 to Pacific 4,842 (1:5,900 people).
 from Pacific 1,383 (1:4,900 Catholics).
Other Catholic 0.1%. 17,000.
Orthodox 2.1%. 560,000. Growth 2.5%. Mainly Greek and southeast European immigrants to Australia.
Marginal groups 2.4%. 650,000. Growth 4.7%. Mormon growth in Pacific islands and among New Zealand Maori is the major contributory factor.

Church groupings

Church groupings	Cong	Members	Affiliated
Protestant	32,600	3,090,000	9,805,000
Evangelical 15.9% of pop		1,366,000	4,204,000
Pentecostal 2.5% of pop		324,000	672,000
Roman Catholic	4,140	4,462,000	6,732,000
Charismatic		est. 67,000	100,000
Orthodox	230	365,000	558,000
Marginal	2,700	340,000	607,000
Total	39,670	8,328,000	17,718,000

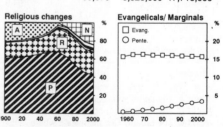

Religious changes

Evangelicals/ Marginals

1. **Praise God for His workings in the Pacific!**
a) **The Pacific was one of the first areas to be evangelized in the modern Protestant missionary era.** Few areas of the world have claimed more missionary lives through disease, violent death and cannibalism. Praise God for the sacrificial labours of those early LMS, Methodist and Anglican missionaries.
b) **Great people movements** over the past 200 years have brought whole people and islands to Christianity. Some of the most strongly Protestant Christian nations in the world are in this region. These people movements continue to this day in Papua New Guinea.
c) **The missionary movement of Pacific islanders** is a dramatic and thrilling story. Many of the island groups were actually pioneered for Christ by these intrepid islanders in the last century.
d) **Recent revivals** and movings of the Holy Spirit stirred the churches in both the Solomon Islands and in New Zealand.

2. **The present spiritual need of the Church,** with decline in commitment, church attendance and spirituality, is sadly the norm in most areas.
a) **Secularism and materialism** in Australia and New Caledonia and dead formalism elsewhere are sapping away the spiritual life of the churches. The need is for revival.
b) **Inadequate teaching** on true repentance, personal faith and a daily walk with the Lord in the island churches had led to a widespread misunderstanding of the true nature of the gospel, syncretic beliefs and, in Melanesia, indigenous cults.
c) **The rapid growth of Mormonism in Polynesia,** winning many nominal Protestants, is a rebuke to the traditional churches. Polynesia is rapidly becoming Mormon – especially Tonga and the two Samoas which are over 20% Mormon.
d) **Concern for missions** had declined for many years in the islands, but a re-awakening is taking place. Pray that Pacific Islanders might once more make an impact on the world. New Zealand's contribution to missions is one of the best for Western nations.

3. **Unreached peoples** are few. Pray for:
a) **Remaining unevangelized and unoccupied tribes** in New Guinea's interior – a few such still exist. Many more are only superficially evangelized.
b) **The few evangelical believers** in parts of New Caledonia, French Polynesia and on many of the nominally Christian island groups. Some areas need to be re-evangelized.
c) **The Indians of Fiji,** the largest unreached people in the Pacific. Pray for the effective evangelization of these Muslims and Hindus.
d) **Bible translation.** This is a major necessity. What remains to be done is being researched, but many hundreds of smaller language groups may still need translators.

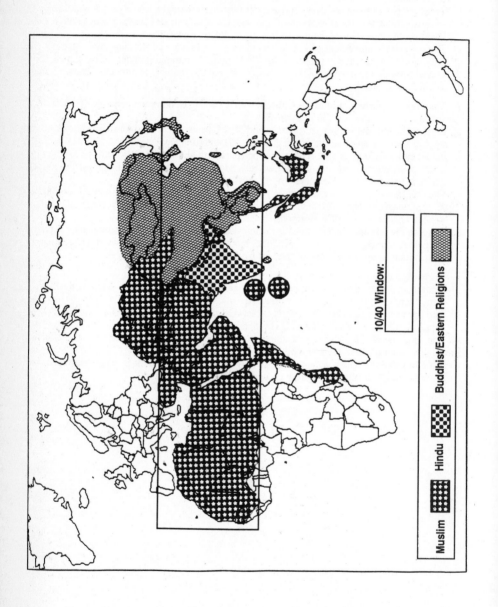

10/40 Window:

Muslim | Hindu | Buddhist/Eastern Religions

Afghanistan
(Republic of Afghanistan)

February 12–13	**A**
Asia	

Area 652,000 sq.km. Dry and mountainous, but with fertile valleys. This strategic land has been called the "Crossroads of Central Asia".

Population	Ann. Gr.	Density
1990	16,557,000	2.7 %	25/sq.km
1995	23,141,000	6.9 %	35/sq.km

Afghanistan's wars created 6.5 million refugees in Pakistan and Iran, and smaller numbers scattered through South Asia, the Middle East and the West.

Peoples:
Indo Iranian 76.3% (41 groups).
 Afghani 46.4% (25). Pushtun 7,490,000 (speaking Pushtu); Nuristani Tribes 195,000.
 Persian 27% (5): Tajik 4,000,000; Farsi/Dari 600,000.
 Other 2.9% (11): Char Aimaq 480,000; Baloch 200,000.
Turkic 23% (12). Hazara 1,800,000 (speaking Dari Persian); Uzbek 1,500,000; Turkmen 380,000.
Other 0.7% (24): Brahui 100,000; Arab 5,000.
Foreign Peoples 0.02%: Russians, Western and Asian relief workers, etc.

Literacy 12%. **Official languages:** Pushtu (used by 50% of population), Dari (35%). **All languages** 50. **Languages with Scriptures** 4Bi 5NT 4por.

Capital: Kabul 3,500,000; many refugees from rural areas. City was extensively damaged in 1992/3 civil war. Urbanization 26%.

Economy: Shattered by 14 years of war. The countryside has been poisoned, bombed and mined; half the housing, most of the complex irrigation systems and a high proportion of the livestock have been destroyed. The most lucrative agricultural crop is now opium (of which Afghanistan is the world's largest producer), which pays for weapons for the warring factions. Recovery will be slow even when warfare ceases. Income/person $230 (1.1% of USA).

Politics: Autocratic monarchy overthrown in 1973. Republican rule ended in a pro-Marxist coup in 1978. The subsequent Soviet invasion was disastrous for the country and ultimately led to the humiliating withdrawal of Soviet forces in 1988–89, and the fall of the Communist regime in 1992. Disunity among the *mujahidin* guerrillas degenerated into civil war between the interim government, largely supported by northern peoples, and the most extreme Islamist faction that is largely Pushtun.

Religion: There was some religious freedom 1964–92. Both main contenders differ only in the extent of application of *sharia* law in the Islamic state declared in 1992.
Muslim 99%. Sunni 79%, Shi'a 20%, Ismaili 1%.
Hindu 0.3%. **Sikh** 2,000.
Christian 0.01%.
 Expatriates. Westerners, some Russians and Asians.
 Indigenous. Maybe 1,000 total.
 Missionaries. None officially permitted, though Christian relief workers are welcome and number over 70.

1. **War's devastation** has brought immense suffering to the nation, yet has been used by God to make people more receptive to the gospel. An estimated 800,000 have lost their lives, a further 1,600,000 have been maimed and 7,000,000 have had to flee their homes. It will take decades to clear the 10–40 million mines and rebuild homes, schools, farms and shattered lives. Pray for peace and deliverance from further tyrannies.

2. **The Civil War** began as an Islamic holy war or *jihad*, but has degenerated into a cruel contest for power, ethnic superiority and religious supremacy. Weapons from Iran and Saudi Arabia and ideological indoctrination have further polarized society to the tragic detriment of the people and surrounding countries. Islam has gained no credit in the hearts of many who claim to be its followers. Pray that the centuries-old powers of darkness that bind this land may be broken, and that many may come to new life in Christ.

3. **Afghanistan is one of the least reached lands in the world.** There are 48,000 mosques but not a single church building, nor a viable fellowship of believers in any but one of the indigenous peoples of the country. Pray for the 88 unreached peoples of this land, especially:
a) The **Pushtuns**, the warlike, vengeful tribes of the Afghan–Pakistan border region. Only a small number of Christians among them.
b) The **Uzbeks** and **Turkmen** of the north.

A

c) The **Tajiks** in the northeast and urban areas.

d) The **Hazara**, Shi'a Muslims of Mongol descent, who have been discriminated against, but who have been more responsive to the gospel.

e) The **Kuchi** nomads in central and western regions who numbered 2,500,000 before the war destroyed their life style. They represent many unrelated tribes and languages. Many fled to Pakistan.

f) The **Char Aimaq** of the west and the **Baloch** and **Brahui** of the south.

g) The **Nuristani** tribes of the much-contested mountains to the north and east of Kabul.

4. **The tragic plight of the refugees** will take years to resolve. Pakistan is urging refugees to return to their homes, and in 1992 about 5,000 were leaving every week. The *mujahidin* (guerrillas) who control the camps have long used Western weapons and aid, but have now become very anti-Western and anti-Christian. Many Christian aid programmes have been abused or stopped, and at least three Christian aid workers have been killed. Pray for Christians who still seek to help and witness tactfully in a hostile environment and atmosphere. Some refugees have become Christians, but open profession has often led to deaths.

5. **Afghan believers** are few and mostly Dari-speaking. Their number in urban and some remote rural areas has multiplied through the witness of expatriates, Afghan believers and even Christian Russian soldiers. The war has given some protection to this small witness. Pray for the continuance and growth of the Church in the '90s; the fundamentalist government could endanger it.

6. **The International Assistance Mission** is an inter-agency Christian organization, supported by 26 agencies and recognized by the government, which has continued to function in the capital through the war. Its loving and dedicated ministry to the blind, maimed, sick, deprived, illiterate and needy has been a commendation of the Christian message that has borne fruit. War conditions and insecurity are not easy for the expatriate 70 staff from many countries; pray for them, and for the recruitment of other dedicated tentmakers with a wide range of skills. This is an unusual day of opportunity.

7. **Distribution of Scriptures.** The new Dari New Testament is available in quantity, and the new Pushtu New Testament in limited numbers. Pray for effective distribution in spite of the difficulties. Pray for the translation of the Scriptures into other languages too; work is in progress in eight, but 29 others may need translators. There has not been a survey of the languages for a long time – this is a great need in the aftermath of the confusion of war.

8. **The Media.** Pray that all appropriate methods of witness may be used effectively.

a) **GRn** has made audio recordings in 38 languages and dialects; nevertheless, there is a shortage of effective gospel cassettes and videotapes. Pray for production and distribution.

b) **Christian radio. FEBA** and **IBRA** broadcast nearly two hours weekly in Pushtu, **FEBA** 50 minutes weekly in Dari, and **FEBC, HCJB** and **TWR** 4.4 hours in Uzbek. Pray for the provision of more Dari- and Pushtu-speaking Christians to prepare programmes. Pray also for programming to commence in the Hazaraqi and Western Pushtu languages.

Albania
(Republic of Albania)

February 14
Europe

Area 28,700 sq.km. A mountainous Balkan state on the Adriatic Sea, adjoining Montenegro, Serbia (Kosova/Illyria), Macedonia and Greece.

Population		Ann. Gr.	Density
1990	3,245,000	1.8 %	113/sq.km
1995	3,521,000	1.4 %	122/sq.km

Peoples:
Albanian 93.5%.
Gypsy 2.5%. **Greek** 2.4%. In the south.
Other 1.6%. Arumun (Vlach) 60,000; Macedonian 30,000; Montenegrin.

Literacy est. 85%. **Official language:** Tosk Albanian. **All languages** 6. **Languages with Scriptures** 2Bi 4NT 6por.

Capital: Tirana 238,000. Urbanization 36%.

Economy: The devastation left by the Communist regime is so great that it will take decades to repair Europe's poorest country. Heavily dependent on Western aid for survival and investment for growth. Virtually the only economic activity is trading in donated and smuggled goods. Unemployment 70%. Income/person est. $250 (1.2% of USA).

Politics: The Communist regime imposed on the country in 1945 crumbled in 1991 soon after Enver Hoxha's death. Two multi-party elections finally resulted in a democratic government in 1992. The restoration of land rights to pre-Communist landowners and the explosive situation in adjoining Kosova, an enclave of Serbia (where 1,800,000 Albanians live), are major policy issues to be resolved.

Religion: The Communists harshly persecuted all religions. All were totally suppressed in 1967. In 1990 the ban was lifted, but pressures from Muslim, Orthodox and Catholic leaders could lead to discriminatory laws against other groups. Religious figures are estimates based on the census percentages of religions before World War II.

Non-religious/other 41.9%.
Muslim 40%. Both Sunni and the deviant Bektashi sect. Albania was Europe's only majority Muslim state.
Baha'i 0.12%.
Christian 18%. Affil 14.2%. Growth 21.3%.
Protestant 0.06%. Growth 39.3%.

Church	Cong	Members	Affiliated
Evangelical groups	17	500	750
Pentecostal groups (6)	12	350	583
Christian Brethren	6	360	550
Denominations (8)	35	1,210	1,883
Evangelicals 0.06% of pop		1,210	1,883

Missionaries to Albania 182 (1:18,800 people) in 32 agencies, mostly short-term at present.

Roman Catholic 7%. Affil 4.62%. Growth 20%.

Catholic Ch	200	90,000	150,000

Orthodox 10.9%. Affil 9.49%. Growth 21.9%.

Albanian Orthodox	200	144,000	240,000
All other (3)		40,800	68,000
Denominations (4)	200	184,800	308,000

Foreign Marginal 0.02%. Growth 35%.

Jehovah's Witnesses	5	250	417
All groups (2)	7	450	717

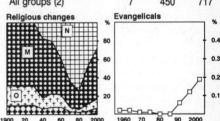

Religious changes   Evangelicals

1. **Praise God for the spectacular changes in Albania.** Hoxha's proud boast of achieving atheism was pronounced by his successor "a mistake" in 1991. Religion is now actively encouraged as an antidote to the crime wave that came with freedom.

2. **Albania's experience with Communism has been economically, morally and spiritually devastating.** The savagery of the repression of all real and imagined opposition to the dictator Hoxha was such that 700,000 were killed or imprisoned for long periods. A high proportion of the population was coerced into spying on neighbours. The democratic government faces an immense task in redressing the injustices of the past, constructing a modern viable state from virtually nothing, initiating a fair programme of land reform, and giving hope to a demoralized people. Pray for wisdom and moderation for the leaders of the nation.

3. **Religious freedom has become a major issue.** Muslims from the Middle East have mounted a massive effort to re-Islamize the country by means of missionaries, scholarships, aid, mosque

building and drawing the country into the Muslim world. Catholics in the north and Orthodox in the south are reasserting their presence where they were once strong, and all three are pressing for stringent legislation to keep out other religions considered un-Albanian. The successes of Mormons and Baha'i could ultimately adversely affect Evangelicals. Pray for balance and wisdom in formulating laws that will grant religious freedom.

4. **Evangelical Christian input** has been swift and the effects dramatic. Within 18 months of the fall of Communism, 16 mission agencies had entered the country for aid projects, evangelism and church planting. By October 1992, there were over 1,000 believers gathering regularly to worship the Lord in 19 congregations and 17 home groups. There is an Evangelical witness in 22 of the 32 districts of the country. Pray for the growth, maturity and legalization of Protestant Christianity in the new Albania. The young church has grown so rapidly that growing pains are acute – how to cope with rich foreign visitors and their aid, fights among members, and preparation of leaders to keep pace with the growth.

5. **Evangelical mission agencies have multiplied since 1990.** There are 32 or more agencies with long- and short-term workers committed to social ministries and to outreach and church planting. The Albanian Encouragement Project is a loose network linking 28 agencies. The larger groups are: **YWAM** (12 workers), **Frontiers** (11), **OM** (10), Ancient World Outreach (7), Brethren (6), **IT** (3). Pray for:
a) **Unity.** There is need for trust, coordination and close fellowship that will set high spiritual standards. It would be tragic if Evangelicals helped to "Balkanize" (fragment) the Church that is beginning to emerge.
b) **Long-term vision and goals.** Much of present work is short-term. Pray for the calling of long-term workers who can learn the language and culture and then contribute to the maturing of churches and training of leaders.
c) **Wisdom in administering aid.** Misuse is rapidly becoming a serious and spiritually-damaging problem.

6. **The unreached.** A toe-hold for the gospel has been established in most major towns, but to reach the rural areas and remote mountain valleys will need a considerable effort. The Swiss Helimission and **MAF** could have a significant role to play. The challenge is to reach **traditional Muslim areas** where folk Islam is more influential, and also the **Gypsy** and **Vlach** minorities.

7. **Albanians abroad.** Nearly half of all Albanians live outside Albania; they need to be evangelized.
a) **Kosova**, part of Serbia, is 92% Albanian. Serbian (Yugoslav) forces have repressed the Albanians, and civil war or even a wider Balkan conflict threatens. The Albanian population is 98% Muslim.
b) **Macedonia** with 700,000 Albanians, and Montenegro with a further 32,000, present challenges to outreach.
c) **European Community** – 320,000 Albanians in Italy are now supplemented by many recent refugees. Albanian guest-workers and refugees now live in Germany, Austria and Switzerland. A further 12,000 in north Greece have been supplemented by many economic refugees since 1990.

8. **Christian help ministries.**
a) **Distribution of the Scriptures is vital.** The Bible in standard Albanian was completed in 1992. Pray for its effective distribution and spiritual impact.
b) **Christian literature** is beginning to flood into Albania. Books, magazines and leaflets are eagerly sought after, be they from Evangelicals, Muslims or cults. Pray that good Christian literature may prevail. *Illyricum/Shigjeta* has been formed to publish Albanian evangelical books. There is a need for a Christian publishing house in the country. There is a dearth of literature suitable for the atheistic and Muslim cultural worldviews of the majority.
c) **The *Jesus* film** in standard Albanian is being widely and effectively used to touch the hearts of many.
d) **Christian radio** over the years through **OD**, **TWR** (**ECM** preparing the programmes), and **IBRA** Radio has prepared hearts for the gospel. Pray for the development and maturation of this ministry. TWR has been granted an extraordinary contract to broadcast 1–3 hours daily in any language and to other lands over the powerful Albanian Radio Tirana built specifically to proclaim atheism!

Algeria

(The People's Democratic
Republic of Algeria)

Area 2,382,000 sq.km. Agriculture is possible on the Mediterranean coast, in the Atlas mountains and oases. 80% is Sahara Desert.

Population	Ann. Gr.	Density
1990 25,364,000	3.2 %	11/sq.km
1995 29,306,000	2.9 %	12/sq.km

Over 90% live north of the Atlas. About 500,000 are nomadic or semi-nomadic in the Sahara. A further two million Algerians or those of Algerian descent live in Europe.

Peoples:
Arabic-speaking 69–82.2%. Many are Arabized Berber.
Berber (up to 17 groups) 17–30%. The actual Berber population is far higher than official figures. Main groups: Kabyle 2,600,000–5,000,000; Tamazight 570,000; Shawiya 480,000–1,000,000; Mzab 220,000; Tuareg 76,000.
Other 0.8% French 110,000; Moroccans 100,000; Xoraxai Gypsy 2,500.
Refugees Western Saharans 165,000 in 26 camps in the southwest Sahara.

Literacy 50%. **Official language:** Arabic. French and, increasingly, English widely used. 25% speak one of the Berber dialects. **All languages** 17. **Languages with Scriptures** 2Bi 2NT 6por.

Capital: Algiers 3,108,000. Other major cities: Oran 628,000; Constantine 440,000. Urbanization 49%.

Economy: Heavily dependent on oil exports. Economic decline due to fall in price of oil, widespread state ownership, a bloated bureaucracy, high population growth and increasing political instability. Unemployment 22%. Public debt/person $940. Income/person $2,170 (10% of USA).

Politics: French colony for 132 years. Independence in 1962 after a bitter war of liberation. A one-party socialist regime backed by the army has held on to power for 30 years. Economic failure and political abuses of power have provoked widespread agitation for change. Democratic elections in 1992 were set to give victory to the Muslim revivalist movement, but an army takeover forestalled this, followed by vigorous suppression of the Muslim party. The polarized and tense political situation could lead to civil war.

Religion: Since independence, the government has actively encouraged the development of an Islamic Arab socialist state. Proselytism is not allowed. The Catholic and the Protestant Church of Algeria are the only Christian bodies officially recognized. Muslim fundamentalists are strongly agitating for the institution of Islamic *sharia* law.
Muslim 99.4%. Sunni Muslims. Polarized between the radicals and secularists. Ibadi sect.
Non-religious/other 0.2%.
Christian 0.40%. Nom 0.14%. Affil 0.26%. Growth 2.7%.
Protestant 0.08% Growth 21.3%.

Church	Members	Affiliated
Indigenous Evangelical Grps	9,000	18,000
Protestant Ch of A	300	750
All other (7)	365	758
Denominations (9)	9,665	19,508
Evangelicals 0.07% of pop	9,000	18,500
Pentecostal/charis 0.02%	2,700	5,500

Expatriate Christians serving in Algeria 25 (1:1,014,000 people).
Missionaries from Algeria 2 (1:10,000 Protestants) 2frn.
Roman Catholic 0.32%. Affil 0.18%
Growth –2.1%.

Catholic Ch	25,700	45,000

Missionaries:
to Algeria 108 (1:240,000 people).
from Algeria 50 (1973 figure).

1. **Opposition to the gospel is intense.** A hundred years of tearful sowing the seed by a tenacious succession of missionaries has borne little fruit. Muslims have a long and bitter memory of "Christian" conquests, colonialism and atrocities, so miracles are needed to overcome the centuries of prejudice. Behind this are the unbound legions of Satan which hold the land in thrall.

2. **Independence and the socialist political system that followed it have failed dismally.** The desire for radical change boosted Muslim extremist opposition as the only viable alternative; the option of the gospel has never been fairly presented. A radical Muslim government would make conditions for gospel proclamation and the lot of the few Christians even more difficult. Pray for God's overruling in the affairs of men and that he may grant democratic moderation and religious freedom to the country. Algeria has become a political time-bomb.

3. **The Berber peoples** may comprise as much as 40% of the population. The Arab majority has long sought to impose their rule, culture and language and resents Berber intransigence. Berber nationalism is becoming a significant force as these peoples seek to reaffirm their identity and return to their cultural roots. Their forebears were once Christian, and many thousands have turned to Christ among the Kabyle – largely through supernatural revelations of the Lord Jesus in the very area where Raymond Lull, the great missionary pioneer, was martyred 600 years ago. Pray for:
a) **The protection of this movement of the Spirit** from external repression. Muslim leaders accuse Christians of poisoning the Kabyle with the gospel.
b) **Spiritual unity and growth in maturity** in the areas where Christians have multiplied. Kabyle history is one of clannishness and divisions. The charismatic issue is controversial and mature leaders are few.

4. **Indigenous Christians in the cities** are relatively less numerous than those in rural areas. Only a few small fellowships exist where Arabic is used; most local Christians tend to use a mixture of French and Kabyle. The easy option is to emigrate to Europe. Pray for:
a) **The establishment of strong indigenous groups** with effective leaders steeped in the Word. There are no Bible schools in the country, and the only alternative for training leaders is the low-key TEE programme, but this is not working as well as it could. Many desire training, but few are willing to take on leadership responsibility.
b) **The protection of believers in persecution.** Threats and intimidation by family, friends, employers and Muslim extremists are a problem. Fear leads to withdrawal from fellowship, compromise and backsliding. Pray for perseverance, willingness to suffer for Jesus and boldness in witness. ·
c) **The few Christian families.** Religious and social pressures force Christian girls into marriage to Muslims. Pray for the few Christian couples, for their strength and endurance, that they may minister to the Church.
d) **Musicians** for worship services and **children's workers** to be raised up.

5. **The unreached** comprise virtually the whole nation.
a) **The growing cities** – the educated elite, the middle classes, and the teeming slums.
b) **Young people** who are frustrated and disillusioned. Two-thirds of the population is under 25; over 50% of the 16–25s are unemployed.
c) **The Berber peoples of the Atlas.** It is mostly the **Kabyle** that have responded. Any overt missionary outreach to the **Kabyle** or to the unreached **Shawiya, Riff** and **Tamazight** would be considered subversive.
d) **The Tuareg.** 1–2 believers known. No continuing work in Algeria.
e) **The Mzab** oasis towns in the Sahara. There are no known Christians and no specific effort has ever been launched to evangelize them in their tight-knit communities.

6. **The active mission force** has steadily declined since 1970 with a number of expulsions. Missionaries are severely restricted in their activities. Most use secular jobs for residency and as a platform for witnessing. Personal witness and discipleship, camps and Bible study groups are the main opportunities for service. What wisdom, tact, courage and faith these servants of God need in the midst of frequent discouragements and insecurity! What sensitivity they need in tactfully helping the few groups of believers to maturity without dominating them!

7. **Bible translation and distribution** is fraught with obstacles and restrictions. Translation work is proceeding in four Berber languages, but nothing has been done for a further ten. Pray for perseverance for translators and for an adequate survey of the unfinished task. One major challenge is for the translation of the whole Bible into Kabyle in the Latin script by 1997.

8. **Christian literature** in the national languages and French is in such demand that supplies do not match it. Pray for the freedom to import and distribute Bibles and teaching materials as well as BCCs. Postal censorship is severe, leading to confiscation of mail and interrogation of recipients; pray for deliverances in this. There is an urgent need for BCCs and other materials in Kabyle.

9. **Algerians in Europe** are numerous; many are there illegally. If civil war or economic collapse comes to Algeria, their numbers may increase dramatically in the 1990s. They are more accessible to the gospel in Europe, but not necessarily more open. Pray for the network of agencies and churches seeking to reach them (**AWM, GMU, WEC** and others). Pray for the discipling of individuals and planting of Arabic- and Berber-speaking congregations which can then be channels for the gospel to their homeland.

10. **Christian media** are important in this internally restrictive situation. Pray for:
a) **Radio.** Both **AWM** (through Arab World Media) and **GMU** have a comprehensive strategy preparing radio programmes, evangelistic and discipling literature, and follow-up programmes (radio, personal counselling, magazines and BCCs). **TWR**-Monaco broadcasts 6 hours/week in Arabic and 1–2 hours/week in Kabyle and **IBRA**-Portugal 3–5 hours/week in Arabic. Thousands have come to faith as a result of this. Pray for the expansion and continued fruitfulness of these ministries.
b) **Audio-visual.** The *Jesus* film on cassette has had a wide impact in Kabyle and also in Arabic.
c) **Use of cassettes.** Music and Scripture tapes are produced and distributed locally.

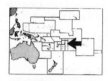

American Samoa
(The US Territory of
American Samoa)

See Pacific
Pacific

Area 200 sq.km. Five small volcanic islands in the Samoan Archipelago.

Population	Ann. Gr.	Density
1990 40,000	2.7 %	201/sq.km
1995 43,000	1.5 %	216/sq.km

There are more than twice as many Samoans living in mainland USA (70,000) and Hawaii (20,000).

Peoples:
Polynesian 89%. Samoan 35,500; Tongan 800.
Euronesian (mixed race) 6%.
Other 5%. Asian (Korean and Japanese) 1,500; American 350.

Literacy 99%. **Official languages:** Samoan, English. **All languages** 4. **Languages with Scriptures** 3Bi.

Capital: Pago Pago 14,000.

Economy: Tourism, fishing, and canning. Income/person $7,000 (33% of USA).

Politics: US unincorporated territory since 1900.

Religion:
Non-religious/other 1%.
Christian 99%. Nom 9.6%. Affil 89.4%.
Growth 2.4%.
  Protestant 52.7%. Affil 44.4%. Growth −1.4%.

Church	Cong	Members	Affiliated
Congregational Chr Ch	22	6,500	11,500
Assemblies of God	18	5,000	7,600
Seventh-day Adventist	3	650	1,300
Methodist Church	2	550	750
All other (7)	19	733	1,320
Doubly counted		−2,400	−4,700
Denominations (11)	64	11,033	17,770
Evangelicals 23.9% of pop		6,100	9,600
Pentecostal/charis 21%		5,500	8,500

Missionaries:
  to Am Samoa 21 (1:1,900 people).
  from Am Samoa 26 (1:690 Protestants) 26frn.
Roman Catholic 19%. Affil 17.5%. Growth 1.7%.

Catholic Ch	5	2,800	7,000

Missionaries to Am Samoa 36 (1:1,100 people).
Marginal 27.3%. Affil 27.3%. Growth 11.2%.

Mormons	23	5,990	9,500
Jehovah's Witnesses	2	199	538
All other (1)		480	960
Groups (3)	25	6,669	10,998

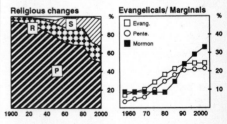

Religious changes   Evangelicals/ Marginals

1. The dominance of the materialistic culture of USA and ease of emigration have weakened the church. Nevertheless, Assemblies of God churches have multiplied over the past generation. Pray for holiness of life and a commitment to discipleship among believers.

2. Spectacular Mormon growth demonstrates that evangelical believers are not meeting evident spiritual needs. Pray that stagnant churches may be roused to evangelize. Pray for the ministry of **YWAM** to simulate this; they have a large base with 33 staff.

Include with Spain
Europe

Andorra

(The Co-Principality of Andorra)

Area 468 sq.km. In the heart of the Pyrenean Mountains between Spain and France.

Population	Ann. Gr.	Density
1990 51,000	4.0 %	109/sq.km
1995 56,000	1.9 %	120/sq.km

Most of the growth is through immigration.

Peoples:
Indigenous Andorran 27.5%.
Foreigners 72.5%. Spanish 28,000; French 3,000; Portuguese 2,100; British 770; Other 2,200.

Literacy 92%. **Official language:** Catalan (Spanish).

Capital: Andorra la Vella 16,000. Urbanization 65%.

Economy: Wealthy through tourism (12 million visitors annually) and also through duty-free trading. Income/person $9,000 (43% of USA).

Politics: Self-governing co-principality since 1278; nominally ruled by the President of France and Spanish Bishop of Urgel. Since 1993 Andorra has had its own constitution, judiciary, foreign policy.

Religion: Official freedom of religion since 1993. The Catholic church remains the established church.
Non-religious/other 5%. **Jews** 200.
Christian 95%. Nom 8.1%. Affil 86.9%. Growth 4%.
Protestant 0.6%.

Church	Cong	Members	Affiliated
Denominations (2)	3	40	70
Evangelicals 0.08% of pop		24	38

Missionaries to Andorra 2 (1:25,500 people) in 1 agency.
Roman Catholic 93.9%. Affil 86.3%. Growth 4%.

Catholic	8	32,120	44,000

Marginal 0.5% Affil 0.5% Growth 10.1%.

Jehovah's Witnesses	2	165	257

1. **Much of the past and present wealth of the country has been based on sin** – smuggling, gambling and international finance as a "tax haven". So, though nominally Christian, Andorra needs a deep work of the Holy Spirit for hearts to be radically changed. There is no known indigenous Andorran evangelical believer.

2. **There are three very small evangelical groups** with a total of 20–30 believers, all being expatriate. There are no resident full-time evangelical Christian workers. Pray for the provision of missionaries. Jesus Is The Answer International Mission is seeking to place a couple to minister in the land.

3. **Christian literature** has been distributed by several evangelical groups, and some witnessing done. Pray for lasting fruit.

Angola

(Republic of Angola)

February 17–18
Africa

A

Area 1,247,000 sq.km. Coastal state that dominates Zaire's and Zambia's trade routes to the Atlantic. Cabinda is an oil-rich coastal enclave to the north of the Zaire River.

Population		Ann. Gr.	Density
1990	10,020,000	2.7 %	8/sq.km
1995	11,531,000	2.8 %	9/sq.km

Peoples:
Bantu 98.5% (36 peoples): Ovimbundu 3,200,000; Mbundu 2,300,000; Kongo (3) 1,300,000; Ovambo-Kwanyama 421,000; Chokwe 420,000; Nyaneka 400,000; Luchazi 240,000; Mbwela 172,000; Nyemba 172,000; Luvale 155,000; Mbundaı 100,000; Herero-Dhimba 100,000; Lunda 90,000; Yaka 80,000.
San-Bushmen 0.5% (up to 6 peoples) 47,000.
Other 1.0% Mestizo 0.5% Portuguese 0.5%.

Literacy 30%. **Official language:** Portuguese. **All languages** 42. **Languages with Scriptures** 12Bi 3NT 13por.

Capital: Luanda 950,000. Many refugees from the interior. Urbanization 26%.

Economy: Potentially wealthy, but the economy is in a state of collapse as a result of the post-independence flight of skilled personnel and 31 years of continual war. An estimated 80% of annual revenue was diverted into the war effort. Income/person $620 (3% of USA).

Politics: A Portuguese colony for 450 years. Independence was won in 1975 after 15 years of warfare. The Marxist-oriented MPLA gained control of the central government with Cuban aid. This rule was contested by the UNITA nationalist movement, supported by the West and South Africa, in a 16-year civil war. A peace agreement was signed in 1991, followed by multi-party elections in which the MPLA won. UNITA would not accept the results as valid, and the civil war resumed with increased severity. By 1993 UNITA controlled 70% of the country.

Religion: The first President, a Marxist, vowed to eradicate Christianity within 20 years, and indeed there have been many incidents of repression and outright persecution of Christians. The harsh realities of war and the ideological collapse of Communism in the '80s have resulted in the ending of nearly all discrimination against Christians. However, in 1988 a law was passed permitting only 12 Christian denominations.

African Traditionalist 13.9%.
Non-religious/other 1.5%.
Christian 84.6%. Nom 16%. Affil 68.6%. Growth 4.9%.
Protestant 19.8%. Affil 14.4%. Growth 6.8%.

Church	Cong	Members	Affiliated
Ev Congregational Ch	1,077	140,000	380,000
Christian Brethren	1,200	125,000	278,000
United Methodist Ch	2,400	120,000	179,000
Ev Ch of SW Angola (AME)	500	40,000	121,000
Seventh-day Adventist	560	67,200	120,000
Assemblies of God	700	26,750	100,114
Evangelical Baptist Ch	55	34,558	50,000
Ev Ch of Angola (AEF)	148	13,300	38,000
United Evang Ch of Angola	197	15,000	25,000
Church of God	100	10,000	25,000
Baptist Convention	85	10,470	20,900
Lutheran Church	68	4,760	11,900
All other (16)	415	51,200	96,315
Denominations (28)	7,505	658,238	1,445,229
Evangelicals 8.4% of pop		364,000	841,000
Pentecostal/charis 1.55%		56,000	155,000

Missionaries:
 to Angola 103 (1:97,000 people) in 27 agencies.
 from Angola 9 (1:160,000 Protestants) 7frn 9xcul.
Roman Catholic 59.3%. Affil 49.6%.
Growth 4.3%.

Catholic Ch	2,848	2,830,000	4,968,000

Many baptised, but commitment is low.
Missionaries:
 to Angola 768 (1:13,000 people).
 from Angola 54 (1973 figure).
Foreign Marginal 0.4%. Growth 18.3%.

Jehovah's Witnesses	221	18,911	39,400

Indigenous Marginal 5.1%. Affil 4.2%
Growth 6%.

Kimbanguist Ch		106,000	320,000
All other (10)		40,000	100,000
Groups (11)		146,000	420,000

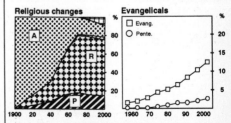

Religious changes

Evangelicals
- □ Evang.
- ○ Pente.

A

1. **The tragic legacy of 31 years of war** will take years to erase once peace is restored. Resettlement of 1.5 million refugees, rehabilitation of 30,000 maimed casualties, care for 20,000 war orphans and reconstruction of roads, railways, homes, hospitals, schools and churches will require enormous resources. Pray for peace and freedom for the gospel. Not all restrictions on Christian activity have been removed.

2. **The church in Angola has multiplied in war and persecution.** Praise God for this. In the first ten years after independence there was intense persecution of Christians, dozens of pastors and thousands of believers were martyred, and many churches were deliberately destroyed. Many simple Christians kept the faith and witnessed. As a result, congregations have multiplied in both the UNITA and MPLA areas in the conflict. Services are packed, and in their desperation and destitution hundreds of thousands have trusted in the Lord Jesus Christ. Pray that this growth may continue and lead to the total evangelization of the country.

3. **Christians will face a new range of moral and ethical challenges** once peace comes. These include granting forgiveness to those who inflicted such suffering and giving loving discipline to Christians who compromised the truth. The government restriction on the legal number of churches poses problems for the more autonomous groups such as Brethren and Baptists; it could also lead to government manipulation or power struggles for church leadership. Pray that Christians may triumph in these areas too. Pray for a Church with holy living, unity in the Spirit, vision for the lost and leaders who truly resemble their Master.

4. **The dearth of trained leadership** is becoming the most critical problem limiting church growth and maturity. For years, little formal training could be given, but now there are seven Bible schools and four seminaries (Ecumenical, Evangelical [at Lubango, **AEF**], Baptist and Catholic). Pray for the provision of funds, buildings, libraries and, above all, godly teachers from Angola and abroad.

5. **The unreached and needy:**
a) Chaos has prevented a survey of needs – this is an urgent requirement, especially for Bible translation. There is ongoing translation work in nine languages, but at least 19 are without either scriptures or translators.
b) Pray for the complete evangelization of the **Nyaneka (Huila)**, **Mbwela, Kwangali** (43,000), **San-Bushmen, Mbukushu** (10,000) – most in the south and southeast where **AEF** has worked.
c) Some 50,000 young people were forcibly taken to Cuba for years of Marxist indoctrination. Pray that their poisoned minds may be cleansed by Jesus, and that they may be reintegrated into their homeland.
d) Towns and cities are circled by large slum areas with many rural refugees. Pray that both spiritual and physical needs may be met.

6. **The life and witness of a depleted missionary force** through the years of suffering was a good testimony. Pray for continued ministry within the churches of **AME** (19), Brethren, British and N. American Baptists (15), **AEF** (13) and others. Pray that a new generation of missionaries may be raised up to reconstruct the country, strengthen the Church and evangelize unreached peoples and areas. Pray for the provision of visas and favour in the eyes of the government.

7. **Young people at school** have had years of Marxist-Leninist teaching. Pray for the ministry of **IFES** (three groups in tertiary institutions and one staff worker) and **SU**. Pray for complete freedom for witness in schools and colleges.

8. **Literature and Bibles are scarce** and in great demand. Pray that supplies entering from Namibia, Canada, Portugal and Brazil may reach those who need them.

9. **Media ministries:**
a) Radio broadcasts reach the land in three indigenous languages from **TWR** in Swaziland and also in Portuguese.
b) The *Jesus* film is available in Portuguese and Kongo.
c) **GRn** has made recordings in 24 languages and dialects.

Anguilla

(The Colony of Anguilla)

See Caribbean
Caribbean

Area 91 sq.km. The most northerly of the Leeward Islands.

Population		Ann. Gr.	Density
1990	6,900	1.0 %	76/sq.km
1995	7,400	1.3 %	81/sq.km

Peoples: Afro-Caribbean 95.4%; Euro-American 4%; East Indian 0.6%.

Literacy 95%. Languages: English, English Creole.

Capital: The Valley 1,100.

Economy: Tourism is virtually the only industry. Income/person $3,890 (18% of USA).

Politics: A British Dependent Territory.

Religion:
Non-religious/other 2.6%.
Baha'i 0.6%. **Muslim** 0.4%.
Christian 96.4%. Affil 94.5%. Growth 0.2%.
 Protestant 91.3%. Affil 89.4%. Growth −0.1%.

Church	Cong	Members	Affiliated
Anglican	5	1,040	2,600
Methodist Church	4	1,050	2,090
Seventh-day Adventist	3	324	540
Baptist Church	3	150	340
All other (5)	3	300	600
Denominations (9)	18	2,864	6,170
Evangelicals 18.4% of pop		620	1,270

Missionaries to Anguilla 2 (1:3,500 people).
Roman Catholic 3.8%. Growth 4.2%.

Catholic Church	2	158	263

Marginal 1.3%. Growth 25.4%.

Jehovah's Witnesses	1	24	90

1. The Christian population is physically isolated from the rest of the world, but needs spiritual separation and consecration as well. The lack of unity or vision for evangelism within or beyond their islands needs to be purged by an outpouring of the Holy Spirit.

See Caribbean
Caribbean

Antigua

(The State of Antigua and Barbuda)

Area: 443 sq.km. Three islands; Antigua volcanic, Barbuda coralline.

Population		Ann. Gr.	Density
1990	86,000	1.2 %	195/sq.km
1995	93,000	1.6 %	210/sq.km

Peoples:
Afro-Caribbean 98%.
European 1%. British, Portuguese.
Other 1%. Lebanese, Syrian, Indo-Pakistani.

Literacy: 90%. **Languages:** English, English Creole.

Capital: St. John's 40,000.

Economy: Dependent on tourism and light industry. One of the few Caribbean states with low unemployment. Public debt/person $2,754. Income/person $3,880 (18% of USA).

Politics: British colony for 349 years; independence in 1981 as a constitutional monarchy.

Religion:
Spiritist 2.5%.

Baha'i 0.8%. **Rastafarian** 0.7%. **Muslim** 0.4%.
Christian 95.6%. Affil 77.3%. Growth 1.2%.
Protestant 83.6%. Affil 67.9% Gr.1.2%.

Church	Cong	Members	Affiliated
Anglican	8	16,200	36,000
Moravian	8	2,700	6,750
Methodist	5	2,000	4,000
Wesleyan	5	1,920	3,200
Seventh-day Adventist	5	580	2,320
Ch of God (Cleveland)	6	504	1,120
Baptist Church (SBC)	3	600	1,000
All other (11)	28	1,895	4,009
Denominations (18)	58	26,399	58,399
Evangelicals 11.7% of pop		4,970	10,000
Pentecostal/charismatic		1,500	3,300

Missionaries:
to Antigua 35 (1:2,400 people) in 7 agencies.
from Antigua 3 (1:20,000 Protestants) 3dom.
Roman Catholic 11.1%. Affil 8.5%. Growth 1.1%.

Catholic Church	6	4,820	7,300

Missionaries to Antigua 30 (1:2,200 people).
Marginal 0.9%. Affil 0.9% Growth 8.6%.

Jehovah's Witnesses	4	303	758
Groups (2)	5	328	808

1. **Christian profession** is rarely accompanied by a holy life among Antiguans. Pray for a revelation of the holiness of God, and a revival. Pray also for the ministry of Christian literature to this end through the CLC bookstore in St. John's.

2. **Oneness in fellowship and vision is the need.** Pray for effective cooperation between the constituent congregations and agencies of the United Evangelical Association.

Argentina
(Argentine Republic)

February 19–20
Latin America

Area 2,777,000 sq.km. Latin America's second largest country with a great range of climate, rainfall and topography.

Population	Ann. Gr.	Density
1990	32,322,000	1.3 %	12/sq.km
1995	34,264,000	1.2 %	12/sq.km

Peoples:
European 84.5%. A fusion of many nationalities, but largely Spanish, Italian and other East and West Europeans. Many minorities have retained a strong cultural identity.
Mestizo 7.0%. Many Bolivian, Chilean and Paraguayan immigrants.
Amerindian 3.7% (18 peoples). Largest: Quechua (3) 1,030,000; Mapuche 51,000; Aymara 26,000; Toba 23,000; Mataco 20,000; Chiriguano 15,000.
Middle Eastern 4.6%. Syrian, Palestinian and Lebanese Arabs 1,000,000; Jews 500,000.
Other 0.2%. Japanese 32,000.

Literacy 95%. **Official language:** Spanish. **All languages** 23. **Languages with Scriptures** 3Bi 7NT 4por.

Capital: Buenos Aires 11,600,000. Other major cities: Cordoba 1,203,000; Rosario 1,170,000. Urbanization 84.6%.

Economy: Blessed with abundant natural resources, and once one of the world's most prosperous nations. Almost a century of government ineptitude brought the nation close to economic collapse with runaway inflation and widespread poverty. Since 1989, the Menem government has persevered with economic reforms and reduced inflation from 200% per month to 7%. By 1993, recovery was well under way. Public debt/person $1,600. Income/person $2,128 (10% of USA).

Politics: Independent from Spain in 1816. Peronist misrule, inflation and increasing leftist urban terrorism provoked the 1976 military takeover. Military incompetence, adventurism and bad record on human rights led to the restoration of democratic rule in 1983. Confidence has gradually returned to the country as the economy improved.

Religion: Roman Catholicism is the official religion, but there is freedom of religion and considerable respect for Evangelicals.
Non-religious/other 2%.
Jews 0.7%. The number of secular Jews is more than double this figure. The sixth largest group of Jews of the Diaspora.
Muslim 1.5%. About half the Arabs are Muslim.

Animist 0.3% A minority within some Amerindian tribes.
Christian 95.5%. Nom 4.6%. Affil 90.9%. Growth 1.6%.
Protestant 8.0%. Affil 7.73%. Growth 6.1%.

Church	Cong	Members	Affiliated
National Union of AoG	825	129,000	415,000
Assemblies of God (indig)	533	80,000	211,000
Visión de Futuro	339	95,000	190,000
Christian Brethren	393	38,478	128,000
Christian Assemblies (Italian)	210	42,000	93,000
Seventh-day Adventist	261	60,000	92,300
Intl Ch of Foursquare Gospel	220	23,200	51,600
Ch of God (Cleveland)	235	21,278	42,600
Ch of God Assoc	99	15,000	37,500
Ev Lutheran Church	241	20,000	30,000
Ch of God (Anderson)	405	17,000	28,300
Ev Union (RBMU/EUSA)	26	2,520	10,100
All other (158)	4,453	382,552	1,022,933
Denominations (170)	9,128	972,028	2,499,533
Evangelicals 6.9% of pop		858,000	2,242,000
Pentecostal/charis 5.63%		698,000	1,818,000

Missionaries:
to Argentina 913 (1:35,400 people) in 76 agencies.
from Argentina 144 (1:17,300 Protestants) in 23 agencies 51frn 81xcul 63dom.
Roman Catholic 85.3%. Affil 81.16%. Growth 1.1%.

Catholic Ch	2,340	20,000,000	29,032,000
Doubly counted		−1,900,000	−2,800,000
Total	2,340	18,100,000	26,232,000

Missionaries:
to Argentina 7,611 (1973 figure).
from Argentina 915 (1973 figure).
Other Catholic 0.12%. Growth 1.7%.

All denominations (4)	28	26,200	40,400

Orthodox 0.6%. Affil 0.45%. Growth 0.9%.

All denominations (7)	1,421	89,000	145,670

Marginal 1.44%. Growth 11.7%.

Jehovah's Witnesses	1,459	96,780	215,000
Mormons	531	85,000	170,000
All groups (6)	2,125	223,780	466,700

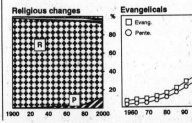

Religious changes

Evangelicals
□ Evang.
○ Pente.

1. **Astonishing reports of the revival in Argentina** are a cause for praise! There has been a tide of conversions in response to every form of evangelism. Some reckon that Evangelicals may even be 12% of the population. Decades of dictatorial and military misrule, the tragic disaster of the Falklands/ Malvinas War against Britain in 1982, and national economic collapse were all factors in making this proud people so responsive.

2. **Church growth among Evangelicals has been dramatic,** especially in the large cities, but less so in the provinces. Growth has been in every evangelical denomination but rather more in those that are Pentecostal. This growth has strained the resources of churches so that conservation and maturation of this harvest of souls has been inadequate; backsliding and loss to cults have been widespread. It is reckoned that only 10% of decisions lead to church membership. Pray for deepening and continuance of the spirit of revival in the '90s to touch every denomination and district.

3. **Spiritual warfare against the forces of darkness** has played a prominent part in Christian ministry, and decisive blows have been struck against bondage, witchcraft and sin, with dramatic results. Pray for the protection and continued spiritual health of all in the forefront of the battle. The dangers are plain – pride in success, an unbalanced ministry, inadequate discipling and emphasis on *doing* rather than *being*. Pray that more Christians may become involved in local and national government where low ethical standards and corruption are rife, and pray for the moral and spiritual reconstruction of society as a result.

4. **Pray for the unity of believers.** Praise God for an estimated 13,000 all-night prayer meetings regularly held in the country. Yet denominational barriers, doctrinal divisions and power conflicts among leaders are damaging the cause of Christ. Pray for the *Pentecostal Federation* and the *Alianza Cristiana de las Iglesias Evangélicas (ACIERA)* in their efforts to bring believers together. Unity is essential for national goals for the '90s to be set and achieved. At present there is little cooperation or visionary planning.

5. **Leadership for the Church** has now become the critical bottleneck for more growth. Lack of finance, facilities and teachers prevent many from being prepared for the ministry. Most Bible schools are full. Some theological colleges emphasize humanism, liberation theology and social action rather than preaching the Word. Pray for the raising up, training and effective deployment of mature Christian leaders who walk humbly with their God.

6. **The immigrant minority Churches** (especially among Italians, Danish, Dutch and Welsh) once made up a significant proportion of Protestants. They attended to the spiritual needs of their own church communities, but did not evangelize the Spanish-speaking majority; however Italian, Russian and Chilean believers have evangelized their own groups. They are in decline, partly because their Spanish-speaking children do not feel at home in the churches. Younger Korean and Chinese ethnic churches are growing.

7. **Lowland Amerindians of the Chaco** in the north have responded to the gospel, and a high proportion are active Christians through the work of **SAMS**, Mennonites, and Pentecostals. Pockets of animism remain, and several indigenous sects have arisen which have led some astray. The coming of the gospel saved both these people and their cultures and gave them a pride and dignity to survive and thrive in the modern world. Pray for:
a) Maturity and growth of these churches and their integration into national life.
b) The ministry of **GRn** recordings – available in 12 languages.
c) Bible translation programmes; work is proceeding in seven languages (**SIL, SAMS**).

8. **Missions.** The greatest need is for mature missionaries able to assist the Church in Bible teaching, church planting and imparting a missions vision. Pray for the church-planting and support work of missionaries with **AoG** USA & Brazil (67), **CBFMS** (38), **Brethren** (30), **CMA** (22), **GMU** (12), and **SBC** (11). Major missionary-contributing nations: USA (517), Germany (104), Brazil (64), UK (55), Sweden (52).

9. **Challenges for evangelism in the '90s.**
a) **Rural and provincial areas,** which have been less touched by the revival.
b) **The estimated 500,000 Jews, most in Buenos Aires,** who are highly secularized but are showing interest in the gospel. Little has been done up till now, but **JFJ**, Chosen People Ministries and 10 other agencies have a ministry to Jews. There are five Messianic assemblies in Buenos Aires.
c) The sophisticated **upper class of the capital,** who have been harder to reach with the gospel.

d) The **urban poor.** Local churches are doing more to address social needs among them, but the challenge is enormous.

e) **University students** who number 902,000, over half being in Buenos Aires. There are few actively witnessing students; pray for the staff and ABUA(**IFES**) groups.

10. **The missionary vision of the Argentinian Church is small but growing** with a significant interest in Spain and North Africa. The economic crisis and hyperinflation have made it hard to maintain missionary support. The COMIBAM committee has a major interdenominational role in stimulating and facilitating the vision for missions. Pray that pastors and churches may gain a vision for the unreached peoples of the world.

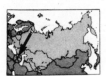

Armenia

(Republic of Armenia; Ayastan)

February 21
Eurasia

Area 29,800 sq.km. Landlocked, mountainous Caucasus state. Armenia claims Nagorno-Karabakh, a 1,750 sq.km. enclave populated by Armenians in neighbouring Azerbaijan.

Population	Ann. Gr.	Density
1990 3,333,000	0.79 %	112/sq.km
1995 3,427,000	0.69 %	115/sq.km

Over 1,300,000 Armenians live in other republics of the former USSR and a further 1,400,000 in 120 other nations around the world.

Peoples: Based on 1989 census.
Armenians 93.3%. A distinctive Indo-European people.
Other 6.7%. Azerbaijani 84,000; Kurds 58,000; Russians 50,000; Ukrainian 8,000; Assyrian 6,000; Greek 4,700.

Literacy 99%. **Official language:** Armenian. **Languages with Scriptures** 1Bi.

Capital: Yerevan 1,300,000. Urbanization 65%.

Economy: Potentially wealthy with minerals, agriculture and hydro power. Crippled by devastating damage in the 1988 earthquake (50,000 killed, 650,000 made homeless) and by the war with Azerbaijan, which controls Armenia's main rail routes to the outside world. Agriculture and industry is being rapidly de-nationalized. Unemployment is high.

Politics: Only at rare points in Armenia's 2,500-year history has it been independent, for the country has been a victim of its location as a strategic buffer between the Byzantine/Turkish, Russian/USSR and Persian empires. Independent as a member of the CIS in September 1991. The conflict with Azerbaijan over the status of Nagorno-Karabakh region dominates the life of the country.

Religion: Religious freedom followed the collapse of Communism, but there is an intimate relationship between the Armenian Apostolic Church and the nation's culture and politics. Armenia was the world's first Christian state (AD 301).
Non-religious/other 17.6%.
Muslim 3.3%. Azerbaijani, Kurds. Reduced since 1990.
Christian 79.1%. Growth 2.5%.
  Protestant 0.56%. Growth 27.4%.

Church	Cong	Members	Affiliated
Pentecostal Ch	80	6,000	15,000
Baptist Ch	10	1,900	3,800
Denominations (3)	91	8,000	19,050
Evangelicals 0.56% of pop		9,400	19,050
Pentecostal/charis 0.45%		7,500	15,000

Missionaries to Armenia est. 10 in 2 agencies.
  Roman Catholic 0.06%.
  Orthodox 78.5%. Growth 2.4%.

Armenian Apostolic Ch	100	1,430,000	2,600,000
Russian Orthodox Ch	3	7,500	15,000
Denominations (2)	103	1,437,500	2,615,000
Evangelicals 4.5% of pop		85,000	150,000

  Marginal 0.01%. Growth 40%.

All groups (2)	3	299	458

1. **Armenia needs peace and good relations with surrounding nations** for survival and economic reconstruction. Centuries of bitter conflict, oppression and massacres have left a legacy of hatred and mistrust of these nations. In 1915 the Turks massacred 1.5 million Armenians because they were Christian and considered a threat. Pray both for forgiveness for the past by all and for wise reconstruction of trust and good neighbourliness by the nation's leaders.

2. **The ancient Armenian Apostolic Church** has long been a cultural refuge in times of persecution, but the old liturgy is not in modern language so is less appropriate for ordinary people. The 1988 earthquake helped to bring about a powerful revival with a sense of national repentance before the Lord and resurgence of interest in the Scriptures. The **Brotherhood** is the evangelical arm of the Apostolic Church which has its roots in the fifth century. The Brotherhood suffered much in past centuries and under Communism, but has been able to operate openly since the late '80s as an autonomous body within the Apostolic Church. Their main emphases are on biblical preaching, personal witness, publishing and distributing evangelical literature and Bibles, and charitable works. They have fellowship meetings in most towns of Armenia. Pray for this movement and its influence for good on the nation.

3. **Communism corrupted public and private morals.** Pray that its deadening influence may be replaced by biblical teaching in homes and schools, and biblical standards in public life and among Christians. The new Armenian Bible was published in 1993 by the Armenian Bible Society (UBS).

4. **All Churches and especially Evangelicals** have grown in numbers since the collapse of Communism, but Baptist and Pentecostal congregations are still relatively few in number. Pray for effective outreach through both the Brotherhood and Protestants to every community and especially to the refugees from the 1988 earthquake and from the war in Nagorno-Karabakh – many are living in great poverty and inadequate housing. A number of new Pentecostal congregations were planted after the earthquake in areas most affected.

5. **Evangelical Christianity has thrived among the Armenians of the diaspora**, with many congregations in the Middle East, North America and elsewhere. Pray that these believers may make a wholesome spiritual impact on their homeland. Most Armenians have retained close links even after many generations.

6. **Christian help ministries.**
a) *Gtutiun* (meaning Compassion) was the first non-government charity allowed to operate. It was set up by the **Brotherhood** with the principal aim of spreading the gospel through evangelists and children's workers, and also engaging in hospital and old peoples' homes' visitation, and medical work. *Gtutiun* also publishes and distributes Christian literature, Bibles and teaching materials through their four bookstores. Pray for *Gtutiun's* 300 workers.
b) **Wealthy expatriate Armenians** are funding production of Christian literature, printing of Bibles and setting up of Christian radio stations to serve Armenia and the surrounding Muslim countries. Pray for a wise integration of all supportive ministries for building up the Church in Armenia, and for the Church to become a light for the gospel to Iran, Azerbaijan, Turkey and beyond.

Aruba

Area 193 sq.km. An island 28 km north of Venezuela. Dry and sandy with no fresh water and few natural resources.

Population	Ann. Gr.	Density
1990 63,000	0.32 %	326/sq.km
1995 64,000	0.32 %	332/sq.km

Peoples:
Antillean Creole 88%. **Dutch** 2.6%.
Other 9.4% (40 nationalities). Spanish-speaking 1,500; English-speaking 1,300.

Literacy 95%. **Official language:** Dutch. Unofficial: Papiamento (a Spanish, Portuguese, Dutch and English Creole).

Capital: Oranjestad 21,000.

Economy: Heavily dependent on tourism and loans from the Netherlands.

Politics: Aruba withdrew from the Netherlands Antilles in 1986. It is an autonomous, self-governing member of the Kingdom of the Netherlands. Independence is planned for 1996.

Religion:
Non-religious/other 1.6%.
Jewish 0.2%. **Other** 1.2%.
Christian 97%. Affil 91.5%. Growth -1.0%.
 Protestant 10%. Affil 9.9%. Growth 0.2%.

Church	Cong	Members	Affiliated
Dutch Reformed	6	900	1,500
Assemblies of God	4	400	1,000
Methodist	3	320	800
Evangelical (**TEAM**)	5	450	750
Baptist (**SBC**)	3	300	500
All other (6)	17	730	1,700
Denominations (11)	38	3,100	6,250
Evangelicals 6% of pop		1,878	3,753
Pentecostal/charis 3.4%		960	2,150

Missionaries to Aruba 2 (1:32,000 people) in one agency.
Roman Catholic 85.1%. Affil 79.7%
Growth −1.4%.

	Cong	Members	Affiliated
Catholic Church		10,900	54,500
Doubly counted		−2,700	−4,200
Denominations		8,200	50,300

Marginal 1.9% Affil 1.9% Growth 8.1%.

	Cong	Members	Affiliated
Jehovah's Witnesses	6	474	1,190

Missionaries: Most figures included with Netherlands Antilles.

1. **There has been considerable growth of the evangelical witness** – predominantly among the non-indigenous. There are over 20 evangelical congregations with outreach, seven being in Dutch/Papiamento and 15 in English. Inter-church rivalry has harmed the overall witness. The major spiritual growth is in **AoG**- and **TEAM**-related churches, though the Methodists too have experienced a strong moving of the Spirit. Pray for a greater impact on the Papiamento-speaking population.

2. **Media.** Radio Victoria (**TEAM**) and the **AoG** station broadcast to the Antilles and to the whole Caribbean in Papiamento and other languages. Pray for enduring fruitfulness for this ministry.

February 23–24
Pacific

Australia
(The Commonwealth of Australia)

Area 7,682,000 sq.km. This island continent is largely grassland and desert in the interior but better watered in the east, southeast and southwest coastal regions, where most live in highly concentrated urban areas. There are three permanently inhabited dependent territories; Norfolk Is. (pop 2,500), Christmas Is. (pop 2,300), Cocos Is. (pop 600).

Population		Ann. Gr.	Density
1990	16,746,000	1.2 %	2/sq.km
1995	17,690,000	1.1 %	2/sq.km

Peoples:
Anglo-Celtic 74.2%. Predominantly British and Irish.
Other European 19.2%. Migrants from nearly every ethnic group in Europe, many still retaining their cultural identity.
Asian 2.3%. Chinese 190,000; Vietnamese 35,000; Malay-Indonesian 35,000; Japanese 12,000.
Middle Eastern 2.0%. Arabic-speaking 250,000; Turkish 40,000; Kurds 11,000; Iranians.
Australian Aborigine 1.5%. 250,000 total, half of whom speak the 111 living languages. (In 1780 approx 300,000 who spoke 260 languages.)
Other 0.8% including Pacific Islanders.

Literacy 99%. **Official language:** English. Nearly 10% of the population do not use English as their first language. **All indigenous languages** 234. **Languages with Scriptures** 1Bi 7NT 26por.

Capital: Canberra 276,000. Other cities: Sydney 3,806,000; Melbourne 3,184,000; Brisbane 1,121,000; Adelaide 1,059,000; Perth 1,020,000. Urbanization 86%.

Economy: Wealthy mixed economy based on industry, agriculture and mining, but world recession, enormous external debt and severe droughts slowed the economy in the '80s. Public debt/person $5,300. Income/person $14,400 (68% of USA).

Politics: Parliamentary democracy, independent of Britain in 1901. A federation of six states and two federal territories.

Religion: A secular state with freedom of religion. Legislation being considered in the state parliament of Victoria could criminalize evangelism of those of other religions or even possessing written materials criticizing other religious beliefs.
Non-religious/other 26.6%.
Muslim 1.5%. Predominantly Turks, Arabs and Yugoslavs.
Jews 0.5%. **Buddhist** 0.8%.
Christian 70.6%. Nom 8.3%. Affil 61.3%. Growth 0.7%.

Protestant 39.6%. Affil 30.4%. Growth –0.5%.

Church	Cong	Members	Affiliated
Anglican Church	1,173	661,000	3,670,000
Uniting Church	3,236	205,700	367,722
Presbyterian Church of A	578	40,156	138,000
Baptist Union	830	61,667	135,054
Lutheran Church	649	72,081	118,341
Assemblies of God	500	27,017	81,440
Seventh-day Adventist	391	46,174	49,226
Churches of Christ	440	35,228	72,591
Salvation Army	553	13,956	70,000
Christian Brethren	290	14,500	32,200
Christian Outreach Centres	170	12,500	25,000
Christian Revival Crusade	100	10,000	13,500
All other (150)	1,962	153,162	282,794
Denominations (162)	10,872	1,353,141	5,085,868
Evangelicals 12.6% of pop		605,761	2,113,701
Pentecostal/charis 2.8%		164,000	474,000

Missionaries:
from Australia 3,543 (1:1,436 Protestants) in 67 agencies 2,005frn 2,053xcul 1,490dom.
to Australia 726 (1:23,100 people) in 79 agencies.

Roman Catholic 26.3%. Growth 1.5%.

Catholic Ch	1,433	3,080,000	4,395,000

Missionaries:
from Australia 1,044 (1973 figure).
to Australia 1,993 (1:8,400 people).

Other Catholic 0.1%. Growth 13.1%.

Denominations (3)	57	4,000	16,000

Orthodox 3.3%. Growth 1.2%.

Greek Orthodox	108	224,000	320,000
Coptic Orthodox	15	35,000	50,000
Antiochan Orthodox (Syrian)	10	29,300	45,000
Russian Orthodox	21	26,400	40,000
All other (29)	73	47,260	98,900
Denominations (33)	227	361,960	553,900

Marginal 1.27%. Growth 7%.

Jehovah's Witnesses	645	53,142	98,489
Mormons	212	53,600	76,575
All other (52)	364	19,100	36,780
Groups (54)	1,221	125,842	211,844

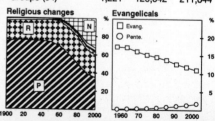

Religious changes

Evangelicals

□ Evang.
○ Pente.

A

1. **Secularism has failed Australians.** Wealth, leisure and pleasure have not satisfied. The economy is in recession with considerable unemployment. Negative attitudes towards authority, tradition and enthusiasms make it hard for the average man in the street to see the gospel as meaningful or the church as relevant. Pray that many Australians might find their solutions to life's problems and identity in a relationship with the Lord Jesus Christ.

2. **The decline in church attendance is causing deep concern** (1966 35%, 1976 18%, 1990 12%). This is most noticeable in some of the larger and more traditional churches. There is some growth in the more evangelical denominations, particularly in the various Pentecostal and charismatic churches and groups. Pray for a growing unity among all evangelicals, and for revival.

3. **Evangelicals are strong in the Sydney Anglican diocese,** and several mainline churches have evangelical majorities while all of the rest have significant and active minorities. However, there has been a drastic drop in Sunday School attendance, and alternative methods must be found to reach the younger generation. Pray that there might be a greater return to biblical truth and holiness, and a resurgent emphasis on evangelism and missions within local congregations.

4. **Missions vision has sunk to a low ebb** in most churches. Giving to missions per capita is possibly the worst of any country in the developed world, so the relatively large number of Australian missionaries suffer from lack of support at every level. The vision for world evangelization has to be imparted to pastors during their theological training. Pray for this and that churches may be enthused thereby. Pray also for the missionary force, especially those who have gone to pioneer areas.

5. **Less reached peoples** are found both among the indigenous inhabitants and the four million non-British post-war immigrants and their families. Pray for those local churches with an active ministry to such communities and also for the work of **ECM** and other agencies among the European minorities.
a) **Aboriginal tribes.** Only a few isolated groups have failed to respond to the very considerable missionary effort now being made all over the country.
b) **Many people in working-class urban areas** and in isolated mining and farming communities in the vast interior, northwest and north have had no vital biblical witness.
c) **Muslims** – around 300,000, with 200,000 living in the Sydney area. Muslims have doubled in numbers in the last decade, and there are now over 50 mosques in use. The majority of this very diverse community is Arabic-speaking; 200,000 are from Lebanon and Egypt; other significant communities are Turkish (40,000), Bosnian and Albanian. Small beginnings are being made to reach these peoples by the Baptist Union, Uniting Church and Stepping Stone Mission's Training Community, resulting in Arabic- and Turkish-speaking groups of believers beginning to emerge. **MECO's** Centres of Fellowship are a significant ministry to Muslims.
d) **Chinese** – 190,000 (60,000 being refugees from Vietnam). About 20% of the Chinese are Christian in name; others are secular or adhere to the various Chinese traditional religions. There are lively groups of believers in the cities and among overseas Chinese students in universities. Pray for the complete evangelization of the non-Christians.
e) **Vietnamese** – 35,000, mostly refugees over the past 15 years. There are a few Christian congregations. **AsEF** is expanding a ministry to meet the spiritual needs of Asian communities in each state.
f) **The diverse peoples from the former Yugoslavia.** Most still retain the use of their mother tongues: Croatian 70,000; Serbian 35,000; Macedonian 8,000; Albanian 4,000. They originate from some of Europe's least evangelized countries, and there are very few believers among them.
g) **Jews** – 80,000; half live in Melbourne. Relatively few have become Christian.
h) **Southern Europeans.** Many second- and third-generation settlers have assimilated into English-speaking Australian society. Many, however, still use their original languages: Italian 450,000; Greek 270,000; Polish 100,000; Maltese 70,000; Spanish 60,000. These represent strategic minorities that, if evangelized and motivated, could make a decisive impact for God on their lands of origin.

6. **The 250,000 indigenous Aborigines** have suffered much in their contacts with Western culture, and their political and land rights have become a major political issue. However, the driving force for these rights is a potent mix of Marxism and liberation theology together with the traditional religions – often exploited by other interest groups. Some have adapted and have been absorbed into the life of the nation, but many have sunk into moral and spiritual degradation, and others have retreated into

A

the more inaccessible and inhospitable parts of the country. In the last eight years an indigenous revival movement in the north has spread through parts of the west and centre of the country with thousands being soundly converted.

a) Pray for the **Aboriginal Evangelical Fellowship,** a key coordinating body of Aboriginal Christians, as it encourages leadership development through its training college, outreach and church planting in every Aboriginal community. Pray that believers may boldly proclaim the liberating power of the gospel in the face of hostility from political activists.

b) Pray for the nearly 500 missionaries in 26 denominational and interdenominational societies working among these people (such as the **Aborigine Inland Mission, United Aborigine Mission, CMS** and **MAF**).

c) Bible translation is in progress in 20 of these small language groups (through the 38 **SIL** and **UBS** workers); 26 languages have a portion of the New Testament. About 12 may still need translators.

d) The use of **GRn** records and cassettes in 86 languages is a vital contribution to the task because of the great linguistic variety among the Aborigines.

7. Witness among the 421,000 students in the 95 universities and colleges is barely adequate. **Students for Christ,** with 1,300 members, is now the largest evangelical campus ministry, followed by AFES (**IFES**) with 70 groups, Student Life (**CCC**), and the **Navigators,** but one of the most active is the Chinese-led **Overseas Christian Fellowship.** Pray for a greater evangelistic zeal, a larger harvest for the Kingdom, and an increased flow of missionaries to the world from these groups.

8. **Young people.** The Inter-Schools Christian Fellowship (**SU**) has a valuable ministry in secondary schools. Many groups, such as Youth For Christ, Crusader Movement, God Squad and the innovative **Fusion Ministries** are seeking to evangelize young people.

9. **Christian Media:**

a) **Christian radio.** This could be more effectively utilized by Evangelicals through the national and local broadcasting networks, which are required, by law, to give a percentage of time weekly to religious broadcasts. Fusion Ministries produces a Christian radio spot that is heard daily by 10% of the population. Funding is a big bottleneck.

b) **Christian literature.** There are 500 Christian bookstores (9 of **CLC**) in Australia, but few Christians read much. Pray that this trend may be reversed and for literature to impact the younger generation of Christians. The evangelistic and teaching materials produced by **The Bible Society, SGM, ACTS International** and **World Home Bible League** are especially worthy of prayer support.

Austria

(The Republic of Austria)

February 25–26
Europe

A

Area 84,000 sq.km. Landlocked; mountainous in the south and west (the Alps), and flat plains along the Danube River in the east.

Population	Ann. Gr.	Density
1990	7,492,000	−0.03 %	89/sq.km
1995	7,479,000	−0.03 %	89/sq.km

Peoples:
Indigenous 96%. German-speaking 7,100,000; Gypsy 9,000.
Immigrant 4%. Slovene 82,000, Turkish 67,000; Polish 39,000; Croat 30,000, Serb 30,000; Kurdish 23,000; Hungarian 22,000; French 15,000; Greek 12,000; Arab 3,000; Iranian 2,000; Chinese 1,200.
Refugees: 380,000 registered from 43 nations. An estimated 600,000 have been absorbed into the Austrian population.

Capital: Vienna 1,875,000 (nearly one quarter of the population). Urbanization 58%.

Literacy 100%. **Official language:** German.

Economy: Predominantly industrial economy. Rapidly developing into a hub for new commercial and trade initiatives with the former Communist states of Central Europe. Unemployment 5%. Income/person $17,360 (82% of USA).

Politics: The heart of the former Austro-Hungarian Empire until 1918. A multi-party democratic republic. A neutral buffer state between West and East between 1945 and 1990. Membership of the EC likely in 1993. The anti-foreign right wing party has gained a growing following.

Religion: The constitution guarantees freedom of religion and also special state church status to both the Roman Catholic and Lutheran *Evangelische Kirche*.
Non-religious/other 8.2%.
Muslim 1.4%. Turks, Yugoslavs, Arabs and Iranians.
Jews 0.08% (2.8% in 1934).
Baha'i 0.02%. **Buddhist** 0.01%.

Christian 90.3%. Active Affil 36%. Growth −0.2%.
Protestant 5.3%. Growth −1.2%.

Church	Cong	Members	Affiliated
Protestant Lutheran Ch	183	180,000	359,400
Protestant Reformed Ch	9	10,600	14,900
Evang Methodists	8	1,100	2,200
Free Christian Chs	31	1,031	2,031
Federation of Baptist Chs (SBC)	11	767	1,700
Evang Free Chs (19)	52	881	1,260
All other (26)	156	8,934	17,504
Denominations (50)	450	203,313	398,995
Evangelicals 0.49% of pop		19,066	36,453
Pentecostal/charis 0.06%		2,700	4,800

Missionaries:
to Austria 588 (1:12,700 people) in 63 agencies.
from Austria 63 (1:6,300 Protestants) 37frn 37xcul 26dom.

Roman Catholic 83%. Growth −0.2%.

Catholic Ch	3,077	2,050,000	6,218,040
Charismatics		8,000	15,000

Other Catholic 0.33%. Growth 0%.

Old Catholic Church	50	8,500	25,000

Orthodox 0.94%. Growth 0.9%.

Denominations (10)	37	47,800	70,210

Marginal 0.74%. Growth 3.1%.

Jehovah's Witnesses	252	18,891	37,800
Mormons	9	3,030	4,100
All other (17)	29	6,568	13,411
Groups (19)	290	28,489	55,311

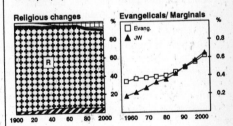

Religious changes

Evangelicals/ Marginals
☐ Evang.
▲ JW

1. **Austria is a cultured nation** famed for music, art and beauty. Yet Austrians need a personal faith in Christ, and only a minority have clearly heard how they may find one. Over 50% of the population is Christian in name, but with no meaningful link with any church, yet an estimated 80% have had dealings with the occult. The high suicide, abortion and alcoholism statistics indicate the spiritual need. Pray for this nation to be set free by the power of Jesus.

2. **The land is nominally Roman Catholic by culture rather than by commitment.** The steady decline in active Catholics and the rapid decline in the number of priests (12% loss in the '80s) is serious. Non-churchgoers shun contact with Evangelicals, who are seen as a foreign sect. There is a small but growing renewal movement in the Catholic Church. Pray that barriers to the entry of the gospel into hearts may be broken down.

A

3. **The Lutheran and Reformed Churches** are declining by 1% annually (2,700 adherents lost every year). Formalism and tradition have little relevance or attraction for the younger generation. There are a number of Bible-believing pastors, and their number is now being increased by graduates of the Free Evangelical Seminary in Basel, Switzerland. Pray for the Pastors' Prayer Fellowship, an evangelical fellowship within the Lutheran Church, and for a move of the Spirit of God in these churches that will make them a force for the evangelization of the land.

4. **Newer evangelical/Pentecostal churches** are few and small in number, but growing. During the '80s, congregations almost doubled in number, rising from 57 to 97, but attendances tripled. Yet born-again believers in these churches and also in the mainline denominations may still be less than 0.3% of the population. Pray for the multiplication of congregations where the Lord Jesus Christ is proclaimed and honoured. Pray also for the efforts of both the **Evangelical Alliance** (ÖEA) and the **Fellowship of Evangelical Congregations in Austria** (ARGEGO) to bring more cooperative action to the fragmented evangelical cause.

5. **Pastors for the congregations** are needed. Too few Austrians enter full-time Christian service, and even fewer for mission work in other lands. Too many rely on foreigners. The first Austrian evangelical, interdenominational Bible school at Ampflwang opened in 1984; graduates from this school could be a decisive factor for church growth in coming years.

6. **Less reached sections of the population.**
a) **Provinces:** Niederösterreich and Burgenland in the east, Steiermark in the centre and Voralberg and Tyrol in the west have fewer Evangelicals.
b) **Towns:** In 1985, there were 55 towns of over 5,000 people without an evangelical witness.
c) **Cultists:** The aggressive activities of New Age movements, Eastern cults, Jehovah's Witnesses and Mormons have gained a considerable following among younger people. Pray both for the nullification of these efforts and for the release of those ensnared.

7. **Missionary numbers** have grown rapidly, major agencies being **YWAM** (with 52 workers), **OM** (47), **CBFMS** (46), **GEM** (34), **Brethren** (33), **TEAM** (30), **ECM** (26), and **IT** (25). Major missionary-contributing nations: USA (310), Germany (57), UK (53), Canada (49). Most are involved in evangelism and church planting, but the work is slow and converts few. Pray for their adaptability and effectiveness in discipling those who will become leaders.

8. **Witness among the 200,000 students** is one of the most fruitful in the land today. Over half of these are in Vienna, where there are also 15,000 international students. Strong groups in the seven universities are growing in depth and outreach. Pray that these young Christians may have an impact on the land and its churches. Pray also for the ministries of ÖSM(**IFES**), **CCC** and **Navigators** on the campuses of Austria. Both **CEF** (with 18 workers) and **SU** have an appreciated ministry to school-age children.

9. **Christian literature** ministries including Scripture distribution of the Bible Society and the literature ministries of Austrian Bible Mission and **CLC** need prayer. The Bible is used as a textbook in schools and supplied free to every child.

10. **Migrant labourers and refugees** need to be reached, the numbers and variety of whom give much scope for cross-cultural ministry. All the states of the **former Yugoslavia** are represented; there is a lively congregation in Vienna where 300 have been converted over the past 20 years. There is a fellowship of ex-Muslims in Vienna, but too little is being done for the Muslim Turks, Kurds, Arabs and Iranians. There are also one Armenian evangelical and two Romanian groups. Pray for the expansion and blessing of these ministries.

Azerbaijan

(Republic of Azerbaijan)

February 27

A

Eurasia

Area 86,600 sq.km. Transcaucasian republic on Caspian Sea, including a 5,632 sq.km. enclave, Nakhichevan, between Armenia and Turkey.

Population	Ann. Gr.	Density
1990 7,129,000	1.32 %	82/sq.km
1995 7,642,000	0.64 %	88/sq.km

Peoples: Figures for 1989.
Azerbaijani 83%. Related to Turkish; 20 dialects. A further one million live in the other republics of the former USSR, 8,130,000 in Iran, 38,000 in Iraq.
Indigenous minorities 3.9%. Lezgin 171,000 (including 4 languages and many dialects); Avar 44,000; Talysh 21,000; Kurds 20,000; Tsakhur 13,000; Tat 10,000.
Foreign minorities 13.1%. Russian 390,000; Armenian 390,000; Ukrainian 32,000; Tatar 28,000; Turks 18,000; Georgian 14,000. Rapid decrease of Russians and Armenians since 1990.

Literacy 98%. **Official language:** Azerbaijani. **All languages** 16. **Languages with Scriptures** 6Bi 1por.

Capital: Baku 1,800,000. Urbanization 55%.

Economy: Oil and mineral wealth was heavily exploited by the Russians. Good economic potential if western expertise revitalizes oil and mining industries. Rapid switch to market economy. Much urban poverty and hampered by cost of undeclared war with Armenia over the Nagorno-Karabakh enclave.

Politics: Long a vassal of surrounding empires. Independent in 1991 from USSR. The old Communist leaders were replaced by nationalists in 1992. Pan-Turkism and affinity with Turkey rather than with Iran, and Muslim resurgence following war with Christian Armenians are determining government policy.

Religion: The nationalists are becoming more Islamic and anti-Christian, but there is officially religious freedom. Religious figures are estimates.
Non-religious/other 17.3%. Many Azerbaijani were non-religious or atheist until 1990.
Muslim 80%. Shi'a 56%; Sunni 24%.
Christian 2.67% (almost all non-indigenous). Growth −10.5%.
Protestant 0.01%. Growth −4%.

Church	Cong	Members	Affiliated
Baptist Ch	6	400	700
All other (5)	2	120	200
Denominations (6)	8	520	900
Evangelicals 0.01% of pop		508	880

Expatriate workers to Azerbaijan est. 20.
Catholic 0.11%. Growth −8%.
Orthodox 2.54%. Growth −10.6%.

Russian Orthodox Ch	7	58,500	90,000
Armenian Apostolic Ch	5	44,000	80,000
Georgian Orthodox Ch		6,000	10,000
Denominations (3)	12	108,500	180,000

1. **Rising nationalism linked with Islamic revival** is making many Azerbaijanis less receptive to the gospel, though in recent years urban youth have shown interest. Pray that hatred and resentment against Christianity will be bound in Jesus' name and many Azerbaijanis will find peace by believing in him.

2. **The Christian population** is almost entirely Russian and Armenian; many have now fled the country. It was a massacre of Armenians in Baku in 1989 that provoked the Armenians of Nagorno-Karabakh to declare independence in 1990, culminating in warfare. Pray for peace between the communities and for a new day of openness among the Muslims.

3. **Azerbaijani Christians** in the country are only around 50 in number out of a possible worldwide total of 200. There are no Azerbaijani-speaking congregations. Pray them into being and for the few believers to stand strong in the Lord.

4. **Foreign Christians** from outside the former USSR can find openings for work and witness. Pray for such to be called and enter into fruitful work in the land. There is a network of concerned Christians who pray and work for the evangelization of this land.

5. **Among the unreached ethnic minorities,** only the **Udi** (6,000) of the many **Lezgin** peoples are Christian; all the other groups are Muslim and without any Scriptures in their languages. The **Talysh, Kurds, Tat, Avar, Tsakhur** and **Tatars** are all unreached. There are at least eight languages without any portion of the Word of God. The **Jews** speaking Kurdish and Tat are also untouched by the gospel.

6. **Christian help ministries.**

a) **Literature** is freely printed in the country, but funds and distributors limit its dissemination. Any Christian literature and Bibles are eagerly received.

b) **Radio** is one of the few media easily applicable to Azerbaijan. Only 2.25 hours/week are broadcast by **IBRA**-Malta, **FEBA** and **High Adventure**, Lebanon. Pray for Azerbaijani preachers and for an increase in their numbers and productivity so that broadcast hours may increase, and pray for lasting impact.

c) **Music and video cassettes in Azerbaijani** are an urgent unmet need.

<table>
<tr><td>

See Caribbean

Caribbean

</td><td>

Bahamas
(Commonwealth of the Bahamas)

</td><td></td></tr>
</table>

Area 14,000 sq.km. An archipelago of 700 coral islands between Florida and Cuba. Forty are inhabited.

Population		Ann. Gr.	Density
1990	260,000	1.4 %	19/sq.km
1995	278,000	1.3 %	20/sq.km

Peoples: Foreign-born 16% of population.
Afro-Caribbean 87%. There are many Haitian refugees who speak French Creole.
Euro-American 12.5%. British, US citizens, Greeks 800.
Other 0.5%. Jews 800; Chinese 500.

Literacy 95%. **Official language:** English.

Capital: Nassau 135,000. Urbanization 54%.

Economy: Prosperous through tourism, oil refining, finance and illegal drug traffic. Public debt/person $2,700. Income/person $10,800 (51% of USA).

Politics: Independent from Britain in 1973 as a parliamentary monarchy. Charges of corruption and drug dealing led to the fall of the government in the 1992 elections.

Religion:
Non-religious/other 4.5%.
Spiritist 1%. **Jews** 0.3%.
Christian 94.2%. Nom 17.5%. Affil 76.7%. Growth 1.2%.
  Protestant 72.2%. Affil 59%. Growth 0.8%.

Church	Cong	Members	Affiliated
Baptist Union	215	22,150	37,000
Anglican Church	96	11,600	27,500
Seventh-day Adventist	37	11,000	15,700
Ch of God (Anderson)	34	3,430	10,400
Ch of God (Cleveland)	72	4,264	8,530
Ch of God of Prophecy	52	3,600	7,200
Methodist Church	69	5,416	7,000
Baptist International Missions	16	3,500	5,390
Christian Brethren	68	2,700	4,910
Assemblies of God	23	1,000	3,750
All other (15)	76	6,355	11,434
Denominations (25)	758	75,015	138,814
Evangelicals 33.2% of pop		46,527	86,365
Pentecostal/charis 8.9%		10,800	23,200

Missionaries:
  to Bahamas 68 (1:3,800 people) in 15 agencies.
  from Bahamas 1 1dom.
Roman Catholic 26%. Affil 16.5%. Growth 3.1%.

Catholic Ch	92	24,500	43,000

Orthodox 0.4%. Affil 0.15%. Growth 3.1%.
Marginal 1.4%. Growth 11.2%.

Jehovah's Witnesses	17	1,213	3,290
All groups (3)		1,531	3,890

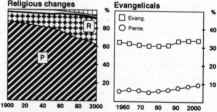

1. **Under a religious veneer, society is sick.** The materialism stimulated by tourism and the corruption sown by trade in hard drugs has deeply affected every level of society. The Bahamas has the dubious reputation of having the highest rate of drug addiction in the world. Pray for God-glorifying changes.

2. **Among Christians, commitment is low** despite the high percentage of Evangelicals in the

country. Few are willing to commit themselves for the Lord's work, and many congregations are without adequate pastoral care. Pray for revival, and for a missionary vision among believers.

3. **Goals for 2000.** Baptists have 215 churches. Their goal is 75,000 believers in 270 churches by the year 2000.

Bahrain

(The State of Bahrain)

February 28
Middle East

Area 691 sq.km. A group of one larger and several smaller islands in the Arabian Gulf between the Qatar peninsula and Saudi Arabian mainland.

Population		Ann. Gr.	Density
1990	515,000	3.7 %	745/sq.km
1995	601,000	3.1 %	870/sq.km

Peoples:
Arab 72.1%. Bahraini 66%. Other Arabs (Palestinian, Egyptian, Saudi, etc.) 6.1%.
Indian, Pakistani 12.7%. Malayali, Tamil, Telegu, Urdu, etc.
Iranian 12%. Farsi, Kurds, etc.
European 2.5%. **Other** 0.7%. Filipino, Korean, etc.

Literacy 75%. **Official language:** Arabic.

Capital: Manama 152,000. Urbanization 79%.

Economy: Has diversified from oil production to some extent to become a major Gulf industrial and banking centre. Income/person $10,360 (49% of USA).

Politics: British protection until 1971. Absolute monarchy since 1975. The Amir rules with the help of an appointed Cabinet and a Consultative Council.

Religion: Islam is the official religion, and all Bahrainis are considered Muslim. No evangelism among them is permitted. Christian expatriate churches have been favourably welcomed.

Muslim 85%. Sunni 21% (largely urban), Shi'a 62% (rural and Iranians), Ismaili 2%.
Hindu 6.2%. About half the Indian community.
Non-religious/other 1.5%.
Christian 7.3%. Nom 2%. Affil 5.3%. Growth 7.5%.
Protestant 1.5%. Affil 1.4%. Growth 3.1%.

Church	Cong	Members	Affiliated
Anglican Church	10	1,100	2,900
National Evang Church	18	972	1,620
Pentecostal groups (6)	6	300	600
All other (8)	13	910	1,966
Denominations (16)	47	3,282	7,086
Evangelicals 0.77% of pop.		1,971	3,959
Pentecostal/charis 0.2%		600	1,000

Expatriate Christians 33 (1:15,600 people).
Roman Catholic 4.5%. Affil 3.4%. Growth 9.1%.

Catholic Church (RC)	11	9,800	17,500
Charismatics		600	1,000

Orthodox 1.3%. Affil 0.53%. Growth 10.6%.

| Denominations (3) | 3 | 1,132 | 2,720 |

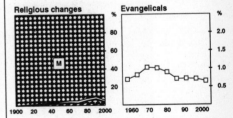

1. **Bahrain has provided a good base for Christian witness** since the beginning of this century. There is opportunity for a tactful witness through the multi-national Christian expatriate community. Pray that individuals may have the courage and wisdom to actually do so beyond their own cultural group.

2. Pray especially for the one **Arabic-speaking evangelical congregation** (mainly expatriates) and their witness to the many Muslims who have never been exposed to the gospel. There are also a few national believers who meet privately in homes.

3. **There are a number of avenues for tactful witness** to the Arab majority.
a) Expatriate Christians employed there – meeting in churches and house fellowships.
b) Expatriate Christian workers serving in the country.

c) The well-known and highly-regarded American Mission Hospital.

d) The Christian bookstore, with a high annual sale of Christian literature.

B

4. **The labour force of nearly 200,000 is 58% expatriate**, and drawn from 45 nations. Amid the prevailing concern for material things, pray that Christians within some of these national groups may win people for Christ. There are over 45 congregations of various denominations and fellowships, nearly half of these being Indian. The less evangelized of these expatriate communities are the Iranians, Hindus and the Muslims from India and Pakistan.

5. **FEBA Radio from the Seychelles is well received**, broadcasting 18 hours in Arabic and 10 hours in English every week. Pray for the financing and production of Arabic broadcasts suitable for breaking down Islamic misconceptions of the gospel.

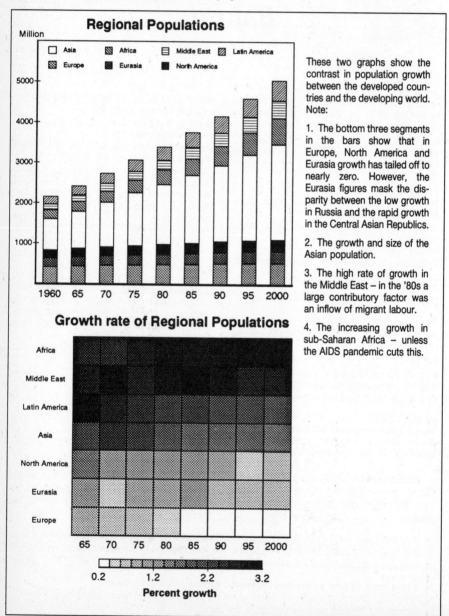

Regional Populations

These two graphs show the contrast in population growth between the developed countries and the developing world. Note:

1. The bottom three segments in the bars show that in Europe, North America and Eurasia growth has tailed off to nearly zero. However, the Eurasia figures mask the disparity between the low growth in Russia and the rapid growth in the Central Asian Republics.

2. The growth and size of the Asian population.

3. The high rate of growth in the Middle East – in the '80s a large contributory factor was an inflow of migrant labour.

4. The increasing growth in sub-Saharan Africa – unless the AIDS pandemic cuts this.

Growth rate of Regional Populations

Bangladesh
(People's Republic of Bangladesh)

March 1–4	B
Asia	

Area 144,000 sq.km. Occupying the delta and floodplains of the Ganges and Brahmaputra Rivers, with high rainfall and frequent flooding.

Population		Ann. Gr.	Density
1990	115,593,000	2.7 %	803/sq.km
1995	132,219,000	2.7 %	918/sq.km

Peoples: All ethnic groups 50.
Bengali 97.3%. Muslim and Hindu Bengalis have distinct cultures and dialects.
Tribal Groups 1.1%. Over 30. Largest: Chakma 352,000; Mogh 185,000; Santal 157,000; Tipera 105,000; Garo 102,000; Tripuri 78,000; Meithei 56,000; Mru 45,000; Hadi 42,000; Usipi 35,000; Bawm 31,000; Oraon 24,000; Dalu 11,000; Pankhu 2,200; Khyang 1,400.
Other minorities 1.6%. Urdu 600,000; Hindi 346,000; Burmese 231,000; Bihari 230,000.
Refugees: 200,000 Rohingya from Arakan, Myanmar.

Literacy 24%. **Official languages:** Bengali, English often used. **All languages** 37. **Languages with Scriptures** 14Bi 3NT 7por.

Capital: Dhaka 6,646,000. Other major city: Chittagong 2,289,000. Urbanization 15%.

Economy: One of the world's poorest nations, suffering from gross over-population and periodic natural disasters such as devastating floods and cyclones with enormous loss of life. There seems little hope that the poverty of this unhappy land will ever be substantially alleviated. Major sources of foreign exchange are aid, textiles and jute. Underemployment 50%. Public debt/person $81. Income/person $180 (0.85% of USA).

Politics: Formerly East Pakistan; independent in 1971 after bitter civil war and defeat of Pakistan by Indian and Bangladeshi forces. Corruption, instability, assassinations and 18 coups have marred the years since then. A nine-year military dictatorship ended in 1991 with restoration of democracy and the election of a government led by a woman, Begum Zia.

Religion: A secular state 1971-88; then the former government declared Islam to be the state religion. This is heightening tensions between Muslims and followers of other religions. Muslim fundamentalists are a vociferous minority.

Muslim 87%. Almost entirely Sunni.
Hindu 11.7%. Decreasing through emigration and lower fertility.
Buddhist 0.6%. Mainly among the Chakma, Mogh and Mru peoples.
Other 0.3%. Non-religious 110,000; Animist 80,000; Baha'i 4,000.
Christian 0.44%. Affil 0.36%. Growth 3.6%.
  Protestant 0.23%. Affil 0.19%. Growth 4.5%.

Church	Cong	Members	Affiliated
Bang Bapt Sangha	230	12,000	25,000
All in One Christ Fellowship	113	9,000	22,500
Bang Baptist Fellowship	242	7,281	20,000
Garo Bapt Union	140	8,740	19,637
Seventh-day Adventist	58	7,000	15,900
Evang Christian Ch	61	5,995	14,600
Ch of Bang (Anglican)	42	4,620	13,200
Evang Lutheran Church	186	4,590	8,200
Presbyterian Synod	84	3,360	6,000
Evang Ch of Bangladesh	53	2,050	5,000
Assemblies of God	102	1,350	5,000
Free Baptists (New Life)	56	1,030	3,430
Assoc of Bapts for World Ev	73	1,600	3,000
All other (19)	508	27,462	53,952
Denominations (32)	1,948	96,078	215,419
Evangelicals 0.08% of pop		39,000	87,000
Pentecostal/charis 0.01%		5,300	14,000

Missionaries:
  to Bangladesh 316 (1:366,000 people) in 50 agencies.
  from Bangladesh 127 (1:1,700 Protestants) 9xcul 118dom.
Roman Catholic 0.21%. Affil 0.18%.
  Growth 2.9%.

Catholic Ch	657	112,000	200,000

  Missionaries to Bangladesh 304 (1:378,000 people).

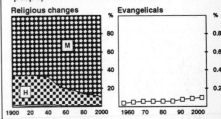

1. **Bangladesh has been a hard field for the gospel.** Revulsion at the cruelty of Pakistan's repression in the name of Islam in the 1971 civil war temporarily weakened Bangladeshi loyalty to Islam, and gave new opportunities for the gospel. However, the rise of extremist Muslim groups pressing for a

more radical Islam is affecting Christian witness in many ways. Pray that the present freedom for all to practise and propagate their own religions be maintained and that the leaders of the nation may handle the many problems with integrity, devotion to duty and fairness. Pray above all that the grip of the powers of darkness may be broken.

2. **Praise God for progress for the gospel despite the increased difficulties.**
a) **Christian aid** since independence and during the nation's frequent natural calamities has been generous and impartial. Non-government organizations such as **HEED** and **World Vision** seek to uphold Christian values and prepare the way for local church and mission involvement. **TEAR Fund** seconds workers and helps in funding projects. Pray for wisdom and sensitivity for all involved in implementing these programmes – that aid not be perceived as manipulative or dependency-producing.
b) **The openness and even responsiveness of whole Muslim families** in some areas to innovative methods of evangelism is encouraging. Pray for strong witnessing churches to be planted and for protection in persecution of all who follow Christ.
c) **Several Hindu castes** have shown marked and continuing response to the gospel. This has mainly been among the Namasudra and, more recently, the Muchi castes.
d) **People movements among tribal peoples** have resulted in nearly all the Bawm and Pankhu becoming Christian, and also 95% of the Garo, 60% of the Oraon, and 50% of the Mahili and Khasi. The turning to the Lord continues among the Santals (25%) and Munda (16%).

3. **Praise God for steady growth in the number of Christians** with ingatherings of both Hindu and tribal people into the churches. The Church has grown at twice the population rate for the last 30 years despite the difficulties. There is rising confidence and faith for that to continue in the '90s. Pray for:
a) **The Bangladesh Baptist Fellowship, Assemblies of God** and the **Bangladesh Free Baptist Churches** who are growing fast and who have set bold church-planting goals.
b) **The Great Commission Movement**, launched in 1991, which has brought together evangelical congregations with the commitment to prayer, research and cooperation to plant a church in every one of the 464 sub-districts and each of the ethnic groups of the country by the year 2000. Pray for the implementation of these goals.

4. **Revival of the church** is the greatest need. Pray that the Holy Spirit may move in these areas:
a) **Nominal Christianity.** Early people movements brought thousands of marginalized sections of society into the Church. Poverty, illiteracy and lack of trained and godly leadership have led to shallowness and nominalism.
b) **Unity.** Imported and indigenous divisions have hindered the effectiveness of the witness in the past. Pray for the **National Christian Fellowship of Bangladesh** as it seeks to encourage evangelical unity and cooperative action in evangelism, teaching and aid programmes.
c) **Missions vision.** After years of little interest, there is growing interest in reaching out to the major non-Christian communities.

5. **Leadership for the churches.** God is raising up a new generation of leaders who exercise a ministry beyond their own community, yet they are few. Pray for the multiplication of leaders:
a) **The Christian Discipleship Centre** and the **Dhaka United Theological Seminary** are the only interdenominational residential schools. The **CDC** also runs TEE and short-term programmes. The CDC had graduated 145 by 1991.
b) Five denominational Bible schools and seminaries (**AoG, ABWE**, Free Baptist, Lutheran and Church of Bangladesh).

6. **Unreached peoples.** Few nations in the world have a larger number of people totally untouched by the gospel. Pray for:
a) **The Muslims.** From among the **100 million** Muslims there are only a few thousand believers, but their numbers are increasing. Pray for the house groups meeting as *Jamat* (Muslim-style congregation) and for their continuing need for discipleship to be met. In 1985 there were only 25 Christian workers among them; the situation has improved, but the vast majority have never heard the gospel. Most are fairly lax in their profession of Islam.
b) **The Hindus** who feel vulnerable as a religious minority. Their insecurity increased during the 1991 Gulf War, when Muslim mobs destroyed Hindu temples. Pray that this may open many to the truth in Jesus. Of the 29 lower castes, only four are over 2% Christian, and in a further six there has been a smaller response. The upper castes have remained resistant to the gospel.
c) **The Bihari** Muslims who, while refusing Bangladeshi citizenship, are denied entry to India and

Pakistan. They live in large refugee camps. Pray that their dilemma may bring an openness to the gospel.

d) **The Rohingya Muslims.** 200,000 became refugees in 1978 and again in 1992 fleeing Myanmar government persecution. They have never been evangelized – pray for those seeking openings to reach them.

e) **The tribal peoples,** some of whom have resisted the gospel, or have not had adequate opportunity to hear: the animist Mru (work by Baptists), the Buddhist Chakma (Baptists), Mogh and Khyang (1,200 Christians).

f) **Students.** There are nine small groups with but 200 Christians linked with the BSFB (**IFES**) for the 458 colleges and 650,000 students. Pray for the two staff workers. In 1992 a **Bangladesh Sports Coalition** was formed for ministry among literate, educated and sports-loving young people.

g) **Young people and children.** Over half the population is under 16. Very little effective outreach is directed to them.

7. **Church planting in the majority community** has borne fruit, and village congregations and indigenous house meetings have multiplied. Pray for great wisdom in nurturing this movement – its leadership, worship patterns, dependence on God in poverty, firmness under persecution from Muslim neighbours, evangelistic vision and relationships with the older Christian community from a different cultural background.

8. **The tribal peoples' very existence** is threatened by the population explosion. The Chakma of the Chittagong Hill Tracts have responded with guerrilla warfare to the destruction of their villages, occupation of their land and even massacres by hundreds of thousands of Bengalis invading their territory. Pray for a just settlement – the granting of limited autonomy to the region has not improved the situation much. Pray also for Christian agencies seeking to bring the tribal peoples to Christ (**ABMS, BMS, SBC**, Presbyterians and Lutherans).

9. **Missions** have been welcomed for their social uplift programmes – hence the emphasis on institutions and aid programmes – but too few are directly involved in evangelistic outreach and church planting. Pray for increased opportunities to fulfil their primary calling. Since 1980 limitations have been placed on missionaries, with all projects, plans and finances needing government approval and strict quotas placed on the number of missionaries allowed. Yet reinforcements are needed. Pray for visas, patience with red tape, and strategic usefulness for the small missionary force in a pressurized situation. The largest agencies are Assoc. of Baptists for World Evangelization (53), Norwegian Santal Mission (49), Scandinavian Pentecostals (36), Mennonite Central Committee (35), **ABMS/BMS** (23), **Interserve** (15), **SBC** (14) and SIM (12).

10. **Christian literature is in great demand** because of the hunger created by:
a) **Mass distribution by Young Christian Workers, EHC, UBS** and **ABWE**, the latter with a large Literature Division.
b) **Bible Correspondence Courses** run by **SIM** and others; the former have a staff of 10 in six centres processing over 2,000 papers a month. Pray for these and all efforts to follow up contacts, and for many to be added to the churches. Pray for inspired, national writers and for efficient production of suitable evangelistic and teaching literature and books.

11. **Distribution of Scriptures** – portions and sales of Bibles have risen year by year. Pray specifically for:
a) **The Bible Society** and its extensive ministry of production and distribution of Scriptures.
b) **The wise distribution of the New Testament in the Bengali Muslim dialect.** Many copies have been distributed since 1981. It has been well received and appreciated by Muslims, but there has been opposition from some churches. A temporary ban on its import in 1990 enhanced sales. Pray for the completion of the Old Testament.
c) **The translation of the Bible into tribal languages.** At least six, possibly nine, translations are needed; work is in progress in three of these.

12. **Christian Media** are important since a high proportion of the population is illiterate. Pray for effective outreach through:
a) **Radio.** Christian broadcasters (**TWR, FEBC** and **FEBA**) transmit eight hours a week in Bengali and 88 hours in English. Pray especially for the production of suitable and sufficient programmes for the non-Christian majority.

B

b) The *Jesus* film. This is available in Bengali, Assamese and Santali, and has been used among Hindus and Muslims with good response. Pray for effective training programmes for those who use the film – both in maintaining the equipment and effectively using the film for church planting. Pray for freedom to show the film in villages and for protection for the operators.

c) **Cassettes. GRn** have a team of recordists working on master tapes in indigenous languages; 21 languages have been recorded. Pray for the completion of the recordings and effective use of the finished product.

See Caribbean
Caribbean

Barbados

Area 430 sq.km. The most easterly of the Windward Islands.

Population		Ann. Gr.	Density
1990	261,000	0.62 %	607/sq.km
1995	272,000	0.83 %	633/sq.km

Peoples:
Afro-Caribbean 95.4%.
European 4%. Asian 0.6%.

Literacy 98%. **Official language:** English.

Capital: Bridgetown 102,000. Urbanization 45%.

Economy: Tourism, sugar and light industries are the mainstays of the economy. Income/person $5,990 (28% of USA).

Politics: Parliamentary government since 1647. Independent from Britain in 1966.

Religion: Complete freedom of religion.
Non-religious/other 9%.
Baha'i 0.6%. **Muslim** 0.36%. **Hindu** 0.25%.
Christian 89.8%. Affil 71.7%. Growth −0.4%.
Protestant 79.3%. Affil 64.35%. Growth −0.6%.

Church	Cong	Members	Affiliated
Anglican	58	21,100	78,000
Methodist	30	4,500	15,000
Seventh-day Adventist	31	7,810	11,000
New Testament Ch of God	48	4,513	10,000
Pentecostal Assemblies of WI	20	4,589	7,400
Wesleyan Holiness	72	3,600	7,200
Ch of God (Anderson)	24	2,800	7,000
Ch of the Nazarene	32	2,003	3,188
Christian Brethren (3)	10	1,040	2,600
All other (53)	99	8,436	26,566
Denominations (64)	424	60,391	167,954
Evangelicals 24.5% of pop		28,375	63,862
Pentecostal/charis 11.6%		14,200	30,400

Missionaries:
to Barbados 26 (1:10,000 people) in 11 agencies.
from Barbados 9 (1:19,000 Protestants) 2frn. 7dom.

Roman Catholic 7.5%. Affil 4.4%. Growth 0.8%.

Catholic Ch	7	7,020	11,500

Missionaries to Barbados 60 (1:4,400 people).

Marginal 3%. Affil 2.9%. Growth 2.4%.

Jehovah's Witnesses	18	1,783	4,600
All other (7)	14	1,350	3,016
Groups (8)	32	3,133	7,616

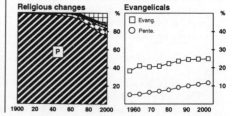

Religious changes

Evangelicals

1. **Since 1627, Barbados has been Protestant.** Despite religious profession and many Evangelicals, real commitment to the Lord Jesus Christ is rare. Materialism, decreasing church attendance, increased violence and crime are the symptoms of spiritual malaise. Pray for the renewal of God's people and a spiritual awakening throughout the country.

2. **Opposition to the gospel is strong.** Sinister attempts have been made by Satanist prayer groups in other lands to destroy churches and pastors in Barbados. Muslim evangelism has become more aggressive, and Eastern religions more vocal. Pray that God's people may have wisdom and courage to counteract these assaults, and may commit themselves to earnest prayer.

3. **Young people** must be transformed by the power of the gospel to lift them above spiritual lukewarmness and the pervasive immorality, for 73% of all births are illegitimate and only 13% of adults are legally married. Pray that churches may offer effective programmes for children and youth. Pray also for the ministry of **CEF** among children, as well as for the efforts of IS/IUCF(**IFES**) in schools and colleges.

B

4. **Goals for 2000.** The New Testament Church of God and Pentecostal Assemblies have set bold church-planting goals. Pray for a greater vision for evangelism and missions within all churches.

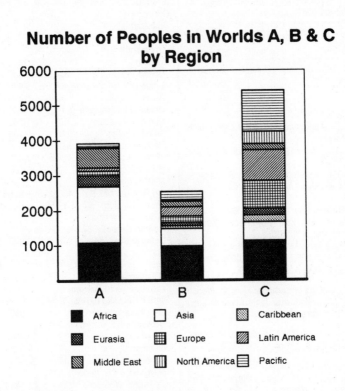

Number of Peoples in Worlds A, B & C by Region

World A: Peoples of the world where %E < 50%.
World B: Evangelized non-Christian peoples where %E > 50% and All Christians < 60%.
World C: Peoples where Christian make up > 60% of the population.

Note:

1. The large number of peoples in Asia, Africa, Middle East and Eurasia that is unreached. This is where pioneer evangelism must be concentrated.

2. The comparatively few unreached peoples in other regions of the world.

3. The large number of Christian peoples in the Pacific.

Compare with diagram in the World section on p 27.

Source: *World Evangelization Database*, D.B. Barrett.

B

March 5
Europe

Belgium
(Kingdom of Belgium)

Area 30,500 sq.km. One of the Low Countries, often called *The Crossroads of Europe*.

Population		Ann. Gr.	Density
1990	9,938,000	0.07 %	326/sq.km
1995	9,980,000	0.08 %	327/sq.km

The second most densely populated country in Europe.

Peoples:
Indigenous 88%.
Flemish 54.7%. Language related to Dutch; mainly in north and west.
Walloon 32.3%. French-speaking; mainly in south and east.
German 0.65%. In districts adjoining Germany.
Jews 0.32%. Mainly in Antwerp.
Foreign 12%.
European Community Citizens 6%. Italian 280,000; French 110,000; Portuguese 80,000; Spanish 70,000; Dutch 70,000.
Other 6%. Arabic-speaking (mainly North African) 150,000; Turkish 60,000; Kurdish 22,000; Chinese 14,000; Zairois 10,000; Albanians 3,000.

Literacy 98%. **Official languages:** Flemish, French and German. **All indigenous languages** 4. **Languages with Scriptures** 3Bi.

Capital: Brussels 1,100,000 – HQ for the European Community and NATO. Urbanization 96.5%.

Economy: Highly industrialized and wealthy, but economy faltering due to weak governments and world recession. Income/person $14,880 (71% of USA).

Politics: Constitutional monarchy since 1830. Political stability imperilled by disagreements between the Walloons and Flemings since the mid-1960s with fragmentation of most political parties along linguistic and regional lines.

Religion:
Non-religious/other 7.2%.
Muslim 3.1%. Mainly North African, Turks and Yugoslavs.

Jews 0.32%. Half the pre-war number. Largely Orthodox.
Buddhist 0.10%.
Christian 89.3%. Attendance 11%. Growth 0.1%.
Protestant 0.8%. Growth 0.5%.

Church	Cong	Members	Affiliated
United Protestant	104	25,000	35,000
Union of Free Ev Chs	67	3,430	6,240
Assemb of God	60	2,320	3,800
Union of Ev Baptists	14	800	2,670
Christian Brethren	22	1,300	1,730
All other (48)	246	19,126	37,816
Denominations (53)	513	51,976	87,256
Evangelicals 0.32% of pop		18,300	32,000
Pentecostal/charis 0.12%		6,700	12,000

Missionaries:
to Belgium 571 (1:17,400 people) in 54 agencies.
from Belgium 60 (1:1,450 Protestants) 17frn 43dom.

Roman Catholic 87.3%. Growth 0.1%.

Catholic Ch	3,976	6,730,000	8,856,000
Doubly counted		−130,000	−175,000
Total	3,976	6,600,000	8,681,000
Charismatics		13,000	17,000

Missionaries to Belgium 2.
Other Catholic 0.04%. Growth −1.1%.

Denominations (4)		1,990	4,430

Orthodox 0.5%. Growth −0.3%.

Greek Orthodox	12	27,700	38,000
All other (3)	5	9,300	15,300
Denominations (4)	17	37,000	53,300

Marginal 0.7%. Growth 2.7%.

Jehovah's Witnesses	325	25,161	50,300
All other (14)	307	9,970	21,050
Groups (15)	362	35,131	71,350

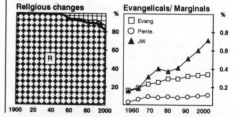

Religious changes

Evangelicals/ Marginals
- □ Evang.
- ○ Pente.
- ▲ JW

1. **For 400 years spiritual darkness has gripped this land.** The Spanish Inquisition destroyed the 600 churches that embraced Reformed teachings in the 16th Century. Pray that the light of the gospel may penetrate that darkness once more.

2. **The great majority of the population is culturally Catholic rather than Christian.** Catholic attendance and adherence to the teachings of the church are stronger among the Flemish than the more lax Walloons. Yet the Church faces four major crises – declining attendances, waning influence,

theological seminaries without students and the invasion of New Age thinking. The charismatic movement has had little lasting impact.

3. **The small Protestant witness** has hardly grown in 20 years; the growth of the Evangelicals and the evangelical wing of the theologically liberal United Protestant Church has offset the liberal decline. Growth has been most marked through the witness of the **BEM/OM** teams, Baptists, Pentecostals in the French-speaking areas and, in the Antwerp area, of the Brethren.

4. **Goals for the year 2000.**
a) There is a growing trans-denominational vision to present the gospel to every Belgian in this decade. Pray for a closer fellowship and unity among believers so that this goal may be achieved.
b) **BEM** plans to plant 47 new churches in the '90s.
c) Cosmopolitan Brussels has nearly 30% foreign residents. It is the HQ of the European Community and NATO. During 1991 many churches cooperated to reach the 400,000 homes in the city. Pray for lasting fruit in the many new churches planted.

5. **Freedom for evangelism has never been greater**, but all outreach is an uphill battle to obtain a hearing. Pray for OM **Love Europe** summer teams in their literature and door-to-door ministry and year teams in evangelism and church planting. **Evangelism Explosion** is a church-based method of evangelism that is attracting interest in a number of churches.

6. **Bible training.** There are four evangelical training schools: the Evangelical Theological Seminary (Heverlee – Dutch and English), Belgian Bible Institute (Heverlee – Dutch), *Institut Biblique Belge* (Ottignies – French) and the Brussels Bible Seminary (French and Dutch). Pray for these institutions, the staff and students.

7. **The missionary force has steadily increased**, the largest being **BEM** with 125 workers. Other missions of note include **AoG** (123), **OM** (61), **GEM** (50), **YWAM** (26), **SBC** (18), Evangelical Free Church Missions (18) and **GMU** (17). BEM aims to recruit 300 new workers in the 1990s. Stress points for missionaries are the hardness of the field, the high cost of living, and the increasing difficulty of obtaining missionary visas for non-EC residents.

8. **A wide range of Christian literature** is being produced by groups such as **SU**, Biblical Literature Fellowship (BLF) with 12 workers, **OM** and **AoG**. BLF has a large printing plant and has published over 500 titles. There are 21 Christian bookstores in Brussels and Wallonia; nationally **BEM** runs seven bookstores and BLF a further five. Pray for the effective use and fruitfulness of these endeavours.

9. **Neglected areas of Belgium:**
a) Of the 2,500 administrative districts in Belgium, 2,200 have no evangelical congregations.
b) There are 140 towns of over 6,000 people without an evangelical congregation.
c) In Flanders (5 million people) there are only 2,000 known evangelical families.
d) Antwerp (660,000) has but 22 small Protestant churches.
e) Luxemburg province (250,000) has nine groups, each with about 30 believers.

10. **Unreached peoples in Belgium:**
a) **North Africans** have grown rapidly through legal and illegal migration, the majority settling in the poorer areas of Brussels. They are almost entirely Muslim and present a unique and urgent challenge for prayer and evangelism. Three **GMU** couples work among these people. "Good News by Telephone" in a number of languages has proved a fruitful method of witness; pray for this and the prospective ministry of "Radio Good News". There is now one congregation of Arab believers in the city.
b) **Turks and Kurds** have proved hard to reach with the gospel. There is now a small Turkish fellowship of seven believers, but the great majority have never heard the good news.
c) **Orthodox Jews** have no long-term ministry specifically directed to meet their need.
d) **The large international body of diplomats** and EC bureaucrats are overpaid and under-evangelized. They present a unique challenge for evangelism, but little has been done to reach them.
e) **The German-speaking cantons** on the German border have been long neglected by evangelicals. Only recently has a beginning been made by German missionaries to plant churches in the area.
f) **The student population** of 176,000 in 17 universities and colleges is a major challenge. **IFES** has a ministry in the five Flemish universities (ESG) and in French universities (GBU), but the total membership in each of the two branches is 50. Pray for the evangelistic ministry of **OM** in cooperation with these groups and in a teaching ministry in the IFES groups; there is one staff couple.

March 6
Caribbean

Belize

Area 23,000 sq.km. A low-lying, swampy enclave to the east of Guatemala on the Central American mainland.

Population		Ann. Gr.	Density
1990	182,000	2.2 %	8/sq.km
1995	201,000	2.0 %	9/sq.km

Peoples:
Afro-Caribbean/Eurafrican 38%. Mainly English-speaking.
Mestizo/Ladino 34%. Predominantly Guatemalans and Hondurans, with considerable illegal immigration in the '80s.
Amerindian 10.5%. Mayan tribes speaking three distinct languages.
Garifuna (Black Carib) 7.6%. Descendants of African slaves and Arawakan Indians.
European 4.2% Mainly German Mennonites and British.
Other 5.7%. East Indian 3,800; Chinese 2,500; Jews 2,100.

Literacy 93%. **Official language:** English; Spanish spoken by 50% of the population. **All languages** 9. **Languages with Scriptures** 2Bi 5NT.

Capital: Belmopan 3,700. Largest town: Belize 74,000. Urbanization 52%.

Economy: Underdeveloped yet relatively prosperous. Public debt/person $694. Income/person $1,600 (7.6% of USA).

Politics: Independence from Britain in 1981 as a parliamentary democracy. British forces remain to prevent annexation by neighbouring Guatemala.

Religion: A secular state with freedom of religion.
Non-religious/other 2.4%.
Spiritist/Animist 2%.
Hindu 1%. **Muslim** 1%. **Baha'i** 1%.
Jews 0.5%.

Christian 92.1%. Growth 3.4%.
Protestant 25.7%. Growth 3.2%.

Church	Cong	Members	Affiliated
Seventh-day Adventist	45	8,600	12,300
Anglican Church	26	3,740	11,000
Methodist Church	5	1,672	5,000
Assemblies of God	40	982	3,000
Ch of the Nazarene	22	1,306	2,023
Baptist Assoc (**SBC**)	10	1,115	1,590
Assoc of Ev Chs (**GMU**)	15	919	1,329
Ch of God (Cleveland)	20	680	971
Mennonite Church	4	500	625
Baptist Chs in Belize	6	400	533
All other (16)	132	4,216	8,392
Denominations (26)	325	24,130	46,763
Evangelicals 11.6% of pop		11,629	21,122
Pentecostal/charis 4.9%		4,100	9,000

Missionaries:
to Belize 105 (1:1,700 people) in 22 agencies.
from Belize 17 (1:2,750 Protestants) in 3 agencies 1frn 16dom.

Roman Catholic 64.3%. Growth 3.3%.

Catholic Church	126	63,200	117,000

Missionaries to B. 56 (1:3,250 people).
Marginal 2.1%. Growth 9.5%.

Jehovah's Witnesses	22	1,004	2,510
Mormons	5	780	1,300
Groups (2)	27	1,784	3,810

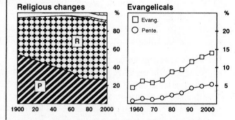

1. **The evangelical witness** is strong, with most of the mission work of the Baptists, Brethren, Mennonites, Nazarenes and Pentecostals being evangelical. Denominational barriers are high; pray for a breakdown of rivalry and mistrust and the growth of a vision for the completion of the evangelization of every ethnic group and immigrant minority. The Catholic Church is growing through immigration from neighbouring Central American lands.

2. **Much of Christianity is nominal and syncretic.** The Spanish-speaking immigrants with their superstitions and superficiality, the Mayans with their underlying paganism, and the Garifuna with their black magic – each need a culturally relevant and sensitive presentation of the gospel. Many settlements still need church-planting ministry, despite the threefold increase in congregations since 1960.

3. **The less reached groups.**
a) The Mayan **Mopan** (2,500) have only a few Nazarene and Mennonite believers.

b) **The Garifuna** have had their own NT since 1983. Their strong animistic culture has only been marginally penetrated (**CoN, Brethren**). There are some Nazarene and Brethren believers among them.

c) **The East Indians and Chinese** have no one focused on their evangelization.

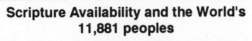

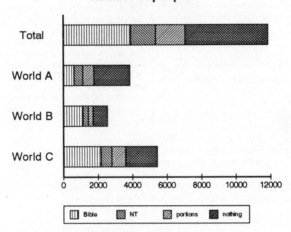

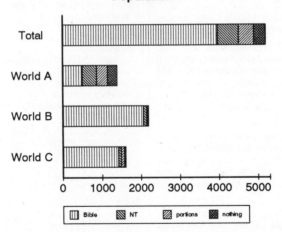

This pair of graphs reveals some interesting facts about the availability of Scriptures.

1. Although 41% of the world's **peoples** have no Scriptures, they constitute only 6% of the world's **population**. Most of the languages that need New Testament translations are spoken by small numbers of people.

2. Although only 619 peoples have the Scriptures (many sharing a common language), they constitute 76% of the world's population.

B

March 7
Benin
(Republic of Benin)
Africa

Area 113,000 sq.km. A long, narrow country wedged between Nigeria and Togo.

Population	Ann. Gr.	Density
1990 4,741,000	3.2 %	42/sq.km
1995 5,573,000	3.3 %	49/sq.km

Peoples: About 57 ethnic groups.
Southern Peoples 69.4%. Fon 1,400,000; Yoruba (8) 465,000; Aja 360,000; Gun 320,000; Ayzo 227,000; Mina 126,000; Wachi 110,000; Mahi 66,000; Tofin 66,000; Xweda 54,000.
Northern Peoples 30.2%. Bariba 460,000; Fula (Fulbe-Borgu) 280,000; Ditammari (Somba) 119,000; Burba 70,000; Boko 70,000; Pila (Yom) 70,000; Lamba 60,000; Gurma 50,000; Nateni (Tayaku) 45,000; Tem (Kotokoli) 43,000; Lokpa (Dompago) 42,000.
Migrants from Niger and Burkina Faso may be 3% or more of the population. Mainly Dyerma (Dendi), Hausa, Mossi.
Other 0.4%.
French 0.3%.

Literacy 28%. **Official language:** French. Trade Languages: Fon in South, Dendi in North. **All languages** 52. **Languages with Scriptures** 5Bi 8NT 4por.

Capitals: Porto Novo 188,000 and Cotonou 501,000. Urbanization 38%.

Economy: Poor and underdeveloped with most people engaged in subsistence farming. Virtually a satellite economy of Nigeria. The stagnation during the years of Marxism is changing with the switch to a free-market economy. Public debt/person $230. Income/person $380 (1.8% of USA).

Politics: Independent from France in 1960. The seventh coup after independence brought a repressive Marxist government to power. The worldwide collapse of Communism in 1989/90 led to the multi-party elections of March 1991 and the first democratic replacement of an African head of state in mainland Africa.

Religion: The application of Marxist ideology between 1972 and 1985 was not harsh, but it bred a spirit of uncertainty and fear that restricted Christian witness and missionary initiative. There is now complete religious freedom.

Tribal religions 54.8%. Strong in all but seven of the peoples in the country – especially the Fon, Lokpa, Boko, Bariba and Egba.
Muslim 17%. While only the Nago, Tem, Dendi and Anii of the indigenous peoples are predominantly Muslim, most northern peoples have a significant minority that is Muslim, and the immigrant Nigerian and Burkinabe are largely Muslim.
Christian 28.2%. Affil 24% Growth 5.5%.
  Protestant 4%. Affil 3.3% Growth 9.9%.

Church	Cong	Members	Affiliated
Methodist Ch	357	25,600	73,000
Assemblies of God	240	19,600	36,318
Nigerian Apostolic Ch	170	8,500	17,000
UEEB (**SIM**)	124	2,970	10,000
Baptist Ch (**SBC**)	21	1,975	9,000
Evang. Bapt Mission	12	1,400	2,800
Ch of Foursquare			
Gospel	29	961	2,402
All other (6)	13	3,826	9,152
Denominations (13)	966	64,832	159,672
Evangelicals 1.96% of pop		41,000	93,000
Pentecostal/charis 1.24%		30,000	57,000

Missionaries:
  to Benin 170 (1:28,000 people) in 24 agencies.
  from Benin 5 (1:40,000 Protestants) in 3 agencies 3frn 5xcul.
Roman Catholic 21.7%. Affil 18.2% Gr 5.3%.

Catholic Ch	1,288	483,000	862,497

Missionaries:
  to Benin 274 (1:17,300 people).
  from Benin 20 (1973 figure).
Foreign Marginal 0.2%. Affil 0.17% Growth 8.8%.

Jehovah's Witnesses	81	2,904	8,180

Indigenous Marginal 2.27%. Affil 2.2% Gr 1.6%.

Groups (20)	269	51,500	107,700

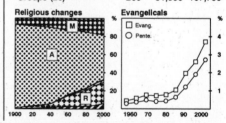

Religious changes

Evangelicals

1. **Praise God for significant changes in the 1980s.** These include the liberation of the country from the ideological bondage and fear of Marxism; the beginnings of a gospel breakthrough among the Fon people; rapid church growth in the country since 1987; and the expectancy of a great harvest in the '90s.

2. **The civilian government** faces an enormous task of reconstructing and developing the country. Pray that an ethnically fair and ethically just democracy might take root in the social fabric of the

B

country, and that the leaders may work for the good of the people rather than for enriching themselves.

3. **Church growth is a new phenomenon.** Historically, the southern Methodist churches have stagnated, and growth elsewhere has been slow. But since 1987, both Evangelicals and Catholics have seen new advances and more rapid growth: in **AoG** churches in the north (Natimba, Burba, Belime, Fulbe, etc) and south (Mina, Nago, Aja, Gun and now the Fon); UEEB/**SIM** in the north and centre (Lokpa, Bariba, Cabe, Fulbe, etc. and now Boko, Ditammari and Fon); **SBC** in the south (the Yoruba-related peoples); and **Evangelical Baptists** in the far north (Dendi and Gurmantche). Pray for:
a) The raising up of more **leaders** of maturity and vision.
b) All **pastoral training** – the AoG Bible Institute (32 students), the ICI Correspondence School, UEEB with one French and seven vernacular primary level Bible Schools (100 students) and 250 studying in a TEE programme.
c) The vision to reach out to every unreached people and community, and the strategy to implement it.

4. **Unreached peoples.** Only a handful of peoples have a Christian majority, and just five have over 5% Evangelicals. Benin has Africa's highest percentage of followers of traditional religions and is the least evangelized non-Muslim country in Africa south of the Sahara. Specific peoples for prayer:
a) **The Fon** – a strategic, well-educated and influential people but in bondage to a fetishism that has remained, until recently, unchallenged by the gospel despite the fact that 20% of the tribe is nominally Christian. The long-awaited breakthrough appears to have begun with rapid church growth since 1987 through the ministry of six missions/churches (including **AoG**, **SIM**, **SBC**). There are now 24 churches with 1,500 adherents; yet this is still but 0.12% of the population.
b) **The Togo border strip** in the west, where the unreached Aguna, Ica, Anii Foodo, Ife, Kabiyu and Anufo total some 130,000. UEEB(SIM) have started work among the 9,000 Soruba.
c) **The middle strip** in the south, where the Mahi, Ayzo, Weme, Idaca and Seto live, and among whom there are no indigenous churches. Total population: 350,000.
d) **The southwest corner** with a complex medley of peoples, including the Wachi, Xweda, Xwla, Ko and Ci totalling 220,000 people.
e) **The Muslim peoples.** No work is being done among the indigenous Tem and Anii, nor among the more urban immigrant Dyerma, Hausa and Mossi. Islam is extending its influence among many of the central and northern peoples, but among the Fulbe (Fula) there has been a breakthrough with nearly 2,000 coming to Christ (**SIM**, **AoG**).
f) **The 800,000 urbanites of the two capitals.** There are 17 evangelical churches with 4,000 adherents and a further 60,000 in African Independent Churches, but the majority have not been reached. Nearly a fifth of the population is Muslim, and no one is working full time for their evangelization.

5. **Missions.** Only since 1946 has the centre and north been penetrated by missions. The largest of these are **SIM** (70 missionaries in 12 peoples) and **EMS**-Nigeria (11), **SBC** (20), **SIL/WBT** (13), Evangelical Baptists (11), AoG (6). Considering the need of the country, the small church-planting missionary force (only 35 in the country!) must be increased. **SIM** runs the only evangelical mission hospital in Benin and has a useful ministry of rural development.

6. **Young people are a vital part of present advance.** Conversions in the towns through youth centres, camps and the extensive use of the *Jesus* film together with good follow-up have often resulted in churches in both towns and rural areas. Pray for adequate resources to be committed to these ministries at a time of unprecedented openness.

7. **Bible translation** is a major unmet need. There are 24 languages without a New Testament. SIM translation teams are working in seven languages and **SIL** in five. Other literature is being translated and printed – TEE materials, Bible commentaries, etc. Pray for a biblically literate Church to be the result. Literature sales are increasing. There are four Christian bookstores.

8. **Media opportunities abound** in the new day of freedom. Pray for:
a) The effective use of **audio recordings** in evangelism and teaching. **GRn** has made recordings in 34 languages.
b) The wise and strategic use of the *Jesus* film in French, Fon and Bariba.
c) **Radio.** The loss of ELWA (**SIM**) radio station in Liberia has forced the churches to look for alternatives. Radio Parakou broadcasts the gospel daily in Fon and Bariba, and weekly in French, with encouraging response (UEEB).

See Caribbean
Caribbean

Bermuda
(Colony of Bermuda)

Area 54 sq.km. About 360 small coral islands in the North Atlantic. The world's most northerly coral reefs.

Population	Ann. Gr.	Density
1990 58,000	0.70 %	1,074/sq.km
1995 60,000	0.68 %	1,111/sq.km

Peoples: About 25% of the population is foreign-born.
Afro-Caribbean 63%.
Euro-American 35.4%. Mainly from UK, USA, Canada and Portugal.
Other 1.6%.

Literacy 97%. **Official language:** English.

Capital: Hamilton 6,000. Urbanization 100%.

Economy: Its superb climate and geographical position makes it a tourist paradise and a lucrative tax haven. There are over 4,500 offshore companies registered in Bermuda. Income/person $26,040 (123% of USA).

Politics: A British Colony; parliamentary democracy.

Religion:
Non-religious/other 10.1%. **Baha'i** 0.5%.
Christian 89.4%. Growth 0.5%.
Protestant 71.7%. Growth 0.2%.

Church	Cong	Members	Affiliated
Anglican Ch	17	3,500	17,500
African Methodist Epis.	10	2,220	5,540
Seventh-day Adventist	8	2,496	3,670
Methodist Ch	3	870	2,900
NT Ch of God (Cleveland)	5	770	1,280
Christian Brethren	9	450	1,050
Baptist Church (SBC)	4	336	1,020
Pentecostal Assemblies	2	440	733
All other (57)	65	4,165	7,917
Denominations (65)	123	15,247	41,610
Evangelicals 17.8% of pop		5,000	10,700
Pentecostal/charis 15.3%		14,150	9,200

Missionaries to Bermuda 13 (1:4,500 people) in 4 agencies.
Roman Catholic 15.5%. Growth 1.3%.

Catholic Ch	8	6,930	9,000

Missionaries to Bermuda 11 (1:5,300 people).
Marginal 2.2%. Growth 3.5%.

Jehovah's Witnesses	4	373	829
All other (3)		220	400
Groups (4)		593	1,229

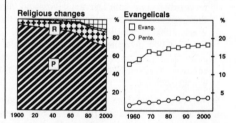

Religious changes / Evangelicals

1. **Bermuda is a materialistic Eden**, but spiritually shallow. The islands are crowded with churches, the airwaves filled with gospel broadcasts, but the message is largely ignored. Pray that the believers may live lives worthy of the Lord, and contribute more to world evangelization.

Bhutan
(Kingdom of Bhutan – Druk Yul)

March 8	B
Asia	

Area 47,000 sq.km. A small kingdom in the eastern Himalaya mountains.

Population	Ann. Gr.	Density
1990 600,000	2.2 %	12/sq.km
1995 671,000	2.3 %	14/sq.km

In 1992 the government announced a population of 600,000 for 1990 instead of 1,516,000. All figures below are estimates based on this.

Peoples: Only rough estimates can be given.
Drukpa 60%. Three major indigenous groups: Ngalong, Kebumtamp, Sharchop, but speaking numerous dialects.
Nepali 30%. Indo-Aryan Paharia and Tibetan Sherpa, Gurung, Rai, Tamang and Limbu. Mainly in the southern lowlands.
Other 8%. Assamese 30,000, Loba, Kirabi, Lepcha, Santali and others.
Expatriates 2%. Mainly Indians, some Westerners.

Literacy 18%. **Official language:** Dzongkha. **All languages** 11. **Languages with Scriptures** 2Bi 1NT 3por.

Capital: Thimphu 28,000. Urbanization 13%.

Economy: Undeveloped subsistence economy but with development potential should the government desire it. Income/person $300 (1.4% of USA).

Politics: Moving from feudalism to a constitutional monarchy. Isolated from the outside world until trade and cultural links with Tibet were severed after the Communist Chinese invasion. India plays a dominant role in foreign affairs of Bhutan and also in its development, but the government fiercely protects its own sovereignty and oppresses those considered non-Bhutanese citizens. Over 70,000 of Nepali descent were forced to become refugees in 1992 due to fighting in the south.

Religion: Unity and independence of the country under state religion of Buddhism. All public worship, evangelism and proselytization by any other religion is illegal.
Lamaistic Buddhist 70.1%. With a strong element of Bon, the animistic pre-Buddhist religion.
Hindu 24%. Mainly Nepali and Assamese.
Muslim 5%. Assamese and Indians.
Animist 0.6%. Predominantly tribes originating from Arunachal Pradesh in India.
Christian 0.33%. Affil 0.13%. Growth 3.2%. Mainly Nepali and Santali.
  Protestant 0.25%. Affil 0.10%. Growth 4.4%.
  Missionaries:
    to Bhutan 72 (1:8,300 people) in 11 agencies.
    from Bhutan 1.
  Roman Catholic 0.08%. Affil 0.03%. Growth 0%.
  Missionaries to Bhutan 10 (1:60,000 people).

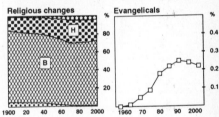

1. **Bhutan was tightly closed to any Christian witness until 1965.** After a very slight relaxation for 25 years, increased success in soul-winning by the few Christians has brought renewed restrictions. National Christians have been denied promotion and overseas training, and pressure has been occasionally brought to bear on any Christian house gatherings. Pray for the opening of this land for the light of the gospel.

2. **The government has pressed the Nepali minority** to assume Drukpa customs, language and clothing. This has provoked a violent reaction with outbreaks of terrorism. Many Nepalis have been expelled, or fled the country to India and Nepal. Pray for the king and his government, and for wise and enlightened rule that gives peace and freedom to all the land's peoples.

3. **The Drukpa majority is strongly Buddhist,** and Christians among them number only about 120-150. Most of these believers are isolated and scattered with little opportunity for fellowship, and some have suffered for their faith. Pray for the emergence of a vital witnessing fellowship in every ethnic group of the Drukpa.

4. **The number of believers among the Bhutanese Nepali** has grown steadily since 1970 through the fervent witness of believers inside Bhutan and on the Indian side of the border. Believers meet in about 20 places but mainly along the southern border. It is not easy for foreign Christians to

fellowship with them. Pray for these believers, who face growing pressure from the authorities.

5. **Missions have been welcomed** to operate leprosy hospitals and be involved in health, agricultural and educational programmes, but only on the condition that they do not proselytize. Leprosy is almost eradicated, and leprosy ministries are being phased out. Small aid projects continue. Pray that aid workers may be called and granted visas. Pray for the silent witness of Christians in various aid missions (**TLM, Interserve**, Norwegian Santal Mission, etc.). Pray for a relaxation of restrictions on entry and witness for missionaries.

6. **Indian believers** in India's border region are active in evangelism and literature distribution among visitors from Bhutan. Many of the Christians in Bhutan have come to the Lord by these means. Pray for conversions among the Bhutanese. Pray also that Bhutanese students in India and lands around the world may hear the gospel.

7. **Christians in government service** – mostly Indians and some Westerners – have good opportunities to witness all over the country. Pray for Christians who work in such frustrating and lonely situations.

8. **Literature distribution** is possible in Bhutan in a limited way, through personal contacts and the mail. Pray for fruit from the literature now spreading through the land.

9. **Bible translation** is making slow progress. Parts of the New Testament have been translated into Dzongkha, but are only in draft form. The main translator has died. Pray the New Testament into print and into the hands and hearts of Bhutanese. Translation is under way in the Kebumtamp and Sharchagpakha languages.

10. **Radio programmes** in Dzongkha and Sharchopkha are being prepared for broadcasting.

Bolivia
(The Republic of Bolivia)

Area 1,099,000 sq.km. Landlocked Andean state. High plateau in southwest, tropical lowlands in north and east. It is one of only two landlocked republics in the Americas.

Population	Ann. Gr.	Density
1990 7,314,000	2.8 %	7/sq.km
1995 8,421,000	2.9 %	8/sq.km

The majority live on the high central plateau.

Peoples:
European 10%. Mainly of Spanish descent; they dominate the political and economic life of the country.
Mestizo 25%. Mixed race, Spanish-speaking, predominantly urban.
Amerindian 64%.
 Highland peoples 62%. Quechua (2 groups) 2,500,000; Aymara (26 sub-groups) 1,889,000; Mixed Quechua-Aymara 227,000.
 Lowland peoples 2%. About 35 groups. A further seven have recently become extinct. Major groups: Chiquitano 47,000; Guarani (2) 33,000; Guarayu 12,000; Tsimane 9,200; Ignaciano 7,700; Trinitario 7,700; Tacana 6,200; Yuracare 4,600; Ayoreo 2,300; Mataco 2,200.
Other 1%. Plaudietsch (dialect of German) 23,000 spoken by Mennonite settlers; Japanese 14,000; Chinese 5,000; Jews 600; Korean.

Literacy 81%. **Official languages:** Spanish, Aymara, Quechua. **All living languages** 38. **Languages with Scriptures** 3Bi 16NT 7por.

Capitals: La Paz (administrative) 1,092,000; Sucre (legal) 93,000. La Paz is the world's highest capital at 3,600 metres. Other major cities: Santa Cruz 467,000; Cochabamba 349,000. Urbanization 49%.

Economy: Decline through frequently corrupt and unstable governments, the fall of worldwide tin and cotton prices, and hyper-inflation (26,000% in 1984), brought the country to its knees. Since 1985 courageous reforms have stabilized the economy. Shared responsibility for ending illegal cocaine exports between the consumers and producers is bringing in foreign aid to build a more healthy agricultural industry. Unemployment 22%. Public debt/person $500. Income/person $600 (3% of USA).

Politics: Independent from Spain in 1825 after a long war for freedom. Since then, over 200 successful coups or revolutions have held back meaningful progress. Since 1985, successive democratic governments have stabilized the country and give cautious hope for improvement.

Religion: The Catholic Church continues to be recognized as the State Church, but the rapid growth of non-Catholic religious bodies has threatened this status. Religious freedom and separation of Church and State is an issue yet to be fully resolved.
Non-religious 5.9%.
Animist 15%. Predominantly Aymara and some lowland peoples. About 58% of the population has been baptized as Catholics, but are practising animists or Christo-pagan, so statistics below must be interpreted in this light.
Baha'i 3%. Strong among the Quechua.
Other 0.4%. Buddhists, Shinto, Muslim 1,000, Spiritist, Jews 600.
Christian 75.7%. Affil 88.5% (see note under Roman Catholic). Growth 3.5%.
 Protestant 9.3%. Growth 8.6%.

Church	Cong	Members	Affiliated
Seventh-day Adventist	119	30,800	68,361
Ev Chr Union (**SIM**)	437	30,120	66,900
Assemb of God of Bolivia	748	29,648	55,268
Evang Methodist	151	11,000	31,400
Baptist Union	150	12,000	30,000
Bol Assembly of God	239	11,114	24,907
Evang Lutheran	120	7,200	24,000
Friends Nat Evang Ch	292	14,000	21,900
Friends Holiness Mssn	200	12,000	20,000
Ch of the Nazarene	137	10,055	14,517
Christian Brethren	145	5,949	11,000
Ekklesia Bolivia	2	6,000	8,570
All other (119)	2,257	142,809	314,261
Denominations (131)	5,062	319,799	680,763
Evangelicals 8.4% of pop		291,600	615,000
Pentecostal/charis 3.5%		119,000	255,000

Missionaries:
 to Bolivia 1,011 (1:7,300 people) in 88 agencies.
 from Bolivia 47 (1:14,500 Protestants) in 8 agencies 7frn 13xcul 34dom.
Roman Catholic 65.2%. Affiliated 77.9%, but of this figure syncretic Christo-pagan are 52.9%, nominal 15%, practising 10%. Growth 2.8%.

B

Catholic Church	836	3,600,000	6,200,000
Doubly counted		−290,000	−500,000
Total	836	3,310,000	5,700,000
Charismatics		3,600	6,200

Missionaries:
to Bolivia 342 (1:21,400 people).
from Bolivia 1,610 (1973 figure).
Orthodox 0.04%. Growth 2.1%.
Marginal 1.17%. Growth 16.3%.

Mormons	157	35,900	69,000
Jehovah's Witnesses	105	7,452	16,600
Groups (2)	262	43,352	85,600

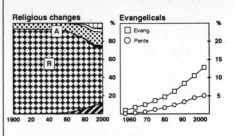

1. **Democracy and freedom are new realities for Bolivia.** The benefits have yet to reach the Amerindian majority that has long been mired in poverty and politically marginalized. Pray for courage and moral integrity for the democratic leaders as they grapple with the immense economic inequalities and social ills of society, not least of the latter being the cocaine "industry". About 50% of the world's cocaine is grown in Bolivia. Bolivian Evangelicals are becoming active in exercising their political responsibility to bring Biblical principles into the government of the country.

2. **The great responsiveness** of many sections of the population is cause for praise to God. The economic and political disasters of the '80s have increased spiritual hunger. Evangelicals have consistently doubled their numbers every ten years since 1960. The major growth has been among:
a) **The Aymara.** A people movement since 1930, with 17% growth per year, has resulted in 20% of these animistic people becoming Evangelicals (Baptist, **AoG**, Friends, Methodist and AEM/**SIM**-related churches).
b) The **urban areas and frontier settlements** in the Amazon lowlands, with many conversions through evangelistic outreach and campaigns among the mestizos.
c) The **lowland Amerindian tribes** (130,000), whose evangelization is nearly complete.

3. **The Catholic Church is confronted by multiple crises.** Its long-held political supremacy is threatened and annual losses to other churches and religions are disturbing. It has failed to develop an indigenous clergy or challenge the rampant paganism within the majority it claims to shepherd. Pray for an outpouring of the Spirit.

4. **Evangelical unity**, a product of a repentance and prayer revival in 1986, has been advanced by weekly prayer meetings among Christian leaders in La Paz. Pray for love and unity of vision among all true believers for the evangelization of the 65% of the population that never goes to church.

5. **The Association of Evangelicals of Bolivia** is sponsoring the launch of the **DAWN programme**. Pray that this may be a sustained, interdenominational, coordinated, country-wide effort which results in:
a) The evangelization of every people group.
b) The tripling of Evangelicals and churches in the '90s.

6. **Territorial powers of darkness** have long held the nation. Only now are Christians coming to grips with the reality of the spiritual battle. Pray that the Lord may rebuke these and liberate millions from fears, bondages, sin and compromise.

7. **The less reached:**
a) **The upper classes** have long held exclusive control of the reins of power, but were shocked by the national disasters of the '80s. Few were Evangelicals before 1985, but all is changing and many are seeking the Lord. The Ekklesia Church came to life in the 1986 revival; many of its members are from this class.
b) **The Quechua** in the high Andes and lowland farming colonies are largely Christo-pagans and have long been indifferent to the gospel. By 1990 only 2% have become Evangelical. About 70% of the Quechua are beyond the reach of present efforts.
c) **The 100,000 tertiary students in the nine universities** are disillusioned with traditional Catholicism, often secular, leftist in political views, and discouraged by interrupted courses and bleak future prospects. About 500 students in eight universities are linked with the CCU (**IFES**); others are linked with the ministry of **CCC** in several universities.

B

d) **The youth** are largely neglected. Few churches know how to meet their spiritual needs. Unemployment, urban violence and increasing drug abuse enhance the growing generation gap. Pray for the work of **SU** and others seeking to reach and disciple the youth.

8. **The lowland tribes** have been largely evangelized at great cost and with considerable success. Praise the Lord for the work of **NTM, AEM-SIM, WGM, UWM,** South American Mission, **SIL** and others. Their ministries have been strongly attacked by anti-Christian anthropologists and others as "genocidal", but in answer to prayer the effects of these attacks have been reduced. Pray for the neutralizing of these assaults, the maturation of indigenous leaders, the integration of these believers into Bolivian life, and the sound conversion of the second generation of Christians.

9. **Leadership training** at various levels is vital for the many growing churches – from jungle village tribal churches to sophisticated elite city congregations. There are over 25 Protestant seminaries and Bible schools as well as a number of TEE institutes and BCCs. All these can never provide maturity and spiritual authority without the deep working of the Spirit of God. Men and women who know their God are needed!

10. **Foreign missions.** Early missionaries struggled long against hostility, persecution and harsh living conditions before the harvest ripened. The contribution of **AEM** (now **SIM**) was unique in pioneering most of the major gospel advances and ministries in the country, but the work of **AoG** and Ekklesia is also significant in new visions and advance. The missionary body now needs to concentrate more on church planting among the Quechua and upper classes and the discipling of the youth. Major missions include **NTM** (130 workers), **SIM** (109), Swedish Pentecostal Mission (65), **WGM** (58), Mennonites (56), Brethren (50), **GMU** (49), South American Mission (47), Norwegian Lutheran Mission (44), **AoG** (35), **SBC** (23), **CBIM** (15), **UWM** (16), Friends (12). Major missionary-contributing nations are USA (557), Norway (75), Canada (73), Sweden (56), UK (53), Brazil (49) and Korea (30). There are six Korean missions in the country, and Koreans have founded two of the three Christian universities.

11. **Bible translation and distribution.** The Bible Society has played a major role in every aspect of Bible work and now has its own press. Over one million New Testaments have been distributed in schools. The Aymara and Quechua Bibles are in great demand. **SIL** has almost achieved the amazing objective of completing the Bible translation programme for all the Amerindian languages that warranted it. May God's Word become part of the life of the entire nation!

12. **Christian Media:**
a) **TV and radio** have made a big impact through six Christian radio and two television networks and also the international stations. The latter include **HCJB, TWR, FEBC,** and High Adventure (USA), among others. Many hours of programmes are broadcast daily in Spanish, with **HCJB** adding eight hours per week in 17 Quechua dialects. The big gap is the lack of broadcasting in Aymara.
b) **Christian literature** – especially tracts, teaching materials and books – is in short supply in Aymara and Quechua. AEM/SIM have a significant ministry in this area.
c) **The *Jesus* film** is being widely used, with considerable impact in Spanish, Aymara and Quechua.

Bosnia and Hercegovina

See under YUGOSLAVIA page 587

B

March 11	*Botswana*
Africa	(Republic of Botswana)

Area 600,000 sq.km. Very dry and prone to severe droughts; mostly the Kalahari Desert.

Population	Ann. Gr.	Density
1990	1,285,000	3.6 %	2/sq.km
1995	1,528,000	3.5 %	3/sq.km

Peoples: Total ethnic groups 83.
Bantu peoples 94%.
   Tswana 70%. Eight major tribes, most living along south-eastern border with South Africa.
   Other 24%. Kalanga 160,000; Yeyi 29,000; Herero 18,000; Ndebele 17,000; Lozi 14,000; Subia 12,000; Pedi 11,000; Shona 10,000.
San (Kalahari Bushmen) 3.4% speaking 32 languages and dialects. Of the 43,000 San, less than 1,000 are still nomadic.
European/mixed race 2%.
Other 0.6% Zimbabweans, Angolans, South Africans and South Asians 1,000.

Literacy 71%. **Official languages:** English, Tswana. **All languages** 26. **Languages with Scriptures** 3Bi 1NT 2por.

Capital: Gaborone 130,000. Urbanization 22%.

Economy: Benign neglect in colonial times. Rapid development since independence through export of meat, diamonds, copper, nickel and gold. Earnings have been wisely used to develop country. Average annual economic growth 13% in '80s despite severe drought. Public debt/person $400. Income/person $940 (4% of USA).

Politics: Independence from Britain in 1966 as a stable, multi-party democracy – a rarity in Africa.

Religion: Freedom of religion. The government has introduced Scripture education into the school curriculum as a compulsory subject.
Tribal religions 37%. A major component within every people, a majority among the San, Yeyi and Mbukushu.
Baha'i 0.8%. A surprisingly strong following among the Tswana.
Muslim 0.2%.
Christian 62%. Nom 13.5%. Affil 47.7%. Growth 4.3%.

Protestant 20.1%. Affil 13.4%. Growth 1.9%.

Church	Cong	Members	Affiliated
United Congregational	200	22,000	50,000
Ev Lutheran in S Af	42	10,600	15,553
Dutch Reformed Ch	60	5,300	14,500
Seventh-day Adventist	31	9,000	12,000
Assemblies of God	31	5,056	9,977
Anglican Church	12	2,990	9,950
United Apostolic Faith Ch	16	4,000	8,000
Ev Lutheran Ch of S Af	17	2,520	7,200
Methodist Church	7	2,700	4,500
Pentecostal Holiness	27	2,097	3,500
Africa Evang Ch (AEF)	15	870	1,000
Baptist (SBC)	14	340	567
All other (30)	164	16,981	35,649
Denominations (42)	637	84,454	172,396
Evangelicals 4.4% of pop		28,413	56,215
Pentecostal/charis 2.6%		17,000	33,700

Missionaries to Botswana 244 (1:5,300 people) in 39 agencies.
Roman Catholic 6.8% Affil 4.2%. Growth 4%.

Catholic Ch	67	31,300	54,000

Missionaries to Botswana 51 (1:25,200 people).
Foreign Marginal 0.17%. Growth 12%.

Jehovah's Witnesses	19	777	2,160

Indigenous Marginal 35%. Affil 30.7%. Growth 5.7%.

Zion Christian Ch of S Af	78	7,000	14,000
Spiritual Healing Ch	80	8,000	12,100
St Peter's Apost Fth Heal Ch	30	6,000	12,000
All other (94)	1,814	177,560	356,900
Groups (97)	2,002	198,560	395,000

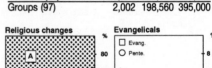

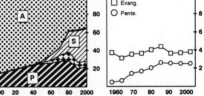

1. **The Tswana** were the first Bantu people in Africa to respond to the gospel, several tribes turning to God in the last century through the LMS from England. Other missions followed. Nominalism soon became a major problem, since each mission planted what became virtually a "state" church for the tribe that received that group. Only a few ageing pastors remain in the United Congregational Church with very few preparing for the ministry. The average congregation today is predominantly composed of women. The majority of Tswana are Christian in name but given over to immorality and drunkenness accentuated by the breakdown of family life. In some areas, over 90% of children are

illegitimate. The AIDS virus had infected at least 6% of the population by 1990. Pray for revival and a reversal of the moral decline.

2. **The growth of African indigenous churches** has been dramatic. Nearly one third of the Tswana are linked to one of these 160 groups, most of which mix Christian truths with traditional religions. Mennonite missionaries are giving Bible teaching to the often-illiterate leaders. Pray for many in these bodies to see the full light of the gospel.

3. **Less reached peoples:**
a) The 50,000 **Bakgalagadi** are mixed Tswana and San, but they speak Tswana. They are partially nomadic, living in the western desert. Little is being done on a permanent basis to reach them.
b) **The Kalanga** resent the cultural dominance of the Tswana. There are few active Christians among them. The New Testament is now being translated.
c) **The Yeyi** of the Okavango Swamp have only been exposed to nominal Christianity in the medium of the Tswana language.
d) The **Mbukushu** and **Subia** in the north are isolated from the main flow of national life and have never received a clear presentation of the gospel.
e) The **Herero** are mostly nominal Lutherans or belong to the fire-worshipping "Oruuano" Church.
f) The **San** have seen their traditional way of life destroyed by drought and modernization. Perhaps 1,000 may now be Christian in about 15 congregations through the efforts of Lutheran, **AEF**, Dutch Reformed and Charles Haupt Ministries workers. Pray that these workers may help the San to adapt to modernity, yet retain their cultural heritage and, above all, find their true identity in Christ.

4. **The last 20 years have been a time of a new evangelical penetration.** The growing work of the Mennonites (32 missionaries), **AEF** (27), **SBC** (21), the Korean Stump Mission (20), **Brethren** (16), **AoG** (4) and others needs prayer. Major missionary-sending nations: USA (108), UK (32), Korea (20), Germany (17), Finland (16), South Africa (13). The spiritual and physical conditions are not easy. Pray for the planting of witnessing churches in which Christians exhibit true holiness and a love for the Scriptures. The impact of Christ For All Nations evangelistic crusades in Gaberone and Francistown since 1975 has been significant.

5. **Young people** under 21 make up half the population, but relatively few are churchgoers. Pray for the ministry of **SU** in providing Christian teaching materials for the schools and nurturing the 30 of the 73 secondary schools that have SU groups. Pray for more part- and full-time workers for this ministry. There is a lively **IFES** group at Gaberone University.

6. **The training and support of pastors and leaders** is a great need. There are few pastors, and the scattered and poor congregations are barely able to support them. Pray for the **AoG** Bible School, and the **AEF** Shashi Bible Training College. Pray for the raising up of men of God able to turn the nation back to Him.

7. **Christian Media Ministries** for prayer.
a) **The Bible Society** oversees the translation programme. Pray for the new Kalanga NT being translated and for wisdom in choice of minority languages for translation projects, the most challenging being the many small San languages.
b) **Radio broadcasts** and Christian TV on the national network are supervised by the International Church Radio Council. **TWR** Swaziland broadcasts 45 minutes daily in Tswana.
c) **Literature** for the rapidly increasing literate population is scarce and often expensive. Little variety is available in Tswana, and virtually nothing in minority languages. Pray for bookstore ministries and the national distribution of evangelistic literature by **EHC**.

B

Brazil
(The Federal Republic of Brazil)

Area 8,512,000 sq.km. One half of the land surface and population of South America. The world's fifth largest country.

Population		Ann. Gr.	Density
1990	150,368,000	2.1 %	18/sq.km
1995	165,083,000	1.9 %	19/sq.km

Peoples: Brazil is a "melting pot" of nations, with much intermarriage, so percentages given below are not meant to indicate rigid categories.
European 53%. Portuguese 15%, Italian 11%, Spanish 10%, German 3% in origin. (Undefined 14%.)
African 11%. Many claim the actual figure is closer to 40%. Descendants of slaves brought from West Africa and Angola.
Mixed race 34.8%. Mestizo and Mulatto.
Asian 1.1%. Japanese 1,200,000; Chinese 160,000; Arab 150,000; Korean 60,000.
Amerindian 0.14%. In 1900 there were 500,000 in 230 tribes, but now there are an estimated 200,000 in 200 tribes, still decreasing through the encroachments of new settlers, loss of land and disease.

Literacy 81%. **Official language:** Portuguese. **All living languages** 208. **Languages with Scriptures** 1Bi 30NT 37por.

Capital: Brasilia 1,950,000. Other major cities: Sao Paulo 18,300,000; Rio de Janeiro 11,700,000; Belo Horizonte 3,640,000; Porto Alegre 3,000,000; Recife 2,700,000; Salvador 2,300,000; Fortaleza 2,300,000; Curitiba 2,170,000. Urbanization 74%.

Economy: Vast economic potential in the developing hinterland of the north and west, rapid growth and industrialization in the '60s and '70s in the south made Brazil one of the leading industrial and trading nations in the world. Massive inflation in the '80s, crippling foreign debts, and gross disparity in wealth between the rich 30% and the poor 70% have blunted growth and increased hardship to many, and hunger encourages violence. There may be 90 million undernourished. Inflation in 1989 was 1,386%, but this fell dramatically in 1990. Public debt/person $565. Income/person $2,550 (12.1% of USA).

Politics: Independent from Portugal in 1822 as a kingdom, it became a federal republic in 1889. Authoritarian military rule between 1964 and 1985 left a legacy of social inequality, bureaucratic inefficiency and state ownership of large parts of the economy. Multi-party democracy restored in 1985. Popular outcry at the corruption of the President forced his resignation in 1992, hopefully strengthening grassroots democracy and forcing on the political system greater accountability to the people they rule.

Religion: Freedom of religion and separation of Church and state. There is still a residual bias to Catholicism in government circles.
Non-religious/other 2.4%. Secularism is on the increase in the middle and upper classes.
Spiritist 4.8%. Spiritist-Catholic 16%. Over 60% of the population are involved in occult practices, most still claiming to be Catholic.
Buddhist 0.2%. **Muslim** 0.1% (though Muslims claim 1.4%). **Jewish** 0.06%.
Christian 92.4%. Affil 91.73%. Growth 1.6%.
  Protestant 21.6%. Affil 19.2%%. Growth 7%.

Church	Cong	Members	Affiliated
Assemblies of God	85,000	6,000,000	14,000,000
Universal Ch of Kingdom of God	10,000	2,000,000	4,000,000
Christian Congregation	15,294	1,560,000	3,120,000
God is Love	3,200	1,600,000	2,670,000
Brazil for Christ	5,000	1,000,000	2,000,000
Baptist Convention	4,492	720,703	1,440,000
Seventh-day Adventist	1,634	482,065	900,000
Lutheran Confession	2,204	595,000	850,000
Foursquare Gospel Ch	2,641	389,266	607,567
National Baptist Conv	720	144,000	360,000
Presbyterian	1,232	190,630	318,000
Evang Lutheran Ch of B	1,426	128,000	216,000
Methodist Church	1,580	79,000	132,000
Indep Presbyterian	420	55,000	91,700
Conv of Ev Baptists	685	37,000	82,200
Chr Ev Alliance	434	8,700	22,900
All other (255)	12,594	1,237,198	2,924,343
Doubly counted		−2,500,000	−5,000,000
Denominations (271)	148,976	13,766,562	28,814,710
Evangelicals 17.8% of pop		12,558,000	26,744,000
Pentecostal/charis 15.6%		11,000,000	23,475,000

Missionaries:
  to Brazil 3,381 (1:44,500 people) in 172 agencies.
  from Brazil 2,755 (1:10,500 Protestants) in 73 agencies 820 frn 1,292 xcul 1,463 dom.

Roman Catholic 68%. Attend 5.3%. Growth 0%.

Catholic	7,466	91,000,000	124,668,000
Doubly counted		−12,000,000	−20,000,000
Total	7,466	79,000,000	104,668,000
Charismatics 0.4%		350,000	600,000

Missionaries:
  to Brazil 3,567 (1:42,200 people).
  from Brazil 975 (1:107,300 Catholics).

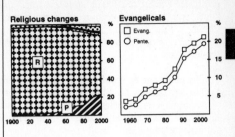

Other Catholic 2%. Growth 1.7%.			
Denominations (2)	308	1,500,800	3,001,600
Orthodox 0.1%. Growth 0.1%.			
Denominations (15)	90	81,620	173,000
Marginal 0.7%. Growth 11.5%.			
Jehovah's Witnesses	5,832	335,039	779,000
Mormons	567	220,000	302,000
All other (57)	510	86,380	195,360
Groups (59)	6,909	641,419	1,276,360

1. **Praise God for the astonishing growth of Evangelicals** – from less than 100,000 in 1900 to four million in 1960, eight million in 1970, 15 million in 1980, and 26 million in 1990, with Pentecostals being 88% of the last total. Brazil has long been known as the largest Catholic country in the world, but it also now has the third largest evangelical community (after the USA and China).

2. **The Catholic Church is in serious trouble**, and faces a discouraging future. There are only 13,000 priests, 46% foreign, and most over the age of 50. About 600,000 Catholics leave the Church every year – 30% turning to spiritist groups and many others to the Evangelicals, provoking tension between conservative Catholics and sections of the Pentecostal movement. Average church attendance is around eight million, but for Evangelicals it is over 20 million. The left wing of the Church has espoused liberation theology and champions the poor and outcast. Yet there are strong renewal movements through both "Base Communities" (one million involved in Bible study groups that work for social and political reform), and also the vigorous 600,000-strong, charismatic movement which are changing the face of the church. Pray for an increasing receptivity to Bible truths that leads to changed lives.

3. **Challenges facing Brazilian Evangelicals.** Intercede for the following needs:
a) **For relevance and a prophetic voice in Brazilian society** – their influence is not in proportion to their large numbers. Evangelistic vision is rarely extended to a vision to bring a message of righteousness to a society ravaged by inequality, injustice, selfishness, crime, immorality and AIDS. Pray that Evangelicals may use their influence to raise the moral tenor of public life rather than for political manipulation.
b) **For spiritual depth.** Pentecostal growth has often been at the expense of adequate discipling, biblical teaching and nurturing of mature leaders. Narrow and petty legalisms concerning dress and social behaviour and a common over-emphasis on physical healing and prosperity have resulted in a high rate of backsliding or membership transfer.
c) **For spirituality** – especially in non-Pentecostal denominations. Liberation theology, with its emphasis on political and social salvation at the expense of personal repentance and faith in Christ, has gained a significant hearing in some churches and seminaries. Pray that theologians may equip the church to maintain loyalty to the Scriptures and balance in teaching its truths. Pray that world evangelization may be *the* priority in the churches.
d) **For leadership for the churches** to maintain growth and retain the fruits of evangelism. There are 27,100 ordained pastors for 150,000 churches. Pray for the 321 seminaries and institutes where over 12,000 men and women are being trained for ministry. The great bottle-neck now is godly, mature, well-trained teachers who are good role models to the students – over 2,000 teachers are needed over the next 10 years.
e) **For unity.** Unresolved divisions weaken the voice of Evangelicals. Pray for the **Evangelical Association of Brazil**, founded in 1991, that it may be a means of fostering unity, fellowship and prayerful cooperation.

4. **Goals for the '90s.** Praise God for denominational goals for prayer mobilization, church multiplication and growth set out by the Assemblies of God, (50,000 new churches and 50 million affiliated to their churches), Baptists, Foursquare Church and others. Pray for denominational barriers to be lowered to enable trans-denominational national goals to be set so that all Brazil be permeated with the gospel.

5. **Spiritism is a dynamic force for evil in Brazil.** It appeals to the emotions and offers physical healing; both traits make it an attractive alternative to traditional Christianity. In 1975 there were at least 14,000 spiritist centres guided by 420,000 mediums. There are seven million Brazilians

B

practising Kardecism ("high" spiritism) and millions more practising Umbanda and Macumba ("low" spiritism with African roots). A majority of Brazilians are involved – most still claiming to be Christian. Pray both for Christians willing and spiritually equipped to minister to those bound by Satan, and for the deliverance of many. Freemasonry among Baptist and Presbyterian pastors is on the increase.

6. **The challenge to reach less evangelized people groups.** Pray for:
a) **The squalid *favelas* (slums), a blight in every major city.** Over 13 million live in such places, where poverty, hopelessness, crime and disease make these people hard to reach. Pray for Christian congregations and agencies to be raised up who will give spiritual and economic uplift to these communities.
b) **The northeast, which is poor and underdeveloped** and also has Brazil's lowest percentage of Evangelicals (5%). There is a great exodus of poor to the Amazon and the cities of the southeast.
c) **An estimated eight million children** who have lost all or most links with their families. Many live on the streets and in the sewers, and live from crime. Prostitution, drug-taking and AIDS are "normal". Pray that Christians may minister love, healing, identity and salvation to these unfortunates.
d) **The secularized, wealthy middle and upper classes.** These have been generally less responsive.
e) **Young people** who face many pressures – especially in university. There are about 1,500,000 students in 871 universities. Pray for more workers to minister to them. The **CCC** and **Navigators** are active, and the ABU(**IFES**) is having a significant impact with groups in most universities. They help students come to the Lord, build them up in the Word and encourage missionary vision. The ABU is also pioneering a ministry to Christian graduates.
f) **The one million Japanese** who are over 60% Roman Catholic and only 3% Protestant. There are 80 evangelical churches with 7,000 adult Japanese believers. Pray for the witness of the Japan Holiness Church (**OMSI**), Japan Evangelical Mission and **UFM**. Pray that these Japanese churches may enter into the mainstream of Brazilian life.
g) **The 160,000 Chinese.** They live largely in Sao Paulo, where there are 12 small evangelical congregations, but the percentage of Christians (1.7%) is low. By contrast, there are 42 churches for the 60,000 Koreans.
h) **The little settlements** along the many rivers in the vast Amazon jungle. These communities are poor and needy – physically and spiritually – and believers are few and often isolated. **UFM** is doing pioneer work in the Lower and Central Amazon region, planting little churches. These churches need prayer – they constantly suffer the loss of key members to the towns and cities. Pray for those engaged in pioneer evangelism by means of river launches – a hard ministry.
i) **Pioneer colonies** along new roads being driven through the virgin jungles of the west and north – the Brazilian Church is seeking to reach out to these rough settlements and plant churches.
j) **The Amerindian tribes yet to be reached.** Possibly about 40 small tribal groups totalling around 5,000 remain to be contacted with the gospel. About 52 tribes are "assimilated" into national life, and a further 45 marginally so. Until curtailed by the government in 1978, **SIL** was working in 41 tribes, **NTM** in 20, **UFM** in five; but in a number of these a viable indigenous church had yet to be planted. Some of these restrictions have since been eased, but international interest in the Amazon makes this a sensitive issue. Pray for the complete evangelization of these tribes and the preservation of the integrity of their societies in the face of disastrous and exploitative invasions into their territories by gold-seekers and settlers.

7. **The role of missionaries** has changed from the past. The most important ministries for missionaries today are in leadership training, missionary preparation for Brazilians and pioneer work in the Amazon region. Missions with the largest number of workers: **NTM** (693 – 30% Brazilian), **YWAM** (610 – 85% Brazilian), **SBC** (292), **SIL/WBT** (208), Baptist Mid-Mission (183), **ABWE** (113), **UFM** (106), Brethren (59), **BMS-UK** (59), **CBFMS** (53), **WEC** (48 – 50% Brazilian), **GMU** (40). Major missionary-contributing nations: USA (2,390), Germany (265), UK (201), Canada (182), Korea (86). Pray for the wise and strategic deployment of the missionary force to the best advantage of the Brazilian church.

8. **Limitations on missionary activity among 48 Amerindian tribes** since 1978 was triggered by a combined assault of anti-Christian anthropologists, development agencies seeking Indian lands, gold-seekers and corrupt officials. Pray that this unholy alliance may be thwarted and that evangelism, Bible translation and church planting may continue unhindered. Brazilian commitment has rapidly increased, with 857 missionaries from national and international agencies serving among

Amerindians. Bible translation is a major unfinished ministry. Work is in progress in 64 languages, but between eight and 70 additional languages may yet require translation teams.

9. **Rapid growth of missions vision** is cause for praise! The AMTB is an evangelical association of cross-cultural missionary agencies that links many of the 1,300 cross-cultural Brazilian missionaries serving in 21 national and 45 international agencies. Pray for:

a) Suitable training and orientation programmes, sending structures and pastoral care for these missionaries.
b) Congregations which have long-term commitment in prayer and giving for their missionaries. Initial enthusiasm has often faded rapidly. Inflation has wrought havoc with the support of missionaries overseas.
c) The *Associação de Conselhos Missionários de Igrejas* (ACMI), founded in 1990 which aims to help local churches set up viable missions structures, programmes and channelling mechanisms.

10. **Christian literature.** Brazil's most widely sold books are about magic and the occult. The evangelical community, as a whole, reads one book per person per year. Pray for change through:

a) Christian publishers such as JUERP (Baptist Conv), EVN (New Life, **CBFMS**), Betania (**Bethany Fellowship**), *Mundo Cristão* (**EUSA**) and ABEB (**IFES**). Most of these are under the umbrella of the Evangelical Literature Committee of Brazil.
b) **Christian distributors. CLC**, with 10 stores and 59 workers is one among many.
c) **The Bible Society**, which distributes over one million Bibles and 142 million portions or leaflets annually.
d) **Gideons International**, who are distributing 10 million New Testaments in six years.

11. **Christian Media** – for prayer:

a) **The *Jesus* film**. Pray for its effective use by film teams all over the country. Over 100,000 see it every year. The video version has been a valuable means of reaching professionals. Pray for those who respond and for their integration into Bible study groups and churches.
b) **Radio.** Brazilian Evangelicals operate four TV stations and 40 radio stations. Internationally, **TWR** Bonaire, **KYFR** USA, and **HCJB** Ecuador beam in 226 hours of broadcasts per week. *Projecto Luz* (700 Club) gains huge audiences across the country. Pray for a lasting impact for the Kingdom.
c) **Cassettes. GRn** have prepared tapes in 80 indigenous languages.

British Indian Ocean Territory

See under MAURITIUS

B

See
Caribbean

Caribbean

British Virgin Islands

(Colony of British Virgin Islands)

Area 150 sq.km. An archipelago of 60 coralline and volcanic islands of which 15 are inhabited. The north-easternmost of the Leeward Islands.

Population	Ann. Gr.	Density
1990 12,257	1.5 %	82/sq.km
1995 12,950	1.4 %	86/sq.km

Peoples:
Afro-Caribbean 90.3% **Euro-American** 7.5%. **East Indian** 0.9%; **Other** 1.3%.

Literacy 98%. **Official Language:** English.

Capital: Road Town 5,200.

Economy: The mainstays are tourism and offshore company registrations. Poor agricultural land. Income/person $10,760 (51% of USA).

Politics: A dependent territory of the UK.

Religion:
Non-religious/other 2.9%.
Baha'i 0.9%. **Hindu** 0.34%. **Muslim** 0.31%.
Christian 95.5%. Affil 90.2%. Growth 0.3%.
Protestant 86.5%. Affil 83.9%. Growth 0.1%.

Church	Cong	Members	Affiliated
Methodist	5	2,475	4,950
Anglican	1	660	2,000
Seventh-day Adventist	2	540	771
Ch of God (Anderson)	3	240	600
Baptist (**SBC**)	2	228	570
All other (12)	15	604	1,397
Denominations (17)	28	4,842	10,288
Evangelicals 25.2% of pop		1,300	3,000

Missionaries to Brit Virgin Is 2 (1:6,000 people).
Roman Catholic 6.3%. Affil 3.6%. Growth -0.4%.

Catholic Ch	2	176	440

Missionaries to Brit Virgin Is 2 (1:6,000 people).
Marginal 2.7%. Growth 7.6%.

Jehovah's Witnesses	3	122	330

1. **The tourist trade** brings large numbers of people seeking fun but whose lives are empty without Christ. Pray that local believers may have a good testimony to them.

2. **The beauty of the islands belies the spiritual need.** There are many churches, and most people profess to be Christian, yet sin mars the lives of many. More than three-quarters of all births are illegitimate. Pray for revival and for Christian families to live exemplary lives.

Brunei

(State of Brunei Darussalam)

March 15

Asia

B

Area 5,800 sq.km. Two small enclaves in Sarawak, East Malaysia on the island of Borneo. Tropical, 70% forest, with heavy rainfall.

Population	Ann. Gr.	Density
1990 266,000	3.5 %	46/sq.km
1995 301,000	2.5 %	52/sq.km

Peoples:
Malay 70.5%. Dominant in government and civil service. Many tribal people who converted to Islam have been absorbed into the Malay population.
Chinese 16%, of which 80% are non-citizen residents. Gradual decline through emigration. Dominant in commerce.
Tribal peoples 5.3%. Predominantly Iban. Also Kedayan, Kayan, Kenyah, Kiput, Murut, Tutung.
Expatriate 8.2%. British 6,000; South Asian 4,200; Gurkha 1,000; Korean; Filipino. Largely involved in the oil industry.

Literacy 85%. **Official languages:** Malay, English. **All languages** 17. **Languages with Scriptures** 9Bi 1NT.

Capital: Bandar Seri Begawan 66,000. Urbanization 59%.

Economy: Entirely dependent on oil, with estimated reserves for 25 years. One of the wealthiest nations in Asia. Income/person $14,120 (67% of USA).

Politics: Refused to join the Malaysian Federation in 1963. A Protectorate of Britain until full independence in 1983. The Sultan rules as an absolute monarch. There are only rudimentary democratic structures.

Religion: Islam is the state religion. Constitutional guarantees for the free practice of other religions are being eroded and limitations on Christian activity are increasing.
Muslim 71%. All Malays, some Iban, Murut and other tribal people.
Chinese Religions 9%.
Non-religious/other 6.5%. Chinese and non-Malay.
Animist/other faiths 5.5%. Mainly tribal peoples. Some Hindus and Buddhists.
Christian 8%. Nom 3%. Affil 5%. Growth 1.6%.
Protestant 3.8%. Affil 2.8%. Growth 2.2%.

Church	Cong	Members	Affiliated
Anglican Ch	3	630	4,400
Tribal churches (4)	4	500	1,000
Brunei Christian F'ship	2	450	900
Bethel Chapel (Brethren)	2	250	625
All other (4)	5	447	763
Denominations (11)	16	2,277	7,688
Evangelicals 1% of pop		977	2,652

Missionaries to Brunei – none.
Roman Catholic 3.9%. Affil 2%. Growth 0.7%.

Catholic Ch	3	2,970	5,300

Missionaries to Brunei 5 (until 1991).
Foreign marginal 0.02%. Growth 5.2%.

Groups (1)	1	13	52

Indigenous Marginal 0.19%. Growth 1.1%.

Groups (1)	3	350	500

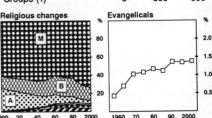

Religious changes   Evangelicals

1. **No evangelism is permitted among Muslims,** and no known believers have come from this community. However, there is a steady stream of conversions to Islam from among tribal and immigrant communities. Pray that through the pure lives of the Christians and the work of the Holy Spirit some may be saved.

2. **The Chinese community feels insecure;** most are still considered foreign, even if they were born in Brunei. Many still follow Chinese religions or are non-religious. About 15% are nominally Christian, but only a small proportion of these are committed to Christ. Pray that neither fear nor materialistic concerns may hold back Chinese from salvation in Christ.

3. **Christians** in the various fellowships have a vigorous outreach through meetings, camps and literature. In 1992, the importation of Christian literature and the public celebration of Christmas were banned and all contacts with Christians in other countries forbidden. Most of the Catholic priests and nuns in the country were expelled at the end of 1991. Pray for Christians in their present predicament and for these unconstitutional edicts to be withdrawn.

B

4. **Tribal peoples** have either been converted to Islam and absorbed into the mainstream of national life, or have remained isolated in jungle villages. Among the latter, many Iban, Kelabit, Murut and others have come to Christ through the witness of the Anglicans, Brunei Christian Fellowship and Bethel Chapel. Pray for the evangelization of each of these communities.

5. **Brunei students** usually complete university education in Malaysia, Britain, Australia or other lands. Pray that they may come into contact with a vibrant Christian witness, be won for Christ, and ultimately return home as witnesses to their Saviour.

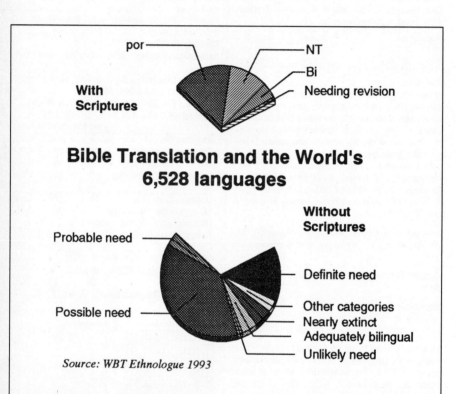

por — NT
— Bi
With Scriptures — Needing revision

Bible Translation and the World's 6,528 languages

Without Scriptures

Probable need —

— Definite need

Possible need — — Other categories
— Nearly extinct
— Adequately bilingual
— Unlikely need

Source: WBT Ethnologue 1993

The WBT *Ethnologue* is the most important source of information on the world's languages and Bible translation status. Note:

1. Less than a third of the world's languages have any of the Scriptures, but the other two-thirds are spoken by only 6% of the world's population.

2. Only 4.2% of the world's languages have the whole Bible, but this 4% constitutes 76% of the world's population.

3. Over 38% of the world's languages need careful linguistic research to determine the need and appropriateness of translating the New Testament into them.

4. There are 925 languages for which translation teams are required for the production of New Testaments.

Bulgaria
(Republic of Bulgaria)

Area 111,000 sq.km. Balkan state adjoining Turkey, Greece, Macedonia, Serbia and Romania.

Population		Ann. Gr.	Density
1990	9,010,000	0.11 %	81/sq.km
1995	9,036,000	0.06 %	81/sq.km

Early returns from the December 1992 census indicate a fall of 5.3% in population since 1985 (not shown here).

Peoples:
Slavic 84%. Bulgarian 6,950,000; Macedonian 225,000; Russian 18,000; Serb 9,000; Czech 9,000.
Turkic 11% (Officially 9%). Turks 990,000; Gagauz 12,000; Crimean Tatar 6,000.
Gypsy 4.6%. Speaking Romani, Turkish or Bulgarian.
Other 0.4%. Armenian 27,000; Greek 11,000; Jews 3,200.

Literacy 90%. **Official languages:** Bulgarian, and locally, Turkish. **All languages** 12. **Languages with Scriptures** 5Bi 3NT 5por.

Capital: Sofia 1,222,000. Urbanization 68%.

Economy: Long one of Europe's poorest countries. Communism left a legacy of inefficient, polluting heavy industry. Since 1990 some progress in liberalizing the economy and adapting to market forces. Much poverty remains, but much potential for growth. Public debt/person $1,220. Income/person $5,300 (25% of USA).

Politics: A nation since the fifth century, but rarely independent. Ruled by the Turkish Ottoman Empire 1396–1878. Communist rule of particular severity 1947–1989. Multi-party democracy instituted in 1990. A see-saw struggle for power since then between the Democrats and Socialists (ex-Communist Party) with the Turkish Party holding a balance of power in parliament.

Religion: Orthodoxy the state religion until 1945. Communist oppression and ruthless control of denominational leadership until 1989. The new democratic constitution proclaims freedom for all denominations, but makes the status of the Orthodox Church one of ambiguous primacy. Statistics below are approximate; the rate of change since 1989 is rapid.
Non-religious/other 17%.
Muslim 13.9%.
Christian 69.1%. Growth 9.9%.
Protestant 1.25%. Growth 17%.

Church	Cong	Members	Affiliated
Pentecostal Union			
(AoG)	280	30,000	43,000
Ch of God (Cleveland)	140	15,000	25,000
Seventh-day Adventist	75	4,500	8,040
Christian Brethren	150	4,500	7,500
Congregational Ch	54	5,000	6,250
Methodist Ch	17	1,700	4,250
Turkish indep. groups	50	4,000	7,000
Baptist Union	30	2,000	3,000
All other (28)	59	5,440	9,400
Denominations (36)	855	72,140	113,440
Evangelicals 1.2% of pop		68,670	107,000
Pentecostal/charis 0.9%		53,000	82,000

Missionaries to Bulgaria 75 (1:120,000 people) in 19 agencies.
Roman Catholic 0.83%. Growth 1.3%.

Catholic Ch	30	30,000	75,000

Orthodox 66.9%. Growth 9.9%.

Bulgarian Orthodox	3,895	4,440,000	6,000,000
Armenian Orthodox	11	14,600	20,000
All other (1)	11	5,500	11,000
Denominations (3)	3,917	4,460,100	6,031,000

Marginal 0.02%. Growth 17.6%.

All groups (3)	13	1,260	1,610

Missionaries to Bulgaria 53 (1:170,000 people).

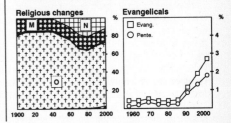

Religious changes   Evangelicals

1. **Bulgaria's political and spiritual transformation** has been one of the most dramatic in the former Communist bloc: from one of the most repressive regimes, with severe persecution of Christians, to multi-party democracy (albeit tumultuous). Across the country is a yearning to fill the moral and spiritual void Marxism created. There is a desire for an identity and a hope. Pray that this may be found in the Lord Jesus through the preaching of the gospel. Many forms of eastern and western cults and also the ancient, but very live, occultism of Bulgaria vie for a following.

B

2. **All Churches have shown dramatic growth.** Many non-religious and atheist Bulgarians have returned to Orthodoxy. The great change is among Evangelicals, who have more than doubled in numbers in three years; in Sofia they have quintupled. Evangelistic outreach among Bulgarians has elicited good response and possibly 4,000–10,000 Turks and Gypsies have come to Christ since 1990. Praise God, and pray for a continued and conserved harvest. There are signs that the initial enthusiasm is wearing off.

3. **The growth has been amidst pain.** The dire effects of outright persecution – with many Christians imprisoned or killed, and manipulation through informers, infiltrators and imposters in the churches – are still to be seen. The subversion of the Orthodox hierarchy was particularly widespread. Some leaders courageously suffered, others compromised – a fact that still breeds division, mistrust and lack of cooperation in Orthodox, Protestant and Pentecostal alike which may lead to new Orthodox and Pentecostal denominations. "Sheep-stealing" – even of whole congregations from one denomination to another – has unfortunately developed into a fine art. Pray for repentance, reconciliation, healing and spiritual unity. These tensions still prevent the formation of a national Evangelical Fellowship. There is a National Committee for the AD2000 Movement linking five denominations and setting goals for the decade.

4. **Maturing the Church is the major challenge for the '90s.** Pray for:
a) **Bible-based teaching of believers.** Only a handful of Christian leaders have had formal Bible training. The hunger of the new Christians is matched only by their ignorance of Scripture and tendency to legalisms.
b) **Leadership training.** Underground TEE programmes of the '80s have blossomed into the interdenominational Logos Bible Academy in Sofia as well as four other Pentecostal denominational schools. Pray for the provision of the right staff, funds and facilities and, above all, spiritual life for these programmes.
c) **The right structures to enhance growth.** The tendency is for autocratic, central leadership and a desire to build mega-churches. Pray for a clearer vision for multiplying churches and plurality of leadership, thus avoiding personality clashes and denominational divisions. Networking and loving communication between leaders is a great need.
d) **The discernment of doctrinal error.** Every modern heresy and cult seems to have targeted the country – Mormons, Children of God, Jehovah's Witnesses, extreme "prosperity" teachings, as well as eastern cults. Christians are being swayed by every wind of doctrine.
e) **The multiplicity of new indigenous agencies that have sprung up** for reaching children, prisons, and ethnic minorities, and for providing literature, Bibles, and Christian teaching in schools and camps. There are also international agencies setting up local branches – **CEF, EHC, TWR,** Gideons, and the Bible Society among others. The need for wise coordination and adequate funding mechanisms is urgent.

5. **Ethnic minorities** need specific prayer.
a) **The Turks** were deeply offended by the Communist campaigns in the mid '80s to impose Bulgarian culture upon them. In 1989, 350,000 fled to Turkey. The collapse of Communism led to the return of half of them and to restitution of their cultural rights. Muslim missionaries from Turkey and Iran have been assiduously seeking to make them stronger Muslims. At the same time there has been a work of the Holy Spirit leading to hundreds of groups of Turkish believers across the country. There were reckoned to be at least 4,000 believers in 1993. This is the first known major spiritual breakthrough among Turks. Pray for Christians with knowledge of Turkish as they seek to disciple the many Pentecostal and indigenous groups (**WEC, OD, OM,** Ichthus Fellowship – the latter three with more short-term involvement).
b) **Gypsies** are generally despised and at the bottom of the social order. Some are Orthodox or Muslim and others still deeply involved in the occult. Among them thousands are turning to the Lord, mainly through the outreach of the Church of God in the Bulgarian language. Others are linked to the indigenous Turkish-speaking movement. A third (180,000) of all Gypsies use Romani as their first language, but lack of a New Testament is a major deficiency. Illiteracy is widespread, and there is a great challenge to patiently teach the fundamentals of the faith.
c) **Pomaks** (300,000) are Bulgarian-speaking Muslims; a specific ministry is needed to reach them. Several congregations of new Christians have been planted in the south of the country.
Pray that there may be warm and close fellowship between the Christians of different ethnic groups. Ancient Balkan inter-ethnic hatreds and mistrust are still potent. Both Turks and Gypsies have formed political bodies to combat discrimination.

B

6. **Foreign missions** have increased personnel committed to Bulgaria. There is great need for long-term missionaries and tentmakers who will learn the culture and language and who earn the confidence of the people through effective role-modelling life and ministry. The need is less for pioneer evangelism than for providing teaching skills and support to an evangelistically-minded church. Pray for:
a) **The calling of the right workers to serve** in this day of extraordinary opportunity. Significant missions: **SBC** (6), **IT** (4), **SEND** (4), **YWAM** (4), **OM** (3), **WEC** (3).
b) **Wisdom in use of short-term visits and ministry.** Too much has been done (and even undone) by enthusiastic but ill-prepared visitors on foray ministries. All needs to be integrated into a wider coordinated strategy that has been developed indigenously. High-powered western evangelism is meeting with rising scepticism.
c) **Sensitive use of foreign funds.** The chronic lack of finance and poverty of those in Christian work makes every infusion of funds a potentially damaging or distorting influence to the spiritual life of churches and individuals. Employment by foreign agencies can easily take away key workers from the ministries most needed by the church. Yet how vital such help is!

7. **Young people.** The authorities are eager to have moral and religious education in schools, so there is freedom for Christian input in many schools. Pray that neither Orthodox sensitivities about Evangelicals nor Western evangelical insensitivities limit opportunities. Millions of Bibles, books and pieces of literature published in the West have been distributed in schools, but not always adequately used. Pray that all this may lead to a good understanding of the things of God and many new Christians.

8. **Christian help ministries.**
a) **Literature.** *New Man* became the first Bulgarian Christian publisher with a wide-ranging vision for producing solid evangelical books, Scripture aids and teaching/evangelistic materials. Pray for viability in the prevailing poverty and flood of Western-produced subsidized literature. **EHC** has plans for a nationwide literature distribution campaign. Effective cooperation between foreign and national literature agencies is needed.
b) **Bible translation and distribution.** The present Bulgarian Bible is archaic; but the new Living Bible soon to be available is not acceptable to some. Pray for consensus among Christians on the issue. Pray for the early availability of an effective modern translation. Distribution of 70,000 of the Cyrillic-script Turkish New Testaments has had a significant impact. Higher levels of illiteracy among Turks and Gypsies are a hindrance. Many Bibles are being printed locally. There is a need for the Scriptures in Romani for the Gypsies.
c) **Radio.** Local television and radio programming is increasing; **TWR** has set up a studio. The potential is enormous; finance and caution about Evangelicals are bottlenecks. Four international broadcasters transmit five hours/week to Bulgaria.

B

March 17	
Burkina Faso	
Africa	

Area 274,000 sq.km. A landlocked country of the Sahel. Prone to drought and famine.

Population	Ann. Gr.	Density
1990 9,007,000	2.7 %	33/sq.km
1995 10,382,000	2.9 %	38/sq.km

Over 1,700,000 Burkinabé (people of Burkina Faso) have migrated to other lands: 80% to Côte d'Ivoire, others to Niger, Mali and France.

Peoples: Over 72 distinct ethno-linguistic groups in four major language families.
Gur-Voltaic (35 groups) 75.7%.
Mossi-Gurma: Mossi 4,541,000; Gurma 533,000. The Mossi are the dominant people in Burkina Faso and comprise 52% of the population.
Gurunsi: Dagaari 287,000; Lyele 225,000; Bwamu 193,000; Kurumba 151,000; Nuna 110,000; Birifor 108,000; Kassena 84,000; Buli 70,000; Gurenne (Frafra) 25,100; Ko 16,200; Puguli 13,200; Kusale 12,600; Sissala 9,000; Pana 7,200.
Senufo (11 groups): Karaboro 64,000; Nanerge 41,500; Tusian 32,000; Tagba 28,000; Bolon 11,000; Tiefo 10,000; Vige 6,700; Wara 4,500.
Lobi-Lobiri: Lobi 175,500; Gouin 53,000; Turka 45,000; Doghosie 14,400; Dyan 14,100; Komono 3,000; Kaanba 7,600.
Mande peoples: 10.8%. Bissa 322,000; Samo 218,000; Bobo 203,000; Marka 158,000; Jula 30,000; Sambla 16,000; Samogho 10,000.
Fula 10%; two groups.
Other African: 3.3%. Songhai 122,700; Tuareg 85,500; Hausa.
Non-Africans: 0.2%. Arab 9,000; French and Westerners 7,000.

Literacy 13%. **Official language:** French, spoken by 10% of the population. **Trade languages:** Moré (the language of the Mossi), Jula in south. **All languages** 72. **Languages with Scriptures** 5Bi 7NT 9por.

Capital: Ouagadougou 437,000. Urbanization 9%.

Economy: 83% of the population is dependent on subsistence agriculture and the intermittent rainfall. Much malnutrition and famine in the centre and north since early '70s. The economic outlook is bleak. Public debt/person $76. Income/person $310 (1.5% of USA).

Politics: Independent of France in 1960. A series of economic disasters destabilized a succession of governments. Six coups since 1966. The 1983 coup brought in a left-wing revolutionary regime which radicalized the structure and foreign relations of the country. The 1987 military coup halted many of the extremes of the former regime, but ambiguously defines itself as "revolutionary, democratic, anti-imperialist and secular".

Religion: The former regime was far less sympathetic to Christian churches and missionaries. The present climate is favourable to Christian outreach and aid programmes.
Traditional religions 33%. Yet most of the population is animistic under a religious veneer.
Muslim 48%. Growing rapidly in some areas. 10% of the country was Muslim in 1900.
Christian 19%. Nom 5.8%. Affil 13.2%. Growth 5.4%.
Protestant 5%. Affil 4.5%. Growth 11.9%.

Church	Cong	Members	Affiliated
Assemblies of God	1,686	83,100	276,907
Chr and Miss Alliance	499	13,400	47,900
Evang Ch Assoc (**SIM**)	255	10,200	30,000
Apostolic Mission	88	5,650	14,120
Baptist Conven (**SBC**)	88	7,920	11,300
Apostolic Church	80	3,150	9,000
Ev Pentecostal Assoc	86	1,880	6,700
Protestant Ev Ch (**WEC**)	38	1,000	3,800
All other (4)	30	844	2,764
Denominations (12)	2,850	127,144	402,491
Evangelicals 4.3% of pop		126,473	400,000
Pentecostal/charis 3.3%		91,000	298,000

Missionaries:
to Burkina 364 (1:24,700 people) in 33 agencies.
from Burkina 141 (1:2,800 Protestants) 136frn 36xcul 105dom.
Roman Catholic 13.9%. Affil 8.6% Gr 2.6%.

Catholic Ch	1,079	451,225	777,975

Missionaries:
to Burkina 579 (1:15,600 people).
from Burkina 56 (1973 figure).
Foreign Marginal 0.02%. Affil 0.02%. Growth 8%.

Jehovah's Witnesses	17	449	1,800

Indigenous Marginal 0.1%. Affil 0.1%. Growth 13.3%.

Groups (9)		3,500	10,000

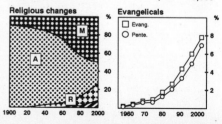

Religious changes | Evangelicals

B

1. **Praise God for growth and advance** in the midst of revolution, drought and famine. Specifically:
a) The spectacular accelerated growth of evangelical churches between 1983 and 1990. Membership more than doubled over that period. By the year 2000 over 14% of the population will be evangelical if this growth is maintained.
b) Significant people movements with thousands of conversions among the Mossi (**AoG**), Lyele (**SBC**), Gurma (**SIM**), Bwamu, Bobo and Samo (**CMA**), Nuna and Sissala (Canadian Pentecostals); all but the Bobo are now over 5% evangelical.
c) The vibrant AoG family of churches, with possibly half its quarter-million following converted out of a Muslim background.
d) The first Burkinabé cross-cultural missionaries sent out to other lands, with **AoG** missionaries moving out to four African countries.
e) Ten peoples without a Christian witness who are now being reached.

2. **The Unreached.** Despite church growth, increased missionary exertions and greater responsiveness, there remain over 28 peoples without an effective witness; 13 of these are Muslim. Most of these lie within the area of witness of existing missions. Pray for the recruitment and deployment of pioneer workers from Africa and the world to evangelize them. Pray also for the Burkina Church to pray and plan together for this. Specific challenges:
a) **Muslims** who are stronger in the north but continue to grow in nearly every ethnic group. Only 20 missionaries are specifically committed to ministering among peoples comprising almost half the population: the urbanized **Soninke, Jula** and the rural **Tuareg** in the north (**WH, AoG**); Bolon in the northwest (**AoG**); Songhai in the northeast; Doghosie, Komono in the south. Strong political ties with Libya strengthen Muslim influence within the country.
b) **The partly nomadic Fulani** who are beginning to respond through the witness of three **SIM** teams, and AoG workers. This outreach needs to be expanded.
c) **Unreached non-Muslim peoples**: the Kurumba with a handful of AoG believers in the north, the Dogon of the northeast, the Bulsa and Gurenne on the Ghana border, the many Senufo sub-groups in the southwest (CMA and Mennonites), and the numerous small peoples of the south (**WEC**).

3. **The power of the occult has yet to be decisively challenged and broken in many peoples of Burkina Faso.** Few countries in West Africa are more dominated by idolatry, fetishism and secret societies. Especially strong is that of the many Lobiri peoples in the southwest (**WEC** area), Gurma (**SIM**) in the east, Gurunsi (Canadian Pentecostals, **AoG**), Senufo and Bobo (**CMA**) in the west. Pray that the power of the risen Christ might be demonstrated for the saving of many.

4. **The Catholics** have grown steadily, but the rate of growth slowed in the '80s. Some 11% of the Mossi and most of the Dagaari are Catholic, yet the strong idolatry and fetishism within the hearts of the converts is often unchallenged.

5. **The dramatic expansion and even local revival conditions** have strained the resources of the evangelical churches to cope with the influx of new converts. Leaders are too few, illiteracy is high, and economic hardship widespread. Pray for church leaders at this significant time. They need wisdom, humility, tact and firmness in the delicate political situation in the country. Pray also for Bible schools run by the major churches and missions in local languages and in French (**SIM, CMA, AoG, WEC** and Pentecostals). Pray for Christian leaders able to stand firm against the idolatrous practices of tribal society and against the demands of non-Christian national leaders. Pray that satanic hindrances to the ongoing growth of the Church in the '90s may be thwarted.

6. **Young people** are better educated than their parents and they enthusiastically supported the failed revolution. Local prospects for employment and advancement are poor, so they are frustrated and disillusioned. Few churches have effective programmes directed at children or young people. Pray for the work of SU in the high schools and the expanding ministry of GBUAF (**IFES**) in the high schools and Ouagadougou University. There are over 1,000 linked with the latter in cell groups around the country and one group of 60 in the university. More staff to expand the work is a great need.

7. **The massive emigration of Burkinabé to the cities and to Côte d'Ivoire** is both a challenge and an opportunity for the gospel. The social upheavals, family breakdowns and economic stagnation caused by the emigration of most of the active men in the community are severe. In 1990 there were estimated to be 1,500,000 Burkinabé in Côte d'Ivoire. It is reckoned that 70% of these convert to Islam within a few months of arrival. Only now are Burkina churches taking up the challenge by sending pastors and missionaries to these people – especially **AoG, CMA** and **WEC**. Pray for an abundant harvest and effective church planting.

B

8. **Missionaries working in Burkina Faso** have a vital role in a land of so much physical and spiritual need. The work has been hard, and victories long in coming. Major missions working in the country are SIL/WBT (66 workers), **CMA** (51), Mennonites (46), **SIM** (41), **WEC** (24), **AoG** (15). Pray for their protection and encouragement. They need to know the Lord's priorities. Missionary reinforcements are needed in a wide range of ministries.

9. **Christian aid and relief** have been coordinated by the Federation of Evangelical Churches. Much is and has been done in alleviating suffering and staving off future disasters. Wisdom is needed by both missions and Christian leaders in the administration of this help. Massive internal migration, poor communications and distortion of the fragile local economy all too easily result. Pray for the hearts of both Muslims and fetishists to be opened to God's Word through such help.

10. **Bible translation is a ministry of major significance.** Only two indigenous languages have the whole Bible – Moré and Bambara. **SIL** has 38 workers committed to 12 language programmes and is surveying the needs of 20 others. Five other missions are involved in translation work in 15 languages. Present and future translators need prayer to complete the immense task. Literacy programmes are needed for many areas so that Burkinabé may read the new translations.

11. **Christian literature ministries** are in the pioneer stage. The Bible Society is now legally registered. The Baptists, CMA and AoG have small bookstores in the capital, but a coordinated nationwide literature publication and distribution network would improve the situation. **CLC** has started ministry in the capital; pray that this and all literature ministries may lead to a literate and well-read church.

12. **Media ministries.** High levels of illiteracy and poverty and the limited availability of literature in local languages enhance the importance of other media.
a) **Radio** is used by some churches for local Christian broadcasts, but lack of equipment and expertise is the bottleneck.
b) **Audio materials** for evangelism and teaching have not been adequately used; **GRn** have made recordings in 40 languages and dialects.
c) **The _Jesus_ film** is proving a key pioneer evangelistic tool in Bambara/Jula and is in use or in preparation in Dogon, Bobo, Dagbani, Fula, Gurma and Soninke.

Burundi
(Republic of Burundi)

March 18

Africa

B

Area 27,800 sq.km. A mountainous country similar to Rwanda to the north.

Population	Ann. Gr.	Density
1990	5,451,000	2.9 %	196/sq.km
1995	6,299,000	2.9 %	226/sq.km

Peoples:
Rundi-speaking 96%. Considerable inter-ethnic mixing.
Tutsi 15%. The politically dominant minority.
Hutu 80%. A further 150,000 live as refugees in Tanzania.
Twa Pygmies 1%. Despised by other groups.
Other African 3.7%. Rwandan 90,000; Zairois 80,000.
Other 0.3%. South Asian 6,500; European 3,000; Arab 1,600.

Literacy 14%. **All languages** 4. **Official languages:** Rundi, French. All speak Rundi. **Languages with Scriptures** 2Bi.

Capital: Bujumbura 272,000. Urbanization 8%.

Economy: One of the world's poorest states. Agricultural economy; coffee provides 90% of export earnings. Dependent on foreign aid. Over-population and lack of natural resources make improvements hard to achieve. Public debt/person $172. Income/person $310 (1.4% of USA).

Politics: For 400 years, Tutsi lordship over the Hutu majority has dominated the political life of Burundi. After the country's independence from Belgium in 1962, the Tutsi constitutional monarchy was replaced by a republican military regime in 1966. Tutsi dictatorship in the '80s led to vigorous and bloody suppression of Hutu uprisings. The Libyan-backed regime was overthrown in 1987, and replaced by a military-civilian government with increased Hutu participation. Conflict between the two groups continues, but in 1992 a multi-party democratic constitution was adopted.

Religion: The previous regime became increasingly hostile against Christians. Meetings were curtailed, missionaries expelled and many ministries closed down. Since 1987, a measure of religious freedom was restored, and the return of missionaries

allowed. During 1992 renewed restrictions on some Christian activities were imposed.
African traditional religions 7.1%.
Muslim 1%. Gradual growth. **Baha'i** 0.1%.
Christian 91.8%. Nom 16.2%. Affil 74.7%. Growth 5.8%.
Protestant 16%. Affil 14.6%. Growth 7.1%.

Church	Cong	Members	Affiliated
Church of Pentecost	2,267	170,000	425,000
Prot Episcopal Ch (MAM)	1,621	48,620	143,000
Methodist Ch Union	244	37,296	70,000
Seventh-day Adventist	81	23,969	43,600
Ev Episcopal Ch (WGM)	160	20,000	40,000
Un of Bapt Chs (SBC)	77	14,527	26,400
Friends (Quakers)	60	6,500	9,500
Christian Brethren	44	3,000	4,000
All other (9)	141	18,150	35,879
Denominations (17)	4,695	342,042	797,379
Evangelicals 14% of pop		323,000	762,000
Pentecostal/charis 8.3%		184,000	453,000

Missionaries:
to Burundi 95 (1:57,400 people) in 13 agencies.
from Burundi 24 (1:33,200 Protestants) in 2 agencies.
Roman Catholic 75.6%. Affil 59.7%.
Growth 5.5%.

Catholic Ch	1,326	1,860,000	3,257,500

Missionaries:
to Burundi 407 (1:13,400 people).
from Burundi 30 (1973 figure).
Orthodox 0.02%. Growth 1.2%.
Foreign Marginal 0.01%. Growth 5.1%.
Indigenous Marginal 0.2%. Growth 10%.

Groups (2)	49	7,700	15,400

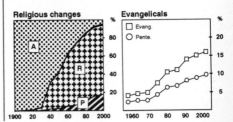

Religious changes   Evangelicals

1. **Government leaders are working to unify the nation,** but centuries of mistrust, enmity and bloodshed cannot be forgotten overnight. The Tutsi military must be placated and the Hutu majority's demands satisfied. Pray for reconciliation and peace – above all at the foot of the Cross. Pray also for full religious freedom to be instituted and maintained.

2. The Burundi Church had a notable revival in the '50s. Subsequent moral and theological compromise harmed the witness, but persecution brought new maturity and spiritual fervour. There is once again revival in many churches. Pray for deep and lasting effects in leaders, laity and young people.

3. Leadership for the churches is in short supply; persecution and closure of Bible schools cut off the supply of newly trained leaders. Pray for the full re-establishment of the Mweya Theological Institute (Friends, Free Methodists and **WGM**), the Pentecostal Bible School and for the effective launching of the Matana Theological College (Anglican-**MAM**). Pray for the provision of staff and the blessing of students as they prepare for the ministry.

4. Missionary personnel are returning to a new situation and a new era. Pray that they may have warm, close relationships with Burundi Christian leaders, and be placed in ministries that will maximize their gifts in the development of the Church. The major ministries are theological education, discipling, media ministries and youth work. The largest missions: Swedish Free Mission (57), Methodists (20), Brethren (5), and **MAM** (CMS-Rwanda Mission) (4).

5. Areas of greater need:
a) **The Twa** are relatively less evangelized, but integrate well into existing churches when converted.
b) A number of **towns** and **rural areas** are less evangelized and without a settled evangelical witness.

6. Refugee resettlement is a major problem in an already crowded land. Pray for wise handling of the 130,000 Burundi refugees in Tanzania – most of whom have put their roots down in that land. There are thousands of believers and churches among them (**WGM**, Pentecostal Church).

7. Young people. The ministry of **SU** in the schools has been used of the Lord. Pray for the establishment and growth of SU groups in each secondary school. There is a small CBU (**IFES**) group in the university. **CEF** also have a ministry among children.

8. Christian Media for prayer:
a) **Literature.** This is scarce and costly, and Christian bookshops are few. There is very little available in Rundi. Christian Literature and Outreach, an agency with which WGM is working, has the vision to rectify this. **SU** has a literature development programme which is supported by **TEAR Fund.**
b) **Radio. TWR** and **SU** have established a communications centre in Bujumbura, where locally-produced programmes are prepared.

Byelarus
(Byelorussian Republic)

Area 208,000 sq.km. Landlocked, fertile agricultural land with extensive forests on the North European plains. Surrounded by Russia, Ukraine, Poland, Lithuania and Latvia.

Population		Ann.Gr.	Density
1990	10,223,000	0.57%	49/sq.km
1995	10,481,000	0.68%	50/sq.km

Peoples: The smallest of the three Slavic nations of the former USSR.
Indo-European 98.4%.
 Slav 98%. Byelorussian 7,905,000; Russian 1,342,000; Polish 417,000; Ukrainian 291,000.
 Other 0.4%. Gypsy 11,000; Lithuanian 8,000.
All other peoples 1.6%. Jews 112,000; Tatar 12,000.

Literacy 99%. **Official language:** Byelorussian, but the majority are still more fluent in the related Russian. **All indigenous languages** 2. **Languages with Scriptures:** 2Bi.

Capital: Minsk 1,650,000. Urbanization 65%.

Economy: One of the most productive agricultural and industrial regions in the former USSR, but collapse of trade between the independent republics and reluctance to modernize and free the economy from state control have forced the country into severe recession and inflation. The Chernobyl nuclear catastrophe in 1986 has made a colossal impact on the Byelorussian economy and health services. Income/person $5,729 (27% of USA).

Politics: Indefensible borders and flat plains have made Byelarus a pawn in international politics and a battlefield in war. Although a separate member of the UN since World War II, it was never an independent state until independence in 1991. Political leadership is cautious, trying to appease both the Communists and democrats and failing to grapple with economic and ecological crises that cripple the new nation.

Religion: Religious freedom after 70 years of Communist repression. Many church buildings were destroyed during that time. Nearly all statistics below are estimates.
Non-religious/other 27.6%. Many non-religious and Marxists have reverted to the faith of their forebears.
Jews 1.1%. **Muslim** 0.2%.
Christian 71.1%. Affil 67.5%. Gro 6.9%.
 Protestant 1%. Growth 15.1%.

Church	Cong	Members	Affiliated
Pentecostal Union	200	16,000	50,000
Baptist Union	150	10,000	32,000
Pentecostal			
– unregistered	38	3,000	10,000
Lutheran Church	3	500	1,000
Adventist Church	2	300	600
All other (10)	30	3,000	7,500
Denominations (15)	423	32,800	101,100
Evangelicals 0.97% of pop		31,800	98,970
Pentecostal/charis 0.61%		21,000	63,000

Missionaries to Byelarus est. 6.
 Roman Catholic 22%. Growth 6.1%.

Roman Catholic		1,300,000	2,167,000
Uniate Catholic		19,800	33,000
Denominations (2)		1,319,800	2,200,000

Missionaries to Byelarus n.a.
 Orthodox 48%. Affil 44.9%. Gro 7.2%.

Russian Orthodox Ch		3,150,000	4,500,000
Old Believers		39,000	60,000
All other (2)		23,100	36,000
Denominations (4)		3,212,100	4,596,000

 Marginal 0.04%. Growth 16.9%.

Jehovah's Witnesses		1,260	4,200

1. **Byelarus stumbled into an unexpected independence** and is searching for a national identity. The cultural dominance of Poland and Russia lasted for many centuries. Even the use of the Byelorussian language has atrophied. Pray for the development of a vigorous evangelical expression of the body of Christ within the culture and a wide range of Christian literature, videos and programmes for radio and television in Byelorussian.

2. **The Chernobyl catastrophe** in the Ukraine blanketed Byelarus with toxic, radioactive debris. Over 20% of the population still lives in areas with radiation levels above the safety limit. USSR and local government response was limited and the long-term effects on health and the economy devastating. This has had a deep effect on the morale of the people and prompted a longing for spiritual answers – many fear premature death. Pray that Christians may minister effectively in this tragic situation and win many to Christ.

3. **It has become fashionable to be Christian.** Many former Communist Party members and fence-sitting non-religious people have returned to Orthodoxy and Catholicism. Real understanding of the

gospel and willingness for true discipleship are lacking. Pray for the Holy Spirit to move through the land.

B

4. **Evangelical Christians** are relatively fewer than in neighbouring Ukraine. Pray for fellowship, understanding and cooperation among Evangelicals – often in short supply. Growth rates in the churches are high among Pentecostals, less so among Baptists, but difficulties with building permits and supplies restrict construction of the required buildings. Lack of mature teachers and structures to cope with new converts also limit retention of those who show interest. More trained leadership is an essential if long-term growth is to be maintained.

5. **Missions.** Russia and Ukraine have attracted far more interest in the West. Pray for helpful supportive relationships with foreign churches and agencies. Too often such contacts have been insensitive and manipulative. Pray for expatriate missionaries to be called to serve long-term in the country.

6. **The less reached.** There are only a few significant non-Christian minorities.
a) **Jews.** 3.5% of Minsk is Jewish. There is a Messianic Jewish group in Minsk, but the majority still need to be reached.
b) **Muslims.** Small communities of Tatar and Azerbaijani exist.

7. **Christian help ministries** for prayer.
a) **The Bible Society (UBS)** has been established in Minsk. Local production of Scriptures is planned. Pray for wide use of the Byelorussian and Russian Scriptures.
b) **Christian literature** is scarce. There is very little evangelistic, apologetic or teaching material available in Byelorussian.
c) **EHC** plans a nationwide distribution of Christian literature to every home.
d) **The *Jesus* film** has been widely shown in Russian and Byelorussian. Resources for follow-up are too limited to help all who are touched.
e) **TWR** has established a base for local programme production.

Cambodia

(State of Kampuchea)

March 20

Asia

C

Area: 182,000 sq.km. Fertile, forest-covered state of southwest Indo-China on the Mekong River.

Population	Ann. Gr.	Density
1990 8,246,000	2.5 %	45/sq.km
1995 9,205,000	2.2 %	50/sq.km

Reduced by 2–3 million in the 1975–79 holocaust and accompanying wars, famines and flight of refugees.

Peoples:
Khmer 85.2%.
Indigenous minorities: 3.6%. Cham 206,000; Mnong 19,000; Paong 19,000; Kui 16,000; Tampuan 15,000; Jarai 10,000; Kru'ng 10,000; Brao 5,000; Chong 5,000; Stieng 3,600; Kravet 3,000; Somray 2,000; Pear 1,400; Lamam 1,000.
Other minorities 11.2%. Vietnamese 600,000 to 1,000,000; Chinese 340,000. Many new immigrants: Lao 17,000. UN personnel 20,000 (in 1993).

Literacy 48%. **Official language:** Khmer. **Languages with Scriptures** 3Bi 1NT 1por.

Capital: Phnom Penh 1,000,000 or more. Urbanization 16%.

Economy: Rich agricultural potential. Reduced to bare subsistence because of the devastation to land and people by war, massacres, political isolation and socialist bureaucracy. The major economic activity is provided by foreign aid and the large UN military presence.

Politics: Powerful kingdoms from first to fourteenth centuries. Thereafter for 500 years a pawn in regional and global conflicts with Thai, Vietnamese, French, Japanese and US invasions or occupations. A tragic victim of the Vietnam War (1970–75) which opened the way for the extreme Marxist Khmer Rouge takeover in 1975. This was followed by one of the most savage slaughters in this century. Almost all former military personnel, civil servants, educated or wealthy people and their families were killed, and the nation turned into a vast labour camp. The Vietnamese army ousted the Khmer Rouge in 1978, but civil war between four contending armies raged with superpower support until 1991. UN-supervised elections in May 1993 were held despite opposition by the Khmer Rouge. Many fear a return to further war and to the "killing fields" of the '70s.

Religion: Buddhism has been the national religion since the 15th century. The Khmer Rouge sought to eradicate all religion. 90% of Buddhist monks and most Christians perished. Since 1978 there have been periods of more tolerance, but only since 1990 have Christians been allowed to worship openly, yet are treated as second-class citizens.

Buddhist 87%. Openly practised and with a revival of interest nationwide.
Non-religious/other 7%. Mainly Marxists.
Animist 2.7%. Mainly tribal peoples.
Muslim 2.9%. Mainly Cham people.
Christian 0.38%. Growth 25.3%.
Protestant 0.10%. Growth 8.8%.

Church	Cong	Members	Affiliated
National churches	61	2,500	6,250
All other (7)	9	900	1,593
Denominations (8)	70	3,400	7,843
Evangelicals 0.08% of pop		3,300	7,600
Pentecostal/charis 0.03%		1,300	2,600

Expatriate workers 105 (1:78,500) in 22 agencies.
Roman Catholic 0.28%. Growth 33.6%.

Catholic Ch		4,000	23,000

Expatriate workers 1.

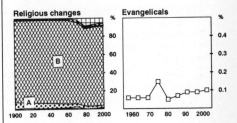

Religious changes

Evangelicals

1. **The terrible genocide perpetrated by the Khmer Rouge** in 1975–1978 and the subsequent civil wars have devastated the people. Their lands are strewn with mines, many are maimed physically and emotionally, with families decimated and numerous widows and orphans. The longing for peaceful transition to democratic government in 1993 is threatened by the continued intransigence of the Khmer Rouge. Pray for a workable and lasting peace with full political and religious freedom.

2. **The election of 1993 may fail to give peace and economic progress.** Violence, intimidation and corruption marked the election preparations. Pray that God may raise up honourable leaders for the nation who will work for reconciliation and the good of the people. Recent governments have been corrupt and have obstructed efforts to alleviate the sufferings of the people.

C

3. **For centuries Cambodia has been in spiritual darkness.** Ubiquitous spirit shrines, strong opposition of Buddhism to any ideological rival, and hatreds generated by 20 years of war all reveal the nature of the conflict. Pray that spirit powers which control the land may be forced to yield to the Lord Jesus.

4. **The Cambodian Church has struggled to survive.** Beginning in 1923, CMA missionaries laboured for 42 years before the breakthrough began. There were only 700 believers in evangelical churches in 1970, but by 1975 this had grown to 9–12,000. Only 2,000 survived the slaughter – many fled to Thai refugee camps where a great harvest was reaped for the Kingdom. Since 1990 the church in Cambodia has had more freedom for worship. By 1993 there were 30 groups or congregations meeting in the Phnom Penh area, others around Battembang and among the Mnong. The fragile young church needs prayer:
a) **For freedom** from government manipulation and interference, and wisdom how to relate to the authorities.
b) **For trained leaders;** lack of maturity leads to quarrelling, divisions and susceptibility to diverting financial offers from Western agencies. There is one Bible school in Phnom Penh.
c) **For effective Christian families** in a nation where family cohesion, trust and love have been severely impaired. To add to the nation's miseries, AIDS is spreading rapidly in the capital.
d) **For ministry to emotional and spiritual needs** of both believers and non-Christians, and vision for evangelism.

5. **Christian ministry to physical needs** is a major concern.
a) **Refugees** poured out of Cambodia between 1975 and 1978. About 700,000 fled to Thailand, where many came to Christ in refugee camps. Many agencies have had a remarkable ministry there (**SAO, YWAM, WV, SBC,** Christian Outreach, **OMF, CMA** and others). Some 350,000 have moved on to USA, France, Canada and other lands, where there are now dozens of Cambodian Christian fellowships. The remaining 350,000 had returned home by 1993 to rebuild their lives; they need much help.
b) **In Cambodia** the needs are enormous. The murder of most of those with skills or an education make expatriate input essential. Rehabilitation, orphanages, reconstruction, health care, projects for agriculture, fisheries, water management and education are all ministries where Christians can have significant input. Pray for World Concern, Christian Outreach, **SAO, CMA, WV, AoG, YWAM,** Mennonites and Servants to Asia's Urban Poor, who are committed to such ministries. **Cambodian Christian Services** has provided a coordinating forum for 12 agencies and overseas Khmer workers. More fellowship and cooperation is needed to avoid wasteful duplication.

6. **Christian workers** are granted visas only for aid and rehabilitation projects. Pray for their health, safety, spiritual freshness and fruitfulness in these ministries. Conditions are difficult and harsh. Pray this land fully open for other ministries – especially pioneer workers, church planters and Bible teachers.

7. **The less reached.** There is a window of opportunity for the land that must be prayerfully kept open. Pray for:
a) **The Buddhist majority.** Though reviving, Buddhism has lost some of its grip.
b) **The Vietnamese,** who have increased in number. They are receptive, there is a growing revival in their homeland, and some are coming to Christ in Cambodia.
c) **The Cham Muslims.** There are several individual believers but no churches known. Refugee communities live in Sumatra (Indonesia), Malaysia and USA.
d) **Tribal peoples.** Among the Mnong there are 700 Christians. Pray for survey and church-planting work to begin.

8. **Christian media ministries for prayer:**
a) **Literature.** CMA missionaries have translated a range of materials, and continue to do so. There is a real need for teaching materials, for false teachings multiply as the doors open wider; few of the believers have the background knowledge of Scripture to combat such error. The **UBS** and others are providing Khmer Bibles and New Testaments. A new Khmer New Testament was completed in 1993. **SGM** Scripture portions are widely appreciated.
b) **The *Jesus* film.** This is available in Khmer and Vietnamese, but has not yet been widely used.
c) **Cassettes.** GRn have scripture messages on cassette in 11 languages.
d) **Radio.** Pray for the considerable input from **FEBC**-Manila in Khmer (2 hours/day), and Vietnamese (3.5). **AoG** also broadcasts in Khmer from Guam. Teaching cassettes are a useful extension of this ministry. FEBC plans to set up a recording studio in the capital.

Cameroon
(The Republic of Cameroon)

March 21
Africa

C

Area 465,000 sq.km. On the continental "hinge" between West and Central Africa. Semi-arid in the north, grasslands in the centre, rainforest in the south.

Population		Ann. Gr.	Density
1990	11,245,000	2.6 %	24/sq.km
1995	12,875,000	2.7 %	28/sq.km

Peoples: Over 260 languages, maybe 500 or more ethnic groups; Africa's most complex country. Only the larger or noteworthy are mentioned here. Major language groups:
Bantu 50.5%. 97 groups: Bamiléké (20) 1,737,000; Ewondo 369,000; Bassa 358,000; Bulu Fang 314,000; Eton 259,000; Nso 231,000; Mum 190,000; Maka 118,000; Kundu 116,000; Kaalong 116,000; Limbum 115,000.
Chadic-Hausa 19.4%. 41 groups: Mandara 393,000; Masa 208,000; Matakam 129,000; Kotoko 116,000; Giziga 102,000; Mose 100,000; Mofu 96,000; Musgu 90,000; Kapsiki 58,000; Gidar 50,000; Gude 46,000; Daba 38,000; Zulgwa 25,000; Mambila 22,000.
Sudanic 10.3%. 41 groups: Gbaya 281,000; Tupuri 277,000; Fali 116,000; Mundang 104,000; Manja 92,000; Mbum 42,000.
West Atlantic 9.6%. Adamawa Fulani, 1,080,000.
Bantoid 8.2%. 42 groups: Bitore 116,000; Kungom 92,000.
Arab 0.7%. Shuwa (Baggara) 69,000; Turku 6,000.
Kwa 0.4%. Igbo 45,000.
Saharan 0.2%. Kanuri 23,000.
Pygmy 0.2%. Two groups: Baka 35,000; Bayaka 11,000.
Other 0.5%. French; British.
Refugees: Chadians fleeing civil war in their land have fluctuated between 50,000 and 200,000.

Literacy 62%. **Official languages:** French, English. **All languages** 275. **Languages with Scriptures** 18Bi 24NT 31por.

Capital: Yaoundé 712,000. Other major city: Douala 1,117,000. Urbanization 42%.

Economy: An agricultural economy, but boosted by oil exploitation in the '80s. The depletion of oil reserves and decline in earnings on cocoa and coffee have put stress on the economy. Political uncertainty has further worsened prospects of improvement. Income/person $1,010 (5% of USA).

Politics: A German colony between 1884 and 1919, then divided between Britain and France. Independence from France in 1960, and union with English-speaking West Cameroon in 1961 as a bilingual one-party republic. The first president, a Muslim Fulani, was replaced by a Catholic southerner in 1982. Popular pressure forced the President to accede to multi-party elections in 1992, but blatant manipulation of the results to prevent change could lead to political upheaval and even civil war.

Religion: Secular state which guarantees religious freedom. Controls on Christian activities in the more Islamized north and promotion of Islam nationwide until the change in leadership in 1982.
Tribal religions 12%. Numerous among central and northern non-Muslim peoples and of considerable influence among Muslims and "Christians".
Muslim 24%. Strong among the Fulani, Mandara, Shua Arab, Kotoko, Kanuri; increasing among the Mbum and Fali.
Baha'i 0.8%.
Christian 63.2%. Nom 17%. Affil 46.2%. Growth 3.3%.
Protestant 22%. Nom 7.1%. Affil 14.9%. Growth 4.3%.

Church	Cong	Members	Affiliated
Ev Ch of Cameroon	1,700	300,000	500,000
Presbyt Church	1,050	179,352	250,000
Presbyterian Ch of C	1,745	113,000	200,000
Cameroon Baptist	720	54,000	106,000
Baptist Union	170	43,000	86,000
Evang Lutheran	248	49,600	82,629
Seventh-day Adventist	494	39,279	74,100
Baptist Conv (NAB)	511	38,538	64,200
Lutheran Brethren	808	18,514	49,433
Un Ev Chs in Nth Cameroon	232	17,400	39,700
Full Gospel Miss (AoG)	272	10,335	15,774
All other (11)	1,567	114,695	208,372
Denominations (22)	9,517	977,713	1,676,208
Evangelicals 4.9% of pop		300,000	550,000
Pentecostal/charis 0.84%		47,000	94,000

Missionaries:
to Cameroon 689 (1:16,300 people) in 48 agencies.
from Cameroon 34 (1:49,300 Protestants) in 3 agencies 2frn 24xcul 10dom.

Roman Catholic 40%. Nom 9.8%. Affil 30.2%.
Growth 2.8%.
Catholic Ch   3,138 2,040,000 3,400,000
Missionaries to Cameroon 1,640 (1:6,900 people).
Foreign Marginal 0.3%. Affil 0.25%.
Growth 1.7%.
Jehovah's Witnesses 481   13,000   26,000
All groups (4)   491   13,836   28,200
Indigenous Marginal 0.9%. Affil 0.81%.
Growth 5.2%.
All groups (50)   398   40,400   91,000

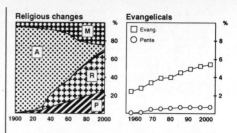

1. **Praise God for present religious freedom**, church growth, and localized touches of revival. Yet the overall situation gives rise for concern:

a) **Political uncertainty** and the danger of civil war. Endemic corruption in government, and unwillingness of the leaders to relinquish power through the ballot box are building widespread resentment. Pray for peaceful change and leadership for the country which will bring unity in a land with such ethnic and religious diversity. Without this, disaster could come.

b) **Spiritual poverty among Christians.** Widespread nominalism and liberal teaching given to church leaders has led to lowering of spiritual standards, pagan practices among Christians, and unchallenged pride, compromise and sin among leaders. Pray for deep repentance, lasting deliverance and true revival, and a restoration of Bible reading, preaching and holiness among Christians.

2. **Christianity is predominant in the centre and south** – the fruit of a century of Presbyterian, Baptist and Lutheran missionary activity. Yet denominational and language barriers have prevented leaders from developing spiritual fellowship and common goals for the advancement of the cause of Christ. Pray for unity and vision for evangelism and missions to transform the church in the '90s.

3. **The north is still a pioneer area** where Christians are relatively few. For years, the Muslim Fulani dominated the trade and politics of the region, but this has been reduced since 1982. The contribution of Lutheran Brethren missionaries from the USA and Norway, the **SUM**, German Baptists and the Full Gospel Mission (**AoG**) has been decisive and the churches have grown faster there than elsewhere in the country. Intercede for these young churches that they may powerfully witness to the pagan and Muslim peoples around them.

4. **Theological training** is the key need. Few outside the north are evangelical. Pray for the provision of born-again, godly national and expatriate staff for the 10 accredited denominational and interdenominational schools in Cameroon. Pray also for a spiritual revolution in these theological faculties and seminaries which will bring new life and biblical standards to churches so long deprived of these.

5. **Bible translation** for Cameroon's 275 languages is an overwhelming task. Only 32 have a Bible or New Testament. **SIL** and **UBS** are involved in 50 translation projects. For 38 more languages, there is a proven need for translation, but further research in another 125 languages may increase that number. Pray for Cameroonian and expatriate translators to be called, trained and deployed. The lack of Scriptures in indigenous languages is a major reason for spiritual poverty in the churches.

6. **The missionary force** is predominantly from USA (303), Norway (99), Switzerland (65), Germany (61) and Nigeria (32). The largest agencies are **SIL** (194), Norwegian Lutheran Mission (95), **SUM** (20), North American Baptist Conference (32) and European Baptist Mission (18). Pioneer missionaries are needed to reach the Muslims and northern pagan peoples, and for Bible translation ministry. Evangelical missionaries could help bring new life and vigour to the more nominal churches – but this requires skills and gifting of a high order.

7. **Less reached peoples.** Pray for careful, in-depth research into the spiritual needs of every people and area in the country.

a) **The many peoples of the Mandara mountains**, 30% Muslim but mostly fetishist, among some of whom **SUM** is beginning to see a breakthrough. The Zulgwa and Mambila are stone-age peoples.

b) **The northern plains peoples** – Giziga, Mofu, Kapsiki, Gude and Gidar among whom Lutheran Brethren missionaries are at work.

c) The less-responsive **Adamawa peoples** – especially the Pygmy Baka (to whom Presbyterians have gone) and Bayaka.

d) **Islam is dominant in eight peoples**, and Christians are few but increasing in numbers. Pray for:
   i) **The Fulani**, with only a handful of Christians.
   ii) **The Kanuri/Kotoko** – a burden for entry for the Lutheran Brethren.
   iii) The Arab **Shuwa** – no Christians and no outreach.
   iv) The Islamized **Fali** and **Mbum**.

8. **Supportive ministries** for prayer:
a) **Christian literature** is not used widely enough. More literature workers, both expatriate and national, are needed for writing, publishing and distributing French, English and local language materials.
b) **Cassette ministries** have been used by churches – **UBS** (Bible reading) and **GRn** with recordings available in 147 languages/dialects. This is a valuable tool in a multilingual land.
c) The **GBEEC** (**IFES**) witness among students is small but vibrant and growing.
d) **Christian radio programmes** may be aired on local stations; few workers have the skills or equipment to prepare quality material. *Sawtu Linjiila* is a studio run by the three Lutheran missions working in Cameroon, Chad and Central African Republic, which produces French and Fulani radio programmes, cassettes, and audio-visual materials. The aim is pre-evangelism among the northern Cameroon peoples who use Fulani as a trade language.
e) There are four **SIM** workers serving with the Swiss-based Helimission, which operates a helicopter service for Christian ministries.
f) **The *Jesus* Film** has been dubbed in the language of the Adamawa Fulani.

March 22–23
North America

Canada

Area 9,980,000 sq.km. The world's second largest country. Wide diversity of mountains, prairie grasslands and forests but much is sparsely populated wilderness and arctic tundra.

Population		Ann. Gr.	Density
1990	26,525,000	0.89 %	3/sq.km
1995	27,567,000	0.77 %	3/sq.km

16% of population born abroad. 80% of population live within 150 km. of the 7,000 km. US border.

Peoples: A mosaic of indigenous and immigrant nations and peoples, many of whom have retained much of their original cultures. The high degree of inter-cultural marriages makes classifications only approximate.
British 37%. Majority in east, centre and west.
French 27.7%. Majority in Quebec Province. Although Canada is officially bilingual with equal rights for all, the French minority includes a considerable separatist segment.
Other European/mixed origin 23.6%. Representing every nation of Europe.
Asian 4.3%. Chinese 780,000; Indo-Pakistani 280,000; Filipino 95,000; Vietnamese 60,000; Japanese 43,000; Korean 29,000.
Indigenous 3.2%. Amerindians (Canadian Indians) 800,000 speaking 65 languages; Inuktitut or Inuit (Eskimo) 32,000.
Middle Eastern 3.2%. Jewish 747,000; Arab 93,000; Iranian 15,000; Turkish 5,000.
African 0.9%. Afro-American, Afro-Caribbean and African.
Latin American 0.13%.

Literacy 96%. **Official languages:** English, French. **All indigenous languages** 78. **Languages with Scriptures** 2Bi 4NT 36por.

Capital: Ottawa 819,000. Major cities: Toronto 3,427,000; Montreal 2,968,000; Vancouver 1,389,000. Urbanization 77%.

Economy: One of the world's leading industrial nations. Over 80% of Canada's trade is with the USA, with which it is closely linked in a free trade agreement. This interdependence moderates trends towards an economic nationalism. Public debt/person $11,760. Income/person $19,020 (90% of USA).

Politics: A federal monarchy with parliamentary government. Independent of Britain in 1867. The unity of Canada is under threat due to increasing polarization between the French-speaking Quebec and the other, English-speaking provinces. A referendum in 1992 on constitutional change rejected government proposals to settle the issue, and the break-up of Canada could be the consequence. Intense negotiations are also under way to restore up to one-fifth of Canada's territory to the indigenous peoples.

Religion: Freedom of religion, but a rapid secularization of every level of society is taking place.
Non-religious/other 12.1%.
Non-Christian religions 4.4%. Jews 1.2%; Sikhs 0.94%; Muslims 0.8%; Hindus 0.75%; Chinese/Buddhist 0.36%; Baha'i 0.2%; Animist 0.1%.
Christian 83.5%. Nom 19.2%. Affil 64.28%. Attend 20.8%. Growth 0.9%.
Protestant 32.2%. Affil 18.07%. Growth −0.5%.

Church	Cong	Members	Affiliated
United Church	4,081	808,441	2,013,256
Anglican Church	3,076	514,475	817,021
Pente Assemblies	1,000	194,972	300,000
Canadian Bapt Fed	1,135	133,032	242,000
Presbyterian Church	1,023	156,513	215,369
Ev Lutheran Ch	654	150,072	207,264
Fell of Ev Bapt Chs	492	60,566	110,000
Salvation Army	407	26,304	94,733
Chr Reformed Ch	235	50,927	88,892
Lutheran Ch – Can	349	65,590	85,584
Chr & Miss Alliance	327	26,794	74,290
Conf of Menns in C	156	28,994	60,400
Gen Conf of Menn Breth	317	27,751	43,452
Pente Assembs of Newfoundland	160	15,707	31,719
Ch of the Nazarene	157	10,844	18,100
Assoc Gospel Chs	123	9,402	17,502
Can Conv of Sthn Bapt	110	6,304	12,600
All other (61)	4,033	277,735	500,349
Denominations (78)	17,835	2,564,423	4,932,531
Evangelicals 7.7% of pop		1,126,000	2,108,000
Pentecostal 1.52%		249,000	415,000
Charismatic est. 2.8%		353,000	778,000

Missionaries:
from Canada 5,432 (1:4,900 Protestants) in 118 agencies 3,760frn 3,567xcul 1,835dom.
to Canada 403 (1:65,800 people).
Roman Catholic 45.2%. Affil 41.67%. Growth 1.7%.

Catholic Ch	5,922	7,510,000	11,375,914
Charismatics 2.9%		525,000	800,000

Majority of French, Spanish, Italian, Portuguese, etc.
Missionaries:
from Canada 2,959 (1:3,800 Catholics).
to Canada 760 (1:35,000 people).
Other Catholic 0.8%. Affil 0.62% Growth −1.8%.
Denominations (4)   904   108,809   171,710
Orthodox 2.9%. Affil 2.23%. Growth 0%.
Greek Orthodox   58   140,000   230,000
Ukrainian Greek
  Orthodox   258   85,200   120,000
All other (37)   211   149,700   258,000
Denominations (39)   527   374,900   608,000
Mostly ethnic minorities of Eastern European, Greek and Middle Eastern origin.
Marginal Groups 2.4%. Affil 1.46%. Growth 3.9%.

Jehovah's Witnesses	1,270	101,713	192,000
Mormons	379	96,300	125,000
All other groups (50)	1,069	83,310	141,000
Total groups (52)	2,718	281,323	458,000

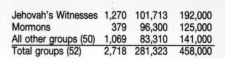

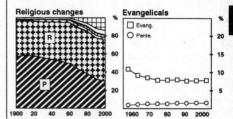

Religious changes   Evangelicals
1900 20 40 60 80 2000   1960 70 80 90 2000

1. **The Christian Church has been marginalized in Canadian society.** Many major denominations have suffered disastrous declines in membership. The loss of biblical roots and lack of vision for evangelism, compromise on homosexuality and moral failure among well-known Christian leaders have all contributed to this tragic situation. Canada needs revival.

2. **The evangelical witness also declined steadily through this century** from 25% of the population in 1900 to about 8% in 1980 and 7.6% in 1990. However, Pentecostal church membership has nearly doubled between 1970 and 1990, and other denominations such as **CMA** have grown even faster. Pray that evangelical Christians may break out of their negative isolationism and unite to make a decisive impact on the nation in its hour of spiritual need.

3. **Vision 2000**, nurtured under the **Evangelical Fellowship of Canada**, was launched by 40 denominations and agencies. The purpose: to serve the Body of Christ in evangelism so that every person in Canada will have the opportunity to see, hear and respond to the gospel by the year 2000; the opportunity being defined as one evangelical congregation for every 2,000 people. This will mean increasing the number of congregations from 8,000 to 14,700. Pray that this big advance may be achieved.

4. **The large number of Bible institutes, colleges and theological seminaries** committed to the orthodox view of Scripture are fulfilling a major role in strengthening the evangelical witness. Most are concentrated in the western Prairie provinces. Pray for those in training and those teaching them, that world evangelization may have priority.

5. **French Canadians** are 85% Catholic in culture, but less than 30% ever attend mass and this percentage continues to fall. Pray for spiritual life and renewal in Catholic institutions and congregations. Evangelicals are only 0.5% of the Francophone population of Quebec, but grew from 150 congregations with 6,000 adherents in 1976 to nearly 400 congregations with 35,000 adherents in 1990. Pray for:
a) **Widespread evangelism** to continue to bear fruit. The rate of conversions slowed in the late '80s.
b) **Increased receptivity** in times of rapid social and political change. For **Vision 2000** to be achieved, 2,300 congregations would need to be started in the provinces.
c) **Quebec separatism** is a potent political movement with unknown implications for Canada's future. Pray that this may stimulate maturity and growth of the churches.
d) **The small, but growing French-speaking Protestant missionary force.**

6. **Canadian Indians** are largely Christian in name, but active evangelistic churches among them are relatively few.
a) **Pray for a moving of God's Spirit** to combat the effects of unintentionally paternalistic missionary work, the high incidence of social and economic problems, and the strident anti-White propaganda that draws many back into old heathen customs.
b) **Pray for the growth of strong, well-led churches** that are culturally Indian. In many parts of Canada a change came after 1981, and hardened communities have been responding to Christ in local revivals.
c) Pray for denominational (Anglican, United Church, **CMA, PAoC,** etc.) and interdenominational (**NAIM Ministries, N. Canada Evangelical Mission,** etc.) missions seeking to evangelize and plant churches – often in the inhospitable northern parts of the country.

d) Although only 25 languages are still actively used, **Bible translation or revision is still needed.** Pray for **SIL** workers and others engaged in 22 language projects.

e) **The one million Canadian Indians living outside reservations** are neglected and needy – especially in the cities.

C

7. **The Eskimos (or Inuit) in the Arctic** are mostly Anglican, but the impact of the worst of Western civilization has greatly altered and harmed the Eskimo way of life. AIDS is a major threat, and the suicide rate is four times the national average. However, since 1982, after a century of nominal Christianity, there has been a wave of conversions and an evident work of the Spirit across the Arctic. Pray that rising nationalistic sentiment might stimulate further spiritual awakening.

8. **Immigrant communities** have multiplied. Toronto lays claim to be the world's most racially diverse city. Vancouver is the world's second-largest Sikh city. Especially significant are:

a) **Asian Indians** (now numbering over 600,000) – 250,000 Sikhs with under 100 Christians, 200,000 Hindus and 150,000 Muslims form the biggest bloc of unreached peoples in the country. **OM** has a team ministering to them in Vancouver and Toronto. Only four known congregations of believers use any of their own languages.

b) **Arabic-speaking peoples,** mostly Muslim or Orthodox Christian; very little specific outreach to them has been undertaken. Most of the few believers are Lebanese or Palestinian.

c) **The Greek, Italian, and Portuguese** communities with few evangelical churches.

d) **The Chinese** (780,000) who will soon number a million people with the influx of immigrants from Hong Kong. There are over 80 growing churches among them.

9. **The missionary vision has been great,** but the number of missionaries has fallen of late. Pray for increased involvement by churches and individuals in the evangelization of the unreached in Canada and around the world. Pray for the stimulation of missionary concern in the many growing evangelical churches among the ethnic minorities; such a vision could be strategic for the evangelization of their lands of origin.

10. Specialized ministries for prayer:

a) **Christian broadcasting.** There are a number of widely appreciated religious programmes on secular radio and TV networks. US Christian stations tend to dominate the airwaves, but recent scandals involving televangelists have brought the medium into disrepute.

b) **Student ministries** in the 266 colleges and universities. These give wide exposure to sections of the campus community. There are three movements linked with **IFES** – IVCF (English), GBU (French) and Ambassadors for Christ Chinese – and also extensive ministries linked with **Navigators** and **CCC.** YFC has a good ministry in high schools. Pray that these and other ministries may make a deep and lasting impact on the 800,000 tertiary students.

Cape Verde Islands

(Republic of Cape Verde)

March 24
Africa

C

Area 4,033 sq.km. Fifteen dry, barren islands 600 km. off the west coast of Africa.

Population	Ann. Gr.	Density
1990 379,000	2.8 %	94/sq.km
1995 444,000	3.2 %	110/sq.km

Peoples:
African 28%; mainly from Guinea-Bissau. **Caboverdian Creole** (mixed race) 71%. **European** 1%.

Literacy 70%, but 84% of adults over 25 have had no formal education. **Official language:** Portuguese. **Trade language:** Portuguese Creole.

Capital: Praia 82,000. Urbanization 35%.

Economy: Deforestation and overgrazing followed by 20 years of drought have devastated the economy. Heavily dependent on aid and remittances from Caboverdian migrants. Unemployment 25%. Public debt/person $292. Income/person $760 (3.6% of USA).

Politics: Independent of Portugal in 1975 as a one-party socialist republic. A revised constitution in 1990 led to multi-party elections and a peaceful change of government.

Religion: The privileged position of the Catholic Church ended in 1975. A secular state with freedom of religion.
Non-religious/other 1.4%.
Christian 98.6%. Affil 95.6%. Growth 2.4%.
  Protestant 3.5%. Growth 5.7%.

Church	Cong	Members	Affiliated
Ch of the Nazarene	23	2,408	9,110
Seventh-day Adventist	27	1,309	3,190
Assemblies of God	3	53	398
God is Love Pente	5	45	345
Baptist Mission Assoc	1	130	260
All other (2)	3	76	115
Denominations (7)	62	4,021	13,418
Evangelicals 2.95% of pop		3,104	11,185
Pentecostal/charis 0.23%		174	858

Missionaries to Cape Verde 22 (1:17,200 people) in 5 agencies.
Roman Catholic 95%. Affil 91.3%. Growth 2.1%.

Catholic Ch	57	163,000	346,000

Missionaries:
  to Cape Verde Is 66 (1:5,700 people).
  from Cape Verde Is 4 (1973 figure).
Marginal 1.12%. Growth 24.1%.

Jehovah's Witnesses	13	642	3,060
Mormons	6	860	1,100
All groups (3)	20	1,552	4,240

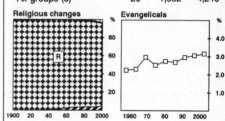

1. **The new democratic leaders** face a daunting task in repairing the damage of years of ecological neglect and socialist planning. Pray for the government, for stability and for social and economic betterment.

2. **Caboverdians are Christian in name,** but in practice are more influenced by superstitions and African fetishism. Pray for true conversions among them. Christian literature in Creole is lacking, most only partially understanding Portuguese.

3. **The steady growth of Evangelicals** has been primarily through the ministry of Nazarene missionaries. There are now churches on most islands with Caboverdian pastors, but the poverty of the islands retards the maturing and growth of the churches.

4. **There are 430,000 Caboverdians** who live in migrant communities, the largest being in New England – USA (250,000), Portugal (50,000), Angola (40,000), Senegal (25,000), Italy (10,000), France (9,000), São Tomé (8,000), Spain (8,000), Brazil (3,000), and Guinea-Bissau (2,000). Pray that many in these communities may become true disciples of Jesus and a blessing to their homeland.

See
Caribbean

Caribbean

Cayman Islands

C

Area 259 sq.km. Three coral islands south of Cuba.

Population		Ann. Gr.	Density
1990	26,000	1.6 %	98/sq.km
1995	28,000	1.5 %	106/sq.km

Peoples. Residents come from 120 nations, 48% being foreign-born.
Afro-Caribbean 59%, including Jamaicans 4,800.
Euro-American 30%. American, Canadian, British.
Latin American/Hispanic 7.9%, mainly Honduran, Cuban, Nicaraguan.
Jews 1.9%.
Asian 1.2%. East Indian, Filipino, Middle Eastern.
Literacy 97.5%. **Official language:** English.

Capital: George Town 13,000.

Economy: Very wealthy through offshore banking and trading. Income/person $19,200 (91% of USA).

Politics: A British dependent territory.

Religion:
Non-religious/other 6%.
Jewish 1.9%; **Baha'i** 0.7%; **Muslim** 0.2%.

Christian 91.2%. Affil 76.9%. Growth 5.6%.
Protestant 81.2%. Affil 74.85%. Growth 5.6%.

Church	Cong	Members	Affiliated
United	20	5,940	9,000
Ch of God (Anderson)	25	1,000	2,500
Ch of God Holiness	15	1,000	2,000
Seventh-day Adventist	7	931	1,550
Baptist Ch	2	166	460
Ch of God (Cleveland)	2	232	387
Baptist Conv (**SBC**)	1	151	252
All other (6)	31	1,628	3,312
Denominations (13)	103	11,048	19,461
Evangelicals 32.3% of pop		4,200	8,400
Pentecostal/charis 1.8%		252	467

Missionaries to Cayman Is 12 (1:2,166 people) in 4 agencies.
Roman Catholic 8.8%. Affil 0.7%. Growth 0%.

Catholic Ch	2	120	200

Missionaries to Cayman Is 4 (1:7,000 people).
Marginal 1.2%. Affil 1.29%. Growth 7.6%.

Jehovah's Witnesses	1	82	205
Other	3	52	130
Groups (2)	4	134	335

1. **The pursuit of wealth and pleasure** is the main preoccupation of the residents. Pray for a spiritual awakening in the churches.

2. **The numerous foreign residents** need to hear the gospel. Pray for effective outreach to those whose first language is not English, for whom little is being done at present.

Central African Republic

(République Centrafricaine)

March 25
Africa

C

Area 623,000 sq.km. A landlocked state in Africa's geographical centre. Variation from tropical forest in the southwest to semi-desert in the northeast.

Population	Ann. Gr.	Density
1990 2,913,000	2.5 %	5/sq. km
1995 3,306,000	2.6 %	5/sq.km

Peoples: Over 100 ethnic groups.
Sudanic 90%. Over 38 languages. Largest: Banda 607,000; Gbaya 542,000; Sango 361,000; Manja 270,000; Mbum 195,000; Kare 72,000; Azande 72,000; Sara 72,000; Tana 63,000; Nzakara 54,000; Maba 44,000; Pana 36,000; Ngbaka 31,000; Kaba Dunjo 31,000; Mbati 27,000; Runga 23,000.
Bantu 3.2%. 11 languages. Largest: Kaka 67,000.
Arab 2.3%. Chad and Baggara Arabs.
West Atlantic 1.9%. Bororo Fulani 58,000.
Chadic-Hausa 1%. Ten languages, mainly on northern borders.
Pygmy 0.8%. Bayaka 18,000; three other small groups.
Other 0.8%. Mainly French.

Literacy 40%, but 73% of population have not had any formal schooling. **Official languages:** French, Sango, the latter a trade language used by most of the population. **All languages** 94. **Languages with Scriptures** 5Bi 4NT 5por.

Capital: Bangui 597,000. Urbanization 41%.

Economy: Underdeveloped subsistence economy due to poor communications with distant seaports. Diamonds and other gemstones are the main exports. Unemployment 30%. Foreign debt/person $264. Income/person $760 (3.6% of USA).

Politics: One-party or military governments 1981–87. A gradually developing multi-party democracy since then.

Religion: Freedom of religion.
Non-religious/other 1.4%. **Baha'i** 0.3%.
Tribal religions 12.3%. Many "Christians" are still following the old ways.

Muslim 3.3%. In the far north, east along the Sudan border, some Fulani in the west and Arabs in towns and capital.

Christian 83%. Nom 40.3%. Affil 42.77%. Growth 2.4%.

Protestant 47.2%. Affil 24.2%. Growth 2%.

Church	Cong	Members	Affiliated
Grace Evang Breth	610	122,000	290,000
Baptist Ch **(BMM)**	118	40,000	100,000
Bapt Ch of the West (Örebro)	712	50,553	95,400
Evang Revival (Elim)	400	18,000	56,300
Cent Afr Ev Ch (AIM)	267	8,000	40,000
Evang Lutheran	215	8,580	22,000
All other (6)	441	40,487	99,880
Denominations (12)	2,763	287,620	703,580
Evangelicals 23.7% of pop		282,000	689,000
Pentecostal/charis 3.1%		33,000	91,200

Missionaries:
to Cent Afr Rep 208 (1:14,000 people) in 24 agencies.
from Cent Afr Rep 14 (1:50,000 Protestants) in 4 agencies 2frn 12xcul 2dom.

Roman Catholic 34%. Affil 17.7%. Growth 2.6%.

Catholic Ch	2,093	299,000	516,000

Missionaries to Cent Afr Rep 504 (1:5,800 people).

Foreign Marginal 0.3%. Affil 0.2%. Growth −4.8%.

All groups (2)	51	1,822	7,030

Indigenous Marginal 1.5%. Affil 0.6%. Growth 15.3%.

All groups (6)	90	9,000	18,000

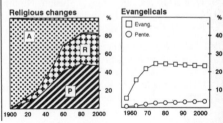

Religious changes   Evangelicals

1. **Few countries have been better evangelized!** Praise God for the massive response to evangelism in the '60s and '70s that brought about rapid church growth. There are now evangelical churches in nearly every tribe and district.

2. **Growth has outstripped the resources of churches to give adequate discipleship to new Christians.** Many are nominal, others are immature in their faith. The lack of Scriptures in local languages, low literacy, and the underlying but often unchallenged powers of darkness have all worked against real depth of commitment or a mature grasp and application of the truths of Scripture. A large evangelical, but often nominal, church is the result. Pray for revival.

3. **Leadership training.** Trained servants of the Lord who are able to give life-changing Bible teaching are in short supply. There are more than a dozen Bible schools for which there is a constant

need for adequate national and expatriate staff. Pray that the right students may be called and that those trained may go out as spiritual and effective Christian workers. The large, underpopulated land makes TEE a key tool for training local leaders, but much work must still be done to develop and maintain this programme all over the country.

4. Mission agencies have played an important role in education and health as well as in planting churches, translating the Scriptures, etc. The largest are Baptist Mid-Missions (55 missionaries), Örebro (40), Grace Brethren (29), Evangelical Lutheran Church of America (13), **AIM** (7). Major missionary sending nations: USA (117), Sweden (40), France (11), Germany (10). Pray for missionaries' health and spiritual fervour in an enervating climate. There are many opportunities for more missionary Bible teachers and those with special skills to help develop a strong indigenous church.

5. There have been tragic divisions between missions and missionaries and between missionaries and local church leaders that have not been a credit to the gospel. Pray for a deeper mutual understanding among the servants of the Lord. Pray for the healing of past wounds, and for cooperation in the building up of the Body of Christ. Pray also that the AEEC (Assoc. of Central African Evangelical Churches) may promote such.

6. The Bangui Evangelical School of Theology opened in 1977 as a result of the initiative of AEAM (Assoc. of Evangelicals of Africa and Madagascar). This was the first theological degree-level school for French-speaking Africa. After many birth pains, this school has now gained stability under African leadership. Pray for this institution and its spiritual impact throughout Africa. Pray for the provision of the right staff and resources. There are now 55 resident students, but it has the capacity to take in 120. The Grace Evangelical Brethren also have a seminary at Bata.

7. The development of secondary and university education means that more must be done to meet the spiritual needs of students. Pray for the GBU (**IFES**) groups in Bangui, and for the Christian Unions now in most of the secondary schools. The Theological Training Secretary of **IFES** for Francophone Africa is based in Bangui. Churches are permitted to organize Bible teaching in school buildings after school hours. Pray that present opportunities may be well used.

8. Bible translation – only four indigenous languages (the trade language, Sango, also Gbaya, Mbai and Zande) have the whole Bible. Pray for effective use of the new revision in Sango. Over one million speak this language, and 200,000 use it as their home language. In seven other languages Bible translation is now being undertaken, but up to 74 may need translators.

9. Unreached peoples. There has been an influx of Muslims who present the greatest challenge at present – a task for which local believers are not yet equipped.
a) **Arabs.** Many are migrants fleeing from Sudan, and most live in the towns. Others are nomadic pastoralists in the north.
b) **Hausa** (10,000) are strongly Muslim. Nothing at present is being attempted to reach them.
c) **Fulani.** Less strongly Muslim – there is now some work by the Baptist Church of the West and Swedish Örebro missionaries.

10. Other less evangelized indigenous groups.
a) **The Pygmy Binga** being evangelized by French and local missionaries.
b) The less evangelized **Sara** groups along the border with Chad. Some are partially Islamized.
c) The partly Muslim **Runga** in the northern tip of the country. Little has been done to reach this tribe, which also lives in Chad and Sudan.

Chad

(Republic of Chad)

March 26
Africa

C

Area 1,284,000 sq.km. Desert in the north, dry grassland in centre, thick bush in the south.

Population	Ann. Gr.	Density
1990	5,678,000	2.5 %	4/sq.km
1995	6,447,000	2.6 %	5/sq.km

Most live in southwest.

Peoples: Ethnic groups: 181. Tribal, cultural and regional differences have dominated the area for centuries. The ethnic and linguistic confusion defies a detailed description! Populations below are estimates.
Sudanic (99 peoples) 44.2%. Largest: Sara and related tribes 1,100,000; Masalit 122,000; Daju (2) 100,000; Karanga 95,000; Mundang 83,000; Bulala 70,000; Bagirmi 67,000; Tana 58,000; Banda 57,000; Tama 50,000; Massalit 75,000; Maba 47,000; Sungor 32,000; Fur 6,000.
Arab 27.3%. Many are nomadic, and live interspersed among other peoples.
Chadic (48 peoples) 19.4%. Marba 100,000; Tupuri 100,000; Tobanga 64,000; Musgu 62,000; Somrai 50,000; Nancere 30,000.
Saharan (9 peoples) 7.8%. Teda/Tubu/Goran 187,000; Kanembu 67,000; Bideyat/Zaghawa 59,000; Kreda 46,000; Daza 34,000.
West Atlantic 0.9%. Fula (6) 51,000.
Other 0.4%. French 3,000.

Literacy 17%. **Official languages:** French (only spoken by the educated), Arabic (spoken by about 60% of the population). **All languages** 126. **Languages with Scriptures** 8Bi 17NT 9por.

Capital: N'Djamena 500,000. Urbanization 24%.

Economy: A subsistence economy due to the lack of rainfall and distance from the sea. The combination of severe droughts and 25 years of civil war has devastated the country. Public debt/person $73. Income/person $190 (0.9% of USA).

Politics: Independent from France in 1960. The non-Muslim Southerners were politically dominant until 1978, but since 1979 northern Muslim factions have fought among themselves for power, with interventions by Libya, France and other powers. There has been a succession of military governments, but with localized rebellions commonplace. The latest regime that seized power in 1990 has promised multi-party elections. A sustained peace in the foreseeable future looks unlikely.

Religion: Muslims dominant in government since 1979, but there has been religious freedom within the constraints of continual civil war. Christians were heavily persecuted between '73 and '75 by the then President, a southerner.
Muslim 45.5%. All the Arab and Saharan groups in the centre and north; a few among Chadic tribes and Sudanic southerners.
African traditional religions 19.1%. Still dominant in many of the Sudanic and some of the Chadic peoples in the south.
Baha'i 0.2%. **Other** 0.1%.
Christian 35.1%. Nom 15.3%. Affil 19.8%. Growth 4%.
Protestant 14%. Affil 13.3%. Growth 4.9%.

Church	Cong	Members	Affiliated
Ev Ch of Chad (EET)	1,030	59,209	329,000
Christian Brethren	600	82,400	230,000
Ev Ch of the Brethren	901	21,300	64,600
Baptist Ch	292	38,000	63,300
Lutheran Brethren	595	17,127	43,827
Ch of God (Cleveland)	76	3,600	12,000
All other (4)	83	4,412	10,610
Denominations (10)	2,766	226,048	753,337
Evangelicals 13.3% of pop		226,000	753,000
Pentecostal/charismatic		6,400	18,600

Missionaries:
 to Chad 249 (1:22,800 people) in 28 agencies.
 from Chad 54 (1:14,000 Protestants) in 2 agencies 2frn 32xcul 22dom.
Roman Catholic 20.5%. Affil 6%. Growth 2.1%.

Catholic Ch	2,378	181,000	341,000

Missionaries:
 to Chad 406 (1:14,000 people).
 from Chad 2 (1973 figure).
Foreign Marginal 0.02%. Growth 11.3%.
Indigenous Marginal 0.6%. Affil 0.5%. Growth 4.4%.

All groups (6)	99	9,900	30,000

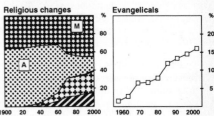

Religious changes

Evangelicals

1. **Civil war and political infighting since independence have fragmented the country** along religious and ethnic lines. Pray for reconciliation and peace, so that the message of the gospel may cross ethnic divisions to the many unreached peoples.

2. **There was rapid church growth in the '60s and '70s.** The work of various missions in the south was blessed by God. During 1973-75 the government severely persecuted Christians who refused to revert to heathen customs. Hundreds were martyred. Church growth slowed in the '80s as nominalism, lack of teaching and legalism sapped the inner life of the church while war, famine and poverty hampered evangelistic outreach. Pray for revival.

3. **The church needs much prayer:**
a) **Growth** has outstripped the availability of resources and trained personnel for discipling. The lack of the Bible in many languages, and illiteracy, make this task the more urgent.
b) **Training of pastors and evangelists** was hindered by war, evacuation of missionaries and the lack of finances to support students in training. Pray for the Shalom Higher School of Theology in N'Djamena and for secondary- and primary-level Bible schools in the south. Pray that the new generation of pastors may be men full of the Holy Spirit. Pray also for refresher courses arranged for those already in the ministry.
c) **Tribalism, syncretic life style and petty legalisms** cripple many congregations. Pray for liberation from all bondages by a deep working of the Holy Spirit in every congregation.
d) **Witness to Muslims is rare.** There are huge cultural, historical and emotional barriers to be overcome. Pray for the vision of EET/MEU to train Chadian missionaries to reach the unreached in the Chari region and beyond. The EET has a missionary society with 26 missionary couples, most of whom are working cross-culturally.

4. There are more **totally unreached** peoples in Chad than in any other African country. AIM and EET have conducted an excellent preliminary survey of the needs. Of the 180 peoples, 30 have strong churches, 30 weaker, and a further 11 Animist and 109 Muslim peoples are still unreached. Praise God for new initiatives by **TEAM, AIM, WEC** and **SUM** to reach them. Pray specifically for:
a) **Arabic-speaking peoples,** hard to reach, specially those that are nomadic. Some are becoming Christians in the east of the country.
b) **Desert tribes of the north** – the Teda, Tubu, and Daza – among whom Frontiers is opening up an outreach, and also the Zaghawa-Bideyat.
c) **Tribes of Lake Chad.** Earlier work started by EET and TEAM missionaries was aborted by war. TEAM has resumed work among the Kanembu and SIL among the Buduma.
d) **Bagirmi** (WEC, Swiss SUM, Lutheran Brethren) among whom there are only five known believers. Pray for their discipling and the planting of a church among the Bagirmi.
e) **The 17 tribes of the Ouaddai** in east central Chad, including the Tama, Massalit, Maba, Daju, Assangori, Massalit, Fur (French **SUM, WEC**). Only about 15 Christians are known in the area.
f) The **Hadjerai** peoples and Daju of the central Guera region. There is a group of churches and a small Bible school in the Mongo and Bitkine area (Brethren and EMET), but most of these peoples are unreached.
g) **N'Djamena,** the only city in the country, is rapidly becoming a centre of Islamic propagation, with many mosques but only 40 or so churches. Many southern Christians gather in these churches, but they make little impression on the Muslim majority. Pray for missionaries working in N'Djamena and for others to be called.

5. **Missionary work** continues despite the upheavals of the past three decades. The main missions groups are *Mission Evangélique Unie* (MEU) with five member missions – TEAM (32 workers), French SUM (9), Swiss SUM (4), WEC (18), EMEK (6) – and other missions who have seconded workers (AP, AIM, etc.), also EMET (8), Lutheran Brethren (8), Grace Brethren (6). Major missionary contributing nations: USA (70), UK (23), Switzerland (19), France (15), Canada (13), Germany (13), Nigeria (10). The need for new workers is obvious, but pray for those with a pioneer spirit and perseverance to give years to language learning, necessary to contribute much to the unreached and to developing churches. Pray also for their daily provision and safety.

6. Specialized ministries:
a) **Bible translation** is a pressing need because of the linguistic diversity. Some church services have to be conducted in three or four languages! The social turmoil and economic difficulties have slowed translation work now being done in 17 languages. Possibly 78 other languages are in need of NTs. The Bible Society is involved in eight projects, and **SIL** is surveying the need and sending in translation teams. Pray for wisdom, perseverance and safety for all involved.
b) **Missionary Aviation Fellowship** with four workers and one plane gives a vital service in a land torn by war and hampered by vast distances and poor communications. Pray for safety, supply of needs, and secure, effective bases for this programme.

c) **GRn** has produced recordings in 50 languages; this is a ministry that could be profitably expanded.

d) **Christian students,** many of whom are affiliated with *Union des Jeunes Chrétiens* (**IFES**), need leadership training and adequate training materials.

Channel Islands

See under UNITED KINGDOM

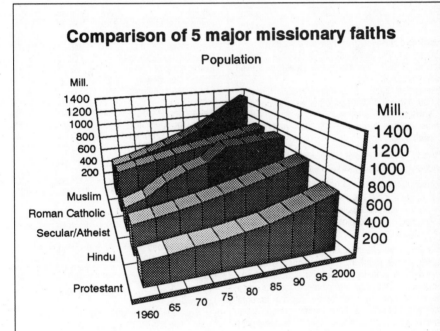

Shown here are five major systems of belief (or unbelief) that contend for the commitment of mankind. These figures are for religious profession and portray the growth of each between 1960 and 2000. Note:

1. The varying growth rates.

2. Muslims are the fastest growing of the major religions, increasing their percentage of the world's population from 12.4% in 1900 to 21.5% in 2000. Yet graphs to follow show that this has been largely due to a higher birth rate.

3. The only belief systems to grow significantly by **change of allegiance** are Secularists and Atheists until 1980 and Protestants since then (see p 183 for the much higher growth of Evangelicals). The change came with the loss of credibility in Communism – the plateau in the Secular/Atheist column shows this.

4. The growth of Catholics has been slower than that of the world's population, so their percentage of the world's population is steadily falling.

March 27	
Latin America	

C

Chile

(The Republic of Chile)

Area 757,000 sq.km. A 4,200-km.-long country wedged between the mountains of the Andes and the Pacific Ocean and averaging only 150 km. in width. Also Easter Island in the Central Pacific. Great extremes of climate from the hot northern Atacama Desert to Antarctic tundra in the south.

Population		Ann. Gr.	Density
1990	13,173,000	1.7 %	17/sq.km
1995	14,237,000	1.6 %	19/sq.km

Peoples: A relatively homogeneous society.
Chilean 91.6%. European 20% (Spanish, Italian, French, British, German, etc.), Mestizo (mixed Spanish/Indian) 71.6%.
Amerindian 6.8%. Mapuche 600,000; Quechua 95,000; Aymara 68,000; six other small peoples.
Polynesian 0.02%. Rapanui 3,500 on Easter Island.
Other 1.6%. European 120,000; Arab 2,600; Chinese 1,500.

Literacy 95%. **Official language:** Spanish. **All languages** 7. **Languages with Scriptures** 2Bi 1por.

Capital: Santiago 5,134,000. Urbanization 84%. 40% of the people live near the capital and 85% in the temperate central provinces. The northern desert, and wet, cold mountains in the south have few inhabitants.

Economy: Mining and export of minerals, especially copper, is the most important economic activity. Considerable industrialization and agricultural development. Draconian implementation of free market policies by the former regime brought economic stability, a trade surplus, and some growth but at great social cost. Unemployment 4.7%. Public debt/person $823. Income/person $2,900 (14% of USA).

Politics: Republic independent from Spain in 1810. The elected socialist government was ousted in a bloody military coup in 1973. The controversial Pinochet regime imposed political conformity and economic change with widespread human rights abuse. The referendum and electoral defeats in 1988/9 opened the way for a democratic government which is cautiously seeking to rectify the damage to health and education and to heal the deep divisions in society.

Religion: The Catholic Church was disestablished in 1925. Freedom of religion, but the period of military dictatorship divided the church – both Catholic and Protestant.
Non-religious/other 9.2%.

Animist 1.4%. On the increase among the nationalistic Mapuche, but occult practices permeate Chilean culture.
Jews 0.24%. **Baha'i** 0.1%. **Muslim** 0.03%.
Christian 89%. Growth 1.8%.
Protestant 27.9%. (Estimates vary from 16% to 30%.) Growth 5.2%. Nearly all Pentecostal figures are estimates; few keep records.

Church	Cong	Members	Affiliated
Pentecostal Methodist	3,250	520,000	720,000
Ev Pente Ch of C	1,680	400,000	571,000
Pentecostal Ch of C	300	150,000	400,000
Seventh-day Adventist	329	69,000	98,600
Evang Army of Chile	722	65,000	92,900
Baptist Convention	225	24,600	40,000
Chr & Missry Alliance	185	11,117	33,350
Methodist Ch of C	77	6,000	25,000
Assemblies of God	445	10,000	24,000
Ch of God (Cleveland)	196	14,324	20,500
Pentecostal Ch of God	37	14,000	20,000
Anglican Ch of Chile	93	6,500	11,500
All other (1,205)	9,100	964,917	1,605,538
Denominations (1,217)	16,639	2,255,458	3,662,388
Evangelicals 26.7% of pop		2,174,000	3,522,000
Pentecostal/charis 25.4%		2,060,000	3,340,000

Missionaries:
to Chile 565 (1:23,300 people) in 56 agencies.
from Chile 102 (1:35,900 Protestants) in 8 agencies 39frn 29xcul 73dom.

Roman Catholic 57.7%. Attend 15%. Growth 0%.

Catholic Ch	3,508	6,230,000	10,388,000
Doubly counted		−1,800,000	−2,787,000
Total		4,430,000	7,601,000
Charismatics		31,000	52,000

Missionaries:
to Chile 135 (1:97,600 people).
from Chile 550 (1973 figure).
Orthodox 0.2%. Growth 0.6%.

All groups (5)	22	14,850	26,115

Foreign Marginal 2.8%. Growth 12.8%.

Mormons	570	160,000	266,000
Jehovah's Witnesses	429	44,067	107,000
All groups (3)	1,003	204,187	373,171

Indigenous Marginal 0.43%. Growth 4.5%.

All groups (6)	193	37,000	57,000

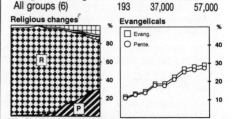

Religious changes

Evangelicals
☐ Evang.
○ Pente.

C

1. **The growth of Evangelicals in Chile is unique.** A Pentecostal revival in 1909 within the Methodist Church gave birth to a dynamic, indigenous Pentecostal movement with great evangelistic zeal. The lower classes were evangelized and churches and denominations multiplied. Possibly one quarter of the population is now affiliated with an evangelical group; 21.5% of these are linked with indigenous Pentecostal groups. Pentecostal growth has pressured the Catholic Church to change; there is a strong Catholic charismatic renewal movement.

2. **The government** faces an almost impossible task in closing the book on the traumatic events of the past 20 years. The just grievances of those who suffered and the fears of those involved in oppression have to be faced. Pray that:
a) People might turn in repentance to God and thereby find healing and unity for the nation.
b) Christians might repent of their carnality in allowing political divisions to divide them and that the prophetic role of the Church to the nation might be restored. Pentecostal enthusiasm for the discredited dictatorship has diminished such a role.
c) God might raise up political and spiritual leaders for the nation who fear him and seek to do his will.

3. **The Roman Catholic Church has been deeply affected** by two major forces:
a) **Social upheaval** and reaction to the excesses of the dictatorship in "Liberation Theology" and the Base Community movement. This led to coldness between Catholic leadership and the former regime.
b) **The widespread distribution and use of the Bible**, the growth of the charismatic movement, and a significant exodus of Catholics to evangelical churches.
Both are being challenged by the conservative Pope John Paul II. Pray that many Catholics may find true liberation and peace through a personal faith in Christ.

4. **Consolidation of the work must follow decades of evangelical growth.** Major areas to cover in prayer – especially for the large number of Pentecostal denominations:
a) **Development of evangelistic strategies for the '90s.** Widespread street preaching harvested many in the past, but no longer. Middle classes have been less affected by the indigenous Pentecostal movement.
b) **Effective teaching of believers.** Personal revelations have often been made equal to the Bible. Preaching can often be unprepared exhortations; general Bible knowledge and understanding are limited among leaders and followers. Petty legalisms often are prized more than holiness of heart. Mormonism has grown rapidly – mainly through winning Pentecostals. Pentecostal nominalism is becoming a problem.
c) **Leadership** which tends to be strong and domineering. Power-seeking and rivalry have sadly led to many divisions. There may be anything from 1,500–5,000 denominations as a result.
d) **Effective grounding of leaders in the Scriptures.** An earlier sentiment against Bible schools is changing. Pray for the **Pentecostal Bible Institute** launched by **AoG** and **PHC** for training pastors of indigenous denominations, and for its acceptance in these denominations.
e) **Local vision to become world vision.** Lack of meaningful fellowship links with other lands has stunted exposure to the world's spiritual needs.

5. **Evangelical denominations** with foreign roots have, generally, been more effective in reaching the middle and upper classes. The Baptists, **CMA**, Anglicans (**SAMS**), **AoG**, **CoN**, **SIM** and others have made some progress in planting churches among them. Pray for every stratum of Chilean society to be reached.

6. **The Chilean missionary movement** has not developed as much as it could. Geographical isolation, political upheaval and lack of exposure have all contributed to this. The sinking of OM's ship MV *Logos* off the southern tip of Chile in 1988 contributed to a new level of interest in missions in the south. The influence of COMIBAM on the Latin American Missions movement and the involvement of **CMA** in their Bible school and **OM** and **YWAM** in setting up missions training programmes have further stimulated interest in missions.

7. **Foreign missions in Chile.** The major agencies are **SBC** (88 missionaries), **SAMS** (36), **ABWE** (32), **YWAM** (30), **MTW** (29), **AoG** (27), Gospel Mission of S. America (26), **CMA** (25), Brethren (21) and BBF (20). Major missionary contributing nations: USA (372), Germany (63), UK (33), Canada (23), Korea (21), Sweden (20), Brazil (18). The major task for missionaries is to serve the large Chilean Church in teaching, developing Chilean leadership and encouraging a missionary vision.

Pioneer work is limited to some peoples listed below and among the upper class and the urban slum dwellers. Pray that the missionaries' contribution may prove vital for maturing the Chilean Church.

8. Unreached Peoples:

a) **The Mapuche (Auracanians)** are the largest and most independent of Chile's indigenous peoples. A strong nationalist movement is agitating for improved land rights. About 70% are nominally Catholic, but the old religion is still the most influential spiritual force. The work of the Anglican Church has resulted in a strong community of 4,000 Christians. **CMA, AoG** and others have also initiated work among them. Two **SIL** workers are translating the New Testament into one of the dialects.

b) **Rapanui** (Easter Islanders) are a largely Polynesian people. One **SIL** couple is translating the NT into their language. Most are nominally Catholic, but there are 50 evangelical believers in two small fellowships.

c) **The Jews of Santiago. SIM** plans a ministry among them.

9. Christian literature is proving a vital evangelistic and teaching tool, but too few Christians have developed a reading habit. Pray that more pastors buy study books. **CLC** is the only major book distributor in the country; pray for the 26 workers, the four bookstores and the large wholesale distribution network.

10. Student witness in the 17 universities and among the 233,000 students is not strong. There are 10 GBU(**IFES**) groups, but only four are viable. **CCC** (40 overseas workers) has a considerable impact on secondary schools and some universities.

11. Christian radio and TV programmes are widely available on national, commercial and Christian stations. **IBRA** radio has continuous transmission from 10 stations. International broadcasts from **TWR**-Bonaire, **HCJB**-Ecuador and others from the USA beam many hours of Spanish programmes.

China

(People's Republic of China)

Area 9,573,000 sq.km. The third largest state in the world, also containing the highest mountains and plateaux in the world. Taiwan, Hong Kong and Macao have separate governments, and are not included here, although Mainland Chinese regard them as an integral part of China.

Population	Ann. Gr.	Density
1990 1,135,496,000	1.4 %	119/sq.km
1995 1,214,221,000	1.3 %	127/sq.km

By far the largest nation in the world with 21.3% of the world's population. Most live in the better-watered central and eastern coastal provinces.

Peoples:
Chinese (Han) 92%. Eight major languages and 600 dialects but one written language common to all. Putunghua (Mandarin) 744 mill., Wu 78 mill., Yueh (Cantonese) 53 mill., Xiang (Hunanese) 45 mill., Hakka 45 mill., Minnan 34 mill., Minpei 23 mill, Gan 22 mill.
Ethnic minorities 8%. Officially recognized 55; but the true total of ethno-linguistic peoples may be closer to 150. Main groups:
  Tai 2.1%. Zhuang 15,490,000; Bouyei 2,545,000; Dong 2,514,000; Li 1,111,000; Dai 1,025,000; Gelo 438,000; Mulam 159,000; Maonan 72,000. Mainly in south and southwest.
  Tibeto-Burman 1.9%. Over 18 peoples: Yi 6,572,000; Tujia 5,704,000; Tibetan 4,593,000; Bai 1,595,000; Hani 1,253,000; Lisu 575,000; Lahu 411,000; Naxi 278,000; Quiang 198,000; Jinpo 119,000. Mainly southwest and west.
  Mongolian 1.35%. Over nine peoples. Manchu 9,821,000; Mongolian 4,807,000; Xibe 173,000; Daur 121,000; Evenki 26,000.
  Miano-Yao 0.84%. Miao (Hmong) 7,400,000; Yao 2,134,000. Mainly in southwest.
  Hui 0.76%. Chinese Muslims 8,603,000.
  Turkic 0.76%. Over six peoples; all Muslim but for Yugur who are Buddhist. Uygur 7,214,000; Kazakh 1,112,000; Kirgiz (Kyrgyz) 142,000; Salar 88,000; Yugur 12,000; Tatar 5,000. Mainly in northwest.
  Mon-Khmer 0.1%. Over six peoples. Wa 352,000; Shui 346,000; Blang 82,000.
  Other 0.25%. Korean 1,900,000; Tajik 33,500; Russian 13,000. Also foreign experts 60,000.

Literacy 73%. **Official language:** Putunghua (Mandarin Chinese); local languages in the five Autonomous Regions. **All languages** 142. **Languages with Scriptures** 15Bi 13NT 26por.

Capital: Beijing (Peking) 10.8 million. Other cities: Shanghai 13.3 mill., Tianjin 8.8 mill., Chongqing 2.9 mill., Guangzhou 3.5 mill., Shenyang 4.4 mill., Wuhan 3.6 mill., Nanjing 2.4 mill. Thirty-four other cities of over one million inhabitants. Urbanization 37%.

Economy: The Cultural Revolution with its application of an extreme Marxist economic system was a fiasco. Since 1978, the see-saw conflict between the hardliners and pragmatists within the Communist government has been reflected in the degree of economic liberalization. The commune system has been partially dismantled with dramatic improvements in agricultural yields. Much of manufacturing and industry has been opened up for privatization and foreign investment with a 14% average growth rate in the '80s. The most rapid growth has been in the special economic zones adjoining Hong Kong and Macao. The restraints of a massive bureaucracy, fear of political liberalization and inefficient state-run industries slowed growth in 1990, but since 1992 the country has moved strongly into growth and a capitalist economic system. Unemployment 2-20% depending on area.. Public debt/person $46. Income/person $360 (1.7% of USA).

Politics: This great and ancient nation has regained its place of importance in the world after nearly two centuries of decline and humiliation at the hands of the Western powers and Japan. Since the final conquest of mainland China in 1949, the Communist Party has remoulded the nation along Marxist lines. The Cultural Revolution (1966–76) was the culmination of Mao's policy. It caused immeasurable suffering and economic chaos. Intellectuals and religious believers were cruelly persecuted. It is estimated that 20 million Chinese lost their lives during that time. The death of Mao Zedong in 1976 and discrediting of radical leftists in 1978 was followed by a more pragmatic leadership under Deng. He initiated a series of economic, political and cultural reforms and developed links with other nations, but all within the limits set by Deng. The crushing of the 1989 student protest in Tiananmen Square in Beijing and also the collapse of Communism in Europe and the USSR left China diplomatically isolated as the oldest surviving Communist regime. The threatened government responded with a reversion to ideological rigidity and repression of all political, ethnic and religious dissent. Economic reform with tight political control emerged as government policy for the 1990s. In 1997 the British return Hong Kong to China and in 1999 the Portuguese Macao.

C

Religion: Elimination of all religious groups has always been the ultimate aim of the Marxist government. In the '50s the government engineered the infiltration, subversion and control of all organized Christianity. By 1958 this had been achieved through the Three Self Patriotic Movement among Protestants, and the Catholic Patriotic Association among Catholics. During the Cultural Revolution even these front structures were banned, and all religious activity forced underground, giving birth to the house church movement. In 1978 restrictions were eased and the TSPM and CPA resurrected as a means of regaining governmental control of the thousands of house churches. This has been only partially successful. The collapse of Communism in Europe is perceived as due to "religion", so strict controls are maintained over Christian and Muslim organizations and all unregistered activity repressed wherever possible. All figures below are estimates.

Non-religious/other 59.1%. Communist Party members are claimed to be about 50 million – all officially atheist. The atheism propagated in the education system ensures that most young people have no religious knowledge.

Chinese religions 27%. A blending of Buddhism, Taoism, Confucianism and folk religion.

Buddhist 3%. **Traditional Buddhists** 24,000,000; strong among the Zhuang, Manchu, Dai, Lahu, Korean, Bulang. Also **Lamaistic Buddhists** 9,600,000; Tibetans, Mongolians, Naxi, Tu Moimba, Pumi, Yugur, Lhoba.

Animist 2.4%. Mainly among the tribal peoples of the south, southwest and far north. Miao, Hani, Yi, Tujia, Yao, Bouyei, Bai, Va Dong, Li, Mulao, She, Gelo, Shui, Qiang, Xibe, Daur, Evenki, etc.

Muslim 2.4%. Dominant in Xinjiang and Ningxia. The major religion of the Hui, Uygur, Kazak, Kirgiz, Tajik, Uzbek, Tatar, Dongxiang, Salar and Bonan. There are now 43,000 officially-allowed mosques.

Christian 6.1%. Growth 7.7%.
 Protestant 5.1%. Growth 7.1%.

Church	Members	Affiliated
Home meetings	18,800,000	47,000,000
Three-Self Patriotic Mvmt	7,000,000	11,000,000
All groups (2)	25,800,000	58,000,000
Evangelicals 5% of pop	25,140,000	57,130,000

Roman Catholic 0.77%. Growth 10.8%.

Roman Catholic Ch	3,500,000	5,000,000
Catholic Patriotic Assoc	2,600,000	3,700,000
All groups (2)	6,100,000	8,700,000

Indigenous Marginal 0.18%. Growth 13.3%.

All groups (est. 200)	1,000,000	2,000,000

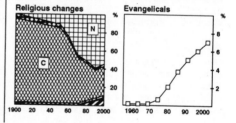

Religious changes   Evangelicals

GENERAL

1. **The growth of the Church in China** since 1977 has no parallels in history. Researchers estimated 30–75 million Christians in 1990 as likely. The State Statistical Bureau in China confidentially estimated 63 million Protestants and 12 million Catholics in 1992. Compare this to the estimated 1,812,000 Protestants and 3,300,000 Catholics in 1949. Most of the growth is in the unofficial house fellowship networks, and through the work of itinerant preachers and numerous local revival movements. Praise God for:

a) **The 140 years of sacrificial seed-sowing** by thousands of missionaries. At one stage there were 8,500 Protestant missionaries, 1,000 of these being with CIM (**OMF**). Their labour was not in vain! Yet it was seen wisest by the Lord to remove them before the harvest that He alone get the glory!

b) **The millions of intercessors** who travailed in prayer for the long-delayed breakthrough. Prayer is changing China.

c) **The manifest bankruptcy of Communism.** Colossal blunders and changes in Party policy over 35 years have disillusioned the people. The fall of personality-cult leaders and the failure of promises for a better future have created a vacuum which only the gospel can fill. The Church of the Lord Jesus is larger than the Communist Party of China. Mao Zedong unwittingly became the greatest evangelist in history. The nepotism, corruption and factionalism of the present Communist Party have become repugnant to the majority.

d) **The Christians who stood firm** in what was probably the most widespread and harsh persecution the Church has ever experienced. The persecution purified and indigenized the Church and has inured it to more recent efforts to weaken and destroy it. In the '60s, Wenzhou City in Zhejiang was selected as a model for the campaign for renouncing religion; it is the most Christian city in China today where Christians officially number 300,000.

e) **The search for Truth among the educated.** The tanks of Tiananmen Square crushed the idolatrous trust in democracy as their solution, and led large numbers of young people to faith in Christ since 1989. The old religions of China have not attracted them, but the claims of Christ have. Until then the growth had been among the poor and the rural population; now every stratum of society has been affected.

f) **The waves of revival** that follow every man-induced or natural disaster. The love and testimony of Christians and the power of the Holy Spirit manifested in miracles, healing and exorcism have played their part.

g) **The fruitfulness of Christian radio** and the remarkable faith of those who broadcast into China for years with little visible evidence of a response.

2. **Barriers to the gospel have been broken down** by the suffering and distress of wars and revolutions this century. The cloying hold of the old religions of idolatrous Taoism, Buddhism and philosophical Confucianism has been broken, and the foreignness of Christianity dissipated. Now is the time of harvest. Pray that the whole land may be evangelized. Over 80% of the population have known only Communism, so the majority has no faith at all. Possibly 500 million Chinese, especially in remote provinces and ethnic minorities, have never heard the gospel. China's 500 million children and young people under 18 are officially forbidden to be exposed to the gospel.

3. **Population control by draconian legislation** and disregard for human rights, family life and moral absolutes have had tragic social consequences with widespread divorce, forced abortion on a massive scale, female infanticide, violence and suicide. Pray for leaders to be raised up for China who will rule with justice. Pray for Christian families to be a light and example to all around. Pray especially that the children of believers may follow in their parents' footsteps, despite mockery, discrimination and a constant barrage of atheistic propaganda.

4. **The Overseas Chinese** number at least 56 million. Of these, 28 million live in the four Chinese-majority territories and states of Taiwan, Hong Kong, Macao and Singapore. The other 28 million live in over 100 nations of the world. Worldwide there has been a significant turning to God among Chinese with highly visible, often wealthy, churches planted within these Chinese communities. Their interest and concern for the spiritual welfare of China has had significant impact – in evangelism, church planting, providing aid and Christian literature. Pray for the growth of overseas Chinese churches, their expansion into unreached Chinese communities around the world and development of China-related ministries.

THE CHURCH IN CHINA

Mar 31–April 2

1. **The TSPM** was reconstituted by the government after 13 years of oblivion. The purpose was to wrest the initiative from the burgeoning house church movement and for the government to gain control of the Church; the amount of political interference has varied widely from district to district. Every form of inducement to extend control over house churches has been used, including coercion, military suppression, threats and promises, but with limited results. In 1991 there were over 7,000 churches linked with the TSPM. Pray for:

a) **Leaders who have compromised** and have been more concerned to implement government policy than obey the Lord Jesus Christ.

b) **Many godly leaders and committed believers** within the TSPM to remain committed to the Truth and fear God more than man.

c) **The 13 officially-sanctioned seminaries**, one of which is specifically for ethnic minority leaders in Yunnan. Much of the instruction is Marxist-oriented and liberal in theology. There are 700 students preparing for ministry, but not all have a call from the Lord. There is a high drop-out rate, and many become enmeshed in administrative work in the TSPM rather than pastoral ministry. Pray that the true believers among them may not lose their faith but be drawn closer to Jesus despite the negative aspects of their training.

2. **The house church movement** and its several networks is the heart of the true Church of China. Its very weakness is its strength. Pray for:

a) **Its commitment to preach Christ and Him crucified** whatever the cost and without compromise. The lack of Scriptures and teaching in depth could affect this.

b) **Its evangelistic outreach.** Witnessing Christians and itinerant preachers have spread the gospel far and wide, but many provinces, districts and towns are still unreached. Yet it is this outreach that is most violently opposed by the authorities. Pray that they may be ever more bold for Jesus and implement their missionary strategy for China.

c) **Its leaders.** Some are old veterans whose ministry began before the Communist takeover. Pray that they may lay the theological foundations for the upcoming generation of young leaders. Most of the latter are in their 20s and 30s and only recently converted. Pray for a right balance between control and freedom in leadership style as the new China emerges.

d) **Its training of leaders.** There are known to be dozens of field/mountain seminaries that gather secretly for three months at a time for fellowship, teaching and preparation for ministry.

e) **Bible study groups on university campuses,** which have multiplied since 1989 with students, graduates, professors and researchers participating. New groups were established in over 12 cities in 1991. This has great significance for the future as a new third wave of church growth in China. Pray for the strengthening and growth of these groups.

3. **Revival and reaction.** Great turnings to the Lord over the past 15 years have deeply affected the provinces of Fujian, Zhejiang, Anhui, Henan and some of the ethnic minorities of Yunnan. In Henan alone, some claim the number of Christians doubled between 1989 and 1991. Pray that other provinces less affected may likewise be touched. The enemy has not been idle. Attacks are coming through:

a) **False teachings.** The many new, untaught and Bible-less converts have easily fallen prey to doctrinal excesses, distortions and error. Millennial extremes and legalistic teachings are common. Exotic names such as *Audible Voice, Queen of the South, Salvation through Knowledge* and the *Shouters* are used. Pray that believers may have discernment and leaders wisdom in correcting these.

b) **Persecution.** This has come in cycles, and was very severe during the Cultural Revolution. Most Bibles were destroyed, believers' homes looted, and believers humiliated. During that time many believers were imprisoned. Between 1983 and 1985, and since 1989, the persecution of unregistered non-TSPM groups and Christian workers has been stepped up. Several thousand believers are known to be imprisoned, and some tortured for their faith since 1989. Pray for the protection and preservation of Christians, and for those imprisoned, and their families, to be upheld. Other Christian workers have been scattered and are in hiding where the pressures have been the most severe. By 1992 it was clear that government policy is to shut down all house churches. The Catholics have suffered particularly severely because of their allegiance to a foreign leader, the Pope. Government control through the puppet CPA has stunted growth and the illegal loyalists have had to carry on very secretively.

April 3–4

CHINA'S LESS REACHED

1. **The Chinese.** The great turning to Christianity has been more among the Han Chinese. By 1992, 6.5–7% were Christian, yet the spread of Christians in society is uneven. Pray for:

a) **Communist Party members.** The official number of 51 million members may be unrealistic. Ideology is a facade to cover self-seeking opportunism. Disillusionment and defection to Christianity have led to many resignations. Pray that the Holy Spirit may convict many more of their sin and need. Among them are also many secret believers!

b) **The armed forces** who are the protectors of the Marxist state, and who jealously guard their privileged position. There are 3,030,000 in uniform, but very few Christians among them.

c) **The "lost generation",** the young people mobilized as the Cultural Revolution Red Guards. The millions involved were morally warped and exploited, losing their youth, education prospects and hopes of betterment in the madness of those years. Pray that they may find hope in Christ.

d) **Those still bound by the idolatrous superstitions** of Taoism, Buddhism and Confucianism. These customs and philosophies are being revived, but young people are not so attracted to them. A new religion, QiGong, is gaining a large following too. Pray for the millions still bound and needing the freedom only the gospel can give.

e) **Students** who are the key for the future. The shock of the events of 1989 have brought many to Christ, but most of the 2,100,000 university students are still unreached. Pray for Christians among them to be built up in their faith and to be fervent witnesses. Pray also for the establishment of Bible study groups on every one of the 1,075 campuses. Pray also for the evangelization of the Chinese sent to study in Japan (90,000), USA (75,000), Australia (40,000) and elsewhere. A number have found the Lord.

f) **The cities.** Some cities in the southeast and centre of the country have many Christians, but the great Chinese cities of Beijing, Tianjin, Taiyuan, Lanzhou and Shenyang have fewer believers and surveillance of their activities is more marked. In these cities alone live 30 million people.

g) **The less evangelized provinces** predominantly in the north and west. Those with possibly less than 1% Christian are **Shanxi, Gansu** and **Jiangxi**. Others with less than 3% Christian are **Qinghai, Hebei, Jilin, Liaoning, Hubei** and **Hunan**. Pray that there may be an outpouring of the Spirit on these less-reached Chinese, and pray for evangelists working in these provinces.

2. **Autonomous regions.** These have been established for five of the most populous ethnic minorities – the Zhuang, Uygur, Tibetans, Mongolians and the Hui – and are the least evangelized areas of China. Massive immigration of Han Chinese has left only Tibet with a clear indigenous majority.

a) **Tibet (Xizang Zizhiqu).** Population 2,200,000. Tibetans 2,100,000. Tibet lost its temporary independence as a theocratic Buddhist state in 1950 when China invaded the land. The Communists have systematically sought to destroy the culture, religion and ethnic identity of the Tibetan people. Resistance to the occupiers has resulted in frequent revolts and unrest. Over one million people may have lost their lives and a further 100,000 may have been forced into exile including the spiritual and political leader of Tibetans, the Dalai Lama.

   i) **Tibetans have long resisted any attempt to bring the gospel to them.** Pray that the present sufferings may be God's means for breaking the demonic bondage of Lamaistic Buddhism. There are no more than a handful of believers in Tibet itself and no known congregations.

   ii) **The political sensitivity and tensions in Tibet** make entry and travel difficult for both Chinese and foreign Christians who desire to witness there. Pray for open doors and freedom to proclaim the gospel.

   iii) **The 2,400,000 Tibetans living in the neighbouring provinces** of Qinghai, Sichuan and Gansu are more accessible for Christian witness, but only a few workers are concentrating on reaching them. Other ethnic groups in the area are more receptive. Pray for the planting of effective Tibetan churches.

   iv) **450,000 Tibetans are in exile.** Nationalism, strong loyalty to Buddhism, and the careful shielding of Tibetans by the Buddhist authorities from any Christian witness make them hard to reach. There are a few congregations among Tibetans in India and a growing responsiveness in Nepal.

b) **Xinjiang Uygur Zizhiqu (Sinkiang):** the vast Central Asian region of deserts, mountains and oases – population 15,155,000 of which the nine Muslim peoples constitute 60% (Uygur, Kazakh, Hui, Kirghiz, Uzbek, Tajik and others); Chinese 39%; Mongolian 1%. There has been a rising level of agitation for independence since the collapse of the USSR in 1990 and considerable resurgence of Iranian-inspired revivalist Islam with many new mosques being built. The proximity of related ethnic groups in the five Central Asian Muslim republics of the former USSR further stimulates nationalistic fervour.

   i) **There were once believers and some churches among the Uygur** in the '30s, but in violence and persecution the churches were destroyed and believers killed or scattered. There are now only a handful of believers among the Uygur. Pray for the completion and distribution of the New Testament and also the dissemination of the *Jesus* film in Uygur.

   ii) **The Muslim Dongxiang, Salar, Bonan, Kazakh, Kirgiz, Tajik, Uzbek and Tatar** in both Xinjiang and the adjoining provinces of Qinghai and Gansu are unreached, with no churches and very little long-term Christian witness to them.

   iii) **The 150,000 Christians in Xinjiang,** almost all Han Chinese, are culturally isolated from the indigenous population. Pray that they may have a vision for and understanding of witnessing to Muslims. Most live in the capital, Urumqi. There are only about 30–40 known Christians among the non-Chinese; their numbers are growing, but they are subjected to heavy pressure by Muslims to return to Islam.

c) **Ningxia Hui.** Population 4,655,000, of which Han Chinese 70%, Muslim Hui 30%. The Hui live in nearly every part of China, but their highest concentrations are in Ningxia and Gansu. They are Han-Chinese-speaking Putunghua but are recognized as a distinct ethnic group. Efforts to reach them have been sporadic. Pray that recent renewed concern for their evangelization will lead to the calling of Christians to serve among them. There are only a scattered few believers known among them.

d) **Nei Mongol (Inner Mongolia).** Population 21,457,000. Han Chinese 86%. Mongolian 11%. Other 3%. The massive influx of Chinese immigrants has swamped and marginalized the indigenous Mongolians, who have clung to their culture and Buddhist religion. The establishment of democracy in the Republic of Mongolia to the north has provoked demonstrations demanding real autonomy for the Mongolians – a desire unlikely to be granted by Beijing. There may be no more than 2,000 Mongolian Christians in China. Pray for an opening up of the Mongolians in China to the gospel. Radio ministry is showing promise. The New Testament in Cyrillic script is available in the republic of Mongolia. Pray for the provision of a Mongolian-script New Testament and for those seeking to plant churches among Mongolians.

e) **Guangxi Zhuang.** The Zhuang are China's largest ethnic minority. For years they were largely neglected by Christians, but over the past seven years great efforts have been made to reach them by means of radio, the *Jesus* film, personal outreach and social programmes. The effects on this Buddhist/animist people have been dramatic, with rapid church growth now taking place. Pray for the complete evangelization of the Zhuang and for the finishing of the New Testament in Zhuang.

3. **Other ethnic minorities.** On average, the percentage of Christians at 1.6% is lower than among the majority Han Chinese. Of the 55 officially-recognized ethnic minorities, 28 are without a known congregation of believers. Some are totally unreached, others have a high proportion of Christians. Pray for:

a) **The Manchu** (9.8 mill. 0.01% Christian) who have lost their language and blended in with the Han Chinese. They live in 15 provinces, but the main concentrations are in Liaoning and Jilin in what used to be Manchuria. There may be no more than 1,000 Christians. Renewed interest is being shown in their evangelization.

b) **The Yi** (6.6 mill. 3% Christian), living mainly in Sichuan and Yunnan. Only since 1949 has a small breakthrough come among the Nosu Yi. The Sani Yi are less reached. Scriptures are needed in at least five of the Yi dialects.

c) **The Tujia** (5.7 mill. 0.2% Christian), **Dong** (2.5 mill. 0.06% Christian), **Bouyei** (2.5 mill. 0.94% Christian), **Li** (1.1 mill; Hainan Is; 0.09% Christian) of the southern provinces who are culturally distinct but beginning to merge into the Chinese culture and losing their languages. Although the first churches were planted nearly a century ago, they have never had the Scriptures in their own tongue.

d) **The unreached peoples of Yunnan.** Ethnic minorities comprise 13 million people in 27 groups without a viable church – Dai, Naxi, Blung, Pumi, Achang, Nung, Jino, Benglong and Drung. Pray that the many Christians among the Lisu (52% Christian), Jingpo (46%), Wa (21%), Lahu (12%), Miao (6%), Hani (4%) and Bai (3%) may catch a vision for the unreached in their area as well as for the relatively few Christians among the Han Chinese of Yunnan.

e) **The unreached of the northern provinces.** Among the following are no known churches: the Buddhist Tu of Qinghai; the Shamanist Xibe of Jilin; the Daur, Oroqen, Hezhen and Evenki of Nei Mongol, the Muslim Salar of Qinghai and Bonan of Gansu.

f) **The Koreans** (1.9 mill., 6.3% Christian) of Jilin and Liaoning, largely unreached, but rapid church growth through evangelism and radio ministry is taking place. Some estimate that there are 130,000 Christians – some reaching out to relatives in North Korea.

4. **Bible translation** is one of the great missions challenges for the '90s. Pray for national and foreign linguists now working on 17 languages, and ask the Lord for translators for the 60 languages for which there is a definite need for a New Testament translation and the 59 others where there may be a need.

April 5–6	SUPPORTIVE MINISTRIES

The rapid growth of the Church and its influence on the democracy movement has heightened the ideological clash since 1989. The Communist Party and the old men that run it feel threatened by the powerful attraction of Christianity. The influence of foreign visitors, students and experts, and the pervasive impact of Christian radio programmes and videos, literature and Bibles have been perceived as decisive in this. Opposition to and vigilance against all activities conducted by foreigners has increased since 1989. Pray that economic desire may overcome ideological fears and keep the door open for Christians.

1. **Missionaries as such are not welcome in China.** Yet China's desire to improve trading relations with the world makes it possible for many Chinese and foreign Christians to enter as:

a) **Tourists.** Over 30 million visited China in 1988. Many Christians were among them. Pray for their ministry of bringing literature, aid, comfort and, in some cases, teaching. Pray also for safety for them and their baggage, tact and wisdom in their contacts and guidance for travel.

b) **Students** – usually for language or culture studies in various universities. In 1991 there were 10,000 from 120 countries. Living conditions are often spartan and uncensored friendships with Chinese hard to maintain. Pray for Christians among them to be used of God to share Christ with those who are genuinely seeking the Lord.

c) **Foreign experts and businessmen.** China aims to recruit about 30,000 experts annually to teach English, Japanese and German as well as other subjects, and also to build up China's technology and industry. Pray that many may be radiant Christians able to impart their faith while on the job.

d) **Chinese family members** who visit their ancestral homes. These have flocked to China in their millions. Christians among them have sometimes seen astonishing results when staying with relatives.

C

2. **Provision of Bibles** is totally inadequate, despite the large increase in the number of copies available. The famine of the Scriptures is most acute in provinces far from ports of entry and for the house churches. In some areas there are reported to be 1,000 or more believers for every Bible. *Amity Foundation,* founded in 1988 and sponsored by the TSPM and the **UBS,** has set up a large printing operation in China, and over 7 million Bibles and New Testaments have been printed since 1981 – nearly all going to TSPM congregations. A further 7 million Bibles and New Testaments are estimated to have been brought in by visitors. Pray that this flow might increase and that every Christian might have access to a copy of God's Word. Importation of Bibles is not illegal but prevented for ideological reasons.

3. **Video and audio tapes.** The increasing availability of play-back machines is making foreign-produced Scripture, song, evangelism and teaching tapes a useful means for disseminating the Truth. Pray for all involved in preparing and distributing these tapes.

a) **The *Jesus* film** is being widely seen on video in homes in 12 completed language versions (eight Chinese dialects and Mongolian, Uygur and Zhuang). A further 14 language editions are planned. Pray that the film may receive official recognition for public showing.

b) **Teaching tapes** that deal with the moral and ethical devastation left by Marxist thought and provide solid biblical teaching are a great need to help the many intellectuals who are coming to faith. Pray for the production of reading materials and tapes to fill this need.

4. **Christian literature.** There is an insatiable demand for hymn books, Bible study and teaching materials, biographies, tracts, and apologetic materials to explain the gospel to students and intellectuals. There are now over 40 titles available (Christian Communications Ltd, **OMF**). Pray for all aspects of publication, entry into China and distribution. Many agencies are involved in this ministry including **AO, CCL OD** and denominational bodies. Pray for many more writers with experience of life in China to be raised up. Pray for wisdom in selection of materials for printing.

5. **Christian radio** has been and still is one of the most potent pre-evangelism and Christian teaching media for China today. Nearly every home now has a radio and a TV. Over 678 hours of broadcasting a week is pouring into China in five Chinese dialects (515 hours in Putunghua alone!) and Akha, Zhuang, Korean, Lahu, Lisu, Mongolian, Miao, Shan, Tibetan, Uygur and Wa. Pray especially for the extensive China-oriented broadcasting of **FEBC** (Manila, Saipan, Korea and Russia), and **TWR** (Guam). There are many major programme producers such as **AO, OMF,** CCRC Seminary of the Air and **CMA.** Pray for wisdom in programme selection and preparation that the message may meet the real needs of the people. There were over 50,000 letters received from listeners between 1979 and 1984, and the volume has continued to increase. Pray for listeners and those who seek to help them. The authorities have fined believers and confiscated radios in some areas for listening to these broadcasts.

Further Prayer Information on China:
1. Asian Report (**AO**).
2. China News and Church report (**CCRC**), PO Box 312 Shatin, N.T., Hong Kong.
3. Chinese around the World (**CCCOWE**), PO Box 98435, Tsimshatsui, Kowloon, Hong Kong.
4. China Prayer Fellowship (**OMF**).
5. Watchman on the Great Wall (**Institute of Chinese Studies, USCWM**).
6. *Pray for China,* Christian Communications Ltd, Box 95364, Tsimshatsui, Hong Kong.
7. News Network International, PO Box 28001, Santa Ana, CA 92799, USA.
8. Chinese Church Support Ministries, 2b Carr Lane, Acomb, York YO2 5HU, UK.
9. *China Insight,* **OMF** China Program, 10 West Dry Creek Circle, Littleton, CO 80120, USA.

C

April 7–8
Asia

China (Taiwan)
(The Republic of China)

Area 36,000 sq.km. A mountainous island 300 km. off coast of mainland China, including the Penghu archipelago, also Matsu and Quemoy Islands near the mainland.

Population

		Ann. Gr.	Density
1990	20,262,000	1.4 %	563/sq.km
1995	21,507,000	1.2 %	597/sq.km

Peoples:

Han Chinese 97.8% speaking three major languages:
  Taiwanese (Hoklo, Minnan) 66.7%. Settled in Taiwan for 300 years.
  Hakka 11%. Settled in Taiwan for 200 years.
  Mandarin 20.1%. Refugees from mainland China 1945–50. Almost entirely urban.
Malayo-Polynesian mountain peoples 1.7% (10 groups). Largest: Ami 153,000; Paiwan 81,000; Tayal 63,000; Bunum 34,000; Taroko 28,000; Drukai 10,000; Yami 2,600.
Other 0.5%. Filipino 50,000; Westerners 25,000; Japanese 10,000; Mongolian 6,000; Tibetan 2,000.

Literacy 92%. **Official language** and language of education: Mandarin. Hoklo and Hakka are widely spoken. **All languages** 21. **Languages with Scriptures** 5Bi 5NT 1por.

Capital: Taipei 2,719,000. Major city: Kaoshiung 1,386,000. Urbanization 74%.

Economy: Rapid industrialization and economic growth to become the world's 14th largest trading power. Unemployment 1.8%. Public debt/person $186. Income/person $7,510 (36% of USA).

Politics: Under Japanese rule 1895–1945, then reverting to China. After the fall of mainland China to the Communists in 1949, Taiwan became the refuge of the Nationalist Chinese government, which still claims to represent all China. This led to international diplomatic isolation and internal political polarization between the mainlanders and many of the indigenous Taiwanese on the issue of continuing part of greater China or independence. Taiwan was effectually a mainlander-dominated one-party republic until the 1987 elections. Since then a more multi-party democracy has emerged. Increasing unofficial trading and tourist links with the mainland, but only if democracy comes would reunification become likely.

Religion: Secular state with freedom of religion.

Non-religious/other 24.2%. Many younger people are secular and abandon their family religions.
Chinese folk religions/Buddhism 70.4%. Blend of Confucianism, Taoism and Buddhism, with strong emphasis on veneration of ancestors.
Muslim 0.4%. Post-war immigrant Hui.
Christian 5%. Affil 4.83% Growth 1.6%.
Protestant 3.1%. Affil 3% Growth 1.9%.

Church	Cong	Members	Affiliated
Presbyterian Ch	1,126	87,500	208,249
Independent Chs	180	36,000	90,000
Little Flock	228	37,440	68,100
Chinese Bapt Conv	100	18,514	37,000
Taiwan Holiness Ch (OMS)	83	10,700	19,400
Ling Leung Tang	8	6,410	15,400
Seventh-day Adventist	41	5,983	15,000
China Free Methodist	53	4,898	7,540
Full Gospel Assembly	75	3,000	7,500
Methodist Church	20	2,543	5,090
Conserv Baptist Assoc	25	1,672	4,780
Fell of Mennonite Chs	20	1,493	4,500
Chr & Miss Alliance	21	1,393	2,090
All other (83)	814	62,773	123,274
Denominations 96)	2,794	280,049	607,923
Evangelicals 2.13% of pop		204,000	431,000
Pente/charis 0.5% of pop		48,000	102,000

Missionaries:
to Taiwan 1,205 (1:16,800 people) in 139 agencies.
from Taiwan 130 (1:4,700 Protestants) in 14 agencies 21 frn 29xcul 110dom.
Roman Catholic 1.6%. Affil 1.52%. Growth 0.6%.

Catholic Ch	782	169,000	307,000

Missionaries to Taiwan 731 (1:27,000 people).
Foreign Marginal 0.1%. Growth 10.3%.

Mormons	47	11,100	17,000
Groups (2)	70	12,790	22,630

Indigenous Marginal 0.2% Growth 1.4%.

True Jesus Church	242	29,400	42,000

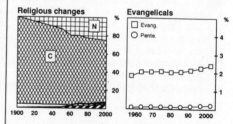

Religious changes / Evangelicals

1. **Taiwan's political future** is a matter for intense political debate and international diplomacy. The growing political power of the Marxist mainland and economic power of capitalist Taiwan are major

factors in the world today. Pray for wisdom and guidance for Chinese and international leaders. The President is a committed Christian.

2. The Church in Taiwan has stagnated for 30 years. After encouraging growth between 1940 and 1960 with a revival and people movement among the mountain people, and many conversions among the Mandarin-speaking mainland refugees, the percentage of Christians has remained static and the Catholics even declined. The breakthrough for the gospel has not yet come. Pray down the barriers to growth:

C

a) **Satanic bondage.** Subjection to the spirit world, gambling and material greed must be broken.
b) **Resurgence of Buddhism and Taoism.** There are over 8,700 temples in the land. Few Chinese want to give up ancestor worship.
c) **Divisions among Christians** – between the older Presbyterian Taiwanese and the newer, more conservative, Mandarin-speaking denominations, and between denominations of Chinese and Western origin.
d) **The lack of pastors and full-time workers.** In most churches the congregation sits back expecting the pastor to do all the work.
e) **Low commitment.** Too few of those converted and baptized ever become active participants in congregational life, and there is a high drop-out rate. Few Christians become soul-winners.

3. The Year 2000 Gospel Movement was born in 1988. The vision and dynamism of this movement has drawn together most of the denominations and Christian workers in a cooperative effort to analyse the need and evangelize the lost by personal witnessing, mass evangelism and use of the mass media. Goals:

a) For every person in Taiwan to have opportunity to hear the gospel in their own language.
b) To increase believers to two million in 10,000 churches. This would mean increasing annual church growth from 2.7% to 16%.
c) Ten percent of the population to be Christian. It is now nearly 5%.
d) To send out 200 cross-cultural missionaries. The present number is around 20.

To achieve this would be a dramatic turn-around in the only major Chinese society where there has not been significant church growth this generation. Pray for a nation-wide prayer movement that can unite and ignite the Church for revival, evangelism and missions.

4. Protestants are unequally distributed among the different linguistic groups. The majority of mountain peoples are nominally Protestant (23% actively so) as are 4.6% of Mandarin, 1% of Taiwanese, and only 0.2% of Hakka. Pray that Hoklo (Taiwanese) and Hakka groups might become more receptive to the gospel.

5. There are 609 mountain churches throughout the tribal areas and some in cities. Most are Presbyterian, though an increasing number are of other denominations or sectarian groups such as True Jesus and Mormons. The breakdown of tribal and family life has been hastened by alcoholism, the drift to the cities, the pervasive influence of TV, increased education of young people, and inability of parents to control and raise their children in a changing society. God gave revival to the Tayal in 1973 and Ami in 1983. Pray for revival that will combat nominalism, spiritual decline and inadequate Bible teaching in these churches. Bible translation work is not yet complete – in six peoples there is a definite need, and in two others a possible need, but work is in progress only in the Yami language on Orchid Island.

6. The lack of pastors is serious but slowly improving. Many rural congregations in Taiwan are without pastors, the critical issue being low levels of giving in churches. There are over 20 seminaries and Bible schools, some with international acclaim, such as the China Evangelical Seminary. Pray for staff and students, and for relevant, spiritual training to be provided. More effective lay training programmes are also essential, so pray for TEE courses with over 800 studying in 60 centres.

7. The witness among students is encouraging. The 576,000 students in 121 universities and colleges are one of the most open sections of the community. Many churches have well-used student centres. Campus Evangelical Fellowship (**IFES**) has an outreach to students with 40 full-time staff workers ministering also in secondary schools. **CCC** also has a large campus ministry. It is now permitted to form Christian groups in middle and high schools. Pray that this golden opportunity may be taken up and for vital, growing groups with the integration of young believers into churches.

8. Missions were pioneered by the Presbyterians, but a great influx of new missions entered after their expulsion from mainland China in 1950. The majority concentrated on the Mandarin minority, and few went on to learn a second or third language. The Taiwanese and Hakka majority have been largely ignored until recently. There are many openings for missionaries in evangelism, church planting, Bible teaching and stimulating local congregations. Teaching English as a foreign language is a useful key for evangelism. The rising cost of living and uncertainty of usefulness in Taiwan has caused many missionaries to leave. Pray in those called of God and willing to identify culturally in this day of opportunity. Some of the largest agencies are: **OMF** (134 missionaries), **SBC** (107), **TEAM** (60), Norwegian Lutheran Mission (52), **SEND** (43), **OMS** (42), Finnish Lutheran Mission (38), Norwegian Mission Alliance (32), **CBFMS** (31), **YWAM** (27), **CMA** (25). Major missionary-contributing nations: USA (638), Korea (94), Norway (86), Finland (59).

9. **Missions vision** was once higher; Taiwan's political isolation has made Christians too introspective. Student missions conferences have created much interest (CEFV-**IFES**). Pray for a reawakening of interest and commitment to pray and send out more missionaries. Training programmes for missionary preparation are increasing in number and scope. There is a growing interest in ministry in Mainland China as political and economic links increase.

10. **Less evangelized areas and peoples:**
a) **The Hakka communities** in the northeast and the southeast. There is now a national group: "The World Hakka Evangelical Association". Several missions have opened a ministry among them (**SEND, OMF, WEC, YWAM**, Presbyterians and others).
b) **The rural areas; mainly Hoklo.** Half of the 369 districts have few churches, 63 have only one church, 11 have none.
c) **The new industrial zones.** Many workers are new to the cities and more responsive. Pray for the Industrial Evangelical Fellowship which encourages an outreach to them, and for **OMF** missionaries who are also involved.
d) **The 60,000 Chinese Muslims** of the Hui minority. There is no outreach to them.
e) **The Penghu Islanders** numbering 97,000. In 1964 there were 17 churches, but now two-thirds are closed. 10,000 Vietnam Chinese have been settled on the islands.

11. **Help ministries:**
a) **Christian literature.** Much is now being published of both local and foreign origin. Pray for efforts by **CEF(IFES)** and others to sell Christian literature through the secular book market.
b) **Radio.** Pray for fruit from extensive coverage by local broadcasters and by **FEBC** and **TWR** from abroad. In 1990 there were 500 hours of Mandarin, six hours of Taiwanese and 1.7 hours of Hakka evangelical broadcasting every week.
c) **Christian video tapes,** a key tool for evangelism. Most of the population has access to a video recorder. Several Christian agencies are seeking to supply good tapes.

Christmas Island

See under AUSTRALIA

Cocos Island
(Keeling Island)

See under AUSTRALIA

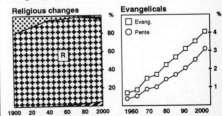

Colombia
(Republic of Colombia)

<table>
<tr><td>April
9–10</td></tr>
<tr><td>Latin America   C</td></tr>
</table>

Area 1,139,000 sq.km. Northwest corner of S. America. The fourth largest country in the continent. Mountains in west, plains and forests in east.

Population		Ann. Gr.	Density
1990	31,819,000	2.1 %	28/sq.km
1995	34,939,000	1.9 %	31/sq.km

Peoples:
Spanish-speaking 98.6%. Estimated composition: Mestizo (Eurindian) 57.6%; European 20%; Mulatto (Eurafrican)14%;African4%;Zombo(Afro-Indian)3%.
Indigenous Amerindian 0.78%. (50% of population in 1850). Still speaking 65 languages in 12 language families. Largest: Guahibo 80,000; Paez 44,000; Catio (Embera) 40,000.
Other 0.6%. Gypsy 39,000; Arab 32,000; English-speaking 13,000; Chinese 7,000.

Literacy 70%. **Official language:** Spanish. **All languages** 79. **Languages with Scriptures** 1Bi 27NT 21por.

Capital: Santa Fe de Bogotá 6,000,000. Other cities: Medellín 2,500,000; Cali 1,630,000; Barranquilla 1,220,000. Urbanization 67%.

Economy: Major export earners: oil and coffee (legal) and cocaine (illegal). Colombia processes 80% of the world's supply of cocaine. A great difference between the incomes of the rich and poor. Unemployment 18%. Public debt/person $534. Income/person $1,190 (5.6% of USA).

Politics: Independent of Spain in 1819 as part of Grand Colombia. A separate state in 1831. Polarization between Conservatives and Liberals has given 150 years of partisan politics, dictatorships and civil war. Those unrepresented by the two contending parties turned to support a variety of violent Marxist guerrilla groups. Some of the latter have aligned themselves with drug cartels who have their own terror groups, leading to a pandemic of assassinations and kidnappings. The constitution of 1991 and elections of 1992 are aimed at bringing the cycle of violence to an end, but the level of violence has continued to increase.

Religion: After years of persecution of and discrimination against religious minorities, the privileged position of the Roman Catholic Church was removed by the 1991 Constitution, which accords greater freedom to ethnic and religious minorities.

Non-religious/other 1.6%. **Tribal religions** 0.5%. **Muslim** 0.2%. **Jews** 0.1%. **Baha'i** 0.1%.
Christian 97.5%. Affil 95.9%. Growth 2.2%.
Protestant 3.8%. Growth 4.6%.

Church	Cong	Members	Affiliated
Seventh-day Adventist	567	83,735	209,000
Pan-Amer Mission	250	25,000	125,000
Ch of Four Sq Gospel	225	31,500	95,500
Chr Crusade Ch	250	30,000	75,000
Assoc of Interamer Ch	71	9,645	48,200
Fed of Evang Min	398	20,000	35,000
Colom Bapt Conv	101	10,398	34,700
Chr & Miss Alliance	341	15,765	23,647
New Tribes Chs (NTM)	21	8,000	20,000
Assemblies of God	445	10,000	19,000
Ev Miss Union (GMU)	207	10,200	15,300
Assoc of Ev Chs (TEAM)	96	3,650	9,130
All other (136)	2,395	182,572	483,663
Denominations (148)	5,367	440,465	1,193,140
Evangelicals 3.1% of pop		359,000	991,000
Pente/charis 2.3% of pop		253,000	724,000

Missionaries:
to Colombia 946 (1:33,600 people) in 72 agencies.
from Colombia 148 (1:8,100 Protestants) in 20 agencies 34frn 18xcul 130dom.
Roman Catholic 93.1%. Affil 91.53%. Growth 2%.

	Cong	Members	Affiliated
Catholic Ch	3,140	15,700,000	29,624,000
Doubly Counted		−240,000	−500,000
Total	3,140	15,460,000	29,124,000
Charismatic		300,000	600,000

Missionaries:
to Colombia 792 (1:40,200 people).
from Colombia 1,452 (1973 figure).
Other Catholic 0.01%. Affil 0.01%. Growth 3.2%.
Denominations (2)   20   1,000   2,000
Orthodox 0.02%. Growth 2.7%.
Marginal 0.6%. Growth 13.1%.

Jehovah's Witnesses	651	46,793	117,000
Mormons	129	45,600	76,000
All groups (7)	790	93,262	194,722

Religious changes

Evangelicals
☐ Evang.
○ Pente.

C

1. **Colombia has a reputation for being possibly one of the most violent countries in the world.** Leftist guerrilla movements and the drug-trafficking "barons" dominate many areas of the country. Corruption, blackmail, kidnapping, assassination and revenge murders have brutalized society, which is fast losing moral values and ethical standards. Pray for the political, legal and spiritual leaders of the nation – for their safety and courage to stand up for the right. Pray that Christians may remain untainted by the evils of their society and become God's instruments for moral, social and spiritual change. Pray that the anger and fear of ordinary people may turn many to personal faith in the Lord Jesus Christ as Saviour.

2. **Satan's hold on Colombia must be broken by prayer.** Widespread occult practices, the web of powers linking corrupt leaders, drug dealers, the private armies and others all conspire to hinder the advance of the gospel through the intimidation of Christians and missionaries and closing areas of the country for the free proclamation of the gospel.

3. **The 1991 Constitution has brought a glimmer of hope** with the opening up of the democratic process to those previously unrepresented, reforming the judicial system damaged by the violence of the drug wars, and granting greater religious freedom. The spate of violence has decreased, but pray for the breaking of the power of the drug syndicates and for alternative employment for the many who have earned their livelihood from drug-trafficking.

4. **The Roman Catholic Church** has exerted an enormous influence on every part of society, but the changing political scene has radically affected it. The main body of the church is strongly traditional, but the charismatic movement has had a wide impact. Yet 70% of all "Catholics" never go to Mass. Pray that the slackening of ties to the state in the new Constitution may open up the way for spiritual renewal.

5. **Evangelical growth has been significant.** In 1933 there were only 15,000 Evangelicals. Subsequent persecution reached a peak in *La Violencia* between 1948 and 1960, when religious bigotry provoked the destruction of churches and the robbery, rape and murder of believers. The last 30 years have yielded a harvest from among a receptive people. Aggressive local, city-wide and national evangelistic outreaches have resulted in an eightfold increase in congregations and Evangelical believers. The level of violence in the country and internal problems have slowed the growth of late. Pray for solutions in:
   a) **The leadership crisis,** which has grown with the growth of the churches. There are too few deeply taught in the Word, too many personality clashes, and a tendency to autocratic leadership which has divided or distracted many congregations and denominations. There are more than 20 theological institutions training pastors.
   b) **The moral crisis.** Fear silences many Christians when confronted by the corruption and violence of their society. Laxity in morals and finance has damaged the effectiveness of many Christian workers and groups. Pray for high standards of biblical holiness among the people of God.
   c) **The disunity crisis.** Divisions within the Body of Christ have become a discredit to the name of the Lord and a poor witness to the government and people. Many denominations have been split over bitter personal rivalries, legal rights, properties and relationships between missionaries and Colombians. CEDECOL, the Evangelical Confederation of Colombia, is a body that links over 50 evangelical denominations and coordinates inter-church action. Pray for a decisive work of healing and spiritual unity.

6. **Missionaries live under great stress** – especially those from the USA. Some have been murdered, others have received death threats and many have had to be withdrawn from ministry in dangerous areas where leftist or narcotics terrorism is rife. Pray for courage and faithfulness to their calling. Internal mission/church relationships have been a source of tension, division and grief. Great humility and sensitivity is required in the complex ecclesiastical scene in order to have a viable, fruitful ministry. Major mission agencies: **SIL/WBT** (278), **NTM** (168), **SBC** (55), **CMA** (37), **AoG** (33), Brethren (29), **TEAM** (25), **OMS** (24), and **ABWE** (19). Major missionary-contributing nations: USA (728), Canada (78), UK (30).

7. **Colombian missionary vision needs stimulation.** Many Amerindian peoples are closed to foreigners, but only a few Colombians have committed themselves to evangelize them. A handful of Colombians have gone to other lands, but church support is limited. The Spanish edition of **Operation World** is published in Colombia. Pray for the ongoing ministry of the COMIBAM committee in inspiring Christians to mission.

8. **Unreached peoples.** Pray specifically for:

a) **Less evangelized cities.** Medellín, with Evangelicals only 0.4% of its population, is renowned for its hardness to the gospel. Medellín is the nation's crime and narcotics capital with 300 gangs of paid killers and 7,000 murders per year. The city of Cali is also a special challenge for the gospel. Cooperation between denominations in Medellín, Barranquilla and Cartagena has led to many conversions (**LAM**).

b) Nearly two million in **Bogotá's slums.**

c) The thousands of *Gamines* or homeless street urchins of the cities. **YWAM** and **WEC** have a ministry to them.

d) **The urban middle class** which has been stricken by the economic and political crises of the past decade. They are possibly the least responsive section of society.

e) **The Syrian-Lebanese Muslim** community, which numbers around 12,000.

f) **Amerindian peoples** closed to evangelical church planters. Possibly 30–40 are in this category – including the Inga, Coreguaje, Cuiba, Desano, Epena, Huitoto, Saliba and Tucano.

9. **Work among Amerindians has been a constant struggle** – travel and living conditions, indifference of the people, opposition of officials and anthropologists, inter-mission rivalry and recently narcotics terrorists who force the Amerindians to grow cocaine and marijuana. The 1991 Constitution grants wide autonomy to tribes in the rain forests. In spite of it all, there has been some response with people movements to Christ. Pray for:

a) **Strong, viable, well-led churches,** able to cope with drug traffickers and modernization.

b) **Church-planting ministries of NTM** (in 10 peoples), South American Mission in three northeastern peoples, **CMA** in two peoples, etc.

c) **Bible translation: SIL** has 145 workers committed to 33 translation projects; a number of NTs are nearing completion, and between four and 13 languages await translators.

d) **GRn** recordings which are available in 58 languages.

e) The opening up of areas and peoples long closed to the gospel by government restrictions or terrorism.

10. **Supportive ministries.**

a) **Literature** is not sufficiently used; few churches have a vision for a literature ministry, yet it could be a major corrective for the lack of Bible teaching. **CLC** has four bookstores, a wide distribution network for literature, and a growing productivity as a publisher of locally-produced Spanish titles. *Desafío*, a WEC magazine, is used for evangelism by 51% of evangelical churches.

b) **Student work** has been slow and hard. Marxist ideology once dominated the campuses, but now a new spirit of enquiry and openness to the gospel prevails. UCU (**IFES**) groups have multiplied, under a vision to see an evangelical group witnessing on each campus.

c) **Christian radio.** Evangelicals have little access to national radio and none to TV networks. However, six evangelical broadcasters – including **HCJB** (Ecuador), **TWR** (Bonaire), **FEBC** and High Adventure (USA) – broadcast 686 hours a week in Spanish. HCJB also broadcasts 1/2 hour per week in the Inga Quechua language.

April 11	*Comoro Islands*	
Africa		

C

Four volcanic islands between Madagascar and Mozambique. The Republic declared itself independent from France in 1975, but one island, Mayotte, seceded to remain a French overseas territory. The Republic still claims Mayotte as part of its territory.

FEDERAL ISLAMIC REPUBLIC OF THE COMOROS

Area 1,862 sq.km. Poor agricultural land but rich marine life in the surrounding seas.

Population		Ann. Gr.	Density
1990	438,000	3.0 %	235/sq.km
1995	509,000	3.1 %	273/sq.km

Peoples:
Comorian 96.9%. Mixed Arab, African and Malagasy ancestry.
Minorities 3.1%. Makua 7,000; French 1,700; Malagasy 700; Arab 500; Réunionese 500.

Literacy 46%. **Official languages**: Arabic, French. Three dialects of Comorian Swahili are widely spoken. **Languages with Scriptures** 2Bi 2por.

Capital: Moroni 23,000. Urbanization 27%.

Economy: Underdeveloped and poor. Vanilla and perfume oils are virtually the only exports, but the collapse of world prices for these commodities has further depressed economic life. Unemployment over 36%. Public debt/person $370. Income/person $460 (2% of USA).

Politics: A one-party state until 1990, when multiparty democratic government was instituted. There have been numerous coups and attempted coups since independence, some involving foreign mercenaries and French military intervention.

Religion: All open witness is forbidden in this Islamic state.
Muslim 98%. Indigenous Comorians are almost entirely Muslim, also some Bantu Makua and Malagasy. There are 780 mosques.
Non-religious/other 1.4%.
Christian 0.6%.
 Protestant 0.16%. Mainly Malagasy in several groups. About 120 Comorian believers.
 Roman Catholic 0.46%. Mainly French, Malagasy and Réunionese.

1. **The islanders were completely unevangelized before 1973.** They are strong Muslims, but also deeply involved in occult practices and spirit possession. Yet many young people are disillusioned with life in Islamic society which offers so little hope. Even today, open Christian witness is forbidden, so intercede for the opening of this land for God's Word.

2. **The quiet witness of 29 AIM medical and veterinary workers** in the Republic and on Mayotte has won credit and public honour as well as opportunities to quietly share the Lord Jesus with the people. Pray for continued and increased opportunities for witness and that such may bear fruit.

3. **Comorian believers** have steadily increased in numbers through the witness and leadership of the first convert. The believers have suffered periods of intense persecution and are not legally permitted to meet openly. Pray for other leaders to be raised up for the several groups of believers. Pray also for the witness of Malagasy and other believers from minority groups.

THE TERRITORIAL COLLECTIVITY OF MAYOTTE

Area 373 sq.km. One larger (Mayotte) and several smaller islands, including Pamanzi.

Population		Ann. Gr.	Density
1990	81,000	3.8 %	217/sq.km
1995	98,000	3.8 %	262/sq.km

Peoples:
Comorian 94.7%. Mainly Maore.
European 2.5%. Mainly French.

Other 2.8%. Mainland African (3) 1,100; Malagasy 1,000.

Literacy 32%. **Official language:** French; shiMaore (the local Swahili dialect) and Malagasy widely used.

Capital: Dzaoudzi 5,400. Mamoudzou (capital designate) 7,325. Urbanization 60%.

Economy: Limited natural resources or exportable

commodities, yet more prosperous than the rest of the Comoros through French aid and military base.

Politics: French rule is challenged by the Comorian government, but neither the local people nor the French administration have shown much enthusiasm for change.

Religion: There is freedom of religion.
Muslim 96.9%. Almost all Comorians, most of the Africans and some Malagasy are Sunni Muslim, but mosque attendance is low.
Non-religious/other 0.4%, mainly French.
Christian 2.7%. Affil 2%. Growth 6.7%.
  Protestant 0.4%. Affil 0.17%. Growth 3.7%.
    Evangelicals 0.04% of population.
  Missionaries to Comoros and Mayotte 37 (1:14,000 people) in 4 agencies.
  Roman Catholic 2.2%. Affil 1.7% Growth 6.6%.
  Missionaries to Comoros and Mayotte 10 (1:61,000 people).
  Marginal 0.1%. Jehovah's Witnesses.

1. **Direct evangelism is permitted**, but not necessarily well received by the Muslim majority. Pray for the witness of **AIM** missionaries on Mayotte and other islands, and for an increase in their numbers to expand both their evangelistic efforts and offers of social help through medicine and teaching.

2. **The only organized Protestant churches** in the four islands are two evangelical groups among the Malagasy on Grand Comore and Mayotte, and isolated Christians elsewhere. Pray for their witness. The few Comorian believers are culturally so different that they cannot easily integrate into these groups. Pray for the right church-planting strategy to be applied.

3. **Christian help ministries** are more easily based on Mayotte. Pray for ongoing **Bible translation** programmes into two of the Comorian dialects. AIM also runs a literacy programme on Mayotte. **FEBA-Seychelles** broadcasts to the islands for ten hours a week in French and three in Swahili.

April 12	***Congo***
C Africa	(Republic of Congo)

Area 342,000 sq.km. Northwest of Zaire. Over 60% of the country is covered with tropical rainforest. Grasslands and bush in the north.

Population		Ann. Gr.	Density
1990	1,994,000	2.8 %	6/sq.km
1995	2,289,000	2.8 %	7/sq.km

Peoples. Over 75 ethnic groups.
Bantu 93.7%. 62 groups. Largest: Kongo (10) 836,000; Teke (15) 490,000; Mboshi (6) 195,000; Mbete (6) 140,000; Sira-Punu (4) 80,000; Bungi 67,000; Lingala 60,000; Maka-Njem (4) 36,000; Kota (5) 9,000.
Adamawa 2.8%. Sango 54,000; Gbaya 2,000.
Pygmy 1.5%. 5 groups. Bayaka 20,000; Monzombo 6,000.
Other 2%. Hausa 4,000; French 28,000; Portuguese 600; Greek 400.

Literacy 63%. **Official language:** French. **Trade languages:** Lingala, Munukutuba. **All languages** 60. **Languages with Scriptures** 4Bi 4NT 12por.

Capital: Brazzaville 800,000. Other city: Pointe Noire 300,000. Urbanization 51%.

Economy: Interior underdeveloped due to limited transportation. Rich oil and mineral deposits, but over-dependence on oil and the fall in world prices, as well as massive embezzlement of government funds, have reduced government spending and living standards. Public debt/person $2,379. Income/person $900 (4.3% of USA).

Politics: Independent from France in 1960. A Marxist-Leninist People's Republic 1968–1991, but in the '80s the ideological rhetoric waned as the economy declined. Constitutional reform opened the way for multi-party democracy in 1992 and elections in 1992 and 1993.

Religion: During the Marxist period, the youth were heavily indoctrinated against religion, 18 denominations were banned and some missions expelled. All restrictions have now been removed and freedom of religion declared.

African traditional religions 10.2%.
Non-religious/other 2.7%. **Baha'i** 0.4%.
Muslim 1.3%.
Christian 85.4%. Nom 7.6%. Affil 75.63%. Growth 3.4%.
Protestant 22%. Affil 20%. Growth 4.8%.

Church	Cong	Members	Affiliated
Evang Ch of Congo	221	155,000	310,000
Salvation Army	242	22,000	62,900
Evang Ch (Likouala) (UWM)	28	3,500	10,600
Baptist Ch (Örebro)	69	2,500	8,330
Assemblies of God	56	3,320	8,300
All other (1)	1	148	296
Denominations (6)	617	186,468	400,426
Evangelicals 18.2% of pop		168,600	363,000
Pentecostal/charis 1.2%		11,000	24,000

Missionaries:
to Congo 118 (1:16,900 people) in 15 agencies.
from Congo 1 (1:400,000 Protestants) 1frn.
Roman Catholic 50%. Affil 44.58%. Growth 2.3%.

Catholic Ch	171	516,000	889,000

Missionaries:
to Congo 337 (1:5,900 people).
from Congo 6 (1973 figure).
Orthodox 0.02%. Affil 0.02%. Growth 0%.
Foreign Marginal 0.38%. Growth 10.7%.

Jehovah's Witnesses	55	2,250	7,500

Indigenous Marginal 13%. Affil 10.78%. Growth 5.2%.

Kimbanguist Church		48,000	80,000
All groups (42)		111,000	215,000

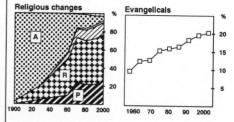

Religious changes

Evangelicals

1. **Praise God that there is once more religious freedom.** Years of intense pressure and discrimination have ended. Pray for stability in the nation in times of painful economic and social transition. Pray that Christians with high moral and spiritual standards may be appointed to positions of influence.

2. **Tribal religions** were encouraged by the former regime, and Christians pressured to compromise with fetishism and ancestor worship. During this period, prophetic-healing syncretic churches multiplied. Pray for revival and restoration of biblical standards where churches have failed, and pray that believers may be bold and forthright in challenging the powers of darkness inside and outside the churches.

3. **Church growth has been dramatic.** There were periods of revival in the '20s and in 1947 which gave stability in the storms of the '70s and '80s. Training of leadership suffered in the time of persecution. Pray for the training of leaders in three Bible schools. **UWM** has a four-year residential Bible training school as well as a TEE programme.

4. **Young people** grew up hearing much anti-Christian propaganda. Church youth work was severely limited for years. Pray that churches may effectively win and disciple the younger generation.

5. **The centre and north of the country** are thinly populated, and many parts are difficult for travel. But there is a growing response to the gospel and a great need for those who can help establish strong, local churches. As a result of economic conditions, the churches generally are financially poor.

6. **Mission work** suffered in the '70s with many workers expelled and institutions expropriated. Pray for the wise resumption of activities that most enhance the growth of God's kingdom. Over half the missionary force is Scandinavian. The largest missions are the Swedish and Norwegian Mission Covenant Church working with the Evangelical Church (54), **WBT/SIL** (16), Salvation Army (9), **AoG** (7), **UWM** (6), and Global Outreach (3). Major missionary-contributing nations: USA (42), Sweden (41), Norway (15).

7. **Unreached peoples.** The needs for evangelization must be better researched.
a) Parts of the large **Teke** tribe in the centre and north are unreached.
b) The **Pygmy** tribes are semi-nomadic jungle groups who are hard to reach. Their numbers are unknown, but may be over 30,000. UWM started work among them in 1991.
c) **Other tribes** – Punu, Nzebi, Pol, Tsaangi, Pande – are believed to be unreached, but there is little information to clarify this.

8. **Bible translation** – the two main languages of communication, Kongo and Lingala, have the complete Bible. Pray for the growing team of 19 SIL workers as they seek to determine which of the 37 languages require a New Testament. Translation projects in hand number 15 and there is a definite need for four more.

<table>
<tr><td>

See Pacific

C

Pacific

</td>
<td>

Cook Islands

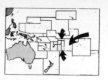

</td></tr>
</table>

In this book, three island archipelagos associated with New Zealand are grouped together.

Area:
Cook: 236 sq.km. Over 100 coral atolls and volcanic islands, 15 of which are inhabited. 3,500 km northeast of New Zealand.
Niue: 260 sq.km; the world's largest coral island.
Tokelau: 10 sq.km. Coral atolls.

Population (1990)		Ann. Gr.	Density
Cook Is	18,300	0.3%	78/sq.km
Niue	2,112	-3.2%	8/sq.km
Tokelau	1,700	0.8%	170/sq.km

Large-scale emigration to New Zealand.

Peoples:
Cook Island: Polynesian (4 languages) 81.6%; Euronesian 15.4%; European 2.4%; Other 0.6%.
Niue: Polynesian 96%; European 2.6%; Other 1.4%.
Tokelau: Polynesian 98%; Other 2%.

Literacy 92% (Cook); 99% (Niue & Tokelau).
Official languages: English, Cook Island Maori. **All languages** 7. **Languages with Scriptures** 4Bi.

Capitals: Avarua 10,000 (Cook). Alofi 1,022 (Niue).

Economy: Heavily dependent on aid from New Zealand and remittances from migrants. Isolation and irregular transport inhibits development. Income/person: Cook $1,250 (5.9% of USA); Niue $1,080 (5.1% of USA); Tokelau $670 (3.2% of USA).

Politics: Cook and Niue Islands are self-governing states in free association with New Zealand. Tokelau is a non-self-governing territory of New Zealand.

Religion: Freedom of religion, but with the Congregational Church in each island group effectively the established Church. Main statistics for Cook Is:
Non-religious/other 1.4%. **Baha'i** 0.8%.
Christian 97.8%. Affil 90%. Growth −0.4%.
Protestant 78.1%. Affil 72.2%. Growth −0.8%.

Church	Cong	Members	Affiliated
Cook Is Christn Ch	94	4,220	10,540
Seventh-day Adventist	14	748	2,200
Assemblies of God	1	75	150
All other (4)	3	165	330
Denominations (7)	112	5,208	13,220
Evangelicals 5.1% of pop		370	940
Pentecostal/charis 1%		90	180

Missionaries:
to Cook Is 10 (1:1,800 people) in 3 agencies.
from Cook Is 11 (1:1,200 Protestants) in 3 agencies 10frn 10xcul 1dom.
Missionaries to Niue and Tokelau: None.
Roman Catholic 13.2%. Affil 12.1%. Growth −1.1%.

Catholic Ch	14	1,110	2,210

Missionaries to Cook Is 15 (1:1,220 people).
Missionaries to Niue 20 (1:200 people).
Marginal 6.5%. Affil 5.7%. Growth 6.9%.

Mormons	6	420	700
Jehovah's Witnesses	3	118	347
Groups (2)	9	538	1,047

Niue: Protestant 74%; Catholic 6.5%; Mormon 16%; Other 3.5%.
Tokelau: Protestant 62%; Catholic 33%; Marginal 5%.

1. **The Christian influence has been strong for 150 years.** The integration of secular and religious leadership has created what are virtually theocratic states. Church attendance is high, but few have assurance of salvation.

2. **Many islands have no known evangelical witness.** There are Evangelicals in several **AoG** churches and small groups within the older churches. Pray for a new infusion of spiritual life.

3. **Migration to New Zealand** for employment has given another means of bringing new life into the islands. 77% of Niue, 66% of Tokelau and 60% of Cook Islanders are now in New Zealand. Pray for the Island churches in Auckland and other New Zealand cities. Blessing there will affect the islands.

4. **Many nominal Christians have been led astray** by Mormons and Jehovah's Witnesses. Pray for an effective discipling and teaching ministry on the Islands.

5. **Bible translation.** A revision of the Rarotongan Bible is needed (**UBS**), and possibly translation into the smaller languages.

Costa Rica
(Republic of Costa Rica)

Area 51,000 sq.km. Rich agricultural land, which straddles the Central American isthmus.

Population	Ann. Gr.	Density
1990 3,015,000	2.7 %	59/sq.km
1995 3,374,000	2.3 %	66/sq.km

Peoples:
Spanish-speaking 95%. European 2,600,000; Mestizo 259,000.
English-speaking 3%. Afro-Caribbean 90,000.
Amerindian 0.43%. Five peoples: Bribri 4,500; Cabécar 4,500; Guaymi 2,400; Burunca 1,200; Maleku 520. Most of these languages are dying out as they are absorbed into the Spanish-speaking population.
Other 1.57%. Chinese 30,000; Europeans 21,000.
Refugees. At one time there were 300,000 Nicaraguans; 60,000 still remain.

Literacy 93%. **Official language:** Spanish. English and Mekitelyu spoken on Caribbean coast. **All languages** 10. **Languages with Scriptures** 2Bi 5NT 6por.

Capital: San José 1,104,000. Urbanization 51%.

Economy: Decline between 1979-88. Main exports are bananas, coffee and textiles. Tourism is also important. Unemployment 6.2%. Public debt/person $1,200. Income/person $1,760 (8.3% of USA).

Politics: Independent of Spain in 1821. A long history of stable, multi-party democratic government. Costa Rica has exercised a stabilizing influence in the conflicts of surrounding lands.

Religion: Roman Catholicism is the official religion, but there is freedom for other faiths. However, other religions are not yet equal before the law, and Evangelicals can be subject to discriminatory legislation and actions by the authorities.
Non-religious/other 5.8%. Baha'i 0.30%.
Chinese Religions 0.27%. Jews 0.2%.
Christian 93.4%. Affil 91.8%. Growth 2%.
  Protestant 10.7%. Growth 8.6%.

Church	Cong	Members	Affiliated
Assemblies of God	169	36,000	55,100
Seventh-day Adventist	63	12,746	29,000
Ch of God (Cleveland)	441	16,087	28,700
Pente Holiness Ch	70	7,000	16,700
Foursquare Gospel Ch	84	3,750	12,100
Assoc of Bible Chs	112	7,200	12,000
Council of National Evang Chs	63	8,000	11,000
Bapt Bible Fellowship	19	5,180	10,400
Ev Assoc of C. Am	70	3,391	9,690
Ch of the Nazarene	32	1,858	7,150
Baptist Conv	32	1,903	3,590
All other (111)	855	61,557	127,927
Denominations (122)	2,010	164,672	323,357
Evangelicals 9.7% of pop		152,000	294,000
Pentecostal/charis 6.8%		108,000	204,000

Missionaries:
  to Costa Rica 452 (1:6,700 people) in 53 agencies.
  from Costa Rica 107 (1:3,000 Protestants) in 16 agencies 99frn 99xcul 8dom.
Roman Catholic 80%. Affil 78.4%. Growth 1.1%.

Catholic Ch	459	1,380,000	2,604,000
Doubly counted		−130,000	−240,000
Total	459	1,250,000	2,364,000
Charismatic 3.3%		53,000	100,000

Missionaries:
  to Costa Rica 33 (1:91,000 people).
  from Costa Rica 234 (1:11,000 Catholics) in 16 lands.
Marginal 2.7%. Growth 7.7%.

Jehovah's Witnesses	228	14,018	35,900
Mormons	51	8,840	13,000
All other (20)	193	16,565	31,990
Denominations (22)	472	39,423	80,900

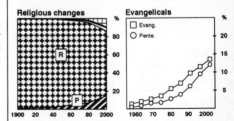

Religious changes   Evangelicals

1. **Praise God for the present time of harvest.** The evangelical population has more than doubled in the '80s through vigorous witnessing to their faith. As a result, a movement of the Spirit has swept through the land.

2. **The Roman Catholic Church** was much influenced by charismatic renewal in the '70s. Many came to a living, personal faith in Christ for salvation. The large exit of Catholics to other churches and sects has provoked others to revert to traditional doctrines and political activism to protect their

C

privileged position. Pray that charismatic and evangelical Catholics may stand firm against these tendencies. Pray for the majority of Costa Ricans who are, at best, nominally Catholic. Many are in great need – immorality, alcoholism and spiritism are rife.

3. **Evangelicals have multiplied in numbers.** Pray that leaders may be filled with wisdom, humility and dependence on God, and for the effective discipleship of new believers. The dangers to pray against are:
a) **A high rate of backsliding.** Former Evangelicals outnumber active ones. Backsliders either return to the Catholic Church, join a sect, or reject religion altogether.
b) **Secularism and materialism** which are sapping the vitality of Christians in urban areas. In rural areas legalism is a real problem.
c) **Disunity.** Polarization and denominational splits are hindrances to cooperative effort and spiritual fellowship.

4. **Improved leadership training** has hastened growth. There are 26 Bible schools and seminaries, and an extensive TEE programme. IMDELA (Missiological Institute of the Americas) has opened a residential and extension programme in missions. Pray for leaders who inspire the churches to missionary vision and outreach.

5. **Costa Rica 2000** is a national saturation church-planting plan coordinated by the Costa Rican Evangelical Alliance and the Evangelism-in-Depth Institute. This seeks to mobilize Evangelicals to reach every sector of society and every area of the country by the year 2000. Pray for close cooperation and a spirit of prayer among Christians that this vision be accomplished.

6. **Alcance 2000** is a focal point of the growing missionary movement in the country. The vision is to mobilize 12,000 prayer warriors, target 50 unreached peoples around the world, and send out 500 cross-cultural missionaries by the year 2000. Pray for the realization of this. Pray also for FEDEMEC (Federation of Evangelical Missions), founded in 1985 and based at the Costa Rican Center for World Mission in San José, which is deeply committed to this vision. Pray for Costa Ricans serving as missionaries in other lands.

7. **Special evangelistic challenges:**
a) **Students** have proved less responsive to the gospel, and drug addiction has become a serious problem. Christian student leadership has been weak in the past. There is a growing national student movement linked with ECU (**IFES**), *Alfa y Omega* (**CCC**), Maranatha (a Pentecostal student work) and others.
b) **All Amerindian tribes** are being evangelized but most are either nominally Catholic or animist. There is, however, a vocal, syncretic, indigenous organization committed to ending missionary work among them. There is a strong indigenous church among the Cabécar, and Evangelical missionary input to the Boruca, Bribri, Guaymi and Maleku, but pray that truly indigenous churches using their mother tongues may be established.
c) **Chinese.** Some have become Catholic, and there are now a few Evangelicals in three small groups. The Chinese Christian Mission started a work among them in 1985. Continued immigration from Asia and emigration to North America make for instability in the congregations.
d) The Mekitelyu **Afro-Caribbean** community on the Caribbean coast is nominally Protestant, but few people have a vital, life-affecting faith in Christ. Pray for ongoing evangelistic campaigns and that these may result in Mekitelyu-speaking congregations.
e) **Muslim immigrants** are few, but increasing. Mainly Arab, Iranian and South Asian.

8. **Missions.** The largest agencies are **LAM** (86), Southern Baptists (33), Calvary Ministries (24), **CRWM** (24), **CAMI** (22), **AoG** (21), **CoN** (18). The stability of the country has made this a good base for many regional and global ministries. Pray for cooperation and close fellowship between agencies, for there is a frustrating duplication of effort and a dominance of North Americans in many supportive agencies. Visas are becoming more difficult to obtain. Major missionary-contributing nations: USA (358), Canada (38).

9. **Christian help ministries:**
a) **Radio and TV.** There are three Christian radio and three TV stations; other secular stations air Christian programmes. Pray that efforts to restrict this ministry may fail. Also pray that broadcasts may lead to conversion among the unsaved and growth among the Christians.
b) **LAM's** "Christ for the City" vision. This has resulted in short-term team ministry in other lands and childcare clinics and outreach in Costa Rican shanty towns.
c) **The Bible Society.** Demand for Scriptures is strong and growing. Pray that no opposition may

succeed in preventing the distribution of Scriptures.

d) **The Spanish Language Institute** where many missionaries learn Spanish. Pray for staff and missionary students.

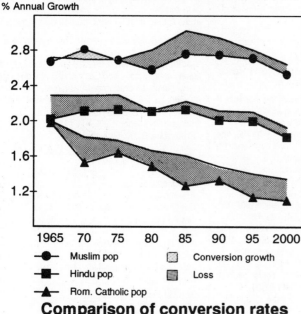

Comparison of conversion rates
Muslims, Hindus and Catholics

% Annual Growth

Muslim pop — Conversion growth
Hindu pop — Loss
Rom. Catholic pop

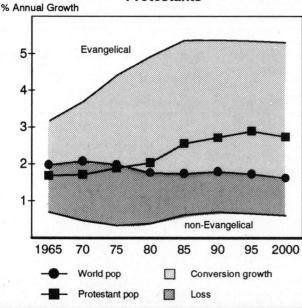

Comparison of conversion rates
Protestants

% Annual Growth

World pop — Conversion growth
Protestant pop — Loss

These revealing graphs show conversion rates by plotting the difference in growth rate of the general population and that of four major faiths. The population curves (simple lines) were obtained by summing the populations of all countries with over 80% of Muslims, Hindus or Catholics. The global growth rate of these faiths was superimposed on these lines. For Protestants, the world population was used.

Observe:

1. Muslims, Hindus and Catholics are all growing more slowly than their surrounding populations.

2. Muslim and Hindu growth as a percentage of the world's population is almost entirely due to a higher birth rate.

3. Muslim "losses" are more due to immigration of non-Muslims into Muslim lands (as in the oil states of the Middle East) and emigration of Muslims to Western lands than to actual losses to other religions.

4. The remarkable contrast within Protestantism between the decline of non-Evangelicals and the rapid growth of Evangelicals.

April 14		
C	*Côte d'Ivoire*	
	(The Republic of Côte d'Ivoire)	
Africa		

Area 322,000 sq.km. On the West African coast between Liberia and Ghana. Rain forest in the south, savannah in the north.

Population	Ann. Gr.	Density
1990 12,596,000	3.8 %	39/sq.km
1995 15,315,000	4.0 %	48/sq.km

Massive immigration from surrounding lands, especially Burkina Faso and Mali.

Peoples: Over 100 ethnic groups; double that if immigrant minority communities are included.
Africans indigenous to Côte d'Ivoire 74.4%.
  Akan 35.3%. 18 groups: Baoulé 1,600,000; the dominant people today. Lagoon peoples (14) 735,000; Agni 487,000; Nzema 47,000.
  Kru 14.6%. 24 groups: Bété 698,00; Guéré 289,000; Dida (2) 178,000; Wobe 170,000; Krou (6) 62,000; Nyaboa 36,000; Godie 28,000; Kouya 11,000.
  Gur 9.9%. 37 groups: Senoufo (32 dialects) 907,000; Kulango 237,000; Lobi 54,000; Téén (Lorhon) 6,000.
  Mande 8.1%. 9 groups: Malinké 639,000; Dioula 179,000; Maou 107,000; Soninké 100,000; Bisa 63,000; Wassulunké 15,000; Bambara 14,000.
  South Mande 6.5%. 9 groups: Yakouba 509,000; Gouro 303,000; Gagou 54,000; Toura 26,000; Yaouré 25,000; Wan 18,000; Mona 8,000.
Foreign Africans 24.9%. Burkinabé 1,600,000; Malian 754,000; Guinean 238,000; other 345,000. In 1993 there were also 200,000 Liberian refugees.
Other 0.7%. French 19,400; Lebanese 9,700.

Literacy 42.4%. **Official language:** French, used by a high proportion of the population. **Trade Language:** Dioula (Jula) in the north and Abidjan. **All languages** 75. **Languages with Scriptures** 4Bi 15NT 16por.

Capitals: Yamoussoukro (political) 120,000, Abidjan (commercial) 3,000,000. Urbanization 47%.

Economy: One of the world's largest producers of cocoa, coffee and palm oil. The post-independence economic boom stimulated both a massive immigration of job-seekers from surrounding lands and a high level of corruption. The collapse of world prices for cocoa and coffee, poor management of the public sector, and spending on prestige projects have more recently put the country under stress. Public debt/person $1,110 (the highest in Africa). Income/person $790 (4% of USA).

Politics: Independent from France in 1960. One-party presidential government under Houphouet-Boigny. Two decades of stability followed by economic recession have given way to increasing unrest and political paralysis because of the aged President's manipulation of the economy and failure to resolve the succession issue. The bloated and corrupt bureaucracy, continuing recession, the unfulfilled expectations of the educated youth, and a high number of foreigners could spell more trouble in the future. In 1990 other parties were legalized.

Religion: Religious freedom. The government is sympathetic to missions.
Traditional religions/other 30.3%. Traditional religions are generally stronger in the centre and west, many tribes still predominantly animist.
Muslim 38.7%. Strong in the northwest and in Abidjan. Africans Sunni, Lebanese Shi'a.
Christian 31%. Nom 15.2%. Affil 20.8%. Growth 4.1%.
Protestant 5.3%. Growth 9.5%.

Church	Cong	Members	Affiliated
Prot Ch of Central C d'I (CMA)	1,550	69,663	189,488
Prot Methodist Ch	750	38,200	131,600
Assemblies of God	760	53,400	89,000
Les Eglises "Reveille" (4)	300	30,000	75,000
Oeuvre Missionaire	54	15,000	30,000
Evang Alliance (WEC)	175	16,100	26,800
Nthn Bapt Chs (CBFMS)	215	4,360	10,900
Baptist Conv (SBC)	116	1,600	8,000
Ind Fund Bapt Chs (BMM)	18	1,470	3,684
Free Will Baptist Ch	42	714	1,786
All other (25)	222	14,619	35,776
Denominations (42)	4,427	266,186	672,034
Evangelicals 4.3% of pop.		228,000	543,000
Pentecostal/charis 1.6%		102,400	203,300

Missionaries:
  to Cote d'Ivoire 897 (1:14,800 people) in 59 agencies.
  from Côte d'Ivoire 26 (1:28,000 Protestants) in 7 agencies 4frn 8xcul 18dom.
Roman Catholic 20.8%. Affil 9%. Growth 3.7%.

Catholic Ch	964	656,000	1,131,719

Missionaries:
  to Côte d'Ivoire 805 (1:15,600 people).
  from Côte d'Ivoire 135 (1973 figure).
Orthodox 0.1%. Affil 0.1%. Growth 8%.
Foreign Marginal 0.1%. Affil 0.08%. Growth 11.3%.

Jehovah's Witnesses	90	3,415	9,760
All groups (2)	93	3,515	9,960

Indigenous Marginal 4.7%. Affil 6.2%. Growth 0.8%.

Harrist Ch	290	58,100	176,000
All groups (138)	1,220	328,200	781,300

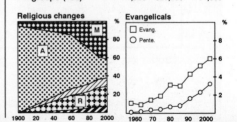

1. **Praise God for the growth of the Church over the past 25 years.** Yet the explosive growth of the population at 3.8% over this period has meant little overall increase as a percentage of the population. During this period most of the peoples in the country have been contacted by missions. Pray that growth in the '90s may be the best yet.

2. **The preaching of Prophet Harris from Liberia in 1914–15 brought over 120,000 coastal people out of fetishism and darkness.** The initiative was lost as missionary help arrived "too little and too late". Many syncretic indigenous churches multiplied and grew out of that movement. The Methodists arrived in 1924 and were once the largest Protestant community, but liberal theology and nominalism are widespread in the churches among the diverse coastal peoples. Pray for a new wave of revival and church planting within every Christianized people in the forest area.

C

3. **The Catholic Church** has made a deep impact through an extensive educational system. Many Ivorians are nominally Catholic as a result. Catholics are a large minority in the south and among the upper and middle classes. The lack is a personal relationship with the Saviour.

4. **Evangelical agencies** had a late and slow start compared to other West African lands. **CMA** entered the land in 1930 and concentrated on the Baoulé in the centre of the country. **MB** began work in 1927 among the Yakouba and Guéré in the southwest, later joined by **UFM**, and **WEC** began in 1934 in between the above among the Gouro and Gagou. Many other missions have entered in more recent years, and growing churches have resulted. Notable among the later arrivals are the **AoG**, with many churches in Abidjan and throughout the country.

5. **The spiritual life of believers** needs prayer. There is tribalism in denominations. Syncretic practices, divisions, leadership power struggles, breakdowns between missions and daughter churches, and often a lack of commitment to full-time service or evangelistic zeal exist in many congregations. Pray for revival for the fragmented Church.

6. **Leadership for the churches** is the big bottleneck. Many denominations have one trained pastor for every 10–20 congregations. Congregational giving has been poor despite relative prosperity, but the recession has decreased giving to even lower levels. Nearly every denomination lacks sufficient pastors, and lay leadership is often ill-trained for pastoral and teaching roles. Many of the larger denominations have French or vernacular Bible schools or TEE programmes. Pray for the calling and training of more leaders of high calibre.

7. **Cooperation between Churches** is essential if unmet challenges are to be tackled. Pray for these cooperative endeavours.
a) **The Evangelical Federation** was founded in 1960 and has become a cooperative fellowship for promoting Bible training, nationwide evangelistic efforts and pastors' retreats, as well as setting up the Evangelical Publishing Centre, but real fellowship between churches and agencies is lacking.
b) **The Lausanne Committee of Côte d'Ivoire** has launched an unreached people research and prayer programme, and is inaugurating an **AD2000 Movement** in the country. Pray that the vision may gain enthusiastic support from pastors and churches.
c) **Missionary training. Calvary Ministries** has established a missions training institute in Abidjan for preparing Ivorian missionaries for service throughout the Francophone region – the first such for Francophone West Africa. The great challenge is to prepare missionaries for Muslim outreach.

8. **The missionary force has grown rapidly.** Now over 20% belong to African missionary agencies or denominations from surrounding countries. Major missions include: **WBT**/SIL (117), **CBFMS** (93), **NTM** (66), **CMA** (59), **WEC** (59), **SBC** (37), **SIM** (33), Free Will Baptists (32), *Mission Biblique* (19) **AoG** (15) and **UFM** (6). Many of these missionaries serve in missionary children's schools (CBFMS, NTM and WEC), or international ministries based in the country, so the need for new long-term missionaries is great – for pioneer evangelism, church planting and a wide range of supportive ministries. Major missionary-sending countries: USA (461), Burkina Faso (120), UK (71).

9. **Peoples that are both unreached and unoccupied** by missions or churches – the Muslim Soninké, Bambara, Wassulunké, Fula-Maasina and the largely traditional Bisa – all peoples with their majorities in Burkina Faso, Mali or Ghana. There are also the Wolof from Senegal, Lebanese Muslims, Tuareg refugees from Niger and a growing number of Chinese business people.

10. **Peoples that are still a pioneer mission field** with no major breakthrough in church planting:
a) **The strongly Muslim peoples of the northwest:** Malinké, Fula and Dioula-speaking peoples, where only a handful have been won through the ministry of **SIM**, **WEC** and **CBFMS**.
b) **Marginally occupied peoples.** For example: in the Free Will Baptist area in the northeast (Birifor, Téén); in the **WEC** area in the centre (Mona, Wan, Yaouré, Kouya, Maou); **MB-UFM** area in the southwest (Toura, Dida, Bété).

c) **The multiplicity of small language groups in the south.** This is so great that present evangelistic, church planting and Bible translation ministries may not cover the need. Pray that this may be adequately researched and every group thoroughly evangelized. **NTM** has targeted the Bakwé, Neyo and Krou in the southeast.

C

11. **Islam has grown rapidly** during this century – from 5% in 1900 to 38% today. Tribal groups in the north and pockets of people in tribes all over the country are becoming Muslim. Urban concentrations of Muslims are high, and so are conversion rates among new immigrants to the cities. Over half of Abidjan's population is Muslim. Pray that Christians may be zealous to win non-Muslims while they can, and also show more concern for the Muslims themselves. Missionary involvement is slowly increasing, but only 33 missionaries are committed to the 3.5 million Muslims.

12. **Abidjan's exploding population**, which doubles every four years, is the strategic key for evangelization of both Côte d'Ivoire and Burkina Faso. Every people of these two lands has a significant community in the city, but most are neglected. There are 53 church-planting missionaries in the city representing 13 churches/missions, but this is not adequate. Over two million Muslims are scarcely touched with the gospel, and only 10 missionaries are seeking to reach them (**SIM, CMA, MTW**). There are only about 100 churches in the city – the more significant being those of the **AoG, SBC**, MB and **CMA**.

13. **The large influx of foreigners** presents unusual opportunities for evangelizing those who are separated from the strong ties of their tribal cultures. Nearly 30% of the population is foreign. AIDS has become a major problem in the country, with 14–16% of Abidjan's population already infected with the HIV virus – few Christians have faced up to this challenge. The whole of West Africa is being rapidly affected because of the migrant population, and little has been done to evangelize the Burkinabé, Malians, Guineans and colonies of Mauritanians in many towns. Pray that churches and missions may send more workers to seize present opportunities before these people become Muslim. The most responsive have been the Mossis from Burkina Faso.

14. **Young people are responsive**, and wherever churches have been willing and able to minister specifically to them, there has been fruit. The liberty for teaching Scripture in public schools is exciting but under-used through lack of qualified personnel. **SU** is making a vital contribution in school evangelism and discipleship. The **IFES** Francophone Africa HQ is in Abidjan, and there is a good GBU group (**IFES**) in the university. IFES aims to set up a nationwide student movement, and Navigators are commencing a student ministry. **CCC** is well established with five full-time Ivorian staff couples.

15. **Literature.** Pray for the bookstores and depots of various missions, including the Bible Society, *Maison de la Bible*, **CLC** (Abidjan), **MB** (Man and Daloa), **UFM** (Gagnoa) and **CBFMS** (Korhogo). Pray also for the inter-mission/church Evangelical Publication Centre in Abidjan, which coordinates much of the production of evangelical literature for all Francophone Africa – publishing books, cassettes and an evangelistic magazine for children. Pray for solutions to problems in these ministries: lack of qualified staff (especially French-speaking), financial pressures and lack of good distribution outlets and marketing strategies.

16. **Bible translation** is one of the most pressing and demanding ministries for Christian workers. A considerable number of national and expatriate workers are involved in 27 translation and literacy programmes linked with **UBS** and various church/mission groups. **SIL**'s contribution in a number of projects is especially significant – many being among the superficially-Christianized people of the south. Possibly 23 other languages will require translators. Pray for newly-translated Scriptures to take root in the hearts of the people. Hosanna Ministries is seeking to record New Testaments in local languages for free distribution in the churches.

17. **Christian Media**
a) **The damage to ELWA radio (SIM)** in Liberia has been a severe blow to Christian work. Pray for an effective Christian radio and TV strategy – involving local radio, national radio and TV networks, and also international missionary stations – to more than replace the loss. The government recently turned down an application for a Christian FM station. Pray for a change of attitude.
b) **AEAM** has launched a project to produce culturally relevant videos for transmission by national television stations across West Africa.
c) **The *Jesus* film** is in use in Dioula, Baoulé and Malinké, and **GRn** audio recordings have been prepared in 49 languages.

Croatia

See under YUGOSLAVIA

C

Cuba
(Republic of Cuba)

April 15
Caribbean

Area 115,000 sq.km. The largest island in the Caribbean.

Population	Ann. Gr.	Density
1990 10,324,000	0.75 %	93/sq.km
1995 10,788,000	0.88 %	97/sq.km

Peoples:
Spanish-speaking 99%. White 66%. Mixed race 21%. Afro-Caribbean 12%.
Other 1%. Indo-Pakistani 31,000; Chinese 15,000; US Military at Guantánamo Military Base 7,000.

Literacy 96%. **Official language:** Spanish.

Capital: Havana 2,077,000. Urbanization 73%.

Economy: Production of sugar and nickel ore have been the mainstays of the economy. Repressive centralized socialist planning, a US trade embargo, and the collapse of Cuba's Communist bloc trade and aid after 1989 have impoverished an already poor country. Rationing, hunger and lack of many essentials are deeply affecting the country. Unemployment 6% but underemployment very high. Public debt/person $626. Income/person $2,690 (13% of USA).

Politics: Independent from Spain in 1898. Castro's revolution brought Communism to power in 1959. After 30 years of vigorously exporting revolution to Latin America and Africa, Cuba is isolated as one of the last protagonists for Communism. The repressive and corrupt police state is diplomatically isolated and politically paranoid, but with no viable alternative government, the old dictatorship continues.

Religion: Strict control of all church activities and repression of religious freedom in earlier years of Communist rule, but since 1990 the Church has enjoyed a greater level of acceptance by the government. In 1992 the constitution was amended making it illegal to discriminate against Christians in Cuban society.

Non-religious/other 30.9%. About 10% of the population is actively linked with the Communist Party.
Spiritist 25%. Widespread occultism of both Afro-Caribbean and European varieties.
Christian 44.1%. Growth 2.4%. Figures below are estimates and may be generally lower than the actual numbers.
Protestant 2.82%. Growth 6.1%.

Church	Cong	Members	Affiliated
Evang Pentecostal	156	28,000	56,000
Assemblies of God	375	30,000	50,000
Assoc of Evs **(WT)**	140	14,000	23,300
Seventh-day Adventist	100	9,991	22,200
Chr Pentecostal Ch	80	8,000	20,000
Bapt Conv of W. Cuba	127	7,600	13,100
Bapt Conv of E. Cuba	134	7,500	12,500
Methodist Ch of C	107	3,200	11,000
Ref Presbyterian	63	1,900	9,050
Free Baptist Conv	15	2,480	4,500
All other (43)	478	34,692	69,758
Denominations (53)	1,775	147,363	291,408
Evangelicals 2.54% of pop		135,200	262,500
Pentecostal/charis		84,000	151,300

Missionaries:
to Cuba 2 (1:5,150,000 people).
from Cuba 2.
Roman Catholic 41.1%. Attend 2%.
Growth 2.1%.
Catholic Ch   618 2,720,000 4,243,000
Missionaries to and from Cuba unknown.
Orthodox 0.01%. Growth 0.7%.
Foreign Marginal 0.13%. Growth 3.9%.
Jehovah's Witnesses   250   8,000   13,300

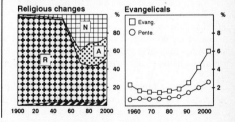

Religious changes   Evangelicals

1. **Fidel Castro clings to power in Cuba** with his battle-cry "Socialism or Death". Christians are proclaiming, "Cuba for Christ". Pray that the inevitable changes may lead to life out of death for

millions of Cubans. Throughout the country there is a suppressed rage. Many fear social chaos or bloody revolution are likely in 1993 or 1994. Hospitals and prisons are full but stores and hearts are empty. Pray for a peaceful transition to democratic freedoms.

C

2. **Few Cubans have had any meaningful contact with Christianity.** The identification of the Roman Catholic Church with Spanish colonial and subsequent repressive governments meant that the church was never strong in Cuban society. The Church suffered a catastrophic loss of influence, numbers and property after the Communist revolution. There are more Evangelicals who attend church than Catholics. Nominal adherence to Catholicism dropped from 85% in 1957 to 38.5% in 1983, with less than 10% of these attending mass. The number of priests dropped from 725 to 200 over the same period. Since the late '80s, a religious resurgence is sweeping Cuba which is affecting every level of society. Evangelical Christians are viewed as having a positive influence on society. Praise God for the change.

3. **The Protestant churches** were decimated by several waves of emigration to the USA, a move encouraged by the authorities. Recovery and growth was slow, but out of the furnace of persecution high-quality leadership and committed membership arose that witnessed fervently. Since 1989 growth has become spectacular. Widespread hunger for spiritual reality is bringing in a great harvest. There were over 1,250 Protestant congregations in 1990. Some estimated that by the end of 1992, Evangelicals might even have reached one million in 6,000 churches and house groups. Pray that this moving of the Holy Spirit may lead to lasting fruit in multiplied churches.

4. **Persecution of Christians** and severe restrictions on street meetings, mass evangelism and the building and repair of church buildings made life difficult for Christians. Discrimination, police informers and possible imprisonment made discipleship costly. All is rapidly changing and persecution has ended, but Christians are still subject to many restrictions. Pray for complete religious freedom.

5. **Leadership for the churches** is a pressing need. Many had to flee or were expelled in the years following the revolution. Praise God for those who stood firm for Jesus. There are now eight Evangelical and two Catholic Bible schools or seminaries. Careful provision of teaching materials and funding from outside is enabling the Church to upgrade its pastors and provide training for leaders of the multiplying house churches. The high educational level of society makes this easier. Many university-trained professionals are coming to Christ, some taking on an active leadership role in the Church. Pray that the many new Christians may be well discipled as a result.

6. **The less reached.**
a) Less than 5% of Cuba's population attends church – the lowest percentage for any country in the Western Hemisphere. Most have no real understanding of the gospel.
b) **Spiritists** have multiplied under Communism. About a quarter of the population is actively involved in the occult *Sanetarie*, which resembles the Haitian *Voodoo.* Pray that Christians may have the love, understanding and spiritual power to see many delivered from this satanic bondage.
c) **The Chinese and Indians** are neglected ethnic minorities. Some of the former are Roman Catholic and Episcopalian, but no specific outreach to them is known.
d) **African school children** were taken from lands considered targets for Marxist revolution to be indoctrinated on the Isle of Pines. In 1989 there were 16,000 from 37 nations. They were isolated from family and all contact with Christianity. Many have now returned to Angola, Mozambique, Namibia, South Africa and elsewhere. Pray that the poison sown in their minds may be neutralized and that God may open their hearts for the light of his Word.

7. **Foreign missions** have been restricted to tactful support and occasional pastoral visits from outside the country. A few were permitted to remain in a low-profile teaching ministry. Pray that missions may plan wisely for the day that Cuba is free once more. The Cuban Church will need humble helping ministries rather than high-publicity, foreign-generated programmes and aid.

8. **There is a famine of the Scriptures.** The Bible Society was closed in 1965 and import of Bibles became very difficult. Some consignments were destroyed by the Marxist authorities. The Cuban Ecumenical Council became the only legal importing and distributing agent for the limited supplies permitted before 1992. Praise God that during 1992 more Scriptures were imported than in the previous 23 years. Pray for the reopening of the Bible Society and the full availability of the Word of God.

9. **Christian help ministries.**

a) **Literature** has been in short supply, but Christian presses are now permitted and, since 1993, government presses have accepted Christian printing jobs. Pray for workers, funds and supplies to print teaching and evangelistic literature as well as Scripture portions. The Bible Society is printing one million of the latter. Pray also for the provision of spiritual study materials for pastors and preachers.

b) **Christian radio** has been a source of strength and encouragement to many. There is no lack of choice with about 2,800 hours of international Christian broadcasting in Spanish every week in Latin America! The main providers are **TWR, FEBC** and **HCJB.**

10. **There are about one million Cuban refugees**, mostly from the white middle and upper classes, living in the USA. Pray for these uprooted people – they have many opportunities to trust in the Lord. It is estimated that 10% of these exiles are now Protestant. Pray that freedom may come to their land again and permit their return, but also that God will enable them to understand and adapt to a very different country from the one they left.

Cyprus

April 16
Europe

Since 1974, the island has been divided into two *de facto* states: the Turkish Republic of Northern Cyprus (TRNC), occupying the northern 36%; and the Republic of Cyprus (RC) the southern 64%. The latter is predominantly Greek and is still recognized internationally as the legal government of the whole island.

REPUBLIC OF CYPRUS

Area 5,896 sq.km. The UN buffer zone and two UK sovereign bases occupy 460 sq.km.

Population	Ann. Gr.	Density
1990 568,200	0.98%	97/sq.km
1995 594,200	0.90%	101/sq.km

Peoples:
Greek 97.1%.
Other 2.9% including British 9,000; Armenian 6,300; Arab 2,500; Turks 100. There are also many Lebanese Arab refugees, and UN Peace-keeping Forces 2,400.

Literacy 94.5%. **Official languages:** Greek; English widely spoken. **All languages** 5.

Capital: Nicosia 236,000. Urbanization 64%.

Economy: Strong recovery after Turkish invasion and well-diversified today. The country's position in the heart of the Middle East and its political stability are major contributing factors for growth. Income/person $7,812 (37% of USA).

Politics: After years of unrest by the Greek majority, independence from Britain was gained in 1960. Subsequent communal conflicts culminated in the 1974 abortive coup (supported by Greece) and subsequent Turkish invasion and partition of the island. As a result, 200,000 people became refugees. All efforts to achieve a settlement have so far failed, and the country remains divided into two states.

Religion: Included with TRNC figures overleaf.

TURKISH REPUBLIC OF NORTHERN CYPRUS

Area 3,355 sq.km.

Population	Ann. Gr.	Density
1990 170,000	0.98%	51/sq.km
1995 177,000	0.90%	53/sq.km

Half the density of the Republic of Cyprus.

Peoples:
Turkish 98.7%. **Greek** 1%. **Other** 0.3%. Turkish troops 27,000.

Literacy 94%. **Official language:** Turkish.

Capital: Leftcosa (Nicosia) 77,000. The city is partitioned between the TRNC and the RC.

Economy: Depressed and stagnating since the invasion.

Politics: Diplomatic isolation of the internationally unrecognized TRNC has crippled development. All attempts to reunify the island have foundered on the intransigence of both governments.

Religion: Open proselytizing is not allowed in either part of the country. In the Greek area the Orthodox Church is influential, and in the Turkish area Islam is dominant. All statistics below are for the whole island.
Muslim 22%. Almost entirely in TRNC; a few Arabs and Turks in RC.
Christian 78%. Growth 0.8%.
  Protestant 1%. Growth 1%.

Church	Cong	Members	Affiliated
Anglican	7	1,400	3,500
Greek Evangelical	3	280	700
Ch of God of Prophecy	3	330	660
Christian Brethren	1	60	120
All other (13)	15	847	1,835
Denominations (17)	29	2,917	6,815
Evangelicals 0.45% of pop		1,300	3,000
Pentecostal/charis 0.1%		330	650

Missionaries:
  to Cyprus 135 (but nearly all are involved in international ministries).
  from Cyprus 2 (1:1,600 Protestants) 2 dom.
Roman Catholic 1.1%. Mainly Lebanese Maronites.

Catholic Ch	10	4,400	8,000

Missionaries to Cyprus 4 (1:355,000 people).
Orthodox 74.8%.

Orthodox	557	278,000	506,000
Armenian Apostolic	5	9,900	18,000
Denominations (3)	563	287,940	524,100

Foreign Marginal 1.1%. Growth 2.4%.

All groups (3)	19	4,223	7,500

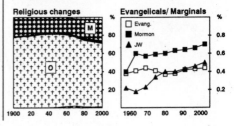

Religious changes   Evangelicals/ Marginals

1. **The Orthodox Church is very traditional,** and while individuals are free to change to another denomination, social pressures are so great that this rarely occurs. Pray for the gospel in its purity to be accepted by the many nominal Christians. Mormons and Jehovah's Witnesses are more numerous than Evangelicals.

2. **The few Evangelicals** are members of the Greek Evangelical Church or belong to several Pentecostal groups, mostly in Limassol and Nicosia. Only two or three missionaries minister to the Greek majority in Greek, and they face opposition from the Orthodox Church. Pray for the witness of Greek and non-Greek believers. Most Evangelicals are from the Armenian minority.

3. **The Logos bookstore (CLC)** is a vital centre for books, tracts and BCCs. Logos is also the core of a range of Christian education ministries that are a boost to the evangelical witness. Pray for the effective use and distribution of literature and also for the nationwide **EHC** tract distribution.

4. **Cyprus (RC) is a major base for Christian organizations** ministering to the surrounding Middle Eastern states. Pray for the stability of the country!
  a) **A number of missions** have HQs or regional centres in Cyprus (**MECO, CCC, YWAM, Interserve,** etc.).
  b) **Arabic literature** is both printed and stocked for distribution throughout the Middle East (**MECO**).
  c) **Christian radio** programmes are broadcast by three Christian agencies over Cyprus Radio in Arabic and Armenian, but not in Greek and Turkish.
  d) **The Logos School of English Education,** started in 1973, has 160 students from all over the Middle East. It has a strong Christian testimony.
Pray that all these operations in Cyprus may be effective throughout the Middle East.

5. **The north (TRNC)** is almost completely Muslim. No open Christian activity is allowed. Praise God for a small group of Turks, converted through literature, who now meet weekly for worship and fellowship. There are reported to be several other small home meetings in two cities. Pray for the crumbling of political, cultural, historical and spiritual barriers to witness and to acceptance of the gospel.

6. **The NATO forces** at the two large military bases are largely British. Pray for the witness of Ministry to Military Garrisons and chaplains. Pray that a clear witness may be given by Christian service personnel to the Cypriots. Pray also for opportunities to share the gospel with the multi-national UN Peace-keeping Force.

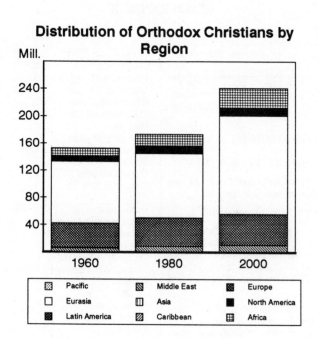

Distribution of Orthodox Christians by Region

▧ Pacific	▨ Middle East	▩ Europe
☐ Eurasia	▥ Asia	■ North America
▦ Latin America	▨ Caribbean	▦ Africa

Orthodox Christianity has had a checkered career in the 20th century.

1. Losses in the Middle East through persecution, massacres and emigration.

2. Slow growth elsewhere – usually lower than population growth.

3. An increase in **Eurasian** growth as Orthodoxy regains some of its old influence in former Communist lands – especially Ukraine, Byelarus and Russia.

C

April 17	*Czech Republic &*
Europe	*Slovakia*

Czechoslovakia ceased to exist at the end of 1992. The two separate states are handled together in this book because economic, political and Christian denominational statistics cannot be fully separated.

CZECH REPUBLIC

Area 78,000 sq.km. Landlocked central European state. Major components: Bohemia, Moravia and part of Silesia.

Population	Ann. Gr.	Density
1990	10,298,000	0.18 %	131/sq.km
1995	10,391,000	0.18 %	133/sq.km

Peoples:
Slavic 98.7%. Czech 9,853,000 (inc. some Slovak); Polish 40,000.
Other 1.3%. Gypsy 50,000; German 47,000.

Literacy 99%. **Official language:** Czech. **All languages** 6. **Languages with Scriptures** 5Bi.

Capital: Prague 1,215,000. Urbanization 76%.

Economy: Highly industrialized but Communism degraded quality. Rapid economic development with considerable German investment since 1990. Rapid privatization of industry, trade and property. Unemployment 3%. Income/person $7,200 (34% of USA).

Politics: Czechoslovakia formed in 1918. A Communist coup in 1948 led to Stalinist repression until 1963. The Dubcek government's attempts at liberalization provoked USSR invasion of 1968 and reimposition of hard-line Communism. Peaceful protests brought about the collapse of the Communist regime in 1989. This "velvet revolution" was followed by rapid democratization and then by the peaceful "velvet divorce" creating two new republics at the beginning of 1993. The Czech Republic aspires to early membership of the EC.

Religion: Communist repression, infiltration and manipulation of the Churches and leadership was particularly severe – and effective. Complete religious freedom in Czech Republic since 1990. Figures below include both republics.
Non-religious/other 26.8%.
Jews 0.03%. Only 5,000 remain of 360,000 in 1938; most killed in Holocaust, some emigrated to Israel.
Christian 73.2%. Nom 18.8%. Affil 54.4%. Growth −1%.
  Protestant 6%. Affil 5.2%. Growth −2%.

Church	Cong	Members	Affiliated
Slovak Ev Ch (Lthn)	327	231,000	330,000
Ev Ch of Cz Breth	600	117,000	192,000
Refmd Chr Ch in Slov	300	101,000	150,000
Silesian Ev Ch (Luth)	40	35,300	49,000
Seventh-day Adventist	170	8,500	15,000
Congregational Ch	222	6,000	12,000
Brethren	43	5,500	10,000
Bapt Unity of Breth	37	4,000	10,000
Pentecostal Ch (AoG)	95	2,200	5,250
Moravian Brethren	18	700	5,000
United Methodist Ch	24	2,000	3,500
Evangelical Free Ch	7	1,400	3,500
All other (7)	163	19,020	28,230
Denominations (19)	2,046	533,620	813,480
Evangelicals 1.5% of pop		146,400	235,300
Pentecostal/charis 0.16%		15,000	26,000

Missionaries:
  to Czech & Slovakia 59 (1:264,000 people).
  from Czech & Slovakia 3 (1:264,000 Protestants).
Catholic 63%. Affil 47.3%. Catholic figures 72.5%. Growth −0.7%.

Roman Catholic Ch	4,391	5,270,000	7,217,921
Uniate Catholic Ch	209	136,000	188,400
Total (2)	4,600	5,406,000	7,406,321
Charismatics 0.1%		10,000	15,000

Missionaries to and from Czech & Slovakia unknown.
Other Catholic 3.4%. Affil 1.2%. Growth -5.9%.

Hussite Ch	432	130,000	185,000
All groups (2)	441	131,500	187,750

Orthodox 0.7%. Affil 0.64%. Growth −8%.

Orthodox Ch	180	54,000	100,000

Marginal 0.12%. Growth 8%.

All groups (9)	230	9,800	18,000

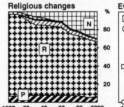

Religious changes

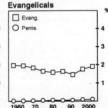

Evangelicals

1. **Praise God for peaceful liberation from the yoke of Communism.** The grim legacy of that system, though discredited, is a moral and spiritual vacuum. Sadly, Marxist propaganda and a generally tamed and compromised church leadership made the Church a less-preferred option to the average secularized Czech (and Slovak) once freedom was restored. New Age and eastern cultic teachings have found a more ready hearing, even among many churchgoers. Pray for spiritual awakening that will restore the tarnished image of the Church.

2. **The wounds inflicted by Communism on the Churches** will take time to heal. Many leaders compromised – often under duress, but this frequently followed theological compromise too. Liberal theology has been widespread in the larger churches, and the majority of adherents are nominal. Of the 73% of those who claim to be Christian, only 16% of Catholics and 14% of Protestants are regular churchgoers. Most active Christians are the old and the young – those in between are few in number. Few churches in the former Communist bloc are more in need of a renewing work of the Holy Spirit.

3. **Czech Protestants** have suffered waves of persecution for nearly six centuries – the great early reformer Jan Hus was martyred in 1415. Culturally and traditionally the Protestant Churches have an important place in the history of the nation. Pray that this may also become true spiritually. Pray also for evangelical congregations within the larger denominations and also for smaller evangelical denominations such as the Baptists and the small, but growing, Pentecostal movements. Charismatic renewal has made considerable progress in some denominations.

4. **Leaders with the precious combination of spirituality and adequate biblical training** are too few. For decades little training was permitted – especially in biblical theology. Pray for the Hus, Comenius and Bratislava Theological faculties where most pastors are trained – but evangelical teachers are few. TEE programmes run by both Evangelicals and Pentecostals for years can now develop into Bible schools. Pray that these may be fully developed and that such schools become a source of godly preachers of the Good News. This is the major area for foreign missionary involvement.

5. **New freedom to evangelize** has not been used as it could have been. The growth in churches has not been large, and initiatives have been fragmented and with little coordination. Pray for the Evangelical Alliance formed in 1991, and for effective cooperation between Evangelicals in leadership training, literature and evangelism. One of the great needs is for a national survey of the churches and the unchurched. Pray for a re-birth of vision among Christians for the complete evangelization of both republics.

6. **Young people** are searching for life-satisfying answers, but are often cynical and apathetic about Christianity. Churches have to redevelop ministry programmes for children and young people – the Baptist churches have made great strides in this. Religious education in schools is required in both republics. Pray that teachers with spiritual life may minister life in the classrooms. **SU** is developing ministry and Bible clubs in schools and **IFES** in universities in both republics, with the beginnings of groups in five of 11 universities in Bohemia and eight out of nine in Slovakia.

7. **Christian literature** may now be freely printed locally and imported, but the range and quality of indigenous writings are still limited. The **Bible Society** has been established, and Bibles and New Testaments have been selling well. The Navrat Christian Publishing House has been set up in Prague. **EHC** plans on a literature distribution to every home in Prague, and then the whole country. Christian literature is being widely distributed in schools. Pray that the impact of the written page may remould the people and build the Church.

8. **Christian radio and television programmes** on national networks are possible, and this ministry could probably be expanded if more personnel with vision and better funding were available. **TWR** is expanding its contacts and programme sources in both republics with 5.5 hours/week in Czech and 4 hours/week in Slovak. HCJB(**WRMF**) Quito also broadcasts 5.5 and 3 hours/week, respectively. Pray that these media might be effectively used to uplift Jesus and counteract error.

April 18
Europe

C

SLOVAKIA
(Slovak Republic)

Area 49,500 sq.km. Landlocked central European state east of Czech Republic. Ruthenia to its east seized by USSR in 1945; now part of Ukraine.

Population	Ann. Gr.	Density
1990 5,287,000	0.18%	106/sq.km
1995 5,334,00	0.18%	108/sq.km

Peoples:
Slavic 81.2%. Slovak 4,981,000 (including some Czech); Ruthenian 100,000; Russian/Ukrainian 60,000; Polish 38,000.
Hungarian 11.2%. In south adjoining Hungary.
Other 7.6%. Gypsy 350,000.

Literacy 99%. **Official languages:** Slovak; locally, Hungarian (still being debated). **All languages** 9. **Languages with Scriptures** 5Bi 1NT 2por.

Capital: Bratislava 440,000. Urbanization 76%.

Economy: Dependent on archaic heavy industry, and hesitant about the heavy social and economic cost of more radical Czech privatization plans. Economy stagnating without foreign investment. Unemployment 11%. Income/person $5,960 (28% of USA).

Politics: Nationalist parties, most being reformed Communists, won elections that led to break-up of federation with Czech Republic. Some fear that a more socialist and protectionist nationalism could lead to economic decline and clashes with Hungary over development of the massive Danube hydro-electric project and restrictions on the culture of the large Hungarian minority.

Religion: There is now religious freedom. About 75% of Slovaks claim to be Christian – mostly Catholic.

1. **Slovakia faces an uncertain future.** Pray that the leaders in addressing the new nation may show restraint and wisdom in solving the severe economic crisis and the question of the large, and anxious, Hungarian ethnic minority. There is a general sense of frustration caused by loss of national identity. Pray that this may cause many to be more open to the Lord.

2. **Protestants** are a small minority in a land that is 60% Catholic. Pray that the witness and outreach of evangelical churches and believers might grow and bear fruit, and that appropriate evangelism will take priority over internal structures and organizational activities.

3. **The despised Gypsy population** is isolated from the mainstream of Slovak life, and is the least reached section of the population. Most are nominal Christians, but there are a few evangelical believers. Pray that Gypsy evangelists and missionaries from other lands may be called for ministry in Slovakia.

Denmark
(The Kingdom of Denmark)

April 19
Europe

D

Area 44,500 sq.km. The most southerly of the Scandinavian countries. See separate entries for Faeroe Islands and Greenland, which are autonomous regions of Denmark.

Population	Ann. Gr.	Density
1990 5,120,000	−0.01 %	119/sq.km
1995 5,129,000	0.04 %	119/sq.km

Peoples:
Danish 96.9% including also German 56,000; Faeroese 6,000; Greenlanders 3,000; Gypsy 3,000. **Foreign** 3.1%. Turks 30,000; Other Scandinavians 19,000; British 10,000; Yugoslavs 10,000; Iranians 9,000; Indo-Pakistani 4,000. 32,000 of these are refugees.

Literacy 99%. **Official language:** Danish.

Capital: Copenhagen 1,378,000. Urbanization 84%.

Economy: Based on services, agriculture and light industry. Strongly export-oriented. Unemployment 10%. Public debt/person $3,710. Income/person $20,415 (97% of USA).

Politics: Stable parliamentary democracy with a constitutional monarchy. A member of the European Community but cautious about implications of too high a degree of federalization of Europe.

Religion: There is complete religious freedom, though the Lutheran Church is recognized as the national Church and is supported out of a state-levied church tax.
Non-religious/other 7.5%. This figure would be much higher if all non-religious "Christians" were included.
Muslim 1%. Predominantly Turks, Iranians, Yugoslavs and Arabs.
Jews 0.16%. About 8,000 in total.
Christian 91.3%. Affil 91.3%. Attend 3%. Growth −0.1%.

Protestant 90.1%. Growth −0.1%.

Church	Cong	Members	Affiliated
Lutheran	2,313	*925,135	4,602,000
Baptist Union	45	5,929	10,000
Pente Mvmt (Elim)	52	5,180	9,090
Salvation Army	39	3,900	5,000
Apostolic	40	2,314	4,881
Danish Covnt Ch	29	1,982	3,150
Methodist Ch	25	1,572	2,540
Danish Moravian Ch	1	275	393
All other (30)	105	7,768	23,812
Doubly Counted		−37,000	−50,000
Denominations (38)	2,649	917,055	4,610,866

* *Danish Christian Handbook estimation 1990*

Evangelicals 4.8% of pop	51,500	246,000
Pentecostal/charis 0.28%	17,500	30,000

Missionaries:
from Denmark 383 (1:13,300 Protestants) in 18 agencies 356frn 37dom.
to Denmark 31 (1:165,100 people) in 8 agencies.

Roman Catholic 0.55%. Growth 0.8%.

Catholic Ch	70	21,400	29,276

Missionaries to Denmark 28 (1:183,000 people).

Orthodox 0.01%. Growth 9.7%.
Foreign Marginal 0.67%. Growth 1.6%.

Jehovah's Witnesses	227	16,120	27,300
Mormons	22	2,750	4,300
All other (9)	122	1,307	2,908
Groups (11)	371	20,177	34,508

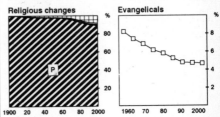

Religious changes / Evangelicals

1. **Denmark needs a fresh visitation from God.** Although 90% of the population still maintain formal links with the national church, church attendance varies between 1% and 4% in most parishes. Pray for an outpouring of the Spirit that will affect Lutherans who have turned to secularism or New Age thinking.

2. **Much of the Lutheran Church is formal,** and the fresh winds of the Holy Spirit must blow through this institution. Some evangelical pastors are committed to renewal of the church. Pray for all who preach the truth within the national church.

3. **The evangelical witness is weak** both within and outside the State Church. Pray that all seeking to live for the Lord may lead many others to a personal faith in Christ. Many groups – like the Lutheran home mission movements, **IFES** student groups and other evangelical groups from both

the Lutheran and Free churches – are becoming concerned for evangelism among secular Danes. The Danish Lausanne group has provided a significant basis for cooperation among all Evangelicals. A **DAWN** movement was launched in 1992 with a united vision in the free churches for planting 2,000 new congregations by the year 2000. Pray for this to be achieved.

4. **Liberal theology** has gained such a dominant position in the State church that it is hard for Evangelicals to find an acceptable ministry. Two conservative Lutheran free theological faculties are expanding facilities and student enrolments. There are also five Bible schools and short-term programmes run by Inner Mission, Lutheran Mission, KFS(**IFES**), the OASE-Movement and **YWAM**. Pray for all graduates of the institutions as they prepare for ministry.

5. **Young people** have been particularly affected by the negative effects of materialism around them, and have become more responsive to spiritual challenges. Only a small minority of children have any practical knowledge of Christianity. Many seek answers in new religious movements.

6. **Eastern religious movements** have gained a large following. Nearly one-third of Danes now believe in reincarnation. The world-renowned **Dialogue Center** in Aarhus and other Christians are doing much to inform churches and schools of these movements and combat their teaching. Pray that churches may provide the spiritual help that many are seeking.

7. **The missionary vision** is relatively weak compared with neighbouring Norway. Most of the 390 Danish missionaries are evangelical, but there has been a steady decline in missionary numbers since 1970. Pray for them and for the growth of interest in and support for world evangelization. Pray also for the unmet spiritual needs among guestworkers and refugees in Denmark. The Muslim Turks, Iranians and Yugoslavs present a particular challenge.

8. **Literature.** The Danish Bible Society published a new translation of the whole Bible in 1992. Pray for the effective entry of God's Word into many homes and hearts. Also pray for a better distribution of Christian books throughout Denmark.

Djibouti

(Republic of Djibouti)

April 20
Africa

D

Area 23,200 sq.km. A hot, dry, desert enclave in Ethiopia and Somalia. It is reputed to be the world's hottest country.

Population	Ann. Gr.	Density
1990 406,000	3.0 %	18/sq.km
1995 473,000	3.1 %	20/sq.km

Peoples:
Issa Somali 45.6% in three major clans: Issa 103,000; Gadaboursi 48,000; Issaq 41,000. But supplemented by many refugees of the same clans from Somalia.
Afar (Danakil) 36%.
Arab 11.5%, many from Yemen.
Other 6.9%. French 12,000; Ethiopian 2,500; Greek 1,600; Indo-Pakistani 400.
Refugees. Up to 50,000 Somalis and Ethiopians.

Literacy 34%. **Official languages:** French and Arabic. **Trade languages:** Somali, Afar. **All languages** 4. **Languages with Scriptures** 2Bi 1NT.

Capital: Djibouti 250,000. Urbanization 75%.

Economy: Plagued by drought, and limited by lack of industry or natural resources. Commerce and the rail link to Ethiopia are the major mainstays of the economy. French aid and military base are important. Unemployment 40–50%. Public debt/person $327. Income/person $475 (2.3% of USA).

Politics: Independent from France in 1977. Politics has been dominated by tensions between the Afar and Somali ethnic groups. Civil war broke out in 1991. The Somali-dominated government was forced by aid donors and Afar guerrillas to legalize multi-party democracy in 1992, but elections brought only cosmetic changes and civil warfare resumed. The government is losing credibility.

Religion: Considerable degree of religious freedom.
Muslim 94.6%. Almost entirely Sunni.
Non-religious/other 0.4%.
Hindu 0.1%. **Baha'i** 0.1%.
Christian 4.8%. Europeans and Ethiopians, very few Somalis.
  Protestant 0.07%. One French Reformed expatriate group, two Ethiopian refugee congregations and a handful of Afar, Somali and Arab believers.
  Missionaries to Djibouti 25 (1:16,200 people) in 3 agencies.
  Roman Catholic 3.7%. French and 600 Somalis. Missionaries to Djibouti 50 (1:6,800 people).
  Orthodox 1%. Ethiopians and Greek Orthodox.

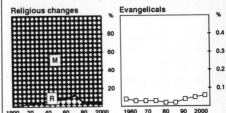

1. **The way opened for the first evangelical witness** in 1975. Praise God for this. Pray for the land to remain open so that strong local churches may be planted among the indigenous peoples.

2. **Missionary work is a tough challenge** in this hot land, and working conditions are extreme. The major agency is **RSTI** with 19 workers. US Mennonite and Baptist workers have joined them. Pray for their ministries in education, public health, agriculture, literature, Bible translation, literacy and youth work. Through these, opportunities to witness abound – pray that these contacts may lead to disciples for Jesus. Pray for the calling of other long-term workers.

3. **The few Somali and Afar believers** are often isolated and suffer many pressures from relatives. Most of the believers are jobless and some are illiterate. Pray for the effective use of literacy programmes and the Scriptures in Somali and Afar. The Somali believers are meeting regularly for Bible study together. Pray that from these believers, leaders for congregations may be raised up.

4. **The less evangelized peoples of Djibouti.**
a) **The Afars'** main territory is in Ethiopia and Eritrea where no evangelism has been permitted for years. The New Testament was published in 1992. Daily Afar broadcasts were resumed by **FEBA**-Seychelles in 1991. Pray for the establishment of the first Afar church.
b) The **Somalis** are a small branch of the larger Somali population in war-torn Somalia. The indigenous and refugee Somalis in Djibouti are a key for the evangelization of their kinsmen across the border. **FEBA** broadcasts 30 minutes daily in Somali.

c) **Arabs,** both local and Yemeni, need a specific approach directed to their spiritual needs.

d) **The ethnic minorities** – Greeks, French and Indians – have little exposure to vibrant Christian witness.

See Caribbean
Caribbean

Dominica
(The Commonwealth of Dominica)

Area 751 sq.km. A hurricane-prone, rugged, mountainous island between the French islands of Guadeloupe and Martinique and ruled by France until 1759. This has determined much of its religious and cultural development.

Population		Ann. Gr.	Density
1990	81,000	1.3 %	108/sq.km
1995	87,000	1.4 %	116/sq.km

Peoples:
Afro-Caribbean 97.2%.
Amerindian 1.5%. Caribs 1,250, the descendants of the original inhabitants, but considerably intermarried with the Afro-Caribbean people.
Other 1.3%. Euro-American 400, East Indian 300, Syrian 200, Chinese 150.

Literacy 94%. **Official language:** English, but 70% speak a French Creole. **All languages** 2. Languages with Scriptures 1Bi.

Capital: Roseau 22,000. Urbanization 30%.

Economy: Heavily dependent on export of bananas and coconuts. Tourism is not a major source of income. Public debt/person $780. Income/person $1,670 (8% of USA).

Politics: Independent from Britain in 1978. A republic with a stormy post-independence political history and a number of attempted coups.

Religion: Freedom of religion.
Non-religious/other 8%.
Christian 92%. Nom 5.7%. Affil 86.3%. Growth 0.7%.
Protestant 17%. Affil 16.9%. Growth 3.6%.

Church	Cong	Members	Affiliated
Seventh-day Adventist	11	2,200	3,140
Methodist	5	1,250	2,080
Chs of Christ	16	900	1,800
Anglican Ch	3	650	1,300
Ch of God of Prophecy	10	300	750
Baptist Conv (**SBC**)	5	152	304
All other (10)	31	2,171	4,649
Denominations (16)	81	7,623	14,023
Evangelicals 9.6% of pop		3,900	8,000
Pentecostal/charis 2.7%		1,100	2,300

Missionaries to Dominica 9 (1:9,000 people) in 4 agencies.
Roman Catholic 74.2%. Affil 68.6%. Growth 0%.

Catholic Ch	43	30,210	57,000

Missionaries to Dominica 55 (1:1,500 people).
Marginal 0.8%. Growth 4.5%.

Jehovah's Witnesses	6	263	658

1. **The Carib Indians** live on an isolated reservation on the northeast coast of Dominica. They are the last of the indigenous peoples in the Caribbean to survive the arrival of colonialism and the wave of immigrants. Most are nominally Christian, but few have a living faith in Christ. Pray that these socially deprived people may find their true identity and fulfilment in him.

2. **The majority of the population** is nominally Catholic. There has been a steady growth in evangelical churches, but the virtual absence of two-parent families and a high rate of illegitimacy makes holy living a rarity. Pray for greater unity among Dominican Evangelicals.

Dominican Republic

Area 49,000 sq.km. The eastern two-thirds of the island of Hispaniola, shared with Haiti.

Population		Ann. Gr.	Density
1990	7,170,000	2.2 %	148/sq.km
1995	7,915,000	2.0 %	163/sq.km

Peoples:
Hispanic 83%. Euro-American 14%; Afro-Caribbean 69%.
Haitian 16%. Dominican-born 500,000; illegal immigrants 500,000.
Other 1%. Chinese 25,000; Jamaicans 22,000; Lebanese 3,000; Japanese 1,500.

Literacy 77%. **Official language:** Spanish. **All languages** 3. **Languages with Scriptures** 2Bi.

Capital: Santo Domingo 2,411,000. Urbanization 56%.

Economy: Growth in the early '70s has been replaced by devastating decline prompted by world recessions, a bloated bureaucracy and a corrupt government spending freely on costly prestige projects. These have resulted in massive poverty, raging inflation, and unemployment at 28%. Public debt/person $498. Income/person $680 (3.2% of USA – it was 10% in 1985).

Politics: Independence achieved four times – twice from Spain (1821/65), once from Haiti (1844) and once from the USA (1924)! Thirty years of repressive dictatorship ended in 1961, but instability and civil war prevailed until 1966. Subsequent democratic governments have not handled the economy wisely, and unrest, rioting and victimization of the Haitians are the consequences.

Religion: Catholicism is the official religion, but there is freedom for other religions.
Spiritist 1%. Half the population is probably involved in occult practices.
Non-religious/other 1.1%.
Christian 97.9%. Nom 7.7%. Affil 84.2%. Attend 10%. Growth 1.7%.
  Protestant 6.1%. Affil 6%. Growth 7.2%.

Church	Cong	Members	Affiliated
Seventh-day Adventist	246	29,000	72,500
Assemblies of God	454	23,378	72,414
Ch of God of Prophecy	172	14,000	40,000
Ch of God (Cleveland)	227	14,170	30,000
Ch of the Nazarene	138	9,902	21,614
Free Methodist Ch	102	9,300	21,100
Moravian	94	6,600	16,900
Defenders of the Faith	24	5,000	16,700
Dominican Evang Ch	146	5,400	15,900
Christian Reformed Ch	95	3,500	11,300
Christian Brethren	100	4,000	8,000
Chr Bible Ch (UFM)	28	2,800	7,000
Ev Temple Assoc (WT)	20	1,400	4,240
Episcopal Ch	28	1,570	4,000
Baptist Convention	19	941	2,050
All other (52)	754	42,666	94,735
Denominations (67)	2,647	173,627	438,453
Evangelicals 5% of pop		142,000	357,000
Pentecostal/charis 3.1%		86,500	212,000

Missionaries:
 to Dominican Rep 174 (1:41,200 people).
 from Dominican Rep 51 (1:8,600 Protestants) in 3 agencies 5frn 5xcul 46dom.
Roman Catholic 91.2%. Affil 77.6%. Practising 7%. Growth 1.3%.

Catholic Ch	1,317	2,900,000	5,570,000
Charismatics 1.2%		43,900	83,500

Missionaries:
 to Dominican Rep 1,561 (1973 figure).
 from Dominican Rep 60 (1973 figure).
Marginal 0.55%. Affil 0.5%. Growth 7.1%.

Jehovah's Witnesses	187	12,108	36,691
Groups (2)	198	13,208	39,441

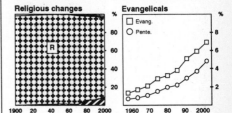

Religious changes / Evangelicals

1. **Protestant churches** have been growing steadily since the '70s after a slow and relatively late start by Protestants. Much of this growth has been in Pentecostal denominations, the Free Methodists and the Seventh-day Adventist Church. The most responsive have been lower and middle classes and especially Haitians. Pray that every level of society and part of the country may experience that growth.

D

2. **Major challenges that confront Christians:**
a) **Retention** of new converts, church members and leaders for the continuing evangelization of the country.
b) **Development** of Christian ethics for Christian involvement in a society where corruption, crime and promiscuity are rampant.
c) **Adaptation** of a largely rural-oriented church to rapid urbanization.
d) **Cultivation** of a missionary vision.

3. **The large Haitian under-class** has been the most responsive of all. The Nazarene and Christian Reformed congregations have multiplied. Haitians are immigrants or descendants of immigrants who are often despised by Hispanics but needed as sugar-cane and manual workers. The government has begun mass deportations of Haitian children and old people to a "homeland" many have never seen. Pray for leaders and congregations witnessing in this tense situation.

4. **Emigration, both legal and illegal,** is relatively easy due to close proximity to the USA. The heavy loss of Christian laymen and leaders has stunted the development and growth of the churches. Pray that the seven accredited theological training schools and the National Evangelical University may provide spiritual, mature and stable leaders for the future.

5. **Missions** are involved in church-planting, evangelistic ministries and technical assistance. Some larger denominational and interdenominational agencies are **SBC** (27 workers), **CRWM** (21), **YWAM** (18), **UFM** (15), **WT** (9) and the **Brethren** (15). The missionary force suffers from a high turnover, and consequent immaturity, lack of adaption to culture and paternalistic attitudes. Pray for stability, maturity and willingness to trust national leaders to lead and give vision.

6. **The less reached** – a target for intercession in the '90s.
a) **Non-churchgoers,** about 90% of the population.
b) **The youth,** scarcely touched by present ministries. ADEE (**IFES**) has two staff workers for the 450,000 secondary school students and 150,000 university students.
c) **The upper class,** from whom most political leaders come.
d) **The Chinese,** who have only two congregations of believers among them.

7. **Goals for the year 2000** – pray for their attainment:
a) A church for every community by the year 2000. There are an estimated 5,000 villages and towns without an evangelical church.
b) A **DAWN** project which has been launched to mobilize national churches and pastors to plant these churches. A national pastors' conference in 1992 gave impetus to this vision. Several denominations are setting courageous goals for growth.

Ecuador

(The Republic of Ecuador)

April 22
Latin America

E

Area 283,600 sq.km. Amazon jungle in east, high Andean Sierra in the centre, fertile coastal plain on Pacific Coast. Also the Galapagos Is. 1,000 km. to west.

Population	Ann. Gr.	Density
1990 10,782,000	2.8 %	40/sq.km
1995 12,314,000	2.7 %	46/sq.km

Peoples: Considerable racial mingling, but approximately:

Spanish-speaking 56.9% (non-Amerindian). Mestizo 2,450,000; Afro-American 610,000; Euro-American 300,000.

Amerindian 42%.

Quichua* 40.9%; non-tribal Quichua 2,707,000 (also Spanish-speaking). Nine other main groups: Chimborazo 1,430,000; Otavalo 89,000; Canari 72,000; Salasca 54,000; Saraguro 45,000; Napo 29,000 and others.

Lowland tribes 1.1%; (11 groups) 119,000. Largest: Shuar 48,000; Orejon 21,600; Cayapa 5,400; Colorado 1,800; Waorani (Auca) 800 and others.

Other 1.1%. English-speaking 65,000; German 32,000; Norwegian 11,000; Chinese 7,000; Arab 1,800.

* Quichua is spelt Quechua in surrounding nations.

Literacy 70%. **Official language:** Spanish. **All languages** 22. **Languages with Scriptures** 2Bi 8NT 5por.

Capital: Quito 1,234,000. Other major city: Guayaquil 1,700,000. Urbanization 53%.

Economy: Unequal distribution of oil wealth has widened the gap between the rich and poor – the latter mainly Quichua. Failure to curb inflation, natural disasters and a high birth rate, combined with declining revenues from oil, bananas and coffee, have lowered living standards for the majority. Public debt/person $1,150. Income/ person $1,040 (4.9% of USA).

Politics: Independent from Spain in 1830. Political stability has been rare, the average government lasting two years. However, the political emancipation of the hitherto downtrodden Quichua over the past 20 years, and democratic changes of government have been major improvements. There are several small anti-government guerrilla movements.

Religion: The culture has been strongly moulded by Catholicism, so though there is freedom of religion, rural populations have not been so receptive to change.
Non-religious/other 0.74%.
Animist 0.5%. **Baha'i** 0.36%.

Buddhist/Chinese religions 0.04%.
Jews 0.01%.
Christian 98.4%. Nom 5.9%. Affil 92.5%. Growth 2.6%.
Protestant 3.8%. Affil 3.5%. Growth 8.4%.

Church	Cong	Members	Affiliated
Assoc of Indian Ev Chs (GMU) (4)	474	61,165	105,141
Independent Chs (30)	178	16,000	35,600
Ch of God (Cleveland)	88	12,434	31,100
Baptist Conv (SBC)	100	9,312	29,100
Chr & Miss All (CMA)	179	12,500	25,000
Foursquare Evang Ch	97	7,000	23,300
Assemblies of God	153	6,130	17,500
Seventh-day Adventist	32	8,250	13,747
Evang Covenant Ch	40	2,970	6,750
Ch of the Nazarene	70	3,125	4,409
Assoc of Miss Chs	12	692	1,540
All other (68)	543	36,585	83,172
Denominations (111)	1,966	176,163	376,359
Evangelicals 3.4% of pop		169,000	363,000
Pentecostal/charis 1.4%		61,000	153,000

Missionaries:
to Ecuador 1,116 (1:9,700 people) in 83 agencies.
from Ecuador 48 (1:7,800 Protestants) in 4 agencies 3frn 3xcul 45dom.
Roman Catholic 93.3%. Affil 87.5%. Christo-pagan 20%. Growth 2.2%.

Catholic Ch	2,206	5,510,000	10,027,000
Doubly counted		−320,000	−590,000
Total	2,206	5,190,000	9,437,000
Charismatics 0.2%		11,000	20,000

Missionaries:
to Ecuador 304 (1:35,500 people).
from Ecuador 120 (1973 figure).
Orthodox 0.02%. Growth 3%.

Orthodox Ch	1	850	1,700

Foreign Marginal 1.3%. Affil 1.29%.
Growth 15.2%.

Jehovah's Witnesses	345	22,763	90,000
Mormons	103	43,400	70,000
All groups (3)	448	66,201	160,089

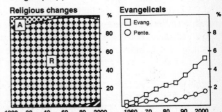

Religious changes

Evangelicals
☐ Evang
○ Pente.

E

1. **Since 1982, the nation has suffered a series of national disasters** – climatic, earthquakes and a cholera epidemic on top of its economic woes. These, together with the breakdown of the old feudal structures of the State and Church, have made Ecuadorians more receptive – especially the Quichua. Praise God for the open doors and hearts, but pray for government leaders courageous enough to confront the entrenched privileged elite and bring meaningful progress and stability to every level of society.

2. **Ecuador had Latin America's smallest percentage of evangelicals in 1960.** Praise God for major breakthroughs and people movements that have brought rapid church growth since then, notably among:
a) **Spanish-speaking urbanites,** with good church growth in the **CMA** and Pentecostal churches.
b) **Quichuas in Chimborazo Province,** and to a lesser extent elsewhere, through the ministry of **GMU.** In 1967 there were only 120 believers among three million people, but now there are over 105,000 in the GMU-related churches. Many other denominations also have seen a harvest among them. In Chimborazo 10% of the Quichuas are Evangelicals. Strong mature leaders and churches have come into being, and an impoverished, downtrodden people is being uplifted by the gospel.
Over the past 30 years, the number of Evangelicals nationwide has grown from 19,000 to 363,000 – a twenty-fold increase. Pray for the unity of believers that transcends class, culture, personalities and denominational labels so that the Body of Christ may exert a decisive influence on the life of the nation.

3. **Vision for further advance in the '90s.**
a) *Ecuador by 2000* plans that everyone in the country be confronted with the claims of the Lord by the end of the century.
b) **The Baptist Convention** aims to have 250,000 members by the year 2000.

4. **Challenges for the church in the '90s.** For continued numerical and spiritual growth, pray for:
a) **Unity in evangelism** to reach the less-reached – especially the very rich and very poor.
b) **Cultural sensitivity** for Spanish-speaking Christians in ministry to the Amerindian Christian majority.
c) **Integration of Quichua and Lowland Indians** into the political, economic and spiritual life of the country, while preserving their cultural integrity.
d) **More and better pastoral training.** Syncretistic beliefs, losses to cults and evangelical nominalism are otherwise inevitable. Bible schools and seminaries are increasing in number, but insufficiently to meet the need. TEE programmes are proving an effective supplement in training lay and pastoral teachers.
e) **Development of missions vision.** Quichua believers are planning missionary outreach to peoples in Peru and Bolivia.
f) **Teaching for the youth** – especially in the area of biblical commitment and relationships. Promiscuity is a serious problem.

5. **Pioneer work among the small jungle tribes** attracted worldwide attention in 1956 when one **MAF,** one **GMU** and three Brethren missionaries were killed by the primitive Waorani (Auca). Nearly all these tribes now have churches and the Scriptures through the work of **Brethren** and **SIL/WBT** missionaries among the Waorani and Colorado, **GMU** among the Shuar, the Quichua churches among the Zaparo, and others. Pray for:
a) **The neutralization of intense anti-missionary propaganda** from humanistic anthropologists, leftist agitators, traders and jungle exploiters. At times opposition has curtailed Christian ministry and Bible translation work.
b) **The efforts by Indian believers** to preserve their lands from irresponsible oil exploration.
c) **The maturing of the jungle churches** to cope with modernity.

6. **Bible translation.** Ecuador is one of the first countries entered by WBT where they have achieved or soon will achieve the goal of a New Testament for nearly every language. WBT has had translators involved in 12 languages, but these are gradually being withdrawn. Pray for the completion of translation programmes in progress, and for the two or three languages where translation work may yet be needed. Pray for the effective use of the Bibles and New Testaments now available.

7. **Missions.** The largest groups are **WRMF** (304 missionaries), **SBC** (89), **CMA** (89), **AoG** (79), **GMU** (55), Norwegian Santal Mission (46), **OMS** (33), **Brethren** (32). Major missionary-contributing nations: USA (799), Canada (62), Norway (46), Brazil (39). There are many

opportunities for missionary recruits in supportive ministries, church planting and pioneer work in the groups mentioned below.

8. **The less-reached:**
a) **The slum-dwellers of Quito and Guayaquil.** Over 60% of the latter's population lives in slums built on a polluted marsh. Few Christian workers have a vision for these deprived people.
b) The **upper and middle classes** who have been relatively unresponsive (**CMA, OMS** and others).
c) **University and school students.** There are over eight agencies involved in campus ministries among the 260,000 students, including **CCC, IFES,** YFC, **LAM** and four denominational groups. The work is small, but an impact is being made on the, often, radical university campuses.
d) The 6,000 people living on the distant and barren **Galapagos Islands,** which have only one evangelical church with two members and six adherents.
e) **The provinces** of Carchi (130,000 people with eight churches) and Loja (361,000 people with only nine churches). The latter is a target for **SIM.** The gold-rush town of Guadeloupe has been described as a "gangster's heaven".
f) **The Chinese** who have no church, though two small Bible study groups serve their community.

9. **Radio.** The ministry of **HCJB** is known and appreciated both in Ecuador and worldwide. The **World Radio Missionary Fellowship** prepares and transmits 900 hours of programmes weekly in 47 languages internationally and 23 Quichua dialects, as well as providing a valuable coverage of Ecuador through radio with 91 hours in Quichua and 450 hours in Spanish. Pray for this ministry and the extensive follow-up work that the large response requires. Pray also for the two Quichua and one Shuar Christian radio stations, under local leadership but started by **GMU,** broadcasting to these indigenous groups. Both the Evangelical Covenant Church and Lutheran Church also run radio stations.

April 23–25
Middle East

Egypt
(Arab Republic of Egypt)

Area 1,001,000 sq.km. 96% desert, and only 3% arable land along the banks of the Nile and around the Western Desert oases.

Population		Ann. Gr.	Density
1990	54,059,000	2.6 %	54/sq.km
1995	60,470,000	2.3 %	61/sq.km

In fertile areas 1,760 people per sq.km!

Peoples
Egyptian 86.4%. Speaking Arabic, but descendants of the ancient Coptic-speaking people of biblical times.
Arab 6.2%. Bedouin 1,081,000; Sudanese 540,000; also Lebanese, Yemeni, Palestinian and others.
Nubian 3%. Arabic-speaking 1,300,000; Nobiin-speaking 350,000; Kenuz-speaking 108,000.
Berber 2%. Nearly all Arabized, a few speaking Zenati at the Siwa Oasis.
Gypsy 2%. Most now Arabic-speaking. Halebi 864,000; Ghagar 216,000.
Other 0.4%. Westerners 250,000; Beja 77,000; Turkish 27,000; Armenian 25,000.

Literacy 45%. **Official language:** Arabic. **All languages** 11. **Languages with Scriptures** 2Bi 1NT 3por.

Capital: Cairo 10,120,000 (unofficial figure nearer 14 million). Other major city: Alexandria 3,162,000. Seventeen other cities with over 100,000 people. Rapid urbanization – now at 49%.

Economy: Poor, and in a state of perpetual crisis. The high birthrate, limited agricultural land and water, world recession and the unresolved tensions between Islamic radicals and the government all conspire to cripple efforts to solve the problems. The Gulf War aid bonanza, remittances from the four to five million Egyptians resident abroad, and revenues from the Suez Canal have enabled the country to survive. Unemployment 17%. Public debt/person $790. Income/person $630 (2.9% of USA).

Politics: President Sadat's diplomacy (1970–81) ended the dominance of the USSR and won control of the valuable Suez Canal and Sinai oilfields from Israel as an outcome of the 1973 Yom Kippur War. The generally popular peace treaty with Israel in 1979 was bitterly opposed by many Arab nations and Muslim extremists within the country and led to Egypt's isolation in the Middle East and Sadat's assassination. Subsequent political reforms have reinstated multi-party democratic government, but Islamic fundamentalism grows with every economic setback. By 1992 the government was forced to crack down on the extremists after the latter had murdered government leaders, Christians and tourists in their efforts to bring about the collapse of the government.

Religion: Islam is the state religion, but until recently the large Christian minority was left in relative peace so long as Muslims were not evangelized. Islamic radicals are successfully forcing a greater Islamization of society.
Muslim 85.4%. Cairo is the intellectual capital of Islam. Muslim fundamentalism has become a significant force over the last 15 years.
Non-religious/other 0.4%.
Christian 14.2%, but officially 6%. Some Christians claim 20%. Growth −1.3%.
Protestant 0.85%. Growth 2.7%.

Church	Cong	Members	Affiliated
Evangelical Ch of E	320	50,000	300,000
Free Methodist Ch	120	12,053	40,200
Assemblies of God	150	15,400	32,000
Pente Ch of God	27	1,300	3,250
Ch of God of Prophecy	13	650	1,630
All other (49)	543	53,379	84,956
Denominations (54)	1,173	132,782	462,036
Evangelicals 0.73% of pop		119,000	396,000
Pentecostal/charis 0.11%		27,000	60,000

Missionaries:
to Egypt 217 (1:249,000 people) in 39 agencies.
from Egypt 135 (1:2,600 Protestants) in 7 agencies 13frn 9xcul 126dom.
Catholic 0.32%. Growth 0.5%.

Coptic-rite Catholic		81,000	140,000
Latin-rite Catholic		8,000	12,000
Other Cath Rites (5)		13,000	23,000
All Catholics (7)	201	102,000	175,000
Charismatics		2,000	3,500

Missionaries:
to Egypt 1,100 (1973 figure).
from Egypt 75 (1973 figure).
Orthodox 13%. Growth −1.6%.

Coptic Orthodox	1,266	4,050,000	6,980,000
Greek Orthodox	25	3,300	14,300
Armenian Apostolic	4	8,450	13,000
All other (4)	3	540	1,238
Denominations (7)	1,298	4,062,290	7,008,538
Orthdx evangs 1.8% of pop		600,000	1,000,000

Missionaries:
from Egypt est. 65 (1:118,000 Orthodox) 6xcul 59dom.

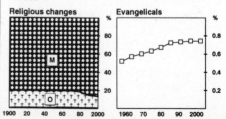

Religious changes

Evangelicals

1. **Islamic fundamentalism** has become a severe threat to the stability of Egypt. Acts of terrorism by extremists, economic sabotage and intolerance are fuelled by economic stresses. Pray for division and confusion to discredit and nullify such plans. The promise of Isaiah 19:19–22 for Egypt must be fulfilled.

2. **Persecution of Christians** became steadily more severe over the '80s. Harassment, severe application of ancient discriminatory laws, destruction of churches and bribery for Christians to adopt Islam are all extensively used to break the morale of Christians. Muslims who have become Christians have been imprisoned and some killed. In 1991 there were 235 Christians known to be imprisoned for their faith. One Muslim leader has publicly exhorted Muslims to *wipe out* all Christians.
a) Pray that Christians may stand firm in their faith and live exemplary lives before their malefactors.
b) Pray for Christians now wavering, for between 15,000 and 30,000 Christians annually are turning to Islam. Many others emigrate to Western countries where they are free to worship.
c) Pray for a change in the law which requires presidential permission to build, repair or even paint a church. Few licences have been granted since 1981 – even when Muslim extremists have destroyed a church building.

3. **The Coptic Church** is by far the largest body of Christians in the Middle East and is a strategic key for the evangelization of the area. Pray that mounting pressures, communal tensions, detention of leaders and persecution may strengthen and enliven the Church. There has been a marked increase in intercessory prayer as a result of these difficulties. The recent wave of persecution has brought together Orthodox and Protestant leaders as never before. In 1992 God stepped in by pouring out the Holy Spirit in revival. Miracles and healings as well as a spontaneous work of the Spirit in hearts in Sunday schools has led to thousands of nominal Christians and even Muslims coming to Christ. Orthodox, Catholic and Protestant churches have been affected. The Assemblies of God report 25,000 new decisions to follow Jesus. Pray that the work of the Holy Spirit may prove irresistible in the midst of opposition.

4. **A biblically-based renewal movement in the Coptic Church** has steadily gained momentum since 1930, and its strong emphasis on Bible study and a warm personal faith has led to many becoming fervent witnesses for the Lord. Pray for the growth and effectiveness of this movement of the Spirit.

5. **The Protestant churches** sprang from the Orthodox minority, and for some decades had not seen significant growth. This is changing: there has been a growing renewal movement since 1973 and many young people are now coming to the Lord. Several Pentecostal and Evangelical denominations are growing significantly. Pray that, despite the difficulties, Muslims may be reached *and* welcomed into the churches. Few Christians would even be open to witness to a Muslim. Many churches have extensive social programmes to help the very poor.

6. **Unreached peoples.** Few Muslims have ever heard a Christian testify. Pray that the Christians may win opportunities to speak through their Christ-like lives. Specific prayer targets:
a) **The urban population** – many are uprooted peasants in squalid slums.
b) **The *fellaheen*** (peasants) in the rural villages of the Nile.
c) **The Nubian people,** largely converted from Christianity to Islam in the 17th century but open to the gospel. Only portions of the Scriptures are available in one of the two languages still spoken by 10–15% of Nubians.
d) **The desert dwellers** – Bedouin, Siwa Berber, and others have had little contact with the gospel.
e) **Arab visitors** to Egypt from many "closed" Muslim lands. They come especially during Ramadan to avoid the rigours of the Muslim month of fasting!

7. **Christian witness among university students** is encouraging. There is a group in many of the faculties of Egypt's four biggest university complexes. Pray that these believers may find open hearts among the 685,000 students in 13 universities and win them in the relatively open spirit of inquiry on the campuses. There are increasing instances of Muslim intimidation and grade discrimination against Christian students. Pray that these believers may be built up in the Lord for future service through the witness of local churches and other students. Work among children and young people in high schools is especially encouraging, with many youth groups in churches, schools, summer conferences and camps.

8. **There is a dearth of volunteers for pastoral and missionary service.** Two-thirds of all evangelical churches have no pastor. Pray for many such to give themselves for the Lord's work. Pray

for many such to give themselves for the Lord's work. Pray also for those in theological training at the Coptic Evangelical Church Seminary (which had only 20 students preparing for the ministry in 1989), the **AoG** and Free Methodist Bible schools, and in institutions abroad.

9. **Openings for Christian service by expatriates are now more numerous than for many years.** There are possibilities for ministry in expatriate community churches and with indigenous churches, as well as in service ministries such as literature and through a variety of professional and business openings which provide opportunities for witness to the non-Christian majority. Pray for labourers!

10. **The missionary vision of the Egyptian church is growing,** but it is limited by lack of funds. Missionaries from Egypt would be more acceptable than Western missionaries in many Muslim lands. Pray that the many Egyptian Christians in the West and Middle Eastern oil states may catch the vision to support such a thrust.

11. **Christian literature** is freely printed and sold. Pray for:
a) **Christian bookstores** (10 in Cairo), and for the effective use of this literature.
b) **More local believers who are able to write** suitable evangelistic and teaching materials.
c) ***Magalla***, the mass-circulation magazine, which has a Christian slant. Over 60,000 copies are sold every issue in 16 Middle Eastern lands. There is also an audio-cassette version. Pray for the magazine's continued publication despite opposition, and for its effectiveness in breaking down misconceptions about the gospel. Pray for all engaged in its publication. Pray also for the West European edition ***Magallati*** and its use among the 2,700,000 Arab speakers living in Europe as well as the numerous Arab tourists.
d) The **SBC** and **AoG** who are working together to produce a three-year Sunday school curriculum in Arabic for use across the Middle East. Pray that it may ground the next generation of Christians in God's Word.
e) **Bible distribution.** The Arabic Living Bible was published in 1988 and has stirred great interest among people of all religions – pray for eternal fruit. In 1992 the revival movement resulted in increased sale of Bibles.

12. **The *Jesus* film in Arabic is being widely shown.** Pray that this vivid portrayal of the Saviour may open many hearts and that there may be freedom for effective follow-up.

13. **Christian radio** is a potent tool. Pray for the various Arabic language studios where programmes are prepared, and for Christian broadcasters and listeners. High Adventure in Lebanon broadcasts over 100 hours per week in Arabic, with **FEBA** 14, **TWR** 8.4 and **IBRA** 3.5 hours each.

El Salvador

(The Republic of El Salvador)

April 26

Latin America

E

Area 21,400 sq.km. The smallest and most densely populated mainland Spanish-speaking state in the Americas.

Population		Ann. Gr.	Density
1990	5,252,000	2.0 %	250/sq.km
1995	5,943,000	2.5 %	282/sq.km

The war displaced over 1,300,000 people, of whom 700,000 took refuge in surrounding lands and the USA. Many of these are returning to their homes.

Peoples:
Spanish-speaking 99.2%. An amalgam of Ladino (Mestizo) 92% Amerindian 5%; White 1.7%; Honduran and Nicaraguan 0.5%.
Amerindian-speaking 0.3%. Kekchi 10,500; Pocomam 5,200. Only 7% of Amerindians still use their original languages.
Other 0.5%. North-American/European 15,000; Chinese 1,300; Turks 500.

Literacy 63%. **Official language:** Spanish. **All languages** 4.

Capital: San Salvador 542,000. Urbanization 43%.

Economy: The 12-year civil war, earthquakes and the collapse of the price of coffee, the country's main export, impoverished the nation. Economic and social inequalities that provoked the war still remain, and have to be tackled now that peace has come. Over 80% live in dire poverty. Unemployment 24%. Public debt/person $312. Income/person $1,040 (4.9% of USA).

Politics: Independent from Spain in 1821 as part of a united Central America and as a separate nation in 1838. All power remained in the hands of wealthy plantation owners allied with the military. A long series of corrupt dictatorships and gross inequalities between the rich and poor provoked armed leftist insurrection in 1981. Over 75,000 were killed in fighting, cross-fire or through right-wing death squads. The ending of the Cold War, revulsion over human rights abuses and international pressure forced through a peace accord in 1992. Steps towards disarmament, effective land redistribution and full democracy have been taken.

Religion: Though Catholicism is the state religion, the Catholic Church opposed the oppression and human rights abuses by the ruling minority. Both Catholics and Evangelicals were martyred.
Non-religious/other 2%. Baha'i 0.5%.
Christian 97.5%. Nom 3.1%. Affil 94.6%. Growth 2%.
Protestant 20.6%. Growth 5.9%.

Church	Cong	Members	Affiliated
Assemblies of God	6,051	108,150	238,900
Prince of Peace	556	50,000	125,000
Apostolic Ch of Apostles & Prophets	300	45,000	100,000
Ch of God (Cleveland)	312	17,808	44,500
Seventh-day Adventist	160	23,000	38,396
Elim Church	71	12,000	30,000
Cntl Am Ch (CAMI)	250	13,222	29,400
Baptist Association	58	7,229	14,500
Baptist Conv (SBC)	47	5,580	12,400
Lutheran Ch (LCMS)	76	7,600	10,000
All other (54)	2,673	182,388	439,918
Denominations (64)	10,554	471,977	1,083,014
Evangelicals 19.8% of pop		445,915	1,038,331
Pentecostal/charis 16.4%		364,000	862,000

Missionaries:
to El Salvador 102 (1:51,500 people) in 31 agencies.
from El Salvador 130 (1:8,300 Protestants) in 7 agencies 38frn 30xcul 100dom.
Roman Catholic officially 88.4%; actually 75.1%. Affil 72.2%. Growth 0.8%.

	Cong	Members	Affiliated
Catholic Ch	246	2,550,000	4,640,000
Doubly counted		−380,000	−848,000
Total	246	2,170,000	3,792,000

Missionaries:
to El Salvador 829 (1973 figure).
from El Salvador 80 (1973 figure).
Foreign Marginal 1.8%. Growth 9.2%.

Jehovah's Witnesses	326	18,445	61,500
Mormons	77	22,400	32,000
All groups (2)	403	40,845	93,500

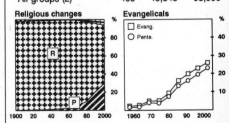

Religious changes

Evangelicals

1. **The fragile peace could easily be broken** and civil war break out once more. Pray for magnanimity, forgiveness and a fair opportunity for all to participate in the economic and political life

of the country. Pray for the election of leaders who will promote this and freedom for the gospel. Pray for the resettlement of the thousands of refugees.

2. **An astonishing spiritual harvest has been gathered** from all strata of society in the midst of the hate and bitterness of war. In 1960, Evangelicals were 2.3% of the population, but today are around 20%. Growth among Pentecostal churches has been dramatic. Pray for the consolidation of this work through effective discipling and motivation of believers for outreach. Pray for evangelistic teams now reaching out – such as the *Cristo es la Respuesta* team with 40 workers. A big problem is the large number of ex-Evangelicals.

3. **Goals for AD2000.** The Salvadoran Evangelical Confraternity, representing 50 denominations, committed themselves in 1987 in a **DAWN** strategy to multiply established congregations from 3,400 to 12,000 by the end of the century. Pray that this may be achieved and that El Salvador may be the Saviour's (*El Salvador* means Saviour).

4. **Suffering and damage to properties, families and lives of Christians** was severe. There were many Salvadoran martyrs. The coming of peace gives an opportunity to rebuild, consolidate, grow and reach out to a physically, morally and spiritually wounded population. Pray that there may be no place for bitterness, carnality and division in the Body of Christ.

5. **Children and young people** have suffered especially. Much could be done by churches and international agencies to both rehabilitate them and win them for Christ. Pray for:
a) **The 350,000 abandoned children** – orphanage, counselling and educational ministries are vital.
b) **The 74,000 university and college students** whose study years have been badly disrupted and politicized. **IFES** has a ministry among them.

6. **Leadership for the churches** must be multiplied. The war, lack of finance, and insufficient staff have crippled what training was available. Pray for the 15 Bible schools, three seminaries and over 12 TEE programmes. Pray for the provision of all material needs for staff and students in this time of economic stress. It is in this ministry that more missionary input is needed. Major missionary-contributing nations: USA (87), Canada (4), UK (4).

7. **Missions interest has grown,** but most believers still find it difficult to imagine themselves as missionaries. Pray for Salvadoran missionaries who *have* been sent and that others may follow.

Equatorial Guinea
(The Republic of Equatorial Guinea)

April 27

Africa

E

Area 28,000 sq.km. A small enclave, Rio Muni, on the African mainland; and several islands in the Gulf of Guinea, including Bioko (2,000 sq.km.) and Pagalu (10 sq.km.).

Population		Ann. Gr.	Density
1990	440,000	2.3 %	16/sq.km
1995	497,000	2.5 %	18/sq.km

The former ruler caused the deaths of about 60,000 people and the flight or expulsion of a further 140,000 between 1969 and 1978.

Peoples:
Bantu 94.3%. Over 10 ethnic groups.
 Mainland. Fang (Ntum, Okak, Maka) 330,000, politically dominant; Seke 11,000; Ngumba 8,900; Ngumbi-Yaka 8,000; Puku 6,600; Benga 3,100.
 Islands. Bubi 24,000 on Biombo Island.
Pygmy 0.7% on Cameroon border.
Spanish-speaking 2.6%. Mixed race 10,500; Spanish 1,000. Mainly on Biombo Island.
Creole-speaking 1.8%. Biombo 4,600; Pagalu 3,000. On the islands.
Other 0.6%. Europeans, Nigerians, Indians.

Literacy 72%. **Official languages:** Spanish and French. **All languages** 9. **Languages with Scriptures** 2Bi 2NT 3por.

Capital: Malabo 73,200. Urbanization 27%.

Economy: Prosperous until independence, but in total collapse by 1979. Great potential for development, but economic recovery is slow. Dependent on Spanish and French aid. Public debt/person $502. Income/person $430 (2% of USA).

Politics: Independence from Spain in 1968. A coup in 1969 brought Macias Nguema to power. This atheist dictator turned his country into a slave-labour camp with Soviet Bloc assistance. A military coup in 1979 resulted in a one-party presidential government economically linked with the neighbouring Francophone states. All dissent and attempts to introduce multi-party democracy continue to be vigorously suppressed.

Religion: In colonial times almost the entire population was baptized as Catholics. The savage persecution of the '70s with the repression of religions has been followed by limited religious freedom. Proselytization and the registration of new denominations are not allowed.
Tribal religion 5.1%. In actual practice, the figure is much higher. Many baptized Catholics still follow the old ways.
Non-religious/other 1%. **Baha'i** 0.4%.
Islam 0.5%. Predominantly Moroccan military and their dependants.
Christian 93%. Nom 15.4%. Affil 77.6%. Growth 2.5%.
Protestant 4.5%. Affil 3.19%. Growth −1.6%.

Church	Cong	Members	Affiliated
Reformed Ch	130	4,000	10,000
Crusade Chs (**WEC**)	20	440	1,100
Methodist Ch	4	300	800
Assemblies of God	8	296	740
Baptist Conv (**SBC**)	40	84	210
All other (5)	13	500	1,171
Denominations (10)	215	5,620	14,021
Evangelicals 0.87% of pop		1,532	3,832
Pente/charis 0.27% of pop		500	1,200

Missionaries to Equatorial Guinea 42 (1:10,500 people).
Roman Catholic 87.8%. Affil 83.86%. Growth 2.7%.

Catholic Ch	88	235,000	325,000

Missionaries to Equatorial Guinea 213 (1:2,100 people).
Foreign Marginal 0.2%. Growth 27.8%.

Jehovah's Witnesses	4	193	1,000
Groups (2)	10	493	1,500

Indigenous Marginal 0.5%. Affil 0.31%. Growth −5.7%.

Groups (1)	5	500	1,350

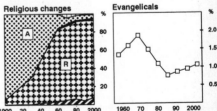

Religious changes   Evangelicals

1. **This ravaged land will need years for recovery** from the effects of economic devastation, murder and exile of virtually all educated citizens. Political rivalries, corruption and attempted coups prolong the agony. Pray for stability and full freedom for the gospel.

2. **The persecuted Church has not emerged unscathed.** Church leaders were forced to compromise or suffer. Tragically, many Protestant church leaders are living in sin and are more interested in power politics than in the spiritual nurture of their flocks. Pray for men of God, fearless for the truth,

to be raised up to lead the churches back to a living relationship with God. Pray for both repentance and revival.

3. **Religious freedom** has yet to come. The newer work of **SBC, AoG** and others has been fruitful despite the restrictions. Pray for these to be removed and for every part of the country to be evangelized. Pray also for missionaries serving in the country. Major missionary-contributing nations: USA (21), Canada (6), Netherlands (5), Nigeria (4), Argentina (3).

4. **There are only 25 trained pastors in the country,** and most of these have been strongly influenced by liberal theological schools in Cameroon. Pray for the two new Bible schools – Crusade/ **WEC** in Bata, and Pentecostal in Malabo.

5. **The less reached.** Almost the whole population is nominally Catholic, but large parts of the country have no evangelical witness – the centre and north of the mainland, and the smaller islands. The ethnic minorities such as the Ngumba, Yaka, Puku and Benga have no known congregations of evangelical believers.

Eritrea

See under ETHIOPIA

Estonia
(Republic of Estonia)

E

Area 45,200 sq.km. Northernmost of the three Baltic states. Separated from Finland by the Gulf of Finland.

Population

		Ann.Gr.	Density
1990	1,581,000	0.69%	35/sq.km
1995	1,636,000	0.40%	36/sq.km

Peoples: Based on 1989 Census.
Finno-Ugric 59.1%. Estonian 963,000; Finnish 17,000.
Indo-European 40% (4% before 1940).
  Slavic 39.2%. Declining slightly. Russian 485,000; Ukrainian 48,000; Byelorussian 28,000; Russian military 70,000.
  Other 0.8%.
All other peoples 0.9%. Jews 4,600; Tatar 4,000; Chuvash 1,200.

Literacy 99%. **Official language:** Estonian; Russian is widely used. **All indigenous languages** 5. **Languages with Scriptures** 4Bi.

Capital: Tallinn 500,000. Urbanization 72%.

Economy: Rapid decline since independence due to breakdown of trading patterns and links with Russia. The country is too small to be viable without close ties with larger economies. Finland is investing heavily in Estonia, but poverty is causing increased Estonian emigration. Income/person $744 (3.5% of USA).

Politics: Long dominated by surrounding nations. Became independent dur 1918–1940. The Soviet invasion in 1940 and subsequent deportation and murder of a large minority of Estonians is still cause of deep resentment against Russia. Became independent during 1988–91 as a multi-party democracy. Strong nationalist sentiment is committed to establishing Estonian identity.

Religion: Severe persecution between 1940 and 1988. Freedom of religion since then. Most figures below are estimates.

Non-religious/other 38.7%. Predominantly Slavs.
Muslims 1%. Immigrant minorities from Central Asia and Urals.
Jews 0.3%.
Christian 60%. Affil 36.8%. Growth 1.2%.
Protestant 38.4%. Affil 15.3%. Growth 3.5%.

Church	Cong	Members	Affiliated
Lutheran Ch	150	75,431	203,968
Ev Chr/Bapt Union	84	6,511	20,000
Pentecostal Chs	10	1,500	5,000
Faith Free Ch	14	2,800	4,300
Methodist Ch	16	1,900	3,330
Seventh-day Adventist	17	1,640	2,000
All other (3)	15	1,200	3,000
Denominations (9)	306	90,982	241,598
Evangelicals 7.5% of pop		44,500	118,000
Pentecostal/charis 0.8%		6,000	13,000

Missionaries:
  to Estonia est.45.
  from Estonia 4 (1:109,000 Protestants) in 2 agencies 4frn.

Roman Catholic 1%. Affil 0.76%. Growth 5.7%.

Catholic Ch	6	1,782	12,000

Orthodox 20.3%. Growth −0.5%.

Estonian Orthodox	35	124,000	310,000
All other (3)		7,150	11,000
Denominations (4)	35	131,150	321,000

Marginal 0.29%. Growth 15.5%.

Jehovah's Witnesses	10	1,260	4,200
Mormons	3	210	350
Groups (2)	13	1,470	4,550

1. **Tiny Estonia's major preoccupation** is to preserve national identity in close proximity to its giant but ailing neighbour, Russia. The Soviet subjugation of Estonia in 1940 was particularly brutal; large-scale enforced settlement of Slavs by Stalin further inflamed Estonian nationalism. Pray for wisdom and sensitivity for the government in handling the ethnic issue – especially the large Russian minority.

2. **God gave revivals** in the Lutheran Church in the past, but a turning away from the Lord preceded the imposition of Communism. There is a strong desire to seek after God once more. Over 90% of Estonian children are sent to Sunday Schools. Churches are growing, and there is great receptivity, but not yet revival. People are discouraged with economic hardship and rising crime.

3. **Estonian churches** lack trained pastors. A Baptist seminary was started in 1988 and graduated its first students in 1992. A Lutheran seminary was started in 1992, also several smaller Bible schools. The Estonian Church needs a new awakening for missions – especially to ethnic minorities in Russia. Two missionaries have gone to the Kumyk people of Dagestan in the Caucasus and won their first converts.

4. **All ministries are now possible for Christians.** Many new initiatives are needed. The Finnish Church has a special concern for Estonia because of the many cultural and spiritual links. Pray that Finnish Christians may be used of God to facilitate these. Pray for the young Estonian **IFES** movement among students, with one full-time worker and 40 part-time. **EHC** plans a nationwide literature campaign in conjunction with local churches. **Christian radio and television** programmes are welcomed on the national system. **TWR** and **IBRA** broadcast a total of 2.5 hours weekly in Estonian.

5. **The less reached.** There are fewer Evangelicals in the north and east and among the Russians. The small Muslim ethnic groups are also without a witness.

Ethiopia and Eritrea

Eritrea became an independent state in May 1993, so both states are handled separately here.

ETHIOPIA
(People's Democratic Republic of Ethiopia)

Area 1,106,000 sq.km. Fertile mountain plateau surrounded by the deserts of the Red Sea coast, and borders on Somalia, Kenya and Sudan. Land-locked since the secession of Eritrea.

Population		Ann. Gr.	Density
1990	45,563,000	3.0 %	41/sq.km
1995	52,569,000	3.0 %	47/sq.km

Peoples:
Semitic origin 45%.
  Ethiopian. Amhara 13,300,000 (North and Central Highlands); Tigrinya 4,150,000 (North and also Eritrea); Gurage (three major dialects) 1,856,000 (South Highlands); Adare (3 groups) 70,000 (East).
  Arab 80,000.
Falashas. A few thousand Black Jews remaining – mainly Christians. Over 70,000 airlifted to Israel.
Cushitic 44%. Over 30 peoples in all areas of the country.
  Oromo 30.1%. Wellega 8,000,000; Borane-Arusi-Guji 3,657,000; Harar-Ittu 2,142,000.
  Somali 3.9%. In Harar and Ogaden.
  Other 10%. Largest: Sidamo 1,261,000; Hadiyya 644,000; Agew 490,000; Gedeo 455,000; Kambaata 443,000; Konso 200,000; Afar 200,000
Omotic 7%. Over 25 peoples in south and southwest. Largest: Wolaytta 1,100,000; Gamo 464,000; Keffa 443,000; Kullo 163,000; Goffa 154,000; Bench 123,000; Yemsa 114,000; Aari 109,000; Basketo 50,000.
Nilo-Sudanic 3.1%. Over 24 peoples in south and west. Related to Sudan peoples. Largest: Anuak 111,000; Gumuz 105,000; Bertha 93,000; Murle 51,000; Me'en 50,000; Koma 50,000; Nuer 40,000.
Other 0.9%.

Literacy 37–50%. **Official language:** Amharic; 65% of population are able to speak it. **All languages** 123. **Languages with Scriptures** 8Bi 11NT 5por.

Capital: Addis Ababa 1,780,000. Urbanization 11%.

Economy: Famine, wars and 17 years of Stalinist Marxism ruined the already weak economy. Poor communications, lack of political unity and severe droughts inhibit rebuilding the economy to pre-revolutionary levels. Unemployment over 35%.

Public debt/person $64. Income/person $120 (0.5% of USA).

Politics: Claimed to be one of the oldest nations known; over 60 references in the Bible. Amhara-dominated Empire 1896–1974, with Italian occupation 1936–41. The Marxist revolution of 1974 overthrew the Emperor Haile Selassie and imposed doctrinaire Marxist ideology on the country with collectivization, nationalization and repression of all dissent and of religion. Regional uprisings together with severe droughts and man-aided famines ultimately led to the collapse of Mengistu's Marxist regime in 1991. The partial failure of the 1992 multi-party elections left the country divided on regional and ethnic lines. The likely alternatives are a loose federal republic of ethnic provinces or the dismemberment of the country into ethnic states.

Religion: Ethiopia was one of the first Christian nations – from the fourth century. The Ethiopian Orthodox Church became the State Church until the 1974 revolution. The Marxist regime persecuted the Church – especially Evangelicals, with many church buildings destroyed and congregations scattered. Since 1991 there has been unprecedented freedom for worship and witness. Religious percentages are approximate.
Non-religious/other 1%. Mainly the urban educated.
Traditional religions 6%. Mainly among peoples of south and west.
Muslim 35%. (Muslims claim 40-50%). Strong in north, east (Afars and Somalis) and southeast (Oromo and Omotic peoples).
Christian 58%. Nom 5.8%. Affil 52.2%.
Growth 1.6%.
  Protestant 14.1%. Growth 11.2%. Some of the denominations listed here include Eritrean statistics which therefore inflate those of Ethiopia.

Church	Cong	Members	Affiliated
Kale Heywet (SIM)	3,000	2,000,000	4,000,000
Evang Ch Mekane Yesu			
(Lutheran)	2,963	400,000	1,000,000
United Pentecostal	1,300	91,000	228,000
Full Gospel – Mulu Wengel	240	60,000	200,000

Seventh-day Adventist	163	57,000	190,000
Heywet Birhane (AoG)	260	65,000	130,000
Sefer Genet (Pente)(FFM)	200	30,000	75,000
Meserete Kristos (Menn)	83	25,000	50,000
Birhane Wengel (Baptist)	75	15,000	45,500
Emmanuel Bapt (BBFI)	12	10,000	25,000
All other (26)	515	50,560	92,533
Denominations (36)	8,811	2,803,560	6,036,033
Evangelicals 13% of pop		2,775,000	5,940,000
Pentecostal/charis 1.7%		421,000	1,070,000

Missionaries:
to Ethiopia 615 (1:74,000 people) in 43 agencies.
from Ethiopia 48 (1:126,000 Protestants) in 6
agencies 5frn 33xcul 15dom.
Catholic 0.75%. Growth 3%.
Coptic- and Latin-rite   154   100,000   170,000
Missionaries to Ethiopia 263 (1:173,000 people).

Orthodox 43.1%. Affil 37.31%. Growth −1.1%.

Ethiopian Orthodox	14,380	10,000,000	17,000,000
All other (2)	2	670	1,550
Denominations (3)	14,382	10,000,670	17,001,550
Charismatic/Evangelical 0.37%.			

Marginal groups 0.03%. Growth 12%.
All groups (7)   7,300   17,000

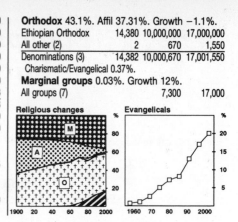

Religious changes   Evangelicals

1. **Ethiopia is in a state of shock.** Her population struggles with the trauma of millions of deaths through repression, famine and war, and of the nation losing its sense of identity and purpose. Communism made many promises, but proved to be a cruel lie that left the land spiritually, economically and agriculturally bankrupt, and in disintegration. Pray for regional and national leaders as they seek to work out a viable political structure that will facilitate peace and economic progress. Pray also that gloom and despair may cause many to take refuge in the Lord Jesus.

2. **Praise God for the thrilling growth of the Protestant churches since 1936.** Two great waves of violent persecution under the Italians in 1936–41 and the Communists in 1974–1990 refined and purified the church, but there were many martyrs. Vision, sacrificial evangelism and courageous witness have characterized Evangelicals of all denominations. There have been great seasons of harvest with millions coming to Christ, the greatest being since the failure and collapse of Communism. Protestants were fewer than 200,000 – and 0.8% of the population – in 1960, but by 1990 this may have become six million and 13% of the population.

3. **The Ethiopian Orthodox Church faces a series of crises.** Centuries of isolation from the rest of the Christian world as an island in a sea of Islam formed its unique theology, traditions and customs. It has to adjust to the dramatic changes of the 20th Century, not least being its loss of political privilege under Communism. The leadership in the post-revolution era feels threatened by massive losses to more vigorous, younger evangelical churches, and there is rising opposition and localised persecution aimed at minimizing that growth. Pray for a greater use of the Scriptures, new life and renewal to come to the Orthodox Church with its millions of nominal adherents. There are small but growing charismatic and evangelical parties within the Church.

4. **The Church faces enormous challenges.** Pray that:
a) **Christians may seize present opportunities for evangelism** and effectively multiply disciples and congregations.
b) **Recovery from the trauma of persecution** may go smoothly. Thousands of places of worship must be built or rebuilt, backsliders and compromisers restored, and families helped after the devastations of famine, separations, bereavements and loss of all possessions.
c) **Effective social help programmes** be expanded to care for the needy and destitute. Western aid agencies such as **SBC, TEAR Fund, WV,** World Relief, World Concern, Lutheran World Relief and others can play a vital role in support of Ethiopian initiatives. The Christian Relief and Development Association coordinates the activities of 88 such organizations. The flood of foreign aid can distort the delicate balance between spiritual and social ministries.
d) **Missions vision may be revived.** Before 1974, thousands of rural missionaries took the gospel to other ethnic groups, but much of this was forcibly stopped. Pray that churches may work together in planning for the full evangelization of every province and people of their land. No such national strategy has ever been launched, nor has there ever been a national survey of the unfinished task. The *Kale Heywet* Church has re-launched its missions programme, sending out 60 pioneer workers to unreached peoples.
e) **Unity among churches** may prevail. Pray for the **Union of Evangelical Churches** formed in 1987.

5. **Leaders in the churches** need prayer for:

a) **Their interactions with the government.** Ethiopia could undergo a tempestuous decade of adjustment, and relationships with churches could become tense.

b) **Their own denominations.** Pray specifically for the *Kale Heywet* Church (Word of Life), the fruit of **SIM** work, now the largest and most widespread evangelical denomination in the country. The *Mekane Yesu* Evangelical Church, the daughter church of Lutheran and Presbyterian missions, is a large, dynamic and charismatic denomination that is growing rapidly. The numerous **Pentecostal churches** are all growing fast.

c) **Their walk with God.** Success following persecution can be a dangerous time – pride, power, fame, and the consequent moral and ethical dangers need to be withstood in prayer.

6. **Leadership training** was severely restricted under Communism. There are too few Christian workers with even a basic Bible training. Pray specifically for staff and students in:

a) **Seminary** level training – at the Evangelical Theological College (*Kale Heywet* and the International Evangelical Church), the *Mekane Yesu* Seminary, and also the Orthodox St Paul's Seminary – all in Addis Ababa. Pray also that more graduates may enter pastoral work rather than filling administrative posts or becoming employed by foreign agencies.

b) **Residential Bible Schools** for various denominations which are multiplying again. The lack of finance for development, for fees and for salaries is a major brake on development. In 1988 the *Kale Heywet* Church had 3,500 students in 105 Bible schools, while the *Mekane Yesu* Church had a further 4,000 students in 24 Bible schools.

c) The network of **local evening and short-term Bible schools**, and **TEE programmes** around the country.

7. **Foreign missions** were forced to close down ministries during the time of Marxist rule. Missionary numbers were reduced to about 400. Since 1991 more missionaries have been able to enter. Pray that the missionary force may be wisely and sensitively deployed to best serve the maturing church. The major ministry needs are in leadership training, pioneer outreach to unevangelized peoples, Bible translation and technical and aid ministries. The largest agencies are: Norwegian Lutheran Mission (152 workers), **SIM** (133), Finnish Lutherans (66), Finnish Pentecostal Mission (29), **SIL** (26), Swedish Pentecostal Mission (23), Danish Lutheran Mission (22), German Lutherans (20), **SBC** (17), and Baptist General Conference (16). Major missionary-contributing nations: USA (165), Norway (159), Finland (100), Germany (50), Sweden (45), Denmark (30).

8. **The Muslim advance.** Muslims strengthened their position under Marxism, and are poised to launch an Islamization of Ethiopia by penetrating Christian areas with the offer of bribes and a mosque-building programme – many were reported to have been built during the time that many Christian churches were being closed. Their numbers are growing significantly, with converts out of both animism and the Orthodox Church. Pray for a definite prayer mobilization that will lead to breakthroughs among Muslim peoples. Converts out of Islam are numbered only in hundreds.

9. **The less reached.** The greatest need is thorough research of the unfinished task. Pray that this may be done. Pray for church-planting in:

a) **The northern provinces** where Evangelicals are few. **Gojam**, **Tigre** and **Gonder** are 95% Orthodox. **Welo** is 65% Muslim, 35% Orthodox. The area has been severely affected by war and two major famines over the past 20 years. The main peoples are Amhara, Tigrinya and Oromo.

b) **The Muslim provinces of the east and southeast.** The Afar, Somali, Oromo and Borane have had minimal contact with missionaries in the past. Pray for the re-entry of workers to reach them, and for the distribution of the Arusi Oromo New Testament.

c) **The south and southwestern provinces** – especially on the Sudan border. All are populated by the Nilo-Sudanic group of peoples. Most of the peoples of special need are small, animistic and isolated. In nearly all there are Christians, but in some the real gospel breakthroughs must still come. Pray for the Basketo (50,000); Dassenach (40,000); Maji (35,000); Suri (30,000); Chara (17,000); Allaaba (5,000); Dime (1,500); Nao (1,000).

d) **Sudanese refugees** from the vicious fighting in the south of that land. Many are housed in large camps. There are over 260,000 refugees in the camp at Itang. Pray for all ministering to these unfortunate people. There are groups of believers among a number of the ethnic groups in these camps.

10. **Young people**, long fed Marxist rhetoric, need purpose and hope in life. Pray for **SU** ministry among young people and for its expansion among teenagers, and for **EVASUE**(**IFES**) with ministry already re-established in 19 colleges. The bottleneck is lack of staff.

11. **Bible translation** is a major missions task to be accomplished. The **Bible Society** is involved in 16 translation projects and training courses for national translators, and **SIL** in survey and in a number of translation teams. KHC/SIM and *Mekane Yesu* Church/Lutheran Missions are committed to translation programmes. Praise God for the completion of the Bench, Hadiyya and Kambatta New Testaments. Major projects needing prayer for completion: Bibles for the Afar, Anuak, Gurage, West Oromo and Wolayta, and New Testaments for the Aari, Amaaro, Burji, Gumuz, Hadiyya, Majang, Kafa, Konso Silti Gurage and Sidamo. There are 17 languages with a definite translation need and a further 39 needing further confirmation of need. Pray for guidance in assessing remaining needs, and resources to start work in those that do (**SIL**).

12. **Christian Help ministries.**

a) **Literature.** Intensive literacy campaigns have created many new readers, but reading materials are scarce. The restrictions imposed on printing and distributing books and magazines have been lifted, but importation and the logistical problems for distribution of literature are still difficult.

b) **Aviation. MAF** have returned after a 14-year absence. The road system, already poor, has been degraded by neglect, so planes are a vital service to Christian work.

c) **Cassettes** with both the Scriptures (Bible Society) and gospel messages (**GRn** in 62 languages). These are a significant means of communicating the Good News. Pray for supplies, distribution, and also planning and implementation of new programmes.

d) **The *Jesus* film.** This is being used in Amharic, Tigrinya, Borane and Turkana. Pray for film teams, travel, safety and follow-up.

e) **Radio. FEBA** broadcasts 11.5 hours/week in Amharic, 6.5 hours/week in Oromo and Tigrinya, and 3.5 hours/week in Afar. Pray for the preparation and impact of these programmes. Pray also for the return of the Lutheran station in Addis Ababa, **Radio Voice of the Gospel**. The Communists seized it after the revolution.

ERITREA

Area 117,000 sq.km. Arid mountainous interior and largely desert along the Red Sea coast.

Population		Ann.Gr.	Density
1990	3,323,000	4.4%	31/sq.km
1995	3,677,000	3.5%	39/sq.km

Peoples: At least nine peoples.
Semitic origin 70.6%. Tigrinya 1,900,000; Tigre and Mensa 683,000; Arab 200,000.
Cushitic 12.8%. Afar 300,000; Saho 144,000; Beja 120,000.
Nilo-Sudanic 14.6%. Kunama 140,000; Nara 63,000.
Other 2%. Mainly Arab and Italian.

Literacy 37%. **Official languages:** English, Tigrinya. **All languages** 9. **Languages with Scriptures** 3Bi 2NT 1por.

Capital: Asmara 600,000.

Economy: Devastated by 30 years of war and drought. In 1992 over 70% of the population was dependent on food aid from abroad.

Politics: Italian colony 1890–1941. UN-arranged federation with Ethiopia in 1951. The war for Eritrean independence began in 1961. All three liberation movements were avowedly Marxist, but since the ending of Ethiopian rule, ideology was forgotten in the effort to rebuild the nation. A multi-party democracy is to be established.

Religion: Secular state but with freedom of religion. Religious statistics are estimates.
Muslim 51%. Dominant among Tigre, Afar, Beja, Saho, and large numbers among all but the Kunama.
Non-religious/other 2.9%. Many influenced by Marxist anti-religious propaganda in the past.
Christian 46.1%. Affil 27.87%. Growth 1%. The Tigrinya has a Christian majority. The Bilen, Mensa and Kunama a minority.
  Protestant 1.5%. Growth 7.8%. The list below is incomplete and Christian figures lower than in reality. Some Ethiopian denominations have an Eritrea membership not listed here. All figures are estimates.

Church	Cong	Members	Affiliated
Faith Ch of Christ	30	3,000	30,000
Evang Ch of Eritrea	117	3,500	10,000
Lutheran Ch in Eritrea	70	3,500	8,750
Full Gospel Ch	3	1,500	3,000
All other (4)	32	1,400	3,100
Denominations (8)	252	12,900	54,850
Evangelicals 1.47% of pop		12,645	54,190
Pentecostal/charis 0.12%		2,000	4,400

Missionaries to and from Eritrea n.a.
Catholic 4.6%. Growth 2.5%.

Coptic- and Latin-rite	99	98,600	170,000

Orthodox 40%. Affil 26.4%. Growth 0.5%.

Eritrean Orthodox	818	572,000	970,000

1. **Long-sought independence won at such cost** could lead to anguish if ethnic and religious divisions polarize the nation. Pray for wisdom, moderation and moral integrity for the new leadership.

2. **Recovery from the devastation of war and drought** will be a long and painful process. Pray for:
a) **Stability and peace** and the rebuilding of the country.
b) **Reintegration of the one million Eritrean refugees** who fled to Sudan during the War and also for Christians among them. A number of refugee churches were planted during the war.
c) **Christian help agencies** who seek to alleviate suffering and set up projects that will improve the lot of the people. They need wisdom and sensitivity in selecting and maintaining projects.

3. **Christians suffered** through warfare in the rural areas and persecution from the Marxist authorities in the cities. The Orthodox are numerous among the Tigrinya; Evangelicals are fewer and confined to the Kunama, Tigrinya, Mensa and the city of Asmara. Congregations were scattered and most social and outreach programmes halted. Pray for churches as they seek to repair and build meeting places, restore fellowship and begin again to reach out in evangelism. Pray also for religious freedom – there are strong pressures from Muslim radicals for Islam to gain political ascendency.

E

4. **Coptic Orthodox and Evangelical Christians** were refined and drawn together in fellowship in the years of suffering. All churches are full, many having daily meetings and nightly prayer meetings. There is a spirit of revival, resulting in concern for both missions and relief and development in their new, but battered, nation.

5. **The return of Christian missionaries** to serve the Church is an urgent need. Every facet of ministry is lacking in skills and gifts – leadership training, media and practical help ministries. Many areas have never been effectively penetrated by missions. The main missions in the past have been Swedish Evangelical (among Mensa, Tigrinya and Kunama), Swedish Lutherans, **SIM** and American Faith Mission, also **MECO** (in the western lowlands) and **RSTI** (among the Afar). Pray also for African mission agencies to take up this challenge.

6. **The less reached.** Pray specifically for:
a) **The Muslim** Beja, Afar, Nara and Saho peoples with no known churches or existing outreach.
b) **The Red Sea coast and cities** of Massawa and Assab where Islam is strongest.
c) **The Tigre** people who are almost entirely Muslim – the only one of the Ethiopian Semitic peoples that is not predominantly Orthodox. There is a Bible in Tigre, but few committed Christians.

<table>
<tr><td>

See under Denmark

Europe

</td><td>

Faeroe Islands

</td><td>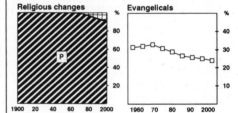</td></tr>
</table>

Area 1,399 sq.km. Archipelago of 18 rugged islands between Iceland and Scotland, 17 of which are inhabited.

Population		Ann. Gr.	Density
1990	47,500	0.43 %	34/sq.km
1995	48,000	0.42 %	34/sq.km

Peoples: Faeroese 97%; Danish 3%.

Literacy 99%. **Official languages:** Faeroese, which is of the Scandinavian family; Danish.

Capital: Tórshavn 14,770.

Economy: Based on the fishing industry. After an economic boom in the '70s and '80s, recession and declining fish yields are raising unemployment levels. Income/person $23,000 (109% of USA).

Politics: Parliamentary democracy; a self-governing region of Denmark, but not a member of the European Community.

Religion: Complete religious freedom, though the Lutheran Church is recognized as the national church and is supported through a tax levied by the State.
Non-religious/other 6.6%.
Christian 93.4%. Growth 0.4%.

Protestant 93%. Growth 0.3%. Most members are nominal.

Church	Cong	Members	Affiliated
Lutheran	57	24,440	37,600
Christian Brethren	27	3,200	5,000
Pentecostal	5	390	600
House Churches	6	180	300
All other (2)	2	138	240
Denominations (6)	97	28,348	43,740
Evangelicals 26% of pop		7,800	12,000
Pentecostal 1.91%		570	900

Missionaries from Faeroe Is 50 (1:874 Protestants) in four agencies.

Roman Catholic 0.1%. Growth 1.4%.
Missionaries to F 1 (1:47,000 people).

Marginal 0.3%. Growth 5%.

Jehovah's Witnesses	4	115	164

Religious changes

Evangelicals

1. **Nominalism and liberal theology** characterize the Lutheran Church, yet within it are strong evangelical movements: the pietistic Home Mission (6,000 affiliated) and the charismatic movement (500). Pray for all who preach the truth within the national Church. Only about 8% of Lutherans are churchgoers.

2. **Evangelicals are a quarter of the population** – a contrast to the few in the mother country, Denmark. The remarkable witness of the Brethren is a major contributory factor. There are also growing Pentecostal and charismatic churches and groups. Yet compromise with a secular society, divisions among believers and a lack of mature leadership in many fellowships tarnish the witness. Pray for a fresh outpouring of the Holy Spirit.

3. **Missions involvement** is high, with 50 Faeroese serving in 14 lands and a further 50 studying in Bible schools in other lands. Pray that the home churches may stand with them as they serve the Lord; few congregations are mission-minded. Christians are trusting for 200 missionaries by the year 2000.

Falkland Islands

(Crown Colony of Falkland Islands)

(Islas Malvinas)

Include with Argentina
Latin America

Area 16,300 sq.km. 200 islands in three groups: Falklands, South Georgia, South Sandwich Is. in South Atlantic.

Population	Ann. Gr.	Density
1990 1,951	0.50%	0.12/sq.km
1995 1,991	0.45%	0.12/sq.km

A further 2,000 British military personnel are based on the islands.

Peoples: British 97%. **Other** 3%.

Capital: Stanley 1,200. Urbanization 56%.

Economy: A forgotten, sheep-ranching colony until the 1982 war. Development, construction, exploitation of fisheries, and tourism have brought sudden wealth to the islanders. Income/person $30,860 (146% of USA).

Politics: Self-governing UK Colony. Argentinian claims on the islands as the **Islas Malvinas** led to 1982 War of South Atlantic.

Religion:
Non-religious/other 13.1%.
Christian 86.9%. Growth 0.8%.
Protestant 76%. Growth 0.9%.

Church	Cong	Members	Affiliated
Anglican	17	170	850
United Free Ch	5	120	560
All other (3)	3	50	70
Denominations (5)	25	340	1,480
Evangelicals 20% of pop		200	400

Missionaries to Falkland Is 5 (1:400 people).
Roman Catholic 10.2% Growth 0%.
Marginal 0.7%. Growth 1.3%.

1. **The traumatic Argentinian invasion,** and Argentina's subsequent defeat by British forces in 1982, decisively affected the economic, political and spiritual life of the once-complacent Falkland Islanders. Praise God for the 150 who made decisions for Christ in a 1991 crusade in the capital. Pray for lasting results in these lives.

2. **There are only three significant Protestant denominations** among the Islanders (Anglican, Tabernacle United Free Church and Baptist) with a few actively witnessing Christians.

3. **The British forces** based on the Islands face a lonely, thankless task. Pray for openness to the gospel and to Christian witness by believers in the forces and **Mission to Military Garrisons.**

F

May 2		*Fiji*		
Pacific		(Sovereign Democratic Republic of Fiji)		

Area 18,274 sq.km. Two larger and 110 smaller inhabited islands, both volcanic and coralline.

Population		Ann. Gr.	Density
1990	749,000	1.6 %	41/sq.km
1995	794,000	1.2 %	43/sq.km

Peoples: Intense ethnic confrontation between the indigenous Fijians and immigrant Indians.
Fijian 47.7%. Speaking 22 dialects; landowners and rulers.
Indian 46.2%. Mainly descendants of indentured labour imported by the British between 1879 and 1916, and also subsequent Gujarati and Sikh immigrants.
  Indo-Aryan 33.3%. Hindi 200,000; Bihari 25,000; Bengali 17,000; Panjabi 7,000.
  Dravidian 12.9%. Tamil 64,000; Telugu 7,000.
Polynesian 1.7%. Rotuman 9,000 on Rotuma Island. Also immigrant Samoans and Tongans.
Other minorities 4.4%. Euro-Polynesian 11,000; Chinese 5,500; European 4,500; Kiribati 2,300.

Literacy 90%. **Official language:** English. Commonly used: Hindustani, Bau Fijian. **All languages** 23. **Languages with Scriptures** 9Bi 1por.

Capital: Suva 180,000. Urbanization 39% (mainly Indians).

Economy: Major export earnings are from tourism and sugar. The Indian community dominates nearly all commercial activities, but has no long-term security, not being permitted to own land. Public debt/person $446. Income/person $1,540 (7.3% of USA).

Politics: British rule 1874-1970. The post-independence balance between Fijians and Indians ended in 1987 with two military coups to prevent power going to a democratically elected part-Indian government. The military government declared Fiji a Republic when the Commonwealth expelled the nation. The 1990 constitution guarantees perpetual Fijian political dominance. Dissension among Fijian leaders, economic decline and inter-communal tensions delayed elections until 1992. A coalition government was then formed. Many Indian professionals have emigrated since 1987. In 1988, Rotuma Island attempted to secede from Fiji.

Religion: Post-coup policy has emphasised the Christian tradition with Sunday observance regulations reflecting strong views of present leaders.
Hindu 37.3%. Over 80% of all Indians.
Muslim 7.5%. 15% of all Indians. Sunni Islam and some Ammadiyah.
Non-religious/other 0.9%. **Sikh** 0.6%. **Baha'i** 0.3%.
Christian 53.4%. Affil 53.1%. Growth 4%.
  Protestant 42.6%. Affil 42.37%. Growth 3.8%.

Church	Cong	Members	Affiliated
Methodist	2,192	57,000	259,000
Assemblies of God	133	9,610	31,000
Seventh-day Adventist	92	8,020	12,330
Anglican	51	3,840	6,200
Chr Brethren	23	650	1,000
All other (14)	33	4,050	7,834
Denominations (19)	2,524	83,170	317,364
Evangelicals 10.4% of pop		23,000	78,000
Pentecostal/charis 5%		13,000	45,000

Missionaries:
  to Fiji 77 (1:9,700 people) in 25 agencies.
  from Fiji 301 (1:1,050 Protestants) in 6 agencies 73frn 74xcul 227dom.
Roman Catholic 9.1%. Affil 9.08%. Growth 4%.

Catholic ch	36	35,400	68,000

Missionaries:
  to Fiji 97 (1:7,700 people).
  from Fiji 5 (1973 figure).
Foreign Marginal 1.4%. Affil 1.35%. Growth 14.1%.

Mormons	19	3,750	6,700
Jehovah's Witnesses	41	1,542	3,430
Groups (2)	60	5,292	10,130

Indigenous Marginal 0.3%. Affil 0.3%. Growth 1.6%.

All groups (5)	28	1,040	2,235

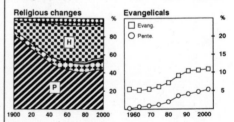

1. **Inter-ethnic conflict**, culminating in the 1987 coup, highlighted the tragic legacy of colonialism. Fijians feared losing political control and their land; Indians feared losing control over their livelihood and future. Since 1987, many Indians with the means to do so have emigrated. A fair political solution looks unlikely at this stage, and increased violence a possibility. Pray that government leaders may act

with wisdom and restraint. Pray that true believers may demonstrate that the Cross has broken down barriers to fellowship.

2. **Fijians embraced Christianity over a century ago**, but this is often cultural rather than spiritual. Legalism, nominalism and failure to confront the ongoing worship of ancestral spirit gods are widespread. Alcoholism and broken homes are major social evils. The dominant Methodist Church is wracked by division over leadership and political involvement. Sadly, some Methodists have destroyed Hindu temples and Muslim mosques. Pray for a deep work of the Holy Spirit in dealing with compromise and ethnic hatred and in bringing revival.

3. **Newer churches with a more strongly evangelical message** are growing, but so too are Mormons and Jehovah's Witnesses. Also within the Methodist, Anglican and Catholic churches are growing evangelical and charismatic groups. However, Vanua Levu and the outer islands need exposure to genuine lived-out Christianity. Pray for agencies involved in church planting and evangelism. The small boat ministry of **YWAM** and **UBS** is unique in taking evangelistic teams and Christian literature from island to island.

4. **Less reached peoples.** The Indians form the largest non-Christian community in the Pacific. Only 4% of the Indians claim to be Christian. Fear and dismay at treatment by Fijian "Christians" have limited and disrupted ministry among them. Pray specifically for:
a) **The Hindus,** who have been patchily evangelized. Yet during the past four decades there has been a steady trickle of converts to Christianity.
b) **The Sikhs** – no specific outreach to them yet.
c) **The 56,000 Muslim community,** tightly knit and very resistant to the gospel. Little is being done to reach them, and the few converted to Christ have suffered considerable persecution.
d) **The Chinese** – mostly Cantonese in origin, but many speaking English. There has been no ministry specifically directed to reach them until 1992 (**WEC**).

5. **Leadership training for the churches.** Fiji plays an important role for the whole South Pacific. Pray for the Methodist Theological College, the **AoG** Bible School (57 students), South Pacific Missionary Village Training Centre (13 students), Ambassadors For Christ Bible School (11 students) and the Baptist Christian Leadership College in Nasinu. Pray also for a stronger evangelical witness in the first.

6. **Missionary vision in the Fijian church is not as strong as it used to be**; pray for Fijians overseas and for a rekindling of enthusiasm for world evangelization. Over 270 Fijians have served as long-term missionaries over the last 120 years. There are two umbrella organizations for Evangelicals – the Evangelical Fellowship of Fiji and the Evangelical Alliance – which seek to draw Christians together in efforts of national, regional and international evangelization and consultations.

7. **Young people and students** are very responsive. Pray for the work of **CCC**, **YWAM**, Youth For Christ, **IFES**, **SU** and **CEF** through whom thousands are being evangelized – both in Fiji and beyond. Pray for the integration of these young Christians in local congregations. Pray especially for the University of the South Pacific in Suva to which students from all over the Pacific come – often from islands where there is only nominal Christianity.

8. **The Bible Society of the South Pacific is based in Fiji.** Pray for their endeavours in undertaking surveys of translation needs (much needed in Fiji's dialects now), translation work, printing and distribution of God's Word throughout the Pacific. Translation and revision work in Fijian and Fiji Hindi are important projects. There is also a dearth of good Christian literature in these two languages.

9. **Christian help agencies** include **WV**, committed to wholistic development, Christian Women Communicating International with their KYB programmes, Bible distribution of Gideons International, the prisoner rehabilitation ministry of Prison Fellowship and the Nurses Christian Fellowship. All need prayer.

May 3
Europe

Finland

(The Republic of Finland)

F

Area 337,000 sq.km. This cold northern land is 70% forest, 10% lake, 8% arable land.

Population	Ann. Gr.	Density
1990	4,975,000	0.30 %	15/sq.km
1995	5,030,000	0.22 %	15/sq.km

Peoples:
Finnish-speaking 93.4%. Speaking a Uralic language.
Swedish-speaking 5.9%. Largely southwest and Eland Islands.
Lapp 0.1%. Total 5,700 with 2,000 still speaking three Same dialects; most living in the Arctic.
Gypsy 0.2%.
Foreign 0.4%. Russians 2,000; Somalis 1,300; Romanians 1,000; Turks 1,000 and others.

Literacy 100%. **Official languages:** Finnish, Swedish. **All languages** 10. **Languages with Scriptures** 4Bi 1NT 4por.

Capital: Helsinki 990,000. Urbanization 63%.

Economy: Specialized, export-oriented economy based on wood products and industry. In deep recession since the economic collapse of its giant neighbour, Russia. Unemployment 18% – the worst in Finnish history. Public debt/person $2,745. Income/person $22,060 (104% of USA).

Politics: Ruled by Sweden for 700 years, then by Russia for a further 100. Independent in 1917. A parliamentary democracy. Applying for EC membership.

Religion: Both the Lutheran and Orthodox churches are folk churches with considerable autonomy yet close ties with the government.
Non-religious/other 9.8%, including Muslim 2,800; Jews 1,000; Baha'i 300.
Christian 90.2%. Affil 89.24%. Growth −0.1%.

Protestant 88.3%. Growth −0.1%.

Church	Cong	Members	Affiliated
Evang Lutheran	1,260	1,740,000	4,472,525
Finnish Pentecostal	206	48,000	68,600
Evang Free Ch	96	13,600	17,600
Salvation Army	56	7,880	10,500
Siloan Pentecostal	1	2,800	7,000
Seventh-day Adventist	68	4,640	6,181
Ch of Sweden (Lthn)	3	1,240	1,800
All other (32)	275	13,482	24,241
Doubly counted		−100,000	−264,000
Denominations (39)	1,965	1,731,642	4,344,447
Evangelicals 16% of pop		345,000	796,000
Pentecostals 1.8% of pop		57,200	89,200
Charismatics 4.9% of pop		99,000	240,000

Missionaries:
from Finland 1,317 (1:3,300 Protestants) in 22 agencies, 1,268frn 49dom.
to Finland 19 (1:261,000 people) in 10 agencies.
Roman Catholics 0.08%. Growth 1.3%.

Catholic Ch	5	2,800	4,000

Missionaries to Finland 58 (1:85,800 people).
Orthodox 1.12%. Growth −0.6%.

Greek Orthdx (Finnish)	128	38,500	55,000
Denominations (3)	130	39,238	55,950

Foreign Marginal 0.71%. Growth 1.8%.

Jehovah's Witnesses	274	17,531	30,200
Mormons	30	2,650	4,200
All groups (9)	315	20,591	35,275

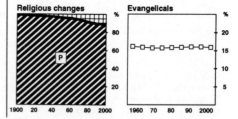

Religious changes

Evangelicals

1. **Praise God for the awakenings and revivals over the past 200 years with a strong emphasis on prayer, repentance and confession.** The last revival occurred during the 1960s. A growing interest in spiritual things could lead to revival again. There is a steady but slow increase in the number of active Christians. Yet Finland has a serious alcohol problem, with all the social tragedies this implies. Secularization and non-Christian religiosity are on the increase – all indicators of spiritual need.

2. **The Lutheran Church** is much more evangelical than most Lutheran churches in Europe – a heritage of the revival movements that have deeply influenced its spirituality. This body is an umbrella for a large number of autonomous fellowships, revival and prayer groups and missions, where most committed Christians find their fellowship and platform for evangelism. About 15–20% of the population would regularly attend such meetings, but average Sunday Lutheran church attendance is only 4%. Pray that this Church may become more meaningful and relevant in society.

3. **The Free Churches, both Pentecostal and non-Pentecostal**, are relatively small but spiritually vigorous and growing. Charismatic renewal has had a marked impact. Pray for greater unity in evangelism and missions among these various bodies.

4. **Young people's work is fruitful.** A high proportion of Finnish young people attend confirmation schools and camps, and thereby many come to a living faith in Christ. Pray for campus ministries of the Evangelical Lutheran Student Mission (**IFES**), EYL, People's Bible Society (CCC) and **Navigators**. These evangelical agencies have also founded a Theological Institute to give a more biblical instruction in parallel with the university theological faculties.

5. **The Finnish Bible Society** has played a significant role in promoting the translation, publication and distribution of the Scriptures. The sudden, explosive demand for Scriptures in the Baltic states and Russia since 1990 has strained its resources and production programmes. Pray for this ministry in a time of such unusual opportunity.

6. **Missionary vision has continued to grow** since the revival in the '60s and early '70s. Many young people have been stirred about the challenge of the unreached but face many obstacles: the high educational and professional requirements of the six recognized missionary societies within the Lutheran Church, the cultural isolation of Finland and the limited vision among believers to support missionaries in interdenominational and international missions. **OM** has sent out over 1,000 Finns in summer or short-term teams all over the world; many are now in full-time ministry. OM aims to send out 100 young people annually on the *Love Europe* outreaches. Pray out many to the needy harvest fields of the world.

7. **The collapse of Communism and of the USSR** has given unprecedented opportunities to Finnish Christians for evangelism and for encouragement of the Christians in Estonia (their ethnic cousins) and in Russia. Pray for numerous evangelistic, discipling, literature and help ministries to these lands that are based in Finland. Many of the less-reached ethnic groups of northern Russia are distantly related to the Finnish people.

8. **Less reached peoples.** Many refugees and asylum-seekers have come to Finland from Somalia, the ex-USSR, Central Europe and elsewhere. Many are Muslims, and few have ever heard the gospel before. Pray for their evangelization.

F

<table>
<tr><td>

May 4–6

Europe

</td></tr>
</table>

France
(The French Republic)

Area 551,000 sq.km. The largest country in Western Europe.

Population	Ann. Gr.	Density
1990 56,173,000	0.36 %	103/sq.km
1995 57,188,000	0.36 %	105/sq.km

Peoples: Indigenous and immigrant ethnic minority figures are approximate due to naturalization, assimilation, illegal immigration and intense anti-foreign propaganda obscuring the issue.
Indigenous 86.3%.
French 74.7%.
Regional minorities 9.7%. Breton 1,900,000; Alsatian 1,517,000; Flemish 780,000; Basque 730,000; Corsican 281,000; Catalan 220,000.
Other national minorities 1.9%. Jews 700,000; West Indian Antillean 250,000; Gypsy 170,000; Réunionese 11,000.
International minorities 13.7%. Many illegal immigrants.
North African/Middle Easterners 7.3%. North Africans 3,700,000 of which over 1,200,000 are Berber (Kabyle, Shawiya, Riff, etc); Lebanese/Arab 180,000; Turks 150,000; Kurds 40,000.
Other European 4.6%. Portuguese 850,000; Italian 600,000; German 560,000; Spanish 480,000; Armenian 220,000; Polish 110,000; Russian 100,000 and others.
Asian 1.3%. Vietnamese 300,000; Chinese 200,000; Lao/Hmong 100,000; Cambodian 70,000; Tamil 25,000.
African 0.5%. Representing every Francophone nation and most West African ethnic groups – Malinke, Soninke, Fula, Wolof, Tuareg, etc.

Literacy 99%. **Official language:** French. Regional languages in decline. Provençal (Occitan) also spoken by up to 10 million in south. French is the first language of 115 million people worldwide. **All languages** 28. **Languages with Scriptures** 12Bi 3NT 11por.

Capital: Paris 10,660,000. Other major cities: Lyon 1,533,000; Marseille 1,227,000. Urbanization 74%.

Economy: Stability and growth leading to a high standard of living. The fifth largest economy in the world with a strong industrial and agricultural base. Government subsidies and social policies funded by high taxation. Unemployment 11%. Public debt/person $4,340. Income/person $17,830 (85% of USA).

Politics: Democratic republic with strong executive presidency. One of core members of EC. There is confusion over France's future international role since the collapse of Communism, vast changes in Eastern Europe, German reunification and the effects of EC legislation on French culture and concerns.

Religion: Secular state with freedom of religion, but with a long history of severe persecution of dissenters and reformers before the 1789 Revolution.
Non-religious/other 19.2%. France has had a strong anti-clerical minority since 1789.
Muslim 7.7%. North Africans, Middle Easterners, West Africans and up to 150,000 French.
Jews 1.1%.
Buddhist 0.3%. **Chinese religions** 0.2%.
Christian 71.5%. Nom 50.5%. Active 21%.
Attendance 13%. Growth −0.6%.
Protestant 1.77%. Growth 0.3%.

Church	Cong	Members	Affil
Reformed Ch	435	21,005	320,000
Ch of Augsburg Confession (Lthn)	250	44,000	220,000
Assemblies of God	650	66,500	133,000
Evang Lutheran Ch	41	4,000	40,000
Reformed Ch of Alsace & Lorraine	78	1,300	32,000
Darby Brethren	101	11,600	23,200
Seventh-day Adventist	123	10,100	15,500
Fed of Baptist Chs	85	5,553	13,400
Full Gospel Fed'n	32	8,000	13,300
Ev Assms (Breth)	110	4,300	7,170
Protestant Ev Ch	22	4,400	5,500
Salvation Army	40	3,180	4,890
Assoc of Ev Menn	28	2,000	3,000
Assoc of Ev Baptist	20	1,100	1,830
All Ind Ev Chs (TEAM)	25	671	1,340
All other (114)	1,114	67,929	161,535
Denominations (129)	3,098	255,638	995,665
Evangelicals 0.63% of pop		167,000	352,000
Pentecostal/charis 0.38%		104,000	218,000

Missionaries:
to France 1,224 (1:45,900 people) in 124 agencies.
from France 452 (1:2,200 Protestants) in 35 agencies 289frn 311xcul 141dom.
Roman Catholic 68.06%. Growth −0.7%.

	Cong	Members	Affil
Catholic Ch	36,689	11,486,137	47,081,000
Doubly Counted		−6,500,000	−8,848,000
Total	36,689	4,986,137	38,233,000
Charismatics		69,000	280,000

Missionaries:
to France 12,409 (1973 figure).
from France 22,754 (1973 figure).
Other Catholic 0.12%. Growth −0.3%.

	Cong	Members	Affil
Denominations (3)	7	40,000	60,000

Orthodox 0.88%. Growth 0.5%.

Armenian Apostolic	115	92,000	230,000
Greek Orthodox	29	48,000	64,000
All other (11)	114	61,800	201,320
Denominations (13)	258	201,800	495,320

Foreign Marginal 0.66%. Growth 3.6%.

Jehovah's Witnesses	1,428	114,308	191,000
Mormons	120	13,000	21,000
All other (22)	290	72,170	161,132
Groups (24)	1,838	199,478	373,132

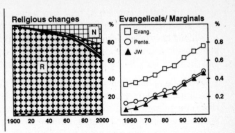

1. **France is a mission field.** This is the opinion both of Catholics and Evangelicals alike – though this suggestion would horrify most French. One of the world's most cultured and sophisticated nations is reaping the barren fruits of 200 years of secularization. Barriers to the gospel are many – intellectualism, rationalism, widespread involvement in the occult, individualism and a nodding acquaintance with institutional Catholicism. These must be broken down by fervent prayer. France is not only needy, but also hardened to the gospel.

2. **The unreached sectors of French society** are many:
a) Over 43 million French people have no *real* link with a Christian church. Many more have a profound ignorance of the gospel.
b) **Large cities** such as Nancy and Nantes have six evangelical churches or less. Many suburbs of Paris and other cities are without an established witness.
c) Of the 38,000 *communes*, 36,000 have no resident evangelical witness.
d) The **Basques** in the southwest are virtually without an evangelical witness in their language.
e) The **Loire Valley** in west central France, and **Brittany**, are particularly bereft of evangelical congregations.
f) **The island of Corsica**, the birthplace of Napoleon, is renowned for its violence. In the population of 240,000, there are 12 small groups with 250 evangelical believers.

3. **The unreached minorities:**
a) **The large Portuguese, Spanish and Italian communities** are more receptive than in their native lands. They have generally not adapted well to French society, but there are few believers who evangelize them in their own languages. There are only seven Portuguese or Spanish congregations for over one million people.
b) **Jews** in France form the fourth largest Jewish community in the world and the largest in Europe with 320,000 in Paris alone and a further 100,000 in Marseille. Eighteen workers in five missions labour among them (**MT, GMU, CWI, JFJ** and the French TMPI). There are about 500–600 believers among them.
c) **North Africans** are almost entirely Muslim, few ever having heard the gospel. The majority live in large low-cost housing areas in larger cities. The growing hostility and racism of French "Christians" have both antagonized them and provoked a strong, well-organised Muslim movement that complicates Christian outreach to them. Pray for French and international churches and agencies seeking to break down these barriers through friendship evangelism, radio, film, BCCs and literature. Agencies involved: **AWM, CCC, WEC, SIM, SBC, UFM, IMI** and **IFES.** Pray also for the 700–1,000 Christians converted from a Muslim background; they face much opposition.
d) **The Berbers** form a large minority among the North Africans and possibly a majority of the Algerians. Kabyle believers have been increasing in number and are active in reaching out to their own people in France and North Africa and producing videos, tapes, radio programmes and literature in Kabyle. The *Jesus* film on video is being used widely in various Berber languages.
e) **Black Africans** have come in large numbers as students, refugees and work-seekers from Muslim areas of Francophone Africa. There is little specific outreach to the Bambara, Wolof, Malinke, Soninke and others. Where are the workers?
f) The large number of **Indo-Chinese** refugees of the '70s and '80s from France's former colony is gradually being absorbed into French life. A small minority have become active Christians – some integrated into French churches, others in their own ethnic churches mainly planted through the ministry of **CMA.** There are now 11 Hmong-Lao groups, seven Chinese, three Cambodian and two Vietnamese congregations, but the few pastors and missionaries can hardly cover the many scattered communities.
g) **The growing Turkish, Iranian and Afghan** communities need to be evangelized.

4. **The Catholic Church** has still a strong cultural and spiritual influence despite two centuries of anti-clericalism, but the majority of the population has deserted the Church, and ordinations to the priesthood have fallen to an all-time low. Tensions exist between conservative traditionalists, liberals, modernists, radicals and charismatics. The latter group has opened many to the truths of God's Word and the need for a living personal faith. Pray that many may embrace these.

5. **Protestants have had a long and glorious history.** At the height of the Reformation 48% of the population was Protestant. Persecution of these Huguenots in the 17th and 18th centuries reduced this to the present 2%. Protestants are more numerous in the southwest and in Alsace, but most are nominal and never attend church. Pastors in the Reformed Church are usually liberal in theology and some are preoccupied with politics. Decline is the norm, but there are staunch evangelical believers in many congregations. Pray for a restoration to the faith and commitment of their martyr forebears in the Reformed and Lutheran Churches.

F

6. **Evangelical Christians** are few, scattered and split up among more than 120 Protestant denominations and nearly 3,000 congregations. Growth has been steady, doubling the number of Evangelicals between 1965 and 1990. Over 1,000 evangelical churches have been planted in the past 20 years. The Pentecostals, and the **AoG** in particular, have grown the fastest, tripling their membership over the same period (see figures above). However, much of that growth has been among Gypsies (with nearly half their number now committed Christians through a remarkable people movement since 1960), Antilleans and other migrants (who form a high proportion of most Parisian evangelical congregations). Pray for:

a) **An impact to be made on the core French population.** To most French people, the evangelical message is still seen as an alien ideology rather than a home-grown faith (Calvin was French).

b) **Unity among true believers.** The diversity and fragmentation of the evangelical witness hinder cooperative effort.

c) **Revival** – few Christians are delivered from spiritual bondages; fear of witnessing, indifference, marriage with unbelievers, and church divisions are the baleful results.

7. **There are over 10 residential Evangelical Bible Schools and Seminaries**, both denominational and interdenominational – and most have a full complement of students. Notable among the latter are the European Bible Institute in Lamorlaye, *Institut Biblique de Nogent*, and the Vaux Evangelical Seminary. There are also denominational seminaries for the Baptists, Pentecostals and the Aix-en-Provence Seminary for Reformed Church students. Pray for:

a) **Full-time workers to be called for ministry** in France. There are only about 3,000 full-time French Protestant workers, and few of these are successful pioneer church planters.

b) **A deep work of the Holy Spirit** to equip those trained with both the theological understanding and spiritual maturity to make an impact for eternity.

c) **The blessing of the whole Francophone world** through French and foreign students who graduate. A high proportion of students are from other lands.

8. **French Evangelicals, though few, have sent out 215 missionaries** into 30 lands. General interest in Protestant churches is low and support small. The largest agencies are: **YWAM** (68 workers), **AoG** (52), *Mission Baptiste Europeéne* (18), **WBT** (18), **OM** (13), **SIM** (11), *Cooperation Evangélique dans le Monde* (11). Pray for the vision for world evangelization to be embraced by the churches. Pray also for the French edition of *Operation World* entitled *Flashes sur le Monde.*

9. **The growth of Islam** has been mainly through immigration and a higher birthrate. However, there may now be as many as 60,000 to 150,000 French who have become Muslim – mostly through marriage. There are probably no more than 70 evangelical Christian workers in full-time evangelism among Muslims. Pray that the need and urgency be seen and present opportunities seized.

10. **Young people are more receptive to the gospel.** Many groups and missions have specialized in this ministry – Youth for Christ, **YWAM**, **CCC**, Young Life, *Eau Vive*, **ECM**, **TEAM** through camps, clubs, coffee bars and ministry in secondary schools; Teen Challenge among drug addicts; **SU** in schools and through Bible reading notes. Pray for many young people to be saved and integrated into good evangelical churches – the latter step usually being much harder than the former!

11. **French and foreign missions have a vital servant role to play in evangelism and church planting.** There are not enough full-time French Christian workers to begin to meet the need. Missionaries find it hard to adapt and win acceptance, and church-planting has had limited effectiveness when foreign patterns are imported. Increasingly missionaries are finding a useful church-planting ministry within indigenous structures (**SBC**, France Mission, *Eau Vive*, **BCU**,

ECM, WT, TEAM, UFM, GEM, GMU, WEC, etc.). Fruit is hard-won, discouragements many, and the missionary dropout rate high. Pray for perseverance, effectiveness, provision of adequate financial support and spiritual power. Largest missionary-contributing nations: USA (759), UK (232), Canada (75), Switzerland (63).

12. **Literature is a valuable tool for evangelism and discipleship.** Literature campaigns by **EHC**, **CCC** and **OM** have been useful to sow the seed widely. Pray for Christian publishing houses and bookstores (70, of which 11 are run by **CLC**) who disseminate Christian literature.

13. **The Bible Society** published the *Good News Bible* in French in 1982. Pray for the impact of God's Word. Only 5% of the population owns a Bible and 80% has never even handled one. The resources of the Bible Society are heavily committed to providing Scriptures for other Francophone lands. A new French study Bible – a big unmet need – is in preparation.

14. **Radio and TV evangelism** has become a new tool since local broadcasting licences were more easily obtained. Pray that Christians may cooperate to make effective use of these media. An association to promote this was started in 1982. Radio Evangile (French branch of **TWR**) is involved in training French believers for local broadcasting. The latter also has a significant radio ministry via **TWR** Monte Carlo (16 hours/month). **HCJB** broadcasts a further 77 hours/month to France from Ecuador. **AWM's Radio School of the Bible**, aimed primarily at North Africans, is aired on five French stations.

15. **There are 68 universities and 1,300,000 students**; 300,000 of these are foreign students. Ministry to these students has national and worldwide implications! The evangelical witness has been slow to develop, but now there are 1,500 students linked with the 55 GBU (**IFES**) groups. Less than half the universities have a GBU group, and most are very small and predominantly made up of overseas students. **CCC** and Navigators also have a growing ministry on campuses. Students are more open than ever, searching for reality in an ideological vacuum.

F

<table>
<tr><td>

May 7–8
Includes French Polynesia, Guadeloupe, Martinique, New Caledonia, St Pierre & Miquelon, Wallis & Futuna

Caribbean
</td></tr>
</table>

French Guiana

(The Department of French Guiana)

Area 91,000 sq.km. Sparsely inhabited jungle territory in northeast South America.

Population	Ann. Gr.	Density
1990	117,000	6.08 %	1.35/sq.km
1995	130,000	2.13 %	1.50/sq.km

Peoples:
Afro-Caribbean 66%. Guianese 41,000, Haitian 20,000; Antillean 6,200; also Suriname refugees 10,000.
European 18%. Mainly French, also including 5,000 in French armed forces.
Other 16%. Bush Negro 7,400; Brazilian 7,000; Chinese 5,000; Hmong from Laos 1,500; Javanese 820; Lebanese 800.

Literacy 82%. **Official language:** French. Guiana Creole widely spoken. **All languages** 12. **Languages with Scriptures** 2Bi 2NT 4por.

Capital: Cayenne 67,000. Urbanization 73%.

Economy: Partially developed coastal strip, and undeveloped jungle hinterland. The Kourou satellite launching site is the major source of income and bringing rapid development. Unemployment 15%. Income/person $12,929 (61% of USA).

Politics: Overseas Department of France. For years infamous as a French penal colony. There is little desire or incentive for independence.

Religion: Secular with freedom of religion. **Non-religious/other** 8.8%.

Spiritist 2%. **Muslim** 1.5%. **Baha'i** 0.8%.
Christian 86.9%. Nom 8.2%. Affil 78.7%. Gr 4.9%.
Protestant 5.8%. Growth 5.9%.

Church	Cong	Members	Affiliated
Seventh-day Adventist	4	803	1,750
Assemblies of God	2	800	1,600
Christian Brethren (3)	10	380	691
Streams of Power	2	260	520
Salvation Army	1	160	267
All other (7)	11	829	1,927
Denominations (14)	30	3,232	6,755
Evangelicals 3.9% of pop		2,150	4,500
Pentecostal/charis 2%		1,200	2,350

Missionaries:
to Fr Guiana 18 (1:6,500 people) in 7 agencies.
Roman Catholic 80%. Affil 71.8%. Growth 4.8%.

Catholic Ch	32	44,520	84,000

Missionaries to Fr Guiana 129 (1:900 people).
Marginal 1.1%. Growth 12.7%.

Jehovah's Witnesses	8	660	1,320

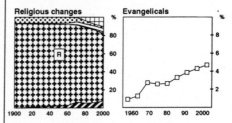

Religious changes   Evangelicals

1. **The penal colony image** is only now wearing off. Yet the economic, moral and spiritual effects remain. Only a handful of the Guianese Creole speakers are active Christians. Over 80% of births are illegitimate, and indifference to spiritual things is widespread. Pray for the **WT** thrust to this specific people group. A translation of the New Testament for this group is definitely needed.

2. **The most responsive peoples** are the Haitians, Antilleans, Hmong and Brazilians, and it is among these peoples that the **AoG**, Baptists (**SBC, CMA**) and **Brethren** are growing. Pray for men and women to be called into the ministry and for the young churches to mature in understanding and vision. There are 18 missionaries – 14 of whom are from USA.

3. **The least reached peoples:**
a) The **Amerindian** tribes – never has any permanent work been established among the inland tribes, but Christians of these tribes in Suriname and Brazil have made evangelistic forays. Pray for the Arawak (320), Wayana (320), Palikur (160), Oyapi (110) and Emerillon (100).
b) The nominally Catholic **Caribs** (1,900).
c) The inland settlements of largely animistic **Bush Negroes.**
d) The **Chinese.** There has been a small outreach by Suriname Chinese Christians.
e) The **French** and **European** communities linked with the space programme – few are active Christians.

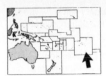

French Polynesia

(The Territory of French Polynesia)

<table>
<tr><td>Include with
French Guiana</td></tr>
<tr><td>Pacific</td></tr>
</table>

F

Area 4,000 sq.km. Five island archipelagos – (Society, Tuamotu, Marquesas, Austral and Gambier) in south-central Pacific. Tahiti is the largest island 1,042 sq.km.

Population	Ann. Gr.	Density
1990	182,000	2.2 %	52/sq.km
1995	200,000	1.9 %	57/sq.km

Peoples:
Polynesian 62.7% speaking 7 distinct languages. Tahitian 76,000; Tuamotuan 16,400; Marquesan 9,100; Tubuaian 9,100; Mangarevan 1,800; Pukapukan 1,100; Rapa 450.
Euronesian 18.3%. Mainly on Tahiti.
French 12%. Many in the armed forces.
Chinese 7%. Controlling the economy.

Literacy 95%. **Official languages:** French and Tahitian. **All languages** 10. **Languages with Scriptures** 2Bi 2por.

Capital: Papeete 104,000. Urbanization 55%.

Economy: Tourism, aid and the French military are the main sources of income, but the wealth generated has not benefited all. The suspension and possible ending of nuclear testing may have a big effect on the economy. Unemployment 15% (unofficially nearer 50%). Public debt/person $2,276. Income/person $12,920 (62% of USA).

Politics: French colony in 1880, Overseas Territory in 1957, increased autonomy since 1977 but with representation in the Senate and Assembly in Paris. The controversial use of Mururoa Atoll for testing nuclear weapons has provoked international opposition and fuelled the Tahitian independence movement.

Religion: Separation of Church and state, religious freedom.
Non-religious/other 14.8%. Mainly French and Chinese.

Chinese religions 0.6%. Baha'i 0.2%.
Christian 84.4%. Growth 1.6%.
Protestant 41%. Growth 0.8%.

Church	Cong	Members	Affiliated
Evang Ch of P'nesia	80	45,100	85,000
Seventh-day Adventist	22	1,960	3,269
Assemblies of God (Frch)	6	600	1,000
Assemblies of God (USA)	1	75	125
All other (3)	13	1,490	2,558
Doubly counted		−9,200	−17,400
Denominations (7)	122	40,025	74,552
Evangelicals 3.1% of pop		3,715	6,660
Pentecostal/charis 1.4%		1,600	2,700

Missionaries:
 to Fr Polynesia 20 (1:9,100 people) in 6 agencies.
 from Fr Polynesia 6 (1:12,400 Protestants) in 2 agencies 2frn 2xcul 4dom.

Roman Catholic 33%. Growth 0.9%.

Catholic Ch	110	36,400	70,000
Doubly counted		−5,200	−9,950
Total		31,200	61,050

Missionaries to Fr Polynesia 92 (1:2,000 people).
Foreign Marginal 7.9%. Growth 11.2%.

Mormons	45	6,820	11,000
Jehovah's Witnesses	19	1,173	3,350
Groups (2)	64	7,993	14,350

Indigenous Marginal 2.5%. Growth 2.2%.

Sanito Church	22	2,200	4,400
Groups (2)	23	2,275	4,627

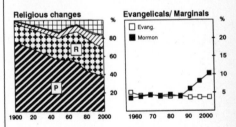

Religious changes

Evangelicals/ Marginals
☐ Evang.
■ Mormon

1. **Tahiti is a paradise gone tragically wrong.** Once a Christian nation that sent missionaries all over the Pacific, Tahiti is now collapsing through promiscuity, prostitution, alcoholism, drug abuse and the breakdown of family life. Young people are frustrated and seeking answers in their confusion, but where are the fervent messengers of the gospel? No longer do Tahitian missionaries leave for other lands as they once did.

2. **Those with a vital personal faith are rare.** As a result, there is a reversion to the bondage of pagan occultism and a multiplication of syncretic and foreign sects – especially Mormons. Pray for a spiritual revolution to take place among the many nominal Catholic and Protestant Christians. Those who migrate to Papeete are usually lost to the churches.

3. **Only a handful of evangelical churches** exist (mainly on Tahiti) and very few evangelical pastors. The main Protestant body, the ECP, is predominantly liberal in theology. However, the French

Assemblies of God has grown fast since 1985. Pray for those national and missionary workers who are preaching the gospel in often discouraging circumstances. There are several missionary workers of the **AoG**, Baptists and **YWAM**.

4. **Unreached peoples.** Almost all adhere to a form of Christianity, but many are without a clear gospel witness – especially the Mangarevans on the Gambier Islands and the Marquesans and Tuamotuans. Biblical Christianity is hardly known in these islands since the people do not fully understand the related Tahitian, the only local language with the Bible. The Chinese are 4% Catholic and 4% Protestant; most are secularists. The French community lives a life apart having minimal contact with any church, and little is being done to evangelize them.

5. **Bible translation** is needed for at least two of the languages spoken in outlying island groups – Marquesas and Tuamotu. **SIL** is looking to God for two linguistic teams to start work.

Gabon

(The Gabonese Republic)

| May 9 |
| Africa |

Area 268,000 sq.km. 80% dense tropical rain forest.

Population	Ann. Gr.	Density
1990	1,171,000	3.5 %	4/sq.km
1995	1,380,000	3.3 %	5/sq.km

Peoples:
Indigenous peoples 84.7%. About 68 ethnic groups.
  Bantu 83.4%. Major groupings of peoples: Fang 427,000; Eshira-Punu 250,000; Kota-Teke 136,000; Ndjabi-Mbete 110,000; Myene 35,000.
  Pygmy 1.3%.
Other African peoples 12%. Cameroonian, Equato-Guinean and West African migrants attracted by job opportunities.
Other 3.3%. French 37,500; Lebanese 1,000.

Literacy 77%. **Official language:** French, which is extensively used. **All languages** 40. **Languages with Scriptures** 2Bi 4NT 8por.

Capital: Libreville 352,000. Urbanization 41%.

Economy: Country underpopulated, yet with immense resources of wood, oil and other minerals. The lack of all-weather roads hinders development. One of Africa's most prosperous and stable economies. Public debt/person $1,817. Income/person $2,770 (13% of USA).

Politics: Retains close economic and political links with France since independence in 1960. A one-party state until the institution of multi-party democracy in 1991. Strikes and political unrest characterized 1992.

Religion: The Catholic Church was dominant until the President's conversion to Islam in 1973. Ten religious organizations were banned between 1984 and 1989, but the banning was never fully implemented. Multi-party democracy has further removed restrictions on religious freedom.
African traditionalist 7.7%, but some estimate this to be nearer 20%.

Muslim 4.2%. Majority foreign, but growing among Gabonese.
Non-religious/other 1%. Mainly French.
Christian 87.1%. Nom 4.9%. Affil 82.2%. Growth 4%.
Protestant 18%. Affil 17.5%. Growth 2.8%.

Church	Cong	Members	Affiliated
Evang Ch of Gabon	500	30,000	150,000
Chr Alliance Ch (CMA)	213	13,975	40,125
Pente Ch of Gabon	20	2,000	10,000
Bethany	7	1,500	5,000
All other (2)	2	109	273
Denominations (6)	742	47,584	205,398
Evangelicals 5.1% of pop		18,000	60,000
Pentecostal/charis 1.6%		4,900	19,000

Missionaries:
  to Gabon 68 (1:17,200 people) in 7 agencies.
  from Gabon 2 (1:103,000 Protestants) in 1 agency.
Roman Catholic 54.8%. Affil 50.3%. Growth 2.9%.

Catholic Ch	83	389,000	589,000

Missionaries:
  to Gabon 213 (1:5,500 people).
  from Gabon 10 (1973 figure).
Foreign Marginal 0.5%. Growth 18%.

Jehovah's Witnesses	15	1,253	6,000

Indigenous Marginal 13.8%. Growth 9.4%.

All groups (10)	193	38,000	161,700

Missionaries to Gabon 7dom.

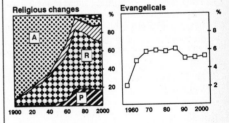

Religious changes   Evangelicals

1. **Gabon is a spiritual battlefield.** The conversion of the President and many government leaders to Islam, the pervasive influence of freemasonry and indigenous secret societies which all government leaders had to join, endemic alcoholism and widespread ignorance of the gospel are all indicators of this. Pray that these influences may be broken down, and all restrictions removed on the preaching of the gospel now that there is more political freedom.

2. **Muslims have multiplied** over the past 20 years: firstly by immigration of Hausa, Fulani and other West African Muslims; secondly by conversions among Gabonese men; thirdly by infusion of Middle Eastern oil money. There are now 30 mosques in Gabon. Pray that this challenge may stimulate vital and effective evangelism among Muslims and non-Muslims alike.

3. **The Catholic Church** has considerable political influence, and the majority of the population were baptized Catholic, but still follow the old ways. After a peak in 1970, the Catholics have lost many followers to Islam and to other churches and sects. Pray that the many nominal Christians may see and embrace the truth – the churches are full, but hearts are empty.

4. **The major Protestant denomination** is the fruit of French missionary work, but the legacy of liberal theology has been a stagnant, nominal daughter church with a leadership more concerned with social issues than evangelism. Pray for a move of God's Spirit.

5. **The evangelical witness** is confined to the Alliance Church (EACG), the daughter church of the **CMA**, and several smaller indigenous Pentecostal denominations. The number of conversions has increased, but the majority lack the discipling they need. Several missions have struggled to establish a presence, but have had to withdraw. Pray for the calling and entry of church-planting and specialized ministry agencies to work together in discipling the peoples of Gabon. UFM is committed to entry for church planting. The only large grouping of evangelical missionaries are the 53 CMA workers. Major missionary-contributing nations: USA (44), Canada (12), South Korea (4), Nigeria (2).

6. **Less reached peoples:**
a) **Of the 68 ethnic groups,** 38 have no evangelical congregation and 25 are marginally reached. CMA and the EACG are targeting 27 but do not have the personnel to work among them all.
b) The **Fang** are the dominant people, largely nominal Protestant and Catholic. The strong Bwiti secret society movement has never been challenged by Bible-believing Christians.
c) **The Provinces of Upper Ogooue and Ogooue-Ivindo** have long been closed for Evangelicals. Born-again Christians are very few among the 17 peoples of the area – notably the Kele, Mbede, Duma, Kota, Kwele, Tsangui, Teke, Obamba and others.
d) **The Babinga, or Pygmies,** live in the virgin forest, despised by other peoples and spiritually neglected. CMA has started a work in one village where 25 have believed.
e) **Libreville** with its wealthy, cosmopolitan population is a challenge for urban church planting. The CMA church is growing and has 6,000 worshippers, but many suburbs and sections of the population are unreached.

7. **Goals for the '90s** set by the EACG:
a) **A complete survey of all the peoples of Gabon** and then church planting initiated.
b) **A Bible teaching church** in every county capital. Of the 43 capitals, 15 now have no such church.

8. **Present opportunities in cities, mining communities, rural areas and schools are being lost because of the lack of workers.** There are two small Bible schools in the country with 40 students so pray for the calling of both pastors and cross-cultural workers for evangelism and church planting. Pray also for the 450 TEE students in 20 centres around the country.

9. **Help ministries** requiring intercession:
a) **Bible translation** is a neglected ministry, and a linguistic survey is required. There may be up to 25 languages for which New Testaments should be provided. Alliance Church and CMA missionaries are working on New Testament translations in three languages.
b) The *Jesus* film in French is being widely used.
c) **GRn** has made recordings available in 24 languages.
d) Both national radio and TV are wide open for evangelism and Bible teaching, but are woefully neglected.

Gambia

(Republic of The Gambia)

May 10

Africa

Area 11,300 sq.km. A narrow enclave within Senegal and extending 400 km. along the Gambia River.

Population	Ann. Gr.	Density
1990 858,000	2.9 %	80/sq.km
1995 983,000	2.8 %	92/sq.km

Peoples: Over 25 ethnic groups that are very intermingled. Largest: Mandingo 332,000; Fula (3) 155,000; Wolof 121,000; Jola 85,000; Tukulor 59,000; Serer 21,000; Manjako 14,000; Soninke 11,000; Aku 6,600.

Literacy 25%. **Official language:** English. **Trade languages:** Mandingo, Wolof. **All languages** 21. **Languages with Scriptures** 2Bi 4NT 4por.

Capital: Banjul 167,000. Urbanization 21%.

Economy: Subsistence agriculture, and dependent on groundnut cultivation and tourism. Public debt/person $340. Income/person $230 (1.1% of USA).

Politics: Independent from Britain in 1965. Senegalese intervention to quell the 1981 coup resulted in abortive efforts to create a Senegambian confederation. A multi-party democracy, but with the ruling party virtually unchallenged.

Religion: Islam has steadily grown in influence. Christian missionaries are restricted to development programmes, but they have considerable freedom to share their faith.
Islam 95.4%. Most Muslims are members of one of three Sufi brotherhoods.

African traditional religions 0.3%. Mainly among the Jola and Manjako, but many of these peoples are becoming Muslim.
Baha'i 0.6%.
Christian 3.7%. Nom 1.2%. Affil 2.5%. Growth 1.5%.
Protestant 1.4%. Affil 0.7%. Growth 3.0%.

Church	Cong	Members	Affiliated
Anglican	6	800	2,700
Methodist	6	1,230	2,234
Ev Ch of Gambia (WEC)	8	70	200
Baptist Conv (SBC)	4	94	162
Ch of Pentecost	7	105	162
All other (8)	14	316	517
Denominations (13)	45	2,615	6,001
Evangelicals 0.19% of pop.		790	1,600
Pentecostal/charis 0.03%		160	250

Missionaries:
  to Gambia 109 (1:7,900 people) in 17 agencies.
  from Gambia 2 (1:3,000 Protestants).
Roman Catholic 2.3%. Affil 1.7%. Growth 0.9%.

Catholic	44	9,240	15,400

Marginal 0.01%. Affil 0.01%. Growth 12.8%.

Jehovah's Witnesses	1	31	78

Religious changes

Evangelicals

1. **Islam is dominant,** yet the land remains open for the gospel. Pray for continued freedom to proclaim the gospel and openness of heart for Muslims to receive it. Little effort was ever directed by the older churches at reaching the Muslim majority – the key people being the Mandingo, a people made famous by Alex Haley's book *Roots*. Converts from Islam have been few, but their numbers are increasing. Nominal Christian girls frequently marry Muslims and become Muslims themselves.

2. **Islam is gradually gaining** ground in the few areas where there are pockets of uncommitted animist peoples. There are many inland villages and towns where there has been little evangelism. The greatest challenge for missions is to see a significant harvest among Muslims.

3. **The churches are largely nominal** and little credit to the gospel. Evangelical believers are few. The new bishop of the Anglican Church is a committed evangelical; pray for him and other evangelical leaders who seek to bring new life to the church. National congresses on evangelization in 1989 and 1991 have helped Christians to cooperatively set evangelization goals – pray for the growth and advance of the late '80s to accelerate.

4. **Missionary work in the Gambia** was pioneered by the Anglicans and Methodists. Much of their work was confined to the Aku (Creole-speaking descendants of freed slaves in Banjul). Catholics and

Methodists have not seen significant results among the other people groups. Methodists have one rural Manjako and Mandingo congregation. **WEC**, with 37 workers, has planted congregations among those from Muslim backgrounds through its medical, agricultural and youth programmes. Other missions include the **ABWE** (18) and **SBC** (12).

5. **Young people** have flocked to Banjul suburban areas seeking work. Pray for ministries directed to them – **SU** in the secondary schools, and the youth work of **SBC**, **WEC**, **YFC** and Korean missionaries. Most youth work is in the capital and outlying area, though **WEC** has youth work inland as well.

6. **Specialized Ministries.**
a) Prison evangelism has been particularly fruitful. Pray both for conversions and the integration of converts into their communities and into their churches when they are released.
b) **GRn** has prepared audio recordings in ten of Gambia's languages.

Gaza Strip

See under ISRAEL

Georgia
(Sakartvelo)

G

Area 70,000 sq.km. Black Sea state between the Caucasus Mountains and Turkey. Three autonomous republics within its borders – Abkhazia in the west, South Ossetia in the north, and Adzharia (Georgian Muslims) in the southwest.

Population		Ann.Gr.	Density
1990	5,441,000	0.69%	77/sq.km
1995	5,595,000	0.68%	80/sq.km

Peoples:
Indo-European 93.3%.
Caucasian 80.2%. Georgian 3,787,000; Armenian 437,000; Abkhazian 96,000.
Iranian 3.6%. Ossetian 164,000; Kurds 33,000.
Slav 7.5%. Russian 341,000; Ukrainian 52,000.
Other 2%. Greek 100,000.
Turkic/Altaic 5.9%. Azerbaijani 308,000.
All other peoples 0.8%. Jews (Georgian) 14,300; Jews (Ashkenazi) 10,300; Assyrian 6,200.

Literacy 99%. **Official language:** Georgian. **All indigenous languages** 8. **Languages with Scriptures** 1Bi 2por.

Capital: Tbilisi 1,279,000. Urbanization 55%.

Economy: Productive soil and good climate for fruit, tea, cotton, wine; the supplier of 90% of the former USSR's tea and citrus fruit. Plentiful hydro-electric power and a well-educated population, but economy in tatters because of civil wars and the general economic collapse of the former USSR. Income/person $3,065 (14% of USA).

Politics: Centuries of domination by surrounding empires. Annexed by Russia in 1801. Briefly independent 1920–21 before conquest by Bolshevik Communists. Independent in 1991, but the first president became dictatorial and stoked hatred against non-Georgian minorities, resulting in three wars – two inter-ethnic and the third a civil war. In

1991 Shevardnadze, the respected USSR Foreign Minister who helped end the Cold War, became President, but by 1993 settlement of the conflicts had not been achieved.

Religion: Over the centuries the ancient Georgian Orthodox Church was the one abiding factor preserving Georgian culture and nationalism. Georgia and neighbouring Armenia are surrounded by Muslim ethnic groups. Since independence, some Orthodox leaders have sought to deny non-Orthodox Christians the opportunity for building churches and open evangelism.

Muslim 21.3%. Mainly Abkhazian, Ossetian, Azerbaijani and Mingrel Georgian. Almost entirely Sunni Islam.
Non-religious/other 20%.
Jews 0.46%.
Christian 58.2%. Affil 56.2%. Growth 5%.
Protestant 0.5%. Growth 8.8%.

Church	Cong	Members	Affiliated
Baptist Ch	23	4,000	16,000
Pentecostal churches	30	2,500	5,000
All other (4)	8	1,600	4,045
Denominations (6)	61	8,100	25,045
Evangelicals 0.43% of pop.		7,400	23,700
Pentecostal/charis 0.1%		3,000	5,350

Missionaries to Georgia est. 8.
Catholic 0.8%. Affil 0.62%. Growth 3.8%.

Catholic – Eastern rite		11,700	18,000
Catholic – Latin rite		10,400	16,000
All Catholics (2)		22,100	34,000

Missionaries to Georgia n.a.
Orthodox 57%. Affil 55%. Growth 5%.

Georgian Orthodox Ch		1,630,000	2,500,000
Armenian Apostolic Ch		238,000	340,000
Russian Orthodox Ch		112,000	160,000
Syrian Orthodox Ch		3,360	5,600
Denominations (4)		1,983,360	3,005,600

Marginal 0.01%. Growth 10%.

Jehovah's Witnesses		150	500

1. **Georgia's independence,** gained with such hope, has degenerated into inter-ethnic hatred and economic collapse. Pray that the leaders of the different factions may achieve a peace that balances Georgian national identity with ethnic minority aspirations.

2. **The Georgian Orthodox Church** has had a glorious past, but compliance of some leaders under Communism effectively turned it into a puppet of the Party. Many others who resisted this were martyred or imprisoned. Pray for renewal to bring spiritual life to a largely nominal Church. Many Georgians have returned to the Church of their forebears and been baptized – including the President.

3. **The small Protestant Church** struggled for survival under Communism, and since independence has battled with its image as being sectarian. Baptists are the largest Protestant body, and they have

grown significantly since the late '80s, but have yet to gain the freedom to build new church buildings or evangelize openly the many Georgians who have no real link with any Church.

4. **The unreached.** Sadly, Georgian racial pride has antagonized the ethnic minorities. They will be better reached by foreigners. Pray for the:

a) **Muslim Abkhazians and Ossetians** who are a minority within their ethnic groups but need to be reached. The majority are Orthodox Christians. Both peoples are embroiled with the Georgian government in bitter secessionary wars. The New Testament is being translated for both peoples.

b) **The Jews;** two distinct ethnic groups. No known witness to them.

c) **Azerbaijanis** who are Muslim; very few, if any, Christians in Georgia.

d) The Muslim **Mingrel** (500,000) and **Laz** (2,000), related to Georgians.

5. **Christian help ministries** for prayer:

a) **EHC** plan a national literature campaign reaching every home.

b) **The Georgian Bible** in current use was translated 900 years ago. Two new translations are being completed – one by the Orthodox Church and one by the **UBS**. Pray that the contents may be more readily understood and heeded by modern Georgians.

c) **Christian radio programmes** prepared in Georgia are broadcast for 30 minutes, six days a week, by **HCJB** in Ecuador.

Germany
(Federal Republic of Germany)

May 12–14

Europe

G

Area 357,000 sq.km, of which the former East Germany constitutes 30%. Strategically placed in the centre of Europe.

Population	Ann. Gr.	Density
1990 79,113,000	0.22 %	221/sq.km
1995 80,000,000	0.22 %	224/sq.km

Large influx of immigrants between 1989–92 from Eastern Europe.

Peoples:
German 93.4%. An estimated five million more Germans live in Eastern Europe and the former USSR.
Indigenous minorities 0.4%. Sorb and Wend 50,000; Jews 40,000; Danish 30,000; Frisian 25,000. Also Austrian 181,000.
European Community 1.74%. Italian 548,000; Greek 314,000; Spanish 134,000; Dutch 101,000; British 86,000; Portuguese 78,000.
Central and East European 1.5%. Russian 360,000 (former USSR military and dependants in East); Yugoslav 652,000; Polish 241,000; Albanian 25,000.
Middle Eastern 2.71%. Turkish 1,204,000; Kurdish 480,000; Arab 177,000; Iranian 90,000; Afghan 29,000.
Asian 0.25%. Vietnamese 60,000; Chinese 40,000; Tamil 35,000; Pakistani 23,000; Japanese 20,000; Korean 14,000.

Literacy almost 100%. **Official language:** German. Worldwide there are 101 million German-speakers. **All languages** 20. **Languages with Scriptures** 6Bi 3NT 5por.

Capital: Berlin (since 1990) 3,410,000. Other major cities: Ruhr area 5,440,000; Hamburg 1,883,000; Cologne/Bonn 1,460,000, Munich 1,211,000. Urbanization 83.7%.

Economy: Dramatic post-war recovery to become one of the world's strongest economies, with huge balance of payments surpluses. The cost of repairing and rebuilding the crippled East German economy is, however, hugely expensive and has forced Germany into recession, dragging much of Europe's economy down with it. Unemployment is rising in the West and East – in the latter it had reached 35% or more in 1993. Public debt/person $4,350. Income/person $18,170 in West, $9,720 in East (86% and 46% of USA).

Politics: The collapse of Hitler's Reich in 1945 was followed by 45 years of partition between the democratic and capitalist Federal Republic (FRG)

and the Communist "Democratic" Republic (GDR). The collapse of Communism at the end of the '80s led to a rapid reunification of the two states – in reality a takeover by the West that is proving socially and economically painful to all. A core member of the EC, and poised to play a dominant role in European affairs.

Religion: Religious freedom, but close cooperation between the government and the Roman Catholic Church and Protestant Established Churches (EKD) in religious education, radio, TV, church taxation through state channels, etc. Under Communism in the GDR, the churches fought for and won considerable freedoms, but the subtle pressures, compromises and infiltration of the leadership by the secret police have spiritually scarred many.
Non-religious 21.6%. Over 69% of the population of the GDR at reunification had no links with any church.
Muslim 2.5%. Mainly Turks, Kurds, Arabs, Bosnians, Albanians. Also 50,000 Germans (80% women married to Turks, etc.).
Other religions 0.1%. Jews 40,000; Buddhist 16,000; Baha'i 12,000; Hindu 4,000; Satanist over 10,000.
Christian 75.8%. Affil 73.7%.
  Protestant 37.1%. Affil 37%.

Church	Cong	Members	Affiliated
Prot Ch in G (EKD)	18,092	22,800,000	29,200,000
F'ship of Ev Free			
(Bapt/Bre)	625	89,500	256,000
Methodist	989	44,500	74,200
Evang Free Ch	321	26,600	60,500
Assoc of Free Pente	350	23,000	60,000
Christian Brethren	173	26,000	59,100
Seventh-day Adventist	346	22,500	45,000
Free Ev congs	140	26,000	43,300
Indep Lutheran Ch	179	25,900	37,000
Christian F'ship	122	11,000	31,400
Moravian Brethren	35	8,000	21,455
All other (171)	2,115	191,441	346,131
Doubly counted		−780,000	−1,000,000
Denominations (182)	23,487	22,514,441	29,234,086
Evangelicals 3.2% of pop		1,709,000	2,516,000
Pente/charis 140,000		262,000	

Missionaries:
  from Germany 3,510 (1:8,300 Protestants) in 119 agencies 2,847frn 2,805xcul 705dom.
  to Germany 1,237 (1:64,000 people) in 127 agencies.

Roman Catholic 36%. Affil 34.9%.

Catholic Ch	12,943	22,100,000	28,300,000
Doubly counted		−530,000	−700,000
Total	12,943	21,570,000	27,600,000

Missionaries:
from Germany 6,873 (1:4,000 Catholics).
to Germany 4,506 (1:17,600 people).

Other Catholic 0.9%.

Denominations (43)	450	43,800	69,970

Orthodox 0.73%.

Greek Orthodox	58	245,000	350,000
Serbian Orthodox	11	75,000	150,000
Russian Orthodox	46	18,500	28,000
All other (12)	89	30,650	49,100
Denominations (15)	204	369,150	577,100

Marginal 1.07%.

New Apostolic	260	286,000	420,000

Jehovah's Witnesses	1,990	154,108	193,000
Mormons	149	14,400	32,000
Church of Scientology		22,500	30,000
All other (42)	635	57,745	174,832
Groups (46)	3,034	534,753	849,832

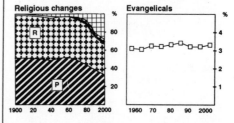

G

1. **The collapse of Communism**, the removal of the Berlin Wall and division between East and West, and the reunification of Germany brought joy and praise to God for answered prayer. Germany's wealth, power and strategic location harnessed for the Kingdom of God would be a blessing to the world. Other European nations fear the abuse of these. Pray that the nation's leaders may wisely use these with sensitivity and restraint.

2. **There are numerous signs of spiritual ill-health** in the nation. Humanism and destructive criticism of the Bible in the 19th Century enfeebled churches, and opened the way to compromise and a pagan Nazi tyranny in the 20th. Post-war wealth in the FRG and Marxist ideology in the GDR gave a further push to secularism, materialism and permissiveness. The loneliness, pointlessness and emptiness of life has driven many to alcohol, drugs, astrology, occultism and New Age thinking. The Church is perceived as no longer relevant to their needs. Blindness to spiritual realities must be removed by believing intercession.

3. **A massive exodus from organized Christianity is in progress.** The drive to opt out of paying church tax has led to an 80% drop in Protestant church membership in the former GDR and 4.5% in the FRG. Actual church attendances tell a more gloomy story, for only 5% of EKD members and 25% of Catholics are active participants in church life. Free churches are just holding their own numerically. The only real growth is among newer, independent and often charismatic churches. Pray that the tragic internal divisions which cripple the witness of Protestants, Evangelicals and Catholics alike may be removed and leaders raised up who emphasize righteousness, holy living and the primacy of evangelism.

4. **The EKD is a federation of Lutheran, Reformed and United State Churches**, but is deeply divided on political, moral and theological issues. The growing number of empty churches is a tragedy. Bible-believing pastors and evangelical/pietistic groups and congregations are more concentrated in Baden-Württemberg, Siegerland and south Saxony in the former GDR. Whole areas of the country have very little evangelical witness – the north, Berlin, Bavaria, Eifel area on the Belgian border, and many cities. Pray above all that the land of Luther may be revived once more.

5. **The radical changes in the former GDR** have been traumatic as the full awfulness and squalor of their society under Communism is revealed. The former Communist elite or secret police are rarely brought to justice for their wrongdoing. Enormous social, economic, political and spiritual changes have required personal choices and provoked stress, and reaction to the changes has emerged in an ugly nationalism and neo-Nazism that is especially evident among the youth. Pray that these changes may open the hearts of the 69% of the population in the former GDR that has no link with a church.

6. **Churches in the former GDR** manifested more vigour under Communism, with large prayer meetings and better church attendances – partly as a protest against the inhumanity and rigidity of Marxism. Now that freedom has come, churches have lost many of these people. Pray that Christians may adapt to the new era and provide an effective witness to their lost countrymen.

7. **Reunification of long-separated denominations** has not been easy. Pray that there may be sensitivity on both sides, sweet fellowship and oneness of heart as ideological, structural, financial and theological differences are ironed out.

8. **In the Free churches,** Evangelicals are proportionally stronger than in the EKD, and church attendance better, but growth in most churches has been minimal and some are declining in number.

Pray that these believers may bestir themselves to permeate their materialistic society with the message of the gospel.

9. **There is a significant evangelical minority in the much larger EKD.**
a) **The Pietist movement** is an influential force within the EKD (especially in Württemberg in the south and in rural areas). The many evangelical fellowships of the **Gnadau Union** within the EKD represent 340,000 Christians and over 63 agencies and institutions.
b) **The Confessional and "No Other Gospel" movements** of the '60's gained good hearing and wide acceptance, and they are making a significant impact on theological thinking and pastoral training.
c) **The Evangelical Alliance** has become a rallying point for over 1.5 million Evangelicals for social action, national weeks of prayer, evangelism and missionary information and outreach. Sadly, there still remains a division between Pentecostals/charismatics and other Evangelicals. Pray for unity among God's people and that this may release rivers of life to the lost.
d) **New evangelical literature and books** covering a wide range of subjects have been a blessing to millions, and a decisive factor in the new evangelical awakening. About 65% of all new Protestant book titles are now evangelical. Pray for writers, publishers and distributors of books. Pray for the impact of more than 150 evangelical magazines with a total circulation of 50 million.

G

10. **Theological education** has proved the major disaster area in the Protestant Church:
a) **The 13 universities** that award theological degrees necessary for acceptance into the EKD ministry have been the preserve of liberal, neo-orthodox and other non-biblical theologies for decades. Pray for more professors who openly proclaim the Truth to be welcomed to teach in these institutions. Students have often emerged with their faith crippled and evangelistic concern stifled. Pray for evangelical students in these spiritual morgues, and pray for those who seek to help them stand true to the Scriptures through pre-university courses and hostels that run parallel courses at university.
b) **German-speaking evangelical seminaries** are limited to Giessen (FTA) and Basel, Switzerland (FETA), and the seminaries of the Free churches; but graduates of these are less acceptable for pastoral ministry in the EKD.
c) **Bible schools** are full, and a stream of young people is moving out to home and foreign fields – pray for such as Adelshofen, Altenkirchen, Brake, Liebenzell, Seeheim, Wiedenest and for the College of Graduate Studies in Missiology established in 1984 in Korntal. A German TEE was launched in 1993.

11. **Missionary vision has long been limited,** with proportionately one of the lowest missionary-sending figures for any country with such a large Protestant community. The total number of missionaries has remained constant for some years, but the proportion of Evangelicals has risen sharply to 80% of the total. Pray for a further increase. Pray for the Association of Evangelical Missions (**AEM**) with 51 members – a catalytic and vital stimulant for training, publicity and sending missionaries. One unique mission is the DMG (German Missionary Fellowship) with 230 missionaries serving with 47 international missions, but with no foreign fields of its own. Other significant German missions: Liebenzell (216 missionaries), *Christoffel-Blindenmission* (189), Wiedenest (128), **WEC** (120), *Allianz-Mission* (78). Pray also for Christians in the ex-GDR to regain a missions impetus after the years of restriction and stifling of the vision.

12. **Student work** is important at this time, with a high proportion of the 1.6 million university students having had no real contact with vital Christianity. There are both denominational and interdenominational student ministries, but full-time workers are woefully few to disciple leaders and launch new groups. Pray for:
a) **SMD(IFES)** with about 50 groups in the 163 universities, and 1,000 groups in the 6,100 secondary schools, and with a heavy camping programme.
b) **CCC** with 80 staff workers in six universities and in churches, and also with wider input into churches with church growth programmes and prayer campaigns.
c) **Navigators** with 55 staff in university witness.
d) ***Wort und Wissen***, a significant new ministry preparing students for university life by giving them good Christian foundations.
e) **Overseas Students** numbering 60,000. Special Bible study groups are organized for them in each SMD group. YMCA and some local churches have also played a significant part in this key ministry.
f) **Missions vision** among students has been rather limited, but there are about 100 serving missionaries who were called through SMD ministry.

13. **Christian radio.** The German branch of **TWR** in Germany, *Evangeliums-Rundfunk*, has made an impressive impact on the German-speaking world with 194 hours of programming every month. Programmes are also provided for Italian, Greek, Spanish, Yugoslav and Turkish immigrant workers within Germany. Pray for the staff, their ministry, and adequate funding – a serious drop in income since 1990 has forced a cut-back in the ministry.

14. **Foreigners.** The flood of immigrants, guest workers, and economic and political refugees since 1989 has overwhelmed German government and voluntary agencies. The economic collapse of the former Communist countries is likely to worsen the problem. Between 1989 and 1992, the annual inflow was 800,000 people. The vast majority have never heard the gospel. There has been a violent backlash against this inflow – especially in the ex-GDR, and these foreigners have often become bitter and resentful over their mishandling. Pray that opportunities to show love and concern and to share Christ may not be lost thereby. Pray also for:

a) The **AFA** (*Arbeitsgemeinschaft für Ausländer*), a fellowship of over 14 mission groups seeking to evangelize through a wide variety of ethnic ministries, with possibly 200 or so workers involved. A number of local congregations also seek to reach these people.

b) **Greater involvement in outreach by German Christians.** Some German congregations are a notable exception to this, but in the main, most missions outreach is by foreigners (US, Swiss and others).

c) **Specific peoples for prayer:**
   i) **Turks,** with over 10 agencies seeking to reach them (including *Orientdienst*, **WEC, OM, CBFMS**). There are no more than 80 believers among them in all Western Europe.
   ii) **Kurds,** with 4–5 agencies seeking to reach them and prepare Scriptures and Christian literature for them.
   iii) **Iranians,** with several Christian groups and localized outreach attempts.
   iv) **North African Arabs and Berbers** – little outreach.
   v) **Albanian and Bosnian Muslims** from former Yugoslavia – no outreach.
   vi) **Southern Europeans** – so many inadequately used opportunities among the nominal Catholic Italians, Spaniards and Portuguese and the Orthodox Greeks. Large areas in their homelands are devoid of an evangelical witness.
   vii) **Gypsies from Central Europe** – many are recent arrivals fleeing discrimination and persecution in Romania and Bulgaria.

15. **The 360,000 ex-USSR military and civilian personnel** are all due to leave the country by the end of 1994. They come from all parts and ethnic groups of the CIS, and have to face the radically new and grim situation in their homelands. They are demoralized, fearful and angry, yet they are open to Biblical truth. Pray that many may return with new life in Christ.

Ghana
(Republic of Ghana)

May 15–16
Africa

Area 238,500 sq.km. Grasslands in north, farmland and forest in south. Centre dominated by the 520 km-long Lake Volta.

Population	Ann. Gr.	Density
1990	15,020,000	3.2 %	63/sq.km
1995	17,543,000	3.2 %	74/sq.km

Higher density in south.

Peoples: About 100 ethnic groups and three major language divisions.
Kwa 74.5%. 5 major sub-groups in centre and south.
Akan (25 groups) 51.5%. Ashanti, Fante, Ahafo, etc. 6,200,000; Abron 606,000; Nzema 285,0000; Wasa 175,000; Anyin 122,000; Ahanta 97,000. Most speak dialects of Twi.
Ewe (3) 11.1%. 1,615,000 in the southeast.
Ga-Adangme (4) 7.7%. 1.300,000 around Accra.
Guan (14) 3.4%. Larteh (4) 156,000; Gonja 138,000; Awutu 85,000 in the centre and north.
C. Togo (14) 0.80%. A medley of small peoples on the eastern border.
Gur 22.6%. 3 major sub-groups in the north. Larger groups: Gurenne (Frafra) 526,000; Dagomba 504,000; Dagaaba 423,000; Konkomba 341,000; Kusasi 255,000; Kulango 255,000; Mamprusi 227,000; Bulsa 131,000; Sisaala 121,000; Wali 99,000; Kasena 78,000; Bimoba 74,000; Birifor 63,000; Nafaanra 51,000; Dega 17,000; Tampulma 11,000; Hanga 7,000.
Mande 0.9%. (2) Busansi 119,000; Ligbi 6,500.
Other 2%. Migrant workers; Fulani 7,300; Westerners; Arab 1,500; Chinese 800.

Literacy 53%. **Official language:** English. **All languages** 72. **Languages with Scriptures** 6Bi 17NT 10por.

Capital: Accra 1,437,000. Other cities: Kumasi 671,000; Sekondi-Takoradi 313,000. Urbanization 32%.

Economy: Slowly recovering from almost total collapse in 1982. Earlier government overspending, mismanagement and corruption reduced this once prosperous land to poverty. Main exports are cocoa, gold and timber. Living standards were further reduced by uncontrolled inflation and periods of drought. A steady economic recovery since 1984 with an average GDP growth of 5% per annum. Public debt/person $151. Income/person $380 (1.8% of USA).

Politics: Independent from Britain in 1957. Nkrumah's "socialist" experiment was a disaster from which the nation is taking years to recover. There have been five military regimes and three short-lived civilian governments since Nkrumah's overthrow in 1966. The revolutionary military government of Rawlings eventually opened up the way for multi-party elections in 1992, and was democratically returned to power but with the majority of the electorate boycotting the election.

Religion: Secular state with religious freedom, but some members of the former military government were hostile to Christianity.
African traditional religions 20%. Mainly among peoples in the northern regions, but many Muslims and Christians continue animistic practices.
Muslim 16%. Sunni 9%, Ahmaddiya 7%. The majority among the Dagomba, Gonja and Wali; growing minority among other northern peoples and in southern cities.
Christian 64%. Nom 19.8%. Affil 44.3%. Attend 12%. Growth 5.3%.
Protestant 27.9%. Affil 20.3%. Growth 8.2%.

Church	Cong	Members	Affiliated
Presbyterian Ch of G	1,791	179,000	814,000
Ch of Pentecost	3,871	240,000	429,000
Seventh-day Adventist	380	130,000	383,000
Methodist Ch	2,467	193,058	330,787
Evang Presby Ch	710	102,000	308,000
Anglican Ch	313	80,000	160,000
Assemblies of God	500	39,600	120,000
Afn Fth Tabernacle Ch	860	92,900	116,000
Apostolic Ch	681	37,500	104,000
Ghana Baptist Conv	180	12,500	20,800
Salvation Army	140	12,200	20,300
Evang Lutheran Ch	100	3,000	10,000
Good News Chs (SIM)	60	2,885	8,740
Evang Ch of G (WEC)	83	1,084	4,520
All other (45)	1,597	108,011	226,966
Denominations (59)	13,733	1,233,738	3,056,113
Evangelicals 9% of pop		630,043	1,344,500
Pentecostal/charis 4.7%		336,000	706,000

Missionaries:
to Ghana 400 (1:37,600 people) in 58 agencies.
from Ghana 672 (1:4,500 Protestants) in 44 agencies 128frn 208xcul 464dom.
Roman Catholic 18.7%. Affil 12.3%. Growth 2.2%.

Catholic Ch	3,080	980,000	1,849,000

Missionaries:
  to Ghana 540 (1:27,800 people).
  from Ghana 60 (1973 figure).
Other Catholic 0.05%. Growth 12.5%.
Foreign Marginal 1.4%. Affil 0.88%.
  Growth 5.9%.

Jehovah's Witnesses	642	37,376	120,000
Mormons	39	5,340	8,900
All other (10)	20	2,000	4,000
Groups (12)	701	44,716	132,900

Indigenous Marginal 16%. Affil 10.6%.
  Growth 3.7%.
  Church of the 12

Apostles	1,500	80,000	125,000
Army of the Cross	1,094	35,000	125,000

Christ Apostolic Ch	500	34,000	40,000
All other (1,113)	7,577	753,100	1,314,000
All groups (1,116)	10,671	902,100	1,604,100

Missionaries from Ghana 666 (1:2,400 affiliates)
38frn 50xcul 578dom.

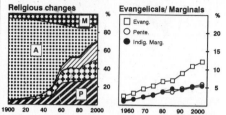

G

1. **A series of economic, natural, and social calamities** reached a climax in 1983/4. This created a spiritual hunger among the people which led to revival and church growth in many areas. Pray that the Holy Spirit may deepen this work.

2. **Pray for the government** – for just rule, wise economic policies, fairness to all religious groups and, above all, that those in authority may subject themselves to the authority of God and his Word rather than human ideologies or demonic influences.

3. **The present spiritual upsurge in Ghana** is in answer to prayer and sacrificial service. The leavening work of literature, Scripture Union in the schools, the Ghana Evangelism Committee and NLFA have brought many thousands to new life and invigorated many Presbyterian and Methodist churches. Numerous evangelical, charismatic and Pentecostal groups and fellowships have sprung up all over the south. In some of these denominations there has been rapid growth. Pray that there may be a growing vision for the evangelization of the whole of Ghana.

4. **For years Christianity has had a large traditional following in the more developed south.** Over 64% of Ghanaians call themselves Christian, but only 40% have any link with a church and only 12% are regular church attenders. Pagan worldviews and practices have gone hand-in-hand with Christian profession. The deadness and formality of many older churches have stimulated rapid growth of the African Independent Churches, which offer excitement, involvement and miracles, but not always salvation by faith. The number of these denominations is in the thousands! Pray that the true gospel may shine into the hearts of those who call themselves Christian but who are not born from above. Pray that a decisive break may be made from all fetishism and pagan bondages, and true liberty in Jesus be found.

5. **Unity among believers is a prerequisite for advance.** This is being promoted by the Ghana Evangelism Committee through national conferences and national evangelistic outreach. The GEC national church survey of 1985–89 culminated in a significant national conference of denominational leaders. The results revealed the spiritual need of Ghana:
a) Nominal Christians number seven million.
b) Of the 26,000 towns and villages, 15,000 have no congregation of Christians.
c) In the less evangelized north there are three million individuals in 40–50 peoples who are unreached or, at best, partially reached.
d) In the heavily evangelized south live two million northerners (18% of the population) that are unreached.
e) The five million adherents of Islam and traditional religions need to be reached.

6. **Outreach goals to be attained by the year 2000** were set at this 1989 conference:
a) To increase congregations from 22,600 to 53,000.
b) To plant 2,000 new churches among northerners in each of the East and West Upper Regions, the Northern Region and northerners in the south.
c) To ensure that there is an active witnessing church for every village, town, urban neighbourhood and ethnic community.
Pray that this vision may become a reality through the mobilization of the church in Ghana.

7. **Mature Christian leaders** are in short supply in this time of rapid growth, economic stress and doctrinal confusion. There are two diploma-awarding schools – Christian Service College in Kumasi

started by **WEC** and Maranatha Bible College (**SIM**) – and Trinity College which awards degrees mainly for mainline churches. There are 27 other accredited denominational and inter-denominational Bible schools as well as a range of TEE and lay training programmes. Pray for the training of many leaders who will live exemplary lives and rightly minister the Word of truth to their people.

8. **The missionary vision of the Ghanaian Church** is held back by the reluctance of Ghanaians to go to the unevangelized peoples in the less developed north. Nevertheless, the proliferation of agencies and increase in number of missionaries is to be commended. Christian Outreach Fellowship has missions outreach in Volta, Western, Northern and Upper Regions. Pray for these and also for the Christian Service College in Kumasi and Maranatha Bible College, both of which train Ghanaian missionaries.

9. **Young people are in the forefront of the move of the Spirit.** Praise God for the impact of **SU** on the secondary schools and GHAFES(**IFES**), **Navigators** and **CCC** on the universities and colleges. Pray that the influence of converted young people may be decisive in church, mission and national affairs. May many hear God's call into full-time service. Very few churches have an effective programme for young people or children; youth under 15 comprise only 30% of the church-going population but 45% of the total population.

10. **Missionary personnel** to serve as Bible teachers, translators, media experts and pioneer evangelists are still needed in this day of opportunity. Visas are hard to obtain, and a quota system is in operation. Pray for missions serving the Lord in the land; the largest: GILLBT/**SIL** (59), **SIM** (36), **SBC** (38), **WEC** (31). Largest missionary-contributing nations: USA (221), UK (45), Germany (44), Nigeria (18).

11. **Non-Christian peoples have never been so receptive.** Pray out labourers to bring the ripened harvest in! Among the 35 or so peoples in the north, only one is even nominally Christian – the Dagari (60% Catholic); in most, less than 2% are Christian of any variety, though only a handful of peoples are without a church in their midst. Most of the churches in the north have been small, weak, largely illiterate, and with a semi-literate leadership; but this is changing.

12. **The less reached peoples of Ghana:**
a) **The traditional peoples of the Upper Region** are beginning to respond through the ministry of expatriate and indigenous missions. Pray for church growth among the Sisaala (**SIM**), Kasena and Bulsa (**SIM**), and Frafra (**SIM, AoG, WEC**). Response is slow among the Bimoba (**AoG**), as well as the Kusasi and Tampulma (**AoG**). Other smaller groups are unoccupied by Christian workers.
b) **The traditional peoples of the Northern Region** are a complex medley of small groups that are scarcely touched by the gospel; over 30 peoples are resident in the region, but there are viable evangelical churches in only 6–7 of these. ECG/**WEC** is planting churches in this area. Response is growing among the Birifor and Konkomba but, though targeted by ECG/**WEC**, there are not adequate labourers for the Nawuri, Nchumburu and others.
c) **The Islamized peoples of the north** have responded only minimally to the gospel, and more input is needed. Examples include the dominant Gonja with only 300 believers (**WEC**), the Dagomba (**AoG, SIM, SBC, WEC**) with 1% Christian, and the Wali (Baptist Mid-Missions). Converts to Christ have often suffered verbal and physical persecution. There is a new openness among the Dagomba in SIM work with many new churches being planted.

13. **Less evangelized sectors of society.**
a) **The cities** which have grown by absorbing many ethnic groups. Northerners in southern cities easily turn to Islam; little has been done by Christians to reach them until recently. Pray that both Ghanaian and expatriate workers may be used of God to increase the number of northern-language congregations in the southern cities.
b) **The many pockets of traditionalists** among the southern peoples; this is especially true among the Ewe sea and river fishermen all over Ghana. The Ghanaian **Volta Evangelistic Association** seeks to reach them.

14 **Bible translation. UBS**, GILLBT and Ghanaian teams are working in 20 languages, but between 11 and 30 other languages are yet to be tackled. Pray for the completion of the Bible translation task.

15. **Supportive ministries.**
a) **Literature:** a chronic shortage due to lack of foreign exchange or printing materials. Pray for the

importation and economic distribution of Bibles (**UBS**) and Christian literature by agencies such as Challenge Enterprises, an indigenous organization backed by **SIM** which handles 90% of Christian literature in Ghana. There are 13 Christian bookstores in Ghana. **Africa Christian Press** publishes a range of good Christian books for distribution throughout Africa. Problems in running an economic indigenous publishing ministry are enormous. Bible Correspondence Courses have been most successful (**SIM, ICI/AoG**).

b) **Christian films (SIM):** used with great effect. The five mobile "cinevans" of Challenge Enterprises have a total audience of over 1.5 million annually. The *Jesus* film is being widely used in Ewe and Twi.

c) **Christian cassettes:** these have only now become more widely used, but a dearth of workers, equipment and batteries limits the growth of what should be a key ministry. **GRn** has recordings in 50 languages.

Include with Spain
Europe

Gibraltar
(Colony of Gibraltar)

Area 6.5 sq.km. A famous rocky peninsula on the south coast of Spain.

Population	Ann. Gr.	Density
1990 30,000	0.68 %	5,172/sq.km
1995 31,000	0.66 %	5,345/sq.km

Peoples:
Indigenous 66%. Gibraltarian – of Italian, Maltese, British, Spanish and Portuguese descent.
Other 34%. British 3,300; Spanish 3,000; Moroccan 2,900 (many more come for temporary employment); Indo-Pakistani 360.

Literacy 80%. **Official languages:** English and Spanish.

Economy: The ending of the British naval dockyard and the reopening of the border with Spain has provoked radical changes. By 1990, there was an economic boom based on financial services and tourism. There are 27,000 companies registered. Income/person $4,550 (21% of USA).

Politics: A British colony since its capture in 1704. It was an important British military base until 1991. The local population has steadfastly resisted Spanish pleas and pressures to return the Rock to Spain. Its future is likely to be resolved within the context of the EC.

Religion: Religious freedom.
Muslim 10% (Moroccan). **Jews** 1.7%. **Hindu** 1.1%.
Christian 87.2%. Nom 11.8%. Affil 75.4%.
Protestant 7.89%. Growth −0.3%.

Church	Cong	Members	Affiliated
Ch of England	3	900	2,000
All other (4)	6	222	368
Denominations (5)	9	1,122	2,368
Evangelicals 1.45% of pop		228	435
Pentecostal/charis 1%		150	300

Missionaries to Gibraltar 2 (1:15,000 people).
Roman Catholic 66.67%. Growth −0.1%.

Catholic Ch	8	12,400	20,000

Missionaries to Gibraltar 4 (1:7,500 people).
Marginal 0.87%. Growth 3.6%.

Jehovah's Witnesses	2	131	262

1. **The Protestant witness.** There are three English-speaking churches (Methodist, Presbyterian and Church of England) and two for the Spanish-speaking – Assemblies of God and Evangelical. The last two maintain a lively witness to the Gibraltarian majority.

2. **The witness to the Muslim Moroccans.** There are about 7,000 migrant labourers from Morocco. Pray that some of these may be won for the Lord. There is a small group of Arab believers who meet regularly.

Greece

(The Hellenic Republic)

May 17–18
Europe

Area 133,000 sq.km. Southernmost point of Balkan Peninsula in S. E. Europe and 150 inhabited islands in the Ionian, Aegean and Mediterranean Seas, the islands constituting 20% of the land area.

Population		Ann. Gr.	Density
1990	10,047,000	0.23 %	76/sq.km
1995	10,124,000	0.15 %	77/sq.km

Peoples:
Greek 92.1%. The descendants of the ancient Greeks whose civilization has so enriched the world.
Indigenous ethnic minorities 4.3%. Most have been largely absorbed into Greek society. Slavic 200,000 (including 20,000 Pomak); Turk 140,000; Gypsy (4 groups) 91,000; Vlach 60,000; Albanian 25,000.
Immigrant and refugee minorities 3.6%. Pontian Greeks (from the former USSR) 200,000; Albanians 100,000; Arabs 28,000; Iranians 10,000; Armenians 10,000; British 8,000.

Literacy 94%. **Official language:** Greek. **All languages** 14. **Languages with Scriptures** 6Bi 2NT 2por.

Capital: Athens 3,027,000. Other major city: Thessaloniki 706,000. Urbanization 58%.

Economy: EC membership has boosted tourism, industrialization and modernization, but failure to enforce discipline in the economy has fuelled inflation and slowed growth. Greece has the largest fleet of merchant ships in the EC. Unemployment 7%. Public debt/person $805. Income/person $5,340 (25% of USA).

Politics: Nearly four centuries of Turkish rule ended with independence in 1827. The last 50 years have been punctuated by two civil wars, two military dictatorships, and tensions with neighbouring Turkey over the political status of Cyprus. A republic with a parliamentary democracy. The collapse of Communist rule in neighbouring Balkan states has created anxiety in Greece. Economic stresses in Albania and threat of war in neighbouring Former Yugoslavian Republic of Macedonia could involve Greece in a wider conflagration.

Religion: The Orthodox Church is recognized and legally protected by the state as the dominant and established religion. The constitution of 1975 removed some of the discriminatory legislation against non-Orthodox bodies, but old laws remain which can be used to hinder non-Orthodox activities and persecute Protestants. There is discussion about the separation of Church and state.
Non-religious/other 0.4%.
Muslim 1.5%. Turks, Pomaks, Gypsy, Arabs.
Jews 0.05%.
Christian 98%. Affil 96.19%. Growth 0.2%.
Protestant 0.2%. Growth 0.3%.

Church	Cong	Members	Affiliated
Greek Evangelical Ch	35	2,000	4,000
Free Evangelical Chs	50	1,380	2,500
Assemblies of God	17	900	1,585
Other Pentecostal (6)	40	1,800	5,000
All other (29)	99	2,168	6,835
Denominations (38)	201	8,248	19,921
Evangelicals 0.14% of pop		6,467	14,500
Pentecostal/charis 0.08%		3,200	7,500

Missionaries:
to Greece 144 (1:69,800 people) in 37 agencies.
from Greece 30 (1:660 Protestants) 5frn 6xcul 24dom.
Roman Catholic 0.53%. Growth 0.3%.

Catholic Ch	77	38,700	53,000

Missionaries to Greece 180 (1973 figure).
Orthodox 96.9%. Affil 95.05%. Growth 0.1%.

Ch of Greece	28,945	6,950,000	9,516,000
Authentic Old Calendar Orth	180	106,000	212,000
Armenian Apostolic	9	4,050	9,000
All other (5)	7	7,840	13,000
Doubly counted		−150,000	−200,000
Denominations (8)	29,141	6,917,890	9,550,000

Foreign Marginal 0.41%. Growth 2%.

Jehovah's Witnesses	332	24,348	40,600
Denominations (2)	335	24,558	40,900

1. **Greece was the first European country to be evangelized** (Acts 16:10), but Christianity is now more cultural than spiritual, with only 2% of the population in church on an average Sunday. Evangelicals number only around 15,000. The Macedonian call is just as valid today.

2. **The Orthodox Church dominates the cultural and religious life of the country.** Orthodoxy was the focal rallying point in the dark years of Turkish occupation, so, to many, to be a Greek is to be Orthodox. All other expressions of Christianity are seen as a threat. Within the Orthodox Church are godly, committed believers, but the majority are bound by traditions and ignorance of the true gospel. Pray for a renewing work of the Holy Spirit.

3. **The last decade has brought increasing liberty to preach the gospel.** However, there are recurring instances of religious persecution and harassment for those who "proselytize" – Pentecostals, Mormons and Jehovah's Witnesses are specifically targeted, and some have been imprisoned. Pray for complete cultural and legal equality for non-Orthodox believers concomitant with Greece's membership of the European Community.

4. **Greek Protestants are few,** and mainly concentrated in the Athens, Thessaloniki and Katerina areas. Pray for:
a) **Unity** in place of the present divisions. Pray for the Pan Hellenic Evangelical Alliance formed in 1977.
b) **Courage to witness** in a society that generally despises and occasionally persecutes them.
c) **Growth** to replace the 30-year stagnation. The newer, mainly Pentecostal, denominations have been growing, but mainly through transfer from other Protestant groups.
d) **A vision for multiplying congregations** in the many centres without an evangelical witness.

5. **Widespread evangelism with effective follow-up discipling is the need.** Specific programmes and visions for prayer:
a) **EHC's** goal to reach every home with gospel literature – only partially complete by 1992.
b) The **Hellenic Mission Union's** (HMU) summer campaigns.
c) The **Love Europe** campaigns of **OM**.
d) The **Thessaloniki Evangelistic Team's** year-round evangelism and summer outreaches.
e) The **AoG Decade of Harvest** goal of 104 churches and 5,000 converts in the '90s.

6. **Theological training** has been a lack. There are two training institutes – **GEM** with 30 students and **AoG** with 15. A seminary to provide advanced training is a real need.

7. Many Greeks have never heard a clear presentation of the gospel. More specifically pray for:
a) **The 150 islands.** The Dodecanese, Cyclades, the Ionian Islands and others are without evangelical congregations. Corfu and Crete are the only exceptions. **HMU** use their yacht *The Morning Star* for evangelizing these isolated communities.
b) **University students.** There is a strong work of **CCC** among them in Thessaloniki and Athens, and a large **IFES** group in the latter, but most of the 197,000 students in tertiary education have little exposure to the gospel.
c) **Albanians** who have flooded into Greece since the collapse of the Communist regime in Albania. Humanitarian aid and spiritual help need to be kept in balance.
d) **Immigrant communities in the Athens area.** There are several outreaches and small Christian groups among the Arabs, Ethiopians and others, but few of the present opportunities are fully used. Greece is a key base for ministry to the Arab world.
e) **Indigenous ethnic minorities** in the north. They are officially ignored, and their cultural identity denied – a reflection of centuries-old Balkan conflicts. Pray for a change in Greek attitudes and fears, and for effective outreach to the Albanians and Vlach and to the Muslim Turks, Gypsies, and Bulgarian-speaking Pomaks.

8. **Foreign missions** have not found Greece an easy field because of strong nationalism, visa restrictions and the high degree of cultural adaptation required. Major ministries are: **GEM** (14 workers), HMU (23 expatriates, 8 nationals), **CCC** (12), **OMS** (8), **AoG** (6). Greece's EC membership facilitates the residence of missionaries from other member states. Pray for labourers and for their adaptation, ministry and fruitfulness.

9. **Literature has been a fruitful form of evangelism.** Tracts are read! Pray for the seed-sowing work of the Greek Bible Society in disseminating all or part of the Scriptures (the whole Bible is being translated into modern Greek), **SU** in producing good Christian Bible Reading aids, and Every Home Crusade. There is little variety in Christian literature available.

10. **Christian Radio and TV.** The legalization of private radio has opened the way for the launching of a Christian radio station in Athens. Some Evangelical Christian TV programmes have also been broadcast. International radio broadcasts by **TWR, High Adventure** and **IBRA** only total 1.5 hours per week. Pray for the most effective use of these media.

11. **The Greek diaspora is large** – USA 2,200,000, Germany 314,000, Australia 300,000, South Africa 70,000, etc. Believers in these lands should be more concerned for evangelization of the Greeks among them.

Greenland

(Kalaallit Nunaat)

Include with Denmark
North America

Area 2,176,000 sq.km. 85% of land is glacial ice-cap.

Population	Ann. Gr.	Density
1990 56,000	1.1 %	0.026/sq.km
1995 58,000	0.70 %	0.027/sq.km

The world's largest island and with the lowest population density of any country.

Peoples:
Greenland Eskimo 88%. **Danish** 10%. **US military** 2%.

Literacy 99%. **Official languages:** Greenlandic, Danish. **Languages with Scriptures** 1Bi 1por.

Capital: Nuuk 12,200. **Urbanization** 80%.

Economy: Based on fishing and mining. Income/person $15,540 (74% of USA).

Politics: Overseas administrative division of Denmark with home rule since 1979.

Religion: Lutheran Church monopoly until 1953.
Non-religious/other 1.4%. **Baha'i** 0.4%.
Christian 98.2%. Nom 30.1%. Affil 68.1%. Growth 1.2%.
  Protestant 97.6%. Affil 67.6%. Growth 1.2%.

Church	Cong	Members	Affiliated
Lutheran	91	26,900	36,400
Pentecostal Ch (AoG)	21	190	970
All other (4)	2	290	457
Denominations (6)	114	27,380	37,827
Evangelicals 3.7% of pop		943	2,047
Pentecostal/charis 1.7%		190	970

Missionaries:
  to Greenland 51 (1:1,100 people) in 10 agencies.
  from Greenland 3 (1:18,000 Protestants) 2frn 1dom.
Roman Catholic 0.2%. Growth 7%.
Missionaries to Greenland 1 (1:55,000 people).
Marginal 0.4%. Growth 8.4%.

Jehovah's Witnesses	7	126	210

G

1. **Greenland has been Christianized**, but not converted. Nearly every settlement has its Lutheran church building – but many are empty of biblical theology, people or life. Pray for renewal, and new life for Dane and Greenlander alike.

2. **The culture of the Greenlanders**, so finely tuned to their inhospitable environment, has been devastated by modernity. The dire results have been widespread immorality, alcoholism, apathy, mental illness and suicide. With home rule, Greenland's culture has revived. Pray that the retranslated Bible may be read, then remould the people and bring to birth a truly Greenlandic church.

3. **Only in the 1950s was an evangelical witness established.** Through the ministry of Scandinavian Pentecostal (14 workers) and Free Church (9) missionaries, and also Faeroese Brethren (8), **AoG** (2) and, more recently, **NTM** (8), some have been won to Christ and churches planted. Travel conditions are harsh and difficult and the communities along the coasts isolated. Pray that "Greenland's icy mountains" may resound with the gospel message!

4. Pray for **Greenlanders to be called and prepared** for Spirit-filled ministry to their country. **YWAM** is setting up a Discipleship Training School in Nuuk.

<table>
<tr><td>See
Caribbean</td><td rowspan="2"></td></tr>
<tr><td>Caribbean</td></tr>
</table>

Grenada

G

Area 344 sq.km. One larger island north of Trinidad and some of the Grenadine islets south of St Vincent. The most southerly of the Windward Islands.

Population	Ann. Gr.	Density
1990 103,000	1.4 %	299/sq.km
1995 110,000	1.3 %	319/sq.km

Peoples:
Afro-Caribbean 96%. East Indian 3%.
Euro-American/Other 1%.

Literacy 85%. **Official language:** English.

Capital: St George's 9,720. Urbanization 27%.

Economy: Already poor and underdeveloped agricultural island at independence, but made poorer by the instability of the past decade and the emigration of the middle classes. A gradual recovery is under way. Income/person $1,900 (9% of USA).

Politics: Independent of Britain in 1974 as a parliamentary monarchy. Independence has proved stormy with bizarre dictatorships, repression, and two increasingly Marxist coups; the last of which provoked the US invasion of 1983 and restoration of democratic government. A political union with other Windward Island states was proposed in 1992.

Religion:
Non-religious/other 0.5%.
Spiritist 0.4%. Muslim 0.2%. Baha'i 0.2%.
Christian 98.7%. Nom 6.6%. Affil 92.1%.
Growth 0.4%.

Protestant 35% Affil 33.6% Growth 0.7%.

Church	Cong	Members	Affiliated
Anglican	25	5,080	14,500
Seventh-day Adventist	28	2,800	5,600
Pentecostal Assemblies	20	1,481	2,470
New Test Ch of God	10	793	1,930
Ev Ch of W Indies (**WT**)	7	330	688
Baptist Conv (**SBC**)	4	205	410
All other (17)	61	4,147	8,313
Denominations (23)	155	14,836	33,911
Evangelicals 12.3% of pop		6,222	12,389
Pentecostal/charis 6.3%		3,400	6,400

Missionaries:
  to Grenada 53 (1:1,900 people) in 8 agencies.
  from Grenada 2 (1:17,000 Protestants) 2dom.

Roman Catholic 61.7%. Affil 56.9% Growth 0.1%.

Catholic Ch	20	31,600	57,500

Missionaries to Grenada 66 (1:1,560 people).

Marginal 2%. Affil 1.6%. Growth 1.6%.

Jehovah's Witnesses	7	409	852
All other (4)	12	480	800
Groups (5)	19	889	1,652

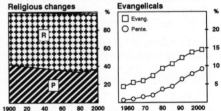

1. **The pain of the events of the last 20 years** has yet to be erased. Pray for the balm of the gospel to bring healing and salvation to the nation. Pray that born-again Christians may be more active in their outreach and witness.

2. **Evangelicals** have no supra-denominational fellowship. Pray for the formation of a national evangelical association.

3. **Missionary vision** is lacking. Pray for the **YWAM** team which is seeking to train and send out West Indian missionaries to unreached peoples elsewhere in the world.

Guadeloupe
(Département de la Guadeloupe)

Include with French Guiana
Caribbean

Area 1,781 sq.km. One larger island and five smaller island dependencies: Marie Galante, Iles des Saintes, La Désirade, St Martin and St Barthélemy.

Population	Ann. Gr.	Density
1990	340,000	0.36 %	191/sq.km
1995	346,000	0.35 %	194/sq.km

Peoples:
Afro-Caribbean 87%.
Asian-Caribbean 10%. East Asians (also mixed with other groups).
European 2%. **Other** 1%.

Literacy 90%. **Official language:** French.
The French Creole Patois is widely spoken.

Capital: Basse-Terre 14,000. Urbanization 46%.

Economy: Agriculture, tourism and light industry supplemented by large subsidies from France help maintain a reasonable living standard. These subsidies are threatened by pressure for a freer market for bananas in the EC. Unemployment 24%. Income/person $4,000 (19% of USA).

Politics: French colony since 1635. Overseas Department of France since 1946.
Religion: Religious freedom, but with a strong secularist tendency.
Non-religious/other 2.8%.
Hindu 0.5%. **Muslim** 0.4%. **Baha'i** 0.4%.
Christian 95.9%. Affil 94.4%. Growth 0.6%.
  Protestant 6.4%. Affil 6.1%. Growth 6.3%.

Church	Cong	Members	Affiliated
Evangelical Ch (WT)	29	3,120	7,000
Seventh-day Adventist	44	4,140	6,900
Assemblies of God	10	1,000	2,500
Evangelical Reformed	7	800	1,400
Ch of God (Cleveland)	8	666	1,400
Baptist Conv (**SBC**)	8	443	695
All other (7)	11	605	1,240
Denominations (13)	117	10,774	20,845
Evangelicals 4.1% of pop		6,700	14,000
Pentecostal/charis 1.27%		2,000	4,300

Missionaries:
  to Guadeloupe 21 (1:16,200 people) in 4 agencies.
  from Guadeloupe 1 (1:20,800 Protestants) 1 frn 1xcul.

Roman Catholic 84.3%. Affil 83%. Growth −0.1%.

Catholic Ch	44	174,000	306,000
Doubly counted		−14,000	−23,800
Total	44	160,000	282,200

Missionaries to Guadeloupe 156 (1:2,200 people).
Marginal 5.2%. Affil 5.2%. Gr 11.4%.

Jehovah's Witnesses	71	6,288	18,000

Religious changes

Evangelicals/ Marginals

☐ Evang.
○ Pente.
▲ JW

G

1. **The evident spiritual need is highlighted** by the breakdown in family life, widespread occultism, secular propaganda in schools and the marked growth of sects. Catholicism is a traditional veneer for most. Pray for a moving of the Holy Spirit to give conviction of sin and true repentance to many.

2. **Areas and peoples less reached with the gospel:**
a) **The outlying dependencies** are less evangelized – St Barthélemy, St Martin and Marie Galante islands. Several missionaries of the Association of Evangelical Churches have recently moved to these islands. Both the Evangelical Church and the Church of God have planted churches on St Martin.
b) The **East Indians** number over 12,000. Most have become nominally Catholic, while retaining many of their Hindu beliefs. Little direct outreach has been aimed at this community.

3. **There were hardly any born-again believers before 1946.** The work of **WT** and **AoG** has been used of God to plant a network of churches. The vital witness of believers, radio and TV evangelism and Christian literature have all played their part. The Evangelical Church has a bookstore on Guadeloupe.

4. **Leadership training** for the growing churches is provided locally through the Evangelical Church's TEE programme with 200 students and School of Discipleship in Guadeloupe. Pray that Christian workers may be called for service at home and in the Francophone lands around the world.

See under Pacific
Pacific

Guam
(The US Territory of Guam)

G

Area 549 sq.km. Most southerly and largest island of the Marianas Archipelago, 6,000 km. west south-west of Hawaii. Also included here are the three tiny US Territories of Johnston Island (2.8 sq.km, 1,300 km. from Hawaii), Midway (5.2 sq.km, 2,350 km), and Wake Island (6.5 sq.km, 3,700 km).

Population		Ann. Gr.	Density
1990	133,000	2.5 %	242/sq.km
1995	150,000	2.5 %	274/sq.km

Johnston Island Pop: 1,000; Midway 13; Wake 300. There are estimated to be a further 26,000 illegal immigrants.

Peoples:
Micronesian 48.6%.
  Indigenous 43.3%. Chamorro 59,600.
  Other islanders 5.3%. Mainly from Palau, Chuuk and North Marianas.
Euro-American 14.3%.
Asian 29.5%. Filipino 30,000; Korean 4,000; Japanese 2,500; Chinese 2,000.
Other 7.6%.
The US Military and dependents are 15% of the total population (both indigenous and USA).

Literacy 96%. **Official languages:** English and Chamorro.

Capital: Agana 4,785. Urbanization 40%.

Economy: Tourism has replaced decades of dependence on US military and federal grants. About 45% of the Guamanian population is in government employ. Income/person $9,885 (47% of USA).

Politics: Spanish rule 1565–1898. US Territory since then. A self-governing, unincorporated territory of the USA. Guamanians are US citizens. Commonwealth status is under negotiation.

Religion: Freedom of religion, though the Roman Catholic Church has been numerically dominant for 400 years.
Non-religious/other 1.3%. **Baha'i** 0.9%.
Buddhist/other Asian religions 3%.
Christian 94.8%. Affil 94.2%. Growth 3.5%.
Protestant 13.7%. Affil 13.7%. Growth 3.6%.

Church	Cong	Members	Affiliated
Seventh-day Adventist	18	1,700	2,430
Assemblies of God	6	1,150	1,640
Baptist Conv (SBC)	3	358	1,190
General Baptist Mission	4	300	667
All other (49)	52	5,465	12,144
Denominations (53)	83	8,973	18,071
Evangelicals 9.7% of pop		6,045	12,745
Pentecostal/charis 3.9%		2,600	5,100

Missionaries:
  to Guam 159 (1:840 people) in 17 agencies.
  from Guam 1 (1:18,000 Protestants) 1dom.
Roman Catholic 78.6%. Affil 78%. Growth 3.2%.

Catholic	27	57,600	103,000

Missionaries to Guam 244 (1:540 people).
Marginal 2.48%. Affil 2.48%. Growth 18%.

Mormons	3	1,320	2,200
Jehovah's Witnesses	4	379	632
Groups (3)		2,000	3,261

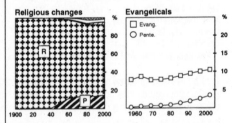

Religious changes   Evangelicals

1. **The Chamorro people** are predominantly Catholic. Scripture reading has increased among them. Pray that there may be many who come to personal faith in Christ.

2. **Most Protestant congregations** are multi-cultural. Pray for a harvest among indigenous and immigrant peoples. Immigrant communities have responded well to the gospel. There are four thriving Korean Presbyterian congregations, one Chinese, and also churches in each of the Micronesian immigrant ethnic groups. The Micronesians with their protected and nominal Christian background have found adaptation difficult, and need prayer for spiritual renewal and social assimilation.

3. **The major thrust of missions** has moved from military ministries to the indigenous and migrant peoples in church planting, Bible teaching and development. Major missions are **AoG** (24 workers), Korean Presbyterians (8), **CRWM** (6), **SBC** (4). There are two Bible Colleges (**AoG** and **Liebenzell/ CRWM**), also a ministry to young people (**Teen Challenge, YWAM**), and to children (**CEF**). Youth problems are multiplying with an estimated 100 youth gangs prone to violence.

4. The Prison Fellowship of Guam has developed a ministry to prisoners which is also penetrating the indigenous population in a significant way. It has fostered a cooperative unity among evangelical churches which is sadly lacking. Pray for resources to develop adequate aftercare programmes for converted prisoners.

5. Christian radio. TWR has a powerful broadcasting station for reaching south and east Asia with 170 hours of programmes per week – 115 of these in five languages of China, as well as in local languages of the Pacific. Pray for the 43 missionaries and staff engaged in this key ministry.

G

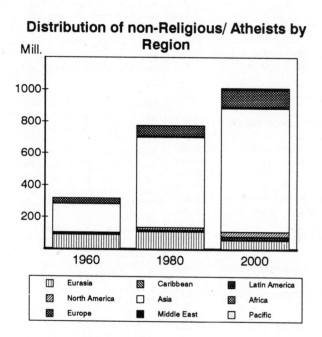

Distribution of non-Religious/ Atheists by Region

In 1980 nearly 20% of the world's population claimed to be non-religious. Note:

1. The rapid rise between 1960 and 1980 due to the combined effects of secularization in Europe (top strips of bar) and Communism in Asia (white).

2. The continued rapid growth of European secularization to AD2000.

3. The collapse of Communism and turning or returning of many peoples under its control to Christianity (bottom strip for Eurasia). The **percentage** of the world's population that are non-religious will decline to AD2000, though **absolute numbers** may continue to increase.

<table>
<tr><td>**May 19**</td><td rowspan="2"></td></tr>
<tr><td></td></tr>
<tr><td>Latin America</td></tr>
</table>

Guatemala

Area 109,000 sq.km. A land of mountains, volcanoes and lakes. Mexico's southern neighbour. Guatemala has a long-standing claim on English-speaking Belize to the east.

Population	Ann. Gr.	Density
1990	9,197,000	2.9 %	84/sq.km
1995	10,621,000	2.9 %	98/sq.km

Many thousands are refugees in south Mexico, fleeing the civil war in Guatemala.

Peoples:
Spanish-speaking Ladinos 43%. Mixed European and Indian.
Afro-Caribbean 2%. Blacks on Caribbean coast.
Amerindian 54%. Descendants of the Mayan civilization. Nineteen peoples speaking 41 languages. Main groups: Quichi 1,200,000; Cakchiquel 781,000; Mam 662,000; Kekchi 542,000; Kanjobal 119,000; Pocomchi 119,000; Tzutujil 118,000; Ixil 110,000; Achi 85,000; Pocomam 50,000; Aguacatec 39,000; Chuj 35,000; Chorti 25,000; Jacaltec 24,000.
Other minorities 1%. Black Carib 37,000; Chinese 15,000.

Literacy 55%. **Official language:** Spanish, but 40% of population do not use it as their primary language. **All languages** 54. **Languages with Scriptures** 4Bi 17NT 19por.

Capital: Guatemala City 1,080,000. Urbanization 38%.

Economy: Predominantly agricultural with 2% of the population owning 80% of the land. This inequitable land use has kept the majority in poverty, and is the root cause of the guerrilla war. Resistance by military leaders to land reform and economic austerity programmes has further hampered development. Cultivation of cocaine and opium has increased massively since 1990. Public debt/person $232. Income/person $290 (1.4% of USA).

Politics: Independent from Spain in 1821, and from the Federation of Central American States in 1838, but controlled by a few plantation owners through a series of dictatorships and military governments. The poor (largely Amerindian) have suffered years of indignity and deprivation. Guerrilla insurgency since 1962 provoked violent reaction, repression and widespread use of death squads by the military. Over 100,000 have been killed. Guatemala's appalling human rights record has only marginally improved since a more democratic constitution was implemented in 1986. Elections in 1990 resulted in the appointment of Evangelicals as President and Vice-President. The extreme right wing of the military remains a threat to the civilian government and a hindrance to attempts to reform society, the economy, the judicial system, and negotiations with guerrilla groups.

Religion: Official separation of Church and state for over 100 years has given great freedom for Evangelicals and increased their influence at the expense of the hitherto dominant Catholic church.
Non-religious/other 1.8%.
Animist/Spiritist 2%. Maybe 25% of Catholics are Christo-pagan. A revival of the ancient Mayan religion has attracted many nominal Christians.
Christian 96.2%. Nom 7.7%. Affil 88.5%. Growth 2.5%.
Protestant 24.1%. Growth 9.2%.

Church	Cong	Members	Affiliated
Assemblies of God	1,385	97,854	224,751
Full Gspl Ch of God	70,872	187,000	
Prince of Peace Ev Assoc	900	72,000	180,000
Ev Ch of C Am (CAMI)	1,167	67,700	169,000
Calvary Chr Min	462	60,000	150,000
Elim Chr Mission	714	50,000	139,000
Seventh-day Adventist	158	40,000	114,000
Ev Miss of the H. Spt	333	30,000	93,800
Christian Brethren	750	30,000	75,000
Voice of God Ev Assoc	274	26,000	65,000
Baptist Conv (SBC)	152	16,500	55,000
National Ev Presby	178	23,000	50,000
Ch of the Nazarene	181	24,014	38,341
All other (35)	3,628	255,413	671,003
Denominations (48)	11,870	863,353	2,211,895
Evangelicals 23.3% of pop		835,000	2,140,770
Pente/charis 15.8%		561,000	1,457,000

Missionaries:
to Guatemala 699 (1:13,200 people) in 68 agencies.
from Guatemala 123 (1:18,000 Protestants) in 21 agencies 36frn 39xcul 84dom.
Roman Catholic 70.7%. Affil 63.03%. Growth 0.2%.

Catholic Ch	640	3,940,000	7,297,000
Doubly counted		−810,000	−1,500,000
Total	640	3,130,000	5,797,000
Charismatics 0.6%		32,000	58,000

Missionaries:
  to Guatemala 97 (1:94,800 people).
  from Guatemala 140 (1973 figure).
Other Catholic 0.1%. Affil 0.07%. Growth 2.8%.
Marginal 1.34%. Growth 19.1%.

Mormons	288	53,500	99,000
Jehovah's Witnesses	184	12,230	24,500
Groups (3)	472	65,744	123,533

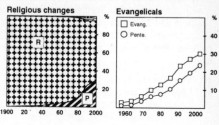

1. **Praise God for evangelical growth.** The enormous missionary input, political instability, the 1976 earthquake, violence and the effective witness of Guatemalan believers have resulted in 23% of the population professing to be Evangelical. Some claim this figure to be nearer 45%. It could be the first Latin American country to have a majority of Evangelicals.

G

2. **Evangelical Christians** have a great responsibility to bring about peaceful, meaningful and lasting change to end the cycle of violence and the selfish, racialist society that caused it. Pray for evangelical leaders.

3. **The Catholic Church** has suffered disastrous decline in influence and numbers. Defection to Evangelicals and, among Amerindians, to a revived Mayan religion, has been massive. Espousal of liberation theology by some priests and the disciplining of the large charismatic renewal movement have further hastened the decline. Pray for new life to permeate the Church, and that the charismatic movement may be rooted in Scripture rather than subjective experience.

4. **Vision for the '90s** has been stimulated by national conferences on evangelism – especially the **DAWN** conference of 1984 in which most of the major denominations set challenging growth goals. Overall, by 1990 the aim was for:
a) Evangelicals to be 50% of the population.
b) 15,000 churches to be functioning – one for each community of 250–1,000 people.
These goals were not met, but they are likely to be achieved by the year 2000. Pray both for their attainment and for adequate discipling and retention of this multitude of new converts. Pray for true unity among church leaders that transcends personality and secondary doctrinal issues.

5. **Evangelistic outreach continues** through a multitude of avenues – wide use of Christian and commercial radio stations, mass evangelism campaigns (such as Luis Palau's 1982 campaign – with 700,000 attending one meeting!), large distribution of Christian literature and tracts (40 Christian bookshops), and, above all, the fervent personal witness of individual Christians. Pray that the fruit will be conserved, the believers matured, and the new generation won for Christ. Shallow professions of faith and an increased rate of backsliding are becoming more common as Evangelicals become more "popular".

6. **Leadership training is well provided for** with six seminaries, (notably the Central American Theological Seminary founded by **CAMI** and now under Guatemalan leadership), 23 Bible schools and six TEE programmes. (TEE was pioneered here by Presbyterians in the '60s and has now spread worldwide.) Pray for humble and effective leaders who will rise above the pettiness, divisions and carnality now all too common in the Body of Christ. Pray also for effective ways of training leaders for rural churches.

7. **Amerindians** have begun to respond in large numbers to the gospel. Churches and missions have reached out into every tribe. Notable in church planting are **CAMI, CoN** and **UWM**. The present guerrilla warfare has brought suffering to the people – with deaths and a massive refugee problem (many fleeing to Mexico, USA and to urban areas). Rural Christians have suffered considerably for their faith during this conflict.

8. **Bible Translation. SIL/WBT** has made a notable contribution to 37 Amerindian peoples in providing New Testaments for many of them. Work is in progress in a further 22. SIL and Bible translation work has come under severe attack by liberal Catholic priests and anti-Christian "experts" seeking to promote Mayan religion. Pray for these attacks to backfire on the critics.

9. **Foreign missions** have lavished attention on the land. The hard battles in faith of the pioneers sowed today's harvest. Special note must be made of the Presbyterians, **AoG, ICFG, CAMI,** Brethren and Nazarene pioneers. The large foreign input needs to be phased out and Guatemalan leadership and missionary outreach to other lands encouraged. There is only a small beginning being made by Guatemalans for missionary work – pray for the 37 Guatemalan Evangelicals serving in other lands.

10. **The less reached.**
a) Amerindian peoples with fewer active believers – the Pocomam, Pocomchi, Ixil (only 1% Evangelical), Jacaltec, Chorti and Upsantec have shown less response to the gospel yet there are active growing churches among them.
b) **Garifuna** (Black Carib) – the *Jesus* film has been dubbed in their language.
c) The **Chinese** – there is only one small fellowship of believers known.

G

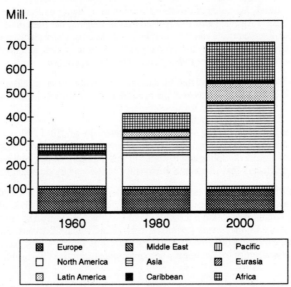

Distribution of Protestants by Region

Legend:
- Europe
- North America
- Latin America
- Middle East
- Asia
- Caribbean
- Pacific
- Eurasia
- Africa

Protestant expansion in the non-Western world came much later than that of the Roman Catholics. Since 1960 that expansion has become dramatic. Note:

1. Numbers in Europe, Pacific and North America have changed little over 40 years. The bottom three tiers in the bar graph show this.

2. Growth has been spectacular in Asia, Latin America and Africa. Protestants in the latter have increased from 19% of the world total of Protestants to 53% in 1990 and possibly 62% in 2000.

Guinea

(Republic of Guinea)

May 20

Africa

Area 246,000 sq.km. On Africa's west coast and between Guinea-Bissau and Sierra Leone.

Population		Ann. Gr.	Density
1990	6,876,000	2.5 %	28/sq.km
1995	7,807,000	2.6 %	32/sq.km

Peoples: Over 40 ethnic groups.
Indigenous:
 Mande 46% (11). Largest: Maninka 1,730,000; Susu 800,000; Yalunka 147,000; Konyanke 128,400; Wassulunke 74,000; Kuranko 55,000; Bambara 34,000; Jakanke 12,600; Lele 10,500; Mikifore 3,600.
 Mande-Fu 11% (6). Kpelle 308,000; Toma 144,000; Dan 71,000; Bandi 50,000; Mano 34,000; Loko 4,000.
 West Atlantic 43%. Fula (3) 2,553,000; Kissi 287,000; Baga 32,000 Landoma 14,000; Nalu 13,000; Bassari 9,000; Badyara 6,000; Limba 4,000; Papel 2,400.
Non-indigenous 0.04%. European, Lebanese.
Refugees: Liberians (250,000 in 1991) mainly Mano, Gio, Bandi in south.
Literacy 28%. **Official language:** French. **Eight national languages:** Fula, Maninka, Susu, Kissi, Kpelle, Toma, Konyagi, Bassari. **All languages** 29. **Languages with Scriptures** 1Bi 6NT 7por.

Capital: Conakry 930,000. Urbanization 23%.

Economy: Potentially the richest state of former French West Africa with abundant land, fertile soil, water and minerals. Reduced to subsistence and destitution by the folly and corruption of successive regimes. Public debt/person $327. Income/person $300 (1.4% of USA).

Politics: French colony until independence in 1958. President Sékou Touré led the unfortunate country into a disastrous flirtation with Marxism which virtually destroyed the country. The cruel, repressive regime was swept away in a military coup in 1984. Basic freedoms were restored, and the military government has been struggling to bring recovery and economic progress but with only partial success. Constitutional reform and a five-year transition to civilian rule by 1995 is being implemented.

Religion: The former government leaders espoused Marxist rhetoric and a pro-Islamic stance. Christians, especially Catholics, suffered considerably at the hands of the authorities. There is now religious liberty for Christian witness and missionary activity.

G

Muslim 83.1%. Strong among the dominant Fula, Maninka and Susu.
Tribal religions 12.4%. Predominant among the forest peoples of the southeast and a few small coastal peoples.
Christian 4.5%. Nom 2.7%. Affil 1.8%. Growth 5%.
 Protestant 0.58%. Affil 0.47%. Growth 5.4%.

Church	Cong	Members	Affiliated
Evang Prot (CMA)	212	7,938	28,000
Anglican Ch	8	555	1,500
All other (9)	23	1,732	2,900
Denominations (11)	243	10,225	32,400
Evangelicals 0.45% of pop		9,625	30,960
Pentecostal/charis 0.03%		1,000	2,150

Missionaries:
 to Guinea 187 (1:36,800 people) in 24 agencies.
 from Guinea 8 (1:4,100 Protestants) in 2 agencies. 2xcul 6edom.
Roman Catholic 3.9%. Affil 1.3%. Growth 4.9%.

Catholic Ch	83	51,900	89,531

Missionaries to Guinea 45 (1:153,000 people).
Marginal 0.01%. Growth 7.9%.

Jehovah's Witnesses	10	278	695

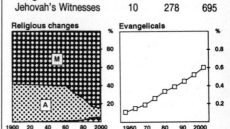

1. **Praise God for the major improvements in the country since 1984:**
   a) **Political liberalization,** but pray for stability, peace between ethnic groups, and political leaders who place national interests above their own.
   b) **Complete religious freedom,** a reaction to the Marxist-Muslim years of terror which has made Muslims more receptive to Christianity.
   c) **The entry or re-entry of more than 10 Evangelical missions** and the beginnings of the evangelization of five hitherto unreached peoples – Fula (**CRWM, CMA, WEC**), Mano (**CMA, AME**), Baga (Open Bible Standard Mission), Landoma (**NTM**), Bullom (**SBC**) and Maninka (**SIM**).

d) The growing expectancy among believers of an abundant harvest.

2. **The Christian population** is concentrated in the southeast and in Conakry, and is almost entirely Kpelle, Toma, Kissi and Mano in composition. They have little vision for evangelizing the Muslim majority. The Evangelical Protestant Church, the fruit of the ministry of **CMA**, has steadily grown, but even so, Christians number only 4% of the population of these four peoples. Pray for both revival and missions vision for these believers.

3. **Guinea is one of the least evangelized countries in Black Africa.** Nearly every people is still a pioneer challenge. The three dominant peoples are all Muslim and have been unresponsive. Pray especially for these:
a) **Maninka.** The radio ministry of **SIM** (ELWA, Liberia) created a good basis for church-planting work and a growing missionary force. **CMA** and *Mission Evangélique* from Switzerland also have an outreach to the Maninka, but converts have been few.
b) **Fula or Futa Jalon**, who are strongly Muslim and known as the custodians of Islam in Guinea. Through the work of **CRWM**, **CMA** and **CM/WEC** there are a few scattered believers. It is hard for new believers to break free from the spiritual bondages of Islam. Praise God for a 1991 conference attended by 30 Fula Christians.
c) **Susu.** Apart from the eight rather nominal Anglican congregations on offshore islands and in Conakry, there is only a handful of believers through the witness of **CMA**, **CM/WEC**, Open Bible Standard Mission, the Nigerian Shekinah Mission and the **SBC**. The breakthrough has yet to come.

4. **Unreached peoples with a minimal missionary presence** number about 20 and comprise 8% of the population. Pray especially for:
a) The Muslim Yalunka, Wassulunke, Jakanke, Kuranko, Dan, Bandi, Tukulor and Badyara. **AME** is commencing ministry among the Kuranko.
b) The northeastern Nalu, Papel, Mikifore and Landoma. **NTM** has opened a work among the Landoma and OBSM has resumed work among the Baga, where there are 150 new believers.

5. **Missions.** For years the only Protestant missionaries were those of **CMA** (1919–1952). In 1967 all Catholic and most Protestant missionaries were expelled. Only 11 CMA missionaries were permitted to remain. Since 1985, CMA and the Evangelical Church have welcomed new evangelical agencies. Most work in close cooperation as members of the *Association des Eglises et Missions Evangélique en Guinée*. Pray for fruitful and close fellowship between missions and also with the national churches. Pray also for courage, stamina and great faith for the growing missionary force in a land of rugged living conditions and poor communications and also for new missionary pioneers to be called. Major missions are **CMA** (41 workers), **SIM** (26), **NTM** (16), **CRWM** (12), **CM/WEC** (12) and **AoG** (6). Major missionary-contributing nations: USA (102), Switzerland (25), Canada (19), Nigeria (8), UK (7).

6. **Leadership training** for pastors and laymen is a great need. Guinea has only one Bible School, operated by the Evangelical Church/**CMA** at Telekoro. Missionaries of the Pentecostal Assemblies of Canada are launching the ICI TEE programme.

7. **Help ministries:**
a) **Christian radio broadcasting** is, at present limited. The national network broadcasts a weekly Christian programme that has a wide audience, but the cessation of programmes from Radio ELWA in Liberia is still keenly felt. Pray for more Christian broadcasting in the major languages.
b) **Literature** is in short supply. There is only one Christian bookstore in the country, but literacy is low.
c) **Cassette ministry** could be vital in this predominantly Muslim and multi-lingual land. **GRn** has made recordings in 20 languages.
d) **Bible translation** is one of the major missionary tasks for years to come. Only Maninka, Kissi and Yalunka have usable New Testaments. The Kuranko and Susu New Testaments need extensive revision (the latter being undertaken). Ten other languages may need translation teams. Work is in progress in seven languages – mostly in surrounding countries.

Guinea-Bissau

(Republic of Guinea-Bissau)

May 21
Africa

G

Area 36,000 sq.km. Coastal state wedged between Senegal and Guinea.

Population	Ann. Gr.	Density
1990 987,000	2.1 %	27/sq.km
1995 1,105,000	2.3 %	31/sq.km

Peoples: Over 27 ethnic groups.
West Atlantic (15 groups) 59.5%. Balanta 250,000; Manjako 102,000; Papel 97,000; Mankanya 31,600; Biafada 32,000; Bijago 24,500; Jola/Felupe 17,000; Nalu 5,500.
Fula (5 groups) 23%. 223,000.
Mande (5 groups) 14%. Mandinga (Maninka or Mandingo) 119,000; Soninke 5,000; Susu 3,000.
Other 3.5%. Creole, Cape Verdians, Guineans, Europeans.

Literacy 6%. All languages 22. **Official language:** Portuguese. **Trade language:** Creole, spoken by 44% of the population. **Languages with Scriptures** 1Bi 5NT 3por.

Capital: Bissau 130,000. Urbanization 29%.

Economy: Little developed in colonial times, and devastated by the long war of independence. Subsequent socialist policies inhibited reconstruction and foreign investment. One of the world's poorest countries with few natural resources. Public debt/person $479. Income/person $180 (0.85% of USA).

Politics: Independent of Portugal in 1974. One-party revolutionary government. Steps initiated in 1991 for introducing multi-party politics, with elections due in 1993.

Religion: Under Portuguese rule the Catholic Church functioned almost as an arm of the colonial government, and Evangelicals were forbidden or discriminated against. Since independence, the measure of freedom for Christian activities has steadily improved, though visa restrictions on new Protestant agencies were relaxed only in 1990.
Animist 48.1%. Predominantly the coastal Balanta and West Atlantic peoples.
Muslim 44%. Fula, Mandinga, Soninke, Biafada are all Muslim; Nalu and Susu are largely Muslim.
Christian 7.9%. Affil 6.2%. Growth 1.9%.
Protestant 0.9%. Affil 0.8%. Growth 7%.

Church	Cong	Members	Affiliated
Evang Ch of G-B (**WEC**)	60	4,500	8,000
All other (2)	2	142	284
Denominations (3)	62	4,642	8,284
Evangelicals 0.84% of pop		4,621	8,242

Missionaries:
to G-Bissau 71 (1:13,900 people) in 13 agencies.
from G-Bissau 4 (1:2,000 Protestants) 1frn 3xcul 1dom.
Roman Catholic 7%. Affil 5.4%. Growth 1.1%.

Catholic Ch	25	31,800	53,000

Missionaries to G-Bissau 74 (1:13,000 people).
Marginal 0.02%. Growth 10.3%.

Groups (2)	3	110	192

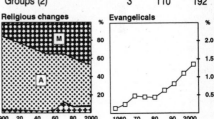

Religious changes   Evangelicals

1. **Praise the Lord for the present openness for the gospel.** The war of independence brought much privation and suffering to the church. The Roman Catholics have not recovered from the taint of links with the Portuguese colonial regime, hence the general percentage decline of Christians since independence (see graph). Yet committed Christians have won a credibility that gives promise of an abundant harvest in the '90s. Pray it in! Pray also that religious freedom may be maintained by the government elected in 1993.

2. **Most Protestant groups** are those which came into being through the ministry of **WEC**. No other missions were permitted between 1939 and 1990, but since then several new groups have commenced work. The Church is stronger among the Balanta and Papel, but spiritually weaker among the Bijago and Manjako peoples. However, there are no more than a handful of believers in the other 23 peoples. Pray for Christians to be confident and effective in reaching out to the Muslim peoples; the latter consider themselves superior.

3. **There are too few missionaries in the country** to cover every unreached ethnic group. WEC has 32 workers in six centres among six peoples supported by three **TEAR Fund** workers. The missionary team is barely coping with existing workloads, and few can give attention to pioneer advance.

Immediate target peoples are the Mankanya, Biafada and Mandinga. Brazilian **YWAM**ers have established a base in Gabu. Pray for reinforcements, the issue of visas and health and strength to work in harsh and often unhealthy living conditions.

4. **Leadership** in the Evangelical Church is mature, many having a great vision for evangelism and missionary outreach to unreached peoples. There are only 36 national pastors; pray for an increase in their numbers. Pray for the one Bible School in the country which is run by the Evangelical Church. Pray also for adequate support for students and pastors; the poverty of believers makes this a major challenge.

5. The unreached for whom prayer is needed:
a) **The Muslim Fula and Mandinga.** These are only now beginning to be reached. Since they are the dominant inland peoples, a breakthrough for Jesus among them would have widespread implications for surrounding peoples and countries. YWAM has seen the first group of Fula converts out of Islam.
b) **Smaller Muslim peoples.** The Nalu, Susu, Soninke, Jahanka, Pajadinka, Maninka and Badyara have never been reached in their own language. Only among the Biafada has an attempt been made (**WEC**).
c) **Traditional peoples.** The Jola/Felupe, Mankanya, Mansoanca, Banyum, Bayot and other smaller groups have never been reached by Evangelicals.

6. **Literature is eagerly sought after,** but little is available in the one Christian bookstore (**CLC**), and few can afford what is.

7. **Bible translation** is a pressing challenge. The Creole, Balanta, Mandinga, Papel and Bijago New Testaments are complete, but literacy programmes need to be expanded. Other languages are without the Scriptures.

8. **A Christian radio programme** aired once a week on national radio has a wide audience. Pray both for quality and lasting response. A cassette ministry for teaching and evangelism needs qualified personnel. **GRn** has produced recordings in 31 languages. The *Jesus* film is being dubbed in Creole.

Guyana

(The Cooperative Republic of Guyana)

May 22
Caribbean

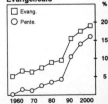
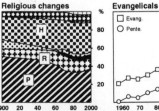

Area 215,000 sq.km. A narrow, developed coastal strip in northeast South America. The hinterland is covered by forest and underdeveloped. Much of the interior is claimed by Venezuela.

Population		Ann. Gr.	Density
1990	754,000	−0.05 %	4/sq.km
1995	754,000	0 %	4/sq.km

Many historical and cultural links with the English-speaking Caribbean islands. Considerable emigration of those with skills, making above population figures optimistic estimates.

Peoples: Colonial importation of labour for the sugar industry has created the present racial diversity and political tensions.

East Indian 51.4%. Predominantly rural farmers.
African/Eurafrican 41.5%. Dominant in government, civil service and in urban areas.
Amerindian 5.1%. The majority live in the sparsely inhabited interior. Two main groups:
  Carib 3.7% (5 tribes). Akwaio 4,800; Patamona 4,500; Macushi 4,000; Waiwai 1,000; Carib 800; Arecuna 500.
  Arawak 1.4% (4 tribes). Arawak 8,000; Wapishana 6,500.
European/Asian 1.8%. Portuguese 9,000; British 2,000; Chinese 1,500.
Chinese 0.2%.

Literacy 91%. **Official language:** English. **All languages** 14. **Languages with Scriptures** 1Bi 2NT 5por.

Capital: Georgetown 237,000. Urbanization 32%.

Economy: After a 20-year flirtation with Marxist economics, living standards plummeted and the country became one of the poorest in the Western Hemisphere. There was a gradual softening of the Communist stance, but state ownership, corruption, and flight of skills slowed development of a more market-oriented economy. Immense potential. Major exports are sugar, bauxite, rice and timber. Unemployment 30%. Public debt/person $1,200. Income/person $310 (1.5% of USA).

Politics: Independent from Britain in 1966. Most of the political parties have been Marxist in orientation, but divided on racial lines. For 28 years an Afro-Guyanese-dominated government held power but during the '80s its Marxist policies moderated, eventually espousing a free-market economy. International pressure resulted in a multi-party election in 1992 in which the opposition party (predominantly East Indian) was elected. Dr Jagan, a former Marxist, has firmly undertaken to continue free market policies in a multi-racial, multi-faith government.

Religion: Atheism promoted until 1985, with considerable tensions between the government and the main churches. A secular state with increased religious freedom since then.
Non-religious/other 2%.
Hindu 34%. All East Indian; brought from India by the British as indentured labour for the sugar industry.
Muslim 9%. Most East Indian, some Afro-Guyanese.
Animist/Spiritist 3%. **Baha'i** 2%.
Christian 50%. Affil 48.31%. Growth 1.5%.
Protestant 35%. Affil 33.3%. Growth 2.3%.

Church	Cong	Members	Affiliated
Anglican Ch	150	19,500	78,000
Assemblies of God	194	14,600	56,285
Seventh-day Adventist	85	13,900	23,105
Lutheran Ch	52	5,210	13,026
Methodist Ch	46	3,658	9,000
Guyana Congreg Union	44	3,100	8,000
Presbytery of Guyana	40	3,360	5,800
Christian Brethren	50	2,700	4,150
Ch of the Nazarene	45	2,184	3,899
NT Church of God	16	1,900	3,500
Presbyterian Ch of G	44	2,033	3,000
Wesleyan Ch	37	1,627	2,500
Bapt Co-op Conv (SBC)	14	980	1,960
All other (39)	306	17,595	39,019
Denominations (52)	1,123	92,347	251,244
Evangelicals 15.5% of pop		43,000	117,000
Pentecostal/charis 11.2%		25,000	84,000

Missionaries:
  to Guyana 47 (1:16,000 people) in 14 agencies.
  from Guyana 11 (1: 22,800 Protestants) in 3 agencies 4frn 4xcul 7dom.
Roman Catholic 13.5%. Affil 11.8%. Growth −0.6%.
| Catholic Ch | 81 | 47,200 | 89,000 |
| Charismatics 0.12% | | 500 | 900 |

Missionaries to Guyana 55 (1:13,700 people).
Orthodox 1.6%. Growth 0.2%.
| Ethiopian Orthodox | 30 | 5,400 | 8,180 |
| Denominations (2) | 64 | 8,090 | 12,380 |

Foreign Marginal 0.75%. Growth 4.4%.
| Jehovah's Witnesses | 30 | 1,651 | 4,720 |
| Groups (8) | 45 | 2,031 | 5,670 |

Indigenous Marginal 0.79%. Growth 0.6%.
| Groups (2) | 15 | 2,990 | 5,980 |

Religious changes

Evangelicals

1. **Official atheism led to pressures on Christian work** and confrontations between the authorities and Christian leaders. This hostility is beginning to backfire to the advantage of the gospel. Pray for all Christians in places of influence, for they need ethical rectitude and divine boldness to demonstrate the power of the gospel. Pray for God-fearing leaders for the country who will rebuild society on the basis of justice and fairness to all.

2. **Inter-racial tensions** are gradually diminishing, but under the surface remains the threat of violence between the Afro-Caribbean urban minority and the East Indian marginalized majority.

3. **The Christian Church** is a mixture of dead nominalism and vital, vibrant evangelical fervour. The last 10 years has seen decline for the older churches, and rapid growth for Pentecostal churches and charismatic fellowships. Evangelical believers are found in all walks of life. Pray that present freedom to worship and witness may be used to the full. Pray for racial harmony and for the diminishing of all cultural barriers to witness and fellowship.

4. **Almost the entire Afro-Guyanese population is "baptized" Christian**, but widespread corruption, witchcraft and immorality show the need of many for a life-transforming meeting with Jesus.

5. **The East Indian majority** – politically marginalized from independence until 1992 – are also spiritually needy. Praise God that over 12% are now Christian – most from a Hindu background. About 70% are Hindu, and 18% Muslim. Among the latter is a strong Muslim revivalist movement. The Muslims are the least reached people in Guyana.

6. **The Amerindian peoples** are largely Christianized and predominantly Catholic. The Wesleyan Church ministers among the Patamona and Akwaio, but results have been meagre. The **UFM** work in the south among the Waiwai, Macushi and Wapishana has resulted in a growing, missionary-minded church despite many government restrictions in the '80s. The Scriptures are being translated in Wapishana and Macushi by **UFM** workers and in Arawak, Akwaio and Carib by **SIL** translators. Pray for the development of mature churches and leadership that can retain their cultural identity and still survive the impact of modernity.

7. **Christian education** at all levels is hampered by severe import restrictions and poverty. Pray for the five Bible schools and for the training of leaders.

8. **Youth work.** The effects of the years of Marxist rhetoric and racial favouritism need to be erased from the education system. Young people face a bleak future with few opportunities for good jobs. Pray for the influential ministry of the 150 Bible Clubs and of the student groups (**IFES**) in nearly every secondary school and college campus with four full-time staff workers.

9. **Christian Missions** have had a long history, but government restrictions and economic collapse reduced the number of missionaries. Conditions are often discouraging. Pray for the church support and pioneering work of the **SBC** (10 workers), **UFM** (7) and Wesleyan Church (5).

Haiti

(The Republic of Haiti)

| May 23 |
| Caribbean |

Area 28,000 sq.km. Western third of the island of Hispaniola; shared with the Dominican Republic.

Population	Ann. Gr.	Density
1990	6,504,000	1.9 %	237/sq.km
1995	7,148,000	1.9 %	261/sq.km

One of the most densely populated countries in the Americas. Many Haitians have fled or emigrated to the USA.

Peoples:
Afro-Caribbean 90%.
Mulatto (Eurafrican) 9.9%.
Euro-American 0.1%.

Literacy 33%. **Official language:** French (10% speak it). **Common language:** Haitian Creole.

Capital: Port-au-Prince 860,000. Urbanization 30%.

Economy: The poorest state in the Western hemisphere, aggravated by over-population, soil erosion, drought and famine. The imposition of sanctions by the USA after the 1991 coup further degraded the economy and enriched the ruling class. Unemployment 60–80%. Public debt/person $103. Income/person $400 (1.9% of USA).

Politics: A slave revolt against the French in 1804 created the first black republic in the world. A troubled history of blood and dictatorships since then. The deposition of the Duvaliers ended a particularly brutal dictatorship in 1986. A succession of coups and military governments aborted all attempts at introducing democracy. The first democratically elected President Aristide only lasted a few months before being ousted by the army in 1991 followed by official corruption on a massive scale and widespread human rights violations.

Religion: Catholicism was the state religion, but the growth of both Voodooism and Protestant Christianity have eroded the influence of the Roman Catholic Church. Official freedom of religion. [*Note: Many Christian statistics are estimates or projections.*]
Non-religious/other 1.4%.
Baha'i 0.2%.
Spiritist. Not officially recorded but approx. 75%, of which nearly all claim to be nominally Christian.

Voodooism is a development of African spiritism and witchcraft.
Christian 98.4%. Nom 10.1%. Affil 88.3%. Growth 0.4%.
Protestant 25.5%. Growth 5%.

Church	Cong	Members	Affiliated
Seventh-day Adventist	262	148,800	298,000
Baptist Convention	89	66,000	220,000
Ch of the Nazarene	287	57,474	140,566
Ch of God (Cleveland)	289	38,569	117,000
Ev Bapt Ch of South Haiti (WT)	275	35,000	100,000
Episcopal Church	324	27,900	93,000
Evang Ch of Haiti (OMS)	120	18,000	60,000
Assemblies of God	151	11,300	56,478
Fth Holiness Miss (WGM)	235	11,000	44,000
Ch of God of Prophecy	206	15,700	39,100
Free Methodist Church	49	8,275	33,100
Evangelical Bapt Miss	345	13,525	28,417
All other (249)	2,520	175,587	430,028
Denominations (261)	5,152	627,130	1,659,689
Evangelicals 20.7% of pop		491,000	1,348,000
Pentecostal/charis 6.5%		150,000	424,000

Missionaries:
to Haiti 473 (1:13,800 people) in 81 agencies.
from Haiti 3 (1:550,000 Protestants) in 3 agencies 3frn 3xcul.
Roman Catholic 72.5%. Affil 62.4%.
Growth −1.1%.

| Catholic Ch | 267 | 2,350,000 | 4,057,496 |

Missionaries:
to Haiti 792 (1:8,200 people).
from Haiti 5 (1973 figure).
Marginal 0.4%. Growth 11.2%.

| Jehovah's Witnesses | 111 | 6,427 | 25,700 |

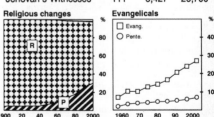

Religious changes

Evangelicals

1. **In 1791 Haiti was dedicated to Satan.** Voodooism is a pervasive evil that affects every level of society. The official recognition of Voodooism, the registration of the National Association of Voodoo Practitioners and nationalistic spirit have led to intimidation of Christians – especially those who speak out against Voodooism. President Aristide re-dedicated the country to Voodooism in 1991 as its "cultural heritage"; shortly afterwards he was deposed. Pray that Christians may be bold to denounce these evils and in the name of Jesus see their destruction.

2. **Two centuries of misrule** have led Haiti to economic, political and spiritual disaster. Pray that leaders accountable to God and those they rule may bring long-denied freedoms to the nation. 85% of the population lives below the poverty line, and malnutrition is widespread.

3. **The Catholic Church** is in crisis with credibility lost and voodooism unchallenged. It is heavily dependent on foreign funds and priests. There is little sign of any effective renewal movements.

4. **The steady growth of Protestant churches** in the difficult economic and spiritual climate is cause for praise. Estimates for Evangelicals vary between 14% and 30%. This has been the result of widespread evangelism, deep commitment to social development and the evident power of Jesus over Satan. Yet there are areas for concern:
a) **The rural poor** have responded more than the urban elite. Illiteracy, marginalization in society and lack of adequate teaching have all prevented Evangelicals from impacting the structures of society.
b) **Church-mission relationships** have often been poor and this has diverted energies from the real battle.
c) **The fragmentation of denominations** on issues of personality, charismatic growth and liberation theology have confused and divided Christians. The Protestant Federation (formed in 1986) and the Council of Evangelical Churches are giving Protestant Christians a platform for speaking with one voice to the government, and for cooperation in social, evangelistic and prayer initiatives.

5. **Leadership training** is too limited because of the poverty of the churches. Many pastors have had little training, some being barely literate themselves. Pray for the 14 Bible schools/seminaries and the many TEE programmes that seek to meet the need. Pray for Haitian leaders to be men of faith and spiritual authority who are not diverted by material inducements.

6. **Desperate physical and social needs** have attracted a wide range of Christian community development agencies such as **WV, TEAR Fund,** World Concern, the Mennonites and many others. Sensitivity and wisdom are needed to preserve the indigeneity, integrity and independence of the churches and their leaders. Pray that every expression of Christian concern in these medical, agricultural, social and literacy programmes may draw folk to the Saviour.

7. **The less evangelized sections of the population:**
a) **The Mulatto elite** are wealthy, French-orientated and isolated from the majority. Few have realized the need for a personal faith.
b) **The youth** are largely rejecting Christianity because of the passivity of the Church in the face of the evident evils of their society.
c) **Refugees** have been fleeing by boat in their thousands – to USA, Cuba, Bahamas and elsewhere. Their destitution and need have made them spiritually receptive. A number of missions (**WT, OMS, CoN** and others) have sought to minister to them in Florida and the Bahamas.

8. **Missions** continue to play an important role, but the political unrest, confrontation with the USA, and also threats and violence against missionaries have forced many to leave. Pray for these servants of the Lord, their witness and example in times of stress, and that they may contribute to the maturing of the church. The larger missions are: Baptists (60 workers in 8 agencies), **UFM** (57), Mennonites (39 in 3 agencies), **WT** (38), **OMS** (27), Wesleyan Church (22), **CoN** (14). Major missionary-contributing nations: USA (384), Canada (33), Germany (14), Netherlands (12).

9. **Christian literature** is not widely available due to poverty, and its value is limited due to illiteracy. The Duvalier regime regarded literacy as a political threat. The Creole Bible was published by the **Bible Society** in 1984. Pray that the Word may begin to transform and revive the flagging Church. Literacy programmes are a prerequisite.

10. **Christian broadcasting** has made a deep impact. A high proportion of the population listens in to Radio Lumière's five stations in the south and centre (Evangelical Baptist Church of South Haiti [WT] and 4VEH in the north [OMS]). Pray for wisdom and safety for staff and producers in the tense political conditions where a wrong word could have dire consequences.

Holy See
(Vatican City State)

See under ITALY

Honduras
(The Republic of Honduras)

May 24
Latin America

Area 112,000 sq.km. A mountainous land with rain forests and fertile coastal plains on the Caribbean and Pacific coasts.

Population	Ann. Gr.	Density
1990 5,138,000	3.2 %	46/sq.km
1995 5,968,000	3.0 %	53/sq.km

Peoples:
Spanish-speaking 92.6%. Mestizo (Ladino) 87.4%; Afro-American 2%; White 2%; Detribalized Amerindian 1.2%.
Amerindians 4.6%, but only 10% use their original languages. Largest: Lenca 206,000; Miskito 15,400; Chorti 12,100; Sumo 2,000; Tol 400.
English-speaking 1.8%. Afro-Caribbean from West Indian islands; American/British 8,200.
Other 1%. Arab 42,000; Garifuna (Black Carib) 30,000; Chinese 2,000; Armenian 1,000; Turk 900.

Literacy 60%. **Official language:** Spanish. **Other languages:** English on the north coast. **All languages** 10. **Languages with Scriptures** 2Bi 3NT 1por.

Capital: Tegucigalpa 800,000. Other city: San Pedro Sula 419,000. Urbanization 41%.

Economy: The broken terrain and unequal distribution of land and wealth have hindered development. Insensitive exploitation by multinationals and corruption of politicians have also helped to keep Honduras poor. Bananas and coffee are the main exports. Unemployment 40%. Public debt/person $533. Income/person $900 (4.3% of USA).

Politics: Independent from Spain in 1821, but 134 revolutions by 1932. Military rule for much of this century. Democratic civilian government since 1984. The nation was deeply affected by US preoccupation with the civil wars in neighbouring Nicaragua and El Salvador. Since 1990, Honduras has sought to lessen dependence on the USA and implement economic reforms.

Religion: The Roman Catholic Church is officially recognized, but there is separation of Church and State and religious freedom.

Non-religious/other 1.4%.
Animist/spiritist 0.6%. **Baha'i** 0.4%.
Christian 97.6%. Affil 94.7%. Growth 3.1%.
Protestant 11%. Growth 6%.

Church	Cong	Members	Affiliated
Christian Brethren	225	20,500	62,100
Ch of God (Cleveland)	463	14,564	44,100
Assemblies of God	825	31,000	43,000
Central Am Ch (CAMI)	251	7,642	26,400
Seventh-day Adventist	75	15,100	25,172
Baptist Convention	83	5,707	19,000
Holiness Ch (WGM)	90	2,500	12,500
All other (82)	2,587	118,029	334,172
Denominations (89)	4,599	215,042	566,444
Evangelicals 10.4% of pop		203,000	537,000
Pentecostal/charis 5.8%		116,000	300,000

Missionaries:
to Honduras 384 (1:13,400 people) in 64 agencies.
from Honduras 58 (1:9,800 Protestants) in 11 agencies 23frn 19xcul 39dom.
Roman Catholic 85.5%. Affil 82.5%. Growth 2.7%.

Catholic Ch	1,468	2,500,000	4,800,000
Doubly counted		−290,000	−560,000
Total		2,210,000	4,240,000
Charismatics 0.47%		12,500	24,000

Missionaries:
to Honduras 113 (1:45,000 people).
from Honduras 50 (1973 figure).
Orthodox 0.13%. Growth 1.1%.

Denominations (4)	3	2,600	6,860

Marginal 1%. Affil 0.98%. Growth 12.1%.

Mormons	84	17,400	29,000
Jehovah's Witnesses	93	5,983	19,900
All Groups (5)	177	24,183	50,500

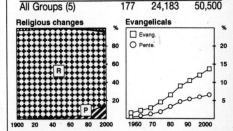

Religious changes

Evangelicals

1. **Response to the gospel in all levels of society has been dramatic over the last 20 years.** This has been brought about by natural disasters, migrations, and social upheavals as well as a massive outreach by churches and missions through evangelism, distribution of Scriptures and literature and extensive use of radio. Pray that the fruit of this harvest may be conserved and mature in the growing churches.

2. **The Roman Catholic Church** has suffered from limited funds and personnel. Over 80% of the latter are foreign. Nominalism, pagan practices and immorality have been widespread, and losses to Protestant churches heavy. Pray that Honduran society may be remoulded by the gospel.

3. **Evangelicals have grown steadily**, but poverty, illiteracy, and paternalistic attitudes among missions have stunted maturity in many denominations. Pray for the ministry of the 16 Bible schools, the one seminary and eight TEE programmes. The ending of the cold war and guerrilla movements in the region have given Evangelicals a window of opportunity to be at the forefront of social and moral change. Pray that they may have a balanced vision for this and for evangelism.

4. **Jealousy and isolationism among Evangelicals is pervasive.** Pray for fellowship and cooperation among Evangelicals. Pray also for the National Evangelical Fraternity organized in 1990 to promote this.

5. **Amerindian ministries**, through both foreign and indigenous missions, have been fruitful. Most Indians have been partially assimilated into the Spanish culture. The Miskito, Garifuna, Sumo and Tol have retained more of a cultural identity, but that is being threatened by extensive, illegal deforestation of their home areas. The Indians have few legal means to prevent this. Pray for Mopawi (Mosquitia Pawisa), an indigenous body founded on Christian principles and dedicated to the development of local cultures and in community development.

6. **The less reached:**
a) **Amerindian peoples.** There has been less response until recently among the Garifuna and Tol, but for both peoples, **SIL** translation teams are working to produce New Testaments. Some humanist groups are seeking to "protect" the culture of indigenous groups from evangelical church planters. Pray that these peoples may both be transformed by the gospel yet retain the uniqueness of their cultures.
b) The minority **Arab** and **Chinese**. There is no known evangelical outreach to them.

7. **Missionaries** still have great influence. Pray that this may be exercised wisely and be supportive of indigenous initiatives and vision for advance. The largest agencies are **SBC** (40 workers), **WGM** (39), **CAMI** (17), **AoG** (17), Brethren (15), **MAF** (15) and **CRWM** (14). Largest missionary-contributing nations: USA (328), UK (16).

8. **Honduran missions vision** is growing. Several Hondurans are serving abroad. **YWAM** is facilitating missionary outreach through short-term exposure, thereby dispelling doubts about its feasibility. An interdenominational missions federation (FEMEH) was formed in 1991 to further a missions vision.

9. **Christian help ministries** are numerous. Pray for **student outreach** (CCC, IFES – 20 groups), **literature agencies** (13 bookstores), **MAF** and others.

Hong Kong

(The Crown Colony of Hong Kong
until 1997, then: Special
Administrative Region of China)

May 25

Asia

Area 1,061 sq. km. A mountainous peninsula and 230 islands on the coast of Gwangdong Province of the People's Republic of China (PRC).

Population	Ann. Gr.	Density
1990 5,841,000	1.4 %	5,633/sq.km
1995 6,159,000	1.1 %	5,939/sq.km

The 1945 population of 600,000 rapidly increased, with over one million refugees and immigrants from the People's Republic of China. One of the most densely populated areas of the world.

Peoples:
Chinese 97%. Yueh (Cantonese) 4,670,000; Minnan 473,000; Hakka 193,000; Putunghua (Mandarin).
Other 3%. Filipino 65,000; English-speaking 59,000; Indian 18,000; Japanese 12,000; Malaysians 12,000.
Refugees: Vietnamese boat people 160,000.

Literacy 88%. **Official languages:** Chinese, English. **All languages** 7. **Languages with Scriptures** 4Bi.

Cities: Victoria 1,269,000; Kowloon 2,163,000; New Territories 2,243,000. Urbanization 93%.

Economy: Rapid growth to become one of the world's leading financial, industrial and trading centres. Hong Kong is the source of nearly half of China's foreign exchange and much of the development of the adjoining Special Economic Zones, where an increasing proportion of Hong Kong's manufacturing is located. Uncertainty about the future dampens the ardour of its ruthless capitalism. Income/person $10,900 (52% of USA).

Politics: British crown colony since 1842. Reverting to China in 1997 as a Special Administrative Region with its government, legal system, finance and international trade guaranteed for 50 years. Recent large-scale emigration of Hong Kong citizens indicates the level of confidence in these guarantees. In 1992 the British Governor, Chris Patten, sought to slightly increase the level of democracy in the colonial administration, but this has led to a breakdown in relations between him and the Chinese government, possibly endangering the 1984 agreement.

Religion: A secular state with religious freedom, but PRC pressures and controls feared by many after 1997 despite official promises to the contrary.
Non-religious/other 15.2%.
Chinese religions 66%. Still fairly popular. Over 360 Taoist and Buddhist temples in Hong Kong.
New religions 3.6%. Syncretic combinations of Chinese and world religions.
Muslim 1%. Predominantly Hui Chinese, also Indians. **Hindu** 0.12%. **Sikh** 0.02%.
Christian 14.1%. Growth 3%.
Protestant 8.5%. Growth 3.9%.

Church	Cong	Members	Affiliated
United HK Chr Baptist	102	44,339	62,228
HK Council of Chs of Christ	35	24,000	34,300
Chr & Miss Alliance	83	20,450	32,828
Anglican Ch	29	15,900	23,000
China Methodist Ch	15	9,017	20,000
Ling Liang WW Ev Miss	15	8,400	16,800
Evang Lthn Ch of HK	54	9,180	13,100
China Rhenish Ch	14	1,983	10,200
Lutheran Ch HK Synod	39	5,000	10,000
All other (36)	609	133,654	272,900
Denominations (45)	995	271,923	495,356
Evangelicals 6.9% of pop		218,000	495,000
Pentecostal/charis 1.6%		45,000	93,000

Missionaries:
to HK/China 761 (1:7,700 people) in 108 agencies.
from Hong Kong 220 (1:2,250 Protestants) in 33 agencies 155frn 93xcul 127dom.
Roman Catholic 4.8%. Growth 0.9%.

Catholic Ch	47	165,000	280,000
Charismatics		350	600

Missionaries:
to Hong Kong 591 (1:9,900 people).
from Hong Kong 60 (1973 figure).
Foreign Marginal 0.42%. Growth 10.5%.

All groups (5)	56	13,573	24,750

Indigenous Marginal 0.36%. Growth 4.2%.

All groups (5)	10	9,000	21,000

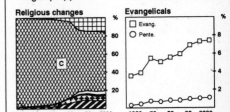

Religious changes

Evangelicals

1. **The countdown to 1997 dominates the thinking of all.** Ambiguities in the 1984 Sino-British accord with subsequent disagreements and the reverberations of the 1989 Beijing massacre have generated fear for the future when China regains control. Pray that politicians on both sides may act

with wisdom and integrity before and after the handover, and that full religious liberty for worship and witness may be maintained.

2. **The tempo of emigration has risen** and 10% of the population (many graduates), 30–40% of the Christians and 50% of the Christian leaders have either left the country or are obtaining foreign passports. Pray that Christians may be guided by the Lord rather than by their fears and also maintain their commitment and credibility during the transition. Pray that churches may be adequately prepared for future ministry in Hong Kong and beyond in the changing situation after 1997.

3. **The Christian community** grew rapidly in the '60s, but growth has slowed because of emigration and a high dropout rate among young adults. Pray that Christians may use these vital years effectively for evangelism, discipleship of converts and laying strong foundations for the Church whatever the future may hold. Christians face many pressures in Hong Kong's crowded and intense atmosphere. Some churches are maintaining vigorous growth through evangelism – such as Ling Liang WWM, Assemblies of God, Baptists, and churches related to **CMA** and **OMS**. Pray for both vitality and growth in the 990 or more churches.

4. **Christian leaders** have a key role to play in the '90s, but workers are too few and large numbers have left the country. There were 849 students in 17 seminaries and Bible schools in 1990, over half being women. Pray for the staff of these seminaries, which include the Alliance Seminary, China Graduate School of Theology and the Baptist Theological Seminary. Pray also for the students and the implantation of a life of holiness and commitment to missions as well as a knowledge of theology and pastoral work.

5. **Hong Kong Evangelism 2000** is a vision for Protestant Christians to double adult membership to 500,000, congregations to 2,000 and workers to 4,000 by the year 2000. Pray that these goals may be achieved.

6. **Hong Kong's underworld of crime and secret societies** (50 Triad societies with 500,000 members – the Chinese equivalent of the Mafia) stimulates the drug addiction, prostitution, theft, gambling and protection rackets that thrive in crowded living conditions in proximity to much material wealth. Christian ministry among the criminals, drug addicts and destitute has increased with considerable success (partly as a result of the work of St Stephen's Society pioneered by Jackie Pullinger).

7. **Less-reached sections of the community.** Fear for the future has increased superstition and idolatry. In 1989, a 30-metre bronze Buddha was built to protect Hong Kong. The spiritual powers behind these must be disarmed to bring release to:
a) **The blue-collar industrial workers,** and the wealthy financiers and businessmen.
b) **The Vietnamese refugees.** Later arrivals numbering 54,000 have been isolated in camps with the likelihood of enforced return to Vietnam. **World Vision** and **YWAM** have a ministry to them.
c) **Immigrants from Mainland China.** Many are housed in squalid squatter settlements, crowded little high-rise flats or boats in the harbours. They are disillusioned and frustrated. A number of churches and missions have sought to alleviate their physical and spiritual needs (**WV, OMF, ECF** and others).
d) **The village farmers and fisher folk.** There are few churches in the rural areas. Pray for the ongoing programmes for their evangelism.
e) The **Muslim and Indian** minorities who are unreached.

8. **Foreign mission agencies** have multiplied since 1950, but over half their workers have ministries directed beyond Hong Kong's borders. Pray that all may be guided in their ministry and location over the transition period, and concentrate on that which is most strategic. Major agencies with ministry in Hong Kong are: **YWAM** (104 workers), **SBC** (62), **OMF** (37), Norwegian Mission Society (34), SDA (34), **CMA** (28), Ev. Free Ch of America (24), **AoG** (23), Finnish Lutheran Mission (23), **PAoC** (17), **OMS** (15), **ABWE** (12), **Asian Outreach** (11). Major missionary-contributing nations: USA (461), Norway (63), UK (40), Korea (33), New Zealand (29), Finland (27).

9. **The missions vision of the Hong Kong Church is growing.** There is widespread interest in ministry to the believers in the PRC and in missionary work abroad. Pray that this burden may grow and not be hindered by fears for the future. The Hong Kong Association of Christian Missions is a focal point for 50 agencies. Pray for adequate sending structures and the sending of quality recruits overseas, and that this may continue after 1997.

10. **Ministry to the mainland Chinese** is fraught with problems yet vital for the believers in unofficial groups in the PRC. Pray for sensitivity, wisdom and boldness for all committed to such outreaches.

11. **Student ministries** show dynamic growth through the HKFES(**IFES**) programmes in evangelism and Bible teaching. Over 5,000 students in secondary and tertiary institutions are involved. Over 12,000 Hong Kong students are studying abroad, where the conversion rate is also high. May the impact of Christian graduates on Hong Kong society be decisive!

12. **Hong Kong is a vital nerve centre for media.** Groups such as Christian Communications Ltd. and **AO** have made significant contributions. **Literature** is written, printed, published and distributed on a massive scale (**CLC, EHC, CMA**). Bibles are printed for the world, and the Bible Society has a key role. **Radio** studios prepare programmes for **FEBC, FEBA, TWR** and many other radio agencies. Pray that this role may continue beyond 1997.

<table>
<tr><td>May 26–27</td></tr>
<tr><td>Europe</td></tr>
</table>

Hungary
(Republic of Hungary)

Area 93,000 sq.km. A landlocked, central European state on the River Danube.

Population		Ann. Gr.	Density
1990	10,552,000	−0.18 %	113/sq.km
1995	10,509,000	−0.08 %	113/sq.km

H

Peoples:
Magyar (Hungarians) 92%. A third of all Hungarians live in other lands: Romania 2,252,000; Slovakia 620,000; Serbia 460,000; Ukraine 160,000; elsewhere 1,400,000.
Minorities 8%. Gypsy 320,000; Ruthenian (Ukrainian) 300,000; German 250,000; Slovak 100,000; Jews 80,000; Croat 25,000; Polish 21,000; Serbian 20,000.
Immigrant groups 0.28%. Chinese 30,000.
Refugees: By 1993, 500,000 Croat, Hungarian, Bosnian and Serb refugees from former Yugoslavia, and 200,000 Hungarian, Romanian and Gypsy refugees from Romania.

Literacy 99%. **Official language:** Hungarian. **Languages with Scriptures** 6Bi 1NT 1por.

Capital: Budapest 2,113,600. Urbanization 62%.

Economy: The first Communist bloc state to begin privatizing the economy, and the first ex-Communist state to record positive economic growth. Poor in natural resources but with a developed industrial base and productive agricultural land. The human cost of change and recovery from the mismanagement and large public debt generated by the previous Communist regime is high; by December 1992 unemployment rose to 11%. Public debt/person $2,050. Income/person $6,100 (29% of USA).

Politics: Hungary lost 60% of its land area at the breakup of the Austro-Hungarian Empire in 1918, leaving large Hungarian minorities in surrounding lands. During World War II the Russian army occupied the land, only leaving in 1991. A Russian-engineered coup brought the Communists to power in 1947. The Hungarian uprising of 1956 brought terrible revenge from the Russians. 80,000 were killed, wounded or deported, and 200,000 fled to the West. The first Communist bloc state to abandon Marxism and institute a multi-party democracy in 1990. The first freely elected government brought economic and political stabilization, but the high expectations of the people can only slowly be realized, causing some disillusionment.

Religion: In 1600, Hungary was 90% Protestant. Many reverted to Catholicism in the Counter Reformation and periods of discrimination that followed. The Communists enforced strict controls on all Christians between 1948 and 1988 through discrimination, intimidation and infiltration. There has been freedom of religion since 1990.
Non-religious/other 12.5%.
Jews 0.8%. **Muslims** 0.1%.
Christian 86.6%. Attend 15%. Growth 0.1%.
Protestant 24.4%. Growth 1.2%.

Church	Cong	Members	Affiliated
Reformed Church	1,133	500,000	2,000,000
Evang Lutheran Ch	341	113,000	450,000
Baptist Ch	400	10,994	25,000
Congregs. of Nazarenes	100	12,000	20,000
Faith Chr Fellowship	8	5,000	13,000
F'ship of Ev Pentes (AoG)	215	4,755	12,000
Seventh-day Adventist	111	5,599	11,200
Apostolic Ch	130	3,000	10,000
Methodist Ch	73	3,000	5,000
Christian Brethren	27	2,000	3,000
All other (9)	213	12,400	23,690
Denominations (19)	2,751	671,748	2,572,890
Evangelicals 4.8% of pop		153,000	510,000
Pentecostal/charis 0.9%		32,000	95,000

Missionaries:
to Hungary 211 (1:50,000 people) in 33 agencies.
from Hungary 46 (1:53,900 Protestants) in 10 agencies 7frn 9xcul 37dom.
Roman Catholic 61.7%. Growth −0.2%.

Catholic Ch	2,265	4,880,000	6,508,000
Charismatic		14,000	20,000

Orthodox 0.3%. Growth 0.4%.

Romanian Ortho Ch	18	10,900	16,500
All other (6)	63	7,100	14,000
Denominations (7)	81	18,000	30,500

Marginal 0.2%. Growth 9.6%.

Jehovah's Witnesses	238	10,647	15,200
All groups (7)	246	13,777	20,500

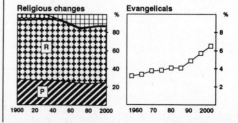

Religious changes

Evangelicals

1. **Praise God for the freedom Hungary has gained.** Pray for God-fearing leaders to be raised up who will guide the nation with wisdom and sensitivity. There is concern about "ethnic cleansing" of Hungarians in Serb-controlled Vojvodina and discrimination against Hungarians in Romanian Transylvania and southern Slovakia. Pray for reconciliation between these minorities and the various national majorities.

2. **The 40 years of bondage are over,** but the moral, social and spiritual damage of Marxism still blights the country and, more sadly, the Church. Although some Catholic and Protestant leaders boldly stood for the Lord and suffered, some official Church leaders only retained their position by compromises with the Communist authorities. A legacy of suspicion, mistrust and division is the result. Pray for a deep work of the Holy Spirit bringing repentance and renewal.

3. **Freedom has brought spiritual interest, a greater responsiveness and steady growth,** but not yet the big ingathering many sought. Hungary had revivals in 1939 and 1946–50 which touched the Reformed and other free churches. There are several strong charismatic and renewal movements in the Catholic Church and in the Baptist, Reformed and Free Churches and also a Pietist Bible Union within the Reformed Church to which 130 of the 850 pastors belong. There are growing independent charismatic congregations and also a flourishing intercessors movement. Pray that reconciliation of the nation to God, spiritual renewal, restoration and revival may affect the whole nation as a result of these.

4. **Hungarians are groping for life solutions.** Economic difficulties have created stress, pessimism and concern for the future. Many fall prey to alcoholism, suicide, burgeoning cults and the occult because of their ignorance of the meaning of sin and the gospel. Pray for more effective local church-based outreach and discipling of enquirers. All too often Christians do not live out the life of the One whose name they bear. There are openings for ministry in schools, hospitals, prisons, and in almost every area of society.

5. **The denominations have a leadership crisis.** Pray for:
a) **Fresh, inspired leadership** able to work together to use the great evangelistic opportunities, and set high ethical and moral standards. Many in leadership have been scarred by the past and are cautious and traditional.
b) **Lack of workers.** The Reformed Church alone needs 600 pastors. Under the Communists the pressure, poverty, low social status and lack of training facilities all helped to limit the number of Christian workers. Pray for more to be called into full-time ministry and for the provision of their needs.
c) **Leadership training.** Seminaries and Bible schools are full and multiplying. Pray for the ministry of the various seminaries and Bible schools and for the provision of godly teachers who love God and his Word. Liberal theology has been a problem in the past. Pray also for the Pentecostal Bible School, the **AoG** ICI TEE programme in Hungarian and also the teaching seminars run by the East Europe Bible Mission and others. The independent charismatic churches also need anointed leadership. Hungary is becoming a centre for Bible training for Central Europe with several English-medium schools (Central European Bible School, Greater Grace Christian Mission and Word of Life).

6. **Ministry to young people** – a day of opportunity but also dearth of trained, Spirit-filled workers for:
a) **Teaching religious knowledge in schools,** where two hours/week are available. Pray for the provision of evangelist-teachers for this opportunity.
b) **Children and youth programmes in churches.** Many have nothing to meet their needs.
c) **University students** (100,000) who are open to both the gospel and to the cults. MEKDsz(**IFES**) has a ministry with 20 groups and 300 students involved.

7. **The less-reached.**
a) **Western Hungary,** especially the urban high-rise apartment dwellers.
b) **The Jews.** Before the Holocaust there were 800,000. Now their numbers are down to 80,000. Anti-Semitism is still a problem that needs to be purged out of the nation. Pray for reconciliation between Jews and non-Jews.
c) **The Gypsy community** which has not seen the same spiritual breakthrough as in Spain, France and Romania, but there are several new charismatic fellowships among them.
d) **The flood of refugees from former Yugoslavia** who need physical and spiritual help.

e) **Chinese** from Mainland China who have increased in number. **COCM** is seeking to begin a ministry to them.

8. **Expatriate missions** are increasing in number. Pray for sensitivity and avoidance of all appearance of control or manipulation in seeking to help the Hungarian Church. The main ministries required of expatriates are in leadership training, teaching English and imparting missions vision. There is little knowledge of missions in churches, but great potential. Largest missions are: Greater Grace Mission (20 workers), **CCC** (14 expatriates, 17 Hungarian staff), **IT** (14), **OM** (13), Word of Life (7 expatriates, 14 Hungarian). Largest missionary-contributing nations: USA (107), Canada (15), Korea (6), UK (5).

9. **Christian help ministries.**

a) **Scripture distribution.** The Hungarian Bible Society was re-established in 1989. Pray for its ministry in distributing the Bible; demand for the Scriptures is greater than the supply not only in Hungary but also in surrounding lands.

b) **Christian literature.** This is in great demand, but too little is locally written and published. Subsidized literature from the West inhibits indigenous literature ministries. Christian bookstores are few and small. **CLC** has opened up a bookstore in Budapest. The Hungarian Literature Mission is a major source of evangelistic materials. **EHC** has plans to reach every home with evangelistic literature.

c) **The** *Jesus* **film.** This is one of the best-selling videos in Hungarian.

d) **Christian radio.** In addition to the few hours a week broadcast in Hungarian by **TWR, IBRA** and **High Adventure**, there are increasing local opportunities for Christian programmes on television and radio. **IT** have set up a music recording studio to serve Central Europe.

Iceland

(Republic of Iceland)

May 28

Europe

Area 103,000 sq.km. A large volcanic island in the North Atlantic; mountainous, largely barren with many large glaciers.

Population	Ann. Gr.	Density
1990	253,000	0.98 %	2/sq.km
1995	264,000	0.85 %	3/sq.km

Peoples:
Icelander 98.5%. Original settlers came from Norway 1,000 years ago.
Foreign 1.5%. US military, a few migrants from Asia and Europe.

Literacy 100%. **Official language:** Icelandic.

Capital: Reykjavik 143,260. Urbanization 91%.

Economy: The fishing industry has been the largest source of income, but conservation measures have limited this. Enormous underused hydro and thermal power resources. Unemployment 3%. Public debt/person $6,000. Income/person $20,160 (96% of USA).

Politics: The world's oldest parliament, established in 930. Under Norwegian and Danish rule 1262–1944. Parliamentary republic, and a member of NATO.

Religion: The Lutheran Church is still recognized as the State Church, but there is religious freedom.
Non-religious/other 1.7%. The old Norse religion has a following of 92 people.

Christian 98.3%. Attend 10%. Growth 1.5%.
Protestant 97.05%. Growth 1.5%.

Church	Cong	Members	Affiliated
National Ch (Lutheran)	310	173,817	236,959
Evang Luth Free Ch	6	5,545	7,159
Pentecostal Movmnt.	12	815	1,050
All other (7)	17	2,319	3,284
Denominations (10)	345	182,496	248,452
Evangelicals 2.85% of pop		5,255	7,200
Pentecostal/charis 1.1%		2,200	2,900

Missionaries:
to Iceland 14 (1:18,000 people) in 7 agencies.
from Iceland 31 (1:8,200 Protestants) in 5 agencies 22frn 22xcul 9dom.
Roman Catholic 0.94%. Growth 4.3%.

Catholic Ch	3	1,757	2,396

Missionaries to Iceland 1 (1:256,000 people).
Marginal 0.26%. Growth 11.8%.

Jehovah's Witnesses	5	246	517
Mormons	3	106	161
Groups (2)	8	352	678

1. **The majority of Icelanders are only nominally Christian.** Prosperity and secularism are causing a drift away from the churches, and there is growing interest in occultism and New Age ideologies. More than 40% of the population has had involvement with the occult. The high level of divorce and illegitimate births (52%) is an indication of need. The New Age, Spiritist, and small but vociferous Norse religion movements are active in seeking to de-Christianize Iceland. Pray that these dark powers may be bound in the name of Jesus.

2. **The Lutheran and smaller, but similar, Free Churches** have few Bible-based congregations where repentance and the new birth are preached. The Lutheran Church has the goal of congregational growth in the '90s (less than 10% are regular churchgoers) culminating in a great celebration in the year 2000, which is also the 1000-year anniversary of the coming of Christianity. Pray for a surge of new vigour and fervour in both the congregations and Theological Faculty where all pastors are trained.

3. **Evangelical believers** may number only 5,000. Under the covering of the State Church, evangelical groups such as the Salvation Army, YMCA and **YWAM** have helped to bring a more biblical perspective to some congregations. There is also a growing charismatic movement. Among the non-Lutheran bodies, the two Pentecostal denominations and the Charismatic Fellowship are the main evangelical bodies. Pray for the growth of this witness.

4. **Evangelistic work** has been discouraging in the prevailing spiritual climate. Since 1980, Pentecostal, charismatic and **YWAM** team evangelism and literature distribution has borne more fruit. **YWAM** has started Iceland's first Bible school and training centre. Pray that these ministries may turn the tide for Jesus.

5. **KSF(IFES) work among the 3,000 university students** is encouraging, with around 200 members. Pray that those who love the Lord may maintain a glowing testimony where indifference is so widespread.

6. **The Bible Society published a new Bible version in 1981.** Pray for the ministry of God's Word through the 10,000 copies already in circulation. Pray also for the Gideons and their Bible distribution ministry.

7. **A vision for missions hardly exists.** Iceland's geographical and cultural isolation hinders the development of such vision. Only 22 Icelanders are serving God overseas.

India

(Republic of India)

May 29– June 2
Asia

Area 3,204,000 sq.km. 25 union states and 7 union territories. Geographically India dominates South Asia and the Indian Ocean.

Population		Ann. Gr.	Density
1990	824,554,000	2.35 %	257/sq.km
1995	904,800,000	2.30 %	282/sq.km

Nearly 16% of the world's population is Indian, living on 2.4% of the world's land surface. In 2020 India will become the most populous country in the world with nearly 1.3 billion people.

Peoples: The great racial, ethnic, religious and linguistic diversity makes a simple subdivision of the population difficult. A 1991 survey identified 4,635 communities or people groups.

Ethno-Linguistic:

Indo-Aryan 73.3%. In north and central India. Hindi 200,600,000; Marathi 81,650,000; Bengali 69,760,000; Urdu 44,542,000; Bhojpuri-Bihari 43,300,000; Gujarati 40,372,000; Oriya 31,000,000; Punjabi 24,330,000; Sindhi 18,760,000; Rajasthani/ Mawari 17,000,000; Assamese 13,947,000; Nepali 6,480,000; Kashmiri 3,817,000; Lambadi/Gypsy 3,624,000; Konkani 2,371,000; Bagri 1,644,000.

Dravidian 24%. Majority in south India. Major groups: Telugu 69,623,000; Tamil 58,547,000; Malayalam 34,166,000; Kannada 33,600,000; Oraon 1,932,000.

Austro-Asiatic 1.6%. Scattered all over India as tribal groups. Over 80 peoples. Major groups (including all related languages): Bhil 10,660,000; Gond 8,349,000; Santal 5,753,000; Kui 2,856,000; Munda 1,200,000; Ho 1,168,000; Khasi 726,000.

Sino-Tibetan 1.0%. Predominantly in northeast India. Over 105 groups; major: Tibetan (16) 1,950,000, Manipuri 1,216,000; Naga (28) 940,000; Tripuri (8) 814,000; Garo 641,000; Mizo 446,000; Kuki-Chin (17) 338,000.

Other 0.1%. British, Chinese, Arabs, Russians, Armenians, Jews.

Caste: A system that perpetuates the racial superiority of Brahmins and other higher castes over the majority. Fundamental to Hinduism, it pervasively influences all religious and social structures in India. Caste discrimination is forbidden by the constitution, but is socially important for over 80% of the population. There are an estimated 6,400 castes. Each functions effectually as a separate group because of the high social barriers that separate them.
High caste 4.9%. Brahmin; the priestly caste.
Forward castes 10.5%. Kshatriya and Vaisya.
Backward castes 47.6%.
Scheduled castes 15%. (Also known as Outcastes, Untouchables, Harijan.) Generally deprived, subjugated and exploited.
Other 22%. Muslims, Christians and Scheduled tribes are not considered part of the caste structure, but are often strongly influenced by caste thinking.
Literacy 52%. Functional literacy nearer 15%.
Official languages: Hindi (the language of the Union), English (legislative and judicial language), 16 other official regional languages (usually of States): Assamese, Bengali, Gujarati, Kannada, Kashmiri, Malayalam, Manipuri, Marathi, Nepali, Oriya, Punjabi, Sanskrit, Tamil, Telugu, Urdu, Sindhi. **All languages** 1,652 (1971 census) of which 33 spoken by more than 100,000 people; 381 are listed in the *SIL Ethnologue*. **Languages with Scriptures** 46Bi 35NT 60por.

Capital: New Delhi 9,252,000. Other major cities (20 over 1 million): Bombay 13,545,000; Calcutta 13,413,000; Madras 5,582,000; Bangalore 4,410,000; Hyderabad 4,280,000; Ahmedabad 3,298,000; Pune 2,485,000; Kanpur 2,111,000; Nagpur 1,661,000; Lucknow 1,642,000. Urbanization 28%.

Economy: Agriculture and industry are both important. 74% of the labour force is agricultural, but rapid industrialization and urbanization is taking place. Economic growth has been offset by the high birth rate, illiteracy, prejudice, resistance to change and bureaucratic inefficiency. The 200 million middle class would benefit most from the market reforms and liberalization being instituted. Over 600 million live in deep poverty, and 300 million live below the bread-line. Population growth will outstrip food production just after 2000. Unemployment 13%. Public debt/person $85. Income/person $350 (1.6% of USA).

Politics: Independent from Britain in 1947. The world's largest functioning democracy. Troubled relations with surrounding nations; two wars with Pakistan and one with China. Internal tensions have steadily increased because of caste, religious and regional loyalties. Secession movements in Kashmir, Nagaland, Manipur, Tripura, Punjab, Assam, and the tribal regions of south Bihar are weakening the union. Religious militancy among Sikhs, Muslims and especially Hindus threatens the survival of secular democracy. The BJP, a radical Hindu political party, became the largest opposition party in the 1991 elections, and then openly provoked confrontation with the government in 1992. This culminated in savage rioting and destruction of Muslim mosques, property and lives, and in destabilizing India's political life and social balance.

Religion: India is a secular state. The rising power of intolerant Hindu factions has caused the passing of anti-conversion laws in some states, discriminatory deprivation of benefits and privileges to the poor who convert to Islam or Christianity, and a rising level of physical violence against both Muslims and Christians. Should the BJP become the government party, federal legislation against minority religions is likely to increase.
Hindu 78.8% (officially 82%). Figure somewhat raised by the automatic inclusion of untouchables and many tribal animists. Hinduism readily absorbs elements of any religion with which it comes into contact. Popular Hinduism is idolatrous with 200 million holy cows and a pantheon of 33 million gods. Intellectual Hinduism is philosophical and mystical and has a growing appeal to Western countries.
Muslim 12% (Muslims claim 14%). A widespread minority, but a majority in Kashmir and Lakshadweep, and growing among scheduled castes. The Muslim secessionist movement in Kashmir is in armed conflict with the government.
Sikhs 1.92%. Majority in Punjab where extremists have waged a bitter guerrilla war against the government for an independent Sikh state. Many Sikhs are in the armed forces.
Tribal religions approx. 1.5%. Among Scheduled tribes.
Buddhist 0.7%. A small minority in the land of its origin. Majority among scheduled castes of Maharashtra and Madhya Pradesh, and Tibetans.
Jain 0.48%. **Baha'i** 0.2%. **Parsi** 0.01%.
Non-religious/other 0.43%.
Christian 2.61% (official)#; possibly 4%. Affil 3.94%. Growth 2.8%. Many denominational figures are estimates.
Protestant 1.91%. Growth 3.4%.

Church	Cong	Members	Affiliated
Ch of South India	9,300	800,000	1,700,000
Council of Bapt Chs of NE India	3,969	488,367	1,630,000
United Ev Lthn Chs (11)	12,392	533,000	1,184,132
Ch of North India	3,300	700,000	1,000,000
Samavesam of Telugu Bapt Ch	1,625	312,000	780,000
Mar Thoma Syrian Ch	900	431,000	718,000
Presby Ch of NE Ind	1,600	234,260	526,503
Ind Pente Ch of God	4,444	120,000	300,000
Salvation Army	3,573	162,000	270,000
Chr Assemblies of Ind	1,200	80,000	267,000
Churches of Christ (6)	3,000	105,000	263,000
Bapt Conv of N Circars	210	125,000	250,000
Seventh-day Adventist	829	160,635	247,000
Assemblies (Jehovah Shammah)	1,350	54,000	216,000
Evang Ch of India	558	73,670	200,000

Baptist Convention	1,023	65,731	164,000
Ch of God (Cleveland)	879	59,022	148,000
Bapt Union of Mizoram	269	41,076	137,000
Pentecostal Mission	1,071	75,000	125,000
Assembs of God (2)	1,392	43,500	124,366
St Thomas Evang Ch	675	54,000	90,000
All other (319)	44,237	2,661,655	5,921,191
Denominations (356)	97,796	7,378,916	16,261,192
Evangelicals 1% of pop		3,601,000	8,307,000
Pentecostal/charis 0.38%		1,364,000	3,181,000

Missionaries:
to India 766 (1:1,076,000 people) in 150 agencies.
from India 11,284 (1:524 Protestants) in 198 agencies 171frn 5,137xcul 6,147dom.
Roman Catholic 1.76%. Growth 2.2%.

Catholic Ch	22,460	8,400,000	15,000,000
Charismatics		15,000	25,000

Missionaries:
to India 2,377 (1:347,000 people).
from India 5,420 (1973 figure).
Other Catholic 0.01%. Growth 10.5%.

All groups (1)	648	27,500	65,500

Orthodox 0.2%. Growth 1.2%.

Malankara Orth Syrian	1,200	1,020,000	1,700,000
All other (5)	90	27,000	45,000
All denominations (6)	1,290	1,047,000	1,745,000

Foreign Marginal 0.01%. Growth 5.1%.

Jehovah's Witnesses	316	10,272	25,700
All other (9)	187	22,727	56,415
All groups (10)	503	32,999	82,115

Indigenous Marginal Affil 0.06%. Growth 4.4%.

All groups (20)		200,000	500,000

 # Note: Census figures are artificially low because only the religion of the head of house was recorded. Also many backward classes and scheduled caste Christians registered as Hindu out of fear.

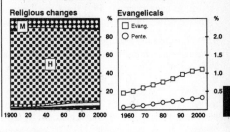

Religious changes / Evangelicals

INDIA GENERAL

1. **Praise God for the 200 years** since William Carey went to India. The Holy Spirit has used the labours of countless thousands of preachers, both Indian and expatriate, to change India and plant the Church. Praise for:
a) **Great freedom to spread the gospel** despite efforts to limit this.
b) **People movements** among the scheduled castes and tribal peoples which continue to this day.
c) **Spiritual stirrings since independence**, manifest hunger for peace with God and response to literature and radio evangelism.
d) **Revivals** in South India, in 1976 in Nagaland, and in the '80s in Mizoram.
e) **New missionary burden** based on prayer that is stirring thousands of churches and resulting in five successive waves of missions, from Kerala, Tamil Nadu, northeast India, Andhra Pradesh and now Orissa.

2. **These advances are being contested by the enemy of souls through:**
a) **Militant Hinduism** which has become a powerful political force, winning four northern states in the 1991 elections. Pray for the preservation of democracy and wisdom for the government in the face of militant violence. The conversion of hundreds of thousands of untouchables to minority religions as an escape from oppressive Brahmin Hinduism has provoked a vigorous response with rising levels of violence against Christian workers and congregations. Pray that Christians may humbly and lovingly commend the gospel to their persecutors without compromise of the truth. Pray also that the Hindu caste system may lose its hold on people.
b) **Discriminatory legislation** in a growing number of states, which inhibits conversions and deprives converts of access as underprivileged classes to government-allocated jobs and funds. Many Christians have succumbed to such blackmail. The law gives inadequate protection to tribals and former scheduled caste underprivileged Christians when Hindu extremists use force to coerce conversion to Hinduism. Pray that Christians may follow Jesus whatever the cost.
c) **Nominalism in the churches.** People movements to Christ were often inadequately discipled. The quality of life of many Christians deters non-Christians from putting their trust in Jesus. Christians have often become just another caste in a Hindu world. Revival is sorely needed to rid the churches of self-seeking, social climbing, petty squabbles and sin; to implant a love for the brethren irrespective of social origin; and to give a burden to evangelize.

3. **Missionary visas for new workers** are hard to obtain, so the missionary force is ageing and in rapid decline. Praise God for the perseverance and dedication of these men and women; pray for eternal fruit through their ministry. Pray that God may raise up a new generation of expatriate workers to gain entrance, develop new ministries and reach the Hindu heartland, unreached cities and peoples for Christ. For too long people have forgotten India's need for workers.

4. **Christians were the fastest growing minority in India until the '70s.** That growth has slowed in many states because people movements were forcibly arrested and also because witnessing to non-Christians is rare; many congregations have no first-generation Christians from a non-Christian background. Nominalism has become a major problem. Newer churches are often more effective in attracting Christians from other churches than winning Hindus or Muslims. Pray for revival that reverses this trend and fires up the believers for outreach and missions.

5. **Caste is one of the biggest issues facing the nation.** Constitutional equality and legal banning of discrimination are provoking intense conflict and violence between the higher castes and untouchables. About 80% of Christians are of backward or scheduled caste and tribal origin, and are not yet liberated from the effects of what is little more than legitimized racism. The ambivalent attitude of Christians is a problem to higher-caste Hindus who are attracted by the gospel but repelled by the low social origin of Christians, and a stumbling block to the untouchables who are put off by castism among Christians. Pray that Christians may both preach and live by biblical standards and set aside the pride and inferiorities of caste, yet reach out sensitively to those still bound by them.

6. **Praise God for growth that is occurring.** In Andhra Pradesh, Orissa, Bihar, Gujarat and in the northeast states hundreds of new village congregations are being planted by indigenous missionaries and local churches. The widespread impact of Christian radio (**FEBA, TWR**) and evangelism through literature (**OM, EHC, International Bible League**) has softened millions to the point of receptivity. OM teams have "graduated" 5,000 young people who are now leaders in pioneer work today. Pray for more to become involved in evangelism, and for better coordinated and more determined evangelism of non-Christians by local churches – even if it does result in discomfort or persecution. A nationwide DAWN movement was launched by most of India's Protestant denominations in 1990 with a vision to plant a church in every one of India's 600,000 unchurched villages. Pray for the Holy Spirit's enabling.

7. **The evangelical witness is a growing force in the Church today.** The proportion of evangelical pastors is steadily increasing in the mainline denominations. Praise God for outstanding, mature leaders of international stature in both the older and newer denominations. Pray for:
a) **The Bible to be given its rightful place** in both the theologically liberal and more evangelical denominations. In the former, dialogue and universalism have replaced evangelism and conversion. In the latter there is little solid teaching, expository preaching or application of teachings to the real and pressing needs of India today.
b) **The Evangelical Fellowship of India** which has a membership of more than 100 evangelical churches and agencies. It is having a significant impact in maturing, stabilizing and mobilizing believers through weeks of prayer and conventions, pastors' retreats, and coordinating missionary outreach, literature production, Sunday School courses and TEE (under title TAFTEE), as well as backing the Union Biblical Seminary.

8. **Training of Christian leaders is of crucial importance.** Syncretism in Catholic, Protestant and evangelical churches is a problem. The lack of dedicated Christian workers prepared to leave all for the sake of Christ is the biggest factor limiting the growth of the Church and causing reversions to Hinduism in rural areas where there is a lack of teaching. There is an average of one pastor for eight churches and 400 villages across the country. Pray for:
a) **Degree-level seminaries,** of which there are over 40. A minority are theologically evangelical. One such is **Union Biblical Seminary** in Pune, with 225 students and from 50 evangelical denominations and agencies. Pray for a stream of warm-hearted workers, anointed by the Spirit, to move out from these institutions to India and beyond.
b) **Bible schools** numbering 150. Evangelical institutions are full. Only 10% of all those trained for Christian work go out into evangelistic or pioneer church-planting ministries. Pray that this percentage may increase.
c) **TEE** – widely used **for training church leaders.** The best known is **TAFTEE** with thousands of students. Multiplication of leaders by all means possible is essential.

9. **Praise the Lord for the growth of Indian indigenous missions.** In 1973 there were 420 missionaries, in 1983, 3,017, and in 1992 over 11,000 in 198 agencies – about half in cross-cultural work. Both denominational and interdenominational agencies have multiplied; most are based in south and northeast India. The **India Missions Association** is a coordinating body for 50 evangelical agencies. The three largest: **India Evangelical Team** (IET) with 575 missionaries, **Friends Missionary Prayer Band** with 474 missionaries working in 60 people groups; **IEM** with 388 missionaries working in 50 people groups. Pray for:

a) **Vision and sensitivity** to the problems of cross-cultural outreach, and dynamic and strategic direction for the mission movement.

b) **Effective training**. The task is so enormous that cooperation is essential.

c) **Adequate cross-cultural preparation** for missionaries. There are a number of cross-cultural training institutes including the inter-mission **Indian Institute of Cross-cultural Communications** begun in 1980, OTI (**IEM**), INCEP (**OM**) and others. Union Biblical Seminary has started a Centre for Missionary Studies.

d) **Missionaries called to go to the Hindu heartlands** of the Ganges plain in the north. Most Indian church-planting missionaries have gone to under-privileged and marginalized people groups. The cultural, linguistic and emotional barriers for south Indian missionaries to reach caste Hindus are high.

10. **Lack of firm information about India's spiritual needs** has crippled prayer, limited recruitment and slowed the evangelization of the country. Pray for completion of the massive analysis of India's Christian resources (**India Christian Handbook**) and research being undertaken into the unreached peoples of India (**India Missions Association** and **India Church Growth Research Centre**). Pray that this information may be widely disseminated and effectively used to mobilize the Church.

11. **India's unreached**. No area of the world has such a diversity and concentration of unreached peoples. Some of the broader categories are mentioned here; others will be found under individual states below.

a) **The North India plains** with their teeming millions. Christians have failed to make a significant impression on the caste Hindu. Pray for the right strategy for evangelizing each caste and planting churches. Of the 6,400 castes, only about 100 have yielded any fruit as a reward for the Saviour's sufferings.

b) **The higher castes** which have shown little open response to the claims of Christ. Pray for the Brahmin (the priestly castes), Kshatriya (the warrior castes) and Vaisya (merchant castes) that pride of descent may be replaced by conviction of sin and faith in the Lord Jesus. Pray for the right approach to win and disciple each group.

c) **The rural population**. Over 70% of Indians live in the 700,000 village communities; only about 65,000 communities would have a Christian congregation – most of these being in south and northeast India, south Bihar and south Gujarat.

d) **The Muslim minority** of 110,000,000 – one of the world's largest and most accessible Muslim communities. Muslims ruled much of India for 600 years. More evangelistic effort and a marginally increased response were evident in the '80s. There may now be a few thousand Muslims who have turned to Christ, but persecution has been severe for many. Pray for the five agencies and 150 or so Indian missionaries labouring among them.

e) **The great cities** with their exploding populations. Many areas are unreached, and few adequate strategies have been proposed to reach them. Many live in abject poverty and have no homes. This is one of the greatest challenges for the gospel in the '90s.

f) **Young people**, neglected in the churches through lack of manpower, training and interest. How much more needy are those who are unchurched! **Youth For Christ, CEF, SU, CCC** and others are seeking to reach out to some.

g) **Students** numbering nearly four million in 176 universities and 6,380 colleges. A high proportion use addictive drugs. Pray for the nationwide ministries of **YFC, Inter-collegiate Pentecostal Fellowship** and the **Union of Evangelical Students of India (UESI-IFES)** with groups and staff workers in most campuses. Pray for a clear, vibrant witness to the thousands of non-Christian students. Pray for their growth and integration into local churches. There are no **UESI** staff workers in Kashmir, Sikkim or Himachal Pradesh.

h) **Tibetan refugees**, possibly numbering 450,000 and scattered through India in special areas and camps where Christian witness is rarely allowed. There are only three churches known with six pastors. The majority remain bound in their superstitions and Lamaistic Buddhism.

i) **AIDS** which has rapidly become a major issue in Bombay and Calcutta. In 1991 there were estimated to be 500,000 HIV virus carriers. The enormity of the disaster that could afflict India has scarcely dawned on the authorities or Christians. Pray that ministry to afflicted families may be initiated.

j) Leprosy sufferers numbering 3.2 million. Christian agencies, especially **The Leprosy Mission**, have a ministry of love to some.

k) **The blind**. India's 10 million blind represent over a quarter of the world total. Few have ever learned the Braille script, nor are there many materials in Braille in Indian languages. The **Torch Trust for the Blind** is committed to producing the whole Bible in Braille in the 12 major languages of India. At present there are some books in nine languages, but none have the whole Bible. Other agencies with ministry to blind people are **Mission to Blind** and **India Fellowship for Physically Handicapped**. Compass Braille is an agency specializing in producing Braille Scriptures in Indian languages by means of computer.

12. **Help ministries**. Pray for the impact of:

a) **Literature distribution**. The prodigious growth of the writing, publishing and distributing of Christian literature has been a major factor in breaking down opposition to the gospel. **EHC** teams are in the process of giving literature out to nearly every home in India for the *third* time. By 1991, 415 million pieces of literature had been distributed with 4.5 million responses and the formation of 8,000 village fellowships. **OM** teams distributed one million Scripture portions or New Testaments and two million tracts in 1989; it is estimated that 250 million or more have been exposed to the gospel through these teams. **SGM** dispatches around five million Scripture portions to India annually.

b) **Christian publishing and bookstores**. Publishers must contend with lack of local writing talent and high costs in a poor land, but many locally-produced books have been printed and sold in large numbers. The Evangelical Literature Fellowship of India is a major coordinating body. Pray for the **Gospel Literature Service** in Bombay (publishing books, tracts, etc.), the **Evangelical Literature Service** (CLC) in Madras (35 full-time workers, eight stores, 45 book titles published annually), and **OM Books** (publishing and nationwide distribution). There are only 260 known Christian bookstores in the country, and 330 Christian literature agencies.

c) **Bible Correspondence Courses** sent out from 60–70 centres. These have proved fruitful. The centre linked with **TEAM** has courses in 22 languages. The **ICI** (AoG) sends out courses in 11 languages, with two million having completed at least one course.

d) **The Bible Society** with its long and remarkable ministry, distributing 90-100 million portions of Scripture or Bibles annually. Other organizations are also supplying and distributing Scriptures – such as **World Home Bible League, Bibles for the World**, and **Bharatiya Bible League**.

e) **Bible translation** – a major need. A new effort as great as that of William Carey and his team 180 years ago should be mounted. At least 13 NTs must be revised and maybe up to 236 languages need translation teams. A new colloquial Hindi Bible has been published. There are 58 languages in which work is in progress. **Indian Institute of Cross-Cultural Communication** (India Missions Association) provides training in linguistics and is monitoring 25 translation projects. **IEM** workers are translating 12 NTs. FMPB, India Bible Translators and others are also involved in translation programmes. Pray for more Indian Bible translators.

f) **The Global Recordings Network** (GRn) with a unique ministry in India's complex linguistic diversity. There are now recordings on cassettes and records in 312 languages and dialects. **World Cassette Outreach** aims to produce the New Testament on cassette for all minority groups by the year 2000.

g) **Christian medical work**. This has had to be streamlined with the reduction in missionary staff. **The Christian Medical Assoc.** has the oversight of 430 institutions with both Indian and expatriate medical workers. **The Emmanuel Hospitals Assoc.** has responsibility for all the institutions that were run by evangelical missions. Pray that the witness going out from these hospitals to the many patients may lead many to seek the Saviour. Pray for the **Evangelical Medical Fellowship of India** and **Evangelical Nurses Fellowship** with groups in many hospitals. All over India the proportion of Christian medical workers is high; pray that many non-Christians may be won to Jesus through them.

h) **Christian radio** which has won a huge audience among Christians and non-Christians. Although there is no Christian broadcasting from stations within India, more than 20 studios prepare programmes for broadcasting by **TWR** Sri Lanka and Guam (24 languages), **FEBA** Seychelles (18 languages and 250 programmes a week) and **FEBC** Manila (4). Weekly there are 295 hours of broadcasting in a total of 35 languages. TWR broadcasts in the early morning have gained an audience of millions. Pray for wise long-term strategies that will lead to effective evangelism and church planting – perhaps by radio alone. Pray also for the inter-agency **World by 2000 radio vision**; there are still 21 languages of over one million speakers without Christian broadcasting and for which talent and resources must be found.

i) **The *Jesus* film**. This is complete or in production in 22 languages, and a further 33 are targeted for 1993. Over 40 teams show the film. Pray for safety for the teams, especially in north India. Pray for the wide dissemination of video cassettes for showing in homes and backyard cinemas.

13. **Indians in other lands** number 13 million. There are large numbers who have emigrated to the Americas (USA 500,000; Trinidad 430,000; Canada 250,000; Suriname 156,000), Europe (UK

800,000), Africa (South Africa 900,000; Mauritius 701,000; Kenya 137,000), Pacific (Fiji 340,000; Australia), Asia (Nepal 3,800,000; Malaysia 1,170,000; Sri Lanka Tamil 1,028,000; Myanmar). A further one million are migrant workers in the Middle East. In some of these communities many have become Christians – as in South Africa, USA and Mauritius; in others there has been relatively little response. Pray that expatriate Indian Christians may be called as witnesses to their land of origin. Visas are easier for them to obtain.

INDIA – STATES

June 3

Most of these states are far larger than the majority of nations dealt with in far more detail elsewhere in this book, yet limitations of space permit only a brief description of each below.

Note: The Peoples/languages percentages do not add up to 100%; there is considerable overlap.

ANDHRA PRADESH

Area 275,000 sq.km. India's fifth largest state – in southeast.

Population 66,355,000. People per sq.km. 241.

Peoples/languages 167. Telugu 85%, Urdu 8%; Hindi 2.6%; Tamil 1.2%; Scheduled castes (59) 15%; Scheduled tribes (33) 5.9%. Largest: Koya 386,000; Konda 245,000; Saora 110,000; Jatapu 100,000; Bagatya 97,000; Goudu 60,000; Kammara 48,000; Gadaba 34,000; Chenchu 33,000.

Religion: Hindu 88%. Muslim 8.5%. Christian 3.5%.

1. **Andhra Pradesh** has the third largest Christian population of any Indian state with a total of possibly 2.3 million (1.4 million officially). 90% of Christians come from scheduled and backward castes. Conversions continue to take place among all castes and tribal peoples. Pray that present outreach by churches and indigenous cross-cultural missions may increase despite opposition.

2. **The unreached:**
a) **Forward castes**. Only a few of these have been penetrated with the gospel.
b) **Muslims**, a close-knit Urdu-speaking community. Little is being done to reach them.
c) **Tribal peoples**. Most are still unreached with no known Christians, with significant breakthroughs only among the Saora (**CBIM**), Koya, Lambadi, Konda and Chenchu (IEM, Christian Outreach, Uplifting New Tribes and others), though Indian missions have commenced work in 11 other tribes.

ARUNACHAL PRADESH

Area 89,000 sq.km. Remote and mountainous, bordering on China and Myanmar. Politically isolated and sensitive.

Population 858,000. People per sq.km. 10.

Peoples/languages 21 tribal groups (many sub-groups). Largest: Adi 186,000; Nissi 150,000; Tagin 57,000; Mishmi 56,000; Wanchoo 54,000; Nocte 51,000; Monpa 32,000; Akpatani 25,000; Tangsa 25,000. Bengali 7.5%. Hindi 4%.

Religion: Est. Animist 68.5%; Christian 5% in 1981 (maybe 10% in 1991); Buddhist 13.7%; Hindu 12%; Muslim 0.8%.

1. **Praise God for the growth of the Church amid severe persecution**. Strenuous efforts by the authorities in the late '70s and early '80s to prevent evangelism and persecute Christians have failed, and persecution has ended. In 1971 only 0.8% of the population was Christian. The Nissi have 220 churches today, the Adi over 300, and the Tangsa may be 30% Christian. However, restrictive legislation has yet to be repealed. Pray that constitutionally guaranteed freedoms may be granted to Christians.

2. **There are plans to reach every tribe by the year 2000**. Pray for Arunachal Pradesh to become majority Christian by then. Indigenous Christians, refugee Christians from Myanmar, and Indian mission agencies from Nagaland, Manipur, Mizoram and other states have planted churches in more than nine peoples. Only the Tangsa and Adi languages have a New Testament. Much translation work is needed.

3. **The unreached.**
a) **The Buddhist peoples** of the west adjoining Bhutan – the Monpa, Memba, Mishmi, Sherdukpen and Sulung – are more resistant to the gospel.
b) **The animist peoples** of the centre and west have a complex and expensive sacrificial system, but are more receptive.

June 4

ASSAM

Area 78,000 sq.km. Dominated by the Brahmaputra River.

Population 22,295,000. People per sq.km. 284.

Peoples/languages 60. Assamese 55%; Bengali 25%; Nepali; etc. 8%; Scheduled castes (16) 6.2%; Namasudra 370,000. Scheduled tribes (23) 12%. Largest: Kumaoni 1,705,000; Munda 1,060,000; Bore 840,000; Boro 510,000; Mizo 371,000; Mikir 244,000; Rabha 191,000; Lalung 131,000; Miri 110,000.

Religion: Hindu 70.9%; Muslim 24%; Christian 4.7% (Catholic 0.9%, Protestant 3.8%); Buddhist 0.3%.

1. **Christian growth has been fast among the receptive tribal peoples.** The largest churches are Baptist, Lutheran and Presbyterian among the Lushai (Mizo), Pawi, Mikir and Garo who are majority Christian. Naga and Mizo missionaries have continued what Western missionaries started and have had success in hitherto unreached groups. Lack of evangelists, church planters, Bible teachers and translators limits faster growth.
2. **The unreached:**
a) **The indigenous majority Assamese** are mostly Hindu. They could one day become a minority in their own state because of illegal Muslim Bengali immigration from Bangladesh. This has resulted in bitter violence and killings, but an amicable settlement was achieved in 1985. Pray that the new climate of peace may be conducive to the spread of the gospel. Pray, too, that the relatively few Christian Assamese and Bengali may exercise a loving ministry among the two estranged peoples, and that effective outreach to Hindu and Muslim alike might be expanded.
b) **Some tribal groups** are only partially evangelized such as the Boro, Miri, Munda, Kachari, yet churches are being planted among them. Other groups such as the Bodo and Rabha remain unreached.

June 5

BIHAR

Area 174,000 sq.km. Ganges plain in north; wooded, mineral-bearing hills in south.

Population 86,339,000. People per sq.km. 497. One of the poorest and least literate populations in India.

People/languages 77+. Hindi 44%; Hindi dialects 35% (Bhojpuri, Maithili, Magai); Urdu 9%; Bengali 2.5%; Scheduled castes (23) 14.1%, most speaking Sadani Bhojpuri; Scheduled tribes (30) 8.5%. Largest: Santal 2,648,000; Oraon 1,288,000; Munda 1,063,000; Ho 742,000; Kharwar 205,000; Kharia 187,000; Bhumij 187,000; Lohara 172,000; Mahli 110,000.

Religion: Hindu 81.5%; Muslim 14.8%; Christian 1.97% (officially 1.06% – Catholic 1.64%, Protestant 0.33%); Animist 1.6%.

1. **North Bihar has been known as a graveyard of missions.** The effort expended has yielded meagre fruit among the Hindu and Muslim peoples of the plains. Strongholds of spiritual darkness are still unchallenged.
a) **The 11.7 million forward caste Hindus** have had exposure to the gospel, but the message has not been socially acceptable. Only 3,000 call themselves Christian (0.03% of total).
b) **The 28 million of the backward castes** are marginally more evangelized; about 0.5% are Christian in 42 of the castes, but in at least 36 others there are no known Christians.
c) **The 12.7 million Muslims** are unreached and gradually increasing as a percentage of the population. No ongoing effort is being made to reach them, and only a handful of converts to Christ are known. As a community they are insecure and subject to Hindu mob violence.
d) **The 11.5 million in the Scheduled castes** are 0.7% Christian, but only three of the 30 castes have more than 1% Christian. People movements earlier this century fizzled out. Pray that these abused, despised, illiterate peoples in grinding poverty might find liberty in Christ. The potential

for a harvest is great, but the biggest barrier is lack of prayer-covered, long-term workers. The **Gospel Echoing Missionary Society** is working among them.
Tribal peoples are agitating for their own state, Jharkand, as a means of escaping exploitation by more powerful Hindu groups.

2. **About 75% of all Christians are southern tribal peoples.** They are isolated by language and culture and despised by other Biharis. A major impact was made by Catholic, Lutheran and Anglican missionaries, but lack of Scriptures and literature in the local languages, low literacy and limited teaching have made nominalism a major problem. Pray for revival among the Santal, Kharia, Munda, Oraon, Lohara and Ho that will bring a missions vision both for the ten animistic tribes with few believers and for all Biharis. There is growth through the pioneer work of the Friends Missionary Prayer Band among the Pahari and Malto. The National Missionary Society, **IMS** and **IBT** also work among the Bihar tribal peoples.

GOA

Area 3,660 sq.km. Portuguese colony 1510-1961. Full statehood 1987.

Population 1,169,000. People per sq.km. 319.

Peoples/languages. Konkani 60%; Marathi 25%; Gujarati 7%; Kannada 3.2%.

Religion: Hindu 64.5%; Christian 31.2% (almost entirely Catholic); Muslim 4%; Other 0.3%.

1. **Traditional Catholicism** is the legacy of centuries of Portuguese rule. Hindu beliefs and customs are interwoven with Christianity. New life in Christ and a clear understanding of biblical Christianity are both urgent needs. Protestants are only around 1,000 in number and churches very few. There is not an adequate Konkani Bible, nor evangelical literature in the language.

2. **Workers** able to communicate in Konkani are a great need. There are few labourers to reach nominal Catholics, Hindus or Muslims.

GUJARAT

Area 196,000 sq.km. Coastal state adjoining Pakistan.

Population 41,174,000. People per sq.km. 210.

Peoples/languages 64. Gujarati 70.7%; Marwari 20%; Sindhi 2.1%; Hindi 2.1%; Urdu 1.8%; Marathi 1.1%. Scheduled castes (30) 7.2%. Scheduled tribes (29) 14.2%. Largest: Bhil 2,500,000; Dubla 534,000; Dhodia 494,000; Garasia 381,000; Gamit 380,000; Rathawas 265,000; Chaudhri 245,000; Kukna 202,000; Dhanka 191,000; Varli 173,000.

Religion: Hindu 89.4%; Muslim 8.9%; Jain 1.2%, Christian 0.5% (Catholic 0.13%, Protestant 0.37%).

1. Gujarat is Gandhi's birth place. Several extremist Hindu groups have polarized society by violent actions against scheduled caste groups, Muslims and Christians. Pray that these events may open the eyes of many to the Truth. Most sections of the community are closed to the gospel. Sadly, the thinking in the traditional Christian community has been Hinduized.

2. **The Christian Church** is predominantly Catholic, Church of North India and Methodist. Many other smaller evangelical denominations are also present (**CMA**, Salvation Army, **TEAM**, Brethren and Pentecostal). Generally, compromise with Hinduism, divisions and lack of outreach have sapped Christian spiritual life. The Christian percentage of the population dropped from 0.44% in 1961 to 0.39% in 1981. The impact of Methodist Church outreach, Salvation Army, **OM** teams, and new Indian missionary efforts (**IEM, FMPB**, IMS, Church Growth Missionary Movement and others) among tribals has reversed this trend, with one church a week being planted in the south. Many Bhil, Kukna, Gamit, Chaudhri, Garasia, Koli, Dhodia and others have come to Christ – possibly increasing the percentage of Christians in the state to 0.5%. Pray that this turning to God may continue unchecked by external opposition or internal failures.

3. **The unreached.** While some tribal peoples are responding to the gospel, much need remains. Pray out labourers for:

a) **Saurashtra,** the southwest peninsula, which has 12 million people and seven Christian congregations. The Amreli district has one million people and just one church.
b) **North Gujarat,** which has more Muslims. There are very few Christians in the area.
c) **Unreached caste groups.** The Scheduled caste groups – the Bhangi, Nadia and Pasi – are urbanized and potentially responsive.
d) **The 20 tribal peoples** with little or no existing outreach – the larger being the Dubla, Dhanka and Rathawa.
e) **The Parsees** (11,000 of India's 75,000 are in Gujarat), a well-educated, wealthy people of Persian origin who follow the Zoroastrian religion. Few have ever believed, and little work has been attempted.

4. **Large Gujarati communities** have grown up in east and central Africa and in Britain. Most have become wealthy traders but, although surrounded by Christians, there has been little success in evangelism.

| June 6 |

HARYANA

Area 44,000 sq.km. Between Delhi and Punjab on plains of Ganges.

Population 16,317,000. People per sq.km. 370.

Peoples/languages. Hindi 88.8%; Panjabi 9.2%; Urdu 1.8%; Scheduled castes (37) 19%.

Religion: Hindu 89.3%; Sikh 6.2%; Muslim 4.1%; Jain 0.27%: Christian 0.08% (Catholic 0.02%, Protestant 0.06%).

1. **Hindu revival movements** are increasingly active, and are very anti-Christian. The church is woefully weak and in gradual decline. Pray that the spiritual powers in this state may be disarmed and captives released, and that revival may come to the churches.

2. **The unreached.** Haryana is one of India's least evangelized states. Indian agencies are pioneering work among the eight million Jat and 1.5 million Chamar castes (**FMPB,** Indian Inland Mission), and the Sikhs (Indian Inland Mission). Pray for a response. Pray also for the unreached Muslims and Jains. There is nothing of the Bible translated into the local language, Haryanavi.

HIMACHAL PRADESH

Area 56,000 sq.km. Mountainous; the foothills of the Himalayas.

Population 5,111,000. People per sq.km. 91.

Peoples/languages (210). Hindi 89%; however most actually speak Pahari, a related language with many dialects but closer to Panjabi. Panjabi 5.8%. Scheduled castes (56) 24.6%. Scheduled tribes (8) 4.6%: Gaddi 129,000; Lahuli 15,000.

Religion: Hindu 95.9%; Muslim 1.7%; Buddhist 1.2%; Sikhs 1.1%; Christian 0.08%.

1. **Himachal Pradesh** is India's least evangelized state. The church is small, weak and not growing. Pray that Christians may mobilize to redress this tragic situation by sending missionaries. It is a centre of Hindu pilgrimages in the Himalayas, so strong spiritual powers need to be bound in Jesus' name.

2. **Christian outreach is limited. IEM** have a pioneer church-planting work in the Kullu district and Shimla, the capital, but there are only three congregations and 50 believers. **FMPB** and Indian Inland Mission are also working in the state. There is a fierce loyalty to idols and animistic Hinduism which needs to be broken. The Buddhist Lahuli are unreached.

| June 7 |

JAMMU and KASHMIR

Area 222,000, but of this 83,000 sq.km. in the north and west was seized by Pakistan in 1947 and 38,000 sq.km. in remote Himalayan Ladakh in 1950 by China. The disputed territory has provoked three wars with Pakistan and a rapidly growing Muslim revolt against Indian rule which, if successful, threatens the integrity of all India.

Population 7,718,700. People per sq.km. 42.

Peoples/languages 74. Kashmiri 52%; Hindi 17%, but many actually speaking Dogri; Panjabi 2.7%. Urdu widely spoken. Scheduled castes (13) 8.3%. Tibetan peoples: Balti 150,000; Brukpa 17,000; Changla 9,000; Zanskar 8,000; Ladakhi 7,000.

Religion: Muslim 64.2%, Hindu 32.2%, Sikh 2.2%, Buddhist 1.2%, Christian 0.16%.

1. **Kashmir has become ungovernable** with numerous Muslim guerrilla groups contesting India's rule. Violence and atrocities have become commonplace. Pray for wise statesmanship to resolve this half-century conflict about Kashmir's future, and for a government for Kashmir that promotes religious tolerance and freedom.

2. **Kashmir is spiritually poverty-stricken.** There are only about 12,000 Christians, most are nominal and either low-caste Hindu or immigrant in origin. Evangelical believers number a few thousand, most being Pentecostal. Pray for workers, open hearts and the planting of new groups of believers.

3. **Missionary activity** has always been limited – Central Asian Mission and **WEC** in the past, but now the **Kashmir Evangelical Fellowship**, Indian Evangelical Team and others are seeking to reach a few of the peoples. Pray for the protection and fruitfulness of these workers living and working in tense and dangerous situations.

4. **Unreached peoples.** All are in this category. Pray for:
   a) **Kashmiri Muslims** who have become more militant for their faith in the uprising. There are a number of smaller Muslim peoples such as the Baltis and Gujars who are unreached. Only about 30 Christians have come from within the Muslim community, and in the Muslim uprising of the late '80s some of these were martyred, and churches destroyed. Helping Hands International has a ministry among them.
   b) **Tibetan Buddhists** from the groups named above in the mountainous north and northeast who have been only marginally evangelized. The Moravians have a small work in Ladakh with three churches and only 150 believers.
   c) **The high-caste Brahmin Pandits of Kashmir**, only 17% of the population but very influential. There are no known Christians. Pull down this stronghold by prayer.
   d) **The Dogras of Jammu.** They have had some Christian outreach, but there are few believers.

KARNATAKA

Area 192,000 sq.km. Southwestern coastal state.

Population 44,806,000. People per sq.km. 234.

Peoples/languages 19. Kannada 66% with many dialect variations; Urdu 9.5%, most speaking Deccani, distantly related to Urdu; Telugu 8.1%; Marathi 3.8%; Hindi 1.8%; Malayalam 1.6%. All castes 250. Scheduled castes (101) 15%. Scheduled tribes (49) 4.9%. Largest: Kol 158,000; Dhodia 145,000; Naikdda 93,000; Zadmali 77,000.

Religion: Hindu 85.4%; Muslim 11.6%; Christian 2.1%, Jain 0.8%.

1. **Karnataka is the least receptive of India's southern states.** Almost all the Hindu caste groups and the Scheduled tribes are unreached. The few Christians are culturally isolated from them, and few have a vision to evangelize outside their community. Almost all Christians are concentrated in Bangalore (6.7% Christian) and the south of the state. The Deccani Muslims number 60,000, but there are only 100 Christians among them.

2. **Bangalore City** is the Indian headquarters for many Christian churches, Indian missions (**IEM**, Quiet Corner) and international agencies (**The Bible Society**, Language Recordings India (**GRn**), **SGM, EHC**, Asia Graduate School of Theology, International Correspondence School of **AoG**, India Bible League, **FEBA**, etc.) and theological institutions. The Methodists and CSI are strong in the area. Pray that Bangalore's privileged Christian community may be revived.

KERALA

June 8

Area 39,000 sq.km. The most southwesterly state.

Population 29,033,000. People per sq.km. 747. India's most literate, prosperous and densely populated state.

Peoples/languages 63. Malayali 96%; Tamil 2.3%. All castes 423. Scheduled castes (68) 10%. Scheduled tribes (35) 1%.

Religion: Hindu 57%; Muslim 23%; Christian 20% (Syrian Orthodox 6.7%, Catholic 8.9%, Protestant and Mar Thoma Syrians 4.4%.)

1. **The Syrian Christians,** with links to the Syrian Jacobite Church, have a tradition that they are direct descendants of those evangelized by the Apostle Thomas. They form the majority of Kerala's Christians and are members of Orthodox, Catholic and Protestant denominations. They have high social status but have become little more than a caste within Hindu society, and few have broken out to become vital witnesses to those of other cultures. There are, therefore, few converts out of non-Christian religions in the churches. Pray that Ephesians 2:13–17 may be true for these Christians.

2. **Kerala has numerous Protestant denominations and evangelistic agencies.** Movings of the Spirit over the last 100 years brought multitudes of both nominal Syrian Christians and low-caste Hindus to faith in Christ. Over the past 30 years the Christian percentage of the population has declined, largely through migration all over India and the world. There are strong mainline, Brethren and Pentecostal congregations. Casteism within the churches is an unmentioned reality, and foreign funds and materialism have provoked divisions. A revived Church in Kerala would have a deep impact on all of India because of the level of education, wealth and dynamism of many Christians – many of whom live all over India.

3. **Unreached peoples.** Some Christians in Kerala are beginning to catch a missionary vision for the unreached religious, caste and tribal groups in their state and beyond. Yet social barriers are high, and believers need to be liberated from the spirit of caste both to evangelize other social groups and welcome converts as brethren in their fellowships.

a) **Of the 35 small tribal groups only three or four have significant Christian groups** and ten others a handful of believers. Most are Hindus, animists or demon worshippers. Only seven have over 10,000 people. Kerala Christians need to catch a vision to reach them – praise God a few have.

b) **The Malabar Muslims or Mapilla** are numerous in the north of Kerala and number 6.6 million. The ministry of **OM, Helping Hands Intl** and others has led to several thousand known conversions and also groups of believers, but resistance to the gospel is high and new Christians have suffered much. Pray for those involved in this arduous and costly ministry.

c) **Of the higher and 68 Scheduled castes of Hindus,** there have been people movements to Christianity from among only six or seven of the latter.

MADHYA PRADESH

Area 443,000 sq.km. India's biggest state; in the centre of the country. Poor and underdeveloped.

Population 66,135,000. People per sq.km. 149.

Peoples/languages 223. Hindi 84%; Marathi 2.3%; Urdu 2.2%; Oriya 1.1%. Scheduled castes (47) 14%. Scheduled tribes (60) 23%. Largest: Gond 4,394,000; Halba 2,341,000; Bhil 2,131,000; Kol 510,000; Oraon 500,000; Dubla 383,000; Seharia 260,000; Baiga 239,000; Bhumia 159,000; Bhatra 96,000; Pardhan 94,000; Patelia 93,000; Korwa 91,000; Nagesia 82,000; Sawar 80,000.

Religion: Hindu 92.4%. (Most of the Scheduled castes and tribes are actually animists.) Muslim 5.2%; Jain 0.85%; Christian 0.70%; Sikh 0.27%; Buddhist 0.14%.

1. **This state was one of the last to open up for missions and is one of the most resistant to Christianity.** It is strongly Hindu with stern laws limiting conversions to Christianity. The small Christian community is growing, but slowly. The great majority of Christians are Catholic; many are in Church of North India or Lutherans and Mennonites, and most are Scheduled caste or tribal in origin. Pray for the overturning of opposition to the gospel in high places and for the frustration of extremist Hindu efforts to "reconvert" Christians – thousands of tribal peoples have been forced to renounce Christianity. The whole state is a pioneer mission field, and could be responsive were there to be more evangelistic outreach.

2. **There are numerous tribal peoples** – especially in the southern three districts where nine tribal groups make up 80% of the population. There are now believers in most of them through the work of **IEM, FMPB,** India Church Growth Mission (ICGM), Evangelical Churches of India, the Discipleship Centre and a number of denominational missions. However, this is still a tough pioneer field with many unbreached strongholds of the enemy of souls.

3. **Bible translation** is a major need. Translation work is in progress in four languages (ICGM), but a further 30 languages await a New Testament translation.

MAHARASHTRA

Area 308,000 sq.km. India's most urbanized and industrialized state.

Population 78,707,000. People per sq.km. 256.

Peoples/languages 226. Marathi 73.6%; Urdu 6.9%; Hindi 6.7%; Telugu 1.5%; Kannada 1.5%. Scheduled castes (59) 7.1%. Scheduled tribes (47) 9.1%. Largest: Bhil 916,000; Gond 447,000; Varli 397,000; Korku 356,000; Thakur 241,000; Kathodi 198,000; Koli 193,000; Gamit 174,000; Malvi 123,000; Andh 103,000.

Religion: Hindu 80.4%; Muslim 10%; Buddhist 6.2%; Jain 1.6%; Christian 1.5% (Catholic 1.35%, Protestant 0.15%).

1. **Bombay** not only has the second highest Christian population of any major city in India (5%), but also has a reputation for vice, child prostitution and a frightening mushrooming of AIDS. There are many Catholics and a growing number of Protestant denominations and churches. Pray that the Christians may be "salt and light" in their city. Bombay New Life Fellowship has won many non-Christians through a massive Scripture distribution campaign.

2. **Christians** are far fewer outside the cities of Bombay and Pune. Some 40% never attend church; court cases, bitterness and quarrelling are common among them. The Protestant community is scattered and very small, and few of them have a personal experience of salvation. In the early '80s **OM**'s Love Maharashtra and in the '90s **EHC**'s F.T.-5000 Project have helped to mobilize many Christians for extensive literature distribution campaigns. Pray that revival, growth and outreach may become part of the life of the churches.

3. **Unreached areas and peoples:**
a) **Rural areas** are neglected and the percentage of Christians is very low.
b) **Many Hindu caste groups, Muslims and Buddhists** are unreached, and little effective evangelism and church planting is being directed to them. Pray for **EHC**, FMPB, Maharashtra Village Movement (MVM), Love Maharashtra and others that are seeking to reach them.
c) **Tribal groups** such as the Gond, Bhil, Korku and Kolam have not responded readily to the gospel. **IEM** has an outreach to them and the Gowli caste group. MVM and a number of other Indian agencies are pioneering another 15 groups; they are joined by international missions such as **TEAM**, IMS, NMS and CNI. Most other tribe and caste groups remain unreached.
d) **The Jains.** 1.2 million of India's 3.5 million live in Maharashtra. This prosperous community with their own religion, derived from Hinduism, has scarcely been touched with the gospel in a culturally appropriate way.

MANIPUR

Area 22,000 sq.km. On Myanmar (Burma) border.

Population 1,827,000. People per sq.km. 82

Peoples/languages: Meitei 1,226,000. Scheduled castes (7) 1.3%. Scheduled tribes (29) 27.3%. Largest: Chin 184,000; Aimol 115,000; Thadou 82,000; Thangkhul 80,000.

Religion: Hindu 59%; Christian 34% (Catholic 3%, Protestant 31%); Muslim 6%; Other 1%.

1. **Nearly all the tribal people have become Protestant over the past 80 years.** Despite some persecution from Hindus, churches have multiplied. Most numerous are Baptists followed by Presbyterians and 14 other denominations. This state has the potential to become majority Christian in the '90s. Pray that this may be so. Drug addiction and AIDS are major problems in the state.

2. **The less reached.**
a) **The majority Meitei are Hindu,** but nationalism is lowering commitment to Indian Hinduism. The number of Christians among them more than doubled to 10,000 in the '80s. The Meitei Bible has recently been published.

b) **Muslims** and **Scheduled caste** groups have been neglected.

c) **Nepalis**. There are some churches among them, but the majority are still Hindu.
There are over 12 indigenous mission agencies ministering in the state.

MEGHALAYA

Area 22,000 sq.km. Mountainous state on Bangladesh's northern border. Average annual rainfall is 12 metres – the world's highest.

Population 1,761,000. People per sq.km. 78.

Peoples/languages. Scheduled tribes (14) 80.6%. Largest: Khasi 630,000; Garo 446,000; Hajong 26,000. Caste Hindus 18.3%; Scheduled castes 0.4%: Bengali 100,000; Assamese 25,000; Hindi 13,000.

Religion: Christian 57%; Animist/other 22%; Hindu 17%; Muslim 4%.

1. **Praise God for the turning to the Lord in Meghalaya.** Most Khasis are Presbyterian and most Garos Baptists. There are a number of other denominations in the state.

2. **The less reached.** Some of the smaller tribes – notably the Hajong, Mikir and others – have been less responsive and remain entrenched in their animism. The Hindu minority has been little affected by the gospel.

June 11

MIZORAM

Area 21,000. Wedged between Bangladesh and Myanmar.

Population 686,000. People per sq.km. 33.

Peoples/languages. Scheduled tribes (14) 94%. Largest: Mizo (Lushai) 340,000; Chakma 31,000; Pawi 28,000; Lakher 18,000.

Religion. Christian 85%; Buddhist 8%; Hindu 7%.

1. **Nearly all indigenous peoples are now Christian**. Great awakenings and recent revival have filled the churches – Presbyterian, Baptist and large indigenous denominations predominating. Secularization and denominational divisions are trends that could hamper vision.

2. **Praise God for the dynamic missions movement** that has blossomed. No nation on earth has sent out a higher proportion of their people as missionaries. There may now be nearly 1,000 Mizo missionaries serving in other parts of India and beyond.

3. **The less reached.** The Buddhist Chakma are being intensively evangelized by Mizo, and churches are multiplying. The **Bangladeshi refugees** and the **Hindu** population are needy.

NAGALAND

Area 16,500 sq.km. Mountainous northeastern border with Myanmar (Burma).

Population 1,218,000. People per sq.km. 73

Peoples/languages: Naga tribes (16 tribes, 60 dialects/languages) 84%. Other 16%; Hindi, Bengali, Nepali, Assamese.

Religion: Christian 85%; Hindu 11%; Muslim 1.8%; Other 2.2%.

1. **The majority of Nagas are Baptists** – in this Nagaland is a state unique in the world. Almost all Nagas are Christian. Revivals since 1976 have brought new life, fervour and a surge of evangelistic and missions outreach. More recently inter-ethnic divisions, compromise over corruption by state leaders, and complacency have dampened spiritual ardour. In-depth Bible teaching is needed; most pastors tend to be evangelists.

2. **Naga Christians are isolated** from the mainstream of Christians due to the geographic and political sensitivity of their area. There is a low-level guerrilla campaign for Naga independence. Pray that Christians may enjoy more helpful interactive fellowship with the Body of Christ worldwide.

3. **Missionary vision blossomed** as a result of revival. Christians made a solemn covenant in 1980 to live for, and further, world evangelization. They are trusting God that 10,000 missionaries will be sent from Nagaland. Pray for Naga mission agencies and missionaries in surrounding states, across India and beyond, and pray that this vision might be fulfilled – there were around 500 Naga missionaries in 1990.

ORISSA

June 12

Area 156,000 sq.km. Eastern coastal state.

Population 31,512,000. People per sq.km. 202

Peoples/languages 68. Oriya 82%; Tamil 2.3%; Hindi 2.3%; Bengali 1.5%; Urdu 1.5%: Telugu 1.4%. Scheduled castes (93) 15.1%. Scheduled tribes (62) 23.1%. Largest: Khond 1,200,000; Gond 686,000; Santal 625,000; Saora 483,000; Kolha 426,000; Shabar 330,000; Munda 305,000; Paroja 285,000; Bhottada 270,000; Bhuiya 260,000; Kisan 250,000; Kol 236,500; Oraon 226,000; Bhumiji 202,000; Siyal 184,000; Bathudi 180,000; Kharia 166,000; Bhumiya 85,000; Koya 81,000.

Religion: Hindu 94.8% (including many animist tribal people), Christian 2% (Catholic 0.8%, Protestant 1.2%), Muslim 1.7%, Animist 1%.

1. **Praise God for steady growth in the number of Christians and churches** despite strong opposition from violent Hindu fanatics. Many churches have been destroyed and converts compelled to revert to Hinduism. Anti-conversion laws are in operation. Pray that Christians may manifest both fortitude and the love of Christ for their persecutors, and that growth may continue.

2. **Tribal peoples of Orissa** are the most responsive to the gospel, as are their brethren in adjoining south Bihar. The Oraon (40% Christian), Kharia (37%), Munda (34%), Binhjia (6.4%), Saora (6%), Kisan (5%), Kol (5%) and Khond (2%) have significant numbers of Christians. Their illiteracy, economic deprivation and political marginalization slow what could be a large movement to Christ. Numerous denominations and agencies work among them. There is an exciting development of missions vision among these believers.

3. **Unreached peoples abound.**
a) **The forward (high) castes** have never been confronted with the claims of Christ.
b) **The 93 Scheduled castes** – all but one are untouched by the gospel.
c) **The tribals.** Of the 62 groups, 20 are less than 0.1% Christian and 42 less than 1% Christian. Pray specifically for a breakthrough among the Bhathudi, Bhottada, Bhuiya, Bhumiji, Gond, Kolho, Paraja, Santal, Siyal and Koya.

4. **Literacy is low** – 52% of the population, 70% of the Scheduled castes and tribes, and 89% of all women cannot read. Pray for effective use of Scripture cassettes, and other audio-visual means of communicating the gospel.

PUNJAB

Area 50,400 sq.km. Northwestern India; one of the most productive agricultural regions of the country.

Population 20,191,000. People per sq.km. 401.

Peoples/languages. Panjabi 85%; Hindi 14.6%; Scheduled castes (37) 27%.

Religion: Sikh 63.6%, Hindu 34%, Christian 1.1% (Catholic 0.18%, Protestant 0.92%); Muslim 1%.

1. **Punjab, India's only state with a Sikh majority,** has been the scene of a violent and bitter guerrilla war with over 15,000 deaths, the assassination of Prime Minister Indira Gandhi in 1984, alienation of the Sikh and Hindu communities and a breakdown of the economic and social fabric of the state. The guerrillas' aim is the establishment of a Sikh state, Khalistan. A solution to the tragedy looks distant, but pray that one may be found. Pray that these events may open the hearts of many to the Prince of peace. It is reported that some Sikh guerrillas have come to Christ.

2. **Most of the Christian community originated in the last century in mass movements** from depressed Chamar and Chuhra castes. Christians are under-privileged, generally nominal and discouraged. May God revive them! Evangelism through Pentecostal churches and the Indian Evangelical Team is bearing fruit, halting the decline in numbers. **IET** has 320 workers in Punjab, Haryana, Orissa, and other states and has already planted 352 churches. The Ludhiana Christian Medical College and Hospital has a worldwide reputation for Christian care and witness. Pray for a dynamic Panjabi Church to emerge.

3. **The unreached.** Only two of the caste groups have shown any response to the gospel. The Sikh Jat have recently become more open, with some churches planted among them through the ministry of Indian Evangelical Team. Slum dwellers in Chandigarh are responding through the ministry of Baptists.

June 13

RAJASTHAN

Area 342,000. An arid state abutting on Pakistan.

Population 43,881,000. People per sq.km. 128

Peoples/languages: Hindi 90%, using the Rajasthani dialect; Urdu 2.2%; Panjabi 2.1%; Sindhi 0.8%. Scheduled castes (81) 17%. Scheduled tribes (12) 12.2%. Largest: Mina 2,070,000; Bhil 491,000; Garasia 71,000; Seharia 36,000; Damor 20,000.

Religion: Hindu 89%; Muslim 7.5%, Jain 1.8%; Sikh 1.5%, Christian 0.12% (Catholic 0.07%, Protestant 0.05%).

1. **Christians are a tiny minority within minority castes and tribes.** There are about 50,000 Christians in the state. Pray for the little CNI, Pentecostal and Brethren congregations. Anti-conversion laws and Hindu pressures have not stopped the steady growth in number of believers through literature distribution, radio evangelism (**TWR** Sri Lanka) and Bible correspondence courses. Most evangelism has been through six Indian missions, **OM**, **EHC**, Rajasthan Bible Institute teams and National Missionary Movement. Only 14 of the 25 districts have any established Christian work.

2. **Unreached peoples:**
a) **The Bhil** (**IEM**), **Mina** (Indian Inland Mission, Pentecostals), Garasia (**IEM**) and others are Hindu/animist and only now beginning to respond to the gospel. Most of the Christians are of these groups.
b) **The Meo** (2,000,000) are Muslim; no Christians are known.
c) **The higher-caste Hindus,** especially the 12 million warlike Rajputs, the Jats and Marwari, have shown no response to the gospel. Entrenched spiritual powers need to be bound.
d) **Jaipur,** the capital, has 1,500,000 inhabitants, but only 8,000 are Christian; half of these are from south India, and the majority are very nominal. There are only five churches in the city.

SIKKIM

Area 7,100 sq.km. Himalayan state sandwiched between Nepal and Bhutan, and long a buffer state between Tibet (China) and India. Annexed by India in 1975.

Population 406,000. People per sq.km. 57.

Peoples/languages: Nepali 75%. The Nepali language is rapidly becoming the *de facto* state language. Lepcha 14% – the original people; Tibetan (Bhutia) 10%.

Religion: Hindu 67%; Buddhist 28.6%; Christian 2.4%; Muslim 1%; Other 1%.

1. **Christians** have steadily grown in numbers despite persecution at times and the exclusion of Western missionaries since 1980. The two main churches are the CNI and the Free Church started by Finnish missionaries. There are also a number of Pentecostal churches. Denominationalism and disunity have harmed the witness of Christians. Several Indian mission agencies have workers in Sikkim. Pray for the complete evangelization of this state.

2. **The less reached.** Most of the Christians are Lepcha and Nepali, with only a few Tibetans. Many

settlements and villages are without a witness. There is a lack of trained full-time workers. Pray for the **Reach Sikkim Movement** launched in 1992.

TAMIL NADU

Area 130,000 sq.km.. The most southeasterly state, well watered and a with strong agricultural economy.

Population 55,638,000. People per sq.km. 428

Peoples/languages: Tamil 85.4%; Telugu 8.4%; Kannada 2.4%; Urdu 1.8%. Upper caste Brahmin 4%; Backward castes (202) 36%. Scheduled castes (76) 18.3%. Scheduled tribes (36) 1.1%; most very small – largest: Badaga 540,000; Irula 123,000; Kurumans 16,000; Kurumba 15,000.

Religion: Hindu 88.6%; Christian 6.0%; Muslim 5.3%.

1. **Christians number nearly 3.5 million**; growth in a number of caste groups has been significant. Pray that high barriers between castes may be broken down for the gospel to permeate every level of society.

2. **There is a spirit of prayer and revival** in both older and newer Evangelical and Pentecostal denominations. The number and variety of Christian denominations, missions and agencies is large. Many are based in Madras, which is nearly 10% Christian and which has doubled in five years to 1,400 churches – the largest number in a south Asian city. One third of Indian missions and numerous interdenominational agencies have their headquarters in the state. Pray that all this vision and activity may result in fruitful outreach to tribal peoples and north India.

3. **The unreached.** There are 28 Indian mission agencies working in Tamil Nadu, including **IEM**, **FMPB** and India Church Growth Mission.
a) **Over 16 large caste groups** have resisted the gospel.
b) **Tribal groups.** There are 15 tribal groups with no known churches. Only among the Badaga (3% Christian) and Kuruman (6.5%) are there a significant number of churches. The Irula, Kurumba and Toda have just a few believers.
c) **The Tamil-speaking Muslims,** the Labbai, are fairly strongly Islamic. Helping Hands International has an outreach to them.

TRIPURA

Area 10,500 sq.km. Almost an enclave within eastern Bangladesh.

Population 2,775,000. People per sq.km. 262.

Peoples/languages: Bengali 70%; Tripuri 16%; Hindi 1.3%. Scheduled castes (32) 15%. Scheduled tribes (19) 28.5%; largest: Tripuri 345,000; Riang 89,000; Jamatia 47,000; Chakma 40,000; Halam 26,000; Mag 18,000; Noatia 14,000.

Religion: Hindu 87.7% – including Tripuri animists as "Hindu"; Muslim 6.8% (Bengalis); Christian 3% (Tribal peoples); Buddhist 2.5% (Chakma).

1. **The indigenous** peoples are now a minority in their own state. Massive Bengali immigration has occurred over the past 30 years, and this group has become politically dominant. Oppression and social exclusion of tribal peoples led to a violent backlash in 1980, with ongoing guerrilla activity against the migrants, but also to an unprecedented openness to the gospel. A dramatic people movement has been taking place since 1970 in all peoples but the Tripuri. Six tribes are now Christian, and at least seven are rapidly becoming so. There are Christians in every indigenous ethnic group, and their numbers exceed official figures.

2. **Christians have been persecuted** both by animists and by extremist Hindu groups. Pray that Christians may thrive and maintain their witness to non-Christians in spite of communal violence.

3. **The unreached:**
a) **The Bengali majority** is unresponsive because of the turning of tribal peoples to Christ. Little ministry is directed to their evangelization.

b) **The Buddhist Chakma** are slowly responding to the gospel. Over 40,000 Chakma refugees from Bangladesh have taken refuge in Tripura.

c) **The Tripuri** have become more open, and there are now some 30 Baptist churches among them. Most are animists, but Hindu coercion and bribery is used to convert them to Hinduism.

June 15

UTTAR PRADESH

Area 294,000 sq.km. India's strategic heartland and most populous state.

Population 139,031,000. People per sq.km. 470.

Peoples/languages 88: Hindi 90%; Urdu 9.7%. Scheduled castes (66) 21.2%. Scheduled tribes (5) 0.2%. Largest: Tharu 94,000; Jaunsari 78,000; Bhotia 47,000; Buksa 32,000.

Religion: Hindu 79.8%; Muslim 19.6%; Sikh 0.4%; Jain 0.13%; Christian 0.12% (Catholic 0.04%, Protestant 0.08%).

1. **Uttar Pradesh is the home of Hinduism, Buddhism and Jainism,** but has given no home to the gospel. It is one of the darkest and most needy parts of the world. Millions of pilgrims visit Varanasi, the "holy" city of Hinduism on the Ganges River, but few find the Living Water that only Jesus can give. Pray that there might be a major mobilization of prayer on this key state, and that God may give the workers who will turn the tide for the gospel.

2. **Christians are a tiny minority** of outcaste (Chamar) and tribal (Dom) origin. Most are nominal and rarely attend church. There is a stream of reversions to Hinduism. There are only 172 little evangelical churches and fellowships and 17 denominations in the whole state – which means there is almost one church per million people. Evangelists and church planters are desperately few, though there are 12 Bible schools in U.P. Pray for the missionaries of **AoG**, the All India Prayer Fellowship, **IEM**, Friends Missionary Prayer Band, Agape and others who are planting churches in the state.

3. **The unreached are many.** The Hindus of Uttar Pradesh are among the world's least-reached mega-peoples. South and northeastern Indian missions have concentrated more on tribal and scheduled caste groups and less on the politically and economically more powerful Hindu castes. Pray that this may be rectified. Pray also for:

a) **The Hindi-related Bhojpuri** (28,000,000) and Kumaoni (2,000,000) in the east of U.P. who are physically and spiritually poor with very few believers.

b) **The Garhwalis** (1,800,000), largely unresponsive. However, the New Testament was recently completed through the work of IEM and Agape and there are now over 100 believers among them. Christian broadcasting has begun in Garhwali.

c) **The tribal Jaunsari, Tharu and Buksa** who are being reached by a number of Indian missions. Lack of workers, indigenous New Testaments, and significant results give stimulus for prayer.

d) **Muslims** who are a large minority of 27 million, and are frequently victims of Hindu mob violence. The destruction of the Babri mosque in Ayodhya in December 1992 provoked nationwide rioting and destruction and seriously damaged India's social fabric. Several Christian agencies are seeking to reach Muslims, but results are yet meagre.

e) **Students.** They are a challenge! UESI(**IFES**) has 12 student groups for the 24 universities and 407 colleges. Pray for these and for the two staff workers.

June 16

WEST BENGAL

Area 89,000 sq.km. Bordering on Bangladesh (which used to be East Bengal).

Population 67,983,000. People per sq.km. 766.

Peoples/languages: Bengali 86.3%; Hindi 5.9%; Urdu 2.2%; Nepali 1.0%. Scheduled castes (59) 22%. Scheduled tribes (38) 5.6%; largest: Santal 1,844,000; Oraon 400,000; Bhumij 233,000; Kora 129,000; Mahali 67,000; Lodha 63,000; Bhotia 47,000; Mal Pahariya 43,000; Lepcha 20,000.

Religion: Hindu 76.5%, Muslim 22.9%, Christian 0.6% (Catholic 240,000, Protestant 70,000).

1. **Christians are a tiny minority among Bengalis.** Hindu reform movements have coopted Christian ethical elements. Christians are largely nominal, and their life style has often deterred Hindus and Muslims from receiving the gospel. Some reckon that in the whole state there are less than 10,000

born-again believers. This is the area where William Carey gave his life for India's evangelization; pray that the work he founded may be revived again. Pray also for the Reach Bengal Movement which has drawn denominations together in fruitful outreach since its inception in 1991.

2. **Calcutta is a huge and tragic slum** with the lowest urban standard of living in the world. It is named after the Hindu deity Kali, the goddess of destruction. Pray for the destruction of Satan's kingdom there. Pray also for Catholics and Evangelicals alike who seek to share their faith in squalid slums where 4.5 million people live, and in streets where a further million eke out an existence. Only 45 of the 163 congregations in the city are Bengali-speaking.

3. **The majority of Christians in the state are tribal**, mainly Santal, Munda and Oraon. Even these groups are only partially evangelized; others have scarcely been touched with the gospel. There are too few workers to reach them.

4. **Muslims** are in the majority in central districts. They are unevangelized.

THE SEVEN UNION TERRITORIES | June 17 |

Mention is made here of three of the more unique Union Territories. The other four are similar to the states of which they are enclaves: **Chandigarh** (capital of Punjab and Haryana 640,000); **Dadra and Nagar Haveli** (Gujarat 138,000); **Daman and Diu** (Gujarat 101,000) and **Pondicherry** (Tamil Nadu 789,000).

1. **Andaman and Nicobar Islands.** 278,000 inhabitants on 35 islands in the Bay of Bengal. Over 25% of the population of mainland immigrants and indigenous Nicobari (25,000) are Christian. The unreached are the four isolated negrito peoples (only 500 people) and the Hindu (64%) and Muslim (8.6%) Bengali, Hindi, Malayali, Telugu and Tamil immigrants.

2. **Delhi, India's Capital** (9,370,000). With its power, wealth and industries, Delhi is a trend-setting city with significant communities from nearly every ethnic group in India. Only 1% of the population is Christian with 220 congregations and 16 denominations.
a) **Outreach ministries** through the CNI, Baptists, Pentecostals, Evangelical Churches of India, Brethren and the Delhi Bible Fellowship (**TEAM**) need to penetrate many of the unreached population segments. **IEM** has a ministry to the Telugu.
b) **Many India-wide Christian organizations** have headquarters in Delhi – notably Evangelical Fellowship of India, All India Prayer Fellowship, Emmanuel Hospital Association, **TWR**-India. Pray that life and blessing may flow from Delhi to the whole country.

3. **Lakshadweep.** 12 coral atolls and 36 islands in the Arabian Sea. 52,000 people live on its 32 sq.km. Over 95% of the population is ardently Muslim; the rest are Hindu (4%) and Christian (0.7%) immigrants from the mainland. No long-term ministry to these Malayali-speaking Muslims has ever been permitted or attempted.

June 18–27
Asia

Indonesia
(The Republic of Indonesia)

Area 1,920,000 sq.km. 13,500 islands (3,000 inhabited), which span 9,500,000 sq.km. of the Indian/ Pacific Oceans, 24 provinces and three special districts.

Population	Ann. Gr.	Density
1990 181,251,000	1.7 %	94/sq.km.
1995 195,623,000	1.5 %	102/sq.km.

The world's fourth most populous nation. Population density varies from Java's 815 people/sq.km. to Irian Jaya's 4/sq.km.

Peoples. Major peoples (see under separate islands for more detail).

Malay 94%. Javanese 75,200,000; Sundanese 31,000,000; Madurese 12,500,000; Minangkabau 5,900,000; Batak 5,800,000; Sumatra Malay 5,200,000; Bugi 5,000,000; Balinese 3,800,000; Acehnese 2,900,000; Dayak 2,900,000; Jakarta Betawi 2,700,000; Banjarese 2,100,000; Sasak 2,100,000; Makassarese 1,600,000; Kalimantan Malay 1,600,000; Toraja 1,300,000.

Chinese 4%. Many are becoming integrated into the Indonesian majority. Only 20% still use Chinese dialects. Scattered throughout the nation. Mainly urban.

Irianese/Papuan peoples 1.2%. In Timor, Alor, Halmahera and Irian Jaya.

Other 0.8%. Arabs, Indians, Europeans, mixed race. See more detail under separate islands.

Literacy 78%; rising rapidly. **Official language:** Indonesian. Its increasing use is both unifying the nation and lessening the importance of smaller languages to the younger generation. **All languages** 701; 17 spoken by more than one million speakers; 247 spoken in Irian Jaya. **Languages with Scriptures** 16Bi 21NT 56por.

Capital: Jakarta 8,670,000. Other cities: Surabaya 3,100,000; Bandung 3,000,000; Medan 2,400,000; Semarang 1,200,000. Urbanization 31%.

Economy: Increasingly diversified economy based on oil, gas, forest products, agriculture and textiles, with large reserves of many minerals. Steady economic improvement, but slowed by over-population in Java, difficult communications by land and sea, as well as a cumbersome democracy. The contribution of the Chinese to Indonesia's economic health is large. Inflation 10%. Public debt/person $228. Income/person $490 (2.3% of USA).

Politics: Colonial rule by Portuguese (1511–1605) and Dutch (1605–1945/9). The abortive Communist coup in 1965 radically changed the political orientation of the country. A strong military-civilian government with a partial democracy. President Suharto has sought to balance tendencies to religious extremism and local nationalisms. To retain power in the parliamentary elections of 1992 and presidential elections in 1993, the Muslim vote was courted by offering a more Islamic state. The political influence of Muslims is rapidly increasing.

Religion: Monotheism and communal peace are the basis for the government ideology of *Pancasila*. All are free to choose to follow Islam, Hinduism, Buddhism or Christianity (Catholic or Protestant); but the numerical and political strength of Islam is frequently exercised to give it preferential treatment, limit Christian expansion, and reduce Christian influence in public life. There are, therefore, some restrictions imposed on open evangelism. Religious statistics are a sensitive political issue, hence the figures given below.

Muslim 79.4–82.9%; officially 87%. These figures need explanation. In 1982 about 29% of the electorate voted for parties that sought to make Indonesia an Islamic state. About 43% could be defined as Quranic Muslims, living by many of Islam's tenets. A further 35% are statistical Muslims who, though enumerated as Muslims in the census, are actually followers of the Javanese mystical religion, *Kebatinan*, that predates Islam, or else animists who have (to a lesser or greater extent) accepted some of the outward aspects of Islam. Islam is strongest in Sumatra, West and East Java, and in many coastal areas in the east of the country.

Animist 1%. Not officially recognised by the government but strong among some peoples in Irian Jaya, East Timor, Sumba, and inland Sumatra, Kalimantan, Sulawesi, etc. Folk Islam followed by the majority is strongly influenced by animism. Nationwide it is still a dominant spiritual force.

Hindu 1.9%. Balinese and the Tengger people of East Java.

Buddhist/Chinese religions 1%. Almost entirely Chinese.

Christian 12.5% (church statistics); 9.6% (official figures). Growth 4.7%. A large number of nominal Christians and other sympathizers would further boost the total – see accompanying graph.

Protestant 9.3%. Growth 4.6%.

Church	Cong	Members	Affiliated
Batak Chr Prot Ch	2,393	1,250,000	2,500,000
Pentecostal Ch of I	1,540	770,000	1,280,000
Bethel Ch in I (CoG)	1,086	253,513	724,000
Bethel Full Gospel	1,200	360,000	600,000
Moluccan Prot Ch	796	371,000	529,845

Evang Chr Ch in I-J	1,052	230,000	460,000
Prot Ch in W.I. (4)	185	171,000	451,000
Nias Chr Prot Ch	578	141,000	312,848
Chtn & Miss Alliance	1,753	155,459	286.967
Indon Prot Chr Ch	797	192,000	286,885
Chr Ch of Java	1,202	156,000	259,871
Toraja Christian Ch	591	123,000	250,000
Evang Ch of I (UFM)	400	35,000	250,000
Ev Chr Ch in Sanghir	355	88,100	220,308
Seventh-day Adventist	1,000	130,000	217,000
Karo Batak Prot Ch	571	82,000	205,000
Ev Ch Kalimantan	908	73,600	184,115
Indep Christian (HKI)	590	68,800	180,950
Chr Ch of Sumba	306	61,200	161,000
Indon Chtn Ch (4)	179	53,600	124,720
Methodist Church	218	37,000	70,874
Ev Chr Ch in Java	60	47,000	67,332
Ev Allnce (TEAM)	289	24,288	60,700
All other (219)	15,864	3,019,057	7,128,754
Denominations (246)	33,913	7,892,617	16,812,169
Evangelicals 4.4% of pop		3,696,000	8,049,000
Pentecostal/charis		2,700,000	5,800,000

Missionaries:
to Indonesia 1,595 (1:114,000 people) in 114 agencies (1986–90 figures; numbers much reduced since).
from Indonesia 1,512 (1:11,200 Protestants) in 39 agencies 62frn 447xcul 1,065dom.
Roman Catholic 3.1%. Growth 4.8%.

Catholic Ch	7,730	3,080,000	5,600,000

Missionaries:
to Indonesia 1,269 (1:143,000 people).
from Indonesia 205 (1973).
Marginal 0.11%. Growth 5.2%.

All groups (8)	351	77,870	196,400

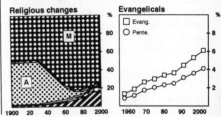

Religious changes

Evangelicals

1. **Praise God for the thrilling growth of the Church!** One of the most significant movements to Christianity in history has been accelerating in this land over the past 30 years. God has used many means to bring this about:
a) **The Communist coup** of 1965 and its bloody aftermath, in which maybe 500,000 Communist sympathizers perished, also led other sympathizers to become Christians.
b) **The fierce Muslim reprisals** on the Communists offended many – especially in Java. Many nominal Muslims turned to Christ.
c) **Harsh extremism of some Muslim groups** has repelled many nominal Muslims, and the legalisms of Islam, such as forbidding the eating of pork, has made Christianity more attractive to animists.
d) **The government recognition** of five religions (Islam, Protestantism, Catholicism, Hinduism and Buddhism) has impelled many animists to consider the claims of the gospel.
e) **The lives of Christians** and their vibrant, fearless witness have made an impact on a society influenced by the power of the occult.
f) **Outpourings of the Holy Spirit brought revival** in the '60s in West Timor, in the '70s in East and Central Java, and '80s in some major cities.
g) **Great people movements to Christ** have occurred in many animistic peoples and also among the Javanese.
h) **The multiplication of evangelistic prayer meetings** has been accompanied by the rapid growth of Pentecostal and charismatic denominations and fellowships.

2. **A spiritual conflict rages for Indonesia, and especially Java.** Java's pre-eminence in population, agriculture, industry and, above all, spiritual influence assures its dominance in national affairs. It is on Java that the most significant turning to Christ has occurred, but it is also the centre of powerful occult powers and of Muslim stratagems to eliminate Christian influence in the country. Pray specifically for the binding of these powers and for continued growth of the Church in the midst of intense opposition.

3. **The external challenge for Christians has grown in the '80s.** The government has tilted policy to favour Muslims in government and military posts, and has funded a massive mosque-building programme in both Muslim and (especially) non-Muslim areas. Muslim intellectuals are aiming to replace Christians in academic institutions and places of influence. There is a creeping Islamization of the nation's institutions and a restriction of Christian evangelism and fellowship meetings in many areas. There have also been outbreaks of violence, church-burnings, and persecution of Christians in areas where there is a Muslim majority. Pray that:
a) **These plans be frustrated,** Muslim extremism discredited, and many followers of Islam re-examine their own religion in the light of Scripture.
b) **The nation's leaders may not bow to Muslim extremist pressure,** which could polarize the nation with disastrous results.
c) **Christians may respond with tact, love and also firmness,** and in all ways commend the gospel.

d) **The 60–70 million nominal and syncretic Muslims** may have their eyes opened to the truth in Jesus, and come to him.

4. The enemy's counter-attack internally within the church is no less severe. While praising God for Christian growth, also pray for the thwarting of these developments:

a) **Too much sensational publicity** which exalts man or the miraculous (as with Timor) or which provokes the attention of those who would oppose the ongoing work of the Spirit.

b) **Too few teachers and disciplers** for those seeking the Lord. Many traditional churches cannot cope with the influx, and new seekers often do no more than increase the population of nominal Christians.

c) **The growth of error.** Inadequate teaching has led to multiplicity of errors, growth of liberal theologies, syncretistic Christianity loaded with occultism and animistic thought patterns and the controversy over "prosperity" theology in more charismatic city churches.

d) **Nominalism and carnality** which have blighted the Church in areas that have been Christian for centuries – Menado in Sulawesi, Timor and Maluku. Many denominations are spiritually lifeless, and riddled with carnality, internal politics, divisions and active practice of indigenous occultism. True conversion experience, renewal and revival are the needs in these bodies.

5. The need for spiritual leaders of maturity for the churches has never been greater. The pastor is of heightened importance in Indonesian church life because the majority of Christians follow the Reformed and Lutheran tradition inherited from the Netherlands and Germany. Yet rapid growth of the Church has far outstripped the supply of full-time workers. So pray for:

a) **The development of effective lay leadership.** Only a third of Reformed/Lutheran congregations have a pastor. Trained lay leadership is therefore essential.

b) **TEE programmes.** These have lost much of their effectiveness by government refusal to recognize credits earned. **CMA** and the Baptists still run TEE programmes. Many pastors have had inadequate training and need to be retrained and fired with new zeal. Many even need to be born of the Spirit.

c) **Primary and secondary level Bible schools** in many parts of the country, many being evangelical and providing pastors for rural congregations.

d) **The 40 degree-level seminaries**, about half being influenced by liberal theology. Pray for the evangelical faculty members. Pray also for the writing and publishing of more evangelical theological works in Indonesian. Pray also for an increase in the number of evangelical pastors in the large and influential regional Lutheran and Reformed churches.

e) **The 18 evangelical seminaries** relating to the Asian Theological Association; all are bulging with students and potential. To mention a few: SEABS in Malang, Java; KINGMI (**CMA**); Baptist (**SBC**); SAN (**OMS**); ETSI Yogyakarta; also Batu, Tanjung Enim and Anjungan of **IMF**, *Institut Theologia Tyranus* and a number of Pentecostal seminaries as well. Pray for an outflow of life through graduates from these institutions to old and new churches and to the mission fields of Indonesia and beyond.

f) **The spiritual quality and commitment of those with theological education** which is becoming more of a problem than finding recruits. Pray for a willingness to go to the less congenial parts of the country for Jesus' sake.

6. The vision for the evangelization of Indonesia is encouraging. A conference in Jakarta in 1988 brought together the three main streams of Protestants – the ecumenicals, Pentecostals and Evangelicals, with vision for outreach. Despite the problems, there is considerable freedom for evangelism and cross-cultural mission outreach throughout the country. Christians need a balance between tact and boldness to exploit this freedom. Many visions are emerging for the '90s:

a) **A church in every village of the country.** Of the 76,000 villages in the country, 50,000 are without a church.

b) **A viable witnessing church for every ethnic group** in the country. About 130 people groups in Indonesia have a Christian population of under 1%. Pray that the Indonesian church may rise to the challenge even as the foreign missionary force is depleted.

7. Development of a missionary vision. The history and background of Indonesian Christianity is unique and can make a significant contribution to world evangelization. Pray for:

a) **Churches to be gripped by the challenge** of hundreds of unreached peoples in their own country and in other lands of Asia and Africa. The financial and manpower resources are there.

b) **The sending out of Christians** as individuals, teams and communities as migrants to unevangelized areas and with a vision for church planting. This is not hard in an increasingly

homogeneous society. Christians will need to be set free from tribalism and local loyalties.
c) **Indonesian missionary agencies**, increasing in number, many being denominationally based. Most are involved in evangelistic and church-planting ministries within Indonesia, and a few have workers outside the country. The largest is **IMF** with 300 workers, 13 serving in other lands. Some Indonesians are also serving with international missions (**YWAM, OM, CLC** and others).

8. **The Transmigration Scheme** is one of the world's largest peaceful resettlements of people ever organized. Vast areas of virgin territory in Sumatra, Kalimantan, Sulawesi and Irian Jaya have been opened up for migrants from overpopulated Java and Bali. Some 6,500,000 were relocated between 1969 and 1991. These new settlements have been hard on the newcomers with harsh conditions, poor soils, and inefficient financing and communications. Yet among these migrants there is an openness to the gospel, and Christian groups have thrived despite the preferential selection of Muslims. Pray that these Christians may be lights for the Lord in areas never before evangelized – especially in Sumatra and Sulawesi. There are also large numbers of migrants to cities. Urban areas are rapidly becoming multi-cultural centres where cross-fertilization of the gospel takes place.

9. **Young people** are a vital mission field, but so little is specifically aimed at evangelizing and discipling them. There are 27 million children in primary and eight million in secondary schools. Response rates at evangelistic outreaches are consistently high.

10. **Students in universities** number 1,200,000 in 792 universities and colleges. There are a further 1,400,000 in tertiary and teacher training colleges. It is estimated that 30% of faculty and students are Christian. A number of specialized agencies have extensive ministry on campuses (**Navigators, PERKANTAS [IFES], CCC** and others). Yet many campuses still lack an organized Christian witness. A new feature is a growing number of Islamic universities. Many Indonesians study overseas – pray that they may be reached in other lands.

11. **The work of missions** has been blessed of God despite the obstacles of geography, bureaucracy and the spirit world. Praise God for the fruitful ministry of Dutch and German missions before World War II and many other international missions since then. Stand with these brethren in the battle for:
a) **Visas** – regular tightening of restrictions on the entry, residence and ministry of missionaries is rapidly reducing their numbers in the '90s. Pray that those the Lord wants in the country may obtain visas.
b) **Innovative ministry alternatives** for those called to Indonesia – as business professionals, teachers, students and so on. Pray for effective development of missionary teams based outside the country but with ministry directed towards the evangelization of unreached peoples. Pray also for the calling of new workers for Indonesia.
c) **The majority of missionaries who are concentrated** in animistic areas of West Kalimantan and Irian Jaya where the young churches are developing to maturity. Church/mission relationships is an area that must be covered in prayer.
d) **The great lack of missionaries** in Sumatra, Nusatenggara, Sulawesi and East Timor. Pray that no island may remain unserved by national or expatriate missionaries.
e) **Major ministries of present missionaries** in teaching, theological training, preparation of Indonesian missionaries and enabling Indonesian media and support ministries (literature, radio, etc.). Pray for vital and effective ministry for them. Major missions in Indonesia are **ABMS, AoG, APCM, CBFMS, CMA, MAF, NTM, OMF, OMS, RBMU, SBC, SIL, TEAM, UFM, WEC.** Major missionary-contributing nations in 1990: USA, Australia, Korea, Canada and Netherlands.

12. **Supportive ministries:**
a) **Bible translation**. The Bible Society, **SIL** and other groups are involved in 124 New Testament translation projects across the country. The rapid reduction in expatriate visas has severely hampered many translations. Pray for their speedy completion. Pray also for the Indonesian indigenous Bible translation agency, *Kartidaya*, and for the calling of many indigenous translators. Indonesia is one of the major unmet Bible translation challenges in the world today, with 129 languages with a definite need and a further 372 with a possible need.
b) **Literature**. There is an insatiable appetite for good Christian literature, but too little is widely available at a price people can afford. Transportation costs can equal production costs. Numerous indigenous and mission groups have an extensive printing and publishing ministry – notably the Christian Publishing Society (with which **OMF** is cooperating), Southern Baptists, AoG and various Pentecostal groups, **CLC** (with eight bookstores), **AO** (concentrating on pastoral teaching and follow-up literature), Bethany House, and Emmaus (widespread BCC

programme). Pray for the provision of literature to meet the need – especially that which is locally written; indigenous authors are few. It is estimated that 1.5 million Christian families do not possess a Bible.

c) **Gospel recordings**, now available in 383 languages and dialects (**GRn**); 183 of these are in Irian Jaya. The potential for using this evangelistic and teaching tool has not been adequately exploited. It is too easy to depend on use of Indonesian, which is often superficially understood.

d) **The *Jesus* film.** This was completed in 16 major languages by 1993. Pray for the liberty to show the film all over the country, and pray for the 30 film teams – their safety, travel, effective links with local churches and good follow-through.

e) **The use of traditional art forms,** such as *Wayang* shadow puppets; a powerful but little-used means of communicating the gospel.

f) **Missionary flying.** This is a boon to Christian workers in this huge, rugged island world, but it is costly and dangerous. In some areas of Kalimantan, Sulawesi and Irian Jaya missionary work would be impossible without it. **NTM, RBMU, SIL**, SDAs, and **MAF** have flying programmes. Pray for the staff and for safety of the planes. Pray also for efforts made to fulfil government requirements in training Indonesian pilots.

g) **Practical ministries.** Development programmes, preventative medical programmes and literacy all provide opportunities for sharing the gospel (**WV** and World Relief Commission).

h) **Christian radio.** There is a rapid development of local language broadcasting in Java, Sumatra and Sulawesi. Pray especially for programmes that are being produced for less-reached peoples on these islands. There are Christian programmes in Indonesian broadcast on the national network. International broadcasters transmit 75 hours/week in Indonesian (**TWR, FEBC**), 3.5 hours/week in Acehnese, Buginese, Sundanese and Javanese (**FEBC**), and 0.5 hours/week in Madurese, Toraja and Balinese (**TWR/IMF**). Languages with over one million speakers but without regular broadcasting are: Balinese, Banjarese, Batak (Toba and Dairi), Lampung, Makassarese, Sasak and Toraja.

June 21

THE ISLANDS OF INDONESIA

Each major island or island archipelago is so unique and complex that some of the more significant are handled separately – from west to east. The map above will help locate them.

SUMATRA

Area 473,500 sq.km. The world's fifth largest island. A vast potential storehouse of minerals and agricultural produce, but much is untamed jungle, swamp and volcanic mountains, with poor surface communications.

Population 36,455,000 in seven provinces: Bengkulu, Jambi, Lampung, Riau, North, South and West Sumatra, and the special autonomous district of Aceh.

Peoples: Major peoples: Acehnese, Batak, Minangkabau, Sumatra Malay, Lubu, Lampung.

Religion (official figures 1985). Muslim 85.9%, Christian 10.7% (Protestant 9.2%, Catholic 1.5%); Buddhist 2.2%, Hindu 0.5%, Other (including Animist) 0.7%.

1. **Sumatra is the home of some of the largest and least reached peoples in the world.** The Dutch colonial administration did not permit the preaching of the gospel to the Muslims, so it was the animistic peoples who were reached and who responded in the last century. These are:
a) **Bataks** speaking seven languages and totalling 5.2 million. The Toba, Dairi, Karo and Simalungun are probably 75% Christian – Lutherans, Methodists and Pentecostals, with some animism remaining. Most of the Angkola and Maindiling are Muslim with only a minority of Christians. The Batak are a dynamic people who have migrated all over Indonesia and who are prominent in the armed forces, police and in business, yet their ethnic pride and strong adherence to old customs often hinders their usefulness as cross-cultural witnesses.
b) **The Nias (480,000) and Mentawei (50,000)** living on islands off Sumatra's west coast. Nearly all are Lutherans, but sadly nominalism and animistic practices are rife. A new and more intelligible Bible translation is being prepared for publication. Pray for a new obedience to its contents.
c) **The Chinese,** mostly in the cities and industrial areas with large numbers of professing Christians today; many still follow the traditional religions and Buddhism.
There is much Christian activity and evangelism by younger and vigorous denominations and agencies within these communities. Pray that these Christians may be revived and break out of their ethnic cocoons to become effective witnesses to the non-Christian peoples around them.

2. **The Muslim majority** has had little exposure to the gospel. There were never more than a few dozen foreign missionaries committed to reach them (**WEC, IMF,** Methodists), but few remain. Pray for Indonesians and others to be called as missionaries for pioneer work and Bible translation and for freedom to witness and disciple these peoples. Pray also for the protection and growth of the few Christians among these peoples. It is only among the 100,000 Serawai of Bengkulu that there has been a significant breakthrough – 3,000 Christians today.

3. **The unreached.**
a) **The Aceh people** of the northern tip of Sumatra are strongly Muslim. There are less than 100 Christians known – almost all resident outside the area. The New Testament was published in 1992.
b) **The Minangkabau of West Sumatra** – a matriarchal society (5.9 million). Many are scattered throughout the country – especially the men! There may be only 1,000 Christians (mostly in Java).
c) **The Malay-related peoples** (10 million) of Jambi, Riau, South Sumatra and beyond. There are few Christians, and few reaching out to them.
d) **The less strongly Muslim peoples of North Sumatra.** There are very few, if any, Christians among the Gayo (180,000) and Simeulue (120,000), but more among the Angkola and Maindiling Batak. There is only a limited outreach to these peoples.
e) **The Muslim peoples of Central and South Sumatra,** 36 of whom are without a congregation of believers. Indonesian churches in the area are increasing outreach to the Kaur (50,000), Bengkulu (25,000), Enim (70,000), Pasemah (400,000), Palembang (400,000), Rejang (250,000) and Semendo (110,000), but, as yet, there are no more than a handful of Christians. There are about 12 peoples with no known outreach; major groups include the Kerinci (250,000), Bathin (100,000), Lematang (100,000), and Rawas (150,000).
f) **The peoples of Lampung in the south.** No churches are known among the indigenous Lampung (2,000,000), Komering (700,000), and Abung (200,000). There are churches among the many Javanese transmigrants in the area.

JAVA

June 22

Area 132,200 sq.km. Fertile; volcanic soil. Many active volcanos.

Population 107,600,000; 60% of Indonesia's population. Densely populated. 815 people/sq.km. Economically, culturally and politically dominant in the nation.

Major peoples: Javanese, Sundanese, Madurese.

Religion: Quranic Muslim approx. 46%, Statistical Muslim/Kebatinan/Animist 50%, Christian 3.6% (Catholic 1.1%, Protestant 2.5% – unofficially considerably higher), Hindu 0.2%, Buddhist 0.6%.

1. **Praise God for the receptivity of the Javanese and Chinese peoples to the gospel.** Since 1965 many churches (Reformed, Pentecostal and other Evangelicals) have been growing in excess of 10% per year. Possibly 40% of the Chinese and over 7% of the Javanese now profess to be Christian. Pray that no effort of the enemy of souls may hinder a continued harvest.

2. **There have been touches of revival among Javanese** in some areas in the past. That is the need today. There is much spiritual life and growth among the urban Chinese with many new churches. Syncretism among the Javanese and materialism among the Chinese are snares. There are also many Minahasan, Ambonese and Batak Christians in the great cities. Pray that pressures from Muslims on the churches may create a greater commitment to the Lord and to the spread of the gospel. In 1992 and 1993 an increasing number of churches were burned by Muslims.

3. **The remarkable response among the Javanese** is in contrast to the lack of response among the other peoples of Java. Now is the time of harvest! Pray for continued outreach to less evangelized towns and villages. The 500,000 Banten Javanese in the northwest of Java are unreached.

4. **Jakarta is a key city for the evangelization of Indonesia.** Almost every ethnic group has a presence there. The city is now over 13% Christian. There are over 730 registered churches and thousands of home meetings. A spiritual awakening in Jakarta could have spiritual impact on the whole country.

5. **Unreached peoples.** The other three major ethnic groups are tragically resistant and neglected:
a) **The Sundanese** – 24 million in West Java – are one of the largest unreached people groups in the world. They are staunchly Muslim, but the underlying animism and the old Sundanese religion are still influential. Several areas still adhere to the latter, resisting Islam but showing response to the gospel since 1978. Christian Sundanese number about 12,000, but most are nominal and culturally isolated from the Muslim majority; the largest church, the Pasundan Church, believes more in coexistence than evangelism. Persecution is assured for those who become Christians. Born-again Christians number but a few thousand. Only about 30–50 workers are committed to their evangelization. There is a dearth of workers, suitable literature and adequate airing of radio programmes. Pray that quickening interest evident among the Sundanese may become concern, conviction of sin and commitment to Christ. The Sundanese Bible was published in 1991.
b) **The Madurese** live in East Java and on Madura Island. This hot-headed, needy people has rejected the few serious attempts to bring them the good news. Each of these attempts has been an object of Satan's strong opposition; the translation of the Bible has had frequent delays but should be published in 1994. Pray for the planting of the first viable church among them. There are only a few hundred scattered Christians and a handful of committed believers.
c) **Tenggerese.** These 400,000 Hindus around Mt. Bromo in East Java have refused Islam and have shown little response to the few attempts to reach them with the gospel. There are some believers in ethnically mixed churches, but a true Tenggerese Church has yet to emerge.

June 23

BALI

Area 5,561 sq.km.

Population 2,778,000; 500 people/sq.km.

Major peoples: Balinese.

Religion: Hindu 92.7%, Muslim 5.6%, Christian 0.9% (Catholic 0.4%, Protestant 0.5%), Buddhist 0.8%.

1. **Bali is an island of great spiritual darkness,** demonic oppression and the occult under a "beautiful" bondage of Hindu culture and intricate ceremonies. There are 49,000 temples but only 36 Protestant and 33 Catholic churches. Some 1.5 million tourists are attracted to this island annually. Balinese need the liberating power of the gospel. The whole Bible in Balinese was published in 1990.

2. **Balinese Christians are few.** The cost of discipleship is high, and converts to Christ have to face much ostracism and persecution when they break with their families' way of life. Pray for the witness of the Christians – mostly of GKII(**CMA**) and the Reformed Church.

3. **Balinese who have migrated** to Sumatra and elsewhere are more open to the gospel. Some

Balinese have come to Christ in Sulawesi and in Bengkulu, Sumatra.

4. **Christian radio programmes** are being prepared for broadcasting in 1993.

W. LESSER SUNDA ISLANDS (Lombok, Sumbawa)

Area 20,177 sq.km.

Population 3,370,000; 167 people/sq.km.

Major peoples: Sasak, Sumbawa, Bima.

Religion: Muslim 96.1%, Hindu 2.9%, Christian 1% (Catholic 0.4%, Protestant 0.6%).

1. **These staunchly Muslim islands are some of the least evangelized in Indonesia.** The 20,000 Protestants are mainly immigrant peoples in the towns (Javanese, Timorese, Chinese). There are no known Indonesian or foreign missionaries seeking to reach the Muslim majority.

2. **The unreached:**
a) **The Muslim** Sasak (2,100,000) on Lombok, and the Sumbawa (300,000) and Bima (500,000) on Sumbawa Island are actually more animist than Muslim. There are just a few little-understood Scripture portions, but outreach has led to a few becoming Christians among the Bima and Sasak.
b) **The Hindu Balinese** – 80,000 on Lombok.
c) **The partly animistic Donggo** (15,000) on East Sumbawa, among whom there are a few hundred Christians (**CMA**).

E. LESSER SUNDA ISLANDS (Sumba, Flores, Lomblin, Alor, Wetar, W. Timor) | June 24

Area 47,876 sq.km.

Population 3,269,000; 68 people/sq.km.

Major peoples: Timorese, Manggarai, Solar, Lio, Roti, Sikka, Sumba.

Religion: Christian 81.8% (Catholic 54.2%, Protestant 27.6%), Muslim 9.8%, Animist 8.4%.

1. **Flores** is 90% Catholic but steeped in pagan and idolatrous ritual involving snake worship. Born-again Christians are very few and largely Timorese. No language of Flores has any Scriptures. The Manggarai (500,000), Lamaholot-Solar (300,000), Ende-Lio (230,000), Sikka (180,000), and Ngada (70,000) need to be evangelized in their own cultural settings and languages. Muslim minorities among the Solorese (140,000) and Manggarai (30,000) are totally unreached.

2. **Sumba** (400,000), long an island known for its animism and resistance to the gospel, has seen a move of the Spirit in the late '80s, with Protestants doubling from 75,000 to 160,000 in five years. Pray that this movement may impact all seven language groups on the island.

3. **West Timor.**
a) **Praise God for the outpouring of the Spirit** in 1965–8, and continued working since then. Miracles, deep repentance and thousands of conversions from occultism and Islam resulted. About 20% of the Timorese were converted. There has been an outflow of life to other parts of Indonesia. Timorese serve the Lord as missionaries on four continents.
b) **The large Reformed Church was blessed by the revival,** and other groups also, such as Pentecostals and **CMA**, have grown as a result. Pray for the consolidation and maturing of the fruit of revival. The majority of the population is Protestant, but witchcraft is still a potent force.
c) **More needy peoples.**
   i) **Sawunese** on Sawu Island and West Timor (100,000) are 80% animist in practice, the rest being nominally Christian, but few with a personal faith. Black magic is widespread.
   ii) **The Ambenu Timorese** and **Belu Tetun** in West Timor are largely nominal Catholic and have few Evangelicals.

4. **The lack of Scriptures** for the languages of this province is a major reason for nominalism, unchallenged witchcraft, and lack of progress for the gospel. Only three of the 60 languages have a

New Testament, though work is in progress in five. A major prayer request is for an adequate survey of translation needs and for provision of translation teams for those languages requiring a New Testament.

EAST TIMOR

Area 14,874 sq.km. For 450 years a rather neglected Portuguese colony. The collapse of the Portuguese empire in 1975 led to civil war as Communists sought to wrest control. In the ensuing anarchy, Indonesia took over the country as its 27th province. The ensuing resistance to Indonesian rule led to 15 years of fighting with considerable loss of life. By 1993 the level of fighting was greatly reduced.

Population 748,000; 50 people/sq.km.

Major people: Tetun.

Religion. Christian 85.1% (Catholic 81.5%, Protestant 3.6%), Animist 12.2%, Islam 2.1%, Hindu 0.3%, Buddhist 0.3%.

1. **East Timor's tragic past** has deeply affected the people. Progress has been made in developing schools, roads and the economy since 1976, but the Timorese are a hurting people. Pray for peace, a workable settlement of the conflict and, above all, that these events may open many hearts for the liberating gospel message.

2. **After years of spiritual neglect**, change has come. A large proportion of the population has turned from animism to the Catholic Church and a smaller number to the Reformed Church. However, understanding of the gospel is limited, and few are free from the fear of the occult. Only on Atauro Island and in Dili, the capital, are there vigorous evangelical groups. Pray for the provision of Christian teachers and leaders to bring the Church to maturity.

3. **Less-reached peoples.** Poverty, illiteracy, lack of knowledge of Portuguese or Indonesian, and lack of the Scriptures have kept most of the 23 ethnic groups in ignorance of the gospel. The Tetun New Testament was completed in 1991 – pray for its impact on the 300,000 Tetun. Pray for the evangelization and provision of Scriptures for the Mambai (80,000), Makasai (70,000), Kemak (60,000), Galoli (60,000), Tukutede (50,000) and Fatakulu (30,000).

June 25

KALIMANTAN

Area 539,000 sq.km. The Indonesian three-quarters of the island of Borneo; shared with Malaysia. An island of tropical rain forest and rivers, but few roads.

Population 9,110,000 in four provinces – West, Central, East and South Kalimantan. 16 people/sq.km.

Major peoples: Malay, Dyak, Iban.

Religion: Muslim 72.8%, Christian 19.3% (Catholic 9.8%, Protestant 9.5%), Animist 3.5%, Hindu 2.5%, Buddhist 1.9%.

1. **The indigenous Dyak peoples** number 2,500,000 and speak a range of nearly 80 languages and numerous dialects. Church growth has been high with large people movements into the churches, but often without a clear break from the spirit world.
a) The **CMA** work in **East Kalimantan** has resulted in a strong church among the Kenyah and Kayan peoples as well as outreach to other ethnic groups.
b) In **Central Kalimantan** many of the 330,000 Ngaju and 80,000 Dohoi are linked with the Reformed Church founded through the work of the Rhenish and Basel Missions. Sadly, few are evangelical in theology.
c) **West Kalimantan** has been the field for **CMA, CBFMS, RBMU**, Go Ye Fellowship and **WEC**. Growing churches have emerged, and over 30% of the population is Christian. The Iban have proved more difficult to win, and most of the Dyak who profess Christianity need a personal encounter with Jesus.

2. **Leadership training** is a major need for the churches, but difficulties in travel, illiteracy, poverty and lack of indigenous Scriptures have all slowed development of mature churches. There are a number of Bible schools. The massive inflow of Javanese and Balinese transmigrants has had an

unsettling effect, but presents a unique opportunity for Christian witness. Pray that these Christians may be inspired and motivated to overcome the cultural, social and religious barriers to evangelize them.

3. **The unreached:**
a) **The large Malay population** of four million along the coasts and up the rivers is strongly Muslim. Nothing is being done to evangelize them, and they have no known churches. Their greatest concentrations are in less-evangelized South Kalimantan.
b) **The transmigrant Javanese** (nominally Muslim), Balinese (Hindu), Bugis (strongly Muslim), and others number over one million. They live in transmigrant settlements and in the oil-boom towns of the east. The growing churches of the Javanese could minister to other ethnic groups around them, but they need the vision to do so.
c) **The animist peoples of the interior** present a challenge. **NTM** has ministry to ten or more tribes in West and Central Kalimantan. The complexities of reaching isolated tribal groups are immense, survey work hard, and living conditions difficult. Pray for more pioneers willing to reach out to these hard-to-access but receptive peoples.
d) **The Chinese**, 25% of the population in West Kalimantan, have proved less responsive to the gospel than elsewhere, though most are nominally Christian. Pray for the witness of Chinese Christians and churches on the coast, in Pontianak and up the Kapuas river.

SULAWESI

June 26

Area 189,300 sq.km. A large crab-like mountainous island, 1,300 km. from north to south. Also many satellite islands. Formerly called Celebes.

Population 12,522,000 in four provinces – Central, North, South and Southeast Sulawesi. 66 people/sq.km.

Major peoples: Bugi, Makassar, Minahasa, Gorontalo, Torajo, Sanghir.

Religion: Muslim 71%, Christian 27.6% (Catholic 1.8%, Protestant 25.8%), Hindu 0.63%, Animist 0.59%, Buddhist 0.17%.

1. **Sulawesi is a patchwork of ethnic groups and of response to the missionary religions** of Islam and Christianity. Generally, nearly all the coastal peoples are Muslim. Christians are in a majority on the two northeastern peninsulas and in the central highlands. The main Christian ethnic groups are:
a) **The five Minahasa peoples of Menado** of the northeast tip of Sulawesi who have been Protestant for three centuries or more. They are among the wealthiest and best-educated peoples of Indonesia, but materialism, nominalism, poor church attendance and occultism are rife. There is little concern for the evangelization of the Muslim and animist majority of the island.
b) **The Sanghir and Talaud Islanders** (210,000) who are found to the north of Menado.
c) **The Toraja** (1,000,000 with eight languages and 30 dialects) who are mostly adherents of the four Reformed Churches. Few have a personal experience of the Lord. Tradition – especially a morbid preoccupation with death – still grips many.
All these peoples need revival. Pray also for lasting fruit through the activities of younger evangelical, Pentecostal and charismatic denominations and agencies.

2. **Less-reached peoples are numerous**, but in most of the larger groups there are small Christian minorities. Pray specifically for:
a) **The Bugis** (3,500,000) and Makassarese (1,600,000) of South Sulawesi with colonies all around the coast. Trading is their major occupation. By Indonesian standards Islam is more orthodox. There are about 800 Buginese Christians and 3,000 Salyar Makassarese Christians – the latter being one of the few significant orthodox Muslim groups responding in any numbers to the gospel.
b) The Muslim **Gorontalo** (900,000), numerous smaller Muslim-animist peoples scattered around the north, and the **Bungku-Mori Toraja** of the southeast, where animistic practices are more prevalent. There are small churches indigenous to these peoples, but response is slow and many areas are untouched.

3. **Bible translation** is an enormous unfinished task. **SIL** researchers spent years surveying the complex linguistic situation and are participating in most of the ongoing 23 New Testament translation projects together with Indonesian translators. Pray that nothing may hinder the publication of these New Testaments. There are only five indigenous languages with a Bible or New Testament, and 28 languages (out of a possible 87) have a definite unmet need for translators.

MALUKU

Area 74,500 sq.km. A medley of over 1,000 small islands scattered over Indonesia's eastern seas.

Population 1,856,000; 25 people/sq.km. There are 128 language groups.

Religion: Muslim 55%, Christian 45% (Catholic 4%, Protestant 41%).

1. **The Moluccan (Maluku) Protestant Church is Asia's oldest Protestant denomination** – founded in 1536. Today, nominalism has crippled the witness of the Church, and Muslims are growing through immigration and conversions of Maluku peoples. Pray for revival.

2. **There are many islands, long Christianized, but where churches stand empty and services are discontinued.** Pray for the re-evangelization of the Maluku islands and for effective means of reaching isolated island communities.

3. **The less-reached** include Ambonese Muslims, the Muslim Ternate (62,000), Tidore (46,000), the seafaring Bajau (25,000), the Makian of Halmahera Island, and numerous other smaller peoples. Pray for an adequate survey of both language and spiritual needs which could motivate missionary endeavour to reach each people. This has partially been done by **SIL**. There are now 23 translation teams active, but a further 39 languages have a definite translation need and yet another 55 a possible need for a New Testament.

June 27

IRIAN JAYA

Area 422,000 sq.km. The western half of the island of New Guinea (see Papua New Guinea for the eastern half). Ruled by Netherlands until 1963, then annexed by Indonesia. It contains some of the wildest and most inhospitable terrain on earth.

Population 1,641,000; 4 people/sq.km. Over 247 languages spoken.

Religion: Christian 83.4% (Catholic 22.9%, Protestant 60.5%), Muslim 16.4%, Animists – not listed but possibly near 10%, Buddhist 0.08%.

1. **Praise God for the people movements that have brought stone-age peoples to faith in Christ from most of the 275 tribes.** Those on the north coast in the last century (Reformed Church), in the more densely populated highlands (**APCM, CMA, RMBU, UFM, ABMS** and others), the "Bird's Head" (**TEAM**), and southern swamps (**TEAM, RBMU**) have responded in this way. Over 90% of the indigenous population is officially reckoned as Christian.

2. **Strong, Bible-centred, maturely led national churches are the great need** as modernization, education and a growing flood of transmigrants, often Muslim, enter the island. Christians must face up to the challenges of tribalism, syncretism and separatist politics which sap the spiritual energies of some churches. Sadly, inter-village fighting has once more become a problem in some Christianized areas.

3. **The missionary force has been depleted over recent years.** Much remains to be done, including pioneer evangelism, church planting, Bible translation and leadership training. Pray for new missionary recruits from other countries as well as Indonesians from outside Irian Jaya. Praise God for the remarkable missionary army that has opened up this island. Pray for **MAF** with planes and seven bases, as well as the essential aviation ministries of **SIL** and **RBMU** in the roadless and dangerous interior. There have been a number of bad accidents in recent years.

4. **The less-reached.** Only in the last few years have virtually all the ethnic groups been located and contacted. Pray that research by **UFM, SIL** and others into unreached peoples may be completed by 1994. Indigenous peoples still requiring pioneer evangelism and church-planting are:
a) **Small peoples east of Cenderawasih Bay** on New Guinea's "shoulder".
b) **Peoples in the northern foothills** of the Eastern Highlands.
c) **Peoples in the southern foothills** of the main range of mountains bisecting the island.
d) **The Baliem Dani** of the Highlands who have not been so responsive as the rest of the Western Dani.
e) **The Muslim population** in the coastal towns – especially Minangkabau and Makassarese.

5. **The Dani peoples** total 300,000. Many turned to the Lord in great people movements over the last decades. At one stage there were 280 Dani missionaries evangelizing other areas. That vision has dimmed. Pray for renewal of life and vision for the Dani churches.

6. **Bible translation** for the many small language groups is an immense task. Only 96 languages have or have had any translation work. There are 49 with a definite need and 130 others with a possible need for a New Testament translation. Pray for:

a) The completion, publication and effective use of the 59 New Testaments in the process of being translated or printed.

b) Cooperation between churches and agencies to have portions of Scripture translated into every vernacular still used as a primary language.

c) The work of **SIL** and other missions in facilitating translation and literacy programmes, by training nationals and helping national workers.

d) Mother-tongue speakers with the skills, gifts, spiritual insight and motivation to tackle the arduous task of translation.

e) The use of cassettes for Scriptures and Christian messages on tape. **GRn** have made recordings in 186 languages.

I

June 28–30
Middle East

Iran

(Islamic Republic of Iran)

Area 1,648,000 sq.km. A central desert ringed by mountains.

Population		Ann. Gr.	Density
1990	56,585,000	3.5 %	34/sq.km
1995	64,525,000	2.7 %	39/sq.km

Peoples: Over 65 ethnic groups, many of which are small nomadic groups.
Indo-Iranian 75.6%. Persian 25,300,000; Kurds 4,670,000; Luri-Bakhtiari 4,280,000; Mazanderani 3,265,000; Gilaki 3,265,000; Dari Persian 1,600,000; Balochi 1,240,000; Tat 620,000; Pathan 113,000; Talysh 112,000.
Turkic 18.8%. Azerbaijani 8,130,000; Turkoman 905,000; Qashqai 860,000; Hazara 283,000; Teymur 170,000; Shahseven 130,000.
Arab 2.2%. Mainly in southwest.
Christian minorities 0.4%. Reduced from 1.5% in 1975 due to emigration. Armenian 170,000; Assyrian 40,000; Georgian 10,000.
Other 3%. Gypsy (Nawar and Ghorbati) 1,188,000; Brahui 149,000; Jews 68,000.
Refugees: Afghans 1.5 million, but decreasing; Iraqi Kurds 120,000 (at one stage in 1991 there were 1.2 million); Shi'a Arabs from Iraq.

Literacy 52%. **Official language**: Persian (Farsi). **All languages** 50. **Languages with Scriptures** 4Bi 1NT 8por.

Capital: Tehran 8,263,000. Other cities: Mashad 1,463,000; Isfahan 1,400,000; Rai 1,310,000; Tabriz 1,038,000; Shiraz 850,000. Urbanization 52%.

Economy: Oil-based. Material progress under the Shah was reversed by the religious bigotry, national paranoia and violence that followed the 1979 revolution. The combination of inefficiency, war damage in the eight-year war with Iraq and run-down of the national economic infrastructure brought Iran to the brink of disaster. Peace, more openness to the outside world, and more market-oriented policies have brought some improvements since 1990. Rapid population growth outstrips the means to feed and employ all, and living standards are being eroded. Unemployment 15–30%. Public debt/person $89. Income/person $1,800 (8.5% of USA).

Politics: The Shah was deposed in the Shi'ite Muslim Revolution, and a theocratic Islamic Republic declared in 1979. Regional loyalties and anarchy brought the country close to civil war and ruin. The Iraqi invasion of 1980 led to eight years of bitter war and maybe 1,000,000 Iranian dead. Less extreme leadership since 1990 has moderated ruinous economic policies, global confrontations and export of Islamic revolution. However, Iran remains a theocratic police state with scant regard for human rights. Iran is extensively re-arming, engaged in diplomatic activity to regain regional superpower status in the Middle East, and vying with Turkey for influence in the Muslim Central Asian States.

Religion: Shi'a Islam is the state religion. All deviations or defections from Shi'a Islam are liable to persecution although constitutionally the rights of Christians, Zoroastrians and Jews are guaranteed. Iran has been the power house for exporting fundamentalist Islam to the Middle East and beyond.
Muslim 99%. Shi'a 87%, Sunni 12% (Kurds, Balochi and Turkoman).
Baha'i 0.5%. 300,000 followers of a Persian world religion founded in 1844. Severely persecuted as a heresy of Islam.
Jews 0.1%. Farsi-speaking Jews (68,000), many of whom are descendants of those exiled to Persia at the time of Daniel.
Parsi (Zoroastrian) 0.04%. 21,000 followers of Persia's ancient pre-Islamic religion.
Christian 0.4%. Affil 0.38%. Growth −1.3%.
Protestant 0.03%. Growth 7.5%.

Church	Cong	Members	Affiliated
Assemblies of God	19	1,600	4,000
Evang Ch (Presby)	10	1,650	3,000
Episcopal Church	4	480	1,200
All other (9)	16	4,733	7,401
Denominations (12)	49	8,463	15,601
Evangelicals 0.3% of pop		7,766	14,432
Pentecostal/charis 0.01%		3,000	6,500

Missionaries:
  to Iran – none known.
  from Iran 7 or more.
Roman Catholic 0.03%. Growth −0.6%.

Catholic	25	7,150	16,500

Orthodox 0.36%. Affil 0.32%. Growth −1.9%.

Armenian	98	112,000	170,000
Nestorian (Assyrian)	9	9,100	13,000
All other (2)	2	363	550
Denominations (4)	109	121,463	183,550

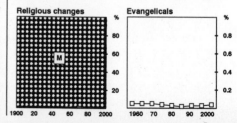

Religious changes

Evangelicals

1. **Islamic revolution** has brought much bloodshed, division and dismay to many in Iran. Huge sacrifices have yielded meagre benefits. Theocratic tyranny has proved more cruel and corrupt than the system it replaced in 1979. Intense anti-Western and anti-Christian propaganda has had an opposite effect by causing many Muslims to seek answers therein. May the pain caused by bigotry, hatred, cruelty and religious extremism open many hearts to the Prince of Peace and doors for the gospel.

2. **The leader of the Islamic Revolution, the Ayatollah Khomeini, died in 1989.** A $9 billion mausoleum and a new "holy" city are being built in his memory. Yet the legacy of his bitterness and anger lives on. Pray that the demonic system underlying Islam may be broken and the people may see the loveliness and grace of Jesus and come to him. Pray for this land to be opened for the gospel.

3. **Many Iranian Muslims have shown marked interest in Christianity since the revolution.** Disillusionment with Islam is muted, but widespread. In 1979, there were 200–300 known believers who had once been Muslim. There are possibly 6,000 in Iran today with about the same number among Iranian refugees. May they be the first fruits of an abundant harvest among Iranians. Many more Iranians have become secret believers.

4. **Over 90% of the Christian community** is from the traditionally Christian Armenian and Assyrian communities which are isolated cultural islands in a Muslim sea. Their existence has been tolerated, but fear, uncertainty, arbitrary arrests, interrogations, enforcement of Islamic dress for women, and Islamic religious education for children have provoked the emigration of a large proportion of their communities. Pray for a work of the Holy Spirit in these churches.

5. **Protestant Churches** were generally small, introspective and struggling before the revolution. Traumatic changes in the country have dynamized them, increasing commitment and church attendance and lowering denominational barriers between Anglicans, Presbyterians and Pentecostals. Some have become fervent witnesses and literature distributors. Of the 12 pastors in the Pentecostal Church, 10 have suffered imprisonment and one has been executed. Yet many believers have been added to these churches despite persecution and steady losses through emigration. For the first time Persian Evangelicals outnumber those from Christian ethnic minorities. Pray for these believers, their steadfastness in faith and growth in grace.

6. **Before 1988, persecution of evangelical Christians was not widespread,** but since the end of the war with Iraq, the pressure has steadily increased. Spies are infiltrated into Christian groups. Conferences are banned, some church buildings have been closed, and all open witnessing declared illegal. Persecution has become particularly severe for Christians who were once Muslims. Pray especially for those who have a non-Christian background. The Episcopal Church, with a majority of ex-Muslims, has suffered particularly severely. Pray also for believers who have had to flee to other lands.

7. **About three million Iranians live outside Iran** in lands where they can be evangelized. The major concentrations are in USA, Western Europe and the Gulf States. Most are refugees, some are students. In many countries little Christian fellowships are springing up as disillusioned Iranians turn to the Lord – the majority from Islam. There are one million Iranians in the USA with about 3,000 believers. *Iranian Christians International* in North America and the *Iranian Christian Fellowship* in the UK (including the Iranian Bible Training and Resource Centre) have become vital coordinating points for evangelizing Iranians, providing literature, programming for broadcasting into Iran and training for Iranian Christian workers. Pray for the Iranian diaspora, its evangelization and its usefulness as a means of strengthening the Church in Iran and evangelizing the nation.

8. **Missions** are no longer free to minister in the land. Pray for those missionaries working among Iranians in Europe, North America and Australia. Pray that the door to Iran and its unevangelized millions may open once more. Some of the largest totally unreached people groups in the world are in Iran. Pray also that agencies around the world may pray, plan and network together and with Iranian believers in preparation for that day.

9. **Unreached peoples.** Pray for each of the larger peoples listed above. Not one of the non-Christian people groups is reached, and in only eight of the 60 or so peoples are there known believers. Pray specifically for:
a) **The peoples of the Zagros Mountains:** the Luri, Bakhtiari and Qashqai peoples are partly nomadic. They are probably the least reached of the world's mega-peoples. There are no known believers, nor has any known sustained effort ever been made to reach them.
b) **The Turkic peoples** numbering 10.5 million, with only a handful of believers. Most of these

peoples have never been exposed to the gospel.

c) **The peoples of the southeast** – the Balochi and Brahui. They are restive and unhappy with Iranian rule. There are no known believers.

d) **The 66,438 villages in Iran**. Only about half-a-dozen have a resident Christian witness.

e) **The 178 towns and cities**. In 1985 there were only 30 organized Protestant churches.

f) **The Baha'i followers**. There are no believers known from this religious group that has suffered so much. Little has been done to specifically evangelize the world's 5 million Baha'i. Pray that God may raise up those with such a vision.

10. **Christian Help ministries** are of special value for the Iran of today – often being the only means of reaching the majority of the population.

a) **Christian literature** is much sought after. Hundreds of thousands of Bibles, New Testaments and pieces of literature were sold and distributed in the years following the revolution. The Bible Society and nearly all Christian literature distribution centres were closed in 1988. Supplies in the country have dwindled away. Pray for ongoing impact from literature already distributed and for new ways to be found to get the Scriptures and Christian literature into the hands of the people. Pray that literature sent through the mail may reach its destination.

b) **Christian video tapes** are popular. There is a large black market for banned Western secular and religious videos, hence their popularity. Pray for the circulation of the *Jesus* film on video tape in Persian, Azerbaijani, Turkish and Turkmen.

c) **Christian radio** has even more importance since the departure of all missionaries. Both **TWR** and **FEBA** broadcast seven hours weekly in Persian. *Radio Voice of Christ* and Radio Voice of the Gospel (**TWR**) are two major programme producers. **TWR** and High Adventure in Lebanon both broadcast in Azerbaijani and Kurdish, with a total of 1.75 hours weekly for each. A cooperative group is developing programmes for the Azerbaijani, Gilaki, Mazanderani and Kurdish languages. Lack of native speakers who know the Lord in these and other mega-language groups hinders further use of radio.

d) **Bible translation** has virtually halted. Very little can be done in Iran for the 35 or more languages with no Scriptures or translation work in progress. Especially urgent is need for the New Testaments in Luri-Bakhtiari and Qashqai.

Iraq
(Republic of Iraq)

July
1–2

Middle East

Area 435,000 sq.km. Fertile plains of the Tigris and Euphrates, high mountains to the north and Syrian desert in southwest. Site of the ancient Sumerian, Assyrian and Babylonian empires.

Population		Ann. Gr.	Density
1990	18,920,000	3.5 %	43/sq.km
1995	22,411,000	3.4 %	51/sq.km

Peoples: Ethnic and religious diversity lies behind much of the agonizing history of Iraq.
Arabs 74.4%. The minority Sunni Arabs have exercised total political domination over the Shi'a, who are twice as numerous. Bedouin 100,000; Marsh Arabs 50,000.
Kurds 19% (though some claim 23%). Mostly Sunni Muslim, some Yezidis, mainly in the mountainous northeast; about 60% in the UN-guaranteed Kurdish Autonomous Region. Four major language groups: Kurmanji, Sorani, Gorani, Luri. Worldwide there are an estimated 25 million Kurds. Their homeland is divided among Turkey, Iran, Iraq, Syria and Azerbaijan.
Turkic 1.4%. Turkmen 227,000; Azerbaijani 38,000; Turk 19,000.
Other minorities 5.2%. Farsi 227,000; Assyrian 65,000; Armenian 37,000; Gypsy (Zott) 20,000; Circassian (Adygey) 19,000.
Migrant labour. A peak of 4 million in Iran-Iraq war. The 2 million Egyptians were partially replaced by Palestinians in the Gulf War. Most of the 500,000 Asians fled at that time.

Literacy 60%. **Official languages**: Arabic, Kurdish in Kurdish districts. **All languages** 19. **Languages with Scriptures** 3Bi 1NT 4por.

Capital: Baghdad 4,706,000. Other major cities: Basra 1,540,000; Mosul 1,220,000; Suleimaniya 1,000,000; Erbil 700,000; Kirkuk 535,000. Urbanization 70%.

Economy: Oil-based economy (since Genesis 11!); profits have been used for industrialization and building military power. War with Iran halted non-military development and UN sanctions brought Iraq to economic standstill. Public debt/person $2,200. Income/person $10,700 (51% of USA) in 1960. Much lower by 1993.

Politics: Monarchy overthrown in a violent revolution in 1958. The Baathist military regime with its secularist, pan-Arab socialism became a repressive dictatorship under Saddam Hussein. A massive military machine was built with the connivance of other Arab oil countries and Western powers greedy for petrodollars, and was used to protect the dictatorship, repress the Kurds and Shi'a, launch a war against Iran (1980–88) and also invade Kuwait in 1990. Although evicted from Kuwait and suffering heavy damage in the 1991 Gulf War, Iraq was not totally defeated. Sophisticated propaganda, ruthless suppression of dissent and evasion of UN sanctions have enabled some restoration of military strength and economic life.

Religion: Pan-Arab socialism rather than Islam is the ideology of the Baathist regime. Religious minorities have been favoured by Saddam Hussein if they demonstrate political loyalty. Christians have had increasing freedom for worship and witness since 1968, but still suffer from discrimination.
Muslim 95.4%. 59.3% Shi'a, 36.1% Sunni. The Sunni Arabs are politically dominant.
Yezidi 0.9%. A Kurdish religion related to pre-Islamic Zoroastrianism.
Non-religious/other 0.5%.
Mandaeans 0.2% Followers of John the Baptist.
Jews 200. (In 1950 there were 250,000, most emigrating to Israel.)
Christian 3.3% Affil 3%. Growth 0.8%.
Protestant 0.03%. Growth 7.1%.

Church	Cong.	Members	Affiliated
Arab Evang Chs	10	1,580	3,500
All other (11)	28	1,368	2,967
Denominations (12)	38	2,948	6,467
Evangelicals 0.03% of pop		2,700	5,900
Pentecostal/charis 0.001%		400	900

Expatriates serving in Iraq: (KAR only) 20+ involved in aid programmes among Kurds.
Roman Catholic 2.25%. Growth 0.7%.

Catholic Ch	55	230,000	425,000

Orthodox 0.75% Growth 1.0%

Assyrian Ch of East	90	45,100	82,000
Syrian Orthodox Ch	36	18,000	30,000
Armenian Apostolic Ch	12	11,000	20,000
All other (3)	7	5,220	9,000
Denominations (6)	145	79,320	141,000

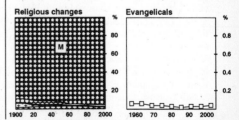

Religious changes

Evangelicals

1. **Modern Iraq has become a byword for repressive dictatorship and crazy military adventures**. The sufferings of the Kurds, Shi'a Arabs, Iranians and Kuwaitis have been headline news for a decade. Saddam Hussein has plans to rebuild the city of Babylon. Pray that the spiritual powers brooding over the land may be bound and that God's purposes for its peoples be fulfilled.

2. **The decade of war and hardship** brought about a significant change in attitudes and lowering of prejudices among Muslims. There is more respect for Christians and a desire to hear the gospel and read the Scriptures. Pray that this might lead to a God-glorifying harvest! The *Jesus* film has been widely and openly shown, and in 1991 the full film was shown on national television.

3. **Christians** are largely Assyrian and Armenian; few are Arab or Kurdish. Catholic and Protestant mission activity in the last century centred on the six Eastern Orthodox Churches resulting in Chaldean Catholics and Evangelicals. Pray for renewal and revival to permeate the entire Christian community. Only in recent years has more effort been directed to the Muslim majority.

4. **Evangelical believers** are mainly confined to the cities. They were persecuted in the '60s and '70s and numbers declined. God gave revivals in the '80s and house groups multiplied – from one in Baghdad to over 300 in that period. Church services are packed in Baghdad, Kirkuk and Basra. Pray for these believers, their walk with the Lord and their witness to non-Christians. A small but growing number of Arabs and Kurds are seeking the Lord, both in Iraq and among Iraqi refugees in Jordan and elsewhere.

5. **Unreached peoples** – all peoples but for the Assyrian and Armenian minorities. Pray specifically for:
a) **The Shi'a Arabs of the south**. The exceptional brutality of the government suppression of the post-Gulf War Shi'ite revolt in 1991 brought devastation and degradation to these people. There is no known direct witness to them at this time.
b) **The Marsh Arabs**, with their distinctive culture at the confluence of the Tigris and Euphrates, who were decimated by government forces driving them from their marshes in 1992. There has been no known outreach to them.
c) **Other unreached minorities** – the Bedouin, Turkmen, Farsi and the Gypsies.

6. **The plight of the Kurds** (see Turkey, Syria and Iran for more information) has caught the attention of the world. They have fought for survival and a national identity for 70 years. The last 10 years have been particularly bloody and cruel. Iraqi atrocities have included the razing of 3,800 villages and towns (including 61 Christian Assyrian villages), destruction of the local economy, mining of fields, deportation of 500,000 to distant camps, and killing of up to 250,000. In the aftermath of the Gulf War in 1991 almost the entire Kurdish population became refugees. UN intervention forced the Iraqi government to concede the formation of the Kurdish Autonomous Region (KAR), which has become a Kurdish state in all but name. Pray for:
a) **A just settlement** of Kurdish desires for freedom and security and of the national sensitivities of Turkey, Syria, Iran and Iraq. Turkey's efforts to control Kurdish guerrilla activity north of its border further isolates Iraqi Kurds.
b) **Economic betterment** – the KAR is isolated and blockaded by Iraq and dependent on Western aid and agencies. Some of these agencies are Christian – pray that their loving ministry may win the hearts of many.
c) **Openness to the gospel** leading to conversions and congregations among the Kurds. There are no known evangelical groups but a growing number of believers and a few Kurdish-speaking Assyrian groups in the KAR.

7. **Christian media**
a) **Christian literature** of all kinds is in great demand – import restrictions and distribution difficulties prevent its wider use.
b) **The Bible Society** was forced to close between 1979 and 1986. Praise the Lord for its reopening and its ministry in distributing tons of Bibles since the Gulf War – demand far exceeds the import quota. Pray for adequate quantities of Scriptures to be made available. Pray also for the completion of the Kurdish Bible translation project to provide the New Testament in Kurmanji and Sorani.
c) **Christian radio broadcasts** are one of the few means available for evangelism. Pray for the Arabic broadcasts of **TWR** (Monaco and Cyprus) and **FEBA** (Seychelles). Many Iraqis have enrolled in Bible correspondence courses as a result. There is only one daily **TWR** 15-minute programme in Sorani Kurdish, but the response has been tremendous.

Ireland

(Irish Republic)

July 3
Europe

Area 70,300 sq.km. 80% of the island of Ireland. Northern Ireland is a constituent part of the United Kingdom.

Population	Ann. Gr.	Density
1990	3,720,000	0.93 %	53/sq.km
1995	3,900,000	0.95 %	55/sq.km

Millions of Irish have emigrated all over the English-speaking world – especially to the USA. (In 1845 the population was 7 million.)

Peoples:
Irish 95.8%. Predominantly of Celtic origin.
Others 4.2%. UK citizens 140,000; Itinerants 7,000.

Literacy 99%. **Official languages**: Irish, English. Irish spoken as first language by 3% of population.

Capital: Dublin 1,024,000. Urbanization 57%.

Economy: Industry, dairy farming and tourism are important. Member of EC. Unemployment 17%. Public debt/person $11,600. Income/person $12,250 (58% of USA).

Politics: For centuries Irish politics have been bloody, complex and emotive because of British involvement. In 1921 Ireland was partitioned between the 26 counties that were Catholic and Celtic and the six Ulster counties that were predominantly Protestant Scots Anglo-Saxon. The south became independent in 1922 and a parliamentary republic in 1949. The partition still deeply affects the political life of both parts. In Northern Ireland, of the population of 1.6 million, approximately 41% are Catholic and look to having closer links with the south, while 54% are mainly Protestant and are determined to maintain their union with Great Britain. Most southern Irish want to see a united Ireland. The IRA, supported by its political wing Sinn Fein – still a legitimate political party in both north and south – aims to achieve a united Ireland through violence. However, their influence in the south is relatively minimal, having received only 2% of the vote in the local elections in 1991, whereas they still achieved 10% of the vote in Northern Ireland.

Religion: There is freedom of religion. The Catholic Church has no official link with the state, but it has a strong influence on all aspects of national life.
Non-religious/other 3.6%.
Muslims 0.2%. **Jews** 0.1%.
Christian 96%. Nom 6.1%. Affil 89.9%.
Attendance 75%. Growth −0.1%.
  Protestant 4%. Affil 3.49%. Attend 82%.
  Growth 0.4%.

Church	Cong.	Members	Affiliated
Ch of Ireland (Ang)	1,041	51,000	95,400
Presbyterian Ch	108	9,150	14,300
Methodist Ch	26	4,700	5,800
House Churches	100	1,550	4,000
Brethren	20	950	1,360
Baptist Union	12	430	1,000
All Other (32)	121	4,010	7,198
Denominations (38)	1,428	71,790	129,058
Evangelicals 0.87% of pop		19,000	32,500
Pentecostal/charis 0.32%		6,200	12,000

Missionaries:
  to Ireland 274 (1:13,600 people) in 43 agencies.
  from Ireland 50 (1:2,600 Protestants) in 14 agencies 39frn 35xcul 15dom.

Roman Catholic 91.6%. Affil 86.13%.
Attendance 81%. Growth −0.1%.

Catholic Ch	1,150	2,790,000	3,204,000
Evang. Catholic 2.6% of pop		83,700	100,000

Missionaries:
  to Ireland 15 (1973 figure).
  from Ireland 4,498 (1:712 Catholics).

Orthodox 0.1%. Affil 0.05%. Growth 0.3%.

Denominations (4)	4	940	1,680

Marginal 0.3%. Affil 0.25%. Growth 3%.

Jehovah's Witnesses	93	3,451	6,280
Mormons	9	1,990	2,800
All groups (5)	105	5,561	9,360

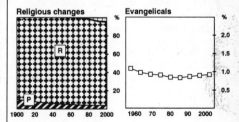

Religious changes

Evangelicals

1. **Praise God for the growth in spiritual concern in Ireland.**
a) **Church attendance**. An estimated 75% of Catholics, and 50% of the smaller Protestant community, attend church at least once a week There is, however, a growing percentage of young people who question the traditional conservatism of the past – and in some urban areas church attendance can be as low as 15%.

b) **The impact of the Scriptures**. The 1962–65 Vatican Council commended the use of the Bible and since then its widespread distribution by the National Bible Society has encouraged a spiritual hunger. There is now a Bible-oriented study/prayer group or fellowship in almost every town – a radical change over the last 20 years.

c) **The Charismatic Renewal movement**. This has given birth to house churches and independent evangelical and charismatic churches in many places in the South, as well as many Catholic charismatic prayer groups. In some instances, these prayer groups have developed into communities that fulfil the function of evangelical churches while remaining part of the Catholic Church or other mainline churches.

d) **The sending of missionaries**. Few countries in the world have such a high proportion of both Catholic and Protestant missionaries to church members.

2. **The Roman Catholic Church retains an influential position in the country** despite a slight decline in numbers. There have been significant renewal movements, such as Charismatic Renewal, Focolare and the Cursillo Movements which have brought new life to parts of the Church. There is a growing focus on an Evangelical Catholic movement, where a group of some 50 Catholic priests and lay-leaders produced a document entitled, *"What is an Evangelical Catholic?"*. The purpose of this document was to clarify aspects of fundamental Christian belief and to build bridges between born-again Christians in all the Christian Churches. However, as Irish Catholicism maintains traditional Catholic positions, pray that God would use the Evangelical Catholic initiative and that many Catholics would come to know Jesus as personal Lord and Saviour.

3. **Protestants** in Southern Ireland have declined over 70 years, from 15% to 4% of the population, through emigration, nominalism and the Catholic Church's policy on mixed marriages. But the Holy Spirit is working in each of the main Protestant denominations. The Church of Ireland (part of the Anglican Communion) is celebrating a Decade of Evangelism and has now at least 20 evangelical ministers. The Presbyterian church is growing and new churches have been built in Lucan and Kilkenny. Lucan is also the home of an Evangelical Reconciliation Centre, run by Presbyterian Youth. Both the Methodist and Baptist churches, under evangelical leadership, have seen growth in some congregations. In the last three years, three new Baptist churches have been formed. Pray that God would raise up more evangelical ministers within the established Protestant churches.

4. **Non-denominational and Pentecostal churches** have experienced strong growth over the last 10 years, birthing new ministries and several Bible colleges, one linked to the International Correspondence Institute in Brussels (**AoG**). A major evangelistic campaign in 1992, led by Luis Palau, was supported by over 60 evangelical churches and drew an attendance of approximately 16,000 people. Pray for greater unity among Irish leaders in non-denominational and Pentecostal churches and between them and evangelical leaders in the mainline denominations.

5. **Young people**: Ireland is a young country, with half its population under 28 years old. They are most responsive to the gospel. Christian camps are run by **Scripture Union** (with some 2–3,000 children per year), **CEF**, Bible Club and others. UCCF(**IFES**) has a ministry in some 20 colleges and universities. There is increasing openness in Dublin to presenting the gospel by street drama and sketchboard. As this new spiritual openness is also being tapped by many cults, pray that many more of Ireland's young people may come to know Jesus, who is the Truth.

6. **Missionaries** in Ireland are working in nearly all of the 26 counties. **GEM**, with 18 workers, has been instrumental in establishing Bible churches in the greater Dublin area with a strong indigenous membership. Other significant missions include **YWAM** (24), Brethren (20), Global Outreach (17), **AoG** (15), **UFM** (14) and Elim (12). Pray for their harmonious integration into the unique Irish scene, and for fruitfulness in ministry. Major missionary-contributing nations: USA (171), UK (71), Canada (20).

7. **Missionaries from Ireland** have gone out all over the world. However, recent years have seen an increase in both long- and short-term missionaries from the Republic. **YWAM** has a thriving base in Dublin and runs retreats and courses all over the South. A number of Evangelical Catholics have become full-time missionaries – some lay-leaders even running retreats for priests and religious workers. However, the lack of a background of tithing causes financial shortages for missionary work. Pray for the release, training and funding of more Irish missionaries and leaders by churches, fellowships and prayer groups.

8. **Less reached groups:**
a) There are approximately **7,000 itinerants** (Travellers), mostly illiterate, increasingly being housed in settled areas.
b) The **Irish-speaking minority,** who live mainly in the rural West, are more traditional, and the evangelical movement is less strong among them.
c) **Muslims are mostly of Arabic origin.** The Islamic movement has recently published a major part of the Koran in Irish and there are now four mosques in the Republic. Pray that God would bring Muslims to know Jesus.

Isle of Man

Included with UNITED KINGDOM

I

<table>
<tr><td>

July
4–5

Middle East

</td></tr>
</table>

Israel

(State of Israel)

Area 28,251 sq.km. – the total area administered by Israel since 1967 including the West Bank of the Jordan, the Gaza Strip and the Syrian Golan Heights.
Israel 20,700 sq.km. (including East Jerusalem).
West Bank (Judea and Samaria) 5,880 sq.km.
Gaza Strip 363 sq.km.
Golan Heights 1,295 sq.km. Annexed by Israel in 1981. Israel and these territories are handled separately below.

Population		Ann. Gr.	Density
1990	4,487,000	*3.9 %	217/sq.km
1995	5,438,000	1.9 %	262/sq.km

* Allowing for immigration.

Peoples:
Jews 81.8%. Immigrants from 102 nations. 450,000 new immigrants 1990–92, most coming from the USSR, before the flow started to slow down.
Arab 15.8%. Israeli Arab 700,000; Bedouin 50,000.
Other 2.4%. Druze 76,000; Egyptian 8,000; Adygey 3,000; Greek 2,700; Samaritan 500.

Literacy 92%. **Official languages:** Hebrew, Arabic. Numerous immigrant languages from all over the world are spoken. **Languages with Scriptures** 7Bi 2por.

Capital: Jerusalem 544,000, but not recognized as such internationally. Tel-Aviv conurbation 1,470,000. Urbanization 90.4%.

Economy: Modern, sophisticated industrial state. The economy is under severe stress because of the wave of new immigrants (25% of population), high military expenditure (29% of government spending), mounting public debt ($16,500/person) and rising unemployment. Income/person $9,750 (46% of USA).

Politics: The founding of Israel in 1948 ended 1,900 years of exile for the Jews. Five wars in 1948, 1956, 1967, 1973 and 1982-5 with surrounding states and also the 1991 Gulf War have exacted a heavy price on Israeli society. Military setbacks in Lebanon, the *intifada* and rapid development of Jewish settlements in the non-Jewish territories have polarized society and brought pressure for a resolution of the Arab-Israeli conflict. The future of the occupied territories – annexation, limited autonomy, or ultimately a Palestinian state – is the subject of intense national and international debate and negotiation. The 1992 elections brought about a change of government with a willingness to consider territorial compromises.

Religion: Freedom for all religious groups to minister within their own communities except for Jewish Christians who are denied any legal standing as a religious body. Proselytization and evangelism are frowned upon but not prevented. Successive coalition governments have obtained the support of smaller Jewish Orthodox parties in return for allowing some limitations on religious freedom.
Jews 81.4% – many divergent forms: Ultra-orthodox, modern Western and Eastern Orthodox, Traditional, Reform, Secular and even atheist. There is division on whether the Karaites (12,000), Samaritans (500) and Jewish Christians (4,000) should be counted. The former two are included here.
Muslims 14.5%. Mostly Sunni Palestinians.
Druze 1.6%. A quasi-Muslim sect with secret beliefs and rituals.
Non-religious/other 0.2% excluding Jews.
Christian 2.34%. Growth 1.4%. Denominational statistics below are for both Israel and the territories under Israeli administration.
Protestant 0.21%. Growth 2.9%.

Church	Cong	Members	Affiliated
Messianic Assemblies	34	2,000	4,000
Baptist Convention	17	842	2,720
Episcopal Ch	6	1,380	2,300
All other (49)	48	1,649	3,681
Denominations (52)	105	5,871	12,701
Evangelicals 0.16% of pop		4,300	9,800
Pentecostal/charis 0.07%		2,000	3,200

Missionaries:
to Israel & Palestine 444 (1:13,800 people) in 80 agencies, though the true number is nearer 1,000.
from Israel 10 (1:1,000 Protestants) 1xcul 9dom.
Catholic 1.3%. Growth 1.5%.

Catholic (5 rites)	89	47,200	80,000

Missionaries:
to Israel & Palestine 350 (1:17,500 people).
from Israel 8 (1:8,200 Catholics).
Orthodox 0.81%. Growth 0.9%.

Greek	23	26,400	44,000
Coptic	6	720	1,200
All other (7)	17	1,893	4,600
Denominations (9)	46	29,013	49,800

Foreign Marginal 0.02%. Growth 6%.

Jehovah's Witnesses	6	380	844
All groups (2)	7	430	924

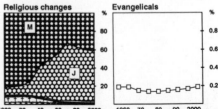

Religious changes / Evangelicals

1. **The return of Jews to Israel** accelerated after the collapse of Communism in East Europe and Ethiopia. Although this was a fulfilment of prophecy (Ezekiel 20:32–34; 36:16–24), most have returned to their ancient land in unbelief. Pray for the nation's spiritual restoration through Messiah Jesus (Romans 11:25,31).

2. **The intense half-century of conflict between Arabs and Israelis** urgently needs resolution. Both sides lay claim to the whole land. Pray for all politicians involved in the negotiating process, and for a just, lasting, adequately guaranteed settlement. Pray for the peace of Jerusalem – the most intractable of all the problems to be resolved, for the city is revered by Jews, Muslims and Christians alike.

3. **Dislike of Christianity is a barrier to be overcome in Jewish minds.** "Christian" nations are seen to be destroyers of the Jewish nation whether by persecution (as in the Holocaust) or by proselytization. Pray that the gospel may be understood as a fulfilment of their Jewish heritage and that a widespread turning to Christ might come. Since 1960, it is estimated that worldwide nearly 100,000 Jews have found the Messiah – mostly in North America.

4. **Praise God for increased boldness to witness** among Jewish Christians leading to a greater response. In 1965 there were but 300 Jewish Christians in Israel. By 1992 there were 3–4,000 who have come from every section of society. Recent immigrants from the former USSR constitute 50–60% of those now coming to the Lord.

5. **Jewish Christians** are often called Messianic Jews – evangelical believers who retain their Jewish identity. Pray for:
a) **Full legal rights of immigration** and social acceptance in the face of national, social and family pressures. Atheist Jews are welcomed, but not Jewish Christians!
b) **Retention of their culture** without compromise of New Testament truth. Indigenous music, hymnology and literature are developing.
c) **Evangelistic outreach** and effective methods to win others to Jesus. More vigorous outreach through these believers is bearing fruit.
d) **Unity.** There has been little real fellowship between the various groups. The **Messianic Jewish Alliance** is becoming a coordinating fellowship for public relations and cooperative efforts, and the **National Evangelistic Committee** for outreach.
e) **Effective leaders**, especially from among younger believers.

6. **The Christian Church in Israel is fragmented** and generally declining in numbers through emigration. It comprises about 85% Arab, 12% expatriate (Egyptian, Ethiopian Greek, Russian, Armenian, Italian, etc.) and 3% Jewish background. There are Catholics (five rites), Orthodox (nine traditions), and Protestants (17 denominations and over 100 mission agencies). Pray for spiritual unity that transcends history, ethnic conflict, national origins, eschatology and secondary areas of theology, and a concern that relatively few Jews and Muslims are being won to Christ – more Christians are becoming Jews and Muslims.

7. **Protestants are more numerous among the Palestinian Arabs.** The largest groups are Anglican, Baptist and Brethren, and most originate from the traditional Christian minority. Born-again Arab believers are a minority among the 6,000 Protestant Arabs, many being more nominal. There is some openness among Palestinian Muslims and freedom to share Christ with them, but there are, as yet, only three groups of believers of Muslim origin. Pray for the outreach of Arab believers to them.

8. **The Protestant missionary force** is estimated at around 1,000; many Christians have entered as individuals to serve the Lord. Some of the larger agencies are **SBC** (49 workers), Church of Scotland (42), Finnish Lutherans (28), **OM** (23), CMJ (Anglican, 21), **AoG** (15), **CMA** (11) and **CWI** (11). Years of seed-sowing and breaking down of long-held prejudices against Christianity are now bearing fruit, but missionary work can be frustrating and discouraging. Many come with exotic ideas about Israel and unrealistic visions, and find little fulfilment or identification with local believers. Pray that all called of God may find viable ministries, effective means of contact with non-Christians and sweet fellowship with local believers. Friendship evangelism, literature distribution and encouragement of believers are the major means of service.

9. **The major evangelistic challenges** are:
a) **Over a third of all Jews were born overseas.** Many still speak the languages of their lands of birth, and are better reached through those languages. Pray for the use of literature and other media among them.
b) **The recent immigrant Jews from eastern Europe.** This flood has strained the nation's resources. Unemployment and culture shock have brought frustration and anger. Many have no knowledge

of Judaism, but have a great spiritual hunger. Some have responded to the gospel. There are several congregations of Russian-speaking believers in Jerusalem. Pray for Russian-speaking Christians to be raised up to help them and to integrate them into Hebrew-speaking congregations.

c) **Ethiopian Jews.** There are 400 Christians among them in Israel. Three thousand were not permitted to immigrate in 1991 because they were Orthodox Christian despite their claim to Jewish identity.

d) **The 100 towns and 800 villages in Israel.** Only a handful have Jewish or Arab congregations.

e) **Palestinian Arabs.** Pray for the evangelization of the 95% who are Muslim. Only a few dozen believers from a Muslim background are known.

10. **Supportive ministries.**

a) **Literature** is of unusual importance for the spread of the gospel due to the multiplicity of languages and paucity of Christians who witness. Pray for the two Christian publishing houses, the production of an increasing selection of Hebrew and Arabic Christian literature, and the nine Christian bookshops. There are three Hebrew Christian periodicals that have a readership beyond the Christian community. Too few believers are engaged in distribution. Pray that Jews may read the NT and find the Living Word. 12% of all homes have a NT.

b) **Student work** is in its infancy. There are five groups with about 100 believers of Arab and Hebrew background linked with **IFES**. Leadership is the key prayer target.

11. **The Jews of the Dispersion** are declining in numbers through a lower birth rate, mixed marriages, secularism, emigration to Israel and conversions to other religions. There are now an estimated 10 million outside Israel. The largest concentrations are in North America six million; former USSR 1,200,000; France 700,000; Britain 330,000; and Argentina 350,000. There are two million Jews in New York. In the USA there is much openness; elsewhere less so. Pray for the ministry of **JFJ**, **MT**, **CWI**, CMJ, etc. Pray for a greater sensitivity on the part of Gentile churches towards the problems of Jewish survival and for the Jewish remnant within the Church. Little is being done for Jews in France and Argentina. The work involves long hours of loving, patient ministry to individuals and families.

GAZA STRIP

An enclave on the southeast corner of the Mediterranean coast.

Population		Ann. Gr.	Density
1990	623,000	3.3 %	1,716/sq.km
1995	719,000	2.9 %	1,980/sq.km

Peoples:
Arabs 96.8%. **Jews** 1.6%. **Other** 1.6%.

Literacy 70%.

Economy: Severe overcrowding, 40% unemployment, increasing poverty and a sense of angry futility and hopelessness.

Religion: Muslim fundamentalism growing and with an anti-Christian bias.
Muslim 98%. **Jew** 1.6%.
Christian 0.39%. Denominational statistics included with Israel.

WEST BANK

Part of what used to be Galilee and Samaria west of the River Jordan.

Population		Ann. Gr.	Density
1990	932,000	2.6 %	159/sq.km
1995	1,050,000	2.4 %	179/sq.km

Peoples:
Arab 88.3%. Palestinians worldwide number five million.
Jews 11%. New settlers.
Other 0.7%.

Literacy 70%.

Economy: Heavily dependent on income earned by Palestinians working in Israel and Arab oil states. Both the *intifada* and the Gulf War of 1990–1 have severely reduced this source. Unemployment is rising.

Politics: The loss of most of their land in 1948 and conquest of the remainder by Israel in 1967 dominates the life of Palestinians. The post-Gulf War international efforts to achieve a compromise settlement of the bitter confrontation between Israelis and Palestinians have only a small chance of success. The possibility of autonomy for the West Bank and Gaza has sparked a bitter power struggle between Islamic fundamentalists and the Palestine Liberation Organization. The Rabin government halted the development of new settlements in 1992.

Religion: Rising fundamentalist Islam and declining Christian population.
Muslim 82.1%. **Jews** 11%.
Christian 6.9% (2.5% including Gaza Strip). In 1940 Palestine was 30% Christian.
Protestant 1.3%. **Roman Catholic** 2.1%. **Orthodox** 3.5%. Denominational statistics included with Israel.

1. **The history of the Palestinian people over the past 50 years is tragic**. They became pawns of international politics, and in the process lost their homes, lands, livelihood and self-respect. 1,800,000 are retained in 61 refugee camps in surrounding Arab lands with little prospect of a return to their former homes or full integration into the host lands. The desire to regain these has led them into wars, globe-encircling terrorism, violence, internal divisions and frustrated hopes. A fair peace with Israel and a reasonable political solution looks unlikely, but not impossible. Pray for the peace of the land and, more, for Palestinians to meet with the Prince of Peace.

2. **The violence of the uprising or *intifada* against the occupying Israeli army** and the growing number of Jewish settlers has brought social disruption and increased poverty. Radical Muslim groups have gained a wide following (50% in Gaza and 30% on the West Bank). Pray that Palestinians may be spared the scourge of yet another tyranny, and that there may be freedom for the proclamation of the gospel whatever the future political direction.

3. **Christian Palestinians** trace their roots back to pre-Islamic times. The antagonisms of the conflict have provoked many to emigrate to Western countries, and their numbers have declined dramatically from 30% in 1940 to 2.5% in 1990. Pray that Orthodox, Catholic and Protestant Christians alike may courageously stand for and witness to the Truth, and be protected in a rising level of intimidation by their Muslim neighbours.

4. **Christian ministry has been restricted** by recent unrest, but continues. Pray for all involved in ministering to the physical and spiritual needs of the people. Especially difficult is work in squalid, prison-like Gaza.

July 6–8
Europe

Italy
(The Italian Republic)

Area 301,000 sq.km. A long, mountainous peninsula that dominates the central Mediterranean Sea. Also two large islands, Sardinia and Sicily.

Population		Ann. Gr.	Density
1990	57,323,000	0.07 %	190/sq.km
1995	57,592,000	0.09 %	191/sq.km

Peoples:
Italian 92.1%. Deep cultural differences exist between the wealthier and more radical northerners and the poorer, more conservative southerners.
Sardinian 2.7%. Speaking four Sard dialects.
Tyrolean 0.5%. In the northeast, speaking Austrian German.
Friulian/Ladin 0.95%. In the northeast.
Other European 1.75%. About half foreign-born. Albanian 320,000; Greek 139,000; French 114,000; Slovenian 96,000; Gypsy 48,000; British 29,000; Maltese 28,000; Croat 25,000.
Middle Eastern/African Est 1.9%. Officially 0.35%. There may be one million illegal immigrants from Africa – especially Arabs, Eritreans and Somalis.
Asians 0.1%. Chinese 40,000 and a growing number of Filipinos.

Literacy 97%. **Official language:** Italian, but vigorous use of nine regional languages akin to Italian. Worldwide there are 64 million Italian-speakers. **All languages** 30. **Languages with Scriptures** 7Bi 3NT 14por.

Capital: Rome 3,300,000. Other cities: Milan 4,600,000; Naples 2,690,000; Turin 1,757,000; Genoa 769,000; Florence 458,000. Urbanization 67%.

Economy: Highly centralized and inefficient government could have brought economic ruin had it not been for the success and drive of the private industrial sector and the initiative of the "black" (illegal) economy. The north is very industrialized. Failure to reform the economy and reduce public expenditure is reducing the country's competitiveness in world markets. Public debt/person $13,600. Income/person $15,150 (72% of USA).

Politics: United as a single state in 1870. Republican democracy since 1946. Weak and unstable succession of 50 governments since World War II but with an underlying social stability. The political paralysis, widespread corruption, economic differences between north and south, unchecked crimes of the Mafia, and the total discrediting of Italy's politicians and political parties came to a head in 1992. Widespread popular outrage and desire for overhaul of Italy's rotten political structures will bring immense changes in the '90s.

Religion: Roman Catholicism ceased to be the state religion in 1984. All religions have equal freedom before the law.
Non-religious/other 17.7%. Almost all were baptized in the Catholic Church.
Muslim 1.9%. **Jews** 31,800. **Baha'i** 5,000.
Christian 80.1%. Growth –0.2%.
Protestant 0.82%. Growth 2%.

Church	Cong	Members	Affiliated
Assemblies of God	1,053	137,000	275,000
Indep Pente Chs	350	70,000	140,000
Waldensian & Meth Ch	200	21,620	29,359
Christian Brethren	230	14,000	25,000
Apostolic Ch in Italy	54	4,700	10,400
Evang Baptist Union	83	4,107	10,300
All other (92)	664	69,868	169,056
Denominations (98)	2,634	321,295	659,115
Evangelicals 1.01% of pop		285,000	579,000
Pentecostal/charis 0.59%		168,000	340,000

Missionaries:
to Italy 462 (1:124,000 people) in 76 agencies.
from Italy 197 (1:3,300 Protestants) in 13 agencies 41frn 41xcul 156dom.
Roman Catholic 78.4%. Growth –0.3%.

Catholic Ch	21,492	34,400,000	45,850,000
Doubly counted		–680,000	–900,000
Total	21,492	33,720,000	44,950,000

Missionaries:
to Italy 8,200 (1973 figure).
from Italy 26,450 (1977 figure).
Other Catholic 0.02%. Growth 0.4%.

All groups (34)	47	5,180	8,780

Orthodox 0.07%. Growth –0.6%.

Denominations (6)	20	18,450	37,300

Marginal 0.73%. Growth 7.9%.

Jehovah's Witnesses	2,419	180,960	377,000
Mormons	89	8,400	14,000
All other (3)		13,064	26,172
Groups (5)	2,508	202,424	417,174

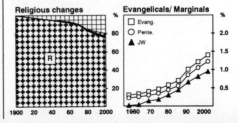

Religious changes

Evangelicals/ Marginals
□ Evang.
○ Pente.
▲ JW

1. **Persecution of Protestants persisted for nearly 800 years**. The last three decades of religious freedom have been met with indifference. Occultism is widespread, and there are reckoned to be 100,000 full-time consulting magicians – three times the number of Catholic priests. Satanism is strong in the north, Turin being one of the major global centres for its activities, which include praying for the removal of all evangelical missionaries from the country. The controlling spiritual powers in Italy have never been fully routed in 2,000 years.

2. **The long-powerful Roman Catholic Church** has lost over nine million members in this generation. Its influence and the number of priests have declined dramatically. Many Italians despise and ignore the Church, nevertheless its traditions and mind-set still permeate every aspect of national life, and church attendance remains one of the highest in Europe. In their disillusionment, many have turned to New Age thinking, cults, the occult and drugs. Pray for spiritual blindness to be removed.

3. **The infamous Sicilian Mafia and Neapolitan Camorra** have infiltrated every level of society. Their power and influence is such that every legal and judicial attempt to tame this monster has failed. Government officials and leaders, and Church authorities, even in the Vatican itself, have been subverted and the attitudes of the general population poisoned by this evil system. Murder and extortion are commonplace – the latter netting an estimated US$23 billion annually. This money and that gained from the lucrative global trade in drugs is used to buy politicians, influence and even industries. Pray for those courageous few who risk their lives to fight this evil system and usher in a new and more effective government system. Pray for Italian society to be freed from this bondage and to be transformed by the power of the gospel.

4. **The most unreached sectors of the population:**
a) **Less than 2,000 of Italy's communities** have an established evangelical witness. The other 31,000 are unoccupied.
b) **The northeastern Veneto Region** with the cities of Venice, Padova and Vicenza has 4,380,000 people, but maybe no more than 400 evangelical Christians – mainly **AoG**, **Brethren** and three congregations related to **ECM**.
c) **Sardinia**, a Mediterranean island with a limited autonomy, has 1,655,000 people with their own language and culture. There are only about 10 evangelical churches, and a few Christian workers. Suspicion of outsiders, fear, vendettas, the occult and the activities of JWs all make any evangelistic outreach difficult.
d) **The materialistic northern cities** of Milan, Turin, Bologna and Venice have few churches. Many cities and towns have no evangelical witness at all.
e) **The 1,147,000 students in 47 universities** are a needy mission field. There are only around 100 students linked to the GBU(**IFES**) in eight cities, and a few others with **CCC**, and with occasional outreaches by **OM** and **YWAM** teams. The second and third largest student bodies (117,000 in Milan, 106,000 in Naples) have no evangelical campus group.
f) **An estimated 400,000 heroin addicts**, with increasing incidence of HIV+ infection, pose a desperate and demanding challenge yet unmet by Evangelicals with the notable exception of those in Naples (**CBFMS** and others).

5. **Unreached minorities:**
a) **Muslims**. They have grown rapidly through legal and illegal immigration to possibly 750,000, 70% of whom are North African. There is little specific outreach to them.
b) **Africans** from all over Africa south of the Sahara who have immigrated seeking work – many congregating in Rome, where there are about 20,000. **SIM** has a small ministry to them.
c) **Albanians**. The long-established Calabrian and Sicilian Albanians speak their own archaic dialects – but little specific long-term outreach has been made. The flood of Albanian young people fleeing chaotic Albania since 1990 number some 30,000. They have responded warmly to material and spiritual help rendered by churches and agencies. Pray for conversions and churches to result.
d) **The minorities in the northeast**. The **Friulians**, **Ladins**, **Slovenes** and **South Tyrolean Germans** all have their own distinctive cultures and languages, but little direct effort is being made to reach these staunchly traditional Catholics with the message of new life in Jesus. The New Life Bible School in Switzerland has developed a good witness to South Tyrolean Germans.
e) **The Greek and Croatian minorities** in the south.

6. **The Protestant Church is weak and divided**, and evidences little cooperative or strategic thinking among leaders, though there are those seeking to change this. Churches tend to be small, introspective and largely ignorant of the biblical challenge to missions. Yet a slow and steady growth

is evident – particularly in the **AoG**, independent Pentecostal churches and the Brethren. Protestantism is still generally perceived as a foreign sect, despite the existence of the indigenous Waldensian Church, the world's oldest Protestant denomination. This latter is now in federal union with the Methodists and some Baptists and, sadly, influenced by liberal theology. Pray for revival that will break down barriers and bring true spiritual unity and a thrust to evangelize Italy.

7. **Evangelism**. Italian believers have shown increased enthusiasm for outreach since 1984. The south has been more responsive, with Sicily being the most fruitful. Here, AoG churches have increased from 150 to 200 in five years. The tireless efforts of Jehovah's Witnesses have made them as numerous as all Pentecostals and Charismatics, and have complicated and hampered personal witness. The AoG *Decade of Harvest*, *Italia per Cristo* and the itinerant tent campaigns of *Christ is the Answer* teams are three significant and praiseworthy initiatives for the '90s. **YWAM** has two bases with a staff of 23.

8. The dearth of mature Italian Christian leaders in Protestant churches at both the national and pastoral level is crippling the advance of the gospel. Internal conflicts and scandals due to pride, money and power-seeking have harmed the witness. Pray for humility, brokenness and unity among the Lord's servants. Pray that the increasing emphasis on preaching inner holiness, family unity and the life of the local congregation may bear fruit in lives. Pray also for the five denominational and two interdenominational Bible schools and seminaries and for an increase in student numbers. The AoG Bible School has 45 students, and the IBE (**GEM**) in Rome a smaller number. YWAM runs a six-month Discipleship Training School.

9. Italy needs missionaries – but of the right calibre. The casualty rate has been unacceptably high in the past, with but 10% on average returning for a second term. Pressures from spiritual forces and entrenched opposition to his message expose any personal inadequacies in a missionary. Pray out to the harvest field those with spiritual stamina, emotional maturity, cultural adaptability and God-given faith. Some significant missionary groups (and number of expatriates) in the country are Brethren (35), **BCU** (28), **CBFMS** (25), **YWAM** (23), **UFM** (21), **CLC** (20), **AoG** (18), **GEM** (17), **TEAM** (15), **SBC** (15), **ECM** (14), and **WEC** (9). Major missionary-contributing nations: USA (277), UK (39), Canada (24), Switzerland (16), Korea (12), Brazil (11). All mission groups, especially the interdenominational, have had traumatic histories. Ministries most needed are in discipleship and planting balanced, Bible-based churches.

10. Literature and Bible distribution have not had a wide impact due to the reluctance of Italians to read. There are about 14 Christian organizations with bookshops – including CLC with 20 full-time workers and seven bookstores. The new common-language Italian Bible was published in 1984. Pray for a hunger for God's Word and a desire for wholesome Christian literature.

11. Christian radio and TV has become an extraordinary tool for evangelism since government control of broadcasting was relaxed. There are now 600 private TV stations in Italy! There are 100 evangelical local radio stations and many other commercial stations that broadcast evangelical programmes. Many churches and missions have developed ministries in radio (including Back to the Bible, ECM, GMU, and **WT**). Pray that in this multiplicity of effort there may be fruitful cooperation to produce relevant, dynamic programmes. Many recent conversions in Italy have been through this medium. Adequate follow-up is a problem. Anarchy on the radio waves has forced a change in the law; pray for the wise use of this medium.

THE HOLY SEE
(State of the Vatican City)

Area 0.43 sq.km. The world's smallest State; an enclave in the heart of the city of Rome.

Population 755. Italian and global composition – almost entirely Catholic hierarchy.

Politics: The Pope is head of State as well as leader of the world's 900 million Catholics.

1. Pray for Pope John Paul II who exercises such an influence within and beyond the Church he leads.

2. The Roman Catholic Church is going through a time of intense turmoil and change. Pray that these changes may be guided by the Holy Spirit. The increasing prominence of the Bible among Catholics is cause for praise – pray that lives, doctrine and structures may be moulded by the Scriptures. There is a small Evangelical Catholic movement within the Church, but it has difficulty in making headway in the face of a conservative hierarchy.

3. Charismatic renewal has had an impact far beyond the 50 million or so who have been or are involved in charismatic meetings. A good proportion of the Catholic missionary force is now charismatic. Pray that the Holy Spirit may bring new life to millions of nominal Catholics.

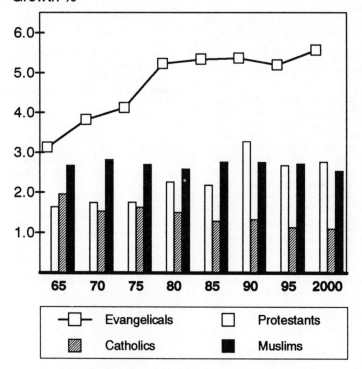

Average Annual Growth Rate
Comparison between Muslims and Christians

Growth %

Legend: Evangelicals, Protestants, Catholics, Muslims

Many have claimed that Islam is the fastest growing religion in the world. This is not wholly correct. Note the annual growth rates above:

1. **The relatively high but consistent growth of Muslims** (the black bar). This is almost entirely due to a high birth rate.

2. **The rising growth rate of Protestants** to equal or surpass that of Muslims – much of this being due to conversions.

3. **The steady decline in growth rate of Roman Catholics.** This is due to large losses to Protestants in Latin America and to secularism in Europe and also due to the lack of manpower in the service of the Church. Ordinations to the priesthood have fallen dramatically worldwide.

July 9	*Jamaica*
Caribbean	

Area 11,000 sq.km. The third largest island in the Caribbean.

Population	Ann. Gr.	Density
1990	2,521,000	1.5 %	229/sq.km
1995	2,706,000	1.4 %	246/sq.km

Emigration 1.1%, mainly to North America.

Peoples:
Afro-Caribbean 93.7%.
Asian/Afro-Asian 5%. East Indian 42,900; Chinese 31,000; Lebanese 2,000.
Euro-American 1.3%. English-speaking 15,000; Spanish-speaking 8,000; Portuguese 5,000.

Literacy 89%. **Official language:** English.

Capital: Kingston-St Andrew 801,000. Urbanization 53%.

Economy: A flirtation with Cuban-style socialism in the '70s damaged the bauxite, sugar and banana industries and drove away the tourists on which the country had depended. Successive governments in the '80s have sought to repair the economy, but a devastating hurricane in 1988 was a further setback. Economic misery, poverty in the urban shanty-towns, a high crime rate, a large foreign debt and 18% unemployment are the result. Public debt/person $1,600. Income/person $1,080 (5% of USA).

Politics: Independent of Britain in 1962 as a parliamentary democracy. Reasonably stable politically despite economic disarray and social violence.

Religion:
Non-religious/other 3.8%.
Spiritist/cultist 9.5%. Rastafarians, Pocomanians, Obeah and many others.
Hindu 0.3%. **Muslim** 0.2%. **Baha'i** 0.2%.
Christian 86%. Nom 35.6%. Affil 50.4%. Attend 36%. Growth 1.7%.
 Protestant 69.8%. Affil 37.9%. Growth 1.6%.

Church	Cong	Members	Affiliated
Seventh-day Adventist	479	67,500	135,000
Jamaica Baptist Un	281	39,991	114,000
Anglican Ch	274	51,500	103,000
NT Church of God	307	35,104	58,507
Methodist Ch	180	18,193	44,500
United Ch	148	16,700	44,000
Ch of God of Prophecy	290	16,000	40,000
Assemblies of God	99	5,200	17,000
Gospel Assemblies	167	8,000	16,000
Moravian Ch	58	3,310	11,037
Int Ch of Foursq Gosp	26	1,770	5,907
All other (325)	1,805	178,543	367,856
Denominations (336)	4,114	441,811	956,000
Evangelicals 18.5% of pop		221,000	467,000
Pentecostal/charis 11%		140,000	279,000

Missionaries:
 to Jamaica 209 (1:12,000 people) in 42 agencies.
 from Jamaica 45 (1:21,200 Protestants) in 8 agencies 23 frn 23xcul 22dom.

Roman Catholic 11.3%. Affil 9.2%. Growth 2%.

Catholic Ch	112	135,140	233,000

Missionaries:
 to Jamaica 167 (1:15,100 people).
 from Jamaica 40 (1973 figure).

Orthodox 0.1%. Affil 0.1%. Growth 0%.

Total	4	2,000	3,330

Foreign Marginal 0.8%. Affil 0.8%. Growth 5.1%.

Jehovah's Witnesses	171	9,166	14,800
Mormons	13	1,260	2,100
All other (7)	20	1,320	3,300
Groups (9)	204	11,746	20,200

Indigenous Marginal 4.1%. Affil 2.2%. Growth 1.3%.

All groups (24)	424	29,320	57,600

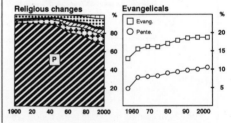

Religious changes   Evangelicals

1. **The country is sinking into a morass of social and economic problems** that appear insoluble. Violence in society is made worse by the powerful drug mafias and their distribution networks in both Jamaica and North America. Pray that government and church leaders may have moral integrity and determination to turn the country back to God.

2. **Spiritual stagnation** has set in. Over a third of the population attends church regularly, but growth in Evangelical and Pentecostal churches is at the expense of traditional churches rather than from among outsiders. There are over 300 denominations in the country. Pray for true revival that breaks down the barriers of sin and separatism.

3. **The spiritual temperature of Jamaica** influences the whole Caribbean. Pray that the Jamaica Association of Evangelicals may be a model of unity and cooperation to weak and struggling associations in other countries. Pray also that the 14 Bible schools and seminaries in Jamaica, which serve the whole Caribbean, may be powerhouses of spiritual life and missions vision.

4. **Stable family life, even among Christians, is a rarity.** Less than 15% of all births are legitimate. Pray for all ministries among children and young people. Pray that the combined ministry of **IFES** and **SU**, with 18 university and 150 high school groups, may result in fellowships that are biblical, evangelistic and courageous. In many schools, 10% of the students belong to these groups. Pray that the seven staff workers and the many Christian teachers may see a radical moral and spiritual uplift among children so that the next generation fares better.

5. **The less evangelized.**
a) **Rastafarians,** a growing force in Jamaica and 12 other Caribbean states. They reject the Western worldview and champion black consciousness, exotic life styles and drug use. They need the Saviour. They number 70,000 in Jamaica, and possibly 180,000 in the Caribbean, USA and UK.
b) **The Chinese.** Most are nominally Catholic, but there is a lively Chinese Christian fellowship on the island.

6. **A missions vision** is largely lacking. Jamaica's illustrious past contribution to the evangelization of West Africa is forgotten. Pray for the Jamaican International Missionary Fellowship, its promotion of missions in churches and schools, its School of Missionary Training and its missionaries sent out into cross-cultural work. Pray for Caribbean churches to once again catch a vision for world evangelization.

7. **Christian help ministries** – many serving the whole Caribbean.
a) **The Bible Society** which is a channel for Scriptures to most of the mini-states of the region.
b) **Literature. CLC** has a notable ministry through four bookstores, a bookmobile and the region-wide distribution of *Caribbean Challenge*. The seven staff are too few to adequately handle the ministry. Pray that more spiritual and teaching literature may be bought and used by Christian leaders.
c) **Operation Saturation,** an **EHC**-sponsored effort to distribute evangelistic and teaching literature to every home in the country.

J

Japan
(Nippon)

Area 372,300 sq.km. A 3,000 km. arc of four large islands (Honshu, Hokkaido, Shikoku, Kyushu) and 3,000 small islands in N.W. Pacific. Mountainous; only 13% can be cultivated.

Population		Ann. Gr.	Density
1990	123,457,000	0.44 %	327/sq.km
1995	126,319,000	0.46 %	334/sq.km

Peoples:
Indigenous 99.3%.
Japanese 99.1%. Sub-groups: Eta (former slave class) 2,470,000; Ryukyuan 148,000; Okinawan 802,000; South American Japanese returnees 150,000.
Ainu 0.2%. The aboriginal inhabitants who have largely lost their original languages.
Foreign 0.7%. Korean 720,000; Chinese 150,000; American 70,000; Filipinos 36,000.
Illegal immigrants: Over 300,000 Pakistanis, Iranians, Bangladeshis, Filipinos, Thai, Malaysians and others.

Literacy 100%. **Official language**: Japanese. There are 125 million Japanese speakers in the world. **All languages** 15 (including 10 Okinawan-Ryukyuan dialects). **Languages with Scriptures** 2Bi 1por.

Capital: Tokyo. Major conurbations: Tokyo-Yokohama-Kawasaki 18,500,000, Osaka-Kobe 5,400,000, Fukuoko-Kita-Kyushu 2,800,000, Nagoya 2,149,000, Sapporo 1,648,000, Kyoto 1,533,000, Hiroshima 1,079,000. Urbanization 77%.

Economy: The world's most powerful export-oriented economy despite lack of oil and raw materials. Low interest rates stimulated a capital investment boom based on high property values. Tokyo became the same "value" as the entire USA. The property crash and Japan's huge trade surplus with the world are stress-points in the world economy and contributory factors in the world recession in the early '90s. Public debt/person $9,464. Income/person $23,730 (116% of USA).

Politics: Constitutional monarchy with a parliamentary democracy. The 45 years of stability and economic expansion have turned Japan into an economic superpower. Rising nationalism and willingness to exert political power in the Pacific causes unease among neighbours. Numerous scandals, corruption and shoddy factional politics discredit the present political system.

Religion: Freedom of religion is guaranteed to all by the constitution, but the rising power of nationalistic Shintoism partly associated with the new Emperor is tarnishing that freedom.
Non-religious/other 12%. Up to 84% of Japanese claim no personal religion, but most follow the customs of Japan's traditional religions. Hence percentages below are only a guide!
Shinto. 80% believe in it; 3% claim to be Shinto. Polytheistic, ancestor-venerating Shintoism has been much modified by Confucianism and Buddhism. Many follow both Shinto and Buddhist customs.
Buddhist 58%, but only 20% practise the religion.
New Religions 24%. Most are Buddhist and Shinto offshoots and increasingly mixed with a New Age worldview. An estimated 100 new religions are founded each year.

Sokka Gakkai	17,000,000
Risshokoseikai	5,500,000
Seicho no Ie	3,700,000

Muslims 0.2%. Mainly South Asians.
Christian 2.5%. Nom 0.91%. Affil 1.59%. Growth 1.8%.
Protestant 1.13%. Affil 0.53%. Growth 1.3%.

Church	Cong	Members	Affiliated
United Ch of Christ	1,445	128,017	202,154
Holy Cath Ch (Anglican)	277	28,972	57,900
Baptist Convention	225	15,088	30,609
Evang Lutheran Ch	155	7,230	21,909
Assemblies of God	165	10,634	16,656
Presb Ch of Christ	143	6,040	13,719
Immanuel Gen Missn	118	7,090	12,436
Ch of Jesus Christ	110	9,293	12,242
Japan Holiness Ch	161	8,130	11,471
Ch of the Nazarene	73	7,187	10,334
Christian Brethren	163	5,550	9,241
Evangelical Alliance	168	6,360	8,694
Jun Evangelical Ch	12	2,350	5,868
All other (128)	3,282	144,037	229,392
Denominations (141)	6,587	391,138	648,829
Evangelicals 0.32% of pop		239,000	389,000
Pentecostal/charis 0.06%		51,000	78,000

Missionaries:
to Japan 3,007 (1:41,000 people) in 194 agencies.
from Japan 407 (1:1,600 Protestants) in 54 agencies 269frn 199xcul 208dom.
Roman Catholic 0.34%. Growth 0.1%.

Catholic Ch	950	290,000	413,766

Missionaries:
to Japan 1,731 (1:72,000 people).
from Japan 170 (1973 figure).
Orthodox 0.02%. Growth 0.2%.

Denominations (2)	86	10,300	25,867

Foreign Marginal 0.56%. Growth 3.6%.

Jehovah's Witnesses	2,355	147,622	246,000
Mormons	264	72,800	91,000
All other (6)	75	283,218	355,478
Groups (8)	2,694	503,640	692,478

Indigenous Marginal 0.14%. Growth 0.9%.

Spirit of Jesus	650	78,000	130,000
Original Gospel Tab	865	22,500	45,000
All other (3)	26	1,050	1,500
Groups (5)	1,541	101,550	176,500

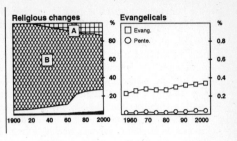

1. **Japan is a mixture of openness and unresponsiveness.** The demonic forces associated with idolatry in temples and ancestor worship in homes have never been decisively challenged. Spiritual warfare is being waged on these fronts:
a) **Social life.** The sincere, polite, hard-working Japanese are too busy to give heed to the gospel and understand little of what is right or wrong or of the meaning of sin because they do not know the Creator God. Most see the value of religion, 30% have a definite religion, but only 10% believe in the existence of a personal God. Pray for the Holy Spirit to bring conviction of sin to the nation.
b) **Resurgence of a nationalistic Shintoism** that is hostile to anything un-Japanese. Pray for Christians to stand firm in Jesus and not compromise their faith under pressure as did many Christians during World War II.
c) **New religions.** The growth of Sokka Gakkai and other religions in the '50s and '60s, as well as the successes of aberrant versions of Christianity such as Moonies, Jehovah's Witnesses and Mormons, is a challenge to Evangelicals who have grown more slowly. An average of 100 new religions are started each year – based on the occult, worship of extra-terrestrial aliens and so on. Pray for the removal of a spirit of delusion.
d) **The youth** who are turning away from the values and work ethic of their parents, and turning to materialistic pleasures, drugs and possessions rather than to the living God. Pray that present economic shocks, instability and fears for the future may shake many out of complacency.
e) **The minimal impact made by the average Japanese Christian** on the centres of power in the land. The lack of radiant witnesses for Jesus in the industrial, commercial and political realms is cause for concern. Nevertheless, Christianity exerts a moral and social influence and attraction far beyond its relatively small presence.

2. **The Church in Japan** experienced good growth between 1945 and 1960, but both Catholic and Protestant percentages have only marginally increased since then, with conversions only just exceeding backslidings. The decisive breakthrough has yet to come, so pray for:
a) **The United Church** – a 50-year-old union of Presbyterian, Methodist and Congregational Churches formed under duress during the war. Liberalism and controversies in the '60s, stirred up by leftist young pastors over social action, blunted evangelistic outreach and caused a decline in membership for a time. Pray for a moving of the Spirit and a return to biblical theology in this and other denominations.
b) **The numerous Evangelical,** and especially Pentecostal denominations, which have grown in numbers and congregations. In 1950 Evangelicals were 20% of Protestants; today they are 65%. The 5,875 Protestant churches had grown to 7,001 by 1990, but most are small. The **Japan Evangelical Alliance** has a membership of 38 denominations, 12 church groupings and 38 agencies. The JEA has sponsored three major national Congresses on Evangelism (1974, 1982, 1991) and other major evangelistic efforts.
c) **Goals for the '90s.**
   i) **One church for every 10,000 people** by the year 2000 – which means 12,360 churches. Humanly speaking, this is unrealistic and the rate of church planting has been slowing.
   ii) **Japan to be 10% Christian** by the year 2000 – this can only happen through a massive mobilization of prayer and outreach hitherto unknown in the country.
   iii) Individual denominations who have set significant growth goals – **AoG, SBC,** and others.
   iv) New writers, evangelists and radio preachers for the next generation.

3. **Bible training for Christian workers** is provided by nearly 100 denominational and interdenominational seminaries and Bible Schools in which over 3,000 are in full-time training. The great hope for the future of the Church is the high quality of many of Japan's pastors and church

leaders. May their numbers be mightily increased! Pray for more men and couples to be called into pastoral and missionary work and to come for training.

4. **Specific weaknesses in the churches:**

a) **Lack of biblical teaching.** Christians need complete renewal of their minds. The pervasive influence of the demonic world, philosophies and superstitions must be replaced by a vibrant theology and a head and heart knowledge of God's greatness and holiness.

b) **The minority complex.** Christians are a tiny minority in a society where consensus is important. Too few families come to faith, and individuals feel exposed.

c) **Non-active membership and backsliding.** Church attendance is low, with only 33% of Protestants attending services weekly. Often Christians are influenced by the Buddhist/Shinto religions which have no regular attendance requirements, and this thinking is carried over into Christian attitudes.

d) **The lack of breadwinning men in the churches.** The drive for success and desire to satisfy the demands of employers make it hard for men to openly identify with and become active in a church. Women are in the great majority in most congregations.

e) **Too few viable, active congregations.** 70% or more of all churches have an average attendance of less than 30. Too much is done by the pastor. Pray for pastors to be willing to activate lay people to work together in persistent, innovative outreach to non-Christians. Lay people's breakfasts in 125 venues is one such effort.

f) **Formality in worship services.** May more life, more joy, and a Japanese hymnology be infused into them!

g) **Lack of understanding about evil spirits and occultism,** and even evangelical theologians who deny their existence.

5. **The missions vision of Japanese Christians** is noteworthy. Over 370 missionaries have been or are serving overseas. There are now 269 serving in 37 lands around the world. Churches have little vision for missions or understanding of the problems of cross-cultural missions and missionaries. There are two small Missionary Training Centres backed by some Japanese churches and missions. The launching of the Tokyo Christian University is expected to play a major role in training future missionaries to serve around the world. The Japanese Overseas Missions Association has a membership of 12 Japanese agencies. One of the big hindrances for long-term Japanese missionary service is the difficulty of re-intergrating children of the missionaries into Japan when they return.

6. **Missions.**

a) **First-term missionaries.** Japan is easy for missionaries to enter, but then the difficulties begin! The difficulty of the language and script, the complexities of the culture, the bewildering strands of a web society, and the pervading influence of the demonic world are all barriers to adaptation and communication. Acculturation takes years, and many missionaries are still in that tearful stage. Pray for them.

b) **Missionary agencies** which are often small and cooperation too limited. Most are involved in church planting and evangelism, but few have found *the* key to growth. Pray for leaders, for the right strategies, and for Spirit-anointed ministries. The profusion of agencies and nationalities defies listing here! There are 466 Baptist missionaries in 16 agencies, 315 Lutherans, 162 Presbyterians, as well as: **TEAM** (163 workers), **OMF** (132), **SEND** (81), **AoG** (50), Liebenzell (28), **OMS** (35), Finnish Free Mission (33), **Brethren** (33), **WEC** (31), **IMI** (21), **CMA** (20), **JEB** (13) and many others. Major missionary-contributing nations: USA (1,753), Norway (173), Finland (104), Germany (102), Korea (94), Sweden (81), Canada (81), UK (76).

c) **Opportunities for missionary service.** These are many, the most needful being evangelism, church planting and teaching. The Japanese Education Ministry hires 2,000 English teachers annually for assisting in high schools; this and private English tuition give good contacts for tentmaking missionaries. Conducting weddings for the one third of Japanese couples desiring a "Christian" wedding gives missionaries and pastors unique evangelistic opportunities at unconverted gatherings!

7. **The less-reached areas and peoples of Japan:**

a) Of the 680 **cities,** there are still eight without a church.

b) Of the 2,597 **towns** of 15,000–30,000 people, 1,823 are without churches.

c) Numerous **country areas** are scarcely touched with the gospel.

d) **The Burakumin** or Eta, descendants of the former outcastes, still suffer some degree of social ostracism. Many have become followers of Sokka Gakkai. Most live in the central Kinki region. There are very few Christians among them, most fearing that becoming one would increase their social ostracism. There is no Christian mission specifically seeking to reach them.

e) **The Ainu**, a non-Mongolian race, first settled in north Japan. They have been partly assimilated into Japanese culture, but a resurgence of Ainu culture may require a specific Christian outreach to them.

f) **Koreans**, descendants of those forcibly brought to Japan between 1903 and 1945, are still classed as resident aliens, despised, poorly paid and usually denied full citizenship rights. The Korean community is sharply divided in their allegiance to either North or South Korea. Korean missionaries have planted over 75 churches among them, but the percentage of Christians among them is lower than that of South Korea.

g) **Chinese**, 60,000 residents, are largely involved in business in the larger cities. The great majority are non-religious or follow the Chinese traditional religions. There are 14 churches among them with 1,100 Christians. There are 90,000 Chinese students in Japan, 50,000 from mainland China – a potentially fruitful field for ministry.

8. **Student witness** is one of the most strategic for the future of the Church. There are 1,123 universities and colleges with 2,500,000 students, but in only 323 of the colleges are there KGK(**IFES**) groups with a total of 1,800 students involved. Japan **CCC** with 20 workers, **YWAM** and **Navigators** (28) also minister on these campuses. Apathy towards religion and scepticism of established religion are widespread, and few make a commitment to Christ, despite the respect for the teachings of Christianity.

9. **Christian literature** – in no other country of the world is literature more suitable for evangelism. A highly literate, reading, commuting society offers excellent publishing and distributing structures for high-quality Christian literature. Pray for:

a) **More Christian writers** of evangelistic and apologetic literature who can communicate with non-Christian enquirers.

b) **Understanding of the Scriptures.** Over three million Bibles are sold annually, and 43% of the under-30s possess a copy, but few understand what they read.

c) **Christian bookstores** which number over 110, with several large networks including Word of Life (**TEAM** 150 workers, 20 stores), **CLC** (80 workers).

d) **Evangelistic literature.** New Life League is a notable producer of literature. **EHC** tracts have been widely distributed.

10. **Christian radio and TV** are useful tools for reaching electronically-minded Japanese. Pray for:

a) **Christian TV programmes** on VHF channels. Dr Paul Yonggi Cho, Pacific Broadcasting Association *Lifeline* and *Harvest Time* are notable examples of ministries with an extensive audience. Satellite TV and cable radio (**TEAM**) broadcasting present a new challenge for Christian broadcasters. Pray that these may be used wisely.

b) **Many radio programmes aired in Japan** (Pacific Broadcasting Association, **TEAM**, **FEBC**, Japan Mission, Lutheran Hour and others).

c) **Foreign short-wave Christian radio stations. FEBC**-Korea, **TWR**-Guam, **HCJB**-Ecuador and others broadcast a total of 60 hours/week in Japanese. Millions of young people belong to short-wave listeners' clubs and listen to these broadcasts.

d) **The *Jesus* film** on video. Over 70% of homes have a VCR. Pray for an effective video distribution plan and for Christians to be trained in the effective use of the *Jesus* video. Video evangelism is proving a key method of outreach – a wider range of videos needs to be produced.

Johnston Island

Included with GUAM

<table>
<tbody>
<tr><td>July 14</td><td rowspan="2">Jordan
(The Hashemite Kingdom of Jordan)</td></tr>
<tr><td>Middle East</td></tr>
</tbody>
</table>

J

Area 88,000 sq.km. Agriculture and population concentrated in the west on the eastern bank of the River Jordan. Most of the country is desert. Jordan has renounced claims on the Palestine West Bank, occupied by the Israelis since 1967.

Population	Ann. Gr.	Density
1990 3,364,000	4.5 %	38/sq.km
1995 3,813,000	2.5 %	43/sq.km

A further 300,000 Palestinians and 80,000 Iraqis have fled to Jordan from Kuwait and Iraq since the start of the Gulf War in 1990.

Peoples:
Arab 96.1%. Palestinian 2,000,000, East Bank Jordanian 1,400,000.
Indigenous minorities 1.6%. Adygey (Circassian) 40,000; Armenian 4,200; Kurd 4,000; Turkoman 4,000; Chechen 3,000.
Other 2.3%. Egyptian 70,000; Greek, Westerner, Pakistani, other Arab nationals.

Literacy 80%. **Official language:** Arabic. **All languages** 6. **Languages with Scriptures** 2Bi 2NT 2por.

Capital: Amman 1,200,000, but supplemented with Gulf refugees since 1991. Urbanization 70%. Nomadic 5%.

Economy: The recovery after the loss of the West Bank in 1967 was good, but the Gulf War and sanctions against Iraq have had a disastrous effect on the economy. Main exports: phosphates, chemicals and fruit. Unemployment over 20%. Public debt/person $1,182. Income/person $1,300 (6.2% of USA).

Politics: Part of Turkish empire until 1918. Independent from Britain in 1946. Constitutional monarchy with King Hussein having executive powers. Involvement with the losing side in three wars with Israel, and in the 1990/1 Gulf crisis and war, have deeply affected every aspect of life due to loss of land, influx of refugees and economic disruption. Jordan relinquished its claim to the Palestinian West Bank, but nearly 2/3 of the present population is Palestinian. The growing power of the Muslim Brotherhood is putting pressure on the government to both permit democratic freedoms and bring in a stronger Islamic system for the country.

Religion: Islam is the state religion, but the constitution prohibits discrimination and promotes the free exercise of religious belief and worship, while prohibiting religious change for Muslims.
Non-religious/other 1.28%
Muslim 94%. Almost entirely Sunni Islam; 3,000 Alawites, a few Druzes and Shi'ites.
Christian 4.69%. Growth –1.3%.
  Protestant 0.46%. Growth 0.3%.

Church	Cong	Members	Affiliated
Episcopal Ch	20	3,900	6,500
Evang Lutheran Ch	5	960	1,600
Baptist Convention	8	580	1,060
Assemblies of God	5	277	990
Evang Ch of CMA	6	219	567
Ch of the Nazarene	7	430	550
Evang Free Ch	9	275	458
All other (13)	19	2,225	3,733
Denominations (20)	79	8,866	15,458
Evangelicals 0.2% of pop		3,750	7,000
Pentecostal/charis 0.03%		277	990

Missionaries:
  to Jordan 103 (1:32,600 people) in over 22 agencies.
  from Jordan 16 (1:1,000 Protestants) 16frn 7stw.
Roman Catholic 1.55%. Growth –2.8%.

Catholic	65	29,600	52,000

Missionaries to Jordan 70 (1973 figure).
Orthodox 2.68%. Growth –0.7%.

Greek Orthodox	32	47,000	84,000
Armenian Orthodox	1	900	1,500
Syrian Orthodox	1	960	4,800
Denominations (3)	34	48,860	90,300

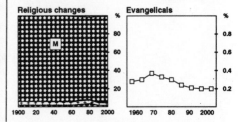

Religious changes | Evangelicals

1. **The Gulf War worsened Jordan's economic crisis** and destabilized political life. Pray for the peace of this land and for the King and government. Pray for the maintenance of religious freedom in the face of rising extremism among some Muslims. Jordan is a centre for many Christian activities – language learning, literature preparation and distribution, and media ministries.

2. **The Christian community** has been in steady decline as a percentage of the population for years, due to lower birth rates, high rate of emigration, and influx of Muslim refugees. Yet Christians are found in all walks of life and often in positions of great influence. Most are Orthodox, Catholic, or mainline Protestant. Pray that Christians may use every opportunity to share their faith with both nominal Christians and non-Christians.

3. **Evangelical churches** are few: 11 in Amman and 18 in the whole country. The most influential are those of **CMA, Nazarenes, SBC**, Free Evangelical and **AoG**. There are less than 7,000 Evangelicals, but there is some growth through effective witnessing. Most conversions are from the nominal Christian community. The constant loss of leadership potential through emigration is a drain on the tiny body of believers. Sadly, of the many who go to other lands for Bible training, few return. Youth work and Christian camp ministries have been fruitful in recent years. Pray for more Jordanian believers to be called to full-time work. A new evangelical theological seminary in Amman is supported by the various churches.

4. **The Gulf War led to deep questioning of the relevance and truth of Islam.** There has been unprecedented openness among Jordanians and refugees (both Palestinian and Asian) which has led to conversions to Christ. The loving and effective aid and witness of Jordanian Christians was a major factor. Pray that this openness may persist and new churches may multiply. Iraqi refugees are still being cared for and some 150 meet weekly for worship and preaching of the Word.

5. **Foreign missionaries** are somewhat limited in range and profile of ministry because of the sensitive religious and political situation, but strategic in supporting and enhancing the ministry of national believers. Pray that their lives may commend the Lord Jesus and gain witness opportunities. Asian missionaries could possibly be more acceptable and welcomed than Westerners. Some of the largest agencies are **SBC** (20 workers) and **CBFMS** (10).

6. **The unreached** are the vast majority of the population. Pray that every Jordanian may have opportunity to hear the gospel by the year 2000. Pray especially for:
a) **The Muslim majority.** Very few have ever heard the gospel clearly presented. Pray for a sensitive witness to Muslims. The most successful methods have been through literature, films, cassettes, friendship evangelism and home meetings. Pray for the happy incorporation of converts from the majority community into fellowships of believers, and their protection in persecution. Pray also for the legal right to convert from Islam.
b) **The Palestinians** who are now a majority in Jordan. Many have been integrated into Jordanian life, but others are still refugees housed in large UN-run camps. Disillusionment, bitterness and frustration have made deep wounds which only the Man of Calvary can heal. Pray for the few Christian Palestinians in the camps.
c) **The 240,000 Bedouin.** Many are still nomadic, and many others are in the army or reachable in cities and hospitals. Believers are very few.
d) **The people in the drier** east and south of the country.
e) **The minorities** – especially the proud and wealthy Adygey, once Christian but now Muslim, and also the Kurdish and Chechen communities.

7. **The missionary vision of the believers is growing,** but more could be done. There are already Jordanian believers serving the Lord in secular work all over the Middle East. Others have become well known all over the Arab World as evangelists and radio preachers.

8. **The ministry of media.** The paucity of Christians and the difficulties placed in the way of open witness to the majority community enhance the importance of radio, cassettes, videos, films and literature. Arabic radio programmes from **FEBA**-Seychelles (18 hours/week), **TWR**-Monaco (2 hours) and High Adventure in South Lebanon (112 hours/week in both radio and TV) have had a significant impact. The *Jesus* film has already been seen by nearly 500,000 people with hundreds of responses. Pray for long-term fruit.

9. **Literature** in Arabic is becoming more widely available. Pray for effective distribution in Jordan and beyond of books, magazines and tracts through two bookstores – a ministry in which **OM** is actively involved. Pray also for the work of the Bible Society in a ministry that is also strategic for the surrounding nations, where restrictions on Christian work are severe.

<table>
<tr><td>

July 15–16

Eurasia
</td></tr>
</table>

Kazakhstan
(Republic of Kazakhstan)

Area 2,717,000 sq.km. Dominating Central Asia and trade routes between east and west. Much of the country is semi-desert.

Population		Ann.Gr	Density
1990	16,662,000	1.05%	6.1/sq.km
1995	17,206,000	1.10%	6.3/sq.km

Peoples: Figures for 1989; many changes by 1992.
Turkic/Altaic 47.7%. Largest: Kazakh 6,535,000; Uzbek 332,000; Tatar 328,000; Uyghur 300,000; Mesketian Turks 125,000; Azerbaijani 90,000. Kazakhs will be about 65% of the population by the year 2000.
Indo-European 51.7%. Many emigrating.
Slav 44.7%. Russian 6,227,000; Ukrainian 896,000; Byelorussian 183,000; Polish 60,000.
Other 7%. German 958,000; Greek 47,000; Moldavian 33,000; Tajik 26,000; Kurds 25,000; Armenian 19,000.
All other peoples 0.6%. Korean 103,000; Mordvinian 30,000; Jews 17,000.

Literacy est 98%. **Official language:** Kazakh; Russian is the language of inter-ethnic communication. **All languages** (indigenous) 5. **Languages with Scriptures** 1Bi 1NT 2por.

Capital: Alma-Ata 1,156,000. Other cities: Karaganda 617,000; Chimkent 369,000; Semipalatinsk 277,000. Urbanization 55%.

Economy: Enormous oil and mineral reserves, large grain producer. Moving to a market economy but somewhat stifled by economic and transportation collapses in Russia. Russian control of production being diminished. Income/household only $500 annually.

Politics: Declared independence after the collapse of the USSR in 1991. The former Communist Party was re-elected in 1991 but vigorously pursues a policy of market liberalization and moderate secularism as an authoritarian democracy. The government has a bias to strengthen Kazakh influence in all levels of government. Though a nuclear power, it has proclaimed its intention of becoming nuclear-free.

Religion: Communist suppression of religion has given way to greater toleration. A strong Muslim minority presses for further Islamization, but the non-Muslim majority and ethnic diversity limit the danger. Likely policy will be of non-interference by the government, but with powers to control inter-religious contacts. All religious figures are broad estimates.

Muslim 40%. Almost entirely Turkic; possibly 5% being practising Muslims. In practice, most Kazakhs are more influenced by folk Islam.
Non-religious/other 32.6%. Russians, Ukrainians, etc.
Buddhist 0.3%. Korean, Buryet, Kalmyk.
Jews 0.1%.
Christian 27%. Nom 15.8%. Affil 11.2%. Growth –5.4%.
Protestant 1%. Growth –16.1%.

Church	Cong	Members	Affiliated
Ev Chr & Baptist Chs	133	20,500	82,000
Lutheran Ch	20	30,000	50,000
Unregistd. Baptists	30	3,600	14,400
Mennonite Ch	20	1,000	3,330
All Pentecostals (5)	53	1,250	3,130
Seventh-day Adventist	3	1,000	2,000
Korean Presby Ch	4	800	2,000
Korean Baptist Ch	3	450	1,130
All other	5	200	500
Denominations (13)	271	58,800	158,490
Evangelicals 0.73% of pop		37,100	122,090
Pentecostal/charis 0.13%		6,000	21,000

Christian expatriates in Kazakhstan est. 50.
Catholic 0.6%. Affil 0.4%. Growth –9.3%.

Ukrainian Uniate Ch	42,000	60,000
Roman Catholic	3,000	4,290
Denominations (2)	45,000	64,290

Orthodox 25.2%. Affil 9.8%. Growth –3.6%.

Russian Orthodox	1,120,000	1,600,000
Armenian Apostolic	6,500	10,000
All other (2)	19,780	28,500
Denominations (4)	1,146,280	1,638,500

Marginal 0.02%. Growth 40%.

Jehovah's Witnesses	1,050	3,500

1. **The future of Kazakhstan hangs in the balance.** For decades Communism blanketed deep divisions within the republic. Many fear that there could be unrest between the Russians, dominant in the north, and Kazakhs in the south, or between the Kazakhs and other Central Asian peoples, or

even between the traditional and progressive Kazakhs themselves. Pray that government leaders may reject ethnic or religious extremism and oppression.

2. **Kazakhs are nominally Muslim**, but fear of spirits is often stronger and has a high profile on national television. Saudi Arabian, Turkish and Iranian Muslim missionaries pour in aid for mosques, Korans and theological education. Only a few Kazakhs have become Christian. Pray that there might be both freedom to proclaim the gospel and for the centuries of spiritual bondage to be broken.

3. **The Kazakh people** have had little valid opportunity to hear the gospel. Now is the time to give it to them! Praise the Lord for the 50–100 who have recently believed. There is more interest among those educated in Russian. Several racially mixed groups of Christians have been started. The four Gospels have been published and portions of the Old and New Testaments are being published as a volume in 1993. Pray for accuracy, wide distribution, and acceptability for the Scriptures. Rural Kazakhs are more traditional and far less evangelized.

4. **Since 1989 there has been dramatic growth in interest among Slavs and Koreans**. Some Russian Orthodox congregations are full and the people enthusiastic for the Scriptures. Charismatic, Pentecostal and some Baptist congregations have grown tenfold or more in a year. There are nearly 20 Korean Presbyterian and Baptist fellowships in the country. The challenges:
   a) **Coping with the hemorrhage of emigrating Christians**. The majority of evangelicals under Communism were German; most have emigrated to Germany. Many Russians and Ukrainians are also leaving.
   b) **Young, trained leadership** which is almost non-existent. There is a danger of young leaders being lured to the West and therefore there is a need for local training programmes for both Russians and Kazakhs.
   c) **Preaching of sound doctrine, holy living, and missions vision**. Few have a concern for the evangelization of the Kazakh or the numerous Muslim ethnic minorities.
   d) **Flexibility to adapt from the days of persecution and German-Russian cultural Christianity**, the latter inappropriate for today's young people and Kazakhstan's culture. Some Baptist and Pentecostal congregations are traditional and legalistic.
   e) **Lack of love and respect between Christian denominations**. Pray for unity among all believers.

5. **Unreached minorities.** Kazakhstan's cultural and religious diversity may make this land most open and strategic for evangelizing most Central Asian non-Christian peoples. Pray that these opportunities may not be lost and that missionaries may be called to serve from former-USSR states and from other parts of the world to reach them. Pray for the peoples listed in the statistics section.

6. **Expatriate workers** have entered as "tentmakers", for which there are numerous opportunities. Most have come for short-term service; the need is for long-term workers who will learn the Kazakh language and culture. By 1993 there were few expatriates who spoke Kazakh. Special needs are for evangelistic discipling, Bible training, Bible correspondence course ministry, and publishing Christian literature. Ten or more expatriate groups are concerned for ministry in the land – four of which are Korean. Pray for more long-term workers to be called, and for a constructive network of cooperation to be deepened among them.

7. **Christian media ministries** for prayer:
   a) **Literature**. The Central Asian Baptist Mission focuses on producing evangelistic, apologetic and teaching literature in Central Asian languages. There is a need for help in all areas of literature. Praise the Lord for the ongoing translation and publication of the Scriptures and other materials.
   b) **The *Jesus* film** which is available in Russian and Kazakh; the film in Kazakh has not yet been widely used. Pray that it may be shown on national television.
   c) **Radio**. Little is yet broadcast in Kazakh. **FEBC**-Saipan and **TWR**-Monaco each transmit three 15-minute programmes weekly.

K

July 17–18
Africa

Kenya
(Republic of Kenya)

Area 582,600 sq.km. Most people live in the better watered plateaus of the south and west. Much of the north and east is desert. Only 9.5% of the land is cultivated.

Population		Ann. Gr.	Density
1990	25,130,000	4.3 %	43/sq.km
1995	30,844,000	4.2 %	53/sq.km

The highest natural increase in the world, with an average family having eight children.

Peoples: Over 117 ethno-linguistic groups.
Bantu 66.6%. 48 peoples. Largest: Kikuyu 5,146,000; Luyia (4) 3,475,000; Kamba 2,829,000; Gusii 1,548,000; Meru 1,378,000; Mijikenda (9) 1,201,000; Giryama 422,000; Embu 296,000; Digo 231,000; Taita 223,000; Kuria 146,000; Tharaka 118,000; Mbere 113,000; Bajun 61,000; Pokomo 36,000.
Nilotic 28.1%. 21 peoples. Luo 3,207,000; Kipsigis 1,055,000; Nandi 596,000; Maasai 382,000; Turkana 340,000; Tugen 296,000; Elgeyo 252,434; Teso 217,000; Pokot 213,000; Marakwet 181,000; Samburu 115,000.
Cushitic 3.6%. 16 peoples. Somali 511,000; Boran 113,000; Oromo (2) 78,000; Gabbra 50,000; Garreh 50,000; Rendille 36,000.
Khoisan 0.3%. 12 peoples.
Asian 0.63%. Mainly Gujarati 104,000; Panjabi 33,000.
Other 0.77%. Arab 64,000; European 60,000.
Refugees: By early 1992 there were over 100,000 Somali refugees in northeast Kenya, fleeing the civil war in Somalia.

Literacy 59%. **Official languages:** English, Swahili. **All languages** 58. **Languages with Scriptures** 13Bi 5NT 13por.

Capital: Nairobi 2,000,000. Other major city: Mombasa 550,000. Urbanization 20%.

Economy: Predominantly agricultural, light industries, and a major tourist country. Post-independence stability aided good growth, but this was not maintained since 1976 because of recession, oil-debt, drought, high population growth and the corrupting influence of one-party-statism. Much unemployment. Public debt/person $350. Income/person $380 (1.8% of USA).

Politics: Independent from Britain in 1963. Virtually a one-party state for much of the time since then. The reluctance of President Moi to open up the political system to Western-style democracy brought pressure from foreign aid donors to permit multi-party elections in 1993. The election was seriously flawed giving a hollow victory to Moi, but leaving the elected representatives of the Luo and Kikuyu, the two dominant peoples, in opposition and parliament suspended. Kenya faces a period of dangerous instability.

Religion: Freedom of religion. Government sympathetic to Christianity. Many Christians in high leadership positions, including the President.
African traditional religions 10%.
Muslim 6%. Majority among coastal Swahili/Arab, Pokomo, Digo and northeast desert Somali, Boran, etc.
Baha'i 1.1%. **Hindu** 0.45%. **Jain** 0.2%. **Sikh** 0.1%. There has been no nationwide analysis of churches or religions since 1972, so most figures are approximate.
Christian 82.1%. Nom 12.5%. Affil 69.6%. Growth 5.5%.

Protestant 45%. Affil 37.3%. Growth 7.1%.

Church	Cong	Members	Affiliated
Africa Inland Ch	4,325	1,000,000	2,000,000
Indep Afr Chs (100)	7,500	600,000	1,500,000
Ch of Prov of Kenya (Anglican)	4,474	850,000	1,450,000
Presbyterian Ch	1,400	480,000	1,000,000
Pente Assemblies	3,900	225,000	500,000
Baptist Convention	1,610	107,395	358,000
Full Gosp Chs	1,857	130,000	325,000
Seventh-day Adventist	1,084	158,000	263,211
Methodist Ch	3,500	140,000	250,000
Ch of God in E Afr	556	89,000	178,000
African Brotherhood	765	76,500	170,000
Salvation Army	1,360	100,000	150,000
Friends (Quaker)	1,667	50,000	111,000
Assemblies of God	900	47,700	90,000
All other (60)	5,931	460,040	1,024,200
Denominations (173)	40,829	4,513,635	9,369,411
Evangelicals 34% of pop		4,079,000	8,538,000
Pentecostal/charis 11.1%		1,240,000	2,860,000

Missionaries:
to Kenya 2,321 (1:10,800 people) in over 176 agencies.
from Kenya 2,166 (1:4,300 Protestants) in 59 agencies 118frn 518xcul 1,648dom.
Roman Catholic 25.9%. Affil 20.1%. Growth 3.9%.

Catholic Ch	2,141	2,680,000	5,050,000
Charismatics		13,000	25,000

Missionaries to Kenya 3,210 (7,800 people).
Orthodox 2.9%. Affil 1.95%. Growth 1.7%.

African Orthodox Ch	456	196,000	490,000

Foreign Marginal 0.2%. Affil 0.15%. Growth 7.5%.			
Jehovah's Witnesses	132	5,600	18,700
All other (11)	76	11,400	19,000
Groups (12)	208	17,000	37,700
Indigenous Marginal 11%. Affil 10.08%.			
Growth 4.3%.			
Afrn Indep Pent Ch	408	204,000	510,000
Ch of Christ in Africa	879	123,000	205,000
All other (232)	11,536	830,600	1,819,000
Groups (234)	12,823	1,157,600	2,534,000

Missionaries from Kenya 109
(1:38,000 Independents).

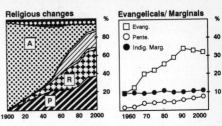

1. **Praise God for the great freedom to preach the gospel since independence,** for the receptivity of the people and for the exciting growth of the Church. Over four-fifths of the population claims to be Christian, and Christians are found in every level of society. Yet there have been growing tensions between the government and church leaders over human rights and the need for political change. Pray that Christians may bring truth and moral uplift to the nation as it edges to the brink of political disaster.

2. **The Protestant churches have grown fast,** and the proportion of Evangelicals is high. The East African Revival (1938–1960) made a deep and lasting impression on the Anglican, Presbyterian and Methodist Churches. The fires of revival were quenched by legalism, divisions, materialism and personality clashes. The growth of evangelical and Pentecostal churches (both international and indigenous) has been dramatic. One of the largest is the **Africa Inland Church,** the daughter body of the considerable missionary input of **AIM.** There have been numerous and extensive evangelistic outreaches (**AE,** CFAN and others) with significant response. Few countries in Africa have been more extensively evangelized.

3. **Rapid growth** has brought its problems:
   - a) **Nominalism** has become a major issue, with a large number of nominal Evangelicals too. Nairobi is 80% "Christian", but only 12% of the population goes to church. Pray for revival to be given again.
   - b) **Tribalism and tribal customs** have caused endless divisions and a multiplicity of independent churches, some theologically orthodox, others little removed from the old tribal religions. Pray for unity based on biblical truth that transcends culture and personalities.
   - c) **The lack of trained leaders** for the 40,000 or more evangelical/Pentecostal congregations gives concern. There are 55 institutions with over 2,000 students where workers are trained for Christian ministry. The Scott Theological College (AIC-**AIM**) and St. Paul's United Theological College (Anglican, Presbyterian, Methodist) are significant institutions. The **Nairobi Evangelical Graduate School of Theology** (with 32 students from 14 countries) and Daystar University College serve all of Anglophone Africa. There are also numerous TEE programmes. Pray for these, and for lives to be set on fire for God through them. Pray for more graduates to be fully and adequately supported by their congregations – a need in all denominations.

4. **Missionary vision among Kenyan Christians** has grown significantly, with over 500 serving in cross-cultural ministries, including a number in other lands. The Africa Inland Church, Anglicans, the Africa Gospel Church and various independent Pentecostal agencies have provided the major thrust for this. The AIC has a Missionary Training College in Eldoret where 15 missionary candidates are trained each year. Pray that churches and agencies may run with this vision.

5. **Foreign missions have had a long and successful involvement in Kenya.** Almost all national ministries are now operating under Kenyan leadership, whether in pioneer outreach, Bible teaching or in service ministries. Many agencies have supportive, global or regional ministries located in Kenya, which partially accounts for the high missionary population. Some major agencies: AIM (463 workers), **SBC** (116), **WGM** (96), Norwegian Lutheran Mission (68), **SIM** (52), **AoG** (52), Finnish Lutheran Mission (55), Finnish Free Mission (46), **PAoC** (46), **CMS** (40), Baptist Bible Fellowship (31), **YWAM** (31), **IMI** (27), Korean Presbyterian (22), **CBFMS** (20), **BCMS** (20). Major missionary-contributing nations: USA (1,382), UK (186), Canada (118), Finland (105), Norway (105), Germany (81), Sweden (55), Korea (48), Australia (42).

6. **Over half the population is under 15.** Youth ministries are vital. **SU** has made a deep impact on secondary schools. **IFES** has lively groups in universities and colleges where over 10% of students are

active believers. Pray for the integration of Christian students into local churches; this is not easy, but their contribution is essential.

7. **Recent breakthroughs** among less responsive pastoral peoples are cause for much praise. The efforts of many Kenyan and expatriate workers in preaching and famine relief have begun to bear fruit. Famines, tribal warfare and radical social changes have been used by God to open hearts among the Maasai, Pokot, Turkana, Mukugodo, Njemps and Samburu and, more recently, the Somalis. The pioneer work of AIC-**AIM** in most of these groups is noteworthy, though numerous other churches and agencies are involved too. Yet, with the exception of the Pokot, less than 10% of these peoples are committed Christians, and churches are still young. Pray for their complete evangelization.

8. **Unreached peoples.** Probably about 12% of the population of Kenya belongs to peoples little affected by the gospel, though only a few are unoccupied by missions. Pray for:
a) **The Somali in the northeast and cities.** The five clans of Somalis are all Muslim. About 20 Christian workers (AIC/**AIM**, **SIM**, **CBIM** and Mennonites) are reaching these people. There are three small groups and 50 believers.
b) **The pastoral tribes of north Kenya** who are predominantly animistic and nomadic. Anglicans, Lutherans, AIC and Pentecostals work among them, but converts are few. Pray for the Boran, Samburu, Gabbra and Rendille, and for the emergence of truly indigenous churches among them.
c) **The tribal peoples of the Muslim coastal strip** including the Digo (0.1% Christian), Bajun (0.01%), Orma (0.01%), Upper Pokomo, Boni of Lamu, and coastal Somalis. The AIC, **CBFMS**, Methodists and Pentecostals are all working in this area. It is reckoned that several thousand Muslims have now believed in Jesus. The Giryama and Duruma are animist, but many are coming to the Lord.
d) **The coastal Swahili and Arab population** which is strongly Muslim. Most are unreached, but Southern Baptist missionaries have seen church multiplication in the largely Muslim city of Mombasa, with over 10,000 baptisms since 1985, many of them from a Muslim background.
e) **The Asian community** which has become insecure since the disastrous expulsion of Asians in Uganda and destructive riots in Kenya in 1982. Over four languages are used. Hindus and Muslims have come to the Lord, and there are now five churches planted among them (**IMI**, **AIM**). IMI has the vision for a church-planting work in every Asian community of East and Central Africa.

9. **Bibles and Bible translation.** Most languages have part of God's Word, and 12 indigenous languages have the whole Bible. Pray for:
a) The valued catalytic ministry of the **Bible Society** (**UBS**) in translation, revision, publishing and distributing the Scriptures.
b) **SIL**, with eight translation teams in Kenya and also serving many churches and agencies in all of East Africa.
c) **Living Bibles International** which has translation projects in seven of Kenya's languages.

10. **Supportive ministries.**
a) **Aid programmes** through many of the above agencies, **TEAR Fund**, **WV**, etc. have played a significant part in opening the way for the gospel in arid and famine-stricken areas. Pray for those involved in a hard and difficult ministry.
b) **MAF**, with 20 workers, has a well-developed ministry, flying to many parts of East Africa and northeast Zaire from their base in Nairobi. Without this ministry much Christian work would come to a halt. **AIM-Air** also has an extensive flying programme in the region.
c) **GRn** has recordings available in 60 languages.
d) The *Jesus* film is being widely shown in English, Gusii, Kamba, Kikuyu, Nandi, Luo and Swahili.
e) **Christian Radio.** There are many Christian programmes aired on the national radio and TV networks, and a Christian radio station may be established. **FEBA**-Seychelles broadcasts ten hours/week in Swahili and has an estimated audience of 650,000. **TWR**-Swaziland has a further 12 hours in Swahili and 20 hours in English.

11. **Nairobi is one of the key communications centres in Africa.** Many international Christian organizations have their continental offices based there. The Ecumenical AACC (All Africa Conference of Churches) and the **AEAM** (Assoc. of Evangelicals of Africa and Madagascar) are two of these. The latter has played a key role in promoting evangelical unity and ministries in theology, training, literature and fellowship. Pray for this work and its extension through Africa.

Kiribati

(The Republic of Kiribati)

See under Pacific
Pacific

Area 849 sq.km. Three archipelagos – Gilbert, Phoenix, and Line, with 33 coral atolls scattered across 2,000,000 sq.km. of the Pacific Ocean.

Population		Ann. Gr.	Density
1990	68,000	1.2 %	80/sq.km
1995	72,000	1.1 %	85/sq.km

Peoples:
Indigenous: Kiribati 96.1%; Euro-Polynesian 2.6%.
Other 1.3%. Tuvaluan 500; European 280.

Literacy 90%. **Official languages:** Kiribati, English. **All languages** 2. **Languages with Scriptures** 2Bi.

Capital: Baraiki/Tarawa 23,000.

Economy: Dependent on copra and fish; subsistence economy, with living standards well below that of other island states. The lack of commercial viability and large distances between islands make improvements difficult to achieve. Public debt/person $676. Income/person $700 (3.1% of USA).

Politics: Independent from Britain in 1979 as a democratic republic.

Religion: Freedom of religion.
Non-religious/other 0.1%.
Baha'i 2.3%.
Christian 97.6%. Growth 1%.
Protestant 44%. Growth 0.6%.

Church	Cong	Members	Affiliated
Kiribati Protestant	124	11,200	26,000
Ch of God (Cleveland)	30	1,035	2,070
Seventh-day Adventist	5	815	1,160
Assemblies of God	7	300	600
All other (2)	2	77	123
Denominations (6)	168	13,427	29,953
Evangelicals 6.2% of pop		2,063	4,211
Pentecostal/charis 3.9%		1,335	2,670

Missionaries:
to Kiribati 6 (1:11,300 people) in 3 agencies.
from Kiribati 2 (1:15,000 Protestants) 2frn.
Roman Catholic 51.5% Growth 0.7%.

Catholic Ch	27	18,900	35,000

Missionaries to Kiribati 16 (1:4,500 people).
Marginal 2.12%. Growth 31.3%.

Mormons	17	780	1,300
Groups (2)	18	816	1,444

1. **The once strong Congregational Church** (Kiribati Protestant) is losing members and pastors to other Protestant groups and also to Catholics, Baha'i, and Mormons. The theological college in Tarawa is not evangelical. Pray for a return to biblical preaching and for New Testament Christianity to counteract nominalism and the underlying power of the occult.

2. **Evangelical Christians are steadily growing in numbers** – largely through the witness of the Church of God with rapidly growing congregations, 33 pastors and a Bible School with 79 students. The **AoG** also has a growing presence. Pray that every island may have a clear, resident gospel witness.

3. **The more needy:**
a) **Migrant labourers** on Nauru.
b) **Migrant communities** moving eastwards to populate the isolated Line and Phoenix Islands.

<table>
<tr><td>July
19–20</td></tr>
<tr><td>Asia</td></tr>
</table>

Korea (North)

(Democratic People's Republic
of Korea)

Area 123,000 sq.km. The larger part of the Korean peninsula, but climate more rigorous than in the south.

Population		Ann. Gr.	Density
1990	22,937,000	2.4 %	187/sq.km
1995	25,548,000	2.2 %	209/sq.km

Peoples:
Korean 99.8%. Chinese 0.2%.

Literacy 91%. **Official language:** Korean.

Capital: Pyongyang 2,355,000. Urbanization 64%.

Economy: Heavily industrialized; vast mineral resources. The centralized socialist economy in steady decline due to the heavy costs of militarization, attempts to become a nuclear power and the ending of aid from China and the USSR. By 1993 the economy was in near collapse with severe rationing of basic foodstuffs. Public debt/person $296. Income/person $919 (4.3% of USA).

Politics: Occupied by Japan 1910–45. On Russian insistence, Korea was partitioned after World War II. A Communist regime was installed in 1948 in the North. North Korea invaded South Korea in 1950 and war dragged on until 1953. The large North Korean armed forces with nuclear capability continue to threaten a second invasion. One of the most repressive regimes in the world, completely dedicated to cultivating the Marxist dynasty of Kim Il-Sung and his son. There are occasional hints of a reunification of the Koreas, but the fortified border between them remains one of the most impenetrable in the world.

Religion: All religions have been harshly repressed. Many thousands of Christians were murdered during and after the Korean War. Religious affiliations are unknown, so the figures given are estimates.
Non-religious/atheist 68%.
Korean religions 29.5% (Shamanism, Confucianism).
Buddhism 1.7%.
Christian 0.6–2%. Figures below are rough estimates.
Protestant 0.4%.

Church	Cong	Affiliated
Secret believers	n.a.	80,000
Korean Christian Fedn.	2	12,000
Total	n.a.	92,000
Evangelicals 0.36% of pop		83,600
Roman Catholic 0.2%.		
Catholic Assoc	1	50,000

Religious changes

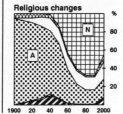

1. **The leader of North Korea and his son** have been almost deified by adulatory propaganda. Pray that the time may soon come when the Lord Jesus, rather than a mere man, may be openly worshipped.

2. **The Church in North Korea** was the birthplace of revival. In 1945, Pyongyang was 13% Christian and in the north there were 400,000 Christians. Most Christians fled to the south during the Korean War or were martyred, and churches were bulldozed. Little is known about the underground church, but only that it has survived and may have grown. There are three propaganda "show" churches in the capital. Pray for grace and endurance for believers and for freedom.

3. **The majority have never heard the name of Jesus.** The knowledge of God has been obliterated for most by an Orwellian nightmare of repression, demands for total conformity, and isolation from the outside world. Pray that the God-shaped hole may be filled within the long-suffering Korean people. The turning to God could be dramatic when Communism collapses.

4. **North Korean students** studying in the USSR and Communist states of Europe heard the gospel when Communism collapsed. Some came to the Lord before their return home. Pray that they may stand firm and grow in spite of the hostile spiritual environment.

5. **Present means of witness are limited:**
a) **Radio**. Many South Korean Christian broadcasts as well as those of **TWR**-Guam and **FEBC**-South Korea reach into North Korea, but nearly all radios are pre-tuned to government stations, and few can hear these gospel broadcasts.
b) **Exotic means.** These include floating literature ashore from the sea, balloon deliveries and some literature infiltrated into the country.
c) **Korean Christians** from China and elsewhere who are able to visit and gain opportunities to witness.
d) **South Korean Christians** who have prayed and prepared for years for the time when the land opens for the gospel. Pray that this may soon happen.

| July 21–22 |
| Asia |

Korea (South)
(Republic of Korea)

Area 99,200 sq.km. Southern half of Korean peninsula. Mountainous; only 22% is arable.

Population		Ann. Gr.	Density
1990	43,520,000	0.98 %	440/sq.km
1995	44,851,000	0.80 %	452/sq.km

Peoples: One of world's most ethnically homogeneous nations.
Korean 99.8%. An ancient and cultured nation.
Other 0.2%. US military and Chinese (24,000).

Literacy 92%. **Official language:** Korean.

Capital: Seoul 10,918,000. Other major cities: Pusan 4,360,000; Taegu 2,286,000; Inchon 1,728,000; Kwangju 1,234,000; Taejon 1,085,000. Urbanization 47%.

Economy: Rapid industrialization and growth since the Korean War. One of the four East Asian "dragons" – the powerful export-oriented nations, with a wide range of sophisticated industries. Unemployment 3%. Public debt/person $493. Income/person $5,569 (26% of USA).

Politics: For centuries, Korea was the "Hermit Kingdom". The attitudes and politics of Koreans have been moulded by the Japanese occupation (1910–1945), the Russian-imposed division of Korea (1945–48) and the devastating Korean War (1950–1953). Strong military-civilian governments held power from 1950 until 1988, when public unrest led to constitutional change and a more open multi-party democracy. The first civilian president in 32 years was elected in 1992.

Religion: There is complete religious freedom. The government has been favourable to Christianity, seeing this as an ideological bulwark against the Communist threat. There is wide variation between government census returns and membership claims by religious groups themselves (represented, respectively, by the two figures listed in parentheses). The first figures are synthesized from a number of sources.
Non-religious/other 20%.
Buddhist 27.7% (19.1%–47%). Strong until 15th century, and with post-war resurgence.
New religions 5.7% (0.8%–15%). Several hundred new syncretic religions, most of recent origin.
Shamanist 10%. Few openly claim to be followers of the ancient religion of Korea, but its influence is widespread.
Confucianist 1.2% (1.0%–24.3%). Official religion until 1910. Both Buddhism and Confucianism have made a deep impact on Korean culture.

Muslim 0.06%. **Baha'i** 0.05%.
Christian 35.3% (19.8%–43.6%). Affil 34.4%. Growth 5.7%.
Protestant 27.1%. Growth 6%.

Church	Cong	Members	Affiliated
Presb Ch of K (Haptong)	4,561	772,000	1,930,596
Presb Ch of K (Tonghap)	5,100	830,000	1,660,248
K Methodist Chs (4)	3,507	503,000	1,048,260
Jesus Assemb. of God	800	400,000	1,000,000
Korea Evang Ch	1,623	301,000	601,801
Korea Baptist Conv	1,740	176,661	556,840
Presby Ch (Reformed)	901	171,000	427,943
Jesus Korean Hol Ch	618	121,408	362,346
G Assembly of Presb Chs in Korea (BoSu)	972	140,000	310,111
Presb Ch in ROK (Hankuk)	1,140	126,000	285,350
Korea Assemb. of God	450	74,200	185,480
Presb Ch of K (Kosin)	1,101	71,500	178,853
Ch of God of Prophecy	88	24,600	123,223
Assoc of Chr Chs	309	56,800	103,265
All other (171)	15,075	1,292,538	3,031,457
Denominations (188)	37,985	5,060,707	11,805,773
Evangelicals 21.1% of pop		3,818,000	9,188,000
Pentecostal/charis 4.5%		743,000	1,860,000

Missionaries:
to Korea 409 (1:106,000 people) in 49 agencies.
from Korea 2,237 (1:5,200 Protestants) in 80 agencies 1,966frn 1,820xcul 417dom. (Recent research indicates 2,956 missionaries overseas by 1992).
Roman Catholic 6%. Affil 5.6%. Growth 4.8%.

Catholic Ch	2,950	1,360,000	2,423,181
Charismatic		21,000	36,000

Missionaries:
to Korea 665 (1,65,000 people).
from Korea 211 (1:11,400 Catholics).
Foreign Marginal 0.6%. Affil 0.6%. Growth 13.6%.

Jehovah's Witnesses	1,055	62,193	138,000
Mormons	146	50,000	105,133
All groups (8)	1,201	115,793	255,133

Indigenous Marginal 1.6%. Affil 1.36%. Growth –0.4%.

Unification Ch (Moonies)	430	140,000	466,914
All groups (5)	3,150	182,900	593,914

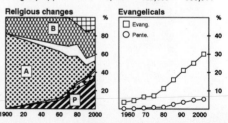

Religious changes   Evangelicals

1. **Praise God for the spiritual awakening in Korea** and the evident work of the Holy Spirit. Here is a selection of the superlatives!
a) The first Protestant church was planted in 1884. By the centenary in 1984 there were nearly 30,000 churches.
b) The capital, Seoul, is almost 40% Christian, with over 7,000 churches, and is also home to ten of the 20 largest congregations in the world.
c) The largest congregation (Full Gospel Central Church), and the largest Presbyterian and Methodist congregations in the world are here.
d) The largest evangelistic campaign (by Billy Graham 1973).
e) The largest Christian mobilization (CCC Explo '74, World Evangelization Crusade '80) with 2,700,000 attending one meeting.
f) The largest baptismal service since Pentecost (in the Army, which is now 65% Christian).
g) The largest theological seminaries in the world.

2. **Praise God for the Korean Church** – founded on sound indigenous principles, blessed with revival, refined by suffering and now becoming a significant missionary-sending body. The well-attended daily early-morning prayer meetings are a notable characteristic. As a result, over 20 churches are planted every day, and the gospel has penetrated every part of society. Pray that wealth, success and cultural acceptability may not stunt this growth or dampen the spiritual energies of Christians.

3. **Spiritual challenges facing the Korean Church** for which intercession is needed.
a) **The discipling of many new Christians** – all coming from a background steeped in Buddhist concepts and structured by Confucian ethics. The Spirit and the Word must bring them into the full liberty of grace in the gospel.
b) **Authoritarian leadership** often bringing formality, legalism and a stifling of expectation for personal guidance among ordinary Christians. The high status of pastors makes it hard for biblical servant leadership to develop.
c) **Cooperation between denominations**. There has been a history of divisions in denominations because of the ecumenism issue, doctrine, regionalism, and personality clashes among leaders. There are over 86 Presbyterian denominations. In recent years there has been increasing willingness to work together in the common cause. Pray that this may continue to develop and enhance the missions thrust of the Korean Church.
d) **Widespread belief that success and prosperity are an indication of God's blessing**. There is often a pride in statistical growth, impressive organization and buildings. It is a temptation for leaders to seek success, wealth and degrees more than lifting up the Cross.

4. **Goals for the Year 2000:**
a) For 50% of the nation to profess Christ.
b) For 20,000,000 Protestant Christians.
c) For at least one Korean missionary to be working in each country of the world, and for a total of 10,000 to be serving as missionaries at that time.

5. **Leadership training is moving into mass production!** Several Presbyterian seminaries and KEC (**OMS**) have over 1,000 students each. The Chongshin College and Seminary has about 2,000 students. There are 283 theological institutions, 38 of which are seminaries turning out over 500 graduates a year. Yet there is a shortage of trained pastors for rural churches and for missionary outreach.

6. **Young people** are a restive yet responsive section of the community. Non-denominational groups such as IVCF(**IFES**), **CCC**, Joy Mission and **Navigators** are all active and making an impact on the 258 colleges and university campuses where there are 1,400,000 students. The University Bible Fellowship is large and has a considerable missions output but has isolated itself from the mainstream of evangelical life. Pray that students may find the delight of personal Bible study. **SU** has a vital role to play in producing Bible study materials. Pray that these ministries may impart:
a) a greater emphasis on expository preaching that addresses real spiritual needs.
b) a leadership model that emphasizes servanthood, holy living, and a close walk with Jesus.

7. **The less reached people groups** are few in number.
a) **The Chinese.** There are nine congregations with 350 believers and a community of around 500. They are 1.4% Protestant.

b) **Korean Muslims.** These are growing as a result of Islamic missionary work among Koreans working in Saudi Arabia. 60% live in Seoul. There are about 40,000 Korean Muslims. A Korea Islamic University is being planned. There is no specific outreach to them, and lack of knowledge of how to reach them.

8. **The missions vision of the Korean Church** has rapidly grown and matured. An increasing number of cross-cultural missionaries is being sent all over the world by 63 Korean and international agencies (sometimes in both!). The larger Korean agencies are: Haptong Presbyterian (313), Methodist (197), Tonghap Presbyterian (197), Ko Sin Presbyterian (113), Korea Harbor Mission (65), Full Gospel Mission Assoc. (58), and Paul Mission (52). There are also large Korean contingents in **YWAM** (272), **OM** (80), **OMF** (35) and **WBT** (25).

a) **Mobilization of young people for missions** has gained momentum. *Mission Korea* is a large biennial nationwide mission movement of various youth agencies (IVCF[**IFES**], Joy Mission, **YWAM** and others). Thousands of young people have been recruited for short-term involvement by **CCC, OM, YWAM,** Joy Mission and others. Pray that these young people may be at the forefront in missions – either in going or supporting those who go.

b) **Preparation and orientation for missions has developed fast.** Many institutions have been founded. To mention a few: The Cross-cultural Missionary Training Institute, Center for World Mission (Presbyterian Tonghap), Global Missionary Training Center, Kosin MTI, the Missionary Training Institute (Presbyterian Haptong), East-West Center, Korea International Mission, the Global Professionals Training Institute (for tentmakers). Pray for effective preparation for Korean missionary trainees.

c) **Cultural adaptation** is hard for Koreans who come from a mono-cultural nation and a language very different in structure from others. The enthusiasm and rugged dynamism of Koreans are valuable assets in pressing through to fruitfulness.

d) **Korean missionaries** serving overseas need prayer – for their adaptation to other missions and missionaries, for effective cooperation, for pastoral care and for adequate education for their children.

9. **The Korean diaspora** – emigration and extensive business interests have multiplied Korean communities around the world. In nearly all, thriving churches have sprung up (over 2,500 in USA alone), and they too are becoming a major factor for sending missionaries.

10. **Missions in Korea** have a valuable servant role in giving a fresh perspective to biblical teaching, personal holiness and, increasingly, training Korean missionaries for cross-cultural work. A number of mission agencies have made a major impact in church planting, including several Presbyterian agencies, **SBC** (112 workers), Baptist Bible Fellowship (32), **TEAM** (13), **AoG** (12) and **OMS** (11). **OMF** (17) loans workers to minister within established churches. **OMS** missionaries have planted the largest denomination in Asia originating from a faith mission.

11. **Christian literature** plays a vital role. The Bible in Korean has gone through many translations and has become a treasured part of the culture. The very active Korean Bible Society has handled a global ministry of Bible printing – making Korea one of the world's major Bible production centres. The range of theological and devotional books is rapidly increasing, and there are many Christian bookstores (including Tyrannus Press, Word of Life Press (**TEAM**), Voice (**CMA**), and **CLC**) and publishers (IVCF[**IFES**], **CLC**). Pray that this ministry may help to form a strong, Bible-literate church.

12. **Christian broadcasting** has a strong base with three large Christian radio networks. All broadcast to both Koreas (415 hours per month). **FEBC**-Cheju and **TEAM**-Seoul broadcast to China, USSR, and Mongolia.

Kuwait
(State of Kuwait)

July 23
Middle East

Area 17,800 sq.km. A wedge of desert between Iraq and Saudi Arabia at the northwest end of the Arabian Gulf.

Population	Ann. Gr.	Density
1990 2,143,000	2.5 %	120/sq.km
1995 1,300,000	−9.5 %	73/sq.km

The loss of 1.1 million expatriates, mainly Palestinian and Asian, during and after the Iraqi invasion has dramatically changed the size and composition of the population.

Peoples (all estimates for 1992):
Indigenous Arab 53% (32% in 1990).
Expatriate 47%. Numbers fluctuating rapidly.
  Other Arab: Egyptian, Syrian, Lebanese, Palestinian 30,000 (400,000 in 1990).
  Asian: Pakistani, Baloch, Indian, Filipino, etc.
  Other: Kurd, Iranian, Westerner.

Literacy 79%. **Official language**: Arabic.

Capital: Kuwait City 145,000. Urbanization 95%.

Economy: 9.4% of world's known oil reserves. Enormous oil income deeply affected by the 1990–91 Iraqi invasion and Gulf War. The loss of skilled labour and management (predominantly Palestinian), an estimated $20 billion damage, and $10 billion loss of oil reserves in oil-well fires have been an enormous setback. Public debt/person $237 (1988). Income/person $15,437 (73% of USA).

Politics: Former British protectorate; became independent in 1961. Constitutional monarchy, but with the Amir and his family exercising quasi-autocratic control. Parliament was suspended and political opposition suppressed in 1986; however, the shock of the Iraqi invasion and occupation in 1990–91 stimulated demands for democratic reforms. The October 1992 elections gave a majority of seats to the opposition in the newly-reestablished parliament, but the cabinet is firmly controlled by the Amir.

Religion: Sunni Islam is the state religion. Immigrant religious minorities are permitted some worship facilities. All figures are 1992 post-Gulf War estimates.
Muslim 89.9%. Sunni 69.9%, Shi'a 20%.
Non-religious/other 1.5%. Predominantly Westerners.
Hindu 2%. Indians.
Buddhist 1%. Sri Lankans.
Baha'i 0.3%. Mostly of Iranian origin.
Christian 5.3%. Nominal 2.3%. Affiliated 3%. Most are Westerners, Pakistanis, and Filipinos, with some Arabs, Egyptians and Palestinians.
  Protestant 0.5%. Affil 0.17%.

Church	Members	Affiliated
Natnl. Evang Ch (25)	294	700
Pentecostal Churches	325	500
Mar Thoma Syrian Ch	310	500
All other (7)	215	510
Denominations (34)	1,144	2,210
Evangelicals 0.13% of pop	870	1,600
Pentecostal/charis 0.06%	470	800

Expatriate Christian workers 8.
Roman Catholic 3%. Affil 2.31%.

Catholic	18,600	30,000
Charismatic	200	300

Expatriate Christian workers 37.
Orthodox 1.7%. Affil 0.5%. These figures could be low.

Coptic Orthodox	1,890	3,000
Armenian Apostolic	1,280	2,000
Syrian Orthodox	496	800
Greek Orthodox	384	600
All other (1)	95	150
Denominations (5)	4,145	6,550

Foreign Marginal 0.1%

1. **The Iraqi invasion** dramatically curtailed Kuwait's profligate spending of its vast oil revenues. Much money had also been invested in promoting Islam – building mosques, buying Bibles for burning, and providing financial incentives for people to become Muslims. The damage to property and ecology will take decades to repair and at enormous cost. Pray that the trauma of invasion may lead Kuwaitis to question the validity of Muslim "brotherhood" and of Islam itself. There are few indigenous believers.

2. **Liberation of Kuwait in 1991** was largely through the efforts of "Christian" nations. Pray that there may be a more receptive attitude among Muslims to true Christians. During 1990 Arab home groups flourished with increased numbers and some conversions. Pray that this may continue.

3. **Many Kuwaitis travel** to other lands as tourists, businessmen, students and, more recently, as refugees. Pray that they may meet Christians who are willing to speak to them of Jesus.

4. **Expatriate ethnic minorities.** The Kuwaitis are determined never to let their country be dominated by foreigners again. Few expatriates are permanent residents – most are on work contracts of two to seven years' duration, and many have to leave their families behind. Over 500,000 new workers have entered Kuwait since the liberation.

a) **Skilled and professional workers,** many nominally Christian, are more concerned with amassing wealth than church attendance or evangelism. Pray that the negative effects of their poor spiritual standards may be nullified by a work of the Holy Spirit, and that true believers may find many opportunities to share their faith in a meaningful way.

b) **Asians** are predominantly from South Asia and the Philippines, and are largely contract labourers or domestic servants. Some live and work in difficult circumstances with incidents of violence and rape perpetrated on them. Pray that there may be an effective witness by Christians to each ethnic group among them.

c) **Middle Easterners.** Most of the ethnic groups represented are unreached – especially the Kurds, Iranians and Baloch. Pray that effective means to reach them may be found.

5. **Expatriate Christians** gained recognition for their prayer and relief aid during and after the Iraqi occupation. Frustrating restrictions imposed on Christian gatherings have since been eased. There are seven sites where churches meet in Kuwait, two of which are Catholic. The National Evangelical Church has become an umbrella for 25 Christian communities, which meet on a former hospital compound. The majority of these are Indian, with some Arab. Main services are held in English, Arabic, Urdu and Malayali. Pray that believers may be granted full freedom of worship and witness and that their lives might commend the Lord Jesus as Saviour.

6. **Christian media** are important means of communicating the gospel in the restrictive situation in Kuwait. Pray for:

a) **Radio broadcasts** – with coverage by **High Adventure** in Lebanon (106 hours/week), **FEBA**-Seychelles (17) and **TWR**-Monaco (16). Pray for a wide audience and a lasting response.

b) **Christian video and cassette tape ministries** – for effective distribution and follow-through. The *Jesus* film on video has been widely and quietly disseminated.

c) **Satellite broadcasting** which could be a potent means for Christian programming, but relevant and meaningful Arabic programmes are few.

Kyrgyzstan
(Republic of Kyrgyzstan)

July 24
Eurasia

Area 199,000 sq.km. Mountainous Central Asian state bordering on China, Kazakhstan and Uzbekistan.

Population	Ann.Gr.	Density
1990 4,338,000	1.78%	22/sq.km
1995 4,696,000	1.60%	24/sq.km

Peoples: Over 80 ethnic groups from all over the former USSR.
Turkic/Altaic 70.1%. Kyrgyz 2,230,000; Uzbek 550,000; Tatar 70,000; Uyghur 37,000; Kazakh 37,000.
Indo-European 28%.
   Slav 24.3%. Steady emigration reducing numbers. Russian 916,000; Ukrainian 108,000.
   Other 3.7%. German 101,000 (virtually all left for Germany by 1993); Tajik 34,000; Kurds 14,000.
All other peoples 1.9%. Dungan (Chinese Muslims) 38,000; Korean 18,000; Jews 6,000.

Literacy 99%. **Official language:** Kyrgyz (full introduction over five years). **All languages** (indigenous) 2. **Languages with Scriptures** 1NT.

Capital Bishkek (Frunze) 631,000. Urbanization 40%.

Economy: Based on wool, tobacco, cotton and agricultural machinery. Good potential for hydroelectricity and mining. Economy being modelled on that of Turkey. Income/person $2,436 (11% of USA).

Politics: The first Central Asian republic to break free from the USSR and one of the closest to a western-style democracy.

Religion: Secular state, but contested by the opposition who want an Islamic state. Full religious freedom of worship, choice and witness constitutionally guaranteed, but with a tilt of deference to Islam.
Muslim 60%. Mainly Sunni Islam. Most Kyrgyz are more followers of folk Islam (influenced by pre-Islamic shamanism).
Non-religious/other 27.9%. Mainly Slav. Some Central Asians.
Buddhist 0.2%. **Jews** 0.14%.
Christian 11.8%. Nom 4.4%. Affil 7.3%.
Growth −1.2%.
   Protestant 0.16%. Growth 10.2%.

Church	Cong	Members	Affiliated
Pentecostal Ch	6	900	3,600
Baptist Chs (5)	13	1,040	2,600
Charismatic Chs	2	240	600
Seventh-day Adventist	1	50	150
Denominations (8)	22	2,230	6,950
Evangelicals 0.16% of pop		2,180	6,800
Pentecostal/charis 0.10%		1,200	4,300

Roman Catholic 0.6%. Affil 0.4%. Growth −1.1%.

Eastern & Latin-rite Cath Ch	11,900	17,000

Orthodox 11%. Affil 6.9%. Growth −1.4%.

Russian Orthodox	176,000	270,000
All other (8)	15,280	24,800
Denominations (9)	191,280	294,800

Marginal 0.01%. Growth 40%.

K

1. **Never before have the Kyrgyz had such opportunity to follow Jesus.** For centuries, foreigners imposed their ideologies on the country – Turkic armies brought Islam in the 17th century, Russians took over in the 19th, and Communism was imposed in the 20th. Though most Kyrgyz are nominally Muslim, the power of the occult and shaman priests, and demon possession has never been broken. These things are openly aired on television and in large public meetings. Pray for spiritual freedom through widespread preaching of the gospel.

2. **Christians** are almost entirely from immigrant ethnic groups, many being German (who have largely left the country for Germany since 1988), Russian or Ukrainian. There is much nominalism among the Orthodox and Catholic. In the unprecedented freedoms since 1990 Baptists, Pentecostals and Adventists have held large evangelistic meetings. Protestant churches are growing and, for the first time, some Kyrgyz have come to faith in Christ too. Pray for:
   a) **Unity among believers.** Serious divisions between Orthodox and Protestant, Baptist and Charismatic do not commend the gospel.
   b) **Leadership and discipleship training for Christians.** Few, if any, leaders have had formal training. This lack could limit present growth.
   c) **Balance in teaching.** Baptists tend to be rigid and traditional, charismatics strong on power but weak on holiness.
   d) **Wisdom in outreach.** Present freedom must be sensitively used; foreign evangelistic methods have provoked concern and opposition. May the only offence be that of the Cross of Christ. Local

Christians are not yet very active in witnessing outside their meeting places.

e) **Sensitivity in helping Kyrgyz believers**. There are at least three congregation of Kyrgyz believers, and a number of Kyrgyz in Russian-speaking congregations. Pray for their protection, as pressures and threats on them could increase. There are between 100 and 200 believers, and their number is increasing weekly – almost the beginning of a people movement among them. Pray for a truly indigenous Kyrgyz church to develop.

3. **The unreached.**

a) **The Kyrgyz majority** lives in rural villages, few of which have ever been reached. There is openness but also a fear to commit themselves to Christ. There are both indigenous and expatriate agencies and workers seeking to reach them, but the ministry is only in its infancy.

b) **Muslim ethnic minorities** are still untouched – Chinese Dungan, Uzbek, Tatar, Tajik, Kurds and others.

4. **Missions.** An informal fellowship of agencies interested in the evangelization of the land has been formed. The number of expatriate Christians serving as tentmakers and witnesses is increasing. Pray for ability to learn the languages and identify with non-Christian ethnic groups. Pray for their safety and spiritual effectiveness in an area where the enemy of souls has never before been challenged. Pray for wisdom – some short-term initiatives have been so bold and public that there could be long-term problems.

5. **Christian help ministries.** There is freedom to develop any ministry in literature, radio, welfare, education or business; finance and personnel are limiting factors. Pray for:

a) **Bible translation and distribution.** The New Testament was published in 1992 (**IBT**), the same time as a Kyrgyz version of the Koran. Many have compared the two and are favourably impressed with the Bible message. Pray for its wide distribution and its message to enter many a heart. **SGA** has produced a well-accepted children's Bible in Kyrgyz.

b) **Christian literature in Kyrgyz**. Literature is limited in quality and range. As the Kyrgyz language gains more prominence and the churches grow, the need for evangelistic, apologetic and teaching materials grow. National Christian writers are few.

c) **The *Jesus* film** and video which is widely used in Russian, and available in Kyrgyz.

d) **Radio. TWR**-Monaco and **FEBC**-Saipan broadcast a total of 1.25 hours a week in Kyrgyz, but shortwave receivers are rare. National radio is an option that needs to be explored. Pray for the means to pursue this.

Laos
(Lao People's Democratic Republic)

July 25
Asia

Area 237,000 sq.km. Landlocked; part of Indo-China between Thailand, Vietnam and China. Mountainous and 70% forested.

Population	Ann. Gr.	Density
1990 4,071,000	2.8 %	17/sq.km
1995 4,583,000	2.4 %	19/sq.km

The majority live in lowlands along the Mekong River.

Peoples: Over 103 ethnic-linguistic groups known; but land inadequately surveyed. During 1975–1979 over 10% of the population fled the country.
Lao-Tai 66.3%. 17 groups. Largest: Lao 2,444,000; Tai (7) 165,000; Phu Thai 128,000; Phuan 96,000; Lue 20,000.
Mon-Khmer 21.4%. 62 groups. Largest: Khmu 384,000; So 102,000; Kui 64,000; Bru 64,000; Kantu 38,000; Ta-Oi 38,000; Laven 32,000; Brao 23,000.
Hmong (Miao) 7.6%. 4 groups. Largest: Hmong (2) 256,000; Mien (Yao) 70,000.
Sino-Tibetan 1.44%. 8 groups. Largest: Phunoi 20,000; Sila 19,000; Akha 6,400.
Other 3.2%. Vietnamese 76,000; Chinese 25,000; Khmer 10,000; Westerners 1,000.

Literacy 43%. **Official language**: Lao. **All languages** 90. **Languages with Scriptures** 6Bi 7NT 10por.

Capital: Vientiane 377,500. Urbanization 16%.

Economy: Subsistence agricultural economy. The Vietnam war, the disastrous implementation of Marxist economics 1975–79, flight of skilled workers, bureaucratic confusion and the lack of cheap communications to the sea all help to make Laos one of Asia's poorest lands. Economic pressure is stimulating sweeping reforms and creating a market economy. Income/person $170 (0.8% of USA).

Politics: Independent from France in 1954. Lao and Vietnamese Communist forces finally conquered the whole country in 1975. There has been considerable anti-government guerrilla activity in the northwest. A pawn in the super-power conflict until 1990. By 1992, the Communist leaders were still in full political control despite economic liberalizations.

Religion: Communist persecution of Christians was harsh between 1975 and 1978. Thereafter, restrictions were eased, though the churches are suspected as potentially subversive, and are watched. There remain restrictions on public evangelism, building of churches and links with foreign organizations. Buddhism is regaining some of its old influence.
Non-religious/other 5.1%. Predominantly Communists.
Animist 33%. Majority of tribal people; also strongly embedded in Buddhist peoples.
Buddhist 58.7%. Majority of lowland Lao.
Chinese religions 0.7%.
Muslim 1%. Cham minority.
Christian 1.53%. Growth 6.2%.
Protestant 0.72%. Growth 13.2%.

Church	Cong	Members	Affiliated
Evangelical Ch (CMA)	160	8,000	16,000
Christian Brethren	90	6,500	13,000
All other (2)	3	220	400
Denominations (4)	253	14,720	29,400
Evangelicals 0.72% of pop		14,600	29,200

Expatriate Christians in Laos 36 (1:113,000 people) in 7 agencies.
Roman Catholic 0.81%. Growth 1.4%.

Catholic Ch	90	19,000	32,800

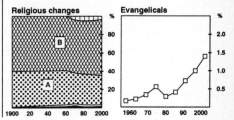

Religious changes

Evangelicals

1. **Much of Laos has yet to be evangelized.** After years of hard work **CMA** and Christian Brethren missionaries saw significant breakthroughs among the Hmong, Khmu and Ngeq (over half the 4,000 Ngeq are Christian). Pray for change that will open the whole land for the preaching of the gospel.

2. **The Church suffered much in the early years under Communism.** Two-thirds of all Christians fled, others backslid, but those who remained stood firm through years of isolation. Many others were converted in the ensuing years, and the Church is steadily growing. Pray for:
a) Complete freedom for evangelism, church planting and building.
b) Effective use of present freedoms for personal witness.
c) A vision for evangelizing the ethnic minorities.

d) An effective unity among the leaders of the nearly 250 evangelical churches in the country.

3. **Leaders for the churches.** Over 90% of all trained leaders left Laos in 1975. Only ten men with Bible training remain. Pray that all informal study programmes (in refugee camps, by radio and through TEE) may help existing leadership be adequately equipped. Pray also that soon there may be permission to build a Bible School.

4. **The Laotian diaspora.** Over 350,000 people fled from Communist rule; 80% now live in North America, Europe, Australia and New Zealand. The remainder live in refugee camps in Thailand.
a) **The 70,000 refugees in Thailand** are slowly returning home as conditions improve. There are 5,000 Christians among them. Pray for ministries to them in the camps and for their witness when they return home.
b) **The Hmong** resisted Communism for years and a high proportion became refugees. Nearly a quarter of these people are now Christian – in over 100 churches in the USA, France and French Guiana. Pray for this scattered people and their complete evangelization. There are only about 1,200 Hmong Christians in Laos itself.
c) **The numerous small colonies of refugees** from other tribal groups are hard to reach, yet vital for the eventual discipling of their homeland communities.

5. **Missionary work** is not officially permitted, but a number of expatriate believers are ministering with considerable freedom through 11 non-governmental organizations administering aid and relief. Pray for a reopened door for Bible translators, pioneer church planters and Bible teachers – the spiritual ministries of greatest need. Pray also for wisdom for expatriates in relating to the Lao church leaders, both in the distribution of aid and in ministry.

6. **Unreached peoples in which there are no known churches.**
a) **The Tai tribes** speaking 15 languages.
b) **The northern peoples,** many of whom have responded to the gospel in neighbouring China and Thailand. Political conditions never allowed missionary penetration.
c) **The small southern tribes** which were being evangelized for the first time between 1957 and 1963, but war prevented the planting of churches among most of these peoples. They are deeply enmeshed in the fear of spirits. In only ten of the 62 tribes have small churches emerged.
d) The **Vietnamese** and **Chinese** which have only been marginally evangelized.

7. **Christian Help ministries.**
a) **Bible distribution** through the **UBS** and the Bible League. Pray for the free and wide dissemination of God's Word.
b) **Bible translation.** Pray that an adequate language survey may soon be possible. The local linguistic situation is highly complex. **SIL, CMA** and **NTM** are all committed to this ministry. There are 13 languages for which there is a definite need for translation teams and a possible total of 66 languages. Pray for the effective use of computer-assisted dialect and script translation programmes in speeding up the process of providing each people with God's Word.
c) **GRn** which has prepared audio-messages in 90 languages of Laos.
d) **Christian Radio.** FEBC broadcasts 16 hours weekly in Lao, Hmong, Khmu and Lahu. Pray for a good reception and spiritual response.

Latvia
(Republic of Latvia)

Area 64,500 sq.km. A fertile plain with 3,000 lakes and indented by the Gulf of Riga. The central Baltic republic.

Population	Ann.Gr.	Density
1990 2,682,000	0.7%	42/sq.km
1995 2,750,000	0.5%	43/sq.km

Peoples:
Indo-European 98.3%.
   Baltic 53.4%. Latvian 1,388,000; Lithuanian 35,000.
   Slav 44.1%. Russian 905,000; Byelorussian 120,000; Ukrainian 92,000; Polish 60,000.
   Other 0.8%. Gypsy 7,000.
All other peoples 1.7%. Jews 23,000; Tatar 5,000; Estonian 3,000.

Literacy 99%. **Official language** since 1989: Latvian; spoken by 62% of population. 82% can speak Russian. **All indigenous languages** 5. **Languages with Scriptures** 3Bi 1NT 1por.

Capital: Riga 915,000. Urbanization 68%.

Economy: The most industrialized of the former Soviet republics, but obsolete machinery and Russia's collapsed economy, which supplied raw materials and markets, have put the Latvian economy into severe decline. The large Russian labour force and military presence still dominate independent Latvia. Income/person $5,689 (26% of USA).

Politics: Since the Middle Ages, Latvia has been ruled by the Germans, Danes, Poles, Swedes and Russians. Latvia had its brief independence from Russia (1917–1940) ended by Stalin's reconquest. Stalin liquidated a fifth of the population, deported many more and forcibly settled Russians in their place. This history dominates modern politics. Independent in 1991 as a multi-party democracy, the first elections were scheduled for 1993. Stringent citizen qualifications disenfranchise most of the Russian settlers.

Religion: Communist repression and control of the Churches was more severe than in other Baltic states because of the large military presence and Russian Communist settlers. Freedom of religion since 1987/88. All figures below are estimates.
Non-religious/other 43.7%. Many Slavs, fewer Latvians.
Jews 0.9%.
Muslims 0.4%. Central Asian and Ural immigrants.
Christian 55%. Affil 37.3%. Growth 2.5%.
   Protestant 20%. Affil 14.7%. Gro 0.7%.

Church		Members	Affiliated
Lutheran Ch		140,000	350,000
Baptist Union	70	7,000	35,000
Pentecostal Chs	30	4,000	10,000
Denominations (3)	100	151,000	395,000
Evangelicals 5.6% of pop		53,000	150,000
Pentecostal/charis 0.57%		5,000	15,000

Missionaries:
   to Latvia 29 (1:92,400 people) in 4 agencies.
   from Latvia 2 (1:200,00 Protestants) in 1 agency 2frn.

Roman Catholic 20%. Affil 14.9%. Growth 5.7%.

Catholic Ch	240,000	400,000

Orthodox 15%. Affil 7.7%. Growth 0.3%.

Russian Orthodox	130,000	200,000
All other (5)	4,680	7,500
Denominations (6)	134,680	207,500

Marginal 0.03%. Growth 20%.

Groups (1)	270	900

L

1. **The ferment and nationalist ardour of 1987–89** have given way to the cold realities of economic privation since independence. There is a widespread sense of need for God to be part of Latvia's future. The devastating moral and social impact of Communist oppression cannot be eliminated without an outpouring of the Holy Spirit. There are, on average, 52,000 abortions annually, compared with only 39,000 live births.

2. **Solutions for the vexed ethnic question are urgently needed**. The anxious Slav population comprises nearly half the population and 70% of that of the capital, yet Latvians need to restore their national pride, culture and language without penalizing ethnic minorities. Pray for the government as the nation's leaders wrestle with these issues.

3. **Religious freedom** has brought many into the churches – and a following for eastern religions and western sects. Lack of teaching, teaching materials in Latvian, and trained pastors hinders growth. Pray for healthy growth in the churches. Evangelicals are relatively few in the rather nominal Lutheran Church, but both the Baptists and Pentecostals are evangelistic and growing. Pray for inter-ethnic harmony among believers.

4. **Leadership training**, so long denied, is now developing apace. Pray for the two Lutheran, Baptist and Catholic seminaries, as well as the Theological Faculty in Riga University.

5. **Youth ministries** were illegal for decades, but are now being resurrected. Pray for church youth activities, camp ministries and campus/school ministries – all in their infancy. Many schools plead for Christian input, but there are few qualified to give it. Pray also for a missions vision to be given to young people.

6. **More spiritually needy sections of the population.**
a) **The Russians** – many are non-religious, and Christians are predominantly Orthodox. Russian Christians are a majority in the Pentecostal churches, but a minority in the Baptist churches.
b) **Many towns and villages** are devoid of an evangelical witness. **EHC** has launched a nationwide literature crusade to reach every home with the Good News.

Lebanon
(Republic of Lebanon)

<table>
<tr><td>July 27</td></tr>
<tr><td>Middle East</td></tr>
</table>

Area 10,400 sq.km. A fertile, mountainous state in the East Mediterranean. An enclave between Israel and Syria. The site of ancient Phoenicia.

Population		Ann. Gr.	Density
1990	2,965,000	2.1 %	290/sq.km
1995	3,286,000	2.1 %	321/sq.km

Since 1975, one-third of the population has been lost through death or emigration. The rate of emigration has been higher among Christians.

Peoples: A melting pot of Middle Eastern peoples. No census for 60 years, so all Lebanon figures are approximate.
Arab 86%.
  Lebanese 68%.
  Other 18%. Syrian 400,000; Palestinian 260,000; Egyptian 79,000.
All other 14%. Armenian 186,000; Kurdish 173,000; Assyrian 14,000.

Literacy 70% and falling because of war. **Official language:** Arabic; French and English are widely used. **All languages** 4. **Languages with Scriptures** 2Bi 2por.

Capital: Beirut 1,418,000. Urbanization 81%.

Economy: Trading, banking and tourism were once profitable and made Lebanon the commercial centre of the Middle East. The sixteen-year agony of civil wars and foreign interventions has reduced part of the land to ruins and poverty. In 1992 recovery began, but it may take a long time before Lebanon regains even a part of its former affluence. Income/person $800 (4% of USA).

Politics: French-mandated territory 1919–1941. Independent in 1941 as a republic, with a constitution based on a delicate balance related to the size of the 17 recognized religious communities. The influx of 400,000 Palestinian refugees between 1948 and 1976 upset the status quo, precipitating the 1975–1992 civil war. The Palestinians seized south Lebanon only to have their power broken by Israeli invasion and occupation (1982–85). Shi'a Muslim and Druze militia improved their political leverage at the expense of the Christians in the subsequent years of bitter fighting, hostage-taking and Syrian efforts to manipulate and control the complex medley of warring factions. The Syrian army imposed a measure of peace in 1992 and opened the way for the Taif agreement of 1992 and a new Lebanese government. The first elections in 20 years were marred by the non-cooperation of Christian factions, but the new government has cautiously begun to exert its control over much of the country but under Syrian oversight. The far south of Lebanon remains under Israeli control; its population is half Christian and half Shi'a.

Religion: Freedom of religion; the only Arab state that is not officially Muslim. The distribution of power according to the size of each community has been frozen at 1932 levels. The rapid increase in size of the Muslim population, and especially of the under-represented Shi'a, is one of the basic reasons for the present conflict. There are 17 recognized religious communities: five Muslim, one Jewish and 11 Christian. All figures are estimates. The last religious census was in 1932, when Christians were 53.7% of the population.

Non-religious/other 1.3%.
Muslim 53%
  Shi'a 33%. Mainly in south, Bekaa Valley in east, and Beirut.
  Sunni 20%. Mainly in Beirut, Tripoli, Sidon and northeast – Syrians and Palestinians.
  Druze 7%. Mainly in Chouf mountains east of Beirut. Their beliefs differ much from the teachings of Islam.
Christian 38.7%. Growth −0.6%. Mainly in East Beirut, central and north Lebanon. Decline from 62% in 1970. Figures below are largely estimates.
  Protestant 0.77%. Growth 0.3%.

Church	Cong	Members	Affiliated
Baptist Convention	22	1,200	3,600
Un of Ev Armenian Chs	5	2,140	2,390
Ch of God (Anderson)	14	1,000	2,000
Nat Evang Synod	13	1,200	1,870
Nat Evang Union	3	1,000	1,300
Seventh-day Adventist	2	500	1,110
Nat Ev Chr Alliance	3	270	992
Christian Brethren (2)	5	340	490
Ch of the Nazarene	2	55	195
All other (9)	17	1,007	2,008
Denominations (19)	86	8,712	15,955
Evangelicals 0.4% of pop		5,921	11,840
Pentecostal/charis 0.05%		750	1,500

Missionaries:
  to Lebanon 16 (1:185,000 people) in 15 agencies, most not living in Lebanon.
  from Lebanon 19 (1:1,200 Protestants) in 4 agencies 16frn 3dom.
Catholic 24.1%. Growth −2%.

Maronite Patriarchate	850	280,000	540,000
Melchite Cath Patr	300	70,200	130,000
Armenian Cath Patr	8	10,100	18,000

Syrian Cath Patriarchate	5	6,720	12,000
Roman Catholic	6	6,720	12,000
Chaldean Catholic	1	1,680	3,000
Denominations (6)	1,170	375,420	715,000

Roman Catholic missionaries:
  to Lebanon 779 (1973 figure) – much reduced in 1990.
  from Lebanon 150 (1973 figure).

Orthodox 13.5%. Growth 2%.

Greek Orthodox Ch	351	133,000	238,000
Armenian Apostolic	280	84,000	150,000
Syrian Orthodox Ch	5	4,800	8,000
Ancient Ch of the East			
(Nestorian)	3	2,850	5,000
All other (2)	3	371	530
Denominations (6)	642	225,021	401,530

Marginal 0.24%. Growth 5%.

Jehovah's Witnesses	56	2,726	6,060
All groups (3)	59	3,211	7,010

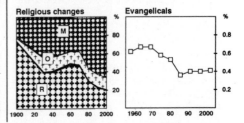

1. **Lebanon's tragedy** – with its communal wars, foreign interventions and hostage-taking – has made world headlines for many years. The fragmentation of the nation has given the world a new word, **Lebanonization**. Its once-wealthy economy is destroyed, its middle class vanished, and its social cohesion unglued. Yet the awfulness of hatred and war has created a search for reality and spiritual hunger. Some nominal Christians and Muslims have come to faith in Jesus, and significant renewal movements are spreading through the ancient Churches. Pray that the work of the Holy Spirit in this land may also create a new set of news headlines.

2. **The fighting has died down,** but the uneasy peace and renewed political activity could easily founder on the hatred and divisions both between and within the different communities. Political fragmentation in the Christian community and deep personal animosities hinder meaningful solutions for the future. Pray for repentance and reconciliation among political and religious leaders, for forgiveness between communities and for trust to be rebuilt.

3. **The government and its leaders** need prayer. No community can command a majority, so a fair compromise solution must be sought so that reconstruction of property, lives and the economy can begin. Most of Lebanon's territory is still under occupation. Pray that religious liberty might be preserved – Lebanon is one of the few countries in the Middle East to have it.

4. **The Orthodox and Catholic Churches are many and varied.** All have a long history of struggle for survival. In the midst of traditionalism and deadness are also significant renewal movements – notably in the Maronite and Eastern Orthodox Churches. Church attendance, especially among the Maronites, is at an all-time high. Pray for new life to infuse these ancient communities.

5. **The Protestant church has struggled to grow** because of centuries of suspicion of Western Christianity and because of the fragmented and divisive message of the many small denominations. More Armenians than Arabs have responded. Conversions have barely replaced losses through emigration. Pray for the ministry of the Baptists, **CMA**, and Church of God – churches that are growing, but relatively few of the new converts are from a non-Christian background. Pray also for greater understanding and fellowship between the churches.

6. **Trained leadership in evangelical churches is at a premium.** The decline in number of residential missionaries, emigration of national leaders, and lack of workers have left many congregations in the region without effective pastoral care. Lebanon has several residential evangelical Bible schools – Baptist (with 28 students), **CMA** (12) in Beirut, the Church of God (32 students) and the Near East School of Theology. Pray for staff, supply of needs and students in these difficult times.

7. **Lebanon has been one of the key centres for Christian ministries to the whole Middle East.** Much of this outreach has been limited or stopped altogether. Pray for the resumption of this role for the blessing of the whole region. Pray especially for these ministries:
a) **The Bible Society** has a vital role in distributing many Bibles to Lebanon and surrounding nations. The war increased circulation and use of the popular 1979 Arabic Bible. A new, modern version was published in 1992. Many Christians of the older churches are reading and studying the Bible.

b) **Christian literature** production has been severely disrupted; much of this ministry has been transferred to Cyprus, Europe and elsewhere. Pray for the Evangelical Carmel Mission, **OM**, **MECO**, Clarion Publishing House, Baptists and others, who are publishing and distributing literature for Lebanon and the Arab world.

c) **Radio**. Both **FEBA**-Seychelles (18 hours/week) and **TWR**-Cyprus (seven hours/week) broadcast into Lebanon. In the Israeli-occupied south Lebanon, the *Voice of Hope* Christian station (**High Adventure**) broadcasts 112 hours/week. This station and its staff have suffered from terrorist attacks. Pray for the safety of the staff, and for spiritual impact.

d) **Student work** in support of the scattered Christian students in the region was halted by the war. An embryo new student movement has been relaunched (**IFES**). YFC and *Grain du Blè* have a ministry in Beirut.

8. **Foreign missions**. The war and the threat of hostage-taking caused most missions to withdraw personnel. Few remain resident in the country; others are based in Cyprus. Pray for more to be called to live and work in Lebanon. Many Lebanese Christians feel forgotten by the outside world. Many opportunities for ministry in teaching, outreach and relief work exist. The enormous task of reconstruction and rehabilitation is an opportunity to demonstrate Christian love and concern. Lebanese churches are heavily committed to relief and development. Pray for good cooperation with international missions and Christian aid organizations – **CMA, MECO, SBC, WV, YWAM** and others.

9. **The unreached**. The social consequences of personal conversion to Christ are immense, so those coming to him have been few, but praise God for greater openness now. So pray for:

a) **The Druze:** a well-organized and close-knit community with a secretive religion steeped in occult practices and the use of curses. There are only one or two known believers.

b) **The Shi'a Muslims**, the most radical of the religious groupings. The Hezbollah faction in South Lebanon is supported by Iran, violently opposed to anything Western, and responsible for most of the hostage-taking in recent years. Pray that they may discover the emptiness of a religion without Christ.

c) **The Kurds:** a despised and ignored but more responsive minority.

d) **The Palestinians:** a tragic, stateless people. There are Christians among them, some evangelical, but the majority are Muslim and unreached.

July 28	*Lesotho*	
Africa	(Kingdom of Lesotho)	

Area 30,400 sq.km. A mountainous, landlocked country completely surrounded by South Africa. Only 9% is arable.

Population	Ann. Gr.	Density
1990	1,774,000	2.9 %	58/sq.km
1995	2,020,000	2.6 %	67/sq.km

Peoples:
Bantu 99.7%. Sotho 1,493,000; Zulu 248,000; Xhosa 18,000.
Other 0.3%. Afrikaans, British, Indo-Pakistani and French.

Literacy 74%. **Official languages:** Sotho, English. **All languages** 4. **Languages with Scriptures** 3Bi.

Capital: Maseru 109,400. Urbanization 16%.

Economy: The mountainous topography, poor communications and lack of agricultural land, together with over-population have kept the country poor and hastened soil erosion. Many seek work as migrant labour in South Africa. Industry is being developed. Export of water to South Africa will soon be a major foreign exchange earner. Unemployment 23%. Public debt/person $152. Income/person $470 (2% of USA).

Politics: A British Protectorate in 1865. Independence in 1966, though heavy economic dependence on South Africa with its political tensions has affected internal policies. A military coup in 1986. King Moshoeshoe was deposed and exiled for seeking a larger political role for himself. A further coup in 1991 led to the opening of the way for multi-party elections in 1993 and the return of the former king – his son is the present king.

Religion: Freedom of religion, but with the Catholic Church having a dominant role. The churches play a major part in providing education and health services.
African traditional religions 6%. **Baha'i** 1%.
Christian 93%. Nom 15.9%. Affil 77.1%. Growth 2.4%.

Protestant 34.8%. Affil 21%. Growth 1%.

Church	Cong	Members	Affiliated
Lesotho Evang Ch	550	67,500	211,000
Anglican Ch	400	60,000	100,000
African Methodist Epis	48	7,319	13,100
Methodist	8	5,000	10,000
Dutch Reformed in Afr	8	2,500	7,396
Assemblies of God	36	2,300	4,266
Seventh-day Adventist	22	2,427	4,050
Full Gosp. (Ch of God)	40	800	4,032
Mahon Mission	15	1,800	3,600
Apostolic Faith Mission	17	800	1,500
All other (19)	40	5,852	13,700
Denominations (29)	1,184	156,298	372,644
Evangelicals 3.9% of pop		29,000	68,500
Pentecostal/charis 1.4%		11,000	24,000

Missionaries:
to Lesotho 143 (1:12,400 people) in 37 agencies.
from Lesotho 47 (1:7,900 Protestants) in 11 agencies 4frn 4xcul 43dom.

Roman Catholic 45%. Affil 43.5%. Growth 3.3%.

Catholic Ch	495	478,000	771,583
Charismatics 0.13%		1,200	2,300

Missionaries:
to Lesotho 140 (1:12,700 people).
from Lesotho 10 (1973 figure).

Foreign Marginal 0.18%. Growth 10.8%.

Jehovah's Witnesses	45	1,304	3,260

Indigenous Marginal 13%. Affil 12.4%.
Growth 1.9%.

All groups (210)	3,333	100,000	220,000

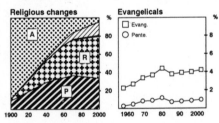

1. **God is beginning to do a "new thing" in Lesotho.** The great pioneering work of the French missionaries of the Paris Missionary Society resulted in the establishment of the Lesotho Evangelical Church which grew nominal and liberal over the years. However, the rapid increase in the number of Pentecostal and charismatic churches is now challenging the mainline churches to make their Christianity more than mere church-going.

2. **The enormous investment of the Catholics has paid big dividends.** Most of the leadership of the country is Catholic by education and profession. This led to discrimination against non-Catholics, but more recently there has been greater unity at leadership level to work together for a democratic and just society.

3. **Praise God for the evidence of his working through the Pentecostal and charismatic churches.**
Pray that the work of God's Spirit will continue, until it has permeated the nominal Christianity
which exists in the majority of churches throughout the land. Pray for:

a) **Bible teaching**. There are four residential Bible schools, the Apostolic Church Mobile Bible
School, *Jesu Evangeli Centre* ministry, and the **AIM** TEE programme with potential to provide
this. Pray for these ministries.

b) **Leadership**. The mainline, Catholic and Pentecostal churches in Lesotho have been under local
leadership for many years, but a new level of leadership is emerging in the charismatic churches
that is cooperating to win the nation for Christ. Church attendance, particularly in the mainline
churches, reflects a preponderance of women.

c) **The Sephiri**, a secret society to which many churchgoers from most denominations belong.
Witchcraft and ancestor worship are taught and practised along with Christian ritual. Pray for
both the exposure of this demonic delusion and for its followers to come to a living faith.

4. **Other supportive and specialized ministries** are contributing to the life and witness of the
Church.

a) **Evangelical witness** has been enhanced through younger ministries – **SBC, AIM, YWAM** and a
number of Pentecostal and charismatic groups.

b) **The ministry of SU among young people** is making a significant impact. Pray for the eight
workers, 63 school groups and six college groups with a total of 2,500 committed members.

c) **The *Jesus* film** is widely used in English and Sotho. It is a significant contributing factor to the
planting of many new fellowships in the mountains.

d) **A nationwide prayer movement** has brought a new dynamism to the witness of believers.

5. **Less evangelized sections of the population.**

a) **The more syncretic indigenous churches.** Many of these groups with their robes, uniforms and
ceremonies have little understanding of the Truth and need to be sensitively helped to a more
biblical theology.

b) **The 500,000 mountain population**, most nominally Christian, but with little contact with the life-
giving gospel. Various evangelical agencies have initiated outreach to them. Major agencies are Joy
to the World, **YWAM**, Fill the Gap Ministries, the Full Gospel Church, Zoe Bible Church and
Global Evangelism Ministries. Many villages are only accessible on horseback, others by **MAF**
plane. The latter also provides a flying doctor service. Pray for this arduous and costly outreach
and for the missionaries involved.

6. **Migrant labourers in South Africa.** Lack of work opportunities in Lesotho forces 37% of the men
to seek employment in the mines and on the farms of South Africa. **AEF** has a fruitful evangelistic
ministry in the mine compounds. Pray for lasting conversions and effective discipling follow-
through.

<table>
<tr><td>

July 29

Africa

</td><td>

Liberia
(Republic of Liberia)

</td><td>

</td></tr>
</table>

Area 111,000 sq.km. Heavily forested coastal state adjoining Sierra Leone, Guinea and Côte d'Ivoire.

Population		Ann. Gr.	Density
1990	2,554,000	3.2 %	26/sq.km
1995	3,005,000	3.3 %	30/sq.km

The disastrous civil war has made these and subsequent figures speculative projections. Maybe 200,000 have been killed and 1,000,000 have fled to surrounding lands.

Peoples: There are 16 major ethnic groups divided in three language families. These figures include refugees in surrounding lands.
Mande 47%. 12 ethnic groups. Largest: Kpelle 487,000, Gio 200,000, Mano 178,000, Loma 142,000; Mande/Mandingo 98,000; Vai 78,000, Gbandi 71,000.
Kru 40.5%. Over 18 ethnic groups. Largest: Bassa 348,000; Grebo (7 languages) 223,000; Klao 184,000; Krahn 95,000.
West Atlantic 7.5%. Kissi 101,000; Gola 99,000.
Other 2.7%. Lebanese 25,000; other West African.
Non-tribal 2.3%. English-speaking.

Literacy 64%. **Official language:** English. **All languages** 34. **Languages with Scriptures** 1Bi 10NT 7por.

Capital: Monrovia 421,000 (1984); now swollen to 1,000,000 with refugees. Urbanization: n.a.

Economy: Mining of iron ore and diamonds, export of rubber, timber and coffee and a large "flag of convenience" fleet of ships could make this land prosper. Yet years of institutionalized corruption, control of trade by Lebanese, and exclusive control of politics by the elite have prevented adequate development. The destruction of the economy in the civil war will take decades to rectify.

Politics: In 1847 Liberia became Black Africa's first independent state. The dominance of the Liberians of American origin ended in the coup of 1980. The military government became increasingly unstable. Massive corruption and repression of the Mano and Gio peoples provoked the 1989 revolution led by Charles Taylor. The war engulfed the country in an orgy of inter-tribal killings and ultimately three armies contending for power. The West African States (ECOWAS) military intervention has proved a costly stalemate, with the Nigerian-led ECOMOG forces controlling Monrovia and Taylor's forces

much of the hinterland. No end was in sight by June 1993.

Religion: Liberia was founded as a Christian state. There continues to be freedom of religion in theory, but in practice there is pressure on Christians to conform to occult secret societies. Figures below are estimates – many nominal Christians and many Muslims have fled the country.
Traditional religions 49.4%, of which maybe 10–15% would claim to be "Christian". Strongly entrenched and institutionalized secret societies. Relatively few Liberians are uninvolved.
Muslim 13.3%. Majority among Mandingo and Vai.
Baha'i 0.3%.
Christian 37%. Nom 12%. Affil 25%. Growth 6.2%.
Protestant 20.6%. Affil 16.4%. Growth 6.2%.

Church	Cong	Members	Affiliated
Baptist Convention	250	59,222	98,700
Lutheran Chs (2)	119	19,100	69,779
Assemblies of God	395	20,000	45,000
United Methodist Ch	420	21,800	43,681
United Lib Inland Ch	71	7,800	20,000
Episcopal Ch	129	13,000	20,000
Assoc of Indep Chs	175	7,000	14,000
Mid-Liberia Bapt Msn	75	3,750	7,500
Presbyterian Ch	15	1,500	3,750
All other (42)	684	42,910	96,786
Denominations (52)	2,333	196,082	419,196
Evangelicals 8.1% of pop		99,000	206,000
Pentecostal/charis 3.6%		42,000	93,000

Missionaries (some figures pre-date the civil war):
to Liberia 353 (1:7,200 people) in 63 agencies.
from Liberia est. 20 (1:21,000 Protestants) 1frn 19dom.
Roman Catholic 3%. Affil 2.4%. Growth 10.8%.

Catholic Ch	156	45,400	73,154

Missionaries to Liberia 212 (1:12,800 people).
Foreign Marginal 0.2%. Affil 0.19%. Growth 9.3%.
Indigenous Marginal 13.2%. Affil 5.5%. Growth 4%.

All groups (est. 110)		77,000	140,000

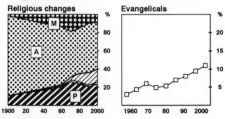

1. **The bloody civil war is a political cancer poisoning much of West Africa.** The military stalemate with mounting casualties, suffering, and 50% of the population living as refugees makes a

compromise solution urgent. Lust for power, deep ethnic hatred, and divisions among West African states about future strategy prevent this. Pray for the humbling or removal of all leaders who prolong the agony for selfish gain and for others to be raised up who will bring peace and foster recovery.

2. **Christianity has compromised with evil on an alarming scale.** Freemasonry imported by the early settlers fused with indigenous tribal secret societies to become a pervasive influence that has corrupted and compromised politics and nearly every denomination, whether mainline, evangelical or Pentecostal. Stagnation, failure of the gospel to advance in Liberia's hinterland, lack of concern for the lost, and spiritual impotence so widespread in the churches are due to condoned sin, witchcraft, alcoholism and polygamy among "Christians". During the war, Christians who refused to compromise were persecuted in some areas. Pray for the binding of these spiritual forces, and for a new day of freedom and power in the Holy Spirit for the Church.

3. **There are signs of hope.** The agony of the nation has driven Christians to new prayer and earnestness for the gospel. Christians have had miraculous deliverances, soldiers have repented of horrible crimes, and there have been localized revivals in the midst of sorrow. The **Association of Evangelicals** has regrouped and begun to lay plans for future reconstruction and evangelization. Pray that out of the fires may come a purified, revived Church that can be a force for reconciliation between ethnic groups, and for the complete evangelization of the country.

4. **Rehabilitation and reconstruction** once peace comes will require years of international assistance. A consortium of mission agencies and churches, the **Christian Health Association of Liberia** (CHAL), is already developing aid programmes, health clinics, rehabilitation projects, counselling of traumatized children and care of orphans. Pray for missionaries and nationals involved in these ministries and for the Christian aid missions who have rallied to raise support for them.

5. **Young people's ministries** have virtually come to a halt. A whole generation of children is growing up in the horrors of war, with little schooling and very little chance to hear the gospel. Pray that **YFC** and **SU** may soon resume their ministries, and for **IFES**, which has continued with ministry to those in distress despite the closure of the university. Many children have been abandoned and orphaned and many others forced to become soldiers – even those as young as eight years of age. Pray for Christians seeking to counsel and rehabilitate the many traumatized by their experiences.

6. **Trained spiritual leaders are few in number**. Many have had to flee or been killed; most Bible training has come to a halt or is struggling to survive with limited resources or personnel. Pray for the resumption of denominational and interdenominational Bible schools – among the latter are the Monrovia and Africa Bible colleges. Pray that a new generation of leaders may be raised up who fearlessly preach the whole gospel without compromise.

7. **Islam's rapid expansion has slowed.** Muslim Mandingo support for the previous, largely Krahn, regime and their relative wealth provoked a cruel response from other tribes. Nearly all the Mandingo have been killed or have fled to Guinea, and up to 1,000 mosques destroyed or damaged. Liberia was to have been a major centre for Islamic growth in West Africa – one of the factors that provoked the war. **SIM**, through Radio ELWA, had begun to see the beginnings of response among the Mandingo. Pray for the evangelization of these refugee communities.

8. **Less-reached peoples.** Of all Liberia's indigenous peoples, only three are majority Christian, despite considerable exposure to the gospel. Most still follow traditional religions; some are Muslim. There are 16 peoples in which there is not yet a viable, growing, indigenous church-planting movement. Pray for:
a) **Muslim groups:** the Vai (**CRWM**) in the west and Mende and Manya (**SIM**) of the northern borders are largely Muslim with few active Christians.
b) **Traditional peoples with growing Muslim influence:** the Dewoin (8,000) near Monrovia and the Gbandi in the north. Both are turning to Islam, and the small Christian community has been shrinking (**SIM**).
c) **Peoples with strong fetish powers** and where a victorious gospel power-encounter must yet come: Krahn in northeast (9% Christian, **AoG**, **SBC**) and Grebo in east (**AoG**, **NTM**).
d) **African independent churches:** these are numerous and highly syncretic, but open for sensitive teaching. **CRWM** has had a ministry to them, helping them to a more biblical faith.

9. **Missionaries** have had a long, hard, uphill struggle to plant churches in the interior – disease, language diversity, entrenched fetishism and now the disruption of war since 1989 have all hampered the work. Some Protestant and Catholic missionaries have lost their lives in the conflict. Most have

had to leave the country, but some minister in Monrovia and among the large refugee communities in surrounding lands. Pray for the return of expatriates to rebuild the work so painstakingly established in the past and also help the Liberian church complete the evangelization of every people. The largest missions before the war were: **SIM** (64), United Methodists (51), **NTM** (41), Baptist Mid-Missions (36), Lutheran Bible Translators (36), North American Lutherans (34), **SBC** (34), **CRWM** (16). Their numbers have been reduced since then. Largest missionary-contributing nations: USA (259), Germany (16), Sweden(12).

10. **Christian help ministries.**

a) **Bible translation** work has been gravely disrupted by the war. Pray for the **Lutheran Bible Translators** and their seven translation projects as well as those of **WEC** and others. There are ten existing translation projects, but a further 11–13 are yet to be tackled.

b) **Christian literature**. Many pastors and Christians have lost all they owned, and there is a great lack of Bibles, New Testaments and Christian literature. **CLC's** bookstore in Monrovia was looted, but is being restocked. Pray for the provision of literature.

c) **Christian radio.** Until its destruction in 1990, SIM's Radio ELWA was Africa's best-known station, with 270 hours/week broadcasting in 44 languages. Praise God for the years of seed-sowing and discipling ministry. By 1993 only a small low-powered transmitter had been brought into operation in Monrovia. Plans were being made for two larger transmitters for broadcasting in 25 languages. Pray for their realization, provision of equipment and funds, and also peace and safety to permit resumption of the ministry.

L

Libya

(Socialist People's
Libyan Arab Jamahiriya)

July 30

Middle East

Area 1,760,000 sq.km. Some agriculture on Mediterranean coast; over 90% is Sahara desert.

Population	Ann. Gr.	Density
1990 4,544,000	3.7 %	2.6/sq.km
1995 5,445,000	3.7 %	3.1/sq.km

Peoples: Indigenous 89% but unofficially nearer 75%.
Arab 77%.
Berber 9.8%. Nearly half are Arabized. About eight ethnic groups. Largest: Zenati 130,000; Jalo 26,000; Zuara 25,000; Tuareg 17,000.
Other 2.2%. Black African 75,000; Teda 9,000; Zaghawa 7,000. Mainly in the southern oases.
Expatriate 11% officially, but unofficially may be over 30%. Many labourers from surrounding lands. Predominantly Egyptian, Sudanese, North African, Chadean, also Korean, European, Pakistani, Bangladeshi.

Literacy 22%. **Official language**: Arabic. **All languages** 11. **Languages with Scriptures** 2NT 1por.

Capital: Tripoli 991,000. Urbanization 75%.

Economy: Transformed by discovery of oil in 1959. Oil wealth has financed revolutionary movements and the promotion of Islam in many nations. The fickle and dictatorial government system has brought patchy development. Widespread subsidies and free handouts limit opposition. 75% of food is imported. The massive Great Man-made River project for transporting Saharan fossil water to the coast is aimed to diversify the economy. Up to 3 million Egyptians may eventually be used for the resulting agricultural development. Public debt/person $400. Income/person $5,410 (26% of USA).

Politics: Ruled by Italy 1911–1943. Full independence in 1951 as a monarchy. The military coup of 1969 led to a revolutionary republic under the leadership of Mu'ammar Ghadaffi. The government has become a cleverly manipulated instrument of policy for its maverick, mercurial leader. No dissent is permitted, and the population has been isolated from outside influences. Diplomatic isolation and economic sanctions imposed by the UN followed years of export of aid to guerrilla movements and terrorism.

Religion: Sunni Islam is the state religion, but secularizing influences are strong. No form of Christian witness to Libyan citizens is allowed, and the worship groups and congregations of expatriates are strictly monitored. All figures below are approximations.
Muslim 96%.
Non-religious/other 0.5%. Westerners, Chinese.
Buddhist 0.5%. Sri Lankan, Korean, Chinese.
Christian 2.2%. Affil 2.1%. Growth 2.1%.
  Protestant 0.2%. Affil 0.15%. Growth 4.1%.

Church	Cong	Members	Affiliated
All groups (6)	93	4,083	6,739
Evangelicals 0.09% of pop		2,600	4,000
Expatriate Christians to Libya 5 (1:909,000 people).			
Roman Catholic 1%. Affil 0.84%. Growth 1%.			
Catholic Ch	10	26,600	38,000
Expatriates to Libya 110 (1:38,000 people).			
Orthodox 1.8%. Affil 1.2%. Growth 2.7%.			
Coptic Orthodox	2	20,000	50,000
Greek Orthodox	3	570	1,900
All other (2)		1,390	2,100
Denominations (4)	5	21,960	54,000

1. **No open evangelism is possible.** The last missionary outpost was closed in 1960. The few foreign Christian workers minister to expatriate communities. Some Catholic medical workers are allowed. The entire population is unreached. There has never been a witness to the Berber or southern oasis peoples. Pray this land open for the King of kings.

2. **The Christian community** is large and foreign. There may be no more than a handful of Libyan believers. Most Christians are nominal; few have opportunity for public worship. There are a few active Protestant and Catholic congregations, and maybe up to 100 informal groups of believers of various nationalities – especially Korean construction workers, Pakistani labourers and Western skilled professionals. Few can communicate with the indigenous Libyans, and any such approach could be dangerous. Pray for the unhindered growth of the witness among expatriates and for outreach to every national grouping among them.

3. **Alternative means for preaching the gospel:**
a) **Radio.** One of the only ways for directly reaching Libyans. Three evangelical stations beam programmes to Libya: **High Adventure**-Lebanon (111 hours/week), **FEBA**-Seychelles (13), and the more clearly heard **TWR**-Monaco (7.5). Radio School of the Bible (**AWM**) is one of the most useful programmes, but follow-up is virtually impossible. Pray for eternal fruit.

b) **Literature and audio and video cassettes.** These may enter only by devious means. Pray for the circulation of Christian tapes in spite of the barriers. Pray for the conversion of censors! BCCs very rarely get through the mail.

c) **Libyans overseas.** Refugees from totalitarianism, diplomats, students and businessmen could be introduced to Christ by believers in other lands.

Include with Switzerland
Europe

Liechtenstein
(Principality of Liechtenstein)

Area 160 sq.km. Mountainous enclave on the Rhine between Switzerland and Austria.

Population	Ann. Gr.	Density
1990 28,452	0.95 %	177/sq.km
1995 30,500	1.40 %	191/sq.km

Peoples:
Indigenous 63.6%. German-speaking Liechtensteiners.
Expatriate 36.4%. Swiss 4,500; Austrian 2,200; German 1,100; Italian 800.

Capital: Vaduz 7,000. Urbanization 30%.

Economy: Wealthy through manufacturing, banking and tourism. Letter box companies are more numerous than inhabitants. Foreign labour force 41% of whole. Income/person $21,000 (99.5% of USA).

Politics: Constitutional principality in customs and monetary union with Switzerland.

Religion: The Catholic Church is the State Church, but freedom of religion guaranteed to all.
Non-religious/other 4.1%.
Muslim 0.5%. **Baha'i** 0.3%. **Jewish** 0.2%.
Christian 94.9%. Nom 10.1%. Affil 84.8%. Growth −0.6%.
Protestant 7.2%. Affil 7.2%. Growth 2.1%.

Church	Cong	Members	Affiliated
Reformed Ch	2	900	1,500
Evang Lutheran Ch	2	304	400
All other (2)	2	65	142
Denominations (4)	6	1,269	2,042
Evangelicals 0.29% of pop		51	82
Pentecostal/charis 0.1%		20	30

Roman Catholic 87.4%. Affil 77.3%.
Growth −0.8%.

Catholic Ch	10	16,700	22,000

Marginal 0.3%. Affil 0.3%. Growth 3.3%.

1. **Liechtenstein has changed** from a feudal backwater in the '30s to a leading banking and industrial centre today. Almost the entire indigenous population is Catholic and the expatriates are nominally Christian with a minority of Protestants. Few in this country have ever been confronted with the necessity of a personal faith in Christ. Church attendance is only a small proportion of those who claim to be Protestant.

2. **The first small evangelical fellowship of believers** was started in 1985 after an evangelistic campaign launched by British, Norwegian and Swiss believers. Pray for the health and growth of this infant work.

Lithuania
(Republic of Lithuania)

July 31
Europe

Area 65,300 sq.km. The southernmost of the three Baltic states.

Population	Ann.Gr.	Density
1990 3,721,000	0.6%	57/sq.km
1995 3,840,000	0.5%	59/sq.km

Peoples:
Indo-European 99.2%.
  Baltic 79.7%. Lithuanian 2,924,000; Latvian 4,200.
  Slav 19.3%. Russian 344,000; Polish 258,000; Byelorussian 63,000; Ukrainian 45,000.
  Other 0.2%.
All other peoples 0.8%. Jews 12,000; Tatar 5,100.

Literacy 99%. **Official language:** Lithuanian. **All indigenous languages** 3. **Languages with Scriptures** 2Bi.

Capital: Vilnius 593,000 (the city was part of Poland until 1940). Urbanization 68%.

Economy: Agricultural and industrial economy, but suffering severe decline along with all former USSR states. Income/person $4,034 (18% of USA).

Politics: Once a powerful duchy controlling much of West Russia, Byelarus and Ukraine. Strong links with Poland. Independent of Russia 1917–1940. Soviet occupation 1940–1990. Independent in 1990 as a multi-party democracy. Intolerant nationalism and hasty privatization of the economy by the party that led the country to independence caused them to lose the 1992 election to the Democratic Labour Party (former Communists), who promised a more cautious reform programme.

Religion: Catholicism was politically dominant before the Soviet conquest. After years of persecution, the Catholic Church is seeking to regain its pre-eminence – some fear that non-Catholics will suffer discrimination and restrictions.
Non-religious/other 13.4%.
Jews 0.33%.
Muslim 0.2%.
Christian 86.1%. Affil 74.4%. Growth 1.1%.
Protestant 1.1%. Affil 1.09%. Growth 5.5%.

Church	Cong	Members	Affiliated
Lutheran Ch	33	12,800	32,000
Reformed Ch in Lith	8	2,100	3,500
Pentecostal Chs	6	1,200	3,000
Baptist Ch	5	600	1,500
Denominations (6)	54	16,900	40,400
Evangelicals 0.32% of pop		4,990	11,950
Pentecostal/charis 0.11%		1,700	4,200
Roman Catholic 80%. Affil 70.5%.			
Growth 0.8%.			
Catholic Ch	668	1,570,000	2,611,000
Orthodox 5%. Affil 3.7%. Growth 5.9%.			
Russian Orthodox	45	71,500	110,000
All other (3)	51	13,775	25,900
Denominations (4)	96	85,275	135,900
Marginal 0.04%. Growth 13%.			

L

1. **Lithuania's long fight for political freedom has been won,** but the people are weary of national politics that cannot grapple with the fall-out of that independence. Economic decline and confrontations with the Russian military and Polish indigenous minority have hampered constructive decision-making. Pray that, in their disillusionment, Lithuanians may seek a personal relationship with the Lord Jesus.

2. **The Catholic Church** plays a key role in Lithuanian society, but it has been weakened by years of persecution. In general, priests are few and old, the Church is locked into a conservatism of another generation, and leaders are afraid of renewal movements that have affected the Polish Catholic Church. In its defensiveness the Church could seek the way of political influence and legal restrictions on non-Catholic Christian ministry rather than spiritual renewal. Pray for both religious freedom and an outpouring of God's Spirit on the land.

3. **Evangelical Christians are very few.** The small Lutheran Church is fairly nominal and Baptists and Pentecostals few. Evangelistic campaigns since 1988 have won possibly 1,000 new converts among young people, who have formed home groups. Pray for strong, evangelistic congregations to be planted in every part of the country.

4. **Ethnic minorities with few Evangelicals.** Both the Russian and Polish communities and also the Muslim Tatar community need prayer.

5. **Expatriate missions.** None, at present, minister long-term in the country. Pray for the right missionaries to be called to serve in this land. Pray also for freedom for them to enter and minister.

6. **Christian media ministries.** There is a lack of radio programmes (**IBRA** and **TWR** broadcast 45 min/week) and evangelical Christian literature.

| August 1 |
| Europe |

Luxembourg
(The Grand Duchy of Luxembourg)

Area 2,600 sq.km. The smallest of the Benelux, or Low Countries, and smallest member of the European Community.

Population		Ann. Gr.	Density
1990	367,000	0 %	142/sq.km
1995	368,000	0.05 %	142/sq.km

Peoples:
Luxembourgers 72.5%
Expatriates 27.5%. Portuguese 50,000; Italian 20,800; French 13,100; Belgian 9,600; German 9,200 and others.

Literacy 100%. **Official language:** None. Letzburgisch (a German dialect) is the national language, German the language of education and newspapers, and French used in official communications.

Capital: Luxembourg 80,000. Urbanization 78%.

Economy: Diversified industrial economy, with banking and finance also important. Public debt/person $1,050. Income/person $24,860 (118% of USA).

Politics: Parliamentary monarchy in economic union with Belgium and Netherlands. A member of EC, and headquarters of many EC institutions.

Religion: Freedom of religion. The Catholic Church is effectually the State Church.
Non-religious/other 1.9%.
Muslim 1%. **Baha'i** 0.3%. **Jews** 0.2%.
Christian 96.6%. Nom 12.9%. Affil 83.7%. Growth 0%.
Protestant 1.25%. Affil 1.2%. Growth 0.8%.

Church	Cong	Members	Affiliated
Protestant Ch of Lux	5	1,400	2,325
Foreign Prot Chs (8)	11	686	980
Mennonite Ch	2	100	167
Free Evang Ch	3	80	119
Assemblies of God	2	47	67
All other (9)	6	377	808
Denominations (21)	29	2,690	4,466
Evangelicals 0.15% of pop		328	535
Pentecostal/charis 0.04%		90	130

Missionaries:
  to Luxembourg 10 (1:36,700 people) in 5 agencies.
  from Luxembourg 1 (1:4,500 Protestants).
Roman Catholic 94.5%. Affil 81.7%. Growth 0%.

Catholic Ch	274	275,000	348,000
Doubly Counted		−38,000	−48,000
Denominations (2)	274	237,000	300,000

Missionaries:
  to Luxembourg 20 (1973 figure).
  from Luxembourg 90 (1:3,300 Catholics).
Marginal 0.85%. Affil 0.8%. Growth 5.1%.

Jehovah's Witnesses	22	1,541	2,570
All Groups (2)	23	1,891	3,008

1. **The land is Catholic by tradition and culture**; revolutionary changes in the Church elsewhere have passed it by, and few have clearly heard the gospel in their own language. Pray that many might come to personal faith in Christ.

2. **The Protestants are a small minority**, and a high proportion are foreigners. Jehovah's Witnesses have had more success among the nationals than Evangelicals. There are small evangelical congregations of the Free Church, Assemblies of God and Mennonites as well as five congregations of the more formal Protestant (Reformed) Church. Pray for expatriate and indigenous pastors and leaders of these groups, and for growth in their congregations.

3. **Foreigners** are a major challenge for evangelization. There are several small Pentecostal churches among the Portuguese and Italians, but the vast majority are in Luxembourg for employment, business or EC affairs, and they show little interest in spiritual things. Pray for both vision and strategy for reaching each group, and for receptive hearts.

4. **A few isolated evangelistic efforts** through **OM**, **AoG** church-planting, Teen Challenge's coffee-bar and others have sown the seed, but growth in evangelistic endeavour is slow.

5. **The Letzburgisch language** is spoken by the majority as their heart language. Most are fluent in French and German, but a Bible in their language could be a key opening for the light of the gospel.

Macao

(The Province of Macao)

August 2

Asia

Area 16 sq.km. A tiny peninsula and two islands 64 km. west of Hong Kong on the coast of Gwangdong Province of China.

Population	Ann. Gr.	Density
1990 401,000	2.2 %	25,062/sq.km
1995 445,000	2.2 %	27,812/sq.km

There is a large, undetermined number of illegal immigrants and tourists in Macao at any one time.

Peoples:
Chinese 93%. Mainly Cantonese. 20% have Portuguese citizenship; over 50% were born in Mainland China.
Burmese 4%. Ethnic Chinese speaking Burmese.
Macanese (Eurasian) 2.7%.
Portuguese 0.3%.

Literacy 61%. **Official language:** Portuguese.
Trade language: Cantonese.

Capital: Macao 380,000. Urbanization 95%.

Economy: Gambling, tourism, light industry and position as a trade gateway to China's special economic zones in the south have generated considerable wealth for some. Public debt/person $64. Income/person $6,300 (30% of USA).

Politics: Rented by the Portuguese in 1577. Became a Portuguese Colony in 1887, considered a Chinese Territory under Portuguese administration since 1974. Macao is to revert to Chinese rule in 1999, but will retain its autonomy for 50 years.

Religion:
Non-religious/other 46.5%.

Buddhist/Chinese religions 44.3%.
Christian 9.2%. Nom 1.9%. Affil 7.3%.
Growth −4.3%.
Protestant 1.8%. Affil 1.78%. Growth 2.5%. The following are estimates.

Church	Cong	Members	Affiliated
Baptist Ch (SBC)	6	616	1,540
Chinese Evang Ch	4	420	1,050
Seventh-day Adventist	2	400	1,000
All other (19)	42	2,000	3,532
Denominations (22)	54	3,436	7,122
Evangelicals 1.5% of pop		2,200	5,130
Pentecostal/charis 0.04%		900	1,500

Missionaries:
to Macao 92 (1:4,400 people) in 15 agencies.
from Macao 33 (1:216 Protestants) all of **CCC** 33dom.
Roman Catholic 7.4%. Affil 5.5%. Growth −6.1%.

Catholic Ch	22	13,000	22,000

Missionaries:
to Macao 10 (1:3,700 people).
from Macao 2 (1973 figure).

M

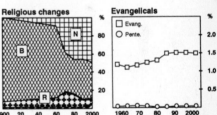

1. **Macao has the dubious distinction of being the first Christian territory in Asia to become non-Christian.** In 1600 Macao was 95% Catholic. By 1990 this had been reduced to about 9%. The Catholic Church has suffered disastrous decline, and Protestant churches have always been small. The number of Protestant churches has grown from 33 in 1986 to 54 in 1990, but growth has been slow. Pray for the people of this territory to be changed by the Word of God.

2. **Macao was the starting point of Protestant missions to China.** There the first Chinese convert was baptised, the first Chinese Bible translated and Robert Morrison, the first missionary, buried. Yet today it is one of the least-discipled communities of Chinese in the world. The Church is small, divided, introspective and weakened by emigration and a high turnover of leadership. Pray for local leaders to be raised up who will help the Church survive and grow after China takes over. The Macao Bible Institute was the first theological school, but there are now three theological institutions for training leaders.

3. **Macao's name means *City of God*,** but it has truly become *City of Sin*. The gambling "industry" employs 10% of the workforce. There are more Thai prostitutes than born-again believers. The influence of sin has brought organized crime, drugs, corruption and deceit to every level of society. Pray for deep repentance and thorough restitution without which little harvest for the Kingdom can be expected.

4. **Evangelical Christians**, both indigenous and expatriate, are cooperating more closely to present a unified witness and avoid duplication of effort. The Macao Christian Church Association and others have developed a set of goals for achievement by the year 2000. The immediate goal is for 20 more churches by 1995.

5. **There has been an influx of missionaries from Hong Kong and other lands**, most being involved in evangelism, church planting, drug rehabilitation and Bible teaching. Major missions are Brazilian and US Baptists (**SBC**) with a total of 35 workers, **YWAM** (10), and **CBFMS** (10). Major missionary-contributing countries: USA (39), Brazil (27), Hong Kong (13). Pray for their effectiveness in this crowded, pressurised and sinful city.

6. **The less-reached:**
a) **The 200,000 recent immigrants** who are legally resident. They are usually too busy to give much thought to eternity.
b) The many **illegal immigrants**. Their insecurity and mobility frustrate long-term outreach and discipling. Several Hong Kong missions are targeting this group.
c) The **12,000 Chinese refugees from Burma**. There is one church among them (Baptist).
d) **Those involved in the entertainment industry**. There are a few seeking to reach them. The Macao Evangelistic Band is one such.
e) **Drug addicts**. Several agencies work for their psychological and spiritual deliverance.

Macedonia

See under YUGOSLAVIA

Madagascar
(Democratic Republic of Madagascar)

August 3
Africa

Area 587,000 sq.km. A 1,600 km.-long island in the Indian Ocean 600 km. off the coast of Mozambique.

Population	Ann. Gr.	Density
1990	11,980,000	3.2 %	20/sq.km
1995	14,074,000	3.3 %	24/sq.km

Peoples:
Malagasy 98.7%. 18 main groups of mixed African, Arab and Indonesian origin speaking a single Indonesian-related language. The Indonesian ethnic element is strongest in the highlands. Largest: Merina 3,200,000 (the dominant ethnic group); Betsimisaraka 1,800,000; Betsileo 1,400,000; Tsimihety 886,000; Sakalava 767,000; Antandroy 635,000; Tanala 473,000; Antaimoro 422,000.
Other 1.3%. Réunionese 40,000; Comorian 25,000; Arab 20,000; French 18,000; Gujarati Indian 17,000; Chinese 16,000; Mauritian 4,000.

Literacy 67%, but functional literacy much lower.
Official languages: Malagasy, French. **Languages with Scriptures** 2Bi 1por.

Capital: Antananarivo 802,000. Urbanization 22%.

Economy: Subsistence agricultural economy. Slash-and-burn farming has destroyed vast areas of forest and caused bad erosion. Poor communications hinder development. Centralized socialist experiments have proved a costly failure. Malaria and malnutrition have become major problems because of the economic slump. A slow economic recovery is under way. Public debt/person $277. Income/person $230 (1.1% of USA).

Politics: For centuries a strong Merina kingdom. Annexed by France in 1896; independent in 1960. A coup in 1972 led to experimentation with Marxism which was a disaster for the country. Popular protest and demands for change were violently suppressed before constitutional change was conceded. Multi-party elections in 1993 gave overwhelming victory to the democratic opposition.

Religion: Under the previous government there was considerable anti-Christian propaganda, but there is now religious freedom.
Traditional beliefs 44.6%. The old Malagasy

religions still have a pervasive power.
Muslim 2.2%. **Chinese religions** 0.1%. **Baha'i** 0.1%.
Non-religious/other 0.3%.
Christian 52.7%. Nom 5.5%. Affil 47.2%.
Growth 3.4%.
Protestant 26%. Affil 24.9%. Growth 3.6%.

Church	Cong	Members	Affiliated
Ch of Jesus Christ	4,492	800,000	1,560,000
Lutheran (ALM, NLM)	4,096	213,000	852,000
Episcopal (Anglican)	978	58,700	163,000
Seventh-day Adventist	144	26,000	65,000
Pente Jesus Saves Ch	200	18,000	40,000
Free Evang Ch	135	10,800	24,000
United Pente. Ch	160	4,800	12,000
Bible Baptist	30	1,200	4,000
Assemblies of God	76	2,280	3,800
All other (19)	1,487	83,600	255,000
Denominations (28)	11,798	1,218,380	2,978,800
Evangelicals 6.3% of pop		287,000	749,000
Pentecostal/charis 1.6%		77,000	188,000

Missionaries:
to Madagascar 186 (1:64,400 people) in 23 agencies.
from Madagascar 42 (1:70,900 Protestants) in 6 agencies 7frn 7xcul 35dom.
Roman Catholic 26%. Affil 21.7%. Growth 3%.

Catholic Ch	6,340	1,430,000	2,600,000

Missionaries:
to Madagascar 1,222 (1:9,800 people).
from Madagascar 100 (1973 figure).
Orthodox 0.01%. Growth −0.3%.
Foreign Marginal 0.07%. Growth 13.6%.

Jehovah's Witnesses	58	3,673	8,160

Indigenous Marginal 0.6%. Affil 0.58%.
Growth 4.4%.

All groups (13)	361	26,550	70,000

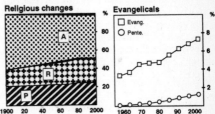

Religious changes | Evangelicals

1. **Praise God for present freedom for the gospel.** Christians were in the vanguard of the democracy movement. Pray that committed Christians may give moral and spiritual leadership to the nation after the years of corruption, economic decline and totalitarianism.

2. **Madagascar's Church** has had a glorious past with persecutions from heathen rulers and then French Catholic colonial authorities. The Protestant Church grew from 5,000 in 1861 to one million in 1900. There have been significant revival movements within the larger churches in 1895, 1941 and

1948, and also touches of revival in the unrest of 1991. Springing from the revival movements have been the indigenous lay movements of "shepherds", which operate within the mainline Protestant Federation Churches from 50 centres across the island. The emphasis on healing and exorcism has led to conversions and some localized church growth. Pray for nationwide revival.

3. **Spiritual deadness rather than revival characterizes the majority of congregations.** Compromise with the old beliefs, veneration of ancestral spirits, and witchcraft are widespread among those who claim to be Christians. The forms of worship remain, but most have no understanding of the biblical message of salvation. Pray that the power of Jesus might be demonstrated as greater, and that many may trust him completely.

4. **Evangelical believers** are predominantly found in the revival movements in the mainline churches – especially sections of the Lutheran Church, and in the Pentecostal and Baptist Churches – most of which are of indigenous origin. Pray for unity among true believers and also for effective evangelism through them. The need for practical training for outreach is great.

5. **Theological training is the greatest source of weakness for the Church.** Most of the seven seminaries and ten Bible schools are theologically liberal and easily accommodate astrology, heathen customs and Marxist social theory. Pray that such schools may return to the biblical theology for which their forebears laid down their lives. The Assemblies of God, Baptists and the Jesus Saves Pentecostal Church have evangelical Bible colleges, and **CBFMS** missionaries have developed a TEE programme. Pray for the provision of well-trained, Spirit-led leaders for the ministry.

6. **Young people** are the key for the future in the rapidly-growing population. **SU**, with 15 full-time workers in school and camp ministries, and UGBM (**IFES**), with four staff workers with 30 groups and 4,000 members, have made a deep impact on young people and seen many conversions. These two movements have had an influence on the country out of all proportion to their numbers. **YWAM** is also having an increasing impact. Pray for these ministries and for the mobilization of young people for evangelism.

7. **The Malagasy Bible has been available for 150 years.** It has a treasured place in the culture. Pray that its message may enter hearts. The Bible Society (**UBS**) has a widely recognized ministry and a vigorous distribution programme, but lack of foreign exchange limits importation and printing of the Scriptures. All Christian literature is in short supply. There are few good, spiritual books in Malagasy. The Lutherans have a large but under-used printing press.

8. **Less-reached areas and peoples** are accessible with difficulty due to the bad state of the road system, so many areas are without any meaningful exposure to the gospel. Pray for:
a) **Thousands of villages** where traditional beliefs remain unchallenged by a Christian presence or church.
b) **Muslims,** who are growing in numbers among the Malagasy Sakalava on the west coast and Antankarana in the north. Specific outreach to them is limited. The **Comorians** and Syrian/Lebanese **Arabs** are unreached.
c) **The Indian/Pakistani-origin Gujaratis** – mostly traders; there are no known believers.
d) **The Chinese** – mostly nominal Catholics. There is no known evangelical witness among them.

9. **The Protestant missionary force** is relatively small, and nearly 65% is Lutheran. More recently-arrived evangelical agencies are the **CBFMS** (8 workers), **AoG** (6), **CCC** (7), **AIM** (4), **AEF** (4). Major missionary-contributing nations: Norway (85), USA (64), UK (14), France (9). **MAF** has one plane serving Christian workers – a much-valued ministry in a land where travel is difficult. Visas are not easy to obtain, but the cross-fertilizing ministry of foreign missionaries in evangelism, literature, church planting and Bible teaching is much needed today.

10. **Christian radio programmes** are aired on national radio, with varying spiritual quality. **FEBA**-Seychelles broadcasts in Malagasy (3.5 hours/week) and French (1.5 hours/week), and **TWR**-Swaziland broadcasts in the same languages (1.75 and 3.5 hours/week respectively).

Malawi

(Republic of Malawi)

August 4

Africa

Area 118,000 sq.km. Central African state extending along Lake Malawi and its outflow river, the Shire. Landlocked and virtually an enclave within Mozambique.

Population	Ann. Gr.	Density
1990 8,428,000	3.4 %	71/sq.km
1995 9,950,000	3.4 %	84/sq.km

Peoples. All indigenous groups are Bantu.
Central peoples 47%. Nyanja-Chewa 3,200,000; Ngoni 758,000 (culturally absorbed Zulu invaders).
Southern peoples 33%. Lomwe 1,550,000; Yao 1,003,000; Sena 255,000.
Northern peoples 15%. Tumbuka 662,000; Nkhonde 300,000; Tonga 220,000; Lambya 41,000; Mpoto 40,000.
Other 5%. Mozambicans, English-speaking 16,000; Portuguese 9,000; Gujarati 5,000; Greek 2,000.
Mozambican refugees 1,250,000 in 1992 – mainly Lomwe, Yao, Sena, Shona in the south.

Literacy 41%. **Official languages:** Chewa and English. **All languages** 14. **Languages with Scriptures** 8Bi 4por.

Capital: Lilongwe 220,300. Largest city: Blantyre-Limbe 402,000. Urbanization 11%.

Economy: Relatively poor, but self-sufficient in food through emphasis on rural development. The long civil war in Mozambique limited direct trade links to the sea and burdened the land with a massive refugee problem. Public debt/person $141. Income/person $180 (0.85% of USA).

Politics: Independent from Britain in 1964. One-party republic under total domination of nonagenarian Dr Hastings Banda, who declared himself Life President in 1971. Banda's rule has brought economic stability but also elimination of all dissent and, increasingly, corruption in the administration. Since 1992, foreign aid was restricted to precipitate change. Multi-party elections are planned for 1993.

Religion: Freedom of religion, but not for religious leaders to question the administration. Persecution of Jehovah's Witnesses followed their banning in 1969.
Muslim 14.5%. Almost entirely Yao people, but also some Asians.
African traditional religions 4.2%; still a potent force for the majority of Malawians.
Baha'i 0.2%. **Hindu** 0.03%, largely Indians.

Christian 81.1%. Nom 13.2%. Affil 67.9%. Growth 7.1%.
Protestant 35.5%. Affil 28.7%. Growth 6.8%.

Church	Cong	Members	Affiliated
Ch of Central Africa, Presbyterian (CCAP)	333	500,000	1,250,000
Seventh-day Adventist	441	84,763	188,000
Anglican Ch	360	66,000	165,000
Bapt Convention	535	70,114	108,000
Church of Christ	2,500	50,000	83,300
African Bapt Assembly	1,160	29,000	72,500
United Evang Ch	106	10,600	32,000
Indep Baptist Conv	100	15,000	30,000
Assemblies of God	600	15,000	30,000
Evang Baptist Ch	130	12,000	26,700
Free Methodist Ch	171	7,624	25,400
Charismatic Chs (5)	48	14,500	22,300
Chr Chs/Chs of Christ	20	12,629	21,000
Christian Brethren	80	4,000	20,000
Apostolic Faith Miss	83	7,500	16,700
Africa Evang Ch (AEF)	50	6,000	15,000
Ch of the Nazarene	81	7,496	14,515
Ch of God (Cleveland)	165	5,366	13,400
All other (31)	1,100	95,307	267,214
Denominations (53)	8,243	1,021,899	2,419,029
Evangelicals 11.3% of pop		438,000	949,000
Pentecostal/charis 2.3%		93,000	195,000

Missionaries:
to Malawi 366 (1:21,200 people) in 55 agencies.
from Malawi 398 (1:6,100 Protestants) in 16 agencies 94frn 77xcul 321dom.

Roman Catholic 26%. Affil 23.7%. Growth 5.3%.

Catholic Ch	2,476	1,040,000	2,000,000

Missionaries:
to Malawi 578 (1:15,800 people).
from Malawi 30 (1973 figure).

Orthodox 0.01%. Growth −1.4%.

Groups	1	325	650

Foreign Marginal 0.59%. Growth 2.1%.

Groups (3)	356	25,000	50,000

Indigenous Marginal 19%. Affil 15%. Growth 11.2%.

Groups (150)	7,031	563,000	1,250,000

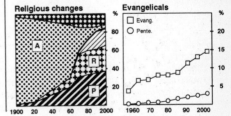

1. **Praise God for the relative peace and freedom for preaching the gospel.** All the surrounding lands have succumbed to devastating wars, economic collapse and famine. Yet the unresolved succession to the present

dictatorship could lead to disaster. Pray for godly, righteous leaders for the nation, and for an orderly change to new political structures. Church leaders are actively involved in the democracy movement.

2. **Malawi has proved to be spiritually the most receptive country in central Africa.** Years of evangelical witness (also **AE**, **DM**, CFAN campaigns), burgeoning youth outreach (**SU**, **IFES**), New Life For All programmes in the churches, multiplied house meetings and prayer groups have all contributed to the blessing. The gospel has penetrated into nearly every section of society, and in places there have been local revivals. Newer charismatic, Pentecostal and evangelical denominations have grown rapidly.

3. **The CCAP is the largest Protestant denomination**: a union of the churches planted by the South African Dutch Reformed Church, the Church of Scotland and the Free Church of Scotland. The three constituent synods need revival. Modernist teaching, nominalism and formalism predominate, yet there are also strong evangelical leaders and congregations. Pray that second- and third-generation Christians may come to personal faith, and for many to be called into full-time ministry.

4. **Full-time workers for rural areas are too few to reap the harvest** and conserve it in the churches. The relative poverty of most rural congregations means that few can afford to support a pastor. There are 13 Protestant and two Roman Catholic seminaries or Bible schools. Pray that the CCAP theological faculty at Zomba might take a more strongly evangelical stand. Pray for many to be called into the ministry, and for the provision of funds to enable them to complete their studies.

5. **Muslim missionary efforts** have been heavily financed by Kuwait and emphasize nationwide mosque-building, strengthening of Islamic institutions and training Muslim Malawians for the spread of Islam. Pray that Malawian Christians may show greater concern for Muslims and their evangelization.

6. **Missions vision in Malawian churches** is growing and is predominantly directed towards the indigenous Muslim Yao, Mozambican refugees, and forays into war-torn Mozambique. Many of these missionaries are sent by churches and agencies to work among those of their own ethnic group. Pray for the maturing and expansion of missions vision.

7. **Less-reached peoples:**
a) **The Yao** are 90% Muslim, though folk Islam is predominant. There is openness for change and new ideas because of the retarding effects of ignoring education in the past. Over 5% of the Yao have become Christians through the CCAP, United Evangelical Church and especially the Evangelical Baptist Church, whose membership is predominantly Yao.
b) **The Nkhonde** in the north are nominally Christian, but evangelical believers are few.
c) **The Sena and Lomwe in the south** are part of larger tribes that live in neighbouring Mozambique. The Sena especially are largely unevangelized in that land. Most of the million or more refugees in the south are of these tribes and also from the unreached Macua people.
d) **Many villages in rural areas** are isolated and untouched by the gospel.
e) **The Gujarati and Tamil** are the main groups of Asians. Only sporadic attempts are made to evangelize these Hindu and Muslim peoples.

8. **Expatriate missionaries** are primarily engaged in supporting existing denominations and agencies in training, outreach and Christian institutions. Pray for a deep heart identification with Malawian believers and fruitful ministries in this day of opportunity. Largest agencies: all Presbyterians (71 – Scots, Irish, US, Canadian, South African, Korean, Welsh), **SBC** (41), **AoG** (34), **AEF** (12) and Anglican. Major missionary-contributing nations: USA (200), UK (62), South Africa (34), Canada (29).

9. **Mozambican refugees** have swamped the southern part of Malawi. Pray for peace in their war-ravaged land, and for their survival and evangelization in Malawi. The inflow of aid has given opportunity for misuse of funds. Pray for the ministry of **World Vision**, Global Ministries, **AEF**, **AoG** and many others in ministering to them. Many congregations have been started as a result. Pray that these may be a major factor in reaching every part of the unreached areas of northern Mozambique.

10. **Christian Help Ministries** for prayer.
a) **Bible translation.** The completion of the whole Bible in Lomwe, Nkhonde, Sena and Yao are the major challenges. Several other languages are without a New Testament and may need translations.
b) **The Bible Society.** There are big demands for Scriptures for local use and for the large refugee community – but limited funds to meet them.
c) **Literature.** This is much sought after, but expensive. **CLAIM** is a joint publishing and distribution venture involving 14 denominations and agencies with 37 outlets and 200 agencies, as well as programmes to train workers. Pray for the adequate supply of quality reading material for the literate, growing, but poor church.
d) **Radio.** The national radio service regularly airs Christian programmes. **TWR**-Swaziland also broadcasts 21 hours/week in Nyanja and **FEBA**-Seychelles two hours/week in Yao.

Malaysia

August 5–7
Asia

Area 330,000 sq.km. Two distinct parts: Peninsular (West) Malaysia on the Kra peninsula of mainland Asia (**PM**), and East Malaysia (**EM**) consisting of the territories of Sarawak and Sabah on the northern third of the island of Borneo. Well-watered; tropical rain forest.

Population	Ann. Gr.	Density
1990 17,339,000	2.3 %	52/sq.km
1995 19,186,000	2.0 %	58/sq.km

Over 82% in **PM**.

Peoples: The Malay population is increasing at the expense of the Chinese and Indian populations.
Indigenous peoples (Bumiputera) 61.4%.
  Malay 52.5%. Predominantly rural but dominating politics, civil service, armed forces and police. A majority in **PM** only.
  Tribal peoples 8.9%. A majority in Sarawak, and largest segment of Sabah's population. Over 130 languages spoken.
Non-indigenous 38.6%.
  Chinese 30%. Speaking over nine major dialects; majority Hokkien, Cantonese, Hakka and Teochew. Influential in commerce and business in **PM** and **EM**.
  Indian 8.1%. Tamil 1,060,000; Panjabi 43,000; Malayali 37,000; Telugu 30,000; etc. Mainly poor estate workers or urban. Almost all in **PM**.
  Other 0.5%. Indonesian, Filipino, British, Thai, Burmese, Sri Lankan, Pakistani.
Illegal immigrants and refugees. Possibly 900,000 Filipinos and Indonesians; mainly in Sabah, also 150,000 Bangladeshi.
Refugees. Filipino Muslims 100,000; Indonesian Acehnese from Sumatra; Vietnamese 22,000.

Literacy 73%. **Official language:** Malay. **All languages** 145. **Languages with Scriptures** 12Bi 10NT 13por.

Capital: Kuala Lumpur 1,475,000. Urbanization 38%. Chinese and Indian majority in urban areas.

Economy: Vigorous growth since independence through the development of logging, oil, mining, agriculture and industry. Development has attracted many illegal immigrants from surrounding poorer nations. Unemployment 8%. Public debt/person $904. Income/person $2,230 (10% of USA).

Politics: Independent from Britain in 1957 as the Federation of Malaya. In 1963, Sabah and Sarawak joined to form Malaysia, a federation of 13 states with a constitutional monarchy. Recent years have been dominated by the efforts of the politically powerful Malays to extend their influence over the non-Malay half of the population in educational, economic and religious life. The growing power of fundamentalist Muslim political parties has further polarized the country, with consequent inter-ethnic and inter-religious tensions.

Religion: Sunni Islam is the official and favoured religion in **PM**, and there is continual pressure to apply the same in **EM** where Islam is a minority. The constitutional guarantee of religious freedom is being ignored. It is illegal to proselytize Muslims, but considerable effort is expended to induce animistic tribal people and Chinese to become Muslim. Some of the figures below are therefore estimates – objective statistics are hard to obtain.
Muslim 55%. Malays, some Indians and a few ethnic minorities in **EM**.
Buddhist 7%. **Chinese religions** 18%.
Hindu 6%. **Non-religious/other** 3%.
Animist 2.4%.
Christian 8.6%. Affil 7.3%. Growth 5.5%.
  Protestant 5%. Affil 4%. Growth 7.1%.

Church	Cong	Members	Affiliated
Evang Ch of Borneo			
SIB (OMF)	510	110,000	190,000
Methodist Ch	300	77,642	150,000
Anglican Ch	322	87,000	150,000
Seventh-day Adventist	200	30,000	50,000
Basel Christian Ch	90	24,000	32,000
Assemblies of God	231	15,000	20,000
Christian Brethren	74	3,000	6,500
Lutheran Ch in M & S	30	2,390	5,320
All other (44)	552	54,111	95,690
Denominations (52)	2,309	403,143	699,510
Evangelicals 3.1% of pop		311,000	541,000
Pentecostal/charis 1.6%		165,000	280,000

Missionaries:
  to Malaysia 189 (1:91,700 people) in 40 agencies.
  from Malaysia 363 (1:1,900 Protestants) in 18 agencies 145frn 145xcul 218dom.
Roman Catholic 3.5%. Affil 3.17%. Growth 3.5%.
Catholic Ch 1,386 291,000 549,000
Missionaries to Malaysia 370 (1973 figure).
Marginal 0.11%. Growth 8.8%.
All groups (6) 7,700 18,700

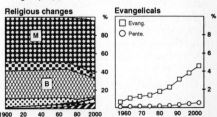

Religious changes   Evangelicals
□ Evang.
○ Pente.

MALAYSIA – GENERAL

1. **The Muslim half of the population** has been politically and socially divided through an extremist minority pressing for radical Islamic reforms and the formation of an Islamic state. This has brought stress to the whole country, an acceleration of Muslim missionary activities among non-Muslims and also discriminatory legislation and actions against non-Muslims. One state is threatening to introduce Islamic law for both Muslims and non-Muslims alike. Pray for inter-racial harmony and true freedom of religion.

2. **All non-Muslims,** and Christians in particular, are suffering a creeping erosion of religious freedom. Intimidation, discrimination and bureaucratic obstructionism are widespread in **PM** but also occur in **EM**. Pray for:
a) **The restoration of full religious liberty,** and that Christians may not be intimidated by threats but rather be bold to stand for their constitutional rights and for their heavenly right to proclaim the gospel.
b) **The restrictions on Christian meetings** to be removed. Worship services in private homes are strongly discouraged, and permits for extending existing church buildings or building new ones are rarely granted. There have been cases of churches being demolished on flimsy pretexts.
c) **Unity among Christians** in the face of persecution. The **Christian Federation** brings together Evangelicals and Protestants, Catholics and Orthodox Christians for cooperation and representation to the government. The **National Evangelical Christian Fellowship** is a more close-knit body to unite Evangelicals for nationwide outreach, spiritual conferences and missions vision.
d) **Courageous Christian leaders** who are prepared, at considerable personal risk, to reason with or confront the authorities over manifest inconsistencies and injustices in the treatment of non-Muslims. Some believers were imprisoned for many months in the '80s.

3. **The DAWN (Discipling A Whole Nation) vision was enthusiastically launched by 14 denominations in 1992.** Pray that this may result in church multiplication. The goals set for the year 2000 are:
a) To plant 4,000 new churches.
b) To see 200 Bahasa Malaysia services being conducted.
c) To raise up 100,000 prayer partners for Malaysia.
Pray for wisdom in their implementation in the charged religious atmosphere in the country.

4. **Leadership training** is of added importance as the missionary force declines. There are about 16 Bible schools or seminaries in the country (six of these being of the SIB in **EM**). Emigration of Chinese Christian professionals and Bible school graduates is a loss the churches can ill afford. Too few are responding to the call to full-time work, and many churches are without pastors.

5. **Since Malay became the only national language,** Christians have been pushed into a series of crises. Pray for solutions to:
a) **The need for Christian literature in the Malay language.** Writers are few and the market is still small, yet all the younger generation are being educated in this medium. Christian literature is widely available in English. There are 24 Christian bookstores and an active Bible society.
b) **The banning of the Indonesian Bible and over 58 Christian books.** A law was passed forbidding Christians from using some religious terms which are used in Islam. The related Indonesian language commonly uses banned terminology in the Bible, so Indonesian Christian literature is not allowed into the country. Pray for a resolution to this issue.
c) **The language of use in church services.** Adaptation to Malay would be wise, but some states have also strongly discouraged the use of Malay in church to inhibit the conversion of Malays to Christ.

6. **Ministry to young people** has been very fruitful with many Indian, Chinese and East Malaysians coming to Christ through agencies such as **YFC, CCC, Navigators, SU, IFES** and others in schools and universities. It has become increasingly difficult to have any ministry within schools in **PM**, making outreach and discipling complicated.

7. **Many Malaysians are studying overseas.** The limited number of higher education opportunities for non-Malays has forced large numbers of Malaysian Chinese and Indians to study in universities across the English-speaking world. There many have come to Christ, where they often become the most enthusiastic Christian group on the campus. Pray that they may retain that enthusiasm when they return home.

8. **Cross-cultural missions** are still needed. The government has further limited the number and duration of missionary visas during the '80s, so the rate of attrition is high. Pray for:
a) **Remaining expatriate workers** and the extension of visas, as well as for useful ministry and

effective preparation of local Christians to take on all ministries. The largest agencies are **OMF**, **SIL** and **SBC**. SIL in Sabah were asked to leave in 1993 and no visas were able to be extended.

b) **Malaysian Christians** to rise to the challenge of cross-cultural missions both within Malaysia and beyond. Pray for the Church in Malaysia to gain a strong missions vision. This is the aim of NECF. **OM**, Navigators, **YWAM, OMF, SIM, WBT** and **WEC** have recruited, trained and channelled Malaysians for missions.

PENINSULAR MALAYSIA

Area 132,000 sq.km. or 40% of the nation.

Population 14,616,000.

Peoples: Malay 55.6%. **Chinese** 33.2%. **Indian** 10.5%. **Orang Asli** (the original indigenous peoples) 0.65%. **Mon-Khmer** (18 peoples) largest: Semai (Senoi) 52,000; Temiar 16,000. **Proto-Malay** (5 peoples) largest: Jakun 33,000; Kensiu 3,000.

Religion: Muslim 59%. **Chinese religions/Buddhist** 29%. **Hindu** 8%. **Christian** 3%, **Non-religious** 1%.

1. **The Church is growing amongst all non-Muslim ethnic groups** – about 10% of the Orang Asli, 10% of Indians and 4% of Chinese are Christian (about half being Catholic). Yet the continual external pressure from Islam at every level, the pressure from non-Christian families to compromise, and the lure of materialism have harmed real commitment. Many young people come to the Lord, but the rate of backsliding after marriage is high. Pray for a deep work of the Holy Spirit in reviving and emboldening the believers.

2. **Worship and witness patterns** may have to be modified to survive and grow under pressure. Greater cooperation, sharing of resources between denominations, and a more vital household worship style must be explored. Pray for guidance for the leaders.

3. **The less-reached.** The task of reaching the many unreached must now be a Malaysian responsibility; the potential in human and financial resources is there! Pray for:

a) **Malays who cannot be evangelized openly.** The 600 or so Malays who have believed have suffered social ostracism and the loss of legal rights, privileges, and jobs; some have had to leave the country. There is more openness among urban Malays and those living in South Thailand and Singapore, but few Christians are actively reaching out to them. Pray for Christians to tactfully, but fearlessly, share the Good News with them. Malay Christians meet together in some house groups or in multi-ethnic churches, but there are no viable Malay churches. Pray for the right evangelistic and church-planting strategy to be revealed and applied.

b) **The Chinese.** The **PM** Chinese have been far less responsive than those in **EM**; materialism and traditional religions are strong. Presbyterian, Pentecostal and charismatic denominations are growing, but mostly among the urban middle-class English-speaking Chinese. There are no churches using Hainanese (200,000 people), and the Hakka, Teochew and Kwongsai are little better served. Rural and small-town Chinese are patchily evangelized. There is religious freedom, but few are using present opportunities for witness and church planting.

c) **The Orang Asli** who are considered by the Malays to be Muslim even though they dislike Islam and its restrictions and remain committed to their traditional ways. In spite of Muslim offers of bribes and obstructions for any Christian witness to them, about 10% have become Christian. Methodists, Brethren, Pentecostal and Lutherans have planted churches among the Orang Asli. However, only the Senoi and Kensiu have any Scriptures – a further 16 languages may need translation teams.

d) **Indians.** There are many Tamil Christians, but few among the poor estate labourers. Other Indian ehtnic minorities are less reached – the 40,000 Panjabis (mostly Sikh) with 62 known believers, and the Telegus. The Indian Muslims number some 50,000; there has been no specific outreach to them. The Tamil Bible Institute (**AsEF**) is training Christian workers to reach Indian communities with the gospel.

SABAH (formerly North Borneo)

Area 74,000 sq.km. Rich in natural resources.

Population 1,470,000 officially; but illegal immigration has increased this.

Peoples – estimates.
Indigenous peoples (38 groups) 26%. Largest: Kardazan, Dusun, Murut Bisaya. Mainly Christian and animist; some Muslim.
Indonesian peoples (4 major groups) 30%. Javanese 300,000; Banjar, Bugis, Wolio. Mainly Muslim.
Filipino peoples (6 major groups) 14%. Tausug, Bajau, Sama, Molbog, Ilanun, Mapun. Muslim.
Chinese 21%. **Malay** 9%.

Religion: est. **Muslim** 55%. **Christian** 30%. **Animist** 7%. **Other** 8%.

1. **The corruption and mismanagement of the state government** with a preponderance of Muslims resulted in their rejection in the 1986 and 1991 elections. Kadazan and Chinese, who are predominantly Christian, have a leading role in the present government. Pray that Christians may use their power wisely for the repair of the economic and spiritual damage of earlier years, and for healing of the tensions between ethnic groups.

2. **Rapid church growth** is taking place among the Chinese, Kadazan, Tagal and Murut peoples through the work of the Basel Mission, Anglicans and **SIB**. The **SIB** has over 300 congregations in Sabah. Some 23% of the Chinese and the majority of the indigenous peoples are now Christian. Nominalism, the drift to the cities of tribal peoples and serious lack of full-time workers are unresolved problems for the churches. The Sabah Council of Churches is a catalyst for fellowship, links with the government, evangelism, conferences and Bible translation. The loss of nearly all missionary visas is a challenge for local Christians to evangelize the unreached in Sabah.

3. **Less-reached peoples:**
a) The Muslim peoples are almost untouched. Pray for specific outreach to:
  i)   The **Filipino**-related peoples, many being refugees from the Muslim Moro uprising in Mindanao, Philippines.
  ii) The **Indonesians**, most being illegal immigrants from Sulawesi and Java. Little is being done to reach them.
  iii) The local **Malays and Muslim tribal peoples**, notably the Bisaya and Bajau.
b) **Some tribal groups**, such as the Kadazan and Dusun, are only partially evangelized, though there have been large people movements among them. The majority of other ethnic groups are now Christian. Few languages have a New Testament; **SIL** have had teams working in 14 languages, but many are being denied visas. There are virtually no other missionary personnel left. Pray for the calling of local Christians for translation work – both to complete the 13 existing NT projects and to start on the 26 languages which may also need to be tackled.

SARAWAK

Area 124,000 sq.km. Forested and under-populated.

Population 1,669,000.

Peoples:
Indigenous peoples (45 groups) 50%. Major groups: Dayak, Iban, Kenyah, Kayan, Penan.

Religion: est. **Christian** 34%. **Animist** 30%. **Muslim** 26%. **Other** 10%.

1. **Sarawak has experienced a series of thrilling movements of the Spirit over the last 50 years.** Through the work of BEM/**OMF** and others, people movements and revivals have taken place in many of the smaller tribes. The SIB (Evangelical Church of Borneo) daughter church has over 260 congregations, six Bible schools and a work in more than 10 peoples, with a vigorous outreach to towns and unreached peoples. Praise God for this, and pray for a retention of the spirit of revival in the up-and-coming generation. The coastal churches among the Chinese are more nominal, though nearly half the Chinese now profess to be Christians.

2. **The Church is under pressure** through materialism in the towns and severe pressure from Muslims in some rural areas. Pray that believers may not only stand firm in their faith, but become more bold in their witness. Pray that many young people may be called and adequately supported in full-time service. Nearly half the SIB churches have no pastor and most pastors are poorly paid and have to seek part-time employment. Pray that leadership in the churches may be able to handle the complexities of national politics and the nurture of churches scattered over a land with many transport difficulties outside the towns.

3. Unreached peoples:
a) **Muslims in the coastal areas** are not open to the gospel, but many Chinese and indigenous Christians live around them.
b) **The Iban** (320,000) and **Melanau** (60,000) have begun to respond to the gospel after years of indifference, but Christians and Christian workers are too few to make use of present opportunities. There are only a few hundred evangelical Christians among them, though 10% would claim to be Christian. The Iban Bible was published in 1988.
c) **Many smaller groups are unevangelized**, and of the 45 languages, two have the Bible, two the New Testament and four have portions only. There is only one other language with ongoing translation work.

Maldives

(Republic of Maldives)

August 8
Asia

Area 298 sq.km. 1,200 coral islands grouped into 19 administrative groups 600 km. southwest of Sri Lanka. 202 islands are inhabited. The entire country is less than two metres above sea level and susceptible to the effects of global warming.

Population		Ann. Gr.	Density
1990	215,000	3.3 %	721/sq.km
1995	248,000	2.9 %	832/sq.km

Peoples:
Indigenous 98.4%. Maldivians of Sinhalese and Dravidian origin with Arab and African admixture.
Foreign 1.6%. Sinhalese 1,400; Indian 1,000; Arab 300.

Literacy 93%. **Official language:** Dhivehi, related to Sinhalese, but with its own script.

Capital: Malé 60,000. Urbanization 26%.

Economy: Fishing and tourism are the significant foreign exchange earners. Lack of fertile soil and fresh water and the high population density keep the people at subsistence level. Public debt/person $406. Income/person $420 (2% of USA).

Politics: Long tradition of isolated independence. The nominal British protectorate terminated in 1965. A non-party democratic republic since 1968.

Religion: Islam is the only recognized religion, and the government is committed to greater Islamization both as an end in itself and as a means of preserving national unity.
Muslim 99.4%.
Buddhist 0.5%. Sinhala.
Christian 0.1%. Almost entirely Sinhala, Indian and Western. No formal meetings.

M

1. **The Maldivians are among the least evangelized on earth.** There have never been any resident missionaries, and there are no officially recognized Maldivian Christians, as the government uses the full power of the state to discourage evangelism and enforce allegiance to Islam. Pray for the deep suspicion of Christianity and the centuries of prejudice against the true message of Christ to be removed, and the gospel to be freely heard.

2. **There are Western and Sri Lankan expatriates** residing in the country. No meetings are officially sanctioned, nor may Christian literature and Bibles be legally imported. Pray that they may not become discouraged but shine for Jesus despite the spiritual pressures under which they live.

3. **Christian media** are restricted. There are no radio programmes, the Scriptures in Dhivehi are not yet available, and all incoming mail is scrutinized for any literature that may propagate anything other than Islamic teaching. Pray that Maldivians may hear the gospel despite these restrictions.

4. **Maldivians travel to other lands** as sailors, students, etc. Maldivians live in several Indian and Sri Lankan coastal cities. Pray that ways and means may be found to bring some to Christ.

August 9		
Africa		

Mali

(Republic of Mali)

Area 1,240,000 sq.km. Landlocked state. Dry southern grasslands merge into the Sahara Desert.

Population		Ann. Gr.	Density
1990	9,362,000	3.0 %	8/sq.km
1995	10,878,000	3.0 %	9/sq.km

Peoples: 33 ethnic groups.
West African peoples 90.9%. Major linguistic groups:
Mande 52.3%. Largest: Bambara 3,000,000; Malinke 668,000; Soninke (Sarakule) 575,000; Kasonke 300,000; Bozo 160,000; Diawara 125,000; Gana 75,000; Duun 70,000; Jula(Diola) 50,000; Marka 25,000; Kagoro 21,500; Yalunka 10,000.
Gur 17%. Senufo 855,000; Dogon 424,500; Bwa (Red Bobo) 306,000.
West Atlantic 15.4%. Fula (Fulbe) 1,106,000; Tukulor 135,000.
Nilo-Saharan 6.2%. Songhai 600,000; Daosahaq 70,000.
Berber 7.3%. Tuareg (speaking three Tamasheq languages) 683,000.
Other 1.8%. French 9,000.
Refugees. Fula from Mauritania 20,000.

Literacy 10%. **Official language:** French. **Trade languages:** Bambara, Fulbe, Songhai. **All languages** 31. **Languages with Scriptures** 2Bi 3NT 9por.

Capital: Bamako 706,000. Urbanization 19%.

Economy: The subsistence agricultural economy has been devastated by drought, famine, desertification and locust plagues since the 1970s. The corruption and mismanagement of post-independence dictatorships worsened the economic disasters. Public debt/person $258. Income/person $260 (1.5% of USA).
Politics: The modern descendant of the great Malian empire. Independent from France in 1960. Popular protests ousted a military dictatorship in 1991. Multi-party democracy instituted in 1991 elections. The Tuareg in the northeast revolted against the central government in 1990 and have gained a degree of autonomy, but unrest continues in the region.

Religion: A secular state with freedom of religion despite the large Muslim majority.
Muslim 86.3%. Strong in north, numerous in centre where Islam and traditional religions are mixed, and slowly growing in the south where traditional religions are stronger.
Traditional religions 11.2%. Strongest among the Dogon (60%), Bwa (70%), and Senufo/Minianka, Shenara and Suppire (65%) in the southeast on the Burkina border.
Christian 3.8%. Nom 0.7%. Affil 1.8%. Growth 5.5%.
Protestant 0.8%. Affil 0.7%. Growth 4.5%.

Church	Cong	Members	Affiliated
Christian Evang Ch	579	14,026	41,700
Evang Protestant Ch	278	14,690	24,200
Assemblies of God	20	500	1,300
Prot Ch Kayes Region	16	300	1,000
Alliance Missn (German)	7	130	325
Evang Baptist Missn	4	70	140
Sthn Baptist Missn	1	46	120
All other (6)	8	108	250
Denominations (13)	913	29,870	69,033
Evangelicals 0.7% of pop		29,870	69,000
Pentecostal/charis 0.01%		500	1,300

Missionaries:
to Mali 309 (1:30,300 people) in 35 agencies.
from Mali 36 (1:1,900 Protestants) in 3 agencies
0frn 2xcul 34dom.
Roman Catholic 1.7%. Affil 1.1%. Growth 6.2%.

Catholic Ch	356	57,700	103,000

Missionaries:
to Mali 257 (1:36,400 people).
from Mali 1 (1973 figure).
Marginal 0.002%. Growth 11.0%.

Jehovah's Witnesses	1	88	238

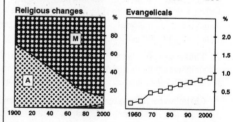

Religious changes — Evangelicals

1. **The progress of the gospel in the 1980s is praiseworthy:**
a) **The Church** has experienced accelerated growth.
b) **The number of missions** and missionaries has doubled.
c) **Islam has proved a disappointment** to many, resulting in a greater openness to Christianity. There have been several large localized people movements to Christ – among the Bambara (**GMU** area) and Bwa (**CMA** area).

d) **National evangelization conferences** have stirred Malian Christians with a vision to reach every ethnic group with the gospel and win 20% of their countrymen to Christ by the year 2000. Pray with them for the realization of these visions.

e) **Five peoples comprising 1.5 million people** that were unreached in 1983 are now being reached, and several remaining untouched groups are now being surveyed for pioneer work to commence.

2. **Missions have multiplied,** and few areas of the country are neither occupied nor targeted. For years there were only four Protestant missions – GMU in the centre among the Bambara, CMA in the east among the Dogon, Bobo, Minianka and Senoufo, UWM in the west among the Maninka and Evangelical Baptists in the north among the Songhai. Only in the GMU and CMA areas have strong churches emerged. Over ten missions have entered since 1980, but this is still a pioneer field. Major mission agencies: CMA (47 workers), Norwegian Lutherans (36), GMU (29), Evang Baptist (18), SBC (16), SIL (15), *Allianz-Mission*, Germany (15), RSTI (14), CRWM (10), AoG (8), UWM (5). Major missionary-contributing nations: USA (165), Norway (39), Canada (27), Germany (20). Pray for missionaries with the gifts needed to complete the evangelization of Mali.

3. **The Sahel famine** brought much help from Christian missions and aid organizations, making many receptive to the gospel. The manifest selfishness and misrule of Muslim leaders brought disillusionment and an even greater receptivity. Pray for the many agencies actively involved in relief, local development to conserve soil vegetation and water, digging wells, and medical outreach. Special mention must be made of WV and MAF, the latter accomplishing much with its full flying schedule. Pray also that the present opportunities may be fully used and that a mature, witnessing church be the outcome.

4. **Both Protestants and Catholics** have grown steadily through the '80s with a significant minority of converts from a Muslim background. Evangelicals are strong only among the Bambara (0.6%), Dogon (3.4%), Senufo/Minianka (3.2%) and the Bwa (6.9%), with small groups of believers in ten other peoples. Material poverty limits funds for training and supporting pastors so Bible schools in the country are struggling. Seventy per cent of believers are illiterate. Pray for the rapid growth of believers in maturity and numbers in this day of opportunity. Pray for a decisive breakthrough among the more Muslim peoples.

5. **Peoples where pioneer work has been established,** but for which prayer is requested:

a) **The Bambara** are a key people for the evangelization of the country, yet they are only 0.6% Protestant. Pray for the work of GMU and, more recently, CMA and AoG among these people. Pray for the Bambara Church. There have been breakthroughs for the gospel since 1974, with churches planted in nearly 300 villages north of Bamako; but follow-up is an urgent need in the light of the activity of syncretic indigenous cults in the area.

b) **The Fula** are scattered throughout the country, but with high concentrations in the south, northwest and centre. The Fulanke and Kasonke speak Malinke, and the Wassulunke and Gana speak Bambara, highlighting the need for distinct church-planting strategies. Of these, only the Kasonke are being reached (Norwegian Lutherans). The first churches are now being gathered by CRWM, CMA, Pioneers and Norwegian Lutherans, in a few sections of the main body of Fulbe-speaking Fula.

c) Among the **Malinke** (UWM, SBC), **Soninke** (RSTI, Frontiers), **Bozo** and **Marka** (CMA) the work is in the early sowing stage, with only a few converts.

d) **The Northern peoples** are more strongly Muslim, yet hard pioneering work has resulted in one or two congregations among the desert Tuareg (Ev. Baptists, WH) and the riverine Songhai (Ev. Baptists). The work among the Tuareg has been gravely impaired by the Tuareg insurrection. The Daosahaq are a distinct Muslim people living among the Tuareg who appear responsive but for whom there are no workers.

6. **Unreached and unoccupied peoples number at least 11.** More specifically:

a) Sections of the **Fula** and the related **Tukulor and Kagoro** in the west.

b) The **Diawara, Soninke** and **Fula** of the Nara area on the Mauritania border.

c) The peoples along the Guinea border – the **Yalunka, Gana, Maninka, Malinke** and **Jula.**

Pray for these peoples to be reached with the gospel and for the right approach to be revealed.

7. **Bamako,** the only major city in the country, has 30 small churches and 18 missionaries. Many suburbs are without a witness. Pray that this strategic centre may be effectively evangelized.

8. **Help Ministries:**

a) **Bible translation.** At least 13 languages may need translation teams, and work is in progress in 13.

M

SIL has 15 workers translating in five languages.

b) **Cassette tapes.** These are a vital evangelistic and teaching tool, and greatly appreciated. **GRn** has made recordings in 23 dialects and languages.

c) **Christian programmes on Radio Bamako.** These have had a wide audience, and have opened many unreached villages to the gospel. Since 1988, national radio and television has offered Christians free TV time on a regular basis.

d) **Literature. GMU** has a literature ministry in the capital and **CMA** in Koutiala. Pray for literacy programmes and the production of suitable reading materials in the various indigenous languages as well as for Bambara Christian literature.

e) **The *Jesus* film.** This has been a major instrument for opening up whole areas for church planting, and is available in Bambara, Bobo, Soninke, Fula and Dogon. Pray for the wise and effective use of this precious resource.

f) **MAF**'s flying and supportive ministries, a boon to the body of Christ. Pray for safety, effectiveness and spiritual life to flow through these ministries.

August 10		
Europe		

Malta
(Republic of Malta)

Area 316 sq.km. Three small but strategic islands in the central Mediterranean. Dry limestone hills with no rivers.

Population	Ann. Gr.	Density
1990 353,000	0.52 %	1,117/sq.km
1995 360,000	0.39 %	1,139/sq.km

Peoples:
Maltese 98.6%. Descendants of Phoenicians, Greeks, Romans, Arabs and others.
Other 1.4%. British 2,400; Arab 250.

Literacy 96%. **Official languages:** Maltese, English. Maltese is related to Arabic with strong Italian influence.

Capital: Valletta 14,800. Urbanization 85%.

Economy: Tourism, ship building and repairing, and light industry. Unemployment 4.4%. Public debt/person $940. Income/person $5,820 (28% of USA).

Politics: Independent from Britain in 1964. Parliamentary republic since 1974. The 1974–87 socialist experiment with international non-alignment was a failure. Since 1987 the nationalist government has freed up the economy and applied for EC membership. Politics is a national obsession!

Religion: The Catholic Church is the State Church, and has regained some of the influence lost during socialist rule. Discriminatory legislation against other religions and denominations was eased in 1989 and 1990.
Non-religious/other 0.9%.
Muslim 0.3%. Mainly Libyans.
Christian 98.8%. Nom 3.6%. Affil 95.2%. Growth 0.4%.
  Protestant 0.6%. Affil 0.48%. Growth −0.1%.

Church	Cong	Members	Affiliated
Ch of England	2	240	1,200
Chr Evang Ch (AoG)	3	72	120
Evang Baptist Ch	1	56	80
Bible Baptist	1	48	80
All other (5)	5	130	221
Denominations (9)	12	546	1,701
Evangelicals 0.12% of pop		230	420
Pentecostal/charis 0.05%		100	190

Missionaries to Malta 11 (1:32,100 people) in 5 agencies.
Roman Catholic 98%. Affil 94.53%. Growth 0.4%.

Catholic	78	210,000	333,700
Charismatic 1.4% of pop.		3,000	5,000

Missionaries:
  to Malta 10 (1973 figure).
  from Malta 746 (1973 figure).
Marginal 0.2%. Growth 8.8%.

Jehovah's Witnesses	5	424	771

1. **Malta was the first nation in Europe to embrace Christianity** – after the Apostle Paul's shipwreck on the island. It has been staunchly Catholic for many centuries with high church attendances. Despite continuing devotion to religion, few Maltese have been confronted with the need for a personal faith for salvation in the living Lord Jesus. Pray for a removal of the barriers of spiritual blindness and fear that hold many from commitment to him.

2. **Protestant activity among Maltese was illegal before 1964.** There is still opposition to the preaching of the gospel by Protestants. Yet there are those in authority who have shown friendship for the cause of the gospel. Pray that this support, and the widespread disillusionment among the younger generation with the hypocrisy of traditional Christianity, may open the land and its people to the message of Life. Some are turning to Jehovah's Witnesses and other cults, and others to evangelical churches.

3. **Maltese Evangelicals** multiplied during the '80s through the witness of the two Baptist groups and the Assemblies of God.
a) **These churches received government recognition** in 1989, but pray for the removal of all remaining discriminatory legislation.
b) **New converts** find it difficult to integrate into these fellowships because of hostile publicity and the social stigma associated with these groups, which are considered "cults".
c) **Bible teaching through BCCs** is offered free of charge by several agencies and many have shown interest in these courses. The AoG are setting up a national ICI (TEE) Centre. Pray that the few believers may become established in the Word.
d) **The AoG**, as part of their **Decade of Harvest**, have set the following goals: ten churches, ten pastors, a Bible School and sending missionaries to other countries. Pray for their achievement.

4. **Catholic charismatic** groups have grown and spread all over the islands. They have considerable evangelistic zeal. Pray that leaders of the groups may centre their ministry on the Bible and resist pressures to compromise basic Scriptural truth.

5. **The older Protestant Churches** have catered for the needs of English-speaking expatriates rather than the Maltese. Their numbers have declined, and there has been little effective outreach to the indigenous population. Pray for new life in these churches and for their ministry to the numerous tourists.

6. **The first one-volume Maltese Bible** was published in 1980. Widespread publicity and controversy was stirred by this edition. A Catholic version was published in 1985. The Gideons have distributed New Testaments widely in hotels, schools and institutions. Pray that many may read the Word with inner enlightenment and outward change.

M

7. **Christian literature** is limited in quantity and variety. Pray that evangelical titles may increase in number, and for the provision of those gifted in writing or translating. Pray for an effective publishing and distribution structure to be established.

8. **Many Maltese have emigrated to other lands** such as Australia (178,000), Britain (40,000) and Canada (20,000) where a number have come to the Lord. Pray that some of these may return to their homeland with the gospel.

Marshall Islands

See under MICRONESIA

Include with
French Guiana
Caribbean

Martinique
(Département de la Martinique)

Area 1,091 sq.km. The most northerly of the Windward Islands; prone to volcanic disturbances.

Population		Ann. Gr.	Density
1990	331,000	0.18 %	303/sq.km
1995	338,000	0.42 %	310/sq.km

Peoples:
Afro-Caribbean 93.7%.
European 2.6%. Almost entirely French.
Asian 2.3%. East Indian 6,300; Arab 500; Chinese 500; Vietnamese 330.
Other 1.4%.

Literacy 93%. **Official language:** French. A French Creole Patois is widely spoken.

Capital: Fort-de-France 108,100. Urbanization 75%.

Economy. Based on bananas, manufacture of rum and tourism. Heavily dependent on French aid. Unemployment 25%. Income/person $5,280 (27% of USA).

Politics. A French possession since 1635. An overseas department of France since 1946.

Religion:
Non-religious/other 3%.
Baha'i 0.4%. **Hindu** 0.3%. **Muslim** 0.3%.
Buddhist 0.1%.
Christian 95.9%. Nom 8.1%. Affil 87.8%.
Growth 0%.

Protestant 8%. Growth 5%.

Church	Cong	Members	Affiliated
Seventh-day Adventist	55	7,360	11,318
Missn Chrétienne Ev	31	4,275	6,110
Assemblies of God	21	1,500	3,000
Free Ev Communities	14	700	1,170
Indep Baptist Ch	10	500	769
Ch of God (Cleveland)	1	261	746
All other (8)	51	1,996	3,245
Denominations (14)	183	16,592	26,358
Evangelicals 5.1% of pop		10,500	17,000
Pentecostal/charis 1.6%		2,700	5,300

Missionaries:
to Martinique 15 (1:22,100 people) in 6 agencies.
from Martinique 3 (1:8,800 Protestants) in 2 agencies 2frn 2xcul 1dom.

Roman Catholic 85.7%. Affil 77.6%.
Growth −0.7%.

Catholic Ch	46	162,000	285,000

Missionaries:
to Martinique 75 (1:4,400 people).
from Martinique 50 (1973 figure).

Marginal 2.2%. Growth 11.5%.

Jehovah's Witnesses	30	2,961	7,402

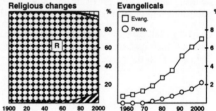

Religious changes / Evangelicals

1. **Martinique** has periodically suffered from major volcanic eruptions and earthquakes. Pray that the population of this beautiful isle may see their basic instability and be shaken out of their carelessness to the things of God.

2. **The churches.** There are growing numbers of evangelical congregations among the Baptist (**SBC**), Assemblies of God and *Mission Chrétienne Evangélique*. Pray for the grounding of these churches in the Word, and the calling of young people into full-time service.

3. **Christian Literature. CLC** operates a well-used bookstore which sells and lends books and tapes. Over 3,000 French Bibles are sold annually through the store. Pray that more local churches may see the value of Christian literature for spiritual growth and use in evangelism.

4. **There are 300,000 Guadeloupans and Martiniquans living in France,** where they are known as *Antilleans*. They comprise a large minority in many Parisian evangelical churches. Pray for the witness of these believers. **WT** has established three churches amongst Antilleans in the Paris area.

Mauritania

(Islamic Republic of Mauritania)

August 11

Middle East

Area 1,031,000 sq.km. The land is entirely desert except for the north bank of the Senegal River on its southern border.

Population		Ann. Gr.	Density
1990	2,024,000	2.8 %	2/sq.km
1995	2,329,000	2.8 %	2/sq.km

75% nomadic in 1970, now less than 25% because of drought which has driven many refugees to the capital.

Peoples: All figures are estimates since ethnicity is a highly sensitive political issue.

Maures 66%.

  White Maures 33%. A mixed Arab/Berber people speaking Hassaniya Arabic. A predominantly pastoral and trading people.

  Black Maures 33%. Also called Haratine; slaves or descendants of slaves.

Black African 28.7%. Tukulor 180,000; Fula 100,000; Soninke 50,000; Wolof 10,000; Bambara. Most are settled farmers in the south and despised by Maures. Numbers reduced by refugees fleeing to Senegal.

Berber 4.8%. Tuareg 60,000 (mostly refugees from Mali); Zenaga 25,000; Masna (speaking Aouker) 7,000.

Other 0.5%. French, Senegalese, Korean, Togolese, etc.

Literacy 28%. **National language:** Hassaniya Arabic. **Official language:** Arabic. **All languages** 6. **Languages with Scriptures** 1Bi 1NT 1por.

Capital: Nouakchott 600,000. Urbanization 34%.

Economy: Unrelenting drought for 20 years has devastated the country and provoked inter-ethnic violence over limited water and usable land. Main export earners are fish and iron ore, but benefits limited by corruption. Public debt/person $912. Income/person $490 (2.2% of USA).

Politics: Independent from France in 1960. Military government: a long succession of military coups that are a continuation of Maure tribal warfare. There is repression of the Haratine, and especially Black Africans. Conflict in 1989 with Senegal led to a two-way exchange of refugees – 200,000 Mauritanians from Senegal and 130,000 Blacks from Mauritania. This conflict, the guerrilla warfare in Sahara/Morocco, together with Mali and Mauritania's siding with Iraq in the Gulf War all harmed the economy and diplomatically isolated the country. In 1992 a civilian government was appointed, and relations with surrounding states improved.

Religion: Islamic republic operating under some *sharia* laws. The constitutional guarantee of freedom of conscience and religious liberty does not extend to Muslims. All proselytization or conversion to another religion is illegal.

Muslim 99.7%. All Sunni.

Christian 0.26%. Growth −3.5%. Almost all expatriates.

  Protestant 0.01%. Mainly expatriates, who number about 200.

  Expatriates serving in Mauritania 30 (1:65,000 people).

  Roman Catholic 0.25%. Growth −3.6%.

Church	Cong	Members	Affiliated
Catholic Ch	7	2,800	5,000

Expatriates serving in Mauritania 50 (1:50,000 people).

M

---

1. **Islam has been entrenched for 1,000 years with little challenge.** Many are the barriers to change – low literacy, no Scriptures yet in Hassaniya Arabic, no radio broadcasts, and laws that forbid Mauritanians from hearing the gospel or converting to Christ. The *strong man* must be bound, his captives released and a truly Mauritanian Church become a reality.

2. **Mauritanians who confess Christ** face the death sentence if discovered, according to Mauritanian law. Some who have shown an interest in the gospel have suffered imprisonment and torture. Pray for freedom of religion in Mauritania. Pray for any believers, that they might be preserved and made strong in persecution, that they might have the courage to meet together, and that they might win others to the Lord.

3. **Expatriate Christians are mainly black African, Westerners and Korean Pentecostals.** Most are involved in technical or professional ministries linked to NGOs. Discouragement is easy because of the harsh climate with sandstorms 200 days in the year, the heat, hostility to anything Christian and severe limitations on sharing their faith. Fellowship opportunities are limited. Pray for steadfastness and consistent witness through their lives that draws non-Christians to enquire about Jesus.

4. **Humanitarian work is being done by a handful of expatriate Christian organizations**. Pray that it may make the love of Christ real to the poor of Mauritania, and that God will use it as a witness.

5. **Mauritanians in other lands** present an opportunity. Mauritanian traders and herdsmen have spread over many countries in Africa – Mali (90,000), Senegal, Gambia, Guinea, Guinea-Bissau, Côte d'Ivoire. Over 200,000 of those in Senegal were forced to flee to Mauritania in 1989; many are still refugees. Pray that these scattered people may be evangelized by all means. It is only in north Senegal that a long-term ministry among them has developed (**WEC**).

6. **Unreached minorities:**
a) **The restive Haratine**, who are Hassaniya by culture and language but also the slave or former slave class of Maure society.
b) **The African peoples** of the Senegal River Valley – the Wolof, Tukulor, Fula, Kasonke and Soninke. A few of these peoples have become believers in Senegal and Mali, but there are no known believers in Mauritania.
c) **The Masna** people of central Mauritania, and the **Zenaga** and **Tuareg** nomads of the desert.

M

Mauritius

August 12
Africa

Area 2,040 sq.km. One larger and three smaller islands east of Madagascar in the western Indian Ocean. One of these, Rodriguez Island, is 500 km to the east of the others. Mauritius also lays claim to Diego Garcia and the Chagos archipelago, which comprise the British Indian Ocean Territory.

Population	Ann. Gr.	Density
1990 1,103,000	1.3 %	541/sq.km
1995 1,172,000	1.2 %	575/sq.km

Peoples: No indigenous peoples; all immigrants.
Indian 64.7%. Hindi/Bhojpuri 330,000; Urdu 64,000; Panjabi 24,000; Tamil 22,000; Marathi 12,000; Telugu 10,600. Many Indians speak only Creole. Politically dominant.
Creole 28%. Mixed African and European.
European 3.8%. French-speaking 37,000. English-speaking 3,000. They control most larger businesses and sugar estates.
Chinese 3%. Prominent in retail trade. Majority Hakka, minorities of Cantonese- and Mandarin-speakers.
Other 0.5%.

Literacy 90%. **Official language:** English, yet the French culture and language is dominant. The most widely spoken language is French Creole. **All languages** 5. **Languages with Scriptures** 4Bi 1por.

Capital: Port Louis 168,000. Urbanization 41%.

Economy: The once-dominant sugar industry has been eclipsed by highly successful diversification and industrialization. Tourism and textiles are now the mainstays of the economy. One of the most successful African economies in the '80s. Unemployment 11%. Public debt/person $572. Income/person $1,950 (9.2% of USA).

Politics: A French colony between 1715 and 1810, and then British until independence in 1968. A parliamentary democracy, but with party politics dominated by ethnic and religious divisions. The Hindu Indian bloc is in the majority, but this is resented by the other groups.

Religion: Freedom of religion compromised by strong tendency for Indianization and, by implication, Hinduism at the expense of Muslims and Christians. All religious and missionary activity directed to evangelizing Hindus is regarded with disfavour.
Hindu 50.3%. A large variety of sects with a weakened Indian caste system.
Muslim 12.5%. Mostly Indian Sunnis, with some Shi'a and Ahmaddiya.
Buddhist/Chinese religions 0.4%.
Non-religious/other 4.1%.
Christian 32.7%. Growth 1.8%.
Protestant 6.7%. Growth 8.1%.

Church	Cong	Members	Affiliated
Assemblies of God	110	29,500	59,000
Anglican Ch	21	3,380	5,200
Presbyterian Ch	5	500	1,000
Evang Ch of M	3	300	600
All other (11)	101	12,636	7,525
Denominations (15)	240	46,316	73,325
Evangelicals 6% of pop		42,000	66,000
Pentecostal/charis 5.7% of pop	39,900	62,000

Missionaries:
to Mauritius 19 (1:58,000 people) in 9 agencies.
from Mauritius 6 (1:11,000 Protestants) 6frn 6xcul.
Roman Catholic 25.8%. Growth 0.4%.
Catholic Ch   308   154,000   285,000
Missionaries to Mauritius 142 (1:7,800 people).
Marginal 0.2%. Growth 7.2%.

Jehovah's Witnesses	13	904	2,100
Groups (4)	16	929	2,350

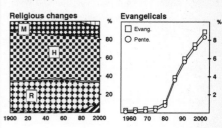

Religious changes   Evangelicals

1. **Ethnic and religious loyalties hinder the progress of the gospel.** There is a strong Hindu revival movement. To the Indians conversion to Christianity is a step loaded with political and ethnic overtones – of "becoming a Creole" – yet praise God that the **AoG** witness has led to large numbers of Hindus coming to Christ.

2. **Most older churches are in gradual decline,** and are traditional and nominal. Few members have a personal faith in Christ. The charismatic movement made a big impact for a while on the Roman Catholic and Anglican churches, but most of those converted have now formed their own independent groups.

3. **Evangelical growth** has been predominantly Pentecostal and charismatic. There are also growing churches through the witness of **AEF** and **SBC** missionaries. There have been a number of unedifying splits, divisions, and displays of doctrinal extremism by immature leaders. Pray for unity and the development of warm evangelical fellowship that overcomes animosities, fears, and divisions.

4. **The training of leaders is of prime importance.** Pray for the **AoG** International Correspondence Institute programme of TEE, and for the several small Bible schools operating in Mauritius.

5. **There is a great openness among young people.** They are less bound by ethnic loyalties, and there are exciting opportunities for witness among them in the multiracial schools. Many have been touched by the gospel but are held back from open commitment by family pressures and liberal church leaders. **YFC** has a good outreach through youth centres, and **IFES** and **CCC** are linked with small evangelical groups in the university. There are too few labourers for this responsive age group.

6. **Missionary work is limited** through lack of personnel with proper experience and the difficulty of obtaining long-term visas. Significant evangelical missions: Presbyterians (7 workers), **SBC** (4), **AEF** (2). Pray that Mauritian believers may become more active in supporting world evangelization. Six Mauritians are serving with **WEC**, **YWAM** and **WH**.

7. **Specific unreached minorities:**
a) **The Muslims.** There are only a few known believers among them, and only one couple is committed to reaching them.
b) **Rodriguez Islanders,** 97% Catholic, isolated, and poor. The **AoG** has started several churches on the island.
c) **The upper-class French community** which is nominally Catholic with very few active believers in their midst.
d) **Speakers of major Indian languages,** Bhojpuri, Hindi and Urdu, all representing large unreached language groups in India. Little evangelism is done in these languages.
e) **The Chinese community.** Most Chinese have become Catholic. Evangelical believers number only around 500 in three to four congregations of the Sino-Mauritian Evangelical Church and Chinese Christian Fellowship. Pray for the removal of the combined barriers of demonic powers and the drive for wealth that keep many from a full commitment to Christ.

8. **Diego Garcia,** in the British Indian Ocean Territory, has been converted into a US-British military base. The original inhabitants were evacuated to Mauritius, where the majority of these 2,100 people live in squalor and deprivation. Most are nominally Catholic.

9. **Help ministries:**
a) **The Bible Society** has a vital role in distributing the Scriptures in all the island territories of the Indian Ocean – Seychelles, Réunion, Comores and others. Pray for translators working on a Creole New Testament.
b) **There are only two Christian bookshops** (one started by **AEF**). Little of their stock is in French or Creole. Pray for the provision and wide distribution of the right Christian literature.
c) **Christian radio broadcasts** from **FEBA** Seychelles are beamed to Mauritius – twelve hours per month in French.

Mayotte

See under COMORO ISLANDS

Mexico

(The United Mexican States)

Area 1,973,000 sq.km. Latin America's fourth largest country. Wide range of topography and rainfall ranging from arid northern plateau, central volcanic plateau and the southern mountains and rain forests. Only 10% of the country is arable.

Population	Ann. Gr.	Density
1990* 88,598,000	2.2 %	45/sq.km
1995 97,967,000	2.0 %	50/sq.km

Note: This is the UN figure. The 1990 census gives 81,250,000.

Peoples:
Mestizo (Spanish/Amerindian) 55%. Many are Amerindian, but now speak Spanish, and are culturally Mestizo.
Amerindian 28%.
  Spanish-speaking 20.5% but still culturally Amerindian.
  Amerindian-speaking 7.5%. Major groupings: Náhuatl (Aztec) 1,197,000; Maya 714,000; Mixteco 384,000; Zapoteco 381,000; Otomí 280,000; Tzeltal 261,000; Tzotzil 229,000.
Euro-American 15.3%. Almost entirely Spanish, also some of American, German, Italian, Russian and Basque origin.
Afro-American 0.5%.
Other 1.2%. Arab 400,000; Gypsy 53,000; Japanese 35,000; Chinese 31,000.
Refugees. In 1990 there were 100,000 Guatemalans and 100,000 Salvadorans.

Literacy 87%. Functional literacy is much lower.
Official language: Spanish, the world's largest Spanish-speaking nation. **All languages** 234. **Languages with Scriptures** 2Bi 91NT 39por.

Capital: Mexico City 15,048,000. Other cities: Guadalajara 3,200,000; Monterrey 2,850,000; Puebla 1,022,000. Urbanization 73%.

Economy: Exploitation of oil and development of industry has benefited the top third of the population, but the poverty of the poorer two-thirds has increased. Massive national debt, inflation, and the deepening economic crisis forced the government to face up to the protectionism, unwise investment policies, entrenched sectional interests, unfairness of existing economic structures, rapid population growth, archaic land-tenure systems and blatant corruption. Mexico's economic turnaround has been spectacular since the end of the '80s. Mexico is likely to become part of a North American Free Trade area in 1993. Unemployment 10%; underemployment 40%. Public debt/person $920. Income/person $1,990 (9.4% of USA).

Politics: Independent from Spain in 1821. The 1910–17 Revolution led to the formation of a one-party federal democracy with power centralized in the President and the Institutional Revolutionary Party. Although the policies and rhetoric of the Revolution still dominate the political statements of leaders, power has been maintained by means of control of the media, manipulation of power groups (unions, police, judicial system, army and others), and electoral fraud. A growing movement for economic reform and political freedoms has led to accelerating government liberalizations and privatization of large state-owned industries and banks. Mexico ratified the North American Free Trade Agreement with the USA and Canada in 1992.

Religion: Secular state with freedom of conscience and practice of religion. No foreign missionaries are officially permitted. The 130-year break between the Mexican government and the Vatican ended with official relations being restored in 1992, and the Catholic Church reasserting its position of dominance. Constitutional changes in 1992 also grant more fair treatment for religious minorities.
Non-religious/other 5.3%.
Jews 0.1%; 57,000. **Baha'i** 28,000. **Muslim** 25,000.
Christian 94.6%. Nom 6.6%. Affil 88%. Growth 1.7%.
  Protestant 5.2%. Growth 7.3%.

Church	Cong	Members	Affiliated
Assemblies of God	3,818	228,000	570,334
Seventh-day Adventist	994	328,000	547,000
Union of Indep Ev Chs	1,000	300,000	500,000
Nat'l Presbyterian Ch	3,250	130,000	433,000
Ind Ev Chs (SFM)	727	80,000	160,000
Ch of God	625	75,000	150,000
Nat Bapt Convention	913	68,497	140,000
Ch of God (Cleveland)	825	41,959	105,000
Indep Pente M'ment	1,567	47,000	85,500
Apostolic Ch of Faith	1,520	38,000	76,000
Methodist Ch	489	44,000	73,300
Nat Chr Ch of AoG	756	34,000	68,000
Ch of the Nazarene	333	27,604	39,340
Foursquare Gospel Ch	120	9,600	32,000
Ch of God of Prophecy	252	8,820	19,600
Episcopal Ch	216	10,800	18,000
All other (306)	15,533	877,473	1,610,655
Denominations (322)	32,938	2,348,753	4,627,729
Evangelicals 4.3% of pop		1,947,000	3,845,000
Pentecostal/charismatic 2.6%		1,119,000	2,280,000

Missionaries:
  to Mexico 1,891 (1:46,900 people) in 173 agencies.
  from Mexico 376 (1:12,300 Protestants) in 30 agencies 84frn 239xcul 137dom.

M

Roman Catholic 87.5% (officially 89.7%). Affil 80.86%.			
Growth 1.2%.			
Catholic Ch	4,662	41,400,000	78,036,000
Doubly Counted		−3,400,000	−6,395,000
Total		38,000,000	71,641,000
Charismatics		700,000	1,600,000
Missionaries:			
to Mexico 354 (1:250,000 people).			
from Mexico 1,990 (1973 figure).			
Other Catholic 0.08%. Growth 0.8%.			
Denominations (2)	528	41,800	75,000
Orthodox 0.1%. Growth 1.1%.			
Denominations (3)	40	59,800	92,000
Foreign Marginal 1.52%. Growth 14.5%.			
Jehovah's Witnesses	8,189	304,756	762,000

Mormons	1,231	285,000	570,000
All groups (11)	9,483	594,982	1,345,000
Indigenous Marginal 0.17%. Growth 2.8%.			
All groups (6)	857	60,000	150,000

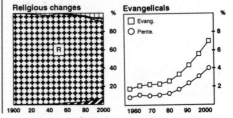

1. **This dynamic, growing nation is searching for an identity** in its Hispanic and Indian roots. This has led to a fierce nationalism and demonstrations of independence from its large northern neighbour, the USA. This is often expressed in anti-Protestant populist propaganda. Pray that Mexicans may find their true identity in a personal faith in Christ.

2. **Unresolved social, economic and political problems** could have dire results if not wisely and speedily addressed. The impoverished rural poor, the exploited urban slum-dwellers, and marginalized Indian communities have too long been ignored. Pray that the leaders of the nation may have courage to deal with centuries of institutionalized graft and privilege.

3. **The Roman Catholic Church** lost much of its political and economic power in the 1910 revolution but retains a visible cultural dominance that could be reinforced by the 1992 religious liberty laws. Most Mexicans are culturally Catholic but still bound by sin, narrow traditionalism and syncretic religious practices, and only 10% are regular churchgoers. The power of the ancient gods and spirit world has yet to be broken in the Spanish-speaking majority and, more especially, in the Christo-pagan Indian minority groups. Pray that Evangelical growth may stimulate reform and renewal rather than persecution!

4. **Persecution of Evangelicals has been a feature of Mexico.** In the last decade this has been sporadic but real – abuse in the media with Evangelicals portrayed as anti-Mexican spies and destroyers of Mexican culture. There have been recent cases, mainly in the rural south, of mob violence, destruction of churches and homes, enforced expulsions of whole evangelical communities from their villages, harassment of evangelistic outreach and arrests of believers on trumped-up charges. Pray that the believers may demonstrate the meekness and love of their Saviour when maltreated. Pray also for the full implementation of religious freedom at both national and local levels.

5. **Evangelical growth** – even under pressure – is cause for praise to God. From the '40s to the '70s this was twice the population growth rate, but in the '80s it rose to three times, mainly in Pentecostal and SDA congregations, through people movements among Indians and through city-wide evangelistic campaigns. Pray for:
a) **A greater harvest in the '90s.** Many believe that the harvest time for Evangelicals has come. Pray, though, for greater love and unity among the multiplying denominations and their leaders.
b) **A healthy growth** in numbers, spiritual maturity, development of leadership and vision for the world.
c) **A penetration of every stratum of society.** Hitherto growth has been among the lower classes, rural Indians, on the northern border with the USA, in the Caribbean coastal states, and latterly among the Indians of the southeast. Wealthier Mexicans and the central and Pacific states have been more lightly influenced.
d) **Unity.** The Evangelical Fraternity of Mexico (CONEMEX) is working to strengthen unity, deal with the government and sponsor important events. A Pentecostal umbrella fellowship is being formed to bring together millions of Pentecostal Christians.

6. **Leadership training is the key to the future health of the Church.** There are well over 100 Bible schools and seminaries training thousands of future leaders at all levels; from indigenous primary-level language to degree-awarding schools, as well as numerous TEE programmes. Pray that spiritual depth and evangelistic vision as well as sound teaching may be imparted to the students. Doctrinal

shallowness, error and also moral and personal relationship breakdowns have impaired the growth of the Church. Pray also for the provision of godly pastors for poor rural and urban slum congregations.

7. **Missions vision in the Mexican Church** has begun to grow over the last decade. There are 81 Mexican Evangelicals serving in 20 countries and others working cross-culturally within Mexico. Pray for these pioneers for the gospel and for a growth in this vision in the churches. **YWAM** runs a Discipleship Training School in Juarez with the specific vision for training Mexican missionaries.

8. **Foreign missionaries'** legal position has been both ambiguous and restrictive. Visas have been a battle to obtain, so most commute on tourist visas. Almost all are US citizens, so they need great sensitivity and tact in their cultural adaptation to overcome the perceived disadvantages of their origin and wealth. Missionaries from outside North America are less than 3% of the total, but face fewer cultural and historical negatives. Openings are many for missionaries in children's and youth work, evangelism and church planting, and especially in leadership training. The largest agencies in Spanish-speaking work are **SBC** (97 workers), **LAM** (75), **AoG** (73), Baptist Bible Fellowship (66), **CAMI** (40), Baptist International Missions (40), **UFM** (29), **GMU** (13), and in Indian work **SIL** (248) and **NTM** (74). Major missionary-contributing nations: USA (1,691), Canada (66), UK (16), Germany (10), Korea (9). Pray that their ministries may assist the Church to be what God desires.

9. **Ministry to young people is vital.** Over 50% of the population is under 20 years of age. This staggering challenge is only being partially met.
a) **Students.** 1,800,000 in over 12,000 campuses with 200,000 in Mexico City alone. Outreach is yielding exciting results. Pray for the wide-ranging ministries of **CCC** (on campuses and among churches), for **IFES**, and for outreach to high school students. Present efforts cannot cover the need and opportunities.
b) **Teenagers.** Few churches have targeted them; most programmes are geared for adults.
c) **Street children**, especially in Mexico City. There may be up to 500,000 who desperately need love and help.

10. **Areas and peoples with few committed Christians.**
a) **There are few strong churches** in the **central states** of Nayarit, Zacatecas, Jalisco, Aguascalientes, Guanajuato, Colima, Michoacan, Queretaro, **the northern states** of Baja California Sur and Sinaloa.
b) **Indian peoples** are largely Catholic in name but pagan in practice. The old pantheon of gods and spirits have been given Catholic names. It has been estimated that of 261 people groups, 129 are without a viable Christian witness and a further 83 are inadequately researched. Vital church-planting ministries must be expanded to build on the impressive Scripture translation programme of **SIL**. Pray for efficient research and analysis of the need for church planting by Mexican and foreign workers, especially in Oaxaca and Guerrero. Pray for the expanding work of **NTM** in five tribes as well as for the extensive work of the Presbyterians and others.
c) **The many conservative Catholic towns and cities**, where evangelical witness is limited and introverted, need to be reached.

11. **Mexico City is a challenge!** By the year 2000 and at present growth rates, it will have 32 million inhabitants, and be the world's largest city. Can it survive the appalling air pollution, unrestricted growth with 5,000 new inhabitants a day, and breakdown of essential services? A 1989 survey revealed that there are only 1,100 churches and 300,000 Evangelicals – about 1.5% of the population – and this has stimulated action improvement. Pray for:
a) **VELA** (Vision for Evangelism in Latin America), a network for churches and agencies to coordinate evangelism and church planting.
b) The many new initiatives of Mexican and expatriate bodies to raise the number of churches to 10,000 by the year 2000.
c) **The 1,000 or so neighbourhoods** without an evangelical congregation – especially needy are the upper-class areas.
d) **The slumdwellers.** Of the 18 million poor, over seven million live in squalid squatter housing in desperate economic conditions. Christian ministry to them is fraught with difficulty and challenge. Few are prepared to commit themselves to it.
e) **The million Indians** representing nearly every language of Mexico. Very little is being done to cater for their spiritual needs.
f) **Evangelism-in-Depth** which is being carried out in parts of Mexico City with encouraging results.

12. **Bible translation and distribution**. Despite centuries of social and cultural pressure, use of indigenous languages is vigorous and varied.

a) **Bible Translation**. The noteworthy work of **SIL** since 1936 is unique. SIL workers have been involved in translation programmes in 126 languages. There are at present 251 workers committed to 68 translation projects. There are 16 languages with a definite translation need and a further 32 where the need has yet to be clarified. The translation of the Maya Bible (**UBS**) was completed in 1991. Pray for the achievement of New Testament and Bible translation goals despite virulent and scurrilous propaganda and agitation for the expulsion of all SIL workers by anthropologists, political factions, and even some Catholic leaders. Pray also for the legalization of their position and provision of visas for ministry. Much of their ministry is now based in the USA.

b) **Bible printing and distribution**. The Bible Society has played an important role in production and distribution of Spanish and indigenous language Scriptures in Mexico and for the whole region. In 1991, the goal was the production of 341,000 Bibles, 212,000 New Testaments and 16 million smaller selections and portions. Pray that the dissemination and reading of the Scriptures may transform individuals, congregations and the nation.

13. **Supportive ministries**.

a) **Christian Radio**. Christian broadcasting was denied Evangelicals in Mexico in 1980, but constitutional changes in 1992 have made it possible for some programmes to be aired locally. There are numerous international broadcasts beamed towards the country with a total weekly input of 1,090 hours! Major contributors are HCJB(**WRMF**, USA and Ecuador), **FEBC** (USA), WYFR (USA), and **TWR** (Bonaire). Pray for relevance, spiritual power, follow-up ministry and lasting fruit. Over 96% of homes have a radio.

b) **The *Jesus* film**. Over 200 agencies use the film in Latin America – many in Mexico. Pray that their ministries may be enhanced through its use. Pray for effective strategies for its use in the large cities, whether by film or video. Pray that the film may be used to make the gospel clear in Spanish and the ten Indian languages in which it has been dubbed.

c) **Cassette recordings. GRn** have messages available in 193 of the 241 languages, a vital tool in the complex linguistic situation. Pray for recordists, new recordings, wide distribution and eternal fruit.

d) **MAF** has a key role in the mountainous and inaccessible regions of the southern part of the country.

e) **Christian literature. *Prisma*** magazine, published since 1969, has been used in evangelism and edifying believers. There is a growing number of Christian magazines and Mexican-authored books. Pray for a literate, well-taught Church to be the result.

f) **Christian camping**. Christian Camping International runs nearly 200 camps around the country. Pray for this well-used and fruitful ministry.

14. **Migrant Mexican labour in California and other border states of the USA** has long been a feature of national life. Their numbers are unknown but may be as many as six to eight million (many illegals). There are many opportunities for them to hear the gospel. Pray for evangelistic and church-planting work in Spanish by **CAMI**, **GMU** and many denominational workers in these areas.

Micronesia

August 15
Pacific

The former US-administered UN Trust Territory is retained here as a single entity because of the small populations and commonalities between the four constituent States.

Area 1,950 sq.km. 2,000 islands of the Caroline, Marshall and Mariana archipelagos in seven million sq.km. of the North Pacific. 100 are inhabited.

Politics: For centuries a strategic global pawn. Ruled by Spain 1710–1897, Germany 1897–1914, and Japan 1914–1945 before the USA took over the administration as a UN Trust Territory. Three republics in free association with the USA have emerged since 1978. Only Palau remains as a Trust Territory.

Religion: During Spanish rule, all islanders were forcibly Catholicized, but the underlying pre-Christian customs and animistic religion remain influential. In each republic there is, theoretically, freedom of religion, but some islands show hostility to variant denominations and religions.

FEDERATED STATES OF MICRONESIA

Area 700 sq.km. Over 600 coralline islands in four main groups – Chuuk, Pohnpei, Yap and Kosrae.

Population		Ann. Gr.	Density
1990	109,000	3.4 %	155/sq.km
1995	118,000	1.6 %	168/sq.km

Chuuk 50.5%; Pohnpei 30.5%; Yap 12%; Kosrae 7% of population.

Peoples:
Micronesian 95.5%. Chuuk (5 dialects) 34,600; Pohnpeian (4) 27,700; Mortlockese 10,600; Yapese 8,000; Kosraean 6,900; Carolinian 4,300; Ulithian (2) 4,100; Woleaian 1,700.
Polynesian 2.1%. Kapingamarangian 1,500; Nukuoro 860 on two atolls south of Chuuk.
Other 2.4%. Japanese, Chinese, US citizens.

Literacy 77%. **Official language** English. **All languages** 19. **Languages with Scriptures** 1Bi 5NT 1por.

Capital: Kolonia (Pohnpei) 6,000.

Economy: Predominantly subsistence farming and fishing. Over 90% of government income comes from US aid. Income/person $1,132 (5.4% of USA).

Politics: A federal republic with four constituent republics with internal self-government since 1986, but with a compact of free association with the USA which administers defence and foreign policy.

Religion: Separation of church and state, with religious freedom. Yap is predominantly Catholic; Pohnpei, Chuuk and Kosrae predominantly Protestant.

Non-religious/other 10%.
Christian 90%. Nom 9%. Affil 81%. Growth 0.8%.
Protestant 40%. Affil 37.6%. Growth 0.7%.

Church	Cong	Members	Affiliated
Prot Ch of East Truk	28	8,350	16,700
Prot Ch of Carolines	100	6,000	12,000
United Ch of Pohnpei	22	5,600	11,200
Assemblies of God	5	195	650
All other (2)	4	200	400
All Denominations (6)	159	20,345	40,950
Evangelicals 14.5% of pop		7,790	15,840
Pentecostal/charismatic 1%		400	1,000

Missionaries:
to Fed St of Micronesia 39 (1:2,900 people) in 11 agencies.
from Fed St of Micronesia 12 (1:3,400 Protestants) in 4 agencies 9frn 9xcul 3dom.

Roman Catholic 47.9%. Affil 41.3%.
Growth 0.5%.

Catholic Ch	24	26,100	45,000

Missionaries to Fed St of Micronesia 20 (1:5,500 people).

Marginal 2.1%. Growth 11.1%.

Mormons	19	1,140	1,900
Jehovah's Witnesses	6	158	395
Groups (2)	25	1,298	2,295

1. **Nominalism** and widespread adherence to magic and animism permeate the population. This, together with Western consumerism fostered by US aid, cripples initiative and spiritual fervour. Alcoholism is a major problem. Pray for revival.

2. **Over a century of Protestant missions** – first through US Congregational missionaries and then the German **Liebenzell Mission** – has resulted in a large part of the population becoming Protestant on some islands. Yap (pop 9,000) is only 5% Protestant; its outlying islands are animistic and closed for evangelical missionaries. There is a need for vision for the lost and for missions. A small **YWAM** base is seeking to stimulate this.

3. **Bible translation and distribution**. The lack of Scriptures in Carolinian and Kapingamarangi, lack of the Old Testament in all but the Chuuk language, and the limited reading of the Bible and understanding of its contents hold back the spiritual development of the largely Christian population, and lay them open for Western cults.

MARSHALL ISLANDS

Area 180 sq.km. There are 34 atolls with 1,156 islands.

Population		Ann.Gr.	Density
1990	46,000	3.9%	254/sq.km
1995	56,000	4.0%	309/sq.km

Peoples:
Marshallese 78.4%. Speaking two dialects.
Other Micronesians and Polynesians 16.6%.
US citizens 5%.

Literacy 86%. **Official languages:** Marshallese and English. **All languages** 2. **Languages with Scriptures** 2Bi.

Capital: Dalap-Uliga-Darrit 13,000, on Majuro Atoll. Ebeye Island is reputedly the world's most densely populated island, with up to 12,000 people on less than 1/2 sq.km.

Economy: Small-scale local agriculture and fisheries are swamped by US aid which inhibits incentive to work. The life of the country is dominated by the payments for reclamation of nuclear bomb-contaminated Eniwetok and Bikini and for compensation to displaced and irradiated islanders. Foreign debt/person $1,600. Income/person $1,180 (5.6% of USA).

Politics: UN Trusteeship ended in 1990. An independent republic in free association with the USA.

Religion: Freedom of religion.
Non-religious/other 2%. **Animist** 4%.
Christian 94%. Affil 73%. Growth 3.7%.
Protestant 80.3%. Affil 61.3%. Growth 3.9%.

Church	Cong.	Members	Affiliated
Assemblies of God	31	7,100	14,200
United Ch of Christ	83	5,000	10,000
Reformed Congreg'l	17	2,000	4,000
Denominations (3)	131	14,100	28,200
Evangelicals 34.6% of pop		8,000	15,900
Pentecostal/charis 30.9%		7,100	14,200

Missionaries:
to Marshall Is 25 (1:1,800 people) in 5 agencies.
from Marshall Is 2 (1:14,000 Protestants) 2frn.
Roman Catholic 10%. Affil 8%. Growth 3.6%.

Catholic Ch	3	2,150	3,700

Missionaries to Marshall Is 59 (1:780 people).
Marginal 3.7%. Affil 3.7%. Growth 0.8%.

Mormons	7	780	1,300
Jehovah's Witnesses	2	167	418
Groups (2)	9	947	1,718

1. **The devastating effects of their war experiences, nuclear testing,** as well as the materialism foreign aid has generated, have left the people without identity or purpose. Drunkenness, drugs, materialism and laziness are widespread. Pray that this nation may truly find fulfilment in following the Lord Jesus.

2. **Protestant Christians** comprise a majority, with the Assemblies of God having won nearly a third of the population. Pray that these Christians may be as salt and light in the midst of a discouraged population.

NORTHERN MARIANAS
(Commonwealth of the Northern Mariana Islands)

Area 477 sq.km. A chain of 14 coral islands 650 km. north of Guam. The southernmost islands – Saipan, Tinian and Rota – are the largest and most important economically.

Population	Ann. Gr.	Density
1990 64,000	14.2 %	134/sq.km
1995 84,000	5.6 %	176/sq.km

Massive influx of migrant labour since 1980.

Peoples:
Pacific Islanders 31%. Chamorro 13,300; Carolinian 2,500; Other Micronesians 4,000.
Asians 64%. Mostly on contract, few long-term, many illegal immigrants. Filipino 28,000; Chinese 5,800; Korean 5,200; Japanese 1,600.
Other 5%. US mainlanders.

Literacy 96% (indigenous). **Official language:** English. Chamorro widely spoken, also some Carolinian. **All indigenous languages** 3. **Languages with Scriptures** 1Bi 1por.

Capital: Saipan 39,000 including migrant labour.

Economy: Tourism, especially from Japan, and US aid are the main sources of national income. More prosperous than the other three Micronesian States. Income/person $7,200 (34% of USA) – including migrant labour.

Politics: A Commonwealth Territory of the USA since 1977. The population was granted US citizenship in 1990.

Religion: Freedom of religion. Almost the entire indigenous population was baptized in the Catholic Church.
Non-religious/other 5%.
Buddhist/Chinese/Japanese religions 10%.
Animist 2%. A high proportion of Catholics are basically Christo-pagans.
Christian 83%. Nom 16.8%. Affil 66.2%. Growth 17.8%.
Protestant 10%. Affil 9.4%. Growth 19.6%.

Church	Cong	Members	Affiliated
Filipino Baptist Chs	2	1,000	1,670
Korean Churches	7	900	1,500
General Baptist Ch	1	250	500
Assemblies of God	1	200	500
Independent Bapts (2)	4	100	222
All other (6)	9	865	1,603
Denominations (12)	24	3,315	5,995
Evangelicals 8.5% of pop		3,053	5,470
Pentecostal/charis 1.2%		360	770

Missionaries to Nthn Marianas 87 (1:736 people) in 7 agencies. 30 workers are involved in FEBC international broadcasting.
Roman Catholic 70.8%. Affil 54.7%. Growth 17.1%.

Catholic Ch	15	20,300	35,000

Missionaries to Nthn Marianas 31 (1:2,100 people).
Marginal 2.2%. Growth 30%.

Jehovah's Witnesses	2	118	1,200
All other (2)	2	620	1,200
Groups (3)	4	738	1,397

1. **The indigenous Chamorro** are Catholic by profession, but animism and folk religion predominate; the majority are non-churchgoers. The Chamorro New Testament is being translated, but only two books of the New Testament are published. Pray that the light of the gospel may shine on this people. Evangelical outreach is only recent. Pray for the ministry of the Baptist and Assemblies of God churches and of the **World Outreach** and **YWAM** teams.

2. **The Asian population** is diverse. There are seven thriving Korean congregations, three Chinese and several Filipino – all with vigorous outreach to their compatriots. However, many of the Asians are culturally isolated and unreached – especially the Japanese and Chinese (both from Mainland China and Taiwan). Many of the Filipinos are involved in the tourist industry; prostitution is a problem.

3. **Over one million Japanese tourists** visit the islands annually – many specifically to worship at Shinto and Buddhist shrines. Pray that they may be reached.

4. **Christian radio.** FEBC has two broadcast services – internationally on short wave to Russia, Central Asia, China, India and South East Asia (25 hours/day), and a local service to the islands in five languages. Pray for deep and lasting impact. Pray for the spiritual and physical protection of both workers and valuable facilities. Saipan is in an area prone to typhoons.

PALAU (BELAU)
(Republic of Belau)

Area 458 sq.km. Eight inhabited volcanic and coral islands.

Population	Ann. Gr.	Density
1990 14,300	0.7 %	31/sq.km
1995 14,800	0.7 %	32/sq.km

Peoples:
Indigenous 92%. Palauan – a mixture of Polynesian, Melanesian and Malay.
Foreign 8%. Other islanders, Chinese, Japanese, US citizens.

Literacy 96%. **Official language:** Palauan; English used widely. **Languages with Scriptures** 2Bi.

Capital: Koror 10,000, on Babelthuap Island.

Economy: Subsistence agriculture, fishing and some tourism. The government is the main employer and relies heavily on US aid.

Politics: The compact of free association with the USA, signed in 1982, has never been implemented because repeated and violently contested referenda have failed to ratify the new constitution.

Religion: Freedom of religion, but the Catholic and Evangelical Churches dominate organized religious life.

Non-religious/other 2%.
Animist 1%. The boundary between animists and nominal Catholics is indistinct.
Baha'i 0.8%.
Christian 96.2%. Growth 0.6%.
  Protestant 25.4%. Growth 2.6%.

Church	Cong	Members	Affiliated
Koror Evangelical Ch	15	1,200	3,000
Seventh-day Adventist	3	500	714
Assemblies of God	2	46	115
Denominations (3)	20	1,746	3,829
Evangelicals 21.1% of pop		1,296	3,186
Pentecostal/charis 0.76%		60	120

Missionaries:
  to Palau 8 (1:2,700 people)
  from Palau 8 (1:480 Protestants) in YWAM 8frn 8xcul.

Roman Catholic 39.7%. Growth −0.6%.

Catholic Ch	12	2,400	6,000

Missionaries to Palau 5 (1:4,400 people).
Foreign Marginal 3%. Growth 8.9%.

Mormons	4	90	300
Jehovah's Witnesses	1	62	155
Groups (2)	5	152	455

Indigenous Marginal 28.1%. Growth 0%.

Modekne		3,000	4,200
Groups (2)		3,025	4,242

1. **Christianity is generally professed,** but nominalism is widespread. Many older people are followers of the Modekne movement, a mixture of Christianity and magic, as well as Catholic. The old animistic religion is also gaining influence. Yet there are the beginnings of spiritual awakening. Pray for the revival of the Evangelical church – the fruit of the work of the **Liebenzell Mission.** The **AoG** have a small but growing work.

2. **Hindrances to the gospel** need to be removed. Closed cultures and strong traditionalism make many villages unwilling for change. The debilitating effects of US aid, material comforts and enormous consumption of beer make discipleship and commitment rare. The whole Bible is not yet available in Palauan, so theological depth is lacking. Outreach to smaller unevangelized island communities is complicated by their geographic isolation.

3. **Missionary vision** for both less-evangelized Micronesian islands and beyond is being stimulated by the **YWAM** base.

Midway Island

See under GUAM

Moldova
(Moldavia)

August 6
Eurasia

Area 33,700 sq.km. Landlocked republic between the Dnestr (Ukraine) and Prut (Romania) Rivers. Formerly Bessarabia, Romania, but seized by the USSR in 1940.

Population		Ann.Gr.	Density
1990	4,377,000	0.84%	129/sq.km
1995	4,544,000	0.75%	135/sq.km

The smallest and most densely populated of the former USSR republics.

Peoples:
Indo-European 94%.
 Latin 64%. Moldavian/Romanian 2,796,000.
 Slav 29.4%. Ukrainian 600,000; Russian 562,000; Bulgarian 88,000; Byelorussian 20,000.
 Other 0.6%. Gypsy 12,000; German 7,000.
Turkic/Altaic 3.7%. Gagauz 153,000.
All other peoples 2.3%. Jews 66,000.

Literacy 99%. **Official language:** Moldovan (Romanian; hitherto in Cyrillic script but reverting to Latin script); in Trans-Dnestria: Moldovan, Russian, Ukrainian. **All indigenous languages** 6. **Languages with Scriptures** 3Bi 2por.

Capital: Chisinau (Kishinëv) 677,000. Urbanization 47%.

Economy: Rich but under-used agricultural land. Most of industry in Trans-Dnestria. The economy is in a state of suspension due to failure to resolve the republic's political future. Income/person $3,600 (13% of USA).

Politics: The USSR's seizure of Bessarabia from Romania in 1940 and its subsequent grotesque dismemberment are the root causes of present conflicts. The north and south were granted by Stalin to Ukraine and the east bank of the Dnestr detached from Ukraine to form the Moldovan republic. Independence declared in 1990. Moldovan desire for reunification with Romania and discrimination against the Slavs provoked secession of Trans-Dnestria in 1991 and six months of bitter war in 1992. An uneasy Russian army-controlled peace prevails, but no political solution is in sight. The Gagauz of south Moldova also voted in 1991 to secede and form their own mini-state.

Religion: The Orthodox Church has regained strong political influence.
Non-religious/other 27.7%.
Jews 1.5%. **Muslim** 0.2%.
Christian 70.6%. Affil 63.4%.
 Protestant 1.7%. Affil 1.68%.

Church	Cong	Members	Affiliated
Baptist Union	185	20,000	50,000
Pentecostal Churches	70	6,000	15,000
Seventh-day Adventist	n.a.	400	1,000
All other (4)	n.a.	3,200	7,000
Denominations (7)	255	29,600	73,000
Evangelicals 1.51% of pop		26,320	65,600
Pentecostal/charis 0.5%		9,000	22,000

Missionaries to and from Moldova n.a.
Catholic 2.5%. Affil 2.11%.

	Members	Affiliated
Eastern-rite Catholic	40,800	68,000
Latin-rite Catholic	14,400	24,000
All Catholics (2)	55,200	92,000

Orthodox 66.4%. Affil 59.6%.

	Members	Affiliated
Romanian Orthodox	1,400,000	2,000,000
Russian Orthodox	364,000	520,000
Bulgarian Orthodox	38,000	57,000
Old Believers Church	6,500	10,000
Other Orthodox (2)	2,630	5,500
All other (1)	1,500	4,000
Denominations (7)	1,812,630	2,596,500

Marginal 0.04%.

	Members	Affiliated
Jehovah's Witnesses	510	1,700

1. **Moldova's future is uncertain and potentially explosive.** The fears and intransigence of the nationalist Moldavians and the Slavs, who have reconstituted the Communist Party, prevent reasoned negotiation of a settlement. Pray for a solution fair to all ethnic groups – all victims of history.

2. **The influence of the Orthodox Church and the prevailing nationalist fervour** make it harder for Evangelicals to receive equal treatment. Christians were severely persecuted under Communism. Three Baptist young men were executed in 1992 because they were conscientious objectors. Pray for full religious freedom.

3. **Evangelical Christians** have multiplied, but they lack so much – meeting places, discipleship materials and funds. Many are very poor. Pray that God may provide their needs. The largest denominations are the Baptists and Pentecostals. There are over 1,000 Baptists among the predominantly Orthodox Gagauz Turks, among whom revival is reported.

4. **Training for pastors** is the greatest need. There are 185 Baptist pastors – none of whom have received any formal training. Pray for the founding of a Bible school. **SGA** is seeking to help in this.

5. **The less reached for prayer:**
a) **1,000 or more villages** have no evangelical witness.
b) **The Gypsy population** is large but statistically included within the Moldovan majority.
c) **The Muslim minorities.** Gagauz believers have a vision to reach them and, beyond, to other Eurasian republics.

6. **Christian help ministries for prayer:**
a) The New Testament is being prepared for the Gagauz.
b) **EHC** reached every home of the capital with Christian literature in 1990. The whole republic is the next target.

Include with France
Europe

Monaco
(The Principality of Monaco)

Area 1.9 sq.km. The second smallest state in the world. On France's south coast.

Population	Ann. Gr.	Density
1990	29,000	1.40 %	15,263/sq.km
1995	30,000	0.68 %	15,789/sq.km

Peoples:
Monegasque 16%. **French** 47%. **Italian** 16%. **Other** 21%.

Literacy 99%. **Official language:** French.

Capital: Monte Carlo 13,100. Urbanization 100%.

Economy: Wealthy as a luxurious holiday resort and tax haven. In customs union with France. Income/person $11,350 (54% of USA).

Politics: Independent city-state with a constitutional monarchy under French protection.

Religion: Roman Catholicism is the state religion.
Non-religious/other 3.9%.
Jews 1.7%. **Muslims** 0.4%.
Christian 94%. Affil 86.2%.
Protestant 3.6%.

Church	Cong	Members	Affiliated
Denominations (2)	2	208	1,040

Missionaries to Monaco 33 (1:900 people) in 2 agencies – almost all associated with TWR ministry.
Roman Catholic 90.1%. Affil 86.2%.

| Catholic Ch | 5 | 18,500 | 25,000 |

Missionaries to Monaco 100 (1973 figure).
Orthodox 0.3%.

1. **Monaco is culturally Catholic, but conspicuously committed to worldly pursuits.** The small Protestant community has little impact on society. Evangelicals are few in number. Both local residents and the many tourists need to hear the gospel.

2. **Christian Radio.** Trans World Radio's ministry from Monaco is widely respected. Powerful medium- and short-wave transmitters broadcast 100 hours of programmes weekly in 27 languages; 17 of these languages are spoken in Europe and ten in North Africa and the Middle East. Pray for:
a) **Spiritual impact** on the materialistic and indifferent cultures of Europe and the resistant and polarized Islamic Middle East.
b) **Effective use of modern technology** – satellite broadcasting, more powerful transmitters, and the means of funding.
c) **The network of studios** producing programmes for transmission from Monaco to the Muslim world (eg. **GMU** and **AWM** for North Africa) and Europe (German **TWR**, etc.). The staff needs prayer, as do the listeners.
d) **The difficult but key follow-up ministries,** which are often the only fellowship links that new believers can enjoy.

Mongolia

(State of Mongolia)

August 17
Asia

Area 1,565,000 sq.km. Grassland, forests in north, three major mountain ranges and the great Gobi Desert in the east. Known as Outer Mongolia before 1911.

Population	Ann. Gr.	Density
1990 2,227,000	3.1 %	1.4/sq.km
1995 2,596,000	3.1 %	1.9/sq.km

Peoples:
Mongolian 91.3%. Halh (Khalkha) 1,614,000. Seven other distinct dialects, but all can speak Halh. Buriat 48,000. A further 4,800,000 Mongolians live in China.
Turkic 6.6%. Kazakh 120,000; Uriankhai (Tuvinian) 27,000; Uighur 1,000. Many of the Kazakhs are emigrating to Kazakhstan.
Other Indigenous minorities 1.8%. Chinese 35,000; Russian 4,000; Evenki 2,000.
Foreigners 0.3%. Chinese, Westerners, Japanese, Korean, others. By 1993 all former USSR troops and dependents had left the country.

Literacy 90%. **Official language:** Halh Mongolian. By 1995 the switch from the Russian Cyrillic to the Mongolian vertical script and traditional spelling system will be well under way. **All languages** 9. **Languages with Scriptures** 2Bi 3por.

Capital: Ulaan Baatar 650,000. Urbanization 58%.

Economy: Pastoral agriculture dominates. Enormous mineral and oil potential. Underdeveloped because of distance from the sea, political and economic isolation and former dependence on the USSR. The collapse of the USSR and the chaos in Russia have crippled the Mongolian economy with massive shortages, inflation and rising unemployment. Unemployment 14–30%. Public debt/person $8,100. Income/person est. $100–200 (0.5–1% of USA).

Politics: The Mongolian Empire of the 13th Century stretched from China to Central Europe. Autonomous from Manchu and Chinese domination in 1911. A revolution supported by the Soviet army in 1921 installed a repressive Communist government. Communism was renounced in 1990 and a multi-party democracy instituted in the 1992 constitution. In the subsequent election, the reformed former Communist party won a landslide victory.

Religion: Lamaistic Buddhism was vigorously suppressed by the Communists. Marxist ideology has been renounced. There was a resurgence of Lamaistic Buddhism, but freedom of religion is guaranteed in the constitution. All religious figures are estimates.
Shamanism/animism est. 50%. The majority of Mongolians are animistic, fearing and appeasing spirits.
Lamaistic Buddhism est. 26%.
Non-religious/other est. 20%.
Muslim 4%. Almost entirely Kazakh and Uighur.
Baha'i is seeking to establish a work.
Christian 0.03%. Affil 0.11%. Growth 37.1%.
Protestant 0.02%. Growth 39.6%.

Church	Cong	Members	Affiliated
Evangelical groups (3)	7	1,000	2,000
Evangelicals 0.02% of pop.		1,000	2,000

Christian expatriates in Mongolia 89 (1:25,000 people) in 14 agencies.
Missionaries from Mongolia 11 (1:200 Protestants) 11dom.
Roman Catholic 0.002%.
Orthodox 0.01%. Russian Orthodox.
Foreign Marginal 0.003%. Jehovah's Witnesses, Mormons, Witness Lee.

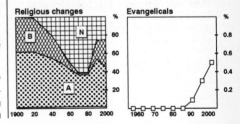

1. **Democratic and religious freedoms** are a new luxury for Mongolians. Pray that these may be retained and that the government may continue to uphold them.

2. **The young Mongolian Church** is a reality for the first time in modern history. The believers are eagerly evangelizing, and new converts are won weekly. By 1993 there were seven autonomous congregations with groups emerging in several towns outside the capital. Pray for:
a) Preservation in the face of opposition.
b) Growth in grace, and maturity.
c) Unity and genuine love for the brethren – already under threat.
d) Discernment of error – sects and new religions have entered and brought confusion.

e) The raising up of leaders of wisdom and humility from among these Christians. Some have already been set aside for full-time ministry. Several Bible school projects for emerging leaders have been started; over 50 Mongolians – all young Christians – were involved in 1993.

3. **Lamaistic Buddhism** has revived. Monasteries have multiplied from one to more than 100. Older people have returned to the beliefs of their forefathers in large numbers. Liberation from one bondage could be replaced by another. Younger Mongolians hanker after material riches and this is possibly the biggest challenge for the gospel. Pray that Mongolians may find complete spiritual liberation in Jesus.

4. **The desperate economic plight** of the nation is leading to suffering, exploitation and social upheaval. Already crime in the capital has become a scourge and alcoholism and promiscuity rife. Pray that the government may handle the situation wisely. Pray also that Christian aid programmes may be carefully implemented for maximum social and spiritual benefit. Most agencies are involved in health, relief, education, and literature programmes.

5. **The opening up of Mongolia for Christian ministries** has been an answer to prayer; pray that this may continue. Christian workers are rapidly increasing in number. Pray for their integration into the culture, adaptation to harsh living conditions, and spiritual effectiveness. Spiritual unity and effective apportionment of ministry responsibilities are two major needs, for there have been breakdowns in relationships. Pray for the calling of Asian and Western missionaries with the gifting and quality needed in this day of opportunity.

6. **The unreached:**
a) **Most of the provinces** have yet to have an indigenous Christian presence though expatriate Christians are moving into many of them now.
b) **Young people and children** are searching for answers for heartfelt needs and are not finding them in Lamaism. Teaching English and other languages by expatriates gives many openings.
c) **The Kazakh** are Muslim in name, but for decades have been denied any religious rights. Muslim missionaries are seeking to re-establish Islam. In 1992 a German team saw a significant number respond to the gospel but there are no long-term church planters.
d) **The ethnic minorities**, such as the Uriankhai, Chinese and Russians, may need specific Christian ministry.

7. **Specific Christian help ministries** for prayer:
a) **Bible translation**. The Mongolian Bible Society has recently translated the Mongolian New Testament which is proving a great success. Ten thousand copies have been sold, and it is being reprinted. The Old Testament is being translated and the New Testament will soon need revision.
b) **Christian literature**. Good discipleship and follow-up literature is needed. Several agencies are working on supplying this.
c) **The *Jesus* film**. This has been widely used. Pray that it may be the means of awakening many across the country to the claims of Christ.
d) **MAF** will commence flying operations in 1994.
e) **Christian radio**. There are no effective Christian radio programmes beamed to Mongolia. Pray for the production of quality programmes for local and international airing.

Montserrat

(Colony of Montserrat)

See Caribbean
Caribbean

Area 102 sq.km. A volcanic mountainous island in the Leeward Islands.

Population	Ann. Gr.	Density
1990 13,000	1.6 %	127/sq.km
1995 14,000	1.5 %	137/sq.km

Peoples:
Afro-Caribbean 97%. **Euro-American** 2%.
Other 1%.

Literacy 77%. **Office language:** English.

Capital: Plymouth 3,500. Urbanization 14%.

Economy: Predominantly agricultural, but growing income from tourism and offshore banking. Income/person $4,540 (21% of USA).

Politics: A dependency of the UK.

Religion:
Non-religious/other 4%.

Christian 96%. Nom 14.9%. Affil 81.1%. Growth 0.8%.
Protestant 81%. Affil 68.6%. Growth 0.8%.

Church	Cong	Members	Affiliated
Anglican	7	1,950	3,900
Methodist	7	700	1,400
Pentecostal Assemb	9	600	1,200
Ch of God of Prophecy	10	300	500
Baptist Convention	1	200	333
All other (2)	4	800	1,229
Denominations (7)	38	4,550	8,562
Evangelicals 21.2% of pop		1,400	2,650
Pentecostal/charis 14%		930	1,750

Missionaries to Montserrat 4 (1:3,300 people) in 1 agency.
Roman Catholic 14%. Affil 11.6%. Growth 0.7%.

| Catholic Ch | 4 | 899 | 1,450 |

Missionaries to Montserrat 1 (1:13,000 people).
Marginal 1%. Affil 0.89%. Growth 4.4%.

| Jehovah's Witnesses | 1 | 30 | 111 |

1. **The newer churches,** mainly Pentecostal, have grown at the expense of the mainline churches – as all over the Caribbean. Pray for renewal in the older churches and spiritual depth in the newer.

| August 18–19 |
| Middle East |

Morocco
(The Kingdom of Morocco)

Area 459,000 sq.km. Northwest corner of Africa. Fertile coastal areas in the north, barren Atlas mountains inland and Sahara Desert to south and southeast. A further 252,000 sq.km. of former Spanish Sahara claimed and occupied by Morocco in 1976.

Population	Ann. Gr.	Density
1990 *25,139,000	2.6 %	55/sq.km
1995 29,116,000	3.0 %	63/sq.km

* Unofficially 30,000,000.

Peoples:
Arabic-speaking 64.7%. Culturally Arab, but predominantly Berber with Arab admixture. Also Jebala 1,081,000.
Berber (Amazightan) 34.8%. Three main language groups: Tachelhait (Southern Shilha) 2,300,000; Tamazight (Central Shilha) 1,900,000; Tarafit (Riff) 1,500,000. There are numerous dialects. Also Ghomara 50,000; Senhaja de Srair.
Other 0.5%. French 80,000; Spanish 20,000; Jewish 12,000, etc.

Literacy 50%. **Official language:** Arabic. French and English are widely used. **All languages** 9. **Languages with Scriptures** 2Bi 4por.

Capital: Rabat 1,063,000. Other cities: Casablanca 4,500,000; Fez 800,000; Marrakech 790,000. Urbanization 45%.

Economy: Agriculture, tourism, and especially phosphate mining are important foreign exchange earners. Morocco and the Western Sahara have 70% of the world's phosphate reserves. The cost of the Sahara war has deeply affected the economy. Unemployment est. 40%. Public debt/person $794; Income/person $900 (4.1% of USA).

Politics: Independent kingdom in 1956. Formerly French and Spanish protectorates. A limited democracy with an executive monarchy that has a poor record for maltreatment of dissenters. The dominant political issue since 1974 has been the occupation of the Western Sahara and the subsequent warfare and political manipulation to retain it.

Religion: Islam is the state religion. The government is committed to the preservation of Islam as the religion of all Moroccans. Other religious groups are tolerated so long as they confine their ministry to expatriate communities.
Muslim 99.8%. Almost entirely Sunni.
Jews 0.05%. 12,000 Sephardic Jews, the remnant of a large community that has emigrated to Israel.
Christian 0.16%. Growth −4.7%.
Protestant 0.01%. Growth 3.9%.

Church	Cong	Members	Affiliated
Evang Reformed Ch	9	280	700
Baptist Convention	3	100	167
All Other (10)	28	732	1,604
Denominations (12)	40	1,112	2,471
Evangelicals 0.010% of pop		615	1,200
Pentecostal/charis 0.001% of pop	90		170

Missionaries:
Christian expatriates in Moroccan ministries inside and outside the country approximately 150.
Missionaries from Morocco 9 (1:270 Protestants) 9frn 3xcul 6dom.
Roman Catholic 0.14%. Growth −5.3%. Almost exclusively French.

Catholic Ch	52	20,200	36,000

Christian expatriates in Moroccan ministries 412.
Orthodox 0.003%. Growth −1.1%
All non-indigenous.

Denominations (3)	2	468	850

1. **Islam** was brought by invading Arab armies in the seventh century. The once-strong North African, and largely Berber, church was blotted out. Pride in Morocco's glorious past as a centre of civilization and Islamic learning and prejudice against the truths of Scripture are barriers to the acceptance of the gospel. Some 80% of the population has had no contact with the gospel. Pray for individual hearts – and the entire nation – to be opened for messengers of the Cross.

2. **The government vigorously opposes a full expression of democracy** and also the rising power of fundamentalist Islam among intellectuals. Yet economic decline and social stresses caused by the Sahara War reinforce the momentum for change. The government refuses to recognize the legality, or even the existence, of an indigenous Moroccan Church. Pray for the king and those in authority, and for a radical change of the situation that will give greater freedom and legal recognition to Christians.

3. **Praise God for a greater interest in the gospel,** but pray that this may lead to concern, conviction, conversion and congregations. Every advance is bitterly contested by the enemy of souls, and every possible obstacle to the witness of national and foreign believers is exploited. Over the land

lies the blanket of a spirit of oppression that grips all but those with a strong faith in the Lord Jesus and his victory.

4. The Church in Morocco has become a reality, but at great cost. Growth has been slow but the momentum has built up. There are possibly 400 indigenous believers who have confessed Christ, as well as other secret believers. There are eight cities in which Christians gather in little groups, yet few could be considered viable, organized churches. Pray for the planting of a church in every city and town. Pray that these believers may radiate the peace and joy of the indwelling Saviour. Pray for deep trust and fellowship to replace the all-too-common fear and mistrust even among believers, so that they may be willing to meet together despite the risk. Pray for an increase in the number of Christian families, and for a vital, vibrant, indigenous Church to take root.

5. Persecution of believers and intimidation of seekers has steadily increased since 1968. Individuals who become followers of Christ are open to charges of treachery and illegal contacts with foreign organizations and are subject to prison sentences for not adhering to Islamic practices such as the fast month of Ramadan. For church groups it is very difficult to find meeting places or to arrange Christian marriages and burials. Persecution has taken many forms: lengthy police interrogations, ostracism, dismissal from employment, family harassment and occasional imprisonment. Believers need encouragement, a strengthened faith, deliverance from the fear of man and a heavenly boldness in the fiery trials they are undergoing.

6. It is hard for leaders to be trained and openly recognized in the hostile environment. Those who obtain training abroad rarely return for ministry in Morocco. There is a low-key TEE programme which is benefiting some mature believers. Pray that there may be God-given, Spirit-gifted leadership for every group of believers.

7. Christian radio and BCCs have been so successful that every effort has been made to hinder or discredit the ministry. **GMU** was forced to move their radio and literature base to Malaga, Spain, and **AWM** to Marseille, France, from where the work continues. Pray for:

a) **GMU, AWM** and **Brethren** missionaries, as well as North Africans, working to write, print, and distribute literature and prepare radio programmes for North Africa.

b) **Christian radio broadcasters:** TWR's six hours a week in Arabic are insufficient for the need. Pray for increased hours on the air at appropriate times and intervals. There are plans for broadcasting in Tachelhait.

c) **A suitable long-term strategy** for effective church planting through radio and literature.

d) **Postal services** to function without interference by the authorities. Many BCCs have been intercepted.

e) **BCC students** to persevere despite difficulties. Over 150,000 have signed on for courses prepared by **GMU, AWM** and others. Since 1988 the number of students has increased dramatically.

f) **Adequate follow-up** that does not put seekers or new believers at risk, and fitting discipleship literature to give them solid teaching. More national believers need to be involved.

g) **Conviction, conversion, cell groups and churches** to be the fruit.

8. Missionary work, as such, is no longer permitted, and all former mission centres were closed. Christian workers remain on in various secular roles as nurses, teachers, etc., and quietly contrive to share their faith and encourage believers. Give praise for others moving out to join them – may their lives radiate the life of Jesus, and may they have a tactful boldness and faith for a harvest despite surveillance, pressure and discouragements. Pray the way open for other Christians to enter to replace the many who have had to leave. Major missions in the past have been **GMU, BCMS, AWM,** Immanuel Mission and **Brethren.** There are over 150 Christian workers whose ministry is directed towards Moroccans.

9. The Berber peoples were nominally Christian until Islam came. Arabization is being resisted, and there is a revival of Berber culture and script. Some are seeking an identity in their Christian past. Pray that many might follow in the faith of their illustrious Berber forebears of the early Church – including Tertullian and Augustine. Pray also for:

a) **Church planting.** In each of the three major peoples there are believers, but, as yet, no established congregations of believers using their languages. Pray for those who have a vision to see this realized, and for wise and creative strategies to achieve it.

b) **Discipling individual believers** amidst all the difficulties – suspicion, fear, isolation, illiteracy together with a lack of Scriptures and teaching materials.

c) **The small communities of Maghreb Jews,** remnants of the 250,000 in Morocco in 1948. Most have emigrated to Israel. There is no known outreach to them at this time.

d) **The nomadic desert tribes** of the south – the Shawiya, Haratine and Tuareg. They have little contact with the gospel.

e) **Bible translation**. The Tifinagh Berber script is now legal in Morocco. Scriptures in Tachelhait, Tarafit and Tamazight are being translated for both Berber and Arabic scripts. Pray for the translators and a wise choice of words in the variety of dialects, and for the dissemination of God's Word among these peoples.

f) **Christian radio**. There have been sporadic efforts to produce programmes in Tamazight, Tarafit and Tachelhait. Pray for regular programmes in all major languages.

10. **The Western Sahara** was a Spanish colony until 1975. The Moroccan annexation is disputed by the Polisario independence movement in a bitter war. The large Moroccan army controls 90% of the territory but only 40,000 of the Sahrawi. Over 150,000 Sahrawi have fled to Algeria where they live in refugee camps. Thousands of immigrants from Morocco have been settled in the Sahara area. The gospel has never been proclaimed to the Arab/Berber Sahrawi people; pray that peace may bring the opportunity to do so.

11. **Moroccans have migrated in large numbers in search of employment**. There are 650,000 in France, 120,000 in Netherlands, 110,000 in Belgium, 76,000 in Spain, 52,000 in Germany and 6,000 in Britain. There are others in Gibraltar and in the Spanish North African cities of Ceuta and Melilla. In only a few centres are they being reached with the gospel (**AWM** in France, **GMU** in Belgium, **YWAM** in various cities, and others).

Mozambique

(Republic of Mozambique)

Area 812,000 sq.km. The Zambezi River divides the 2,800 km-long land into the widely differing north and south.

Population		Ann. Gr.	Density
1990	15,663,000	2.7 %	20/sq.km
1995	17,913,000	2.7 %	22/sq.km

At the height of the war in 1992 nearly 40% of the population were refugees – internally four million and in surrounding lands 1,800,000. Deaths in the war had mounted to more than one million.

Peoples:
Estimates – inadequately surveyed.
Indigenous Bantu peoples 99.1%. Over 38 ethnic groups:
  Northern peoples 50.1%. Makua 4,950,000; Lomwe 1,347,000; Chwabo 627,000; Makonde 360,000; Yao 313,000; Maviha 110,000; Matengo 110,000; Mwani (Swahili) 70,000; Akoti 35,000; Sangage 18,000.
  Central peoples 20%. Sena-Nyungwe 1,227,000; Shona-Ndau 1,100,000; Nyanja 423,000; Kunda 157,000; Nsenga 141,000; Podzo 86,000.
  Southern peoples 29%. Ronga-Tswa 1,848,000; Tsonga (Shangaan) 1,503,000; Chopi 760,000; Swazi-Zulu-Ngoni 141,000; Tonga 19,000.
Other 0.9%. Euro-African 200,000; Portuguese 30,000; Indian 15,000; Chinese 7,000.

Literacy 33% (official), 20% (actual and still declining). **Official language:** Portuguese (understood by 60% of population). **All languages** 244. **Languages with Scriptures** 9Bi 2NT 7por.

Capital: Maputo 1,300,000. Other major city: Beira 1,000,000 – vastly swollen with refugees. Urbanization 18%.

Economy: The world's poorest country; the result of centuries of colonial neglect, overhasty application of Marxist economic theories and 30 years of intense guerrilla warfare. Climatic extremes of flooding and droughts have further impoverished the desperate population. Fertile agricultural land and large mineral wealth were under-utilized, and most rural areas became a depopulated no-man's-land. Road and rail links are few and barely usable. Heavily dependent on foreign aid. Reconstruction of the country will take years. Public debt/person $300. Income/person $80 (0.38% of USA).

Politics: A Portuguese colony for 470 years. Independent in 1975 as a Marxist-Leninist state after a long and bitter war for independence. The anti-government movement, Renamo, subsequently spread rural devastation to most of the country in an exceptionally brutal guerrilla war. The war and international pressure encouraged the Frelimo government to end the flirtation with Marxism in 1988 and

to institute a multi-party democracy and a market economy in 1990. After much negotiation a peace accord was signed in October 1992 and by April 1993 an uneasy peace prevailed.

Religion: Government policy between 1975 and 1982 was the exclusive propagation of Marxism, "all-out war on the churches" and "destruction of religious superstitions". A steady lessening of restrictions since then led to religious freedom by 1990. Religious figures are estimates.
African traditional religions 40%.
Non-religious/other est. 5%.
Muslim 13%. The majority among the Yao in northwest and coastal Makonde, Makua and Mwani.
Christian 42% Nom 14.2%. Affil 27.8%.
Growth 7.6%.
Protestant 14%. Affil 10.8% Growth 13.7%.

Church	Cong	Members	Affiliated
United Bap Ch (AEF)	1,778	170,000	400,000
Assemblies of God	396	95,000	380,000
Ev Assemb of God	600	60,000	150,000
Presbyterian Ch	1,049	43,000	100,000
Seventh-day Adventist	402	49,323	82,200
Anglican Ch	118	20,000	75,000
United Methodist Ch	900	30,000	60,000
Full Gosp Ch of God	149	18,113	51,800
Assmbs of God, Afr	120	30,000	50,000
Reformed Ch in M	121	14,500	30,000
New Alliance (Brethen)	120	12,000	30,000
Ch of the Nazarene	214	13,734	28,907
Ev Ch of Christ in Zambezia	75	10,000	25,000
Free Methodist Ch	93	10,218	20,000
Baptist Convention	17	5,492	12,200
All other (26)	1,539	90,246	191,000
Denominations (41)	7,691	661,626	1,686,207
Evangelicals 8.9% of pop		529,000	1,400,000
Pentecostal/charis 4.7%		246,000	733,000

Missionaries
  to Mozambique 293 (1:53,500 people) in 47 agencies.
  from Mozambique 5 (1:337,000 Protestants) in 1 agency.
Roman Catholic 22.5%. Affil 11.7%. Growth 0.6%.
Catholic Ch   4,132   1,120,000   1,829,000
Missionaries to Mozambique 648 (1:24,000 people).
Foreign Marginal 0.5%. Affil 0.40%. Growth 10.0%.
Jehovah's Witnesses   300   25,000   62,500
Indigenous Marginal 5%. Affil 4.95%. Growth 16.7%.
All Groups (200)   2,533   385,000   775,000

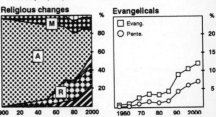

Religious changes | Evangelicals

1. **Mozambique has religious freedom for the first time in its history**. The Catholic monopoly under Portuguese rule was only breached in the southern third of Mozambique. Protestant ministries were severely restricted or forbidden. Sporadic but severe persecution of evangelical believers occurred. Under Marxism all Christians suffered. Missionaries were expelled, Christian leaders intimidated and imprisoned, and many churches and institutions seized or destroyed. Discriminatory legislation was passed to limit Christian gatherings to recognized church buildings and prevent evangelism. Increasing freedoms since 1982 have led to unprecedented growth among nearly all groups. Praise God for the freedom, but pray that this may be maintained when peace eventually comes.

2. **The long succession of political, military and natural calamities** has created a great hunger for reality and unprecedented responsiveness to the gospel. Yet the awful realities of suffering and destitution continue with scant prospect of change. Pray for the peace settlement to endure, for an effective national government, and for wise leaders who will enable the people to rebuild their lives and repair the shattered economy.

3. **Suffering has strengthened Christians for the present harvest**. Yet lack of education and holy living is making the church prone to strife, shallowness and low standards. Before independence Protestant denominations were largely restricted to the three southern provinces, where there was much nominalism, but massive movements of population have enabled Christians to bear witness to people from all parts of the country. Pray for the continued multiplication of believers and congregations in:

a) **The cities** of Maputo and Beira where there has been more stability and a huge influx of refugees, and where Anglican, Nazarene, Baptist and various Pentecostal churches have grown.

b) **The refugee camps in Malawi** where Malawian and Mozambican workers have won many to the Lord.

c) **The Lomwe people of Zambezia in the north** where the United Baptist Church, the fruit of **AEF** work, has grown from 1,500 believers in 1959 to 170,000 today in a remarkable people movement to Christ.

d) **The "Beira Corridor"**, a 280-km strip of territory on either side of the road and rail links between Zimbabwe and the sea, which was guarded by Zimbabwean troops and where 20% of the country's population found some protection and food. Zimbabwean and Mozambican Christian workers have planted many churches among these unfortunate people.

4. **The Catholic Church**, long associated with colonial repression, suffered particularly severely after independence. Huge defections, widespread nominalism and lack of Africanization with a dearth of indigenous clergy led to a big drop in numbers. Renewal movements among Catholics elsewhere have had little impact.

5. **Training of church leadership is an urgent priority**. Most congregations are led by men and women with little or no education, and very few by those with theological training of any kind, nor are there funds or adequate facilities to provide it. The government insists that each group provide adequate training for their leaders. Pray for:

a) **The seminaries and Bible colleges**. One in Ricatla, operated by the Christian Council for Mozambique for the more traditional churches, has 42 students, but liberal teaching is predominant. The Nazarene (40 students) and United Baptist Colleges (11) are evangelical. The **AoG** has two Bible schools with 140 students. However, there is no Bible school in the northern half of the country.

b) **Non-formal training** which has proved successful – TEE (United Baptists, **AEF**) and correspondence courses (Emmaus Bible School of the Brethren and Global Literature Lifeline based in Zimbabwe).

c) **African independent churches**. These have mushroomed in numbers and size over the past 10 years. A medley of syncretic teachings, legalisms and false teachings together with a great desire for help and teaching characterize many of their leaders. **AIM** in Beira and others in Maputo are seeking to fill this gap with gratifying results with many of these groups centering more on the Bible.

6. **Mozambique has had the largest concentration of unreached peoples in Africa south of the equator**. This is still true, but it may not be so for much longer. Despite the violence, the spread of the gospel to nearly every part of the country has continued through the courageous activities of Mozambicans. Large gaps remain:

a) **The two northern provinces** of Cabo Delgado and Niassa. These have few Christians and churches.
b) **The northern coastal Muslim peoples** – little has ever been done for their evangelization – pray for the Mwani (**SIL** now translating the NT), Makonde (part Muslim, some Brethren believers), Koti and Sangage. **AIM** is targeting this area.
c) **The Yao of Niassa** among whom the Anglicans have a growing work. A further six agencies have sent missionaries to work among them in Mozambique and Malawi. Pray for good teamwork. The New Testament has just been completed.
d) **The Makua**, the largest animistic unreached people in Africa, possibly the world. Some 20% are Muslim, 10% Catholic, and about 5,000 are believers (**AoG** and United Baptists), but the more Muslim areas towards the coast are unreached.
e) **The peoples of the Zambezi valley** – especially the Sena, Kunda, Podzo, Nyungwe, Chwabo and Mazaro. Only in the last few years have Sena churches and some Chwabo churches been planted. Many of these peoples are refugees today.

All these areas and peoples need pioneer missionary input, but unless peace is maintained this will be impossible.

7. **Expatriate missionaries** were expelled in 1975/76, but since 1982 the doors have begun to open once more. Missionaries have been obliged to confine their activities to the cities and safer areas. Conditions are harsh. The disease, starvation and despair of the destitute majority, the danger to life and property, and frustration and disappointments have to be faced. The loss rate is high, and few push through to learn both Portuguese and a local language. Pray for their survival, adaptation and fruitfulness. The ministries for which missionaries are needed: leadership training, initiating youth and children's work, pioneer church planting and Bible translation in association with Mozambican Christians, aid and reconstruction work. Major missions include: **AIM** (22 workers), Mozambican Christian Fellowship (20), NGK (18), **WV** (14), **AEF** (11), Jesus Alive Ministries (10), **SBC** (6), **SIL** (6), **TEAM** (6), **PAoC** (4), **YWAM** (3). Major missionary-contributing nations: USA (82), Malawi (81), South Africa (39), Brazil (17).

8. **Bible translation and distribution.** The Mozambique Bible Society has a bookshop and great freedom to operate, but lack of Bibles, foreign currency and means of distribution limit this ministry. Projects for new translations or revisions have also been hampered. The government changed its language policy in 1982 to actively encourage the use of local languages, but a nationwide policy on orthography is needed. **SIL** has workers to promote the study of Mozambican languages and to help in Bible translation. This is needed in at least five and possibly 10 languages – especially in Makua, kiMwani and Sena. A number of other languages with inadequate New Testaments require new translations. Pray for the five translation projects in progress, one being the Lomwe Old Testament.

9. **Christian help ministries**
a) **Literature** is easily imported but in short supply. Distribution and high costs are major problems, and Christian bookstores are limited in number and in range of stock. People are eager for literature. Agencies outside the country have done much to send in good evangelistic literature (All Nations Gospel Publishers, South Africa; Global Literature Lifeline, Zimbabwe; **Open Doors**; **SGM**; Frontline Fellowship) and the gospel broadsheet *CEDO* (**WEC**). **SU** has started work in Mozambique with the aim of providing good Bible reading aids.
b) **Radio** has been used of God for both church planting and teaching. **TWR** in Swaziland broadcasts in Portuguese, Lomwe, Shona, Tswa and Shangaan for a total of 26 hours/week and **FEBA**-Seychelles in Portuguese, Swahili and Yao (16 hours). Pray for the provision of programmes in Makua, Sena and other languages of Mozambique. The shortage of radios and batteries limits the audience. A FEBA/TWR studio has been opened in Maputo.
c) **Films** have been highly successful evangelistic tools among refugees. The *Jesus* film is widely used in Portuguese and Shona, but Shangaan and Makua/Lomwe versions are an urgent prayer need. The Yao version was made available in 1992.
d) **GRn** have prepared messages in 21 of Mozambique's languages.
e) **Relief and development programmes** by Christian agencies are welcomed by the government because of widespread hunger and destitution. Half the population in 1992 was dependent on aid for survival. ACRIS, a Christian medical association formed in 1991, is taking over administration of hospitals and clinics and providing Christian medical personnel. **WV** and others have been engaged in supplying basic needs to many. **MAF** has several planes involved in these programmes, but flying conditions are tricky. Pray that these efforts may strengthen believers and stimulate evangelism.

August 22–23	
Asia	

Myanmar (Burma)
(The Union of Myanmar)

Area 677,000 sq.km. Basin and delta of the Irrawaddy River ringed by a horseshoe of high mountains that isolates the country from India, China and Thailand.

Population	Ann. Gr.	Density
1990 41,675,000	2.1 %	62/sq.km
1995 46,275,000	2.1 %	68/sq.km

Peoples:
Burmese (Bama) 63.1% The dominant people.
Minorities 19.3%, each with numerous sub-groups. Karen (15) 2,600,000; Arakanese (Rakhine) 1,875,000; Chin (4 languages, 40 dialects) 916,000; Kachin 625,000; Taungyo 265,000; Lisu 125,000; Intha 125,000; Lahu 125,000; Rawang 100,000; Akha 67,000.
Tai 8.4%. Shan (3) 2,920,000; Tai (3) 570,000.
Mon-Khmer 4.4%. Mon 792,000; Wa 558,000; Palaung 400,000.
Other 4.8%. Chinese 1,051,000; Rohingya 550,000; Bangladeshi/Indian 500,000; Malay 21,000; Moken 7,000.

Literacy 78%. **Official language:** Burmese. **All languages** 90. **Languages with Scriptures** 12Bi 10NT 16por.

Capital: Yangon (Rangoon) 2,674,000. Other major city: Mandalay 725,000. Urbanization 30%.

Economy: One of the world's poorest nations despite the wealth of its natural and human resources. Few countries have had their economies so effectively plundered and destroyed by those claiming to rule the land. The only successful export industries are illegal – opium and teak from the so-called Golden Triangle in the Lao and Thai border region. Underemployment and economic stagnation have become normal. Income/person $400 (1.8% of USA).

Politics: The country has known little peace since the Japanese invasion in 1942. Independent from Britain in 1947 as a Federal Union of seven districts and seven ethnic minority states. Insensitivity of the central government to the aspirations of ethnic minorities has provoked unrest and bitter ethnic wars in nine areas. Popular demands for democratic rule opened the way for elections in 1990. The opposition party won 85% of the seats, but the military regime refused to hand over power. In the subsequent repression, democracy leaders were arrested, exiled or killed.

Religion: There is freedom of religion. Buddhism is no longer the state religion, but it still has great influence in governmental affairs.

Buddhist 87.8%. Mainly Burmese, Shan, Mon and many Arakanese. There are reputed to be over 1 million pagodas (Buddhist temples) in the country. Many tribal groups are claimed to be Buddhist, but are more animist in practice.
Muslim 3.8%. Rohingya in Arakan; many fled to Bangladesh in 1991/2. Also some Bengalis.
Animist 1.1%.
Hindu 0.5%. Indians.
Non-religious/other 0.3%
Christian 6.5%. Affil 6.3%. Growth 5.1%. 95% from an animistic and 5% from a Buddhist background.
Protestant 5.2%. Affil 5.18%. Growth 6%.

Church	Cong	Members	Affiliated
Baptist Convention	3,417	477,723	1,500,000
Assemblies of God	750	82,319	123,000
Churches of Christ	1,000	51,889	104,000
Methodist Ch of M	215	43,004	71,700
Ch of Prov of M (Ang)	611	22,995	44,290
Presbyterian Ch of M	200	25,000	50,000
Lisu Christian Church	233	14,000	35,000
Seventh-day Adventist	139	12,798	32,000
Self-Supp Karen Bapt	105	10,500	21,000
Evang Free Ch of M	352	8,000	20,500
Mara Christian Ch	50	10,000	20,000
Christian Brethren	41	4,085	10,200
Chr Reformed Ch	65	3,420	5,700
Meth Ch of Union of M	25	3,104	5,540
All other (22)	657	59,322	115,746
Denominations (36)	7,860	828,159	2,158,676
Evangelicals 3.6% of pop		580,000	1,483,000
Pentecostal/charis 0.27%		66,000	113,000

Missionaries:
to Myanmar 20 (1:2,100,000 people) in 8 agencies.
from Myanmar 2,313 (1:930 Protestants) in 22 agencies 39frn 783xcul 1,530dom.
Roman Catholic 1.3%. Affil 1.15%. Growth 1.3%.

Catholic Ch	875	298,000	480,000

Missionaries:
to Myanmar 155 (1:274,000).
from Myanmar 25 (1973 figure).
Foreign Marginal 0.01%. Growth 6.2%.

Jehovah's Witnesses	86	1,763	6,080

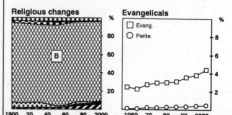

Religious changes

Evangelicals

1. **Three decades of military rule have brought the country to destitution.** Widespread despair and resentment followed the repression of democracy in 1990, but the courage of the leader of the main opposition party, Aung San Suu Kyi, was recognized in her award of the 1991 Nobel Peace Prize. Pray for an orderly transfer to a just and democratic government that will rebuild the country with both democratic and religious freedom.

2. **The isolation of the church in Myanmar has lasted for 30 years.** All Protestant and most Catholic missions were expelled in 1966. Praise God for foundations laid by Adoniram Judson, the famous American Baptist missionary, and those who followed – for on these foundations the Church has continued to grow and become a strong missionary-sending body, despite the limitations and isolation. Pray for the removal of restrictions on fellowship with Christians from other lands.

3. **Growth continues in the churches.** Christianity has been deeply rooted and has grown stronger in adversity. Many Christians are well educated and are in positions of responsibility all over the country. However, growth slowed during the '80s because of liberal theology and is now most marked in the smaller, newer denominations. The most growth has been among ethnic minorities – and now the majority of the Kachin, Mara, Rawang, Lisu, Lahu, Lushai, the northern Chin and 40% of the Karen are Christian. Pray that they may continue to evangelize every sub-group in their respective peoples and reach out to other unreached peoples and to the Bama majority.

4. **The challenges facing the Church in Myanmar:**
a) **Nominalism** among third- and fourth-generation Christians is widespread. Pray for revival.
b) **Liberal theology** in some of the larger seminaries is creating a church leadership that scorns evangelicals and the message of new birth. Pray that the Bible may retain its rightful place in the affections of both leaders and church members. There are a number of seminaries and Bible colleges in Burma; only the Evangelical Bible Seminary in Yangon is interdenominational.
c) **Most Christians are from minority groups** which are embroiled in military actions against the central government. Pray that this may not cause bitterness, hatred of other peoples, compromise of their faith, or blunting of a missions vision.
d) **Unity among believers** that transcends ethnic origins and denominational ties. Pray for the ministry of the **Myanmar Evangelical Christian Fellowship** in promoting this.
e) **Economic hardship** is so great that many Christians in the Golden Triangle area are tempted to grow opium.

5. **The spiritual fortress of Buddhism** has yet to be breached. Pray for the breaking down of the intellectual, philosophical and demonic strongholds where, as yet, the penetration of the gospel has been minimal. Buddhist revivalism is making the situation more difficult for religious minorities.

6. **Unreached peoples.**
a) **The Bama (Burmese) peoples.** There are only 40,000 Protestants among them. It is not easy for tribal believers to witness to them because of the years of mistrust, nor is it easy for the politically dominant Bama to receive the gospel from them without prejudice. Pray for conversions among this staunchly Buddhist people.
b) **The Buddhist ethnic minorities** – especially the sophisticated but resistant Shan (0.6% Christian), Palaung (0.96%), Mon (0.9%), Taungyo (0.5%), Mogh of Arakan (0.1%), Intha (0.1%) and other smaller peoples.
c) **The animist peoples** – Moken (Sea Gypsies), Southern Chin, Dai, Tiddim, Naga, the Wa and many others.
d) **The Chinese in the cities** who are more reached with 62 churches and 10,000 believers. However, only 2% of the total Chinese population professes to be Christian. Less reached are the Hakka and Cantonese in the cities and the Chinese settlements in the mountainous north where there are many refugees and illegal immigrants from Yunnan Province in China.
e) **The Chettiyars, an Indian minority**, who originated from the former French enclaves in India, and other Indians from many states in India. Among them are Muslims and Hindus. Very little outreach has been directed towards them.
f) **The Rohingya of Arakan**, Muslim descendants of Arabs, Moors, Moghuls and Bengalis who settled in Arakan 1,000 years ago. The Myanmar military regime has denied them citizenship, and in both 1978 and 1991 over 250,000 were driven from their homes and forced to become refugees in Bangladesh. There are no known Christians among them, and little Christian ministry is offered to them.

M

7. **The missionary vision of the Church in Myanmar** has been an inspiration to many around the world. Missionaries from ethnic minority churches have spread the gospel to many hitherto unreached peoples throughout the mountain fringes of the country. There are over 2,000 missionaries sent out to evangelize and plant churches in areas hitherto unreached – though many question this high figure. About a third of these are working cross-culturally. The largest agencies are: the Baptist Convention (1,400 workers), Assemblies of God (120), Presbyterian Church of Myanmar (58) and the Churches of Christ (35). Pray for this vision to be sustained and expanded and so lead to a harvest of souls being gathered into churches.

8. **Christian help ministries:**

a) **There is a shortage of Bibles** and all forms of Christian literature in Burmese and minority languages because of import restrictions. Some Burmese Bibles and NTs are being printed in Burma, but funding and supplies are difficult to obtain.

b) **Bible translation** is a major challenge. There are teams working on 13 NT translations, but at least 18 and possibly up to 62 languages need translation. Most of the work will need to be done by Myanmar translators. Pray for evangelical translators to be raised up to continue existing programmes and for an adequate survey of the remaining unmet need.

c) **Christian Radio** has been effective with 172 hours of broadcasting in 16 languages. Major radio agencies and their broadcasting languages: **FEBC** (Akha, Burmese, Jingpo, Chin (4), Karen (2), Lahu, Lisu, Lushai, Palaung, Rawang and Chan) and **TWR** (Burmese, English). Pray for the production of programmes and provision of equipment.

Namibia
(Southwest Africa)

August 24

Africa

Area 823,000 sq.km. A predominantly desert land. Most people live on the central plateau and the better-watered northern border regions adjoining Angola.

Population		Ann. Gr.	Density
1990	1,876,000	3.2 %	2/sq.km
1995	2,191,000	3.2 %	3/sq.km

Peoples: Five races, 11 groups speaking 21 languages.
Bantu peoples 70.7%.
  Ovambo 49.6% (6 groups) in north; politically dominant.
  Others 21.1%. Kavango 174,000; Herero 141,000; Caprivi peoples (4 groups) 70,000; Tswana 11,000.
Khoisan 7.7%. Nama 90,000; San (Bushmen – 5 groups) 38,000.
Damara 7.5%. 141,000. Speaking Nama.
European origin 4.7%. Afrikaner 30,000; German 20,000; English 6,000.
Mixed race 7%. Coloured 70,000; Rehoboth Basters 46,000. Speaking Afrikaans.
Other 2.4%.

Literacy 72% but much lower in practice. **Official language:** English, though few understand it, most speaking Afrikaans. **All languages** 21. **Indigenous languages with Scriptures** 6Bi 1NT 5por.

Capital: Windhoek 152,000. Urbanization 32%.

Economy: Mining of diamonds, uranium and other minerals is the chief source of income. Agriculture and fisheries are important. Economic prospects are good if the independent government can both make the distribution of wealth fair to all ethnic groups and avoid nepotism, corruption and heavy-handed state control. Unemployment around 50%. Public debt/person $1,000. Income/person $1,300 (6% of USA).

Politics: A German colony 1883–1915. Ruled by South Africa 1915–1990. Independence gained in 1990 after a long, costly war which severely disrupted the social and economic fabric of the country. The major party, SWAPO, renounced Marxism and has espoused multi-party democracy and a mixed economy. A member of the British Commonwealth.

Religion: Secular state with freedom of religion. Despite the high profile of Christian denominations, non-Christian religions are being granted similar opportunities in schools and in the media. Africa's only country with a Lutheran majority.

African traditional religions 5%.
Non-religious/other 3.9%.
Jews 0.1%. **Baha'i** 0.02%. **Muslims** 0.01%.
Christian 91%. Affil 63%. Growth 2.5%.
Protestant 67.9%. Affil 44.4%. Growth 1.3%.

Church	Cong	Members	Affiliated
United Evang Luth Ch	119	229,000	573,000
Anglican Ch	123	16,000	80,000
Evang Reformed (NGK)	88	27,500	44,000
Seventh-day Adventist	38	5,700	19,000
Rhenish Ch in N	10	5,700	19,000
Full Gosp Ch of God	44	6,509	13,000
African Meth Epis Ch	44	3,500	10,600
German Lutheran Ch	21	5,000	10,000
Baptist Union	37	3,084	7,710
Evangelical Bible Ch	25	2,500	5,000
United Congregational	33	2,160	3,600
All other (25)	416	28,315	53,370
Denominations (36)	998	336,768	834,280
Evangelicals 8.9 % of pop		78,200	166,000
Pentecostal/charis 2.5%		19,500	47,000

Missionaries:
to Namibia 177 (1:10,600 people) in 28 agencies.
from Namibia 26 (1:32,100 Protestants) in 3 agencies 22frn 22xcul 4dom.
Roman Catholic 16%. Affil 12.7%. Growth 6.1%.

Catholic Ch	125	143,000	238,000
Charismatic 0.03%		300	500

Missionaries to Namibia 281 (1:6,700 people).
Foreign Marginal 0.6%. Affil 0.55%.
Growth 3.9%.

Jehovah's Witnesses	15	644	2,150
All other (2)	28	4,130	8,186
Groups (3)	43	4,774	10,336

Indigenous Marginal 6.5%. Affil 5.3%.
Growth 5.4%.

Protestant Unity Ch	174	17,400	29,000
Ovambo Indep Ch	39	5,850	13,000
Herero Church	54	5,400	9,000
All other (97)	447	27,800	48,000
Denominations (100)	714	56,450	99,000

Religious changes   **Evangelicals**

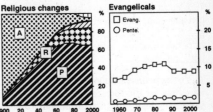

1. **Peace and independence have been gained,** but the preceding war left 90,000 dead, the problem of reintegration of the combatants and 50,000 refugees, and massive unemployment. Great maturity,

moderation and restraint is required of the government – pray for the leaders. The lasting reconciliation needed to heal the deep divisions within society and the church caused by apartheid can only be meaningfully gained through the forgiveness that the gospel brings. Pray that God's Word may continue to be freely preached and gladly embraced, and that it may become the foundation for the whole nation.

2. **Namibia has the highest percentage of Christians for any country in Africa.** The early labours of German and Finnish Lutheran and then Anglican missionaries gave birth to large denominations. The influence of liberal and then black theology eroded that spiritual heritage, and true discipleship and holy living are now in short supply. During the strife preceding independence the Church became deeply divided between those who supported armed struggle and those who did not. Pray for a unity, based on Scripture and bathed in the Spirit, that will bring reconciliation and revival.

3. **The evangelical witness has been strengthened** in recent years through new missionary thrusts by the **NGK, AEF/AIM, YWAM**, Baptists and Pentecostals to areas and peoples only superficially touched by the gospel. Charismatic fellowships – both independent and within many denominations – have brought new life and fervour. The Namibia Evangelical Fellowship, formed in 1989, already has 180 members. Pray for healthy and effective cooperation among believers in evangelism, deepening the spirituality of the churches and speaking out as a prophetic voice to the nation.

4. **Leadership training.** The major seminary in the country has been much influenced by black and liberation theology to the spiritual impoverishment of students going into the ministry. The result: accelerated nominalization of the churches, lowering of moral standards for leaders and followers, and reliance on occultism rather than the Lord. The two evangelical seminaries in Windhoek started by the **NGK** and **AEF/AIM** united in 1992 to form the Namibia Evangelical Theological Seminary. The Namibia School of Theology in Windhoek is run by the **AoG**. The latter has an innovative range of study programmes to provide advanced theological studies for pastoral work and special courses for African independent churches which are revolutionizing these often syncretistic denominations. There is a lower-level Bible school at Rundu (**AEF/AIM**). Pray for staff and students and for the spiritual impact to affect the nation for good. A missions vision is growing.

5. **Christian radio programmes** on the national network have had a remarkable impact counteracting liberal theology, restoring evangelicalism to mainline churches, and opening up resistant peoples such as the Herero to biblical teaching. Most of the 60 hours of religious programming every week has been evangelical in content, but since 1991 this has been reduced with mainline churches taking control of content. Media for Christ have permission to start a Christian radio station. Pray for the protection of this ministry.

6. **Pressing social issues** must be addressed by Christians; the government has not the resources for adequate answers to:
a) **Full rehabilitation of combatants** and returned exiles from the independence conflict. Widespread economic stagnation and unemployment hinder this. Deep emotional scars and sin need to be faced. The San provided the South African army with some of the best bush fighters in the war, but their lot since independence has been one of tragic neglect and marginalization.
b) **Ovamboland**, where nearly half the population lives. It is on the Angola border and was particularly affected by the war. There is virtually no paid employment in the area. Unrest continues. There was revival in the area a generation ago.
c) **The multiplying urban shanty towns,** as unemployed flock to the cities.

7. **African Independent Churches** are strong among the Herero, Basters, Damara and Nama, bringing compromise with the ancestor worship and witchcraft of their forebears and hostility to the gospel. Pray for the tactful ministry of the **NGK, AIM** and **AEF** missionaries and Namibian Christians by means of teaching, radio and help ministries which are bringing many leaders to a living faith in Christ.

8. **Young people** clamour for education, but the education system suffered damage and decline in war. Pray for the spreading work of **SU** in secondary schools and for an effective discipling and teaching ministry that will shape tomorrow's leaders.

9. **Missionaries in both older and newer missions** need acute sensitivity and understanding as they minister within the new context of independence. Major missions are: Finnish Lutheran (47 workers), **AEF/AIM** (35), **SBC** (12), NGK (12), **YWAM** (9). Major missionary-contributing nations:

South Africa (51), Finland (47), USA (37), Germany (14), UK (11).

10. **The less-reached peoples:**
a) **The San** (Bushmen) – much romanticized but in reality a suffering people, marginalized, often landless farm labourers or squatters and affected by alcoholism. They need spiritual and physical help. The **NGK** has laboured for years, and there are five congregations among the Heikum, Mbarakwena and Kung. There are six trained pastor among them.
b) **The peoples of the Kavango and Caprivi Strip** in the northeast – the Yeyi, Mafue, Subiya and Mbukushu. Many are animists or Adventists. **AEF/AIM** have planted four churches in the area.
c) **The Himba** or Kaokoveld Herero are 94% animist, and about 5% are at least nominally Christian (Lutheran and **NGK**).
d) **The German- and English-speaking communities** are more influenced by secular humanism. Over 60% of the Germans have no link with a church. Pray for the evangelical churches among them.

11. **Christian help ministries**
a) **Bible translation.** All the major languages have full Bibles. The Namibia Bible Society is involved in revisions of these and also the completion of the Mbukushu Bible and translation into one of the San languages.
b) **Christian literature** for local languages and away from main centres is scarce. Christian Mobile Literature, **SU** and **YWAM** all have bookstores.
c) **MAF** is commencing a flying ministry. Pray for its development as a service to the church.
d) **The *Jesus* film** sound-tracks have been prepared by Media For Christ in five Namibian languages. Pray for lasting results from the showing of this film.

Nauru
(The Republic of Nauru)

	See Pacific
	Pacific

N

Area 21 sq.km. A single coral island once covered with phosphate 300 km. west of Banaba, Kiribati.

Population		Ann. Gr.	Density
1990	9,000	2.4 %	425/sq.km
1995	10,000	2.1 %	472/sq.km

Peoples:
Indigenous Nauruan 58%. Micronesians.
Other Micronesians 24%. Kiribati 1,600; Marshallese, Kosraean.
Other 18%. Chinese 750; European 720; Tuvaluan 280; Fijian 180.

Literacy 99%. **Official languages:** Nauruan, English. **All languages** 9. **Languages with Scriptures** 6Bi 1por.

Economy: Nauruans are among the richest peoples in the world. Phosphate mining is the source of this wealth, which is being invested in shipping, air transport, insurance and offshore banking. The phosphate reserves will be exhausted by 1995 leaving 80% of the island uninhabitable. Public debt/person $3,645. Income/person $20,000 (95% of USA).

Politics: German rule 1888–1914. UN Trusteeship administered by Australia and Britain until independence in 1968. Nauruans resisted invitations for resettlement in 1964.

Religion: Freedom of religion.
Non-religious/other 4%.
Buddhist/Chinese religions 4%.
Baha'i 1.6%.
Christian 90.4%. Affil 84.2%. Growth 2.7%.
Protestant 60%. Affil 67.7%. Growth 2.8%.

Church	Cong	Members	Affiliated
Congregational Ch	18	1,580	3,500
Anglican Ch	2	122	270
All other (4)	4	640	1,433
Denominations (6)	24	2,342	5,203
Evangelicals 6.8% of pop		326	626
Pentecostal/charis 4.2%		220	390

Roman Catholic 30%. Affil 27.3%.
Growth 2.5%.

Catholic Ch	1	1,450	2,500

Missionaries to Nauru 14 (1:650 people).
Marginal 0.4%. Affil 0.22%. Growth −3.6%.

1. **The wealth of Nauruans** contrasts markedly with the relative poverty of surrounding island states. Materialism has sapped the people of spiritual concern. Church life is at a low ebb. There are few evangelical believers. This isolated island paradise of materialism, where everything has been free, may end with the exhaustion of the source of their wealth. There is low life-expectancy because fresh food cannot be grown locally. Pray that the shock may cause a turning to God.

2. **The only clearly evangelical witness** is through the small but growing Pentecostal Nauru Independent Church. The *Jesus* film is being used in both English and Nauruan.

3. **The workers attracted to Nauru** by phosphate mining have the instability of impermanence – many live in temporary accommodation, and little is done to evangelize them.

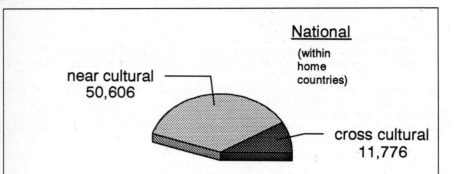

National
(within home countries)

near cultural
50,606

cross cultural
11,776

The World's Protestant Missionary Force in 1992

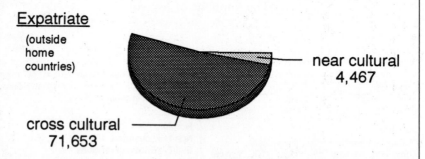

Expatriate
(outside home countries)

near cultural
4,467

cross cultural
71,653

Widely divergent understandings of what constitutes a missionary have complicated a unified tally of missionary numbers (see the World section and Appendices 2, 3 and 5). This gives a summary:

1. Of the 76,120 missionaries and their wives serving in other lands for one year or more, about 4,500 are working in their own or similar cultures – such as chaplains, pastors in emigrant communities (especially Chinese and Koreans) and teaching missionaries' children.

2. Of the 138,500 missionaries, 45% are serving within their own countries. Most in this subset are serving in a supportive role for overseas operations (North America, Europe) or are serving in a near-cultural situation. In some countries these figures are suspect and need verification.

Nepal

(Kingdom of Nepal)

August 25–26
Asia

Area 141,000 sq.km. A mountain-ringed Himalayan state between China (Tibet) and India.

Population		Ann. Gr.	Density
1990	18,195,000	2.1 %	129/sq.km
1995	20,188,000	2.1 %	143/sq.km

Very unevenly distributed. Most live on the overpopulated hills and in the Kathmandu valley; many are migrating to the Terai lowlands in the south.

Peoples:
Indo-Aryan 80.6%. 23 peoples in south and west in major groupings: Nepali 9,900,000; Maithili 2,260,000; Bhojpuri 1,370,000; Tharu 776,000; Awadhi 540,000; Rajbansi 94,000; Dhanwar 16,000.
Tibeto-Burman 18.8%. 54 peoples in north and east in major groupings: Tamang 946,000; Newari 775,000; Magar 491,000; Rai 400,000; Limbu 291,000; Gurung 180,000; Sunwar 34,000; Sherpa 29,000.
Other 0.6%. Santali 35,000; Munda 5,700; Indian, European.

Literacy 20%. **Official language:** Nepali, the first language of 55% of the population and widely spoken by the remainder. **All languages** 99. **Languages with Scriptures** 6Bi 4NT 16por.

Capital: Kathmandu 500,000. Urbanization 9%.

Economy: An isolated subsistence economy. The terrain is difficult and in habitable regions there is a high population density. The development of roads, agriculture and social projects has been slow. Main foreign exchange earners are tourism, agriculture and Gurkha soldiers. Heavily dependent on foreign aid and good relations with India. Income/person $170 (0.9% of USA), with 40% living below the poverty line.

Politics: Political isolation from the outside world ended in 1951. In 1962, the King assumed executive power in a government system with no political parties. Massive civil unrest in 1990 brought about extensive liberalizations, multi-party elections, and a victory for the Congress Party in 1991.

Religion: The world's only Hindu kingdom. Hinduism is the state religion. Since 1991 there has been freedom for all to profess and practise their religion, but not to proselytize.
Hindu 89%. Much intertwined in Buddhism and a strong, underlying animism. A complex caste system exists despite its illegality since 1963.
Buddhist 7%. Lamaistic Buddhism is dominant among the Tibeto-Burman peoples. The Buddha was born in Nepal.
Muslim 3.5%. Predominantly in the Terai.
Christian 0.58%. Growth 13.4%.
Protestant 0.56%. Growth 13.5%.

Church	Cong	Members	Affiliated
Indig Nepali Chs (3)*	1,000	50,000	105,000
All other (3)	30	2,015	3,400
Denominations (6)	1,030	52,015	108,400
Evangelicals 0.56% of pop		51,910	108,250
Pentecostal/charis 0.33%		30,000	63,000

* *Nepal Church Fellowship, Assemblies of God, Agape Fellowship.*

Missionaries:
to Nepal 582 (1:31,000 people) in 2 large intermission fellowships and a number of independent agencies.
from Nepal 155 (1:700 Protestants) in 3 agencies (mainly **CCC**) 2frn 2xcul 153dom.
Roman Catholic 0.02%. Growth 8%.

Catholic Ch	19	2,100	3,000

Missionaries to Nepal 118 (1:161,000 people).
Marginal 0.002%. Growth 16.1%.

All groups (2)	10	200	286

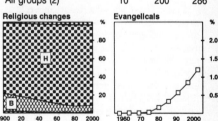

Religious changes

Evangelicals

1. **Praise the Lord for the growth of the Church in Nepal** in the midst of persecution. For years witness among Nepalis was only possible in north India, but in 1951 the first opening for the gospel came. In 1960 there were 25 baptized believers, in 1985 there were 25,000, and by 1991 there were 50,000 or more. In the new freedoms, churches are springing up all over the country, and worship buildings are being erected. Most ethnic groups and castes are represented in this movement to Christ – a great contrast to north India.

2. **Pray for political stability,** and for the government to be both just and fair in interpreting the ambiguously-worded constitutional guarantee of religious freedom.

3. **Official persecution ended** with the change of government in 1990, an amnesty for all religious prisoners and dismissal of outstanding court cases. Before then, between 300 and 400 pastors and believers suffered terms of imprisonment for either changing religion or baptizing new believers. Local pressure and persecution will probably continue as long as the churches multiply and grow. Pray that Christian leaders may be both wise and united in their response to the new social and political conditions.

4. **There are three major groupings of churches in Nepal** which are recognized and which cooperate in specific projects and goals – Nepal Church Fellowship, Assemblies of God and Agape Fellowship. The diversity of the body of Christ will surely increase as the Church grows. Pray for unity in that diversity to achieve the evangelization of their nation. One goal is to evangelize all 94 major towns – there were 66 still unreached in 1992.

5. **Freedom has opened the doors to a variety of sects and denominations** intent on building their own kingdoms. Pray that the church may be kept from error, ethnic division, doctrinal disputes and the beguilements of foreign money.

6. **Leadership is the critical bottleneck.** For years, no training institutions were allowed. This has rapidly changed with four Bible training institutions, the three larger being **AoG** (10-month courses), Nepal Bible Ashram (2-year courses), Nepal Theological Seminary (founded by Korean missionaries and aiming for accreditation to award degrees). Short-term and mobile training by **CCC, YWAM** and **OM** is also a vital contribution. The few full-time leaders must itinerate widely, and little consistent teaching can be given to the multiplying groups of believers. Pray for more leaders and effective teaching.

7. **The less-reached peoples.** Pray that an adequate survey of the country may stir the church to reach out to every community and people. Many peoples are only marginally reached, with very few believers. Of special note:
a) **Few of the Awadhi and Maithili** of the Terai lowlands on the Indian border have heard the gospel and these few have been unresponsive.
b) **The numerous Tibeto-Burman, and frequently Buddhist, peoples** are often isolated in mountain communities that have not been exposed to the gospel. There are a few dozen believers among the Sherpa of the Mt Everest area. Thousands are coming to Christ among the Tamangs.
c) **Tibetans**, both refugees (100,000) and those in the little "kingdom" of Mustang in the north need to be reached.
d) **The peoples of the far West** are mostly unreached.
e) **The Muslims** are untouched. Some claim that the Muslim population is twice as large as reported.
f) **University students** have been in the forefront of political change. There are 400 students linked to the ministry of **IFES** and staff workers ministering among them. **CCC** also have workers committed to student ministry.
g) **North India** is a spiritual desert and the church nominal and in decline. Pray that the Nepali church may become a means for evangelization there.

8. **Missions have played a remarkable role** in improving health, agriculture and education in a land hampered by disease, low life expectancy and illiteracy. Relationships with the government can be delicate, and visa applications are carefully screened. Pray for wisdom and grace for leaders and missionaries, and for the entry of called workers. Pray for radiance of life and continued freedom to share the gospel in all contacts with Nepalis as the medical workers minister in hospitals, dispensaries, leprosy and health programmes, and others in educational institutions. Many Nepali Christians owe their conversion to the loving practical ministries of expatriates and the fervent witness of local believers. Pray also that the missionaries may be a blessing to the Nepali believers. The **United Mission to Nepal** is the largest body with 300 missionaries representing 40 agencies from 18 countries. The **International Nepal Fellowship** has a further 121 (including workers from 10 seconding agencies and 12 nations) in the west of Nepal. Several other foreign and Indian agencies also work in the country.

9. **Nepalis outside the country:**
a) About seven million live in India, Bhutan and other lands, where numerous groups of Christians have come into being. There is a Nepali Bible school in Darjeeling, West Bengal.
b) **Gurkha soldiers** are world-renowned for their bravery. Thousands serve in the Indian and British armies, and other security forces in Hong Kong, Britain, Brunei, India, Singapore and other countries. All are recruited in Nepal and Darjeeling, many being Gurung, Magar, Limbu and Rai. Pray for outreach to these soldiers – some have been converted while in service and returned to spread the gospel in their villages.

10. **Other help ministries** for which prayer is requested:

a) **Bible translation** is in progress in 15 languages, but practical and spiritual obstacles to their completion are many, one being the low literacy and lack of literacy programmes in local languages. Pray for all who are committed to complete these projects. There are 72 languages without any Scriptures at all and 20 for which there is a definite need for translation.

b) **The Bible Society's** ministry has expanded after years of great difficulties. Distribution of Scriptures, especially the New Testament in Nepali, has mushroomed.

c) **Christian literature** can now be freely printed, imported without restriction, and distributed without censorship. Pray for the Bible Society bookshop in Kathmandu, **OM's** assiduous literature distribution teams, and **EHC's** ambitious house-to-house literature campaigns, the latter having covered 30% of the homes of Nepal. Pray that these burgeoning literature ministries may enhance spiritual and church growth.

d) **The Christian Arts Association of Nepal** seeks to promote the expression of the gospel through indigenous arts, drama, music and literature.

e) **Cassette tapes** are a useful evangelistic and teaching tool, but players are not widely available. **GRn** has recorded 88 languages and dialects.

f) **Bible Correspondence Courses** have long been a key means of outreach, but the programme lacks funds and personnel to continue effectively. The response since 1990 has overwhelmed the resources of the three correspondence schools.

g) **Radio** is under-utilized, and Christian broadcasts are little known in Nepal. Pray for effectiveness for the 15-minute daily broadcasts from **FEBA** Seychelles and a total of one hour a week from **TWR** Guam. There are reception and publicity problems which limit audiences.

h) **The _Jesus_ film** is being widely used in Nepali; pray for fruit.

N

August 27
Europe

Netherlands

(The Kingdom of the Netherlands)

Area 41,800 sq.km. Over 30% is below sea level.

Population	Ann. Gr.	Density
1990	15,010,000	0.45 %	*442/sq.km
1995	15,312,000	0.40 %	*450/sq.km

* Excluding inland water areas.

Peoples:
Indigenous 93.4%. Dutch 13,450,000; Frisian 525,000.
Ex-colonial 2.3%. Surinamese 225,000; Antilles/Aruban 60,000; Moluccan (Indonesia) 45,000; Javanese 7,500; other Indonesian 10,000.
Other 4.3%. Turks 192,000; other EC nations 151,000; North African (Arab, Berber) 160,000; Chinese 70,000; Kurds 40,000; (former) Yugoslavian 16,000; Cape Verdian 12,000; Gypsies 8,000; Vietnamese 8,000; Tamil 7,000; Iranian 5,000.

Literacy 95%. **Official languages:** Dutch (Nederlands), Frisian. English is in wide use.

Capital: Amsterdam 700,000. Seat of government: The Hague 700,000. Other major city: Rotterdam 1,100,000, the world's busiest seaport. Urbanization 88%.

Economy: Strong industrial, agricultural and trading economy. One of the world's leading exporting nations. Member of the EC. The generosity of the social security system has eroded the work-ethic; one-seventh of the working population is now registered unfit for work and dependent on the State. Unemployment 4.4%. Public debt/person $10,200. Income/person $16,010 (73% of USA).

Politics: Protestant-led revolt against Spain established Dutch independence in 1568 and led the country to become one of the world's great commercial nations. Stable, democratic, constitutional monarchy. There is a strong Christian coalition of Roman Catholic and Protestant parties; socialist parties are in decline.

Religion: Freedom of religion, but steady secularization and anti-discrimination legislation threaten Christian liberties in the name of tolerance.
Non-religious 30.6%. Mostly "secularized" Christians. Real percentage probably nearer 35%.
Muslim 2.7%. Turk, North African, Middle Eastern, Indonesian and some Surinamese.
Hindu 1%. Surinamese Asian and Sri Lankan Tamil.
Buddhist 0.9%. Chinese and others.
Jews 0.10%. Before World War II it was 1.4%.

Christian 64.7%. Growth 0%.
Protestant 28.3%. Growth −0.6%.

Church	Cong	Members	Affiliated
Neth Rfmd Ch (NHK)*	1,546	572,000	2,600,000
Reformed Ch (GK)*	1,000	470,000	784,000
Reformed (Liberated)	270	62,000	116,000
Rfmd Chs in N	165	42,000	84,000
Chr Reformed (CGK)	194	45,000	76,000
Mennonite Brotherhd.	150	18,000	32,700
Apostolic Ch	40	10,000	25,000
Lutheran Ch*	40	12,000	24,700
Baptist Union	86	12,676	21,100
Moluccan Chs (3)	85	9,900	18,000
Free Evang Chs	80	12,000	16,000
Assoc of Free Ev Congs	46	7,302	13,500
Salvation Army	89	12,000	12,000
F'ship of Pente Chs (AoG)	65	7,000	11,700
All other (95)	1,506	178,747	323,117
Denominations (111)	5,362	1,470,625	4,157,817
Evangelicals 5.1% of pop		372,000	755,000
Pentecostal/charis 2.24%		154,000	336,000

[* These churches unite in 1994.]
Missionaries:
from Netherlands 1,187 [many agency figures for 1986 only].
to Netherlands 363 (1:41,300 people) in 45 agencies.
Roman Catholic 35.6%. Growth 0.3%.

Catholic Ch	1,674	3,720,000	5,320,000
Charismatic 0.7%.		75,000	106,000

Missionaries:
from Netherlands est. 5,000 (1:1,100 Catholics).
to Netherlands 1,559 (1973 figure).
Orthodox 0.06%. Growth 0.4%.

Denominations (6)	48	6,000	8,570

Marginal 0.8%. Growth 1%.

Jehovah's Witnesses	329	31,359	53,200
Mormons	33	4,760	6,800
All other (40)	347	34,530	58,071
All groups (42)	709	70,649	118,071

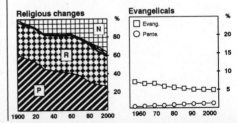

Religious changes

Evangelicals
☐ Evang.
○ Pente.

1. **The Netherlands has two major claims to fame:**
a) **A glorious history as a Christian nation** – its fight for religious freedom, ministry to refugees and Jews, and overseas missions.
   b) **A decadent present as a secular society** that has turned its back on its past. The dramatic decline in the number of Christians in this generation and the openly permissive society that is replacing it with few restrictions on drugs, deviant life styles, prostitution, homosexuality, abortion and euthanasia has led to the deterioration. Pray for revival, renewal of Christian traditions and structures, a return to biblical standards and church planting among ethnic minorities.

2. **The larger Protestant churches** have either damaged their credibility by their deadening traditionalism, formalism and theological disputes or abandoned their biblical vision for evangelism and missions in favour of free-thinking liberalism, pluralism and secularism. As a result they have declined from 61% of the population in 1900 to 25% in 1990. There is no prophetic voice to speak against the tide of New Age thinking, the occult, eastern and western cults, militant feminism and immorality, nor a message to touch the real needs of young people today. Dialogue and compromise are prized more than soul-winning. Some of the older free churches have also lost much of their vitality. Yet there are many congregations that hold a more reformed and biblical position in most mainline denominations; the charismatic renewal movement has had a positive impact among traditional reformed pastors.

3. **The Roman Catholic Church** is likewise in decline with fewer members, priests and missionaries every year. The liberal wing is opposed by the hierarchy but has a strong influence in bending the Church into a liberal direction. However, the growing charismatic and evangelical movements within the Church, with a widespread Bible study and home prayer cell network, are cause for thanksgiving to God. The south of the country is more strongly Catholic with relatively few Protestant evangelical groups.

4. **Signs of hope for spiritual awakening** are nevertheless there. For this praise God! Home cell groups, new free churches, and great international congresses hosted by the Netherlands have multiplied. Innovative outreach to young people on the streets, ministry to prostitutes and drug addicts, and the success of evangelical Christian broadcasting on the national radio and TV networks are encouraging.

5. **Dutch Christians** need prayer for:
a) **A revitalization of the church's structures and leadership** to make them relevant to today's generation. Too much of vital Christianity has had to operate outside the present system in a multiplicity of agencies. There is not yet enough church planting among those alienated from traditional Christianity, many having no real concept of the gospel.
   b) **Spiritual unity** with a drawing together of denominations, institutions, agencies and ethnic groups with a single vision for reaching the nation and the world, and the willingness to financially support this with generosity. Pray for the **Evangelical Alliance**, **Evangelical Missionary Alliance**, and the **Lausanne** and the **AD2000** Movements in their catalytic work to bring this about. The evangelical world is fragmented and individualistic in orientation.
   c) **Christian media.** Almost unique in Europe is the large input of Christians into the national radio and TV networks. *Evangelische Omroep* (EO), an interdenominational evangelical broadcasting organization, has become a strong binding factor for Christians and has given life and hope to non-Christians. EO has 13 hours of air time on TV and 62 hours on radio every week. Pray that the biblical approach may not be compromised by liberal or worldly trends, yet be effective in reaching heart needs with relevant programming and in a vocabulary non-Christians will understand.
   d) **Theological training** that is biblical and relates to both churches and overseas missions. This balance is often missed. Pray for more students and a higher proportion committed to missions.
   e) **Christian literature:** there are over 120 Christian bookshops, and a growing variety of good literature and good Bible versions. **CLC** has three shops and a bookmobile.

6. **Young people's ministry** has become harder through indifference and an interest in non-Christian religious experiences. Christianity is perceived as no longer relevant. Pray for:
a) **Parents** to see the need to witness to their children.
b) **Schools** to provide adequate Christian education.
c) **Churches to gain the interest of young people** by addressing their felt needs.
d) Street evangelism, coffee bars, camps and outreach to drug addicts through *Jong en Vrij*, **YWAM**, Agapé (**CCC**) and **YFC**.

e) **University students** who live in a high-pressure ideological battle zone where it is hard to stand for Jesus. Pray for **Navigator** and **IFES** groups on many campuses. About 1,000 students are affiliated to groups linked with the latter.

f) **A challenge to missions and outreach** that will give young people a cause for which to live and die. The cost of commitment is too high for most. Triennial Europe-wide missions conferences hosted in the Netherlands have had a significant impact on young people.

7. **Dutch missions,** long eclipsed, are gaining new workers and increased interest. The EMA has grown to a membership of 80 agencies. A better understanding of unreached peoples and of the need of the former Communist world and the Middle East has increased recruitment and prayer. Many Dutch missionaries are involved in Bible translation and evangelical aid programmes.

8. **The spiritually needy and less-reached.**

a) **The cities are highly secularized.** Amsterdam has become a byword for godlessness. Over half the population claims no religious affiliation. The large drop-out population and the moral collapse hamper witness to the unconverted. Over 75% of the Arab, Asian and Southern Europe migrant population lives in Amsterdam, Rotterdam, The Hague and Utrecht. A number of churches and agencies have ministry to these sections of the community, but most such work is on a small scale. Notable are the efforts of international movements such as **YWAM**, Agape Movement (**CCC**), **YFC** and **OM**, as well as Dutch agencies. Pray for the turning of the tide of permissiveness in these cities.

b) **The Muslim minority.** Moroccans and Turks are the largest communities. All are "guest workers" and have many problems with housing and unemployment. Specialized efforts and committed friendship are needed to reach them. Pray for those seeking to reach them, such as SVEOM, Gospel for Guests, **YWAM** in Amsterdam, and various churches. Only a few have come to the Lord, and lack of nurture and care means a high casualty rate. There are two groups of Turkish believers and several other small fellowships for other minorities.

c) **Hindus.** Little has been done to evangelize Suriname Asians, most of whom are Hindu. **IMI** has launched an outreach to them.

d) **Over 139 language groups** are represented among the guest workers, refugees and migrants. Pray that they may hear the gospel rather than be swallowed up in materialism and sin. Specialized efforts for many of these groups are needed – especially the Chinese (nine known churches), Tamil, Iranian, Vietnamese and Southern Europeans. Pray that churches may "adopt" some of these peoples and enter into partnership plans for their evangelization.

N

Netherlands Antilles

Include with Aruba
Caribbean

Area 800 sq.km. Two larger, barren islands, Curaçao and Bonaire off the coast of Venezuela, and two and a half smaller islands in the Leeward islands 800 km. to the northeast. St Maarten is shared with France. In 1986, Aruba withdrew from the Netherlands Antilles as an autonomous territory of the Netherlands.

Population	Ann. Gr.	Density
1990	183,000	0.90 %	229/sq.km
1995	185,000	0.22 %	231/sq.km

Peoples:
Afro-Caribbean/Creole 91.8%. A blend of African, Amerindian, Dutch, Surinamer and 40 other nationalities.
European 6.1%. Mainly Dutch.
Other 2.1%. Chinese, Jews, Arabs.

Literacy 95%. **Official language:** Dutch. **Common languages:** Papiamento (84% of the population) in the southern two islands, English in the northern two and a half islands.

Capital: Willemstad 139,000. Urbanization 92%.

Economy: Heavily dependent on extensive oil refining industries and tourism, but made wealthy thereby. The closure of most of the refineries during 1983–85 created a major economic crisis for the territory. Income/person $7,060 (36% of USA).

Politics: Integral part of Kingdom of Netherlands with domestic autonomy and parliamentary democratic government. Relationships with the mother country and between the islands is a matter of intense political debate.

Religion:
Non-religious/other 5%.
Jewish 0.3%. **Muslim** 0.2%.
Christian 94.5%. Growth 0.8%.
Protestant 12.9% Growth 1.9%.

Church	Cong	Members	Affiliated
Anglican Ch	1	840	2,400
Evangelical Ch	12	472	1,200
Assemblies of God	15	394	1,160
All other (45)	88	7,546	18,830
Denominations (48)	116	9,252	23,590
Evangelicals 4.7% of pop		4,000	8,600
Pentecostals/charis 0.85%		600	1,560

Missionaries to Neth Antilles 145 (1:1,260 people) in 11 agencies, half being **TWR** workers on Bonaire.
Roman Catholic 78.3%. Affil. 78.1%.
Growth 0.4%.

Catholic Ch	24	84,400	143,000

Missionaries to Neth Antilles 259 (1:706 people).
Marginal 3.3%. Affil 3.2%. Growth 7.3%.

Jehovah's Witnesses	26	2,085	5,960

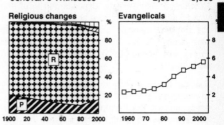

Religious changes / Evangelicals

1. **Openness to the gospel has not resulted in a great harvest.** Moral laxity, superstition, and the growing marginal sects show how few understand the message of salvation. Major church-planting missions: **TEAM** (21 workers), **SBC** (10), **AoG** (6).

2. **Evangelical witness has progressed slowly.** A vital, growing church in every island is a target for prayer. **TEAM** has concentrated on evangelism and church planting among the Papiamento-speaking majority, and the 12 daughter churches are a large part of the evangelical witness.

3. **The Old Testament in Papiamento** was completed by **TEAM** missionaries in 1990, and the revised New Testament in 1993. Little Christian literature is available in this language. Pray for the ministry of the TEAM bookshop on Curaçao.

4. **Christian radio** is a significant ministry which involves most of the Protestant missionary force. **TEAM** concentrates on local Papiamento broadcasts from Radio Victoria, and **TWR** on Latin America and the world from their powerful station on Bonaire. Pray for the relatively isolated TWR missionary community of 76 expatriate workers on Bonaire occupied with the practical drudgery of maintaining the radio ministry, often with little visible encouragement, yet much fruit.

Include with French Guiana
Pacific

New Caledonia

(Territory of New Caledonia and Dependencies)

Area 18,700 sq.km. One large 400 km-long island, the Loyalty Islands, and other smaller coral islands 1,400 km. northeast of Australia.

Population		Ann. Gr.	Density
1990	165,000	1.5 %	9/sq.km
1995	178,000	1.5 %	10/sq.km

Peoples:
Indigenous (Kanak) 45%. Melanesian (27 languages) 73,600; Polynesian (1) 3,000.
Other Pacific islanders 13%. Wallisian 10,200; Futunan 3,000; Vanuatan 2,400; Tahitian 2,100.
European 37%. Caledoche (settlers) and metropolitan French.
Asian 5%. Javanese 5,500; Vietnamese 2,500; Chinese 500.

Literacy 89%. **Official language:** French. **All languages** 41. **Languages with Scriptures** 4Bi 1NT 4por.

Capital: Nouméa 88,000. Urbanization 61%.

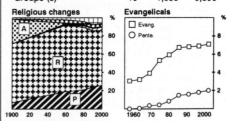

Economy: Rich mineral deposits (40% of the world's nickel reserves) have brought prosperity to the immigrant peoples, but little of the wealth has percolated through to the indigenous peoples. Public debt/person $1,900. Income/person $10,140 (48% of USA).

Politics: French Colony in 1853; overseas territory of France since 1946. Exploitation of and discrimination against the Kanaks provoked an independence movement which led to violence in 1985. Agreement reached for three regional governments in 1988 and a commitment to a referendum on independence in 1998.

Religion: Freedom of religion in an increasingly secularized society. The majority of the non-

Melanesian population has no meaningful contact with a church.
Non-religious/other 7.6%. Mainly French.
Muslim 3.8%. **Baha'i** 0.4%. **Buddhist** 0.2%.
Christian 88%. Nominal 9%. Affil 79%. Gro 0.6%.
Protestant 23.6%. Affil 19.7%. Growth 0.1%.

Church	Cong	Members	Affiliated
Autonomous Evang Chs	121	4,600	20,000
Free Evangelical Ch	70	3,520	8,800
Assemblies of God	35	1,300	2,600
Seventh-day Adventist	4	339	800
All other (5)	5	156	260
Denominations (9)	235	9,915	32,460
Evangelicals 6.8% of pop		4,293	11,246
Pentecostal/charis 1.64%		1,350	2,700

Missionaries:
to New Caledonia 51 (1:3,200 people) in 7 agencies.
from New Caledonia 2 (1:16,000 Protestants) in one agency.
Roman Catholic 62%. Affil 57%. Growth 0.5%.

Catholic Ch	167	40,000	94,000

Missionaries:
to New Caledonia 205 (1:800 people).
from New Caledonia 6 (1973 figure).
Marginal 2.4%. Affil 2.36%. Growth 9.6%.

Jehovah's Witnesses	11	1,165	2,840
Mormons	4	280	700
Groups (3)	19	1,638	3,890

1. **The political future** is cause for concern. The violence of the '80s could recur. The population is fairly evenly divided between those desiring independence and those who desire to retain links with France.

2. **The Melanesians** are Christianized, and nearly every village has a Catholic or a Protestant Church. However, for the vast majority, Christianity is a veneer over the underlying demonic influences and bondages. Even some evangelical pastors fail to discern the difference between demon-influenced practices and the gospel. Many of the leaders in the main Protestant churches are influenced by liberation theology, though in recent years the Free Evangelical Church has become more evangelical. Pray that these churches may discover the power of the gospel and see many delivered from the power of the evil one. Praise God that there are significant revivals taking place in Free Church congregations.

3. **Missions.** The first missionary was a Rarotongan from the Cook Islands. Later LMS work was taken over by the PEMS. The entry of the **AoG** and a clear preaching of the gospel was controversial. Their ministry has affected the non-Kanak urban population more than the indigenous Kanaks. Pray for expatriate missions into the churches to be fruitful and blessed of God.

4. **Less reached-peoples:**
a) **The 6,000 Muslims** of Javanese and Arab descent retain their religion, but are losing their languages. Little has been done to reach them.
b) **Polynesian Islanders** retain their own culture and language. There are a few evangelical believers among the Wallisians and Futunans; most are traditionally Catholic.
c) **The Caledoche** are descendants of convicts and settlers who arrived in the last century. Most live in and around Nouméa. They are fairly closed to outside influence, and there are very few evangelical believers among them. The **AoG** have won some to Jesus.
d) **The Metropolitan French** are usually only in the country for a few years as bureaucrats or business people. Very few have any interest in or contact with a church during their sojourn.

5. **Bible translation** is a major challenge. Through the encouragement of **WBT-SIL**, the indigenous *Association Calédonienne de Linguistique et de Traduction* was formed. There are four SIL couples seconded to the ACLT. Translation work is under way in six languages, but several others definitely require translation teams. Pray that the Scriptures may root the gospel in each ethnic group.

N

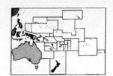

August 28	*New Zealand*
Pacific	

Area 268,000 sq.km. Two main mountainous islands 1,800 km. southeast of Australia.

Population	Ann. Gr.	Density
1990	3,379,000	0.80 %	13/sq.km
1995	3,507,000	0.75 %	13/sq.km

75% of population lives on the North Island.

Peoples:
European 73.8% of which 4.1% are not of English-speaking origin.
Polynesian 13.2%. Indigenous Maori 321,400; immigrant Pacific Islanders 124,000 (Samoan, Tongan, Cook Islanders, Niue Islanders, etc.).
Euro-Polynesian 5.6%.
Other 7.4%. Chinese 36,600; Indian 27,000; Arab 4,000; Japanese 3,000.

Literacy 99%. **Official language:** English; Maori increasingly prominent. **All languages** 17, two of which are indigenous.

Capital: Wellington 325,000. Largest city: Auckland 885,000. Urbanization 84%.

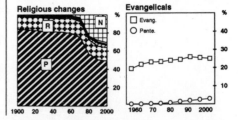

Economy: Highly efficient export-oriented agricultural industry, but worldwide subsidized overproduction forced the economy into recession. Recovery being painfully won by dramatic deregulations and partial dismantling of the welfare state. Over 10% of the work force emigrated to Australia in the '80s. Public debt/person $5,700. Income/person $11,800 (56% of USA).

Politics: The Waitangi Treaty between the Maori and British in 1840 granted the latter the right to settle in exchange for guarantees of Maori land and natural resources. The present dispute is concerning the degree of sovereignty the treaty granted the British. Independent of Britain in 1907. A stable parliamentary democracy with the British Monarch as head of state.

Religion: Freedom of religion; no established church.
Non-religious/other 28.7%.
Other religions 1.5%. Hindu 17,700; Buddhist 12,700; Muslim 5,800; Jews 3,120; Baha'i 2,900.
Christian 69.9%. Growth 1%.
  Protestant 50.3%. Growth 0.2%.

Church	Cong	Members	Affiliated
Anglican Ch	807	102,000	732,048
Presbyterian Ch	706	60,000	540,675
Methodist Ch	197	20,800	138,705
Baptist Union	217	24,600	70,155
Christian Brethren	240	13,200	20,337
Salvation Army	102	6,400	19,992
Assemblies of God	149	10,300	17,226
Seventh-day Adventist	87	9,750	13,005
Apostolic Ch	74	3,740	6,804
Elim Pentecostal Ch	47	1,650	2,352
Assoc Chs of Christ	39	760	1,767
All other (60)	1,065	84,222	136,236
Denominations (71)	3,730	337,422	1,699,302
Evangelicals 25.6% of pop		196,000	864,000
Pentecostal/charis 7.6%		88,000	257,000

Missionaries:
  from New Zealand 1,701 (1:1,000 Protestants) in 77 agencies 1,333frn 1,112xcul 589dom.
  to New Zealand 221 (1:15,300 people) in 37 agencies.
Roman Catholic 14.8%. Growth 1.39%.

Catholic Ch	344	334,000	498,612
Charismatic 0.57%		13,000	19,000

Missionaries:
  from New Zealand 292 (1:1,650 Catholics).
  to New Zealand 553 (1:6,100 people).
Orthodox 0.13%. Growth 1.2%.

Denominations (3)	5	2,810	4,260

Foreign Marginal 3%. Growth 9.8%.

Mormons	158	50,900	76,000
Jehovah's Witnesses	151	11,515	19,182
All other (14)	42	2,991	5,002
All groups (16)	351	65,406	100,184

Indigenous Marginal 1.7%. Growth 3.2%.

Ratana Church	143	28,600	47,595
Ringatu	32	4,830	8,052
All groups (2)	175	33,430	55,647

1. **Praise God for the evident moving of the Spirit in the churches since the '60s.** Charismatic renewal brought widespread changes – a newness of worship, freedom in fellowship across denominational lines and a reversal of the 70-year decline in the number of committed Christians. Every denomination has been affected by the ongoing revival. Theologically liberal congregations have decreased in numbers, and evangelical Christians have multiplied in the Anglican and

Presbyterian churches. The most dramatic growth has been in the indigenous charismatic groups, Pentecostal denominations and the Baptist Union.

2. **New Zealanders have increasingly turned away from God and to secularism**, a trend that continues. Yet economic shock, social upheavals, Maori nationalism and increased immigration of Polynesians and Asians have shaken people out of the complacency of the '60s and prepared them to receive the gospel. Pray that Christians may live lives that commend the truth to an unbelieving and disturbed generation, and also courageously testify to them.

3. **Revival** has not solved all spiritual problems! It has virtually stopped the decline in overall membership, but winning back the outsiders must also be achieved. Pray for:
a) A return to **expository preaching and solid Christian teaching** in churches and Bible schools after the emotion and excitement of recent years, yet at no sacrifice of spiritual fervour.
b) A wise application of **NT church growth principles** to conserve the fruit, stabilize congregational leadership and expand evangelistic outreach.
c) **The implementation of the vision of the New Zealand DAWN movement** launched in 1987 following extensive research. This will mean commitment to double church attendance to 500,000 and increase congregations from 2,962 to 4,100 by the year 2000. The Baptists have targeted 40,000 members in 300 churches by that date. Pray that pastors and congregations may rise up in faith to take these advances by faith and action.

4. **The missions vision of the New Zealand Church is an example to many other lands.** A new surge of interest has followed the *Perspectives on the World Christian Movement* courses, and many new candidates for missions are coming forward. Pray for these and their full preparation for cross-cultural service; there are 19 residential Protestant Bible schools and eight part-time; the best known is the Bible College of New Zealand in Auckland. Pray also for this vision to be nurtured by pastors and embraced by whole congregations.

5. **A Maori cultural revival** and demands for compensation under the 1840 Treaty have shocked the white majority. The Maori resent their cultural dislocation which has put them at a social disadvantage – high unemployment, relative poverty, crime, youth gangs, welfare needs are the result. Many are Christian in name, but the Church is not indigenous enough and often in non-Maori hands. Syncretic sects such as Ringatu and Ratana as well as the Mormons have gained a large following. Pray that Maoris may find their full cultural blossoming in embracing the fullness of the gospel.

N

6. **New Zealand's increasing diversity** in cultures presents new challenges:
a) **Polynesians** have immigrated to NZ seeking employment. Large communities of Samoans, Tongans and islanders from the NZ-administered Cook, Tokelau and Niue Islands live in the cities. Auckland has the largest Polynesian population of any city in the world with over 100,000. The Congregational and other Pacific Island churches have high attendances but a low level of commitment. Pray that the Holy Spirit may break through the barriers of nominalism, tradition and pride to bring a revival of the knowledge of God and a zeal for evangelism.
b) **Indians** are increasing in numbers, especially from Fiji since the 1987 coup. There is some outreach, but there is a lack of Indian Christian leadership.
c) **Chinese** immigrants have a long history in New Zealand. Recently immigration has increased, mainly from Hong Kong. Although 75% claim to be "Christian", only 12% of these attend church regularly. There are about 15 churches with a large Chinese membership. May they be challenged to daring discipleship and missions.
d) **Southeast Asian refugees and the Japanese community** are predominantly Buddhist. Attempts have been made to reach them and there is one Japanese congregation in Auckland.
e) **The 6,000 Jews** have one **CWI** couple seeking to reach them.
f) **Muslim** outreach is being developed.

7. **Christian supportive agencies** are numerous and influential – **YWAM**, **ICF** and TSCF (**IFES**), Navigators and **YFC** among youth, **World Vision**, Radio RHEMA with its wide coverage and large listenership, Open Air Campaigners and others are all deserving of prayer as they seek to strengthen the church and enable it to reach out to the lost.

August 29	# Nicaragua
Latin America	(Republic of Nicaragua)

Area 130,000 sq.km. The largest of the Central American republics; poor communications with the sparsely populated eastern half of the country.

Population	Ann. Gr.	Density
1990	3,871,000	3.4 %	30/sq.km
1995	4,540,000	3.2 %	36/sq.km

Most live in the Pacific lowlands and adjacent highlands.

Peoples:
Spanish-speaking 83%. Ladino (Eurindian) 68%, European 14%, Amerindian 1%. Three Hispanicized Amerindian peoples: Matagalpa 20,000; Monimbo 10,000; Subtiaba 5,000.
English/Creole-speaking 12%. African and Afro-Indian 390,000; Black Carib 8,000; Rama (Amerindian) 1,900.
Amerindian dialects 4.7%. Miskito 160,000; Sumo 7,000.
Other 0.3%. Chinese 7,000; North American 1,500; Arab 400; etc.

Literacy 74%. **Official language:** Spanish. English-speaking communities on Atlantic coast. **All languages** 7. **Languages with Scriptures** 1Bi 2NT.

Capital: Managua 875,000. Urbanization 60%.

Economy: Potentially rich, fertile land with low population density, but brought to destitution by the depredations of dictatorships and revolutionary wars. The combined effects of the imposition of Marxist economic policies and the crippling confrontation with the USA during the '80s led to hyperinflation and collapse in 1990 and a painfully slow recovery. The democratic government has not the means to fulfil promises to the former combatants. Inflation has been slowed, but at a big social cost. Unemployment 40–50%. Public debt/person $1,860. Income/ person $840 (3.8% of USA).

Politics: Independent republic since 1838. The rather brutal and corrupt Somoza dictatorship ended in 1979 after a bitter civil war. The Sandinista government imposed Marxist ideology and economic principles despite much internal resistance and US-supported subversion from surrounding lands. Economic distress and Sandinista arrogance unexpectedly lost them the 1990 election. President Violeta Chamorro has sought to hold a balance between the angry right and obstructionist Sandinista left, the latter still controlling the armed forces, police and unions. The fragile peace could break down into civil war once more.

Religion: Secular state with some abuses of religious freedom under the Sandinista government. Complete religious freedom since 1990.
Non-religious/other 3%
Christian 97%. Nom 6%. Affil 91%. Growth 3.3%.
Protestant 17.31%. Growth 7.8%.

Church	Cong	Members	Affiliated
Assemblies of God	1,370	40,000	100,000
Apostolic Ch of Faith	263	21,000	80,800
Seventh-day Adventist	48	27,000	51,900
Ch of God (Cleveland)	281	14,121	40,300
Moravian Ch	135	12,100	36,596
Ch of God of Prophecy	177	9,500	23,800
National Bapt Conv	79	8,000	20,000
Good Samaritan Bapt	100	8,000	20,000
International Bapt Ch	42	6,000	9,380
Brethren in Christ	55	2,360	7,870
Ch of the Nazarene	75	4,166	6,428
Fed of Central American Chs (CAMI)	70	2,900	5,800
All other (148)	1,821	99,786	267,354
Denominations (160)	4,516	254,933	670,228
Evangelicals 15.1% of pop		219,000	585,000
Pentecostal/charis 11%		155,000	424,000

Missionaries
to Nicaragua 108 (1:35,800 people) in 34 agencies
from Nicaragua 34 (1:19,700 Protestants) in 3 agencies 9frn 9xcul 25dom.
Roman Catholic 79.4%. Affil 73.4%. Growth 2.3%

Catholic Church (RC)	690	1,610,000	3,031,000
Doubly Counted		−95,000	−190,000
Total	690	1,515,000	2,841,000
Charismatics 1%		50,000	90,000

Missionaries:
to Nicaragua 36 (1:108,000 people).
from Nicaragua 70 (1973)(1:41,000 Catholics).
Marginal 0.28%. Growth 0.1%.

Jehovah's Witnesses	104	4,900	8,910
All other (1)	9	1,110	2,110
All groups (2)	113	6,010	11,010

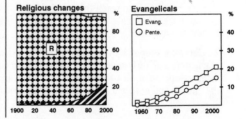

Religious changes

Evangelicals

1. **Nicaragua is a deeply divided nation.** The traumatic events of the past 20 years have divided politicians, unions, churches and families. Pray for the government as it seeks to reconcile the

opposing factions, set right the gross injustices of past regimes and reintegrate the 50% of the population that became refugees during the war. Failure could lead to civil war and a new totalitarianism of the right or the left. The next elections are due in 1996.

2. **Suffering has brought a turning to God of remarkable proportions.** God used many means:
a) **Earthquakes and volcanoes** – the destruction of Managua in 1972 brought churches and agencies together for evangelism and multiplied conversions.
b) **Evangelism** through Evangelism in Depth, mass crusades, and church outreach.
c) **The violence and despair** of years of war, the failure of the revolution of 1979 and the 1990 elections to bring improvements.
Evangelicals grew from 1.9% in 1960 to 7% in 1980 and at least 15% in 1990. Some claim that Evangelicals may now be 20–30% of the population.

3. **Lack of spiritual unity is the major crisis facing the church.** The battle areas:
a) **Theology.** Liberation theology has divided Catholics and a number of Protestant denominations. Pray for a healthy biblical balance in teaching and action.
b) **Relationships to the state** – cooperation or separation? Both Catholics and Protestants were divided on the issue. There are two major groupings within the Protestant camp – CEPAD (The Evangelical Committee for Relief and Development) which cooperated with the Sandinistas and CNPEN (The Council of Evangelical Pastors) which stressed independence from any government. Several other alliances of pastors were formed in 1992. Pray for discernment, restraint and love for believers in the confusion, and the wise use of their enhanced voting power. There are some committed believers in the government.
c) **Teaching on the Holy Spirit.** Catholics are split between the conservative traditionalists and more evangelical charismatics. Protestants are likewise divided, though Pentecostals and charismatics have grown steadily from 20% to 75% of all Protestants.

4. **Leadership for the churches.** The number of churches has increased beyond Nicaragua's capacity to train new leaders. Over 70% of the pastors have had little or no formal training. Most are very poor, receiving inadequate support from their congregations. Pray for the eight Bible schools and a variety of TEE and mobile training schemes in operation. **YWAM** plans on setting up a Discipleship Training School for Christian workers and developing a University of the Nations. Pray for existing leadership in a time of harvest and also for protection from pride, power struggles, doctrinal excess and heresy.

5. **Vision for the future.** There is much for the church to do:
a) **Vision 2000** – many churches and agencies are working together to ensure that there are churches planted in every town and village during this decade. The **AoG**, **CAMI** and the **Baptists** have set bold advance goals for this period.
b) **Missions vision** – in its infancy; delayed by the political and economic setbacks. **YWAM** is being used of God to stimulate this.
c) **Revival** – especially among the English/Creole and Miskito Christians on the east coast where there is much nominalism in the churches.

6. **Christian care for the needy** with two-thirds of the people living in poverty. The major challenges for care are:
a) The **returning refugees** – many are destitute, and their homes and lands stolen from them.
b) The **urban poor** facing high unemployment and inflation with meagre prospects of early improvement.
c) The **sick** – the health care service has almost collapsed.

7. **The less-evangelized sections of the population:**
a) **Young people** who have grown up in the midst of war, hatred and Marxist propaganda. Pray that Christian ministry among young people and children might not only win them to Christ but also instil Christian moral, social and work standards.
b) **The Sandinista and "Contra" soldiers** who are frustrated by having lost loved ones, disillusioned and often landless. They need those who can minister love and spiritual healing after the bitter war with many atrocities meted out to opponents and innocent civilians alike.
c) **The Hispanicized Indians.** These are nominally Catholic, and few active evangelical congregations exist among them.
d) **The Black Caribs,** still largely animist, though there are churches among them.

8. **The expatriate missionary force** was greatly reduced in the '80s. Some are now returning. Pray for good sympathetic understanding as they seek ministry openings in a radically changed land. Pray that mistakes and attitudes of the past may be rectified and that they might be used of God to strengthen the maturing church. The major task for missionaries is in Bible teaching and preparing men and women for Christian leadership. The largest agencies are Mennonites (17), US Presbyterians (12), United Methodists (10) and **SBC** (6). The largest missionary-contributing nation is USA (95).

9. **Christian help ministries.** A multiplicity of high-tech and sophisticated expatriate agencies could flood the country with ideas and expensive gimmicks. Pray for those who will enhance the indigenous work of the Spirit in the churches – whether through literature, Bible distribution, mass media or other means.

N

Niger
(Republic of Niger)

August 30
Africa

Area 1,267,000 sq.km. Sahara desert in centre and north. Only the southwest and a narrow strip along the Nigerian border in the south are savannah grasslands.

Population		Ann. Gr.	Density
1990	7,109,000	3.1 %	6/sq.km
1995	8,313,000	3.2 %	7/sq.km

Peoples: All peoples 27.
Chadic 52.8% Hausa 3,600,000. Also the less Islamic Mauri 127,000; Kurfey 50,000; Tyenga 5,000.
Fula-Fulbe 9.8%. The more settled Islamic Sokoto Fula and nomadic Wodaabe Fula.
Nilo-Saharan 26.1%. Songhai, subdivided in the Djerma, 1,106,000; Kado 335,000; Dendi 40,000; Kurtey 32,000; Wogo 28,000. Also Kanuri-Manga 325,000 and related Mober 50,000 and Kanembu 11,000. Teda/Tubu 32,000; Zaghawa 35,000.
Gur 0.3%. Gurmantche 20,000; Mossi 11,000.
Tuareg 10.6%. Three groups (and languages): Tamahaq (Tahaggart); Tamashek (Tawellemmet); Tamajeq (Tayert).
Arab 0.3%. Nomadic Shua, North African Arab.
Other 0.1%. French 6,000.

Literacy 10%. **Official language:** French. **Trade language:** Hausa. **All languages** 21. **Languages with Scriptures** 3Bi 3NT 5por.

Capital: Niamey 400,000. Urbanization 21%.

Economy: Mining of uranium and other minerals has brought some economic development to this impoverished land, but in the '80s the Sahel famine, collapse of the uranium market and Nigeria's closure of the common border devastated the economy. Ninety per cent of the population live at bare subsistence level at the best of times. Income/person $290 (1.5% of USA).

Politics: Independent from France in 1960. Military regime between 1974 and 1991. Economic stresses and the global popularization of democracy led to the suspension of the constitution in 1991, a transitional government and adoption of a multi-party constitution in December 1992. There has been Libyan-backed Tuareg insurgency in the north for some years.

Religion: A secular state with strong Islamic tendencies. There have been some restrictions on the extent and nature of missionary activity, but there is religious freedom.
Islam 90.5%. Sunni Muslims, many linked with Sufi brotherhoods. Islam is strongest among the settled Fulani, Kanuri, Hausa city dwellers and Tuareg.
African traditional religions 9%. Only two peoples have resisted Islam: the Kurfey and Maouri.
Christian 0.38%. Affil 0.38%. Growth 4.2%.
Protestant 0.10%. Affil 0.10%. Growth 5.9%.

Church	Cong.	Members	Affiliated
Evangelical Ch	80	1,000	5,500
Evang Baptist Ch	9	500	1,000
All other (5)	5	198	418
Denominations (7)	94	1,698	6,919
Evangelicals 0.10% of pop.		1,658	6,838

Missionaries:
 to Niger 264 (1:26,900 people) in 22 agencies.
 from Niger 1 (1:7,000 Protestants).
Roman Catholic 0.25%. Growth 3.6%.

Catholic Ch	26	9,540	18,000

A high proportion are French expatriates.
Missionaries to Niger 138 (1:51,500 people).
Indigenous Marginal 0.03%. Growth 3.4%.

Groups (5)		950	1,900

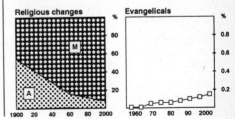

Religious changes / Evangelicals

1. **This Muslim land is open for the gospel,** and Muslims are more receptive than ever before, yet response has been very small. Islam is strong and well-organized. There is an Islamic university near Niamey. Pray that the land may remain open, and that every social, religious and spiritual barrier to the knowledge of the Lord may be removed. In 1981 some restrictions were placed on the preaching of missionaries; new missions have had to limit their activities to social welfare, but this restriction is being eased.

2. **There are too few missionaries to cover all the opportunities,** especially in the eastern half of the country. Pray labourers into this difficult and long-resistant land. The loving ministry of missionaries in over ten Christian aid agencies and missions through health education, rural improvement and

other aid programmes has won credibility for the gospel and created a new interest among Muslims and animists. **SIM** has 197 missionaries and is by far the largest agency, with a wide range of ministries in Niger and serving all of West Africa, including the only mission hospital in the land. Other significant agencies: **EMS**-Nigeria (10), **SBC** (9), Sahara Desert Mission (7), **YWAM** (5). The largest missionary-contributing nations: USA (136), UK (28), Canada (22), Nigeria (18). There is a growing contribution from other Nigerian missions (**CM, CMF**). Pray for sensitivity in helping the small, young churches and their leaders to maturity.

3. **The Christian Church in Niger** is the only one in Africa south of the Sahara where numbers have declined since 1960. The Catholic Church, the major part, is predominantly expatriate and has not really made an impact on the indigenous population. Evangelicals are a very small minority, but have doubled in numbers and congregations in the '80s. Only among the Hausa (**SIM**) and the Djerma and Gurmantche (Evangelical Baptists) have viable and stable congregations been established. Believers are often isolated and widely separated; few are literate or have received consistent Bible teaching.

4. **Leadership in the churches.** There have been problems due to lack of fellowship, coordination and maturity, and divisions have occurred in the small church – pray! There are several lower-level Bible schools initiated by **SIM**. Pray for the emergence of a mature, educated, articulate leadership.

5. **Pioneer ventures worthy of much prayer among:**
a) **The Tuareg,** once rich, now impoverished and resentful due to drought, famine, changing trade patterns and political marginalization. The selfless ministry of missionaries from **SIM**, Baptist International Missions and Sahara Desert Mission has opened the hearts of some, and there are four small groups of believers. **SIM** and **SIL** missionaries are translating the Scriptures; the Tayert New Testament was published in 1991. **YWAM** and **WH** also have a commitment to reach these people.
b) **The Djerma,** still 25% animist, with only 50 believers. Evangelical Baptist missionaries have laboured long, but no breakthrough has yet come among this resistant people.
c) **The Kanuri-Manga** and related peoples, the Yerwa, Mober and Kanembu, numbering over 400,000. Only six missionaries (**SIM, SIL, CMF**) are committed to this ministry. There are only about 10 believers, and only a few portions of Scripture (**SIL**).
d) **The Fulbe** (Fulani), both the settled Sokoto and nomadic Wodaabe Fulani of the west, and the less Islamized nomadic Fulani across the whole country. **SIM** has 10 workers committed to the Fulbe. There have recently been an increasing number of conversions among the Wodaabe; there were over 60 believers in 1991, with one Bible school graduate among them.
e) **The Songhai** who have no known believers. Six **SIM** missionaries have been committed to their spiritual welfare since 1989.
f) **The unreached Tubu** of the east. **SIM, SIL, YWAM** and **Frontiers** are all seeking to develop ministry to them.

6. **Unreached and unoccupied peoples** number 19. Major groupings are given here together with missions investigating entry: the Western Sokoto Fulbe, the Mober (**SIM**), the Arabs, Zaghawa (**YWAM**), Kurfey, Mauri, Tyenga, Dendi, Kirtey, Wogo, Kado, Kanembu. There are hardly any missionaries in the east of the country.

7. **Young people** have been the most responsive, yet little has been done to minister to this key section of the nation. There is a small GBU(**IFES**) group in the university, but most of the believers are from other African lands; pray for the calling of a national staff worker.

8. **Bible translation and distribution.** The Djerma Bible was published in 1991. Pray for an impact to be made; 25% of the population understand Djerma. **SIL** workers committed to translation programmes in Tamachek, Manga and Fulbe (Fulfulde). There are at least six other languages, and possibly several others, into which translation is necessary.

9. **Media Ministries**
a) **Christian literature.** Poverty and illiteracy are severe limitations. There are three Christian bookstores in the country.
b) The **audio-media** which has been inadequately funded or exploited. **GRn** have prepared messages in 22 languages of Niger.
c) **The *Jesus* film.** This is only available in Hausa.

Nigeria
(The Federal Republic of Nigeria)

**August 31–
September 1**

Africa

Area 924,000 sq km. Tropical forest in south, merging into savannah in the north. Desert encroachment in the north. Previously divided into 12, 19, and now 30 states to minimize the impact of ethnic loyalties on national politics and to accelerate development.

Population: No reliable census since independence, and the figures below, based on the 1991 census, are widely disputed but more realistic than earlier exaggerations.

Population		Ann. Gr.	Density
1990	85,580,000	3.3 %	92/sq.km
1995	100,580,000	3.3 %	108/sq.km

Peoples: Over 426 ethnic groups. All numbers below are estimates; ethnicity is a sensitive political issue.
Indigenous peoples: Hausa 18,850,000; Yoruba 18,850,000; Ibo 16,000,000; Fulani 9,912,000; Ibibio 5,000,000; Kanuri 3,717,000; Edo 3,000,000; Tiv 2,000,000; Ijaw 1,800,000; Anang 1,088,000; Nupe 1,062,000; Igala 565,000; Urhobo 546,000; Isoko 321,000.
Others 0.2%. European, Lebanese, Chadian Arab.

Literacy 51%. **Official language:** English. **Trade languages:** Hausa in north and middle belt, Yoruba in the west, Ibo in east and Pidgin English all over the south. **All languages** 427. 96% of the population use 21 major languages. **Languages with Scriptures** 16Bi 39NT 57por.

Capital: Abuja 379,000. Other major cities: Lagos 5,686,000 (the capital until 1991); Ibadan est. 2,000,000. About 41 cities of more than 100,000. Urbanization 17%.

Economy: Rich in agricultural land and mineral resources. Vast oil wealth squandered on grandiose prestige projects such as the new federal capital and wasted through incompetent management, corruption and neglect of agriculture and infrastructure. This mismanagement led to economic collapse and high inflation. Public debt/person $356. Income/person $319 (1.5% of USA).

Politics: Independent from Britain in 1960. A federation of 30 states. The wide differences between the cultures of the feudal and predominantly Muslim north and the entrepreneurial largely Christian south and the manipulations of the Muslims to retain political control are the main causes of the turbulent post-independence history of tension, violence, coups and civil war. There have been a succession of Muslim-dominated military governments since 1983, but a controlled transition to civilian democratic government has been set in motion. After several false starts, the changeover is expected in 1993. The root problem of dishonest politics and corrupt government has not been squarely faced.

Religion: Freedom of religion, but most post-independence governments have given preferential treatment to Islam and have ignored incidents of Muslim persecution of Christians. Nearly all the statistics for religions and churches given below are estimates; few denominations maintain records.
Muslim 40%. Muslims claim up to 60%, non-Muslims as low as 30%. Dominant in federal and military leadership and in northern states.
Traditional religions 10%. Mainly among the peoples of the middle belt and minority peoples in the north. Still influential in both Muslim peoples of north and west, and Christian peoples of the south.
Christian 50%. Nom 9.1%. Affil 40.9%. Growth 5.5%.
Protestant 26.5%. Affil 22.4%. Growth 5%.

Church	Cong	Members	Affiliated
Anglican Ch	1,300	900,000	4,500,000
Ev Chs of W Af (SIM)	2,547	700,000	2,500,000
Methodist Ch	3,000	600,000	1,500,000
Christ Apostolic Ch	4,952	520,000	1,300,000
Baptist Convention	4,400	501,236	1,250,000
Ch of God Miss Intl	3,200	480,000	1,200,000
Ch of Christ in N	1,300	400,000	1,000,000
Apostolic Ch	5,135	380,000	844,000
Assemblies of God	3,957	274,000	685,745
Deeper Life Bible Ch	4,733	348,980	612,641
Qua Iboe Ch (QIF)	1,065	150,000	429,000
Luth Ch of Christ	1,240	171,000	342,254
Gospel Faith Mission	300	42,000	185,000
Seventh-day Adventist	434	80,648	161,000
Lutheran Ch of N	320	29,000	68,000
All Other (514)	14,043	1,347,237	3,265,133
Denominations (529)	51,926	6,924,101	19,842,773
Evangelicals 15.9% of pop		4,993,000	14,046,000
Pentecostal/charis 9.2%		3,224,000	8,164,000

Missionaries:
to Nigeria 768 (1:111,400 people) in 76 agencies.
from Nigeria 2,873 (1:6,900 Protestants) in 68 agencies 238frn 1,254xcul 1,619dom.
Roman Catholic 13%. Affil 10.2%. Growth 7.8%.

Catholic Ch	12,375	4,950,000	9,000,000
Charismatics 0.2%		100,000	180,000

Missionaries:
to Nigeria 923 (1:92,700 people).
from Nigeria 80 (1973 figure).

Orthodox 0.004%. Growth 1%.

Denominations (3)	2	2,090	3,800

Foreign Marginal 0.5%. Affil 0.47%.
Growth 4.8%

Jehovah's Wit-nesses	2,681	142,073	355,000
All other (21)	72	25,200	57,000
All groups (22)	2,753	167,273	412,000

Indigenous marginal 10%. Affil 7.8%.
Growth 4.3%.

All groups (est. 1001)	3,975	3,212,000	6,900,000

Missionaries from Nigeria 70, of which 58frn.

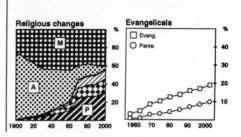

NIGERIA GENERAL

1. **The growth and dynamism of the Church,** in spite of the negative economic and political stresses, is cause for praise. This growth has accelerated over the past 15 years. There have been three great waves of growth: first in the last century on the coast through denominational missions; the second in this century through predominantly interdenominational agencies, such as **SIM** and **SUM**, in the Middle Belt; and since the '60s and '70s, among the more educated through a large number of indigenous denominations and independent fellowship groups. Much of the latter is charismatic in emphasis and has deeply rooted the gospel in Nigerian cultures. Indigenous denominations such as Deeper Life Bible Church and Church of God Mission have grown dramatically, as have the denominations related to international agencies, such as the Assemblies of God and ECWA.

2. **Nigeria is a key state in Africa,** so the devil contests every gospel advance.
a) **On the religious level Islam is seeking to gain full control** through the systematic Islamization of the north and intense missionary activity in the south. Christians in the north have been restricted in their activities, and victimized by rioting, looting and destruction of churches in many areas. Many Christians have been killed. Pray that Christians may be led of the Lord in persecution and learn to use spiritual weapons for this spiritual warfare.
b) **On the political level,** structures where deception and greed reign unchallenged make it hard for any committed Christian to be involved. Pray that God may raise up spiritual, God-fearing leaders for the nation who have the moral integrity and courage to tackle the economic situation, root out the culture of corruption and establish true religious freedom.
c) **On the spiritual level** the rapid growth of indigenous *spiritual* churches which mix Christianity with traditional fetish beliefs, and the invasion of foreign cults affecting the educated, are drawing many away from the Truth. Pray that the spirit of compromise and error might be exposed and rejected.

3. **The Nigerian church** has grown with an influx of millions of non-Christians over the past three decades. Pray for discernment in dealing with inherent dangers:
a) **Widespread evangelism is not accompanied by sufficient follow-up and balanced teaching.** Numerous doctrinal distortions and emphases – often from abroad – such as an over-emphasis on material prosperity or undue stress on certain gifts, are bringing dissension to the Body of Christ.
b) **Materialism, seeking after position and power, and selfishness** have further harmed the spiritual impact of churches. Divisions, fragmentation and a profusion of indigenous denominations and sects are the results. Pray that Christian leaders may set a good example in humility, simplicity of life style and holiness.
c) **Second-generation nominalism** in both traditional and younger churches is becoming a big problem. Double standards are widespread, and immorality, membership in secret societies, and compromise with the world bring strife, division, and disrepute for the gospel.
d) **The indigenous syncretic groups** are numerous and widespread, but little has been done to bring the light of God's Word to bear on their incomplete grasp of the Truth.

4. **Praise God for Nigerians raised up to lead denominations** and agencies. Yet the rapid growth of the Church in times of social change, economic hardship and continual pressure from Muslims have placed unusual strains on leaders. Pray for:
a) **A multiplication of leaders** well versed in the Scriptures, skilled in disciple-making and steeped in the knowledge of God and the power of prayer.
b) **The numerous seminaries and Bible schools** providing residential courses and also the TEE programmes run by many denominations. Pray that head and heart knowledge be kept in balance.

There are over 160 accredited seminaries and Bible schools in Nigeria.

c) **The bridging of the generation gap.** Older pastors with less education and more caution find it difficult communicating with the younger, more educated generation who seek more freedom in worship. Many of the young turn to Pentecostal and charismatic groups who provide such freedom.

d) **Greater love and fellowship between leaders**, with Christ-likeness and mutual submission replacing rivalry, strong individualism and a tendency to dictatorial leadership styles. There needs to be a greater willingness for accountability to the Body of Christ – leaders to the led and ministries to the wider Church.

e) **Leaders who help others to be prepared for leadership.** One-man-ministries, empire-building and unwillingness to delegate responsibility to the upcoming generation are common weaknesses.

f) **The growth in missions vision.** Many young people, especially graduates, are giving up their jobs to go into cross-cultural missions.

5. **Nationwide interdenominational movements** have been used of God to make a deep impact on specific sections of the community. Of note:

a) **Secondary schools. Scripture Union** in the south and **Fellowship of Christian Students** in the north have had a big impact through a network of groups in most schools. Pray for the overworked travelling secretaries, Christian teachers who act as advisors, and the student leaders themselves. The work needs a new infusion of the Spirit for the '90s.

b) **Universities and colleges.** NIFES is the largest member body of **IFES**, with 40,000 evangelical student members on over 300 campuses. Their impact on non-Christians has been significant, with many Muslim students being won to Jesus. Pray that the national executive and campus leaders may give both vision for evangelism and missions and spiritual depth and sound teaching to the members. Pray also that Christian graduates may maintain the vision, contribute actively to the life of local churches, and be willing to go into full-time pastoral or missionary service. Multiplication of students' fellowships has greatly fragmented Christian student witness.

c) **The upper and business class.** The Full Gospel Businessmen's Fellowship, Pan-Africa Christian Women's Alliance, Nigerian Women for Christ and others exert influence in much of the country. Pray that Christians may win many influential people to Christ and that the whole nation may be thereby uplifted.

6. **Expatriate missionaries** are welcomed by Nigerian churches and missions. Visas are hard to obtain for Christians, but not for Muslims. Pray for the removal of discriminatory treatment in visa applications. Nigerian Christians are rising to the challenges of the '90s, but rapid church growth and the large number of unreached areas and peoples are stretching their resources. Key ministries for expatriates include Bible teaching and leadership training, teaching Bible knowledge in schools, a wide range of supportive and aid ministries, and training Nigerian missionaries. Pray for the safety, health and effectiveness of the missionary force – each of these factors has become even more of a spiritual battleground in today's Nigeria. Some of the larger agencies are **SIM** (180), **(SBC)** (119), **SUM/AP** (71), **CRWM** (51), **QIF** (23), **CMS** (13). Major missionary-contributing nations: USA (506), UK (76), Canada (42), Denmark (39), Netherlands (21), Germany (17), Korea (12).

7. **Mission vision.** Nigeria has become one of the major missionary-sending countries of the developing world. The stimulus of Lausanne 1974 and the Nigeria Congress on Evangelization 1975, as well as the founding of the **Nigeria Evangelical Missions Association** (NEMA) in 1982, have helped to push this vision. Pray for:

a) **The ministry of NEMA**, with a membership of over 30 agencies, in coordinating the missions thrust to the unreached in Nigeria and beyond and as a forum for sharing skills, resources and vision.

b) **Denominational agencies with a strong missions programme.** The **Evangelical Missionary Society** of ECWA has by far the largest number of cross-cultural missionaries (830 in 1991). The Deeper Life Bible Church has sent out 72 missionaries to 32 nations. Anglicans (90), His Grace Evangelical Movement (22), Baptists (20), Churches of Christ in Nigeria (TEKAN) and others also have missionary sending programmes. Pray that other denominations may catch the vision.

c) **Interdenominational agencies** have multiplied – such as **Calvary Ministries** (77 workers), **Christian Missionary Foundation** (50), **Missionary Crusaders Ministries** (9), **Nations for Christ** and others. Pray for the defining and clarifying of long-term goals.

d) **Missionary support.** Few congregations really understand their responsibility to support mission agencies by praying, giving and going. Pray for Nigerian support agencies which seek to address this problem and act as a bridge between churches and missionaries on the fields. There are about 240 Nigerian missionaries serving in other lands, mainly in West Africa, where they face difficulties in receiving funds to provide for their material needs and educate their children.

e) **The goal for the year 2000** – that 75% of the population be Christian.

8. **Nigeria's unreached peoples.** Hitherto no national survey of either the harvest force (the statistics and spread of the church) nor the harvest field (unreached peoples and areas) has ever been made. This is essential for the complete covering of the nation in pioneer evangelism and church-planting ministries. Pray specifically for the NEMA-sponsored *Searchlight* project in carrying out a state-by-state survey of churches and peoples, and for an army of dedicated researchers to bring the survey to successful completion. Initial results reveal that there are more than 80 unreached peoples, of which 28 have no known groups of Christians, mostly in the North, Middle Belt and the riverine areas.

9. **Literature is vital for the growth of the Church.** It is avidly sought but in short supply. Pray for:
a) **Authors** who can creatively cover a wide range of issues in a culturally relevant way. Much that is produced is only addressing the popular issues of the moment rather than dealing with the deeper issues.
b) **The printing** of affordable Christian books and literature. Printing materials and paper are very expensive.
c) **Publishing.** Christian publishers – such as ECWA Productions, TEKAN Publications, Baraka Publications, Calvary Ministries Media Services and **SU** – publish books, magazines, Sunday School materials and Bible-reading notes, but all face frustrating limitations because of the economic situation and need prayer.
d) **Distribution.** Although there are well over 300 Christian bookstores in Nigeria, turnover and stock range are severely limited by the price and lack of foreign exchange. Major distribution agencies are the 36 Challenge Bookstores (ECWA), and 30 bookstores affiliated with TEKAN and **SU**.

10. **Christian media** for evangelism and teaching is important in today's Nigeria.
a) **GRn** has provided recordings in 443 languages and also innovative cassette and record playback machines for ease of use. Pray for their widespread use in evangelism.
b) **Television** is used by many Christian groups, but creative and diverse programming is a great need. NLFA, ELWA, Baptist Media, *Muryar Bishara*, and FGBFMI all have studios. There is a need for greater cooperation between groups to cut high costs.
c) The *Jesus* film is complete or in production in 19 Nigerian languages. Pray for preparations to be completed as soon as possible. Pray that the film may also be aired on television. ECWA and Baptist Media have produced other films and filmstrips; pray that many churches and agencies may use these tools effectively.
d) **Christian radio** suffered a grievous blow by the loss of Radio ELWA in Liberia. Pray for adequate substitutes – either through the lifting of the ban on private ownership of radio stations in Nigeria, or through use of existing local radio facilities, or through an alternative site for the resumption of programming and broadcasting. Both ELWA (**SIM**) and Muryar Bishara (**SUM/AP**, Lutheran) have studios.
e) **Drama using traditional themes** is useful in evangelism and teaching. Mount Zion Ministries, Peace Foundation Ministries, and others promote this medium – pray for its wide application.
f) **Bible translation is still a massive task.** Nigerian and expatriate translators are working on 37 NT translation projects overseen by the Bible Society. At least 61 other languages definitely need such ministry to begin. The Nigerian Bible Translation Trust, a continuation of the work of **SIL**, is working in 10 languages. There are 253 languages in which adequate linguistic survey work is still needed. Pray for the finishing of this enormous task, and pray for the calling of more Nigerians into translation ministry.

September 2   **NIGERIA REGIONS**

We have divided Nigeria into three regions to help in understanding the highly complex social and religious situation. Religious percentages are approximations.

THE SOUTH

States: Abia, Akwa-Ibom, Anambra, Cross River, Delta, Edo, Enugu, Imo, Lagos, Ogun, Ondo, Osun, Oyo, Rivers.

Population 41,253,000.

Major peoples: Yoruba, Ibo, Urhobo, Edo, Isoko, Efik, Ijaw, Ibibio, Anang and other indigenous peoples – about 150.

Religion: Christian 73%, Traditional religions 17%, Muslim 10%.

1. **The region was pioneered** by Anglicans, Methodists and Southern Baptists in the west, by Presbyterians, Catholics, **QIF** and others in the east and by UMS-UMCA in the whole region. Christians are in the great majority. Pentecostal churches are now the predominant influence and the fastest growing – ranging from small groups meeting in garages to mega-churches. Cities are better served with an average of four churches per sq.km., but rural areas lack dedicated pastors because of the relative poverty. Pray for sacrificial concern among Christians for the less reached and less privileged areas. Pray also for revival to make the Christians into true disciples of Jesus.

2. **The less-reached peoples and areas:**
a) **The Muslim suburbs** (*sabongari*) in southern towns and cities where Northerners congregate. Very little prayer concern or evangelism has been directed to these difficult areas.
b) **Muslim groups among Southern peoples.** The Yoruba Muslims are influential and make up about 25% of all Yoruba. Muslim missionary efforts and enticements with money and favours have brought pockets of other southern peoples to Islam. Pray for specific outreach to these Muslims.
c) **The Niger Delta.** Many small peoples live in these virtually inaccessible swampy areas largely bypassed by missions. **CMS** has a church-planting ministry in the area.
d) **The Benin border area.**
e) **Coastal areas:** Lagos lagoon, Ondo, Ogun, Edo and Delta states where the Christian presence is not strong.

THE MIDDLE BELT
(the southern half of the pre-independence Northern Region)

States: The new federal Capital Territory (Abuja), Plateau, Benue, Niger, Kogi, Taraba and Kwara. The southern parts of Kaduna, Bauchi and Adamawa are culturally also part of the area.

Population 17,300,000.

Major peoples: No dominant group, but a medley of over 230 languages, most using Hausa as a trade language. Largest: Tiv 2,000,000; Nupe 1,800,000.

Religion: Muslim 20%, Traditional religions 20%, Christian 60%. Both Islam (through political influence) and Christianity (through evangelism) are growing.

1. **The area was pioneered by SIM in the centre and west and SUM/AP in the centre and east.** Their ministries have now largely been integrated into their large daughter churches – Evangelical Churches of West Africa (SIM) and Fellowship of Churches of Christ in Nigeria – COCIN/TEKAN (SUM/AP). Pray for the ministry of missionaries serving these churches.

2. **The churches have grown dramatically** over the last 30 years. They are almost entirely evangelical with a vigorous evangelistic outreach. New Life For All proved most successful in this area, and many believers were mobilized for profitable outreach. Pray for the spiritual growth of believers and also for the conversion of the younger generation – evangelical nominalism is becoming a problem. Newer Pentecostal churches from the south have made rapid progress in the past decades. Pray for revival and a vision for cross-cultural outreach – present growth is not revival.

3. **Muslim missionary activity** has intensified in the region. Considerable efforts are made to win over pagans and backsliding Christians. Pray that these attempts may be frustrated by conversions to Christ. Pray that Christians may overcome historic hatreds and personal fears for courageous witnessing to Muslims in love.

4. Less-reached peoples. There are still 60–70 peoples in the region who have shown only a small response. This is changing with increased Nigerian research and missionary outreach. There are four main areas of particular need:

a) **The Gwoza Hills in the northeast** (Adamawa and Taraba States and the south of Borno State). The area has become a spiritual battleground, with some peoples turning from paganism, others to Islam and yet others to Christ. Over 23 peoples live in the area. Pray for the peoples in the heart of the battle – Guduf, Hidkeala, Dghwede and Matakam.

b) **The mountain regions in the east around Yola in Adamawa State.** These are the home of numerous peoples, some scarcely touched by civilization. Over 50 peoples live in the area, many unreached. Pray especially for pioneer outreach to the Mumuye 500,000, Chamba 150,000 and Bata 50,000.

c) **Plateau State.** Many peoples have turned to the Lord, but some are more resistant, such as the predominantly animist Rubassa 120,000.

d) **Along the Niger River and Benin border** where there are numerous unreached and partially-reached peoples. Pray for the Muslim Nupe, pagan Kambari 200,000, Gbari Yamma 40,000, Dukawa 50,000, Busa 60,000 and Kamuku 25,000. The Dukawa and sections of the Kambari are now turning to Islam in large numbers. Only a handful of Christian workers are attempting to reach them (UMCA, **CMF**, **CM**, ECWA, CRWM).

September 3	**THE NORTH**

States: Sokoto, Kaduna, Kano, Bauchi, Bornu, Katsina, Jigawa, Kebbi, Adamawa and Yobe.

Population 33,191,000.

Major peoples: Hausa, Fulani, Kanuri. About 40 other smaller groups north of the Middle Belt, many of which are still following traditional religions.

Religion: Muslim est. 77%, Traditional religions 15%, Christian 8%. Latter mainly in Kaduna and cities.

1. **There have been great gospel advances into this Muslim area** over the last 25 years. Muslims are coming to the Lord and churches are being planted in both the Muslim centres of Sokoto and Kano as well as in the rural areas where groups of animist people live. Pray for a greater harvest in coming days. Converts out of Islam face considerable opposition and hostility from relatives. Most of the Christians are from further south; pray for their witness to be effective among their Muslim neighbours.

2. **Persecution of Christians** has increased over the '80s with certain Muslim extremists violently opposing Christian activities and even their presence in the north. There have been a number of serious riots in which many hundreds of Christians have lost life and property and in which churches have been destroyed. Pray that Christians may retaliate with love and win the right to testify to Muslims.

3. **The need for missionaries continues. SIM** and **SUM/AP** have sought to evangelize in this area for many years, but the work has been hard. Praise God for the increasing concern of the Nigerian church for the evangelization of the north. Pray for the calling of ex-Muslims into full-time service, and also for their training as missionaries to Muslim peoples.

4. **Unreached peoples:**

a) **The Fulani** are a strategic people right across Africa. Their origin was in Senegal, but their greatest number is in Nigeria, where 10 million of the possibly 29 million Fulani live. They form both the strongly Muslim ruling class in Nigeria and also the nominally Muslim nomadic cattle grazers over much of Nigeria and the Sahel. Pray that Nigerian and expatriate Christians may catch a vision for their evangelization. Pray that God may give the right strategies for reaching both groups – the nomadic cattle people being a particular challenge. About 93% of Nigerian Fulani are Muslim. There has been a growing response through ECWA-**SIM** and others, and there may now be 2,000 Christians. In 1983 the **Joint Christian Ministry in West Africa** was formed to specifically coordinate evangelism, literature, radio and training ministries. Pray that Christians in West Africa might be enthused to reach them. If the gospel gripped the Fulani, all West Africa would be affected! Many of the urban Fulani speak only Hausa and must be reached through this language.

b) **The Hausa** are known as Muslims, but maybe 30%, while claiming to be Muslim, actually follow their traditional religion. The majority of these are known as **Maguzawa**, a people with their own distinctive culture, and among them an exciting turning to Christ is going on. Many new ECWA, Anglican, Baptist and other churches are being planted in rural areas. The Isawa, a Hausa Muslim sub-group that give high honour to Jesus, are responding to the gospel (ECWA). Pray for large numbers of Hausa to be won to Christ in this day of opportunity.

c) **The Kanuri of Borno State** are strongly Muslim, and have been so for 1,000 years. There are about 25 known believers among the 3,700,000 Kanuri after years of witness by TEKAN-SUM/ AP missionaries. Bible translation is progressing, but the key to the hearts of the Kanuri has yet to be found. Pray that the breakthrough may soon come.

Niue Islands

See under COOK ISLANDS

Norfolk Island

See under AUSTRALIA

Northern Mariana Islands

N

See under MICRONESIA

September 4
Europe

Norway
(Kingdom of Norway)

Area 324,000 sq.km. A long, mountainous, fjord-indented land. One of the four Scandinavian countries. Also included are the Arctic dependencies of Jan Mayen and Svalbard (Spitzbergen) Islands 62,000 sq.km.

Population	Ann. Gr.	Density
1990 4,212,000	0.28 %	13/sq.km
1995 4,271,000	0.28 %	13/sq.km

Peoples:
Norwegian 95.7%.
Other indigenous 1%. Same (Lapp) 23,000; Gypsy 3,500.
Other European 2.2%. Swedish 21,000; Finnish 12,000; Danish 12,000; Russians (on Svalbard) 3,000.
Other 1.1%. Pakistani 14,000; Vietnamese 9,000; Africans 7,000; Latin Americans 6,500; Chinese 3,000; Kurds 3,000.

Literacy 96%. **Official language:** Norwegian (Bokmaal and Nynorsk). **All languages** 13. **Languages with Scriptures** 6Bi 1NT.

Capital: Oslo 458,000. Urbanization 71%.

Economy: Strong and wealthy industrial state with high earnings from oil, mining, fishing and forest products. Income/person $13,820 (66% of USA).

Politics: Independent from Sweden in 1905 as a parliamentary monarchy.

Religion: The Lutheran Church is the official religion of the state, but there is complete freedom for other denominations and religions.
Non-religious/other 4%.
Muslim 0.5%. Pakistanis, Turks, Kurds, Arabs.
Jews 0.02%. **Buddhist/Chinese** 0.04%.
Baha'i 0.04%.
Christian 95.4%. Nom 5.2%. Affil 90%. Growth 0.2%.
 Protestant 94%. Affil 88.7%. Growth 0.1%.

Church	Cong	Members	Affiliated
Lutheran Ch	1,340	2,740,000	3,700,000
Pentecostal Mvt	279	40,200	61,800
Salvation Army	128	27,900	42,900
Free Evang Lutheran	72	7,200	20,600
Independent Chs (19)	58	10,361	18,800
Mission Covenant Ch	133	8,110	16,200
Methodist Ch	56	6,300	14,700
Baptist Ch	59	5,900	11,800
Seventh-day Adventist	72	5,450	6,990
All other (32)	144	13,480	23,405
Doubly counted		−130,000	−180,000
Denominations (59)	2,341	2,734,901	3,737,195
Evangelicals 9.8% of pop		277,000	411,000
Pente/charis 3.3% of pop		92,000	140,000

Missionaries:
to Norway 53 (1:79,400 people) in 17 agencies.
from Norway 1,654 (1:2,260 Protestants) in 21 agencies 1,517frn 1,517xcul 137dom.

Roman Catholic 0.7%. Growth 11.5%.

Catholic Ch	18	21,500	29,000

Missionaries:
to Norway 476 (1973 figure).
from Norway 20 (1973 figure).
Orthodox 0.04%. Growth −3%. Mainly Greeks.
Marginal 0.52%. Growth 3.7%.

Jehovah's Witnesses	176	9,671	17,600
Mormons	23	2,410	3,700
All groups (5)	204	12,549	22,080

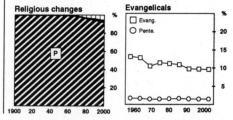

Religious changes

Evangelicals
□ Evang.
○ Pente.

1. **Norway has a rich spiritual heritage.** The influence of Pietism, prayer and revival movements within the State Church over the past 300 years are still strong. Although 90% are members of the Church of Norway, only 15–20% would claim to be committed, and Sunday church attendance represents only 3% of the population. Non-Christian immigrants in the last two decades and the importation of new religious groups and ideas have helped to erode confidence in the uniqueness of Christianity. Pray for a fresh outpouring of the Holy Spirit.

2. **The Lutheran Church** is unique in Europe, for although it is the State Church, many of the pastors are theologically evangelical. Out of revival and persecution have sprung up many voluntary organizations within the Church – agencies, prayer-houses and fellowships – which have been the source of good in Christian schools, theological education and foreign missions. Pray that this large

Church may not be moved from its biblical basis, and that it may be continually freshened by the work of the Holy Spirit.

3. **The Free Churches** are a small but significant minority, yet only a few of the Pentecostal groups and Baptists are showing any growth at all. Pray that this stagnation may end, and that a new vision for evangelism may emerge. The **Storbue Project** is a Free Church initiative in Oslo to reach secularized urbanites.

4. **Theological training** is largely in the independent and evangelical faculties of Oslo and Stavanger, ensuring the strength of the evangelical position in the churches. Pray that many may be called into Christian service at home and abroad.

5. **More needy areas and peoples:**
a) **Oslo and the surrounding area** has a lower number of evangelical Christians but this is where over half the population lives.
b) **The Same** (Lapps) are nominally Lutheran, but committed believers are relatively few. Their language and culture are very different from Norwegian. EMF has a work among them.
c) **Immigrant minorities** need to be reached. There are 20,000 Muslims, mainly from Pakistan and the Middle East. A number of Latin American refugees have settled in Norway.

6. **Norway has made a great contribution to world evangelization.** This land has sent out proportionately more Protestant missionaries than almost any other nation in the world. There are about 14,000 mission support groups for the many denominational missions, but many of these groups are ageing and not attracting younger members. The Pentecostal Movement alone has sent out 300 missionaries – over 1% of its adult members. The land has the potential to send and support more – pray them out! There is a new concern for evangelizing unreached peoples.

N

Oman

(The Sultanate of Oman)

Area 212,000 sq.km. A mountainous land on the southeast coast of Arabia and the strategic tip of the Musandam Peninsula that dominates the entrance to the Arabian/Persian Gulf.

Population		Ann. Gr.	Density
1990	1,468,000	3.4 %	5/sq.km
1995	1,735,000	3.4 %	6/sq.km

Peoples: About 15% of the population and 70% of the work force are foreign. Percentages below are estimates.
Arab 64.4%. Omanis, Gulf states Arabs, Saudi Arabians, Jordanians, Palestinians. Also Zanzibari (Swahili-speaking) 34,000.
Balochi 18%. The majority are Omani citizens.
Mahra 7.6%. Two non-Arab speaking minorities.
Iranian 3%.
Other expatriates 7% (estimate but likely to be much higher). Pakistani, Indian, Filipino, Sri Lankan, Westerners.

Literacy 41%. **Official language:** Arabic. **All languages** 8. **Languages with Scriptures:** 3Bi 1NT 1por.

Capital: Muscat 120,000. Urbanization 9%.

Economy: A latecomer as a Middle Eastern oil producer. Oil revenues are financing agricultural and industrial diversification. Oil wealth has been distributed wisely for the improvement of living standards. Income/person $5,220 (24% of USA).

Politics: A feudal monarchy until 1970, absolute monarchy since then. No political parties permitted, but there is considerable personal freedom and political stability.

Religion: Ibadi Islam is the state religion. Churches for the expatriate communities are permitted.
Muslim 95.5%. Ibadis in majority, minorities of 7% Shi'ites (many being Iranian), 4% Sunni.
Hindu 1.6% Indians, some Pakistanis and Sri Lankans.
Baha'i 0.2%. Mainly Iranians.
Non-religious/other 0.2%.
Christian 2.5%. Nominal 0.8%. Affil 1.7%. Growth 11.7%.
Protestant 0.4%. Affil 0.28%. Growth 4.9%.

Church	Cong.	Members	Affiliated
English-speaking groups (4)	5	700	1,400
Mar Thoma Ch	4	500	1,300
Ind/Pakistani Prot grps (5)	5	300	600
Ch of South India	4	300	429
Pentecostal grps (6)	6	210	280
Arabic-speaking chs (3)	3	70	117
Denominations (20)	27	2,080	4,126
Evangelicals 0.16% of pop		1,175	2,280
Pentecostal/charis 0.06%		500	900

Christian workers est. 20. Ministering to expatriate communities.
Roman Catholic 1.6%. Affil 1.3%. Growth 12.4%.

Catholic Ch	11	12,200	19,000
Charismatics		600	950

Christian workers 1.
Orthodox 0.5%. Affil 0.14%. Growth 24.0%.

Denominations (3)	8	1,500	2,000

Christian workers est. 2.

1. **Rapid social change since 1970 has transformed Oman.** Oil wealth, rising education levels and the opening up to the wider world have broadened the minds of Omanis. Pray that many may become receptive to spiritual change too.

2. **Indigenous believers** may number no more than 20. There were once two groups that met together, but those that remain are scattered and without fellowship. Pray for Omani churches to be planted.

3. **The Unreached.** The entire Muslim majority is the big challenge. There are no known believers among the Mahri of Dhofar, the Balochi of the eastern coasts, the Zanzibaris, or the Gujarati traders.

4. **Almost the entire Christian population is expatriate.** There are four centres where Christians of many denominations meet and services in many languages are held. There are no restrictions on evangelism among expatriates, and there is a steady stream of conversions among Asians in both the newer and more traditional churches. Pray for a pure life style and a glowing witness by believers to their own communities, as well as to the indigenous population. There are Western and Indian Christian workers serving these communities.

5. **Christian professionals and workers.** Pray that they may win the right to share the gospel effectively through their exemplary lives and also have the boldness to do so. The Reformed Church

of America has maintained a good medical work since 1890, when Samuel Zwemer, the famous missionary to Muslims, began his mission work in Oman. The hospital, clinics and missionary workers have been incorporated into the government health service. Pray that by all means the gospel may be proclaimed.

6. Other means of witness.
a) **Five family bookshops** (Danish Reformed Church) have a literature outreach in many languages.
b) **The Bible Society** has a good ministry in distributing the Scriptures in many languages to the expatriate communities. Distribution in Arabic requires more innovation – pray for this to happen.
c) **Christian radio broadcasts in both Arabic and English** are clearly heard from **FEBA**-Seychelles. There is a sizeable audience, and some have come to the Lord as a result.
d) **Over 1,600 Omanis are studying in the West.**

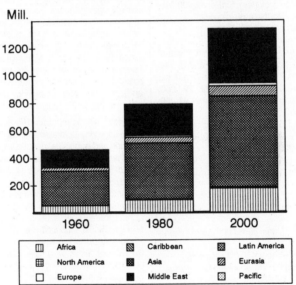

Distribution of Muslims by Region

Legend:
- Africa
- North America
- Europe
- Caribbean
- Asia
- Middle East
- Latin America
- Eurasia
- Pacific

O

The global growth of Muslims is plain. The patterns of growth vary:

1. **Conversion to Islam** has been a larger factor in Africa (the Sahel and West Africa), less so in Asia and among Afro-Americans in North America.

2. **Immigration** to non-Muslim regions is the larger factor in Europe and North America.

3. **High birth-rate** is the dominating cause of growth.

September 6–9
Asia

Pakistan

(Islamic Republic of Pakistan)

Area 880,000 sq.km., which includes 83,700 sq.km. of the third of Kashmir controlled by Pakistan. Arid mountains in the north and west. Sindh desert in southwest. Vast irrigation schemes in the fertile Indus valley.

Population		Ann. Gr.	Density
1990	122,666,000	3.5 %	154/sq.km
1995	141,599,000	2.9 %	178/sq.km

Peoples: Over 170 ethnic groups, six major language families and numerous dialects.
Indo-Iranian 85%.
  Panjabi 61%. Also including Siraiki 12,400,000; Hindko 3,000,000. Northern plains; political dominance resented by other groups.
  Sindhi 12%. In south and Karachi.
  Urdu 9%. Mohajirs – Indian Muslim immigrants at time of independence. Mainly Karachi and Sindh.
  Northern peoples 2%. Numerous smaller groups. Largest: Kohwari 263,000; Kohistani 220,000; Shina 215,000; Kashmiri 105,000; Gujuri 81,000; and Torwali 60,000.
  Tribal peoples of Sindh 1%. Major groups: Koli 750,000; Mawari 208,000; Bagri 200,000; Od 50,000; Datki 34,000.
Iranian 13.6%.
  Pathan (Pukhtun who speak Pushtu)/Afghan 10.1%.
  Baloch 3%.
  Other 0.5%. Hunza (Burusha) 75,000; Dari/Farsi; Wakhi 6,000.
Dravidian 0.74%. Brahui 908,000 living among Baloch.
Tibetan 0.34%. Balti-Purik 400,000; Kashmir.
Turkic 0.1%. Hazara 70,000, speaking Dari Persian. There are possibly 50,000 Central Asian Uzbeks among the Afghan refugees.
Other 0.3%. Arab 122,000; British 10,000; Chinese 6,000.
Refugees Afghan (Pukhtun, Turkic, Hazara) 3,500,000; Iranian.

Literacy 26%. **Official language:** Urdu, which is becoming widely used by all. **All languages** 68.
Languages with Scriptures 5Bi 4NT 13por.

Capital: Islamabad 245,000. Other major cities: Karachi 16,000,000; Lahore 4,250,000; Faisalabad 1,300,000; Rawalpindi 985,000; Peshawar 700,000. Urbanization 30%.

Economy: Much of the agricultural land and commerce is controlled by a few wealthy families. The economy is under siege from the combined assault of uncontrolled population growth, lack of water and land, 40% of government income squandered on the military, the effects of the Afghanistan wars and refugees, and a spectacular level of world-affecting corruption (the collapse of the BCCI bank). The implementation of Islamization policies could tip the nation into economic disaster. Unemployment is officially 3%, but actually nearer 40%. Public debt/person $121. Income/person $370 (1.7% of USA).

Politics: Independent from Britain at the partition of India in 1947, but little stability since. There have been three wars with India and a succession of inept civilian governments and autocratic military regimes. The dismissal of Benazir Bhutto's government followed by a rigged election gave increased powers to extremist Islamic elements. Since 1979 the war in Afghanistan, influx of refugees, and growth of armed Islamic guerrilla movements have increased Pakistan's internal instability and are inhibiting economic development and affecting the whole region.

Religion: Islamic republic. The government is pursuing its policy of Islamization of the legal system, taxation and public life, despite widespread popular misgivings. The government appears weak in the face of pressure from extremist Islamic groups. The steady implementation of *sharia* law is in direct conflict with the constitution and provides numerous opportunities to extremist Muslim groups for the oppression and persecution of religious minorities.
Muslim 96.7%. Sunni 67.6%, Shi'a 26.1% (including the unorthodox Ismaili), Ahmaddiya officially 0.13% but unofficially 3%. The latter are not considered Muslims by the government and are persecuted. Many have been driven underground.
Hindu 1.5%. Tribal peoples of Sindh and some Sindhis and Panjabis. Attrition through emigration and conversions to other religions.
Other 0.1%. Baha'i 25,000; Animist 20,000; Parsee 6,000; Buddhist 2,000.
Christian 1.7%, but unofficially 2–3% Affil 1.66%. Growth 3.9%.
  Protestant 1.06%. Growth 3.1%.

Church	Cong.	Members	Affiliated
Ch of Pakistan	736	184,000	460,000
Presbyterian Ch of P	200	44,800	332,000
Assoc Ref Presb Ch	176	26,400	110,000
Salvation Army	668	25,200	42,000
United Ch in Pakistan	82	14,000	40,000
National Meth Ch	148	13,300	38,000
Christian Brethren	73	8,000	32,000
Seventh-day Adventist	45	6,579	18,800

Full Gospel Assembly	63	5,000	16,100
Indus Chr Fell	6	1,208	3,020
International Missions	36	900	3,000
Pakistan Chr F'ship	6	397	1,590
Evang Alliance Chs	8	240	1,200
All other (38)	636	80,133	208,450
Denominations (51)	2,883	410,157	1,306,160
Evangelicals 0.29% of pop		111,000	352,000
Pentecostal/charis 0.08%		36,000	102,000

Missionaries:
to Pakistan 736 (1:167,000 people) in 72 agencies.
from Pakistan 137 (1:9,500 Protestants) in 11
agencies 6frn 13xcul 124dom.

Roman Catholic 0.59%. Growth 5.3%.

Catholic Ch	659	389,000	720,000

Missionaries to Pakistan 455 (1:277,000 people)
Marginal 0.01%. Growth 2.9%.

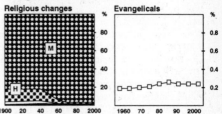

Religious changes

Evangelicals

1. **Pakistan faces a daunting array of problems.** Dissension, corruption and inability to address adequately the nation's social, economic and ecological problems have plagued the present elected government and its predecessor. Treading a middle path which satisfies liberals and fundamentalists has proved difficult. Many people are disillusioned and fearful. Pray that there may be a thirst for reality and an openness to the gospel resulting in discipling and church growth.

2. **Islamization is posing problems for minorities**, and their constitution rights are being eroded. Implementation of the *sharia* laws with a mandatory death sentence for "disrespect to the Prophet" has become the means for Muslims to bring false charges against Christians. Several have been martyred and others are in prison as a result. Pray for the preservation of basic human rights for all citizens of Pakistan regardless of religion, sex or status.

3. **Persecution of religious minorities by Muslim extremists has rapidly increased since 1988.** Christians are barred from some professions and the most menial tasks reserved for Christians alone. They have been politically marginalized by voting on separate electoral rolls. Their testimony in court is half the value of a Muslim's – meaning there is little redress in the courts and little publicity in the Press for violence and blatant discrimination against them. Beatings, imprisonments and even some cases of murder go unpunished, as well as the destruction of property and churches. Fear and dismay have gripped the Christian community. Pray that these sufferings may draw Christians close to the Lord and strengthen them in faith and courage so that they may bear a pure testimony to those who oppress them.

4. **Christians who come from a Muslim background are particularly under threat** with the implementation of *sharia* law. There are possibly thousands of secret believers, but only a handful have confessed Christ and identify openly as Christians – for it could lead to their martyrdom. Pray for their protection and multiplication and for their integration into Christian fellowships. All too often such believers have the double trauma of rejection by their community and then non-acceptance by the Christian community.

5. **Christian missions have been working in the land since 1833.** Christian standards and institutions have had a deep impact on the country – a fact which Muslim fundamentalists want to ignore. Presbyterians, Anglicans, Methodists and, later, Salvation Army missionaries pioneered the work. There was a great turning to the Lord from six of the 30 scheduled Hindu castes between 1890 and 1930. This was accompanied by revival in 1904. Other missions, predominantly evangelical, entered Pakistan around the time of independence. Most of the latter work together in the Pakistan Evangelical Fellowship and in a number of inter-church/mission projects. Some larger missions are **Interserve** (73 workers), **TEAM** (72), **CMS** (66), **SIM** (28), **OM** (26), **IMI** (21), **CBFMS** (17), **RSTI** (7). Major missionary-contributing countries: USA (244), UK (158), Canada (77), Australia (49), Germany (34), New Zealand (28), Finland (26), Sweden (25), Korea (24). The great majority of missionaries are serving within existing church structures; only a minority work in pioneer outreach and church planting. The wave of violence, death threats, kidnappings of foreigners, and increasing pressures from the authorities has complicated their ministries. Pray for their protection and for creative opportunities to reach the numerous unreached peoples and areas. Most missionaries are from the West, but an increasing number come from Asian lands. Pray for both the calling of others to serve in the land and the issue of visas for them to enter.

6. **The Church needs prayer today as never before.** The great majority are Panjabis of low-caste Hindu origin and most of the remainder are Hindu tribal peoples of the Sindh, and therefore often

despised and oppressed by the Muslim majority. Pray for:

a) **Revival.** Lack of teaching, poverty and illiteracy have hastened the lowering of spiritual standards, nominalism and the practice of occultism among those who profess to be Christians. There has been little significant church growth for several decades except among the Mawaris and Koli in the Sindh desert.

b) **Spiritual leadership in the churches.** There has been a tragic history of leadership struggles, court cases, factionalism and divisions in some denominations. God is raising up many fine younger leaders. Pray that they may be models of spirituality and godliness.

c) **Courage to share their faith with non-Christians.** Everything conspires to make Christians fearful, introspective and silent. Only a few have a burden for reaching Muslims. **OM** teams have challenged many believers to become involved in outreach – pray that this challenge may affect whole congregations, too.

d) **A missionary vision.** Some Pakistani believers have started fellowship groups in a number of Middle Eastern lands, some with an outreach to non-Christians. Pray for those involved in such ministry, which is often at considerable personal risk.

7. **Leadership training.** There are 12 Protestant and six Catholic theological colleges and Bible schools, the best known being the inter-church/mission theological seminary and United Bible Training Centre at Gujranwala. Pray for this and also the **TEAM**-related Bible Institute in Attock City. Too few prospective leaders respond to the call of God, and lack of finance limits many. Pray that a higher proportion of Pakistani Christian leaders may be able to serve in national churches without needing the support of foreign agencies. Several denominations use TEE courses from the Open Theological Seminary which has 900 students in 60 centres.

8. **The unreached.** Over 160 ethnic groups and 40 language groups are without viable, indigenous congregations and an effective cross-cultural missions initiative. Few countries present a greater challenge for missions. Pray specifically for the larger groups mentioned in the lists above. Also pray for:

a) **Baloch and Brahui.** Some 75% of the world's 4,500,000 Baloch live in Pakistan. There are only about 10 known Christian Baloch in the world. Over one million live and work in Karachi. Balochistan is largely desert and not open for expatriate workers. There are no known Christians among the Brahui, who live among them. Pray for the inter-agency fellowship that is reaching out to this strategic and restive people.

b) **The Pukhtun** of the North West Frontier with Afghanistan who are famed for their combativeness and clannishness. They control the lucrative drug and weapons trade in Pakistan and Afghanistan. Over two million live in Karachi. There are only two known Pushtu-speaking congregations, and just a few believers. A handful of expatriate workers are committed to ministry among them (**TEAM, RSMT**, NW Frontier Fellowship and others).

c) **The peoples of the far north.** Over 27 smaller peoples live in the mountain valleys of Kashmir, Kohistan, Swat, Dir, Chitral, Gilgit and the Hunza. The Kalash are largely animist, but turning to Islam since 1975. All the other peoples are Muslim – Sunni, Shi'a and Ismaili. Pray especially for the Burushas of the Hunza, the Tibetan-related Balti, the Khowaris of Chitral, the Shina, as well as the numerous smaller groups. There is not one known church among any of these peoples and only a handful of Christians. The medical work of the Brethren has been the means of many openings for the gospel.

d) **The Sindhi and Panjabi majority** on the Indus plain. Christians are almost exclusively from the Hindu minorities that were originally at the bottom of the social order; **IMI, CBFMS, SIM** and **CMS** have planted growing churches among them. Few Muslims have been reached. **CBFMS** has a ministry in the area but, as yet, there is no truly Sindhi congregation of believers.

e) **Karachi** with its huge population (double official figures) which is a violent and ethnically divided city. Inter-ethnic conflicts, kidnappings and violent crime are endemic, yet it is a key to reaching the country. There are an estimated one million drug addicts in the city, and **CMS** and others have commenced a ministry to them. The 30 churches of 120,000 Christians in the city are almost entirely Panjabi and Goanese. Pray for outreach and church-planting teams to be set apart for every ethnic group in the city – especially for the Urdu-speaking Mohajirs, the 500,000 Ismaili Muslims and numerous Afghan refugees.

f) **Afghan refugees** in Pakistan who reached a peak in 1990 of about four million. Their numbers are slowly going down as some move back to their shattered land still torn by civil war. There are 330 registered refugee camps, nearly half the population being children and the rest predominantly women. Most are Dari- and Pushtu-speaking, but there are also many Uzbek, Tajik and other groups represented. For years Christian aid organizations provided valuable material and spiritual aid, but the ministry has been greatly reduced due to extremist Muslim pressure, persecution, kidnapping, and even murder of Christian workers. Pray for those who continue this thankless task for Jesus' sake, and pray for eternal fruit.

g) **The Ahmaddiya.** This is a militantly missionary-minded sect but largely driven underground by intense Muslim persecution. Few of the three million Ahmaddiya worldwide have ever come to Christ, but their sufferings are making them more open for the good news.

9. **Young people** are a major target for prayer since 50% of the population is under 15. Yet very few ministries major on either Christian or non-Christian youth. Good work is being done by **SU**, **CEF**, **CCC**, Church Foundation Seminars and **YFC**, but the labourers equipped for these specialized ministries are few. Pray for the ministry of SU staff workers. Pray for PFES(**IFES**) who have 19 staff workers and an expanding ministry in universities and colleges. Six of the 12 universities have groups.

10. **Pakistanis have emigrated all over the world in recent years** – especially to the Middle East, North America, Britain and Australia. Very few Muslims of Pakistani origin have come to Christ in these lands, and Christians have done relatively little to reach out to them. This is particularly true for the 450,000 living in Britain.

11. **Christian help ministries.**

a) **Literature production.** The MIK Christian Publishing House was pioneered by Brethren missionaries. Here a wide range of Christian literature, including **SGM** publications, is translated, edited and published. Pray for vision and faith for writers, staff and readers alike.

b) **Literature distribution. The Bible Society** has a vital Bible printing, translating and distributing network. **CLC** has a bookshop and literature outreach in Karachi. **OM** teams have distributed millions of leaflets and books around the country. Despite low literacy, there is much interest – pray that hearts may be touched by the Holy Spirit.

c) **Bible translation.** This is a big challenge with only nine languages having a NT. Translation teams are working on 18 languages, and a further three need extensive revision (Balochi and Pushtu being key). Research may reveal that up to 38 languages require NT translation teams. The Hindko NT was published in 1990 (**TEAM**). Pray for expatriates and nationals to be called and equipped for translation work.

d) **Bible Correspondence Courses.** These have proved a useful means for teaching Christians and non-Christians. Pray for the inter-mission Pakistan Bible Correspondence School – with five regional centres and 40 staff with 9–10,000 students actively involved. Also pray for courses run by the Swedish Pentecostals. Pray for the staff and students, and that there may be eternal fruit.

e) **The *Jesus* film.** This is in use in both 16mm and video cassette in Urdu and Pushtu. Muslim fanaticism and limited church and agency cooperation and support lessen its wider use. Pray for safety and freedom to show the film and distribute the video cassette widely.

f) **Radio.** The lack of Christians and churches among the larger peoples hinders development of adequate daily programming. **FEBA** broadcast in Urdu (six hrs/wk), Panjabi (2), Pushtu (1.5), Sindhi (1.2), Hindko (0.4), and Siraiki (0.2). **TWR**-Swaziland also covers Urdu (2–3 hrs/wk). Pray also that the "World by 2000" partnership of **TWR**, **FEBA**, **FEBC** and **HCJB** will develop these broadcasts further and will provide programmes in the Balochi and Brahui languages.

g) **Cassettes.** LRI(**GRn**) have prepared recordings for distribution in 56 languages.

Palau (Belau)

See under MICRONESIA

Palestine, West Bank

See under ISRAEL

<table>
<tr><td>September 10</td></tr>
<tr><td>Latin America</td></tr>
</table>

Panama

(Republic of Panama)

Area 77,000 sq.km. The narrowest point of the Central American isthmus, and bisected by the Panama Canal.

Population	Ann. Gr.	Density
1990 2,418,000	2.1 %	31/sq.km
1995 2,659,000	1.9 %	34/sq.km

Peoples: Considerable racial intermingling.
Spanish-speaking 79%. Ladino (Eurindian) 1,500,000; Afro-Caribbean 240,000; Euro-American 136,000; Amerindian 75,000.
English-speaking 9%. West Indians, US civilians and military; both groups declining through assimilation and emigration.
Amerindians 5% speaking eight languages. Guaymi (2) 50,000; Kuna (2) 37,000; Embera 6,600; Buglere 3,300; Bribri 1,700; Waunana 1,670; Teribe 1,660.
Asians 7%. East Indians 96,000; Chinese 60,000; Arab 15,000; Japanese 1,200; Korean.

Literacy 88%. **Official language:** Spanish. **All languages** 13. **Languages with Scriptures** 3Bi 2NT 6por.

Capital: Panama City 665,000. Urbanization 53%.

Economy: Petroleum products, agriculture and revenues from the canal and large "flag of convenience" fleet of ships are the main sources of income. Widespread corruption, US sanctions (1988–90) and US invasion of 1990 brought the economy close to collapse. Recovery is slow and unemployment is 25%. Public debt/person $1,450. Income/person $1,780 (8.1% of USA).

Politics: Republic which seceded from Colombia in 1903 with US encouragement in order to facilitate the building of the canal. A succession of strong military and weak civilian governments. The USA returned the Canal Zone to Panama in 1979 while retaining some controls until 2000. The Noriega military dictatorship was ended by the US invasion of December 1989. The subsequent civilian government has lost public support because of widespread corruption and its unpopular austerity programme.

Religion: A secular state with religious freedom.
Muslim 4.5%. East Indians and Arabs.

Baha'i 1.2%.
Buddhist/other 0.8%. Chinese, Japanese, Korean.
Animist/Spiritist 0.7%. Amerindians, Afro-Carib.
Non-religious/other 2%. Jews 0.1%.
Christian 90.7%. Affil 90%. Growth 1.9%.
  Protestant 16.7%. Growth 8.8%.

Church	Cong.	Members	Affiliated
Assemblies of God	258	34,500	115,000
Seventh-day Adventist	120	30,000	50,000
Intl Ch Four-Sq Gosp	327	24,500	49,000
Ch of God (Cleveland)	122	7,833	26,100
Baptist Convention	85	8,511	21,300
Episcopal Ch	25	6,000	20,000
New Tribes Mission	46	4,000	10,000
Methodist Chs (3)	91	4,102	10,000
Evang Miss Union	42	855	1,282
All Other (64)	507	35,317	100,013
Denominations (75)	1,623	155,618	402,695
Evangelicals 13.7% of pop		120,000	330,000
Pentecostal/charis 10.6%		89,000	257,000

Missionaries:
  to Panama 228 (1:10,600 people) in 34 agencies.
  from Panama 26 (1:15,500 Protestants) in 4 agencies 1frn 3xcul 23dom.
Roman Catholic 72.5%. Affil 71.8%. Growth 0.5%.

Catholic Ch	171	1,110,000	1,978,000
Doubly Counted		−150,000	−242,000
Total		96,000	1,736,000
Charismatic		3,300	6,000

Missionaries:
  to Panama 141 (1:17,500 people).
  from Panama 350 (1973 figure).
Orthodox 0.06%. Growth 1.5%.
Marginal 1.5%. Growth 10.7%.

Jehovah's Witnesses	133	6,451	21,500
Mormons	37	7,950	15,000
All groups (2)	170	14,401	36,500

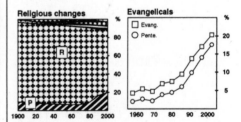

Religious changes

Evangelicals
☐ Evang.
○ Pente.

1. **Panama is a divided and despairing nation.** Civil war is not out of the question. Its famous canal is both the cause for its existence and the occasion of its manipulation by greater powers. Noriega's corrupt rule and spectacular drug-running operations provoked the confrontation with the USA which helped to destroy both the economy and the self-confidence of the people. Pray for honest government accountable to those it rules.

2. **The nation is morally in ruins.** Though Panama is nominally Catholic, Catholicism is often an irrelevant cultural heritage and the church seen as a supporter of the blatantly corrupt ruling class. There is a widespread breakdown of law and order, and of moral and family life. Common law marriages and a 72% illegitimacy rate are indicative of this. Pray for the spiritual restoration of a society that has lost its values and its identity.

3. **Spiritual hunger has increased** since the traumatic events of 1988. This has benefited Evangelicals, and especially the four largest Protestant denominations listed above. In 1935 there were 38 Protestant congregations; in 1990 there were over 1,600. However, the **Catholic Church** has suffered large losses and appears not to have the vitality or the manpower (70% of priests are foreign) to halt the decline. The English-speaking **Afro-Caribbean churches** are more nominal and losing their young people, who are being assimilated into the Spanish culture. Pray for the Holy Spirit to convict many of sin and lead them to the Saviour.

4. **The major challenges facing Evangelicals:**
a) **Spiritual unity.** The Church is as divided as the nation – both within and between denominations. No trans-denominational fellowship structure has succeeded, and no long-term cooperative plans for outreach have developed.
b) **The loss of youth.** The strong emphasis on Sunday schools and youth work has brought many young people into the churches, but there is a high drop-out rate after marriage.
c) **Theological training that encourages holiness of life and spirituality.** There are 11 Bible schools and seminaries, as well as four TEE programmes. Pray for more Panamanians to be called into full-time service. Strong, mature leadership is needed to energize the church and combat widespread activities of cultic groups.

5. **Amerindians** have been responding to the gospel. The extensive church-planting ministries of numerous denominations and missions have been fruitful. All eight peoples now have viable churches. The Bible translation programme of **SIL** in seven languages is nearing its goal of a NT for each. SIL workers have had many frustrating delays – pray for the completion of the remaining three NTs. Pray also for the full flowering of a vital and truly indigenous church in each people, and for the work of **NTM** and **GMU** to this end.

6. **The less-reached sections of the population:**
a) **The upper-middle classes** remained aloof from the gospel until the mid '70s. A number of lively charismatic fellowships have been started since then.
b) **The Chinese** are rapidly being assimilated, but many still speak Cantonese and Hakka, and few have been evangelized. Most are nominal Catholics or follow traditional Chinese religions. There are four Chinese missionaries ministering to them, and two small congregations.
c) **The East Indians** are mostly Muslim, though some are Hindu. There is no specific outreach to them.
d) The 3,200 **Jews** are unreached.
e) **University students.** Of the 51,000 in higher education, only a few students are involved in a campus witness. Men are conspicuously few among them. The campus ministry Minamundo (**LAM, IFES**) has still a pioneer challenge.

7. **Over 90% of the missionary force is from North America.** The confrontation with the USA made their presence or ministry in Panama more difficult. Pray for great sensitivity and humility as well as an appreciation for their Panamanian co-workers. A large proportion of the missionaries work among the Amerindians. Colombia's drug wars are affecting rural work. Some **NTM** missionaries were kidnapped in the border area in 1993. The largest agencies: **NTM** (84 workers), **SBC** (33), **AoG** (16), **GMU** (11), **WBT** (9), Lutheran Church, Missouri Synod (7), **CAMI** (5). Major missionary-contributing nations: USA (182), Canada (13).

8. **Christian help ministries**
a) **Literature.** This is distributed by the Bible Society and a dozen bookstores (one of **CLC**) – almost all in the Canal Zone. Poverty, illiteracy and low interest in reading limit the impact. Pray for the dissemination of literature nationally and internationally from these centres.
b) **Radio.** As well as the large coverage of HCJB(**WRMF**) Ecuador, **TWR**-Bonaire and others, there is also a local station sponsored by **LAM**.

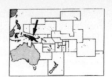

<table>
<tr><td>

September
11–12

Pacific

</td></tr>
</table>

Papua New Guinea

(Independent State of Papua New Guinea)

Area 463,000 sq.km. Eastern half of New Guinea, the second largest island in the world, also many smaller islands in the north and east which make up the nation of Papua New Guinea. The other half of the island (lying just north of Australia) is Irian Jaya, part of Indonesia. PNG is a land of high mountains, dense forests, lowland swamps, coral islands, torrential rainfall, many rivers, and beautiful flora and fauna including the bird of paradise – the national emblem.

Population	Ann. Gr.	Density
1990 4,011,000	2.7 %	9/sq.km
1995 4,553,000	2.6 %	10/sq.km

Peoples: About 1,000 peoples speaking 862 languages. Ethnically and linguistically the world's most complex nation, whose cultures have been moulded by geography, successive immigrations, sorcery, fear and warfare, and more recently by Christianity, colonialism, World War II and modernization.

Melanesian 98%. Numerous tribal groups, over half of which are less than 1,000 in population. Largest: Enga 195,000; Chimbu 142,000; Melpa 101,000; Tolai 93,000; Huli 90,000; Wahgi 66,000; Kamano 64,000; Boikin 52,000; Kaugel 47,000.

Other 2%. Caucasians 58,000; Chinese 10,000; Polynesians (on outlying atolls), Filipino, Indians, etc.

Literacy 43%. Official language: English. Trade language: Tok Pisin (neo-Melanesian) in centre and north, and increasingly used in southwest. All languages 854. Languages with Scriptures 8Bi 99NT 116por.

Capital: Port Moresby 155,000. Urbanization 14%.

Economy: Predominantly subsistence agricultural/fishing economy, supplemented by cash crops (tea, coffee and copra), an expanding mining industry and increasing local manufacture. Good economic growth although the closure of mining on Bougainville (North Solomons) has affected the economy. Many problems (land compensation claims, rugged terrain, earth-tremors, aggressive multinational corporations) complicate the wise management of the land's rich mineral, timber, fish, oil and gas resources. Public debt/person $350. Income/person $990 (13% of USA).

Politics: The north and east parts (called German New Guinea) were under German control until World War I and the south (called British New Guinea) was under British rule until 1901. The latter then came under Australian rule and was called Papua. Australia continued to administer Papua and New Guinea until independence in 1975 when Papua New Guinea became a state within the British Commonwealth. The nation is governed by a democratic parliamentary system and administered on a decentralized basis by 19 provincial governments. The violent attempt on Bougainville to declare independence remains unresolved in 1993 and is unsettling the nation.

Religion: Freedom of religion. Many Christians are in government, and the whole country is permeated with Christian values. Local nationalists and humanist anthropologists are exerting pressures to limit the activities of churches and missions.

Animist 2.1%. The roots of this are still evident, even in Christianity.

Non-religious/other 0.4%. **Baha'i** 0.7%. Islam is beginning to have an influence.

Christian 96.8%. Nom 15.2%. Affil 81.6%. Growth 2.8%.

Protestant 61.7%. Affil 48.6%. Growth 1.7%.

Church	Cong	Members	Affiliated
Evangelical Lutheran	2,050	358,000	550,450
United Ch	3,000	90,000	300,000
Anglican Ch	667	80,000	200,000
Seventh-day Adventist	484	62,100	103,546
Bethel Pente Tab	267	40,000	80,000
Bapt Union (W High)	321	35,270	78,400
Gutnius Lutheran Ch	417	33,081	60,000
Apostolic Ch	300	25,000	50,000
Evang Ch of PNG	160	19,500	48,800
Christn Revival Crusade	138	18,000	45,000
Christian Brethren	200	17,000	42,500
Assemblies of God	350	18,000	37,000
Int Ch of Foursq Gosp	328	20,004	33,300
Indigenous Chs (NTM)	109	13,100	32,700
All other (64)	1,808	117,227	286,170
Denominations (78)	10,599	946,282	1,947,866
Evangelicals 22.3% of pop		414,210	894,269
Pentecostal/charis 10.4%		180,000	419,000

Missionaries:
to PNG 2,278 (1:1,760 people) in 82 agencies.
from PNG at least 222 (1:8.800 Protestants) in 11 agencies 40frn 191xcul 31dom.

Roman Catholic 32.8%. Affil 30.7%.
Growth 4.6%.

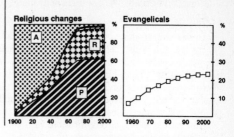

Catholic Ch	1,649	726,000	1,230,000
Charismatic		14,500	25,000

Missionaries to PNG 1,157 (1:3,170 people).
Foreign Marginal 0.3%. Growth 7.9%.

Jehovah's Witnesses	94	2,471	11,200
Mormons	13	1,260	2,100
All groups (2)	107	3,731	13,300

Indigenous Marginal 2%. Growth 2.6%.

All groups (45)	267	32,000	80,000

1. **The government faces a daunting task** of uniting such a variety of peoples into a single nation. Tribal fighting and revenge killings still occur, especially in the Highlands. Social dislocation caused by the drift of people to the cities, and unemployment for the educated youth, have caused serious problems, including crime and violence. Pray that the leaders of this land may seek the guidance of God in the affairs of their nation.

2. **Missionaries** both from the South Pacific and the West suffered disease and martyrdom at the hands of cannibals during the early days of church planting just over 100 years ago. The large investment of missionary personnel in evangelism, church planting, health, education and development has significantly changed the land and its people. Many missionaries continue to work in these areas as well as translation, teaching, discipling, leadership training and support work. The larger mission agencies are **SIL** (771 workers), **NTM** (399), Lutheran agencies (172), **APCM-UFM** (158), Baptist groups (106), Pentecostal missions (76), Nazarenes (74), **MAF** (41), **SSEM** (30). Major missionary-contributing nations: USA (1,194), Australia (392), New Zealand (145), Germany (137), Canada (106), UK (98), Finland (42), Korea (31).
Pray for:
a) Good relationships between expatriate and national workers.
b) A greater emphasis on relating the gospel to local cultures in order to see a more indigenous expression of Christianity.
c) Those committed to strengthening the church through various ministries.
d) Those involved in translation and literacy programmes. A great deal of work is still to be done in these areas.
e) Those involved in health, education and community development programmes.

3. **Over the past 120 years the gospel has spread throughout PNG,** first along the coast and then inland, and finally in the past 40 years into the Highlands. Nearly all the tribes have been reached. In some there have been mass movements to Christianity. Today over 96% claim to be Christian. Praise God for the miracles already seen in the lives of many, and for the presence of an alive, vibrant church today. But the ready acceptance of the gospel has resulted in a nominal and superficial Christianity of the majority without a radical transformation of basic values and beliefs. True discipling is an urgent need. In some areas there is already disillusionment and a turning back to traditional customs, drunkenness, gambling, cargo cults or other syncretic groups. Pray for revival and deep repentance which will result in true disciples and transformed cultures. Revivals have occurred in many areas (e.g. East and West Sepik, New Britain, North Solomons and Highlands areas) but follow-up discipling in these situations is greatly needed. There is also vigorous growth in Pentecostal and charismatic fellowships in many areas, especially the towns.

4. **The PNG Church faces challenging problems.**
a) Nominalism is the major problem facing the church today. Discipling is the urgent need.
b) Diversity of languages and strong tribal ties often make it hard for the emergence of trans-cultural fellowships and hinder the flow of blessing from one area to another.
c) Illiteracy and lack of Scriptures in many local languages can result in spiritual apathy, slow growth, and vulnerability to error. Translation and literacy programmes and the provision of appropriate and relevant Christian literature are important. The indigenous Bible Translators Association is a developing ministry encouraging translation by nationals. The Bible Society has a goal of distributing one million New Reader Scriptures.
d) Denominational rivalry at local church level confuses the people and prevents spiritual unity. There is good cooperation between main denominations at national level. The Melanesian Council of Churches was the first ecumenical body in the world to include the Roman Catholic Church

along with Protestants. The main body linking evangelicals is the National Council of Evangelical Churches.

5. **Leadership training is a priority.** Many small Bible schools are run by churches and missions. There are also many denominational theological colleges. The well-known interdenominational Christian Leaders' Training College (CLTC), with 120 full-time students and an international faculty, trains leaders for churches from all over PNG and the Solomon Islands. Churches are recognising the value of TEE as a tool for training the many marginally-literate rural pastors and church workers who have received minimal training. Pray for:
a) Men and women called of God to full-time service as pastors, missionaries, etc. The lure of highly paid secular jobs is strong for those with good education.
b) Bible teachers who can impart a love of God's Word to students and the desire to apply its truths to their own cultures.
c) The provision of many more mature, articulate Christian leaders who will significantly influence the spiritual life of the nation, and establish the church on biblical foundations.
d) Specialised Urban Training programmes to prepare leaders for urban ministries e.g. CLTC Centres in Port Moresby and Lae; Baptist Urban Pastoral Training Centre (BUPTC) in Port Moresby.
e) The excellent TEE programme in English run by CLTC to serve PNG and the Pacific, and development of more TEE programmes in Tok Pisin in the country.

6. **There is an increasing missionary vision in the country.** The indigenous PNG Missionary Association is being used of God to stimulate mission awareness and prepare and send missionaries overseas. It also coordinates a national prayer movement called Global Prayer Warriors. Christian Leaders' Training College runs an annual missions conference called Launch Out. Operation Mobilisation have a base in PNG and many nationals have already served on the MV *Doulos*. Many denominations have sent or are planning to send overseas missionaries. Many are working cross-culturally within the country. The **NTM** Missionary Training Centre provides a two-year course for prospective PNG missionaries.

7. **Aircraft of missionary organizations are essential for the work of missions.** Many areas are only accessible by air. Flying conditions are some of the worst in the world, with thick forests, high mountains, dense clouds and treacherous weather conditions. Pray for the flying staff of **MAF** (with 54 workers, 20 planes and a helicopter), of **SIL** (with four planes and two helicopters), of **NTM** (with three planes and one helicopter), and all who service these planes and travel in them. Several aircraft have crashed with loss of life. Helimission have recently established a ministry with helicopters.

8. **Young people's ministry** is encouraging. **SU** has a good ministry among students in high schools and is seeking to expand through regional workers. TSCF (**IFES**) is doing a noteworthy work on the 21 college campuses in PNG. **YWAM** has valuable input in youth training and mobilization for evangelism and missions. Camps (especially at Easter) are very significant in youth ministry. The government openly encourages youth work through the church. Pray for the many "graduates" of these ministries that they may impact their nation for good.

9. **Peoples and areas of special spiritual need.** Few PNG peoples are unevangelized and unoccupied by missions but there are several groups and areas of special need.
a) **Unreached people groups.** Some tribes are only now being discovered and opened up in isolated parts of the country, e.g. the Star Mountains on the Irian Jaya border, and some Fly and Sepik River valleys and swamps.
b) **Cargo cult followers.** Of the people groups who are affected by cargo cults, some within the groups have turned back to biblical Christianity (e.g. on Manus Island). Pray for those pockets where cargo cults are still firmly entrenched (e.g. some parts of Manus Island, Bougainville and Madang Province).
c) **Squatter settlements.** Increasing numbers of people live in squatter settlements outside towns and cities; they are places of poverty and social unrest.
d) **Prisoners.** They tend to be very open to Christian witness. **Prison Fellowship International** has a well-established ministry which is bringing hope and blessing to many.
e) **Chinese.** The Chinese merchant community are often third- or fourth-generation in PNG, and are still resistant to the gospel.

10. **Bible translation** in the many languages of PNG is an uncompleted task; it is time-consuming and demanding. Translation teams are definitely needed for 133 languages and possibly for a further

488. **SIL** members have already completed 79 New Testaments and are working on a further 220. Others are also involved in translation supported by the Bible Society. The publication in 1989 of the Tok Pisin Bible was a major step forward. Pray for all involved in translation, literacy and distribution programmes.

11. **Christian help ministries** for prayer:
a) **Local radio** is a vital link used by churches and Christian workers to exchange news and spread the gospel, and *Kristen Radio* has a modern studio for national and regional Christian broadcasting on the national radio network. EM-TV is now operating throughout the country; Christians have input through the Churches' Council for Media Coordination.
b) **Christian Radio Missionary Fellowship** (CRMF) serves the churches by providing two-way radio contact for those in isolated areas.
c) **Christian cassettes** are an effective tool for evangelism and teaching, especially for the large group of illiterates, many of whom speak only their tribal language. Language Recordings (**GRn**) has produced materials in 567 languages and dialects, and flip charts are widely used in conjunction with them.
d) **Christian literature.** There are four main publishing groups: Christian Books Melanesia (Brethren), Evangelical Brotherhood Church (Swiss Missions), *Kristen Press* (Lutheran), and the Bible Society. Much excellent material is being produced, and there are Christian bookstores in most towns.
e) **Films and videos.** Several Christian film libraries have been operated over the past years, and many churches use films regularly. Video is increasingly popular, and *Kristen Komunikaisen* in Lae are planning involvement in this ministry. The *Jesus* film is extensively used in English and Tok Pisin.

P

<table>
<tr><td>

**September
13**

Latin America

</td>
<td>

Paraguay
(Republic of Paraguay)

</td>
<td></td></tr>
</table>

Area 407,000 sq.km. Landlocked nation. The Paraguay River divides the more fertile and developed east from the forests, marshes and ranches of the Gran Chaco.

Population	Ann. Gr.	Density
1990 4,277,000	3.0 %	11/sq.km
1995 4,893,000	2.7 %	12/sq.km

Peoples:
Spanish/Guaraní-speaking 81.8% of mixed Spanish and Guaraní descent. About 8% speak only Guaraní.
Portuguese-speaking 13%. Mainly in the northeast.
Minor Amerindian peoples 1.5%. Mainly in the sparsely populated Chaco. Over 17 groups. Largest: Chulupe 15,000; Lengua 13,000; Chiriguano 8,500; Sanapana 7,400.
Immigrant minorities 3.7%. German 72,000; Italian 26,000; Ukrainian 26,000; Japanese 12,000; Chinese 7,500; Korean 6,000; Greek 1,800.

Literacy 90%. **Official languages:** Spanish, Guaraní: 90% of population speak the latter. **All languages** 21. **Languages with Scriptures** 1Bi 9NT 3por.

Capital: Asunción. 980,000 (including satellite towns). Urbanization 46%.

Economy: Apart from agriculture and hydro-electric power, there are few natural resources. Development hindered by distance from the sea and lack of mineral resources. The completion in 1988 of the world's largest hydro-electric project – on the Paraná River – has boosted the economy. Unemployment 15%. Public debt/person $417. Income/person $1,030 (4.9% of USA).

Politics: Independent from Spain in 1811. Devastating wars with surrounding nations in 1864–70 and 1932–35. Corrupt military dictatorship 1954-89. Since then economic and democratic reforms have reintegrated Paraguay into the world's political and trade network.

Religion: Complete separation of Church and State and equality before the law of all religious bodies was declared in 1992.
Non-religious/other 0.8%.
Animist 0.7%. **Buddhist** 0.2%. **Baha'i** 0.1%.

Christian 98.2%. Nom 1.2%. Affil 97%. Growth 3.1%.
Protestant 5.95%. Affil 5.4%. Growth 8.3%.

Church	Cong	Members	Affiliated
Mennonite grps (12)	111	20,575	54,376
Baptist Convention	73	5,201	22,275
Pentecostal grps (15)	116	8,144	21,000
Assemblies of God	172	6,450	14,950
Seventh-day Adventist	23	5,200	13,000
Anglican Ch	30	5,178	12,015
Evang Ch of River Plate (Luth)	100	8,000	12,000
Grace and Glory Ch	43	2,990	8,775
Ch of God (Cleveland)	80	3,471	7,800
Assoc of United Christians	12	1,725	5,130
Christian Brethren	45	1,380	4,050
Slavic Baptist Ch	12	1,093	3,645
Korean Prot Chs (3)	8	1,183	3,240
New Tribes Mission	34	581	2,025
All other (58)	260	17,506	48,356
Denominations (99)	1,119	88,677	232,637
Evangelicals 4.3% of pop		68,457	185,000
Pente/charis 2% of pop		33,500	84,500

Missionaries:
to Paraguay 522 (1:8,200 people) in 63 agencies.
from Paraguay 15 (1:15,500 Protestants) in 6 agencies 10frn 11xcul 4dom.

Roman Catholic 91.7%. Affil 91%. Growth 2.8%.

Catholic Ch	362	2,060,000	3,892,000

Missionaries:
to Paraguay 51 (1:83,800 people).
from Paraguay 180 (1973 figure).
Orthodox 0.18%. Growth 2.1%.

Denominations (3)	3	4,130	7,800

Marginal 0.39%. Growth 11%.

Mormons	46	5,830	11,000
Jehovah's Witnesses	49	3,501	5,840
All groups (2)	95	9,331	16,840

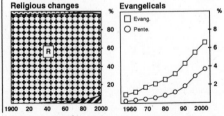

Religious changes   Evangelicals

1. **Paraguay still suffers the effects of two centuries of tyranny, war and government incompetence.** Pray for the government as it seeks to build the nation's institutions and infrastructure on the basis of democracy, truth, justice and religious freedom. These virtues have been in short supply in the past.

2. **The Roman Catholic Church** has long dominated the spiritual and political life of Paraguay. A superstitious traditionalism and bondage to many pre-Christian deities and customs keep many from liberty in the Lord Jesus. This bondage must be broken by prayer. Only a minority of believers are of the Spanish-Guaraní Mestizo majority. Paraguay has never had a true spiritual awakening.

3. **Many of Paraguay's Protestants** are German-speaking Mennonites and Lutherans, Ukrainian Baptists and Korean Presbyterians. These immigrant communities are often culturally isolated from the mainstream of national life. Pray that these communities may integrate into Paraguayan society and contribute towards its evangelization.

4. **Evangelical church growth** has been slow, but numbers have more than doubled in the '80s. Hitherto most of the converts were poor and illiterate Mestizo and Amerindians, and dependence on missionary initiative and programmes and lack of effective leadership were brakes to progress. This is changing, and evangelistic crusades, a wide distribution of the Scriptures, a greater openness and rising faith that God's time has come encourage many to trust for a breakthrough. However, more aggressive, purposeful evangelistic zeal is needed if Paraguay is to be affected. Most church growth over the past decade has been in the Pentecostal and Baptist churches.

5. **Evangelical Christian leaders** have increasingly worked together over the past decade to promote large evangelistic crusades and the evangelization of the country. The great needs in prayer for leaders are:
a) Better training and preparation for the ministry. There are 250 students in the nine seminaries and Bible institutes and a further 1,250 TEE students.
b) Boldness in evangelism – setting a good example to their flocks.
c) More time for prayer and Bible study.
d) Men and women of courage and strong faith to reach the whole land and every community with the gospel.
e) The impartation of a missionary vision to the church – small beginnings have been made in the formation of a National Committee for Missions.

6. **Work among the Indian minority peoples** has been fruitful. A majority have become Christians through the work of **SAMS** among the Lengua Guaraní and Sanapana, **NTM** in seven tribes, the **Mennonites** among the Lengua and Chulupe, and the German Indian Pioneer Mission among four others in the southeast. Missionary aid projects – providing education and the Scriptures, and initiating agricultural programmes – are helping many to become viable and self-sufficient. However, **NTM** and other missions have been subjected to vicious and distorted publicity of involvement in man-hunts and genocide. Pray that such attacks may be blunted, and even prove a blessing in disguise. Pray for the young churches as they adapt to the national culture.

7. **Missionary help is needed**, and there is an open door for those who can humbly work alongside Paraguayan brethren and strengthen national leadership. The main ministries needing personnel are church planting, leadership training and Bible translation. The largest agencies are **NTM** (72 workers), **SBC** (36), German Indian Pioneer Mission (29), **AoG** (24), **SAMS** (21) and **SIM** (12). There are 51 Korean and 49 Brazilian missionaries.

8. **Outreach target for the '90s. SIM** is planning ministry to 30 towns and cities in the northeast, where there is little gospel witness.

9. **Student ministry.** The GBU (**IFES**) ministry was formed in 1981, and has since spread to three cities and 300 students involved in groups, but this is only 1% of the total student body.

10. **Christian help ministries.**
a) **The Bible Society.** An extensive distribution of the Scriptures without precedent in the history of the country has created a receptiveness to the gospel in every section of the literate population. Pray that many lives may be changed through reading God's Word.
b) **Bible translation.** The Bible Society is supervising the Guaraní Bible translation, and three other indigenous New Testaments, but at least eight languages still lack a New Testament.
c) **Christian literature.** The five evangelical bookstores are all located in the capital; other centres lack effective literature outlets.
d) **EHC** has launched a nationwide campaign to reach every home with evangelistic literature.

September
14–15

Latin America

Peru
(Republic of Peru)

Area 1,285,000 sq.km. Three zones – dry coastal plain in the west where most of the cities and industry are located, high Andean plateau which is more agricultural, and upper Amazon jungles in the east.

Population		Ann. Gr.	Density
1990	22,332,000	2.5 %	17/sq.km
1995	25,123,000	2.4 %	20/sq.km

Peoples:
Spanish-speaking 44.5%. Mestizo 7,300,000; White 2,745,000; Black 114,000. A further six to seven million Amerindians use Spanish.
Amerindian 54.2%.
  Highland peoples 52.5%. Quechua 10,800,000; Aymara 1,235,000;
  Lowland peoples 1.7%. 390,000 speaking 41 languages.
Other 1.3%. Japanese 109,000; Chinese 100,000; Westerners 27,000.

Literacy 67%. **Official languages:** Spanish, Quechua. **All languages** 91. **Languages with Scriptures** 4Bi 23NT 28por.

Capital: Lima (and its port, Callao) 6,600,000. Other major cities: Arequipa 1,250,000; Trujillo 532,000. Urbanization 70%.

Economy: Climatic changes, world recession, cholera epidemics and, above all, the devastation of guerrilla insurgency led to the collapse of the fishing and mining industries and reduced the majority of the population to desperate poverty with raging hyper-inflation. Fujimori's government brought down inflation from 120% per month to 10% per month in 1992. Peru is claimed to be the world's riskiest country for business. Unemployment could be well over 50%. Public debt/person $555. Income/person $1,090 (5% of USA).

Politics: Fully independent from Spain in 1824. A long history of dictatorships and repressive military rule. Democratic government between 1980 and 1991 was not able to reform the gross inequalities in society nor deal with the corrupt judiciary and police. Two violent extreme Maoist terrorist movements gained much influence in 12 years of war in which 26,000 lost their lives and which inflicted $10 billion in damage. In 1992, President Fujimori suspended the constitution and took over the running of the country in an attempt to break the cycle of repression, violence and economic collapse – to the hope of some and dismay of others. A return to constitutional government is promised in 1993.

Religion: Religious freedom guaranteed in 1978 constitution, but in practice the Catholic Church still tends to be favoured and exercises a decisive influence.
Non-religious/other 1%.
Animist 1%, though at least 30% of nominal Catholics are in reality Christo-pagan.
Other religions 0.5%, including Buddhist, Sokka Gakkai, Baha'i, Jews, Muslims.
Christian 97.5%. Nom 4.6%. Affil 93%. Growth 2%.
Protestant 7.1%. Affil 7%. Growth 7.7%.

Church	Cong	Members	Affiliated
Seventh-day Adventist	424	187,151	374,000
Assemblies of God	1,511	204,750	341,000
Evangelical Ch of P	1,600	80,000	250,000
Ch of the Nazarene	296	22,917	52,734
Chr & Miss Alliance	176	20,730	37,313
Ch of God of Prophecy	191	7,260	20,700
Methodist Ch	70	5,600	18,700
Ch of God (Cleveland)	127	4,866	12,200
All other (110)	2,705	126,654	455,922
Denominations (118)	7,110	659,928	1,562,569
Evangelicals 5.6% of pop		512,000	1,259,000
Pentecostal/charis 2.5%		270,000	564,000

Missionaries:
  to Peru 1,039 (1:21,500 people) in 89 agencies.
  from Peru 190 (1:8,200 Protestants) in 9 agencies 58frn 73xcul 117dom.
Roman Catholic 89%. Affil 84.6%. Growth 1.5%.

	Cong	Members	Affiliated
Catholic Ch	2,070	10,700,000	19,395,000
Doubly Counted		−280,000	−500,000
Total		10,420,000	18,855,000
Charismatic 0.26%.		32,090	50,000

Missionaries:
  to Peru est. 1,600 (1:14,000 people).
  from Peru 250 (1973 figure).
Marginal 1.5%. Affil 1.44%. Growth 13.5%.

	Cong	Members	Affiliated
Mormons	370	87,500	159,000
Jehovah's Witnesses	721	34,978	117,000
Israelite Ch of New Covenant	170	17,000	34,000
All other (1)	2	83	172
Groups (4)	1,263	139,561	310,172

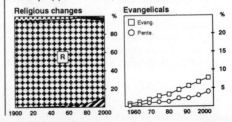

Religious changes

Evangelicals
□ Evang.
○ Pente.

1. **Peru is a nation under economic, political and military siege.** The ferocity and cold-blooded cruelty of the *Sendero Luminoso* Maoist terrorist movement and the over-reaction of the security forces have brought economic ruin, social disruption, uncertainty and fear, but not the meaningful changes required to address fundamental wrongs. Spectacular successes in capturing the leaders of the *Sendero Luminoso* in 1992 have raised hopes of an end to the ongoing guerrilla war. Pray that the government may have the courage and integrity to lay the foundations of a more just, fair and economically viable society with democratic and religious freedom. Evangelicals are increasingly prominent in voting power and in government leadership. Pray that they may use their new-found influence wisely. Pray also that the two major terrorist movements may be thwarted in their attempts to establish a Marxist state.

2. **The Catholic Church is in a crisis.** Over 80% of its clergy are foreign. It is polarized between the traditionalists and those who espouse liberation theology. The charismatic movement has had a deep impact, but those touched have often formed autonomous groups or joined evangelical churches. There has been large loss of numbers to indigenous religious movements and foreign sects, as well as to the Evangelicals. Pray that all churches may faithfully proclaim the attractiveness of Christ and the fulness of the gospel.

3. **The national crisis has provoked a massive growth in evangelical churches** – especially in the rural areas most affected by social breakdown. Evangelicals have become a significant source of leadership, stability, social aid and hope, and have grown seven-fold since 1960 and from 0.8% to 5.7% of the population. In many rural areas there has been purification through suffering, revival and miracles. However, in the cities there is more superficiality, spiritual lethargy and need for revival. There has been marked growth in the **AoG**, **CMA**, IEP (**SIM-LL**), **CoN** and other Pentecostal groups, but inadequate inter-denominational fellowship and goal-setting for the future. Pray for unity and continued growth.

4. **The National Evangelical Council of Peru** (CONEP) has a commendable record in bringing Evangelicals together for coordinating disaster relief, social help to war refugees, speaking out on human rights issues, communication between evangelicals and the authorities, and also research into the spiritual needs of the nation. Various aid organizations (**WV**, **TEAR Fund** and others) have done much to support relief programmes. Pray that all national and foreign workers and these programmes may be protected and maintained. They are seen as a threat to the Marxist goal of restructuring society according to their ideology, and some workers have been murdered.

5. **The Quechua and Aymara peoples,** the descendants of the Incas, have begun to emerge from centuries of oppression, cultural deprivation, grinding poverty and isolation. Quechua was recognized as an official language in 1975. There is new growth, optimism and blossoming of Christianity in Quechua culture, with revival in some areas. Pray for:
   a) **Millions of mountain Quechua and Aymara** who are still bound by superstitions of pagan and "Christian" origin. Several million more are landless or war refugees and are migrating to the cities in large numbers.
   b) **Bible translation work for the 31 distinct languages in the Quechua family.** Cuzco, Ayacucho and Arequipa have the whole Bible (**UBS**, IEP), Ancash the NT (**SBC**, **SIL**), these being avidly bought and read. SIL teams are working on a further 15 of these languages, but the work is hampered in many areas by terrorism and drug trafficking.
   c) **Believers in the Spanish-speaking churches to accept Quechua Christians.** Centuries of resentment and prejudice need to be overcome.
   d) **The development of an indigenous, biblical expression of the Body of Christ** in hymnology, worship, literature and outreach. The rapid growth of syncretic indigenous groups is becoming a matter for concern.

6. **The Lowland Amerindians** have responded to the preaching of missionaries of South American Mission, Swiss Indian Mission, **RBMU** and others. The three Lowland provinces of the upper Amazon have the highest percentage of evangelical believers in the country. The *Sendero Luminoso* has infiltrated some areas and brought terror to many of these simple villagers. **The Association for Evangelism and Social Action** has been formed specifically to help them. Pray that the churches among them may become strong and enable these peoples to withstand the destructive impact of the outside world on their cultures. Only a few isolated groups are yet untouched by the gospel message, but considerable work in Bible translation must yet be completed. **SIL** has been involved in 20 New Testaments for non-Quechua peoples, and has teams committed to a further ten. New Testaments may be needed for a further 11 languages.

7. **Persecution of believers** at the hands of both the terrorists and the army has become severe since 1980. An estimated 800 Christian leaders have been martyred, and a number of massacres of congregations perpetrated. One victim was the well-known Quechua translator of the Ayacucho Bible. Especially exposed are Christians in areas of fighting, drug growing and where they provide social help – both sides view their ministry as a threat. Pray for:
a) Courage, consistent Christian living and uncompromising commitment to the Lord in the face of persecution.
b) Protection and preservation of Christian leaders and their families.
c) The ministry of AMEN (a Peruvian mission), CONEP, **WV**, **TEAR Fund** and many others in providing food, counselling of war victims and rehabilitation programmes. Workers have been threatened and killed and their ministry to the needy restricted.

8. **Christian leaders are in short supply.** Doctrinal confusion, deficient theology and the multiplication of sects must be answered by clear biblical teaching, but few pastors have the gifts and training. Pray for:
a) **Leadership training.** The interdenominational Lima Seminary is strategic for Spanish-speaking countries (**LL, SIM**, etc.). At least 20 other Bible schools are preparing workers for the ministry. TEE programmes are so necessary, but are hampered by a lack of missionary and Peruvian personnel and adequate teaching materials. There is a lack of enthusiasm among those who would most benefit from them. Pray for the provision of more missionary Bible teachers with sufficient theological training and maturity.
b) **Balance in preaching the gospel and addressing social concerns.** Most evangelical leaders have had no guidance from missionaries on how to handle the burning social issues of the day and have become impressed with the apparent relevance of the theology of liberation without always seeing its pitfalls.
c) **Sunday school teachers and youth leaders.** The majority of congregations provide no special teaching or programmes for young people – a major deficiency that must be rectified.

9. **Coastal cities** have a lower percentage of Evangelicals than the national average. The war has accelerated migration to cities of the displaced and destitute, and Lima is ringed by sprawling slums in which over three million people live, to which 350,000 new migrants are added annually. Abject poverty, unemployment and malnutrition are the lot of the majority. Few have found the key to the evangelization of the sprawling slums of Lima and the nurture of churches in that difficult environment, though the Pentecostals and **SAMS** have made a good beginning. The infiltration of terrorists into these slum areas in recent years has seriously hampered Christian work. Praise God for remarkable church growth in Lima through the ministry of **CMA**, AoG, Baptists, **SAMS**, and **TEAM** over the last 15 years.

10. **Foreign Missions** have passed through difficult times, especially those from USA (68% of the missionary force); anti-American press reports, spy scares, and the widespread activities of Mormons and Jehovah's Witnesses have not helped. The spreading scourge of terrorism adds new perils for the life and ministry of missionaries. The majority of the missionary effort is directed to pioneer work in the eastern jungle, Bible translation and leadership training. Reinforcements are needed, but restrictions on their ministry are numerous because of the war. Some larger agencies are **SIL/WBT** (300 workers), **SBC** (71), Swiss Indian Mission (55), South American Mission (41), **CMA** (36), **LL** (36), **MTW** (29), Brethren (27), Evangelical Free Church of America (21), **AoG** (21), **SIM** (19). Major missionary-contributing nations: USA (701), UK (73), Germany (67), Switzerland (53), Canada (45), Brazil (24).

11. **The less-reached.** Despite church growth, parts of Peru are still a pioneer field.
a) Many towns and villages on the **high plateau** (Aymara and Quechua), **the coastal provinces** and **lowland settlements** of Spanish-speaking farmers. All are relatively less covered by Evangelicals.
b) **The upper classes.** They are staunchly traditional Catholics and few have a personal relationship with the Lord Jesus, and are rather isolated from existing evangelical witness.
c) **Ethnic minorities.** The 7,000 **Gypsies** (many still speaking Romany and with one congregation of believers), the **Chinese** with several small congregations, and the Japanese (many now returning to Japan).
d) **The terrorists** (numbering around 6,000 with 40,000 supporters), their lives blighted and warped by Marxist indoctrination and murder. They will need special care and loving ministry when peace comes. Pray for conversions among them.
e) **The traumatized victims of war and oppression,** including many children. There are an

estimated 120,000 child refugees without support and 50,000 orphans. There are reported to be thousands of children who have been sold into slavery to work in remote mines.

12. **Student ministry** is strategic for Peru's future. The present guerrilla movements were born in the violent, Marxist-oriented state universities, where political agitation and strikes lengthen student careers for years. There is widespread disillusionment and frustration, and Christian students need great courage to stand out for Jesus. Pray for the ministry of AGEUP (**IFES**) with four staff workers and 28 groups in the 46 universities. The 431,000 students have a lower proportion of Evangelicals than any other section of the population.

13. **Peruvian missions interest is growing**, but lack of knowledge and funds limits that growth. The **CMA** and Baptists have launched a missions programme. There is a post-graduate faculty of Mission in Lima – Latin America's first. AMEN (*Asociación Misionera Evangélica a las Naciónes*) with 135 workers, is a young, interdenominational mission with great vision; some of their workers have gone to serve the Lord in Europe and other parts of Latin America.

14. **Christian media.**
a) **Radio** has a wide audience, both the local *Radio del Pacifico* (**TEAM**) in Lima, and the large international stations of HCJB(**WRMF**) Ecuador (Spanish and Quechua) and **TWR** Bonaire (Spanish), with thousands of hours of broadcasting per week in Spanish, and 100 in 17 Quechua dialects!
b) **The *Jesus* film** is widely shown in Spanish, Quechua and Aymara, and has made a deep impact – even on hardened terrorists!
c) **GRn** have made recordings in 40 of Peru's languages.

P

September 16–18
Asia

Philippines
(Republic of the Philippines)

Area 300,000 sq.km. 73 provinces; 7,250 islands, of which over 700 are inhabited, the largest being Luzon (116,000 sq.km) in the north and Mindanao (102,000 sq.km) in the south.

Population		Ann. Gr.	Density
1990	62,409,000	2.5 %	208/sq.km
1995	69,922,000	2.3 %	233/sq.km

Peoples:
Malayo-Indonesian Filipinos 95%.
 Major peoples 92.2%. Cebuano 15,230,000; Tagalog 14,850,000; Ilocano 8,000,000; Hiligaynon 6,000,000; Waray (Samar/Leyte) 3,000,000; Iranun 241,000; Kankanay 220,000; Ifugao 111,000; Yakan 70,000.
 Tribal peoples 2.8%. In the more inaccessible mountainous areas of Luzon (46 tribes) 1,083,000; Mindanao (43 tribes) 570,000; Mindoro (6 tribes) 58,000; Palawan (6 tribes) 35,000.
Mixed race 3.5%. Filipino, Spanish, American, Chinese, many speaking Tagalog.
Chinese 1.3%. Urban; extensive involvement in commerce and industry.
Other 0.2%. US citizens, Vietnamese, Arab, Japanese, Korean, etc.

Literacy 89%. **Official languages:** Filipino (based on Tagalog), English. **All languages** 168. **Languages with Scriptures** 13Bi 42NT 45por.

Capital: Metro-Manila 10,000,000. Urbanization 41%.

Economy: A mixed agricultural and industrial economy. High population growth, widespread corruption, social and political unrest, two guerrilla wars and a series of natural disasters have played havoc with the economy, causing widespread poverty and unemployment. The closing of US military bases in 1992 and the uncontrolled crime wave have cut aid and inhibit foreign investment, prolonging the agony. Public debt/person $371. Income/person $709 (3.2% of USA).

Politics: A Spanish colony from 1565 to 1898; hence the Catholic majority and many Spanish customs. Ruled by the USA until independence in 1946. Martial law imposed in 1971 to combat Communist subversion; the country became virtually a one-party republic. Political manipulation, mismanagement and abuse of civil liberties stimulated antipathy to the government and led to its downfall in 1986. The first democratic government survived seven coups, but was powerless to address the serious economic situation, tame the excesses of the military or lessen the impact of the Communist and Muslim secessionist guerrilla wars. Fidel Ramos was elected President on a minority vote in 1992 – the first democratic change of government for 26 years. The Republic is a member of ASEAN.

Religion: Freedom of religion. Asia's only country with a Catholic majority. The election of a Protestant president in 1992 is likely to further weaken the strong political influence of the Catholic Church.
Non-religious/other 1.3%.
Animist 0.7%. Many nominal Catholics are still animist at heart. Majority among many of the tribal peoples.
Muslim 8%. Sunni Islam. Almost all in southwest, Mindanao, Sulu Is. and Palawan. Strong among the Maguindanao, Maranao, Iranun, Samal and Tausug; less strong, but in the majority, among eight other peoples.
Christian 90%. Affil 88.5%. Attend 4.9%. Growth 2.5%.
Protestant 7.5%. Growth 5.1%.

Church	Cong	Members	Affiliated
Seventh-day Adventist	2,405	438,329	548,000
United Ch of Christ	1,600	200,000	333,000
United Methodist Ch	1,120	155,000	282,000
Assemblies of God	1,251	80,000	197,840
Phil Bapt Miss (SBC)	1,578	84,138	187,000
Conv of Phil Bapt	441	83,000	166,000
Chr & Miss Alliance	1,592	80,847	143,342
Evang Methodist Ch	295	44,964	112,000
Episcopal Ch	457	48,000	100,000
Conserv Baptist Assoc	258	30,000	75,000
Int Ch of Foursq Gosp	745	35,836	70,000
March of Faith	208	25,000	62,500
Ch of God (Cleveland)	305	24,222	60,600
Assoc of Bible Chs of P (OMF, SEND)	232	15,000	37,500
All other (256)	18,896	1,283,227	2,322,100
Denominations (270)	31,383	2,627,563	4,966,882
Evangelicals 5.1% of pop		1,684,000	3,184,000
Pentecostal/charismatic 2.8%		954,000	1,766,000

Missionaries:
 to Philippines 2,957 (1:21,000 people) in 170 agencies.
 from Philippines 2,159 (1:2,200 Protestants) in 62 agencies 173frn 735xcul 1,424dom.
Roman Catholic 65%. Affil 63.5%. Growth 2.1%.

Catholic Ch	2,504	26,000,000	48,120,000
Doubly counted		−4,600,000	−8,500,000
Total	2,504	21,400,000	39,620,000
Charismatic		100,000	190,000

Missionaries:
  to Philippines 247 (1:252,000 people).
  from Philippines 850 (1973).
Other Catholic 8.1%. Growth 1.4%.

Phil Independent Ch	8,571	3,000,000	4,800,000
All other (100)	500	100,000	250,000
Denominations (101)	9,071	3,100,000	5,050,000
Foreign Marginal 1.04%. Growth 9.3%.			
Jehovah's Witnesses	2,981	104,519	348,000
Mormons	638	149,000	213,000
All groups (11)	3,971	287,668	646,208

Indigenous Marginal 8.4%. Growth 4%.

Iglesia ni Cristo	8,400	1,050,000	1,750,000
All groups (282)	18,617	2,985,000	5,225,000

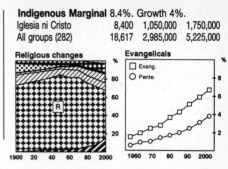

Religious changes

Evangelicals
□ Evang.
○ Pente.

1. **Praise God for answered prayer in giving dramatic growth in Protestant churches since 1974.**
The turmoil, suffering and rapid changes in the nation have prepared millions to seek a personal faith
in Christ. Growth has been marked in all evangelical groups, but more especially among the
Pentecostal and charismatic fellowships, many of which are indigenous in origin. The number of
congregations in denominations that had gathered statistics doubled from 10,000 to over 20,000 in the
'80s.

2. **The Roman Catholic Church** faces the end of privileged influence. The election of a Protestant
president is an indication of this. The Church faces three critical issues:
a) **Response to the gross inequalities and corruption in society.** There is deep division between
   conservatives and those who support leftist revolution. Pray for a return to biblical values and
   priorities.
b) **The successes of Evangelicals** which have provoked opposition, especially to the DAWN
   church-planting movement and the New Life 2000 campaign of **CCC**. Pray that this may not
   affect the freedom to evangelize and that Evangelicals would respond courageously, wisely and
   gracefully.
c) **The need for renewal.** Many Catholics are practising animists and spiritists. Yet the study of
   Scripture and charismatic renewal have touched hundreds of thousands, many of whom have
   come to personal faith in Christ. Pray that the Church may be invigorated and renewed by the
   Holy Spirit.

3. **Bold goals for achievement by the year 2000** have been set by many denominations and agencies.
The influence of the Church Growth movement on Filipino Christian leaders, the impact of
international, regional and national congresses between 1966 and 1980, and the Christ Only Way
home Bible study movement of the '70s all laid the foundation for this vision for growth through
church multiplication. The **Discipling A Whole Nation** (DAWN) vision was taken up by many
leaders in 1979–80 with the overall goals:
a) At least one church in each of the 42,000 barangays (neighbourhoods) by 2000; about a third now
   have a Protestant church; the greatest challenge to achieve this goal is in Mindanao – mainly in the
   Muslim areas.
b) Increase congregations from 10,000 in 1979 to 50,000 by 2000. The multiplication of
   congregations was almost on target in 1992, but not for planting churches in **every** barangay.
Praise God for the degree of cooperation this national strategy has stimulated, but pray for the
attainment of these goals.

4. **Danger points for the Filipino Church.**
a) **Rapid growth with inadequate discipling.** Many are prone to delusion by erroneous teachings.
b) **Poverty leading to dependency on foreign funds**, with all the abuses and spiritual
   impoverishment that can follow. Pray for reliance on God in the churches, and for sensitivity on
   the part of funding agencies.
c) **Insufficient leaders.** Praise God for outstanding Filipino leaders, but their numbers are too few.
   The frequent divisions in denominations and the proliferation of new groups often led by those
   with minimal training, and almost no accountability, have given rise to doctrinal distortions,
   fanciful interpretations and moral failures. Pray for the 100+ seminaries and Bible Schools from
   primary to postgraduate level. Some key seminaries: The Alliance Biblical Seminary (**CMA**),
   ATS, FEBIAS (**SEND Int**) and FEAST (**AoG**). TEE programmes are many and vital if run well.
   Many of the better-qualified Christian workers emigrate to the USA.

P

d) **Lack of spiritual unity** across denominational lines. Pray for the work of the Philippines Council of Evangelical Churches in its ministry of promoting unity, cooperation, and confirmation and proclamation of the gospel.

5. **The democratic government** needs prayer. Courageous and unpopular decisions on moral, social and economic issues will have to be taken if the underlying causes for Communist and Muslim insurgency are to be tackled. The corruption, self-seeking and greed of the powerful will have to be confronted and the wave of violence, crime and extortion (often aided and abetted by the army, police and judiciary) ended. Pray that Christians in positions of power and influence may be incorruptible, valiant for Truth, and fervent in righting these social evils. On some islands churches are still closed due to guerrilla warfare – notably in Panay, Samar, parts of Luzon and Mindanao. There have also been some brutal killings of Christians by both Communists and Muslims.

6. **Praise the Lord for the missionary burden of Filipino Christians!** Cultural flexibility, use of English and simplicity of life style have helped Filipinos to adapt well as missionaries. Their numbers have grown to nearly 2,200, of which over 700 are known to be in cross-cultural ministry and 170 or more overseas. The **DAWN** movement has set the goal of 2,000 cross-cultural missionaries by the year 2000, half of which are to be overseas. Poor church backing, lack of finances, visa difficulties, and Asian class structures inhibit the development of this movement. Pray for Bible school educators, denominational leaders and local pastors who are the ones who will have to recruit, train and send missionaries. Some significant agencies with Filipino cross-cultural workers are: **YWAM** (125 workers), Philippines Missionary Fellowship (**PMF**) (87), **NTM** (66), Translators Assoc. of Philippines (47), **OM** (40), United Evangelical Church Mission (22), **OCI** (15), **OMF** (11), **CMA** (11). **PMF's** Missionary Training Institute and the Asian Center for Missionary Education specifically provide cross-cultural preparation for would-be missionaries.

7. **The multiplication of foreign mission agencies** has continued. There are many opportunities for service: pioneer evangelism, the urban poor, Bible teaching, student work and technical ministries. Pray for a humble sensitivity on the part of missionaries in a time when Filipino Christians are seeking an identity of their own rather than adopting North American culture. Some larger agencies are: **NTM** (388 workers), **SIL** (344), **OMF** (171), **SBC** (168), **AoG** (108), **CBFMS** (79), **SEND** (77), **CMA** (75), **ABWE** (56), **RBMU** (43), **IMI** (31). Major missionary-contributing nations: USA (207), Canada (201), Korea (199), New Zealand (100), UK (93), Australia (53), Germany (50). Safety is a major prayer item. A number of missionaries have been kidnapped, violated and even killed by guerrillas and criminal gangs.

8. **Less-reached peoples.** A surge of interest has produced advances to unreached areas and peoples in the '80s. Both expatriate and Filipino missionaries have seen breakthroughs with new churches planted. The major challenge is for the evangelization of the nearly four million Muslims in 14 ethnic groups and of small tribal peoples yet unreached. **SIL** and others have achieved the remarkable record of completing 42 New Testaments by 1992, with teams continuing work in a further 56 (and targeting another 13 or more). There are yet five more languages with a definite need and a further 45 with a possible need of a New Testament translation. Pray for the completion of this task, and that the Bible might enter into the culture and hearts of every people. Pray for the less reached on these islands:

a) **Mindanao.** The **Muslim Maranao**, **Magindanao** and **Iranun** live in central Mindanao. Several churches have been planted through the work of a combined **OMF**, **SEND**, **RBMU**, **IMI**, **TEAM**, **UFM** and **SIM** team as well as through Filipino and Indonesian missionaries, but these successes have provoked reaction, with one church building in Zamboanga being razed and the congregation scattered. The 18 **Manobo** tribal peoples are isolated, and outreach to them is limited by warfare and intimidation. Nevertheless, the number of Christians has increased markedly in some groups. **CMA**, **OMF**, Baptist, **NTM** and Filipino agencies minister to some of these peoples. Pray for churches to be planted that will be spiritually strong and maturely led to cope with the influx of colonists, guerrillas and materialism that encroach on their old life styles and lands. Lowland Filipinos have often exploited the mountain peoples.

b) **The Sulu Islands** in the far south, the home of the **Muslim Tausug, Samal and Yakan** peoples. Opposition to Christians has been severe, and fruit of **CMA** work slow to develop. There are four Samal churches and a few groups of Tausug and Yakan believers. The Muslim Sama are former pirates and slave traders, but civil unrest has made the southern Sama more open; there are now four churches among them. Among the Sama Bajau (30,000) Islam is less strong, but there is only one known family of believers.

c) **Palawan,** a long, isolated, underdeveloped island in the southwest, only partially evangelized. It is home to the **Muslim Palawani** (45,000), **Molbog** (5,600), and **Jama Mapun** (15,000) on nearby Cagayan Island. **NTM** have seen some Molbog come to faith in Christ. **SIL** and others have translation teams working in these languages, and **Brethren** and **NTM** workers are pioneering among groups of the Palawani, but, to date, no churches have been planted. **NTM** also has a pioneering work among six of the small isolated animist tribes in the mountains.

d) **Luzon,** the largest island. It has a number of less reached peoples – mainly the settled central mountain peoples. The Ifugao, Tinggian Bontok (85,000), Kankanay, Kalinga (70,000) and Isnag (15,000) are largely animist, and have only recently begun to see the first breakthroughs and respond to the gospel. Pray for the continuing translation and literacy work of **SIL** and other missions such as **NTM** and **RBMU** who are working to establish or strengthen the young churches. Many small, semi-nomadic hunter-gatherer Dumagat Negrito peoples live on the typhoon-lashed, rugged north and northeast coastal mountains of Luzon. Few have become Christian, and the task of church planting is complex. **NTM** has made a large investment of personnel among these peoples.

e) **Mindoro.** The seven Mangyan tribes of the mountainous interior are no longer unreached, though pockets of animism and opposition to the gospel remain. **OMF**'s work has resulted in a network of tribal churches that have begun sending missionaries to tribal peoples on Luzon. Second-generation Christianity is now the problem. New Testaments are completed in three languages and soon will be available in three others.

f) **Samar and Leyte Islands,** the home of the **Waray-Waray.** Most of the land area is overrun by Communist guerrillas, poverty is desperate, Catholicism nominal and less than 1% are Evangelicals. Conditions are harsh for Christian witness, but the spiritual need is great.

9. **Manila** may now be the home of over 10 million people – three million of whom live in squalid shanty-town slums, some living on and from the six city rubbish dumps. There are 900 depressed areas in the city, 400 of which have no church. Most of the churches are in the more affluent areas. A massive effort with worldwide prayer has brought significant improvements since 1985, with a doubling of the number of churches by 1990 and a far greater effort to reach the poor. Special mention must be made of the innovative ministries of **Action International** (85 workers) and **Servants to Asia's Urban Poor** (24). The problems in planting viable autonomous churches in the midst of such deprivation and moral degradation present a challenge to prayer.

10. **The Chinese** number 800,000, but only 3% are Protestant. Many more are Catholic. There are only about 58 predominantly Chinese congregations; most are wealthy, but few Chinese are prepared to volunteer for full-time service. The wave of crime and kidnappings has unsettled the community; their relative wealth makes them prime targets. Pray that this may lead many to the security found in Jesus.

11. **Student ministry** among the 1,200,000 students in the many universities has developed well despite the strong leftist element which inhibits open evangelism. Many groups are involved – **CMA, CCC, Navigators, AoG** and also the IVCF(**IFES**) (**OMF**-assisted) with 40 keen staff workers and 150 associates. Pray for the development of strong witnessing groups in the universities and high schools – the latter a major thrust of IVCF(**IFES**).

12. **Christian media ministries.**

a) **Literature** is extensively used by Christians. There are over 44 denominational and non-denominational literature agencies for printing, publishing and distribution. Pray for the work started by **OMF** (publishing house and network of bookstores), **CMA, CLC** and others. There are more than 100 Christian bookstores in the country. The use of Bible comic books is proving effective in reaching youth.

b) **Christian radio and television.** Extensive use of radio and TV is made by Christians. Few countries are better served. The former President, Corazon Aquino, even declared the first week in June as "National Gospel Broadcast Week". A Christian TV channel is also planned.

c) **FEBC Philippines** has 20 stations from which 2,200 hours of programmes per week are broadcast in 61 languages and dialects to the Philippines and other parts of Asia. Pray for:
   i) The 200 (mainly Filipino) staff, that they may know the blessing of the Lord in ministries that are often behind the scenes.
   ii) The programming studios and programme producers, smooth running of broadcasting equipment, printing presses, and follow-up ministries.

   iii) The spiritual impact on Filipino audiences. Many local stations are used for smaller language groups.

   iv) The fruitfulness of international ministries to Asian countries and regions more difficult to access – especially China, Siberia, Indo-China and Myanmar.

d) **The _Jesus_ film** has had an immense impact. Millions have been confronted with the claims of Christ but need to be gathered into congregations where they can be discipled. The film is available in Bicol, Cebuano, Hiligaynon, Ilocano, Maranao, Pampangan, Pangasinan, Tagalog and Waray as well as in English.

e) **GRn** have prepared messages in 118 languages of the nation.

Pitcairn Island

See under PACIFIC Region

Poland

(The Republic of Poland)

Area 313,000 sq.km. Central European plain.

Population	Ann. Gr.	Density
1990	38,423,000	0.65 %	123/sq.km
1995	39,365,000	0.49 %	126/sq.km

Peoples:
Slav 97.9%. Polish 365,000; Ukrainian 260,000; Byelorussian 230,000; Kashubian 200,000; Russian 60,000; Slovak 38,000.
Other 2.1%. German 310,000; Greek 114,000; Gypsy 81,000; Lithuanian 11,500.

Literacy 99%. **Official language:** Polish. **All languages** 10. **Languages with Scriptures** 4Bi 1por.

Capital: Warsaw 1,700,000. Other major cities: Lodz 900,000, Kraków 850,000. Urbanization 60%.

Economy: The centralized command economy under Communism impoverished and polluted the country. Since 1989 the gradual transition to an export-oriented market economy has been slowed by world recession and the difficulty of restructuring unprofitable heavy industry. The painful reform programme is bearing fruit, and by mid-1993 Poland was the first post-Communist economy to show real growth through private enterprise. Unemployment 14% (1993). Public debt/person $912. Income/person $4,560 (21% of USA).

Politics: Centuries of conflict and occupation by surrounding regional superpowers – Austria, Russia, Germany, France. One quarter of the population died in World War II. The Soviet army imposed a Communist regime in 1945. Popular discontent and the grass-roots Solidarity movement helped to bring democracy to Poland in 1989. A multi-party democracy with 29 parliamentary parties. Unstable coalitions to mid-1992 and disputes over the division of powers between parliament and president delayed implementation of some reforms. More stability since then as economic improvements become more obvious. Membership of the EC is being sought.

Religion: Since the collapse of Communist rule, the Catholic Church has reasserted its traditionally strong role in national affairs and its desire to establish a state based on Catholic principles and theology. Non-Catholics fear the erosion of their present freedoms that could lead to discrimination and even intolerance.
Non-religious/other 2.4%.

Jews 0.02%. The 3.5 million Jews in 1939 are reduced to 9,000 today.
Muslims 0.01%. Descendants of Tatars.
Christian 97.6%. Affil 96.6%. Growth 0.9%.
Protestant 0.49%. Growth 2.9%.

Church	Cong	Members	Affiliated
Ev Ch of Augsburg			
Conf	352	68,300	91,000
Seventh-day Adventist	130	10,000	40,000
Assemblies of God	143	12,400	16,500
Methodist Ch	50	3,500	7,000
Polish Baptist Union	56	3,150	5,000
Reformed Evang Ch	17	2,800	4,000
All other (16)	310	14,550	23,000
Denominations (22)	1,058	114,700	186,500
Evangelicals 0.15% of pop		38,460	59,360
Pentecostal/charis 0.06%		16,600	23,000

Missionaries:
to Poland est. 77 (1:500,000 people) in 25 agencies.
from Poland 67 (1:2,800 Protestants) in 5 agencies
6frn 6xcul 61dom.
Roman Catholic 94.3%. Affil 93.4%. Growth 0.8%.

Catholic Ch	8,573	23,700,000	35,377,000
Cath – Eastern-rite	50	250,000	500,000
Denominations (2)	8,623	23,950,000	35,877,000
Charismatic 1.6%		300,000	600,000

Missionaries:
from Poland 1,028 (1973 figure).
Other Catholic 0.21%. Growth −1.3%.

Polish Nat Cath Ch	67	20,100	38,000
All other (5)	232	27,950	43,600
Denominations (6)	299	48,050	81,600
Orthodox 2.1%. Growth 2.6%.			
Orthodox Ch	451	496,000	800,000
Denominations (4))	456	499,840	806,600
Marginal 0.43%. Growth 7.7%.			
Jehovah's Witnesses	1,248	96,841	161,000
All other (12)	15	2,230	4,500
Denominations (13)	1,263	99,071	165,500

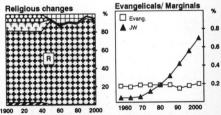

Religious changes

Evangelicals/ Marginals
☐ Evang.
▲ JW

1. **Hard-won political and religious freedoms are savoured with delight** – but so easily could be lost. Pray for political and economic stability and progress that would give no opportunity for a new dictatorship of the right. Above all, pray that repentance from sin and personal faith in Christ may be freely preached and welcomed in every part of the nation. Pray also that the leaders of the land may be wise and far-sighted in directing the country's affairs.

2. **The Catholic Church** was the custodian of Polish culture and nationalism in the face of Russian imperialism and Soviet Communism. It successfully blocked all efforts by the Communists to deprive it of its independence and foist atheism on the nation. It is theologically conservative and has regained a powerful political influence since the fall of Communism.

a) **Pray that new-found political power may be sensitively exercised.** Much resentment has been generated by its strong stand on moral issues and by compulsory religious education in schools. Attendance at mass has plunged from 90% to 15–20% in three years.

b) **Pray that Poland's religious leaders** may be men who know a life of holiness and a walk with God. The election of Polish John Paul II to the papacy and the large number of candidates for the priesthood (25% of Europe's total) are indicative of the influence religious leaders can exercise in coming years.

c) **Oasis is an evangelical movement within the Catholic Church.** Hundreds of thousands of nominal Catholics have come to a warm personal faith in Christ as a result of the Bible study groups, camps, publishing house and network of bookshops. Informal fellowships and Bible study groups continue to multiply in the cities. Pray that the leadership may retain and develop a sound, healthy biblical orientation despite pressures to conform to traditional teachings. Pray also that those in the movement may grow in their knowledge of the Lord and be a blessing to others.

3. **Freedom has caused an explosion of new movements and activity** – some good, some harmful.

a) **Evangelism has increased.** Local churches have reached out in the streets, public places and prisons. Tent missions have been conducted. **EHC** reached one million homes with literature in 1992. Pray for lasting fruit and church growth, and that present opportunities might be used to the full.

b) **Church growth has been strongest** in Pentecostal denominations and the Adventists. Pray for warm fellowship and cooperation between churches at the national and local levels. Many new church buildings are being erected.

c) **Evangelical unity** has been limited. The years of freedom have brought both a multiplication and division of denominations. Pray that the Holy Spirit may bring reconciliation, love and unity of vision at the foot of the Cross. There is a slowly dawning realization that Evangelicals need each other. In 1992 the first **March for Jesus** was organized in major cities.

d) **The multiplication of foreign sects and religions** has brought confusion. Jehovah's Witnesses are more numerous than Evangelicals (see graph above). New Age and eastern religious movements have rapidly gained a following. Occultism and materialism are on the rise. Pray for the disarming of every ideological assault and a demonstration of the power and lordship of Jesus Christ.

4. **Bible training for leaders** is developing fast. By 1993 there were 20 Protestant institutions ranging from seminary level to part-time or correspondence Bible schools – remarkable for a land with so small a Protestant presence! Pray for biblical faithfulness, spiritual power and missions vision to be the hallmark of the ministry of graduates.

5. **University students** – 362,000 in 92 universities and colleges – are receptive to the gospel. The Christian Students Association (**IFES**), with its flourishing international links, has groups in 22 of the 30 universities and is seeking to develop a high school ministry.

6. **The less-reached:**

a) **The Jews and Muslims** are the only unreached peoples in the country, but their numbers are small. There is a sad rise in anti-Semitism.

b) **The evangelical witness** is limited. Thousands of towns and villages have no evangelical presence at all, but the nation needs to be researched and Christian resources wisely deployed for maximum effectiveness.

Pray that Polish believers may gain a vision for missions and develop structures to send their own missionaries to Central Europe and beyond.

7. **Foreign mission agencies** long had a supportive role in Communist days. Many agencies now have workers based in Poland. Pray that cultural sensitivity, humble servanthood to the small but developing evangelical cause, and spiritual fruitfulness may characterize their ministry in the new Poland. Agencies include **OM** and **ECM**.

8. **Literature** ministries have multiplied – publishers, printers and distributors (Baptists, **CLC**). The amount of Christian literature has increased substantially. The major limitation is lack of funds in the inflated economy with rapid price rises. Pray for the work of the Bible Society, which has a key role in both Poland and surrounding lands. Demand for Bibles outstrips supply – the Bible Society prints on average 1,000 Bibles a day.

9. **Christian radio and television programmes** may be aired on national and local networks; **TWR**-Monaco also broadcasts daily for 24 hours/week in Polish. Pray for the provision and preparation of high-quality programmes that will change lives (Baptists and **AoG**).

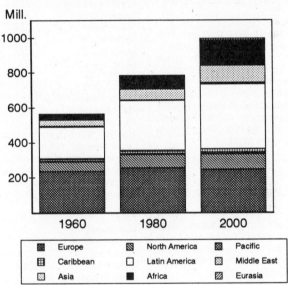

Distribution of Roman Catholics by Region

Catholic growth is slowing. Note:

1. The decline in numbers in Europe.

2. Growth in North America – mainly through immigration.

3. Growth in Latin America, but slower than population growth; large losses to Pentecostals and, in Brazil, to spiritism.

4. Strong growth in Africa and Eurasia.

P

<table>
<tr><td>September
21

Europe</td></tr>
</table>

Portugal
(Portuguese Republic)

Area 92,000 sq.km. Occupying 15% of the Iberian Peninsula, which is shared with Spain. Also the Atlantic islands of the Azores (2,247 sq.km, 9 islands) and Madeira (794 sq.km, 2 islands).

Population	Ann. Gr.	Density
1990 10,285,000	0.25 %	111/sq.km
1995 10,429,000	0.28 %	113/sq.km

Peoples:
Portuguese 96.6%. Nearly 900,000 refugees from African colonies were added to the population at their independence in 1975. 1,300,000 Portuguese are guest-workers in other European countries.
Other indigenous minorities 0.9%. Gypsies 84,500; Galician 10,400.
Immigrant minorities 2.5%. Brazilians 103,000; Angolans and Mozambicans 100,000; Spanish 41,000; Cape Verdians 31,000; Arabs 27,000; Goanese 20,000; Timorese 3,000.

Literacy 84%. West Europe's lowest level. **Official language:** Portuguese. **All languages** 5.

Capital: Lisbon 1,705,000. Urbanization 30%.

Economy: The poorest country in the European Community, but EC aid and trade is bringing rapid development and modernization of industry. Living standards are rising and unemployment decreasing – now at 4.6% of the work force. Public debt/person $2,800. Income/person $4,260 (20% of USA).

Politics: Independent kingdom from 1143. A republic in 1910. 48 years of dictatorship ended in a revolution in 1974 in which a socialist democracy was instituted. All Portugal's African colonies (Mozambique, Angola, Guinea-Bissau, São Tomé and Cape Verde) were hastily granted independence in 1975. Membership of the EC since 1986 has brought stability and moderation in politics.

Religion: Freedom of religion since the 1974 revolution, and a rapid secularization and pluralization of religious attitudes. Traditional Catholicism remains influential.
Non-religious/other 3.8%.
Muslim 0.2%. Arabs, Africans.

Christian 96%. Nom 4.7%. Affil 91.3%. Growth 0.3%.
Protestant 1.24%. Growth 5.7%.

Church	Cong	Members	Affiliated
Assemblies of God	497	25,000	33,300
Manna Christian Ch	31	10,000	25,000
Seventh-day Adventist	100	7,000	16,000
Christian Brethren	117	4,000	6,670
Baptist Convention	58	3,943	5,260
Presbyterian Ch	35	1,700	5,000
Methodist Ch	19	1,260	5,000
Lusitanian Ch	17	1,250	5,000
Congregatn. of Christ	102	3,000	5,000
All other (46)	338	12,918	21,597
Denominations (55)	1,314	70,071	97,262
Evangelicals 0.95% of pop		58,000	97,000
Pentecostal/charis 0.69%		43,000	71,000

Missionaries:
to Portugal 335 (1:30,700 people) in 60 agencies.
from Portugal 168 (1:760 Protestants) in 18 agencies 123frn 112xcul 56dom.

Roman Catholic 93.9%. Affil 89.2%.
Practising 25%. Growth 0.2%.

Catholic Ch	4,339	6,600,000	9,300,00
Doubly Counted		−85,000	−120,000
Total	4,339	6,515,000	9,180,000

Missionaries:
to Portugal 260 (1973 figure).
from Portugal 2,309 (1973 figure).
Orthodox 0.01%. Growth 0%.

Greek Orthodox Ch	1	600	1,200

Marginal 0.9%. Affil 0.85%. Growth 10%.

Jehovah's Witnesses	546	38,071	64,500
Mormons	105	11,500	23,000
Groups (3)	651	49,613	87,572

Missionaries to Portugal 600 (nearly all Mormons).

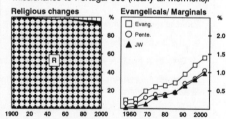

Religious changes — Evangelicals/ Marginals

1. **Political upheavals and social changes since 1970** have transformed the nation from a backward, dictatorial colonial power to a modern industrial democracy. With this has come unprecedented religious liberty. Sadly, this has not resulted in a large number coming to personal faith in Christ. The old bondages remain – the veneration of Mary is a "Christian" veneer over the old paganism, and an

estimated 90% of the population consult spiritist mediums and witches. To this are added the new bondages of materialism, alcoholism, drug abuse, New Age movements, Mormonism and Jehovah's Witnesses – the latter two being almost as numerous as Evangelicals. Pray for the spiritual liberation of Portugal.

2. **The Roman Catholic Church** is strongly traditional, and needs renewal. The north is more loyal to the Church, but in the centre and south the Church is becoming irrelevant to the secularized majority of the population. Pray for a renewing work of the Holy Spirit in which many are opened to the illumination of the Scriptures, freed from traditionalism and introduced to a warm personal relationship with Jesus.

3. **Evangelicals** have had two decades of freedom to proclaim the gospel after years of restrictions and discrimination. Growth has generally been slow, but among Pentecostal denominations there has been significant growth of late – especially in the Assemblies of God and newer charismatic fellowships. What are some of the constraints?
a) **Lack of a united vision** to reach the nation for Christ.
b) **Lack of full-time Christian workers.** There are only 350 pastors for the 1,168 churches. Many congregations are very small and hardly viable.
c) **Doctrinal confusion.** The strong emphasis on prosperity teaching in one charismatic group has divided and devastated a number of evangelical congregations and ultimately caused disillusionment and backsliding to many who were ensnared.
Pray for cooperative efforts being launched such as the **March for Jesus** and the possibility of a DAWN programme for the nation. Pray for the mobilization of all believers for outreach.

4. **Bible training is a key ministry** in the light of the lack of full-time workers with adequate theological depth. Pray for the nine seminaries, including Assemblies of God, Portuguese Bible Institute founded by **GEM**, Word of Life, Presbyterian, Baptist and Bethel Bible Institutes founded by Brazilian missionaries. A number of significant TEE programmes fill a real need for those already involved in leadership, including *Núcleo* and ICI (**AoG**).

5. **The less-reached.** Pray for:
a) **The seven northern and northeastern provinces** which are strongly traditional Catholic; relatively few evangelical churches exist. Brethren, Baptists, **AoG**, *Missão Antioquia*, **GEM** and **WEC** have commenced church-planting programmes.
b) **The four provinces of the south** which are poor, with few people ever going to church. Attendance at mass by people in Beja province is less than 3% of the population. Evangelical churches are few.
c) **The 316 counties, 73 of which have no evangelical congregation.** In these counties live 800,000 people.
d) **The 4,400 localities.** Only 768 have a resident evangelical witness.
e) **Madeira Island** (273,000) which has only 16 small evangelical churches, and the **Azores** (253,000) with a further 29, most being Assemblies of God and Baptist. Three of the nine islands have no churches.
f) **Outreach to minorities** – Goanese, Arabs and others – which is limited. Possibly 100,000 Macao Chinese will migrate to Portugal before China takes over this colony in 1999. Few are Christian.
g) **Marginalized youth.** Some estimate that 50% of young people have experimented with drugs. Many need deliverance. Teen Challenge has a ministry directed to their need.

6. **The 1,300,000 Portuguese migrant workers** in other countries of Europe need the gospel. Many live in difficult conditions with little thought for anything but making money. It is difficult to reach them with the gospel and to plant churches among them. Pray for workers to evangelize the 1,000,000 in France, 80,000 in Belgium, 78,000 in Germany, 50,000 in Luxembourg and 30,000 in Britain.

7. **Since 1974 missionary workers have increased**, but evangelical missionaries are half as numerous as the 600 Mormon missionaries. Portugal is not an easy field for foreigners to find acceptance so pray for their perseverance and fruitfulness. Workers of quality are needed in the many unreached areas for ministry in evangelism, church planting, Bible training and music. Short-term team evangelism by young people could also be productive. Some significant missions: AoG (26 workers), **Word of Life** (24), **WEC** (15), **GEM** (14), **CoN** (12), Bethel (11), **TEAM** (11), **BCU** (9). A growing number of Brazilian missionaries are entering the land (58 in 1991) and finding acceptance once they realize that Portugal is different from Brazil. Major missionary-contributing nations: USA (175), Brazil (58), UK (44).

8. **Student work** is still in a pioneer stage. GBUP(**IFES**) has a ministry that is established in eight universities and also in some high schools. **CCC** also has a ministry on one campus. **SU** and **CEF** have small, but useful, ministries among school children. **YWAM** is launching **Kings Kids** and a Discipleship Training School to challenge young people for missions. Pray for a more extensive and effective outreach to the youth.

9. **Christian Media**
a) **Literature:**
   i) The growing ministry of Bible production and distribution by the **Bible Society**.
   ii) *Núcleo* which has a vital coordinating ministry for the Body of Christ in research, publishing, printing tracts and distributing cassettes and films.
   iii) **CEDO**, the quarterly gospel broadsheet ministry of **WEC**, with 40,000 going out each edition all over Portugal and 60 nations around the world. Response is heavy from Mozambique and Angola.
   iv) Eight **Christian bookstores**, one run by **CLC**.
b) **Christian radio and TV.** Pray for greater access for Evangelicals to radio and for openings on Portuguese TV stations.

P

Puerto Rico

Area 9,100 sq.km. Greater Antilles; between Dominican Republic and the Virgin Islands.

Population	Ann. Gr.	Density
1990 3,709,000	1.5 %	407/sq.km
1995 3,958,000	1.3 %	435/sq.km

Peoples:
Euro-American 74.7%. Spanish-speaking 2,690,000; English-speaking 82,000.
Afro-Caribbean 25.2%. Mostly Spanish-speaking; a few French- and English-speaking.
Asian 0.1%. Chinese 2,000.

Literacy 89%. **Official Languages:** Spanish, English.

Capital: San Juan 1,253,000. **Urbanization** 71%.

Economy: Densely populated with few natural resources but much aid from USA. Industry and tourism are the main sources of income. Unemployment 15%. Income/person $6,010 (30% of USA).

Politics: A Spanish colony for 400 years. Conquered by USA in 1898. Became self-governing Commonwealth associated with the USA in 1952. There is hot debate on the nation's future – independence or statehood within the USA.

Religion: Freedom of religion is a constitutional right. All media, state facilities and public schools are open for the free exercise of religion.
Non-religious/other 2%.
Christian 98%. Affil 90.1%. Growth 1.2%.
  Protestant 28%. Affil 26% Growth 4.7%.

Church	Cong	Members	Affiliated
Pente Ch of God	480	66,953	112,000
Seventh-day Adventist	247	29,950	74,900
Assemblies of God	146	39,000	70,900
Baptist Convention	82	27,000	54,000
United Methodist Ch	70	10,000	25,000
Ch of God (Cleveland)	199	14,689	24,500
Defenders of the Faith	123	12,000	24,000
Chr & Miss Alliance	51	5,631	14,100
Other Pentecostal (22)	2,102	256,000	410,000
All other (52)	985	85,201	156,066
Denominations (82)	4,485	546,424	965,466
Evangelicals 22.5% of pop		484,000	834,000
Pentecostal/charis 19%		421,000	703,000

Missionaries:
  to Puerto Rico 141 (1:26,300 people) in 31 agencies.
  from Puerto Rico 65 (1:14,900 Protestants) in 5 agencies.

Roman Catholic 66.6% (officially 91%).
Affil 60.7%. Growth −0.2%.

Catholic Ch	316	1,580,000	2,771,930
Doubly Counted		−296,400	−520,000
Total		1,283,600	2,251,930

Missionaries:
  to Puerto Rico 1,650 (1973 figure).
  from Puerto Rico 520 (1973 figure).

Marginal 3.4%. Affil 2.43%. Growth 6.1%.

Jehovah's Witnesses	293	24,042	68,700
Mormons	49	11,200	16,000
All other (5)	23	2,750	5,500
Groups (7)	365	37,992	90,200

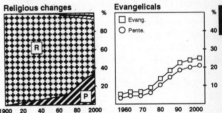

1. **Praise God for the growth of evangelical churches over the past generation.** Widespread evangelism, a large missionary input and a responsive people has resulted in nearly 30% of the population becoming Protestant. There is also a strong charismatic movement within the Catholic Church. Pentecostals make up 84% of all Evangelicals.

2. **Anglophone North American culture has made a deep impact on Hispanic Puerto Ricans.** Although creating fertile soil for change, this impact has also provoked an identity crisis which affects politics, the Catholic Church and church/mission relationships. Pray for maturity and vision for indigenous leadership in the churches. There are over 12 seminaries or Bible schools in the Commonwealth.

3. **The Puerto Rican Church** faces three major challenges:
a) Evangelicals need to play a bigger and more positive role in society by tackling social evils such as crime, divorce, drug and alcohol abuse and suicide. Puerto Rico has some of the highest rates for these evils in the world.

b) Rivalry between denominations.

c) Sharpened missionary vision. Most of Puerto Rico's missionaries are involved in ministry to Puerto Ricans in the USA. Most of the cross-cultural missionaries are with **YWAM** or **OM** and several indigenous Pentecostal Churches.

4. **Over-population and unemployment have forced over 1.5 million Puerto Ricans to emigrate to the USA.** Sixty per cent live in New York, where they form the lowest income group. Many live in Hispanic ghettos, where frustration has driven large numbers to violence, drugs and immorality. Pray for all specifically ministering to this community.

<table>
<tr><td>

September 23

Middle East

</td><td>

Qatar

(The State of Qatar)

</td><td></td></tr>
</table>

Area 11,400 sq.km. Arabian Gulf peninsula that is almost entirely desert.

Population		Ann. Gr.	Density
1990	444,000	8.2 %	39/sq.km
1995	516,000	3.1 %	45/sq.km

Peoples:
Indigenous Qatari Arab 20%.
Other Arab 25%. Lebanese, Syrian, Palestinian and Egyptian.
South Asian 34%. Pakistani (Urdu, Baloch), Indian (Tamil, Malayali, etc.), Sri Lankan.
Other 21%. Iranian 73,000; Westerner 9,000.

Literacy 76%. **Official language:** Arabic.

Capital: Doha 217,000. Urbanization 88%.

Economy: Petroleum products are 82% of exports. Qatar has some of the world's largest gas reserves. Oil wealth used to diversify the economy. Public debt/person $2,400. Income/person $9,920 (47% of USA). The Qataris live in great wealth, but the Asians in considerable poverty.

Politics: Part of Turkish-Ottoman Empire until 1918, then under British protection until independence in 1971. An absolute monarchy, but growing protests from Qataris at abuses of power by the Emir.

Religion: The strict Wahhabi form of Sunni Islam is the state religion. Proselytism of Muslims is forbidden, but expatriate Christians are allowed to meet informally.
Muslim 91.4%. Sunni 80.4%; Shi'a 11%.
Hindu 2%. **Baha'i** 0.2%.
Non-religious/other 0.4%.
Christian 6%. Nom 3.5%. Affil 2.5%. Growth 0.1%.
  Protestant 2.5%. Affil 1.1%. Growth 0.7%.

Church	Members	Affiliated
Anglican	40	300
All other (5)	1,300	4,500
Denominations (6)	1,340	4,800
Evangelicals 0.53% of pop	700	2,300

Roman Catholic 3%. Affil 1.13%. Growth 0%.

Catholic Ch	3,500	5,000

Orthodox 0.5%. Affil 0.29%. Growth −1.4%.

Denominations (3)	858	1,300

1. **There were no Qatari believers** before 1985. Several have come to the Lord outside the country, but have suffered much for him. Pray that they may become the nucleus of a Qatari Church.

2. **Expatriates are drawn from many nations by the high earnings in Qatar.** Christians are restricted in their witness because of the strict control of the authorities. Only the Anglican Church has official status. All other Catholic and Evangelical groups have to meet in homes. Pray that the small groups of believers among Indians, Pakistanis, Egyptians and Westerners may bear fruitful witness to their own communities. Pray also that there may be opportunities to share with non-Christians of all unreached people groups.

Réunion

(French Department of Réunion)

September 24

Africa

Area 2,510 sq.km. Volcanic Indian Ocean island 700 km. east of Madagascar. The largest of the Mascarene Islands which include Mauritius.

Population	Ann. Gr.	Density
1990	595,000	1.7 %	234/sq.km
1995	641,000	1.5 %	252/sq.km

Peoples: A high degree of cultural integration makes an ethnic analysis difficult. Over 80% of the population speaks Creole in the home.
Creole 42.6%. **European** 25.6%.
Indian 23%. Tamil and Gujarati.
Other 8.8%. Chinese 21,000; Comorian 17,000; Malagasy 8,000; French 2,400.

Literacy 83%. **Official language:** French. Common language: French Creole.

Capital: St. Denis 132,000. Urbanization 53%.

Economy: Overdependent on production of sugar. A subsidized outpost of the European Community and the French welfare state. Unemployment over 40%. Income/person $5,990 (28% of USA).

Politics: Overseas Department of France, hence a *de facto* member of the European Community.

Religion: Freedom of religion.
Non-religious/other 0.5%. **Baha'i** 0.8%.
Hindu 6.7% (nearer 15% unofficially). Tamil, some Gujarati.
Muslim 4.2%. Comorians, Gujarati.
Christian 87.8%. Affil 83.5%. Growth −0.6%. Possibly 50% are more animist than Christian in practice.

Protestant 5%. Affil 4.8%. Growth 12.2%.

Church	Cong	Members	Affiliated
Assemblies of God	130	12,000	20,000
Evang Ch (AEF/AIM)	12	730	3,170
Seventh-day Adventist	15	1,200	3,000
Baptist Convention	8	625	1,040
Reformed Ch	1	400	800
All other (4)	4	350	583
Denominations (9)	170	15,305	28,593
Evangelicals 4.3% of pop		14,000	25,400
Pentecostal/charis 3.45%		2,300	20,500

Missionaries to Réunion 20 (1:29,800 people) in 8 agencies.
Roman Catholic 81.9%. Affil 77.8%. Growth −1.3%.

Catholic Ch	73	259,000	463,035
Charismatic 3.1% of pop		10,400	18,000

Missionaries:
to Réunion 126 (1:4,700 people).
from Réunion 5 (1973 figure).
Marginal 0.9%. Affil 0.88%. Growth 14.6%.

Jehovah's Witnesses	19	1,833	4,950
All groups (2)	22	2,013	5,250

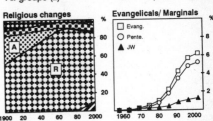

1. **The Réunionese are spiritually needy.** High unemployment and frustrated dependency on metropolitan France generate inferiority and even hatred. Over 50% of births are illegitimate, and family structures are breaking down. Alcoholism is a blight. Pray that this sick society may find hope and purpose in believing in Jesus.

2. **Although Catholicism is the professed religion** of over 80% of the population, the Malabar religion – a synthesis of Hinduism and African witchcraft – is the real faith of half the population. Since Vatican II, Bible reading has been promoted in the Catholic Church, and there is now a vigorous charismatic renewal movement. Pray for the eyes of many nominal Christians to be opened to their need and to the Saviour.

3. **Praise God for dramatic growth** in a receptive population. Since 1966 French Assemblies of God and since 1970 **AEF/AIM** missionaries have seen significant response. The Assemblies of God have been successful in seeing many freed from occult bondage. Pray for growth in grace, numbers, and spiritual understanding in these young and enthusiastic churches.

4. **Mature leadership** for the young and rapidly growing churches is a priority. The Evangelical Church commenced a Bible school in 1984. This school has had more of an impact on Madagascar; there is a lack of students from Réunion. **YWAM** has set up a Discipleship Training School in St.

Pierre to prepare young people for service throughout the Francophone Indian Ocean nations (Réunion, Mauritius, Comores, Seychelles, Madagascar).

5. Less-reached peoples:

a) **Young people.** Increased efforts to reach them are bearing fruit. Pray for the outreach and discipling ministry of **YWAM** and ministry in schools and on the university campus of *Jeunesse en Action*. Pray for a turning to the Lord, a high standard of holy living among them and for spiritual leaders for the future to be raised up.

b) **The Hindu,** most nominally Catholic but Hindu in practice.

c) **The Chinese,** also nominally Catholic, but Buddhist in worldview. **CMA**-Hong Kong have commenced a ministry among them. There are not yet any Chinese churches.

d) **The Muslims, mainly Comorians and Gujarati.** No outreach to them is known. Pray that Réunionese believers may catch the vision for their evangelization and be adequately prepared for such ministry.

6. Christian media. Pray for impact through:

a) **Christian literature and Bible distribution.** There is only one Christian bookstore; nevertheless, much has been distributed around the island.

b) **Radio.** There are private radio stations run by the Catholics, SDA and **AoG**. There is an encouraging response to **FEBA**'s daily broadcasts in French from Seychelles.

R

Romania

September 25–26
Europe

Area 237,500 sq.km. Baltic state on the lower River Danube. Adjoining Republic of Moldova, seized by the USSR in 1940, has expressed desire for reunification with Romania.

Population	Ann. Gr.	Density
1990 23,272,000	0.48 %	98/sq.km
1995 23,816,000	0.46 %	100/sq.km

Peoples:
Romanian 81%. A Latin people descended from Romans settled in Dacia.
Hungarian 7.9%. In Transylvania; restive because of Romanian efforts to suppress their culture.
Gypsy 9%. Severely persecuted by Romanians for decades. Many have fled to Germany since 1989.
Germans 0.6%. In Transylvania. Over 70% of the community has emigrated to Germany since 1988.
Other 1.5%. Turk 150,000; Serb 80,000; Ukrainian 67,000; Slovak 34,000; Jews 21,500.

Literacy 96%. **Official language:** Romanian. **All languages** 13. **Languages with Scriptures** 8Bi 1NT 4por.

Capital: Bucharest 2,231,000. Urbanization 51%.

Economy: A land rich in agriculture, minerals and oil but plundered, impoverished and polluted under Communism for the benefit of the elite. Economic liberalization since 1990 has been slow because of government reluctance and a bureaucracy that strangles progress. Public debt/person: none. Income/person $1,640 (8% of USA).

Politics: Communist coup in 1947 with Russian support. One of the Communist bloc's most oppressive and cruel regimes. The 1989/90 revolution and two democratic elections failed to unseat the leadership with their Communist past. The refurbished secret police still exercise a pervasive control. There is a revival of anti-minority nationalism against Hungarians and Gypsies. The wars in neighbouring former Yugoslavia and Moldova could deeply affect Romania.

Religion: Under Communism, manipulation and control of the churches was oppressive, with severe persecution for those who refused to submit. Religious freedom has been promised, but 1991 legislation recognizes 14 religious bodies as eligible for state subsidies and institutes a system that could be used to exert government controls on denominations and evangelism.

Non-religious/other 14%.
Muslim 1%. Turks, some Bulgarians and Gypsies.
Jews 0.1%. Declining through emigration.
Christian 84.9%. Growth 0.8%.
Protestant 8%. Growth 0.9%.

Church	Cong	Members	Affiliated
Reformed (Hussite)	1,786	500,000	715,000
Rom Bapt Union	1,300	230,000	330,000
Pentecostal Chs	1,740	208,000	320,000
Christian Brethren	571	80,000	160,000
Seventh-day Adventist	521	65,000	130,000
Ev Ch of Augsburg Confession	141	73,500	105,000
Hung Bapt Union	200	20,000	33,300
Ev Luth Synod	30	15,000	32,000
All other (6)	186	15,675	24,590
Denominations (14)	6,475	1,207,175	1,849,890
Evangelicals 4.9% of pop		739,000	1,142,000
Pentecostal/charis 1.52%		23,000	355,000

Missionaries:
to Romania 165 (1:141,000 people) in 38 agencies.
from Romania 9 (1:205,000 Protestants) in 4 agencies 2frn 2xcul 7dom.
Catholic 7.09% Growth 5.6%.

Roman Catholic Ch	1,151	756,000	1,050,000
Greek Catholic Ch	140	100,000	600,000
Denominations (2)	1,291	856,000	1,650,000

Missionaries to Romania n.a.
Orthodox 69.5% Growth 0.3%.

Rom Othdx Ch	12,347	11,900,000	17,000,000
The Lord's Army		300,000	750,000
Old Ritual Ch		46,900	70,000
Armenian Apos Ch	19	8,400	12,000
All other (6)	3	110,850	152,500
Doubly counted		−1,300,000	−1,800,000
Denominations (10)	12,369	11,066,150	16,184,500
Evangelicals 3.2%		300,000	750,000

Marginal 0.41%. Growth 3.2%.

Jehovah's Witnesses	228	19,030	29,300
All other(2)		13,450	65,900
Groups (3)	228	32,480	95,200

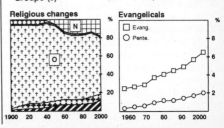

Religious changes   Evangelicals

R

1. **The 1989 revolution** removed the Ceausescu "dynasty", but not Marxist controls or attitudes. There remains a heaviness and pessimism because of unrelieved poverty and the deep wounds caused by the excesses and cruelty of the Ceausescu regime. Pray that godly rulers may address serious economic and ethnic breakdowns and also make a clean break with the tyrannies of the past.

2. **Communism created a great spiritual thirst.** Growth among Baptists, Pentecostals and Brethren has been marked for the past two decades, and greatly accelerated since 1989 with possibly 1,600 churches being planted in three years. There is a spirit of revival in many areas. Every evangelistic outreach creates much interest and yields new converts. There were over two million Protestants by 1993. Pray that no action by the enemy or man may quench the work of the Holy Spirit, and that every denomination in every part of the country may be affected.

3. **Religious freedom** is a treasured, but threatened gain. Millions have grown up with no meaningful exposure to the gospel. Some leaders in the Orthodox Church oppose Protestant and foreign evangelistic outreach. One Orthodox leader has called Protestantism "the biggest heresy in Europe". Pray that there may be full freedom for the proclamation of the gospel. Pray that relationships between the major Christian bodies may be based on respect and trust.

4. **Praise God for the harvest being reaped.** Luis Palau and other Western evangelists have been used of God to win many, but the majority of those who seek the Lord are not being integrated into Bible-believing congregations. Pray that Christians may be freed from a passive survival instinct to a joyous outreach to their countrymen.

5. **The Lord's Army** is a remarkable, unofficial renewal movement within the Orthodox Church with about 300,000 converted members and many more sympathizers. This evangelical movement is strong in the northern rural areas. It was severely persecuted by both the Communists and the Orthodox hierarchy. Pray that this movement may act as leaven in the whole Orthodox Church with its large nominal membership. The Church was compromised by some leaders who bowed to serve Communism and today by those who seek political rather than spiritual power.

6. **The challenges facing the Church.**
a) **The transition from severe persecution and restrictions to freedom** to worship and witness has been difficult. Pray for flexibility and vision for the leadership and also wisdom in handling those of their number who openly or secretly served the atheist authorities in the past.
b) **There is need for biblical teaching.** Few pastors have had formal training. The Pentecostal churches are in a theological crisis; 80% of their number have had no formal training. The result is often petty legalism, despising of sermon preparation and placing the prophetic word higher than the Scriptures.
c) **Ethnic divisions infect Christians too.** The poisoned relationships between Romanians and Hungarians and condoning the shameful treatment of Gypsies need an application of the Cross of Christ to heal these breakdowns.
d) **Materialism imported from the West** has damaged spirituality. Unwise dispensing of material help and funds in the widely publicized aftermath to the revolution in 1989 often provoked jealousy, quarrelling and division. Sadly, spirituality plummeted as links with Western agencies and congregations multiplied. Pray that these links may be developed in a way that enhances spirituality, maturity and outreach.
e) **Nominalism among the German and Hungarian Protestants.** Many of the Lutheran and Reformed Churches need renewal.
f) **The Evangelical Alliance (EA) formed in 1991** brings together five main Protestant bodies and The Lord's Army. Pray that effective, united fellowship and cooperative evangelism may be promoted.

7. **Bible training for existing and future leaders is the greatest need.** Some 90% of new churches have no pastor.
a) **Bible schools and seminaries** have been launched by the Baptists, Pentecostals, Brethren and also by the **Romanian Missionary Society** in Oradea. It is aimed that the latter eventually become a Christian university with an emphasis on preparing Christian teachers. Pray for provision of godly teachers, spiritual theological writings, and calling of the right students to prepare for Christian work.
b) **BEE** (Bible Education by Extension), a movement started from Vienna by a group of evangelical agencies (**SEND** Int, **ECM** and others), was pioneered in Romania and spread to many Communist Bloc countries. The work continues but has now become the basis of extensive

R

development of Bible training in the denominations and is now entirely run by Romanians. Pray for the hundreds of evangelical leaders studying part-time in BEE and other TEE courses.

8. **Foreign missions**, notably **Open Doors**, provided a spiritual lifeline to the believers under Communism in providing Bibles, Christian literature and practical help. After Communism's collapse, a profusion of agencies, congregations and individuals rushed in to help. Amidst much that was good and worthwhile, many went in with little tact and less wisdom to "teach", dispense favours and seek to manipulate or hire Christian workers. Pray that expatriates called to serve may show sensitivity, humility and an ability to learn from and work alongside Romanian Christians. Long-term incarnational ministry for the upbuilding of the Church, rather than much short-term foray work, is the ongoing need.

9. **Young people are numerous, families are large and schools now open for Scripture teaching**, but Christians trained for school and church work among them are few. Pray for the provision of Christian teachers so that this generation of children may be discipled. Pray also for the establishment of specialist interdenominational agencies able to minister to them – **CEF**, **YFC** and others. Strong independent groups are springing up in universities (**IFES**).

10. **Christian outreach.** Pray for a missions vision to blossom in Romania, both for the country itself and abroad. There are areas of concentration of churches such as Transylvania, but other areas with few churches. Pray for:
a) **The ministry of the *Jesus* film**, being shown all over the country by EA-appointed evangelists. Response to the message of the film is spectacular. Pray for conservation of new believers in Bible-believing churches.
b) **The Gypsy community.** Many live in ghettos and isolated villages. They are despised and neglected. An estimated 150,000 fled to Germany to escape persecution during 1991–2. Among them are some large evangelical churches, but many Gypsy communities still need to be reached.
c) **The Muslims**, predominantly Turks, Tatars and some Bulgarians. Most live in the southeast province of Constanta. Very little has been done to reach them.

11. **Christian media ministries.**
a) **Literature.** For years Romania has depended on free Western-produced Bibles and literature. Pray for the indigenous International Literature Associates Printing House in Cluj, the Romanian Bible Society, the **CLC** literature distribution base and many others, as they seek to establish a viable, indigenously-funded literature ministry. There is enormous demand despite the poverty. There is a great need for locally written literature and theological works. Few pastors have a theological library.
b) **Radio.** The EA is sponsoring television and radio programming. The Romanian Missionary Society and HCJB(**WRMF**)-Ecuador plan a network of 12 Christian radio stations to cover the country.

R

<table>
<tr><td>September
27–October 1

Eurasia</td></tr>
</table>

Russia
(Russian Federation)

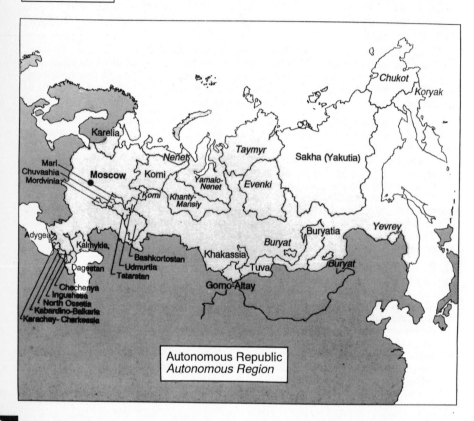

Autonomous Republic
Autonomous Region

R **Area** 17,075,000 sq.km. The world's largest country, extending across 11 time zones between the Baltic and the Pacific. The federation consists of Russia (12,439,000 sq.km.), eight European/Uralian autonomous republics (Bashkortostan, Chuvashia, Karelia, Mari, Komi, Mordvinia, Tatarstan and Udmurtia), eight Caucasus republics (Adygea, Chechenya, Dagestan, Ingushetia, Kabardino-Balkaria, Kalmykia, Karachay-Cherkessia, North Ossetia), and five Siberian republics (Buryatia, Gorno-Altay, Khakassia, Tuva and Sakha [Yakutia]). There are a further 11 autonomous regions.

Population		Ann.Gr.	Density
1990	147,970,000	0.76%	8.7/sq.km
1995	153,646,000	0.50%	9.0/sq.km

Only a third of the population lives in Siberia (Asia), where many areas are only sparsely populated.

Indo-European 89.3%. Many peoples below represent families of languages and ethnic groups.

Slav 85.5%. Russian 120,000,000; Ukrainian 4,363,000; Byelorussian 1,206,000; Polish 94,000.
Caucasus peoples 2.2%. Chechen 908,000; Avar 544,000; Kabardin 386,000; Dargin 353,000; Lezgin 257,000; Ingush 215,000; Adygey 123,000; Lak 106,000; Tabasaran 94,000; Cherkess 51,000.
Iranian 0.32%. Ossetian 402,000; Tajik 38,000.
Other 1.3%. German 842,000; Armenian 532,000; Moldavian 178,000; Gypsy 152,000; Georgian 130,000; Greek 92,000.
Turkic/Altaic 8%.
Turkic 7.6%. Tatar 5,522,000; Chuvash 1,774,000; Bashkir 1,345,000; Kazakh 636,000; Azerbaijani 336,000; Kumyk 277,000; Karachay 268,000; Khakass 79,000.
Altaic 0.4%. Buryat/Mongolian 420,000; Yakut 380,000; Tuvin 206,000; Kalmyk 166,000; Nogay 74,000; Altai 69,000; Evenki 30,000.
Finno-Ugric 2.1%. Mordvinian 1,072,000; Udmurt 714,000; Mari 644,000; Komi 336,000; Karelian/

Finnish 172,000; Komi-Permyak 147,000.
Semitic 0.38%. Jews 550,000; Assyrians 10,000.
Other Siberian peoples (15) 0.1%. Nents 34,000;
Chukchi 15,000.
Other 0.1%. Korean 107,000.

Literacy 98%. **Official language:** Russian; local
languages in autonomous republics. **All indigenous
languages** 101 (59 in Europe, 42 in Siberia).
Languages with Scriptures 6Bi 6NT 29por.

Capital: Moscow 9,000,000. Major cities: St.
Petersburg 5,035,000; Nizhniy Novgorod 4,467,000;
Novosibirsk 1,443,000; Yekaterinburg 1,375,000.
Urbanization 74%.

Economy: Russia's potential wealth is enormous.
The long-term effects of a Marxist centralized
command economy have been devastating. Industrialization and collectivization of farms were
achieved at enormous cost and with great cruelty.
Extraordinary contradictions, inefficiency and ecological neglect are bearing bitter fruit today. The
Chernobyl nuclear catastrophe in 1986 was possibly
the final trigger for the collapse of the economy and
of Communism itself. Efforts by the Russian
government to liberalize the economy and reduce
state ownership have faltered due to resistance of
the vast bureaucracy and old leadership structures
which are threatened by the changes. Hyper-
inflation and disastrous decline have been the
results.

Politics: Russia has known only autocracy or
tyranny since it became a country in the eighth
century. The Tsarist Empire collapsed in 1917
followed by the Bolshevik Communist revolution.
Russia dominated the USSR from its founding in
1922, and the Communist leadership exploited both
the ordinary Russian people, the many ethnic
groups, and client satellite states it seized or controlled. The resentment of the oppressed hastened
the dismemberment of the USSR once central
control in Moscow was weakened. Multi-party
democracy was instituted in 1990, but a failed
Communist coup in 1991 led to the subsequent
banning of the Communist Party. The battle
between the reformist democrats supported by
President Yeltsin and the ex-Communist leadership
and bureaucracy supported by Prime Minister Cher-
nomyrdin led to a stalemate in 1993, preventing
constitutional reform, delaying economic reforms
and hastening the collapse of central government. A

number of the constituent republics are seeking
total independence from Russia.

Religion: For 70 years the expressed policy of the
Communist Party was the elimination of religious
"superstition". Atheism was promoted and all open
expression of faith forbidden. All religions were
vigorously repressed, restricted, persecuted, sub-
verted or manipulated to further Communist goals.
Millions died or were imprisoned for their faith, and
thousands of churches destroyed. Religious free-
dom is now constitutionally guaranteed.
All figures below are estimates.
Non-religious/other 32.7%.
Muslim 8.7%. Mainly Turkic and Caucasus peoples.
Buddhist 0.6%. **Hare Krishna** 0.47%. **Jews** 0.4%.
Shamanist/animist 0.8%. Significant growth.
Christian 56.3%. Affil 51.6%. Growth 16.5%.
 Protestant 0.7%. (Possibly much higher.)
 Growth 4.1%.

Church	Cong	Members	Affiliated
Eurasian Bapt F'ship	1,200	150,000	429,000
Lutheran Ch		102,000	170,000
Pentecostal Union	400	35,000	130,000
Unregd Pentecostals	250	30,000	107,000
Seventh-day Adventist	205	38,000	90,000
Other Pentecostal		15,000	60,000
Indep Baptist Congs	80	10,000	30,000
Unregistered Baptist	125	10,000	20,000
Reformed Church		3,000	5,000
Denominations (9)	2,260	393,000	1,041,000
Evangelicals 0.56% of pop		278,200	831,000
Pentecostal/charis 0.23%		96,000	343,000

Missionaries:
 to Russia 473 (1:312,000 people) in over 40
 agencies.
 from Russia est. 500.
Catholic 0.48%. Growth 10.3%.

Eastern-rite Catholic	320,000	493,000
Latin-rite Catholic	143,000	220,000
All Catholics	463,000	713,000

Missionaries to Russia n.a.
Orthodox 55%. Affil 50.36%. Growth 16.8%.

Russian Orthodox Ch	8,000	46,800,000	72,000,000
All Old Believers (3)	310	1,210,000	1,700,000
Armenian Apostolic		270,000	450,000
Georgian Orthodox		42,300	65,000
All other (13)		166,450	303,000
Denominations (19)	8,310	48,490,750	74,518,000

Marginal 0.08%. Growth 19.4%.

Jehovah's Witnesses	16,800	56,000
All other (5)	36,000	60,000
Groups (6)	52,800	116,000

R

1. **The spectacular demise of Communism took the world by surprise.** The ideology that sought to
destroy Christianity and promised to parade the USSR's last Christian on television was defeated by
Christians who prayed. **Open Doors** and others called for a **seven-year campaign of prayer for the
Soviet Union** in 1984 with the specific goal of complete religious liberty and Bibles available for all.
This was achieved in 1990/91! Praise God!

2. **The Church in Russia** was the object of the most severe and sustained persecution of any nation in
recent history. Martyrs could be numbered in millions, 90% of church buildings were seized or
destroyed, structures and ministries emasculated or manipulated, leadership cowed into compliance
and compromise, Christians discriminated against, their children harassed and denied education

opportunities, and millions consigned to years of imprisonment, exile or psychiatric "treatment". Give thanks to God for his protection and enablement of his Church to survive, grow and triumph in the end. Praise God also for many agencies in the West who did so much to maintain links between the persecuted Church and Christians in the free world, and to provide Bibles, literature and practical help. Of special mention: **UBS, Open Doors, Light in the East** (Germany), **SGA** and Keston College (now Keston Research) in England, Swedish Slavic Mission, Bibles to All (Sweden) and *Avainsanoma* (Finland).

3. **Russia is still threatened by the possibility of a new tyranny.** If democracy fails, the economy continues to deteriorate, and the Russian mafia remain unchecked, an explosion could occur. Pray that leaders may have the courage and unity to give the nation stability as well as freedom, and then to address the disastrous state of the country – the result of 75 years of greed and callous thoughtlessness of past dictators and their minions.

4. **The power, ability and numbers of Russians ensure them a key role in the world's future.** There are 151 million in the world, 120 million of whom live in Russia itself and 25 million in the other republics of the former USSR. Loss of super-power status and sense of purpose has deeply affected the people. Russian nationalism has gained a strong following and is frequently expressed in anti-Semitism, religious bigotry and threats to regain territory they once ruled.

5. **The Russian Federation is a ferment of ethnic confusion.** Millions of Russians have returned to their motherland from the European satellite states and other republics of the former USSR. Resentment by ethnic minorities at past cruelties, deportations, discrimination and exploitation and the collapse of central government has allowed local nationalisms to flourish. The very existence of the Russian Federation is in peril. Pray that Russian and other ethnic leaders may show wisdom, sensitivity, moderation and forgiveness for the past as they seek to rebuild the country. Inflamed nationalisms could seriously delay the evangelization of the many unreached peoples in the country.

6. **Disillusionment, fear for the future and a feeling of helpless anger** at the breakdown of even the meagre security under Communism, together with the ideological vacuum has created an enormous interest in religion – whether it be Christianity, Western or Eastern sects, occultism, parapsychology or even Satanism. The promulgation of laws giving complete religious freedom in 1991 has given unprecedented opportunities for the true and false to gain a hearing and following. Pray for the exposure and neutralization of Satan's lies and for the embrace of the gospel.

7. **Freedom for the gospel is unprecedented.** Since 1991, schools, the media, public places and institutions have been open for presentation of the Good News. There are more open doors than can be entered. Any evangelism gains a dramatic response. Pray for:
a) **Appropriate evangelism.** Mass evangelism through Billy Graham, Luis Palau and many Western Pentecostal evangelists has created enormous interest and high publicity, but massive response to appeals has yielded relatively few disciples and new church members. Glowing reports in the West of conversions are premature! There are simply not the resources in counsellors, disciplers, follow-up materials or congregations able to lead these enquirers from total ignorance of the gospel to a living, life-changing faith.
b) **Local church mobilization.** Evangelical churches have little experience or understanding of aggressive evangelism outside church meetings or of total mobilization of members for evangelism. The mindset generated by a century of persecution takes time to change.
c) **Effective use of the media.** Articles and advertisements in the Press and openings for Christian programmes on radio and television are boundless. A high proportion of the Russian-speaking population is being exposed to the gospel. Pray for the fog of Marxist dogma to be dispelled and for the Lord Jesus to be revealed to millions.

8. **A massive turning to Christianity is under way** – but few firm statistics are available. Even from the '70s nearly 70% of all Russian children were baptized in the Orthodox Church. The Catholic Church gained credibility in its opposition to Communism and is gaining numerous converts. Evangelical congregations are multiplying. Praise God for this growth, but pray that the Holy Spirit may be poured out in revival.

9. **The Orthodox Church** has been at the heart of Russian culture, but emerged from under Communism battered and discredited. Some of its leaders have been exposed as willing tools of the atheists. Compromise brought deep divisions that are still very real. There are growing demands for the Orthodox hierarchy to regain its pre-Communist political dominance. Yet within Orthodoxy are vital renewal movements and leaders who maintained their integrity. Pray both for renewal and

reconciliation. There were only three seminaries in 1988 with 2,500 students training for the priesthood, but teaching was much tainted with Marxist ideology. Pray that biblical theology may replace this.

10. **Evangelical Christians** are multiplying, but face serious challenges. Pray for:
a) **Practical holiness to be preached and lived out.** Communism created a society where deceit, fear, low moral and work standards, and unwillingness to make decisions became normal. This spirit affects many Christians too.
b) **Wisdom in handling Christians who compromised,** collaborated and even betrayed fellow believers. Pray for firmness, justice and loving forgiveness to heal the wounds of the past.
c) **Unity.** Denominational barriers are high, especially between Pentecostal and non-Pentecostal. Lack of cooperation and fierce competition – especially for links with Christians in the West – have not glorified the Lord. Nearly every denomination suffered division through Communist policy of registration of congregations that submitted to severe restrictions and persecution of those who would not. These divisions remain. There is a great need for an Evangelical Fellowship that brings together all Evangelicals for fellowship and coordination of ministry.
d) **Provision of theological training** – so long denied. Under Communism limited TEE and correspondence courses for pastors were begun. Since 1990 the number and variety of residential and TEE/BEE courses have multiplied, but Russia's vast distances, shattered economy, and lack of trainers inhibit expansion. By 1993 there were an estimated 25 Protestant seminaries and Bible schools functioning (mainly through Russian partnerships with North American and Korean missionaries and seminaries). A further 13 are expected to be launched in 1993. The Russian Orthodox Church has now 13 seminaries and the Catholics one. Pray for the increase and fruitfulness of this ministry and for the hundreds of expatriate agencies contributing funds, personnel and expertise to develop these programmes. Pray also for upgrading programmes for pastors. Many feel threatened by better-educated young pastors who are beginning to graduate with theological qualifications.
e) **Cultural sensitivity.** For years Russian culture and language dominated and those of ethnic minorities was suppressed. Over 18% of the population is non-Russian and speak over 100 languages. Pray for a missions vision in the Russian church and ability to bridge the cultural and social barriers Russian missionaries face. Praise God for the founding of hundreds of mission agencies within Russia and in Ukraine, many with a cross-cultural vision – but in the main few churches share that vision.

11. **Christian missions from other lands.** Sudden open doors stimulated an enormous response from the free world. Some estimate over 6,000 missions and church-based agencies initiated ministry – delivering aid, support, preaching, evangelizing and Bible teaching. There were no structures and fellowship mechanisms in the country to coordinate or give guidance to this astonishing inrush. Much good was achieved, but also much bad perpetrated – importation of Western and Asian cultural forms or denominational differences, insensitivity to indigenous culture and leadership, unwise use of funds, and ecclesiastical empire-building. Most of these initiatives were short term. Pray for:
a) **Long-term missionaries.** By 1992 there were an estimated 400 in the country, 250 being based in Moscow. Pray for their adaptation to culture and living conditions, efficient acquisition of language fluency, and safety in a violent, crime-ridden society. Pray for an increase in their number and for effective deployment to needy areas and peoples in Russia.
b) **Relationships with Russian Christian leaders** to be based on respect, equality and deference to indigenous culture and visions. The poverty of most churches makes employment by a foreign agency an enticing option, and high-powered foreign methods can all too often overwhelm indigenous structures.
c) **Relationships with government authorities.** Bureaucratic incompetence and passing up decision-making can frustrate. The old structures are little changed from Communist days.
d) **Relationships with other agencies.** WV has set up a New Independent States Christian Resource Centre to facilitate this. More sharing of visions and cooperation in their implementation are needed.

12. **Sections of the population in special need for prayer.**
a) **Young people.** Schools had to change from Marxist textbooks full of distortions and propaganda to providing education with a moral basis. Western Christians have had astounding requests for help in teaching, providing children's Bibles and literature, and developing new curricula for state schools. C-Mission is an umbrella for many agencies working together on a five-year plan to

place Christian teachers in every school of the country. A Christian university has been launched to help meet the need for such teachers.

b) **Students.** Various international agencies (**IFES, CCC, Navigators** and others) are establishing networks of Christian groups on campuses across the country. Pray for national leaders to be raised up and for a significant impact on intellectuals through these ministries.

c) **Those influenced by new religions.** Hare Krishna followers are said to number 700,000. New Age ideas permeate the thinking of millions. Jehovah's Witnesses, Mormons, Moonies and others are rapidly gaining in numbers and influence. Few Christians are prepared for ministry to such.

d) **Occultists.** Millions are ensnared by parapsychologists, sorcerers and even Satanism. Such activities are widely publicized on television.

13. **Russia's unreached.** For years the country's ethnic minorities were out of reach of any mission activity. In the last century Orthodox missionaries influenced many of the northern and Siberian peoples but largely through the Russian language only. For many decades church activity among most of these was eliminated by the Communists. Many remain animists or shamanists with a superficial adherence to Orthodoxy. Little impact was made on the Muslim and Buddhist ethnic groups. A tremendous missionary challenge lies before the Russian Church and expatriate mission agencies to reach each one. A significant proportion of the completely untargeted and unreached peoples of the world are in Russia. For special mention:

a) **The Caucasus peoples.** In the northern valleys of the Caucasus and between the Black and Caspian Seas live a complex medley of 30-60 Caucasus, Iranian and Turkic peoples, many very small. Most live in the eight Caucasus Autonomous Republics named above. Nearly all are Muslim and only among the Ossetians are there a few Christians. There are no known indigenous churches for *any* of the remainder of these peoples. Some Russian and Ukrainian missions are beginning to target some of these; only a handful of expatriate agencies have done so. Through the ministry of **IBT** there are, or soon will be, New Testaments for the Adygey, Kabardian, Ossetian and Karachai; translation proceeds in Chechen, Nogay, Avar, Lezgin, Kumyk, Lak, Dargin, Tabasaran, Tsakhur, Rutul, Agul, Andi and Bezhti; but churches have yet to be planted that will use them.

b) **The Buddhist peoples.** The **Kalmyk** are the only European Buddhist people, living to the northwest of the Caspian Sea. A Ukrainian mission is working among them and there are some believers and churches. The four Gospels are being translated. The **Buryat Mongolians** around Lake Baikal in Siberia were briefly evangelized by the LMS from England 170 years ago. There are only a handful of Christians, and Buddhism is being revived. The **Tuvinians** have declared Lamaistic Buddhism the state religion in the Tuva Republic. One of the first Tuvinian Christians was martyred, but in 1990 his wife was baptized; the event was televised, creating much interest. There is a small fellowship of believers among them, and the New Testament is being translated.

c) **The Siberian peoples** – 20 ethnic groups among one million indigenous people scattered through Siberia's forests, mountains and tundra. Climatic and living conditions are harsh in the extreme. Most are animist/shamanist with a superficial veneer of Orthodoxy. Ukrainian, Russian, Western and Asian missions are exploring possibilities for church-planting and Bible translation ministry among them. The first evangelical congregations have recently been planted among the **Yakut** and **Evenki** by Slavic and Estonian missionaries. Western missions are also participating. **IBT** has supervised the commencement of translation of the New Testament in at least nine of these languages. These small, isolated peoples will need hardy pioneer missionaries – pray for such to be called.

d) **The Ural Turkic peoples.** Most of the **Bashkir** and **Tatar** peoples are nominally Muslim; some are Orthodox. There may be several hundred Tatar Evangelicals; however, these make up only 0.05% of the population. The New Testament must still be completed for both Tatar and Bashkir. The **Chuvash** people are superficially Orthodox, but superstition and secularism predominate today. There are only a few hundred Evangelicals among them. They have never had the Scriptures in their own language.

e) **The Finno-Ugric peoples of Arctic Europe.** These are nominally Orthodox, but very few are Evangelicals. The Komi and Permyak are 0.5% Evangelical, but among the Mari, Mordvin, Karelians, Udmurt, Khant and Vogul the percentage is far lower. Finnish missions are expanding ministry to these peoples with whom they have a distant kinship.

f) **The Jews.** Many are emigrating to Israel, but there are important concentrations in European Russian cities. Though many are secularized, many others have been open to the gospel and come to Christ – a large proportion of Messianic Jews in Israel are of recent Russian and Ukrainian

R

origin. There are also pockets of Georgian, Tat and Hill Jews in the Caucasus region totalling 14,000 who are still unreached.

g) **The Gypsy peoples.** These live scattered over European Russia with many in the Urals. In some areas there has been an awakening and churches have been planted. About 5% of Russian Gypsies are Evangelicals.

14. **Bible Translation.** Much research remains to be done on the translation needs of Siberian and Caucasus languages. There are at least 30 and possibly 58 languages which will require New Testament translations. The persevering, single-minded work of the **Institute of Bible Translation**, based in Sweden, has been remarkable with its vision to provide the Scriptures for all the non-Slavic peoples of the USSR. Many translation projects were started in very restrictive conditions under Communism. Today **UBS** and **IBT**, together with other agencies and churches, are involved in 61 new translations or revisions in the Eurasian region. Pray for the teams of translators and for the provision of mother-tongue Christian speakers in many of these peoples where few, if any, Christians are known.

15. **Christian media ministries** for prayer:

a) **The Russian Bible Society** (**UBS**) which is once more active. Bibles and the Children's Bible (**IBT/OD**) are freely available at last. There is a need for a good modern Russian Bible; the current version is being revised (UBS).

b) **Christian literature. Protestant Publishing** is a Christian (mainly Baptist) publishing house in Moscow which published 150 Russian book titles (25% locally written) in 1992. They also run three Christian bookshops in Moscow and 20 elsewhere. There are Christian presses in several cities – most helped or donated by Western Christians. Praise God for these developments, but pray for literature ministries in a time of great demand. Follow-up materials are in short supply.

c) **The *Jesus* film.** This is available in 45 languages of Russia alone. By 1991, 15-20 million Gospels of Luke had been distributed to viewers of the film – 70 million on Russian television. By 1993 it was estimated that 125 million people in the former USSR had seen the film. Pray for lasting impact, funding for projectors and training for projectionist evangelists.

d) **GRn** which had recordings in only 21 languages in 1991. There is great scope for developing this ministry for smaller language and dialect groups.

e) **Christian radio and television.** The national and local radio and television networks are willing to broadcast Christian programmes, and ministry is also gaining in importance over the Christian stations. The influence of broadcasts by interdenominational Christian agencies such as **TWR**, **FEBC**, HCJB(**WRMF**), **IBRA** and Christian programmes put out on secular and denominational networks during the time of Communist rule cannot be underestimated. Present interest and growth in Russia is, in part, attributable to the years of radio ministry. Seven international Christian radio stations broadcast over 300 hours of programming every week in Russian. The influence of Earl Poysti and **Russian Christian Radio** is noteworthy – an audience of millions was gained in the '80s.

R

October 2
Africa

Rwanda

Area 26,000 sq.km. A mountainous country similar to its southern neighbour, Burundi.

Population	Ann. Gr.	Density
1990	7,232,000	3.5 %	275/sq.km
1995	8,582,000	3.5 %	326/sq.km

Peoples:

Hutu 87.3%. The dominant people since 1959.

Tutsi 10%. The former feudal ruling people. A further 250,000 living as refugees in southwest Uganda.

Twa (Pygmy) 1%.

Other 1.7%. Rundi refugees, Westerners, Zaïrois.

Literacy 50%. **Official languages:** French, ki-Nyarwanda.

Capital: Kigali 300,000. Urbanization 7%.

Economy: Fertile agricultural land with few natural resources. Main sources of foreign exchange are coffee, tea and aid. Over-population and distance from the sea inhibit development. The civil war has crippled the economy and brought chronic hunger to some areas. By 1993 there were an estimated one million refugees within the country. Public debt/person $122. Income/person $310 (1.5% of USA).

Politics: A feudal Tutsi monarchy which continued through German colonial occupation (1899–1916) and Belgian Mandate (1916–1962). A Hutu revolt overthrew the Tutsi government in 1959 with many Tutsi killed or driven into exile. A Tutsi invasion from Uganda in 1990 led to conflict, many deaths and the displacement of thousands of people. In 1992 the Hutu-dominated military government opened the way for the institution of a multi-party democracy, but the rising level of warfare hinders this.

Religion: There is freedom of religion.

Traditional religions 9.8%.

Muslim 10%. **Baha'i** 0.2%.

Christian 80%. Nom 3.5%. Affil 76.5%.

Growth 5.6%.

Protestant 30%. Affil 29.2%. Growth 9.2%.

Church	Cong	Members	Affiliated
Anglican Ch	2,000	180,000	600,000
Seventh-day Adventist	770	208,000	520,000
Presbyterian Ch	51	120,000	400,000
Pentecostal Ch	1,741	131,000	272,000
Baptist Union (SBC)	486	35,572	123,000
Free Methodist Ch	38	22,800	120,000
Assoc of Ev Bapt Chs (CBFMS)	67	17,913	60,000
All other (8)	86	6,563	16,770
Denominations (15)	5,239	721,848	2,111,770
Evangelicals 20.2% of pop		482,000	1,459,000
Pentecostal/charis 4.5%		146,000	316,000

Missionaries to Rwanda 150 (1:48,200 people) in 18 agencies.

Roman Catholic 49.9%. Affil 47.2%.

Growth 3.7%.

Catholic Ch	1,173	1,880,000	3,412,000

Missionaries:

to Rwanda 753 (1:9,600 people).

from Rwanda 70 (1973 figure).

Orthodox 0.02%. Growth 2.8%.

Foreign Marginal 0.02%. Growth 4.9%.

Indigenous Marginal 0.08%. Growth 8.4%.

All groups (6)	24	2,400	6,000

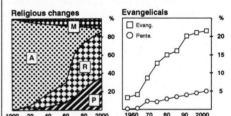

Religious changes   Evangelicals

1. **For centuries the tensions and bitterness** between the Hutu and Tutsi have dominated the country. The efforts of the military government during the '80s to rebuild harmonious relationships between the two peoples, commitment to multi-party civilian government, and freedom of the press was damaged by the invasion in 1990. Pray for real reconciliation and the raising up of godly leaders who will establish peace and promote economic and spiritual growth.

2. **The Rwanda Revival** of the '30s onwards that began in the Anglican Church deeply affected many denominations in Rwanda, East Africa and beyond. The after-glow remained, but a new generation needed a fresh touch of the Spirit. The inter-ethnic conflict has recreated a widespread spiritual hunger, and the last few years have been ones of harvest and church growth once more. Pray for revival that will truly nail tribalism and carnal living to the Cross of Christ.

3. **A spontaneous movement of the Spirit in the Roman Catholic Church** during the '70s led to an extensive network of prayer and Bible study groups springing up all over the country. This emphasis

on the Scriptures has gradually been replaced by increasing structure and control and by a reversion to a more traditional theological stance. Pray for the born-again believers within this church.

4. Christians have suffered much in the conflict. Some have been killed because of their ethnic origin, and many have lost all their meagre possessions. Adversity has driven many to seek God in a new way. Pray that Christians may be a means of bridging the ethnic divide and providing aid and encouragement to those who have been made destitute.

5. Christian leaders of vision and spiritual calibre are needed. Pray for those in training at the inter-church seminary in Butare and elsewhere in Africa and the West. All too often those who are highly trained find it hard to be satisfied with their ministry and support in a land of poor rural churches. Pray for the training of local leaders for the churches. Pray also for a deeper fellowship across denominational barriers.

6. Scripture Union has a blessed ministry among young people of all churches, thus helping to lessen denominational rivalry. Pray for blessing on the daily Bible-reading notes and extension of this ministry to the churches, for this is often the only systematic Bible training most people get. Pray also for the SU programme to develop follow-up materials for new converts – few churches have a vision for this.

7. Missionaries have persevered in the midst of the national trials, but their ministry has sometimes been hampered. Pray that their life and witness may be a blessing and example to all. There is unprecedented freedom for new religious agencies to register, and this is bringing in new initiatives and ways of proclaiming the gospel. Most are evangelical; some of the larger agencies are: Swedish Pentecostal Mission (25 workers), **SBC** (18), **Mid-Africa Ministry** – formerly Rwanda Mission – (12), Free Methodists (12), **CBFMS** (11). Major missionary-contributing nations: USA (86), Sweden (28), UK (16), Denmark (7).

8. Less-reached peoples:
a) The Muslims are a growing community. Much money for mosque construction has been poured into the country by Libya. Few Christians have either the burden or the knowledge to approach them with the gospel. Some Muslims have, however, become Christians.
b) The 25,000 Twa remain largely unreached, and few Christians are concerned for them.

9. Specialized ministries.
a) **Student work.** There are 2,000 tertiary students on three campuses. GBU (**IFES**) has a group on each and one staff worker.
b) **The *Jesus* film.** This is in circulation in French, kiNyarwanda and kiRundi.

Sahara, Western

See under MOROCCO

S

October 3	*Samoa (Western)*
Pacific	(The Independent State of Western Samoa)

Area 2,831 sq.km. Two large volcanic islands, Savai'i and Upolu, and seven small islands covered by lush tropical rainforest.

Population	Ann. Gr.	Density
1990 170,000	0.84 %	60/sq.km
1995 178,000	0.92 %	63/sq.km

Over 200,000 Samoans live in American Samoa, USA, New Zealand and Australia.

Peoples:
Indigenous Polynesian 98.8%. Samoan 151,000; Euronesian 17,000.
Other 1.2%. Other Polynesian, European.

Literacy 99%. **Official languages:** Samoan, English. **Languages with Scriptures** 2Bi.

Capital: Apia 35,700. Urbanization 21%.

Economy: Decline since independence; an agricultural subsistence economy. Heavily dependent on remittances from Samoans abroad, and on tourism. Income/person $720 (3.4% of USA).

Politics: German rule 1900–1914, thereafter New Zealand UN trusteeship until independence in 1962. Parliamentary democracy of the elite until 1991, when universal suffrage was introduced.

Religion: Constitutional freedom of religion is often not upheld at a local village level.
Non-religious/other 0.14%.
Baha'i 1.9%.
Christian 98%. Growth 0.8%.
Protestant 53.3%. Growth −2%.

Church	Cong	Members	Affiliated
Congregational Ch	244	15,000	57,700
Methodist Ch	113	11,899	19,200

Assemblies of God	45	7,000	12,000
Seventh-day Adventist	20	3,070	5,677
Ch of the Nazarene	11	456	783
Ch of God (Cleveland)	2	114	228
All other (6)	21	1,715	3,200
Doubly counted		−4,900	−8,200
Denominations (12)	456	32,754	90,588
Evangelicals 11.2% of pop		9,694	19,052
Pentecostal/charis 8.5%		8,900	14,500

Missionaries:
to Samoa 10 (1:17,000 people) in 6 agencies.
from Samoa 74 (1:1,200 Protestants) in 3 agencies 59frn 32xcul 42dom.

Roman Catholic 20.5%. Growth 1.2%.

Catholic Ch	67	18,000	36,000
Doubly counted		−600	−1,200
Total	67	17,400	34,800

Missionaries to Samoa 117 (1:1,480 people).
Foreign Marginal 23.8%. Growth 8.5%.

Mormons	93	28,000	40,000
All other (1)	5	226	452
Groups (2)	98	28,226	40,452

Indigenous Marginal 0.47%. Growth 5.7%.

Groups (2)	4	400	800

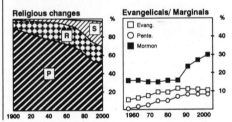

Religious changes

Evangelicals/ Marginals
□ Evang.
○ Pente.
■ Mormon

1. **The Samoans have been Christian** for over a century, and every village has at least one church, but the traditional class structure and pre-Christian cultural standards were not necessarily transformed by the gospel. Pride, political manipulation, formalism, ignorance, division and compromise have weakened the Church before the challenge presented by the influx of cults, high teenage suicide, and the need to provide a future and a hope for the next generation. Pray for both government and church leaders of Samoa; there are committed Evangelicals among them.

2. **The growth of Mormonism** has been both spectacular and relatively unchallenged. Pray for all seeking to enlighten Samoan Christians of Mormonism's errors, and to win Mormons to Jesus. Pray for renewal and revival. The whole nation has an obligatory quiet time for prayer and Bible reading at dusk.

3. **The growth of Evangelicals** has been predominantly through the Assemblies of God. They and other evangelical agencies, such as Youth For Christ, have met with opposition, and individual Christians have faced pressure from traditional leaders who also lead mainline churches. Pray for complete freedom for the gospel and for harmony between the newer and more traditional branches of the church.

4. **Unity among Evangelicals** has long been lacking. Pray that the Samoan Evangelical Alliance, formed in 1991, may be a means to overcome the prevailing nominalism, underscore personal commitment to Christ, and further the cause of the gospel.

5. **Samoan missionaries** played a major role in evangelizing the Pacific in the last century. Most Samoans serving abroad today are pastoring Samoan migrant congregations. An exception to this is the contingent of 19 Samoan **YWAM**ers serving around the world. Pray for them and their ongoing influence in their home churches.

6. **Christian radio and TV**. Pray that Radio Rhema may be launched. This Christian station could have an impact for Jesus on the 400 villages of Samoa.

San Marino

(Most Serene Republic of San Marino)

Include with Italy
Europe

Area: 62 sq.km. An enclave in North Central Italy.

Population	Ann. Gr.	Density
1990 23,000	0.89 %	377/sq.km
1995 24,000	0.85 %	393/sq.km

Peoples:
Sammarinese 83.8%. **Italian** 15.7%.
Other 0.5%.

Literacy 98%. Offical language: Italian.

Politico-economic: Independent republic since AD 301. In customs union with Italy. Main foreign exchange earners are tourism (two million visitors annually) and postage stamps. Income/person $8,590 (41% of USA).

Religion: No official religion; freedom of religion, but almost the entire population is Catholic.
Non-religious/other 4.6%.
Baha'i 0.6%.
Christian 94.8%. Nom 2.3%. Affil 92.5%.
 Protestant: None known.
 Roman Catholic 93.6%. Affil 91.3%.

Church	Cong	Members	Affiliated
Catholic	12	13,900	21,000

Missionaries to San Marino 20 (1973 figure).

Marginal groups 1.15%.

	Cong	Members	Affiliated
Jehovah's Witnesses	2	132	264

1. **Although Catholic by tradition and culture** San Marino has been heavily influenced by the Communist party and secularism. Pray for the Sammarinese to have life-changing encounters with the Lord Jesus Christ.

2. **There is no known evangelical witness;** the Baha'i and Jehovah's Witnesses are the only non-Catholic faiths represented. Pray for the establishment of born-again groups of believers.

S

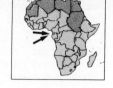

Include with Equatorial Guinea
Africa

São Tomé & Príncipe

(Democratic Republic of São Tomé and Príncipe)

Area 964 sq.km. Two larger and several smaller islands in the Gulf of Guinea 200 km. west of Gabon.

Population		Ann. Gr.	Density
1990	112,000	2.9 %	112/sq.km
1995	129,000	2.9 %	129/sq.km

Peoples:
Forro and Angolares 80%. Descendants of African slaves. The Forro are politically dominant, the Angolares more rural.
Fang 10% from Equatorial Guinea.
Mestizo 7%. Mixed race.
Portuguese 2%. Other 1%.
Also many contract labourers from Cape Verde, Angola and Mozambique.

Literacy 34%. **Official language:** Portuguese.

Capital: São Tomé 35,000. Urbanization 41%.

Economy: Subsistence agriculture; cocoa the major export. Unemployment 31%. Income/person $360 (1.7% of USA).

Politics: Settled by Portuguese in 1493, and became a major slave transhipment centre. Independent from Portugal in 1975 as a Marxist republic. A multi-party democracy was instituted in January 1991.

Religion: Secular state with freedom of religion.
Non-religious, traditional religions, etc. 3%.
Christian 97%. Nom 6.3%. Affil 90.7%.
Growth 4.7%.
Protestant 4.9%. Growth 7.9%.

Church	Cong	Members	Affiliated
Assemblies of God	12	1,400	3,500
Seventh-day Adventist	1	430	1,080
Methodist Ch	1	140	280
All other (3)	3	260	590
Denominations (6)	17	2,230	5,450
Evangelicals 3.7% of pop		1,700	4,200
Pentecostal/charis 3.4%		1,540	3,850

Missionaries:
to ST & P 17 (1:6,600 people) in 3 agencies.
from ST & P 7 (1:7,700 Protestants) 7dom all in YWAM.
Roman Catholic 91.9%. Affil 85.7%.
Growth 5.5%.

Catholic Ch	12	58,600	96,000

Missionaries to ST & P 27 (1:4,100 people).
Marginal 0.13%. Growth 18.9%.

Jehovah's Witnesses	1	56	140

1. **Evangelical growth has accelerated** since independence – mainly through the work of the Portuguese Assemblies of God and more recently through **YWAM** Brazilian missionaries and Deeper Life Nigerian missionaries. There were few born-again believers 20 years ago. Pray for the development of locally-led congregations and effectively trained Christian leaders.

2. **Less-reached sections of the population** are the Príncipe islanders, the rural Angolares and the contract labourers – each group having its own distinct Creole language. Pray for their salvation.

S

Saudi Arabia

(Kingdom of Saudi Arabia

October 4–5

Middle East

Area 2,240,000 sq.km. The main portion of the Arabian Peninsula; almost entirely desert but containing 25% of the world's known oil reserves.

Population	Ann. Gr.	Density
1990 14,131,000	4.0 %	6/sq.km
1995 17,118,000	3.9 %	8/sq.km

In 1974, 27% of the population was nomadic; this percentage is dropping rapidly through settlement plans and industrialization.

Peoples (figures approximate):
Indigenous 75%. Arab 10,240,000; Shahara 28,000; Mahra 14,000.
Foreigners 25%.
Arab 16%. Yemeni 500,000 (1 million expelled in 1990); Egyptian, Jordanian, Lebanese, etc. 800,000.
Asian 7%. Pakistani 382,000; Filipino 132,000; Indian 120,000; Iranian 102,000; Korean 66,000; Chinese 58,000; Indonesian 37,000; Bangladeshi 15,000.
African 1.4%. Nigerian, Sudanese, Somali, etc.
Western 0.6%. American, British, Italian, French, etc.

Literacy 38%. **Official language:** Arabic. **Indigenous languages** 4. **Languages with Scriptures** 1Bi 1NT 1por.

Capital: Riyadh 1,308,000. Other cities: Jiddah 1,600,000; Mecca 550,000. Urbanization 77%.

Economy: Oil wealth is used to improve services and communications, develop industries and finance Islamic expansion around the world. The combined effects of profligate spending, spectacular corruption of the large royal family and the heavy cost of the Gulf War (at least US$50 billion) have enforced a measure of austerity since 1990. Public debt/person $131. Income/person $6,230 (28% of USA).

Politics: Absolute monarchy and a semi-feudal state with administration, diplomacy and commerce tightly controlled by the large royal family. Since the Gulf War there has been pressure from democrats to liberalize the country and from fundamentalists to exert more control, resulting in some changes.

Religion: An Islamic state committed to the preservation of traditional Islam. All other religions are prohibited. Expatriate Christian gatherings are not allowed. All non-Muslim figures are estimates.
Muslim 93.4%. Sunni 79% mainly of the strict Wahhabi sect; Shi'a 13.4% mainly Arabs on Gulf coast and Iranians; Ismaili 1%.
Non-religious/other 1.4%. Westerners, Chinese.
Hindu 0.7%. **Buddhist** 0.5%. Migrant Asians.
Christian 4%. Affiliated 3.2%. The estimated 580,000 Christians can meet for worship only on an informal basis. Expatriates are 98% of the total Christian population, which is mainly Filipino, Korean, Indian, Arab and Western.
  Protestant 1%. Affiliated 0.6%.
  Roman Catholic 2.6%. Affiliated 2.3%.
  Orthodox 0.4%. Affiliated 0.2%.
Christian workers are not legally sanctioned.

1. **Saudi Arabia** once had a large Christian population. They were expelled when Islam gained control 1,300 years ago. It is now one of the least evangelized nations on earth. No Christian workers are permitted and all Christian "propaganda" banned. No Christian is permitted to set foot in Islam's holiest city, Mecca. Pray that one day soon the land may have many Christians praising the Lamb that was slain.

S

2. **The world's one billion Muslims are required to pray towards Mecca five times daily.** Every year over two million make the *Hajj* or pilgrimage to the city. Pray that many may have their eyes opened to see the emptiness and bondage under which they live, and embrace the freedom that there is in Christ. Praise God a small but growing number are doing just that – even in Saudi Arabia!

3. **The pervasive abuse of human rights**, the arrogance of the religious police and the stifling control of government, the media, the judicial system, and any form of democratic dissent is building up a tide of desire for change. Yet very few Saudis have heard the Good News, seen a Bible or met a true believer.

4. **The massive Islamic missionary effort** is coordinated by the Muslim World League in Mecca. Vast sums of money are used to propagate Islam around the world – aid to countries considered sympathetic, building mosques, sending missionaries, literature, radio, etc. The Saudi government denies Christians the liberty to share their faith, yet demands it for Muslims elsewhere. The world's largest printing presses were set up in this country and churn out 28 million Korans annually for

worldwide distribution. Pray that "Christian" nations may have the courage and moral integrity to insist that Saudi Arabia's leaders grant their Christian minority the rights that were agreed upon when they signed the UN Charter.

5. **Any Saudis who confess Christ** face the death sentence if discovered, yet a growing number are both seeking and finding him. One Saudi believer was publicly beheaded in 1992. Pray for the preservation and multiplication of believers, and legalization of Christianity for Saudis. Pray also that they may be able to meet together in safety and have access to God's Word.

6. **Expatriates** are often hard, materialistic, isolated and frustrated. The poorer Asian labourers must leave families for years in order to earn money for their support. Pray for an adequate witness to each in spite of the seemingly insuperable obstacles. The communities devoid of a witness are the Yemenis, many of the Pakistanis and the Iranians. Some Koreans have been converted to Islam. Yet there are disciples of Jesus among the Korean construction workers, Filipino workers and nurses, Pakistani labourers and Western professionals. Pray for their witness to their own communities and beyond.

7. **Expatriate Christians** live under strict surveillance. Secret gatherings are hunted down with increasing diligence and the leaders subjected to humiliating beatings, imprisonment and expulsion from the country. This is particularly so for the Asian Christians who have often been the most effective witnesses for Jesus. Few expatriates have meaningful contacts with Saudis under these conditions. Pray that no threat may quench Spirit-inspired witnessing.

8. **Witnessing by other means:**
a) **Saudis abroad.** Students, businessmen and tourists visit the West, where they can be reached. Many prefer to travel abroad during the month of fasting!
b) **Christian radio.** Over 146 hours of broadcasting weekly in Arabic are available through **FEBA**, High Adventure, **TWR**, **IBRA** and HCJB(**WRMF**). Many listen secretly.
c) **Christian literature and video cassettes**. These are banned, and are therefore in great demand. Many copies of the Scriptures and the *Jesus* video are in surreptitious circulation.

S

Senegal

(Republic of Senegal)

October 6

Africa

Area 196,000 sq.km. Much of the land is arid with few natural resources.

Population	Ann. Gr.	Density
1990 7,369,000	2.7 %	37/sq.km
1995 8,448,000	2.8 %	43/sq.km

The majority live on the coast and in the area around the capital.

Peoples: Over 50 ethnic groups in three main linguistic families.
West Atlantic 84.5%.
  Wolof 36% (2). Wolof 2,520,000; Lebu 100,000. Politically dominant, staunchly Muslim.
  Fula 27.4% (4). Fulacunda 935,000; Tukulor 661,000; Fula Jeeri 350,000.
  Serer-Cangin 12.6% (6). Serer 848,000; Cangin (5) 88,000.
  Bak 6.7% (17). Jola (14) 405,000; Balanta (2) 78,000; Bayot 5,000.
  Other 1.8% (9). Manjak 70,000; Bainuk 21,000; Mankanya 19,000; Bassari 6,500; Badyara 6,500; Konyagi 4,000.
Mande 12.7% (7). Mandinka 445,000; Malinke 259,000; Soninke 140,000; Bambara 55,000; Jahanka 22,000; Yalunka 13,000; Kassonke 6,000.
Arab 1.6%. Hassaniya Mauritanians 40,000, greatly reduced from 300,000 since the inter-racial strife of 1989; Lebanese 43,000.
Other 1.2%. Mainly French and Cape Verdians in Dakar.

Literacy 23%. **Official language:** French. **Trade language:** Wolof. **All languages** 37. **Languages with Scriptures** 2Bi 4NT 6por.

Capital: Dakar 1,800,000. Urbanization 39%.

Economy: Agricultural base, heavily dependent on unreliable rains, groundnut cultivation and foreign aid. Income/person $650 (3.3% of USA).

Politics: Independent from France in 1960. Multi-party democracy. The southern province, Casamance, destabilized since 1983 by a Jola secessionist guerrilla movement.

Religion: A secular state with freedom of religion. The three Muslim Sufi brotherhoods – the Mouride, Tidjane and Qadiri – are influential in political and economic life.
Muslim 90.8% (Muslims claim 95%). Sunni Islam, but over 85% of Muslims are members of the three Sufi brotherhoods. Strongest among the Fula, Tukulor and Wolof.
Traditional religions 3.6%. Predominantly Serer (44%), Jola (10%) and smaller peoples of the Casamance in southwest.
Christian 5.6%. Affil 5%. Growth 5%.
Protestant 0.1%. Affil 0.1%. Growth 5.4%.

Church	Cong	Members	Affiliated
Lutheran Ch (Finnish)	37	1,800	3,000
Assemblies of God	43	815	2,910
Baptist Ch (CBFMS)	9	94	235
Evang Church (WEC)	7	70	230
Baptist Convention	3	101	168
All other (9)	25	835	2,113
Denominations (14)	124	3,715	8,656
Evangelicals 0.07% of pop.		2,000	5,400
Pentecostal/charis 0.04%		800	2,900

Missionaries:
  to Senegal 463 (1:15,900 people) in 31 agencies.
  from Senegal 4 (1:2,200 Protestants) in 3 agencies.

Roman Catholic 5.4%. Affil 4.9%. Growth 5%.

Catholic Ch	238	211,019	363,826

Missionaries to Senegal 644 (1:11,400 people).
Marginal 0.1%. Growth 6.4%.

Jehovah's Witnesses	14	585	1,950

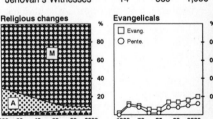

Religious changes

Evangelicals

1. **Islam has grown over the last 50 years** to about 90% of the population, yet the land is wide open for the gospel! The highly organized and politically powerful Sufi brotherhoods claim 85% of all Muslims as members. To this point tolerance for other religions has been a point of pride. Pray for such tolerance to continue; extremists could insist on setting up a narrow, bigoted Islamic state. Pray for a breakthrough for the gospel among Muslims, and for a spiritual impact to be made on the Muslim brotherhoods, of whom the strongest are the Tidjane and the Mouride.

2. **Christians are few,** though their influence is disproportionately great through their input into education. Most of these Christians are nominal and their life style gives little credit to the cause of Christ. Almost all are originally from a non-Muslim background and from the Cape Verdian, Serer

and Jola peoples, but among them freedom in Christ and victory over the powers of darkness have yet to be demonstrated. Muslims refer to Christians as "those who drink" rather than those who follow Christ.

3. **Evangelical believers are few**, the rate of growth slow, and only among the Serer (FLM, **AoG**), Bassari (AoG), Balanta (**WEC, AoG, NTM**), and Jola (**WEC, SBC, SIL**) has there been any significant church planting. Believers are scattered, often poorly taught and under constant pressures from Muslim or animistic relatives to conform. The lack of believing girls tempts many young men to marry unbelievers or to immorality. Pray for a strong church with a backbone of Christian families to be planted in each ethnic group. Sadly, liberal teaching is affecting the young Lutheran Church, with increasing nominalism among members.

4. **Christian leaders are few**, but an increasing number of young men are taking up theological studies. There are probably no more than 100 full-time national Christian workers. The **AoG** runs a Bible school, and **CBFMS** a TEE programme. **YWAM** runs a biennial six-month discipleship course. Pray that men of God may be raised up who can pastor believers and lead them out in effective evangelism.

5. **Missions in Senegal have struggled for years without much fruit** in the adult population, but among young people results have been more encouraging. **WEC** entered the Casamance in the south in 1936 among the Fula, in the '50s to the Jola and Balanta, and later the predominantly Muslim Senegal River Valley in the north. Other pioneer missions have followed, and there are now 25 church-planting missions serving in the country. The largest are **NTM** (115 workers), **WBT/SIL** (54), **WEC** (53), Finnish Lutherans (52), **SBC** (32), **UWM** (22), **AoG** (18). Major missionary-contributing nations: USA (263), Finland (52), UK (46), Canada (19), Switzerland (14). Pray for more church planters called of God to serve in this needy but open land. Pray also for encouragement among the missionary teams; most are young, inexperienced and short on leadership in a difficult, unresponsive field.

6. **Major areas of the country are virtually untouched with the gospel.**
a) **Dakar, the burgeoning capital**, is a medley of peoples with only about 15 evangelical groups. There is a wide-open door to evangelize indigenous ethnic communities. Most missionaries in the city are in administrative work serving missionaries and projects or in ministry to overseas students or expatriates. **SBC, UWM, AoG**, Brethren and Apostolic Church missionaries have planted churches; others are now joining them.
b) **The Senegal River Valley** in the north and northeast is a major development zone. Only a few missionaries are working on this strategic frontier with closed Mauritania, among the Tukulor, Maure, Wolof, Fula and Soninke (**WEC**, Lutherans and others). There is no viable church in the entire area, and up-river only a handful of missionaries.
c) **The central and eastern areas of Senegal** are sparsely populated and unevangelized, as is the territory along the frontier of north Gambia. There is an **AoG** church in Tambacounda, but the members are mostly Bassaris who have migrated there from another area seeking employment.

7. **Unreached peoples.** Pray for the:
a) **Wolof.** Despite much effort by missionaries of **AoG, CBFMS, SBC, Brethren, WEC, SIM** and others, results have been meagre. There are possibly only 150 believers and the beginnings of several congregations. Pray that the advent of the Wolof New Testament, *Jesus* film and the patient friendship evangelism of Christian workers may break down the barriers preventing this proud people from seeking Jesus.
b) **Serer.** Strongly fetishist until this century, now many are becoming Muslim and Catholic and a good number Protestant – FLM, **AoG, CBIM** and **SIM** have seen an encouraging response. **SIL** and recently **NTM** are working among the related Cangin language groups.
c) **Fula.** A pastoral people, some nomadic. Nearly all are Muslim. Lutherans work among the northern Fula, and **WEC**, with eight workers, in the Casamance. There are two small groups of believers in the latter area, but overwhelming family pressures and ostracism have held back many from wholehearted commitment. WEC aims to complete the Fula New Testament by 1997.
d) **Tukulor.** Muslim for 900 years, and considering themselves as the defenders of that faith. It is a miracle that there are now 15 believers (**WEC**, Lutherans, **SIL**).
e) **Jola,** speaking 14 major dialects and languages. In Fogny in the Casamance many are nominally Muslim, and in the south strong fetish worshippers. The Roman Catholics have gained many followers through their social work and failure to speak out against the use of palm wine. There are only about 100 or so committed believers in five churches (**WEC, SBC** and **SIL**). The

breakthrough has yet to come to this, the last large animistic pocket of people in the country.

f) **Maures.** All are Muslim, with only one known believer. The majority live in inaccessible Mauritania, though many can be reached in the Senegal River Valley (**WEC**).

g) **The smaller peoples on the southern border** who are animistic or nominally Muslim. **NTM** has a major thrust to evangelize the Balanta-Ganja, Manjak, Budik, Bainuk, Badjaranke, Malinke and Jalonke, with plans also to reach the Mankanya. Some work has been done among the Konyagi (**AoG**), but the fetishist Mankanya, Bayot, Bainuk and Ganja are unreached.

h) **Muslim peoples still totally unreached** in Senegal, though with most there is mission work among them in neighbouring countries: Mandinka, Jahanka, Bambara and Kassonke. A beginning has been made to reach the Soninke (**SIL**, Pioneers, Korean Methodists) in the east.

8. **Young people.** Many have flocked to the cities in search of education and employment. Their commitment to conservative Islam is not so great, and **YWAM**, Gideons and some churches are seeking to reach them. **SBC**, **UWM** and others have a youth work in Dakar. The **IFES** group in Dakar University is small but fervent; however, most of the members are non-Senegalese. Recent political unrest and student dissatisfaction have restricted evangelistic outreach. Pray for an impact for God to be made on children and young people.

9. **Bible translation.** Much was achieved in the '80s. Four long-awaited New Testaments were published, namely Wolof (**CBIM**, Brethren), Serer (Finnish Lutheran), Mandinka (**WEC**, Gambia) and Bassari (**AoG**); pray for a wide dissemination and deep impact on readers. Work on 15 other New Testaments is in hand; pray especially for work on Tukulor, several Jola languages (**WEC**, **SIL**) and Fulacunda (**WEC**) to be completed.

10. **Help Ministries for which to pray:**

a) **Reading rooms** have been a major outreach tool to Muslims in many urban centres. Pray for meaningful conversations with enquirers. Pray for the publication and distribution of effective Christian literature.

b) **The *Jesus* film** is available in Wolof and Serer, but its use has been limited so far. The French version has been broadcast twice on television. Results have not been as great as anticipated.

c) **Cassette/tape ministries.** GRn has recordings available in 27 languages. Scripture on tape has been particularly effective for the Wolof and Serer.

d) **Christian radio programmes** can be broadcast on national and local stations. Pray that churches and missions may use this medium more (**SBC**, **WEC**, Brethren).

S

October 7	
Africa	

Seychelles
(Republic of Seychelles)

Area 453 sq.km. 92 granite and coral islands spread across 400,000 sq.km of the Indian Ocean, 1,600 km east of Kenya.

Population	Ann. Gr.	Density
1990 69,000	1.2 %	152/sq.km
1995 72,000	0.85 %	159/sq.km

Peoples:
Creole 89.1%. Predominantly of African and European and some Asian origin.
Asian 6.3%. Tamil, Hindi and Gujarati from India 3,000; Chinese 1,000.
African 3.1%. Malagasy, Réunionese, Swahili, Guinean.
European 1.5%. British, French.

Literacy 62%. **Official languages:** Seychelles Creole, English, French. **Languages with Scriptures** 2Bi 1por.

Capital: Victoria 35,000. Urbanization 47%.

Economy: Tourism is the source of 48% of foreign earnings and 30% of all employment. Fishing is also important. Development choked by excessive state control. Foreign debt $0.122 billion. Unemployment 20%. Income/person $4,170 (19% of USA).

Politics: French colony 1756–1814, then British-ruled until independence in 1976. The coup of 1977 resulted in a one-party socialist government and the crushing of all dissent. The collapse of Communism elsewhere and the choking off of foreign aid brought about a multi-party election in 1992 – won by the ruling party – and efforts to re-write the constitution.

Religion: Both Catholics and Anglicans openly challenged one-party rule.
Non-religious/other 1.5%.
Hindu 0.6%. **Muslim** 0.3%. **Baha'i** 0.3%.
Christian 97.3%. Affil 92.3%. Growth 0.4%.
Protestant 9.5%. Growth 3.1%.

Church	Cong	Members	Affiliated
Anglican Ch	11	1,910	5,030
Evangelical Ch	2	423	650
Pentecostal Ch	1	325	650
Seventh-day Adventist	4	143	239
Denominations (4)	18	2,801	6,569
Evangelicals 4% of pop		1,300	2,800
Pentecostal/charis 1% of pop		350	700

Missionaries to Seychelles 35 (1:2,000 people) in 5 agencies, but 28 of these are operating the FEBA international radio station.
Roman Catholic 87.6%. Affil 82.6%. Growth 0.8%.

Catholic Ch	17	36,000	61,000
Doubly Counted		−2,100	−4,000
Total	17	33,900	57,000

Missionaries to Seychelles 44 (1:1,500 people).
Marginal 0.2%. Affil 0.2%. Growth 8%.

Jehovah's Witnesses	1	81	162

Religious changes

Evangelicals

□ Evang.
○ Pente.

1. **Nearly all Seychellois claim to be Christian**, but are steeped in superstition and depend on the outward rites of baptism and confirmation. Immorality is a serious problem, and few have a saving knowledge of Christ. Pray that full freedom for the preaching of the gospel may be granted, and pray that many within the recognized churches may be converted.

2. **The arrival of FEBA missionaries in 1971** gave openings for an evangelical witness to be established. Subsequently, **AIM** and **PAoC** missionaries and indigenous Christians were able to help in establishing new evangelical and Pentecostal congregations. At the same time, the evangelical witness in the Anglican Church grew strongly. Praise God for these developments. Pray for spiritual life to be maintained and deepened and for the provision of Seychellois leaders for the congregations.

3. **Evangelical missionary work** has been somewhat restricted to technical and help ministries in the past. **AIM** missionaries run the Christian Resource Centre as a means of helping in leadership development for the churches. Pray for strategic ministry openings for missionaries.

4. **Less reached peoples:**
a) **The outer and less-populated islands** are isolated and have had little challenge to a personal commitment to Christ.

b) **The youth** have been hardened against biblical truth by rigorous Marxist teaching while on military service and by a promiscuous life style. Pray for effective ministries to be developed to win them for the Lord.

5. **The Seychelles Creole NT** is being translated through the Bible Society of Mauritius. Pray for the rapid completion of this project and for the Word to make a deep impact on Seychellois society.

6. **FEBA has a radio ministry on Mahé.** The strategically-placed islands enable 400 hours of broadcasting per month in 14 languages of South Asia, 300 hours in eight languages of East Africa, and 100 hours in two languages of the Middle East. Many of these lands are not open for residential missionary work. Pray for:
a) **The preparation of programmes** in receiving areas in India, the Middle East and Africa.
b) **Continued permission to broadcast** and for good reception in the target areas.
c) **Financial provision and efficient performance.** Equipment and operating costs are expensive.
d) **The expatriate and national staff** to run the station and for their physical and spiritual health in a hot, humid climate.
e) **The growing response** from Muslims and Hindus in India and Pakistan and for adequate follow-up among these enquirers.
f) **The Arabic broadcasts to the Middle East** and also for a settled studio in the area. (The Lebanese civil war frequently disrupts the work of the Beirut studio.)
g) **Expansion of the African outreach** and news service in English, which draws many listeners.

S

October 8	*Sierra Leone*
Africa	(Republic of Sierra Leone)

Area 72,000 sq.km. Small coastal state between Guinea and Liberia.

Population	Ann. Gr.	Density
1990 4,151,000	2.5 %	58/sq.km
1995 4,726,000	2.6 %	66/sq.km

Peoples: All ethnic groups approx. 74.
West Atlantic peoples (11) 45.5%. Temne 1,170,000; Limba 326,000; Sherbro (3) 153,000; Fula 166,000; Kissi 90,000; Krim 9,000; Gola 7,600.
Mande peoples (8) 43.8%. Mende 1,249,000; Kuranko 209,000; Kono 176,000; Loko 95,000; Maninka 89,000; Yalunka 31,000.
Kwa peoples (3) 1.3%. Bassa 29,000; Kru 7,600.
Krio (Creole) 8.6%. Descendants of released slaves and detribalized urbanites.
Other 0.8%. Lebanese, 25,000, Indo-Pakistani 8,000; Greek 700.
Refugees Liberians 125,000 in 1991.

Literacy 17%. **Official language:** English. **Trade language:** Krio (Creole) spoken by 10% of the population as first language and 90% as second. **All languages** 23. **Languages with Scriptures** 1Bi 8NT 9por.

Capital: Freetown 469,000. Urbanization 28%.

Economy: The potential wealth of the land from diamonds, iron ore and bauxite has been squandered through corruption and mismanagement at every level. The economy is at the point of collapse, and the local currency valueless. Inflation, foreign debt, and massive smuggling networks are the result. Income/person $200 (1% of USA).

Politics: Founded as a home for freed slaves in 1797. Independent from Britain in 1961. A one-party republic with frequent periods of instability. The Liberian civil war which started in 1990 has further destablized the country with large parts of the south affected. A military coup brought in a new government in 1992 that promised to deal with corruption, ending the activities of Liberian rebels, and introducing multi-party politics, but popular support and hopes for improvement had decreased by 1993.

Religion: Freedom of religion, but Islam has been growing in influence.
Traditional religions 48%, although over 90%

would still be animistic in their world view. Strongest among the Kono, Kissi, Koranko, Limba and Loko.
Muslim 43.1%. Growing among most tribes, especially the Temne and Mende, the two largest peoples.
Christian 8.9%. Nom 2%. Affil 7%. Growth 2.9%.
Protestant 6.8%. Affil 5.1%. Growth 3.1%.

Church	Cong	Members	Affiliated
United Methodist Ch	226	27,733	46,200
Anglican Ch	49	13,000	25,040
W Africa Methodist Ch	42	10,000	19,000
Wesleyan Ch	108	4,850	15,090
Natnl Pentecostal Ch	20	5,930	9,890
Seventh-day Adventist	117	5,320	8,859
Assemblies of God	109	1,285	6,679
Baptist Convention	36	3,805	6,340
Afr Methodist Episc Ch	9	1,355	3,000
All other (28)	582	36,913	72,042
Denominations (37)	1,298	110,191	212,140
Evangelicals 2.19% of pop.		42,000	91,000
Pentecostal/charis 0.8%		16,000	34,000

Missionaries:
to Sierra Leone 233 (1:17,800 people) in 37 agencies.
from Sierra Leone 131 (1:694 Protestants) in 8 agencies 2frn 3xcul 128dom.
Roman Catholic 1.9%. Affil 1.7%. Growth 2.3%.

Catholic Ch	790	41,800	72,000

Missionaries to Sierra Leone 234 (1:17,800 people).
Orthodox 0.01%. Predominantly Lebanese. Growth 8.7%.
Foreign Marginal 0.06%. Growth 2%.

Jehovah's Witnesses	30	752	2,510

Indigenous Marginal 0.14%. Affil 0.1% Growth 5.6%.

Groups (44)	86	2,100	5,700

African indigenous missionaries to Sierra Leone 7.

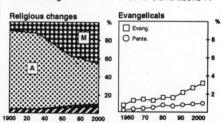

Religious changes / Evangelicals

1. **Sierra Leone was the first West African country to be evangelized,** but after nearly 200 years of effort, less than 10% of the nation even claims to be Christian. The slow growth inland is offset by decline in the capital and there is no single denomination, Pentecostal or mainline Protestant, that has ever made a lasting spiritual impact on the country. Pray that the Christians may be electrified by the ministry of the Holy Spirit!

2. **The decay of public and private morality** has been so severe that the land faces a grim future despite its economic potential. Pray for the emergence of wise and godly political leaders with foresight and courage to make amends for past failures. Pray for freedom to preach the gospel.

3. **Witchcraft and the pervasive secret societies** have hardly ever been challenged and defeated by the power of the Cross. Both Islam and churches in general have avoided the confrontation that must come before breakthroughs can be seen.

4. **There are about 150 churches in Freetown,** but there is much nominalism, worldliness and sin among professing Christians; only 34% of Christians go to church. Almost the entire Krio population professes to be Christian, but their pride and lack of consistent Christian living are major factors hindering the spread of the gospel to the tribal peoples they despised in the past.

5. **Churches in the hinterland** are a small minority surrounded by a sea of Muslim and animistic peoples. Illiteracy, feelings of inferiority, denominational rivalry, and lack of vibrant, growing churches have all combined to depress Christians. Pray for revival, and pray for the emergence of vital local leadership.

6. **The serious lack of trained and spiritual leadership** needs to be speedily rectified. There is little encouragement or incentive for young people to go into full-time service. There are Roman Catholic, Anglican and Methodist seminaries, but only one interdenominational, evangelical, post-secondary institution – the Sierra Leone Bible College. There are two English/Krio and three vernacular Bible Schools, three being run by the **AoG**. The ICI-TEE system of the AoG has 15,000 enrolled students. Pray for spiritual life and vision to be imparted to the students.

7. **The first Protestant churches began in 1785,** yet after 200 years the land is still very much a pioneer mission field. A new beginning is required in many areas. The hardness of the field, the cultural inflexibility of earlier presentations of the gospel, and an over-emphasis on institutions and schools have combined to limit the impact of earlier missionary efforts; many missionaries have been discouraged. Pray for a new day of trust and respect between missionaries and nationals as equal partners – there is a legacy of a paternalistic past to be removed. Some major agencies are: the Missionary Church (25 workers), Lutheran Bible Translators (23), Wesleyan Church (19), United Brethren Church (18), United Methodist (17), **AoG** (10), United Pentecostal Mission (5). Major missionary-contributing countries: USA (147), UK (30), Germany (12), Sweden (10), Korea (6), Nigeria (6).

8. **The less-reached.** Islam is spreading faster than Christianity among the **Temne** (70% Muslim), **Mende** (50%), **Yalunka** (80%), **Kuranko** and **Loko** (40%). Yet in each of these peoples many denominations are represented. Pray for both vision and cooperative outreach to the many villages without a church. Most Christian converts come from an animistic background. Pray for a greater impact for God among Muslims. There is only one people, the **Kono** (11% Muslim), that is more than 10% Christian.

9. **The Unreached.** Despite a relatively high number of missions and denominations, the Muslim Fula, Susu, Malinke and Vai, and the traditional North Kissi, Klao and Bom have not yet been reached. Pray that national churches and missions may soon rectify this. These peoples represent 10% of the nation's population.

10. **Young people's work** has been fruitful, but not enough of that fruit has been conserved and matured in existing churches. **SU** and **YFC** have had a decisive impact on the more educated. **IFES** groups function on nine university and college campuses.

11. **A Vision for the '90s** was born at a national evangelization conference sponsored on the basis of good preliminary research done by both **YWAM** and the **Evangelical Fellowship of Sierra Leone**. Pray for the realization of these goals:
a) Research the strength, size and variety of the church in Sierra Leone, and also the unchurched and unreached areas and peoples so as to motivate the church to see major advance by the year 2000.
b) Motivate, train and mobilize a task force to be deployed for this advance.

12. **Media Ministries**
a) **Radio.** The gap left by the destruction of Radio ELWA (**SIM**, Liberia) in 1990 has yet to be filled. Pray that regular vital radio ministry may once more be launched.
b) **Literature. CLC** has a strategic and well-used bookstore in Freetown. Pray for the ministry of

the written page. Pray also for the granting of permits to import literature – these are often hard to obtain, and there are severe shortages of stock; literature and Bibles are prohibitively expensive as a result. The EMA-CLC Book Aid project importing second-hand Christian books is a spiritual lifeline.

c) **GRn** has audio recordings in 19 languages; the *Jesus* film has narration in both Temne and Mende.

13. **Bible translation** is still a major need. At least three languages need to be translated. Translation teams, notably the Lutheran Bible Translators, are active in six other languages, but these need to be backed by effective literacy programmes.

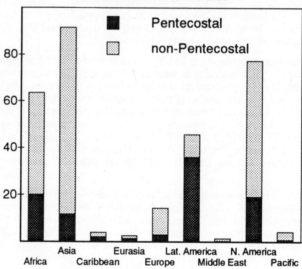

The distribution of Evangelicals worldwide in 1990 is a measure of their success since 1960. Observe:

1. The few Evangelicals in Europe and Eurasia.

2. The extraordinary numbers of Evangelicals in Asia (mainly China and Korea) and Africa.

3. There are more Asian than North American Evangelicals, and soon African Evangelicals will also surpass those of North America.

4. The uneven distribution of those in Pentecostal denominations. Little impact has been made by Pentecostals in Europe or Asia, but a large proportion of Evangelicals in Latin America, the Caribbean and increasingly Africa and North America are Pentecostals. These figures do not include charismatics in non-Pentecostal denominations.

Singapore

(Republic of Singapore)

October 9

Asia

Area 620 sq.km. One larger and many smaller islands off the southern tip of Peninsular Malaysia, and strategically located for communications and trade.

Population	Ann. Gr.	Density
1990	2,702,000	1.10 %	4,344/sq.km
1995	2,836,000	0.97 %	4,559/sq.km

Population: Multi-racial and multi-lingual society.
Chinese 77.7%; language origin: Hokkien 884,000; Teochew 452,000; Cantonese 338,000; Hakka 151,000; Hainanese 146,000; and others.
Malay 14.1%. Both of Malay and Indonesian origin.
Indian 7.1%. 95% speak English; ethnic origin: Tamil 111,000; Malayali 14,000; Panjabi 14,000; Bengali 12,000; Sindhi 5,000; Hindi 5,000; etc.
Other 1.1%. Filipino 50,000; Thai 30,000; Japanese 20,000; Sri Lankan 12,000; Indonesian 8,000; Korean 3,000; Jews 300.

Literacy 90%. **Official languages:** Mandarin (Chinese), English, Malay and Tamil Indian. **All languages** 24.

Capital: Singapore is a city-state. Urbanization 100%. Reputedly Asia's greenest and cleanest city.

Economy: Dramatic growth since independence to become one of the world's most efficient trading and financial centres. The world's second busiest port after Hong Kong. The economy is tightly controlled with clear, long-term strategies for development of high-tech industries and services. Unemployment 2%. Public debt/person $1,140. Income/person $10,450 (48% of USA).

Politics: British rule 1824–1963. Part of Malaysian Federation 1963-65. Independent as a parliamentary democracy in 1965. The strong, paternalistic government of Prime Minister Lee and his successor, Goh Chok Tong, have provided direction and stability for spectacular economic growth. There has been little viable political opposition to challenge autocratic tendencies.

Religion: Freedom of religion, but concerns to maintain ethnic and religious harmony are expressed in legislation limiting public proclamation of religious belief. Religious education in schools is being phased out. All religions are enjoined not to be involved in politics.
Chinese religions 52.4%. A blend of Buddhism, Taoism, Confucianism and ancestor worship.

Non-religious/other 14.2%. Mainly Chinese.
Muslim 15.4%. Malays and 26% of Indians.
Hindu 3.3%. 53% of Indians.
Sikh 0.5%. **Baha'i** 0.2%.
Christian 14%.* Affil 12.32%. Growth 5%.
Protestant 8%. Affil 7.8%. Growth 7%.

Church	Cong	Members	Affiliated
Methodist Ch	39	21,707	46,200
Assemblies of God	36	11,000	25,119
Anglican Ch	24	10,657	23,700
Presbyterian Ch	36	10,248	18,600
Baptist Convention	30	6,264	15,700
Bible Presby Ch (3)	25	6,079	13,500
Christian Brethren	20	5,243	10,500
Lutheran Chs (2)	6	1,910	3,180
CNEC Churches	11	1,107	2,460
Evang Free Ch	12	980	2,300
All other (60)	154	22,950	49,448
Denominations (73)	393	98,145	210,707
Evangelicals 6.7% of pop		84,000	182,000
Pentecostal/charis 2.63%		35,000	71,000

Missionaries:
to Singapore 385 (1:7,000 people) in 62 agencies
– many serving in regional or global offices based in Singapore.
from Singapore 567 (1:371 Protestants) in over 33 agencies 354frn 354xcul 213dom.
Roman Catholic 5.7%. Affil 4.26%. Growth 1.8%.

Catholic Ch	29	80,500	115,000

Missionaries:
to Singapore 165 (1:16,400 people).
from Singapore 2 (1973 figure).
Orthodox 0.1%. Affil 0.08%. Growth 1.9%.

Denominations (3)		440	2,200

Marginal 0.2%. Affil 0.19%. Growth 4.9%.

All groups (6)	15	3,040	5,000

* Note: The 1990 Census gives 12.6% and an official survey in 1988 gives 18.7%. There are compelling reasons to doubt both figures.

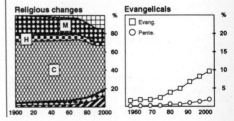

Religious changes

Evangelicals

1. **The dynamism and growth of the Church in Singapore** over the past 20 years is cause for much praise to God. Rapid social change, economic development and increasing use of English are human factors in this growth. The receptivity of Chinese and Indian Singaporeans, active evangelism of

churches and agencies, and the concentration of committed, giving Christians in the little state are spiritual factors.

a) **The responsiveness of the educated** is exceptional. The population is 15% Christian, but among those who have completed high school it is 30%, among university students it is 41%, and among medical students 73%. Christians have influence far larger than their national percentage – this must be used wisely. In 1992 there were 312,700 foreign workers and students in Singapore.

b) **Church growth is vigorous** with nearly 400 Protestant congregations in 1992 (270 English-speaking, 100 Chinese-speaking, 20 Indian-speaking). The fastest-growing are the Methodists, charismatic churches and Assemblies of God. Worship services are packed with young people, most being first-generation Christians. Yet the drop-out rate is high as young people marry and enter the materialistic rat-race.

c) **Liberal theology** has rapidly declined in mainline denominations, with most congregations being evangelical and evangelistic. The Anglican Church has become charismatic. Pray that this dynamism may be directed to the blessing of the world.

2. Major challenges facing the Church:

a) **Coping with affluence** – maintaining a spiritual cutting edge, and using wealth effectively for God's Kingdom.

b) **Handling restrictive government legislation limiting outreach.** Christians need sensitivity in Singapore's multi-faith context, but also boldness to stand firm when fundamental issues of freedom of speech are challenged. Doctors and medical students may not share their faith at work, and Christians are exhorted to cease aggressive evangelism.

c) **Maintenance of adequate family life and witness** in high-rise flats and with high employment.

d) **Unity among churches.** Since 1980 the Evangelical Fellowship of Singapore has been a means for drawing churches together. The Chinese-speaking Christian Churches of Singapore brings together those churches that do not use English.

3. Goals for the 1990s. Many Singaporean Christian leaders have committed themselves to pray and work for:

a) **Singapore to be 30% Christian** by the census in 2000.

b) **Every people group in Singapore to be reached** and to have a viable witnessing body of Christian believers.

4. The less-reached.

a) **The Malay population.** All are considered Muslim by birth, and for years the community was economically isolated. Christians of other ethnic groups are hesitant to evangelize for fear of upsetting intercommunal relationships. A small number of Malays have become Christians.

b) **Sections of the Indian community** – predominantly the older non-English-speaking. There is little consistent outreach to them. The Sikhs, Sindhi and Hindi communities are the least exposed to the gospel.

c) **The Chinese community,** the lower-paid and non-English speakers. They have shown less response to the gospel in the past, but this is changing. Language groups with fewer churches are the Teochew (one church for 50,000) and Hakka (one for 76,000).

d) **Migrant workers.** A number of Singaporean churches encourage outreach to and church meetings for Filipinos, Thai, Japanese and others. There are some lively congregations of Koreans, Filipinos and Indonesians. Pray for an effective long-term strategy for fully evangelizing and discipling these communities before they return home.

e) **Drug addicts** – a growing problem, with an estimated 15,000 addicts. Eight Christian groups are involved in drug rehabilitation programmes. Teen Challenge has a notable ministry among them.

5. Singapore could well claim to be the *Antioch* of Asia. Its dynamic, missions-minded church and unrivalled facilities make it a major base for international Christian organizations such as World Evangelical Fellowship, Evangelical Fellowship of Asia, SU, YFC and the Bible Society. Many international missions have training and sending bases in Singapore, notably: **AsEF**, International Service Mission (**Interserve**), **Navigators, TLM, OM, OMF, SIM, WEC, SIL/WBT, YWAM**.

6. Bible training in the 16 seminaries, Bible schools and missions training schools is becoming a key ministry for Christians all over Asia. Worthy of particular mention are the **Singapore Bible College**, Trinity Theological College and Tung Ling Bible School and the specifically missions preparation institutions of **YWAM, SIL** for linguistics, Asian Cultural Training Institute and Bethany School of Missions. **The Haggai Institute** has provided stimulating short-term courses for pastors and

Christian workers from all over the world, especially Asia and Africa. Many churches run their own theological training programmes.

7. **The blossoming of missions vision in Singapore** is cause for much praise. The seminal impact of OM and its ship ministry was a significant factor. **The Singapore Centre for Evangelism and Missions** has played a catalytic role in unifying and mobilizing the Singaporean missions enterprise. The number of churches with an active missions programme is an example other nations should emulate. Singaporean missionaries overseas increased from 140 in 1988 to 381 in 1992! Nearly 60% of these have been sent directly by their congregations to the field. **Church in Missions Association** links 15 such churches. Many others serve with international missions such as **OMF** (22 workers), **CCC** (18), **YWAM** (18), **WEC** (15), **WBT** (14), **OM** (10). Some of the goals agreed at the National Missions Consultation in 1991 to be achieved by the year 2000 are:
a) 500 Singaporean missionaries overseas, 200 of them serving in the unevangelized world.
b) Half of Singapore's churches to be sending churches, two-thirds to be giving over 10% of their budget to cross-cultural missions.

8. **Young people** are open to the gospel, and are the dynamic future of the country. The impact of youth ministries has been decisive. Among undergraduates, 40% are involved in VCF (**IFES**), **CCC** or Navigators groups. The Navigators, with 65 staff workers, have had a unique contribution in discipling thousands in educational institutions and in the armed forces. **Eagles Evangelism** has used effective and innovative evangelistic outreaches. **Youth For Christ** also has had an extensive ministry, as does **Boys Brigade**. Pray for the effective integration of young people into local churches and for their mobilization for world evangelization.

9. **Foreign missions.** Western missionaries helped to plant churches and sow a missions vision. As a result, many churches have taken up that vision. The major ministries of expatriate missionaries today are in international ministries based in Singapore, and in Bible and missionary training. The largest missions are: **OMF** (57, most of whom are working in their mission headquarters), **YWAM** (38), **SBC** (32) and **AoG** (22).

10. **Christian support agencies.**
a) **Literature** is widely available. There are more than 37 Christian bookstores (7 of **SU**) and over eight publishers of books, magazines and tracts. Much literature is printed in Singapore and distributed in lands around the world.
b) There are over 176 para-church agencies involved in a large variety of spiritual and technical ministries.

Slovakia

See under CZECH REPUBLIC & SLOVAKIA

Slovenia

See under YUGOSLAVIA

October 10		
The Pacific		

Solomon Islands

(The Solomon Islands)

Area 28,370. Six of the seven major volcanic islands of the Solomon Islands, also numerous smaller coral atolls. Bougainville Island is, at present, part of Papua New Guinea. The major islands are Guadalcanal, Choiseul, New Georgia, Santa Isabel, Malaita and San Cristobal.

Population		Ann. Gr.	Density
1990	329,000	4.1 %	12/sq.km
1995	389,000	3.4 %	14/sq.km

Peoples: Over 90 ethnic groups.
Indigenous 97.9%.
  Melanesian 290,000 speaking 66 languages – none spoken by more than 10,000 people.
  Polynesian 11,400 speaking five languages – mainly on outlying coral islands.
Expatriate 2.1%. Other Pacific Islanders 4,300; English-speaking 1,200; Chinese 600.

Literacy 54%. **Official language:** English. Trade language: Solomons Pidgin, spoken by half the population. **All languages** 65, but up to 120 if distinct dialects included. **Languages with Scriptures** 2Bi 6NT 13por.

Capital: Honiara 32,000 on Guadalcanal Island. Urbanization 16%.

Economy: Over 90% of the population depend on subsistence agriculture and fishing. Rich mineral resources remain to be exploited. Fishing and forestry are the main export earners. Public debt/person $330. Income/person $570 (2.7% of USA).

Politics: Independent from Britain in 1978 as a parliamentary monarchy. The secessionist movement in the Northern Solomons, which are part of Papua New Guinea, is also a source of destabilization to the Solomon Islands.

Religion: Freedom of religion but with a strongly Christian emphasis.
Tribal religion 2.9%.
Cargo cult movements 2.7%, animist with Christian accretions.
Baha'i 0.4%.
Christian 94%. Affil 92.4%. Growth 4.3%.
  Protestant 73%. Affil 71.9%. Growth 4%.

Church	Cong	Members	Affiliated
Ch of Melanesia (Ang)	1,120	67,200	112,000
Sth Seas Evang Ch	415	26,000	42,600
United Church	440	23,000	38,300
Seventh-day Adventist	138	18,394	30,700
Assemblies of God	30	528	1,600
All other (6)	63	6,392	11,350
Denominations (11)	2,206	141,514	236,550
Evangelicals 26.8% of pop		52,400	88,000
Pentecostal/charis 7%		13,300	23,000

Missionaries:
  to Solomon Is 81 (1:4,100 people) in 17 agencies.
  from Solomon Is 158 (1:1,500 Protestants) in 2 agencies.
Roman Catholic 19.2%. Affil 18.8%. Growth 5.5%.

Catholic Ch	144	36,000	62,000

Foreign Marginal 1.2%. Growth 4.5%.

Jehovah's Witnesses	35	805	4,030

Indigenous Marginal 0.6%. Growth 7%.

Groups (1)	7	660	2,000

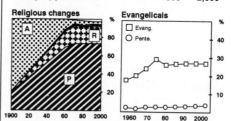

Religious changes

Evangelicals

1. **Praise the Lord for the work of the Spirit in reviving power** in the SSE Churches in 1935 and 1970 and in nearly all Protestant denominations in the '80s. People in all walks of life are coming to the Lord in churches, house groups and prayer meetings. There are strong, growing churches, dynamic leaders, and a missionary outreach to surrounding lands.

2. **Island and tribal loyalties and the turmoil on neighbouring Bougainville could create difficulties for the government.** Pray for wise leadership and continued freedom for the gospel. Its impact on the land has been great.

3. **Inadequate training of pastors** is the biggest bottleneck for the Church's growth in maturity and expansion. Pray for the six SSEC Bible Schools, the Anglican Theological College, and also TEE programmes.

4. **Missions.** The work of **SSEM** (10 workers), as well as that of the Methodists and Anglicans, is praiseworthy. Missionary personnel are needed for specialized ministries – above all in teaching and

training ministries, and also in Bible translation, for which **WBT** has committed 26 workers.

5. Unreached peoples. The land has been so exposed to the gospel that only pockets of resistant animists on Guadalcanal and Malaita hold out against the gospel. Yet the continued influence of syncretic or almost pagan "cargo cults", which have prompted an exodus from churches in the past, shows the need for a personal appropriation of the gospel by each generation.

6. Youth ministries. These are important with the rapid population growth and numbers of third- and fourth-generation Christians. **SU** has vital groups in many of the high schools.

7. Bible translation. National believers are taking the initiative, and this long-underestimated ministry is now receiving the attention it deserves. Pray for the 17 translation projects by **UBS** and **SIL**; 28 more languages may still need to be tackled. The major need is for the completion of the Bible in Pidgin (the trade language). Only six languages of the 65 have a New Testament.

Somalia
(Somali Democratic Republic)

October 11

Africa

Area 638,000 sq.km. The semi-arid Horn of Africa east of Ethiopia and Kenya.

Population	Ann. Gr.	Density
1990 7,555,000	3.4 %	12/sq.km
1995 8,505,000	2.4 %	13/sq.km

Of these 1,000,000 have fled to other lands, and by April 1993 possibly another 250,000 had died of famine and war.

Peoples:
Somali 98.5%.
 Northern Somali 77.5%. Four major clan families: Dir, Daarood, Hawiye, Isxaaq. Numerous clans and sub-clans; largely semi-nomadic.
 Southern groups 21%. More despised; some mixed with Bantu ex-slaves, more agricultural. Main clan families: Digil and Rahanwiin, speaking five languages related to Somali.
Other minorities 1.5%. Mainly Bantu peoples: Mushungulu 50,000; Bajun and Baraawe Swahili 40,000. Most of the Arab and all of the Indian and Italian communities have left the country.

Literacy 24% but in decline. **Official languages:** Somali, English (in north), Italian (more in south) and Arabic (few speak it). **All languages** 14. **Languages with Scriptures** 6Bi.

Capital: Mogadishu 500,000 in 1989, but possibly 1,500,000 in 1993. Urbanization n.a.

Economy: Subsistence pastoral economy – largely camel or cattle herding; some agriculture in south and northwest. Economy in ruins, and controlled by warlords trading in narcotics, arms and food aid. Majority of population totally dependent on food aid and likely to remain so through 1994.

Politics: United as a single country in 1960 soon after the British (in north) and Italians (in south) granted independence to their respective fiefs. Cold war rivalries provided Somalia with ample weapons – first from the USSR, then from the USA – for wars against Ethiopia and clan fighting. These have brought the country to destitution. The corrupt and repressive dictatorship of Siyaad Barre ended in bloody civil war in 1991 but with no viable alternative. The country slid into clan warfare with warlords vying for power – a direct cause of the appalling famine and destruction of 1991/3. UN intervention in 1992 was an effort to permit aid to reach starving population. The former British Protectorate declared its independence from Somalia in 1992, but no state has recognized the new Somaliland.

Religion: Islam is the official religion and has regained its former prominence after the Marxist orientation of the government in the '70s.
Muslim 99.96%. Almost all Somalis are Sunni.
Christian 0.04% in 1990; the number of Christians has been reduced since then to a handful of expatriates and a few hundred Protestant and Catholic Somalis.
Christian expatriates serving in Somalia: some in NGOs.

S

1. Somalia, as a viable state, exists no more. Its future size, composition and leadership are shrouded in doubt. Pray for UN, international and national leaders to agree on Somalia's future. Pray that its future rulers may learn from the past and govern the nation for the good of its people with respect of human rights – including religious freedom. Pray that militant Islamic groups may not gain control.

2. **Islam has failed the country**. Pray that its inadequacies may be apparent to all, and that in the new Somalia the nation may be free to hear the gospel and believe. Most of the country has never been exposed to the gospel.

3. **The work of missions** has been limited, dangerous and hedged with restrictions, and in 1974 forced to cease. Swedish Lutherans won a few hundred to Christ in the south between 1898 and 1935. Mennonites and **SIM** (1953–74) also saw a few hundred turn to the Lord. Pray for workers for the Somali to be called, prepared and ready for the opening of these defiantly closed doors.

4. **Somali Christians** have experienced intense opposition; many are unmarried men – there being few Somali Christian women. In 1991 there were about 500 Somali Catholics and several hundred Evangelicals – most being secret believers. Some have since fled the anarchy, taking refuge in Kenya, Ethiopia, Yemen and elsewhere. Pray for their protection, growth in the faith and boldness to witness when opportunities arise.

5. **Christian ministry to the suffering is a great need**. Some estimate that by the time peace comes 25% of the population will have died and 30% will be permanently damaged through trauma, malnutrition and maiming, the majority being children. Pray for:
a) **Aid workers**, some Christian, who face danger, enormous stress and frustration. Pray that Christian aid organizations may be able to enter, help in the rebuilding of lives and find opportunity to share their faith.
b) **Refugees** and ministry to them in Kenya (500,000). There is need for ministry to the refugees in Ethiopia (200,000), Yemen (60,000), the Gulf and the West.

6. **About 3.5 million Somalis live in surrounding lands:** Ethiopia (approx 2,800,000); Kenya (511,000); Djibouti (192,000). **SIM**, **SBC**, Life Ministries, **CBIM** and others have a ministry to Somalis in Kenya, and **RSTI** in Djibouti. Pray for Christian aid workers and their tactful witness. Pray that all these ministries may have an impact on Somalia itself and that viable Somali churches may be planted.

7. **The Somali Bible** was published in 1977. Many NTs were handed out just before the expulsion of missionaries in 1974, and Bible and literature distribution has quietly continued in refugee camps and in response to radio broadcasts since then. CNC (Somali Voice of New Life) runs follow-up Bible correspondence courses with students in 13 countries. The collapse of the postal services in Somalia has hindered the work there.

8. **Radio broadcasts** are prepared by CNC in Kenya and transmitted daily by **FEBA** Seychelles. Response to the daily half-hour broadcasts is good. This is the main way of reaching directly into the country.

S

South Africa

(Republic of South Africa)

Area 1,222,000 sq.km. This includes:
1. **Four quasi-independent states:** Transkei 45,000 sq.km; Bophuthatswana 40,000 sq.km.; Ciskei 9,000 sq.km.; Venda 6,500 sq.km. These 'TBVC' states are not internationally recognized and are likely to be reincorporated into South Africa at any time from 1993 onwards.
2. **Walvis Bay**, an enclave on Namibia's coast, 1,124 sq.km. Its future is a matter for intense negotiation between South Africa and Namibia.

Population		Ann. Gr.	Density
1990	35,248,000	2.2 %	29/sq.km
1995	39,189,000	2.1 %	32/sq.km

Population growth differences: White 1.6%; Asian 1.9%; Coloured and Black 2.9%. The four TBVC states 7,200,000; the six self-governing homelands 9,500,000.

Peoples:
Black 72.5%.
 Nguni 43.6% (5 groups). Zulu 6,820,000; Xhosa 6,734,000; Swazi 1,025,000; South Ndebele 470,000; North Ndebele 318,000.
 Sotho 23.7% (3 groups). Tswana 3,440,000; North Sotho/Pedi 2,818,000; South Sotho 2,091,000.
 Other 5.2%. Tsonga/Shangaan 1,196,000; Venda 642,000.
White 14.2%. Afrikaner 2,565,000; English-speaking 1,709,000; Portuguese 617,000; Greek 70,000; German 45,000.
Coloured (mixed race) 10.1%. 90% live in the Western Cape Province. The Cape Malays are considered part of this community.
Asian 3.2%. Indians 916,000; Chinese 15,000.
Migrant labour from surrounding lands. est. 2,700,000.
Refugees: Mozambicans maybe 500,000.

Literacy 64% and falling. **National languages:** Afrikaans, English. The ten Black national and TBVC states each use their majority language as the official language. **All languages** 32. **Languages with Scriptures** 18Bi 2NT 1por.

Capitals: Pretoria (administrative) 865,000; Cape Town (legislative) 1,740,000; Bloemfontein (judicial) 220,000. **Other major cities:** Johannesburg/ Soweto 3,500,000 (6,600,000 live in the Witwatersrand and South Transvaal industrial complex); Durban 1,100,000; Port Elizabeth 680,000. These figures do not include millions of squatters who have moved to the cities since 1989. Urbanization 56% (Asians 93%, Whites 89%, Coloureds 78%, Blacks 40%).

Economy: The richest and most industrialized country in Africa (25% of GNP, 40% of industrial output). The world's biggest exporter of non-petroleum minerals – especially gold, platinum, chrome, diamonds and coal. Lack of water and erratic rainfall limit growth. World recession, drought and worldwide opposition to the racial policies have stunted growth and raised unemployment. Government overspending on defence and the cumbersome bureaucracy have also helped to put the economy into severe decline since 1982. Public debt/person $837. Income/person $2,460 (11% of USA).

Politics: The Union of South Africa was formed in 1910. A white minority parliamentary republic was created in 1961. The 1984 constitution extended a limited sharing of power with the Coloured and Asian minorities but excluded Blacks from national politics. The worsening economic crisis, deteriorating security situation, and the ending of the Cold War have all helped to trigger rapid changes in the '80s. The de Klerk government took bold steps to end apartheid and initiate serious negotiations towards setting up a fully democratic, multi-racial country. Most of the apartheid laws were repealed by July 1991. However, the battle for power and influence between the ANC, the Inkatha Freedom Movement, the Pan-African Congress and the government has contributed to an interminable cycle of intimidation and violence with a mounting death toll. The violence is pushing all sides to seek a viable solution so that rebuilding the new South Africa can begin. The first multi-racial election is expected in 1994. The ten ethnic homelands are enclaves within South Africa. Four opted for political independence: Transkei 1976, Bophuthatswana 1977, Venda 1979, Ciskei 1981. All but Bophuthatswana have military regimes. They constitute 13% of the land area but half the population. Their general poverty, over-population and economic dependence on South Africa will inevitably mean their full political reincorporation in South Africa.

S

Religion: Freedom of religion. Government statistics and some denominations omit the figures for the TBVC states. An attempt has been made below to include them. The future government is likely to have a strong humanist slant; racial and religious tolerance may include a law against proselytizing children under 18.
African traditional religions 17.7%. The peoples more strongly so are Venda 62%; Shangaan 48%; Zulu 27%; Xhosa 25%.

Non-religious/other 6.5%. Satanists number over 100,000.

Hindu 1.7%. Indians, mainly in Natal.

Muslim 1.25%. Cape Malays, Indians, Zanzibaris and some Zulu.

Jews 0.25%. About 86,600, over half in the Rand area of South Transvaal. There are 2,000 Black Jews.

Christian 72.6%. Growth 2.7%.

Protestant 38.4%. Growth 2.6%.

Church	Cong	Members	Affiliated
Methodist Ch	6,450	758,178	2,500,000
Ch of Prov of SA (Ang)	1,200	520,000	2,000,000
Dutch Ref Ch (NGK)	1,203	955,794	1,403,180
Dutch Ref Ch of Af (NGK-ZA)	468	293,000	892,000
Evang Lutheran Ch	1,612	422,000	703,349
Intl F'ship of Charis Chs	600	400,000	700,000
Apostolic Faith Mission	2,787	369,000	615,000
Dutch Ref Miss Ch (NGSK)	257	225,000	470,000
Presby Ch of Africa	413	231,000	400,000
Full Gospel Ch of God	850	260,000	350,000
Dutch Ref Ch (NHK)	303	193,561	326,652
Presbyterian Ch of SA	220	75,000	300,000
Assemblies of God	2,000	250,000	300,000
Reformed Ch (GK)	417	95,800	159,618
Reformed Presby Ch	980	50,000	150,000
Seventh-day Adventist	571	63,065	145,292
Pentecostal Prot Ch	500	88,000	135,000
United Congreg Ch	660	96,113	127,035
Moravian Ch (2)	82	40,800	102,003
Ch of England in SA	160	32,000	100,000
Baptist Convention	634	35,572	71,100
Baptist Union (2)	489	38,175	64,000
Pente Holiness Ch	435	35,808	59,700
African Evang Ch	210	16,500	55,000
Ch of the Nazarene	308	20,538	50,155
All other (158)	7,627	808,766	1,349,141
Denominations (185)	31,436	6,373,670	13,528,225
Evangelicals 16.6% op pop		3,418,000	5,847,000
Pentecostal/charis 8.5%		1,931,000	3,007,000

Missionaries:
to Sth Africa 1,294 (1:27,200 people) in 113 agencies.
from Sth Africa 2,509 (1:5,400 Protestants) in 86 agencies 653frn 1,856 local (both xcul and dom).

Roman Catholic 7.8%. Growth 1.1%.

Catholic Ch	2,800	1,650,000	2,750,000

Missionaries:
to Sth Africa 2,589 (1:13,600 people).
from Sth Africa 100 (1973).

Orthodox 0.34%. Growth 22.3%.

Denominations (1)	19	48,000	120,000

Foreign Marginal 1.83%. Growth 5.9%.

New Apostolic Ch	1,500	250,000	455,000
Jehovah's Witnesses	1,063	48,590	139,000
All other (12)	242	30,462	52,028
Groups (14)	2,805	329,052	646,028

Indigenous Marginal 24.3%. Growth 3%.

Zion Christian Ch		1,000,000	2,000,000
All groups (est. 4,000)		3,634,000	8,556,700

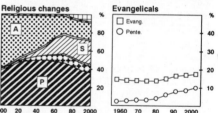

Religious changes / Evangelicals

1. **The political and spiritual future of South Africa** hangs in the balance, and therefore on the prayers of God's people. Pray for:

a) **The political future**, which could be catastrophic with years of bloodshed and chaos. Pray for sensitivity, moderation and wisdom for leaders of all races as they negotiate a suitable government system for the country which will give ethnic harmony, economic stability and equitable distribution of opportunity and resources to all races. Pray also that the post-settlement election may be free, fair and without intimidation, and may bring many Christians into positions of influence.

b) **The spiritual direction of the nation.** The high proportion of committed Christians in all racial groups is an asset, but humanist and socialist values could become the basis of the first post-apartheid government. Pray that political leaders may establish the new South Africa on principles compatible with the Bible and maintain full freedom of religion.

c) **Reconciliation between the races.** The legacy of contempt, mistrust, fear, injustice, violence, intimidation and deep hurt has scarred the soul of the nation.

2. **Praise for the positives:**

a) **The strength of biblical Christianity** despite the widely publicized negatives. The Spirit of God is moving in all major racial groups, and with touches of revival in some areas. There are large numbers of evangelical believers in the country.

b) **The increasing prayer concern** among Christians, and growth of interracial and interdenominational prayer movements. There is a groundswell of spiritual earnestness as the political crisis comes to a head – may it lead to a spiritual awakening.

c) **The spectacular growth of Pentecostals** from 0.5 million adherents in 1960 to 2.5 million in 1990 and of the **newer charismatic churches** – notably Hatfield Christian Church and the Rhema Bible Church – to 250,000. Most of the latter are part of a loose fellowship, the International Fellowship of Christian Churches, with 700,000 adherents.

3. **Missions involvement for South Africans** was severely affected by diplomatic isolation between 1961 and 1991 and the worsening economic crisis. Past South African missionary commitment and mission agencies have become internationally renowned – including the **NGK**(DRC) with a major outreach for many years to a number of African nations, South Africa General Mission (now **AEF**), **IHCF** (with a worldwide ministry to and through medical workers), Africa Evangelistic Band, **Dorothea Mission**, and more recently **African Enterprise** and Christ For All Nations (linked with the name of Reinhard Bonnke). Pray for:
a) **A new wave of mission thrusts** from South Africa with the ending of visa restrictions to many lands. Pray especially for an emphasis on the unreached areas and peoples of the world. There is considerable interest in the tragic need of neighbouring Mozambique.
b) **The Evangelical Fellowship of South Africa, the South African Missions Association** and **South African Action for World Evangelization**. These all play varied roles in coordinating, providing fellowship and encouraging missions vision. **Reachout** is an innovative and comprehensive mobilizing mechanism for recruiting many short-term worker teams sponsored by SAAWE. An African Society for Frontier Missions has been formed.
c) **The effective development of Coloured and Indian missionary vision**. A number of Christians from these communities have moved overseas as missionaries – notably with **OMF**, **WEC**, etc. to Asia, Pacific, Europe and Latin America.
d) **The emergence of missionary outreach from the Black churches**. There is great potential, but obstacles for its realization are enormous, and the relatively few missionaries from this community have a hard task to convince the leadership of the validity of missions, let alone raising missionary support. **YWAM** has a strong burden to facilitate this vision.
e) **African Enterprise** which has an energetic outreach and teaching ministry to other parts of the world – but especially Africa.
f) **The provision of funds for South African missionaries serving abroad**. This has become a major issue because of the decline in value of the local currency.

4. **Black African communities**
Population 26,224,000.
Religion: Christian 76% (Protestant 35%, African Independent Churches 32%, Roman Catholic 8.6%).
African traditional/no religion 24%.
a) **Black nationalism** is on the verge of achieving its long-cherished goal of political power. The violent decades of protest against white political dominance and repression have left a legacy of urban neglect with inadequate housing and services, rural impoverishment and a bad educational system rendered virtually useless. Meaningful development has been set back many years. Inflated expectations of rapid economic improvement following political emancipation are likely to be dashed, causing enormous social upheavals and the resumption of old ethnic hatreds. Pray for the peace of South Africa.
b) **Missionary work** began among the Blacks in 1799. Nearly every major denomination in Europe and North America has played a part in their evangelization. Heroic effort and tragic mistakes have marked its progress. The missionary force has reduced in numbers as mature churches have emerged, and most existing ministries are in church development, leadership training, youth, literature and radio ministries. Pray for fruitful ministries for them in times of great difficulty, ministry restrictions, and discouragement.
c) **The Church** is an extraordinary mixture. The rapid growth of the African Independent Churches is a challenge to more orthodox churches that have often suffered considerable decline and loss of spiritual vitality. Among more evangelical groups, growth has been marked among the various Assemblies of God groups, Pentecostals, Church of the Nazarene and, more recently, charismatic churches. Major prayer points:
  i) **The mainline churches**. These became the only legal voice for political action for Blacks. The politicization of the gospel has further impoverished spirituality. Pray for renewal that will restore the balance and deal with nominalism, sin and traditional practices common among professing Christians.
  ii) **Leadership**. Pray for God to raise up deeply spiritual and biblically-centred leaders for the coming generation who will be able to address the total needs of all, especially the poor and marginalized, with the teaching and life style of Jesus. Political activism and Black or liberation theology with its Marxist presuppositions have all too often supplanted the preaching and living out of the Word of God.
  iii) **The African Independent Churches** (AICs). These have grown to include almost one-third of

S

the Black population. Some are highly syncretic, while others are more biblical in orientation but in need of teaching. Efforts by a number of agencies to provide theological training for AIC leaders have borne some fruit.

iv) **Effective and close fellowship links** to be strengthened between Black and other racial Christian groups, and between mainstream churches and AICs.

d) **The urban areas** present a challenge. Over ten million Blacks live in satellite townships of the cities. Some have become household names because of the violent events of the past three decades – Soweto and Alexandra (Johannesburg), Kwa Mashu (Durban), Gugulethu (Cape Town), Sharpeville, Boipatong being but some of these. Soweto itself has over three million inhabitants. To these urban areas have been added millions in squatter areas that have sprung up overnight since the repeal of apartheid legislation. Pray for:

i) **The churches, believers and their witness** in a society full of social stress, where tribal and family authority have broken down, and where political, ethnic and criminal violence is commonplace. Rape, teenage pregnancies and murder are perpetrated unchecked, and AIDS is becoming a scourge. Believers have been subjected to intimidation and violence for their faith. Pray that they may be protected, given grace to stand for Jesus and be lights for him in these very places.

ii) **Young people and children** who have become pawns in the revolutionary war for political power. Many have had their education ruined, millions are ill-equipped for any training or employment, and their anger could be a threat to stable government for decades to come. Many have become fiercely hostile to Christianity as the religion of the oppressors. Pray for all efforts to meet their spiritual needs – through the evangelical SCM, **Youth Alive, SU, Youth for Christ, YWAM,** Africa Youth Evangelism and others.

iii) **Evangelistic outreach** through churches and mass evangelism agencies (Assemblies of God, African Enterprise, Dorothea Mission, Samaria Mission, Africa for Christ Evangelistic Association, Evangelistic Christian Outreach and Gospel Ambassadors for Christ). The major new challenge is the evangelization of the new squatter settlements. Much is being done locally, and church growth in them is fast.

iv) **The multiplication of efforts made by Islam** and other "-isms" which are making inroads into city areas. Several mosques have been built of late.

e) **Migrant labourers** are a major feature of South African life because of earlier restrictions on population movement. Over 2,700,000 people are in this category. Many men live separated from their families for long periods. It was armed clashes between migrant labourers and resident urbanites of differing political loyalties that led to the thousands killed in township violence between 1990 and 1993. Effective evangelism and church planting are hard because of their social disruption as a transient society. About 280,000 migrants come from other lands such as Lesotho (150,000), Mozambique (60,000), Malawi (30,000) and Botswana (29,000), and many more from the 10 national states. The mines draw workers from all over South Africa and beyond for longer or shorter periods. At any one time 400,000 are living in the large mine compounds of the Transvaal and Orange Free State. Pray for the outreach of the Mission to Miners (**AEF**), NGK and others to these migrant workers. Pray that those won to Christ may be so effectively discipled that churches may be planted and strengthened in their home areas when their contract period ends.

f) **The political future of the ten Self-governing/Independent States** is a major point for negotiation. It is almost inevitable that this patchwork of largely unviable, overcrowded enclaves will be fully reintegrated into South Africa in the near future. Pray for wise solutions. There is a massive exodus of people from these areas to the cities. Pray for these entities:

i) **Bophuthatswana:** population 2,000,000; 40% of all Tswana. West Transvaal and North Cape Province. Fairly viable economy. **Christian** 90.4%, of which AICs form 24%. **Non-Christian** 9.6%.

ii) **Ciskei:** population 830,000; 12% of Xhosa. East Cape Province. Independent 1981; the dictatorial government has a poor record on human rights. **Christian** 75%, **non-Christian** 25%.

iii) **Gazankulu:** population 1,060,000; 40% of Shangaan/Tsonga. Northeast Transvaal. Economically backward. **Christian** 51%, **non-Christian** 49%. Only AICs and RCs growing significantly; mainline churches generally in decline.

iv) **Kangwane:** population est. 600,000; 16% of Swazi. Northeast Transvaal. **Christian** 68%, **non-Christian** 32%. Massive growth of AICs from 28.6% in 1970 to 48% in 1980.

v) **KwaNdebele:** population 560,000; 35% of S. Ndebele. North Transvaal. **Christian** 85%, much nominalism; **non-Christian** 15%. AICs 50% of population.

vi) **KwaZulu:** population 5,053,000; 60% of Zulu. Natal. Has refused independence. Very fragmented geographically. **Christian** 75%, **non-Christian** 25%.

vii) **Lebowa:** population 2,826,000; 60% of Pedi. North Transvaal. Poor and economically unviable. **Christian** 57%, **non-Christian** 42%. Rapid growth of AICs and RCs. The Zion Christian Church, the largest AIC, is predominantly Pedi.

viii) **Qua-Qua:** population 320,000; 9% of South Sotho. East Orange Free State. Very poor and over-populated. **Christian** 88%, **non-Christian** 12%.

ix) **Transkei:** population 3,280,000; 43% of Xhosa. Between Natal and east Cape Province. Independent 1976, one-party state. Good potential for economic viability. **Christian** 67%, **non-Christian** 33%.

x) **Venda:** population 600,000; 68% of all Venda. Independent 1979, now a one-party state. **Christian** 55%, **non-Christian** 45%. Pray for:
  * **The complete evangelization of pockets of non-Christians** – especially among the Venda, Shangaan, Pedi, and parts of Zulu and Xhosa.
  * **The enlivening of Protestant churches**. The RCs and especially AICs are growing. The discouraging economic and political situation and the absence of a considerable part of the active male population as migrant labour make effective church development very difficult. Lack of finance, dynamic leadership and spiritual vitality are prayer challenges.

5. The White community. Population 4,530,000.
Religion: Christian 92.1% (Protestant 83%, Roman Catholic 8.8%).
Non-religious/other 6%. **Jews** 1.9%.
The dramatic events of the past three decades have shaken the complacency, materialistic affluence and even the spiritual credibility of this community as Christians. Pray for:

a) **A rekindling of spirituality and faith** in the midst of traumatic change, and the courage to take bold decisions, for they still hold the reins of economic and political power.

b) **The Afrikaners.** Among them are many committed believers and outstanding Christian leaders. The influence of Andrew Murray, an NGK minister, lives on. Over half of all Afrikaners are members of this church, and a high proportion are active churchgoers. Nominalism is affecting the NGK. Pray for revival once more.

c) **The English-speaking people** who tend to be less religious than the Afrikaners. There is more liberal theology in the major denominations, yet significant changes are occurring in the Anglican Church through the charismatic movement, with a return to a more biblical theology and personal faith by a large minority. Evangelical denominations such as the Baptists, Church of England in SA, Assemblies of God, and especially the charismatic churches are growing steadily (though the largest growth in these denominations is outside the White community). However, many English-speaking people are alienated from the churches and need to be confronted with the gospel.

d) **The less reached: The Jews,** among whom there is a small, but growing number of Hebrew Christians (**CWI, JFJ**). **The Portuguese** are nominally Catholic and very conservative, but response through Pentecostal and **NGK** missions is increasing. The **Greeks** are neglected.

e) **Young people.** There are many denominational and interdenominational groups seeking to witness among them: Youth For Christ, SU, Student Christian Assoc., **His People, YWAM, CCC** and others among young professionals and teens. Pray for young people to be won for Christ and to hear God's call into Christian service.

6. The Coloured community. Population 2,929,000 (mainly West Cape Province).
Religion: Christian 86% (Protestant 72%, Roman Catholic 10%, Other 4%).
Non-religious/other 7.8%. **Muslim** 6.2%.

a) **The churches** need revival. To most, religion and daily life are not closely related. Churches are often weak in leadership, nominal and introspective, and there has been a large defection to sectarian groups. However, the development of vital evangelical congregations with evangelistic and missionary outreach is moderately encouraging – especially among Pentecostal, **NGK** (NG Mission Church), **TEAM** and independent charismatic churches.

b) **Outreach.** Charismatic churches have grown rapidly with many thousands coming to faith. Bethel evangelists of the AEB have seen much fruit from evangelistic outreach. Some churches and missions have a fruitful ministry among sailors in Cape Town. The rural areas are the least touched by present evangelistic outreach. Pray for many dedicated young people to be called into full-time Christian work.

c) **The Cape Malays** (almost all in Cape Town) are considered part of the Coloured community and speak Afrikaans. They are predominantly Malay and Muslim. They cling tenaciously to their customs and religion. Teams of Coloured Christians linked with **Life Challenge** (**SIM**) are saturating Muslim areas with the gospel, and a few are coming to Christ.

S

7. **The Asian community.**
Population 931,000 (81% Natal, 14% Transvaal, 3.9% Cape Province). Predominantly Indian; some Chinese.
Religion: Hindu 61%. **Muslim** 19.5%. **Christian** 13% (Protestant 10.4%, Roman Catholic 2.6%). **Non-religious/other** 6.5%.
The Indian community has gone through traumatic social and economic changes since their arrival in Natal a century ago. Many are very Westernized.

a) **The bondage of Hinduism** is still very real despite a significant response to the gospel. A number of denominational and interdenominational agencies seek to reach them – such as the Pentecostals, **AEF, NGK, TEAM** and Church of England in SA.

b) **The growth of the Church** was rapid during the '70s, but has slowed more recently. The major impact has been through the Bethesda Temple Full Gospel Churches (50,000 adherents), Apostolic Faith Mission (11,000), Baptist (3,500), **AEF**-related churches (3,000), and Reformed Church in Africa (**NGK**) (2,400). The weaknesses evident are Hindu thought patterns and practices, and often a weak and divided leadership. There are at least three good Bible schools – pray for the calling and equipping of Indian pastors and missionaries.

c) **The Indian Muslims** (198,000) are a generally wealthy, tightly-knit community that has been fairly successful in resisting Christian evangelism, yet about 40% no longer believe Islam to be unique. Over the last 10 years Full Gospel Churches, Baptists, **AEF** and **SIM** have developed specific ministries to them. **Jesus to the Muslims** is an agency committed to enable Christians to reach Muslims through literature, seminars, etc. There are only about seven full-time workers committed to Muslim outreach. About 200 have come to Christ from out of the Muslim community – they need prayer.

d) **The Chinese** (15,000) live mainly in Transvaal; most are secularized, nominal Christians. Five denominations have Chinese membership.

8. **Christian literature.** The production and distribution of literature is prodigious! There are over 60 Christian publishers. Of note are **All Nations Gospel Publishers** (with a worldwide distribution of tracts and booklets), Emmanuel Press, Africa Christian Literature Advance (**AEF**), and **NGK Press**. There are nearly 200 Christian bookstores. **The Bible Society** has a well-developed programme for improved translations of the Scriptures – the last major languages to receive the Bible being the South Ndebele and Swazi. **SU**'s ministry through literature and to young people has been noteworthy. Few countries are better served with Christian literature, but pray that what is distributed may be eternally fruitful.

9. **Christian radio and television.** The South African broadcasting corporation airs 23 radio services in 19 languages and four television services in seven languages. Over 12 million listen or watch religious broadcasting. Radio and Television Pulpit on the national network have a large audience. **TWR** broadcasts 46 hours per week in six European languages and a total of 16 hours per week in Zulu, Ndebele and Tswana. Pray also for agencies who prepare these programmes, including **AEF**, **CoN**, Dorothea Mission and MEMA(NGK). Pray that Christians may continue to have access to these media in the future.

S

Spain

(Kingdom of Spain)

October
15–16

Europe

Area 505,000 sq.km. The major part of the Iberian peninsula and Balearic Islands in the Mediterranean. Also included are the Canary Islands off northwest Africa and the enclaves of Ceuta and Melilla on the North African coast.

Population	Ann. Gr.	Density
1990 39,333,000	0.38 %	78/sq.km
1995 40,060,000	0.37 %	79/sq.km

Peoples:
Indigenous 98.9%.
  Spanish 91.6%. Major languages: Castilian 28,900,000; Catalan 6,512,000; Galician 3,236,000; Aragonese 30,000.
  Basque 5.7%. Euskara, the Basque language, is the primary language of 40% of the Basques (918,000).
  Gypsy 1.6%. Calo Romani 163,000; Vlach Romani 1,000.
  Spanish living overseas 2,000,000; half in Latin America.
Foreign 1.1%. North African/Arab 200,000; Latin Americans 150,000; EC citizens 100,000; Chinese 20,000.

Literacy 93%. **Official language:** Castilian Spanish. Catalan, Galician and Basque are the official languages in the respective autonomous regions. Spanish is the first language of 280,000,000 people – the world's third most widely-used language. **All languages** 11. **Languages with Scriptures** 4Bi 2NT 2por.

Capital: Madrid 4,200,000. Other major cities: Barcelona 2,600,000; Valencia 800,000; Seville 680,000. Urbanization 77% (some claim 91%).

Economy: Decades of instability and isolation prevented economic expansion. Tourism and industry together with integration into the EC have transformed Spain into a progressive, modern, industrial economy. Unemployment 20%. Public debt/person $5,000. Income/person $9,150 (42% of USA).

Politics: Spain's tumultuous past moulds the present. The Muslim Moorish occupation lasted 700 years, ending in 1492. The worldwide Spanish Empire lasted for three centuries. The last two centuries have been marked by instability, civil wars and dictatorships; the latter under General Franco lasted from 1939 to 1975. Constitutional monarchy with wide powers given to 17 autonomous communities as a means of preserving national unity. The left-wing Basque ETA terrorist campaign for full Basque independence has plagued Spain since 1961.

Religion: During Franco's dictatorship, Catholicism was the state religion. Non-Catholics, especially Evangelicals, were subject to discrimination and even persecution. The 1978 Constitution guaranteed equality of rights for all ideologies and religions, and no single faith has national status. Full equality for Evangelicals, Muslims and Jews was only fully established in 1992.

Non-religious/other approx 20%. Rapid secularization with large losses from the Catholic Church – many to New Age and sects.
Muslims 0.5%. Mainly North Africans.
Jews 0.03%; 15,000.
Christian 79.5% (officially 93.5%). Affil 87.7%. Growth −1.2%.
Protestant 0.89%. Growth 10%.

Church	Cong	Members	Affiliated
Philadelphia Ev Ch	363	30,990	200,000
Christian Brethren	175	9,768	20,800
Seventh-day Adventist	61	5,671	18,900
Baptist Union	63	7,405	13,500
Spanish Evang Chs	35	2,277	10,000
Assemblies of God	86	4,123	6,566
All other (88)	671	29,267	79,209
Denominations (94)	1,454	89,501	348,975
Evangelicals 0.79% of pop		80,000	312,000
Pentecostal/charis 0.6%		49,000	238,000

Missionaries:
  to Spain 1,109 (1:35,500 people) in 144 agencies.
  from Spain 48 (1:7,300 Protestants) in 19 agencies.
Roman Catholic 78% (officially 92%). An estimated 50% of Catholics have no meaningful link with the Church. Affil 86.19%. Practising 27%. Growth −1.3%.

Catholic Ch	21,730	9,402,317	36,200,000
Doubly counted			−2,300,000
Total	21,730	9,402,317	33,900,000
Charismatic 0.02%		3,000	7,000

Missionaries:
  to Spain 1,280 (1973 figure).
  from Spain 21,000 (1:1,600 Catholics).
Orthodox 0.01%. Growth 3.8%.
Marginal 0.62%. Growth 7.3%.

Jehovah's Witnesses	1,079	84,562	211,000
Mormons	129	11,900	17,000
All other (6)	18	2,000	16,000
All groups (8)	1,226	98,462	244,000

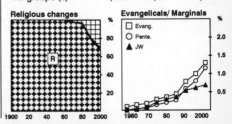

Religious changes

Evangelicals/ Marginals
  □ Evang.
  ○ Pente.
  ▲ JW

S

1. **The changes in Spain since 1974 are astonishing** – from tyranny to liberty, poverty to wealth, isolation to integration in Europe, religious discrimination to rampant secularism. Yet freedom has not brought the awaited ingathering of Spanish people to Christ. The one exception is the remarkable outpouring of the Holy Spirit on the Gypsies of Spain; the Philadelphia Church has multiplied to embrace a third of all Gypsies. Some 60% of all Evangelicals in Spain are Gypsy!

2. **The shadow of the Inquisition still lies over Spain**. Pray for the removal of its consequences in the life of the nation. In the name of Christ hundreds of thousands of innocent Spanish Jews and Evangelicals and then American Indians were tortured and burned at the stake during and after the time of the Reformation. The Church became associated with tyranny and bigotry, and this is one of the underlying causes of the widespread disillusionment with religion. Over 50% of those baptized as Catholics no longer retain links with the Church.

3. **The Catholic Church faces a crisis**. In a few years 20% of its members, mostly young people, have turned to secularism and religious indifference. The number of priests is declining at nearly 2% every year. Renewal movements have hardly affected the Church. Pray for spiritual life to burst forth.

4. **The spiritual vacuum is being filled by:**
a) **Foreign cults**. There are almost as many active Jehovah's Witnesses as Protestant church members. The Mormons are doubling their numbers every five years. There are estimated to be 300 cults active – 30 being Satanist.
b) **Drugs**. There are reckoned to be 300,000 addicted to heroin and cocaine, a major factor in the AIDS epidemic. In 1992 there were estimated to be 100,000 carrying the HIV virus, and AIDS victims are more numerous than in any other European country. RETO, REMAR (Pentecostal) and **Bethel** (WEC-related) have had success in rehabilitating drug addicts in centres in many parts of the country. The Bethel converts have planted four churches and are extending their ministry to other lands.
c) **Gambling**. This is a major obsession, with 11% of private-sector spending misused at great social cost to families.
Pray for spiritual power, love, and wisdom for all seeking to minister to these people bound by Satan's wiles.

5. **The growth of Evangelicals has been steady** but not as fast as expected. The 6,000 Protestant church members in 1932 had increased to 20,000 in 1963, 36,000 in 1980 and 89,000 in 1990, but they are very unevenly distributed. Most churches are concentrated in Catalonia (especially Barcelona), Andalucia and, to a lesser extent, around Madrid. Pray for changes:
a) **Freedom from the effects of being a despised and rejected minority** in order to make full use of today's freedom and equality by vigorous outreach.
b) **The Spanish evangelical churches to be freed from their foreignness**. Many missionaries have unwittingly imported their national and doctrinal idiosyncrasies and tried to control the churches they planted, stunting indigenous expression and leadership.
c) **Greater cooperation between denominations in fellowship and evangelism**. There is an individualistic independence and mistrust of others that has long inhibited cooperation.
d) **The development of a Spanish missions vision** recently begun. The **Llamada** conferences every three years and the ministry of **OM**, **WEC** and Latin American missions have inspired young people to go to the Middle East and Africa, in spite of the shortage of sending structures and supportive churches. *La Gran Comision* is a bulletin that imparts this vision and is distributed in Spain and other lands. Pray for the vision to mature. Pray also for the growth and development of several young Spanish mission agencies.

6. **Leadership training**. The small size of the evangelical community and the high level of unemployment make it difficult for small congregations to support full-time workers or for Christians to commit themselves to the work of the Lord. In 1990 there were about 1,350 pastoral workers – but only a minority working full-time in the ministry. Many young people have been enthused for Christian service and missions through the ministry of **OM** and **YWAM**. There are 14 seminaries and Bible schools – one of each initiated by **GEM**. **TEAM** has launched a seminary specifically to train church planters. (To graduate, a student must show effectiveness in winning people to the Lord and planting a church.) **TEAM**, **OMS**, **AoG**(ICI) and **Open Bible Standard Mission**(INSTE) run or have initiated TEE programmes. Pray that from this input there might be a good supply of godly men and women to further the gospel in Spain and beyond.

7. **There has been a considerable increase in missionaries and agencies since 1975**, yet the unoccupied areas are numerous. Two-thirds of the missionary force is concentrated in Madrid or

around Barcelona. Proliferation of agencies and lack of coordination are issues for concern. Pray for:

a) **Missionaries** to be called to less-evangelized areas.

b) **Good relations between expatriate and national workers**. Missionary and nationals are about equal in number, but missionaries have the financial freedom to work full-time, which many of the nationals cannot do. The potential for pain in relationships is obvious.

c) **Missionaries to be able to integrate fully into Spanish culture and life**. Many new missionaries remain aloof and need pastoral care and encouragement to adapt and then become effective church planters. There is much pioneer evangelism but little fruit in churches planted.

Some larger missions are: **AoG** (95 workers from 9 nations), Brethren (57), **SBC** (50), **WEC** (47), Finnish Free Mission (32), **OMS** (32), **YWAM** (32), **GEM** (30), **GMU** (29), **TEAM** (28), **OM** (27), **ECM** (18), **WT** (18), **ABWE** (17), **CAMI** (15), **SEND** (12). Most are engaged in evangelism, church planting and Bible teaching. Major missionary-contributing nations: USA (590), UK (125), Latin Americans (57), Canada (46), Finland (34), Sweden (33), Korea (27).

8. The need of Spain is enormous.

a) **Over** 15,000,000 live in towns, villages and districts where there is no evangelical church.

b) **Of the 15 regions**, three have less than 10 Protestant churches – Cantabria (9), La Rioja (8) and Navarra (8). In these regions live 2,500,000 people.

c) **Of the 50 Provinces**, 16 have very few evangelical churches or believers.

d) **Of the 8,046 municipalities**, only 435 have an evangelical witness.

9. The less-reached minorities.

a) **The Basques** – an ancient and proud people without a single Euskara-speaking Protestant church. The few churches in the four provinces (Guipúzcoa, Vizcaya, Alava and Navarra) where Basques live are Spanish-speaking. There are about 50 scattered evangelical believers who find it difficult to worship or witness in Basque. Only the beginnings of evangelistic and literature ministries have been made (**CAMI**, Baptists). The widely-differing dialects in an already difficult language complicates the task. Pray for the indifference of this people to be broken down.

b) **The Muslims**. Much of Spain was ruled by the Moors for 700 years. Muslims want to re-win the land. There are groups of Spanish converts to Islam in Granada and Cordoba. Saudi Arabia funded the building of Europe's largest mosque in Madrid. Pray for an effective strategy to win Muslims for Christ and for those called to implement it.

c) **The flood of illegal immigrants from North and West Africa**. Numbers are unknown but Spain is a preferred route into Europe. Pray for ways and means to evangelize them – it will need those with a special calling; most are Muslim.

d) **The Chinese**. Many are refugees from China; 12,000 live in Madrid. There is a small outreach to them (COCM).

10. **The one million students** are largely unevangelized. In 1967 there were but 12 known evangelical students in universities. Today there are over 500 linked with **IFES** groups served by six staff workers. There are 15 university towns without an evangelical student witness. Pray for the consolidation of existing work and expansion to other campuses and to secondary schools.

11. **Ceuta and Melilla** (123,000) are small Spanish enclave towns on the north coast of Morocco. Forty per cent of the population is Muslim, half speaking Cherja, a Berber language. There are six small evangelical churches, three of which have some former Muslims in their membership. This is a strategic bridgehead for the gospel in North Africa. Pray for those seeking to use it for such.

S

12. **The Canary Islands** form an archipelago of seven larger islands off Africa's northwest coast. Among the 1,560,000 inhabitants are but 2,000 believers in 59 small churches and fellowships – most being on the two larger islands. There is need for more evangelism on the smaller islands of Lanzarote, Fuerteventura, Gomera, La Palma and Hierro and for more teaching for the scattered groups of believers.

13. **Christian literature** has been a major factor in church growth, yet the Spanish are poor readers, making literature work expensive and bookstores hard to finance. Pray for the 21 bookstores; **CLC** has one centre and a distribution network serving evangelical bookstores throughout Spain. Christian books are both imported and published in Spain, but too few are written by and for Spaniards.

14. **Christian radio and TV**. Local radio stations carry evangelical programmes, and the national TV network broadcasts a 15-minute evangelical programme once every three weeks. There are also numerous opportunities for evangelical broadcasts on local radio. Pray that these means of proclaiming Christ may be effectively used.

<table>
<tr><td>

October 17–18

Asia

</td><td>

Sri Lanka
(Democratic Socialist Republic of Sri Lanka)

</td><td>

</td></tr>
</table>

Area 65,600 sq.km. Large island 80 km. southeast of India.

Population		Ann. Gr.	Density
1990	17,209,000	1.3 %	262/sq.km
1995	18,320,000	1.3 %	279/sq.km

There are 1,500,000 Sri Lankans in other lands.

Peoples:
Sinhalese 74%. An Aryan people; largely Buddhist. Many castes – unusual for Buddhist societies.
Tamil 18.2%. Declining through war and flight of over 700,000 refugees from the country. Over 90% Hindu.
  Lanka Tamil 2,160,000. Resident for over 1,000 years in Jaffna in north and on east coast.
  Indian Tamil 950,000. Descendants of imported labourers in 19th and 20th centuries; mainly in highland tea plantations.
Moor 7.1%. Arab-Tamil descent 950,000, Tamil descent 28,000.
Malay 0.25%.
Burgher 0.22%. European-Asian descent. Once privileged; many emigrating to Australia. Nearly all live in Colombo.
Veddah: Only 300 left of the original inhabitants. Most speak Sinhala.

Literacy 86%. **Official language:** Sinhala and Tamil, with English as the link language. **All languages** 6. **Languages with Scriptures** 3Bi.

Capitals: Colombo 1,886,000 (administrative). Sri Jayewardenepura Kotte 107,000 (legislative). Urbanization 21%.

Economy: Agricultural with tea and rubber the most important export commodities. Increasing industrialization since 1977 – especially textiles. The ten-year civil war has damaged trade and development, and destroyed the tourist industry. The spiralling cost of the war is crippling the economy. Unemployment 15%. Public debt/person $247. Income/person $470 (2.1% of USA).

Politics: Independence gained in 1948, as a parliamentary democracy, after 450 years of successive colonial administrations by the Portuguese, Dutch and British. Attempts to Sinhalize national life in 1956 and the attendant discrimination against ethnic and religious minorities provoked increasing communal violence and efforts by extremists to fight for an independent Tamil state in the north and east. A bitter civil war broke out in 1983, but all efforts to settle the conflict by local politicians and an aborted three-year Indian military intervention (1987–89) failed because of the intransigence of the extremists

on both sides. The assassination of the President by Tamil separatists in May 1993 has further escalated the intensity of the warfare.

Religion: Buddhism is the state religion and, as such, is protected and promoted. Although freedom for other religions is assured, there has been some discrimination against minority religions in taxation, employment and education, and since 1988, a rising anti-Christian feeling. Christianity is perceived as foreign and a colonial imposition (sadly a partial truth under Portuguese and Dutch rule).
Buddhist 70.3%. Almost entirely of the Sinhala community. Resurgent since 1956, actively seeking the conversion of Christians, and stimulating Buddhist missionary activity round the world.
Hindu 14.3%. Almost entirely Tamil.
Muslim 7.8%. Moors, Malays and some Tamil.
Christian 7.6%. Growth 2.9%.
  Protestant 0.92%. Growth 4.4%.

Church	Cong	Members	Affiliated
Ch of Ceylon (Anglican)	137	20,500	50,000
Methodist Ch	100	15,500	26,200
Assemblies of God	151	6,000	15,521
F'ship of Free Chs	100	8,000	11,000
Ceylon Pente Msn	53	4,200	7,000
Foursquare Gosp Ch	80	4,000	6,200
Ch of South India	32	3,850	5,500
Salvation Army	183	2,000	4,000
Baptist Union	20	2,027	3,000
All other (43)	263	14,550	30,497
Denominations (52)	1,119	80,627	158,918
Evangelicals 0.44% of pop		39,000	75,700
Pentecostal/charis 0.36%		31,500	60,000

Missionaries:
  to Sri Lanka 117 (1:147,000 people) in 38 agencies.
  from Sri Lanka 159 (1:476 Protestants) in 11 agencies 3frn 11xcul 148dom.
Roman Catholic 6.6%. Growth 2.7%.
| Catholic Ch | 489 | 636,000 | 1,135,800 |

Missionaries:
  to Sri Lanka 1,208 (1:14,200 people).
  from Sri Lanka 30 (1973 figure).
Marginal 0.03%. Growth 7.4%.
| All groups (2) | 37 | 1,598 | 4,930 |

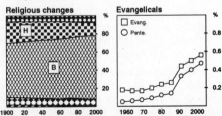

Religious changes

Evangelicals

S

1. **Claimed by some to be the site of the Garden of Eden, Sri Lanka is now an island of tears.** The ugly conflict between the Buddhist Sinhala and Hindu Tamil has brought great suffering with 25,000 killed, 700,000 Tamil refugees in India and the West, and 700,000 displaced in Sri Lanka. Pray for peace and communal harmony for this war-torn land.

2. **Buddhists long prided themselves on their non-violent religion** and their missionary activity in the Western world. The civil war has shattered that image, and there is widespread disillusionment in both Buddhism and Hinduism and a search for meaningful answers. Praise God for a significant increase in conversions to Christ. Yet both main religions are idolatrous, and most of their followers are bound by fear and appeasement of the spirit world. Intercede, claiming deliverance in Jesus' name.

3. **After centuries of decline, the Church is beginning to grow again.** A drop in the Christian percentage from 21% in 1722 to 7.4% in 1985 is tragically unique in non-Muslim Asia. **The causes of decline:** nominalism, Western worship patterns and use of European languages, and the renaissance of indigenous cultures and religions. **The result:** a ghetto-mentality, middle-class Church that did not evangelize and that suffered a steady loss of numbers by emigration and to Buddhism and Hinduism. Praise God for significant changes in more evangelical churches to rectify these failures and for a new urgency to win non-Christians. Pray that the Holy Spirit's stirring might become his outpourings on this needy church.

4. **There is need for change in the Church.** The more traditional denominations are some of the most nominal in Asia. Praise God for an evangelical minority among the Anglicans, Methodists, Baptists and Salvation Army which prays for revival and works for winning the lost, but radical transformations must be prayed into being:

a) **A return to biblical theology and holiness in the major seminaries and in the congregations.** Liberal theology has emphasized dialogue, compromise and social engineering rather than evangelism, confrontation of error and personal faith in Christ.

b) **Cultural adaptation** to make worship, hymnology, language and structures relevant and welcoming to non-Christians.

c) **A vision for evangelism and outreach** to non-Christians whatever the cost. Large areas of the country are without a gospel witness; nearly all Christians are concentrated in the Colombo and Jaffna urban regions; few live in the rural areas. Many trained workers emigrate, and few are willing to work in the less-privileged rural areas.

d) **Integrity in finance.** Too many individuals seek foreign support for their own ministries without any accountability to the Body of Christ in Sri Lanka – a fertile field for abuse, ministry distortion, and personal greed.

5. **There is a surge of spiritual life and vision** that is bringing a sense of expectancy among born-again Christians. There has been a significant increase in conversions to Christ among Buddhists and Hindus.

a) **The growth of Pentecostal, charismatic and some evangelical groups,** first in the cities and now in rural areas, is a new thing for the country. The **AoG** work is the most widespread and vigorous.

b) **The missions vision of YFC, Margaya Mission, Gospel Ministries and Lanka Village Ministries,** all Sri Lankan indigenous agencies, is bearing fruit. These agencies are seeking to plant churches in Buddhist and Hindu areas through literature outreach and church-planting teams. The 420 rural churches in 1983 had doubled by 1991.

c) **Christian media** outreaches are getting response – **EHC** literature evangelism with every home being visited for the third time, and **CCC**'s showing of the *Jesus* film and vision for reaching every village in the country.

d) **Evangelical theological education** has increased through the AoG Bible School, Lanka Bible College, the Salvation Army Officers Training School, the Association for Theological Education by Extension and others.

e) **Cooperation and unity of purpose among Evangelicals** is replacing mistrust and extensive sheep-stealing. The **Evangelical Alliance** and the *Navodaya* **Committee** are being used of God to promote fellowship among churches, concerted outreach and communications with the authorities. The *Navodaya* Conference in 1992 was a time of revival and commitment to the Lord and to missions outreach. *Navodaya* means "Dawning of a New Era" – pray that this may be so for the Church.

6. **Evangelical success has stirred a vigorous reaction.** This is seen in rising opposition from both Buddhists and Hindus in a propaganda press war, accusations of inducements to convert people, pleas for imposing restrictive legislation on church buildings, and a number of cases of open

S

persecution and burning of churches – at least eight in 1991/92. Pray that Christians may fearlessly, yet lovingly, commend and preach the gospel and thereby win their persecutors.

7. **Missionary work** has been restricted by the authorities. New visas have been extremely hard to obtain. Pray for a change – the needs are so numerous that the resources of the Sri Lankan Church are inadequate for evangelism, church planting and other ministries. **TWR** has 16 workers, but deployed in their international broadcasting ministry; other missions such as the Salvation Army, Methodists, **AoG**, **BMS**, **SBC** and **WEC** have just a handful of workers each. Pray in a new generation of missionaries able to culturally identify with Sri Lanka's present need.

8. **The Lanka Tamil community**, once relatively prosperous, but now impoverished, angry and fearful, needs prayer. Large numbers have had to flee the violence of both the Tamil Tiger guerrillas and the Sri Lankan army. Over 300,000 have fled to nearby India and over 100,000 to Europe and North America. Pray for Christian ministry to spiritual and social needs both in Sri Lanka and in the lands of refuge. The Christian community is the only structure in Sri Lanka that has not been polarized by the war. Pray that the church may be a bridge for wider reconciliation. Pentecostal churches in the Jaffna area are seeing many conversions among Hindus.

9. **The less-reached:**
a) **The villages** present a challenge. Throughout the land are rural communities that have never heard the gospel. Twelve million people live in the 25,483 villages of Sri Lanka, but only 900 villages have Protestant Christian groups. Many areas are devoid of any witness. The ravaged villages of the north and east are particular needy (**AsEF** and others).
b) **The urban slums** are little evangelized. Most Christians are among the more prosperous. A few churches and groups are taking up this challenge – pray for the expanding work of **Jesus Lives Ministry** with Sri Lanka's largest congregation (3,000) and various Pentecostal outreaches.
c) **Youth programmes are limited;** few agencies are making more than a localized impact. FOCUS (**IFES**) now has groups functioning in five universities, but the work has been severely hindered by the national unrest. A number of urban evangelical churches have large youth fellowships; **YFC** and **CCC** have had considerable influence on the youth of the main cities. The vast majority of children and young people in rural areas are out of reach of the gospel.
d) **Indian Tamils** on the tea estates are a deprived and despised community. Little interest has been shown in their evangelization until recently. By 1985 there were 2,500 believers, and since then a mass awakening has brought many more into the Church through **AoG**, Methodist and Smyrna Church outreaches.
e) **The Moors** are generally traders, bureaucrats and farmers. Until recently there were few converts out of Islam, but through one indigenous ministry over 100 Muslims have believed in Christ. The **AoG** has a good ministry among economically depressed Muslims in Colombo.
f) **The Malays** are syncretic Muslims, and potentially more open. Pray for a specific ministry to them.
g) **Other unreached social groups:** the educated Buddhists, coastal-belt fishing communities, the Tamil and Sinhala refugees, villages being set up under the Village Re-awakening programme, and the Tamil and Sinhala militants who continue to polarize the country.
h) **Tribal groups** such as the Rodhiyas (7,000) and Gypsies (1,000). **YFC** has some work among the former.
i) **Students**. The universities are hotbeds for Marxism. FOCUS (**IFES**) has a good discipling ministry, but there is little meaningful evangelism on the campuses.

10. **Christian help ministries:**
a) **Literature**. This is in great demand. Literacy is high, but good, inexpensive and culturally relevant literature is not being printed and distributed in sufficient quantities to make use of the opportunity. The main publishers – Pragma Publishers, Gospel Ministries, **YFC**, Lanka Bible College (evangelism and discipleship), **SGM** (Scripture portions) – have published much, but too few committed colporteurs are available. There is a dearth of good pre-evangelism literature for Buddhists and Muslims. New Life League have a printing press in Colombo which is much used for printing gospel literature.
b) **Radio**. Sri Lanka is thinly covered by international broadcasters – **FEBA**-Seychelles broadcasts 10.5 hours/week in Tamil and two hours in Sinhala. However, **TWR's** ministry from Sri Lanka to India and Bangladesh on medium- and short-wave is highly successful. There are large audiences for 19 languages and 66 hours/week of broadcasting. Over 300 Indian follow-up workers respond to listeners' questions and seek to channel them into existing churches.

St Helena and Ascension

Include with UK
Africa

Area 412 sq.km. St Helena (122 sq.km) 2,000 km. west of Angola in the south Atlantic. Two dependencies: Ascension Island (90 sq.km) 600 km. to the northwest, and Tristan da Cunha (100 sq.km) 1,200 km to the south. There are also several uninhabited islands.

Population		Ann. Gr.	Density
1990	7,000	3.1 %	17/sq.km
1995	8,000	2.7 %	19/sq.km

St Helena 78%; Ascension 17%; Tristan 5% of pop.

Peoples:
St Helenan 91%. Predominantly British but also Chinese, African, Malay.
Expatriate 9%. British and US administrative, scientific and military personnel – mainly on Ascension Island.

Literacy 97%. **Official language:** English.

Capital: Jamestown (St Helena) 3,253.

Economy: Heavily dependent on income from communications and military installations on Ascension. There is a growing fishing industry. Income/person $2,345 (10% of USA).

Politics: Dependent Crown Colony of the United Kingdom.

Religion:
Non-religious/other 2.8%. **Baha'i** 0.5%.
Christian 96.7%. Nom 17.2%. Affil 79.3%. Growth −0.6%.
Protestant 90.4%. Affil 73%. Growth −1%.

Church	Cong	Memb	Affiliated
Anglican Ch	16	3,900	4,820
Salvation Army	1	70	108
Baptist Ch	1	50	77
All other (1)	1	70	108
Denominations (4)	19	4,090	5,113
Evangelicals 3% of pop		170	238

Missionaries to St Helena 3 (1:2,300 people).
Roman Catholic 1.43%. Growth 2.1%.

Catholic Ch	4	65	100

Missionaries to St Helena 1 (1:7,000 people).
Other Catholic 0.86%. Growth 13.3%.
Marginal 3.96%. Growth 5.7%.

Jehovah's Witnesses	2	109	182
Other (1)	1	57	95
Groups (2)	3	166	277

1. **There has been a dramatic decline in church attendance** over the past 30 years. On the other hand, sects such as Jehovah's Witnesses and The Way International have been aggressively propagating their message and gaining a significant following. St Helenan society is hedonistic and indifferent to the claims of the gospel. Pray for the full evangelization of this generation of islanders.

2. A large proportion of the working population lives and works on the communications and military bases of **Ascension** and the **Falklands** because of the lack of employment opportunities. Pray both for the evangelization of these transient communities and for a restoration of strong Christian family units, the latter being adversely affected by the unstable patterns of their society.

3. **Evangelicals** are a mere 3% of the population. There have been periods of revival in the 1850s and 1910, but the islands are spiritually dead today. Pray for a fresh outpouring of the Holy Spirit.

S

See Caribbean
Caribbean

St Kitts and Nevis

(The Federation of St Kitts and Nevis)

Area 269 sq.km. Two volcanic islands in the Leeward Islands.

Population	Ann. Gr.	Density
1990 43,000	0 %	161/sq.km
1995 44,000	0.46 %	165/sq.km

Peoples:
Afro-Caribbean 95%.
East Indian 3%. **Euro-American** 1.5%.

Literacy 88%. **Language:** English.

Capital: Basseterre 20,000. Urbanization 50%.

Economy: Dependent on sugar and fishing and, since the collapse of the world sugar prices, also on foreign aid. Income/person $2,770 (13% of USA).

Politics: Associated state of UK in 1967. Anguilla protested and reverted to British colonial status in 1980. Independence in 1983.

Religion:
Non-religious/other 3.1%. **Baha'i** 0.4%.
Christian 96.5%. Nom 17.1%. Affil 79.4%. Growth 0.5%.
  Protestant 82.5% Affil 67.3%. Growth 0.4%.

Church	Cong	Members	Affiliated
Anglican Ch	13	6,270	12,540
Methodist Ch	30	5,900	11,800
Moravian Ch	4	980	3,270
Wesleyan Ch	22	780	1,420
Baptist Convention	5	900	1,290
Ch of God of Prophecy	13	700	1,270
Seventh-day Adventist	9	720	1,200
Ch of God (Cleveland)	9	674	1,120
All other (19)	41	2,378	4,778
Doubly counted *		−5,400	−9,000
Denominations (27)	146	13,902	29,688
Evangelicals 25.3% of pop		6,100	11,153
Pentecostal/charis 8.7%		2,000	3,800

Missionaries to St Kitts & Nevis 5 (1:8,600 people) in 3 agencies.
Roman Catholic 10%. Affil 7.9%. Growth 1.1%.
| Catholic Ch | 5 | 2,450 | 3,500 |
Missionaries to St Kitts & Nevis 10 (1:4,300 people).
Foreign Marginal 1%. Growth 4.8%.
| Jehovah's Witnesses | 3 | 216 | 480 |
Indigenous Marginal 3%. Growth 0.4%.
| All groups (6) | 8 | 800 | 1,330 |

* Emigration, inclusion of Anguillan statistics and dual membership.

1. There is much hardening to the gospel among the unconverted due to their ample exposure to a luxuriant variety of denominations, competing outreach ministries and Christian radio programmes. Few respond. Pray for revival and for unity among believers that will impact their unconverted compatriots.

S

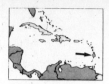

St Lucia

(The State of St Lucia)

See Caribbean
Caribbean

Area 619 sq.km. Windward Islands, between Martinique and St. Vincent.

Population	Ann. Gr.	Density
1990 153,000	4.3 %	248/sq.km
1995 164,000	1.4 %	266/sq.km

Peoples:
Afro-Caribbean 96.1%.
East Indian 2.6%. **Euro-American** 1.3%.

Literacy 90%. **Official language:** English, but French "Patwa" or Creole widely used.

Capital: Castries 54,000. Urbanization 52%.

Economy: Manufacturing and tourist industries rapidly growing but with decline in agricultural exports. Unemployment 25%. Income/person $1,540 (7.2% of USA).

Politics: Independent from Britain in 1979 as a relatively stable parliamentary democracy.

Religion: Freedom of religion.
Spiritist 2%. **Baha'i** 1.2%. **Hindu** 0.9%.
Muslim 0.5%. **Rastafarian** 0.3%.

Christian 95.1%. Growth 2.5%.
Protestant 18.2%. Growth 5.1%.

Church	Cong	Members	Affiliated
Seventh-day Adventist	35	5,200	7,831
Anglican Ch	2	2,070	4,130
Pentecostal Assemb	15	1,500	2,500
Apostolic Faith Ch	4	800	2,000
Baptist Churches (3)	13	625	1,250
Evang Ch of WI	11	543	1,085
All other (22)	75	4,910	9,002
Denominations (30)	155	15,648	27,798
Evangelicals 10.3% of pop		8,500	15,700
Pentecostal/charis 5.1%		4,200	7,740

Missionaries:
 to St Lucia 6 (1:25,600 people) in 3 agencies.
Roman Catholic 75.7%. Affil 73.6%.
Growth 1.9%.

Catholic Ch	22	63,600	120,000
Doubly Counted		−4,240	−8,000
Total	22	59,360	112,000

Missionaries to St Lucia 39 (1:3,900 people).
Marginal 1.2%. Affil 1.1%. Growth 4.5%.

Jehovah's Witnesses	6	460	800
All other (4)	5	382	915
Groups (5)	11	842	1,715

1. **The large nominal Christian population** needs liberation from the deadening blanket of religion without life in a society where 80% of all children are born out of wedlock. Pray for a spiritual awakening among them.

2. **The number of churches alive in the Spirit** have multiplied – but so have the divisions. Pray for unity among believers.

3. **The upper strata of society** are less influenced by vital Christianity; materialism is becoming a major block to spiritual life as the economy improves. **IFES** has pioneered a work in secondary schools with encouraging results and launching of five ISCF groups. Pray for Christians to be guided in how to meaningfully communicate the good news to them.

4. **The majority of St Lucians and Dominicans speak a French Creole.** A **WBT** couple is facilitating translation of the New Testament for them. Pray that the Word of God may thereby become more precious, understood, and applied in daily life.

S

<table>
<tr><td>Include with
French Guiana</td></tr>
<tr><td>North America</td></tr>
</table>

St Pierre & Miquelon

(Territorial Collectivity of St Pierre and Miquelon)

Area 242 sq.km. Eight rocky islands at the mouth of the Canadian St Lawrence River, and 25km south of Newfoundland.

Population	Ann. Gr.	Density
1990 6,300	0.4%	25/sq.km
1995 6,400	0.4%	25/sq.km

Peoples: French of predominantly Breton and Basque origin.

Literacy 99%. **Official language:** French. **Languages with Scriptures** 2Bi 1NT.

Capital: St Pierre 5,400. Urbanization 80%.

Economy: The partial collapse of the fishing industry has left these islands heavily dependent on French economic aid. Income/person $2,495 (12% of USA).

Politics: An overseas department of France; the last vestige of France's once vast North American possessions.

Religion: Freedom of religion.
Non-Christian 2% including Baha'i.
Christian 98%. All Roman Catholic but for a small group of Jehovah's Witnesses and a few Protestants.
  Catholic Missionaries to St Pierre 17 (1:370 people).

1. **This is the only territory in the Americas without a known evangelical congregation of believers.** Pray for the evangelization of these French fishing communities. **EHC** literature has been distributed. This is a possible field for French Canadian believers. Pray that the difficult economic present and future may cause many to seek a living relationship with Jesus.

S

St Vincent

(St Vincent and the Grenadines)

<table>
<tr><td>See Caribbean</td></tr>
<tr><td>Caribbean</td></tr>
</table>

Area 389 sq.km. Windward Islands; located between St. Lucia and Grenada. One larger island and the majority of the Grenadine islets to the south.

Population	Ann. Gr.	Density
1990 116,000	2.2 %	298/sq.km
1995 120,000	0.68 %	308/sq.km

Peoples:
Afro-Caribbean 84.5%. **East Indian** 5.5%.
Carib (with much African intermarriage) 2%.
Euro-American 3.5%, many Portuguese.
Other 4.5%.

Literacy 85%. **Official language:** English.

Capital: Kingstown 20,000. Urbanization 26%.

Economy: Agriculture and tourism are the mainstays of the economy. Underemployment and overpopulation becoming acute. Income/person $1,200 (5.6% of USA).

Politics: Independent from Britain as a parliamentary democracy in 1979.

Religion:
Hindu 2%. **Spiritist** 2%. **Muslim** 1%.

Baha'i 0.3%. **Other** 1%.
Christian 93.7%. Nom 25.5%. Affil 68.2%. Growth 1.4%.
Protestant 72%. Affil 54%. Growth 1.3%.

Church	Cong	Members	Affiliated
Anglican Ch	23	4,000	20,000
Methodist Ch	29	4,320	12,000
Seventh-day Adventist	15	3,000	4,250
Evang Ch of W Indies	9	1,200	3,000
Ch of God (Cleveland)	19	1,330	2,960
Christian Brethren (2)	10	950	1,580
Baptist Ch	10	900	1,500
All other (24)	91	10,710	17,363
Denominations (32)	206	26,410	62,653
Evangelicals 24.7% of pop		16,086	29,000
Pentecostal/charis 14.5%		10,500	17,000

Missionaries:
to St Vincent 18 (1:6,400 people) in 6 agencies.
from St Vincent 4 (1:15,723 Protestants) 4frn.
Roman Catholic 20.5%. Affil 12.9% Growth 1.3%.

Catholic Ch	15	9,000	15,000

Missionaries to St Vincent 27 (1:4,300 people).
Marginal 1.2%. Growth 10.4%.

Jehovah's Witnesses	4	200	400
All other (3)	6	520	1,040
Groups (4)	10	720	1,440

1. **There is little active cooperation between denominations**. Pray for the revitalization of the Association of Evangelical Churches.

2. **Vincentians have been described as a nation of backsliders**. Pray for restoration.

3. **A Bible teaching ministry is a rare gift in the churches**. Pray for the encouragement of such through the three Bible School extension programmes (**AoG**, Church of God, **WT**).

S

<table>
<tr><td>

October 19–20

Middle East

</td><td>

Sudan

(Republic of the Sudan)

</td></tr>
</table>

Area 2,504,000 sq.km. Africa's largest country. Desert in north, merging into grasslands in the centre and tropical bush in south; straddling the Nile Rivers.

Population		Ann. Gr.	Density
1990	25,195,000	2.9 %	10/sq.km
1995	29,116,000	2.9 %	12/sq.km

These figures are approximate.

Over 1.5 million deaths through war, genocide and famine since 1985. Over 5,000,000 southern Sudanese internally displaced as refugees and a further 200,000 in surrounding lands.

Peoples: Over 140 ethnic groups.
Sudanese Arab 36%. Many tribes and clans. Numerous non-Arab groups such as Nubians, and the peoples of Darfur and Kordofan have been Arabized, bringing Arabic-speakers to an estimated 49% of the population.
Non-Arab 64%.
  Nilotic 31.6%. 30 peoples. Largest: Dinka (5 groups) 2,900,000; Nuer 1,138,000; Bari 546,000; Toposa 301,000; Lotuko 295,000; Shilluk 244,000; Kakwa 135,000; Didinga 128,000; Lwo 126,000; Atuot 111,000; Anuak 90,000.
  Eastern Sudanic 10.2%. 22 peoples. Largest: Fur 744,000; Masalit 400,000; Nubian 258,000; Maba 191,000; Berta 131,000; Daju 116,000; Murle 111,000; Midob 100,000; Tama 96,000.
  Nuba 6.5%. 42 peoples; most small in number. Largest: Koalib 380,000; Moro 160,000; Kadugli 133,000; Krongo 122,000; Wyimang 92,000.
  Niger-Congo 2.8%. 12 peoples. Largest: Zande 521,000; Bviri 100,000.
  Central Sudanic 1.7%. 19 peoples. Largest: Moru 104,000; Madi 83,000.
  Other 11.3%. Beja 1,585,000; Fula 420,000; Hausa 418,000; Zaghawa 236,000; Kanuri 195,000.

Literacy 27%. **Official language:** Arabic. **All languages** 117. **Languages with Scriptures** 8Bi 17NT 12por.

Capital: Khartoum. Khartoum-Omdurman conurbation 1,676,000 but supplemented by an estimated 2,800,000, mainly southern, refugees. Urbanization 30%.

Economy: Enormous agricultural and mineral resources. A small group of Islamists seized control of the economy, forced through Islamic reforms, and sought to impose these on the non-Muslim south bringing the whole country to economic ruin. Only massive aid from Libya and Iran enables the government to survive. An estimated 60% of the population suffered malnutrition or starvation in 1992 due to famine induced by drought and war and made worse by the government's denial of its severity and refusal to allow adequate aid to reach its victims. Unemployment: very high. Public debt/person $328. Income/person $420 (2% of USA).

Politics: Joint Egyptian and British control 1899–1956. Since independence in 1956 there have only been seven years of civilian rule. Bitter fighting between Arab northerners and southern secessionists 1955-1972. After 12 years of uneasy peace, and a degree of autonomy for the south, fighting broke out again in 1983. The ascendency of extremist Muslim groups forced through the implementation of Islamic law on all citizens in 1991. Sudan has become a base for Iran to extend fundamentalist revolution to the south by military force and to Egypt and all North Africa by subversion. The southern armies of rebels are badly divided on the issue of secession or federalism and power struggles for leadership. They are more isolated since they lost their support base in Ethiopia in 1991.

Religion: Declared an Islamic Republic in 1983 despite the 1972 peace agreement and protestations of offended southerners who are largely Christian or traditionalists. The threatened application of Islamic law to Muslims and non-Muslims alike was a direct cause of renewed fighting. Crude and forceful attempts at Islamizing non-Muslims have been cloaked under the guise of subduing political rebels. Suppression of moderate Muslim groups is also severe. Nearly all figures below are estimates.
Muslim 70%. Sunni Islam, with several powerful Sufi religious orders, the largest being Ansar, the followers of the famous Mahdi. Almost the entire indigenous northern population is Muslim.
Traditional religions 9.9%. Predominantly among southern tribes, Nuba Mountain peoples and some Darfur peoples.
Non-religious/other 1.1%. Mainly urban intellectuals.
Christian 19%. Predominantly in south, in Nuba mountains and Khartoum's southerners. Affil 14.4%. Growth 10.9%.
  Protestant 7%. Affil 5%. Growth 9.1%.

Church	Cong	Members	Affiliated
Episcopal Ch of S	143	350,000	1,000,000
Sudan Ch of Christ	63	10,000	100,000

Presbyterian Ch in S	286	40,000	100,000
Africa Inland Ch	13	3,000	620,000
Sudan Interior Ch	35	1,554	8,000
All other (8)	60	12,105	28,728
Denominations (13)	600	416,659	1,256,728
Evangelicals 3.1% of pop		246,700	782,400
Pentecostal/charis 0.44%		39,000	110,000

Missionaries:
to Sudan 162 (1:155,500 people) in 24 agencies. Many have had to leave since 1990 or are based in Kenya.
from Sudan 16 (1:78,500 Protestants) in 4 agencies. 4frn 4xcul 12dom.
Roman Catholic 12%. Affil 8.7%. Growth 13.3%.

Catholic Ch	654	1,280,000	2,200,000

Missionaries:
to Sudan 371 (1:68,000 people).
from Sudan 55 (1973 figure).
Indigenous marginal 0.03%. Growth 10.9%.

All groups (est.8)		2,800	7,000

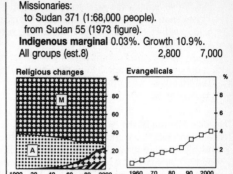

1. **Sudan's leaders proudly boast that they are the leaders of the Islamic Revolution in Africa.** In fact, an Arab minority have used this as a tool to strengthen their personal control of the economy and political power. The tragic cost is a million dead, an economy devastated and a country divided. Suffering and disruption of lives appear unending. Pray for the disarming of the spiritual powers that have held the land in centuries of bondage and that a fair and durable peace be established. There was once a strong Christian presence in northern Sudan, but this area gradually became Muslim between the eighth and fifteenth centuries – a process now being extended to the non-Muslim south.

2. **The sufferings of the southerners and also of moderate Muslims have been little noticed by the outside world** because of the exclusion of foreigners from the areas of worst violence. In addition, well-publicized crises in nearby Ethiopia and Somalia have dominated the media. Most international aid agencies have been expelled or severely hampered in their efforts to alleviate suffering and save thousands from death. Pray that world leaders may prevail upon the government to change its policy or that it may be removed and replaced by those who will seek the good of all Sudan's peoples.

3. **There has been persecution of the Church** over much of the past 40 years, but much more since 1985. Deliberate attempts to eliminate a viable Christian presence have been extreme, and have included bombing of Sunday church services, destruction of churches and Christian villages, massacres with even mass crucifixions in some areas, killing of pastors and leaders and a food-for-conversion policy for refugees banished to desert areas around Khartoum. Persecution has been especially severe in the Nuba mountains, and a *jihad* or holy war was declared by Muslims against the Nuba peoples. Whole areas have been laid waste and lands seized and given to Arabs. Pray that Christians may bear good witness to their persecutors in these sufferings and become spiritually strong as a result.

4. **The Church has grown in the midst of suffering.** Catholics, Anglicans and the Church of Christ in Sudan (fruit of **SUM-AP** ministry in the Nuba Mountains) have reported multiplied conversions in a receptive population. Massive movements of population have broken down barriers of customs and languages to bring people to Christ from hitherto unreached peoples. For many, becoming Christian is an expression of opposition to Islam and nominalism is still a problem, but for many others it is a genuine work of the Holy Spirit. The Anglican and Presbyterian Churches have experienced revival, and there have been significant people movements among the Nuer (Presbyterian), Mabaan, Uduk (Sudan Interior Church), Dinka (Episcopal), Toposa, Acholi (Africa Inland Church), and some of the Nuba tribes (Sudanese Church of Christ). Pray that Christians may demonstrate a love and concern for others that transcends ethnic and racial divisions – political differences and bloody fighting have deeply divided southerners along tribal lines.

5. **Pressing needs of the Christians.** Pray for:
a) **Physical needs.** Many Christians have taken refuge in Khartoum, Juba (the southern capital), surrounding lands or in the bush. Many are destitute and largely dependent on aid which rarely reaches them. Diseases are endemic and medical treatment is rarely available. The Sudan Council of Churches is struggling to help some but with slender resources through the **Sudan Emergency Operations Consortium**. Outside help needs to be fully restored. The New Sudan Council of Churches operates from Nairobi representing churches in southern Sudan.
b) **Leadership.** There are too many young converts for the pastoral care and teaching available. A number of Bible schools function under considerable difficulty and many disruptions. Pray for the

S

AIC Bible School, the Anglican Seminary, the SIC/**SIM** and SCOC/SUM-**AP** joint Theological College now based in Omdurman, and a Pentecostal Bible school in Juba. Pray for the provision of adequate facilities, staff and Sudanese leaders for the churches. Many Sudanese are studying in other lands.

c) **Unity in the midst of tribal and denominational diversity.** The political divisions within the southerners is also reflected in the Church. Pray that Christians may be delivered from hatred, unforgiveness and bitterness. Praise God for many who demonstrate great faith and joy in hazardous times.

6. **The Church in the Arab-speaking north is minute.** There are very few Christians among the Arabic-speaking northerners. There are a number of Coptic Orthodox churches in the towns, but probably no more than 200 ethnic Arab evangelical believers. There are hundreds of thousands of southern Christians in the Khartoum area, but establishing new congregations is hard in the face of uncertainty, harassment by the authorities and lack of resources, yet many new churches are springing up. Most use Arabic as their language of worship. Pray that Christians may make an impact for Jesus on the Muslim majority in the north. The Sudanese **OM** team has had an unusual literature ministry in the area and has been able to show the *Jesus* film fairly extensively.

7. **Missionary activity on the part of expatriates has steadily decreased**, and few expatriate Christian workers remain. In 1964 missionaries were expelled from the south, and limited ministry had been permitted in the Khartoum area (**SIM, CMS**), Nuba Mountains (SUM-**AP**) and among Ethiopian refugees. The **ACROSS** programme run by **SIM, AIM**, SUM-**AP**, **TEAR Fund** and others carried on a vital range of help ministries between 1972 and 1988 before the enforced closure of its ministry. Since then only a low-profile spiritual ministry and aid programme has been permitted in Khartoum and a few outlying areas. The rate of expulsions and refusals of visas has been stepped up since 1990. Pray for:

a) **The few Christian agencies still able to carry on in the north.**

b) **Input to the south** where the Khartoum regime is not in control; this is largely based in Kenya. ACROSS is able to carry on an extensive ministry with the churches and in aid programmes in these areas – and workers are needed for these ministries.

c) **The reopening of the land** so that outside help may be given to help the battered Church repair the immense emotional and physical damage to lives and property, and to train a new generation of leaders.

d) **The calling and preparation of indigenous and expatriate workers** to evangelize the many peoples of the north who have never had the opportunity to hear the gospel.

8. **The less-reached.**

a) **Sudanese Arabs,** few of whom have heard the gospel. In only 4–5 centres has there ever been consistent outreach; Christians are very few.

b) **Unreached non-Arabic peoples.** There may be 60–80 peoples less than 2% Christian. A survey of spiritual and Bible translation needs is a priority once peace comes. Pray that this may be accomplished.

c) **Darfur** in the west which never had a Christian presence until 1984, when Chadian famine refugees poured into the area. For a limited time ACROSS had workers in some of the camps. There is not a single known indigenous Christian among the Fur, Masalit, Zaghawa, Daju, Tama, Bideyat, Meidob, and Fulani, who make up 50% of the region's population.

d) **The eastern region on the Red Sea coast** has never been reached except for a brief **RSTI** effort (1978–84) to reach the hard and suspicious **Beja.** There may be no more than 2–3 Christians among them.

e) **The eastern border with Ethiopia.** The Berta, Burun and Gaan are largely traditional with some Muslim chiefs; the next few years are critical. Pray that they may turn to Christ rather than to Islam.

f) **The Nuba Mountain peoples,** an island of non-Muslims in a sea of Islam. Whole tribes have turned to Christ (Episcopal Church, Sudanese Church of Christ); a few others have become Muslim. There are a number of unreached groups. It appears that government policy is to eliminate the Nuba peoples by destruction of their villages, murder and their relocation as slave labour.

g) **The southern provinces.** There are still some peoples among whom the spiritual breakthrough has yet to come.

9. Bible translation is still a major unmet need. At least 21 and possibly 70 languages will need to be tackled. Various translators are working in 22 languages, but some work has had to be continued elsewhere due to the closure of the south to translators. **SIL** entered in 1976 and has many openings for developing literacy and translation programmes; 26 projects are contemplated, 13 others initiated. Pray for the **SIL** staff of 50 involved and for the work of the **UBS** in five translation projects. Pray also for the newly formed indigenous Sudan Bible Translation and Literacy Association.

10. Christian media.
a) **Literature.** This is in woefully short supply – lack of foreign exchange for importing literature and lack of a distribution network exacerbate the problem. Pray for Bible distribution for the Christians – many of whom have lost all they possess.
b) **Cassette ministry** – both for Scriptures and **GRn** recordings (in 112 languages). This could be a vital tool with the high levels of illiteracy, but the lack of play-back equipment and batteries limits its application.
c) **Radio. FEBA**-Seychelles broadcasts daily in Arabic 18 hours/week. Pray for the development of broadcasts in Beja.

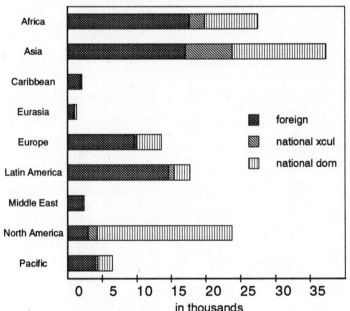

Composition of Protestant Missionary Force Serving in Each Region

in thousands

Legend: foreign, national xcul, national dom

Active missionaries serving in each region are divided into:

1. Expatriates serving as foreign missionaries (both cross-cultural and in a near culture).

2. Nationals working within their own country. Those working cross-culturally (xcul) and mono-culturally (dom) are a further subdivision.

Observe:

1. Over half of Asia's missionaries are indigenous.

2. Most missionaries serving in North America are servicing missions thrusts in other regions.

S

October 21
Latin America

Suriname
(Republic of Suriname)

Area 163,000 sq.km. Northeast coast of South America between Guyana and French Guiana.

Population	Ann. Gr.	Density
1990	403,000	1.5 %	2/sq.km
1995	435,000	1.5 %	3/sq.km

Peoples: Few nations can rival Suriname's ethnic diversity.
Asians 56%. Indian (mostly originating from Bihar) 156,000; Indonesian (predominantly Javanese) 62,000; Chinese (Hakka, Yueh, Putunghua) 12,000; Hmong (from Laos) 1,500.
Afro-Caribbean 41.5%. Creole (mixed race) 127,000; Black and Bush Negro 43,000.
Amerindian 1.5% in six ethnic groups.
Other 1%. Dutch, Guyanese, Portuguese.

Literacy 95%. **Official language:** Dutch. Trade language: Sranang Tongo (Taki-taki). **All languages** 17. **Languages with Scriptures** 3Bi 4NT 5por.

Capital: Paramaribo 246,000. Urbanization 65%.

Economy: Good potential, but ruinous policies of the military regime caused widespread decline through government controls, neglect of infrastructure, mismanagement and cutting off of Western aid. Main exports are bauxite, aluminium, rice and forest products. Unemployment 25%. Public debt/person $169. Income/person $3,020 (14% of USA).

Politics: Independent from Netherlands in 1975. A leftist military coup in 1980 with Cuban and Libyan help brought instability, repression and suffering to the country. A succession of coups, uprisings and abortive elections followed. An internationally supervised election in 1991 and gradual return to peaceful conditions may lead to improvement.

Religion: Freedom of religion – unaffected by recent political upheavals.
Muslim 24%. Most of Indonesians, 20% of Indians.
Hindu 23.6%. Majority of Indians.

Spiritist/animist 2.9%. Mainly Bush Negroes.
Non-religious/other 3%. **Baha'i** 1.2%.
Christian 45.3%. Affil 39.5%. Growth 0.5%.
Protestant 21.7%. Affil 17.6%. Growth 0.3%.

Church	Cong	Members	Affiliated
Moravian Ch	55	34,900	47,745
Dutch Reformed Ch	9	3,640	6,500
Evang Lutheran Ch	7	2,200	4,000
Seventh-day Adventist	11	2,097	3,000
Evang Ch of W Indies	14	1,100	2,440
Chr & Miss Alliance	2	240	343
Assemblies of God	6	122	340
All other (16)	46	3,112	6,499
Denominations (23)	150	47,411	70,867
Evangelicals 2.9% of pop		6,200	12,000
Pentecostal/charis 0.6%		1,100	2,400

Missionaries:
to Suriname 160 (1:2,600 people) in 22 agencies.
from Suriname 2 (1: 35,000 Protestants) 1frn 1xcul 1dom.
Roman Catholic 22.8%. Affil 21.09%.
Growth 0.4%.

Catholic Ch	354	44,200	85,000

Missionaries:
to Suriname 107 (1:3,800 people).
from Suriname 10 (1973 figure).
Foreign Marginal 0.64%. Growth 8.3%.

Jehovah's Witnesses	23	1,539	2,570

Indigenous Marginal 0.17%. Growth 3%.

All groups (3)	3	280	700

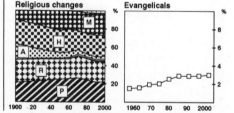

Religious changes   Evangelicals

1. **Suriname's post-independence experience has been disastrous.** Pray for peace, godly leaders, stable government, economic improvement, and, above all, for spiritual awakening. The young nation is compartmentalized by race and religion, and the potential for further conflict remains.

2. **Christian leaders** with a warm personal faith and biblical message are rare. Pray for the three small **Bible schools** (two Pentecostal and one Baptist), and also for the ministry of Christian leaders in **re-laying biblical foundations and standards** in a nation that has lost its way morally and ethically in the confusion of the past decade.

3. **Both the Moravian and the Catholic Churches have a large following** in many ethnic groups. Few from these denominations know of the new birth, and Christian belief is often mixed with

spiritism. However, there are several key evangelical leaders in the Moravian Church, revival prayer groups and a spiritual awakening among the youth. Pray for revival to sweep through the traditionalism of the majority of Christians. There are a number of small but growing evangelical and Pentecostal groups, but the number of born-again people is relatively low. The completion of the Sranang Tongo and Sarnami Hindi New Testaments could be a significant means of bringing renewal to the churches. **SIL** workers had completed 48% of the latter in 1992.

4. **Most of the six Amerindian peoples are now Christian. WT** has seen people movements among the Wayana, Akurio and Trio. The coastal Carib and Arawak are more needy. Pray for stability, maturity and indigenity to be maintained in the tribal churches; the pressures of the missionary and the coastal cultures are overwhelming, and recent rebellions have been extremely disruptive. Some have reverted to old customs. Pray for the service of two **MAF** planes that make the ministry of **WT** practicable.

5. **Missions** have suffered limitations in movement and facilities because of the political situation, but have been free to minister. The major ministry challenges are for more effective discipling of new leaders, Bible translation (five NTs are being translated – mainly through the 42 **SIL/WBT** workers in Suriname) and pioneer outreach to non-Christian peoples. Other larger agencies include: Independent Faith Mission (21 workers), **IMI** (11), **WT** (11), **SBC** (10). Major missionary-contributing nations are USA (115) and the Netherlands (21).

6. **Less-reached peoples.**
a) **Javanese** are Muslim, though often nominally so. The work of **IMF**, **IMI** and others has resulted in the fastest-growing churches in Suriname, but the majority are still unreached. The NT is being translated into the local derivation of Javanese.
b) **The Indian community** has shown little response to the gospel. The ministry of **IMI** and **WT** has led to the planting of two small congregations largely made up of former Hindus. The Muslim community is unreached. The *Jesus* film is available in the Sarnami language. Pray for barriers of occultism, prejudice and misunderstanding to be broken down.
c) **Chinese** are responding to the ministry of two Chinese **CMA** missionary couples, and there are two growing congregations.
d) **Bush Negroes** are descendants of escaped slaves who formed their own distinctive communities, but many of these communities have been decimated and scattered in reprisals for local uprisings against the military regime. Six groups and languages have developed. Bible translation work is in progress in Aukaans and completed in Saramaccan. Witchcraft and fear of spirits is widespread, but there are some strong Christians among them (**WT** and **Baptists**). Many communities are only superficially evangelized. Pray for decisive breakthroughs in these peoples bound by the occult.
e) **Guyanese refugees** number 20,000. There are five small churches among them (**WT**).
f) **The Laotian Hmong** live in several villages. **CMA** missionaries have planted one congregation among them, but the lack of Hmong pastors cripples the work.

7. **Bible distribution** has increased greatly since independence. The **Bible Society** has a unique ministry in both disseminating the Scriptures and producing a popular daily 20-minute TV programme. Pray that the people may be blessed and enriched through the entrance of God's Word. Christian literature is available only in limited quantities because of economic impoverishment.

8. **Bible translation** continues through the ministry of the Bible Society and **SIL**. Seven translation projects are being tackled. The Sranang Tongo language is spoken by 80% and Sarnami Hindi by 38%.

Svalbard

Included with NORWAY

October 22	*Swaziland*
Africa	(Kingdom of Swaziland)

Area 17,400 sq.km. Small, fertile, well-watered, landlocked enclave between Mozambique and South Africa.

Population	Ann. Gr.	Density
1990	789,000	3.5 %	45/sq.km
1995	938,000	3.5 %	54/sq.km

Peoples:
Nguni 90.2%. Swazi (Swati) 650,000; Zulu 76,000.
Other African 5.8%. Tsonga 19,000.
Other 4%. European 17,000; Eurafrican 8,000; Indian 6,000.

Literacy 67%. **Official languages:** siSwati, English. **All languages** 4. **Languages with Scriptures** 3Bi 1NT.

Capital: Mbabane 40,000. Largest city Manzini 52,000. Urbanization 26%.

Economy: Mostly pastoral and agricultural, but also some mineral production. Main exports: sugar, citrus, timber, paper pulp. Some manufacturing. Not highly populated in some areas. Part of Southern African Customs Union and Rand Monetary Area. Unemployment 27%. Public debt/person $337. Income/person $900 (4.2% of USA).

Politics: A British protectorate 1899–1968. A monarchy with democratic government suspended pending agreement on a new, but much-disputed constitution. The major issue is between the traditionalists and the modernists over the extent of the King's powers.

Religion: Freedom of religion, but criticism of non-Christian traditions is not welcomed. Figures for religions are estimates.
Traditional religions 17.6%, but in practice it is much higher.
Muslim 0.8%. East Africans, Comorians, Indians.
Baha'i 0.4%.

Non-religious/other 1%. Europeans.
Christian 80.2%. Nom 9.7%. Affil 70.3%. Growth 5.4%.
Protestant 21.5%. Affil 16.6%. Growth 2%.

Church	Cong	Members	Affiliated
Ch of the Nazarene	101	7,041	18,752
Methodist Ch	231	4,269	18,000
Full Gospel Ch	43	6,317	15,800
Assemblies of God	140	7,000	14,000
Anglican Ch	96	6,000	12,000
Evang Ch (TEAM)	111	5,000	11,100
Africa Evang Ch	41	2,000	7,000
All other (32)	338	17,247	34,830
Denominations (39)	1,101	55,234	131,482
Evangelicals 11.9% of pop		40,000	94,000
Pentecostal/charis 5.5%		18,400	43,000

Missionaries:
to Swaziland 220 (1:3,600 people) in 34 agencies.
from Swaziland 31 (1:4,200 Protestants) in 3 agencies 26frn 27xcul 4dom.
Roman Catholic 6%. Affil 5.1%. Growth 1.5%.

Catholic Ch	20	22,000	40,000

Missionaries to Swaziland 222 (1:3,600 people).
Foreign Marginal 0.5%. Affil 0.46%. Growth 10.3%.

Jehovah's Witnesses	51	1,235	3,530
All groups (2)	52	1,295	3,630

Indigenous Marginal 52%. Affil 48.2%. Growth 7.2%.

All groups (70)		152,000	380,000

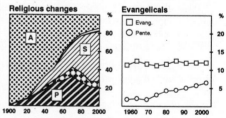

Religious changes   Evangelicals

1. **Few countries have been more saturated with the gospel,** but biblical Christianity has been compromised with entrenched traditional religions. Although 80% of the population is Christian, the church is in need of revival. The demonic powers that have long held the land have yet to fully yield to the Lord Jesus Christ.

2. **Nearly all the Protestant denominations are evangelical in theology,** but stagnation and even decline for decades has been the norm. A large missionary input and much activity has not produced a committed, well-taught Church. Congregations are predominantly composed of women – the men are often in the syncretic independent churches. Pray for a new spirit of prayer, vision for evangelism, and courage to deal with the root causes of the spiritual weaknesses.

3. **The African independent church movement** has grown to gain a following of over half the population – especially among men. The degree of compromise with polygamy, witchcraft, ancestor veneration and appeasement sacrifices varies widely. The "Ethiopian" Churches broke away early from the mission-planted churches and tend to be oriented to the Old Testament. The large "Zionist" movement has a strong emphasis on both pentecostal gifts and traditional customs. Pray that these many congregations may be exposed to the truths of God's Word and come to a biblical theology and faith. The Mennonites have a teaching ministry to this end – with some successes and also frustrations.

4. **Renewed vision for evangelism** has led to church growth through the ministry of the Church of the Nazarene and also the South African-related Assemblies of God, Full Gospel Church of God and, more recently, the Deeper Life Bible Church from Nigeria. Major crusades conducted by Christ For All Nations and **AE** have brought evangelical churches together. The AEAM/WEF-linked **Swaziland Conference of Churches** has sponsored nationwide outreaches and coordinated radio and television broadcasting on the national networks. Pray for unity, growth, and holiness to characterize the Church in Swaziland. Pray also for effective ministry to the men, Mozambican refugees, and the Muslim community.

5. **Quality Christian leadership is in short supply.** The multiplicity of small congregations means that most pastors are poorly trained and paid and therefore part-time in the ministry. Few congregations are confident to confront either traditionalists or intellectuals, and so have little impact on the unchurched. Pray for changes in attitudes, patterns of giving, and the level of commitment among leaders and led alike. There are seven Bible schools or seminaries in Swaziland.

6. **Most Protestant missions and missionaries are evangelical**, the largest agencies being **CoN** (45 workers), **TWR** (39), Swedish Holiness Union (15), **Mennonites** (10), Swedish Alliance Mission (10) and **AEF** (6). Major missionary-contributing nations: USA (110), Norway (25), Sweden (21), South Africa (18). The majority are heavily committed to institutional programmes and to radio ministry, and only a minority are in direct church development. Pray for a happy and close relationship between expatriates and national believers – there has been a history of breakdowns and divisions.

7. **Young people** are torn between the old ways and the new. Pray for a decisive impact on young people through the ministry of **SU** in secondary schools and INCOSCM (**IFES**-related) in the university, and pray that this impact will lead to spiritual changes in the nation.

8. **Christian literature** in siSwati is a vital need – after years of linguistic domination by the related isiZulu. The siSwati New Testament was published only in 1981. Pray for the production, distribution and impact of the siSwati Bible when it is published in 1994.

9. **Christian radio** and television:
a) **In Swaziland** the national network is free for Christians, and well used.
b) **To other lands**, through **TWR's** powerful radio station, go programmes in 23 languages and with a potential audience of 350 million people in south and central Africa and also Pakistan. Pray especially for the provision for programmes in languages of areas of great poverty and devastation by war and drought.

S

October 23		*Sweden*
Europe		(Kingdom of Sweden)

Area 450,000 sq.km. The largest of the Scandinavian countries, a land of mountains and forests. Only 10% of the land is cultivated.

Population		Ann. Gr.	Density
1990	8,339,000	−0.03 %	19/sq.km
1995	8,326,000	−0.03 %	19/sq.km

Peoples:
Indigenous 91%. Swedish 7,741,000; Saami (Lapp) 17,000; Gypsy 3,000.
Other Scandinavian/Baltic 3%. Finnish 123,000; Estonian 60,000; Danish 35,000; Norwegian 28,000; Latvian 6,000.
Other Foreign 6%. Mainly migrant workers and refugees: Serb/Croat/Bosnian 120,000 (many new arrivals); Greek 50,000; Latin American 35,000; Iranian 35,000; Turk 20,000; Assyrian 15,000; Kurdish 10,000; Iraqi 6,000; Albanian 4,000. Also Eritrean, Somalis, North African, Chinese.

Literacy 99%. **Official language:** Swedish. **All languages** 15. **Languages with Scriptures** 6Bi 1NT 3por.

Capital: Stockholm 2,290,000. Urbanization 83%.

Economy: Highly developed and industrialized. The cost of the extensive social welfare system, worldwide recession and impending membership of the EC have forced painful adjustments on the country. Unemployment 5.4% (1992). Public debt/person $11,100. Income/person $21,710 (99.5% of USA).

Politics: Parliamentary government with a constitutional monarchy. The 175 years of strict neutrality and 50 years of almost uninterrupted social democracy and welfare statism has moulded Swedish society. The retreat from socialism since 1990 is beginning to break that mould. EC membership is expected in about 1995.

Religion: The Lutheran Church is the State Church, but a gradual separation is taking place. All Swedish citizens are automatically members by birth unless they or their parents request otherwise. There is freedom of religion for other denominations and religions.
Non-religious/other est 34.9%; though 94% of the population was, by default, born "Christian".
Muslim 0.8%. **Almost entirely immigrant. Bosnians, Albanians, Middle Easterners and North Africans.**
Jews 0.19%.

Christian 64.1%. Affil 59.3%. Att 5%.
Growth −2.7%. A high proportion have no continuing link with Christianity, hence the large *Doubly counted* figure below.
Protestant 60.4%. Affil 55.7%. Growth −3.1%.

Church	Cong	Members	Affiliated
Ch of Swed (Luthrn)	2,565	2,975,276	7,301,665
Pentecostal Movmt	2,115	97,282	155,778
Swed Miss Cov Ch	1,056	77,058	154,400
Finnish Lutheran Ch	20	20,000	50,000
Estonian Luth Ch	64	15,250	50,000
Swed Evang Missn	288	23,006	46,301
Örebro Mission Ch	362	20,272	33,233
Baptist Union	359	20,796	31,554
Salvation Army	470	9,984	29,511
Swed Alliance Missn	279	11,712	23,739
Swed Holiness Un	418	5,021	8,986
All other (49)	336	28,277	55,209
Doubly Counted		−2,275,276	−7,301,665
Denominations (60)	8,332	1,013,934	4,640,376
Evangelicals 6.8% of pop		237,500	565,000
Pentecostal/charis 3.7%		170,000	210,000

Missionaries:
to Sweden 99 (1:94,800 people) in 20 agencies.
from Sweden 1,749 (1:2,700 Protestants) in 31 agencies.
Roman Catholic 1.7%. Growth 2.6%.

Catholic Ch	39	109,000	140,120

Missionaries:
to Sweden 347 (1:25,000 people).
from Sweden 20 (1973 figure).
Orthodox 1.3%. Growth 4.9%.

Serbian Ortho Ch	4	14,400	28,833
Syrian Orthodox Ch	17	17,100	26,272
Greek Orthodox Ch	6	11,600	17,500
Finnish Orthodox Ch	10	3,000	5,980
All other (10)	22	12,578	24,686
Denominations (14)	59	58,678	103,271

Marginal 0.64%. Growth 2.7%.

Jehovah's Witnesses	338	22,742	39,200
Mormons	40	4,540	7,700
All groups (8)	378	30,532	53,400

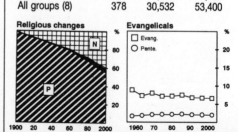

Religious changes

Evangelicals
□ Evang.
○ Pente.

S

1. **In the last century Sweden was noted for its revivals,** but in this century for its permissive society and materialism with all the dire consequences for the social fabric. After Denmark, Sweden is the most secularized country in Europe and in great need of re-evangelization. Pray for the government and leaders of the nation, as years of permissive legislation and erosion of respect for the things of God need to be reversed. Pray for revival that will sweep through the nation.

2. **The spiritual need of the country** is shown by the decline of professing Christians from 99% of the population in 1900 to 64% today. Only 5% of the population regularly goes to church. Over half the population has no real knowledge of the Christian faith, which is perceived as a pleasantly impersonal cultural heritage with little practical relevance. Pray especially for the institutions and leaders of the State Church, and for a fresh moving of the Spirit within it. There is a growing evangelical minority among the pastors of the State Church.

3. **The Free Churches** are larger than in any other Scandinavian country. Although the fruit of revivals in the last century, most are in decline, whether evangelical or Pentecostal in theology, and have lost 25% of their membership in 15 years. Pray that these churches may become relevant and effective in their witness in today's Sweden. The fading of the welfare state dream is causing many to be open to spiritual things, but the message embraced is that of the New Age rather than the gospel.

4. **Spiritual renewal is evident in some areas.** Newer charismatic churches are growing. Informal home gatherings are being used of God in winning the unchurched. Greater cooperation between churches is leading to increased outreach. The Pentecostal movement airs programmes on 100 radio stations, produces a newspaper, and runs drug rehabilitation programmes that are proving fruitful. SESG (**IFES**), one of many Christian agencies among youth, reports great openness for Evangelicals to share their faith in schools. Praise God for good signs, but pray for the spirit of indifference and spiritual lethargy to be lifted.

5. **Theological training** is a key prayer target. There are two main theological faculties at the universities, where many pastors are trained; this education is affected by the humanistic influence of the universities in general. However, the Johannelund Seminary is conservative evangelical with 130 students; many graduates become Lutheran pastors. The Free Churches run eight theological schools with one- to four-year courses, including Örebro (170 students), Swedish Mission Covenant Church (Lidingö, 120), Baptist Union (Bromma, 80), Pentecostal Movement (Bromma, 65), and Alliance (Kortebo, 50). There are also many short-term Bible courses offered by most denominations. Besides these, there are independent Bible schools that run one- to three-year courses. Over 150 young people are trained annually in short-term courses held by **YWAM**. **OM** also has done much to motivate young people for evangelism and missionary service.

6. **Missionary outreach from Sweden** has been outstanding. The contribution of the Lutheran Church and all the Free Churches in nearly 100 countries has been used of God. Pentecostal missionaries make up nearly half of all present missionaries from Sweden, with one missionary for every 130 adult members. Pray for a quickening of this vision among young people for short-term and, even more, for long-term work. Pray for the notable work of the **Institute of Bible Translation** in Stockholm with the vision to provide a translation of the NT in every non-Slavic language of the former USSR.

7. **More needy areas and peoples.**
a) **There are rural and urban areas** with few evangelical churches; the latter are unevenly distributed due to localized revivals in the past.
b) **Political and religious refugees** from the Middle East, Latin America and the former Communist Bloc have been given a home in Sweden. They are frequently the section of the community most open to the gospel. Many of these minorities are unevangelized. There are few workers among them.
c) **Croatian, Bosnian and Albanian refugees** flooded into Sweden during 1992 with possibly 300,000 seeking refuge since hostilities began in former Yugoslavia. Pray that these destitute, distressed people will find consolation through faith in Jesus.
d) **Muslims** have grown from a handful in the '50s to 68,000 in 1992. Pray for workers to be called to reach each significant ethnic group and to be provided with the tools to assist them: literature, the *Jesus* film and Scriptures.
e) **The 5,000 Chinese** have two churches and several home groups of believers. COCM has an outreach among them.

October 24		
Europe		

Switzerland
(Swiss Confederation)

Area 41,300 sq.km. Mountainous land; 26% unproductive, yet the Swiss Alps are one of the greatest tourist attractions in the world.

Population	Ann. Gr.	Density
1990 6,521,000	0.16 %	158/sq.km
1995 6,552,000	0.09 %	159/sq.km

Peoples:
Indigenous 82.6%. Swiss German 4,125,000; French 1,128,000; Italian 253,000; Rheto-Roman 50,000; Gypsy 21,000.
Foreign 17.4%. Italian 381,500; ex-Yugoslavian 142,000; Spanish 117,000; Portuguese 86,000; German 84,000; Turk 53,000; French 52,000; Asian 39,000; Austrian 29,000; Kurdish 13,000; Tibetan 1,500.

Literacy 99%. **Official languages:** German, French, Italian, Rheto-Roman. **Languages with Scriptures** 4Bi 1NT 1por.

Capital: Bern 146,000. Other major cities: Zürich 368,000; Basel 181,000; Geneva 158,000. Urbanization 58%.

Economy: A strong and wealthy industrial state. Both tourism and banking are important foreign exchange earners. Loss of business confidence in recession of early '90s was a factor in the Swiss rejection of closer ties with the EC. Unemployment 3.6% (1992). Public debt/person $3,100. Income/person $35,160 (160% of USA).

Politics: Independent in 1291. Federal democratic government with the constituent 20 cantons and 6 half-cantons retaining a high degree of autonomy and power. Policy of non-involvement in world politics likely to be retained because of the fears of uncontrolled immigration.

Religion: The federal constitution guarantees religious freedom, but relationships between cantonal governments and the churches are decided locally. The post-Reformation confrontations between Catholics and Protestants helped determine the majority religion of each canton.
Non-religious/other 7.7%. In practice, probably 20% or more of the population is secular.
Muslim 1%. Mainly Turks. Also Bosnians, Albanians, Arabs and Kurds.
Jews 0.3%.
Christian 92% (actually nearer 40%). Attend 6%.

Growth 0%.
Protestant 42%. Growth −0.4%.

Church	Cong	Members	Affiliated
Fed of Protestant Chs			
of Switz (13)	2,101	2,150,000	2,828,678
F'ship of Pentecostal			
Free Chs (20)	400	15,000	29,000
Methodist Ch	253	10,300	21,400
St Chrischona Pilg Miss	216	5,300	17,200
Lutheran Chs (2)	16	9,380	13,401
Salvation Army	91	6,100	9,390
F'ship of Free Ev Congs	101	5,800	9,000
Evang F'ship of Bern	220	4,200	6,000
Mennonite Ch	15	3,000	4,290
F'ship of Baptist Chs	15	1,382	2,300
All other (102)	678	42,636	77,485
Doubly counted		−240,000	−346,000
Denominations (144)	3,908	2,013,098	2,672,144
Evangelicals 5.4% of pop		237,000	349,000
Pentecostal/charis 1.4%		60,000	91,000

Missionaries:
  to Switzerland 219 (1:29,800 people) in 40 agencies.
  from Switzerland 1,341 (1:2,000 Protestants) in 57 agencies 1,073frn 1,056xcul 285dom.
Roman Catholic 47.22%. Growth 0.1%.

Catholic Ch	1,703	2,340,000	3,079,000

Missionaries:
  to Switzerland 845 (1:7,700 people).
  from Switzerland 1,804 (1973).
Other Catholic 0.33%. Growth −0.1%.

Denominations (33)	54	14,950	21,400

Orthodox 1.07%. Growth 5.9%.

Denominations (10)	49	49,000	70,000

Foreign Marginal 1.43%. Growth 1.2%.

Jehovah's Witnesses	297	16,552	29,600
Mormons	32	4,340	6,200
All other (29)	208	22,846	57,130
All groups (31)	537	43,738	92,930

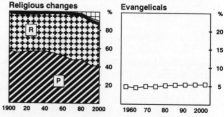

Religious changes

Evangelicals

1. **The great reformers, Calvin and Zwingli,** expounded the great truths of Scripture in this land, but few today have any interest or understanding of what real Christianity is. Wealth, comfort,

indifference and a vague religiosity have become the norm. The socio-political upheavals of the '90s have stirred an uncertainty, fear and identity crisis in the hearts of many, but it is the occult and eastern religions that the younger generation are exploring. Many baptized as children no longer retain any link with a church, and enrolled membership has halved in 30 years. Pray that the Swiss may find the true way in Jesus Christ, and that the nation might be stirred again by the Holy Spirit.

2. **The falling away of the Swiss from the churches is gaining momentum.** Lack of clergy in the Catholic Church and widespread espousal of liberal and neo-orthodox theology in many of the Cantonal Reformed Churches have sapped the spirituality of many congregations. This is partially offset by the growth of Pentecostal, charismatic and evangelical free churches. Pray:
a) **That prayerful men and women of God** in both the leadership and the congregations may be used to bring revival to the whole Swiss nation.
b) **That Spirit-filled pastors** within French, German and the few Italian Cantonal churches may be used to bring spiritual renewal to the many formal and shrinking congregations. Only 8% of Reformed Church members go to church.
c) **That theological students** may become enthused by the Word of God, aim for a spiritual ministry, and not be ensnared by dead theologies and human psychologies so often taught in the theological faculties of the universities.

3. **In the Catholic cantons**, predominantly in the south and centre of the country, the small evangelical witness is growing, and the centuries-old prejudices and religious polarization are breaking down. Among both priests and laity there is a search after biblical truth. Pray that many may find it in a personal relationship with Jesus and come to assurance of salvation, and that a living fellowship of believers may come into being in every community.

4. **Praise God for signs of hope.** There is growth and expectation for a new day for the churches. Pray for:
a) **Congregational outreach** through home Bible studies and personal evangelism, the most fruitful method today. Pray that true believers in both the Cantonal and Free Churches may be more effectively motivated and activated for outreach.
b) **Saturation church planting.** Since 1989 an interdenominational working group has the goal of launching a DAWN-type saturation church-planting programme. The vision is to multiply new congregations and increase church attendances, and was warmly endorsed by many younger leaders in 1991. Interest in church planting is increasing in all the major denominations.
c) **The Fellowship of Pentecostal Free Churches** which aims to double the Francophone churches from 60 to 120 in the decade. The Federation of Free Evangelical Churches also aims to double congregations and church attendances over this period. Pray for a combined strategic effort in this area.
d) **Outreach through agencies** such as **New Life, Christ For All** (EHC), *Christliche Kontaktgruppe,* **OM,** Open Air Campaigners and **YWAM.**
e) **Ministry to young people** (**SU** in schools and with a good camp ministry), students (with small **IFES** groups in French- and German-speaking universities), drug addicts and alcoholics, children (**CEF**) and others.

5. **Bible training** is provided by a number of institutions. From them graduates have gone out for Christian service all over Europe and the world. Remember the:
a) **German-speaking seminaries:** FETA (*Freie Evangelisch-Theologische Akademie,* Basel), St. Chrischona, and Bible schools in Aarau, Beatenberg, and Walzenhausen; and shorter-term Bible schools in Bienenberg and Gunten/Emmetten.
b) **French-speaking Bible schools:** Emmaus, *Le Roc, Institut Biblique et Théologie d'Oruan* (Pentecostal) and **YWAM.** Pray that these may retain their spiritual cutting edge, and become a means of blessing and revival in Switzerland. Pray also for many to be called into full-time work.

6. The *Arbeitsgemeinschaft Evangelikaler Missionen* (AEM) was formed in 1972 to strengthen and coordinate missionary vision and outreach – especially in the Free Churches; 33 agencies are members. The *Fédération des Missions Evangéliques Francophones* (FMEF) has the same vision for the French-speaking Protestant churches in Switzerland and France. The *Communauté de Travail des Eglises Chrétiennes de Suisse* links together eight denominational missions. Pray for a greater awareness and sense of responsibility in Swiss churches for world evangelization, and support of the commendably large missionary force.

S

7. **Peoples and areas where the evangelical witness is small:**
a) **Cantons.** The German-speaking cantons of Luzern, Zug, Schwyz and Uri, the largely Francophone Valais and Fribourg, and the Italian-speaking Ticino are culturally Catholic.
b) **The foreign communities.** Switzerland has the highest proportion of foreign residents and guest workers of any major state in Europe. The major cities are rapidly becoming internationalized. This has generated fear and resentment. Pray that Christians may actively and effectively reach out to the 25 or more distinct ethnic minorities. The major groupings are the Catholic Italians, Spanish, Portuguese and Croats, the Orthodox Greeks, Romanians and Serbs, the Hindu Tamils, and the Muslim Turks, Kurds, Arabs, Albanians and Bosnians. There are a number of agencies and churches committed to this ministry; most are linked together in the ***Arbeitsgemeinschaft für Ausländermission*** of the Swiss Evangelical Alliance.

8. **Local radio and TV stations** are well used by several Swiss Christian agencies, and have great potential for reaching the population, but pray for more openness on national radio and television.

S

Syria

(Syrian Arab Republic)

October 25

Middle East

Area 185,000 sq.km. Fertile plain on Mediterranean coast; 60% desert in centre and east but crossed by Euphrates River.

Population		Ann. Gr.	Density
1990	12,501,000	3.6 %	68/sq.km
1995	14,904,000	3.6 %	80/sq.km

About 80% live on or near the Mediterranean coast.

Peoples:
Arab 85%. Bedouin 927,000; Palestinian 489,000. **Other** 15%. Kurds 960,000; Turks/Turkmen 500,000; Armenian 320,000; Assyrian 54,000; Cherkess (Circassian) 50,000; Domari Gypsy 28,000.

Literacy 65%. **Official language:** Arabic. **All languages** 11. **Bible translations** 2Bi 1NT 4por.

Capital: Damascus 1,850,000. **Other major city:** Aleppo 1,216,000. **Urbanization** 50%. Damascus and Aleppo are reputedly the oldest continually inhabited cities in the world.

Economy: Oil and agriculture are important. Heavy military spending in decades of confrontation with Israel have hampered development. The dramatic fall in trade and aid from the former USSR has led to severe economic problems only alleviated by benefits accruing from Syria's cooperation in the Gulf War against Iraq. Public debt/person $995. Income/person $1,020 (4.8% of USA).

Politics: Independent from France in 1946. Continuous internal upheavals until the coup in 1970. Relative internal stability under an Alawite minority, military-civilian socialist government. Since 1973, Syria has sought to gain political dominance in war-torn Lebanon and now exerts a strong influence over its small neighbour. The southwest Golan Heights have been occupied by Israel since 1967 and formally annexed in 1981. Peace talks with Israel have been initiated.

Religion: Prior to 1973 Islam was the religion of the state. Since then it has been a secular state with Islam recognized as the religion of the majority, and all other minorities accorded definite rights and privileges.

Muslim 90.5%. Sunni 75.1%, Alawite 11.7%, Druze 2.7%, Ismaili 1%, Yezidi 0.2%. The Druze and Yezidi are not considered Muslim by many.
Non-religious/other 1.5%.
Jews 4,000. Many want to emigrate.
Christian 8%. Affiliated 6.45%. Growth 2%.
Protestant 0.23%. Growth 1.9%.

Church	Cong	Members	Affiliated
Un of Ev Armenian Chs	29	7,150	13,000
Nat Evang Synod of Leb & Syria	38	4,800	7,600
Nat Ev Alliance Ch	19	807	3,230
All other (15)	41	2,630	5,204
Denominations (18)	127	15,387	29,034
Evangelicals 0.1% of pop		5,977	12,624
Pentecostal/charis 0.02%		1,000	2,300

Christian expatriates:
to Syria 12 (1:1,000,000 people).
from Syria 5 (1:6,000 Protestants).
Roman Catholic 2.9%. Affil 2.32%. Growth 3%.

Catholic Ch	203	162,000	290,000

Missionaries to Syria 81 (1973).
Orthodox 4.9%. Affil 3.9%. Growth 1.4%.

Greek Orth	149	134,000	240,000
Armenian Apostolic	24	66,000	120,000
Syrian Orth (Jacobite)	24	47,600	85,000
Assyrian Ch (Nestorian)	22	22,000	40,000
All other (2)	3	812	1,450
Denominations (6)	222	270,412	486,450

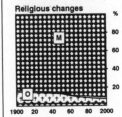

Religious changes

1. **The Alawite minority regime** has retained power by disallowing all political dissent. The country has been involved in wars and confrontations with surrounding states for the last 50 years. Pray for both political and religious freedom.

2. **Christian minorities** are tolerated and have freedom to worship and witness within their own community, but all activities that could threaten the government or communal harmony are watched. Christians find it hard to witness freely in these conditions, even when given the opportunity.

3. **The Muslim majority has a false conception of what a true Christian is.** Pray that they may be enlightened by contacts with believers who have a holy life style and radiant witness. Many Muslims are in daily contact with Christians, as are Syrian soldiers based in Lebanon.

4. **Syrian Christians have been a respected minority** since the time of the church in Antioch (Acts 13). They survived the onslaught of militant Islam in AD 636. Most Christians are Arab and 25% are Armenian, descendants of a multiplicity of Orthodox and Catholic traditions. Christians are an influential minority in the cities, professions, politics and the armed forces, but are a shrinking percentage due to a high rate of emigration to the Americas and Africa. Pray that believers may recapture the zeal of the church of Antioch, and reach out to their compatriots with the gospel.

5. **The Protestant witness is small,** but churches are slowly growing. Almost all new converts are from the traditional Christian minority which, in turn, has been challenged to become more Bible-oriented, with increasing interest in the study of the Scriptures. There are churches in most cities, but the lack of full-time workers and availability of training for leadership are serious limitations. Pray that believers may be both ambitious and original in seeking out opportunities to win non-Christians, despite official pressures.

6. **Conversions out of Islam are few and far between.** Spiritual bondages, social barriers and religious prejudices must be broken down before some will make the decisive step. For such individuals pray for perseverance in persecution, acceptance into fellowship by other believers and growth to maturity.

7. **Unreached peoples** to pray for:
a) **The Sunni Arab majority,** very few of whom have heard the gospel.
b) **The Alawites** are a rural community, but influential in the army and government. Their beliefs differ much from orthodox Islam. Little specific effort has been directed to them.
c) **The Druze** in the far south are a heretical and secretive offshoot of Islam; they have been unresponsive.
d) **The Kurds** of the north and northwest might be more receptive. Some are Orthodox Christian, others are Yezidis and Shi'a, but most are Sunni Muslim.
e) **The Bedouin, Cherkess, Turkmen and Gypsy** minorities are solidly Muslim with no known Christians.
f) **The dwindling Jewish community** is declining through emigration and because of many restrictions imposed on them.

8. **Missionaries** as such are not allowed to reside in the country. Pray for those who pay occasional pastoral visits, and for a more open door to this needy land. Pray for Christian professionals living in the country.

9. **Christian media.**
a) **Literature** has been freely available for a decade, and there is a brisk sale of Bibles from the two Bible Society bookrooms. Pray for its impact on Christian and non-Christian alike.
b) **The *Jesus* film** is widely circulated on video cassette in Arabic. Pray for many non-Christians to follow him as a result.

S

Tajikistan

Area 143,000 sq.km. The southernmost republic of the former USSR bordering on Afghanistan, China, Uzbekistan and Kyrgyzstan. The Pamir and Tien-Shan Mountains are 93% of the surface area.

Population	Ann.Gr.	Density
1990	5,294,000	3.6%	37/sq.km
1995	6,311,000	3.5%	44/sq.km

The Tajik themselves grew at 4.55% annually during the '80s.

Peoples. Figures for 1989. Since then nearly all Germans, 40% of Russians, and many Uzbeks have left the country. Only larger groups are mentioned.
Indo-European 72%.
  Iranian 62.5%. Tajik 3,172,000; Farsi 31,000; Ossetian 8,000. 6 Pamir peoples est. 60,000. Yagnob 2,000.
  Slav 8.6%. Russian 388,000; Ukrainian 41,000.
  Other 0.9%. German 33,000; Armenian 6,000.
Turkic/Altaic 27.2%. Uzbek (in the north) 1,198,000; Tatar 72,000; Kyrgyz 64,000.
All other peoples 0.8%. Jews 15,000; Korean 13,000; Galcha, Hazara, Arab.

Literacy: 99%. **Official language:** Tajik. **All indigenous languages** 10. **Languages with Scriptures** 2Bi 1NT.

Capital: Dushanbe 602,000. Other major cities: Khojent 163,000; Kulyab 100,000. Urbanization 33%.

Economy: Rich in minerals, coal, oil and hydroelectric power, but the effects of 70 years of Communist mismanagement have been an ecological and economic disaster. The collapse of the USSR, loss of Russian technocrats, poor communications with the rest of the world, and civil war have reduced much of the population to poverty and starvation. Unemployment in rural areas 70%. Income/person $1,613 (8% of USA) – the poorest of the former USSR republics.

Politics. The northern portion of the Persian Empire until the 12th century. Russian colonial rule from the mid-19th century. Stalin arbitrarily defined the republic's borders in 1929 – described as a mixture of tragedy, farce and chaos. The Tajik cities of Samarkand and Bukhara were placed in Uzbekistan and the Uzbek population of Khojent in the north included in Tajikistan. After the collapse of the Soviet empire, civil war broke out between the Tajik of Dushanbe and the east (who were more strongly Muslim or democratic), and the Tajik of Kulyab and Khojent (allied with Uzbeks and Russians as reconstituted Communists). The latter had regained control of most of the country by early 1993. The war in Tajikistan could destabilize all of Central Asia.

Religion: The battle between Communists and the alliance of fundamentalist Muslims and democrats prevents a definition of government policy. Muslims have increased the number of mosques from 120 in 1991 to 2,100 in 1993. A few Orthodox churches have also been built.
Muslim 82.3%. Sunni 80.7%; Ismaili 1%; Shi'a 0.6%. Much folk Islam and Zoroastrian religious symbolism.
Non-religious/other 13.2%. Mainly Slavic, some Tajik.
Jews 0.3%.
Christian 4.2%. Nom 1.9%. Affil 2.3%. Growth −4.9%.
Protestant 0.04%. Growth −24.5%.

Church	Cong	Members	Affiliated
Lutheran Ch		600	1,000
Baptist Ch	7	374	500
Pentecostal Ch	3	150	375
Korean Pentecostal	1	50	300
Denominations (4)		1,175	2,175
Evangelicals 0.02% of pop		635	1,275
Pentecostal/charis 0.01%		240	725
Roman Catholic 0.12%. Affil 0.12%.			
Growth −1.4%.			
Catholic Ch		3,900	6,500
Orthodox 4%. Affil 2.1%. Growth −4.2%.			
Russian Orthodox Ch		70,000	100,000
All other (4)		6,500	10,000
Denominations (5)		76,500	110,000

T

1. **The civil war** has brought suffering, bitterness and hatred to the newly independent nation with 20,000 killed and 500,000 refugees in early 1993. The causes are not only ideological and ethnic, but also clan divisions within the Tajik themselves. This land has never been exposed to the gospel since the advent of Islam. Pray for these tragic events to pass, but leave a people open to receive the gospel. Pray that the Lord Jesus may reveal himself to Muslims in a supernatural way.

2. **The Christian Church** is almost entirely composed of Russians and Ukrainians (Orthodox) and Germans (Protestant). The majority have left the country since 1989. Evangelicals only number a few hundred Russians, Germans and Ukrainians, and a sprinkling of other ethnic groups. Pray for the

establishment, in each city, of a strong multi-ethnic Christian witness which can then reach out to rural areas.

3. **Islamic fundamentalism**, amply supported by Iranian propaganda and Afghan arms, could bring bigotry and another ideological tyranny to the land. Pray for extremism to be restrained and Muslims to meet with Christ.

4. **Missions.** Pray for this land to be opened up for Christian ministry. There is a network of agencies concerned for Tajikistan, but entry and residence of expatriates is hindered by the disturbed situation. There are two ex-USSR mission agencies seeking to reach the Tajik. Pray for the calling and entry of long-term personnel who will master the language and be used of God to establish a Tajik Church.

5. **The unreached.** Indigenous peoples have had minimal opportunity to hear the gospel. Pray specifically for the conversion of Tajik and Uzbek leaders. Pray also for the mountain peoples of the Pamirs in the east. In that region live six Ismaili Muslim peoples – the Ishkashimi, Roshani, Bartangi, Shughni, Wakhi and Yazgulyam, who have never been reached.

6. **Tajik** number nearly 10 million in Central Asia. Believers are very few in the former USSR; only in Afghanistan has there been a significant turning of Tajik to the Lord. Pray for the multiplication and spread of Tajik believers throughout the area. Pray also for good cooperation among all concerned for the Tajik. There is a growing interest among a number of evangelical agencies.

7. **Christian media ministries.**
a) **The whole Bible in Tajik** (Cyrillic Script) was completed in 1992 (**IBT**). Praise God for this, but pray for its effective dissemination. There are between five and seven indigenous languages that will need Bible translation. There is also a children's Bible in Tajik, but little else in Christian literature.
b) **The *Jesus* film** and video have been prepared in Tajik and shown on national television.
c) **Christian radio. HCJB(WRMF)** Ecuador broadcasts in Tajik; the four daily programmes broadcast by **TWR**-Monaco and **FEBA**-Seychelles in Farsi and Dari can be understood, but few have short-wave receivers.

T

Tanzania

(United Republic of Tanzania)

October 27–28

Africa

Area 943,000 sq.km. Mainland Tanganyika and Zanzibar (two offshore islands of 2,460 sq.km.).

Population	Ann. Gr.	Density
1990 27,328,000	3.7 %	29/sq.km
1995 32,892,000	3.8 %	35/sq.km

Peoples: Indigenous ethnic groups 160. Widespread use of Swahili has lessened tribal divisions.
Bantu peoples 90.9%. Over 130. Largest: Sukuma 5,000,000; Haya 1,200,000; Gogo 1,000,000; Chagga 990,000; Nyamwezi 926,000; Makonde 900,000; Ha 800,000; Hehe 650,000; Nyakyusa 600,000; Bena 568,000; Nyaturu 556,000; Shambala 550,000; Ruguru 520,000; Asu 400,000; Mwera 400,000; Yao 400,000; Makua 360,000; Zigula 355,000; Langi 310,000.
Nilotic 4%. Eight groups. Largest: Maasai 430,000; Luo 223,000.
Cushitic 2.2%. Six peoples. Largest: Iraqw 365,000.
Khoisan 0.3%. Two groups. Sandawe 70,000; Kindiga 4,000. Related to San (Bushmen) of Southern Africa.
Sudanic 0.1%. Five groups.
Other 2.5%. Indian 250,000 (predominantly Gujarati); Arab 195,000; Eurafrican 80,000; European 70,000; Chinese.
Refugees: Burundi Hutu 180,000; Rwandans 25,000; also many Mozambicans.

Literacy est. 80%. **Official languages:** Swahili, English. 1.8% of population speak only Swahili but 94% are bilingual. **All languages** 131. **Languages with Scriptures** 18Bi 16NT 18por.

Capital: Dar es Salaam 1,500,000. Capital designate Dodoma 204,000. Also Zanzibar 158,000. Urbanization 27%.

Economy: Agricultural subsistence economy. Inefficient, centralized bureaucracy, an over-zealous nationalization of businesses, and collectivization of rural communities into *ujamaa* villages have led to costly failure. Foreign investment has dried up and inefficiency and corruption have led to a run-down of industry, agriculture and infrastructure and a serious reduction of living standards. Liberalizations first in Zanzibar and then on the mainland are gradually bringing improvements. Public debt/person $192. Income/person $120 (0.5% of USA).

Politics: Tanganyika gained independence from Britain in 1961, Zanzibar in 1963. The two countries united as a one-party federal socialist republic in 1964, though Zanzibar has retained a considerable degree of autonomy. Legislation passed in 1992 permits multi-party elections. The country has a Muslim Zanzibari President and a Christian Prime Minister. There has been considerable pressure by

Zanzibar for more privileges and even political separation from the mainland.

Religion: Religious freedom for worship and witness, but Muslims are favoured in provision of building sites for mosques and in the application of anti-blasphemy laws.
Muslim 35% (Zanzibar 98%). The majority in Zanzibar, along the coastal belt, and some peoples on the Mozambique border.
Traditional religions 13.2%.
Baha'i 0.4%. **Hindu** 0.1%. **Other** 0.3%.
Christian 51%. Nom 14.4%. Affil 36.6%. Growth 5%.
Protestant 19%. Affil 14.7%. Growth 5.2%.

Church	Cong	Members	Affiliated
Evang Lutheran Ch	4,868	463,000	1,156,000
Anglican Ch	4,869	390,000	950,000
Africa Inland Ch (AIM)	1,000	300,000	600,000
Seventh-day Adventist	505	106,000	265,000
Moravian Ch	177	115,000	230,000
Baptist Convention	1,046	92,117	167,000
Pentecostal Chs in T	700	56,000	160,000
Assemblies of God	650	34,200	90,000
Christian Brethren	70	12,000	66,000
Pente Holiness Ch	90	29.000	56,000
Mennonite Chs (2)	196	20,078	47,000
Pente Assemb of God	510	12,500	38,000
All other (28)	1,170	85,31818	203,000
Denominations (41)	15,841	1,714,213	4,028,000
Evangelicals 9.7% of pop		1,136,000	2,638,000
Pentecostal/charis 2.4%		254,000	647,000

Missionaries:
to Tanzania 1,367 (1:20,000 people) in 107 agencies.
from Tanzania 211 (1:21,000 Protestants) in 14 agencies 38frn 72xcul 139dom.
Roman Catholic 31.2%. Affil 21.1%. Growth 4.9%.

Catholic Ch	6,480	3,110,000	5,760,000

Missionaries:
to Tanzania 1,908 (1:12,800 people).
from Tanzania 92 (1973 figure).
Orthodox 0.04%. Growth 0%.
Foreign Marginal 0.04%. Growth 10.2%.
Indigenous Marginal 0.73%. Growth 7%.

All groups (40)	1,600	80,000	200,000

T

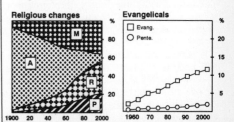

Religious changes

Evangelicals

☐ Evang.
○ Pente.

1. **Tanzania is spiritually responsive.** Economic crises and the social disruption caused by the collectivization of rural communities have broken down traditional structures and opposition to the gospel. Churches in many parts of the country are full to overflowing. Pray that pressures to increase Islamic influence across the country may fail and that Christians may exert a wholesome and moral influence at every level of society.

2. **The growth of the Church has been good but patchy.** Revival movements in both the Lutheran and Anglican Churches have brought life to traditional congregations; most of the bishops are Evangelicals. Evangelicals, and especially Pentecostals, have multiplied in numbers during the '80s. However, there are problems that limit growth in numbers and spirituality.
a) There are extensive areas where the churches have stagnated and where many potentially open villages are unreached. There are too few evangelists and church planters.
b) Western cultural forms combined with African worship patterns of singing, choirs and collections leave little time for biblical teaching.
c) There is a critical lack of trained, mature leaders. Many pastors have to care for 20 or more congregations.
d) **The spread of AIDS** has been especially bad in the northwest and in the 15-30 age bracket, and is beginning to deeply affect the country. Pray for church teaching programmes aimed at slowing the spread of the disease and for counselling clinics and care structures for victims.

3. **Leadership training** needs to be given top priority in the churches. Training facilities and funding are limited. Pray for the 15 or so Bible schools and seminaries in the country. Many need upgrading to higher levels to prepare leaders for an increasingly literate population. Extensive use is made of short-term residential training courses, **TEE** and also **cassette Bible schools** for training local leaders. The AIC is planning to found a missionary college for workers to reach unreached tribal areas.

4. **Response among young people** has been particularly encouraging. Over 50% of the population is under 15.
a) **Schools are obliged to provide religious education**, but there are 53 schools for every qualified RE teacher. Christian teachers can and do have a big impact. Pray for church programmes to equip teachers for this key role.
b) **Scripture Union** has had a major impact, but leadership and vision is the need. Pray for a fresh anointing of the Spirit and a new cutting edge.
c) **FOCUS groups (IFES)** in universities and colleges are large and evangelistic. Many students are being converted, including Muslims. Lack of staff workers is a hindrance to better national coverage and coordination of outreach and discipling. Pray for the four staff workers.

5. **Missionaries** have a key role in equipping and motivating Tanzanians for Bible teaching and outreach to Muslim areas and in working in partnership with them. The largest group of missionaries are Lutherans (340; mainly Scandinavian and German), Swedish Free Mission (176), Anglicans (141 in **CMS** and Crosslinks), **AIM** (105), **SBC** (90), and **Brethren** (53; from Germany and Britain). Major missionary-contributing nations: USA (329), Sweden (253), Germany (209), UK (153), Finland (130).

6. **The Muslim challenge.** Islam grew rapidly between 1880 and 1960 and again since 1980. Muslim political power is being expanded as much as possible. Extensive use of the mass media, Middle Eastern oil wealth for mosque construction, and influence in the administration have been responsible for the latest surge. Some Muslims have come to Christ, but decisive breakthroughs are prayerfully awaited. Pray that Tanzanian Christians may be given a vision for their evangelization, and that Tanzania's secular constitution may be preserved.

7. **The less reached.** Great areas of need remain.
a) **Zanzibar** with three distinct ethnic groups on the two islands of Zanzibar and Pemba. There are two Anglican, two Lutheran and six Pentecostal congregations on Zanzibar, and one Anglican and two Quaker congregations on Pemba. Most of the believers are descendants of slaves or mainlanders. Islamic resurgence and anti-Christian propaganda have slowed outreach. Pray that economic and political liberalization may be accompanied by spiritual liberation.
b) **The Muslim coastal peoples.** Zaramo, Langi, Ruguru, Shambala, Zigula, and the many urban coastal Swahili are almost entirely Muslim. Pray that Christians may learn how to reach them and love them into the Kingdom. **AIM** is to launch a new church-planting thrust in this area, and **RSTI** is planning the same.
c) **The peoples on the Mozambique border.** The Brethren from Germany have worked and prayed

for a breakthrough among the Islamized Makonde and Yao, and have only now begun to see the beginnings of a harvest. **AEF** has assigned workers to assist in this outreach because this is a key area for evangelizing unreached northern Mozambique.

d) **Peoples in which many still follow traditional religions.** In nearly all there is a significant Christian presence. AIC/AIM are reaching the Sukuma and Zinza (120,000), with new advances to the Sandawe. In the Lutheran areas of the north are the Maasai, Iraqw, Nyaturu and Barabaig (80,000); the publication of the whole Bible in Maasai has led to significant numbers coming to Christ, and in the Lutheran areas of the southwest are the Nyakyusa and Safwa (180,000).

e) **Urban areas.** These are growing but churches are less equipped to evangelize them.

8. **Bible translation** is a partially-met challenge. The increasing use of Swahili lessens the need for translation into some languages. However, there are at least 61 languages that definitely require a NT translation and possibly a total of 89. Pray for Tanzanian translators to be trained to meet the need. Bible and teaching cassettes have been widely used. **GRn** has recordings available in 72 languages. Totog, the language of the Barabaig, is a high-priority target of **SIL**.

9. **Christian literature** is vital for an increasingly literate nation, yet the poverty and difficulty of obtaining foreign currency to buy supplies hamper printing and distribution on a larger scale. Pray for more Tanzanians with the gifts and calling to write appropriate Christian articles and books. Pray also for the **Central Tanganyika Press** (Anglican) and **Africa Inland Press**, and for effective distribution of their products. **SU**, the Bible Society and the AIC have thriving Christian bookstores. The **Gideons** are active in placing New Testaments in schools.

10. **Missionary flying is an essential service ministry to the Church because of the few and poor roads.** **MAF**-Europe has its biggest operation in Tanzania – 12 aircraft based at Dodoma and seven satellite bases – involved in moving Christian workers and maintaining medical programmes and outreach to the Maasai, Iraqw and Barabaig. Evangelism and the showing of the *Jesus* film at airstrips is one evangelistic spin-off!

11. **Christian radio** has more potential in Tanzania than in many African countries. The Lutherans and **IBRA** have recording studios. **FEBA** (Seychelles) broadcasts 21 hours per week in Swahili and has a regular half-million listeners, and also airs a daily 20-minute programme in Yao. **TWR**-Swaziland broadcasts 19 hours per week in English.

T

October 29–30
Asia

Thailand
(Kingdom of Thailand)

Area 514,000 sq.km. A fertile and well-watered land bordering on Myanmar, Laos, Cambodia and Malaysia.

Population		Ann. Gr.	Density
1990	55,702,000	1.5 %	109/sq.km
1995	59,605,000	1.4 %	116/sq.km

Peoples: Four major peoples and numerous smaller groups, most of the latter being small mountain tribal groups.
Thai 77.7%. Four main groups. Central 21,000,000; Isan (Lao-Thai) 15,000,000; Northern 6,000,000; Southern 5,000,000.
Chinese 12.1%. Thai-speaking 80%. A minority still use over six Chinese languages, mostly Swatow/Teochew.
Malay 4%. In the extreme south adjoining Malaysia.
Mon-Khmer 3.7%. Over 14 peoples. Largest: Khmer 1,500,000; Kuy 234,000; So 55,000; Phay 31,000; Khmu 15,000; Lawa 14,000.
Other Tai 0.6%. Over 10 peoples. Phu Thai 156,000; Lu 78,000; Shan 56,000; Nyaw 50,000; Saek 11,000.
Meo-Yao 0.48%. Four peoples. Meo (Hmong) (3) 80,000; Yao (Mien) 16,000.
Tibeto-Burman 0.92%. Over 15 groups. Karen (9 groups) 380,000; Lahu 28,000; Akha 25,000; Lisu 16,000.
Other 0.5%. Westerners, Burmese, Japanese, Pakistani, Vietnamese.
Refugees. Cambodians 100,000 and decreasing; Hmong Laotians; Karen from Myanmar.

Literacy 89%. **Official language:** Thai. **All languages** 81. **Languages with Scriptures** 18Bi 7NT 15por.

Capital: Krung Thep (Bangkok) 6,450,000. Urbanization 19%.

Economy: Productive agricultural economy. Main exports are rice, sugar, pineapples and rubber. The depletion of forest cover is worsening the cycle of droughts and floods. Rapid industrialization and development of mineral resources. The government is trying to eradicate drug trafficking from the "Golden Triangle" in the far northwest of the country. Public debt/person $221. Income/person $1,170 (5.5% of USA).

Politics: A kingdom since the 13th Century, and never ruled by a Western power. Constitutional monarchy, with the popular king having a strong unifying and stabilizing role. The powerful army dominated politics and commercial life for 60 years. Corrupt, selfish practices of army leaders spread corruption to all levels of society and served to protect crime, prostitution, drug-dealing and arms rackets. The army's violent suppression of pro-democracy demonstrations in 1992 led to its humiliation. Subsequent election of a civilian government committed to dealing with corruption and diminishing army influence in politics.

Religion: Buddhism is the state religion. Foreign religions are protected under the monarchy.
Buddhist 93.4%. Thai, Lao, Shan, some Chinese, etc. Much syncretism with spirit worship.
Muslim 4%. Malays and some Thai in the far south.
Chinese religions 1.6%. Many Chinese are included with the Buddhist figure.
Christian 1%. Affil 0.84%. Growth 3.9%.
Protestant 0.43%. Growth 7%.

Church	Cong	Members	Affiliated
Ch of Christ in T	380	45,308	82,400
Karen Baptist Conv	182	11,079	19,000
Seventh-day Adventist	33	8,740	16,800
Lahu Baptist Conv	76	6,000	15,000
Chs related to OMF	188	6,200	12,400
Finnish Free Mission	58	3,500	8,750
Thai Baptist Chs Assoc	39	3,203	7,120
Hope of Bangkok	100	3,000	6,000
Full Gospel Ch Foundn	21	2,846	5,690
Gospel Ch of Thai	107	3,153	5,148
Evang Covenant Ch	74	3,000	5,000
Full Gospel Fell Ch	35	2,040	4,080
Bonds of Fellowship (WEC)	60	1,200	3,000
All other (43)	463	17,604	36,115
Denominations (56)	1,816	116,873	226,503
Evangelicals 0.3% of pop		82,000	162,000
Pentecostal/charis 0.08%		10,800	46,300

Missionaries:
to Thailand 1,293 (1:43,100 people) in 104 agencies.
from Thailand 117 (1:2,000 Protestants) in 10 agencies 4frn 14xcul 103dom.
Roman Catholics 0.6%. Affil 0.42%. Growth 2.1%.

Catholic Ch	620	127,000	236,078
Charismatics		400	700

Missionaries:
to Thailand 401 (1:140,000 people).
from Thailand 5 (1973 figure).
Marginal 0.01%. Growth 12.8%.

Mormons	18	2,210	4,100
Jehovah's Witnesses	37	1,310	3,120
All groups (3)	56	3,591	7,319

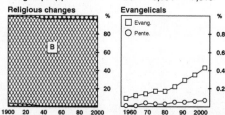

Religious changes   Evangelicals

1. **Thailand means *Land of the Free*** because it successfully retained its freedom when surrounding countries were colonized by Western powers. It is believed that a special guardian angel, ***Phra Sayam Devadhiraj***, protected the land, and a golden image of this spirit being was made. Ever since it has been worshipped. The land is in bondage to a complex web of culture, spirit appeasement, occult practices and Buddhism, with a social cohesiveness out of which few dare come. Many Thai Christians fast and pray one day a month for the spiritual breakthrough so that the Thai may be free indeed through the Lord Jesus.

2. **The rottenness at the core of Thai society** can only be fully excised and cleansed through a turning to God. Corrupt leaders have protected the large sex industry, drug networks, crime syndicates, and ecological degradation of the country. Pray that honest, just leaders may be raised up who will also lay legal and social frameworks that will limit corruption.

3. **The growth of the Church has been disappointing**. After four centuries of Catholic and 160 years of Protestant work, Thai Christians are only 1% of the population. The Catholic Church's percentage has scarcely increased in 40 years. Only in the '80s did Protestants begin to do any better. Much of the growth has been among the Thai-speaking Chinese in the cities and the marginalized tribal peoples. Pray for:
   a) **The Church of Christ in Thailand,** the largest denomination (within which many denominational missions serve). There have been touches of revival in the north, but nominalism and theological compromise are problems, leaving growth marginal since 1960.
   b) **The Evangelical Fellowship of Thailand.** This links the majority of evangelical bodies in fellowship. In 1992 there were over 1,200 congregations, 56 national ministries and 53 expatriate organizations linked with the EFT.
   c) **High standards of holiness in church life.** Church leaders need to squarely face syncretism, a high rate of backsliding, misuse of church funds, and a tolerant condoning of sin resulting in failure to discipline those who err.
   d) **New spiritual vitality and vision.** Many congregations are poor, rural, and often highly illiterate.

4. **A vision for advance and growth in the '90s has been launched.** The Thai Protestant Coordinating Committee – linking the CCT, **SBC** and EFT – is setting the goal of 600,000 members, 6,000 pastors, 600 in home missions and 60 overseas missionaries by the year 2000. Of these, half are targeted by the EFT, which means that they hope to increase their 900 churches with 15 members or more in 1990 to 3,000 churches in ten years. Missions vision is slow to develop, yet **OMF** has set up a Thai Home Council, and there are three small indigenous Thai missions. Pray for vision to become reality, and for breakthrough.

5. **Leadership training** is vital. There are 17 Bible schools, most with a full complement of students, and a further seven TEE programmes operating in the country. Many graduates do not go into full-time church-planting or pastoral work. Pray for the **Bangkok Bible College** (initiated by **CMA** and **OMF**, with 140 graduates), **Phayao Bible Training Centre (OMF)** and many denominational Bible colleges. Praise God for fine evangelical leaders in churches, but those who are adequately trained and mature are few – the many rural churches have little Bible teaching as a result. Deference given to older pastors inhibits the development of younger workers.

6. **Missions** have considerable freedom for ministry despite a quota system which somewhat restricts the number of visas. Major involvement in the past was institutional; medical work and schools playing an important role in winning the first converts and planting the first churches in many parts of the land. The major emphasis is now on urban and rural evangelism, church planting and Bible teaching. Pray for:
   a) **The calling, entry and preparation of new workers** to this exacting field. For many, two difficult languages must be mastered for effective communication.
   b) **Safety.** Disease, road accidents and insurgency have led to the loss of a number of missionaries.
   c) **Effective partnership** with Thai believers in strategic outreach.
   d) **The major agencies. OMF** has 209 missionaries in five fields (among tribal peoples in the north, Thai in the centre, south and Bangkok, and Malay in the south). Other major agencies: **YWAM** (101 in refugee work and evangelism), **SBC** (86 missionaries), **NTM** (96 in tribal work), **CMA** (61 in the east and Bangkok), **SIL** (59), FFM (53), **WEC** (44 in the northwest and Bangkok) and AoG (40). There are 837 missionaries linked with the Evangelical Fellowship of Thailand. Major missionary-contributing nations: USA (603), UK (99), Finland (87), Canada (74), Korea (59), New Zealand (58), Australia (53).

7. **The unfinished task.** Pray for these challenges to be met:

a) **Of the 73 provinces,** 14 have fewer than 1,000 Christians of any type, and three have less than 100 (Phangnga, Ranong and Angtong); four have no evangelical congregations.

b) **Bangkok,** *the sin capital of Asia.* Most of the country's estimated 100,000 male and 700,000 female prostitutes operate in this city. Over two million people derive their income from the sex industry. Many girls are kidnapped or sold into prostitution slavery. Most of the 35,000 street children of the city end up in this evil. AIDS has become a major scourge, with at least 500,000 infected by 1992 and a projected four million by the year 2000. Pray for all who seek to minister to these tragic people. A number of expatriate and indigenous workers are committed to urban church planting (Servants to Asia's Urban Poor, **AoG, SBC, CMA, WEC** and others). Most of the 109 Protestant congregations have little contact with the poorer areas of the city.

c) **The middle and upper classes,** wealthy and well educated, but showing little response to the gospel. By contrast, interest in the occult and necromancy is reported to be strong.

d) **Student witness,** small but growing. Twelve Christian hostels for students, run by six agencies, have proved valuable for discipling students and initiating Christian campus groups. **YFC,** TCS(**IFES**), **CCC** and an indigenous movement called *Yuwakrit* have seen conversions and growth of groups on campuses. The vast majority of the one million students remains unevangelized.

e) **Refugees.** Thailand has provided a refuge or conduit to new homelands for hundreds of thousands of refugees from the decades of fighting in Laos, Cambodia and Vietnam. As peace is gradually restored, their numbers are diminishing. Most that remain are Hmong Laotians and Cambodians, among whom there are a number of churches. Pray for the reintegration of these unfortunate people in their lands of origin, the survival and growth of Christian groups and ongoing Christian ministries to the remaining 200,000 or so (estimate for 1993) refugees (**YWAM, WV, CMA, SAO** and others). There is a growing refugee problem on the Myanmar border, with many Karen and Burmese seeking refuge from repression.

8. **The Chinese** are an influential minority. They make up nearly half the population of Bangkok, and control about 85% of the economy. Chinese form a significant majority of Christians in urban Thai-speaking congregations. There are also 69 Chinese-speaking congregations with 9,150 members. The dynamism and financial clout of this community, if fully activated, could be a significant force for evangelization. There are too few ethnic Chinese full-time workers.

9. **Of the 2,500,000 Muslims, 90% are Malays.** Nearly all live in the five southernmost provinces, where there has been political tension and guerrilla activity by Communists (until 1992) and Muslim separatists. This is the only major Malay community in Asia open for evangelism, but after years of hard work **OMF** missionaries have seen only about 100 turn to Christ. The upsurge in Islam in Malaysia to the south is affecting the Thai Malays and complicating outreach. Many seekers are held back by fear. Pray for the local believers and missionary team, and for their outreach through postal outreach, radio and literature. The Jawi Malay New Testament is being distributed to Malays, as well as a new BCC in Thai and Malay especially written to help Malay Muslims.

10. **The tribal peoples** are beginning to respond in large numbers. This follows years of hard work by Baptists among the Karen, and **OMF** among eight tribes in the north. The younger work of **NTM** in 11 tribes around the country is still in its early stage. Many workers are needed to win and disciple tribal peoples. Pray for:

a) **The multiplying, but scattered congregations** among the northern Hmong, Lahu, Lisu, Akha and Karen peoples. Lack of leaders and second-generation nominalism are problems. The Buddhist Shan and Taoist/animist Yao have been less responsive.

b) **The pioneering work of NTM** among the Phu Thai, So, Thin and Chaobon. Breakthroughs have yet to come.

c) **The Kui, Khmu and Khmer peoples in the east who are unreached. CMA** works in the area, but there are insufficient workers to concentrate on them, especially the newly responsive Northern Khmer. The Kuy New Testament was nearing completion in 1992 (CMA).

d) **The Golden Triangle.** Opium poppies are the only lucrative cash crop for most of the northern tribes. Cultivation is an acute temptation for Christians and a formidable barrier to repentance for non-believers. The narcotics trade breeds insecurity and violence. Pray for believers and missionaries in sensitive areas.

11. **Bible translation** is still a major target for prayer. Work is in progress in 21 languages – main agencies being **SIL, NTM** and **OMF.** Between 16 and 34 languages may need translators. There are four different versions of the Thai Bible in circulation.

12. **Media evangelism and discipleship** have been well developed in Thailand. Pray that the following may prepare millions for the gospel and edify the Church:
a) **Traditional drama** with Christian themes is highly effective.
b) **Radio** has had a wide impact. Forty-nine Thai stations air many hours of Christian programmes every day. **FEBC, OMF**, Full Gospel Mass Communications and Voice of Peace Studio prepare a wide range of programmes. **OMF/FEBC** have built up a significant listenership among Buddhists with promise for eternal fruit.
c) **Cassette ministries** were first widely used in Thailand. The **Voice of Peace Studio** pioneered the use of evangelistic and teaching cassettes, which are most effective in rural areas.
d) **Christian literature** is increasing. Over 1,000 Thai book titles have been published. There is increasing cooperation between publishers (such as **CLC, OMF** [*Kanok*], **CMA**). There are more than 20 Christian bookstores in the land, five of which are run by **CLC**.
e) **The *Jesus* film** is widely used in Thai, Vietnamese and Hmong.

T

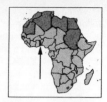

October 31
Africa

Togo
(Togolese Republic)

Area 57,000 sq.km. The Atlantic coastline is only 56 km. long, but the little land stretches 540 km. northwards to the Sahel. Wedged between Ghana and Benin.

Population		Ann. Gr.	Density
1990	3,455,000	3.1 %	61/sq.km
1995	4,038,000	3.2 %	71/sq.km

Peoples: About 78 ethnic groups in 2 major language groups.
Kwa 55%. Largest: Ewe 861,000; Waci 365,000; Mina 201,000; Aja 111,000; Akposo 95,000; Ife 74,400; Anufo 42,000; Akebu 41,000; Fon 36,000; Mahi 25,000; Anyanga 7,200; Adele 7,000; Igo 6,300; Hwe 4,200; Akpe 3,400; Kpessi 3,100; Anii 700.
Gur 42.8%. Largest: Kabiye (Kabré) 489,000; Tem (Kotokoli) 204,000; Moba 189,000; Nawdm 146,000; Gurmantche 121,000; Lama 117,400; Ntcham (Bassari) 62,000; Konkomba 50,100; Akasalem 34,000; Ngangam 33,500; Taberma 20,000; Mossi 20,000; Bago 6,100; Delo 5,000.
Other 2%. Fula 48,200; Bisa 10,300; Hausa 9,600.
Non-African Peoples 0.2%. Lebanese 3,500; French 3,000.

Literacy 39%. **Official language:** French. **All languages** 43. Only two indigenous languages used in education system: Ewe/Mina and Kabiye. **Languages with Scriptures** 5Bi 5NT 4por.

Capital: Lomé 450,000. Urbanization 24%.

Economy: Mining phosphates and agriculture are important sources of foreign currency, and economic growth has been moderate. The south is more prosperous than the drier north. Public debt/person $273. Income/person $370 (1.7% of USA).

Politics: Independent from France in 1960. One-party military-civilian regime in power since 1967. Pressure internally and externally to open up the country to multi-party democracy led to a national conference in 1991 in which Eyadema, the President, was stripped of his powers and a transitional government installed. A referendum in 1992 confirmed a multi-party constitution, but its provisions were eroded in a contest of power between Eyadema and the transitional government that degenerated into anarchy and virtual civil war between the southern and central peoples.

Religion: A period of intense anti-Christian rhetoric in the '70s has cooled to an official indifference. In 1978, 20 religious groups were banned; only Muslims, Catholics and five Protestant churches were legally permitted to function. In 1990, a greater freedom for other churches and missions to minister was granted.
Traditional religions 36%. Still a major spiritual force in nearly every people.
Muslim 21%. Continued growth throughout this century. Muslims were only 4% in 1900.
Christian 43%. Affil 28.9% Growth 5.7%.
Protestant 9%. Affil 5.4% Growth 5.4%.

Church	Cong	Members	Affiliated
Evangelical Ch	200	28,800	120,000
Baptist Assoc. (SBC)	157	8,447	21,000
Assemblies of God	259	10,800	18,000
Methodist Ch	25	3,750	7,500
Lutheran Ch	31	1,750	3,500
Evang Baptist Ch	22	1,750	3,500
All other (4)	230	5,122	12,286
Denominations (10)	924	60,669	184,436
Evangelicals 1.84% of pop		29,000	64,000
Pentecostal/charis 0.93%		16,000	32,000

Missionaries:
to Togo 275 (1:12,600 people) in 23 agencies.
from Togo 16 (1:11,700 Protestants) in 4 agencies.
Roman Catholic 32%. Affil 21.3%. Growth 4.9%.

Catholic Ch	725	406,000	738,000
Charismatics 0.11%		2,000	3,500

Missionaries
to Togo 249 (1:16,000 people).
from Togo 32 (1973 figure).
Foreign Marginal 0.3%. Growth 14.9%.

Jehovah's Witnesses	78	5,318	13,300

Indigenous Marginal 1.7%. Growth 17.1%.

All groups(27)	554	36,000	60,000

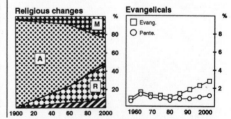

Religious changes   Evangelicals

1. **The political crisis** has brought anarchy and violence to the country, half the population of Lomé fleeing to Ghana and Benin. Pray for peace and a government that promotes the common good.

2. **The Church in Togo stagnated between 1960 and 1985.** The long established *Eglise Evangélique*

became theologically liberal and nominal and remained confined to the Ewe, while the Methodists remained among the Mina. The Catholics likewise only grew slowly. The newer evangelical groups have begun to grow – the **AoG** (once mainly in the north and now predominantly in the south), the Baptists (**SBC** and **ABWE** in the south) and the Missouri Synod Lutherans among the Moba in the north have all seen encouraging results. Pray for the establishment of strong indigenous congregations with visionary leadership in both the younger and older denominations.

3. **Praise God for a significant improvement in the spiritual life of Togo.** There is now greater freedom for churches and missions than for many years. Unevangelized peoples have been entered (Gourmantche, Lama and Ngangam), the Scriptures are being translated (work in 14 languages), Christian bookshops have opened (**CLC**), and new evangelical agencies entered (**SIM** and others).

4. **The strongly entrenched powers of darkness** have scarcely been challenged through intercessory prayer and confrontation with the power of the gospel. The two major forces to be tackled:
a) **The idolatry and strong secret societies** of the Ewe, Fon and other tribes. Christians cannot grow in their faith until they have fully repented and renounced the works of darkness.
b) **The growing strength of Islam.** There is a steady stream of conversions to Islam throughout the country, yet there is not one mission or Christian worker focused on Muslim evangelism in the eight Muslim peoples or the high concentrations of Muslims in urban areas – a total of 700,000 people.

5. **The Unreached of Togo.** Togo and Benin have the highest percentage of unevangelized traditionalists in Africa. Only 15 of Togo's peoples have evangelical congregations within their cultures. There are 25 unreached with no congregations known, or 21% of the population. The major challenges:
a) **The eight Muslim peoples** – the Tem, Anufo, Akaselem, Bago, Akpe and Anii as well as the more dispersed Fula and Hausa. A special effort must be made to reach these almost totally unreached peoples. **SIM** is eager to commence ministry to the Muslim peoples.
b) **The northern traditional peoples** – the Nawdm, Konkomba, Tamberma, Sola, Lokpa, Mossi and Bisa. There is a sprinkling of **AoG** churches in the area, but the vast majority have yet to hear the Good News.
c) **The south-central traditional peoples** – the Akebu, Anyanga, Adele, Delo and Kpessi.
d) **The southern coastal area** which is poorly researched. There are likely to be many unmet needs among the Fon, Mahi and others.
Many of these peoples could be best reached by Ghanaian and Benin believers who are of the same language group.

6. **Leaders for the young churches are few**, and training facilities in Togo limited. Pray for appropriate vernacular and French Bible Schools and TEE programmes to be launched. The Baptist School of Theology and Assemblies of God Advanced School of Theology in Lomé serve Francophone countries all over West Africa. Pray for Spirit-filled Togolese leaders to be raised up.

7. **Goals for AD2000.** The Assemblies of God are aiming for 300 churches and 36,000 members, and the Baptist Association for 500 churches. Pray that these advances may be achieved.

8. **Young people** were adversely affected during the '70s by the godless and anti-Christian atmosphere in the schools, and Christian staff and students are few. With greater liberty, Christians are free to minister, but the work of **SU** among young people and GBU(**IFES**) in the university have grown slowly and are still in their infancy. There is a pressing need for a vital, nationwide outreach to high schools. Pray for a radical improvement in the situation. The Baptists have a youth programme in Lomé, but generally speaking, the churches are ill-fitted to address the needs of children or young people.

9. **Evangelical missions** are few, but their number could be augmented by those committed to plant churches among the unreached. Church planters and disciplers are the great need. The largest missions are: **SIL/WBT** (75 workers), Association of Baptists for World Evangelism (**ABWE**) (57), **SBC** (39), **AoG** and Ministry of Jesus (35), **YWAM** (28). Many of these workers are, however, committed to teaching, translation and media ministries that cover West Africa. Major missionary-contributing countries: USA (185), France (15), Ghana (13), Switzerland (12).

10. **Bible translation** is a major need. Pray especially for the completion of the Kabiye Bible now that Kabiye is one of the two indigenous languages used in education. There are at least seven and possibly 19 languages into which the NT should be translated. Work is in progress in 14 languages, 10 of

which are in the hands of the 47 **SIL** workers. Pray that there might be adequate teaming up of translators with evangelical church planters.

11. **The Media tools** that should be covered by prayer:
a) **Christian literature** is in great demand. Pray for the ministry of both the Bible Society and **CLC**.
b) **GRn** have prepared materials in 21 languages.
c) The *Jesus* film is being translated into Kabiye, the key language of the north. Pray for lasting impact.

Tokelau Islands

See under COOK ISLANDS

See Pacific
Pacific

Tonga
(Kingdom of Tonga)

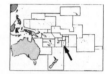

Area 779 sq.km. Archipelago of 171 coral and volcanic islands 600 km. east of Fiji, 36 being inhabited.

Population	Ann. Gr.	Density
1990 96,300	-2.5 %	125/sq.km
1995 98,000	0.41 %	131/sq.km

Much emigration to Australia and New Zealand.

Peoples:
Polynesian 98.3%. Tongans speaking three related languages.
Other 1.7%. English-speaking 600; Other Pacific Islanders 400; Chinese 200.

Literacy 100%. **Official language:** Tongan. **All languages** 5. **Languages with Scriptures** 3Bi.

Capital: Nuku'alofa 24,000. Urbanization 32%.

Economy: Agriculture, tourism and sale of passports to Chinese are the main sources of income. Public debt/person $456. Income/person $910 (4.3% of USA).

Politics: British Protected State 1900–1970. Constitutional monarchy with the king and nobles having the predominant influence. Since 1990 there has been a growing movement to curb the power of the aristocracy and make the constitution more democratic.

Religion: Freedom of religion. The Free Wesleyan Church enjoys a privileged position with the king as titular head.
Non-religious/other 0.1%. **Baha'i** 0.3%.
Christian 99.6%. Affiliated 98%. Growth 1%.

Protestant 51%. Affil 49.7%. Growth −1.1%.

Church	Cong	Members	Affiliated
Free Wesleyan	190	11,400	40,664
Free Church of Tonga	81	7,320	10,458
Ch of Tonga	41	4,140	6,903
Seventh-day Adventist	15	2,190	3,130
Tokailolo Fellowship	10	1,530	3,059
All other (8)	39	1,609	3,192
Doubly counted		−12,000	−19,700
Denominations (13)	376	16,189	47,706
Evangelicals 11.9% of pop		5,100	11,400
Pentecostal/charis		2,360	4,900

Missionaries:
to Tonga 18 (1:5,300 people) in 7 agencies.
from Tonga 48 (1:1,100 Protestants) in 4 agencies 23frn 23xcul 25dom.

Roman Catholic 16%. Affil 15.8%. Growth 0.2%.

Catholic	14	8,800	15,176

Missionaries to T 38 (1:2,500 people).
Foreign Marginal 32.5%. Growth 5.5%.

Mormons	117	11,483	31,000
Groups (2)	118	11,546	31,191

Indigenous Marginal 0.06%.

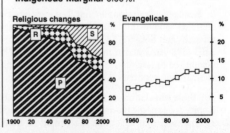

Religious changes

Evangelicals

1. **The Tongan church** has had a glorious history of missionary outreach. Pray that the vision may be restored. Pray for Tongan missionaries serving in seven other lands.

2. **This last century has been one of spiritual decline**, bitter schisms within the Methodist groups (the first three listed above), and the rapid growth of Mormons to almost a third of the population. Pray both for the spirit of error to be bound and for the fragmented church to be united in revival.

3. **Leaders anointed of God** to proclaim the truth in love must be raised up. Unity among the evangelical groups is hampered by doctrinal extremes, politics and personalities.

4. **Scripture Union** has had considerable impact on nominal Christians, with many coming to the Lord. **SU** has branches in nearly every village of Tonga.

5. **The less-reached.** The growing Chinese community is the only unreached people group, some immigrating from Hong Kong and China.

6. **Help ministries.** Pray for the lasting impact in lives of:
a) **The *Jesus* film** which is being used in Tongan.
b) **Literature.** Both the **Bible Society** and **SU** distribute Bibles and other Christian materials widely.

T

<table>
<tr><td>November
1

Caribbean</td><td colspan="2"><h1>Trinidad and
Tobago</h1>(The Republic of Trinidad and Tobago)</td></tr>
</table>

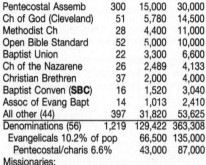

Area 5,128 sq.km. Two islands off the coast of Venezuela.

Population	Ann. Gr.	Density
1990 1,321,000	2.2 %	258/sq.km
1995 1,451,000	1.9 %	283/sq.km

Peoples:
Afro-Caribbean 57.1%.
East Indian 40.7%.
Euro-American 0.9%.
Other 1.3%. Chinese 6,500; Lebanese 2,600.

Literacy 96%. **Official language:** English.

Capital: Port-of-Spain 300,000. Urbanization 57%.

Economy: Export earnings heavily dependent on oil, but the sharp fall in world prices has caused severe unemployment and economic decline. Unemployment 22%. Income/person $3,160 (15% of USA).

Politics: Independent from Britain in 1962 as a parliamentary democracy. Prolonged economic recession in the '80s provoked political and ethnic tensions culminating in an abortive coup by militant black Muslims in 1990. The political climate continues to be unsettled.

Religion:
Non-religious/other 9.1%.
Hindu 24.3%.
Muslim 5.9%. Mainly East Indian with some Afro-Caribbean converts.
Baha'i 0.9%.
Christian 59.8%. Affil 56.7%. Growth 0.5%.
Protestant 28%. Affil 27.5%. Growth 0.8%.

Church	Cong	Members	Affiliated
Anglican Ch	83	29,070	153,000
Presbyterian Ch	115	14,000	40,000
Seventh-day Adventist	78	14,000	31,000
Pentecostal Assemb	300	15,000	30,000
Ch of God (Cleveland)	51	5,780	14,500
Methodist Ch	28	4,400	11,000
Open Bible Standard	52	5,000	10,000
Baptist Union	22	3,300	6,600
Ch of the Nazarene	26	2,489	4,133
Christian Brethren	37	2,000	4,000
Baptist Conven (**SBC**)	16	1,520	3,040
Assoc of Evang Bapt	14	1,013	2,410
All other (44)	397	31,820	53,625
Denominations (56)	1,219	129,422	363,308
Evangelicals 10.2% of pop		66,500	135,000
Pentecostal/charis 6.6%		43,000	87,000

Missionaries:
to Trin & Tobago 96 (1:13,800 people) in 19 agencies.
from Trin & Tobago 32 (1:11,400 Protestants) in 5 agencies 9frn 9xcul 23 dom.
Roman Catholic 29.9%. Affil 27.2%. Growth 0%.

Catholic Ch	61	205,000	360,000

Missionaries:
to Trin & Tobago 85 (1:15,500 people).
from Trin & Tobago 33 (1973 figure).
Orthodox 0.5%. Affil 0.5%. Growth 1.4%.

Denominations (2)	25	4,880	7,020

Foreign Marginal 1%. Growth 8%.

Jehovah's Witnesses	61	5,749	12,800
All groups (2)	63	5,999	13,255

Indigenous Marginal 0.4%. Growth 1.7%.

Total	25	3,000	6,000

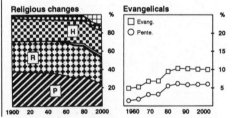

Religious changes   Evangelicals

1. **The increasing violence and breakdown of social stability and family life,** together with rising ethnic tensions and unemployment, bode ill for the future. Pray for government and religious leaders as they seek to bring harmony to the nation. The Prime Minister is a committed Christian.

2. **The East Indians** are the largest non-Christian community in the Caribbean. Ties with their cultural and religious roots have loosened, and about 14% of the population would claim to be Christian. Little has been done to evangelize the Muslims, but from among the Hindus there has been fruit; the Presbyterians, **WT** and **TEAM** have all planted strong churches. Pray for the harvest to increase, and for those reaping it.

3. **Religious instruction in public schools** presents an exciting opportunity for the gospel. In 1981 there were 118 Trinidad Christians engaged in this ministry. Pray for the young people of all races. **YFC, CEF** and **IFES** have work among students. Little is done in the churches to disciple children.

4. **A cross-cultural vision** is lacking in most churches. Pray for a greater awareness of local and world needs, and for effective training to be given in cross-cultural outreach. Only a handful of Trinidadians have gone overseas as missionaries – mostly with **OM** and **YWAM**.

5. **Help ministries:**
a) **Christian literature. CLC** operates three bookstores that are widely appreciated and extensively used. Pray for the 13 workers.
b) **Christian radio and TV programmes** broadcast on the national network. **TWR** and other Christian agencies also broadcast radio programmes from outside the country and have a large audience. Pray for the production of programmes that are relevant and spiritually effective.

Tunisia
(Republic of Tunisia)

November 2
Middle East

Area 155,000 sq.km. Mountainous and agricultural in north, Sahara Desert in south. The site of notable civilizations: Carthaginian, Berber Christian and Arab Islamic. The smallest of the Maghreb nations of North Africa.

Population		Ann. Gr.	Density
1990	8,169,000	2.4 %	53/sq.km
1995	9,019,000	2.0 %	58/sq.km

Peoples
Arab 98.3%. Mixed Berber and Arab descent.
Berber 1.2%. Few remain who speak the six Zenati/ Berber dialects.
Other 0.5%. French 11,000; Jews 3,000; some Italian, Maltese, Greek, etc.

Literacy 42%. **Official language:** Arabic; French is widely used. **All languages** 11. **Languages with Scriptures** 1Bi 2NT 1por.

Capital: Tunis 1,225,000. Urbanization 53%.

Economy: Rapid development after independence. Oil, tourism, agriculture and industry are all important foreign currency earners. Unemployment 11%. Public debt/person $745. Income/person $1,290 (6.1% of USA).

Politics: Independent from France in 1956. A republic with strong presidential government and little freedom for viable opposition parties. The repression of fundamentalist Muslims has been severe, with many reports of serious human rights abuses. Multi-party elections are promised for 1994.

Religion: Islam is the state religion. The secular tone of the government has been moderated in the face of rising Muslim fundamentalism. Not favourable to any form of Christian proselytism, but tolerance shown to foreign religious minorities.
Muslim 99.5%. Sunni, with minority of Ibadi Kharija on Djerba Island.
Non-religious/other 0.1%.
Jews 0.04%.
Christian 0.25%. Affil 0.19%. Growth −1.2%.
Protestant 0.005%. Growth −2.2%.

Church	Cong.	Members	Affiliated
Denominations (7)	7	200	371
Evangelicals 0.002% of pop		122	225

Expatriate Christians serving in Tunisia 37.
Roman Catholic 0.18%. Growth −1.2%.

Catholic Ch	15	8,700	15,000

Missionaries to Tunisia 430 in 1973; fewer today.
Orthodox 0.004%. Growth 0.7%.

Religious changes

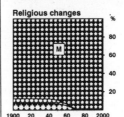

1. **In earlier centuries the Christian Church was strong,** producing such leaders as Tertullian and Cyprian. Schism, heresy, foreign invasions and finally Islam brought about its demise. There are only about 50 indigenous evangelical believers today; less than half come together for worship. Pray that a living, growing Church might become a reality again in this land.

2. **A century of missionary involvement has produced meagre fruit.** The powers that have bound and blinded Tunisians for centuries have not yet been disarmed through believing intercession. The barriers of apathy, materialism, occult practices and conformity to the outward trappings of Islam

must be pulled down by a concerted effort of praying people around the world. As elsewhere, radical solutions offered by revivalist Muslims are being embraced by the youth.

3. **Indigenous believers** are often isolated, fearful, weak in their faith and prone to backslide or to marry a Muslim. To some, emigration is an easy option. Only a few have dared to openly share their faith. Pray for deep commitment to Jesus – few Tunisian believers have stood in the faith for more than 10 years. Pray also for trust among believers, deliverance from fear of man and courage to witness.

4. **There is a leadership crisis,** with no mature leaders for the two small groups of indigenous believers. Pray that some may be raised up for the upbuilding of the Church. TEE courses are available and could be a useful training tool.

5. **The Christian population** is almost entirely expatriate and predominantly Catholic, and is now one-tenth of its size in 1960. There are two functioning Protestant congregations – Anglican and French Reformed, both with a lively ministry. Pray that expatriate Christians may discover quality opportunities to share their faith with non-Christians, encourage seekers and disciple young believers. Pray also for sensitivity and a persevering, servant spirit in a humanly discouraging situation. Pray for others to be called of God into this ministry.

6. **Specific unreached areas and peoples:**
a) **The young people** are disillusioned with the existing situation and negative about their own land; many seek for answers in extremism or materialism. Over 50% of university students support the cause of fundamentalist Islam.
b) **The southern part of the country** is a spiritual desert. Sfax, a city with nearly 500,000 people, has no group of indigenous believers.
c) **The Berber communities** maintain some of their distinctives even though they have largely lost their languages. Their ancestors were Christian. The island of Djerba with 65,000 people, mostly Berber, is a specific challenge with its unique culture and with no known Christians. There are also two Jewish settlements.

7. **Reaching Tunisians by other means.**
a) **The 300,000 Tunisians** in France, 24,000 in Germany and 7,000 in Belgium are being reached by a number of agencies, but more could be done.
b) **Christian radio** has had little impact. **TWR**-Monaco and **IBRA** Radio broadcast nine hours/week in Arabic. Many listen, but meaningful response and follow-through with BCCs has been slight. **GMU** in Spain and **AWM** in France are deeply involved in radio programming and BCC ministry in Arabic.
c) **Christian literature** is not openly sold or distributed. Pray that a Christian bookstore may be permitted, and also the dissemination of Christian literature throughout the land. Pray for the development of a good Christian cassette and video programme.

T

Turkey

(Republic of Turkey)

November 3–5

Middle East

Area 780,000 sq.km. The country straddles two continents – 3% in Europe (Thrace), 97% in Asia (Anatolia) – and controls the Bosphorus and the Dardanelles, the vital sea links between the Black Sea and Mediterranean. Its strategic position has made the area of prime importance through history.

Population	Ann. Gr.	Density
1990 55,616,000	2.0 %	71/sq.km
1995 61,151,000	1.9 %	78/sq.km

Peoples: There has been continued pressure on the ethnic minorities to conform to Turkish culture. Ethnic populations are therefore hard to tabulate.
Turks 76.1–81.1%. A Central Asian people that conquered and largely absorbed the indigenous peoples of the land from the eleventh century onward. The Turks are ethnically diverse, but culturally fairly homogeneous. Distinctive sub-groups: Azeri 530,000 in the east, Crimean Tatar 400,000, Yoruk 320,000 on the west coast.
Kurds 14–19%. (The Kurds claim 21–25%). An Indo-Iranian people in southeast Anatolia, probably related to the ancient Medes. Many Kurds use Turkish as their primary language. Main language groups: Kurmanji 5,000,000; Kirmanjki 1,500,000; Dimli (Zaza) 1,000,000.
Arabs 1.6% in South Anatolia adjoining Syria.
Muslim minorities 1.8%. Gypsy (Turkish, Arjila, Domari) 355,000; Kabardian (Circassian) 202,000; Adyghe 130,000; Laz 92,000; Pomak Bulgarian 70,000; Albanian 65,000; Bosnian 50,000; Abkhazian 35,000.
Refugees 1.3%. Iranians 500,000; Bulgarian Turks 200,000; Central Asians 50,000.
Non-Muslim minorities 0.2%. Armenian 45,000; Jews 20,000; Assyrian 10,000; Greek 4,000. Rapid decline through emigration. Note religious graph. There were 1,750,000 Armenians and 1,500,000 Greeks in Turkey in 1900.

Literacy 76%. **Official language:** Turkish. **All languages** 35. **Languages with Scriptures:** 6Bi 4NT 13por.

Capital: Ankara 2,560,000. Other major cities: Istanbul (Constantinople) 7,200,000; Izmir (Smyrna) 1,757,000; Adana 916,000; Bursa 835,000. Urbanization 45%. Rapid growth of cities.

Economy: Tourism, agriculture and industry are all important to the economy; rapid development in '80s. It is self-sufficient in agriculture. Remittances from the 2.5 million Turks working in Western Europe are a significant source of foreign exchange.

The collapse of the USSR in 1990 and Turkey's subsequent cultural and economic ties with Central Asian Turkic republics (Azerbaijan, Kazakhstan, Kyrgyzstan, Turkmenistan, Uzbekistan) are of deep future significance. Turkey is, at the same time, one of Europe's poorer nations and the richest and most developed of the six Turkic nations of Central Asia. Unemployment est 20%. Foreign debt/person $611. Income/person $1,360 (6.2% of USA).

Politics: The Turkish Ottoman Empire once stretched across North Africa, Arabia, Western Asia and Southeast Europe. Its demise and final fragmentation in World War I led to revolution and the formation of a republic in 1923. Periods of social disorder and military rule led to a return to a democratic government in 1983, but with the military still retaining considerable influence. Turkey is a member of NATO, but is in dispute with fellow NATO member, Greece, for long-standing historic reasons and over territorial rights in the Aegean Sea and the division of Cyprus. Suppression of the large Kurdish minority has been moderated, but an intensifying guerrilla war fought by a Marxist Kurdish liberation movement since 1985 has disrupted life in the east of Anatolia. Turkey's cultural links with Central Asia and proximity to conflicts in Iraq and the Balkans have enhanced Turkey's strategic importance.

Religion: Turkey's Ottoman Empire was for centuries the guardian of all the holy places of Islam and its chief protagonist. Since the sweeping reforms of the 1920s Turkey has officially been a secular state. In recent years Islam has become a more important political factor, making the lot of non-Muslim minorities more difficult despite the constitutional guarantee of religious freedom.
Muslim 99.8%. Sunni Muslims 83%. Alevi Shi'a 14% predominantly among Zaza Kurds. Shi'a 2% among Azeri and Iranians. There are also Yezidis among the Kurds.
Jews 0.04%.
Christian 0.2%. Rapid decline. Almost entirely confined to national and foreign minorities. Growth −6.5%.
Protestant 0.02%. Growth 0.8%.

Church	Cong	Members	Affiliated
Foreign Protestants	32	3,500	10,000
Minority Indig Groups	17	950	1,700
All other (2)	4	520	864
Denominations (4)	53	4,970	12,564
Evangelicals 0.01% of pop		1,700	3,500

Christian expatriates approx. 350 (1:160,000 people).

T

Catholic 0.03%. Growth 0%.				Jehovah's Witnesses	14	1,013	1,690
Cath – Eastern rite (6)	24	6,600	11,000	All groups (3)		2,063	3,590
Cath – Latin rite	13	3,600	6,000				
Total	37	10,200	17,000				
Christian expatriates 240 (1:240,000 people).							
Orthodox 0.13%. Growth –10.7%.							
Armenian Orthodox	35	27,000	45,000				
Assyrian Orthodox	24	6,000	10,000				
Greek Orthodox	11	4,900	7,000				
All other (7)		6,000	10,000				
Denominations (10)	70	43,900	72,000				
Marginal 0.01%. Growth 1.2%.							

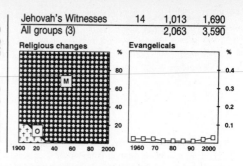

Religious changes — Evangelicals

1. **Turkey remains the largest unreached nation in the world.** Once a bastion of Christianity, it became a strong propagator of Islam. The Christian population has declined from 22% to 0.2% since 1900 – most of these Christians being non-Turkish. Few of the 55 million Muslims have ever heard the gospel.

2. **Turkey is a nation torn in opposite directions.** Some seek closer ties with the West and membership in the EC; Islamists desire to develop links with the Muslim world, and nationalists with Central Asia. The constitution and the judiciary are predominantly secular and support religious freedom, but the majority of the politicians, police and also the growing Muslim fundamentalist movement are aggressively hostile to anything Christian. Pray for the wise provisions of the constitution to be upheld and for all attempts to restrict religious freedom to be frustrated.

3. **The barriers of prejudice and hatred of the gospel can appear insurmountable.** Pray for the following barriers to be broken down:
a) **History.** Turkey's long association with Islam and bitter wars with "Christian" European nations make conversion appear almost an act of treachery.
b) **Culture.** To be a Turk is to be a Muslim, even if nominally so. Fear of family pressure, police intimidation and threats from Muslim extremists keeps many from coming to Christ.
c) **Attitude.** A deep-seated resistance in the general public to anything Christian makes any form of witnessing difficult. A radical change in public attitudes must be prayed for.
d) **Wrong understandings.** Evangelical Christians are lumped together with Armenian terrorists and Jehovah's Witnesses. Sensational articles in the Press spread untruths about Christians, further inflaming public opinion. Muslim misconceptions about Christian doctrine present another major barrier.
e) **The violent suppression of Christian minorities.** The turbulence and political instability before and after World War I brought about widespread violence and forced deportation for many Armenians. Armenian nationalists, urged on by Russian agents, fought for a homeland. The horrific Turkish response resulted in the virtual elimination of Armenians through expulsions or massacres. Some estimate 1.5 million died. Pray that the cloud of prejudice and darkness might be lifted and many might find joy and peace in the forgiveness offered by the Lord Jesus.

4. **The Christian Church** as a whole is declining because of the emigration of Armenians, Greeks and Assyrians who are predominantly members of the ancient eastern Churches. There is revival within the Armenian Orthodox Church. Christians are often regarded as second-class citizens because of their ethnic and religious background. Evangelical believers are few – possibly 800 among ethnic minorities and 500–600 Turks or Kurds. However, there is significant growth in indigenous fellowships which is cause for praise.

5. **Praise God for the emergence of a Turkish Church.** In 1960 there were less than 10 known believers; today there are 12 Turkish-speaking fellowships with around 500 Turkish believers. The exciting news of 4,000 or more new believers among Turks and Turkish-speaking Gypsies in neighbouring Bulgaria has raised expectations of harvest in Turkey. Pray for:
a) **Turkish leaders** as they seek to work together to establish their own identity and plan their own future – the high proportion of expatriates among believers can inhibit this. A national advisory board of Turkish leaders was established in 1990.
b) **Believers** who are often isolated, fearful of pressure from family and friends, and suspicious of other believers. Most go through a severe identity crisis after coming to Christ. Backsliding has been common, compromise in marrying non-Christians frequent, and relationship breakdowns

between believers disheartening. Pray for warm, caring fellowships that provide encouragement, a sense of belonging, and joyful worship.

c) **Perseverance.** Emigration is often a way to escape persecution, find a good paying job, or find a foreign marriage partner. A strong, growing Church must become a reality in Turkey.

d) **Courage in persecution.** A wave of arrests of believers in 1988 led to harassment and interrogation, but every charge brought to court was dismissed or the defendants acquitted, thereby encouraging the believers to be more assertive in claiming their civil rights.

e) **Boldness in witness.** Increasingly, Turkish believers take on the work initiated by expatriates and also start new ministries. Pray for a vision to see a living congregation planted in every province of Turkey.

f) **Legal recognition.** This is slowly being gained through a number of court cases, but equality for all religions is yet to be obtained.

g) **Leadership training** which is difficult to provide in Turkey; a TEE programme has started in Ankara and Istanbul, and a Bible school in Istanbul.

6. **Missionary work** began in 1821, but was soon directed to the more receptive non-Muslim minorities as a means of reaching the majority. Since 1960 renewed prayer and effort is slowly yielding fruit among Muslims. All expatriates have long lived under the threat of police harassment and expulsion from the country, but earlier expulsions were quashed and declared illegal in three court cases in 1992. Pray for:

a) **Those called,** equipped and gifted for tentmaking ministries in this land where vital opportunities to share one's faith are hard to find.

b) **The right ministry opportunities** and strategy that will enable the whole country to be exposed to the gospel. Most are engaged in teaching, study, or business, or on tourist visas.

c) **The right relationship** with indigenous believers – too many foreigners in an area can stifle the development of mature leadership.

d) **The 20 or so agencies** with a specific burden and calling to minister to Turks, and for the continuance of fruitful cooperation among them.

e) **Vision for the evangelization of the whole land.** For years little was done for eastern Anatolia, the Black Sea coast or the interior provinces. Pray for the implementation of strategies for their evangelization.

7. **Other means of witness** are profitably employed, and need prayerful support:

a) **Literature.** About five million pieces of literature have been distributed over the past few years in door-to-door work, postal evangelism, advertisements in the Press, etc. **Call of Hope, Friends of Turkey,** and **OM** have done much to develop this ministry. Pray for fruit and for the development of effective follow-up.

b) **Postal evangelism.** Through pen-pal letters, magazines and broadsheets a growing response has been produced. 250,000 "gospel letters" were sent in 1992 alone. Requests for Bible Correspondence Courses have escalated to over 500 every month. Turkish believers have set up the *Holy Books Research Association* as a route to obtain legal recognition for BCC ministry. Pray that this may be granted.

c) **Christian radio programmes,** broadcast by five international stations – **FEBA,** High Adventure, **IBRA** (now on medium wave from Russia), **TWR** and ECR-Italy. The 12 hours/week are mainly in Turkish, some in Azerbaijani and Kurmanji. Pray for favourable reception in radios and hearts.

d) **Ministry to the 2.5 million Turks and Kurds in Western Europe.** Migrant labourers in Germany (1,684,000), France (190,000), Netherlands (192,000), United Kingdom (150,000), Austria (90,000), Belgium (82,000), Switzerland (66,000) and Sweden (30,000) are far more accessible to Christian workers. A number of local churches and international agencies are seeking to evangelize them, but local hostility to migrant workers does not help this outreach. Among such are **OM, WEC, Friends of Turkey** and *Orientdienst*. There are possibly 100 converted Turks as a result of this ministry. There is also a work among the 51,000 Turks in Australia. Pray for the multiplication of Turkish and Kurdish Christian groups in these areas and for these to make an impact on their homelands.

e) **Ministry to Turks in the Balkans.** There are opportunities for ministry among Turkish minorities in Bulgaria (1,100,000), Macedonia/Serbia (250,000), Romania (150,000) and Greece (140,000). The opening up of Bulgaria and Bulgarian Turks to the gospel may be of great significance for the Church in Turkey. Over 5,000 Turks and Turkish-speaking Gypsies have come to Jesus through spontaneous and miraculous events since the late '80s. Pray for ministry directed to teaching and mobilizing these believers.

f) **Use of audio-visual media.** Cassette and video tapes are valuable tools, but more good relevant materials must be produced and distributed – some are actively working to do this. After years of effort, the *Jesus* film was approved by the censors. Pray for wide circulation and deep impact as it is distributed in video shops, and pray that it may be shown on national television.

8. **Unreached peoples:** For years the few Turkish Christian groups were limited primarily to Istanbul and Ankara with a small presence in Izmir (Smyrna in the NT) and Adana. This is changing, and small groups are emerging in other centres. Specific challenges to prayer:

a) **The goal of a living, growing fellowship of believers** in every one of the 71 provinces – possibly only nine have such. Especially needing prayer are the turbulent eastern Anatolian provinces and the Black Sea coastal provinces, where the Kurdish and Laz peoples live.

b) **The Kurds** are a majority in east and southeast Turkey. Suppression of their language and political aspirations as well as the violent secessionist movement has made specific outreach in Kurdish a sensitive matter, but the Kurdish language was legalized in 1991. Many Kurds in the north of their area are followers of Alevi teachings (which give high regard to the Lord Jesus Christ) and are only nominally Muslim; some are Yezidis (a religion based on Zoroastrianism involving occultism). There may be now 200 or more Christians. Pray for those tactfully seeking to reach out to them, translate the Scriptures and provide literature, the *Jesus* film and radio and cassette materials in Kurmanji and Dimili, both inside and outside the country. About 25% of all Turks in Western Europe are, in fact, Kurds.

c) **The ethnic Muslim minorities** listed under **Peoples** above. None of these peoples have been evangelized; many live in communities, though use of their languages is declining.

d) **Iranian refugees** who fled the violence and Islamic extremism of the 1979 Revolution. Up to 500,000 still remain in the country – many in Istanbul, while many others have moved on to Western countries. There has been a response to the gospel in Istanbul and Ankara and small Farsi-speaking congregations established.

e) **Central Asian refugees** from Communism; many are from the unevangelized areas of Afghanistan and the former USSR. There are Uzbeks, Kazakhs, Kyrgyz, Tatars, Turkmen and others.

f) **University students.** There are 500,000 students in 343 universities and colleges, but there is no specific campus ministry, though a number of students have come to the Lord.

9. **Bible translation** is a vital ministry. Two versions of the Turkish New Testament were published in 1988/89. Both have proved popular, and there is an annual distribution of 25,000 copies. Pray for the completion of the new version of the Old Testament. Translation into minority languages is a sensitive issue – most of the ongoing 14 translation projects are furthered in the West or in surrounding lands.

10. **Christian literature** may be legally written, printed and distributed, but negative publicity, official intimidation, obstructionism and restrictions make life difficult for all involved. The Bible Society has a bookstore in Istanbul and is able to distribute Bibles and Christian literature to secular bookstores. There are several Turkish Christian publishing houses established, and the quantity and variety of books available are increasing, but the greatest need is for mother-tongue writers to produce culturally relevant literature. By 1993 there were 40 book titles available, but more literature written by national believers is needed.

T

Turkmenistan

<table>
<tr><td>November
6</td></tr>
<tr><td>Eurasia</td></tr>
</table>

Area 488,000 sq.km. Two populated strips of irrigated land on its northern and southern borders separated by the barren Kara-Kum Desert. 80% of the republic is desert, 1% irrigated arable land.

Population	Ann.Gr.	Density
1990 3,622,000	2.2%	7.4/sq.km
1995 4,039,000	2.3%	8.3/sq.km

Peoples: Numerous ethnic minorities from all over the former USSR are represented.
Turkic/Altaic 86%. Turkmen 2,537,000; Uzbek 317,000; Kazakh 88,000; Tatar 39,000; Azerbaijani 33,000.
Indo-European 13.9%.
  Slav 10%. Russian 334,000; Ukrainian 36,000.
  Iranian 2.3%. Baloch 28,000; Persian 8,000.
  Other peoples 1.6%. Armenian 32,000; Lezgin 10,400.
All other peoples 0.1%.

Literacy 50%. **Official language:** Turkmen using Cyrillic script, but changing to Latin-based as used in Turkey. **All indigenous languages** 2. **Languages with Scriptures** 1NT 1por.

Capital: Ashkhabad 407,000. Urbanization 45%.

Economy: Famed for its carpets, camels and desert, but oil and gas production are the major sources of wealth, followed by production of cotton. The country is almost entirely dependent on water from the Amu Darya River, which is already over-used. Gas and oil revenues have prevented economic collapse and perpetuated Marxist economic structures. Trade and communication link being proffered by Iran, which exerts an increasing influence on the country. The majority of the population is poor and suffering health problems because of pollution. Income/person $700 (3.3% of USA).

Politics: Nomadic tribal past; only united as a country under Russian Tsarist rule in 1881. A Soviet Republic until independence in 1990. The shock of unexpected independence has frozen the state structures. The Communist Party changed its name to become the Democratic Party. The leaders are having difficulty coming to terms with independence and what degree of freedom to grant the people.

Religion: Government policy is a secular state with freedom of belief. Islamization proceeds, but at a slow pace. The government leans more to Turkey than to Iran in religious preference. Figures below are estimates.
Muslim 76%. Almost all Turkmen are Sunni; those in Iran are Shi'a. Sufi secret sects are strong.
Non-religious/other 18.2%. Many non-Turkic, some Turkic peoples.
Jews 0.07%.
Christian 5.7%. Nom. 2%. Affil 3.7%.
Growth −1.2%.
  Protestant 0.01%. Growth −2.7%.

Church	Cong	Members	Affiliated
Baptist Ch	3	80	200
All other (2)	1	110	265
Denominations (3)	4	190	465
Evangelicals 0.01% of pop		900	465

  Catholic 0.1%.
  Orthodox 5.6%. Affil 3.66%. Growth −1 2%.

Russian Orthodox		70,000	100,000
Armenian Apostolic Ch		18,900	27,000
All other (1)		3,850	5,500
Denominations (3)		92,750	132,500

  Marginal 0.01%.

1. **Turkmenistan** is still not fully open for the gospel. Pray that there may be full religious freedom and opportunity for people to hear the gospel.

2. **Islamization of the state** continues apace as links with neighbouring Iran become closer. Pray for this land to be delivered from another tyranny.

3. **Christians are few** and mainly Russian, Ukrainian or Armenian. Their numbers are decreasing through emigration. Pray that the few evangelical believers may be more free to witness and reach out to the unevangelized majority. There is only a handful of Turkmen believers known.

4. **The land is for the first time opening for the gospel.** There is a group of evangelical agencies cooperating for the evangelization of the Turkmen people. Pray for an even greater open door for entry of expatriates to serve in this land.

5. **Witness by other means.**
a) **The *Jesus* film** and video is available in Turkmen, and it is gaining a good response. Pray for its showing widely across the country.

b) **Bible translation.** The New Testament was published in 1993, and parts of the Old Testament are in draft form. Pray for its distribution – not so easy at this time.

c) **There are no radio broadcasts** yet in the Turkmen language.

<table>
<tr><td>See
Caribbean

Caribbean</td><td colspan="2"><h1>Turks and Caicos Islands</h1>(Colony of Turks and Caicos Islands)</td><td></td></tr>
</table>

Area 430 sq.km. An archipelago of 30 coral islands at the southeastern end of the Bahamas.

Population		Ann. Gr.	Density
1990	9,351	2.9 %	22/sq.km
1995	10,730	2.4 %	25/sq.km

Peoples:
Afro-Caribbean 95%. Including a growing number of Haitian refugees.
Euro-American 5%.

Literacy 87%. **Official language:** English.

Capital: Cockburn Town 3,200. Urbanization 60%.

Economy: Until 1986, the islands were a major staging post for shipping drugs to the USA, and also for laundering the financial profits. Tourism, offshore financial services, and fishing are the main legal sources of income. Income/person $4,510 (21% of USA).

Politics: A dependency of the United Kingdom with considerable local autonomy until 1986. Direct rule was imposed by Britain for two years to combat drug-related corruption in the government.

Religion:
Non-Religious/other 1%.
Christian 99%. Nom 21.4%. Affil 77.6%. Growth 1.8%.
Protestant 84.5%. Affil 63.6%. Growth 1.4%.

Church	Cong	Members	Affiliated
Baptist Union	13	511	1,280
Methodist Ch	4	480	960
Anglican Ch	3	322	870
Ch of God of Prophecy	6	250	490
NT Ch of God (Cleveland)	2	153	340
All Other (2)	13	1,080	2,117
Denominations (7)	41	2,796	6,057
Evangelicals 37% of pop		1,600	3,500
Pentecostal/charis 15.6%		700	1,500

Roman Catholic 12%. Affil 11.5% Gr 1.9%.

Catholic Ch	3	770	1,100

Missionaries to Turks & Caicos 1 (1:10,300 people).
Marginal 2.5% Growth 14.8%.

Jehovah's Witnesses	1	72	240

1. The corruption and drug scandals rocked the church-going islanders. Pray that Christian values may permeate every level of society.

T

Tuvalu

(The State of Tuvalu)

See Pacific
Pacific

Area 26 sq.km. Nine low coral atolls in the central Pacific, eight of which are inhabited.

Population	Ann. Gr.	Density
1990 9,100	2.0 %	350/sq.km
1995 9,900	1.7 %	380/sq.km

Peoples:
Indigenous 96.6%. Polynesian 91.2%; Euro-Polynesian 5.4%.
Other 3.4%. Kiribati 100; Micronesian, British, Chinese.

Literacy 96%. **Official languages:** English, Tuvalu.

Capital: Fongatela 2,120.

Economy: Main sources of income are from fishing licences, postage stamps, an international trust fund and remittances from the 1,500 Tuvaluans who live outside the country. Income/person $420 (2% of USA).

Politics: independent from Britain in 1978 as a parliamentary monarchy.

Religion: Strongly Protestant; other religions not granted freedom until 1964.
Baha'i 3.4%.
Christian 96.6%. Growth 2%.
  Protestant 93.8%. Growth 1.8%.

Church	Cong	Members	Affiliated
Tuvalu Ch	12	3,270	8,164
Seventh-day Adventist	1	192	274
Pentecostal groups (2)	3	65	100
Denominations (4)	15	3,527	8,538
Evangelicals 5% of pop		210	450
Pentecostal/charis 1.1%		65	100

Missionaries to Tuvalu 2 (1:4,500 people).
Roman Catholic 1.1%. Growth 4.4%.
Missionaries to Tuvalu 1 (1:9,900 people).
Marginal 1.7%. Growth 13.3%.

Jehovah's Witnesses	1	50	152

1. **Tuvalu** may be the first nation to disappear as a result of global warming and the rise in the level of the oceans. Pray that the uncertainty of the future may bring spiritual earnestness.

2. **The Tuvalu Church** (Congregational) is, in effect, the established church; nominalism and tradition are brakes on spiritual life and fervour. The new work of **AoG** and Church of God of Prophecy is the only distinctly evangelical ministry on the islands. Pray for spiritual life for all groups.

T

November 7–8	*Uganda*
Africa	(Republic of Uganda)

Area 241,000 sq.km. Much of the land is fertile and well-watered. The climate is temperate in the highlands. Long known as the "Pearl of Africa".

Population	Ann. Gr.	Density
1990	18,442,000	3.5 %	77/sq.km
1995	22,012,000	3.6 %	91/sq.km

No one can estimate with accuracy the numbers who perished during Amin's dictatorship and the subsequent civil wars, famines and tribal killings. Estimates vary from 800,000 to 2,000,000. The long-term effects of AIDS on the population are likely to be devastating; above numbers and growth-rate estimates could be significantly affected.

Peoples. Over 55 ethnic groups; four major divisions:
Bantu 65.6%. Largest: Ganda 3,015,000; Nyankore 1,643,000; Kiga 1,391,000; Soga 1,370,000; Gisu (Masaba) 751,000; Nyoro 495,000; Tooro 488,000; Nkonjo 364,000; Nyarwanda (Tutsi/Hutu) 358,00; Gwere 278,000; Dama 247,000; Nyole 229,000.
Nilotic 28.2%. Largest: Iteso 1,021,000; Lango 978,000; Acholi 735,000; Alur 420,000; Karamojong 346,000; Khumam 113,000; Kakwa 87,000.
Sudanic 4.7%. Largest: Lugbara 589,000; Madi 179,000; Sabiny 110,000.
Other 1.5%. Zairois, Rwandan, Kenyan, Sudanese, etc.
Refugees. Many Zairois and Sudanese arrived in 1992.

Literacy 57%. **Official language:** English. **All languages** 43. **Languages with Scriptures** 16Bi 4NT 8por.

Capital: Kampala 773,000. Urbanization 10%.

Economy: A healthy economy in the 1960s, but spoiled by Amin's expulsion of the Asian business community in 1972, then ruined by years of warfare. Good soil and two annual growing seasons make Uganda fertile, but 90% of export income is from coffee, the value of which has halved in three years. Attempts to reduce military spending and curb corruption have had meagre success. The death rate from AIDS among people of working age will have a serious effect on the economy. Public debt/person $161. Income/person $250 (1.2% of USA).

Politics: Independent from Britain in 1962. An attempt to delicately balance the political powers of the southern Bantu kingdoms and northern Nilotic peoples ended in 1967, when the northerner Milton Obote took complete control, favouring his own tribe, the Lango. Anarchy increased until Idi Amin seized power in 1971. The crazed dictatorship of Amin brutalized the country as the army pillaged and murdered with impunity. Amin's invasion of north-west Tanzania in 1978 provoked a vigorous response, and in 1979 Tanzanian and Ugandan exile troops deposed the military regime, restoring Obote to power. Continued inter-tribal warfare and government incompetence racked the country. Yoweri Museveni gained power in 1986 and has gradually brought a measure of stability unknown for 25 years. A paternalistic partial democracy, but with the large army wielding considerable influence. A new constitution was being hotly debated in 1993, and a full-fledged multi-party system will probably soon be adopted.

Religion: Under Amin there were restrictions and intense persecution of Christians. For a time the Muslim minority was favoured. There is now freedom of religion. Most figures below are estimates:
Traditional religions 5.9%. Throughout the country, but a majority in four or five northeastern peoples, the Karamojong, Pokot, etc.
Muslim 8%. Most live in the northwest, but some are sprinkled all over the country. No group has a Muslim majority, but there are large minorities among the Kakwa, Madi and Soga.
Baha'i 2.7%.
Christian 83.4%. Nom 13.8%. Affil 69.6%. Growth 4.2%.
Protestant 30%. Affil 27.6%. Growth 4.6%.

Church	Cong	Members	Affiliated
Anglican Ch	20,000	1,040,000	4,500,000
Pente Assemb of God (**PAoC**)	700	52,000	130,000
Seventh-day Adventist	399	65,000	110,000
Elim Pentecostal Fell	1,125	45,000	100,000
Ch of the Redeemed	400	40,000	80,000
Deliverance Church	120	18,000	36,000
Ch of God (Anderson)	262	12,000	30,000
Baptist Ch of U	360	11,000	22,000
Assemblies of God	30	1,900	3,050
All other (25)	764	35,412	80,693
Denominations (34)	24,160	1,320,312	5,091,743
Evangelicals 24.7% of pop		1,161,000	4,547,000
Pentecostal/charis 5.9%		336,000	1,080,000

Missionaries:
to Uganda 382 (1:48,200 people) in 75 agencies.
from Uganda 920 (1:5,500 Protestants) in 11 agencies 20frn 23xcul 897dom.
Roman Catholic 52%. Affil 40.7%. Growth 3.7%.

Catholic Ch	3,288	4,280,000	7,500,000	

Missionaries:
 to Uganda 779 (1:23,700 people).
 from Uganda 110 (1973 figure).
Orthodox 0.14%. Growth 4.4%.
Denominations (2)   15,000   25,000
Foreign Marginal 0.02%. Growth 22.3%.
Jehovah's Witnesses   19   999   4,000
Indigenous Marginal 1.19%. Growth 10.2%.
All groups (est. 40)   121,000   220,000

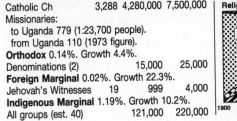

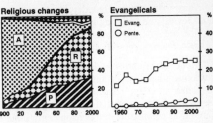

1. **Uganda, famed for revival, has suffered a spectacular moral collapse.** The devastation of 20 years of unrestrained terror, murder, tribal warfare and corruption destroyed much of the social fabric of the nation and hastened the spread of the AIDS virus to an estimated 25–30% of the population by 1992. Uganda has the highest known incidence of this terrible disease of any nation in the world. Only a spiritual transformation can reverse present trends. Pray for this.

2. **Praise God for the impact of the East African Revival over a period of 60 years.** It brought new life and evangelical fervency to the large Anglican Church, and in the '80s fresh growth and spiritual life in the smaller and younger Pentecostal, Baptist and charismatic groups. The centrality of Christ expressed in the stressing of repentance, brokenness and walking in the light kept the fire of revival burning, but divisions have arisen over teaching on spiritual warfare, worship and spiritual gifts. Pray for evidence of the fruit of the Spirit – especially humility. Pray also for the Decade of Evangelism launched by the Church of Uganda (Anglican) and African Evangelistic Enterprise (**AE**).

3. **The '70s were a time of terrible persecution for Christians.** Nominalism, formalism and failure to check tribalism in the churches prevented the Church from unitedly standing for the truth. The result was the banning of many smaller denominations, destruction of many churches and institutions, heavy loss of life among Christians and the loss through murder and exile of some of Uganda's finest Christian leaders. These sufferings brought many believers back to renewed commitment and earnest prayer, but also left a legacy of problems that need prayerful resolution:
    a) **Forgiveness for perpetrators of the suffering**; bitterness and backsliding have harmed the spiritual life of many Christians.
    b) **Reconciliation among Christians.** The sharp divisions between Protestant and Catholic, revived and non-revived, charismatic and non-charismatic have not been a credit to the gospel.
    c) **Facing up to tribalism**; much of the anarchy of recent years was caused by inter-ethnic hatreds. This also infected the Church.
    d) **Dealing with nominalism.** Most of the population claims to be Christian, but the continuation of polygamy and widespread promiscuity belies this claim. Pray for evangelism and discipleship to have high priority in churches.
    e) **Training of a new generation of leaders.** The Bishop Tucker Theological College, once strongly evangelical, has some liberal teachers on the faculty. There are several Pentecostal Bible schools and a Baptist Seminary. **YWAM** has the vision of providing short-term training for 2,000 by the year 2000 in their Discipleship Training School. Pray for the provision of spiritual, godly leaders.

4. **The AIDS disaster** is of such magnitude that the breakdown of economic life and society is threatened. Some project that by 1997 one-third of Uganda's population may die or have developed full-blown AIDS symptoms. Much of the economically active population could be wiped out. It is estimated that war created 800,000 orphans, but now AIDS could create many more. Pray for:
    a) **The churches to promote and live out Christian chastity** before marriage and faithfulness in marriage as the only acceptable life style.
    b) **Christian education and help ministries** to destitute orphans and old people as well as to victims of the AIDS pandemic. Government policy is now for chastity outside marriage, loyalty within it.
    c) **Various expatriate agencies** who are also playing an important role.

5. **Ministry to young people** is fundamental for rebuilding the country in the wake of the devastation of AIDS. Pray for the extensive ministry of **SU** in schools and for FOCUS(**IFES**) in Makerere University (where the Christian Union has a membership of 500 among the 9,000 students) with also a developing ministry in other colleges through the five staff workers. Life Ministry (**CCC**), with eight workers on the university campus, disciples faculty and students and challenges those with the maturity for involvement in world missions. Pray also for effective youth programmes in churches – not a priority in the past.

6. Missionaries from Uganda. The large number of committed Christians and the experience of both revival and suffering give Ugandans a unique basis to share the gospel elsewhere. A growing number are serving abroad – most short-term (Life Ministries). Pray for UEMA (Uganda Evangelical Mission Agency) recently formed to send missionaries to full-time service abroad.

7. Most missionaries had to leave the country during Amin's dictatorship. Many have been welcomed back. Uganda's economic and social condition makes for many opportunities for expatriate Christian ministry. The dominance of Western agencies belongs to the past, so pray for a close fellowship between expatriates and Ugandan believers and the calling of those eager to serve the Church in reconstruction, development, Bible training and other ministries. Some of the larger missions: **CMS** (54 workers), **SBC** (24), Finnish and Swedish Pentecostals (23), **TEAR Fund** (16), **YWAM** (15 and 53 nationals), **MAF** (8), **CCC** (6 and 54 nationals). Major missionary-contributing countries: USA (149), UK (106), Kenya (39), Sweden (17), Canada (17).

8. Outreach challenges. Much of the country has been well evangelized, but pray for these peoples:
a) **The northeast peoples** – Karamojong, Pokot and Jie, who are only partially-reached nomadic peoples. In the last few years many Karamojong have turned to the Lord after years of vicious tribal warfare and severe cattle disease. The big challenge is to plant viable congregations that fit the life style of a semi-nomadic people.
b) **Muslim communities.** These are scattered across the country and have become aggressive in winning non-Muslims. Arab states are pouring large sums of money into education. The Muslim University in Kampala is one part of their strategy. There have been few converts to Christ – and those that have been saved have suffered persecution. Few Christians have taken up the challenge of ministry to them.
c) **Ministry to refugees.** There remain 87,600 Rwandan refugees in the southwest – the source of the ongoing civil war in Rwanda. There is a growing flood of Sudanese refugees fleeing the civil war and famine in that land. The Ugandan Church must play an increasing role in ministering to these people.

9. Christian support ministries.
a) **Christian literature** is in great demand, but poverty and lack of local supplies, facilities and foreign exchange limit its availability.
b) **Bible translation** is an unfinished task. Seven languages are identified as needing a New Testament translation team – but this could rise to 12 on further research. There are teams working on 10 New Testaments. **SIL** have sent their first five translators to Uganda.
c) **The *Jesus* film** is being widely shown in Ateso, Luganda, Lugbara, Lunyoro and Lunyankole.
d) **MAF** has a valuable ministry in flying Christian workers and aid – especially in the dry northeast.
e) **Christian radio and TV programmes** are aired on the national network and are widely appreciated. Pray for effective programming and lasting fruit.

U

Ukraine

November 9–10
Eurasia

Area 604,000 sq.km. Formerly the granary of the USSR. A flat, fertile, forested plain with no natural borders.

Population	Ann.Gr.	Density
1990 51,820,000	0.74%	86/sq.km
1995 53,770,000	0.50%	89/sq.km

Europe's fifth most populous nation.

Peoples: 1989 figures.
Indo-European 97.8%.
 Slav 96.3%. Ukrainian 37,419,000; Russian 11,355,000; Byelorussian 440,000; Bulgarian 234,000; Polish 219,000.
 Other 1.5%. Moldavian/Romanian 460,000; Greek 99,000; Armenian 54,000; Gypsy 48,000; German 38,000 (increasing); Georgian 24,000.
Turkic/Altaic 0.8%. Tatar 87,000; Crimean Tatar 46,000 (rising to 200,000 by 1993).
All other peoples 1.4%. Jews 487,000; Hungarian 187,000; Mordvinian 19,000.

Literacy 99%. **Official languages:** None. Ukrainian and Russian widely spoken. **All indigenous languages** 9. **Languages with Scriptures** 5Bi 1NT 2por.

Capital: Kiev 2,635,000. Other major cities: Khar'kov 1,587,000; Dnepropetrovsk 1,182,000; Odessa 1,141,000; Donetsk 1,090,000; Lviv (Lvov) 767,000. Urbanization 60%.

Economy: An important industrial and agricultural power. Rich reserves of coal, iron ore, oil and natural gas. 50% of USSR's total agriculture production was from Ukraine. After a faltering and painful start to economic reform, the economy collapsed with hyper-inflation in 1992 with reduction to a partially barter economy. By 1993 the government had had to reverse policy and is working hard to establish a viable market economy.

Politics: For centuries Ukraine has been dominated and fought over by the Russians, Lithuanians, Poles, French and Germans. Independence was declared in 1991, signalling the end of all hope of retaining even a modified form of the USSR. The Ukrainian Communist Party was banned, its leaders switched to become nationalists, but the old state apparatus and bureaucracy remained in place within the multi-party democratic system. Long-term commitment to reforms, the future of its large stockpile of nuclear weapons, the status of Crimea and the large Russian minority are issues that will soon have to be faced.

Religion: The Church was severely persecuted under Communism. Freedom of religion since 1990.
Non-religious/other 25.5%.
Jews 0.94%. Many emigrating to Israel and the West.
Muslim 0.47%. Mainly Turkic peoples.
Shamanist/animist 0.1%.
Christian 73%. Nom 7.9%. Affil 65%. Growth 8.5%.
Protestant 3.2%. Growth 9.2%.

Church	Cong	Members	Affiliated
Ev. Chr & Baptists (3)	1,400	162,000	492,000
Pentecostal Union	900	100,000	333,000
Unregd Pentecostals	700	80,000	320,000
Reformed Ch	95	130,000	200,000
Seventh-day Adventist	230	69,000	138,000
Other Pentecostal (5)	100	25,000	100,000
Lutheran Ch	16	16,300	25,000
Chrtn Charismatic Ch	30	5,000	8,330
All other (22)	72	11,945	26,363
Denominations (36)	3,543	599,245	1,642,693
Evangelicals 2.74% of pop		468,000	1,418,600
Pentecostal/charis 1.6%		230,000	819,000

Missionaries:
 to Ukraine over 48 (1:1,079,000 people) in at least 19 agencies.
 from Ukraine est. 330 (1:5,000 Protestants) 30frn 34xcul 296dom.
Catholic 15%. Affil 11.4%. Growth 7.9%.

Eastern-rite Catholic	2,000	3,710,000	5,300,000
Latin-rite Catholic	420	400,000	615,000
All Catholics	2,420	4,110,000	5,915,000

Orthodox 55%. Affil 50.3%. Gro 8.6%.

Ukrainian Ortho Ch	7,500	17,300,000	25,000,000
Autocephalous Ortho	1,200	360,000	554,000
Old Believers Ch	60	240,000	400,000
Armenian Apos Ch	3	26,000	40,000
All other (9)	2	45,900	65,800
Denominations (13)	8,765	17,971,900	26,059,800

Marginal 0.21%. Growth 11.7%.

Jehovah's Witnesses		30,000	100,000
Mormons		6,000	10,000
All groups (2)		36,000	110,000

1. **Chernobyl in north Ukraine has become known around the world.** The nuclear catastrophe that poisoned much of Europe deeply impacted Byelarus and north Ukraine with long-term consequences of apocalyptic proportions in contamination of ground, water, food and health problems. Chernobyl was the site of a massacre of Jews by the Nazis in 1942; the power station was built on the mass graves. In

Ukrainian, Chernobyl means *Wormwood* – mentioned in Revelation 8:10–11; this is an appropriate parallel that was recognized by many across the USSR. Pray that this terrible event may bring many anxious people to Christ – millions could be affected or even die as a result of the radiation.

2. **Ukraine is a key state,** a spiritual bridge between east and west. Kiev was where Russian Christianity was born 1,000 years ago. For centuries the loyalty of Ukrainians has been sought or demanded by Catholics to the West and Orthodox to the East. Most Ukrainians are of the Russian Orthodox Church, a minority of the Roman Catholic Church. Many others are of the Greek or Uniate Catholic Church, which follows the Orthodox liturgy and structure but accepts the leadership of the Pope. Under Communism the Uniates were forced underground because they refused to join the Orthodox Church, but now are free once more. Pray that spiritual life and renewal rather than power-politics may govern structures and relationships within these large bodies. Much superstition and superficiality exist, but also a spiritual minority with a love for the Scriptures.

3. **The moral and ethical vacuum created by Communism** has had devastating social consequences – deceit, fear, unwillingness to make decisions, and, with freedom, crime, drugs, murder, sexual promiscuity and pornography, have further degraded society. A deep yearning after something better has swept through the land. It has become popular to be a Christian and all churches are growing rapidly, but any sect, psychic manipulator, or evangelist can find a following. Pray that present hunger may be sated with the Word of Life rather than another spiritual bondage.

4. **Ukraine has a strong Christian heritage,** but suffering under Communism was severe. Millions of Christians were killed by collectivization or imprisoned and murdered in the *gulags* of Siberia. Pray that full freedom of religion for all groups may be enshrined in the constitution, and that Christians may jealously guard and make full use of that freedom.

5. **Evangelical Christians** have emerged stronger and more numerous from 130 years of unrelenting persecution – Ukraine was the ex-USSR's "Bible Belt" with over half its Baptists and Pentecostals. Pray that nothing may prevent the free flow of the Holy Spirit in the growing revival. The dangers:
a) **The need for full restoration and reconciliation.** Communist persecution, manipulation of leadership and blackmailing Christians to become informers has left a deep problem handling those Christians who bowed, compromised, collaborated, or even joined the persecutors. Orthodox, Catholic and Protestant Churches all face this. Pray for firmness, fairness and forgiveness in handling all who failed.
b) **Lack of unity.** Communist subterfuge brought division and chaos between registered and unregistered congregations of nearly all denominations. Since freedom came, disputes have come into the open. The registered Baptist and Pentecostal Christians were forced into one body, but have now gone their separate ways, with little fellowship or love between them. Pray for removal of prejudice, mistrust, personality clashes, and structures that prevent fellowship and promote competition – especially in tapping Western funds and aid.
c) **Lack of flexibility.** Many leaders have been made timid by unrelenting persecution, so they fear to go out aggressively to win the lost and often discourage younger believers with the vision for evangelism.
d) **The lack of resources for maximizing the present harvest.** Almost any outreach brings overwhelming response, but church buildings, discipleship materials, disciplers and basic equipment are in short supply.

6. **Good, spiritual, theological training** is the great need. Virtually no pastors in evangelical churches have had any training at all; preaching quality amply demonstrates the lack. Numerous Bible schools, evening seminars, and BEE/TEE programmes have been launched since 1989. By 1993 there were 11 residential Evangelical/Pentecostal seminaries or Bible schools functioning with a further four planned. There were also three Orthodox and two Catholic seminaries. BEE has established 25 Bible Training Institutes – one for each of the 25 regions of the country, and linked to the Association of Ukrainian Bible Training Institutes. Pray for wise, helpful coworking with expatriate bodies and staff to provide trained workers for Ukraine and all the former USSR.

7. **Expatriate agencies.** Some such as **OD, Light in the East, SGA** and many others faithfully served the persecuted church before 1989. Hundreds of others have flocked in to the country since then, but all too often with short-term goals, little cultural understanding, less consultation with others, and unimagined "wealth". Foreign ideas, methods, theological fads and empire-building methods have often harmed more than helped. Yet there is a great need for long-term workers who learn the

language and culture to serve the Ukrainian Church in Bible teaching, role-model life style in family and ministry, and helping Ukrainian missions outreach.

8. **Outreach challenges:**
a) **The middle class and educated.** These require different evangelistic initiatives and methods – a special challenge to Evangelicals, who are predominantly poor and less educated because of past restrictions on known believers.
b) **Students. IFES, CCC** and others have developed campus ministries, and student groups are multiplying. Pray for effective indigenous structures to be planted. IFES has three full-time workers.
c) **Crimea.** This was donated to Ukraine by Khruschev but differs from Ukraine. It has remained a bastion of Communism and the base of the former USSR naval fleet. Yet over 200,000 exiled **Crimean Tatars** have been welcomed back from Central Asia by Ukraine. They are all Muslims, with no known Christians. There are five Russian and Ukrainian and one Western mission seeking to reach them. The New Testament is being translated. Pray a Tatar Church into being.
d) **Ukrainian Jews.** Many have emigrated to Israel and the West. **Chosen People Ministries** have seen fruit in outreach to them.

9. **Missions vision.** Hundreds of new mission agencies have been started since 1989, some small and localized, others growing and successful – in evangelism, literature work and cross-cultural outreach. Ukrainian missionaries serve in many ex-USSR republics – even in east Siberia. One such agency is *Svet Evangelia* with missionaries serving in eastern Siberia. Pray for development and maturing of this vision.

10. **Christian media ministries** for prayer:
a) **Bible ministries.** The Ukrainian Bible Society (**UBS**) was restarted in 1991. Many realize the need of the Bible for restoration of moral and absolute values in society. The Children's Bible in Ukrainian is very popular (**IBT/OD**).
b) **Literature evangelism. EHC** plans a distribution of 13 million pieces of literature to every home.
c) **Radio and television.** These are open for Christian programmes. One series (Christian Broadcasting Network) elicited four million letters, swamping the postal system and follow-up plans. Baptismal services on television have stirred much interest.

U

November 11
Middle East

United Arab Emirates

(The United Arab Emirates)

Area 77,700 sq.km. of desert and mountains on the Arabian Gulf and the Gulf of Oman. Seven emirates: Abu Dhabi, Dubai, Sharjah, Ras al Khaimah, Ajman, Umm al Qaiwain and Fujairah.

Population		Ann. Gr.	Density
1990	1,881,000	6.9 %	24/sq.km
1995	2,176,000	3.0 %	28/sq.km

Peoples: Figures below are approximate.
Arab 76.3%.
Indigenous 30.7% including Bedouin 183,000.
Expatriate 45.6%. Lebanese 324,000; Omani 156,000; Egyptian 100,000; Saudi 95,000; Yemeni 78,000; Palestinian 64,000.
Asians 16.7%. Indians 120,000; Pakistanis 100,000; Filipinos 50,000; Baloch 20,000; Sri Lankan 20,000.
Africans 5%. Somali 100,000.
Other 2%. Iranians 20,000; Westerners 49,000.

Literacy 73%. Lower among nationals. **Official language:** Arabic. **All languages** (including expatriate communities) 20. **Languages with Scriptures** 13Bi 2NT 1por.

Capital: Abu Dhabi 730,000. Urbanization 87%.

Economy: Breathtaking advance from poverty to fabulous wealth in 20 years. Massive development schemes funded by oil wealth. Abu Dhabi has enormous oil reserves. Dubai's and Fujairah's are much smaller, and the other four emirates have little or no oil. Natural gas is also being exported. Dubai has become an important commercial and industrial centre. Rate of growth has slowed since 1978. Public debt/person $4,800. Income/person $18,430 (87% of USA).

Politics: The British-protected Trucial States became a confederation of monarchies in 1971. No political parties or elections are permitted. The Amir of Abu Dhabi is President of the Supreme Council which rules the country.

Religion: Sunni Islam is the religion of state. There is freedom to worship and witness within the expatriate communities, but no outreach to the indigenous population is officially permitted. Religious figures are estimates.
Muslim 84.6%. Sunni 67.7%. Shi'a 16.9%.
Hindu 4.7%. Mainly Indian.
Buddhist 1%. Sri Lankan, etc.
Non-religious/other 1%.
Christian 8.7%. Many nominal Christians.
Protestant 1%. Affil 0.69%.

Church	Cong	Members	Affiliated
Anglican Ch	7	1,050	3,500
TEAM	10	58	450
All other (33)	31	3,869	8,994
Denominations (35)	48	4,977	12,894
Evangelicals 0.33% of pop		2,856	6,172
Pentecostal/charis 0.04%		250	800

Expatriate Christian workers to UAE 70 (1:28,000 people).
Roman Catholic 4.5%.

Catholic Ch	12	59,500	85,000

Expatriate Christian workers to UAE 34 (1:57,000 people).
Orthodox 3.2%.

Armenian Apostolic Ch	2	3,000	5,000
All Orthodox (6)	7	11,000	55,000
Denominations (7)	9	14,000	60,000

1. **The radical changes of the last two decades** have made UAE citizens more cosmopolitan and open to new ideas, yet Islamic fundamentalism has increased restrictions. Many are in daily contact with foreign Christians, but not all believers have opportunities to share their faith because of the possible results. Pray for courage, wisdom and open hearts.

2. **Several Christian medical agencies** have been invited to serve the people – notably the **TEAM** hospital and clinic at Al Ain and a Worldwide Services maternity clinic in Fujairah. The continuance of these ministries is dependent on good relationships with the authorities. Christians serve in difficult conditions with little visible fruit. Pray that their faith for a harvest may be abundantly rewarded.

3. **Expatriate Christians** have considerable freedom for witness and worship. Pray for the many English, Arabic, Urdu, Filipino and Indian language worship groups and congregations. In a materialistic society they need grace to evangelize their own ethnic groups; there are some conversions, and some fellowships are experiencing revival. They need even more grace to evangelize across cultural barriers to unreached peoples. There are several TEE programmes active in UAE for training leaders.

4. **The unreached:**
a) **The indigenous Arab population** – both urban educated and rural illiterate have had little exposure to the gospel. Educational standards are rising rapidly, and there are 10,000 university students; most of the staff are expatriates.
b) **Many expatriate communities** – the migrant Irani (Persian, Kurd, Baloch), Pakistani (Panjabi, Pushtun and Baloch), Somalis, Sudanese and Thai have no known groups of believers among them.

5. **Media available for outreach** – several bookshops stock Christian literature. Video tapes can be widely used. Arabic broadcasts from **FEBA** Seychelles reach the UAE. Pray for the effective use of all means to evangelize all people groups.

U

United Kingdom
(United Kingdom of Great Britain and Northern Ireland)

Area 244,000 sq.km. Two main islands: Britain and the northeast of Ireland. A union of four kingdoms: England 130,400 sq.km, Scotland 78,800 sq.km, Wales 20,800 sq.km, and Northern Ireland 14,100 sq.km. Also three small autonomous states which are dependencies of the British Crown: Isle of Man 588 sq.km. (island in the Irish Sea); Guernsey 78 sq.km. (five Channel Islands); Jersey 116 sq.km. (one Channel Island).

Population		Ann. Gr.	Density
1990	57,411,000	0.19 %	235/sq.km
1995	58,210,000	0.28 %	238/sq.km

England 83.1%; Scotland 9.2%; Wales 5%; Northern Ireland 2.7%.

Peoples:
Anglo-Saxon/Celtic 92.1%. English 74.1%; Scots 8% (88,000 speaking Gaelic); Welsh 5% (580,000 speaking Welsh); Irish 5% – including the million or more Irish Republic citizens working in Britain.
Asian 4%. Indian 1,100,000 (Panjabi, Gujarati, Tamil, Malayali, Hindi); Pakistani 600,000 (Urdu, Panjabi, Pushtun); Chinese 200,000 (Cantonese, Hakka); Bangladeshi 120,000 (Bengali, Sylheti); Filipino 74,000; Vietnamese 22,000; Japanese 12,000.
Afro-Caribbean/mixed 1.7%. West Indian origin; many are British-born.
European Community 1%. Greek 200,000; Italian 200,000.
Middle Eastern 0.45%. Arabs 150,000 (Yemeni, Iraqi, Moroccan, etc.); Turks 60,000; Iranians 12,000; Kurds 6,000; Assyrians 5,000.
African 0.3%. Nigerian, Ghanaian, Somali, etc.
Other 0.75%. Jews 330,000; Gypsies 80,000 (Romany, Irish Travellers).

Literacy 97%; functional illiteracy 12%. **Official language:** English; in Wales both English and Welsh. English has become the primary language of 800 million in the world as well as the major language of international communication. **All languages** 15 indigenous, over 200 immigrant languages. **Indigenous languages with Scriptures** 7Bi 2NT. There have been more translations of the Scriptures into English than in any other language.

Capital: London 9,046,000. Other major cities: Birmingham/West Midlands 2,770,000; Manchester 2,576,000; Liverpool/Merseyside 1,448,000; Glasgow 1,391,000; Sheffield 1,306,000; Leeds/Bradford 1,173,000; Newcastle 1,140,000. Urbanization 91%.

Economy: An industrialized economy – the world's first. Decades of decline through poor management, low investment, labour unrest and high levels of public ownership. During the '80s some of these problems were resolved and reversed the trend for a few years. Recession since 1989 has brought further decline and an erosion of confidence for the future. Unemployment 10%. Public debt/person $5,500. Income/person $14,570 (69% of USA).

Politics: Parliamentary, constitutional monarchy. The UK was formed in 1801 as a Union of Great Britain and Ireland. Southern Ireland formally seceded from the Union in 1921. The British Empire, which once covered one quarter of the world, has become 60 independent states, most being members of the British Commonwealth. Since 1945 the transition from a world power to a European state linked to its own continent has not been easy. Low-level but costly and interminable IRA guerrilla insurgency has caused damage and distress in Northern Ireland and on the British mainland.

Religion: There is religious freedom. The Church of England (Anglican) is recognized as the Established Church in England, and the Church of Scotland (Presbyterian) in Scotland. The Sovereign is recognized as the titular head of the Church of England.
Non-religious/other 28%. Numerous "Christians" are secular and have no meaningful link with a church.
Muslim 2.5%. Predominantly South Asian, Middle Eastern and a few thousand indigenous British.
Sikh 0.8%. **Hindu** 0.7%.
Jews 0.6%. **Buddhist** 0.15%.
Other 0.7%. Occultists, Satanists, Hare Krishna, etc.
Christian 66.5%. Attend 11%. Growth −0.4%.
Protestant 53.2%. Growth −1.1%.

Church	Cong	Members	Affiliated
Ch of England	106,268	1,542,000	23,800,000
All Methodist Chs (6)	7,500	483,387	1,200,000
Ch of Scotland	1,700	800,000	1,000,000
Ch of Ireland	475	150,000	660,000
Baptist Union of GB	1,960	158,000	600,000
Ch in Wales (Ang)	1,178	108,431	439,000
All New Chs (20)	1,400	120,000	400,000
Presby Ch in Ireland	456	253,700	330,000
Afro-Carib Chs (166)	965	69,658	279,000
United Reformed Ch	1,800	117,900	187,000
Christian Brethren	1,537	63,200	126,000
Assemblies of God	605	48,000	107,000
Salvation Army	923	62,063	95,000

Bapt Union of Wales	560	27,700	83,900			
Presby Ch of Wales	1,034	63,214	83,000			
Scottish Episc Ch	310	36,000	80,000			
Elim Pentecostal	429	35,724	79,400			
Baptist Union of Scot	167	16,212	40,500			
Friends (Quakers)	480	18,500	30,300			
All Lutheran (6)	95	13,964	19,900			
All other (76)	6,420	365,904	646,166			

Orthodox 0.83%. Growth 4.6%.

All Orthodox (19)	205	265,258	470,000

Marginal 2.46%. Growth 8.2%.

Ch of Scientology	13	75,000	600,000
Jehovah's Witnesses	1,311	120,611	241,000
Mormons	400	97,000	149,200
All other (34)	1,595	166,357	410,200
All groups (37)	3,319	458,968	1,400,400

Denominations (290)	46,262	4,553,557	30,288,166
Evangelicals 7% of pop		2,000,000	4,000,000
Pentecostal/charis 3.5%		490,000	1,984,000

Missionaries:
to UK 1,021 (1:56,200 people) in 131 agencies (many serving in global ministries based in UK).
from UK 7,012 (1:4,300 Protestants) in 153 agencies 5,368frn 5,500xcul 1,512dom.
Roman Catholic 10%. Growth 1.4%.

Catholic Ch		4,457 1,945,626	5,700,000

Missionaries:
to UK 3,074 (1973 figure).
from UK 1,432 (1:4,000 Catholics) 1,227frn 205dom.

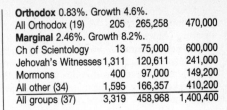

Religious changes

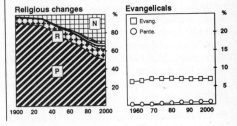

Evangelicals

UK GENERAL

1. **Britain needs prayer.** The social breakdown, economic decline and the impotence of politicians to deal with the malaise in society has also deeply affected spirituality. Areas of concern:

a) **Spiritual need** is highlighted by increasing violence in the cities, the high divorce, suicide and illegitimacy rates, and drug abuse which is paralleled by a growing number of younger people who have no contact with or knowledge of Christianity. Without a radical change disaster looms. Pray for national repentance and restoration to spiritual vigour that once made Britain a blessing to the world.

b) **Strident propaganda of New Age and eastern mystical cults** has eroded the Judeo-Christian heritage to the point that public opinion is no longer Christian. Christians have been marginalized in the media, public life, government legislation and school curricula. Religious pluralization has sapped the confidence of many Christians to testify boldly and even believe that Jesus is the *only* way to the Father. Revival is the need once more – many believe changes in recent years could herald a spiritual transformation. There has been a national awakening every century for the last 800 years; the last was in 1859–60. Pray for a greater prayer burden to unite Christians to seek that blessing.

c) **The lethargy and complacency** of Christians at the spiritual and moral collapse around them has changed to a determination by many to reverse the situation. The disastrous decline in attendances in the United Reformed, Methodist, Catholic and Anglican churches continues apace – of special concern is the loss of young people. The blanket of materialism and the television culture have deadened the sensitivity of Christian and non-Christian alike.

d) **The influx of non-Christian religions** has affected the worldview of the population. Many of the spokesmen of Islam, Buddhism, etc. push for legislation that will favour their religions, and demand freedoms they would never grant Christians in their lands of origin. Occultism, astrology, reincarnation and even Satanism have become popular, with a massive increase in literature promoting their ends. The mission field has come to Britain, but few stir themselves to win these people to Christ.

2. **The signs of hope for which praise can be offered to God.**

a) **The century-long decline** in church attendances is slowing – mostly because of the growth of the more charismatic churches and congregations, also Pentecostal, Baptist and independent churches.

b) **Traumatic social change,** increasing violence and the breakdown of moral standards before the tide of secular humanism have shocked many to realize that something has gone seriously wrong. There is a willingness among young and old to consider the claims of Christ. Pray that millions may yield to him!

c) **The renewal movement of the 1960s** brought radical changes. Charismatic renewal brought hundreds of pastors and congregations from dead liberalism and traditionalism to lively worship and a love for the Bible. Mainline churches have been affected, and a whole new family of fast-growing churches has come into being – often rather inappropriately named "house churches". These newer churches have become a significant spiritual force in the nation, deeply affecting church structures, fellowship patterns and worship style in other denominations. There are over 20 different "streams" within this movement as well as hundreds of autonomous congregations.

d) **Evangelicals** have become more committed to socio-political involvement, determined to act as "salt" and "light" in society.

3. **The future of the Church of England is crucial for the country.** This composite body is an umbrella under which Anglo-Catholics, broad churchmen, liberals and Evangelicals co-exist and where, tragically, equivocation on homosexuality, Freemasonry and the basic tenets of the Christian faith are condoned. Fragmentation of the Church over the issues of the ordination of women, ecumenism and disestablishment is possible. Yet Evangelicalism is a growing force and gaining centre stage, with 27% of bishops, 53% of clergy, 60% of ordinands, and 40% of church-goers espousing its cause. The charismatic movement has also contributed to an extensive renewal movement in the Church. Pray that the leadership of the church might regain a prophetic role and speak with clear biblical authority to a nation that is morally and spiritually adrift.

4. **Evangelical Christians** are steadily growing in numbers in contrast to overall Christian decline. Pray for:

a) **More effective outreach. The Decade of Evangelism,** launched with enthusiasm, is being mired in theological fuzziness, loss of confidence about the need to evangelize those with other religions, and apathy. Pray that dynamic leaders with vision may lead the churches into action, wrest victory from the jaws of defeat, and make an impact on the nation.

b) **Greater unity. The Evangelical Alliance** has done much to encourage cooperative programmes, outreach and fellowship. **Mission England** (1982–85) was a time of drawing many believers together. **Spring Harvest** has become one of the world's largest inter-church annual events, drawing 90,000 Christians together and thereby disseminating biblical teaching, hymnology, vision and cooperative evangelism across the denominational spectrum. **March for Jesus** has drawn a growing number of Christians onto the streets in an open commitment of faith – 200,000 in 250 centres in 1992. The **Disciple A Whole Nation** (DAWN) movement has drawn together many congregations with a church-planting vision – to double the number of Evangelicals and also double evangelical congregations to 20,000 by the end of the century.

c) **New evangelistic initiatives.** The Billy Graham and Luis Palau campaigns of the past decades have been fruitful, but innovative methods used by **Saltmine Trust, Oasis, YWAM, SU,** British **YFC** and **OM** are making more effective inroads for the gospel among the unchurched.

d) **A better biblical and theological base.** Fervour in worship and subjective experience have often been at the expense of good expository teaching and challenge to missions.

e) **A right balance between biblical separation and social involvement.** Too many Evangelicals turn a blind eye to the very real and serious social problems of the day. In the past Evangelicals have been the moving force for moral uplift and social change.

5. **Membership of the European Community** and all this implies for the future is a matter for intense public concern and debate. Pray for politicians involved in the lengthy cycle of compromises – that spirituality and witness may not be compromised too. Pray that British Christians may make full use for Christ of the mobility and religious tolerance that the EC confers.

6. **Theological training** is a key ministry. There is a shortage of trained pastors and Christian workers, but the great majority of those entering the ministry are evangelical believers. There are 78 denominational and 53 interdenominational training institutions. Evangelical denominational colleges are generally over-subscribed and bringing a stronger evangelical impact on their denominations. Pray for many university theological departments and denominational theological colleges where liberal theology is often still taught – frequently to evangelical students. Pray also for the Bible schools such as: London Bible College, All Nations Christian College, Northumbria Bible College, Moorlands College, Glasgow Bible College, Birmingham Bible Institute and others where many are prepared for both home and overseas service.

7. **Young people** have become more responsive, but many come from a background of drugs, child abuse, broken homes, immorality and abortions and therefore need intensive discipling. Pray for:

a) **Commitment** to the life and work of local congregations. Great celebrations, Christian music and enthusiastic worship draw them, but discipline and dedication to the will of God are needed.

b) **Youth ministries.** Many congregations lack the right leadership or the vision to run effective youth and children's programmes that inspire. **British Youth for Christ** and **Frontier Youth Trust** have had a widespread impact on urban young people.

c) **A re-introduction of missions vision.** A missions vision is rarely given to young people, and Sunday School programmes seem to have forgotten that Jesus gave the Great Commission for young people too. Pray for the restructuring of church programmes to rectify this. Pray also for the ministry of **YWAM** (King's Kids, Discipleship Training Schools), **OM, World Horizons** and **British YFC** in recruiting, training and mobilizing young people for short- (and then longer-) term missions.

d) **Children.** Only 14% under 15 years of age are involved in church-related activities. Pray for children's ministries such as Covenanters, Crusaders, **SU** and others.

8. **Students** are exposed to great pressures in the secular education system. Many schools have little religious activity, and much that exists is formal and humanistic. A largely godless and materialistic younger generation is being formed by it. Relatively few secondary schools have a live, outgoing witness from staff or student groups. Pray for:

a) **The SU and Christian Union groups** in schools – for their growth and multiplication, and for Christian teachers to be used of God to help launch such groups.

b) **The campus Christian groups** among the 900,000 full-time students in colleges and universities. Their growth and diversity is encouraging, the main ones being: Agape (**CCC**), **Navigators** and UCCF(**IFES**). The oldest and most widespread is the work of **UCCF** with CUs in nearly 600 colleges and universities, but a further 300 have no permanent group. Pray for mature, stable leadership, effective support and advice from the 45 travelling secretaries, and establishment of a viable witness in every college. The student population is one of the more receptive segments of society.

c) **Overseas students.** Over 400,000 overseas students are granted visas every year – 80,000 to do university degrees. Outreach to them is varied but too limited, and many return home without ever hearing the gospel. UCCF(**IFES**), International Student Christian Services (**ISI**), In Contact Ministries, and others have ministry to them.

9. **Missionary interest** has waned, and many congregations have never sent out their own missionary. There is a widespread conviction that either the job has been done or that efforts should be concentrated on Britain's need. Pray for:

a) **A renewed commitment** by local congregations to world evangelization, to pray out their members to the areas of greatest need, and to care adequately for those who go.

b) **The 5,400 British Protestant missionaries** around the world, and that their numbers may be increased by dedicated long-term missionaries (in 1972 there were 7,000 missionaries). About 16% of all UK missionaries are short-term workers.

c) **The Evangelical Missionary Alliance** in its coordinating role in world missions in and from the UK.

10. **Unreached immigrant minorities.** Extensive post-war immigration from the New Commonwealth (Third World states formerly ruled by Britain) has brought in many ethnic minorities, some of which are from lands with minimal exposure to the gospel and where entry for missionaries is restricted or forbidden. The majority have settled and found employment in the inner cities of England. London itself is nearly 17% non-white. Ethnic minorities have become a majority in many inner-city areas. There are 350 schools in the country with over 75% ethnic minorities. Cultural distance, discrimination and even open hostility have antagonized many to "Christianity". Pray for:

a) **Local congregations** in multi-ethnic areas to open their doors, homes and hearts to this mission field on their doorstep, and to find effective ways of making friendships, meeting felt needs and winning some for the Lord.

b) **Specialist cross-cultural workers** to be called both for training churches and ministering to specific ethnic groups. Unique ministries: **South Asian Concern**, **OM** (Turning Point), **YWAM** teams, **In Contact Ministries**, and also missionaries linked with **Interserve, ECM, MECO**, BCMS Crosslinks, **WEC, IMI, IT, RSTI** as well as Third World mission agencies.

c) **Better coordination of effort and research of the need.** South Asian Concern has completed a detailed survey of the 1.5 million South Asians. Many ethnic minority communities are completely unreached because of lack of information to mobilize a ministry to reach them.

d) **Effective use of literature and other media.** Some **CLC** bookstores stock minority language literature. **WEC**'s broadsheet ministry in English, Panjabi, French, Hindi, Swahili, Urdu and

Arabic reaches many. **In Contact Ministries** specializes in literature on Islamics and in ethnic minority languages.

11. **Specific ethnic minority groups** that need intercession:
a) **Caribbean and African peoples.** There are over 166 denominations; 20% of the population is church-going. In the past these churches have been somewhat isolated from the mainstream of evangelical Christianity. The African Caribbean Evangelical Alliance (ACEA) is committed to creating an equitable partnership through their programmes of networking and community building. Pray that ACEA may be able to continue giving a sense of unity to these churches and help them to combat the growing social and economic problems faced by the black community in general.
b) **South Asians.** There are possibly 500 or so Christians from the Hindu and Sikh communities, and the rate of conversions is increasing. There are some thriving congregations in the Midlands and London area. The Muslim community is more difficult, increasingly organized. Pray for the breaking down of spiritual, cultural and emotional barriers that hold back many from believing. Pray for more workers committed and culturally prepared for this outreach. The Bangladeshi and Pathan communities are unreached.
c) **Middle Eastern peoples.** All outreach is largely localized and sporadic. Many wealthy **Arabs** come as tourists, businessmen and students; a few have come to faith, and there are several Arab Christian fellowships. There is only one Christian fellowship for each of the **Turks**, **Kurds** and **Iranians**. For the latter there is also a Bible Training School for preparing Iranians for ministry – the only one in the world. The **Yemenis** and 50,000 **Moroccans** are unreached.
d) **Chinese**, mainly from Hong Kong and some from Vietnam. They are steadily increasing in number. **The Chinese Overseas Christian Mission** has a good work among them. There are now 62 churches, 7,500 members and a Protestant community of about 7%.
e) **The Jewish community.** This is slowly declining through assimilation (80% have no religious commitment to Judaism) and marriage. Many are disillusioned by the rigid legalism and internal squabbling of communal leaders. Many of the believers integrate into Gentile churches, though there are also eight fellowships of Messianic Jews and possibly about 2,000 believers altogether. Pray for the ministry of CMJ, **MT**, **CWI** and **Jews for Jesus**. There is increasing opposition from Jewish anti-missionary and Christian liberal circles.
f) **Gypsies.** Many have been turning to Christ in large numbers since the initial breakthrough through French Gypsy missionaries in 1952. There are 50,000 Romany and Kale Gypsies and a further 30,000 Irish Traveller Gypsies. There are 5,000 committed Christians linked with the **Gypsy and Travellers Evangelical Movement.** Literacy is low and full-time workers are few.

12. **The rising challenge of Islam.** Growth comes more through immigration and a higher birthrate, but there are about 6,000 Anglo-Saxon Muslims – most through marriage. Muslim communities have become highly organized and press constantly for legislation that will favour Islam. There are 1,800 mosques (many no more than a room in a house) and 3,000 Koranic schools in Britain today. Yet Christians have been apathetic or fearful to witness to Muslims, and conversions have been few. Many church leaders espouse a fuzzy pluralism and denounce those who give a clear-cut Christian message. Pray that God may give the key for their evangelization, the discipling of converts and their protection in persecution. The Islamic Council of Europe is based in London. Oil-wealth funding and considerable missionary effort is directed to winning England for Islam.

13. **Christian literature and Bibles.** Few nations have such an extensive range of Christian literature, Bible versions and the facilities to acquire them. **The Gideons International** have distributed 20 million New Testaments and Bibles in their 40 years of ministry. In 1991 there were 594 **Christian bookstores** carrying an average of 3,500 titles! There are over 100 **Christian publishers** publishing 2,400 new titles annually. **The Bible Societies** not only have a ministry of Bible translation, publication and distribution in Britain and around the world, but also a wide range of catalytic ministries to stimulate Christian growth. **Bookaid** (EMA-CLC) has a remarkable ministry of exporting annually one million surplus and second-hand Christian books to poorer countries. Pray for these ministries and for Christians to become more avid readers.

14. **Christian broadcasting.** The 1990 Broadcasting Act opened unprecedented opportunities for Christians to own local radio stations, satellite and cable TV stations. Pray for wisdom and balance in the face of the opportunities; for many Christians active in secular broadcasting; for religious programmes on national radio and television – over six million view *Songs of Praise* every week.

ENGLAND

Area 130,400 sq.km.

Population 46,161,000. People per sq.km. 354.

Capital: London 9,046,000.

1. **Only 10% of adults and 14% of children are in a church service on an average Sunday**, although 65% would claim to be Christian. Nominalism and notional Christianity are enormous problems to overcome. A nodding acquaintance with the structures and trappings of Christianity and basking in the afterglow of Christian influence anaesthetize the majority. Pray that the Holy Spirit may break down the barriers and bring a sense of the holiness of God.

2. **Over 60% of the English** people have no real knowledge of the contents of the Bible, hence what the gospel really is. England is the most secular of the four kingdoms.

3. **The inner cities of urban England**, and especially London, are spiritual wastelands from which evangelical Christians have fled and then forgotten. Dying congregations, closed churches, and churches converted into Muslim mosques or Hindu temples are commonplace. Pray that God may raise up an army of workers to tackle the desperate needs of these polyglot, polycultural areas.

4. **The rural areas** present a challenge. Many villages have had no resident evangelical witness for a century or more. The **Datchet Evangelical Fellowship** and others are seeking to revive discouraged congregations and open closed chapels.

NORTHERN IRELAND

Area 14,100 sq.km.

Population 1,570,000. People per sq.km. 111.

Capital: Belfast 449,000.

Politics: The problems of Northern Ireland are but a continuation of the centuries-old tension between the Celtic Irish and Anglo-Saxon Scots-English. It is a historical coincidence that the former are Catholic and the latter largely Protestant. The partition of Ireland between the 26 counties of the South and six counties of Ulster did not solve the problem, for an indigenous and dissatisfied minority of Catholics who remained in Ulster under the British Crown still aspired to an all-Ireland Republic while the majority of the people adhered strongly to the British link. The civil rights campaign of this minority in the late '60s degenerated into civil violence by extremist factions on both sides; violence continues to the present. The Province (of Ulster) is ruled directly from London, and political attempts at finding solutions founder on the intransigence of both sides, but signs of change are appearing.

1. **The tragic cycle of violence, revenge and communal fears** must be broken. Pray for forgiveness and reconciliation between the communities. Pray also for the local, Irish and British politicians and church leaders who must tactfully and sensitively move toward a workable solution.

2. There has been much seed-sowing of the Word of God by local believers and by agencies such as the Faith Mission, **OM**, and many others. Fruit is beginning to appear in unexpected places!

3. **Within a 50-km radius of Belfast** is a higher concentration of evangelical churches than possibly anywhere in the world. These churches are full, and there are many committed, praying believers in all denominations. All Protestant denominations are generally far more evangelical than their counterparts in Britain. Pray that:

a) **Christians may be a means of reconciliation** and reconstruction in a province seriously harmed socially and economically by the "troubles".

b) **There may be a greater Bible-based spiritual unity and depth among believers.** A united witness to the life-changing power of the gospel is so necessary because the communal violence is perceived by those outside the church to be caused by "religion". Pray that the Northern Ireland Evangelical Alliance may increasingly draw Evangelicals together.

c) **Christian leaders** may set an example in Christ-likeness and not play on sectarian fears for political advantage.

4. **The missionary burden of Northern Ireland churches** is higher than elsewhere in the UK. Pray that this generosity in giving of money and personnel for world evangelization may continue!

SCOTLAND

Area 78,800 sq.km.

Population 4,957,300. People per sq.km. 63.

Capital: Edinburgh 433,000.

1. **Revivals** in past centuries and the localized revivals of the northeast coast in 1925 and Lewis in the Hebrides in the 1950s need to be repeated on a national scale.

2. **Scotland has sent out great men and women to bless the world** such as David Livingstone, Robert Moffatt, Mary Slessor and Eric Liddell. May this good tradition continue!

3. **The stirrings of new life in the Church of Scotland is encouraging.** Some 15% of the adult population is in a church service each Sunday, and the rapid increase in numbers of evangelical theological students and ministers is changing the church. Yet nominalism remains a major problem, liberalism is still the major theological emphasis, Freemasonry influences many churches, and the general decline in membership and church attendance has not been halted. Roman Catholic churches have changed their emphasis to one of evangelization and have had some success. Pray that the call to re-evangelize Scotland may be heeded.

4. **Of all the larger denominations, the Baptists, Pentecostals and, even more, the Charismatics and New Churches have shown an increase in membership and congregations.** Pray for church growth all over Scotland, especially the areas where Protestant numbers are low. Strathclyde, Scotland's most densely populated area, has the lowest percentage of Protestants, and the Aberdeen area the highest percentage of non-church goers.

WALES

Area 20,800 sq.km.

Population 2,798,000. People per sq.km. 135.

Capital: Cardiff 482,000.

1. **Wales is known as the land of revivals.** From early in the 18th century Wales experienced a consistent series of revivals. The last of these, and in many ways the least significant, occurred in 1904. Pray that revival will come again – many groups in Wales are praying!

2. **Economic changes have had a profound impact.** The decline of the coal and slate industries has led to massive depopulation and depression in industrialised areas. Coupled with an acceptance of the social gospel, this has led to empty chapels and a hardened population. Pray for the many small evangelical fellowships that are seeking to maintain their witness in these hard and unreceptive areas.

3. **Wales has preserved its own language and culture.** Some 20% of the population still speak Welsh. However, areas where Welsh is spoken by the majority are being flooded by English immigrants. Pray that the severe tension this is causing may not lead to escalating violence.

4. **New life is springing up in many parts of the Welsh church** – godly pastors are increasing in number and evangelistic work among young people is expanding. Pray that Christians will be able to unite so that the gospel can make a significant impact on the life of the nation once again.

U

United States of America

November 15–20
North America

Area 9,529,000 sq.km. The world's third largest nation in area and in population.

Population	Ann. Gr.	Density
1990 249,235,000	*0.82 %	26/sq.km
1995 258,204,000	0.71 %	27/sq.km

* Immigration accounts for 0.54% growth.

Peoples: A nation of immigrants with a greater diversity of ethnic origins than any other on earth. There are approx. 670,000 legal immigrants annually, and over 700,000 illegal immigrants.
Native Americans 0.8%. Major groups:
Amerindians 1,760,000 in 266 ethnic groups.
Hawaiian 200,000; Polynesians in Hawaii.
Eskimo 37,000 in Alaska.
Aleut 2,000 in the Alaskan Aleutian Islands.
Euro-American 70.5%. The ethnic mix is so great, the relative contributions of different peoples are hard to determine. Probably German 20%, Irish 17%, English 16%, Scots 7%; Other 10.5%.
Afro-American 12.1%. Most of their forebears came to America as slaves. Increasing immigration from Caribbean and Africa, including possibly 450,000 Haitians.
Hispanic 9.4% officially, but with illegal immigration from Mexico and Central America it may be 11%. Over 25 ethnic groups identifiable, who all speak Spanish. Mexican 12,600,000; Central and South American 2,500,000; Puerto Rican 2,300,000; Cuban 1,100,000; Other 1,600,000. Also Portuguese-speaking Brazilians 1,140,000.
Asian/Pacific 3%. Rapid increase in immigrants – 42% of all immigrants in '80s were Asian. Chinese 1,645,000; Filipino 1,405,000; Vietnamese 859,000; Japanese 804,000; Korean 800,000; South Asians 634,000.
Other 4.2%. Jews 5,900,000; Arabs 3,000,000; Armenian 1,100,000; Iranian 900,000.

Literacy 95.5% (functional literacy 85%). **Official language:** English. There is continuing debate concerning the possible use of languages of ethnic minorities in the education system – especially Spanish. **All indigenous languages** 189, of which 77 are close to extinction. Numerous languages and dialects still used by immigrants from all continents. About 13% of the population use a language other than English in the home. **Indigenous languages with Scriptures** 5Bi 8NT 48por.

Capital: Washington DC 3,288,000. There are 44 mega-cities (over one million). Largest conurbations: New York 17,100,000; Los Angeles 11,640,000; Chicago 7,660,000; Philadelphia 5,118,000; San Francisco 4,623,000; Detroit 4,346,000; Houston 3,468,000; Boston 3,454,000; Dallas-Fort Worth 3,152,000; Cleveland 3,070,000; Miami 2,954,000; Pittsburgh 2,538,000; St Louis 2,534,000; Minneapolis 2,335,000; Seattle 2,312,000.

Economy: The most powerful economy in the world with immense agricultural and industrial production. The state of health of the US economy has worldwide repercussions. Massive government deficits and adverse trade balance could precipitate future crises for the world economy, as well as for the nation itself. A North American Free Trade area is being created between USA, Canada and Mexico. Unemployment 5.4%. Public debt/person $14,300. Income/person $21,100.

Politics: Independent from Britain in 1776 as a federal republic. The number of states increased from the original 13 to 50 as the nation expanded westwards across the continent and Pacific. The strong democratic tradition, emphasis on private initiative and civil liberties have helped to make the nation great. The USA emerged from World War II as the leading industrial and military power in the world – but for 40 years in cold-war confrontation with the USSR. The costly Vietnam war was a trauma from which the USA slowly began to recover in the 1980s. The collapse of the USSR over 1989-91 left the USA as the only global power but unsure of how to use that power in multiplied local conflicts around the world.

Religion: Freedom of religion is written into the constitution. No state in the world has been so strongly influenced by biblical Christianity. The separation of State and Church enshrined in the constitution has been misused by liberal and anti-Christian minorities to limit the public exercise of religion and to promote permissive legislation.
Non-religious/other 8.7%.

Jews 2.4%. One third of all Jews in the world. Many new immigrants from ex-USSR.
Muslim 1.8% (estimates vary between 0.5% and 2.4%). About a third are Afro-American.
Buddhist 0.4%. East Asians.
Hindu 0.2%. **Baha'i** 0.02%.
Christian 86.5%. Nom 14.9%. Affil 71.6%. Growth 0.3%.
  Protestant 51.3%. Affil 43.2%. Growth 0.3%.

Church	Cong	Members	Affiliated
Southern Baptist Conv	37,922	15,032,798	21,500,000
United Methodist Ch	37,238	8,849,803	11,091,032

Nat Baptist Conv USA	44,444	8,000,000	9,410,000
Evang Lutheran Ch	10,912	3,889,462	5,226,798
Charismatic f'ships	22,727	2,500,000	5,100,000
Nat Bapt Conv of Am	19,774	3,500,000	4,270,000
Ch of God in Christ	15,000	1,200,000	4,000,000
Presbyterian Ch	11,433	2,847,329	3,553,335
African Meth Epis	10,789	2,050,000	2,800,000
Luth Ch Missouri Synod	5,964	1,955,008	2,600,846
Episcopal Church	7,333	1,695,878	2,445,286
Amer Baptist Chs	5,801	1,504,573	2,280,000
Assemblies of God	11,149	1,280,760	2,161,610
United Ch of Christ	6,260	1,599,539	1,993,459
Chs of Christ (non-inst)	13,097	1,280,000	1,681,013
Chr Chs/Chs of Christ	5,238	966,976	1,213,188
Chtn Ch (Disciples)	4,035	677,223	1,037,757
Seventh-day Adventist	4,214	717,443	957,000
Amer Baptist Assoc	1,849	270,000	900,000
Ch of the Nazarene	5,158	561,253	864,703
Ch of God (Cleveland)	4,996	555,828	855,000
Salvation Army	1,122	115,320	445,566
Reformed Ch in Amer	917	196,953	362,932
Free Will Baptist Ch	2,461	234,508	345,000
Gen Assoc of Reg Bapts	1,582	216,408	333,000
Conserv Bapt Assoc	1,121	204,496	292,000
Chr & Miss Alliance	1,797	132,112	271,865
Pente Holiness Ch	1,490	125,940	262,000
Christian Brethren	820	52,740	85,600
All other (1,158)	86,685	11,575,019	19,332,264
Denominations (1,187)	383,328	73,877,369	107,661,254
Evangelicals 30.3% of pop		49,344,000	74,000,000
Pentecostal/charis 13.4%		19,430,000	33,300,000

Missionaries:
to USA 2,320 (1:107,000 people) in 78 agencies.
from USA 59,074 (1:1,800 Protestants) in 614 agencies
39,916frn 40,574xcul 18,500dom.

Roman Catholic 28%. Affil 21.42%. Growth −0.2%.			
Catholic Ch	22,441	38,300,000	53,385,998
Charismatic		2,300,000	3,200,000
Catholic Evangelicals		736,000	1,068,000
Missionaries:			
to USA 10,582 (1:23,500 people).			
from USA 5,595 (1:9,500 Catholics).			
Other Catholic 0.2%. Affil 0.19%. Growth −0.2%.			
All groups (61)	151	290,140	476,211
Orthodox 3%. Affil 2.84%. Growth −0 5%.			
Greek Orth AD of N & S			
Amer	575	1,400,000	1,750,000
Ortho Church in America	426	616,000	880,000
All other (68)	767	2,894,610	4,443,216
Denominations (70)	1,768	4,910,610	7,073,216
Charismatic		35,000	48,000
Foreign Marginal 4%. Affil 3.94%. Growth 4.2%.			
Mormons	9,035	2,920,000	4,175,000
Jehovah's Witnesses	9,782	904,963	2,260,000
All other (356)	23,822	2,056,150	3,377,000
All groups (358)	42,639	5,881,113	9,812,000

Missionaries from USA est. 45,000.

Religious changes

Evangelicals

1. **The awesome solemnity of the role of the USA** in the post-"cold war" world is only now beginning to dawn on many. US leadership politically, economically, morally and spiritually will be tested as never before. Pray that the inscription on every US coin, *In God We Trust*, may be a reality for the nation's leaders in each of these realms.

2. **The Pilgrim Fathers**, the first English-speaking settlers, were determined to establish a land in which they were free to exercise their Christian faith. On that heritage has developed one of the largest and most dynamic Christian movements in history. In the USA are 23% of the Protestant congregations in the world, 24% of the Evangelicals and 52% of the world's Protestant foreign missionary force. Evangelistic vitality, generosity and vision have been major factors in the surge of gospel advances since 1945. Give praise to God for this!

3. **The spiritual heritage of the USA is being steadily eroded** – its loss would impoverish the world. The spiritual attacks are on two major fronts:
a) **External.** An unholy alliance of minority rights groups such as humanists, homosexuals, New Age enthusiasts and pro-choice abortionists exploit the provisions of the constitution and control of the media to disparage and mock Christians and limit or remove anything Christian in public life. The aim is to replace "intolerant" Christian values with a permissive pagan culture. Intercede for the land and in Jesus' name bind these powers.
b) **Internal.** The greater challenge is for commitment among Christians. Lack of it has had devastating consequences – a respect for the Bible without knowledge of or obedience to its contents and an interest in religion without a holiness to recommend it. The tragic fall of famous televangelists has proved this and provided ammunition for the enemies of the gospel. The word "revival" has been debased to mean slick mass evangelism – the need of the hour is a true revival with conviction of sin, repentance and an outpouring of the Holy Spirit.

4. **There are stirrings of spiritual awakening.** Pray this into a movement of the Spirit.
a) **The growth of Evangelicals.** This has been gaining momentum since the mid '70s. Evangelical

denominations are growing but at the expense of more liberal and traditional denominations which have been in decline. The political influence of Evangelicals has grown too, but needs to be used wisely.

b) **Widespread evangelism.** Major evangelistic campaigns by Billy Graham and many others have won respect and credibility for the gospel. A multiplicity of local outreaches, congregational mobilization methods, evangelistic tools, and imaginative use of the media have won millions to a living faith. The USA is one of the most evangelized nations on earth.

c) The rapid growth of **Pentecostalism** and, in more recent years, the explosive growth of **charismatic** groups within and outside nearly every denomination – Protestant, Catholic and Orthodox. These are dynamic new factors in the Christian scene which have reversed the decline in some major traditional denominations. Figures above are an attempt to indicate that growth, which has yet to be objectively measured.

d) **A strong movement against the evils of society** – drug abuse, promiscuity and pornography, permissive legislation, abortion and crime. These are what the media (especially films) portray, giving the distorted image of the USA presented to the world. Pray for such movements as Traditional Values Coalition, Christian Coalition, Concerned Women for America and Citizens for Excellence in Education.

e) **A burgeoning prayer movement across the country.** Millions are committing time and effort to city-wide Concerts of Prayer, Marches for Jesus, community prayer meetings and prayer walks. Pray for the nurture and growth of this vision, and that this may bring about the long-awaited revival.

5. **Specific challenges facing the Church**, and especially Evangelicals:

a) **Spiritual unity.** Oneness in the Lord among those who are committed to him is needed. The luxury of perpetuating strong divisions over secondary issues such as church government, gifts of the Spirit, eschatology, definitions of biblical inerrancy, methods of evangelism and social issues is hampering the energetic furtherance of world evangelization. Pray for the National Association of Evangelicals, which links 50,000 evangelical congregations and 77 denominations in fellowship and cooperative action.

b) **Christian church leadership** with high moral principles, a servant spirit and ability to disciple successors. Pyramid church structures more akin to business corporations are common, yet they often enhance the pastor and diminish lay initiative.

c) **Effective Bible exposition and teaching** that activates believers. This is not as common as it should be: spiritual entertainment can often be a substitute. Many of the Lord's people are over-evangelized and underfed!

d) **A clear biblical stand and appropriate involvement in the burning social issues of the day** such as the high rate of divorce (among Christians too), the collapse of the public education system, inner-city poverty, drug abuse, homosexuality and the failure of the health-care system.

6. **Leadership training possibilities abound.** The variety and number of theological training possibilities defies full analysis! There are 644 institutions that award theological degrees! The American Association of Bible Colleges includes 89 accredited evangelical colleges. Pray for a deeper level of commitment to Christian service and to world evangelization among students.

7. **Young people** present one of the major areas of spiritual battle today. The bitter fruits of humanistic philosophies are now being harvested in disorientation, spiritual vulnerability, moral decay, rejection of authority, widespread drug abuse and mindless violence. Yet God has raised up youth movements to combat this confusion and make a mighty impact on the world. To mention a few: **OM, YWAM, CCC**, Teen Challenge. Pray for the youth; the next generation could be America's most traumatic ever if there is not a decisive work of God's Spirit.

8. **Student ministries** have flourished in recent years. The impact of the complementary ministries of IVCF(**IFES**), **Navigators**, **CCC** and others has led to effective discipleship and outreach on campuses. The large Urbana conferences of IVCF and CCC efforts such as **Explo-86** have challenged many students with the needs of a lost world. The ministries of the **Navigators** and **CCC** have diversified into a wide range of activities in the USA and around the world.

9. **The 30 million Afro-American community** is a victim of its origins in slavery and discrimination. The civil rights movement achieved much in changing structures and attitudes, but the cycle of unemployment, poverty, family instability and crime is unbroken for many. Pray for:

a) **Young people** – especially in the decaying inner cities – 23% of those in their 20s are in prison. Drug abuse and AIDS are rampant, and murder is the major cause of death for 15- to 34-year-olds.

b) **Black Muslims** – multiplying in protest against a white Christianity with which the black community has few meaningful ties. Estimates of their number range from 800,000 to 1,500,000. Most come from a Christian background. Pray for ministry to reach them.

c) **The Afro-American churches.** Many of the largest and most vigorous evangelical churches are Black, but they are isolated from the mainstream of evangelical Christianity. Pray for a unity among believers that transcends race, and pray for a moving of the Spirit of God in the many churches with little spiritual life. Some of these have been deeply impacted by the charismatic movement.

d) **Greater missions vision among the Christians.** The Destiny Movement (with conferences in 1987 and 1992) is helping to redress this, but most churches lack the structure and practical experience to become effective sending churches.

10. **Church growth among ethnic minorities** is the growing edge of US Evangelicalism today. This is an urban phenomenon – minorities comprise a majority in 25 US cities, and by the year 2000 this will have risen to 50. There are an estimated 125 ethnic communities that maintain their cultural cohesion – very few without growing churches. In 10 years Hispanic Evangelicals have increased from 4% to 20% of the community. Dynamic networks of congregations have sprung up among Koreans, Chinese, Filipinos, Arabs and even Iranians. Pray for:

a) **The effective evangelization and discipling of every ethnic minority,** both new immigrants and those largely integrated into US life, and development of vision and outreach to evangelize their lands of origin through radio, literature and personal evangelism. The major challenge is to mobilize Christians for this who originate from the Middle East, and from South, Central and East Asia.

b) **The growth and maturation of these churches** – in language use and in keeping the balance between cultural integrity and integration into the mainstream of US life – especially as second- and third-generation numbers increase. Pray for the provision of wise and forward-looking leaders. There is generally a lack of pastors, but a danger that the gaps be filled by those drawn from their more needy lands of origin.

c) **Effective strategies and cooperation between Anglo-American and ethnic minority churches and agencies** to ensure these minorities are discipled in what is a highly fragmented ministry. The **SBC** has 250,000 believers in 4,600 congregations and 87 languages; 40% of new churches of **AoG** are among ethnic minorities; **CMA** has a vigorous church-planting ministry among them too.

d) **Growth of missions vision.** Notable in this is the Korean-American **Korean World Missions Council** – an interdenominational association linking nearly 600 North American Korean churches. In conferences in 1988 and 1992 goals for the future were established – including the sending of 1,000 missionaries by the year 2000. May this vision be emulated by other groups.

11. **Native Americans** have suffered intensely in their encounter with centuries of European immigrants. They have lost almost all their lands, their self-respect and much of their culture, and they still face prejudice and insensitivity to their plight. Poverty, disease and unemployment are common among those on Indian reservations and among the 50% or so who have migrated to the cities. There is a vigorous movement across the country to revive indigenous cultures; this is successfully demanding the honouring of treaties protecting Indian lands and rights that have rarely been kept by the government in the past. Pray for:

a) **Vitalization of Christianity** among native Americans. A profusion of missionary efforts over the centuries has yielded meagre fruit. In the early '80s there were 2,500 congregations and 320,000 Christians of all kinds, but syncretic indigenous sects and cults as well as reversions to pre-Christian beliefs are widespread. Only about 17% of the total population is affiliated with churches. The largest group, the Navajo (200,000), has begun to respond after years of indifference; now believers are 10% of the population.

b) **Bible translation,** which has regained importance as local languages are revived. Over 50 languages are in common use, and **SIL** and others have teams working in 27.

c) **The evangelization of every reservation.** Of the 300 Indian reservations, 54 were surveyed in 1979 and only 20% had a church led by a native American. The situation has only slightly improved since then.

d) **The indigenous peoples of Alaska,** who have retained their identity far more than those in mainland USA. Over 16 missions and churches have ministry among them. To name three: **SEND** with 91 missionaries, **Interact Ministries** (formerly Arctic Missions) with 75, and **GMU** with 17. The harshness of the climate, geographical isolation and economic stresses complicate the work of bringing churches to maturity. Many of the Aleut and Eskimo are traditionally

Orthodox Church Christians, a legacy of the time when Russia ruled Alaska. Over 71% of the 65,000 indigenous people profess to be Christian.

12. **The less-reached.** The variety and effort expended to evangelize the majority of US residents who do not regularly go to church means that few are unreached, but there are some groups which need missions input.

a) **The six million Jews** are an influential minority, and the largest concentration of Jews in the world. New York is estimated to be 10% Jewish. A growing receptivity and response to the gospel has been evident since 1970, and more Jews are being won to Christ in the USA than since New Testament times. There are variously estimated to be between 30,000 and 100,000 Messianic Christians; about 15–20,000 have retained their cultural distinctives and meet in Messianic congregations. An estimated 600–1,100 come to the Lord each year. There are more than 48 agencies and 325 full-time workers committed to Jewish evangelism – one of the most dynamic and innovative is **Jews for Jesus**. Pay for the maturation of the work after the euphoria of the '70s.

b) **The sects** pose a challenge. Most of the more aggressively missionary sects such as Christian Science, Mormonism, Jehovah's Witnesses and Scientology have originated in the USA. There are reckoned to be 2,500 such sects and exotic cults. Specific efforts to reach such people must be made. Some successes have been seen among both Mormons and Jehovah's Witnesses. [*See page 615 for more details.*]

c) **Foreign students** number over 400,000 and come from 181 countries; 56% from Asia (China 40,000; Taiwan 34,000; India 30,000); 30% are Muslim. Many come from lands with few Christians and are unreceptive to missions. Over 37 agencies and many local congregations are involved in ministry to them, and response has been remarkable. The Association of Christian Ministries to Internationals is an umbrella body linking ministries such as **ISI**, IVCF (**IFES**), **CCC**, **Navigators** and others. Pray for conversions and a discipling ministry that will enable these students to be effective witnesses when they return home.

13. **The US missions force.** Major umbrella bodies for Evangelical agencies are **EFMA** and **IFMA** and for more charismatic agencies **AIMS**. The **ACMC** (Advancing Churches in Missions Commitment) acts as a coordinating support structure for local church missions programmes. The largest sending agencies are: **SBC** (4,684), **WBT/SIL** (4,440), **NTM** (2,440), **YWAM** (2,232), **AoG** (1,918). Pray for:

a) **Missions vision** to become deeper and more prominent within local churches.

b) **Realistic support mechanisms** to be developed by churches and agencies. Unnecessary expenses and extravagant budgets bring discredit to the missions movement, stress for field workers and limitation on numbers sent out.

14. **Christian media ministries** are available in such profusion, only brief mention for prayer is made for:

a) **Christian literature.** In the '80s there were massive increases in sales of Christian literature through the 5,000 Christian bookstores and through secular outlets – but the subject matter was more often for the "fad" market. Pray for a more discerning and book-loving Christian public.

b) **Christian radio and television** which have developed dramatically since 1961. The National Religious Broadcasters links together 1,400 Christian broadcasting bodies which produce 75% of all religious programmes in the USA. There are over 1,100 Christian radio stations and over 350 Christian TV stations in the USA. Pray for:

i) **Wise and sensitive use of these powerful media.** The credibility of all such ministries was damaged by the distorted, fraudulent and immoral life styles of certain televangelists.

ii) **A balance in use of funds** for what is a very expensive ministry.

iii) **Programming that uplifts the Lord Jesus** rather than personalities, products or organizations and that promotes morality, family cohesion and biblical holiness.

<table>
<tr><td>

November 21

Latin America

</td><td>

Uruguay
(Eastern Republic of Uruguay)

</td><td>

</td></tr>
</table>

Area 176,000 sq.km. Located between Brazil and Argentina on the east bank of the River Plate estuary.

Population	Ann. Gr.	Density
1990 3,128,000	0.76 %	18/sq.km
1995 3,246,000	0.74 %	18/sq.km

Peoples:
Spanish-speaking 92.9%. Majority of Spanish origin, Italian origin 25%, Mixed race 5%.
Other ethnic minorities 7.1%. Italian 79,000; Jews 50,000; German 28,000; Brazilian 28,000; Russian 14,000; and other.

Literacy 95%. South America's most educated population. **Official language:** Spanish.

Capital: Montevideo 1,550,000; about half the country's population live in the area. Urbanization 86%.

Economy: Once prosperous through agriculture. Loss of markets, economic stagnation and expense of maintaining a welfare state have lowered living standards but the population is unwilling to pay the high cost of restructuring the economy and trimming the cost of the social security system. Ranching, tourism and agriculture are still the highest export earners. Inflation for 1990 was 129%. Reform, some privatisation of industry, and membership of *Mercosur*, the Southern Cone Common Market, are bringing positive change. Unemployment 8%. Public debt/person $974. Income/person $2,620 (12% of USA).

Politics: Independent from Spain in 1828. A long tradition of democracy and civil liberties was interrupted between 1973 and 1985 when Communist guerrilla activity provoked a military take-over. A civilian government was elected in 1985.

Religion: Separation of church and state in 1918, with no preference given to any religion. The most secular state in South America. The present government has given a higher profile to the Catholic Church.
Non-religious/other 37.2%.

Jews 1.7%. Montevideo is 3% Jewish.
Christian 61.1%. Affil 56.2%. Growth −0.9%.
Protestant 3.63%. Affil 3.54%. Growth 3.3%.

Church	Cong	Members	Affiliated
Assemblies of God	540	7,800	17,527
Waldensian Ch	15	3,350	12,000
Seventh-day Adventist	36	6,013	12,000
Baptist Convention	46	3,836	9,590
Ch of God (Cleveland)	44	2,151	5,380
Lutheran Ch	10	2,000	5,000
Ch of the Nazarene	20	1,209	2,444
Chr & Missn Alliance	15	990	1,200
All other (43)	229	19,579	45,986
Denominations (51)	955	46,928	110,727
Evangelicals 2.2% of pop		30,700	68,800
Pentecostal/charis 1.55%		20,500	48,400

Missionaries:
  to Uruguay 218 (1:14,300 people) in 43 agencies.
  from Uruguay 63 (1:1,800 Protestants) in 10 agencies 54frn 45xcul 9dom.
Roman Catholic 48.3%. Growth −1.8%.

Catholic Ch	224	1,730,000	2,400,000
Doubly counted		−640,000	−890,000
Total		1,090,000	1,510,000

Missionaries:
  to Uruguay 1,447 (1973 figure).
  from Uruguay 350 (1973 figure).
Orthodox 0.93%. Growth 2.1%.

Denominations (6)	7	17,400	29,000

Marginal 3.5%. Growth 9.1%.

Mormons	118	42,000	56,000
Jehovah's Witnesses	106	7,755	25,900
New Apostolic Church	115	17,300	23,000
All groups (8)	339	68,635	108,400

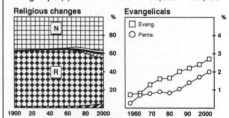

Religious changes — Evangelicals

1. **Uruguayan society has been characterized by secularism** and hope in man throughout this century. During the '70s disillusionment set in, and by the '90s the manifest failure of secularism created a desperate search for the transcendent. Brazilian Spiritists, long banned, are now significant opinion-shapers. New Age thinking is filling the vacuum among the agnostic middle-class and intelligentsia. Evangelical groups who have recognized this have found unprecedented spiritual openness.

2. **Lack of knowledge of God has given opening to a spirit of error.** Brazilian spiritism has made a big impact on the country; there are now 1,200 registered occult centres – more than the number of Protestant churches. The largest non-Catholic religious bodies are the sectarian Mormons, Jehovah's Witnesses and New Apostolic Church. Pray for these delusions to be exposed and the demonic powers behind them defeated.

3. **Protestant churches** have struggled throughout this century to make an impact on Uruguayan society, but evangelistic crusades and big efforts have garnered meagre fruit in converts. However, since 1986 the growth of some Pentecostal groups and Baptists has suddenly accelerated. Pray for this awakening to continue and that all churches may find ways to exploit this new spiritual interest.

4. **Church leaders** need prayer – that there be more fellowship and cooperation across denominational barriers. Pray also for leadership training in the 20 or so seminaries and Bible schools. Liberal theology has limited the effectiveness of some denominations.

5. **Ministry among young people** is vital in a land where no religious instruction is given in public schools. There is a need for leaders for young people – within congregations and for interdenominational movements. Campus Crusade, CBUU(**IFES**), **AoG** and Baptists have established small university ministries. A Catholic University was allowed to open in 1984 – an historic first.

6. **Missions vision** has been limited but is experiencing a flowering of interest. Two Uruguayan mission agencies have been formed (*Avance* and *Desafio Mundial*). The Uruguayan COMIBAM sponsored a Congress on Missions in 1993.

7. **Missions to Uruguay.** This has been a discouraging field of service. The pioneer stage is past and there are few unreached areas. Those called to minister in a loving servant role to the Church have much to offer. Larger missions are **SBC** (42 workers), **AoG** (23), Finnish Free Mission (11), WEF Ministries (8) and Gospel Mission of S. America (6). Teams of church planters from other Latin American countries are having some success. Major missionary-contributing countries: USA (137), Brazil (23), Canada (13), Finland (11), UK (10).

8. **The less-reached.**
a) **The Jews** are concentrated in Montevideo. JAMI has a small witness among them. There is an openness to the gospel.
b) **The Chinese and Japanese communities.** There is no church among them.
c) **The Palestinians** living in several border towns. *Desafio Mundial* is focusing on them.
d) **The upper middle class** living along Montevideo's coast are possibly the largest unevangelized group in one location in South America. Argentinian Baptist missionaries are targeting them and have begun one church.

9. **Christian support ministries.**
a) **Literature.** This is a vital Christian ministry in this highly literate land. **CLC** has a ministry through its two bookstores and bookmobile ministry through the country. **SBC** and the Bible Society have an extensive literature and Bible distribution ministry. **EHC** has a vigorous tract distribution ministry. Pray that the written Word may make a lasting impact. The recession has hindered sales.
b) **Radio.** There are several groups producing radio programmes which have given Evangelicals more exposure. **TWR** broadcasts from Montevideo to Uruguay, Argentina and Paraguay.

U

November 22–23
Eurasia

Uzbekistan

Area 447,000 sq.km. Fertile, irrigated mountain valleys in east – notably the Ferghana Valley. Desert and the Aral Sea in the west.

Population		Ann.Gr.	Density
1990	20,446,000	2.7%	46/sq.km
1995	23,377,000	2.7%	52/sq.km

Peoples: Every ethnic group but one of the former USSR is represented in Uzbekistan.

Turkic/Altaic 83%. Uzbek 14,200,000 (some are actually ethnic Tajik); Kazakh 808,000; Tatar 468,000; Karakalpak 412,000; Turkmen 228,000; Crimean Tatar 189,000; Kyrgyz 175,000; Azerbaijani 44,000; Uyghur 36,000; Bashkir 35,000.

Indo-European 14.9%. Many emigrating.
Slav 9.3%. Russian 1,653,000; Ukrainian 153,000; Byelorussian 29,000.
Iranian 4.9%. Tajik 934,000; Persian 25,000; Ossetian 6,000.
Other 0.7%. Armenian 50,000; German 40,000.
All other peoples 2%. Korean 183,000; Jew 94,000; Mordvinian 12,000.

Literacy 99%. **Official language:** Uzbek; Russian widely used. **All indigenous languages:** 8. **Languages with Scriptures** 2Bi 1NT 1por.

Capital: Tashkent 2,500,000. Other major cities: Samarkand 500,000; Bukhara 220,000. Urbanization 25%.

Economy: Great potential for growth with large oil fields, and the world's biggest gold mine. The lack of water is one of the critical limiting factors for growth. The world's third largest cotton producer. Yet the Marxist command structure with its patronage, corruption and ecological insensitivity remains little changed in independent Uzbekistan. Unemployment 27%. Income/person n.a.

Politics: Samarkand was the 14th century capital of Tamarlane's vast Mongol/Turkic empire. Uzbekistan's key position ensures its ongoing political importance in Central Asia. Russian colonial rule 1868–1917. Created a Socialist Republic 1924. Independent as a democratic republic in 1991, but the People's Democratic Party (former Communist Party) banned the Islamic Fundamentalist Party, and other parties are not permitted to function freely. Tokens of ethnic and Islamic culture were adopted as cover for a policy of no change.

Religion: The government declared a secular state with no official ideology or religion, but Islamic influence is steadily growing.

Muslim 68.2%. Sunni Muslims and a few Shi'a. Zoroastrian concepts, animism and wearing of charms are incorporated into local Islamic beliefs.
Non-religious/other 26.1%.
Jews 0.46%. **Buddhist** 0.3%. **Baha'i** 0.2%.
Christian 4.7%. Nom 3.2%. Affil 1.5%.
Growth –15.9%.
Protestant 0.13%. Growth 5.2%.

Church	Members		Affiliated
Registered Pentes (3)	3	2,000	6,670
Korean Presbyterian	20	2,500	6,250
Baptist Union	10	2,000	6,000
Unreg. Pentecostals	15	1,500	5,000
Korean Baptist	15	1,500	3,000
Denominations (7)	63	9,500	26,920
Evangelicals 0.13% of pop		9,500	26,920
Pentecostal/charis 0.06%		3,500	11,700
Roman Catholic 0.2%. Growth –35.7%.			
Catholic Ch		9,000	15,000
Orthodox 4.4%. Affil 1.28%. Growth –9.1%.			
Russian Orthodox		163,000	250,000
Denominations (2)		170,150	261,000
Marginal 0.01%. Growth 5.2%.			
Jehovah's Witnesses		520	1,300

1. **Independence has not brought freedom,** but left an ideological void and disillusionment. Lenin's statue in Tashkent was replaced with a globe – the globe's ideologies are seeking to fill that void. Fundamentalist Islam daily gains a bigger, but underground, following. Occultism attracts a wide interest, and the sects have arrived – Moonies, JWs, Hare Krishna. Pray that the Uzbek people may not be ensnared by yet another tyranny but find freedom and truth in the Lord Jesus Christ.

2. **Political changes will inevitably come.** Pray that the nation's leaders may govern without exploiting ideological, ethnic or religious passions. There is a developing contest between democracy and Islamic fundamentalism. Uzbekistan's future direction could be determinative for all of Central Asia.

3. **Ecological disasters Communism left to develop unchecked will have to be faced.** The lack of water and its misuse in agriculture have poisoned the soil and the people with chemicals as well as hastened the rapid disappearance of the Aral Sea with frightening impact on the environment. Pray that impending crises may turn many to seek God.

4. **Tashkent is the Islamic capital of Central Asia** – the other five Muslim-majority republics look to the Muslim *mufti* (leader) based there. Yet, for most, Islam has more a cultural than a religious significance – especially among the youth. This could change. Saudi and Iranian Muslim missionaries assiduously work to rebuild mosques, distribute Korans and increase commitment to Islam. Behind this activity is that of the satanic forces that use layers of false religions to bind and blind the people. Pray for release for his captives in a way that will cause a rapid disintegration of the barriers and lead to many conversions.

5. **Christians are almost all of immigrant minorities** – many of whom are emigrating. Between 1985 and 1991 over 800,000 Russians left Uzbekistan. There are 35 Korean congregations in the country, and more Korean than Russian Evangelicals. Evangelical churches are growing – Baptist, Pentecostal and especially Korean denominations. Their situation is not easy. Pray for:
a) **Freedom for church construction and evangelistic outreach.** The authorities have been obstructive.
b) **Bridging of the cultural divide** between Russians, Koreans and Uzbeks. The differences, history, insensitivity in the past and fears for the future all make outreach to the majority population hard. Pray for grace and for the right approaches to reach Muslims.
c) **The Uzbek believers** – probably still only a few in number. Praise God for them and the pastors among them that he has raised up. Pray for their protection, growth in grace and freedom to develop an authentic Uzbek Christian literature, music, worship style and fellowship structure.

6. **Expatriate Christians** serving the Lord in Uzbekistan have increased in number. There are a number of agencies concerned for the spiritual need of the land. Pray for effective, fruitful cooperation, and provision of safety, health, physical needs and proficiency in the language – all tested constantly. Pray also for viable witness-giving job opportunities. There are strict controls and limitations on the lives of expatriates, which can be irksome. Pray for grace and greater liberty in outreach. Some are trusting God for 500 workers to be called during this decade.

7. **The unreached.** Only a small fraction of the Muslim majority has ever had the opportunity to believe. Pray specifically for the:
a) **Uzbek.** Most of those who have heard are in Tashkent, but few in the rural areas where 75% of the people live. Pray especially for the Ferghana Valley, where Islam is being revived.
b) **Karakalpak,** who live south of the Aral Sea and who suffer most in health because of salt storms and polluted water. Pray for a strong church among this people and for the completion of the New Testament; only the Gospel of Matthew was finished by the end of 1992.
c) **Persians,** Shi'a Muslims who live in the cities but now speak Uzbek while retaining their original customs. No Christians are known.

8. **Christian media ministries.**
a) **Bible translation and distribution** is an ongoing task. The New Testament, together with Genesis and Psalms, was published in 1992. Pray for its wide dissemination, acceptance and impact on the Uzbek.
b) **Christian literature in Uzbek** is limited. Pray for mother-tongue writers, poets and hymnologists to be raised up and their works printed.
c) **The *Jesus* film** in Uzbek was banned from public showing after public oppposition. Pray for wide circulation and use of the video.
d) **Christian radio** is limited in programming hours (1.75 hours/week by **FEBC**, HCJB(**WRMF**) and **TWR**), in listeners, and response. Pray for effective ways of communicating the Good News by this medium. There are possibilities for Christian programmes on local television and radio.

U

See Pacific
Pacific

Vanuatu
(The Republic of Vanuatu)

Area 12,190 sq.km. Twelve larger and 70 smaller islands southeast of Solomon Is. in S.W. Pacific. Formerly New Hebrides.

Population	Ann. Gr.	Density
1990 164,000	2.9 %	13/sq.km
1995 191,000	3.1 %	16/sq.km

Peoples: Around 112 indigenous languages and numerous dialects. Only 35 languages have over 1,000 speakers, none over 6,000.
Indigenous 91.8%. Melanesian (102) 147,600; Polynesian (3) 2,900.
Other Pacific Islanders 2.5%. From Wallis, Kiribati, Fiji, Tonga, etc.
Other 5.7%. French 6,300; English-speaking 1,900; Vietnamese 770; Chinese 330.

Literacy 61%. **Official languages:** Bislama (Pidgin English), English, French. **All languages** 111. **Indigenous languages with Scriptures** 4Bi 4NT 38por.

Capital: Vila 20,000 (on Efate Island). Urbanization 23%.

Economy: Over 80% of population involved in subsistence agriculture. Main exports copra, beef, timber, cocoa. Public debt/person $94. Income/person $860 (4.1% of USA).

Politics: Bizarre Anglo-French Condominium 1914–1980 with duplicated administration, police and education. Independent in 1980 as a parliamentary republic but politics still affected by the impact of dual colonialism with tensions between Francophone and Anglophone political parties.

Religion: Religious freedom.
Non-religious/other 1.2%.
Animist and Cargo cultists 14.7%.

Christian 84.1%. Nom 9.9%. Affil 74.2%. Growth 2.2%.
Protestant 65%. Nom 5.5%. Affil 59.5%. Growth 2.1%.

Church	Cong	Members	Affiliated
Presbyterian Ch	304	13,300	51,000
Ch of Melanesia (Ang)	167	17,500	25,000
Seventh-day Adventist	41	6,878	8,000
Churches of Christ	49	2,450	4,900
Assemblies of God	74	2,460	4,100
Free Evangelical Ch	21	1,250	1,900
Apostolic Ch	14	850	1,700
All other (2)	11	270	510
Denominations (9)	681	44,958	97,110
Evangelicals 21.7% of pop		15,400	35,500
Pentecostal/charis 4%		3,600	6,400

Missionaries:
to Vanuatu 32 (1:5,200 people) in 5 agencies.
from Vanuatu 2.
Roman Catholic 16.2%. Nom 4.3%. Affil 11.9%. Growth 2.1%.

Catholic Ch	26	11,300	19,500

Missionaries to Vanuatu 43 (1:3,800 people).
Foreign Marginal 0.51%. Affil 0.51%. Growth 23%.

Mormons	1	140	200
All groups (2)	3	329	1,145

Indigenous Marginal 2.4%. Growth 2.6%.

All groups (6)	32	1,600	4,000

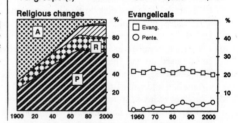

Religious changes   Evangelicals

1. **Vanuatu's motto is "*In God we stand*".** Pray that the leaders of this complex little nation may be an example in doing so. Christians played a major role in the attainment of independence and in subsequent governments.

V

2. **The Protestant church is numerically strong** – mainly Anglicans in the north and Presbyterians in the centre and south. Some islands have been touched by revival; however, in other islands spiritual life is at a low ebb, few having heard a clear gospel presentation. Pray for the training of leaders in the one **AoG** and two Presbyterian Bible colleges. Pray for Spirit-filled leaders who know how to apply Scripture to life.

3. **Missionary martyrs in evangelizing these islands have been many.** On Erromanga alone six died. Today the Church welcomes missionaries in a supportive role for teaching the Word; the largest agencies are **WBT** (13 workers), Australian Churches of Christ (10), and US **AoG** (6). Pioneer work is

also still needed for a number of smaller, superficially evangelized peoples, especially in Bible translation.

4. Cargo cults and reversion to paganism have been major problems over the past 40 years. There are also many nominal Christians who follow "custom". Pray for decisive demonstrations of God's power among the largely traditional peoples of Tanna, Aniwa, Santo and Vao.

5. Bible translation is the major unfinished task. At least eight, and possibly 81, languages may require New Testament translations or revisions. **UBS** and **SIL** are involved in 13 projects. Pray for wisdom as to which of the small language groups warrant the effort, and for translation teams of expatriates and nationals.

6. Christian media.
a) **GRn** have made recordings in only 11 of the languages – much more could be done to develop an effective audio ministry.
b) **EHC** have seen good response to their nationwide literature distribution campaign since 1986.

V

<table>
<tr><td>**November 24–25**

Latin America</td><td><h1>*Venezuela*</h1> (Republic of Venezuela) </td><td></td></tr>
</table>

Area 912,000 sq.km. 80% of the population lives along the Caribbean coastal belt in the north; centre and south are grasslands and tropical forest. A further 230,000 sq.km. of Guyana to the east is claimed by Venezuela.

Population		Ann. Gr.	Density
1990	19,736,000	2.6 %	22/sq.km
1995	22,213,000	2.4 %	24/sq.km

Peoples:
Spanish-speaking 96.7%. Approx. composition: Mestizo 66%, European 20%, African 10%. The large Italian community has been almost entirely absorbed into the majority.
Amerindian 2%. About 38 peoples. Largest: Guajiro 84,000; Warao 28,000; Piaroa 14,000; Yanomamo 14,000.
Other 1.3%. Arabs 110,000; Chinese 40,000; Jews 20,000, English-speakers 20,000.

Literacy 91%. **Official language:** Spanish. **All languages** 40. **Languages with Scriptures** 1Bi 11NT 9por.

Capital: Caracas 3,600,000. Other major cities: Maracaibo 1,207,000; Valencia 955,000; Maracay 900,000; Barquísimeto 723,000. Urbanization 84%.

Economy: One of the world's largest oil producers. Oil wealth has benefited the rich elite at the expense of the poor. Some attempts are being made to diversify the economy. Large-scale corruption, exposed by falling revenues from oil, has created resentment and instability. Unemployment 9.6%. Public debt/person $1,305. Income/person $2,450 (11% of USA).

Politics: Independent from Spain as part of Gran Colombia in 1821; and as a separate state in 1830. A succession of revolutions and harsh dictatorships ended in 1958. Stable democracy for 30 years until economic stress and disillusionment with corrupt government provoked a number of civilian riots and political coups which have weakened the government. The ruling party was rejected by the electorate in the December 1992 elections, but the results have been widely disputed, causing considerable unrest in the country.

Religion: Religious freedom is guaranteed in the constitution. The Catholic Church regained official recognition in 1964 after years of strained Church-State relations, and has a strong influence which sometimes causes difficulties for foreign missions – especially in reaching the indigenous Amerindians.

Spiritist/animist 2.4%. If baptized Catholics who are practising Spiritists are included, probably nearer 12%.
Non-religious/other 2.3%.
Muslim 0.42%. Predominantly Arabs and Turks.
Baha'i 0.2%. **Buddhist** 0.12%. **Jews** 0.10%.
Christian 94.5%. Affil 91%. Growth 1.8%.
Protestant 5.34%. Growth 10.3%.

Church	Cong	Members	Affiliated
Seventh-day Adventist	175	47,000	118,000
Assemblies of God	250	30,000	62,965
Light of the World	300	35,800	60,000
Baptist Convention	186	15,769	45,100
OVICE (TEAM)	665	21,320	35,500
Christian Congregation	63	7,500	25,000
Christian Brethren	78	7,800	19,500
Assoc of Evang Chs	84	6,720	15,000
Natnl Assemb of God	80	7,000	14,000
Indigenous Indian Chs	74	2,590	10,800
United World Mission	21	3,000	10,000
All other (80)	3,007	277,645	638,220
Denominations (91)	4,983	461,344	1,054,085
Evangelicals 4.8% of pop		414,070	940,720
Pentecostal/charis 3.43%		290,000	675,000

Missionaries:
to Venezuela 637 (1:31,000 people) in 53 agencies.
from Venezuela 131 (1:8,000 Protestants) in 7 agencies 12frn 50xcul 81dom.
Roman Catholic 87.7%. Affil 84.1% Attend 10%. Growth 1.2%

Catholic Ch	1,145	9,130,000	16,606,000

Missionaries:
to Venezuela 150 (1:132,000 people).
from Venezuela 480 (1973 figure).
Other Catholic 0.02%. Affil 0.01%. Growth 1.2%.

All other (1)		1,250	2,500

Orthodox 0.15%. Affil 0.13%. Growth 9.5%.

Denominations (6)		13,800	26,000

Marginal 1.36%. Growth 17.5%.

Jehovah's Witnesses	770	60,444	201,000
Mormons	135	31,000	62,000
All other (4)		2,656	5,400
All groups (6)	905	94,100	268,400

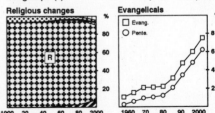

Religious changes

Evangelicals
☐ Evang.
○ Pente.

1. **Venezuela is at a critical point in its history.** Economic mismanagement of its oil wealth has enriched a minority at the expense of the majority, fuelled unchecked corruption, stimulated the use of Venezuela as a drug-trafficking conduit, and eroded the credibility of existing democratic structures. Pray for leaders to be raised up who honour God and value fairness, and that justice may be done in the nation.

2. **Venezuela's evangelical breakthrough only really began in the '80s.** Before then growth was slow, but most indigenous Pentecostal and missions-planted churches (especially those linked with the work of **TEAM**, Baptists and **AoG**) have begun to grow at 10% a year. There are still obstacles that need to be removed in intercession:

a) **An entrenched spiritism** that permeates the life of the country. Occultism is openly practised, and there are thousands of spiritist shops openly marketing charms, medicines, idols and literature.
b) **A traditional Catholicism** that jealously guards its privileged position by encouraging official discrimination against other denominations in hindering building permissions, degree validation in seminaries, issuance of visas and evangelization of the Amerindians.
c) **The insidious effects of drug trafficking** on the economy, society and individuals. Much of this influence comes from Colombia, where the war against the traffickers has intensified.
d) **Moral breakdown in society**, reflected by many single-parent families. Fatherhood is too often associated with abuse, violence, drunkenness and irresponsibility. Those who come to Christ often take years to work through the negatives of their past.
e) **Rapid growth** of New Age influence and worldview, making it harder to reach young people. Also, Mormons and Jehovah's Witnesses are growing at almost double the rate of Evangelicals.

3. **Challenges facing the churches.** The need is:
a) **For true discipleship.** Many new Christians come from tragic, muddled backgrounds and need much help.
b) **For commitment** in a society ensnared in materialism or poverty. Relatively few are therefore willing to commit themselves for full-time ministry, and the loss-rate of pastors going back into secular employment is high.
c) **For unity.** Divisions still hold back effective cooperation in many areas, though there are increasing levels of cooperation.
d) **For petty legalism** in some Pentecostal churches to be broken. This has brought many into bondage rather than the true liberty there is in Christ.
e) **For missions vision in churches.** The first missions congress was held in 1985. Since then many young people have been enthused for world evangelization, with involvement in short-term cross-cultural outreach and a growing number for full-time Bible school training for missions. Yet few congregations have the vision to support them.

4. **Leadership training** is fundamental if present growth rates are to be maintained and urban areas evangelized. There are three seminaries. The ***Seminario Evangélico Asociado***, started by **TEAM** and the Evangelical Free Church, has grown rapidly and serves many denominations. The **Evangelical Seminary of Caracas** serves both mainline and Pentecostal churches. The Baptists also have a Seminary. There are also a number of Bible Institutes and Schools (**UWM**, **AoG** and others).

5. **The evangelization of Amerindian tribal peoples** by Evangelicals has been intensely opposed and their work slandered with unfounded accusations by an assorted group of anthropologists, leftist politicians and some Catholic priests. In 1993 legislation was being considered to ban new work and limit existing work among tribal peoples. The homeland of the largest group, the Yanomamo on the Brazilian border, has been declared a special reserve where no outside influence will be allowed. This deeply affects the work of **NTM** (in eight peoples, including the Yanomamo) and **TEAM** (in a further six). Pray for:

a) **The defeat of all attempts** to prevent Amerindian people from having a chance to hear the gospel – few still live in the old traditional ways.

b) **The Evangelical Council of Venezuela** as it seeks to resolve the issue with the authorities.
c) **The opening up of the few remaining unevangelized tribes** for evangelical missionaries – possibly Venezuelan missionaries would be preferable.
d) **The continued ingathering** of Amerindians among the Guajiro, Maquiritare, Yanomamo, Panare, Motilone, etc. into culturally-appropriate churches. Most of the larger tribes have significant and growing churches.
e) **Bible translation work,** which continues in 13 languages. Translation work may only be needed in an additional 4–10 languages. Pray for the impact of God's Word to be such that these peoples may

be spiritually mature enough to cope with the inevitable encroachment of Spanish culture and all the trappings of civilization.

f) **MAF**, which has two planes serving missionaries living in isolated jungle areas.

6. **The work of Protestant missions** has not been easy. To obtain visas is often a battle in faith. Comity agreements between the early missions hindered advance. Vigorous opposition by the Catholic Church earlier in the century, as well as the strong anti-foreign feeling, created barriers to harmonious relationships among missionaries and nationals. Renewed public denunciation of missionaries in general continued in the '90s. Pray for more missionaries for urban church planting and Bible teaching ministries, and for close and harmonious cooperation between expatriates and national workers. The largest missions: **NTM** (151 workers), **TEAM** (103), **SBC** (80), Evangelical Free Church (36), **AoG** (18), **LCMS** (17), **CMA** (16), Christian Brethren (13), **WEC** (12), **CCC** (11).

7. **The less-reached sections of society:**
a) **The upper and middle classes** have been less evangelized. A number of missions and churches are concentrating efforts to reach these important groups.
b) **Caracas**, the capital, is less evangelized than the Amerindian tribes. In 1985 there were only about 25,000 Evangelicals in 165 churches for a city of 3,600,000; the situation was not markedly improved in 1992. However, in 1939 there were only two churches! Pray for a concerted effort to plant churches in every part of the growing city (**CMA**, **TEAM** and Pentecostal churches have set goals for the '90s). There are about one million living in the *ranchos* (slums).
c) **Students** have been neglected. Christian groups on campuses are generally small. More needs to be done to evangelize and disciple students (**CCC**, **IFES**).

8. **The unreached minorities:**
a) **Italian and Portuguese** immigrants are hardly touched by Evangelicals.
b) **The Arab** community has become prominent in commerce. Some are Orthodox and Maronite Catholics, but many are Shi'a and Sunni Muslims. No direct effort to evangelize them has been made. There are also growing communities of Iranians and Turks.
c) **The Jews** number 20,000. There is no permanent ministry directed towards them.
d) **The Chinese** are growing in numbers. There are only two small congregations of believers for the 40,000. Several missions have a ministry among them (Canadian Chinese, **CMA** and **WEC**).

9. **Christian literature is in demand.** Economic conditions are adversely affecting costs and distribution. Both **TEAM**/Evangelical Free Church and the Baptists founded publishing houses which are now run by Venezuelans. **CLC** has a growing wholesale and retail distribution network with six centres. More literature workers are needed.

10. **Christian radio** is a strategic ministry. **TWR** Bonaire has a wide audience, and many have been won to Christ and edified. Venezuelan Christians plan to start Christian FM and AM commercial stations for radio and, later, TV. Pray that needed permits may be granted.

V

Vietnam
(Socialist Republic of Vietnam)

November 26–28
Asia

Area 330,000 sq.km. Long, narrow country occupying the entire 3,444 km. eastern and southern coastline of Indochina.

Population		Ann. Gr.	Density
1990	67,171,000	2.3 %	203/sq.km
1995	75,030,000	2.2 %	226/sq.km

Possibly two million have fled Vietnam since 1975.

Peoples:
Vietnamese 86.7%. Predominantly coastal people; large cultural differences between northern and southern Vietnamese.
Mon-Khmer 5%. Over 44 ethno-linguistic groups. Largest: Khmer (Cambodian) 1,030,000; Muong 800,000; Koho 186,000; Mnong 180,000; Bahnar 158,00; Hrey 149,000; Stieng 81,000; Sedang 75,000; Bru 50,000.
Thai-Dai 3.9%. Over 17 ethno-linguistic groups. Largest: Tho 900,000; Nung 600,000; Tai Dam 500,000; Tai Don 190,000; Phu Thai 150,000; Tai Daeng 100,000.
Miao/Yao 1.6%. Over seven groups. Largest: Hmong 1,032,000; Miao 650,000; Mien (Yao) 326,000.
Malayo-Polynesian 1%. Over five groups. Jarai 304,000; Cham 143,000; Radey 120,000; Roglai 86,000; Haroi 33,000.
Chinese 1%. About two-thirds of the 1975 Chinese community has fled to China and the West.
Other 0.8%. Hani 37,000; Mixed race, etc.

Literacy 88%. **Official language:** Vietnamese. **All languages** 88. **Languages with Scriptures** 4Bi 12NT 20por.

Capital: Hanoi 4,500,000. Other cities: Ho Chi Minh City (Saigon) 3,300,000, Urbanization 20%.

Economy: Over 44 years of war played havoc with the economy. Recovery has been slow because of the Vietnamese military intervention in Cambodia, the economic collapse of its main supporter and trading partner, the USSR, and inefficient centralized control of the country by a heavy-handed Marxist bureaucracy. Public debt/person $139. Income/person $189 (0.9% of USA).

Politics: Communist republic declared in North Vietnam in 1945. There was continuous warfare between 1941 and 1985, under the Japanese, and then against the French, South Vietnam, USA and all surrounding lands. North Vietnam finally conquered the South in 1975, and Cambodia in 1978-85. Vietnam's poverty and diplomatic isolation has only marginally modified its Marxist policies. Vietnam's attempts to liberalize the economy in the late '80s were only partially successful.

Religion: Constitutional guarantees of religious freedom are meaningless; actual government policy is to control all religious movements. Pressures on Christians continue to be harsh, and particularly severe for unregistered churches. Persecution markedly increased during 1991 but has lessened since then.
Non-religious/other 29.8%.
Buddhist 52%. Numerous sects, and strongly permeated with Confucianism, animism and magic.
New religions 5.2%.
  Cao Dai 2,000,000; a syncretic Buddhist-Catholic religion.
  Hoa Hao 1,500,000; an offshoot of Buddhism.
Animist 3%. Among tribal groups.
Muslim 0.2%. Mainly the Cham people.
Christian 9.8%. Growth 6.2%.
Protestant 0.8%. Growth 12.5%.

Church	Cong	Members	Affiliated
Evangelical Ch (CMA)	260	160,000	350,000
Unregd. house chs	253	38,000	95,000
Montagnard churches		18,000	60,000
Seventh-day Adventist	23	4,000	6,670
Assemblies of God	46	2,100	3,000
All other (5)		11,500	22,140
Denominations (10)	632	233,600	536,810
Evangelicals 0.78% of pop		225,900	524,000
Pentecostal/charis 0.18%		48,000	115,000

Missionaries:
  to Vietnam 19 (1:3,500,000 people).
  from Vietnam 3 (1:180,000 Protestants) 3frn.
Roman Catholic 8.9%. Growth 5.7%.

Catholic Ch		3,900,000	6,000,000

Missionaries:
  to Vietnam 1.
  from Vietnam 340 (1973 figure).
Marginal groups 0.07%.

All groups (8)		22,000	50,000.

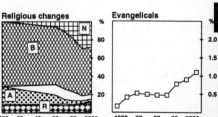

1. **Vietnam remains one of the few avowedly Communist nations in the world.** The North Vietnamese conquest of South Vietnam in 1975 ended the war but brought great hardship to the population. Repression of religious, economic and political freedoms continues. Pray that Vietnam might emerge from its long night of suffering, freed from past demonic and ideological bondages, and open for the gospel.

2. **All open missionary work ceased in 1975. CMA** laboured for 64 years in Vietnam (for 50 years as the only Protestant mission). Other agencies arrived in the late '50s, notably **WEC, UWM** and **SIL** among the tribes, and Southern Baptists in the cities. In 1974 there were 280 missionaries in the land. The years of sowing are beginning to reap an abundant harvest.

3. **A triumphant, growing Church is emerging from years of persecution.** In the late '80s it was apparent that a large-scale turning to God was taking place, with reports of rapid growth in both registered and unregistered churches, in the Catholic Church and especially among the mountain tribal peoples of central and southern Vietnam. Praise God for preservation and growth. As in China, Communism failed to stamp out the witness, but rather strengthened and spread the flame of the Spirit! Statistics are scarce, but between 1985 and 1992 Evangelicals may have more than doubled in number.

4. **Christians continue to suffer for their faith.** The Marxist regime fears the influence of Christians – especially that of the mushrooming house church movement, perceiving the demise of Communism elsewhere attributable to the role played by Christians. Repression, interrogations and imprisonments have increased since 1990. Lack of news from Vietnam, sad memories of the Vietnam war and euphoria over the collapse of Communism elsewhere have caused this land and its suffering Church to be forgotten by believers elsewhere. Pray for:
   a) **Those in prison for their faith.** In 1992 there were possibly 60 or more Christians incarcerated. Pray for their witness in prison – many have come to faith because of it in the past. Pray also for their grieving, often destitute families.
   b) **Registered churches.** Pray that pastors and believers may withstand unrelenting government pressures to compromise and conform to strict regulations. The Church in the north has suffered much longer, and controls by the authorities there are more strict. Meetings are only permitted in recognized church buildings – but many have been closed or destroyed. All open evangelism, itinerant ministry or printing of literature is forbidden and contact with foreign Christians restricted. Yet these churches have grown, especially the Evangelical Church (CMA), among the mountain peoples or Montagnards, and more recently in **AoG** churches.
   c) **Unregistered churches.** These are harried by the police, with meetings frequently broken up and leaders arrested. Yet the courage and tenacity of these believers under pressure rarely fails and growth continues. There are tensions between leaders of registered and unregistered churches.
   d) **The *Montagnard* churches** among the Hrey, Jeh, Roglai, Toho, Jarai, Radey and many others. They have suffered particularly savage persecution – churches razed, congregations scattered, Christians killed. Yet continuing people movements to Christ are reported. Maintaining adequate fellowship is hard where meetings are illegal and little of the Scriptures in their languages survive. This has led to schisms and false teaching in some areas.

5. **Leadership training is the urgent need.** Many of the Evangelical Church pastors are old, and younger churches are often led by those with no opportunity for theological study and therefore susceptible to error or bias in their teaching. Pray for an increase in the importation of study materials, theological books and commentaries – all in short supply. Pray also for informal study programmes and several unofficial Bible schools in Hanoi, Ho Chi Minh City, Danang and elsewhere. The Catholics have reopened four seminaries, but student selection and graduation is monitored by the Marxists.

6. **Vietnam's flood of refugees** has become a trickle as countries make immigration more difficult, but over two million have fled amidst terrible suffering. Who will easily forget the tragic *boat people*, many of whom perished in their attempts to reach freedom? (A high proportion were of the ethnic Chinese minority.) Pray for those still in camps in Indonesia, Malaysia, Thailand, Hong Kong and elsewhere, with little chance of resettlement. Pray for those settled in the USA 859,000, France 300,000, China 250,000, Australia 37,000, Canada 33,000, and about 25 other lands. Pray for Christian workers seeking to meet their spiritual and material needs. Praise God for the steady stream of conversions to Christ among them. Pray also for the Vietnamese churches in North America and Europe.

7. **Vietnam is gradually opening up to the outside world.** The desperate need for economic development and trade is giving opportunities for tentmaker missionaries in business and teaching English. The **AoG** have been invited to set up a drug rehabilitation centre and orphanages. The Mennonites and others have been asked to develop social programmes for the poor. Pray that this land may be fully opened once more for missions input and that even now there may be those called and prepared to go to Vietnam. There remains much land to be possessed.

8. **The less-reached.** The present growth of the Church is not universal – many sections of the community and numerous ethnic groups remain scarcely touched by the gospel. Pray for:
a) **The Muslim Cham and Buddhist Khmer** of the Mekong Delta; only a handful have believed. **FEBC** broadcasts twice a week in Cham and twice daily in Khmer.
b) **The northern ethnic minorities** which have been beyond the reach of missionaries for 50 years because of war and Communism. Most are Buddhist or animist, and are without any known believers. Pray especially for those of the Dai and Miao-Yao peoples listed above and also for the Khmu, Khang, Khao, Muong and Pong. Only those for whom Christian radio broadcasts are provided have opportunity to hear. **FEBC** broadcasts in **White** and **Black Tai** and also **Nung**; there have been conversions as a result.
c) **Central highland ethnic minorities** such as the Hung, Nguon, May, So and others which have never been reached.
d) **Communist officials and government leaders.** The perfect Communist state for which they fought and suffered has proved a grim failure. Disillusionment is widespread.
e) **The Cao Dai and Hoa Hao religionists** who strongly resisted Communism. They are declining in numbers. Christians need to be aware of their unique cultures and beliefs and reach them in a relevant way.

9. **Bible ministries:**
a) **Only 20,000 Bibles have been legally imported into Vietnam since 1975.** Pray for these restrictions to be removed. Pray also for Bibles and New Testaments to be brought into the country overtly or covertly and for effective distribution networks to be set up. Only about 10% of Vietnamese believers in the south have copies of the Scriptures; the number is far less in the north.
b) **Bible translation** is an ongoing task. Christians in the north are working on a new translation of the Vietnamese Bible. At the fall of South Vietnam in 1975, **SIL** members were working on 24 translation projects; work continues in seven languages, but between 44 and 63 have a definite translation need. Pray for the completion of this task.

10. **Christian media ministries:**
a) **Christian literature** production is strictly monitored and effectually banned. Christians have set up some secret presses, and a little literature is surreptitiously carried into the country. Pray for the provision of evangelistic, follow-up and teaching literature.
b) **The *Jesus* film** and video is available in Vietnamese and Hmong, but lack of freedom and equipment limit the use of the video.
c) **GRn** have prepared recordings in 55 languages of Vietnam. Pray that these may be circulated throughout the country.
d) **Christian radio programmes** of **FEBA** from Manila and Saipan have been remarkable in their scope and impact. They are a source of strength to tribal and Vietnamese believers, and widely heard despite shortage of batteries and radios and the persecution of those discovered listening in. **FEBA** broadcasts 24 hours/week in Vietnamese and one or two programmes/week in 23 other minority languages. Pray for first-language speakers – for their provision and preservation to keep up the flow of programmes.

<table>
<tr><td>

**See
Caribbean**

Caribbean

</td></tr>
</table>

Virgin Islands of the USA

(The Territory of the Virgin Islands of the USA)

Area 352 sq.km. In the Leeward Islands lying between Puerto Rico and British Virgin Islands. Three larger and 50 smaller islands.

Population	Ann. Gr.	Density
1990 113,000	1.5 %	321/sq.km
1995 121,000	1.4 %	344/sq.km

Very rapid growth in '60s and '70s through immigration from other Caribbean islands.

Peoples:
English-speaking 83.7%.
 Afro-Caribbean 69.4%. **Euro-American** 12.5%. **Other** 1.8%.
Hispanic-speaking 16.3%.
 Afro-Caribbean 10.3%. **Euro-American** 2.3%. **Other** 3.7%.

Literacy 90%. **Official language:** English, but Spanish widely spoken.

Capital: Charlotte Amalie 13,600. Urbanization 45%.

Economy: Tourism is the mainstay of the economy, with over one million visitors a year. A growing industrial base, with the ninth largest oil refinery in the world. About half the working population is poor and foreign, creating tensions in society. Income/person $11,740 (56% of USA).

Politics: Danish colony until 1917, when purchased by the USA. A self-governing unincorporated US territory.

Religion:
Non-religious 1.5%. **Baha'i** 0.5%.
Spiritist/Rastafarian 0.5%. **Jews** 0.3%.
Christian 97.2%. Affil 81.8%. Growth 1.7%.
Protestant 58.7%. Affiliated 49.7%. Gr 1.9%.

Church	Cong	Members	Affiliated
Episcopal Ch	8	6,875	13,800
Seventh-day Adventist	15	4,500	7,500
Moravian Ch	8	2,200	6,290
Methodist Ch	8	2,250	4,500
Baptist Intl Mission	5	1,800	3,000
Ch of God of Prophecy	4	700	2,800
Ch of God (Cleveland)	5	1,118	2,240
Assemblies of God	4	1,000	1,670
Ch of the Nazarene	4	305	699
All other (30)	127	10,865	20,371
Denominations (39)	188	31,613	62,870
Evangelicals 22.7% of pop		13,000	25,600
Pentecostal/charis 15%		8,500	17,000

Missionaries to Virgin Is 39 (1:2,900 people) in 6 agencies.
Roman Catholic 34.4%. Affil 27.8%. Growth 0.9%.

Catholic Ch	5	18,000	31,500

Missionaries to Virgin Is 39 (1:2,900 people).
Orthodox 0.6%. Affil 0.6%. Growth 1.4%.

Total	1	290	725

Marginal 3.5%. Affil 3.5%. Growth 4%.

Jehovah's Witnesses	8	481	1,200
All other (7)	14	1,640	2,859
Groups (8)	15	2,121	4,055

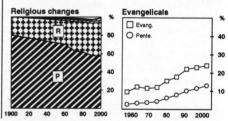

Religious changes

Evangelicals

1. **Tourism and the inflow of wealth have played havoc with the moral and social fabric of society.** Crime is widespread. Pray for the evangelization of tourists, those involved in the crime "industry", the many Hispanics and the local islanders themselves.

2. **The great need is revival.** Many Christians are very nominal. The Moravians had a glorious past, but need a renewed singleness of love for Christ. The growth of the sects, the New Age movement and the Rastafarian movement among the youth are symptoms of spiritual poverty.

3. **There is conversion growth** through the witness of the two Church of God groups, Assemblies of God and the Nazarenes. The Catholic Church grows through immigration and the influence of the charismatic movement. Pray for unity and shared vision for the '90s among evangelical leaders.

4. **The Christian Church has become nominal and lacking in vitality.** The Evangelicals are no exception to this malaise. Though some islanders are coming to Christ, the majority of the inhabitants, who live in an earthly paradise, are not heading in the direction of the heavenly one.

V

Wallis and Futuna Islands

(French Territory of Wallis and Futuna)

Include with French Guiana
Pacific

Area 274 sq.km. Three groups of coral islands 300 km. west of Samoa.

Population	Ann. Gr.	Density
1990 15,000	4.6 %	55/sq.km
1995 16,000	1.3 %	58/sq.km

A further 14,000 work in New Caledonia.

Peoples:
Polynesian 98.4%. Wallisian (Uvean) 9,900; Futunan 4,750.
Other 1.6%. French 120.

Literacy 95%. **Official language:** French.

Capital: Mata-Utu 600.

Economy: Based on export of labour and coconuts.

Politics: An overseas territory of France.

Religion: Roman Catholicism is the only recognised religion. Virtually a Catholic theocracy. Almost the entire population is church-going.
Non-religious/other 1.1%.
Christian 98.9%.
  Protestant 1.5%. Mainly Futunans.
  Roman Catholic 97.4%.
  Missionaries:
    to W & F 3 (1:5,000 people).
    from W & F 14 (1:1,100 Catholics).

1. **The Catholic Church** and Polynesian culture and social structures have become so interwoven that adherence to Christianity is often more outward than through a living, personal faith. Pray for first-hand faith for these two island peoples.

2. **Until 1985 this territory was one of the few countries of the world without a congregation of evangelical believers.** Then a converted Futunan was used of God to plant a vigorous, though persecuted, church in his homeland. There has been good growth, the New Testament is being translated, and outreach to the Wallis Islands has begun. On one there are several Wallisian and one Vietnamese family of believers. Pray for them.

3. **Many islanders have migrated to New Caledonia and Vanuatu** seeking work. Pray that some may be won to a personal commitment to Christ there, and thereby bring blessing to their homeland.

<table>
<tr><td>

November 29–30

Middle East
</td></tr>
</table>

Yemen
(Republic of Yemen)

Area 472,000 sq.km. (532,000 sq.km. if the disputed border area with Saudi Arabia is included). Mountainous south and south-western portion of the Arabian Peninsula.

Population	Ann. Gr.	Density
1990 12,756,000	4.77 %	27/sq.km
1995 16,102,000	3.36 %	34/sq.km

About one million Yemenis expelled from Saudi Arabia and Gulf states during the 1990 Gulf crisis.

Peoples:
Arabs 97.2%. Over 1,700 clans or tribes.
Other 2.8%. Somali 230,000 (also 60,000 or more recent refugees). Mahri and Soqotri 31,000; African 28,000; Indian and Pakistani 65,000; Jews 2,000.

Literacy 39%. **Official language:** Arabic. **All languages** 6. **Languages with Scriptures** 2Bi 1NT 3por.

Capital: Sana'a 427,000. Other city: Aden 318,000. Urbanization 25%.

Economy: Agricultural and pastoral economy. Increasing export of oil. Aden is a key international port. Major foreign currency earnings came from Yemeni workers in Saudi Arabia – this ceased with their expulsion in 1990, a major blow to the economy. Public debt/person $386. Income/person $640 (3% of USA).

Politics: A turbulent history of wars and conquests. The North was an isolated feudal theocracy until 1962's republican revolution. The North remains conservative. The South was ruled by Britain until independence in 1967, but soon afterwards a Marxist coup ousted traditional rulers, imposing a leftist regime. The two disparate countries united in 1990. After two years of violent electioneering, peaceful elections for a unitary government were held in April 1993.

Religion: Islam is the official religion, but there are tensions between the North, wanting the full implementation of Islamic law, and the South, wanting a more moderate stance.
Muslim 99.9%. Sunni 62% (centre and south); Shi'a Zaidi 37% (northeast); Ismaili 0.9%.
Jews 0.02%. A few remaining in north – once a large population.
Christian 0.06%. Largely expatriate.
Protestant: A few hundred expatriates and some Yemeni secret believers. Expatriates in NGOs 60.
Catholic: About 5,000 expatriates. Expatriates serving in Yemen 60.
Orthodox: Ethiopian refugees.

1. **Yemen once had many Christians.** The Muslim conquest in the time of Mohammed was followed by the conversion of Yemenis to Islam. Pray that Jesus may reign in many Yemeni hearts once more.

2. **The nation's stability and social structure are threatened** by tensions between North and South, influx of refugees, inter-tribal feuding and widespread use of the narcotic *qat*. The latter debilitating habit has diverted much valuable agricultural land into the cultivation of its leaves. May Yemenis, like their illustrious ancestor the Queen of Sheba, seek for wisdom from the One greater than Solomon!

3. **For 1,300 years, the North was sealed from the gospel.** In 1964 the government asked some Christian agencies to initiate health and educational projects. Only three remain in a low-profile ministry with opportunities to tactfully share their faith. Pray for spiritual liberation; as yet very few Yemenis have ever heard the gospel.

4. **The South had longer exposure to the Christian message,** and several groups of Yemeni believers came into being. In 1972 the Marxist government nationalized all mission and church property, and Christian workers had to leave, only one Catholic priest remaining to minister to a few Christians of Indian origin. There are signs of change since the union; the Anglican church is likely to be returned to the few remaining believers. Pray for a new day of freedom for worship and witness.

5. **There are expatriate Christians living for their Lord** in their secular jobs as well as those in non-government agencies. Pray that they may maintain their spiritual glow in the face of many attacks from the enemy of souls through discouragement, sickness, isolation from the wider Christian family, and constant threats to their presence in the land. Pray for greater freedom for them to share their faith by word and through literature. Pray also for others to be called to serve in the many existing openings in health, water engineering and education.

6. **Yemeni believers** rarely have any opportunity for real fellowship, and are under continual pressure from relatives and persecution from the authorities. There are only a handful known in the North, but possibly more in the South. Pray that they may be strong in their faith, growing in grace and used of the Lord to win others.

7. **Unreached peoples**. Yemen is one of the world's least evangelized countries. Specific peoples for prayer:
a) **Large areas of the Hadhramaut** in the southeast and mountain areas of the North have never been evangelized.
b) **The non-Arab indigenous minorities** – the Mahri in the interior mountains of the Hadhramaut and the indigenous Soqotri on the Indian Ocean island of Socotra. No Christians are known, though centuries ago the Soqotri were Christian.
c) **The refugee Ethiopians and Somalis**. Few Christians are known among the latter, but there is a large fellowship of evangelical Christians among the Ethiopians.

8. **Christian media**.
a) **Bibles**. There is a need for an Arabic translation in Yemeni Arabic.
b) **Video and audio cassettes** of music, preaching, Scripture portions and parables are available in Yemeni Arabic, but the **Jesus** film is not yet available in Yemeni Arabic; this could make a big impact.
c) **Christian radio programmes** from **FEBA**-Seychelles are clearly received. Many listen. Pray for lasting fruit and fellowships of believers to result. There are 18 hours/week broadcast in Arabic and 3.5 hours/week in Somali.

Y

<table>
<tr><td>**December
1**</td><td rowspan="2">*Former
Yugoslavia*</td><td></td></tr>
<tr><td>Europe</td></tr>
</table>

April 1993. Only Serbia and Montenegro remain as a federal republic under the name Yugoslavia. The other republics of the former Yugoslavia declared their independence during 1991 and 1992. Bosnia and Hercegovina, Croatia, Macedonia and Slovenia are still retained under Yugoslavia in this book **only** because of their entanglements in the wars and distress that followed its dismemberment. General information and prayer points are given first, followed by descriptions of each of the newly constituted republics.

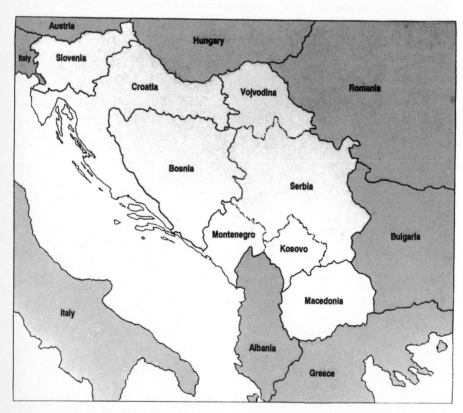

Total area 256,000 sq.km. On the Adriatic Sea in the southwest Balkans.

Population		Ann.Gr.	Density
1990	23,345,000	0.25%	91/sq.km

Peoples: Europe's most complex mosaic of peoples after the Caucasus region in Russia.
National groups 89%. Considerable intermingling in the different republics. Serbs 36.3%; Croats 19.7%; Bosnians 8.9%; Slovenes 7.8%; Albanians 7.7%; Macedonians 6%; Montenegrins 2.6%.

Other major groups 11%. Gypsy 834,000; Hungarian 549,000; Turk 143,000; Slovak 110,000; Bulgarian 79,000; Romanian 76,000; Arab 72,000; Czech 34,000. Large movements of population since 1991.

Politics: The division of the Roman Empire nearly 1,700 years ago created a major cultural and religious fault-line between northwest and southeast of the former Yugoslavia. Successive ethnic and imperial conquests further helped to make the Balkans a byword for ethnic hatreds and political intrigue. Modern Yugoslavia developed from fragments of the Austro-Hungarian and Ottoman Turkish empires between 1878 and 1921. Ethnic nationalisms helped trigger World War I and provoke genocidal civil war during World War II. Communism imposed by President Tito in 1945 blanketed deep ethnic hatred between Serb and Croat and Serb and Albanian. Tito's death in 1980 exposed the nation's festering wounds and loosened the bonds within the federal republic. By 1991 the break-up of the country erupted in civil wars that have threatened to entangle surrounding nations.

Religion: The media portray Yugoslavia's conflicts as religious – but they are more ethnic and ideological. Religion is manipulated because of ethnic linkages with Catholicism, Orthodoxy or Islam. Estimates for 1990:

Non-religious/other 14.3%.
Muslim 11%. Mainly Bosnians and Albanians.
Christians 74.7%.
  Protestant 0.7%. Mainly among ethnic minorities.
  Catholic 33%. Mainly Croat, Slovene, Czech, Slovak.
  Orthodox 41%. Mainly Serb, Montenegrin and Macedonian.

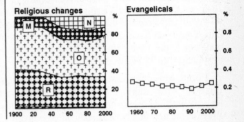

1. **The Balkan conflict could ignite a regional war** in which Serbia is supported by Orthodox Christian nations, Bosnia by Turkey and Muslim lands, and Western nations siding with Croatia or attempting to quell the conflagration. Pray that world leaders may be wise to know when courage or caution is needed in momentous decisions that must be made.

2. **"Ethnic cleansing" is new to the vocabulary of world politics, but not new to the nations that comprise the old Yugoslavia.** During Germany's occupation in World War II, Croatian nationalists slaughtered between 60,000 and 750,000 Serbs. The large Serbian minorities in Bosnia and Croatia fear a repetition, and launched a pre-emptive war to link Serbian enclaves and eliminate other ethnic groups within those links. The savagery, atrocities and duplicity of those involved in the fighting have shocked the world. The hatreds generated could sour yet further generations without a deep repentance and forgiveness that can only come through a personal relationship with the Lord Jesus Christ. There has been an unprecedented openness to the gospel since 1991.

3. **The Church is one of the most traditional in Europe** – this includes Orthodox, Catholic and most Protestant denominations, though small renewal movements among Romanian Orthodox and Catholics are significant. A recent increase in religious fervour is little more than a reinforcement of ethnic prejudices. Most denominations are restricted to one or two peoples. Pray for an outpouring of the Spirit that will halt the decline, enliven traditional congregations, replace liberal theology with fervent biblical preaching and bring unity to the body of Christ.

4. **Protestants number 83,000,** and of these Evangelicals number only 18,000 or so, a tiny minority more concentrated in north Croatia and Vojvodina in Serbia among the Hungarian and Slovak minorities. Yet in the fragmentation of Yugoslavia they remain one of the few bodies that is not tied to a single ethnic group, though this can still be an issue among them. Pray specifically for:
a) **Spiritual effectiveness** in a time of unprecedented stress and openness.
b) **Unity.** Protestant churches can be as *Balkanized* as their nations. Divisions because of strong personalities, ethnic and denominational exclusivism and doctrine have often limited effective cooperation and witness. Only in Croatia has an Evangelical Alliance been formed.
c) **Growth.** Stagnation and decline in the Protestant churches have been the pattern for decades. Pray that there may be revival in these churches. There are signs of hope – Slovak evangelical churches are full and vibrant, the Evangelical Church (Pentecostal) is evangelistic and growing in nearly every republic, and evangelical churches in Croatia are winning new converts.

5. **The spiritual need of these nations is great.** Since Albania's opening to the gospel, and planting of evangelical churches there, Macedonia, Montenegro, Bosnia, southern Serbia and Dalmatia in Croatia are now Europe's areas with the fewest evangelical believers. Over 90% of former Yugoslavia's evangelical churches are north of Belgrade. Pray specifically for:
a) **War refugees.** Some estimate that by mid-1993 there were 120,000 killed and 2 million refugees both within former Yugoslavia and in other European countries – most in Germany (250,000). The personal tragedies caused by torture, rape, split families and orphaned children are overwhelming aid organizations, Christian agencies and churches. This is especially true in Croatia. Pray that many may come to a living faith. Pray for local and expatriate churches and agencies seeking to meet physical, emotional and spiritual needs.

b) **The cities.** There are 36 cities of over 50,000 inhabitants without an evangelical congregation. The **Balkan Mission** and *Iliricum*, two indigenous agencies, have the vision to plant churches in each of these cities.

c) **Ethnic groups.** Some of the least evangelized peoples on earth are the Bosnians, Gypsies (no evangelical churches or outreach), and Albanians (one small evangelical church) of the former Yugoslavia.

6. Peoples from former Yugoslavia working in Western Europe number over 1,000,000. Pray for their evangelization in Germany (652,000), Austria (160,000), Switzerland (142,000), Sweden (120,000) and France (70,000) – supplemented by 500,000 refugees, mainly Croatians, Bosnians and Albanians from Kosova. Among them are communities representing all of the diverse peoples of the country. Some have come to Christ and returned home with a testimony. The work has been especially fruitful in Sweden.

7. Foreign missions have many openings for long-term ministry – the degree of openness for overtly Christian work varying. Much done hitherto has been short term, but long-term workers who identify with the people and their language and also with indigenous believers are the greatest need. Pray for the few who have already become involved in ministry in these republics in a time of danger and distress. There are an estimated 60 foreign missionaries assigned to the republics of the former Yugoslavia.

8. Christian help ministries for prayer:

a) **Bible printing and distribution** have been complicated by the breakdown of communications in the wars. The Bible Society has had to set up separate agencies in each republic. Demand for the Scriptures has never been greater.

b) **Christian literature** could be a vital tool. There are two key Christian bookstores – in Belgrade and Zagreb – but stocks are limited and the variety poor – even poorer in Cyrillic script, Serbian and Macedonian. Good evangelistic, apologetic and teaching literature is needed.

c) **Christian radio programmes** are prepared by **ECM** and other agencies, and transmitted by **TWR**, **IBRA**, High Adventure and others in Serbian (7 hours/week), Albanian (5), Croatian (4.5) and Slovenian (1.7). This is too little for major impact, but resources are limited and producers few.

December 2

BOSNIA & HERCEGOVINA
(Republic of Bosnia & Hercegovina)

Area 51,000 sq.km. Landlocked mountainous Balkan state.

Population		Ann.Gr	Density
1990	4,308,000	0.53%	84/sq.km
1995	4,422,000	0.52%	86/sq.km

1.5 million refugees due to the war.

Peoples: Figures for 1991; subsequent large displacements of people in the Bosnian war.
Bosnian Muslim 38.3%; **Serb** 30.1%; **Croat** 17.3%; **Other** 13.2%. Rumelian Turks 1.1%. No ethnic group has a majority.

Literacy est. 92%. **Official language:** Serbo-Croat.

Capital: Sarajevo 319,000 in 1991; devastated by besieging Serb forces and population reduced since then.

Economy: Small-scale farming and light industry. War has led to massive destruction of villages, towns and cities.

Politics: Bosnia became separated from Serbia in 960, and during the 500-year Turkish occupation many Bosnian Serbs became Muslim. The breakup of Yugoslavia led to a Croat-Muslim alliance in support of independence in March 1992. This was immediately followed by Serbian military action to increase their area to 70% of Bosnia, thus linking all Serb majority areas in Croatia, Bosnia and Serbia. All efforts by UN and other mediators to stem Serbian aggression and "ethnic cleansing" have failed to deliver a solution acceptable to all warring parties. By May 1993 Serbian and Croatian forces had seized most Muslim-majority areas.

Religion: No religious group could claim dominance, though Islam was the largest minority.
Muslim 40%.
Non-religious/other 18%.
Christian 42%. Growth −0.2%.
  Protestant 0.04%. Growth 0.8%.

Church	Cong	Members	Affiliated
Seventh-day Adventist	21	673	1,040
Ev Chr Ch of Bosnia (Luth)	2	385	550
Evangelical Ch (Pente)	3	80	123
Baptist Ch	1	40	62
Christian Brethren	1	25	42
Denominations (5)	28	1,203	1,817
Evangelicals 0.01% of pop		318	490

Roman Catholic 14%. Growth −0.8%.
Roman Catholic   350   416,000   603,000
Orthodox 27.9%. Growth 0%.
Serbian Orthodox   360   828,000   1,200,000
Marginal 0.02%. Growth 5.2%.

1. **The tragedy of the Bosnian people** has been vividly shown to the world. The destruction of villages and towns, expulsion of their inhabitants, systematic looting, and rape of women have left deep scars and an abiding hatred between communities that once lived together and even intermarried. Pray for peace and a just settlement.

2. **Bosnia has fewer evangelical believers than any other country in Europe.** Only 3–4 evangelical congregations were known to exist before 1991. Pray for a strong, effective witness to develop in every Bosnian town. The Evangelical Church in Croatia has opened a work in three Bosnian cities since 1991.

3. **Bosnian Muslims are Europe's least evangelized people.** Little has ever been done to give them the gospel, and there are no known churches or believers. Christianity is seen to be partly to blame for their agony – the Serbs being Orthodox and Croats Catholic. Both Serbs and Croats have been seizing Bosnian Muslim villages and towns. Pray for Christians to be called to minister to the needs of this abused people in Bosnia and in all the countries into which they have been forced to flee.

CROATIA
(Republic of Croatia)

December 3

Area 56,500 sq.km. Crescent-shaped country between the Danube River and Adriatic Sea. The land is almost bisected by Bosnia and the Serbian-controlled Krajina area of Croatia.

Population		Ann.Gr	Density
1990	4,747,000	0.36%	84/sq.km
1995	4,832,000	0.32%	85/sq.km

Peoples: Croat 78%; Serb 8.6%; Gypsy 2.7%; Other 10.7%.

Literacy est. 97%. **Official language:** Croatian – closely related to Serbian but written in Latin rather than Cyrillic script.

Capital: Zagreb 931,000; a further 150,000 refugees.

Economy: Devastated by loss of territory to Serbians, immense destruction of property and industry, cessation of income from tourism, and the cost of purchasing weaponry for war. Inflation high. Income/person $7,110 (32% of USA).

Politics: Yugoslavia's short history has been dominated by bad relationships between the Serbs and Croats. Declaration of independence from (a Serb-dominated) Yugoslavia in 1991 was followed by invasion and months of bitter warfare in which Croatia lost a third of its territory to the Serbians – largely Serbian-majority areas. An uneasy armed truce supervised by the UN was still holding in April 1993. A multi-party democracy, but stunted by war and authoritarian nationalism.

Religion: The new constitution is likely to grant complete religious freedom. Croatia is traditionally Catholic.
Non-religious/other 6.8%.
Muslim est. 5%. Mainly Bosnians – supplemented by refugees.
Christian 88.2%. Growth 0.6%.
Protestant 0.6%. Growth 0.1%.

Church	Cong	Members	Affiliated
Slovak Ev Chr Ch (Luth)	13	7,140	10,200
Evn Ch in Croatia (Luth)	13	2,250	4,500
Evangelical Ch (Pente)	24	1,500	2,500
Baptist Church	34	1,200	2,000
All other (7)	117	5,028	7,971
Denominations (11)	203	17,118	27,171
Evangelicals 0.18% of pop		5,189	8,700
Pentecostal/charis 0.09%		2,600	4,500

Roman Catholic 72.5%. Growth 1.3%.

Catholic Ch	1,500	2,370,000	3,440,000

Other Catholic 0.16%. Growth −0.2%.

| Denominations (2) | 11 | 3,500 | 7,800 |

Orthodox 14.8%. Growth −2.6%.

| Serbian Orthodox | 300 | 483,000 | 700,000 |

Marginal 0.15%. Growth 6.5%.

| Jehovah's Witnesses | 69 | 3,609 | 7,080 |

1. **The issue of Serb-Croat relationships** and past atrocities perpetrated by both sides has to be faced if lasting peace is to be attained. Only through Christ can true reconciliation be achieved. Pray for this.

2. **Dislocation and suffering** have caused many to seek peace with God, and churches are beginning to grow after decades of decline. Among Protestants, the Lutheran, Baptist and Pentecostal churches have been encouraged by conversions among unchurched.

3. **The refugee situation** is difficult. Many families have suffered bereavements or have been split because of the war. Croatia hosts 700,000 of its own people ejected from their homes as well as many thousands of Bosnians. Croatian churches together with expatriate agencies have done much to alleviate their sufferings and give spiritual help. Many Muslim refugees have been drawn to Christian meetings as a result. This situation has given great impetus to Protestant churches and agencies and fostered a new sense of commitment.

4. **Evangelicals are few on the Adriatic coast.** Pray for more outreach and church planting in Istria, Zagorje and Dalmatia. The Evangelical Church aims to plant churches in every city of over 20,000.

5. **Leadership training.** The Evangelical Theological Seminary (Pentecostal) has returned to its Croatian home in Osijek after a war-exile in Slovenia. There are 120 residential and 160 extension students from all over the Balkans and former USSR as well as former Yugoslavia. About 80% of all former Yugoslav full-time evangelical workers were trained there. Pray for the staff and students and also the provision of all their needs.

December 4

FEDERAL REPUBLIC OF YUGOSLAVIA
(Montenegro & Serbia)

Area 102,000 sq.km comprising two republics, Serbia and Montenegro.

Population		Ann.Gr.	Density
1990	10,338,000	0.85 %	101/sq.km
1995	10,787,394	0.80 %	105/sq.km

Serbia comprises 94% of the population.

Peoples:

Serbia. Serbian 66.4%; Albanian 14% (in Kosova 90%); Hungarian 5.3% (in Vojvodina 19%); Bosnian 2.3%; Croat 1.6%; Other 10.4%.

Montenegro. Montenegrin 62.9%; Bosnian 14.6%; Serb 9.3%; Albanian 6.6%; Croat 3.6%; Gypsy 3%.

Literacy 93%. **Official language:** Serbian. **All languages** 16. **Languages with Scriptures** 8Bi 1NT 4por.

Capital: Belgrade 1,600,000. Belgrade has been destroyed 40 times in its history. Urbanization 50%.

Economy: Slow move away from centralized Communist economy. Massive inflation, trade sanctions and costs of war have crippled the economy. Unemployment 16% and rising. Income/person $2,490 (11% of USA) but ranges from Vojvodina ($6,790) to Kosova ($1,520).

Politics: With Communism discredited, Serbian leaders became strident nationalists but did little to change economic or political structures.

Religion: Since 1990 the Serbian Orthodox Church has sought to regain its former political influence. Other denominations and religions could be disadvantaged. Figures below are largely estimates.

Non-religious/other 9%.

Muslim 17%.

Christian 74%. Growth 2.2%.

Protestant 0.82%. Growth −0.3%.

Church	Cong	Members	Affiliated
Slovak Ev Chr Ch (Luth)	52	28,700	41,000
Reformed Ch	56	8,500	21,250
Evang Ch (Pente)	47	4,000	6,150
Seventh-day Adventist	69	2,923	4,500
Methodist Ch	14	1,200	2,000
Baptist Church	36	800	2,000
Church of God	11	400	615
Christian Brethren	4	100	154
All other (5)	32	3,165	5,758
Denominations (13)	321	49,788	83,427
Evangelicals 0.19% of pop		11,469	19,700
Pentecostal/charis 0.08%		5,300	8,200

Catholic 6.1%. Growth −0.1%.

Latin-rite	200	391,000	567,000
Byzantine-rite	50	38,000	55,000
Denominations (2)	250	429,000	622,000

Orthodox 67%. Growth 2.4%.

Serbian Orthodox	2,300	4,690,000	6,800,000
Bulgarian Orthodox	4	7,000	10,000
All other (2)	25	4,495	9,500
Denominations (4)	2,329	4,701,495	6,819,500

Marginal 0.03%. Growth 6.4%.

Jehovah's Witnesses	32	1,681	2,800

1. **Serbian nationalism** has become a potent weapon in the hands of politicians. The whole of the Balkans has been destabilized. Pray that the spirit of vengefulness and paranoia – based on centuries of perceived victimization – that has gripped leaders and people may be bound. Pray also for full religious freedom to be instituted and preserved.

2. **The Serbian Orthodox Church** has a large and growing influence in both republics, but there is more nationalism than spirituality in that growth. Pray for new life within this ancient Church; there are few signs of a renewal movement.

3. **Evangelical believers** among the Serbs are few, and congregations are small and scattered and often characterized by spiritual mediocrity, personality clashes, petty legalisms and rivalry. There are only seven small congregations in Belgrade and very few south of the city. Present freedoms for open-air evangelism and witness are underused. Pray that the Holy Spirit may bring believers to unity and powerful witness. The majority of Evangelicals are Hungarians and Slovaks in Vojvodina.

4. **Montenegro** is largely Orthodox by tradition and fiercely independent. There is only a small handful of Evangelicals – one small Baptist group and the beginnings of a Pentecostal group. Pray for the calling of workers to this needy republic.

5. **Kosova** is 90% Albanian, who are almost completely Muslim. The only Christians are a 2% Catholic remnant and a small Pentecostal church in the capital, Pristina. Kosova was the cradle of Serb culture, but lost to the Turks after a well-remembered battle in 1389 and only regained after World War I. The Serbian minority has suppressed Albanian culture, expelled many Albanians from employment and children from schools, and instituted "ethnic cleansing" by severe discrimination. Albanians see themselves as suffering more than the Jews ever did under Nazi Germany. Serbian armed forces exert a tight control, but the coming explosion could mean worse fighting than that seen in Bosnia. Pray for:
a) **Peace for Kosova**, and a just political settlement. Mistrustful Albanians seek union with adjoining Albania.
b) **Openness to the gospel**, and for people to proclaim it.

MACEDONIA

December 5

Area 25,700 sq.km. Landlocked state between Serbia, Bulgaria, Greece and Albania.

Population	Ann.Gr.	Density
1990 2,009,000	1.2%	78/sq.km
1995 2,130,000	1.1%	83/sq.km

Peoples: Macedonian 66%; Albanian 20% (estimates vary between 7.2% and 30%); Turk 4.5%; Gypsy 5.3% (possible 8%); Serb 2.1%; Bosnian 2.1%.

Literacy: est. 85%. **Official language:** Macedonian; related to Bulgarian.

Capital: Skopje 600,000.

Economy: One of the poorest regions of former Yugoslavia. Further impoverishment has followed a Greek blockade and UN sanctions against Serbia.

Politics: Macedonia is a melting pot of nations and subject to territorial claims by all its neighbours. Its declaration of independence in 1992 was vigorously contested externally and also internally by its restive and politically-marginalized Albanian minority. If war comes to neighbouring Serbian Kosova, Macedonia could face invasion, civil war and partition in a multi-nation Balkan war. Macedonia is a multi-party democracy, but with the old Communist leaders still retaining control.

Religion: The Orthodox Church has a strong influence. Religious policy has yet to be clarified.
Non-religious/other 8.3–13.3%.
Muslim 25–30%.
Christian 62.8%. Growth 1.6%.
  Protestant 0.18%. Growth 2.3%.

Church	Cong	Members	Affiliated
Methodist Ch	10	1,000	3,000
Seventh-day Adventist	5	200	308
Evangelical Ch	1	120	200
Congregational Ch	1	60	86
Baptist	2	33	50
Denominations (5)	19	1,413	3,644
Evangelicals 0.07% of pop		550	1,300
Pentecostal/charis 0.01%.		120	200
Roman Catholic 2.3%. Growth 0%.			
Catholic	25	32,200	46,700
Orthodox 60.3%. Growth 1.7%.			
Macedonian Orthodox	900	816,000	1,200,000
Albanian Orthodox	7	4,200	6,000
Bulgarian Orthodox	2	3,500	5,000
Denominations (3)	909	823,700	1,211,000
Marginal 0.05%. Growth 4.4%.			
Jehovah's Witnesses	8	400	1,000

1. **Macedonia's future** is clouded with uncertainty, most wondering *when* rather than *whether* war will begin. Pray for ethnic harmony and sensitivity on the part of ethnic leaders.

2. **The Macedonian Orthodox Church** is spiritually weak and steeped in tradition, yet vigorously opposes any evangelical or evangelistic ministry. Pray for new life to touch this Church. Many Macedonians are bound by superstition.

3. **The evangelical witness is very small.** The Methodists are growing, as is the Evangelical Church, but the small Baptist fellowships are stagnant. Pray for unity among believers and active vision for outreach. There are only 3–5 full-time evangelical Christian workers in the country.

4. **The unreached** are numerous.
a) **Skopje, the capital,** has only four small evangelical churches, none ministering to the 60,000 Gypsies or 200,000 Albanians.
b) **Ten cities of 50,000** lie within 100km of Skopje – none of these have an evangelical witness.
c) **The large Gypsy population** may number 160,000. Skopje is the largest Gypsy city in the world. No permanent ministry has ever been directed at their evangelization.
d) **Albanians** are rapidly increasing through both a higher birth rate and thousands of refugees fleeing persecution in Kosova. Nearly all are Muslim. There are no known Christians or Christian ministries among them.

e) **The Turkish community** mostly live in the western city of Debar (84% Muslim). There are no evangelical Christians in the area.

5. **Foreign missions** are only now investigating ministry possibilities. Macedonia may be the European land most needing pioneer missionaries, yet the challenge of this land will make it a hard field of service.

6. **The Macedonian Bible** published in 1988 is rejected by most Christians as inaccurate and difficult to understand. Pray for the completion of a new translation now being undertaken.

SLOVENIA
(Republic of Slovenia)

Area 20,300 sq.km. Alpine state adjoining Italy and Austria.

Population		Ann.Gr	Density
1990	1,943,000	0.3%	96/sq.km
1995	1,979,000	0.4%	98/sq.km

Peoples: The most homogeneous of the republics of former Yugoslavia.
Slav 97%. Slovene, a few Croats, Serbs and Czech.
Other 3%. German, Hungarian, Italian.

Literacy: 98%. **Official language:** Slovenian. **All languages** 5. **Languages with Scriptures** 2Bi 1NT 1por.

Capital: Ljubljana 323,000.

Economy: The most prosperous of former Yugoslav republics – it produced 23% of its exports with 8% of its population. Independence caused slight loss of markets to the south. Income/person $12,520 (56% of USA).

Politics: Dominated for centuries by Austria. Part of Yugoslav federation in 1918 until independence established in 1991 after a brief war with the Serbian/Yugoslav army. There is a strong desire for democratic government and membership in the EC.

Religion: Freedom of religion, but with the Catholic Church having an influential role.
Non-religious/other 17.5%.
Christian 82.5%. Growth 0.3%.
Protestant 1.3%. Growth −0.2%.

Church	Cong	Members	Affiliated
Ev Ch of Augsburg Conf (Lutheran)	30	7,600	19,000
Seventh-day Adventist	93	3,318	5,110
Evangelical Ch (Pente	7	580	967
Baptist Ch	6	300	500
All other (2)	4	180	300
Denominations (6)	140	11,978	25,877
Evangelicals 0.18% of pop		1,949	3,400
Pentecostal/charis 0.05%		600	1,000
Roman Catholic 81%. Growth 0.3%.			
Catholic Ch	1,000	1,100,000	1,588,000
Other Catholic 0.09%. Growth 0%.			
Marginal 0.13%. Growth 6.5%.			
Jehovah's Witnesses	29	1,496	2,500

1. **Slovenia has a strong Catholic tradition.** Pray that knowledge about Christianity may lead Slovenians to the Scriptures and to a relationship with the Living Word.

2. **Bible distribution** is a major task. The Bible Society has the vision that all the 500,000 school children and every home in Slovenia have access to a Bible. Pray for this goal to be achieved. Bibles are being distributed in school libraries and through the 164 secular bookshops.

3. **Slovenia has had a Protestant witness** since the Reformation, but there are few evangelical churches. Pray that local and expatriate Christians may join together in planting churches in every Slovenian town.

Y

Zaire

(Republic of Zaire)

(Possible reversion to Republic of Congo in 1993)

December 6–7
Africa

Area 2,345,000 sq.km. Covering much of Central Africa's rain forest. The heavy rainfall and extensive river systems complicate communications.

Population	Ann. Gr.	Density
1990	35,990,000	3.14 %	15/sq.km
1995	41,813,000	3.24 %	18/sq.km

Large areas are sparsely populated.

Peoples: Estimate of 450 ethnic groups; numerous sub-groups.
Bantu 83.3%. Centre and south. Over 220 ethnic groups. Largest: Luba 6,480,000; Kongo 5,900,000; Mongo 4,860,000; Rwanda 3,600,000; Bangi and Ngale 2,090,000; Rundi 1,370,000; Teke 971,000; Nandi 800,000; Tetela 750,000; Lendu 700,000; Chokwe 504,000; Sanga 431,000; Phende 420,000; Lega 400,000.
Sudanic 13.3%. In the north; over 40 peoples. Largest: Azande 730,000; Mangbetu 650,000; Lugbara 288,000; Ngbandi 210,000.
Nilotic 1.43%. Four peoples. Largest: Alur 500,000.
Pygmy 0.46%. Eleven peoples. Largest: Mbuti 76,000; Efe 67,000.
Other 1.4%. Westerners, other Africans, Greeks, Indians.

Literacy 61% (functional literacy much lower). **Official language:** French. **Trade languages:** Lingala-Bangala in north and northwest, Swahili in east and south, Luba in centre and Kongo-Tuba in west. **All languages** 212. **Languages with Scriptures** 23Bi 12NT 36por.

Capital: Kinshasa 4,200,000. Other major cities: Lubumbashi 700,000; Kisangani 315,000; Kananga 300,000. Urbanization 44%.

Economy: Vast mineral resources and agricultural potential. Post-independence chaos, widespread maladministration and corruption have enriched the powerful elite but impoverished the nation. The road system hardly functions, trade is reduced to a trickle and profitable agricultural estates have reverted to forest. Africa's potentially most wealthy nation can no longer feed its own people, and is dependent on foreign aid. President Mobutu has been unwilling to distinguish between state finances and his own – a root cause of Zaire's dire straits. Hyper-inflation averages 1,000–3,000% annually. Public debt/person $246. Income/person $260 (1.2% of USA).

Politics: In 1960 Belgium hastily granted independence to an ill-prepared people, which led to eight years of violence, anarchy and secessionist wars. A military coup in 1965 brought General Mobutu to national leadership. For nearly 30 years he has ruled as a virtual dictator, all opposition being repressed or subverted. Mobutu and those around him have shamelessly enriched themselves – an action condoned by Western nations because of his support in the Cold War. The collapse of Communism has brought pressure for reform and democracy, but Mobutu has successfully manipulated, bribed or suppressed all efforts to dislodge him from power. By early 1993, constitutional talks were at a stalemate, and confrontation between the President, with his well-armed presidential guard, and the Prime Minister and the majority of the people has brought chaos, rioting, anarchy and a virtual cessation of trade.

Religion: In 1972 the President decreed that only six organized religions were permitted to operate and own property: Catholic, one Protestant Church (ECZ), Kimbanguist Church, Orthodox, Muslims and Jews. The authenticity programme of the government between 1971 and 1978 placed increasing controls and limitations on Christian institutions and activities. Economic and social disasters forced a dramatic reversal, so that by 1980 there was considerable religious freedom once more, with a resumption of Christian control of many schools and institutions that had been seized and plundered by the state.
Traditional religions 2.7%. Pockets of peoples and areas where response to the gospel has been less.
Muslim 1.4%. Sunni Muslims, predominantly in eastern towns.
Christian 95.9%. Affil 92.3%. Growth 3%.
Protestant 36%. Affil 35.4%. Growth 5.7%. Almost all of the 97 Protestant Churches are member communities of the *Eglise du Christ au Zaire* (ECZ). Most are evangelical, some more liberal, and others marginal in their theology.

ECZ Communities	Cong	Members	Affiliated
Disciples of Christ	1,217	280,000	700,000
Presbyterian	470	270,000	600,000
Seventh-day Adventist	970	230,000	575,000
Bapt-West (CBIM, ABFM)	505	227,159	568,000
United Methodist	2,432	291,883	550,000
Pente (AoG-UK)	2,111	190,000	543,000
Bapt-River (BMS-UK)	221	176,944	442,000
CECCA (WEC)	1,545	80,000	230,000
Evang Covenant	1,157	96,000	214,000
Assemblies of God	595	97,660	182,860
CECA (AIM)	1,575	66,133	176,000
Free Methodist	540	52,631	150,000

Z

Mennonite Brethren	228	46,906	125,000
Bapt-Kivu (CBFMS)	1,099	50,313	107,000
Eg Ev du Lubongo (RBMU, now AP)	577	70,000	103,000
Chrtn & Miss All	526	50,347	94,258
Ev Free Ch (Ubangi)	450	42,000	80,000
All other (80)	16,903	2,520,019	7,304,100
Denominations (97)	33,530	4,838,995	12,718,218
Evangelicals 21% of pop		2,969,000	7,598,000
Pentecostal/charis 12.4%		1,700,000	4,450,000

Missionaries:
to Zaire 1,406 (1:25,000 people) in about 93 agencies.
from Zaire 2,086 (1:6,100 Protestants) in 34 agencies 33frn 94xcul 1,992dom.

Roman Catholic 42.1%. Affil 41.68%. Gro 1.3%.

Catholic Ch	10,500	9,500,000	15,000,000
Charismatic		10,000	15,000

Missionaries:
to Zaire 4,366 (1:8,200 people).

from Zaire 830 (1973 figure; much lower today).
Orthodox 0.02%. Growth −2.3%.
Foreign Marginal 0.82%. Growth 14.2%.

Jehovah's Witnesses	1,327	67,917	295,000

Indigenous Marginal 17%. Affil 14.34%. Growth 1.3%.

Kimbanguist Church	12,000	3,000,000	5,000,000
All other (est.20)	1,000	80,000	160,000
Denominations (21)	13,000	3,080,000	5,160,000

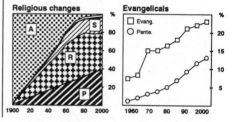

Religious changes / Evangelicals

1. **For centuries Zaire has been plundered for its wealth** – by Arab and European slave traders, Belgian colonial rulers and, latterly, the "lootocracy" that has ruled the nation for the sole purpose of self-enrichment. That spirit of greed and corruption has rotted the fabric of society and tainted Christians too. Pray for:

a) **A successful transition** to democratic rule with leaders accountable to the people, and with the ability to further the reconstruction of the country. The opposition is deeply divided.

b) **The spirit of greed and corruption** to be rooted out of society, and that Christians may set a good example in high ethical standards. An outpouring of the Holy Spirit is needed.

c) **Ethnic discord** not to mar future development of the nation or the Church. The breakdown of the economy has caused tensions to rise. There is ample opportunity for "ethnic cleansing" – actually occurring in Shaba province in the south with the oppression and expulsion of the Kasai peoples.

2. **In the midst of Zaire's disasters God has been working.** Praise Him for:

a) **The massive turning to Christ** (see graph!). The number of Christians has grown from 1.4% of the population in 1900 to 96% today. Though much of this would be nominal, there have been powerful revivals in some areas before and after independence.

b) **The many who gave their lives for this harvest.** Thousands of Christians and hundreds of Catholic and Protestant missionaries were martyred in the Simba Rebellion of 1964. Serving the Lord in Zaire is still fraught with perils.

c) **Persecution and pressures** that have refined the Church and brought a new spiritual earnestness, which has increased since the rioting and disasters of 1991. Churches are overflowing, and in many areas weekly all-night prayer meetings for the nation are being held.

3. **The Christian Church** remains the only viable national social structure for rebuilding the nation. Pray that its leaders may be uncompromising in moral and ethical issues. The manipulation and battering that the Church has endured have led to compromises and lowering of standards in some cases. Pray for revival in all main Christian bodies. The Kimbanguists are members of a large indigenous Church, with 5–6 million members, which began in 1921 as a messianic sect but which has gradually moved to a more biblical theology.

4. **The Church of Christ in Zaire (ECZ)** came into being through both government edict and pressure from some church leaders, though many evangelical leaders are now in favour of their membership in the ECZ. There have been positive benefits: the divisiveness of tribalism has been diminished, unnecessary competition reduced, administration rationalized and cooperation in training schemes and media increased. However, in the new Zaire, restructuring, change and renewal are imperative to face the daunting challenges of the '90s. Pray for:

a) **Biblical leadership patterns.** Centralization of leadership has harmed local congregational life and initiative, stimulated hierarchical structures, power-seeking, pride of position and misuse of funds, and compromised the Church's prophetic role. Changes must come – but may they not be at the expense of unity, fellowship and cooperation.

b) **Commitment to the authority of Scripture.** Evangelical, liberal and even syncretic indigenous

Z

churches were brought under the same umbrella. The evangelical majority has been pushed aside, and more outspoken and less Bible-committed leaders have often taken the limelight, helped by many smaller non-evangelical groups who have been invited as participating communities.

c) **Nominal Christians** to find real life in Christ. Over 30% of "Christians" no longer attend church. Large numbers have no clear grasp of repentance and faith in Christ. Animistic thought patterns, fear of witchcraft and syncretism are major problems. Pray that believers may recognize their inheritance in Christ and confront the forces of darkness in the power of the Spirit.

d) **Biblical holiness among Christians.** Believers must repent of corruption and moral permissiveness. AIDS has become a terrible threat to society – 20% of Kinshasa's population carries the virus. Moral purity and care for AIDS sufferers are major issues to be faced.

e) **The need for a vision for the lost.** Without this vision the churches will perish. Local and cross-cultural evangelism and missionary vision must be stimulated. Praise God for small beginnings by some Protestant communities in this respect (**CMA, CECCA/WEC,** Baptists and others).

f) **The effectual geographic compartmentalization** of the country by the ECZ which has often blunted evangelistic zeal, left many areas devoid of any evangelical witness, and hindered cross-cultural outreach. Spiritual monopolies can be just as inefficient as state monopolies.

5. **Leadership training** at every level must be a priority.

a) **Lay leadership** was neglected for years, and TEE programmes were few and localized. In 1985 a dramatic change came with the launch of the Portable Bible Schools movement. Two-month intensive training courses for lay leaders and sending them out as church planters to unchurched villages have transformed the spiritual situation since then. Pray for this vision to be implemented throughout the country.

b) **Bible Schools** abound. There are large numbers of primary local-language and trade-language Bible Schools, and a smaller number of French ones. They often function with slender resources and inadequate staff. Pray that spiritual and material standards may be constantly improved.

c) **The higher-level institutions** need prayer support. Some important ones are: *Institut Supérieur de Théology* in Kinshasa, the Bunia Seminary (**AIM, UFM, Brethren, WEC, CBFMS**), as well as several denominational schools. These are strategic for the provision of a new generation of well-educated pastors and leaders. Pray that spirituality among students and graduates may be more marked than intellectual pride or a nationalistic spirit that rejects anything foreign.

6. **The less-reached are few,** but superficially Christianized peoples are more numerous. Special targets for prayer:

a) **Rural villages.** The shocking realization that villages with a resident Protestant pastor had been reduced from 50% of the total in 1960 to 15% in 1985 galvanized many for action. At that stage 18 million people lived in villages without a functioning church. The Portable Bible Schools movement has radically changed this, with lay church planters starting congregations in 15,000 villages between 1986 and 1990. The vision is to see every one of the 70,000 villages in Zaire with a congregation by the year 2000.

b) **Young people's ministries.** These need new life breathed into them. The crumbling of the education system through lack of funds and limited prospects for employment has blighted the future of the next generation. The vast size of the country, poor communications and limited funds have also limited the effectiveness of national movements such as GBU(**IFES**) in the universities and **SU** in secondary schools. Pray that effective evangelism and discipleship programmes may be re-established and expanded.

c) **The intellectuals and the elite.** Many in the cities have little contact with a living witness to biblical Christianity, many living in wealth far removed from the real world around them.

d) **The vast swamplands northeast of Kinshasa,** which are sparsely populated and under-evangelized. Many other similar pockets of neglect exist. Pray for more concerted research in locating these areas, and for church planting to be initiated.

e) **The peoples who have been less responsive,** and have a high proportion of non-Christians: Hunde (200,000), Bira (58,000) and the many Pygmy groups in the north and northeast (**EHC** "Every Tree Campaign", **CECCA/WEC** and others are seeing conversions among them).

f) **The Swahili-speaking Muslim communities** (500,000) in eastern towns, Kinshasa and along the eastern border. There is little outreach to them. There is a considerable missionary effort by Muslims to spread Islam.

7. **Missionary involvement** is most needed in Bible teaching and discipling ministries, but is most demanded in development programmes, health and education. Pray for:

a) **A wise deployment of expatriate workers** and for the most effective use of their gifts.

Z

b) **Harmonious relationships** between national and expatriate workers. There were many strains during the anti-foreign emphasis of the authenticity campaign. Missions are now, to a large degree, integrated into their daughter churches.

c) **Safety.** Lawlessness and violence have increased as the economic situation has declined. It is not easy to work under the constant tension that a swift escape may be necessary. There have been several temporary evacuations of missionaries from whole regions since 1991.

d) **Provision of supplies and wisdom** in their use when so much needs to be done.

e) **The right strategy** for mission agencies. Some larger groups: Pentecostal agencies (197), **AIM** (98), United Methodist (81), **BMS** (67), Mennonite agencies (62), **WBT/SIL** (57), Brethren (56), Presbyterians (46), **CMA** (42), **CMS** (41), **CBFMS** (25), **WEC** (17), **UFM** (15). Major sending countries: USA (797), UK (216), Sweden (136), Canada (69), Norway (69), Germany (58).

8. **Help ministries** have once more become a major responsibility for the churches and related missions. The government takeover of hospitals and schools in the 1970s was a disaster from which the health and education system is only slowly recovering. The administration and financing of these institutions is a constant drain on the time and energies of key personnel, yet their pressing needs cannot be ignored. There have been severe losses of equipment and buildings through looting and violence since 1990. Pray for right priorities, and effective use of:

a) **Health services.** There are a number of major and smaller hospitals run by different communities/missions such as **BMS**, ABFMS and **CMA**. One such is the inter-community/mission hospital at Nyankunde in the northeast (**AIM, Brethren,** Mennonites, **UFM, WEC** and others). Expatriate personnel are in constant demand.

b) **Education.** Many of the better schools are church-run. The Catholics have made an enormous effort in this field; Protestants are under much pressure to do the same, but resources are limited, and committed Christian staff hard to find and retain. Pray that the educational system may also produce fine Christian leaders for the future.

c) **Transportation.** The breakdown in surface transportation has enhanced the importance of **MAF** and seven other flying agencies. Without the 38 aircraft and 34 flying personnel, missionary involvement, health programmes and lay-training schemes would be seriously limited or even close down. Pray for safety in flying – much is over trackless forest – and for the provision of fuel, finance and personnel. **MAF** suffered enormous losses in 1991 due to rioting in Kinshasa.

9. **Bible translation** is a major unfinished task. The profusion of languages led to an emphasis on trade-language evangelism which limited gospel penetration and stunted the development of indigenous Christian life styles, music and worship.

a) **At least 29 and possibly 123 languages** are in need of translation programmes by Zairois or expatriate believers.

b) **The Bible Society** is supervising 22 Bible translation programmes.

c) **Research into translation is still needed. SIL** has done much towards this, and has involvement in ten translation projects and a consultancy ministry in a number of others.

10. **Christian media.**

a) **The *Jesus* film** is available in the languages of the Azande, Bemba, Kongo, Nyarwanda and Rundi, but lack of equipment, electricity supplies and reliable transportation limit its use.

b) **Christian literature** distribution is a problem. **EHC** is actively seeking to reach every home with Christian literature, also to reach those affected by the AIDS epidemic with suitable literature.

c) **GRn** has messages available in 252 languages and dialects – a valuable resource in this land of many languages.

Z

Zambia

(Republic of Zambia)

Area 753,000 sq.km. Landlocked country; still heavily forested.

Population		Ann. Gr.	Density
1990	8,456,000	3.8 %	11/sq.km
1995	10,174,000	3.8 %	14/sq.km

Peoples: There are 82 ethnic groups.
Bantu peoples 97%. Major groups. Bemba 2,000,000; Tonga 990,000; Nyanja 989,000; Lozi 473,000; Lala-Bisa 439,000; Nsenga 427,000; Tumbuka 406,000; Nyika 320,000; Mambwe 262,000; Kaonde 240,000; Lunda 220,000; Lamba 211,000; Luvale 203,000; Lenje 169,000; Mwanga 169,000; Mbunda 126,000.
Foreign 3%. Europeans 30,000; Asians 20,000 (mainly Gujarati Indians). Also many refugees from Angola and Mozambique.

Literacy 76% (functional literacy 25%). **Official language:** English. **Trade language:** Both Bemba and Nyanja spoken by large minorities of the population. **All languages** 36 indigenous languages. **Languages with Scriptures** 15Bi 7NT 5por.

Capital: Lusaka 1,100,000. Urbanization 43%.

Economy: Copper mining and refining has long been the major source of foreign exchange. Post-independence prosperity was squandered by heavy-handed socialism, neglect of agriculture and widespread corruption. Wars and unrest in surrounding lands of Angola, Rhodesia/Zimbabwe, Mozambique and South Africa helped to drive the nation to virtual bankruptcy. The new government is pledged to reinstitute a free market economy and stamp out corruption. Public debt/person $484. Income/person $1,390 (6.6% of USA).

Politics: Independent from Britain in 1964. One-party democracy under President Kaunda's leadership until 1991. Growing corruption, economic collapse and the ending of the cold war prompted multi-party elections and led to a change of government.

Religion: The official philosophy of former President Kaunda was socialist – humanism was made government policy. President Chiluba's first official act was to declare unilaterally that Zambia is a Christian country, but with the assurance that there would be freedom of religion.
Traditional religions 23%. Widespread, but in rapid decline; stronger in some western and southwestern ethnic groups.
Non-religious/other 0.5%.

Muslim 1%. Some Asians and immigrants from Tanzania and Malawi, and a growing number of Zambians.
Baha'i 0.3%. **Hindu** 0.2%.
Christian 75%. Nom 20.2%. Affil 54.8%. Growth 3.3%.
Protestant 27%. Affil 22.11%. Growth 11.3%.

Church	Cong	Members	Affiliated
United Ch	850	300,000	750,000
Seventh-day Adventist	522	120,000	218,000
Rfrmd Ch in Zambia	65	55,900	133,000
Baptist Convention	500	43,000	108,000
African Meth Episc	193	16,400	82,000
Christian Brethren	1,000	37,500	75,000
Ch of God (Cleveland)	348	40,736	75,100
Anglican Ch	198	18,000	45,000
Pentecostal Holiness	261	25,506	42,500
Evang Ch in Z (AEF)	494	15,200	31,600
Pente Assemb of God	111	10,500	25,000
Baptist Assoc of Z	150	7,000	18,000
Apostolic Faith Missn	180	9,000	18,000
Brethren in Christ	116	6,632	16,632
All other (44)	1,598	103,043	232,882
Denominations (58)	6,586	808,417	1,869,714
Evangelicals 12.5% of pop		456,000	1,056,000
Pentecostal/charis 2.74%		118,000	240,000

Missionaries:
to Zambia 626 (1:13,500 people) in 68 agencies.
from Zambia 353 (1:5,300 Protestants) in 17 agencies 44frn 85xcul 268dom.
Roman Catholic 32%. Affil 19.24%. Growth −4.4%.

Catholic Ch	2,800	944,000	1,627,000

Missionaries:
to Zambia 1,066 (1:7,900 people).
from Zambia 30 (1973 figure).
Orthodox 0.04%.
Foreign Marginal 8%. Affil 7.4%. Growth 6.4%.

New Apostolic Ch	435	174,000	434,510
Jehovah's Witnesses	1,800	73,729	184,000
All groups (7)	2,235	249,829	622,010

Indigenous Marginal 8%. Affil 6.1%. Growth 5.6%.

All groups (71)		257,500	515,000

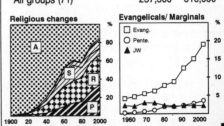

Religious changes

Evangelicals/ Marginals
- □ Evang.
- ○ Pente.
- ▲ JW

Z

1. **The Christian President**, at the time of his inauguration, prayed on television before the nation a prayer of national repentance and renounced the sins of idolatry, witchcraft, occultism, injustice and corruption, asking God's forgiveness through the blood of Jesus. Pray that the leaders of the land may live this out and not use their power for personal gain or sectional interests.

2. **Praise God for the impact of the gospel in Zambia.** Protestant Christians have grown from 700,000 to 1,870,000 in ten years as the Spirit of God has moved through the country with many coming to personal faith in Christ – in urban areas, among educated young people and increasingly in the rural areas. The United Church (from the work of LMS, Paris Evangelical Missionary Society, Church of Scotland and Methodist Missionary Society) has a growing evangelical witness and is bringing new life and outreach in once dead and formal congregations. The economic crisis, poverty, unemployment and the AIDS epidemic have all prompted a search after God that multiplied conversions in the late '80s.

3. **The maturing of the Church in urban areas is encouraging.** Strong, well-led English-speaking Baptist and Pentecostal Churches have developed over the last 15 years; although few older people are responding, many educated young people and professionals are coming to Christ. Pray that some of these may also be called into full-time work.

4. **Rural churches vary widely in spiritual quality and vigour.** Pray for:
a) **The many thriving evangelical congregations in the northwest** among the Luvale, Chokwe, Lunda, and other peoples (**Brethren**), Kaonde, Mbwela and Nkoya (**AEF**) and Lamba (Baptist). The area has a high concentration of evangelical believers, but they need a greater vision for cross-cultural outreach to other areas of the land.
b) **The work of the Brethren in Christ and Churches of Christ among the Tonga peoples** in the south, which has been fruitful; but some areas are only partially evangelized.
c) **The Reformed Church among the Nyanja peoples in the east,** which is theologically evangelical but formal and growing more slowly than other denominations.
d) **The Lozi and southwestern peoples and Bemba and northern peoples,** who have very few evangelical congregations. Many have become nominally Christian, but because of unclear teaching, vast numbers have been swept into sectarian or syncretic indigenous churches. Pray for the planting of churches in these spiritually needy areas. The **PAoC**, Pentecostal Holiness Church, **AEF**, **Brethren** and Churches of Christ have commenced work in the northeast.

5. **The Evangelical Fellowship of Zambia** (EFZ) has become an important focal point of fellowship for denominations and agencies and for cooperative efforts. Pray that God may give united vision to Christian leaders as they tackle the daunting problems facing Zambia.

6. **Challenges for the Church in the '90s.**
a) **The discipling of Zambia.** A nationwide survey sponsored by the EFZ is being used to stimulate churches to multiply and plant new congregations in every community of the country.
b) **The AIDS catastrophe** which is rapidly developing. Some estimate 22% of the urban population carry the HIV virus, and the death rate is mounting monthly. Pray that Christians may set moral standards that will minimize the spread of the disease, and care for and minister to those afflicted. Immorality is so widespread that new moral foundations have to be laid.
c) **To develop effective missions programmes for envisioning,** training and sending Zambian Christians. Few Christians realize the Great Commission is for them too.

7. **Leadership training.** This is a priority in a land where nominalism and syncretism have led large numbers of people into indigenous and sectarian groups. The EFZ has sponsored the Theological College of Central Africa in Ndola, which is the first evangelical degree-awarding theological institution in Central Africa. The TCCA, Justo Mwale Theological College, Apostolic and Pentecostal Bible Schools are full to capacity. There are a total of 17 Bible schools. Pray for spiritually and educationally qualified mature leaders to be prepared through these institutions. TEE is widely used, but has only been partially effective. Lay training is a must, for most of the church planting has been done by lay people.

8. **Young people.** SU has had a significant impact in the secondary schools, with large, lively groups in most of them. Many missionaries and Zambian believers have an extensive ministry in teaching the Scriptures in government schools. ZAFES(**IFES**) has four staff workers and groups in almost every post-secondary institution.

Z

9. **Missions.** There is an open door, but the emphasis is on working within the structure of the national churches, or in preparing Zambians for leadership. The largest are: **Brethren** (127 workers), **AEF** (77), **SBC** (43), Brethren in Christ (24), Christian Churches/Churches of Christ (24), Swedish Baptist Union (18) and **ABMS** (16). Pray for wisdom, tact and humility for these brethren as they seek to help the Zambian Church. There are many opportunities for service: Bible teaching in schools, leadership training and the use of technical skills such as in radio, and literature production and distribution.

10. **The less-reached.**
a) **Many smaller peoples**, especially in the southwest, are minimally reached.
b) **The urban satellite towns** of Lusaka, the Copperbelt and Kabwe are spiritually needy. Many are squalid shanty settlements. Pray for the work of **DM** and others in evangelizing these areas where sin is rife.
c) **The Indian community** is largely Gujarati. There is a South African **AEF** couple of Indian ethnic background working among them, but there is no church as yet.
d) **Muslims** are active in propagating their religion and making liberal use of funds to entice non-Muslims into their sphere of influence. Pray for effective outreach to Muslims.

11. **Christian help ministries:**
a) **The Bible Society (UBS).** This has a key role in Bible translation and distribution. In 1987 over 206,000 Bibles were distributed. There are still a few languages without a New Testament.
b) **Christian literature.** EHC has reached one million homes with evangelistic literature. There are 16 Christian bookstores, but the quantity, range and local applicability are limited. Lack of foreign exchange, local supplies and authors are big limitations.

Z

December 9		*Zimbabwe*
Africa		(Republic of Zimbabwe)

Area 391,000 sq.km. Landlocked and dependent on surface routes through war-torn Mozambique and troubled South Africa for imports and exports.

Population		Ann. Gr.	Density
1990	9,721,000	3.2 %	25/sq.km
1995	11,352,000	3.2 %	29/sq.km

Peoples:
Shona 69.1%. Karanga 2,250,000; Zezuru 1,800,000; Manyika 1,100,000; Rozvi 700,000; Ndau 332,000; Korekore 300,000; Nambya 64,000.
Nguni 17%. Ndebele 1,485,000; Kalanga 161,000 (a Shona group being absorbed by Ndebele).
Other indigenous peoples 4.7%. Tswana-Sotho 157,000; Shangaan-Tsonga 117,000; Tonga 112,000; Venda 71,000.
Malawian and Mozambican 6.7%. Chewa 470,000; Sena 87,000; Yao 38,000; Kunda 29,000.
Other minorities 2.5%. European 90,000; Coloured 30,000; Asian 19,000.
Refugees: Mozambicans 200,000.

Literacy 76%. **Official language:** English. **Trade languages:** Shona is widely spoken, Ndebele in the west. **All languages** 19. **Languages with Scriptures** 12Bi 2NT 2por.

Capital: Harare 1,316,000. Other major city: Bulawayo 879,000. Urbanization 27%.

Economy: One of Africa's more advanced economies with mining, commercial agriculture and industry contributing to foreign earnings. The post-independence boom is fading through the combined effects of severe drought, massive population increase and economic mismanagement. Large sums spent on education with few employment possibilities and the looming disaster of death through AIDS (between 10% and 30% of the population carries the HIV virus) bode ill for the future. Unemployment 31%. Public debt/person $264. Income/person $640 (3% of USA).

Politics: The Rhodesian declaration of independence from Britain by the white minority in 1965 led to intense guerrilla warfare and eventually independence as Zimbabwe in 1980. Ideological commitment to Marxist-Leninism and a one-party state has been watered down by economic and political realities, enabling the land to recover from the effects of war.

Religion: Religious freedom.
Traditional religions 32.6%. Strong in all areas but in a majority among the Tonga, Kunda and Ndau. Many indigenous churches are syncretic.

Non-religious/other 4%. Baha'i 27,000. Hindu 6,500. Jews 1,200.
Muslim 1.6%. Malawian Yao, Indians and some Shona-speaking Remba.
Christian 61.7%. Nom 13%. Affil 48.7%. Growth 5.6%.
Protestant 33%. Affil 24.06%. Attend 15%. Growth 8.5%.

Church	Cong	Members	Affiliated
Z Assmbs of God, Afr	1,709	300,000	600,000
Seventh-day Adventist	395	166,617	278,000
Anglican Ch	500	95,100	237,848
United Methodist Ch	650	65,000	163,000
Salvation Army	687	60,075	150,000
Methodist Ch	1,116	78,000	101,000
Ch of Christ	115	14,000	70,000
Baptist Convention	320	31,678	63,400
Evang Lutheran Ch	200	27,200	60,500
Reformed Ch in Z (NGK-SA) (3)	756	25,000	60,000
Chs of Christ (CC-NZ)	120	14,100	40,300
Assemblies of God – Back to God	120	20,000	40,000
Brethren in Christ	173	12,039	26,200
All other (66)	1,426	212,151	448,775
Denominations (81)	8,287	1,120,960	2,339,023
Evangelicals 14.3% of pop		656,000	1,386,000
Pentecostal/charis 9.7%		469,000	946,000

Missionaries:
to Zimbabwe 630 (1:15,400 people) in 68 agencies.
from Zimbabwe 240 (1:9,700 Protestants) in 18 agencies 49frn 77xcul 163dom.
Roman Catholic 12%. Affil 8%. Gro 0%.

Catholic	1,488	412,000	777,600
Charismatic		2,000	4,000

Missionaries:
to Zimbabwe 905 (1:10,700 people).
from Zimbabwe 10 (1973).
Foreign Marginal 1.57%. Gro 5.3%.

Jehovah's Witnesses	557	18,382	40,800
All groups (10)	934	74,422	152,400

Indigenous Marginal 15.12%. Growth 4.7%.

African Apostolic Ch J Marange	183	220,000	550,000
All groups (181)	1,130	496,000	1,470,000

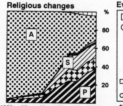

Religious changes

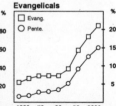

Evangelicals

Z

1. Praise God for the miracles he has performed in Zimbabwe despite the serious problems in the nation.
   a) **The unexpected and unprecedented freedom to preach the gospel** in public, on the media, in schools and in prisons since political independence has led to hope and life. Many had feared persecution and repression.
   b) **Spectacular church growth** in the '80s has replaced decline due to war in the '70s. The launching of the DAWN vision has further spurred growth among a population made receptive by suffering and social stress. Evangelicals grew at over 10% a year in the '80s. The growth has been greatest in the urban Pentecostal and charismatic churches.
   c) **Large evangelistic outreaches and crusades** by **Christ for All Nations, AE, DM** and others have brought many into the Kingdom and birthed a number of churches.
   d) **Massive distribution of Christian literature and the Scriptures** has fed a literate population hungry for reading materials.

2. **Severe socio-economic problems** threaten the stability and progress of the nation. These are a call to urgent prayer and action.
   a) **Unemployment** has become a major social problem; less than 3% of the 300,000 who leave school every year find a permanent job. The severe droughts of the past 12 years have brought great suffering to the rural areas and a huge influx of destitute people to the cities. Frustration, social breakdown and crime are the results.
   b) **AIDS is beginning to reap its grim harvest of deaths.** With present trends, an otherwise-expected 16,700,000 population in 2012 could be 7,800,000. Pray that the Christians may both set high moral standards and be ready to provide the loving care and spiritual help that are soon to be required. The impact of AIDS on such a scale could tear apart the structures of society.

3. **For years the majority of churches stagnated.** Emphasis on institutional work, the lack of clear biblical teaching, and failure to ensure that pastors and church leaders had a vital living faith in Christ resulted in a large number of nominal, compromised Christians. The war changed that. In the sifting process many fell away and reverted to the old ways, but a stronger church has emerged that has returned to an emphasis on spiritual ministry, evangelism and church planting. Pray for:
   a) **A clear stand against witchcraft and demonic powers** or veneration of ancestors in the guise of nationalism. Pray that Christians may not compromise, but know the power in the name of Jesus to both protect and deliver from fear and bondage.
   b) **Spiritual unity. The Evangelical Fellowship of Zimbabwe** links together 40 churches and organizations, and the **Pentecostal Fellowship of Zimbabwe** has brought together ten denominations.
   c) **A credibility in national affairs** and with the government so that the church may boldly and effectively speak out against moral and social wrongs.
   d) **A growth in missions vision** and the means to send and support Zimbabwean missionaries in other lands. Strict exchange controls hold back many who testify to God's call into missions. A major challenge is the spiritual need of neighbouring Mozambique, where Zimbabwean missionaries have already had a significant impact.

4. **Leadership training.** Pray for:
   a) **The 22 or more seminaries and Bible schools.** Few have attained degree level – a great need with the increasing sophistication and education of city congregations. Churches lack means for giving further study opportunities to existing pastors through TEE or residential courses.
   b) **The bridging of the generation gap** between the more cautious, less trained, older pastors and the dynamic, impatient younger leaders.
   c) **Mature, evangelical theologians,** able to present a biblical theology that addresses the real needs of Africa – death, sickness, the spirit world, corruption in society and so on.

5. **Vision 2000** is a national initiative developed since 1985. Most of the Protestant denominations were drawn together in a 1992 Congress to set church-planting goals for the '90s. Pray for:
   a) The ongoing research programme to reveal the areas and people in need of ministry.
   b) The vision to double the number of congregations from nearly 10,000 congregations to 20,000 in this decade, and to give every person an opportunity to respond to the gospel.

6. **Young people** brought up on the idealistic visions of independence have been disillusioned by empty political slogans, the greed of the powerful and the dearth of jobs. They have become the most receptive section of the population. Some 48% of the population is under 15 years of age. Pray for the ministry of:

Z

a) **Scripture Union**, which has had a decisive impact on the educated by their work in the secondary schools. The number of these schools increased from 250 in 1980 to 1,517 in 1989, and there are large active outgoing Christian groups in most of them. The camp ministry has been signally blessed. A smaller work in the primary schools is getting under way – pray that it may grow through an extensive programme of weekend camps. Pray for more Christian teachers to be raised up to nurture this work in their spare time.

b) **FOCUS(IFES)**, which is responsible for Christian Unions among the 10,000 students in universities and colleges, has 11 lively, growing groups. Pray that Christian graduates may become key leaders in the nation.

7. **The less-reached.** Zimbabwe has been extensively evangelized, but areas of need remain:

a) **The rural areas.** In many districts churches are few and full-time workers even fewer. Pray for the calling of pastors and evangelists willing to serve in rural areas. Pray also for evangelistic outreaches specifically to these areas. Especially effective have been teams showing the *Jesus* film and **Operation Foxfire** teams of **AE**.

b) **The burgeoning cities**, swelled by hundreds of thousands of rural migrants looking for non-existent jobs. Squatter settlements are multiplying and crime is on the increase. Outreach to the unemployed is a major challenge.

c) **Less-reached peoples.** There are congregations in every indigenous people, but relatively fewer among the Tonga, Nambya and Dombe of the Hwange-Kariba area in the northwest (where the Assemblies of God have made a significant impact), the Kunda in the northeast, and the Ndau (**AEF**) in the east. The Kalanga and Ndebele have been exposed to the gospel for 130 years but have been less responsive than the Shona peoples.

d) **Farming areas.** About one million labourers and their dependents live on the 4,200 commercial farms, many owned by whites. Over half are from Malawi and Mozambique. The CCAP(**NGK**), Salvation Army and others maintain an extensive ministry to these communities – especially to the Malawian Chewa-Nyanja speakers, but many farm communities are without an evangelical congregation of believers.

e) **Muslims.** They are few in number, but the least reached of all Zimbabwe's peoples. Most are Yao from Malawi (40,000), many are Indians in the main towns, and some are of the indigenous Shona-speaking Remba. They have energetically sought to build mosques all over the country and attract Zimbabwean converts. Little Christian outreach has been made to win them.

f) **Mozambican refugees** fleeing the ongoing civil war in central Mozambique who live in camps on the eastern border. Many are destitute and without Christ. Pray that many may be saved and return with the good news to their sparsely-evangelized home areas.

8. **Protestant missionaries** numbered 996 in 1975, but because of the war were reduced to less than 250 in 1980. Numbers have slowly climbed to 630, but visas are harder to obtain or renew. The need for missionary input is less and only essential for specialized or international ministries; the church in Zimbabwe is well able to handle the remaining task. Major agencies are: **SBC** (85 workers), **TEAM** (32), **AEF** (26), Swedish Lutherans (25), Salvation Army (20), **YWAM** (17), Brethren in Christ (15), Elim Pentecostal Mission (13).

9. **Christian literature** has become a major ministry in Zimbabwe and beyond (especially Mozambique). Pray for:

a) **Scripture distribution.** The **Bible Society** has a huge Scripture printing and distribution programme. The government ruling for compulsory religious education has led to a massive distribution of Bibles, NTs and Scripture portions. In June 1985 a new start was made to revise the Shona Bible; a reliable revision is long overdue. **Bibles for Africa** printed two million booklets containing Luke and Acts for distribution in schools.

b) **Gospel Literature Lifeline** which has developed a successful tract and follow-up literature ministry with correspondence courses. Two and a half million tracts were distributed in 1981, five million in 1984, much being printed for Mozambique.

c) **Christian bookstores** in nearly all the major centres. The shortage of foreign exchange and lack of variety of good locally-produced materials limits stock and impact.

d) **CAVA** (Christian Audio Visual Action) which is, at present, the only major publisher of literature in Shona to counteract the renewed challenge offered by traditional animistic religion. About 25 books have been written and 90,000 copies printed in 1990 and distributed widely. Audio-visual materials are also produced.

e) **EHC**, which has covered all the homes of the country one and a half times, gaining one million responses.

Z

10. **Christian electronic media:**
a) **Radio and TV** programmes are broadcast on the national networks. International broadcasts are also received from **TWR** Swaziland in English (33 hours/week), Shona (10 hours), Ndebele (7 hours) and Tswana (5 hours). There is a large audience.
b) **The *Jesus* film** is widely used for church planting in Shona, Ndebele and Tonga.

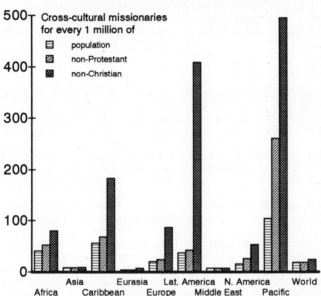

Protestant Missionary Presence by Regions of the World

Cross-cultural missionaries for every 1 million of

- population
- non-Protestant
- non-Christian

Regions (left to right): Africa, Asia, Caribbean, Eurasia, Europe, Lat. America, Middle East, N. America, Pacific, World

This graph portrays the final columns of Appendix 3 and also the Protestant to population ratio in the country surveys. It is an attempt to show Protestant missionary **density** by region and by three measures:

1. **The whole population** (column 1 in each group) – the number of missionaries for every million people. This is not an absolute figure, but a figure derived to make comparisons. The higher density of missionaries in the Pacific, Caribbean and Africa is shown.

2. **The non-Protestant population** (column 2 in each group) – whether non-Christian, Catholic or Orthodox.

3. **The non-Christian population** (column 3 in each group). Where there is a large difference between columns 2 and 3, much of the outreach is directed to evangelizing those who claim to be Christian (especially true for Latin America and Europe). There is considerable discussion among Evangelicals as to whether these constitute needy fields.

Note:

1. The final group of bars representing the world average. All regions with lower values are less well served with missionaries.

2. The lack of missionaries for Asia, Eurasia and the Middle East. All regions with low values in **all three** bars represent **World A** – the least-reached and most spiritually-needy parts of the world.

3. The high concentration of missionaries in the Pacific and Caribbean – two of the most Christianized regions in the world.

Z

December 10	**AD 2000**	Special Ministries

The end of the century and the millennium has become a motivating challenge to make a concerted effort to achieve the goals set by the Lord Jesus in the Great Commission. For the first time in history that is within our grasp. Let us not grieve the Holy Spirit by disobedience.

In 1988 David Barrett and James Reapsome catalogued some 700 plans through history launched for evangelizing the world of which 387 were still being pursued – some with great vigour. Many are denominational (**SBC** Bold Mission Thrust, **AoG** Decade of Harvest and others), media-oriented (The World by 2000 – radio agencies [*see Christian Radio on p 603*], The Bible Societies, The *Jesus* Project CCC [*see* Jesus *film p 605*], **GRn** [*see next section*] etc.), or agency initiatives by such as **CCC**, **YWAM**, **WEC**, etc.

Pray for:

1. **Effective cooperation** in achieving the goal. Praise God for new cooperative networks that are emerging, covering nearly every major least-reached mega-people or groups of related peoples. However, these delicate plants need careful, prayerful nurture. In some newly-opened areas of the world the situation is better described as confusion, anarchy, division and duplication.

2. **Effective use of resources and tools.** A new vision is for the non-residential or coordinator missionaries that, under God, seek to orchestrate multi-media, multi-agency efforts to reach the least-reached peoples of the world. Pray for these leaders and emerging cooperative networks.

3. **Specific global evangelization plans** known to you. Various such movements have been mentioned in both the country section as well as subsequent pages in this specialized ministry section.

4. **The AD2000 and Beyond Movement** which is one significant umbrella movement worthy of prayer. This is an outgrowth of the LCWE movement and is a coordinating hub for connecting networks (specialized "tracks") concentrating on specific Great Commission ministries or targets – Radio, Saturation church planting (**DAWN**), March for Jesus, Cities, Unreached peoples, Bible translation, Literature. The heart of the focus is the 10/40 Window (see p 82). Pray for:
a) **The leadership and coordination role** of Luis Bush and Thomas Wang.
b) The effective dissemination of the vision for the goal of world evangelization by AD2000 and continuing the momentum beyond that date until Jesus comes again.
c) **The coordination of large global ministries** and national and international networks springing up in many parts of the world.
d) **The achievement of the motto of the movement:** *A church for every people and the gospel for every person by the year 2000.*

December 11	**TAPE, RECORD AND CASSETTE MINISTRIES**	Special Ministries

The arrival of cheap cassette tape recorders has made it possible to distribute Christian tapes widely to both Christians and the unconverted. This has become a valuable tool for evangelism, teaching and the encouragement of believers. Numerous local and international agencies have been founded for the production and distribution of cassette tapes. Pray for:

1. **Skilled labourers** who can handle the expensive equipment necessary to make good recordings, maintain cassette playback machines and effectively distribute the tapes. Few mission agencies have grasped the significance of this ministry or exploited its potential.

2. **Evangelism through tapes. Global Recordings** (**GRn**) pioneered the use of simple messages on gramophone records for evangelizing minority people groups and more inaccessible populations. These messages are now usually produced on tapes. Often these records and tapes are the *only* means available to communicate the gospel to these peoples in their own languages. Recordings can be made far more speedily than sending in a missionary to learn the language or complete translation of portions of God's Word. This is a vital tool for evangelism among unreached peoples. Pray for:

a) **An increase in the numbers and availability of recorded messages.** In 1993 there were recordings made in 4,562 languages and dialects, but at least 2,438 other languages and dialects could be recorded to great benefit. Most of these are in Africa, South Asia, China and the Pacific.

b) **Field recordists** – both from **GRn**-related agencies and mission and church workers committed to multiply the ministry in producing both evangelistic and teaching tapes. The work is often arduous and difficult, requiring much travel and hard living conditions. Pray for the right language informants, preparation of texts, recording and production of tapes. Pray for the protection of delicate equipment handled in situations of geographical and climatic extremes.

c) **The Global Recordings network** which is a fellowship of 21 national agencies (see some names and addresses in Appendix 2). Pray for the strategic development of the vision for reaching every tongue with the gospel by means of recorded messages.

d) **Field distributors.** They have a key role in all the complexities of importation, distribution, teaching effective use of tapes, care of machinery and follow-up teaching. More workers are required.

3. **Teaching and church growth through tapes.** In many spiritually hard areas of the world, the few Christians are isolated and have little opportunity to learn new hymns and choruses or receive adequate teaching. Messages on tape can fill that void. Pray for the provision of the equipment, batteries and relevant messages. Much useful material is generated for this through tapes prepared for Christian radio programmes. Many TEE courses make extensive use of tapes for teaching purposes.

4. **Bible tapes.** Many new translations of the Scriptures are first circulated on tape with great blessing (**UBS, WBT**). This is particularly useful for the world's 1.1 billion illiterate people, for those who have no written Scriptures and for areas where there is a real threat that political events may prevent the printing and distribution of the Word of God.

5. **Effective use of new technology.** Various Christian agencies are developing innovative new technologies for communicating the gospel, such as **Galcom** in Canada with cheap miniature solar-panel radios and cassette players and also credit-card-size microchip players. Pray that such may multiply opportunities for the least-reached to understand and respond to the gospel. Bibles and concordances on computer and effective computer programmes to rapidly compile concordances in new languages are becoming a valuable means for building up the Church.

<table>
<tr><td>

**Special
Ministries**

</td><td>

CHRISTIAN RADIO
AND TELEVISION

</td><td>

**December
12**

</td></tr>
</table>

This is potentially one of the most useful aids for world evangelization but, as yet, is inadequately exploited. Give praise for the role of Christian radio in:

1. **Bringing light and hope** to Communist-ruled lands. Many churches owe their beginnings and individuals their conversion to radio broadcasts. Christian radio also played an important role in the ultimate opening up of European and Eurasian lands for the gospel in 1989. Byelarus, Ukraine and Russia are rapidly becoming *sources* of Christian radio broadcasts today!

2. **Being one of the few means of sharing the gospel** in closed Muslim lands. In some of these, audiences are fairly large.

3. **The continuing ministry to restricted-access Communist states of Asia.** The ministry of **FEBC** to China has been unique.

Pray for:

1. **Christian radio agencies.** There are over 13 major Evangelical agencies involved in international broadcasting. The volume and variety of broadcasting is now huge – in 1990 Christian broadcasting by these agencies attained 8,485 hours/week in 211 languages. Some larger agencies are: **WRMF** (HCJB-Ecuador with 450 workers); **TWR** (seven transmitters around the world and 339 workers); **FEBC** (Philippines and Micronesia with 96 workers); **FEBA** (Seychelles with 77 workers); also **SIM** (ELWA Liberia), **IBRA** (Sweden), High Adventure (Lebanon and elsewhere with 26 workers). These agencies are frequently mentioned throughout the book.

2. **The World by 2000 vision.** This was launched by four radio agencies (TWR, FEBA/FEBC, HCJB and SIM) in 1985 with commitment to work together to produce a daily 30-minute programme in every language spoken by more than one million people by the year 2000. Of the total of 300 languages in this category, the 107 languages served in 1985 had increased to 154 in 1992. The planning, research, funding, search for native-language speakers for programmes (in many of these languages there may be few, if any, Christians), studio facilities and all the complexities of maintaining and expanding this ministry need to be covered in prayer.

3. **Good reception in target areas.** The wave bands are increasingly crowded. More and more powerful transmitters are needed to "shout down" competing stations. Technical skill is needed to transmit effectively. Short programmes in the minority languages of closed countries are hard to publicize in order to build up a committed audience.

4. **The listeners.** There are 1,200 million radio receivers in the world and, potentially, most of the world's population could have access to a set. Pray for spiritual fruit in souls saved, Christians strengthened and churches planted.

5. **Follow-up.** Many stations and programming agencies have a large staff to handle the four to five million letters sent in by listeners annually. Pray for the protection of senders and letters in the post – in many Muslim and Communist countries there is heavy censorship and only a small proportion of the letters get through. Pray for personal letters, literature and BCCs sent out in return. Pray for new converts to be linked up with groups of other believers.

6. **The ICRE project** (International Communication Research for Evangelism) initiated by **FEBC**. This project aims at a long-term strategy for using radio (and other means where possible) for evangelism and church planting among unreached peoples. Pray for research, pilot programmes, effective evaluation and a radical step forward in the strategic use of radio through the ICRE project.

7. **Effective use of television and video recorders.** Television has been the source of much evil, yet good Christian programmes can be uplifting. Pray for more Christians to become actively involved in secular broadcasting as well as on Christian channels where allowed. The expanding use of satellites for broadcasting means that there are few barriers to reception for those with the right equipment. Good, marketable Christian programmes, especially in languages other than English, are a major lack.

8. **Nullification of the negatives** in Christian broadcasting:
a) **The highly-publicized moral failures of some televangelists** which brought dishonour to the Lord and shame to Christians. The impact of the medium is highlighted by the fame such ministries gain, but pray that there might be adequate pastoral and financial accountability in these ministries. Pray also that lost credibility of Christian programmes may be regained through the spirituality and quality of both workers and programmes.
b) **The bias against evangelical programming on many national networks.** Anything evangelistic is seen as proselytizing, recruiting or manipulating people. The widespread pluralism and lack of ethical absolutes causes Evangelicals to be denied reasonable access and their message diluted or denied air time.

Special Ministries	THE *JESUS* FILM	December 13

The *Jesus* Film Project is a ministry of Campus Crusade for Christ. This literal portrayal of the life of Jesus according to the Gospel of Luke has become one of the most powerful evangelistic tools of recent times and the most watched film in history. By 1991 more than 440 million had seen it; the response is enormous. **CCC** estimates an initial response from 31 million people.

Pray for:

1. **The year 2000 vision**: that all of the world's 300 languages spoken by more than one million people, and many of the smaller ones, will have a version of the film available and in use by then. The intermediate goal was to have 271 translations ready by the end of 1993.

2. **Churches and agencies using the *Jesus* film** – these number more than 260. Pray that they may be creative in its use and work together with other churches to reach target areas.

3. **Film teams.** These work at New Life Training Centres around the world (as of 1990 there were more than 200 training centres). Plans call for New Life Training Centres to be responsible for presenting the gospel to 100,000 people each year for at least five years and for training at least 100 small group Bible study leaders each year.

4. **Follow-up.** Failure to plan for this can dissipate the impact of the film. Pray for many churches to be planted both by agencies and churches and also through CCC New Life 2000 workers in New Life Groups.

5. **Public showings in cinemas, theatres and television.** Millions see the film in this way around the world. Audiences in former Communist countries have been spectacular and by 1993 an estimated 125 million people had seen the film in the republics of the former USSR. Pray for continued opportunities to show the film on national television networks – especially at Christmas and Easter. Pray also for adequate mechanisms for helping those touched.

6. **Video cassettes of the film.** These have become an outstanding tool for home evangelism in repressive situations. Response has been beyond expectations! In many a Muslim land the film is banned – an excellent recommendation for the quiet circulation of thousands of video cassettes in every part of the Muslim world. Pray that this may be part of the opening up of Muslim lands for the gospel.

Special Ministries	BIBLE SOCIETIES AND BIBLE TRANSLATION	December 14

The provision of God's Word in the mother tongue of each people of the world is fundamental to world evangelization. Many agencies are committed to various aspects of making the Scriptures available to all. Special mention must be made of the **United Bible Societies** (**UBS**).

Pray for:

1. **The national Bible Society members** – in 1993 there were 111 societies working in 200 countries and territories. Pray for their staff with their specialized skills for the many tasks. Pray for their walk with God, for guidance in what translation and printing projects to tackle and for relations with other Christian bodies.

2. **Translation and revision work.** UBS staff workers give much encouragement and advice to missionaries and nationals in new language and modern speech translation programmes. Much wisdom is needed in the many problems that arise. The **UBS** was involved in 609 translation projects in 1992, 410 of them being first-time translations.

3. **The printing of the Scriptures.** This presents many problems – in some areas it is high costs, in others it is the lack of facilities or materials. The price of Bibles is reduced through subsidies. Pray for the provision of large sums of money needed. The **UBS** budget for 1992 was $53 million.

4. **Importation and distribution.** Much trouble and effort is expended on importing paper, machinery and completed Bibles. War, political crises and unsympathetic or hostile governments make for long and difficult negotiations. Pray for those involved. Sometimes the **UBS** depot or bookstore is the only source of Christian literature and Bibles in a country. In others a vast network of churches, shops and local distributors moves out millions of portions of the Scriptures. In 1992 worldwide distribution was 17 million Bibles, 14 million New Testaments and 618 million portions of the Scriptures. What a spiritual impact this could have!

Other specialized agencies to mention for prayer.

1. **Wycliffe Bible Translators/SIL** has a remarkable record in singleminded dedication to the completion of translating the New Testament into the languages of the world. By 1992 **WBT** translators had completed 333 New Testaments and were involved in a further 863 projects. Their staff numbers 6,267, but many more translators, advisers, literacy workers and support personnel are needed.

2. **Scripture Gift Mission** (**SGM**) distributes superbly produced Scripture portions, selections and Gospels. This has been a remarkable ministry around the world. Often an **SGM** Scripture portion is used and treasured for years. In many languages an **SGM** booklet is the first portion of the Scriptures ever published. In 1992 over 17 million portions in 357 languages were distributed in 173 countries.

3. **The Bible League** has an unusual record in strategic Bible distribution to enable church planting around the world. In 1992 over 900,000 Bibles, 4.4 million New Testaments and a total of 27 million Scriptures were distributed, major countries being Taiwan, Thailand, Philippines, Russia, Brazil and Ukraine. It is estimated that through this work 133,000 people came to Christ and became church members and at least 870 churches were planted in that year.

4. **Gideons International** have a remarkable ministry in placement of free Bibles and New Testaments in hotels, schools, hospitals, prisons and other public institutions, together with personal testimony where possible. The work has spread to 146 countries with membership and financing almost entirely indigenous to those countries. Countless millions have found comfort, deliverance, challenge and salvation through Gideon Bibles.

5. **The Pocket Testament League** has a ministry of distribution of Gospels and New Testaments in 100 or more countries in many languages. These are compiled in a manner to facilitate soul-winning and discipleship.

Vision for AD2000

A Forum of Bible Agencies was formed in 1992 linking together the efforts of 17 Bible translation and distribution agencies. The aims are courageous and need to be covered in prayer. These are:

1. **The whole Bible translated** into all languages spoken by five million or more by the end of 1999. There are 33 languages in this category that need to be translated.

2. **The New Testament translated** into all languages spoken by over 500,000 people by the end of 1998 – 77 languages that need to be translated.

3. **Some Scriptures in audio or written form** for all languages spoken by more than 250,000 by the end of 1997 that need to be translated.

4. **Translation begun in all languages** spoken by over 100,000 people by the end of 1997.

Of the world's 6,528 languages, at least 925, and possibly over 2,000 languages, still have a need for New Testament translation work.

<table>
<tr><td>Special
Ministries</td><td># THEOLOGICAL
EDUCATION
BY EXTENSION (TEE)</td><td>December
15</td></tr>
</table>

TEE was one of the significant missiological breakthroughs of recent decades. The Western pattern of residential seminaries and Bible colleges for training Christian workers was proving too costly, slow and not necessarily training those best fitted for the ministry in the rapidly growing Church in other parts of the world.

TEE started in Latin America as a means of training pastors while in the ministry. It has rapidly spread round the world and diversified into distant learning courses at all levels from basic to degree-earning, often supplemented by travelling lecturers, cassettes, videos and a wide range of relevant biblical, pastoral and social concern courses. By 1980 there were 250 known evangelical TEE centres with over 27,000 students around the world.

Pray for:

1. **Development of TEE at a global level** – international coordination, sharing of materials, standardization of qualifications and integration of TEE into national theological education systems. In some countries TEE has lost credibility and effectiveness for this lack. Pray for key international TEE agencies, some listed below.

2. **Provision of trained writers of courses and coordinators** to make TEE effective at a local level. Adaptability to different levels of education of TEE students and flexibility in travel arrangements can make this a demanding ministry as they seek to encourage and help their students.

3. **TEE students** who often live in less than ideal study situations – poverty, hard manual work in the day, lack of study facilities and ongoing demands for ministry. Pray for motivation, discipline, openness to the instruction of the Holy Spirit and, ultimately, more fruitful ministry.

Each of these are listed because of their unique contribution to the advancement of TEE and widespread acceptance of the quality of the ministry.

1. TAFTEE (India), PO Box 520, Bangalore 520–005, India. Over 4,000 students.

2. SEAN International, The Pound, Whitestone, Exeter, Devon EX4 2HP, England. Materials used worldwide.

3. LOGOI, 13200 SW 128th Street, Suite D-1, Miami, Florida 33186, USA. Mainly Latin America, with 14,000 students.

4. LOGOS, Potsdamerstr. 115, 4800 Bielefeld 17, Germany. Russia/Eurasia.

5. ACTEA, PMB 2049, Kaduna, Nigeria. Linked with AEAM and with a commission for coordinating TEE in Africa.

BIBLE CORRESPONDENCE COURSES (BCCs)

This ministry has grown and become one of the most effective means for following up contacts from literature distribution and Christian radio programmes. The relative ease in using the post in sensitive areas of the world and the emphasis on studying the Word of God has had a great impact on BCC students – some being converted and others being strengthened in their Christian life. This has proved the best single means for winning Muslims.

1. **There are reckoned to be over 300 centres sending out evangelical BCCs.** Pray for the workers involved in preparation of materials and helping the students through the post.

2. **Pray for the publicizing of BCCs** through tracts, radio programmes or through other students in lands where there are few believers and doors are closed to missionaries.

3. **Pray for effective personal follow-up of students** by local Christians and for their integration into Christian fellowships.

| December 16 | CHRISTIAN LITERATURE | Special Ministries |

Literature has played a major role in changing the world for good or bad.

1. The little *Red Book* of Mao Tse Tung and its 740 million copies blighted a whole generation of Chinese.

2. Saudi Arabian printing presses churn out millions of Korans to strengthen and extend Islam.

3. More than half of all evangelical Christians attribute their conversion, in part, to Christian literature.

4. The flow of *samizdat* (illegal, underground) literature in the USSR and smuggling in of Christian literature and Bibles played a major role in the demise of Communism there.

Some prayer points.

1. **Crash literacy programmes** in many parts of the world create an immense desire for *any* literature among new literates. Pray for a greater interest among churches in this ministry. Pray for more and better Christian literature. There are over one billion illiterate people, and the number is increasing.

2. **The glut of Christian literature in English, Spanish and German is in contrast to the famine in most other languages.** Much of what is available is translated from English, but is an inadequate substitute for locally written materials. Pray for mature Christian writers to be raised up all over the world.

3. **Evangelistic literature.**
a) **EHC** has a global vision to distribute good Christian literature to every home, nation-by-nation. An estimated 39,000 homes are reached daily. **EHC** is operating in 68 countries and in 1990 distributed 29 million pieces of literature. Remarkable results have been achieved. Mention is frequently made in the text of the countries. Pray for the global direction of this ministry.
b) **Gospel broadsheets** have had an amazing growth since God called **WEC** to this ministry. The *SOON* broadsheets are produced bi-monthly in English, French, Portuguese, Spanish, Arabic, Urdu, Thai, Hindi, Bengali, Swahili, etc. and distributed free by hand and post. The testimonies,

short articles and offers of BCCs have brought a dramatic response. Over 1.5 million copies are printed every issue and penetrate into some of the least accessible and unevangelized nations on earth.

4. **Supply of Christian literature** is hindered in the places of greatest need because of poverty, difficulty of distribution, cost of printing using expensive materials from the West and rampant inflation. Pray for adequate funding mechanisms in Eurasia, Africa and poorer parts of Asia so that indigenous publishing and printing operations can become viable. Pray also for **BookAid** (**CLC**), an innovative method of donating second-hand Christian books to poor countries for sale and support of indigenous literature agencies.

5. **Literature missionaries are too few.** Pray for the calling of those with the right qualities and qualifications for this ministry – in journalism, printing, publishing, writing, distribution, etc. Few Bible schools give adequate attention to the training of literature missionaries.

6. **Distribution** is made through various methods – Christian bookstores, colportage, Bible vans, etc. Pray for opportunities for personal witnessing and counselling in this distribution work and for fruit from the literature sold or handed out. One mission worthy of prayer is **CLC** with 143 Christian bookstores in 44 countries. **CLC** urgently needs 200 more workers!

7. **Christian magazines** have had a valuable ministry in many parts of the world, both evangelistically and in helping Christians. Heavy production costs now harm sales and threaten viability. Pray for guidance for those who have to make difficult decisions. Pray also for spiritual fruit from this ministry.

Special Ministries	# RELIEF AND DEVELOPMENT	**December 17**

The magnitude of suffering and disasters afflicting many areas appears to increase by the year. The ubiquity of the television camera vividly portrays suffering caused by wars, famines, natural disasters and man's cruelty to man.

Consider the following:

1. **Population growth** of 90 million annually is straining food resources to the extent that increased poverty is inevitable.

2. **The selfishness of rich trading nations** is denying the poorer nations the chance to develop their economies to viability. Most aid does not achieve this. The dumping of food-surplus aid damages local agriculture in the long term.

3. **The difference of income/person** between "north" and "south" over the last century has increased from 2:1 to 70:1. Inevitably this will increase the flow of refugees, the impact of natural disasters and the likelihood of conflict.

4. **The impact of the AIDS pandemic**, the revival of resistant strains of malaria, tuberculosis and other diseases as well as the effects of environmental pollution will steadily degrade world health – especially in the poorer countries – and reduce the ability to survive economically.

An adequate Christian response to human suffering is needed. Pray:

1. **That generous giving by Christians** to aid programmes be wisely used. Prestige projects, lack of long-term strategy, inefficient communications, self-seeking bureaucracies and corruption can gobble up vast sums of money with little material or spiritual benefit to the sufferers and even bring about an unhealthy dependency on the donors.

2. **For those who administer the aid** and resettlement programmes. Many agencies have sprung up to channel the giving of Evangelicals – there are over 100 such in North America. Some of the better known are **World Vision**, **TEAR Fund** and MAP International, but there are many others from all over the world. Pray for the provision of the right personnel, a balance between physical and spiritual

needs and for evangelism and church planting to be furthered. Praise the Lord that where care and tact has been exercised and a loving Christian testimony shared, there has been a harvest of souls in a number of countries.

3. **For the right balance in giving.** Christian donors need to be guided by the Lord rather than by their emotional response to physical suffering. The famine of the Word of God is a far more serious problem than that of food in Africa today. The giving by Christians to the sufferers of famine in Ethiopia and Somalia was commendable, but must be matched by a similar generosity to train spiritual leaders for the under-taught church in Africa.

An adequate Christian involvement in development to deal with the causes of suffering is also needed. Pray for:

1. **Development projects** run by Christian agencies and churches. Many agencies have been specifically set up to fund and initiate such schemes. Pray that all projects selected may be those most beneficial to local communities and pray for a wise selection of appropriate technology that can be continued and expanded locally without foreign input.

2. **Christian workers.** Honest, humble, dedicated expatriate and national workers who have both the technical expertise and the love of Christ are in great demand. Pray for many to be called and equipped for such ministries and that their labours may win opportunities to share the gospel. Agriculture, development of effective markets for products, provision of clean water, literacy campaigns, preventive medicine, etc. are all key areas of need in many parts of the developing world.

3. **The planting and strengthening of local churches** through these projects. The whole ministry should be geared to bring the gospel to the people helped and to plant churches or, where churches already exist, to enable them to raise the finances to support local and missionary work and workers.

December 18	**MEDICAL MISSION WORK**	Special Ministries

This ministry has been one of the major Christian ministries on the mission field for many years. Appalling suffering and total lack of any medical attention in many fields impelled pioneer missionaries to expend much labour and money in developing clinics, hospitals, leprosaria, etc. This ministry needs prayer in these days of change, for:

1. **Adaptability.** Governments demand higher standards, and in some lands, are taking over all non-government health services. Medical missionary work must constantly be assessed for usefulness in changing circumstances. The present trend is for fewer, but better equipped and staffed, mission hospitals, and an emphasis on preventive medicine.

2. **Supply of needs in funds and personnel** – that mission boards and national churches responsible may know how best to apportion them in accordance with the spiritual benefits to be reaped. Such programmes can too often become the master rather than the servant.

3. **Usefulness in winning people to the Lord and for the churches.** The primary aim of medical missionary work can sometimes be forgotten in the busyness of a large institution. Yet many can be and are won by this means. Pray for the right balance between medical and spiritual needs.

4. **The opening of doors to the gospel.** In many lands this is the only means for entry and witness; for example, in Yemen, Afghanistan and Bhutan. Pray that the witness of these medical missionaries, albeit tactful, may lead to the conversion of some, and also the planting of churches.

5. **Leprosy work.** This will probably long remain a ministry for which Christians will have a large input, for the disease is unpleasant and the psychological and social problems many. There are over 18 million leprosy sufferers in the world, but only 20% are receiving treatment. There has been an increase in the incidence of this disease over the last 20 years in spite of the ready availability of drugs

to combat it. Pray for the work of **The Leprosy Mission**, and others, in seeking to alleviate the sufferings of these unfortunate people and win them for the Lord. Pray for the conversion of some and also that they may reintegrate into their communities as witnessing Christians and become the means of starting new congregations.

6. **The AIDS pandemic.** This is becoming a terrible threat to whole nations – especially in central and southern Africa, India, Thailand and Brazil. This is likely to become the new frontier in medical missions and in the ministry of local churches in the '90s. A range of new skills and spiritual gifts will be needed to cope with the stress and demands of ministry to the sick and bereaved.

7. **Health field workers.** Because more people pass through the hospitals of the world than through its churches, the **HCFI** seeks to win for Christ and train medical personnel – doctors, dentists, nurses, para-medicals, etc. – to share their faith with those whom they serve medically. Pray for:
a) **The conversion to Christ** of many health field workers.
b) **The witness of Christians** in the health field to be both wise and bold to patients and colleagues.
c) **Christian medical workers serving in hazardous circumstances.** In restricted countries where churches are closed, hospitals remain open – hence the strategic value of this work.
d) **HCFI staff workers round the world.** Pray for additional staff. Pray also for the HCFI Training Centres and training ministry in Europe, Africa, Asia, North and South America and for the International *HEARTBEAT* magazine which circulates in over 100 countries.
e) The increasing infiltration of deceptive forms of Alternative Medicine and New Age, false religions, and humanistic and secular influences in the health field to be exposed and thwarted.

Special Ministries	**MISSIONARY AVIATION**	December 19

What an essential means for evangelism and church growth the Christian "air force" has become! In many areas access is difficult by any other means. In 1984 there were about 476 aircraft in 48 lands used to transport Christian workers, supplies, hospital patients and aid. No more recent survey has been made, but this number has not changed much. Without this service, ministries would be slowed or stopped. Some 90 mission agencies have their own aircraft, but other agencies exist solely for the purpose of serving churches and missions. Pray for:

1. **The staff.** There are about 600 missionary pilots, mechanics and support personnel serving the Body of Christ. Their exacting ministry demands high technical ability and efficiency. They also can have a vital spiritual ministry for which they have many unique opportunities. Pray for the provision of workers technically and spiritually equipped for this ministry.

2. **Mission Aviation Fellowship**, which is unique and deserving of special prayer as the pioneer of this ministry and the largest agency, with four branches operating 140 aircraft in over 25 countries, flying over 30,000 hours per year.

3. Other significant flying agencies:
a) **Jungle Aviation and Radio Service** (JAARS) is a vital component of **WBT/SIL**'s Bible translation ministry in 11 lands. JAARS operates 47 aircraft.
b) Other agencies with a large flying programme are **AIM**-Air in Kenya, Wings of the Morning (US Methodist, Zaire) and Tribal Air (**NTM**) in 10 countries.

4. **The supply of all needs.** Although the overall savings in time and finance are enormous, this is high-tech ministry and costly for both the operators and users.

5. **Safety.** The record has been good, but there have been a number of tragic accidents. Pilots must often operate from primitive airstrips in wild terrain and dangerous climatic conditions. A single mistake by a mechanic or pilot can have tragic consequences.

MISSIONARY NAVY

The rapid development of a significant variety of Christian ships with a mobile ministry has proved one of the major means the Holy Spirit has used to spread missions vision, cross-pollinate evangelistic methods, bring spiritual life and renewal in churches and give a unique discipling ministry to young Christians in lands where little of such depth is available.

Pray for the following:

1. **OM's ship ministry** through the **MV *Doulos*** (the oldest passenger liner afloat today) and **MV *Logos II*** with an average of 450 personnel at any one time. Major ministries include evangelism, literature and book exhibition ministry.

2. **YWAM's** Mercy Ships **MV *Anastasis*** and the smaller **MV *Good Samaritan*** with an average of 600 personnel involved in discipling, Christian aid and mobile medical work.

3. **The Pacific Ocean fleet** of small vessels. The thousands of isolated island communities spread over the vastness of the Pacific need encouragement, renewal in lifeless churches and new vision. God is raising up a variety of ministries:
a) **Daystar III** based in New Zealand with an extensive ministry of Bible and Christian literature distribution.
b) **The Korean Hannah Mission's vessel MV *Hannah*** with 30 crew and personnel involved in evangelism, church planting, training in missions and discipleship in Asia and the Pacific.
c) **Boat Ministry, Singapore** using ferro-concrete yachts for the islands of Indonesia.
d) **YWAM** prayer flotillas for the Pacific based in New Zealand.

4. **The Inland Waters flotilla.** Many missions are expanding this type of ministry:
a) On the Amazon in South America (**UFM**, Brazilian Bible Society, Costa Rican Amazonian Mission with three launches and reaching 19 tribes, **SIM** in Bolivia).
b) **BEM** on Belgian canals and **GMU** in southwest France.
c) **Hellenic Missionary Union** boat *Morning Star* in the Greek islands.

5. **The Gospel of Christ** Christian yacht with text-emblazoned sails. A globe-encircling, well-publicized voyage envisaged to uplift the Lord Jesus is planned for June 1994 in connection with the worldwide **March for Jesus**, as well as participation in international races. Ministries anticipated include evangelism in ports and among boating people as well as intercession at sea.

Pray for:

1. **Provision of funds** for these expensive yet strategic ministries. Costs have risen dramatically over the past decade.

2. **Provision of technically qualified crew and staff** without whom ships may not sail. This is a constant need.

3. **The spiritual health, growth and safety of all involved** in this demanding ministry. People from many nations have to live and witness together. The loss of the **MV *Logos I*** near Cape Horn in 1988 highlights the potential for danger.

4. **The ministry of the ships** to stimulate world vision, local evangelism and holy living in ports of call.

5. **Seamen's missions around the world.** There are an estimated 10 million seafarers and fishermen – increasingly non-Western and non-Christian – who have little exposure to the gospel. Missions such as Korea Harbour Evangelism with workers in many lands have a caring ministry to them.

| **Special Ministries** | **SHORT-TERM WORKERS (STWs)** | **December 21** |

More and more young people (and some older ones too!) have been serving the Lord in a cross-cultural situation for periods of a few weeks to three years. This is a significant worldwide development. It is impossible to assess how many believers all over the world give some or all of their time during any one year to missionary work, for this may equal the world's entire full-time missionary force! Many thousands of young people in Europe, Africa and Asia move out every year with such groups as **YWAM, CCC, OM, TEEN Missions** and **World Horizons** as short-term literature missionaries, evangelists, etc. Others serve the Lord for special projects with missionary societies. Pray for:

1. **A deep sense of God's calling to service.** Inexperience, immaturity, or lack of cross-cultural exposure can make the experience traumatic. Unsuitable STWs can divert Christian leaders from their ministry and slow the advance of the gospel rather than furthering it.

2. **Spiritual growth.** Often the greatest permanent results of a short-term ministry are what the Holy Spirit does in the life of the short-term worker. Pray for sufficient pastoral care, adequate fellowship, worthwhile in-service teaching and training and also fruitfulness.

3. **Protection.** Our world is more dangerous than in past decades; wars, kidnappings, resurgent diseases and spiritual attacks from the enemy need to be prayed against.

4. **Long-term ministry** after the short-term experience. Pray that the short exposure may have a positive influence in bringing many STWs into long-term overseas ministry or fruitful home involvement for the Lord.

| **Special Ministries** | **STUDENT MINISTRIES** | **December 22** |

The tertiary students of the world constitute one of the most strategic mission fields. Consider:

1. Worldwide there are 37 million students in universities and colleges. Many will be in leadership roles in 20 years' time.

2. In some areas the percentage of evangelical students is generally lower than in the general population. This is true in Latin America and many countries in Europe and China. Whole student cultures remain little influenced by biblical Christianity.

3. The student world has radically changed over the past decade. The militancy and espousal of left-wing causes has waned and a self-seeking hedonism become prevalent. Christian ministry should address needs generated by this culture shift.

Many agencies have been raised up to reach students. A few key ones are mentioned below, though some have diversified into ministries that have outgrown the student arm of the work.

1. **International Fellowship of Evangelical Students** (**IFES**) has become a worldwide fellowship of autonomous national movements in universities, with a wide variety of local names. The emphasis of this ministry is evangelism, Bible study groups, literature and missions. This vital field needs much prayer:
   a) **For the extension of the evangelical witness to universities where, to date, none exists.** Areas of special need: Latin America, Muslim world, French-speaking Africa, Eurasia.
   b) **For the right leadership** in the rapidly changing population of the student world – for adult

advisers, travelling secretaries and student leaders.

c) **For Christian students and their growth in the Lord** and that from their number some may go into full-time service for the Lord.

2. **The Navigators** with their unique personal discipleship programmes have made a deep impact on many. Their work began among the military in the USA, but in 1985 they ministered among university students at 298 locations in 34 countries; that number has since been increased. Their emphasis is upon multiplying spiritual labourers through disciplined study and application of God's Word. They are moving out increasingly into local church-related ministries.

3. **Agencies specializing in ministry among international students,**such as **ISI** and **IFES**, have developed effective outreach to some of the 450,000 international students in English-speaking nations. In other language areas the coverage is poorer – especially in Francophone universities. Many of these students come from lands closed to the gospel and sadly, the majority are repelled by the coldness and lack of concern of "Christians" and return home disillusioned. Others have been wonderfully converted. Students converted in the West could become a decisive factor for the spread of the gospel when they return home.

4. **Campus Crusade** began and continues as a campus ministry but the ministry has broadened out into a multi-dimensional thrust for world evangelization. (See p 605 for the *Jesus* film ministry.) Over 11,000 workers serve in 105 countries. Pray for their evangelistic, discipling and mobilizing ministry among students.

5. **Student missions conferences** have been used for many years to inspire students with a vision for the world. Some of the more significant are the triennial Urbana conference of IVF(**IFES**) in USA and the triennial conferences for European young people in Utrecht, Netherlands. Other significant conferences are developing in size and sophistication in Nigeria, Korea and Latin America. Pray that these may be the source of many becoming committed to world evangelization.

6. The rapid development of Christian student movements in Central Europe, Ukraine, Russia and other former Communist countries is cause for praise, but needs also to be covered in prayer.

<table><tr><td>December 23</td><td># CHRISTIAN TENTMAKERS</td><td>Special Ministries</td></tr></table>

Since the time of Paul, the "original" tentmaker, it has often been expedient or essential to use a secular skill or profession as a platform for sharing the gospel (Acts 18:3). Great movements of people seeking employment or education opportunities since 1950 have enabled Christians to use the same means to evangelize nations, peoples and strata of society otherwise closed to full-time Christian workers. There are about 60 nations in the world where this is the major means for gaining entry into a country and in 33 of these it is the *only* way.

1. **Hundreds of thousands of Western, Middle Eastern, Asian and African Christians** have sought education opportunities or employment as doctors, nurses, paramedicals, lecturers, teachers, engineers, agriculturalists, house servants, road sweepers, etc. Most have done it for personal reasons. Pray that they may be stirred to witness to non-Christians as they observe the darkness, need and misconceptions of the indigenous populations around them.

2. **Pray for the specific calling of Christians** with the necessary qualifications and spirituality to serve in "closed" lands, specifically the Muslim heartlands and Communist lands of Asia.

3. **Adequate cultural and spiritual preparation** is hard to obtain while retaining the necessary expertise, yet it is essential. Pray for good, appropriate training and screening of this special type of worker.

4. **These tentmakers frequently go to areas where the authorities or the people are hostile to Christianity.** Fellowship and pastoral care are vital ingredients in their ability to survive spiritually and be fruitful, but are often hard to provide. Pray especially for those living in lonely, pressurized situations where every action can be carefully monitored. Pray for their protection as they challenge

the entrenched powers of darkness. Asian Christians working in the Middle East have been effective tentmakers, but a number have suffered as a result.

5. **Strategic deployment and fruitful service** is a major area of weakness. Too often the long hours of work, isolation and lack of an effective strategy for church planting mean little long-term fruit. There are relatively few success stories. Pray that the work of Christian tentmakers may be integrated into ministry networks (local church, mission or inter-agency) which provide continuity in contacts, direction in ministry and result in churches being planted. Many mission agencies have adapted their structures to facilitate tentmaking and provide the necessary accountability and continuity.

6. **Wisdom and tact, together with a holy boldness,** are needed where active proselytization is forbidden so that there may be conversions and the establishing of fellowships of believers.

7. **The right use of time** is important. Appropriate employment that gives opportunity both for doing the job in a Christ-uplifting way and for friendship evangelism is not easy to procure.

8. **Pray for the conversion of prominent citizens** of these countries through the witness of tentmakers. This could totally change the attitudes of governments and open the doors for other Christian workers.

Special Ministries	OUTREACH TO SECTS OR CULTS	December 24

The worldwide growth and spread of missionary cults of western and eastern origin has been a striking phenomenon in the 20th century. This has accompanied a global pluralization of religions. The religion graphs throughout this book vividly show that the relative simplicity of 1900 has given way to the medley of beliefs in 2000. Note the following developments:

1. **Jehovah's Witnesses** have grown worldwide from 916,000 members in 1960 to 4,313,000 in 1992. There are over 11,431,000 adherents today. Many give sacrificial hours in door-to-door work to proclaim a false message in 224 nations. In some nations – such as Poland, Belgium and Guadeloupe – Jehovah's Witnesses outnumber Evangelicals.

2. **The Mormons** (The Church of Jesus Christ of Latter Day Saints) have similarly grown from 1,408,000 adherents in 1960 to 7,301,000 in 1990. The short-term missionary work of the Mormons puts many Protestant churches to shame. Many parts of Polynesia are rapidly becoming majority Mormon. Mormon missionaries numbered 44,000 in 1990 with work in 256 countries and territories.

3. **Hindu-Buddhist cults** have made astonishing inroads among young people in the West – some *gurus* gaining large followings. Many lives have been damaged by aberrant practices – use of drugs, promiscuous sex and exposure to demonic influences. The *Hare Krishna* movement has rapidly gained a large following in Russia since the ending of Communist rule.

4. **New Age** has swept through modern cultures in the West and East. In the West a worldview shift to acceptance of eastern mysticism, reincarnation and "self" awareness together with interest in old Western occultism has posed a serious challenge to Christianity and the whole basis on which Western culture has been founded. A large minority of churchgoers would accept some New Age premises.

5. **New religious movements** that mix Christian concepts and terminology with indigenous non-Christian beliefs and practices have gained followings of millions – **Christo-paganism** in Latin America, **Indigenous syncretic churches** in Africa (with a following of over 34 million), new movements in China and others too.

Pray for:

1. **Those who have been led astray** into quasi-Christian movements – often through ignorance and the failure of born-again Christians to reach them first. Praise God for thousands who have left such cults and found liberty in Christ.

2. **The bias in Western media towards New Age and Eastern religious concepts** and against biblical Christianity to be removed. Pray that Christians may be well-taught and discerning concerning these errors.

3. **The spiritual vacuum in the former Eurasian and European Communist states** which has not only been filled by true Christians but also by numerous eastern and western sects. Pray for the truth to be proclaimed so that all can see what is erroneous.

4. **Preparation of suitable literature** in all main languages to help Christians understand these cults and how to witness to cultists. The need for apologetic literature in Eurasia is particularly acute. The organizations below can provide help.

5. Specific organizations needing prayer and offering help:
a) **Christian Research Institute International** (Pseudo-Christian sects), Box 500, San Juan Capistrano, CA 92693, USA.
b) **MacGregor Ministries** (Pseudo-Christian Sects, New Age), Box 73, Balfour, BC V0G IC0, Canada. Also Box 538, Prospect East, SA 5082, Australia.
c) **Reachout Trust** (Pseudo-Christian Sects, New Age), Alpha Place, Garth Road, Morden, Surrey SM4 4LX, UK.
d) **Free Minds, Inc.** (formerly Bethel Ministries – Jehovah's Witnesses), PO Box 3818, Manhattan Beach, CA 90266, USA.
e) **Concerned Christians and Former Mormons** (Mormons), Information and Research Center, 14106 Whittier Blvd., Whittier, CA 90605, USA.
f) **Watchman Fellowship**, PO Box 556, Muldersdrift, Transvaal 1747, South Africa.

<table>
<tr><td>December
25</td><td><h1>MINISTRY TO
CHILDREN</h1></td><td>Special
Ministries</td></tr>
</table>

The importance of ministry to children and young people cannot be overestimated. They are the potential Church of tomorrow. Consider the following:

1. **Over 140 million children were born in 1992.** Of these, only 17 million were born in more developed countries.

2. **There are 1,510 million children under 15 in less developed countries.** (Half of Africa south of the Sahara is under 15.) Over 35% of these will grow up illiterate, most will be poor, 40% in Asia and 26% in Africa will be malnourished.

Pray for:

1. **The preservation of the family.** This is under threat worldwide.
a) **In the West** stable two-parent families are becoming the exception and few children have any contact with the gospel. The legacy of rejection, spiritual ignorance and deprivation of real love is beginning to bear bitter fruit. Pray for Christian families as they seek to bring up their children in the fear of the Lord when all around them society is disintegrating and hostile.
b) **In poor countries** parents can do little for their children because they are caught in the cycle of poverty, disease, illiteracy and instability. Debt encourages slave or child labour, poverty and social breakdown.

2. **The children themselves.**
a) **Non-Christian children.** Only in a few lands is there a wide range of evangelistic and discipling ministries for children. They are often ignored or treated as if adults. Children in special need of prayer are:
i) An estimated 50–100 million indentured or slave children sold to settle debts.
ii) The estimated 30 million street children in the world without any family contacts – many in Latin America.
iii) The seven million child-refugees as of 1992.
iv) The 400,000 African children carrying the HIV virus. It is estimated 2.5 million African children will die with AIDS and five million become AIDS orphans by AD2000.
v) The 120 million blind or deaf children – most of whom will never receive special help.
b) **Non-Christian children of Christians.** Numerous children do not follow in the faith of their

parents. Many churches do not provide spiritual care and nurture. Too few Christians are trained to reach out to the children of church members and few churches see the need. Pray for the development of good teachers and materials for successful ministry among such children. **CEF** has a notable record in providing this.

c) **Christian children.** They are the best evangelists of their peers. Pray for many in schools with a non-Christian and often hostile environment. Pray for international agencies with specific discipling ministries among children such as **YFC**, **SU**, Boys' Brigade and Crusaders.

3. **Literature for children** – a big need in many countries. Only in a few languages is there a wide variety of good literature for this age group.

4. **Bible camp ministries.** These have been much used of God and have possibly been one of the more fruitful ways of evangelizing and teaching young people. Many churches and agencies run such camps, but there are rarely enough spiritual leaders for this ministry.

5. **Missionary children (MKs).** The witness of Christian families on the mission field is a significant aspect of witness and teaching by example for many cultures. Yet the personal and educational needs of children is a major factor in terminating or suspending the cross-cultural ministry of their parents at their peak of usefulness.

a) **MKs** grow up bi-cultural or even tri-cultural, but often without a sense of belonging to any culture. This enriches some and embitters others. Pray that parents might have great wisdom in keeping ministry and family in balance and give the children a sense of privilege in their enriching experiences. Pray that parents and children might be a united team for the spread of the gospel.

b) **Education is always a costly challenge** – in parental time if home schooling is pursued, in much travel and strong emotions if the only option is boarding school away from home, or in costs if secular schooling is used. Pray for wise decisions for each child as to the option used. Pray for MK schools in various parts of the world and the provision of funds and missionary staff. Pray that home churches may understand this crucial issue as an integral part of missionary support.

c) **The growing non-English-speaking missionary force** is having to face the challenge of the danger that their children may lose contact with their home cultures. They can face enormous emotional and educational problems when they return to their home countries. This problem is particularly acute for non-Western children in Western-based mission schools.

d) **Missionary children need fulfilling careers** – pray that MKs may find a deep and satisfying relationship with Jesus and then careers enriched by their childhood experiences. Pray that many may become active servants of God.

| Special Ministries | # SATURATION EVANGELISM AND CHURCH PLANTING | December 26 |

Saturation evangelism is the total mobilization of the active membership of a church or group of churches to cover an entire area with the gospel. This has had many titles and forms over the past 30 years.

1. **Evangelism in Depth** (EiD) pioneered in the '60s by **LAM** in Latin America.

2. **New Life For All** (NLFA) in Africa (**SIM** and others).

3. **Evangelism Explosion** (EE) in the USA and beyond.

The effects have been beneficial in areas where there were strong young evangelical churches (as in parts of Latin America and central Nigeria), but less so in other areas. More recent expressions of this vision have had more lasting benefits for local churches – especially in EE.

During the 1980s the concept of saturation **church planting** came to the fore – especially in Ghana and the Philippines. This has resulted in a growing movement to mobilize the Church in a country to plant churches in every community. This has become known as the **DAWN Movement** (Discipling **A** Whole Nation) and the vision has rapidly spread to many lands.

1. **The DAWN vision** has led to a dramatic turn-round for the good in Ghana and the Philippines. Pray that many other lands may see churches revived and moving out with a vision to multiply churches in unreached areas and peoples.

2. **The key to saturation church planting is adequate research** of both the harvest field and the harvest force. Pray that nations which have set up such a function may press it through to conclusion. Many countries are engaged in this arduous process. Pray that the results may motivate the Church to action and implementation.

3. **Specific DAWN goals for the future.**
a) Every nation in the world to initiate a saturation church-planting vision by AD2000.
b) Ten million evangelical churches or worshipping groups in the world by the end of AD2000. The present number is hard to determine but may have been around 4–5 million in 1990.
c) A congregation in existence for each cluster of 500–1,000 people in every village and city neighbourhood in the world by 2015.
Humanly speaking, these goals would be impossible to achieve globally, but it puts a major challenge before the Church!

<table>
<tr><td>December
27</td><td># URBAN
EVANGELIZATION</td><td>Special
Ministries</td></tr>
</table>

For the first time in history over half the world's population lives in or near a city. By AD2000 there will be 21 cities of over 10 million, 93 over five million and 433 over one million. Most of these cities are in the non-Western world and a growing number are non-Christian. Africa's cities are growing at 10% every year. Generally speaking, Christians are not advancing in the major cities in the same way as elsewhere. The cities are one of the biggest challenges for missions for the '90s.

Pray for:

1. **Adequate strategies** for the evangelization of the major non-Christian cities of the world. The racial, ethnic, linguistic, social and religious complexities of modern cities make an all-out effort essential to reach each cultural unit of these cities.

2. **The urban poor**, the biggest single challenge. Vast slums and squatter camps are mushrooming all over Latin America, Africa and many parts of Asia. Appalling conditions and squalor make any Christian ministry difficult and complex – how to combine evangelism and social betterment without creating dependency or churches filled with those seeking escape from the system. Pray for the urban poor and for God's guidance as to how to work most effectively.

3. **The decaying inner cities of the Western world.** In the midst of affluence many cities have a rotten core. Unemployment, poverty, drug abuse, crime and despair are widespread. Most Christian congregations have migrated to the more comfortable suburbs, leaving these areas with inadequate Christian input. Many of these inner cities have become the home of many immigrant ethnic minorities who need to be reached with the love of Christ. Pray for bodies such as the Salvation Army, Association of Rescue Missions (USA), Ichthus (UK), Bethel (Spain) and many others with commitment to these needy peoples.

4. **Major international and regional conferences** which will increasingly focus on urban ministries over the coming decade. Pray that these may lead to effective cooperation among churches and agencies, without which the task will be impossible to achieve.

5. **The mobilization of a trained and efficient work force.** Christian workers, in general, fear the cities, especially the less comfortable slums and inner cities, and do not know how to handle the high costs, complexities and tensions of city ministry. Pioneer work in concrete jungles and vast squatter

settlements has to be seen as just as valid as pioneering in rural areas. God is raising up new agencies specifically to reach the urban poor such as Servants to Asia's Urban Poor.

6. **The essential and effective use of all modern methods of communication.** Millions need to be confronted with the claims of Christ in as short a time as possible. No one medium can achieve this, but a combination of all in a concerted effort could decisively change the spiritual climate of a city.

Special Ministries	# INTERNATIONAL COOPERATION FOR WORLD EVANGELIZATION	**December 28**

The growth and expansion of the Church worldwide has built up such momentum and grown in such complexity that close cooperation at every level has become essential. No longer is the missions movement Western but global, and the potential for disastrous confrontations and relationship breakdowns grows greater.

There are three major international evangelical bodies with closely overlapping constituencies and similar but not identical aims. These are:

1. The **World Evangelical Fellowship** – representing national and regional Evangelical Fellowships around the world and with a wide range of commissions and interests to further world evangelization.

2. The **Lausanne Movement** – representing Evangelicals in both evangelical denominations and agencies and also Evangelicals in other Protestant Churches. The 1974 Lausanne Congress gave its name to the movement and also was pivotal in giving a new impetus for world evangelization with special focus on the unreached.

3. The **AD2000 and Beyond Movement** (see p 602) which was an outgrowth of the 1989 Singapore GCOWE and the 1989 Lausanne Congress in Manila. The constituency is more a range of task- and ministry-oriented agencies and churches committed to the major goal of focusing on the world evangelization goals for the year 2000 after which point the Movement will disband.

Pray for:

1. **Effective cooperation between Evangelicals** around the world to best enhance the move to complete the evangelization of the world as soon as possible (Matthew 24:14). Pray that personalities, nationalities and secondary doctrines may not hinder this.

2. **The leaders of the above organizations and their walk with God** – that they may be an example in vision, Christ-likeness and the power of the Cross to bring such a diversity of Christians to unity in him.

3. **Wise use of funds for convening international and regional conferences.** The speed and ease of international air travel makes such congresses, consultations and conferences possible. They are expensive yet they provide a forum for fellowship, cross-fertilization of ideas and cooperative action. Pray for lasting results from such conferences. Specific events to come:
a) GCOWE II in June 1995 (AD2000 and Beyond Movement).
b) Numerous conferences being considered for the turn of the millennium. May only those on God's agenda be launched!

4. **Effective networking among churches and agencies in pioneer areas.** Recent openings in former Communist lands have been abused by lack of it to the detriment of the indigenous churches and the credibility of the gospel. Pray that as other bastions of resistance to the gospel crumble through prayer, Christians may relate more effectively. Praise God for countries where this networking has been implemented.

<table>
<tr><td>December
29</td><td>**PRAYER – A
GLOBAL MINISTRY**</td><td>Special
Ministries</td></tr>
</table>

Give praise to the Lord for the rapid spread and growth of movements for prayer and intercession around the world. A list of some significant networks and their addresses is given in Appendix 2, but over 100 are known. God is stirring Christians on every continent to pray and exercise their throne-authority in Christ for revival, spiritual awakening and world evangelization. God has used and is using these movements to accelerate the expansion of his kingdom.

Pray for:

1. **The spiritual vitality and growth of existing prayer movements,** and effective strategic networks to develop which will span not only the world but the different major languages used by Christians. Pray for development at every level – local church, community, city, country and continent.

2. **Fellowships of believers and Christian ministries.** Pray that their corporate life and ministry might be *the* priority rather than an optional extra. Too many centre on activity and thus on human energy. Ask God for a spirit of repentance for the sin of prayerlessness where this has happened.

3. **Prayer Coordinators.** God is raising up significant leaders with ability to write about and motivate for intercession. Pray for these men and women to be inspired by the Holy Spirit, their numbers multiplied and discernment given as to major targets for intercessory warfare.

4. **Local churches and their leaders** to teach and demonstrate in their lives and ministries the importance and efficacy of prayer. The local church prayer meeting is, in many countries, the most poorly attended in the church programme; many evangelical churches no longer even have one. Pray that God may renew this vision with a spirit of faith, expectancy and power among his people.

5. **Families.** Few Christian families maintain a time of prayer and worship together. Pray that Christians may restructure their lives and renew their commitment to enable this to be restored and their children enthused with a world vision.

6. **Courses on prayer** to be incorporated into required curricula of Christian seminaries, colleges and schools. Rarely-found prayer courses are generally only an elective. A change in this could deeply affect the Church and progress of world evangelization.

<table>
<tr><td>December
30</td><td>*OPERATION WORLD*</td><td>Special
Ministries</td></tr>
</table>

Response to the previous four editions of *Operation World* has been encouraging. Many have faithfully prayed through the book. Hundreds have written to testify to God's guidance for ministry or call to missionary work. Areas and peoples hitherto unevangelized have been prayed open, entered and churches planted.

We estimate that over 600,000 copies of the earlier editions have been distributed – over 80% in English; also in Dutch, French, German, Korean, Portuguese and Spanish. We are grateful for reports that the Spanish and Portuguese editions have had a major input into the development of missions vision in Latin America, where information on the need of the world was previously limited.

Pray for:

1. **The fifth English edition.** Pray for the bold distribution plans to get the book into the hands of Christians, enhanced circulation in English-speaking nations and subsidized editions for countries with economic problems in Africa and Asia. Pray for more vision, prayer and mobilization to be the outcome.

2. **The first edition of** *You Can Change The World* to impact a new generation of children for missions. Pray that this book may restore missions to the heart of children's and young people's ministries in local churches. Many have neglected such an emphasis.

3. **Other language editions of both** *Operation World* **and** *You Can Change The World*. Plans are being implemented for possible publication of either or both books into Afrikaans, Chinese, Dutch, French, German, Indonesian, Korean, Portuguese, Spanish and possibly others too. Pray that these editions may be used of God to give missions vision to growing churches around the world and further enhance the development of the global missions movement, especially in Latin America, Africa and Asia.

4. **The electronic edition of** *Operation World* to become a valuable information, research and motivation tool for those with access to computers.

5. **The work of the author and his fellow-workers in the WEC International Research Office** in England in collecting, collating, storing and disseminating information on world evangelization. Pray also for guidance about any possible future editions of this book.

6. **The army of helpers and informants** around the world who contributed to the present volumes. Pray that their ministries might be blessed in a very special way. Pray also for the flow of vital information from them to continue and enable a more accurate picture of the spiritual needs of the world to be given.

7. **The hastening of world evangelization** through these ministries.

Special Ministries	**THE LORD'S RETURN**	**December 31**

The last prayer in the Bible is "Come, Lord Jesus" (Revelation 22:20). Peter tells us that we should be "looking for and hastening the coming of the day of God" (2 Pet. 3:12). How better can we do it than by praying for the fulfilment of Genesis 12:3, Revelation 7:9–10 and Matthew 24:14? Pray for:

1. **The speediest possible evangelization of the world** – of every unreached people group, area, city and nation.

2. **The Great Commission** to be restored to its rightful centrality in the ministry of the Church worldwide.

3. **Your part in achieving this.** What is God's will for *your* life? In the coming year are you willing to do whatever he commands regarding the need of the world? Is it possible God is calling *you* to a specific ministry in praying, supporting, or even personally going to the ends of the earth for your Master?

4. **Your local church's part.** Pray that your fellowship may grow in missionary zeal and commitment in the coming year.

APPENDIX 1
LEADERS OF THE WORLD'S NATIONS

Political changes in the world today are so rapid that the names of leaders have not been included in the text for individual countries. This would date the information too fast! Yet these leaders need prayer as the Scriptures exhort us (1 Samuel 12:23, 1 Timothy 2:1–4).

This list comprises the most important decision-makers in the country in June 1993 and not necessarily the titular head of state, who often plays a more ceremonial role. Usually this has meant one leader, but in a few countries we have given two. See p 30 in the section on the WORLD for prayer points.

The final column is left blank. Any leadership change can be entered there.

State or Territory	Title	Name	Changes
Afghanistan	President	**Rabbani**, Burhanuddin	
Albania	President	**Berisha**, Sali	
Algeria	Head of State – Acting	**Kafi**, Ali	
American Samoa	Governor	**Lutali**, A. P.	
Andorra	President of Executive Council	**Ribas Reig**, Oscar	
Angola	President	**dos Santos**, José Eduardo	
Anguilla	Chief Minister	**Gumbs**, Emile	
Antigua and Barbuda	Prime Minister	**Bird Sr.**, Vere C.	
Argentina	President	**Menem**, Carlos Saúl	
Armenia	President	**Ter-Petrosian**, Levon	
Aruba	Prime Minister	**Oduber**, Nelson	
Australia	Prime Minister	**Keating**, Paul	
Austria	Chancellor	**Vranitzky**, Franz	
Azerbaijan	President	**Elchibey**, Abulfaz	
Bahamas, The	Prime Minister	**Ingraham**, Hubert Alexander	
Bahrain	Amir	**Khalifa**, Isa bin Suluman al-	
Bangladesh	Prime Minister	**Khaleda Zia**, Begum	
Barbados	Prime Minister	**Sandiford**, Erskine	
Belgium	Prime Minister	**Dehaene**, Jean-Luc	
Belize	Prime Minister	**Price**, George	
Benin	President	**Soglo**, Nicéphore	
Bermuda	Premier	**Swan**, John	
Bhutan	King	**Wangchuck**, Jigme Singye	
Bolivia	President	**Paz Zamora**, Jaime	
Bosnia	President	**Izetbegovic**, Alija	
Botswana	President	**Masire**, Ketumile	
Brazil	President	**Franco**, Itamar	
British Virgin Is	Chief Minister	**Stoutt**, H. Lavity	
Brunei	Sultan and Prime Minister	**Hassanal**, Bolkiah	
Bulgaria	President	**Zhelev**, Zhelyu	
Burkina Faso	President	**Compaoré**, Blaise	
Burundi	President	**Ndadaye**, Melchior	
Byelarus	President	**Shushkevich**, Stanislav	
Cambodia	Head of State	**Sihanouk**, Norodom (Prince)	
Cameroon	President	**Biya**, Paul	
Canada	Prime Minister	**Campbell**, Kim	
Cape Verde Islands	President	**Mascarenhas Monteiro**, Antonio	
Cayman Islands	1st Elected Member Exec. Council	**Bodden**, W. Norman	
Central African Rep	President	**Kolingba**, André	

State or Territory	Title	Name	Changes
Chad	President	**Déby**, Idriss	
Chile	President	**Aylwin Azocar**, Patricio	
China, People's Rep	Premier, State Council	**Li**, Peng	
China, Taiwan	President	**Lee**, Teng-hui	
Colombia	President	**Gaviria Trujillo**, Cesar	
Comoros	President	**Djohar**, Said Mohammed	
Congo	President	**Lissouba**, Pascal	
Cook Islands	Prime Minister	**Henry**, Geoffrey	
Costa Rica	President	**Calderon Fournier**, Rafael Angel	
Côte d'Ivoire	President	**Houphouët-Boigny**, Felix	
Croatia	President	**Tudjman**, Franjo	
Cuba	President	**Castro Ruz**, Fidel	
Cyprus	President	**Clerides**, Glafkos	
Czech Republic	Prime Minister	**Klaus**, Václav	
Denmark	Prime Minister	**Rasmussen**, Poul Nyrop	
Djibouti	President	**Gouled Aptidon**, Hassan	
Dominica	Prime Minister	**Charles**, Mary Eugenia	
Dominican Republic	President	**Balaguer Ricardo**, Joaquin	
Ecuador	President	**Durán** Ballén, Sixto	
Egypt	President	**Mubarak**, Mohammed Hosni	
El Salvador	President	**Cristiani Burkard**, Alfredo Felix	
Equatorial Guinea	President	**Nguem Mbasogo**, Teodoro Obiang	
Eritrea	President	**Issayas**, Aferworki	
Estonia	President	**Meri**, Lennart	
Ethiopia	President	**Meles**, Zenaawi	
Faeroe Islands	Prime Minister	**Dam**, Atli	
Falkland Islands	Chief Executive	**Sampson**, Ronald	
Fiji	Prime Minister	**Rabuka**, Sitiveni	
Finland	President	**Koivisto**, Mauno	
France	President	**Mitterrand**, François	
	Prime Minister	**Balladur**, Edouard	
French Guiana	President of General Council	**Castor**, Elie	
French Polynesia	President of the Territorial Govt	**Flosse**, Gaston	
Gabon	President	**Bongo**, Omar	
Gambia, The	President	**Jawara**, Dawda Kairaba	
Georgia	Head of State	**Shevardnadze**, Eduard	
Germany	Chancellor	**Kohl**, Helmut	
Ghana	President	**Rawlings**, Jerry	
Gibraltar	Chief Minister	**Bossano**, José	
Greece	Prime Minister	**Mitsotakis**, Constantine	
Greenland	Prime Minister	**Johansen**, Lars Emil	
Grenada	Prime Minister	**Brathwaite**, Nicholas	
Guadeloupe	President of General Council	**Larifla**, Dominique	
Guam	Governor	**Ada**, Joseph F.	
Guatemala	President	**de León Carpio**, Ramiro	
Guinea	President	**Conté**, Lansana	
Guinea-Bissau	President	**Vieira**, Joao Bernardo	
Guyana	President	**Jagan**, Cheddi	
Haiti	President	**Aristide**, Jean-Bertrand	
Holy See (Vatican City State)	Pope	**John Paul II**	
Honduras	President	**Callejas Romero**, Rafael Leonardo	
Hong Kong	Governor	**Patten**, Chris	

State or Territory	Title	Name	Changes
Hungary	Prime Minister	**Antall**, József	
Iceland	Prime Minister	**Oddsson**, David	
India	President	**Sharma**, Shankar Dayal	
	Prime Minister	**Rao**, Narasimha	
Indonesia	President	**Suharto**	
Iran	President	**Rafsanjani**, Hashemi Ali Akbar	
Iraq	President	**Hussein**, Sadisavam Saddam	
Ireland	Prime Minister	**Reynolds**, Albert	
Israel	Prime Minister	**Rabin**, Itzhak	
Italy	Prime Minister	**Ciampi**, Carlo Azeglio	
Jamaica	Prime Minister	**Patterson**, Percival James	
Japan	Prime Minister	**Miyazawa**, Kiichi	
Jordan	King	**Hussein** ibn Talal	
Kazakhstan	President	**Nazarbayev**, Nursultan	
Kenya	President	**Moi**, Daniel arap	
Kiribati	President	**Teannaki**, Teatao	
Korea, Dem. People's Rep	President	**Kim**, Il Sung	
Korea, Republic of	President	**Kim**, Young Sam	
Kuwait	Amir	**Sabah**, Jabir al-Ahmad al-Jabir as-	
Kyrgyzstan	President	**Akayev**, Askar	
Laos	Prime Minister	**Khamtay**, Siphandon	
Latvia	President	**Gorbunovs**, Anatolijs	
Lebanon	President	**Hrawi**, Elias	
	Prime Minister	**Hariri**, Rafiq al-	
Lesotho	King	**Letsie III**	
	Chairman of Military Council	**Ramaema**, Elias	
Liberia	President – Interim	**Sawyer**, Amos	
Libya	Chief of State	**Ghadaffi**, Mu'ammar al-	
Liechtenstein	Prime Minister	**Büchel**, Markus	
Lithuania	President	**Brazauskas**, Algirdas	
Luxembourg	Prime Minister	**Santer**, Jaques	
Macao	Governor	**Vieira**, Vasco Rocha	
Macedonia	President	**Gligorov**, Kiro	
Madagascar	President	**Zafy**, Albert	
Malawi	Life President	**Banda**, Hastings Kamuzu	
Malaysia	Prime Minister	**Mahathir**, Mohamed	
Maldives	President	**Gayoumm**, Maumoun Abdul	
Mali	President	**Konare**, Alpha Oumar	
Malta	Prime Minister	**Fenech-Adami**, Edward	
Marshall Islands	President	**Kabua**, Amata	
Martinique	President of General Council	**Maurice**, Emile	
Mauritania	President	**Taya**, Moaouia Ould Sidi Mohammed	
Mauritius	Prime Minister	**Jugnauth**, Aneerood	
Mayotte	President of General Council	**Bamana**, Younoussa	
Mexico	President	**Salinas** de Gortari, Carlos	
Micronesia, Fed. States of	President	**Olter**, Bailey	
Moldova	President	**Snegur**, Mircea	
Monaco	Chief of State	**Rainer III** (Prince)	
Mongolia	President	**Ochirbat**, Punsalmaagiyn	
Montserrat	Chief Minister	**Meade**, Reuben	
Morocco	King	**Hassan II**	
Mozambique	President	**Chissano**, Joaquim Alberto	
Myanmar	Prime Minister	**Than Shwe**	
Namibia	President	**Nujoma**, Sam	

State or Territory	Title	Name	Changes
Nauru	President	**Dowiyogo**, Bernard	
Nepal	King	**Birendra**, Bir Bikram Shah Deva	
	Prime Minister	**Koirala**, Girija Prasad	
Netherlands	Prime Minister	**Lubbers**, Ruud	
Netherlands Antilles	Prime Minister	**Peters**, Maria Liberia	
New Caledonia	President of Territorial Congress	**Loueckhote**, Simon	
New Zealand	Prime Minister	**Bolger**, Jim	
Nicaragua	President	**Chamorro**, Violeta Barrios de	
Niger	Prime Minister	**Cheiffou**, Amadou	
Nigeria	President	**Babangida**, Ibrahim	
Niue Islands	Premier	**Louis**, Frank	
Norfolk Island	Administrator	**Macdonald**, H.	
Northern Mariana Is	Governor	**Guerrero**, Lorenzo de Leon	
Norway	Prime Minister	**Brundtland**, Gro Harlem	
Oman	Sultan	**bin Said**, Qaboos	
Pakistan	President	**Khan**, Ghulam Ishaq	
Palau	President	**Nakamura**, Kuniwo	
Panama	President	**Endara Galimany**, Guillermo	
Papua New Guinea	Prime Minister	**Wingti**, Paias	
Paraguay	President	**Wasmosy**, Juan Carlos	
Peru	President	**Fujimori**, Alberto Keinya	
Philippines	President	**Ramos**, Fidel	
Pitcairn Islands	Island Magistrate	**Young**, Brian	
Poland	President	**Walesa**, Lech	
	Prime Minister	**Suchocka**, Hanna	
Portugal	President	**Soares**, Mario Alberto Nobre Lopes	
Puerto Rico	Governor	**Rossello**, Pedro J.	
Qatar	Amir	**Thani**, Khalifa ibn Hamad al-	
Romania	President	**Iliescu**, Ion Russia	
Russia	President	**Yeltsin**, Boris	
Rwanda	President	**Habyarimana**, Juvénal	
Réunion	President of General Council	**Boyer**, Eric	
Sahara	n.a.	n.a.	
Samoa	Prime Minister	**Alesana**, Tofilau Eti	
San Marino	Captains-Regents	Rotating leadership	
São Tomé & Príncipe	President	**Trovoada**, Miguel	
Saudi Arabia	King	**Saud**, Fahd ibn Abd al-Aziz	
Senegal	President	**Diouf**, Abdou	
Seychelles	President	**René**, France Albert	
Sierra Leone	President	**Strasser**, Valentine E. M.	
Singapore	Prime Minister	**Goh**, Chok Tong	
Slovakia	Prime Minister	**Meciar**, Vladimir	
Slovenia	Prime Minister	**Drnovsek**, Janez	
Solomon Islands	Prime Minister	**Mamaloni**, Solomon	
Somalia	President - Interim	**Mahdi Mohammed**, Ali	
South Africa	State President	**de Klerk**, F. W.	
Spain	Prime Minister	**González Márquez**, Felipe	
Sri Lanka	President – Acting	**Wijetunge**, Dingiri Banda	
St Kitts and Nevis	Prime Minister	**Simmonds**, Kennedy Alphonse	
St Lucia	Prime Minister	**Compton**, John	
St Vincent	Prime Minister	**Mitchell**, James F.	
Sudan	Prime Minister	**Bashir**, Omar Hassan Ahmad al-	

State or Territory	Title	Name	Changes
Suriname	President	**Venetiaan**, Runaldo R.	
Swaziland	King	**Mswati** III	
	Prime Minister	**Dlamini**, Obed	
Sweden	Prime Minister	**Bildt**, Carl	
Switzerland	President	**Ogi**, Adolf	
Syria	President	**Assad**, Hafiz al-	
Tajikistan	President – Acting	**Rakhmanov**, Imamoli	
Tanzania	President	**Mwinyi**, Ali Hassan	
Thailand	King	**Bhumibol**, Adulyadej	
	Prime Minister	**Chuan**, Leekpai	
Togo	President	**Eyadema**, Gnassingbe	
Tokelau Islands	Administrator	**Walter**, N. D.	
Tonga	King	**Tupou** IV, Taufa'ahau	
Trinidad & Tobago	Prime Minister	**Manning**, Patrick	
Tunisia	President	**Benali**, Zine el-Abidine	
Turkey	President	**Demirel**, Suleyman	
	Prime Minister	**Ciller**, Tansu	
Turkmenistan	President	**Niyazov**, Saparmurad	
Turks and Caicos Is	Chief Minister	**Missick**, Washington	
Tuvalu	Prime Minister	**Paeniu**, Bikenibeu	
Uganda	President	**Museveni**, Yoweri	
Ukraine	President	**Kravchuk**, Leonid	
United Arab Emirates	President	**Al-Nahayan**, Zaid bin Sultan	
United Kingdom of GB & NI	Prime Minister	**Major**, John	
United States of America	President	**Clinton**, William Jefferson	
Uruguay	President	**Lacalle Herrera**, Luis Alberto	
Uzbekistan	President	**Karimov**, Islam	
Vanuatu	Prime Minister	**Carlot**, Maxime	
Venezuela	Interim President	**Velasquez**, Ramón	
Vietnam	President	**Le**, Duc Anh	
Virgin Is of the USA	Governor	**Farrelly**, Alexander	
Wallis and Futuna Is	President of Territorial Assembly	**Uhila**, Soane Mani	
Yemen	President	**Salih**, Ali Abudullah	
Yugoslavia	President	**Milosevic**, Slobodan (Serbia)	
Zaire	President	**Mobutu** Sese Seko	
	Prime Minister	**Tshisekedi**, Etienne	
Zambia	President	**Chiluba**, Frederick	
Zimbabwe	President	**Mugabe**, Robert	

APPENDIX 2
AGENCIES
Abbreviations and Addresses

The information in *Operation World* gives a general overview of the world and the growth of the Kingdom of the Lord Jesus Christ, but for more detail and updated information you need to receive regular information for effective prayer. To enable this, we have indicated many agencies in **bold type abbreviations** throughout the book. Our prayer is that you may make use of the addresses of these agencies and publishers of information. Every Christian with a heart for the evangelization of the world ought to subscribe to several or more publications. Why not write to some of the addresses listed below?

Four categories of names and addresses of evangelical publishers and agencies are given. The list is not complete, but representative, and deemed helpful for a worldwide readership. Most of those listed below have asked to be included, but we could not include all. Both denominational and interdenominational agencies have been listed, but the emphasis has been more on the latter because of the broader interest to the majority of readers.

I

Publications providing Worldwide Prayer Information in English

Here follows a brief list of publications which are wholly or partially given to the provision of such information.

Publication	Type
United States of America	
AD 2000 Global Monitor Global Evangelization Movement, P.O. Box 129, Rockville, VA 23146, USA	Newsletter
Church Around the World Tyndale House Publishers, P.O. Box 80, Wheaton, IL 60189, USA	Leaflet
DAWN Report DAWN Ministries, 7899 Lexington Drive, Suite 200B, Colorado Springs, 80920, USA	Magazine
Evangelical Missions Quarterly Evangelical Missions Information Service, PO Box 794, Wheaton, IL 60189, USA	Journal
FrontierScan U.S. Center for World Mission, 1605 Elizabeth St., Pasadena, CA 91104, USA	Leaflet
Global Prayer Digest U.S. Center for World Mission, 1605 Elizabeth St., Pasadena, CA 91104, USA	Magazine
International Journal of Frontier Missions International Student Leaders Coalition for Frontier Missions, PO Box 27266, El Paso, TX 79926, USA	Journal
Mission Frontiers U.S. Center for World Mission, 1605 Elizabeth St., Pasadena, CA 91104, USA	Magazine

Publication	Type
News Network International News Service News Network International, PO Box 28001, Santa Ana, CA 92799, USA	News service
Pulse Evangelical Missions Information Service, PO Box 794, Wheaton, IL 60189, USA	Newsletter
World Christian News YWAM International Research and Information, PO Box 26479, Colorado Springs, CO 80936–6479, USA	Newsletter

United Kingdom

Facts Evangelical Missionary Alliance, 9 Anwyll Close, Caerleon, Gwent NP6 1TJ, United Kingdom	Magazine
FFM Prayer Bulletin (Emphasis on Muslims) Fellowship of Faith for the Muslims, P.O. Box 58, Wakefield, W. Yorks WF2 9YD, United Kingdom	Newsletter
World Report United Bible Societies, 7th Floor, Reading Bridge House, Reading RG1 8PJ, United Kingdom	Newsletter

Other Western Nations

FFM Prayer Bulletin (Emphasis on Muslims) Fellowship of Faith for the Muslims, PO Box 21, Station "J", Toronto, ON M4J 4Y1, Canada	Newsletter
IDEA German Evangelical Alliance, Postfach 1820, D-6330 Wetzlar, Germany	Newsletter

Asia

Asian Action Asia Evangelistic Fellowship, Balestier Estate, PO Box 485, Singapore 9132	Newsletter
Asian Church Today Evangelical Fellowship of Asia, c/o WEF, 141 Middle Road, #05–05, GSM Building, Singapore 0718	Magazine
Asian Report Asian Outreach, GPO Box 3448, Hong Kong	Magazine
Berita NECF – Malaysia National Evangelical Christian Fellowship of Malaysia, 11M Jalan SS21/56B, Damansara Utama, 47400 Petaling Jaya, Selangor, Malaysia	Newsletter

Africa

AEAM – Prayer Bulletin and Afroscope Association of Evangelicals of Africa and Madagascar, PO Box 49332, Nairobi, Kenya	Newsletter

Publication	**Type**
	Newsletter

Missions Update – Nigeria
   Christian Missionary Foundation,
   U.I.P.O. Box 9890, Ibadan, Oyo State, Nigeria

II

Interdenominational Inter-mission Agencies

Significant national, regional and international evangelical bodies, in mainly English-speaking missionary-sending countries, are given below as representative of a large number of smaller mission agencies based in these lands that are too numerous to be included here. Many produce useful prayer information.

Global

AD2000 **AD 2000 and Beyond Movement,**
   2860 S. Circle Drive, Suite 2112, Colorado Springs, CO 80906, USA
LCWE **Lausanne Committee for World Evangelization,**
   PO Box 300, Oxford OX2 9XB, United Kingdom
WEF **World Evangelical Fellowship,**
   141 Middle Road, #05–05 GSM Building, Singapore 0718

Africa

AEAM **Association of Evangelicals of Africa and Madagascar**
   PO Box 49332, Nairobi, Kenya

Asia

AMA **Asia Missions Association**
   PO Box 1, Takaku, Nasu, Japan 325–03
EFA **Evangelical Fellowship of Asia**
   31-A, Lorong Mambong, Singapore 1027
   EFA Missions Commission
   PO Box 1416, Manila, Philippines

Australia

AEA **Australian Evangelical Alliance**
   PO Box 536, Camberwell, Vic. 3124

Brazil

AMTB *Associaçao de Missoes Transculturais Brazileiras*
   c/o CP 582, 01051 – Sao Paulo
BAM **Brazilian Association of Missions**
   Caixa Postal 1316, 13001–970 Campinas, S.P.
COMIBAM Caixa Postal 49, 09001 Santo André, S.P.

Caribbean

EAC **Evangelical Association of the Caribbean**
   41 Elizabeth Park (2), Worthing W9, Barbados

Europe

EEA **European Evangelical Alliance**
   Postfach 23, A-1037 Wien, Austria
TEMA **The European Missionary Association**
   Koopmansgoed 9, 3771 MJ Barneveld, The Netherlands

Germany

AEM   *Arbeitsgemeinschaft Evangelikaler Missionen*
Hindenburgstr 36, 7015 Korntal-Munchingen 1

Hong Kong

HKACM   **Hong Kong Association of Christian Missions**
PO Box 71728, Kowloon CPO, Hong Kong

India

EFI   **Evangelical Fellowship of India**
803/92 Deepali, Nehru Place, New Delhi 110 019
IMA   **India Missions Association**
Post Box 2529, Madras 600 030

Netherlands

EZA   *Evangelische Alliantie*
Hoofdstraat 51-A, 3971 KB Driebergen-Rijsenburg

New Zealand

EMA   **Evangelical Missionary Alliance**
PO Box 68-140, Auckland 1032

Nigeria

NEMA   **Nigeria Evangelical Missions Association**
UIPO Box 9890, Ibadan, Oyo State

Pacific

EFSP   **Evangelical Fellowship of the South Pacific**
PO Box 670, Honiara, Solomon Islands

Philippines

PCEC   **Philippine Council of Evangelical Churches, Inc.**
PO Box 10121 QCPO (Main), 1100 Quezon City

Singapore

EFS   **Evangelical Fellowship of Singapore**
141 Middle Road, #05–05 GSM Building, Singapore 0718
SCEM   **Singapore Centre for Evangelism and Missions**
116 Lavendar Street, #04–07 Pek Chuan Building, Singapore 1233

South Africa

EFSA   **Evangelical Fellowship of South Africa**
P/Bag X1 Mayor's Walk, Pietermaritzburg 3208

United Kingdom

EMA   **Evangelical Missionary Alliance**
Whitefield House, 186 Kennington Park Rd., London SE11 4BT

United States

AAPC   **Adopt-a-People Clearinghouse**
PO Box 1795, Colorado Springs, CO 80901–1795
AIMS   **Association of International Mission Services**
PO Box 64534, Virginia Beach, VA 23464
EFMA   **Evangelical Fellowship of Mission Agencies**
1023 15th Street, NW, Suite 500, Washington, DC 20005–1922
IFMA   **Interdenominational Foreign Mission Association**
PO Box 398, Wheaton, IL 60189–0398

MARC-WV   **Missions Advanced Research and Communications Center**
919 W. Huntington Drive, Monrovia, CA 91016
USCWM   **U.S. Center for World Mission**
1605 Elizabeth St., Pasadena, CA 91104

III

Mission Agencies and Their Addresses

Mission agencies in **bold type abbreviations** in the text are listed below, together with some contact addresses and statistical information.

We regret that space only allows a representative selection of Protestant ministries mainly from around the English-speaking world. We have selected 116 agencies and over 300 national offices on the basis of size, type of ministry and fields of service, from over 2,500 agencies and 4,200 national offices in our database. The agencies listed below have more than 74,382 missionaries in active service, which is over half of all known Protestant missionaries. See Appendix 3 for a national and regional itemization of missionaries.

We have grouped together similar missions from different nations, even if there is no direct organizational link: for instance, **AoG, Brethren, EF, GRn.**

Explanation of columns.

1. The addresses are as up to date as we can ascertain, but not all addresses of the agency are given because of space. The address is preceded by an abbreviated country name.

2. After the full name of the agency the **World** total of missionaries is given, followed by the number of countries of ministry (both sending and receiving).

3. The second column lists the agency's largest sending countries and missionary numbers sent.

4. The third column lists the largest fields of service with number of serving missionaries.

Abbrev. Mission name and addresses		Lands of origin		Fields of service	
ABMS	**Australian Baptist Missionary Society**	**World:**	**132**	**in 9 countries**	
	Aust. PO Box 273, Hawthorn, Vic 3122.	Australia	132	Pap N G	39
ABWE	**Association of Baptists for World Evangelism**	**World:**	**769**	**in 29 countries**	
	USA PO Box 5000, Cherry Hill, NJ 08034.	USA	715	Brazil	117
AE	**African Enterprise**	**World:**	**59**	**in 7 countries**	
	S.Afr. Africa Enterprise, Box 647, Pietermaritzburg 3200.	S Africa	20	S Africa	25
	UK 41 Dace Road, London E3 2NG.	USA	20	Kenya	6
	USA PO Box 727, Monrovia, CA 91016.	UK	5	Zimbabwe	6
AEF	**Africa Evangelical Fellowship**	**World:**	**385**	**in 22 countries**	
	Aust. PO Box 292, Castle Hill, NSW 2154.	USA	121	S Africa	121
	Canada 470 McNicoll Avenue, Willowdale, ON M2H 2E1.	Canada	71	Zambia	92
	S.Afr. PO Box 23913, Claremont 7735.	UK	46	Zimbabwe	29
	UK 30 Lingfield Rd., Wimbledon, London SW19 4PU.	Australia	29	Botswana	28
	USA PO Box 411167, Charlotte, NC 28241–1167.	S Africa	22	UK	20
AIMI	**Africa Inland Mission International**	**World:**	**836**	**in 23 countries**	
	Aust. 36 Hercules Street, Chatswood, NSW 2067.	USA	432	Kenya	412
	Canada 1641 Victoria Pk Ave, Scarborough, ON M1R 1P8.	UK	147	Tanzania	105
	S.Afr. PO Box 109, Plumstead 7800.	Canada	80	Zaire	98
	UK 2 Vorley Road, Archway, London N19 5HE.	Tanzania	70	Namibia	23
	USA PO Box 178, Pearl River, NY 10965.	Australia	37	Mozam.	22
AM	**Antioch Mission**	**World:**	**46**	**in 16 countries**	
	Brazil Cx Postal 582, Sao Paulo, CEP 01051.	Brazil	43	UK	9
	UK 149 Rosefield Road, Smethwick, Warley, West Midlands B67 6DZ.	UK	3	Portugal	8
				Mozam.	5

Abbrev.	Mission name and addresses	Lands of origin		Fields of service	
AoG	**Assemblies of God**	**World:**	**3,256**	**in 134 countries**	
Aust.	PO Box 229, Nunawading, Vic 3131.	USA	1,918	Côte d'Iv	138
NZ	PO Box 8023, Tauranga.	Brazil	412	Belgium	126
UK	Hook Place, Burgess Hill, W Sussex RH15 8RF.	Burk. Faso	132	Mexico	125
USA	Div. of Foreign Missions, 1445 Boonville Ave,	Myanmar	120	Myanmar	120
	Springfield, MO 65802.	UK	118	Philippines	112
AOI	**Asian Outreach International Ltd**	**World:**	**36**	**in 8 countries**	
HK	Int'l Headquarters, GPO Box 3448, Hong Kong.	New Z'land	18	Hong Kong	16
Aust.	PO Box 167, Park Holme, SA 5043.	USA	8	Mongolia	6
Canada	PO Box 939, Cambridge, ON.	Australia	8	Asia (Gen)	6
NZ	PO Box 2160, Tauranga 3000.			New Z'land	3
Sing.	Maxwell Road, PO Box 3038, Singapore 9050			Australia	2
UK	2 Kingswood Close, Lytham, Lancs FY8 4RE.				
USA	PO Box 9000, Mission Viejo, CA 92690.				
AP	**Action Partners:** See **SUM** Fellowship.				
APCM	**Asia Pacific Christian Mission**	**World:**	**250**	**in 5 countries**	
Aust.	Box 276, 345 Bell Street, Preston, Vic 3072.	Australia	192	Pap N G	175
NZ	35 Karaka Street, Auckland 1.	New Z'land	36	Indonesia	47
AsEF	**Asia Evangelistic Fellowship**	**World:**	**112**	**in 11 countries**	
Sing.	Balestier Estate, PO Box 485, Singapore 9132.	Malaysia	30	Malaysia	30
Aust.	PO Box 122, Epping, NSW 2121.	India	22	India	16
India	6 Farida Villa Road No I, TPS IV, Bandra,	Indonesia	15	Indonesia	15
	Bombay 400050.	Philippines	12	Philippines	12
AWM	**Arab World Ministries**	**World:**	**272**	**in 24 countries**	
UK	PO Box 51, Loughborough, Leics., LE11 0ZQ.	USA	154	N Afr/M E	116
Canada	PO Box 3398, Cambridge, ON N3H 4T3.	UK	54	France	91
USA	PO Box 96, Upper Darby, PA 19082.	Canada	30	USA	22
BCMS	**BCMS Crosslinks (prev. Bible Churchmen's Miss. Soc.)**	**World:**	**87**	**in 13 countries**	
UK	251 Lewisham Way, London SE4 1XF.	UK	87	Tanzania	32
BCU	**Bible Christian Union, Inc.**	**World:**	**134**	**in 14 countries**	
Canada	1428 Sandhill Drive, Ancaster ON L9G 4V5.	USA	87	Italy	28
USA	PO Box 410, Hatfield, PA 19440–0410.	Canada	27	France	24
BCWM	**Brethren in Christ World Missions**	**World:**	**85**	**in 9 countries**	
US	PO Box 390, Mount Joy, PA 17552–0390.	USA	81	Zambia	24
Canada	2519 Stevensville Rd, Stevensville, ON L0S 1S0.	Canada	4	Zimbabwe	15
BEM	**Belgian Evangelical Mission**	**World:**	**126**	**in 2 countries**	
UK	20 Vicarage Farm Road,	Netherlnd	36	Belgium	125
	Hounslow, Middlesex TW3 2EZ.	Belgium	27	Int'l	1
BFM	**Bethany Fellowship Missions**	**World:**	**124**	**in 16 countries**	
Sing.	Raffles City PO Box 143.	USA	112	Brazil	47
USA	6820 Auto Club Road, Minneapolis, MN 55438.	Brazil	7	Mexico	16
BMM	**Baptist Mid-Missions**	**World:**	**816**	**in 41 countries**	
USA	PO Box 308011, Cleveland, OH 44130-8011.	USA	808	Brazil	183
BMS	**Baptist Missionary Society**	**World:**	**206**	**in 14 countries**	
UK	PO Box 49, Baptist House, 129 Broadway,	UK	206	Zaire	67
	Didcot, Oxfordshire OX11 8XA.			Brazil	59
CAMI	**CAM International**	**World:**	**202**	**in 8 countries**	
USA	8625 La Prada Drive, Dallas, TX 75228.	USA	195	Guatemala	52
CBFMS	**CBFMS (prev. Conservative Baptist For. Mission Soc.)**	**World:**	**677**	**in 38 countries**	
USA	PO Box 5, Wheaton, IL 60189.	USA	677	Côte d'Iv	93
CBIM	**Canadian Baptist International Ministries**	**World:**	**118**	**in 16 countries**	
Canada	7185 Millcreek Dr., Mississauga, ON L5N 5R4.	Canada	118	Bolivia	15

Abbrev. Mission name and addresses		Lands of origin		Fields of service	
CBr	**Christian Brethren**	**World:**	**1,363**	**in 86 countries**	
Aust.	Aust. Missionary Tidings (CMML), PO Box 400, Chatswood, NSW 2057.	USA	433	Zambia	127
		UK	421	France	120
Canada	Missionary Service Committee, 1562A Dunforth Ave., Toronto,	Canada	225	Zaire	59
		New Z'land	147	Brazil	59
	ON M4J 1N4.	Australia	104	Philippines	52
UK	Echoes of Service, 1 Widcombe Crescent,	Faeroe Isl	17	S Africa	50
	Bath, Avon BA2 6AQ.	S Africa	13	Bolivia	50
NZ	Missionary Funds (NZ) Inc., PO Box 744,	Netherlnd	2	Spain	46
	Palmerston North.			Argentina	37
USA	CMML Inc., PO Box 13, Spring Lake, NJ 07762.			Austria	37
CCC	**Campus Crusade for Christ International**	**World:**	**11,043**	**in 105 countries**	
USA	100 Sunport Lane, Orlando, FL 32809.	USA	5,218	USA	4,670
Canada	PO Box 300, Vancouver, BC V5J 1R1.	S Korea	1,606	S Korea	1,554
UK	Agapé (formerly CCC), Fairgate House,	India	475	India	475
	Kings Road, Tyseley B11 2AA.	Indonesia	394	Indonesia	394
CEF	**Child Evangelism Fellowship Inc.**	**World:**	**2,621**	**in 60 countries**	
USA	PO Box 348, Warrenton, MO 63383.				
Canada	PO Box 165, Winnipeg, MB R3C 2G9.				
UK	64 Osborne Road, Levenshulme, Manchester M19 2DY.				
CLC	**Christian Literature Crusade**	**World:**	**598**	**in 43 countries**	
UK	51 The Dean, Alresford, Hampshire SO24 9BJ.	UK	115	UK	86
Aust.	PO Box 91, Pennant Hills, NSW 2120.	Brazil	68	Japan	46
USA	PO Box 1449, Fort Washington, PA 19034.	Japan	44	India	33
CM	**Calvary Ministries**	**World:**	**138**	**in 7 countries**	
Nigeria	PO Box 6001, Jos, Plateau State.	Nigeria	138	Nigeria	115
CMA	**Christian and Missionary Alliance**	**World:**	**1,119**	**in 52 countries**	
USA	PO Box 35000, Colorado Springs, CO 80935.	USA	735	Indonesia	104
Aust.	PO Box 336, Curtin, ACT 2605.	Canada	226	Ecuador	89
Canada	Box 7900, Station B, Willowdale, ON M2K 2R6.	Australia	80	Philippines	79
UK	PO Box 320, Oxford OX2 7JJ.	Netherlnd	27	Australia	64
CMF	**Christian Missionary Foundation**	**World:**	**55**	**in 10 countries**	
Nigeria	PO Box 9890, UIPO, Ibadan.	Nigeria	49	Nigeria	24
CMS	**Church Missionary Society**	**World:**	**751**	**in 33 countries**	
Aust.	93 Bathurst St., Sydney NSW 2000.	Aust	220	Tanzania	106
				Nigeria	103
				Pakistan	66
NZ	CMS House, 167 Wairakei Rd., Christchurch 5.	New Z'land	54	Uganda	54
				Zaire	41
				Kenya	41
UK	Partnership House, 157 Waterloo Rd.,	UK	338	Israel	35
	London SE1 8UU.	Ireland	43	Nepal	29
CN	**Christian Nationals: See PI**				
CoN	**Church of the Nazarene**	**World:**	**596**	**in 55 countries**	
USA	6401 The Paseo, Kansas City, MO 64131.	USA	484	Pap N G	75
CRWM	**Christian Reformed World Missions**	**World:**	**259**	**in 19 countries**	
USA	2850 Kalamazoo Avenue, S.E.,	USA	197	Nigeria	63
	Grand Rapids, MI 49508.	Nigeria	12	Philippines	32
CWI	**Christian Witness to Israel**	**World:**	**22**	**in 6 countries**	
UK	Seven Trees, 44 Lubbock Road,	UK	19	UK	13
	Chislehurst, Kent BR7 5JX.	New Z'land	2	Australia	3
NZ	PO Box 6455, Auckland.	Hong Kong	1	France	2
DLBC	**Deeper Life Bible Church**	**World:**	**74**	**in 31 countries**	
Nigeria	PO Box 59, University of Lagos PO,	Nigeria	72	USA	10
	Akoka, Yaba, Lagos.	Togo .	2	France	7

Abbrev.	Mission name and addresses	Lands of origin		Fields of service	
DAWN	Dawn Ministries	World:	6	in 2+ countries	
USA	7899 Lexington Dr, Suite 200B, Colorado Springs, CO 80920.	USA	6	Africa	4
DM	Dorothea Mission	World:	126	in 10 countries	
S.Afr.	PO Box 219, 0001, Pretoria.	S Africa	70	S Africa	47
UK	44 Navigator Close, Hilperton,	Zimbabwe	18	Zimbabwe	41
	Trowbridge BA14 7QA.	UK	16	Zambia	11
ECF	Evangelize China Fellowship, Inc.	World:	5	in 1 country	
USA	PO Box 418, Pasadena, CA 91102.	USA	5	USA	5
ECM	European Christian Mission	World:	105	in 17+ countries	
UK	Int'l Ofc, 50 Billing Rd, Northampton NN1 5DH.	UK	53	Spain	18
Aust.	PO Box 15, Croydon, NSW 2132.	USA	30	Greece	13
Canada	1077 56th St., Suite 226, Delta, BC V4L 2A2.	Canada	12	Italy	12
NZ	PO Box 8749, Auckland.	New Z'land	1	Eurasia	9
USA	PO Box 1006, Point Roberts, WA 98281.	Netherlnd	1	Europe	9
EF	Elim Fellowship/Elim Pentecostal Churches	World:	161	in 29 countries	
NZ	Elim Church of NZ, PO Box 68 148,	USA	120	Kenya	23
	Newton, Auckland 2	UK	41	Mexico	19
UK	Elim Int'l Missions, PO Box 38, Cheltenham,			Tanzania	17
	Gloucestershire GL50 3HN.			USA	10
USA	Elim Fellowship, For. Missions Dept.,			Zimbabwe	9
	7245 College Street, Lima, NY 14485–0815.			Colombia	8
EHC	Every Home for Christ	World:	56	in 4 countries	
USA	7899 Lexington Dr., Colorado Spgs, CO 80920.	USA	54	USA	52
EMS	Evangelical Missionary Society – ECWA	World:	832	in 5 countries	
Nigeria	PO Box 63, Jos, Plateau State.	Nigeria	832	Nigeria	801
USA	c/o SIM International, PO Box 7900,			Benin	11
	Charlotte, NC 28241.			Niger	10
F	Frontiers	World:	365	in 39 countries	
Canada	6240 London Road, Richmond, BC V7E 3S4.	USA	276	Mid E/N Afr	161
Switz	PO Box 351, CH-9424 Rheineck, Switzerland	Canada	32	Asia	116
USA	325 N. Stapley Drive, Mesa, AZ 85203.	Switz	34	Eurasia	70
FEBA	FEBA Radio (Far East Broadcasting Associates)	World:	77	in 12 countries	
Canada	6850 Antrim Avenue, Burnaby, BC V5J 4M4.	UK	49	Seychelles	25
UK	Ivy Arch Road, Worthing, W Sussex BN14 8BU.	Canada	14	Canada	11
FEBC	Far East Broadcasting Company, Inc	World:	96	in 9 countries	
Aust.	PO Box 183, Caringbah, NSW 2229.	USA	46	N Marianas	30
NZ	PO Box 4140, Hamilton 2001.	Australia	13	Philippines	24
USA	15700 Imperial Highway, La Mirada, CA 90638.	New Z'land	8	USA	16
FFM	Fellowship of Faith for the Muslims	World:	5	in 1 country	
Canada	PO Box 221, Postal Sta J, Toronto, ON M4J 4YI.	Canada	5	Canada	5
UK	PO Box 58, Wakefield, West Yorkshire WF2 9AN.				
FM	France Mission Trust	World:	78	in 2 countries	
UK	The Old Chapel, Chapel Lane, Michinhampton,	France	38	France	77
	Stroud, Gloucestershire GL6 9DL.	UK	16	UK	1
FMPB	Friends Missionary Prayer Band	World:	477	in 1 country	
India	1/9 Baracah Rd, Kilpauk, Madras 600010.	India	477	India	477
GEM	Greater Europe Mission	World:	337	in 21 countries	
USA	PO Box 668, Wheaton, IL 60189-0668.	USA	311	Belgium	50
Canada	PO Box 984, Oshawa, ON L1H 7N2.	Canada	19	France	42
GMU	Gospel Missionary Union	World:	451	in 24 countries	
USA	10000 N Oak Trafficway, Kansas City, MO 64155.	USA	301	Ecuador	59
Canada	2121 Henderson Highway, Winnipeg,MB R2G 1P8.	Canada	109	Bolivia	49
GRn	Global Recordings network	World:	189	in 19 countries	
Aust.	Language Recordings Int'l, Priv. Mail Bag 19,	USA	57	Australia	25
	Castle Hill, NSW 2154.	Australia	32	India	21

Abbrev.	Mission name and addresses	Lands of origin		Fields of service	
Canada	Language Recordings Int'l, 1059 Upper James St, Suite 210, Hamilton, ON L9C 3A6.	India	21	Indonesia	13
India	GR Associates, 7/4 Commissariat Road, Bangalore 560025.	Indonesia	13	Nigeria	12
		Canada	11	S Africa	11
		S Africa	10	Pakistan	7
Kenya	Language Recordings Int'l, Box 21244, Nairobi.	Nigeria	8	Philippines	6
Nigeria	GRWA, PMB 2201, Jos, Plateau State.	Pakistan	7	Canada	6
Philip.	Gospel Recordings, PO Box 50, Valenzuela, Metro Manila.	Philippines	6	Pap N G	6
		Pap N G	4	Int'l	6
Sing.	GR Ltd., Serangoon North, PO Box 512 9155.	Bangladesh	4	Kenya	5
S.Afr.	Language Recordings Int'l, PO Box 62, Observatory, Cape Town 7935.	New Z'land	4	Mexico	4
		Singapore	3	Bangladesh	4
UK	Language Recordings Int'l, PO Box 197, High Wycombe, Bucks. HP14 3YY.	Sierra Leone	3	Singapore	3
		Kenya	2	Sierra Leone	3
USA	Gospel Recordings, 122 Glendale Blvd., Los Angeles, CA 90026–5889.	Germany	1	Africa (Gen)	2
		UK	1	Cameroon	1

HCFI	**Hospital Christian Fellowship International**				
Neth.	Noordersingel 90, 3781 XK Voorthuizen.				
USA	PO Box 4004, San Clemente, CA 92674.				

I	**INTERSERVE**	**World:**	**501**	**in 24 countries**	
UK	325 Kennington Road, London SE11 4QH.	UK	182	Nepal	91
Aust.	PO Box 320, Box Hill, Victoria 3128.	Australia	96	Pakistan	77
Canada	#200–4030 Sheppard Ave. East, Agincourt, ON M1S 1S6.	USA	51	India	66
		New Z'land	50	UK	49
NZ	PO Box 10–244, Auckland 3.	Netherlnd	34	Mid East	31
USA	PO Box 418, Upper Darby, PA 19082.	Canada	30	Asia (Gen)	22

IBRA	**International Broadcasting Association**				
Swed	S-105 36 Stockholm.				

IBT	**Institute for Bible Translation**				
Swed	Box 20100, S-104 60 Stockholm.				

IEM	**Indian Evangelical Mission**	**World:**	**410**	**in 6 countries**	
India	7 Langford Rd, Pst Bag 2557, Bangalore 560025.	India	410	India	398

IET	**Indian Evangelical Team**	**World:**	**575**	**in 1 country**	
India	126 Andheri More, New Delhi 110 030.	India	575	India	575

IFES	**International Fellowship of Evangelical Students**	**World:**	**102**	**in 20 countries**	
UK	55 Palmerston Road, Wealdstone, Harrow, Middlesex HA3 7RR.	USA	48	Brazil	19
		Australia	17	Australia	17
Aust.	129 York Street, Sydney, NSW 2000.	Brazil	17	Austria	9
NZ	PO Box 9672, Wellington.	UK	9	UK	9
USA	PO Box 7895, Madison, WI 53707.	Canada	2	Spain	7

IHCF	**International Hospital Christian Fellowship: See HCFI.**				

IMF	**Indonesian Missionary Fellowship**	**World:**	**263**	**in 10 countries**	
Indon.	PO Box 4, Batu 65301, East Java.	Indonesia	263	Indonesia	242

IMI	**International Missions, Inc.**	**World:**	**291**	**in 18+ countries**	
Canada	Box 2064, St Catharines, ON L2M 6P5.	USA	247	Mid East	52
USA	PO Box 14866, Reading, PA 19612–4866.	Canada	20	USA	47

INF	**International Nepal Fellowship**	**World:**	**112**	**in 4 countries**	
Aust.	PO Box 1340, Chatswood, NSW 2057.	UK	47	Nepal	104
NZ	PO Box 144, Wellington 1.	Germany	19	Australia	6
UK	69 Wentworth Road, Harborne, Birmingham, West Midlands B17 9SS.	New Z'land	16	New Z'land	1
		Australia	12	UK	1

ISI	**International Students, Inc.**	**World:**	**167**	**in 4 countries**	
USA	PO Box C, Colorado Springs, CO 80901.	USA	166	USA	162
Canada	Int'l Student Ministry, Box 3980, Station B, Calgary, AB T2M 9M5.	India	1	Japan	2
				Canada	2
UK	Int'l Student Christian Services, 22 Amersham Road, London SE14 6QE.			India	1

Abbrev.	Mission name and addresses		Lands of origin		Fields of service	
IT	**International Teams**		**World:**	**226**	**in 19 countries**	
	USA	PO Box 203, Prospect Hgts., IL 60070.	USA	143	Austria	51
	Canada	625 Wabanaki Dr. #4, Kitchener, ON N2C 2G3	Canada	57	Philippines	34
JEB	**Japan Evangelistic Band**		**World:**	**15**	**in 4 countries**	
	Aust.	PO Box 1031, Glen Waverley, Vic 3150.	UK	13	Japan	9
	Canada	3841 W. 38th Ave., Vancouver, BC V6N 2Y5.	Canada	1	UK	4
	UK	275 London Road, North End, Portsmouth,	USA	1	Canada	1
		Hampshire PO2 9HE.			USA	1
	USA	PO Box 33201, Seattle, WA 98133.				
JFJ	**Jews for Jesus**		**World:**	**52**	**in 5 countries**	
	USA	60 Haight Street, San Francisco, CA 94102.	USA	49	USA	45
LAM	**Latin America Mission**		**World:**	**302**	**in 13 countries**	
	Canada	3075 Ridgeway Drive, Unit #14,	USA	178	Costa Rica	105
		Mississauga, ON L5L 5M6.	Canada	28	Mexico	75
	USA	PO Box 52–7900, Miami, FL 33152–7900.			Colombia	17
LCMS	**Lutheran Church-Missouri Synod**		**World:**	**274**	**in 27 countries**	
	USA	1333 S. Kirkwood Rd, Saint Louis, MO 63122.	USA	229	S Africa	31
LL	**Latin Link (formerly EUSA, RBMU of UK)**		**World:**	**72**	**in 5+ countries**	
	UK	185 Kennington Park Road, London SE11 4BT.	UK	72	Peru	36
LRI	**Language Recordings International: See GRn.**					
MAF	**Mission Aviation Fellowship**		**World:**	**493**	**in 31 countries**	
	Aust.	PO Box 211, Box Hill, Vic 3128.	USA	238	Indonesia	73
	Canada	PO Box 368, Guelph, ON N1H 6K5.	UK	72	Tanzania	58
	NZ	591 Dominion Rd, Balmoral, Auckland 4.	Australia	59	Pap N G	51
	UK	Ingles Manor, Castle Hill Avenue,	Canada	46	Zaire	31
		Folkestone, Kent CT20 2TN.	New Z'land	29	USA	26
	USA	PO Box 3202, Redlands, CA 92373-0998.	Netherlnd	10	Ecuador	21
0MECO	**Middle East Christian Outreach**		**World:**	**158**	**in 15+ countries**	
	Cyprus	PO Box 662, Larnaca.	UK	30	Asia	75
	Aust.	PO Box 59, Moreland, Victoria 3058.	Australia	24	Mid East	45
	Canada	PO Box 245, Mississauga, ON L5A 3A1.	USA	11	Cyprus	19
	UK	22 Culverden Park Road,	S Africa	10	Australia	7
		Tunbridge Wells, Kent TN4 9RA.	Costa Rica	4	USA	3
	USA	PO Box 502, Le Mars, IA 51031.				
MT	**Messianic Testimony**		**World:**	**30**	**in 6 countries**	
	S.Afr.	PO Box 23749, Claremont, 7735, Cape.	UK	20	UK	13
	UK	93 Axe St., Barking, Essex IG11 7LZ.	France	6	France	11
MTW	**Mission to the World – Presbyterian Ch in America**		**World:**	**552**	**in 56 countries**	
	USA	PO Box 29765, Atlanta, GA 30359.	USA	552	Mexico	46
					Japan	42
N	**The Navigators**		**World:**	**3,376**	**in 52+ countries**	
	Aust.	PO Box 265, Blaxland, NSW 2774.	USA	2,055	USA	1,759
	Canada	Box 27070, London, ON N5X 3X5.	Canada	149	Philippines	141
	NZ	PO Box 1951, Christchurch 1.	S Korea	136	Canada	126
	UK	Rear Mews 17D, Coombe Road,	UK	135	S Korea	122
		New Malden, Surrey KT3 4PX.	Philippines	127	Asia	113
	USA	PO Box 6000, Colorado Spgs, CO 80934.	Singapore	71	UK	105
NGK	**Nederduitse Gereformeerde Kerk (Dutch Reformed Ch)**		**World:**	**124**	**in 15 countries**	
	S.Afr.	PO Box 433, 0001 Pretoria.	S Africa	124	Malawi	35
NTM	**New Tribes Mission**		**World:**	**3,356**	**in 25 countries**	
	Aust.	Box 84, Rooty Hill, NSW 2766.	USA	2,440	Brazil	693
	Canada	PO Box 707, Durham, ON N0G 1R0.	Canada	286	Pap N G	488
	UK	Derby Rd., Matlock Bath, Matlock,	Brazil	204	Philippines	388
		Derbyshire DE4 3PY.	UK	141	Colombia	168
	USA	1000 E 1st St., Sanford, FL 32771.	Australia	114	Venezuela	159

Abbrev.	Mission name and addresses	Lands of origin		Fields of service	
NWFF	**North West Frontier Fellowship**	**World:**	**7**	**in 2 countries**	
UK	26 Wigmore Ave., Swindon, Wilts. SN3 1ET.	UK	5	Pakistan	6
NZ	89 Masters Avenue, Hamilton.	New Z'land	2	UK	1
USA	5736 Hebron Lane, Lakeland, FL 33813.				
OCI	**OC International**	**World:**	**357**	**in 23 countries**	
Ger	European HQ, Pechhuettenstr. 4,	USA	218	Philippines	47
	67105 Schifferstadt.	Philippines	17	USA	39
Sing.	Bras Basah, PO Box 0311, Singapore 9118.	Canada	12	Brazil	28
USA	PO Box 36900, Colorado Spgs, CO 80936.	Brazil	10	Guatemala	25
OD	**Open Doors with Brother Andrew**				
Neth.	PO Box 47, 3840 AA Harderwijk.				
S.Afr.	PO Box 990099, Kibler Pk 2053.				
UK	PO Box 6, Witney, Oxfordshire OX8 7SP.				
USA	PO Box 27001, Santa Ana, CA 92799.				
OM	**Operation Mobilization**	**World:**	**2,234**	**in 57+ countries**	
Aust.	PO Box 32, Box Hill, Vic 3128.	UK	355	On ships	546
Canada	PO Box 9, Port Colborne, ON L3K 5V7.	USA	347	India	332
Sing.	PO Box 805, Orchard PO, Singapore 9123.	India	307	UK	208
S.Afr.	PO Box 30221, 0132 Sunnyside, Pretoria.	Germany	124	Mid East	126
UK	The Quinta, Weston Rhyn,	Canada	109	USA	74
	Oswestry, Shropshire SY10 7LT.	Switzerlnd	94	Austria	71
USA	PO Box 444, Tyrone, GA 30290–0444.	Netherlnd	84	Belgium	60
OMF	**Overseas Missionary Fellowship**	**World:**	**1,077**	**in 21+ countries**	
Sing.	Int'l HQ, 2 Cluny Road, Singapore 1025.	USA	292	Thailand	212
Aust.	PO Box 849, Epping, NSW 2121.	UK	263	Philippines	172
Canada	1058 Avenue Road, Toronto, ON M5N 2C6.	Canada	110	Japan	136
NZ	PO Box 10159, Balmoral, Auckland.	Switzerlnd	73	Taiwan	98
S.Afr.	PO Box 41, Kenilworth 7745.	Australia	60	Indonesia	70
UK	Belmont, The Vine, Sevenoaks, Kent TN13 3TZ.	New Z'land	60	Singapore	56
USA	10 W Dry Creek Circle, Littleton, CO 80120.	Germany	45	USA	40
OMS	**OMS International**	**World:**	**414**	**in 21+ countries**	
Aust.	PO Box 195, North Essendon, Vic 3041.	USA	315	Taiwan	34
Canada	PO Box 33522, Dundurn Postal Outlet,	UK	27	Ecuador	33
	Hamilton, ON L8P 4X4.	Canada	12	Japan	32
NZ	GPO Box 962, Hamilton.	New Z'land	12	Spain	30
S.Afr.	Box 640, Roodepoort TVL 1725.	S Africa	11	Colombia	24
UK	1 Sandileight Avenue, Didsbury,	Australia	5	Haiti	20
	Manchester M20 9LN.	Ireland	4	Indonesia	20
USA	941 Fry Road, Greenwood, IN 46142.			Brazil	18
P	**Pioneers**	**World:**	**150**	**in 18 countries**	
USA	PO Box 725500, Orlando, FL 32872-5500.	USA	148	Indonesia	43
PAoC	**Pentecostal Assemblies of Canada**	**World:**	**209**	**in 29 countries**	
Canada	6745 Century Ave, Mississauga, ON L5N 6P7.	Canada	201	Kenya	46
PI	**Partners Int'l/Christian Nationals Evang. Commission**	**World:**	**54**	**in 5 countries**	
USA	PO Box 15025, San Jose, CA 95115	USA	49	USA	46
Canada	CNEC, 8500 Torbram Road, Unit #48,	Canada	4	Canada	4
	Brampton, ON L6T 5C6.	Singapore	1	Indonesia	2
UK	Christian Nationals, Bawtry Hall, Bawtry,			Philippines	1
	Doncaster, South Yorkshire DN10 6JH.				
PMF	**Philippine Missionary Fellowship**	**World:**	**87**	**in 1 country**	
Philip.	PO Box 3349, Manila.	Philippines	87	Philippines	87
QIF	**Qua Iboe Fellowship**	**World:**	**33**	**in 3 countries**	
UK	7 Donegall Square West, Belfast BT1 6JE.	UK	22	Nigeria	24
RBMU	**RBMU International**	**World:**	**151**	**in 8+ countries**	
Aust.	720 High St., Reservoir, Vic 3073.	USA	84	Indonesia	49
Canada	101 Queen Street So., Suite 10,	Canada	52	Philippines	43
	Mississauga, ON L5M 1K7.	Australia	15	Peru	15
USA	8102 Elberon Ave., Philadelphia, PA 19111.			Cameroon	14

Abbrev.	Mission name and addresses		Lands of origin		Fields of service	
RSMT	**Red Sea Mission Team** (also **RSTI**)		**World:**	**82**	**in 11 countries**	
	Aust.	GPO 3302, Sydney, NSW 2001.	UK	21	Mid East	18
	UK	33 The Grove, Finchley, London N3 1QU.	Germany	13	N Africa	16
	USA	PO Box 16227, Minneapolis, MN 55416.	Canada	12	UK	12
SA	**Salvation Army**		**World:**	**568**	**in 63+ countries**	
	UK	Int'l Headquarters, PO Box 249,	UK	187	S Africa	41
		101 Queen Victoria St., London EC4P 4EP.	USA	123	Zambia	33
	Aust.	39 Park Street, S Melbourne 3205.	Canada	71	Australia	29
	Canada	PO Box 4021, Postal Station A,	Switzerlnd	50	Zimbabwe	28
		Toronto, ON M5W 2B1.	New Z'land	42	Brazil	20
	NZ	204 Cuba Street, Wellington.	Australia	22	Canada	16
	USA	PO Box 269, Alexandria, VA 22313.	Sweden	19	Chile	16
SAMS	**South American Missionary Society**		**World:**	**225**	**in 17 countries**	
	UK	Allen Gardiner House, Pembury Road,	UK	116	Chile	36
		Tunbridge Wells, Kent TN2 3QU.	Australia	59	Paraguay	25
SAO	**Southeast Asian Outreach**		**World:**	**12**	**in 2 countries**	
	UK	90 Windmill St, Gravesend, Kent DA12 1LH.	UK	6	Cambodia	9
SBC	**Southern Baptist Convention**		**World:**	**4,735**	**in 135 countries**	
	USA	PO Box 6767, Richmond, VA 23230–0767.	USA	4,654	Brazil	292
			S Korea	32	Philippines	170
			Nigeria	22	Japan	169
SEND	**SEND International**		**World:**	**471**	**in 12 countries**	
	Canada	7–998 Coldstream Road, R.R.3,	USA	334	Japan	139
		Komoka(London), ON N0L 1R0.	Canada	43	Philippines	77
	USA	PO Box 513, Farmington, MI 48332.	Germany	16	Taiwan	36
SGA	**Slavic Gospel Association**		**World:**	**39**	**in 4+ countries**	
	Aust.	PO Box 396, Noble Park, Vic 3174.	USA	30	USA	27
	UK	37a The Goffs, Eastbourne, E Sussex BN21 1HF.	Australia	8	Australia	5
	USA	PO Box 1122, Wheaton, IL 60189–1122.	New Z'land	1	Europe	3
SGM	**Scripture Gift Mission**		**World:**	**38**	**in 2+ countries**	
	UK	Radstock Hse, 3 Eccleston St, London SW1W 9LZ.	India	9		
	Aust.	PO Box 688, Castle Hill, NSW 2154.	S Africa	6		
	Canada	300 Steelcase Road W., Unit 32,	USA	5		
		Markham, ON L3R 2W2.	Canada	5		
	India	18/1 Cubbon Road, Bangalore 560 001.	Australia	4		
	NZ	PO Box 10.274, Auckland 3.	Ireland	3		
	USA	PO Box 250, Willow Street, PA 17584–0250.	Singapore	2		
	S. Afr.	PO Box 1187, Johannesburg 2000.	New Z'land	2		
SIL	See WBT.					
SIM	**SIM International**		**World:**	**1,490**	**in 40 countries**	
	USA	Int'l Office, Box 7900, Charlotte, NC, 28241.	USA	770	Niger	197
	Aust.	PO Box 371, Miranda, NSW 2228.	Canada	198	Nigeria	180
	Canada	10 Huntingdale Blvd, Scarborough, ON M1W 2S5.	UK	124	Ethiopia	158
	NZ	PO Box 38588, Howick.	Australia	92	Bolivia	108
	Sing.	116 Lavender St., Pek Chuan Bldg. # 04–09.	New Z'land	78	Benin	79
	S.Afr.	Private Bag X1, Clareinch 7740, Cape Town.	Germany	62	Canada	66
	UK	Joint Mission Centre, Ullswater Crescent,	Switzerlnd	49	Liberia	50
		Coulsdon, Surrey CR3 2HR.	S Korea	27	Kenya	48
SSEM	**South Sea Evangelical Mission**		**World:**	**66**	**in 5 countries**	
	Aust.	PO Box 368, Clayfield, QLD 4011.	Australia	31	Pap N G	23
	NZ	PO Box 19-202, Avondale, Auckland.	New Z'land	18	Solomon Is	16
SU	**Scripture Union**		**World:**	**152**	**in 10 countries**	
	UK	130 City Road, London EC1V 2NJ.	Australia	130	Australia	130
	USA	7000 Ludlow St, Upper Darby, PA 19082.	Lesotho	6	Lesotho	8

Abbrev.	Mission name and addresses	Lands of origin		Fields of service	
SUM	**SUM Fellowship**	**World:**	**206**	**in 12+ countries**	
	Aust. PO Box 237, Baulkham Hills, NSW 2153.	UK	64	Nigeria	69
	Nigeria Church of Christ in Nigeria, PMB 2127,	Denmark	63	Cameroon	61
	Jos, Plateau State.	Switzerlnd	43	Chad	15
	UK Action Partners, Bawtry Hall, Bawtry,	Australia	20	Kenya	14
	Doncaster, South Yorkshire DN10 6JH.	France	6	Sudan	7
TBL	**The Bible League**				
	USA 16801 Van Dam Road, South Holland, IL 60473.				
TEAM	**The Evangelical Alliance Mission**	**World:**	**1,034**	**in 34 countries**	
	Aust. 26 Homebush Rd., Homebush, NSW 2140.	USA	846	Japan	153
	Canada PO Box 155, Sub. 158, Calgary, AB T1Y 6M0.	Canada	111	Venezuela	103
	USA PO Box 969, Wheaton, IL 60189–0969.	Portugal	11	USA	94
TEAR	**TEAR Fund**	**World:**	**166**	**in 30+ countries**	
	UK 100 Church Rd, Teddington, Mx. TW11 8QE.	UK	105	Nepal	23
TLM	**The Leprosy Mission**	**World:**	**194**	**in 25+ countries**	
	Aust. 7 Ellingworth Parade, Box Hill, Vic 3128.	UK	48	S Africa	42
	Canada 40 Wynford Dr, Ste 216, Don Mills, ON M3C 1J5.	S Africa	43	USA	30
	UK Goldhay Way, Orton Goldhay, Peterborough,	USA	33	Bhutan	14
	Cambridgeshire PE2 0GZ.	Australia	24	Australia	14
TMI	**Teen Missions International, Inc.**	**World:**	**20**	**in 9 countries**	
	USA 885 East Hall Rd, Merritt Island, FL 32953.	USA	14	Zimbabwe	4
TWO	**Teen World Outreach**	**World:**	**170**	**in 13 countries**	
	USA 7245 College Street, Lima, NY 14485–0815.	USA	170	Grenada	18
TWR	**Trans World Radio**	**World:**	**339**	**in 15 countries**	
	UK 45 London Road, Biggleswade,	USA	254	Neth Antil	95
	Bedfordshire SG18 8ED.	S Africa	10	USA	80
	USA PO Box 700, Cary, NC 27512–0700.	UK	9	Swaziland	39
UBS	**United Bible Society**				
	UK Reading Bridge Hse, Reading, Berks. RG1 8PJ.				
UFM	**UFM International (USA) & UFM Worldwide (UK)**	**World:**	**575**	**in 28+ countries**	
	UK 47a Fleet St., Swindon, Wiltshire SN1 1RE.	USA	443	Brazil	119
	USA PO Box 306, Bala Cynwyd, PA 19004.	UK	53	Haiti	50
UWM	**United World Mission, Inc.**	**World:**	**154**	**in 16 countries**	
	USA PO Box 250, Union Mills, NC 28167-0250.	USA	123	USA	56
WBT	**Wycliffe Bible Translators**	**World:**	**6,267**	**in 65 countries**	
	Aust. Graham Road, Kangaroo Ground, Vic 3097.	USA	4,540	USA	1,171
	Canada PO Box 3068, Station B, Calgary, AB T2M 4L6.	Canada	436	Pap N G	726
	NZ Fareham House, PO Box 10, Featherston.	UK	302	Philippines	345
	S.Afr. PO Box 548, Kempton Park 1620.	Australia	300	Peru	306
	USA PO Box 2727, Huntington Bch, CA 92647.	Switzerlnd	129	Indonesia	302
	UK Horsleys Green, High Wycombe,	Germany	108	Mexico	248
	Bucks. HP14 3XL.	Netherlnd	81	Brazil	237
WEC	**WEC International**	**World:**	**1,511**	**in 51 countries**	
	UK Bulstrode, Oxford Road,	UK	401	Côte d'Iv	62
	Gerrards Cross, Bucks. SL9 8SZ.	Australia	250	Senegal	59
	Aust. 48 Woodside Avenue, Strathfield, NSW 2135.	USA	216	Mid East	57
	Canada 37 Aberdeen Avenue, Hamilton, ON L8P 2N6.	Germany	128	Brazil	48
	HK PO Box 73261, Kowloon Central PO, Kowloon.	New Z'land	107	Indonesia	48
	NZ PO Box 27264, Mt Roskill, Auckland 4.	Canada	100	Spain	47
	Sing. PO Box 185, Raffles City, Singapore 9117.	Switzerlnd	71	Thailand	44
	USA PO Box 1707, Fort Washington, PA 19034.	Netherlnd	62	Ghana	39
WGM	**World Gospel Mission**	**World:**	**401**	**in 19 countries**	
	USA PO Box 948, Marion, IN 46952.	USA	373	Kenya	89
		UK	13	Bolivia	58

Abbrev. Mission name and addresses		Lands of origin		Fields of service	
WH	**World Horizons**	**World:**	**283**	**in 22+ countries**	
Aust.	PO Box 690, Baulkham Hills, NSW.	UK	185	UK	98
UK	Glanmor Road, Llanelli, Dyfed SA15 2LU.	Brazil	26	Mid East	28
WRMF	**World Radio Missionary Fellowship (HCJB)**	**World:**	**450**	**in 9+ countries**	
UK	HCJB, 131 Grattan Road, Bradford,	USA	276	Ecuador	318
	West Yorkshire, BD1 2HS.	Canada	40	USA	91
NZ	Box 38–776, Howick, Auckland.	UK	15	Australia	8
USA	PO Box 39800, Colorado Springs, CO 80949.	Australia	12	UK	8
WT	**WorldTeam USA**	**World:**	**175**	**in 13 countries**	
USA	PO Box 143038, Coral Gables, FL 33114.	USA	130	Haiti	32
WV	**World Vision**	**World:**	**1,287**	**in 32 countries**	
Aust.	Box 399-C, GPO, Melbourne, Vic 3001.	USA	769	USA	701
Canada	6630 Turner Valley Road,	Australia	237	Australia	237
	Mississauga, ON L5N 2S4.	Canada	161	Canada	156
NZ	Private Bag 92078, Auckland 1020.	Philippines	10	Cambodia	30
UK	Dychurch House, 8 Abington Street,	India	6	Romania	29
	Northampton NN1 2AJ.	Singapore	2	Mozam.	25
USA	919 W. Huntington Drive, Monrovia, CA 91016.	Hong Kong	1	Eurasia	9
YFC	**Youth For Christ**				
Sing.	YFC Int'l, Raffles City, PO Box 214, Singapore 9117				
Aust.	50 Morrie Crescent, Blackburn, Vic 3130.				
Canada	YFC Americas, PO Box 20411, Upper James Postal Outlet, Hamilton, ON L9C 7M8.				
UK	Cleobury Place, Cleobury Mortimer, Kidderminster, Worcestershire DY14 8JG.				
USA	PO Box 228822, Denver, CO 80222.				
YWAM	**Youth With A Mission**	**World:**	**7,076**	**in 106 countries**	
	"The GO Manual": a full list of addresses &	USA	2,232	USA	1,912
	opportunities: YWAM Publishing, PO Box 55787,	Brazil	592	Brazil	612
	Seattle, WA 98155, USA (tel 206–771–1153).	UK	380	Australia	420
Aust.	Pac & Asia Office: Box 61, Watson, ACT 2602.	Australia	377	UK	364
Brazil	Evangelism & Frontier Missions:	New Z'land	370	Netherlnd	291
	Cx Postal 2024, 30.161 Belo Horizonte, MG.	Canada	340	Canada	227
UK	Europe, Mid E & Africa Ofc (GO Manual avail.):	S Korea	272	S Korea	221
	13 Highfield Oval, Ambrose Lane, Harpenden,	Germany	224	Switzerlnd	212
	Herts. AL5 4BX (tel 0582–765–481).	Switzerlnd	222	Philippines	191
USA	Ofc of the Pres.; University of the Nations:	Netherlnd	206	Germany	172
	75–5851 Kuakini Hwy, Kailua-Kona, HI 96740.	S Africa	176	India	164
	Americas Office: Box 4600, Tyler, TX 75712.	Norway	149	New Z'land	162
	King's Kids: Box 117, Kailua-Kona, HI 96745.	Philippines	125	S Africa	144
	Mercy Ships: Box 2020, Lindale, TX 75771.	Indonesia	112	Norway	117
Kenya	E Africa Area Office: PO Box 76046, Nairobi.	Fiji	94	Indonesia	110
S.Afr.	S Africa Area Office: Private Bag 10,	Sweden	84	Hong Kong	104
	Garden View 2047, Johannesburg.	India	78	Thailand	101

IV

International Prayer Networks

Below are details of some of the significant prayer networks God is raising up to push the battle for world evangelization to the enemy's gates. Please make contact with any with whom you would like to establish an ongoing prayer fellowship and receive regular information to stimulate your praying.

Network and Addresses	Type of Participants	Prayer Focus
1. **AD2000 and Beyond Movement, Prayer Track**	Coordinators of Prayer Networks	10/40 Window Spiritual Warfare
USA c/o Peter & Doris Wagner, 215 N. Marengo Avenue, #151, Pasadena, CA 91101. Tel 1–818–577–7122. Fax 1–818–577–7160		

Network and Addresses	Type of Participants	Prayer Focus

Nigeria:
c/o W. F. Kumuyi, PO Box 59,
University of Lagos PO, Akoka, Yaba, Lagos.
Tel 234–1–82–3264. Fax 234–1–82–2990

2. **Campus Crusade for Christ** — All — New Life 2000 / World evangelization

USA:
c/o Ben Jennings, Campus Crusade for Christ,
100 Sunport Lane, Orlando, Florida 32809.

Germany:
Agape Europe, Lettenbuck, D–7841 Auggen-Hach.

Philippines:
ACPO Box 51, 1109 Quezon City.

3. **Concerts of Prayer International** — Multi-denominational / Multi-ethnic / City-wide prayer movements — Spiritual awakening / World evangelization

USA:
David Bryant, Concerts of Prayer International,
Pentagon Towers/Box 36008, Minneapolis,
MN 55435.
Tel 1–612–853–1740. Fax 1–612–853–8474

4. **Daniel Prayer Groups, Kings' Kids** — Children, Teens, Families — World revival

USA and Asia:
Carol Kauffman, 75–5851 Kuakini Highway,
Kailua-Kona, Hawaii 96740, USA
Tel 1–808–326–4454. Fax 1–808 326–4453

UK:
Wynne Stearns, 22 Lawn Street, Paisley PA1 1HF.
Tel 44–41–554–7251. Fax 44–41–550–2292

5. **Esther Network International** — Goal: one million young prayer warriors — World / Spiritual warfare / 10/40 Window / Muslim nations

USA:
Esther Ilnisky, 854 Conniston Road, West Palm
Beach, Florida 33405.
Tel 1–407–832–6490. Fax 1–407–832–8043

6. **Every Home for Christ** — All / Change the World School of Prayer — World evangelization / 10/40 Window

USA:
PO Box 35930, Colorado Springs,
CO 80935–3593.
Tel 1–719–260–8888. Fax 1–719–260–7408

UK:
71 Clifton Rd, Shefford, Bedfordshire SG17 5AG.
Tel 44–462–81–5389. Fax 44–462–81–7384

India:
PO Box 1719, Secunderabad 500–003.
Tel 91–842–76–028

South Africa:
PO Box 7256, Hennopsmeer, 0046.
Tel 27–12–663–4587. Fax 27–12–663–4589

Network and Addresses	Type of Participants	Prayer Focus
7. **End-Time Handmaidens and Servants** **USA:** Gwen R. Shaw, PO Box 447, Jasper, Arkansas 72641. Tel 1–501–446–2252. Fax 1–501–446–2259	All	Nations of World Israel
8. **LCWE Global Prayer Network** **USA:** Glenn Sheppard – LCWE Senior Associate for Prayer 3322 Irvin Bridge Rd, Conyers, GA 30207, USA LCWE office 5970 Fairview Rd, Suite 514, Charlotte, NC 28210–3196.	All Around the Clock Prayer	World evangelization
9. **Intercessors International** **Germany:** Johannes Facius, Markgrafen 19, D–7272 Altensteig. Tel 49–7–453–7076. Fax 49–7–453–1385	All	Nations of World
10. **Lydia Fellowship International** **UK:** Mrs Shelagh McAlpine, PO Box 85, Waterlooville, Hampshire PO7 7QU. **USA:** PO Box 20236, San Jose, CA 95160. **Australia:** PO Box 95, Gordon NSW 2072.	Christian Women	Church Communities Countries

11. **March for Jesus**
 	
UK:
Gerald Coates, Roger Forster, Lynn Green, Graham Kendrick
PO Box 39, Sunbury on Thames, Middlesex TW16 6PP.
	Participants in mass
	  prayer and praise on
	  the streets
		The World
		The Nations

12. **Watchman Prayer Alert** **USA:** Dr T W Hunt or Mary Betts, 127 Ninth Avenue North, Nashville, TN 37234.	All	Spiritual Awakening

APPENDIX 3

THE WORLD'S PROTESTANT MISSIONARY FORCE

These tables give an analysis of foreign and indigenous missionaries received and sent for each country of the world. They also give a measure of the missionary need in the final two columns. Truly we are living in a day of the globalization of the missionary force!

Explanation of columns

Column 1 – Countries grouped by region. Data is only given where it is expedient to do so.

Column 2 – Foreign missionaries. These are expatriate workers and their wives (if not indigenous). These figures include short-term workers of over one year's service and furloughing missionaries assigned to these countries. They also include 3,000–4,000 working in countries where missionary work is not allowed as such. The number of the latter may be double this figure.

Columns 3–6 – Indigenous missionaries. See definitions for missionary and indigenous missionary in Appendix 5. The total includes all cross-cultural and near culture (xcul + dom) missionaries within their own country and abroad. Column 3 = Column 5 + Column 6.

Column 7 – All cross-cultural missionaries. This includes:

1. All foreign workers (Column 2). Also included are 4,467 foreign workers working in a near-cultural situation; this latter is derived from the difference between columns 5 and 7 in the world totals.

2. All indigenous cross-cultural workers ministering in their own country. This is derived from Column 5, which also includes cross-cultural workers in other countries. (This subset is not tabulated here because of space limitations. Fuller details are available in the electronic *Operation World*.)

The sum of these two gives the total number of expatriates and indigenous workers serving cross-culturally within the given country.

Column 8 – Protestant Missionaries (column 7) per million non-Christians. Derived by dividing the number of missionaries by the population of non-Christians and multiplying by one million. This creates a *statistical comparison, or construct*, rather than *actual number* of missionaries. The lower the figure the greater the need for missionaries. The world average is 24 Protestant missionaries for every million non-Christians. Any figure below that reflects special need of missionary input (see also bottom line in regional tables, which gives the number of countries below the world average).

Column 9 – Protestant missionaries (column 7) per million non-Protestants. This is derived in the same way as the previous column, only replacing non-Christians with non-Protestants. The world average is 18 Protestant missionaries for every million non-Protestants. Contrast the figures between columns 8 and 9 for countries with large non-Protestant Christian communities! There is controversy among Christians as to whether such lands constitute needy mission fields or not. The primary pioneer countries are those with low Christian populations and low missionary figures in both columns 8 and 9.

Continental region	Expatriate miss. to region	Indig. missionaries from countries in region				All xcul miss to region	Statistical construct: Missionaries per 1 million	
		Total	In other lands	Cross-cultural	Near culture		non-Christians	non-Protest.
Africa	17,646	12,829	1,665	3,713	9,116	19,864	80	52
Asia	17,059	23,681	3,461	9,593	14,088	23,828	9	8
Caribbean	1,985	262	125	83	179	1,988	183	68
Eurasia	1,035	351	31	39	312	1,073	7	4
Europe	9,685	19,564	15,671	15,780	3,784	9,961	86	24
Latin America	14,620	4,482	1,364	2,126	2,356	15,409	408	42
Middle East	2,210	277	70	61	216	2,211	7	7
North America	2,942	64,378	43,554	44,168	20,210	4,253	53	26
Pacific	3,941	6,211	3,672	3,773	2,438	4,348	494	260
Other[1]	4,997	6,457	6,457	4,129	2,328	4,997	n.a.	n.a.
WORLD	76,120	138,492	76,070	83,465	55,027	87,932	24	18

(1) Includes all missionaries with international or global ministries or where field of service is unknown.

AFRICA

Country	Foreign miss. to country	Indig. missionaries from country				All xcul miss. to country	Statistical construct: Missionaries per 1 million	
		Total	In other lands	Cross-cultural	Near culture		non-Christians	non-Protest.
Angola	115	9	7	9	0	117	37	14
Benin	171	5	3	5	0	173	48	38
Botswana	249	0	0	0	0	249	370	221
British Indian Ocean	n.a.							
Burkina Faso	364	141	136	36	105	364	47	42
Burundi	95	24	2	2	22	95	69	20
Cameroon	689	34	2	24	10	711	118	74
Cape Verde	22	0	0	0	0	22	1,434	60
Central African Rep	208	14	2	12	2	218	131	99
Chad	197	54	2	32	22	227	50	46
Comoros	Included with Mayotte							
Congo	116	1	1	1	0	116	241	73
Cte d'Ivoire	900	26	6	8	18	902	90	76
Djibouti	28	0	0	0	0	28	71	69
Eq Guinea	42	0	0	0	0	42	428	99
Eritrea	Included with Ethiopia							
Ethiopia	623	48	5	33	15	651	29	16
Gabon	68	2	2	2	0	68	326	70
Gambia	109	6	2	0	6	109	130	128
Ghana	400	672	128	208	464	484	58	40
Guinea	199	8	0	2	6	201	30	29
Guinea-Bissau	72	18	1	18	0	89	96	91
Kenya	2,322	2,166	118	518	1,648	2,723	356	173
Lesotho	142	47	4	4	43	146	359	104
Liberia	353	290	1	1	289	353	184	165
Madagascar	192	42	7	7	35	192	30	21
Malawi	385	398	94	77	321	422	156	70
Mali	315	36	0	2	34	317	34	34
Mauritius	19	5	5	5	0	19	26	18
Mayotte	4	0	0	0	0	4	92	91
Mozambique	285	5	5	5	0	285	25	20
Namibia	190	26	17	22	4	195	281	187
Niger	264	1	1	1	0	264	37	37
Nigeria	768	2,878	243	1,259	1,619	1,784	34	26
Réunion	22	0	0	0	0	22	224	39
Rwanda	150	0	0	0	0	150	86	29
São Tomé & Príncipe	17	7	0	7	0	24	2,305	225
Senegal	468	4	1	2	2	469	67	64
Seychelles	35	0	0	0	0	35	6,643	561
Sierra Leone	233	131	2	48	83	279	72	71
Somalia	n.a.							
South Africa	1,294	1,866	651	908	958	1,556	161	72
St Helena	3	0	0	0	0	3	1,765	1,404
Swaziland	220	31	26	27	4	221	945	336
Tanzania	1,367	217	44	78	139	1,401	81	60
Togo	275	16	3	3	13	275	112	84
Uganda	382	920	20	23	897	385	69	29
Zaire	1,470	2,086	33	96	1,990	1,533	551	66
Zambia	626	353	44	87	266	669	175	102
Zimbabwe	630	240	45	139	101	724	145	98
TOTAL(1)	17,646	12,829	1,665	3,713	9,116	19,864	80	52
Number of countries below world average							0	2

(1) This includes 512 missionaries working in unspecified countries.

ASIA

Country	Foreign miss. to country	Indig. missionaries from country				All xcul miss. to country	Statistical construct: Missionaries per 1 million	
		Total	In other lands	Cross-cultural	Near culture		non-Christians	non-Protest.
Afghanistan	n.a.							
Bangladesh	316	132	0	9	123	325	3	3
Bhutan	72	0	0	0	0	72	120	120
Brunei	0	0	0	0	0	0	0	0
Cambodia	105	0	0	0	0	105	13	13
China, PRC	n.a.							
China, Taiwan	1,209	131	22	21	110	1,209	63	62
Hong Kong	767	220	155	93	127	767	153	143
India	775	11,284	171	5,137	6,147	5,746	7	7
Indonesia	1,599	1,518	68	450	1,068	1,992	13	12
Japan	3,015	409	271	201	208	3,019	25	25
Korea, North	0	0	0	0	0	0	0	0
Korea, South	409	3,957	2,032	1,601	2,356	409	14	13
Laos	36	0	0	0	0	36	9	9
Macao	93	33	0	0	33	93	250	236
Malaysia	189	363	145	145	218	193	12	12
Maldives	n.a.							
Mongolia	89	11	0	0	11	89	40	40
Myanmar	22	2,313	39	783	1,530	791	20	20
Nepal	584	155	2	2	153	584	31	31
Pakistan	736	137	6	13	124	743	6	6
Philippines	2,958	2,164	178	742	1,422	3,543	493	61
Singapore	385	567	354	365	202	396	167	159
Sri Lanka	117	159	3	11	148	125	8	7
Thailand	1,293	117	4	11	106	1,301	24	23
Vietnam	19	3	3	3	0	19	0	0
TOTAL[1]	17,059	23,681	3,461	9,593	14,088	23,828	9	8
Number of countries below world average							16	12

(1) Including 2,271 missionaries working in Asia in general or in sensitive countries.

CARIBBEAN

Country	Foreign miss. to country	Indig. missionaries from country				All xcul miss. to country	Statistical construct: Missionaries per 1 million	
		Total	In other lands	Cross-cultural	Near culture		non-Christians	non-Protest.
Anguilla	2	0	0	0	0	2	5,305	2,740
Antigua	35	3	0	0	3	35	1,796	1,268
Aruba	Included with Netherlands Antilles							
Bahamas	68	1	0	0	1	68	920	561
Barbados	26	9	2	2	7	26	352	279
Belize	105	17	1	1	16	105	7,278	776
Bermuda	13	0	0	0	0	13	1,575	703
British Virgin Is	2	0	0	0	0	2	1,668	1,016
Cayman Is	12	0	0	0	0	12	1,999	1,835
Cuba	2	2	2	2	0	2	0	0
Dominica	9	4	2	2	2	9	793	130
Dominican Rep	216	51	5	5	46	216	192	32
French Guiana	18	0	0	0	0	18	722	163
Grenada	53	2	0	2	0	55	6,930	820
Guadeloupe	21	1	1	1	0	21	1,108	66
Guyana	47	11	4	4	7	47	121	93
Haiti	473	3	3	3	0	473	621	98
Jamaica	209	45	23	24	21	210	168	134
Martinique	15	3	2	2	1	15	373	49
Montserrat	4	0	0	0	0	4	1,693	1,020
Netherlands Antilles	161	4	4	4	0	161	15,811	1,010
Puerto Rico	141	65	61	16	49	141	385	51
St Kitts & Nev	5	0	0	0	0	5	549	347
St Lucia	6	3	1	1	2	6	556	48
St Vincent	18	4	4	4	0	18	488	337
Suriname	156	2	1	1	1	156	640	470
Trinidad	94	32	9	9	23	94	165	98
Turks & Caicos	0	0	0	0	0	0	0	0
Virgin Is – US	39	0	0	0	0	39	2,817	778
TOTAL[1]	1,985	262	125	83	179	1,988	183	68
Number of countries below world average							2	2

(1) Including 35 missionaries working in un specified countries

EURASIA

Country	Foreign miss. to country	Indig. missionaries from country				All xcul miss. to country	Statistical construct: Missionaries per 1 million	
		Total	In other lands	Cross-cultural	Near culture		non-Christians	non-Protest.
Armenia	10	0	0	0	0	10	14	3
Azerbaijan	n.a.							
Byelarus	6	0	0	0	0	6	2	1
Georgia	8	0	0	0	0	8	3	1
Kazakhstan	n.a.							
Kyrgyzstan	n.a.							
Moldova	0	0	0	0	0	0	0	0
Russia	505	14	0	4	10	509	7	3
Tajikistan	n.a.							
Turkmenistan	n.a.							
Ukraine	48	330	30	34	296	82	5	2
Uzbekistan	n.a.							
TOTAL[1]	[2]1,035	351	31	39	312	1,073	7	4
Number of countries below world average							12	12

(1) Total incomplete due to inadequate or confidential data.
(2) Including 458 missionaries working in Eurasia or in sensitive countries.

EUROPE

Country	Foreign miss. to country	Indig. missionaries from country				All xcul miss. to country	Statistical construct: Missionaries per 1 million	
		Total	In other lands	Cross-cultural	Near culture		non-Christians	non-Protest.
Albania	182	0	0	0	0	182	65	56
Andorra	2	0	0	0	0	2	300	39
Austria	593	64	37	37	27	593	819	84
Belgium	572	65	22	22	43	572	550	58
Bosnia[1]	2	0	0	0	0	2	1	0
Bulgaria	77	0	0	0	0	77	28	9
Channel Is	Included in UK						4	0
Croatia[1]	2	0	0	0	0	2	886	197
Cyprus	137	2	0	0	2	137	12	6
Czech Rep	87	3	1	1	2	87	70	61
Denmark	31	387	342	342	45	31	45	34
Estonia	45	4	4	4	0	45	0	0
Faeroe Is	0	43	43	43	0	0	37	32
Finland	20	1,323	1,278	1,278	45	20	85	25
France	1,348	456	293	315	141	1,373	62	26
Germany	1,247	3,524	2,861	2,819	705	1,293	271	72
Gibraltar	2	0	0	0	0	2	384	15
Greece	144	33	8	9	24	147	0	0
Holy See	0	0	0	0	0	0	151	27
Hungary	213	46	7	9	37	215	4,463	2,647
Iceland	20	31	22	22	9	20	729	76
Ireland	274	50	39	39	11	274	0	0
Isle of Man	0	0	0	0	0	0	41	8
Italy	462	198	42	42	156	462	17	13
Latvia	29	2	2	2	0	29	0	0
Liechtenstein	0	0	0	0	0	0	4	1
Lithuania	4	0	0	0	0	4	168	28
Luxembourg	10	1	1	1	0	10	0	0
Macedonia[1]	0	0	0	0	0	11	654	31
Malta	11	0	0	0	0	33	11,498	1,180
Monaco	33	0	0	0	0	378	70	35
Netherlands	367	1,193	866	876	317	52	123	110
Norway	52	1,635	1,498	1,498	137	77	96	2
Poland	77	67	6	6	61	339	382	33
Portugal	333	174	129	116	58	165	47	8
Romania	165	9	2	2	7	0	0	0
San Marino	0	0	0	0	0	10	n.a.	n.a.
Slovakia	10	1	1	1	0	0	0	0
Slovenia[1]	0	0	0	0	0	1,126	233	29
Spain	1,109	133	62	63	70			
Svalbard	Included under Norway					88	26	24
Sweden	88	1,739	1,652	1,652	87	226	386	59
Switzerland	219	1,351	1,083	1,066	285	1,167	61	44
UK of GB	1,021	7,012	5,368	5,500	1,512	66	25	7
Yugoslavia[1]	53	18	2	15	3			
TOTAL	[2]9,685	19,564	15,671	15,780	3,784	9,961	86	24
Number of countries below world average							12	19

(1) Incomplete information; Yugoslavia figures include whole of former Yugoslavia.
(2) Including 644 missionaries with a wider ministry in Europe or in no specific country.

LATIN AMERICA

Country	Foreign miss. to country	Indig. missionaries from country				All xcul miss. to country	Statistical construct: Missionaries per 1 million	
		Total	In other lands	Cross-cultural	Near culture		non-Christians	non-Protest.
Argentina	913	144	51	82	62	944	321	32
Bolivia	1,010	48	7	13	35	1,016	1,203	15
Brazil	3,397	2,768	832	1,304	1,464	3,871	311	32
Chile	565	102	39	29	73	565	389	59
Colombia	947	148	34	59	89	974	750	32
Costa Rica	452	107	99	99	8	452	1,832	168
Ecuador	1,151	48	3	15	33	1,163	1,441	112
El Salvador	113	130	38	41	89	116	409	28
Falkland Is	5	0	0	0	0	5	19,608	10,638
Guatemala	612	123	36	39	84	620	585	89
Honduras	384	58	23	19	39	388	1,415	85
Mexico	1,891	376	84	239	137	2,046	192	24
Nicaragua	108	34	9	9	25	108	310	34
Panama	228	26	1	3	23	230	953	114
Paraguay	520	15	10	11	4	521	4,079	129
Peru	1,043	190	58	73	117	1,058	676	51
Uruguay	217	34	28	28	6	217	158	72
Venezuela	637	131	12	63	68	688	387	37
TOTAL[1]	14,620	4,482	1,364	2,126	2,356	15,409	408	42
Number of countries below world average							0	0

(1) Including 427 missionaries working in Latin America in general.

MIDDLE EAST

Country	Foreign miss. to country	Indig. missionaries from country				All xcul miss. to country	Statistical construct: Missionaries per 1 million	
		Total	In other lands	Cross-cultural	Near culture		non-Christians	non-Protest.
Algeria	n.a.							
Bahrain	n.a.							
Egypt	n.a.							
Gaza Strip	n.a.							
Iran	n.a.							
Iraq	n.a.							
Israel	434	10	0	1	9	435	73	71
Jordan	n.a.							
Kuwait	n.a.							
Lebanon	42	29	15	15	14	42	23	14
Libya	n.a.							
Mauritania	n.a.							
Morocco	n.a.							
Oman	n.a.							
Palestine-West Bank	n.a.							
Qatar	n.a.							
Sahara	Included with Morocco							
Saudi Arabia	n.a.							
Sudan	162	16	4	4	12	162	8	7
Syria	n.a.							
Tunisia	n.a.							
Turkey	n.a.							
UAE	n.a.							
Yemen	n.a.							
TOTAL[1]	2,210	277	70	61	216	2,211	7	7
Number of countries below world average							23	23

(1) Including 1,572 missionaries/expatriates serving in Middle East – many in sensitive countries.

NORTH AMERICA

Country	Foreign miss. to country	Indig. missionaries from country				All xcul miss. to country	Statistical construct: Missionaries per 1 million	
		Total	In other lands	Cross-cultural	Near culture		non-Christians	non-Protest.
Canada	408	5,336	3,636	3,627	1,709	515	53	23
Greenland	50	3	2	2	1	50	2,799	2,751
St Pierre & Martinique	0	0	0	0	0	0	0	0
USA	2,484	59,074	39,951	40,574	18,500	3,688	52	26
TOTAL	2,942	64,378	43,554	44,168	20,210	4,253	53	26
Number of countries below world average							1	1

PACIFIC

Country	Foreign miss. to country	Indig. missionaries from country				All xcul miss. to country	Statistical construct: Missionaries per 1 million	
		Total	In other lands	Cross-cultural	Near culture		non-Christians	non-Protest.
American Samoa	21	26	26	26	0	21	4,962	945
Australia	743	3,598	2,062	2,241	1,357	969	149	83
Christmas Is	Included with Australia							
Cocos Is	Included with Australia							
Cook Is	10	11	10	10	1	10	5,470	1,967
Fiji	78	301	73	74	227	79	225	183
French Polynesia	20	6	2	2	4	20	704	186
Guam	159	1	0	0	1	159	20,736	1,396
Johnston Is	0	0	0	0	0	0	0	0
Kiribati	6	2	2	2	0	6	3,743	158
Marshall Is	25	0	0	0	0	25	2,019	1,404
Micronesia	38	12	9	10	2	39	1,879	573
Midway Is	n.a.							
Nauru	0	0	0	0	0	0	0	0
New Caledonia	51	2	2	2	0	51	1,472	385
New Zealand	218	1,715	1,347	1,126	589	229	224	136
Niue Island	0	3	3	3	0	0	0	0
Norfolk Is	Included with Australia							
N Mariana Is	86	0	0	0	0	86	3,980	1,483
Palau	8	8	8	8	0	8	13,817	709
Papua New Guinea	2,278	222	40	191	31	2,429	3,283	1,177
Pitcairn Is	0	0	0	0	0	0	0	0
Samoa	10	74	59	32	42	10	2,976	126
Solomon Is	81	161	6	23	138	98	4,013	1,060
Tokelau Is	0	0	0	0	0	0	0	0
Tonga	18	48	23	23	25	18	9,641	373
Tuvalu	2	0	0	0	0	2	6,452	3,559
Vanuatu	37	0	0	0	0	37	876	553
Wallis & Futun	0	0	0	0	0	0	0	0
TOTAL[1]	3,941	6,211	3,672	3,773	2,438	4,348	494	260
Number of countries below world average							7	7

(1) Including 52 missionaries serving in more than one country or in Pacific generally.

WORLD (1)   (2) 76,120 138,492   76,070   83,465 (2) 55,027 87,932   24   18

(1) The world totals include those serving as missionaries but not assigned to a specific field or with a global ministry.

(2) The totals in Columns 2 and 4 differ by 50. They should be identical, but prolonged checking in our databases has failed to unearth the small error.

(3) The totals in Columns 5 and 7 differ by 4,467. This represents foreign missionaries working in near cultures, which were included in the latter total.

APPENDIX 4
OTHER ABBREVIATIONS

$	USA dollars
ABFMS	American Baptist Foreign Mission Society (USA)
AEB	Africa Evangelistic Band (South Africa)
AEE	African Evangelistic Enterprise; see **AE**
AEM	Andes Evangelical Mission; amalgamated with **SIM**
AIC	African Independent Church(es) Africa Inland Church (**AIM**-related)
ALM	American Lutheran Mission
AME	African Methodist Episcopal Church
AMEN	*Asociacion Misionera Evangélica a las Naciones* (Peru)
AMG	American Mission to Greeks
Ang.	Anglican
ASEAN	Assoc. of South East Asian Nations
BBFI	Baptist Bible Fellowship International
BCC	Bible Correspondence Course(s)
BCMS	Bible Churchman's Missionary Society; now Crosslinks
BEM	Borneo Evangelical Mission; see **OMF**
BGC	Baptist General Conference
Bi	Bible
BMMF	see **Interserve** or **I**
CAPRO	See Calvary Ministries (**CM**, Nigeria)
CBIM	Canadian Baptist International Ministries; formerly CBOMB
CCAP	Church of Central Africa, Presbyterian (Malawi, C. Africa)
CFAN	Christ For All Nations
Ch	Church
CIM	China Inland Mission; now **OMF**
CMJ	Church Mission to the Jews (Anglican)
CMML	Christian Missions in Many Lands, see Christian Brethren
CNEC	Christian Nationals Evangelism Commission, see Partners Int'l
CNI	Church of North India
COCM	Chinese Overseas Christian Mission

COMIBAM	*Congreso Misionero Ibero Americano* (1988)
cong.	congregation
CSI	Church of South India
CU	Christian Union
DAWN	Discipling A Whole Nation Movement
dom	Missionaries working within their own or a near culture
DRC	Dutch Reformed Church (South Africa, Netherlands)
EA	Evangelical Alliance
EC	European Community
ECWA	Evangelical Church of West Africa (SIM-related)
EEC	European Economic Community
EFT	Evangelical Fellowship of Thailand
EHC	Every Home for Christ; formerly Every Home Crusade
EiD	Evangelism in Depth
EKD	*Evangelische Kirche in Deutschland* (Germany)
EMF	European Missionary Fellowship
Ev	Evangelical
FEBIAS	Far East Bible Institute and Seminary (Philippines)
FFM	Finnish Free Mission (Pentecostal), also Fellowship of Faith for Muslims
FGBMFI	Full Gospel Business Men's Fellowship International
FLM	Finnish Lutheran Mission
frn	Foreign missionaries – those working in other lands
GDR	German Democratic Republic (East Germany)
HCJB	Radio Voice of the Andes (**WRMF**, Ecuador) IEP
HMU	Hellenic Missionary Union
HQ	Headquarter(s)
ICFG	International Church of the Foursquare Gospel
ICI	International Correspondence Institute (**AoG**)
IEP	*Iglesia Evangélica Peruana* (**SIM**-related)
IMS	Indian Missionary Society
Ind.	Independent
ISCF	International Student Christian Fellowship

JW	Jehovah's Witnesses
LMS	London Missionary Society (UK)
LRI	Language Recordings International; see **GRn**
MB	*Mission Biblique* (France/ Switzerland)
MKs	Missionaries' children
NATO	North Atlantic Treaty Organization
NGK	*Nederduits Gereformeerde Kerk*; (Dutch Reformed Church, S. Africa)
NGO	Non-Governmental Organization
NLFA	New Life For All
NLM	Norwegian Lutheran Mission
NMS	National Missionary Society
NT	New Testament
PEMS	Paris Evangelical Missionary Society; now DEFAP
PFI	Prison Fellowship International
PHC	Pentecostal Holiness Church
por	portion (of Bible)
RC	Roman Catholic
SAM	South American Mission; formerly South American Indian Mission
SCM	Student Christian Movement
SDA	Seventh-day Adventist Church
SFM	Swedish Free Mission
SIB	*Sidang Injil Borneo* (Malaysia, BEM-**OMF**)
sq.km.	square kilometres
stw/STW	Short-term worker
SwAM	Swedish Alliance Mission
TEE	Theological Education by Extension
TSPM	Three Self Patriotic Movement (China)
UCCF	Universities and Colleges Christian Fellowship (**IFES**)
UK	United Kingdom of Great Britain and Northern Ireland
UN	United Nations
USPG	United Society for the Propagation of the Gospel (Anglican)
UVM	Upper Volta Mission (Burkina Faso)
WCE	World Christian Encyclopedia
xcul	Missionaries working cross-culturally (in homeland or abroad)
YMCA	Young Men's Christian Association
ZEM-NM	Zambesi Evangelical Mission and Nyasa Mission (Malawi)

APPENDIX 5

DEFINITIONS

Here are a few definitions of terms used throughout the book.

10/40 Window. The area of the world between latitudes 10° and 40° north of the equator covering North Africa, Middle East and Asia. The window has in view most of the world's areas of greatest physical and spiritual need, most of the world's least-reached peoples and most of the governments that oppose Christianity. See map on p 82.

adherent. A follower of a particular religion, church or philosophy. This is the broadest possible category of such followers and includes professing and affiliated adults and also their children (practising and non-practising) who may reside in a given area or country. As it refers to those who, if not under coercion, would claim to have a religion even if their adherence is only nominal, it is the only figure that can be used to adequately compare the relative numbers of followers of different religions and Christian traditions.

adult members. Adult church members over 12–18 years of age (depending on the denomination) who are communicants or full members. Adult members are given in the second column of statistics in the denominational tables.

affiliated Christians. All who are considered as belonging to organized churches. This includes full members, their children and other occasional attenders considered as part of the church community. These figures represent the whole Christian community or inclusive membership. Affiliated Christians are given in the third column of statistics in the denominational tables.

Black theology. Christian theology as interpreted from the viewpoint of the oppressed Black race.

born-again believer. Those who by grace and through faith in the atoning work of Christ have been regenerated by the Holy Spirit. However, in common usage it often includes those who claim an evangelical conversion experience.

Catholic (non-Roman). Numerous, generally small, secessions from the Roman Catholic Church over the past 300 years but which retain many elements of traditional Catholic dogma. Also Protestant and mainly Anglican secessions that have Catholic-type sacramentalism and hierarchy.

Charismatics. Those who testify to a renewing experience of the Holy Spirit and present exercise of the gifts of the Spirit such as *glossalalia*, healing, prophecy and miracles. This neo-Pentecostalism, Charismatic Renewal or "Second Wave" Pentecostalism has generally remained within mainline denominations. There is a further "Third Wave" renewal movement with many characteristics of the Second Wave but with less open identification with Pente-

costalism or the Charismatic Movement. Second and Third Wave Charismatics are counted as a single entity in this book. In my global survey of denominations I have assessed percentages of affiliated Charismatic Christians for each of the 23,000 denominations in the world for 1990 only. Barrett's figure for 1990 of 174 million Second and Third Wave charismatics also includes 91 million post-charismatics, thus giving a total of 83 million active charismatics (70 million Protestant, 11.7 million Catholic, 0.5 million Orthodox). My independent assessment of active Charismatics gives a total of 65 million Protestant and 10 million Catholic. The correlation between these two surveys is gratifying.

Church (with capital C). A particular denomination, or the universal visible Church at a national or worldwide level. Where a denomination's name is followed by initials in brackets, the parent mission is indicated (this is to identify the ecclesiastical origin or current affiliation for the reader and does not mean present control!).

church (with a small c). A local fellowship of believers. The word is commonly used to mean a church building or church service, but here this usage has usually been avoided. The starting of churches is termed **church planting.**

creative-access countries. See restricted-access countries.

cross-cultural missionaries. Full-time Christian workers sent by their churches to work among peoples of a different culture, either within their own nations or abroad. In missionary statistics the abbreviation "**xcul**" has been used.

ethnolinguistic people. An ethnic or racial group speaking its own language. A people group distinguished by its self-identity with traditions of common descent, history, customs and language.

Evangelicals. The subdivision of Protestantism (including Anglicans and non-Western evangelical groups) which generally emphasizes:

1. The Lord Jesus Christ as the sole source of salvation through faith in him.

2. Personal faith and conversion with regeneration by the Holy Spirit.

3. A recognition of the inspired Word of God as the only basis for faith and Christian living.

4. Commitment to biblical preaching and evangelism that brings others to faith in Christ.

Note:

1. The definition of Evangelicals and the statistics

relating to them are so fundamental to the contents of this book that it is important for the reader to understand the implications. It enables a measurement of the size and spectacular numerical growth of evangelical Christians over the last few decades.

The noun "Evangelical" is capitalized since it represents a body of Christians with a fairly clearly defined theology (as also Orthodox and Catholic bodies, etc.). Evangelicals are here defined as:

1. All affiliated Christians (church members, their children, etc.) of denominations that are evangelical in theology as defined above.

2. The proportion of the affiliated Christians in other Protestant denominations (that are not wholly evangelical in theology) who would hold evangelical views.

3. The proportion of affiliated Christians in denominations in non-Western nations (where doctrinal positions are less well defined) that would be regarded as Evangelicals by those in the above categories.

Note: *This is a theological and not an experiential definition. It does **not** mean:*

1. That all Evangelicals as defined above are actually born-again. In many nations only 10–40% of Evangelicals so defined may have had a valid conversion and also regularly attend church services. However, it does show how many people align themselves with churches where the gospel is being proclaimed.

2. That those of evangelical persuasion are confined to Protestant denominations, for an increasing number of Catholics, Orthodox and others have a clear testimony to a personal meeting with the Lord and hold an evangelical position regarding the Bible. See below for Evangelical Catholics and Evangelical Orthodox.

Evangelical Catholics. A growing number of individual Catholics are openly subscribing to a doctrinal position close to that defined above for Evangelical Protestants. Some estimates for numbers of Evangelical Catholics have been given (Ireland, USA and in the World overview sections), but these are incomplete. These statistics are not included with those of Evangelical Protestants, who are the primary focus throughout this book.

Evangelical Orthodox. Revival and renewal movements have deeply influenced sections of some ancient Orthodox Churches. Some of these would be termed theologically evangelical – even if they themselves may not use this term. In several countries statistics have been given for such. For example, in Romania the Lord's Army, an Orthodox body, is a member of the national Evangelical Alliance.

evangelized. The state of having had the gospel communicated and offered in such a way that the hearer becomes aware of the claims of Christ, and the need to obey and follow Him. Possibly over two billion have been exposed to the gospel but are not linked with any Christian church.

indigenous missionary. One working in or sent from his/her homeland as a missionary.

Liberation theology. Christian theology redefined on the basis of sociological, and often Marxist, presuppositions of oppression, thereby motivating the poor to claim equal participation in society.

marginal groups. A general term used in this book to describe all semi-Christian or fringe groups, sects and cults that accept certain Christian features and parts of the Scriptures, together with supplementary revelations claimed to be divine. Most claim that they alone have the "truth". Many readers may understandably question the validity of including these groups as Christian. However, we consistently classify a person's religion according to his or her self-assessment. All of these groups claim allegiance to Christ even if their theological understanding of his person, deity, atoning work or resurrection may be defective. See prayer items for ministry to these groups given for December 24.

missionary. One who is sent with a message. This word of Latin derivation has the same basic meaning as the wider use of the term "apostle" in the New Testament. The Christian missionary is one commissioned by a local church to evangelize, plant churches and disciple people away from his home area and often among people of a different race, culture or language. Modern usage varies widely with strong regional preferences:

1. **The stricter North American usage** – all sent to evangelize, plant churches or minister **outside their homelands.** We have abbreviated this category as "frn".

2. **The wider European and Latin American usage** – all sent to evangelize, plant churches or minister **cross-culturally** whether in other lands or in their homelands. Abbreviated in statistics as "xcul".

3. **The even broader African and Asian usage,** which is closer to the biblical concept indicated above and which encompasses all those sent to evangelize, plant churches and minister away from their home areas whether cross-culturally or not and whether in their own countries or abroad. (This is the definition of "indigenous missionary" used elsewhere in this Appendix and in Appendix 3.) However, such breadth in the use of "missionary" makes it harder for the researcher to specify the cultural or geographical distance a Christian worker must cover in order to be properly categorized as a missionary (as contrasted with an evangelist). It is especially helpful in such a case to be able to identify the sub-division of missionaries working within their own or a near culture (abbreviated here as "**dom**").

In this book we have sought to synthesize differing perspectives in dividing all missionaries of each country and region into the three categories of "**frn**", "**xcul**" and "**dom**". **Total = xcul + dom**. Most, but not all, foreign missionaries are cross-cultural, for many are actually working within expatriate communities of their own culture.

Pentecostals. Those affiliated to specifically Pentecostal denominations committed to a Pentecostal theology usually including a post-conversion experience of a Baptism in the Spirit, present exercise of the gifts of the Spirit and speaking in tongues. David Barrett's remarkable survey of 20th century Pentecostal/Charismatic renewal in the *International Bulletin of Missionary Research* of July 1988 includes numerous other streams such as non-white indigenous quasi-Pentecostals, Catholic Apostolics, Chinese house-church Pentecostals and other non-affiliated Pentecostals. All these are generally grouped under the category of "First Wave" or Classical Pentecostalism. Barrett's total for 1990 of 194 million First Wave Pentecostals becomes 85 million if the categories I have omitted from this assessment in *Operation World* are subtracted. This accords remarkably with my figure of 93 million derived by a completely new global survey of denominations.

people group. A significantly large sociological grouping of individuals who perceive themselves to have a common affinity with one another. From the viewpoint of evangelization, this is the largest possible group within which the gospel can be spread without encountering barriers of understanding or acceptance. There are basically three types:

1. **Ethnolinguistic people group**, which defines a person's identity and primary loyalty according to language and/or ethnicity. This is the category that has been emphasized in this book. We have reserved the word **people** rather than people group for this type. **Cross-cultural** church-planting teams of missionaries are needed for peoples in this category. Of the estimated 12,000 ethnolinguistic peoples, probably over 9,000 already have at least one or two viable indigenous churches within their culture.

2. **Sociological people group** – a grouping defined by its long-term relation to the rest of society, such as by migration or traditional occupation or class, but not having a self-contained culture or identity as an ethnic group. In most cases local church outreach is required – either to plant daughter churches or to incorporate converts into multi-social congregations. There are probably hundreds of thousands of such people groups.

3. **Incidental people groups** – casual associations of individuals which may be temporary and usually the result of circumstances rather than personal choice. Examples of such groups are high-rise flat dwellers, drug addicts, occupational groupings, commuters, etc. These groupings present unique problems and opportunities for evangelism, but only rarely will it be appropriate for specific churches to be planted for the sole benefit of such groups.

people movement. A movement of a large number of non-Christians in a particular people into the Church. This is frequently a group decision. It presents a wonderful opportunity to win and disciple many for the Lord by leading them into a personal faith in the Lord Jesus Christ. Failure to do so can soon lead to nominalism or syncretism.

post-charismatics. Those once involved but no longer active in Charismatic Renewal. Barrett estimates that for 1990 there were 32 million Protestant and 60 million Catholic post-charismatics in the world.

professing. A claim of allegiance to a religious belief – whether known to or listed in the records of an organized religion. Professing Christians usually number more than affiliated Christians. Where the difference is significant, this is included in the statistical section of the text for each country as nominal.
Professing = affiliated + nominal.

reached/unreached. A term that is widely used today to describe people groups and areas that have or have not responded to the preaching of the gospel. The use of the term has been continued in this book despite the faultiness of the terminology. Strictly, it should be a measure of the **exposure** of a people group to the gospel and not a measure of the **response**.

renewal. A quickening or enlivening in personal commitment to Christ in the churches. Charismatic renewal in the historic denominations is an example. See above under Charismatics.

restricted-access countries. States that limit or prevent Christian ministry by expatriates as missionaries. Alternatively they are called **creative-access countries**, where expatriates must seek secular avenues of entry – business, medical work, teaching, as house servants and other means. Most countries in this category have been Communist and Muslim, but today are predominantly Muslim.

revival. The restoring to life of believers and churches which have previously experienced the regenerating power of the Holy Spirit but have become cold, worldly and ineffective. The word is often wrongly used of evangelistic campaigns, but it really means a sovereign act of God and an answer to prayer in bringing about a religious awakening and outpouring of the Spirit on his people.

Syncretism. The attempt to synthesize elements of different religious systems into a single body of belief and practice. **Baha'i,** for instance, is a synthesis of Islamic, Christian and other religious tenets. Some **African Indigenous Churches** have sought to synthesize elements of Christianity with pre-Christian traditional beliefs.

Universalism. The belief that ultimately all people will be saved irrespective of religious belief or lack of it while on earth. The underlying premises are that many have an implicit awareness of a supernatural being to which they respond by doing good to others and that a loving God could not consign people to eternal punishment for sin – non-biblical teaching rejected by nearly all Evangelicals.

unreached people. An ethnolinguistic people among whom there is no viable indigenous community of believing Christians with adequate numbers and resources to evangelize their own people without outside (cross-cultural) assistance. Other researchers have adopted the terms "hidden people" or "frontier people group".

World A. Nations and peoples in the least evangelized world. Defined as those nations and peoples that are less than 50% evangelized as defined in the World Evangelization Database compiled by Dr David Barrett and team.

World B. Nations and peoples in the evangelized non-Christian world. Defined as those nations and peoples that are more than 50% evangelized and less than 60% Christian (including all major Christian groups).

World C. Nations and peoples in the Christian world. Defined as those nations and peoples that are more than 60% professing Christian. This includes all nominal and affiliated Christians of all ecclesiological traditions and not only Protestants.

World Evangelization Database. A large research database on missions and resources for research use, with four information-retrieval library versions, compiled by Dr David Barrett and team.

APPENDIX 6
CHURCH STATISTICS

The *Operation World* denominations database

In 1984–86 we developed a denominational database for the analysis of global church growth. The starting point was the data assembled by Dr David Barrett in the early '70s for the production of the *World Christian Encyclopedia* in 1982. We conducted a wide-ranging search for data to cover the period 1960–1985 for the fourth edition of *Operation World*, which was published in 1986.

For this fifth edition we expanded the data to include four basic denominational figures.

1. **Number of congregations.** The results have proved variable due to the wide differences in definition of what constitutes a congregation both between denominations and within a denomination from year to year.

2. **Adult membership.** Where denominations only give inclusive membership, we have had to derive a figure to enable comparison with those that only give adult membership.

3. **Affiliated or inclusive membership.** Where denominations only give adult membership, again we have had to derive a figure for inclusive members. Data collected over 30 years show that many denominations are inconsistent from year to year in sometimes giving affiliated and at other times adult membership!

4. **Church attendance** has been a major data item collected by recent researchers – especially by **DAWN** programmes in countries with a saturation church-planting initiative and also in the MARC *Europe Christian Handbook* series for that continent. We have added this data to our database, but could not use it consistently for all countries, so these figures have not been included in the text of this edition.

The denominations database has individual entries for 5,300 specific denominations and totals covering an overall 24,000 denominations in the world. This means a total input of 500,000 pieces of data!

This database enabled us to make interpolations for missing data, extrapolations of earlier data to 1990 and 2000 and derivations of national, regional and global totals for six ecclesiological branches of Christendom. We were also able to make a denomination-by-denomination assessment of the growth of the Evangelical Movement and of Pentecostals within that Movement as well as to derive an estimate for the strength of the Charismatic Movement in non-Pentecostal denominations in 1990.

The entire database system will be available for users of the electronic *Operation World*. Corrections and updates would be appreciated!

Modifications to the World Christian Encyclopedia approach in handling denominational data.

The sophisticated statistical analysis of the WCE has had to be simplified for such a volume as this. However, the WCE gave us a valuable starting point for the construction of our denominational database. We have made the following adaptations:

1. The seven ecclesiological types of the WCE have been slightly adjusted. The seven types are Anglican, Catholic (non-Roman), Non-White indigenous, Marginal Protestant, Orthodox, Protestant and Roman Catholic.
a) In *Operation World*, Anglicans have been included with Protestants.
b) "Non-White indigenous" is a classification based on non-Western origin of such denominations – a useful concept to quantify the strength and variety of such movements, but not adequate for our purposes. These denominations have been redistributed among the other ecclesiological types according to church structure and doctrine – and only more marginal or syncretic non-Western groups have been retained under this classification so that the term becomes "indigenous marginal".

2. We have only retained the concept of professing Christians (those known to the government or public as such) and affiliated Christians (those known to the churches). We have adjusted the statistics

of professing and affiliated Christians to allow for dual membership, secret believers, and apostates and backsliders still on church rolls.

Please refer to the WCE for more information.

Methodology for *Operation World*

1. **Sources of statistics** have included denominational handbooks and reports, a questionnaire sent to church-planting mission agencies, national surveys and Christian handbooks, voluminous correspondence around the world and also scraps of data picked up in our culling of hundreds of magazines, circulars and surveys. Each item entered was tagged with source, as were derived and estimated figures.

2. **Data for each five-yearly period between 1960 and 1990** was entered – often from a variety of sources. Growth curves enabled interpolation or extrapolation of data where missing.

3. **Use of ratios unique to each denomination** helped us to fill out missing data. Rarely was there full information for any given year covering congregations, membership, affiliation and attendance. Reasonable ratios establishing a link between each were calculated using every available piece of information – past statistics, growth, age structure, family size, etc. This enabled more sober estimates of Christians, especially Evangelicals, than some figures that have been bandied about.

4. **Evangelical percentages** were derived as follows:
   a) All denominations claiming or estimated by us to be **theologically conservative Evangelical** were entered as 100% evangelical (see definitions in Appendix 5). This means that all affiliated with an evangelical denomination are considered theologically evangelical. It is not a measure of personal faith.
   b) **Pluralistic denominations** (those with a variety of theological views other than evangelical – such as sacramentalist, liberal, etc.). The estimated percentage of Evangelicals in the denomination in 1960 and 1990 was entered and this was used to calculate the Evangelicals affiliated to that denomination. Incremental changes between 1960 and 1990 were calculated from there.
   c) **National, regional and world totals** could then be derived from the results.

5. **Pentecostals** were totalled on the denominational tag using WCE nomenclature – as also could be done for any type of denomination.

6. **Charismatic** totals were calculated for 1990 only. An estimated denominational percentage for charismatics in non-Pentecostal denominations was entered and this used to calculate national, regional and global totals.

The purpose of this methodology is that the whole system be transparent with every estimate, derivation, assumption and source known and verifiable and, where necessary, rectifiable.

APPENDIX 7

STATISTICAL SOURCES

A complete bibliography is impossible to provide here! Only some of the more significant sources can be given.

Primary sources

1. Personal correspondence. For the production of the last two editions we have sent out approximately 10,000 personal letters and questionnaires for information and checking of data and the text. We have preferred nationals to expatriates, but often the latter have been in a better position to respond. The response rate has been well over 50% and most encouraging.

2. Personal conversations around the world in many providential times of fellowship with key informants.

3. Numerous surveys and documents as well as circulars and reports produced by individuals and mission agencies. Much of the more significant information gathered has been collated in subject and date order in our Research Office. Approximately 500,000 pages of this material has been put on to microfiche film (70 frames per fiche requiring a fiche reader with 24× magnification lens). Fuller details are obtainable from the International Research Office, WEC International, Bulstrode, Gerrards Cross, Bucks, SL9 8SZ, England.

Secondary sources.

1. General

Encyclopedia Britannica Book of the Year 1990, 1991, 1992, 1993. ISBN 0–85299–585–5.
The World Factbook, CIA, USA 1989.
Royal Mail International Business Travel Guide 1990/91, London. ISBN 0–946393–11–7.
Area Handbook Series, US Government Printing Office.
World Population Data Sheets 1990–1992, Population Reference Bureau, 1875 Connecticut Ave NW, Suite 520, Washington DC 20009, USA.

2. Religions

National Censuses where available.
National Christian Handbooks (Europe), MARC Europe.
Encyclopedia Britannica Book of the Year.
World Christianity Series. 1979–1991. MARC/World Vision, USA.
World Christian Encyclopedia, David B. Barrett, Ed. (Oxford University Press 1982) ISBN 0 19 572435 6.
World Christian Handbooks 1962, 1967. World Dominion Press, London, UK.

3. Statistics for specific items (where supplementary to the above).
a) **Area**
   The above.
b) **Population**
   World Population Prospects 1990, United Nations. ISBN 92–1–151223–9.
   Target Earth, Kaleb Jansen, 1989. Global Mapping/University of the Nations. ISBN 0–027545–01.2.
   Government Censuses, when available.
c) **Peoples**
   World Evangelization Database, 1992, Dr David Barrett, Hon. Research Advisor, United Bible Societies, PO Box 6767, Richmond, VA 23230, USA.
   Adopt-a-People Clearinghouse, Kaleb Jansen.
   PeoplesFile Index
   Unreached Peoples Annuals, MARC, USA.
d) **Literacy**
   The above.

e) **Languages**
Ethnologue 11th and 12th Editions, Barbara F. Grimes, Ed. (WBT/SIL 1988/1992). ISBN 0 88312 815–2
f) **Bible Translation**
Ethnologue 1992.
World Translations Progress Report, UBS (1992).
g) **Economic data**
The above.
h) **Urban statistics**
World Evangelization Database, D Barrett 1992.
AD2000 List of Cities, Viv Grigg 1992.
United Nations Projections 1980.
i) **Denominations**
Denominational statistics, handbooks and responses to questionnaires.
World Christian Encyclopedia
National surveys, handbooks, etc. from numerous countries, notably DAWN/Saturation church planting surveys.
Church growth books, Wm. Carey Library, etc.
World Christianity Series, 1979–1991, MARC/World Vision, USA.
j) **Missions**
North American Protestant Ministries Overseas, MARC 1980. ISBN 0 912552 1 34 4.
UK Christian Handbook 1992/93, Peter Brierley, Ed. MARC Europe, ISBN 0 947697 95 0.
From Every People, Larry Pate, MARC 1989, ISBN 971–511–162–9.
The Last Age of Missions, Lawrence E. Keyes, Wm. Carey Library, 1983. ISBN 087808 4355.
Mission Handbook USA/Canada Protestant Ministries Overseas 14th ed 1989. 15th ed. 1993. J Siewert, MARC/World Vision, USA.
Christian Handbooks (Europe), P. Brierley, MARC Europe 1985–1992.
Guida delle Missioni Catholiche, 1989, Vatican, Rome.
Numerous questionnaires and surveys.
Mission journals and publications.

APPENDIX 8
OTHER OPERATION WORLD RESOURCES

Other Resources

Overhead transparencies

A wide range of maps, graphs and photographs are availiable from

WEC International Research Office, Bulstrode, Gerrards Cross, Bucks SL9 8SZ, England
Global Mapping International, PO Box 25399, Colorado Springs, CO 80936–5399, USA

A new series of maps and diagrams, using information from this edition of *Operation World*, will be available in June 1994. Write to the above addresses for complete lists.
The WEC and GMI productions are complementary and different from one another.

Operation World information on Microfiche

WEC International Research Office
Large holdings of data, articles, surveys and clippings gathered for the production of *Operation World* have been collated by country or region, subdivided into subject and date, and put on microfiche film. This is a unique collection of information relating to world evangelization.
Sujects: Politico-economic, Christian survey, Church and mission, Peoples, Media, Religion.
Range: Covering 1980–1986, 1987–1989 and 1990–1992.
Quantity: Approx 500,000 pages of information.
Format: 72 frames per fiche.

People Profiles

Adopt-a-People Clearinghouse, P.O. Box 1795, Colorado Springs, CO 80901–1795, USA.
The Clearinghouse distributes two series of people profiles:
  1. Four-color profiles of unreached peoples.
     Format: multi-fold glossy card with text, photographs and maps. They can be customized.
  2. Profiles, submitted by mission agencies of some of the 6,000 "unreached and adoptable" peoples.
Format: wide variety of size, length and complexity.
Send for list of available profiles.

Country Passports

Adopt-a-People Clearinghouse, P.O. Box 1795, Colorado Springs, CO 80901–1795, USA. Kaleb Jansen and his team have begun to produce a series of country profiles in the size and format of passports, providing information more detailed than that presented in *Operation World*.

Send for list of passports available and planned.

Other expressions of Operation World

Electronic Operation World

See behind the scenes how **Operation World** was produced. The entire text of the book and the extensive global database from which the data was derived is now available for your computer.

Extract the information you need and pray more effectively and push forward the task of world evangelization.

Available from: **Global Mapping International,**
Box 25399, Colorado Springs, CO 80936–5399, USA
To be published early in 1994. Please write details for special pre-publication offer.

You Can Change the World
by Jill Johnstone

A Children's Version of Operation World
An A-Z to help children to pray for the world.
Covering 26 peoples and 26 countries. 128 pages A4 format.
Full-colour illustrations, stories, information, rhyme-raps and daily prayer points

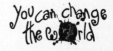

A wide variety of supporting resources – Sunday School packs, inflatable globes, stickers, etc are available from your Christian bookstores or the publishers of **Operation World** or from WEC International.

Other language versions planned.

Other language versions

In preparation:

Chinese, Dutch, French, German, Korean, Spanish and Portuguese.

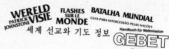

Contact OM Publishing for details. See addresses below.

Operation World Maps and Prayer Cards

Prayer card packs (74) – rewritten using the new statistics from *Operation World*.

Operation World World map – newly designed, including all new countries up to May 1993.

Available from your Christian bookstore or from OM Publishing
USA: Box 28, Waynesboro, GA 30830–0028
UK: PO Box 300, Carlisle, Cumbria CA3 0QS.